Standard Catalog of
HANDGUNS
THE COLLECTOR'S PRICE AND REFERENCE GUIDE

JERRY LEE

Published by

Gun Digest® Books, an imprint of F+W Media, Inc.
Krause Publications • 700 East State Street • Iola, WI 54990-0001
715-445-2214 • 888-457-2873
www.krausebooks.com

To order books or other products call toll-free 1-800-258-0929
or visit us online at www.gundigeststore.com

ISBN-13: 978-1-4402-3009-7
ISBN-10: 1-4402-3009-9

Cover Design by Al West
Designed by Kara Grundman, Paul Birling,
Sandi Carpenter and Tom Nelsen
Edited by Jerry Lee and Jennifer Pearsall

Printed in the United States of America

CONTENTS

INTRODUCTION

A GUIDE TO PRICING

Prices shown in the *Standard Catalog of Handguns* are designed as a *guide*, not as a quote, and the prices given reflect *retail* values. This is very important to remember. You will seldom realize full retail value if you trade in a gun or sell it to a dealer. In that situation, your gun will be valued at its *wholesale* price, which is generally substantially below retail value to allow for the seller's profit margin.

Prices for firearms can vary with the time of the year, the geographical location and the general economy. It is not practical to list prices in this book with regard to time of year or location. What is given is a reasonable price based on sales at gun shows, auction houses, and information obtained from knowledgeable collectors and dealers. In certain cases there will be no price indicated under a particular condition but rather the notation "N/A" or the symbol "—." This indicates that there is no known price available for that gun in that condition or the sales for that particular model are so few that a reliable price cannot be given. This will usually be encountered only with very rare guns, with newly introduced firearms, or more likely with antique firearms in those conditions most likely to be encountered. Most antique firearms will be seen in the good, fair and poor categories.

Standard Catalog of Handguns can be used as an identification guide and as a source of starting prices for a planned transaction. If you start by valuing a given gun according to the values shown in this book, you will not be too far off the mark.

In the final analysis, a firearm is worth only what someone is willing to pay for it. New trends arise quickly, and there are many excellent bargains to be found in today's market. With patience and good judgment—and with this book under your arm—you, too, can find them.

ABOUT THE EDITOR

Jerry Lee has been editor of several leading magazines in the firearms field including *Guns, Petersen's Handguns, Rifle Shooter*, and *Wing & Shot*. For many years he also was editor of the *Guns & Ammo* and *Shooting Times* specialty and annual publications. These include such titles as *Book of the 1911, Book of the AR-15, Combat Arms, Surplus Firearms, Book of the Model 70, Firearms for Law Enforcement, Gun Guide*, and many others. He was also responsible for editing the content of custom magazines and catalogs for Smith & Wesson, Remington, Ruger, Mossberg, CZ, Hornady, Nikon, and other manufacturers. Jerry is an NRA Life Member and has written several articles for that organization's website. His passion in firearms mainly centers around Colt handguns, rimfire rifles and 20-gauge shotguns. Jerry and Susan, his wife of more than 40 years, live in West Virginia.

AUCTION HOUSES

Among the many resources used by the editors to determine trends in firearms values are the prices realized at recent auctions. These include the following auction houses, which are considered to be among the very best in the field of modern and antique firearms.

Amoskeag Auctions, 250 Commercial Street, Suite 3011, Manchester, NH 03101; **www.amoskeag-auction.com**
Bonhams & Butterfields, 220 San Bruno Avenue, San Francisco, CA 94103; **www.bonhams.com**
Heritage Auctions, 3500 Maple Avenue, 17th Floor, Dallas, Texas 75219; **www.ha.com**
James D. Julia, Inc., 203 Skowhegan Rd., Fairfield, ME 04937; **www.juliaauctions.com**
Little John's Auctions, 1740 W. La Veta Ave., Orange, CA 92868; **www.littlejohnsauctionservice.com**
Rock Island Auction Co., 7819 42nd Street West, Rock Island, IL 61201; **www.rockislandauction.com**

GRADING SYSTEM

In most cases, the condition of a firearm determines its value. As with all collectible items, a grading system is necessary to give buyers and sellers a measurement that most closely reflects a general consensus on condition. While all grading systems are subjective, the system presented in this publication attempts to describe a firearm in universal terms. It is strongly recommend that the reader be closely acquainted with this grading system before attempting to determine the correct value of a particular firearm.

NIB (NEW IN BOX)

This category can sometimes be misleading. It means that the firearm is in its original factory carton with all of the appropriate papers. It also means the firearm is new, that it has not been fired, and has no wear. This classification brings a substantial premium for both the collector and shooter. It should be noted that NIB values are not the same as MSRP (manufacturer's suggested retail price), but rather are "street prices" that can be considerably lower than the MSRP. A NIB value should closely represent the selling price for a new, unfired gun in the box.

EXCELLENT

Collector quality firearms in this condition are highly desirable. The firearm must be in at least 98 percent condition with respect to blue wear, stock or grip finish, and bore. The firearm must also be in 100 percent original factory condition without refinishing, repair, alterations, or additions of any kind. Sights must be factory original, as well. This grading classification includes both modern and antique (manufactured prior to 1898) firearms.

VERY GOOD

Firearms in this category are also sought after both by the collector and shooter. Modern firearms must be in working order and retain approximately 92 percent original metal and wood finish. It must be 100 percent factory original, but may have some small repairs, alterations, or non-factory additions. No refinishing is permitted in this category. Antique firearms must have 80 percent original finish with no repairs.

GOOD

Modern firearms in this category may not be considered to be as collectible as the previous grades, but antique firearms are considered desirable. Modern firearms must retain at least 80 percent metal and wood finish, but may display evidence of old refinishing. Small repairs, alterations, or non-factory additions are sometimes encountered in this class. Factory replacement parts are permitted. The overall working condition of the firearm must be good, as well as safe. The bore may exhibit wear or some corrosion, especially in antique arms. Antique firearms may be included in this category if the metal and wood finish is at least 50 percent of the factory original.

FAIR

Firearms in this category should be in satisfactory working order and safe to shoot. The overall metal and wood finish on the modern firearm must be at least 30 percent and antique firearms must have at least some original finish or old re-finish remaining. Repairs, alterations, non-factory additions, and recent refinishing would all place a firearm in this classification. However, the modern firearm must be in working condition, while the antique firearm may not function. In either case the firearm must be considered safe to fire if in a working state.

POOR

Neither collectors nor shooters are likely to exhibit much interest in firearms in this condition. Modern firearms are likely to retain little metal or wood finish. Pitting and rust will be seen in firearms in this category. Modern firearms may not be in working order and may not be safe to shoot. Repairs and refinishing would be necessary to restore the firearm to safe working order. Antique firearms in this category will have no finish and will not function. In the case of modern firearms their principal value lies in spare parts. On the other hand, antique firearms in this condition can be used as "wall hangers," or might be an example of an extremely rare variation or have some kind of historical significance.

Example prices are shown for the conditions described above in this format:

NIB	Exc.	V.G.	Good	Fair	Poor
2250	1800	1500	1250	1000	700

PRICING

Prices given in this book are designed as a guide, not as a quote, and the prices given reflect retail values. This is very important to remember. You will seldom realize full retail value if you trade in a gun or sell it to a dealer. In this situation, your gun will be valued at its wholesale price, which is generally substantially below retail value to allow for the seller's profit margin.

It should also be remembered that prices for firearms can vary with the time of the year, geographical location, and the general economy. As might be expected, guns used for hunting are more likely to sell in late summer or early fall as hunting season approaches. Likewise, big-game rifles chambered for powerful magnum cartridges will likely have more appeal in western states than in the

Deep South, while semi-automatic rifles or shotguns will not sell well in states where their use for hunting is prohibited, such as is the case in Pennsylvania.

It is not practical to list prices in this book with regard to time of year or location. What is given here is a reasonable price based on sales at gun shows, auction houses, and information obtained from knowledgeable collectors and dealers. In certain cases there will be no price indicated under a particular condition, but rather the notation "N/A" or the symbol "—." This indicates that there is no known price available for that gun in that condition or the sales for that particular model are so few that a reliable price cannot be ascertained. This will usually be encountered only with very rare guns, with newly introduced firearms, or more likely with antique firearms in those conditions most likely to be encountered. Most antique firearms will be seen in the Good, Fair and Poor categories.

Standard Catalog of Firearms can be used as an identification guide and as a source of starting prices for a planned firearms transaction. If you begin by valuing a given firearm according to the values shown in this book, you will not be too far off the mark.

In the final analysis, a firearm is worth only what someone is willing to pay for it. New trends arise quickly, and there are many excellent bargains to be found in today's market. With patience and good judgment—and with this book under your arm—you, too, can find them.

ADDITIONAL CONSIDERATIONS

Firearms have been admired and coveted, not only for their usefulness, but also for their grace and beauty. Since the beginning of the 19th century, gun makers have adorned their firearms with engraving, fine woods or special order features that set their products apart from the rest. There is no feasible way to give the collector every possible variation of the firearms presented in this book. However, in a general way, certain special factors will significantly influence the price of a firearm.

Perhaps the most recognizable special feature collectors agree that affects the price of a rifle or shotgun is engraving. The artistry, beauty and intricate nature of engraving draw all collectors toward it. But firearms engraving is a field unto itself requiring years of experience to determine proper chronological methods and the ability to identify the engraver in question.

Factory engraving generally brings more of a premium than after-market engraving. To be able to determine factory work is a difficult task, and can be full of pitfalls. In some cases, factories like Colt and Winchester may have records to verify original factory engraving work, whereas other manufacturers such as Parker, Remington or Savage may not. Whenever a firearm purchase is to be made with respect to an engraved gun, it is in the collector's best interest to secure an expert opinion and or a factory letter prior to the purchase. Engraved firearms are expensive. A mistake could cost the buyer or seller thousands of dollars; proceed with caution.

The 19th and 20th centuries were times when guns were purchased by or given to historically important individuals. Firearms have also been an important part of significant historical events such as the Battle of the Little Bighorn or the Battle of Bull Run. Many of these firearms are in museums where the public can enjoy, see and appreciate them. Others are in private collections that seldom, if ever, are offered for sale. If the collector should ever encounter one of these historically important firearms, it cannot be stressed strongly enough to secure an expert determination as to authenticity. Museum curators are perhaps the best source of information for these types of firearms. As with engraved guns, historical firearms are usually expensive, and without documentation their value is questionable.

Special features and variations are also a desirable part of firearms collecting. As with engraving, special order guns can bring a considerable premium. The Colt factory has excellent records regarding its firearms and will provide the collector with a letter of authenticity. Winchester records are not as comprehensive but rifles made prior to 1908 may have documentation. Other firearm manufacturers either do not have records or do not provide the collector with documentation. This leaves the collector in a difficult position. Special order sights, stocks, barrel lengths, calibers, gauges and chokes must be judged on their own merits. As with other factors, an expert should be consulted prior to purchase. Experienced collectors, researchers, and museums will generally provide the kind of information a collector needs before purchasing a special order or unique firearm.

Perhaps the best advice is for the collector to take his time. Do not be in a hurry, and do not allow yourself to be rushed into making a decision. Learn as much as possible about the firearms you are interested in collecting or shooting. Try to keep current with prices through this publication and the auction houses listed nearby. Go to gun shows, not just to buy or sell, but to observe and learn. It is also helpful to join a gun club or collector's association. These groups have experienced members who are glad to help the beginner or veteran.

Firearms collecting is a rewarding hobby. Firearms are part of our nation's history and represent an opportunity to learn more about their role in the American experience. If done skillfully, firearms collecting can be a profitable hobby as well.

A

A.A.
Azanza & Arrizabalaga
Eibar, Spain

A.A.

A 6.35mm and 7.65mm caliber semi-automatic pistol with a 6- and 9-shot magazine. Many of these pistols are identifiable by the trademark "AA" on their frames.

Courtesy James Rankin

NIB	Exc.	V.G.	Good	Fair	Poor
—	300	175	150	100	50

Reims

A 6.35mm or 7.65mm caliber semi-automatic pistol with 6- or 8-round magazine capacity. Most of the pistols have their slides marked "1914 Model Automatic Pistol Reims Patent."

NIB	Exc.	V.G.	Good	Fair	Poor
—	200	175	150	100	50

A.A.A.
Aldazabal
Eibar, Spain

Modelo 1919

A 7.65mm semi-automatic pistol with 9-round magazine capacity. The trademark of a knight's head over three A's is on the side of the slide and the grips.

Courtesy James Rankin

NIB	Exc.	V.G.	Good	Fair	Poor
—	200	175	150	100	50

A & R SALES SOUTH
El Monte, California

NOTE: A&R Sales South also made frames for custom 1911 builds.

45 Auto

An alloy-frame version of the Colt Model 1911 semi-automatic pistol.

NIB	Exc.	V.G.	Good	Fair	Poor
475	325	200	150	125	100

A. J. ORDNANCE

A delayed blowback action that is unique in that every shot was double-action. This pistol was chambered for the .45 ACP cartridge and had a 3.5" stainless steel barrel with fixed sights and plastic grips. The detachable magazine held 6 shots, and the standard finish was matte blue. Chrome plating was available and would add approximately 15 percent to the values listed.

NIB	Exc.	V.G.	Good	Fair	Poor
1950	1300	800	400	250	175

ABADIE
Liege, Belgium

System Abadie Model 1878

A 9mm double-action revolver with a 6-shot cylinder, octagonal barrel and integral ejector rod.

NIB	Exc.	V.G.	Good	Fair	Poor
—	550	350	175	125	90

System Abadie Model 1886

A heavier version of the above.

NIB	Exc.	V.G.	Good	Fair	Poor
—	575	400	200	125	90

ACCU-MATCH
Mesa, Arizona

Accu-Match Custom Pistol

This is a competition pistol built on the Colt 1911 design. Chambered for the .45 ACP it is fitted with a 5-1/2" match grade stainless steel barrel, stainless steel slide and frame with extended slide release and safety. Fitted with a beavertail grip safety and wraparound finger groove rubber grips, this pistol has a threaded three port compensator and dual action recoil spring system with three dot sight system.

NIB	Exc.	V.G.	Good	Fair	Poor
1050	750	550	400	300	175

ACCU-TEK
Chino, California

AT-380SS

Introduced in 1991 this semi-automatic pistol is chambered for the .380 ACP cartridge. Fitted with a 2.75" barrel with adjustable for windage rear sight. Black composition grips. Stainless steel construction. Furnished with a 5-round magazine. Weight is about 20 oz.

NIB	Exc.	V.G.	Good	Fair	Poor
245	165	100	75	50	25

AT-380 II

Introduced in 2004 this pistol is chambered for the .380 ACP cartridge. It is fitted with a 2.8" barrel. Magazine capacity is 6 rounds. Stainless steel. Magazine release is on bottom of grip. Weight is about 23 oz.

NIB	Exc.	V.G.	Good	Fair	Poor
255	175	125	100	75	35

CP-9SS

This semi-automatic double-action-only stainless steel pistol is chambered for the 9mm cartridge and is fitted with a 3.2" barrel with adjustable for windage rear sight. Magazine capacity is 8 rounds. Grips are black checkered nylon. Weight is about 28 oz. Introduced in 1992.

NIB	Exc.	V.G.	Good	Fair	Poor
295	225	150	100	75	50

CP-45SS

Similar to the Model CP-9SS but chambered for the .45 ACP cartridge. Furnished with a 6-round magazine. Introduced in 1996.

NIB	Exc.	V.G.	Good	Fair	Poor
300	245	195	150	125	75

CP-40SS

Introduced in 1992 and similar to the CP-9SS but chambered for .40 S&W cartridge. Furnished with a 7-round magazine.

NIB	Exc.	V.G.	Good	Fair	Poor
300	245	195	150	125	75

BL-9

This is a semi-automatic double-action-only pistol chambered for 9mm cartridge and furnished with a 5-round magazine. Barrel length is 3". Grips are black composition. Finish is black. Weight is approximately 22 oz. Introduced in 1997.

NIB	Exc.	V.G.	Good	Fair	Poor
295	225	150	100	75	50

BL-380

Similar to the Model BL-9 but chambered for the .380 ACP cartridge. Also introduced in 1997.

NIB	Exc.	V.G.	Good	Fair	Poor
255	175	125	100	75	35

HC-380SS

This .380 ACP semi-automatic pistol has a 2.75" barrel. Stainless steel finish. Weight is about 28 oz. Furnished with a 10-round magazine. Introduced in 1993.

NIB	Exc.	V.G.	Good	Fair	Poor
255	175	125	100	75	35

AT-32SS

Similar to the Model AT-380SS but chambered for the .32 ACP cartridge. Introduced in 1991.

NIB	Exc.	V.G.	Good	Fair	Poor
225	175	110	75	50	40

ACHA
Domingo Acha
Vizcaya, Spain

Atlas

A 6.35mm caliber semi-automatic pistol manufactured during the 1920s in the style of the Model 1906 Browning. Grips are plain checkered hard rubber. Some grips had the ACHA trademark of the Count's head. The name Atlas appears on the slide. Later models incorporated a grip safety.

Courtesy James Rankin

NIB	Exc.	V.G.	Good	Fair	Poor
—	250	175	100	75	50

Looking Glass (Ruby-Style)

This is a 7.65mm semi-automatic pistol in the Ruby-style. These pistols were furnished with a 7-, 9-, or 12-round magazine.

Courtesy James Rankin

NIB	Exc.	V.G.	Good	Fair	Poor
—	265	195	100	75	50

Looking Glass

A 6.35mm or 7.65mm caliber semi-automatic pistol. Various markings are seen on these pistols and their grips as they were sold in both France and Spain by different distributors. The pistol pictured has two trademarks: Domingo Acha on the grips and Fabrique D'Arms de Guerre De Grande Presision on the slide.

Courtesy James Rankin

NIB	Exc.	V.G.	Good	Fair	Poor
—	295	175	110	75	50

ACME ARMS
New York, New York

A trade name found on .22 and .32 caliber revolvers and 12 gauge shotguns marketed by the Cornwall Hardware Company.

.22 Revolver

A 7-shot single-action revolver.

NIB	Exc.	V.G.	Good	Fair	Poor
—	375	275	175	125	75

.32 Revolver

A 5-shot single-action revolver.

NIB	Exc.	V.G.	Good	Fair	Poor
—	400	300	200	150	100

ACME HAMMERLESS
Made by Hopkins & Allen
Norwich, Connecticut

Acme Hammerless

A .32 or .38 caliber 5-shot revolver with either exposed hammer or enclosed hammer. Sometimes known as the "Forehand 1891."

NIB	Exc.	V.G.	Good	Fair	Poor
—	295	225	175	50	25

ACTION
Eibar, Spain
Maker—Modesto Santos

Action

A 6.35mm or 7.65mm semi-automatic pistol marked on the slide "Pistolet Automatique Modele 1920." Often found bearing the trade name "Corrientes" as well as the maker's trademark "MS."

NIB	Exc.	V.G.	Good	Fair	Poor
—	275	175	115	80	60

ACTION ARMS LTD.
Philadelphia, Pennsylvania

AT-84, AT-88

This pistol is the Swiss version of of the CZ-75. It is built at ITM, Solothurn, Switzerland. The AT-84 is chambered for the 9mm cartridge. The AT-88 is chambered for the .41 Action Express. Both have a 4.75" barrel. The 9mm pistol has a magazine capacity of 15 rounds while the .41 AE has a capacity of 10 rounds. Finish is either blue or chrome with walnut grips.

Courtesy James Rankin

NIB	Exc.	V.G.	Good	Fair	Poor
750	550	450	375	300	150

AT-84P, AT-88P

As above, with a 3.7" barrel and smaller frame.

NIB	Exc.	V.G.	Good	Fair	Poor
750	550	450	375	300	150

AT-84H, AT-88H

As above with a 3.4" barrel and smaller frame.

NIB	Exc.	V.G.	Good	Fair	Poor
750	550	450	375	300	150

ADAMS
Deane, Adams & Deane
London, England
London Armoury Co. (After 1856)

Revolvers based upon Robert Adams' patents were manufactured by the firm of Deane, Adams & Deane. Although more technically advanced than the pistols produced by Samuel Colt, Adams' revolvers were popular primarily in England and the British Empire.

Adams Model 1851 Self-Cocking Revolver

A .44 caliber double-action percussion revolver with a 7.5" octagonal barrel and 5-shot cylinder. The barrel and frame are blued, the cylinder case hardened and the grips are walnut. The top strap is marked "Deane, Adams and Deane 30 King William St. London Bridge." This revolver does not have a hammer spur and functions only as a double-action.

NIB	Exc.	V.G.	Good	Fair	Poor
—	4000	2975	1475	775	400

Adams Pocket Revolver

As above, in .31 caliber with a 4.5" barrel.

NIB	Exc.	V.G.	Good	Fair	Poor
—	3750	2875	1375	750	400

Beaumont-Adams Revolver

As above, fitted with a Tranter Patent loading lever and the hammer made with a spur.

NIB	Exc.	V.G.	Good	Fair	Poor
—	2500	1950	950	695	300

ADLER
Engelbrecht & Wolff
Blasii, Germany

An extremely rare and unusually designed semi-automatic pistol adapted for the 7.25mm Adler cartridge. This is a striker-fired blowback pistol with a 3.4" barrel. Single-column magazine has an 8-round capacity. Weight is approximately 24 oz. Produced in very limited numbers, probably only a few hundred, between 1906 and 1907.

Courtesy James Rankin

NIB	Exc.	V.G.	Good	Fair	Poor
—	—	10000	8750	2750	1250

ADVANCED SMALL ARMS INDUSTRIES
Solothurn, Switzerland

one Pro .45

Introduced in 1997 and built in Switzerland by ASAI, this pistol features a 3" barrel chambered for the .45 ACP cartridge. It is based on a short recoil operation and is available in double-action or double-action-only. Also available is a kit (purchased separately) to convert the pistol to .400 Cor-Bon caliber. The pistol weighs about 24 oz. empty.

NIB	Exc.	V.G.	Good	Fair	Poor
1000	725	595	425	195	100

ADVANTAGE ARMS U.S.A., INC.
Distributed by Wildfire Sports
St. Paul, Minnesota

Model 422

A .22 or .22 Magnum caliber four-barrel derringer with 2.5" barrels. Entirely made of an aluminum alloy. Finished in either blue or nickel-plate. Manufactured in 1986 and 1987.

NIB	Exc.	V.G.	Good	Fair	Poor
225	125	100	85	65	45

AERO
Manufactura De Armas De Fuego
Guernica, Spain

Model 1914 (Aero)

A 7.65mm caliber semi-automatic pistol with a 3.25" barrel in the Ruby design. The Aero name is on the slide along with an airplane. Magazine capacity is 7 rounds, weight is about 23 oz.

Courtesy James Rankin

NIB	Exc.	V.G.	Good	Fair	Poor
—	350	250	200	125	95

AETNA ARMS CO.
New York

A .22 caliber spur trigger revolver with an octagonal barrel and 7-shot cylinder. The barrel marked "Aetna Arms Co. New York." Manufactured from approximately 1870 to 1880. Copy of the S&W No. 1.

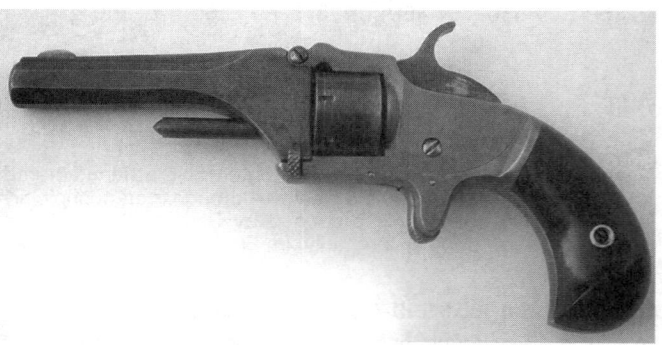

NIB	Exc.	V.G.	Good	Fair	Poor
—	—	550	375	150	100

AFC
Auguste Francotte
Liege, Belgium

This was one of the most prolific makers of revolvers in Liege during the last half of the 19th century. It is estimated that over 150 different revolvers were made and marketed by them before they were forced out of business by the German occupation of 1914. Francotte produced many variations from Tranter copies to pinfires, early Smith & Wesson designs to the 11mm M1871 Swedish troopers revolver. They made break-open revolvers and produced only one semi-auto, a 6.35mm blowback design. A good portion of their pistols were produced for the wholesale market and were sold under other names. These particular revolvers will bear the letters "AF" stamped somewhere on the frame. Because of the vast number and variety of pistols produced by this company, cataloging and pricing is beyond the scope of this or any general reference book. It is suggested that any examples encountered be researched on an individual basis. For more information on Francotte see the information under that listing.

Model 1895

One of the earliest Francotte pistols. Chambered for the 8mm cartridge, it is a lever-operated repeater. Marked "A. Francotte & Co. Makers" on the top of the slide.

Courtesy James Rankin

NIB	Exc.	V.G.	Good	Fair	Poor
—	7000	5500	4150	2300	1500

Trainer

A single-shot target pistol made for competition in .22 caliber short. AFC trademark on the left side of the frame. This model was probably not made by Francotte, but sold by that firm and others.

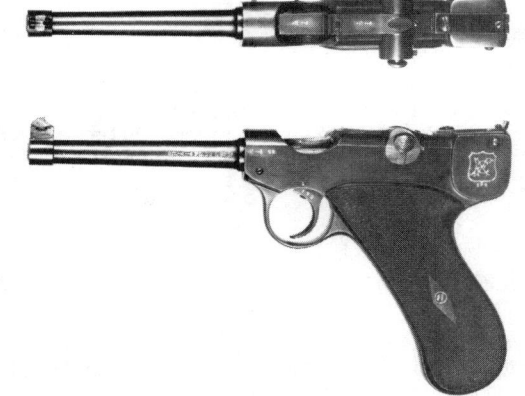

Courtesy James Rankin

NIB	Exc.	V.G.	Good	Fair	Poor
—	3800	3150	2700	2175	1500

Semi-Auto

A 6.35mm, 6-shot detachable magazine pocket pistol with blue finish. This model was marked "A. Francotte A Liege" on the frame.

Courtesy James Rankin

NIB	Exc.	V.G.	Good	Fair	Poor
—	425	300	195	125	90

AFFERBACH, W. A.
Philadelphia, Pennsylvania

This maker is known to have produced copies of Henry Derringer's percussion pocket pistols. Though uncommon, their values would be approximately as listed.

NIB	Exc.	V.G.	Good	Fair	Poor
—	—	2750	2200	995	300

AGNER (SAXHOJ PRODUCTS INC.)
Copenhagen, Denmark

Model M 80

A .22 caliber single-shot stainless steel target pistol with a 5.9" barrel, adjustable sights and walnut grips. This pistol is fitted with a dry fire mechanism. Also available in a left-hand version. Imported from 1981 to 1986.

Courtesy James Rankin

NIB	Exc.	V.G.	Good	Fair	Poor
—	1250	875	600	450	200

AGUIRRE
Eibar, Spain

A Spanish manufacturer of pistols prior to World War II.

Basculant

A 6.35mm semi-automatic pistol marked on the slide "Cal. 6.35

NIB	Exc.	V.G.	Good	Fair	Poor
—	275	150	125	75	50

LeDragon

As above, with the slide marked "Cal. 6.35 Automatic Pistol LeDragon." It is patterned after the Browning Model 1906. A stylized dragon is molded into the grips.

Courtesy James Rankin

NIB	Exc.	V.G.	Good	Fair	Poor
—	275	150	125	75	50

AIR MATCH
Paris, Kentucky

Air Match 500

A .22 caliber single-shot target pistol with a 10.5" barrel, adjustable sights and adjustable front-mounted counterweights. Blued with walnut grips. Imported from 1984 to 1986.

NIB	Exc.	V.G.	Good	Fair	Poor
775	595	425	300	250	125

AJAX ARMY

A spur-trigger, single-action, solid-frame revolver that was chambered for the .44 rimfire cartridge. It had a 7" barrel and was blued with walnut grips. It was manufactured in the 1880s.

NIB	Exc.	V.G.	Good	Fair	Poor
—	750	450	365	275	200

ALAMO RANGER
Spain

A double-action Spanish copy of the Colt SAA, chambered for the .38 Long Colt or .38 Special. The cylinder held 6 shots. The finish was blued; grips were checkered hard rubber. The maker of this pistol is unknown.

NIB	Exc.	V.G.	Good	Fair	Poor
—	350	225	115	75	45

ALDAZABAL
Eibar, Spain
Aldazabal, Leturiondo & CIA

Model 1919

A vest pocket semi-automatic pistol copied from the FN Browning Model 1906. Caliber is 6.35mm.

Courtesy James Rankin

NIB	Exc.	V.G.	Good	Fair	Poor
—	295	175	125	75	50

Military Model

A semi-automatic pistol in the Ruby-style. Caliber is 7.65mm with a 9-round magazine.

Courtesy James Rankin

NIB	Exc.	V.G.	Good	Fair	Poor
—	375	275	195	125	75

Aldazabal

Another typical low-quality, "Eibar" -type semi-automatic. It was a Browning blowback copy, chambered for the 7.65mm cartridge. It had a 7-shot detachable magazine and blued finish with checkered wood grips. This company ceased production before the Spanish Civil War.

NIB	Exc.	V.G.	Good	Fair	Poor
—	295	165	115	65	40

ALKARTASUNA FABRICA DE ARMAS
Guernica, Spain

This company began production during World War I to help Gabilondo y Urresti supply sidearms to the French. After the hostilities ceased, they continued to produce firearms under their own name. They produced a number of variations in both 6.35mm and 7.65mm marked "Alkar." Collector interest is very thin. The factory burned down in 1920, and by 1922 business had totally ceased.

Alkar

A 6.35mm semi-automatic pistol with a cartridge counter in the grip plates. One variation of many built in either 6.35mm or 7.65mm.

Courtesy James Rankin

NIB	Exc.	V.G.	Good	Fair	Poor
—	295	250	195	125	100

Alkar (Ruby-Style)

A 7.65mm semi-automatic pistol built in the Ruby-style. This pistol was supplied to the French government during World War I.

Courtesy James Rankin

NIB	Exc.	V.G.	Good	Fair	Poor
—	295	225	165	100	90

ALL RIGHT FIREARMS CO.
Lawrence, Massachusetts

Little All Right Palm Pistol

Squeezer-type pocket pistol invented by E. Boardman and A. Peavy in 1876, was made in .22 cal. and had a 5-shot cylinder with a 1-5/8" or 2-3/8" barrel. The barrel is octagonal with a tube on top of it which houses the sliding trigger. The finish is nickel. The black hard rubber grips have "Little All Right" & "All Right Firearms Co., Manufacturers Lawrence, Mass. U.S.A." molded into them. There were several hundred produced in the late 1870s.

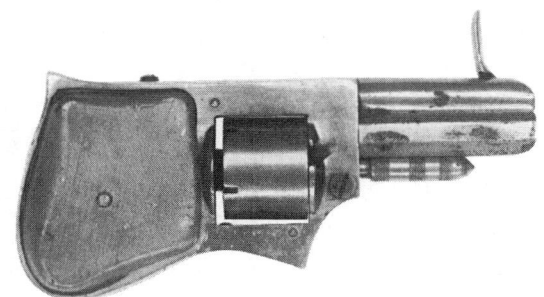

Courtesy Milwaukee Public Museum, Milwaukee, Wisconsin

NIB	Exc.	V.G.	Good	Fair	Poor
—	4000	3250	2950	1050	300

ALLEN, ETHAN
Grafton, Massachusetts

The company was founded by Ethan Allen in the early 1800s. It became a prolific gun-making firm that evolved from Ethan Allen to Allen & Thurber, as well as the Allen & Wheelock Company. It was located in Norwich, Connecticut, and Worcester, Massachusetts, as well as Grafton. It eventually became the Forehand & Wadsworth Company in 1871 after the death of Ethan Allen. There were many and varied firearms produced under all of the headings described above. If one desires to collect Ethan Allen firearms, it would be advisable to educate oneself, as there are a number of fine publications available on the subject. The basic models and their values are listed.

First Model Pocket Rifle

Manufactured by Ethan Allen in Grafton, Massachusetts. It was a bootleg-type, under-hammer, single-shot pistol chambered for .31 percussion. Larger-caliber versions have also been noted. It had barrel lengths from 5" to 9" that were part-octagon in configuration. It had iron mountings and was blued with walnut grips. The barrel was marked, "E. Allen/ Grafton/Mass." as well as "Pocket Rifle/Cast Steel/ Warranted." There were approximately 2,000 manufactured from 1831 to 1842.

NIB	Exc.	V.G.	Good	Fair	Poor
—	—	—	1650	750	200

Bar Hammer Pistol

A double-action pistol with a top-mounted bar hammer. It was chambered for .28 to .36 caliber percussion. The half-octagon barrels were from 2" to 10" in length. They screwed out of the frame so it was possible to breech load them. The finish was blued with rounded walnut grips. They were marked, "Allen & Thurber/ Grafton Mass." There were approximately 2,000 manufactured between the early 1830s and 1860.

NIB	Exc.	V.G.	Good	Fair	Poor
—	—	—	1650	725	200

Tube Hammer Pistol

This version was similar to the Bar Hammer with a curved hammer without a spur. There were only a few hundred manufactured between the early 1830s and the early 1840s.

NIB	Exc.	V.G.	Good	Fair	Poor
—	—	—	2900	1300	400

Side Hammer Pistol

A single-shot, target-type pistol that was chambered for .34, .41, and .45 caliber percussion. It had a part-octagon barrel that was from 6" to 10" in length. There was a wooden ramrod mounted under the barrel. This model had a good quality rear sight that was adjustable. The ornate trigger guard had a graceful spur at its rear. The finish was blued with a rounded walnut grip. The barrel was marked, "Allen & Thurber, Worchester." There were approximately 300 manufactured in the late 1840s and early 1850s.

NIB	Exc.	V.G.	Good	Fair	Poor
—	—	—	1400	650	200

Center Hammer Pistol

A single-action chambered for .34, .36, or .44 percussion. It had a half-octagon barrel from 4" to 12" in length. It had a centrally mounted hammer that was offset to the right side to allow for sighting the pistol. The finish was blued with walnut grips. It was marked, "Allen & Thurber, Allen Thurber & Company." Some specimens are marked, "Allen & Wheelock." There were several thousand manufactured between the late 1840s and 1860.

NIB	Exc.	V.G.	Good	Fair	Poor
—	—	—	1400	650	200

Double-Barrel Pistol

A SxS, double-barrel pistol with a single trigger. It was chambered for .36 caliber percussion with 3" to 6" round barrels. The finish was blued with walnut grips. Examples with a ramrod mounted under the barrel have been noted. The flute between the barrels was marked, "Allen & Thurber," "Allen Thurber & Company," or "Allen & Wheelock." There were approximately 1,000 manufactured in the 1850s.

NIB	Exc.	V.G.	Good	Fair	Poor
—	—	—	1250	600	150

Allen & Wheelock Center Hammer Pistol

A single-action pocket pistol chambered for .31 to .38 caliber percussion. It had octagon barrels from 3" to 6" in length. The finish was blued with square butt walnut grips. The barrel was marked, "Allen & Wheelock." There were approximately 500 manufactured between 1858 and 1865.

NIB	Exc.	V.G.	Good	Fair	Poor
—	—	—	1100	550	100

Allen Thurber & Company Target Pistol

A deluxe, single-action target pistol that was chambered for .31 or .36 caliber percussion. It had a heavy, octagon barrel that was from 11" to 16" in length. There was a wooden ramrod mounted underneath the barrel. The mountings were of German silver, and there was a detachable walnut stock with a deluxe, engraved patchbox. This weapon was engraved, and the barrel was marked, "Allen Thurber & Co./Worchester/Cast Steel." This firearm was furnished in a fitted case with the stock, false muzzle, and various accessories. It was considered to be a very high grade target pistol in its era. The values listed are for a complete-cased outfit. There were very few manufactured in the 1850s.

NIB	Exc.	V.G.	Good	Fair	Poor
—	—	—	9000	4000	1000

NOTE: For pistols without attachable stock deduct 75 percent.

Ethan Allen Pepperboxes

During the period from the early 1830s to the 1860s, this company manufactured over 50 different variations of the revolving, pepperbox-type pistol. They were commercially quite successful and actually competed successfully with the Colt revolving handguns for more than a decade. They were widely used throughout the United States, as well as in Mexico, and during our Civil War. They are widely collectible because of the number of variations that exist. The potential collector should avail himself of the information available on the subject. These pepperboxes can be divided into three categories.

No. 1: Manufactured from the 1830s until 1842, at Grafton, Massachusetts.

No. 2: Manufactured from 1842 to 1847, at Norwich, Connecticut.

No. 3: Manufactured from 1847 to 1865, at Worchester, Massachusetts.

There are a number of subdivisions among these three basic groups that would pertain to trigger type, size, barrel length etc. It would be impossible to cover all 50 of these variations in a text of this type. We strongly suggest that qualified, individual appraisal be secured if contemplating a transaction. The values of these pepperbox pistols in excellent condition would be between $1,500 and $5,000. Most examples will be seen in the fair to good condition and will bring $1,000 to 2,000 depending on variation.

Large Frame Pocket Revolver

A double-action pocket revolver that was chambered for .34 caliber percussion. It had an octagon barrel from 3" to 5" in length. There were no sights. The 5-shot, unfluted cylinder was game scene engraved. The finish was blued with rounded walnut grips. It had a bar-type hammer. This was the first conventional revolver manufactured by this company, and it was directly influenced by the pepperbox pistol for which Ethan Allen had become famous. It was marked, "Allen & Wheelock" as well as "Patented April 16, 1845." There were approximately 1,500 manufactured between 1857 and 1860.

Courtesy Milwaukee Public Museum, Milwaukee, Wisconsin

NIB	Exc.	V.G.	Good	Fair	Poor
—	—	—	1400	700	350

Small Frame Pocket Revolver

This version was similar to the Large Frame Pocket Revolver except chambered for .31 caliber percussion, with a 2" to 3.5" octagon barrel. It was slightly smaller in size, finished and marked the same. There were approximately 1,000 made between 1858 and 1860.

NIB	Exc.	V.G.	Good	Fair	Poor
—	—	—	1400	700	350

Side Hammer Belt Revolver

A single-action revolver chambered for .34 caliber percussion. It had an octagon barrel from 3" to 7.5" in length. It featured a hammer that was mounted on the right side of the frame and a 5-shot, engraved, unfluted cylinder. The cylinder access pin is inserted from the rear of the weapon. The finish is blued with a case-colored hammer and trigger guard and flared butt walnut grips. It is marked, "Allen & Wheelock." There were two basic types. Values for the early model, of which 100 were manufactured between 1858 and 1861, are listed.

NIB	Exc.	V.G.	Good	Fair	Poor
—	—	—	1500	750	300

Standard Model

The second type was the Standard Model, with a spring-loaded catch on the trigger guard as opposed to a friction catch on the early model. There were approximately 1,000 manufactured between 1858 and 1861.

Courtesy Milwaukee Public Museum, Milwaukee, Wisconsin

NIB	Exc.	V.G.	Good	Fair	Poor
—	—	—	1200	595	200

ALL RIGHT FIREARMS CO.
Lawrence, Massachusetts

Little All Right Palm Pistol

Squeezer-type pocket pistol invented by E. Boardman and A. Peavy in 1876, was made in .22 cal. and had a 5-shot cylinder with a 1-5/8" or 2-3/8" barrel. The barrel is octagonal with a tube on top of it which houses the sliding trigger. The finish is nickel. The black hard rubber grips have "Little All Right" & "All Right Firearms Co., Manufacturers Lawrence, Mass. U.S.A." molded into them. There were several hundred produced in the late 1870s.

Courtesy Milwaukee Public Museum, Milwaukee, Wisconsin

NIB	Exc.	V.G.	Good	Fair	Poor
—	4000	3250	2950	1050	300

SIDE HAMMER POCKET REVOLVER

This version was chambered for .28 caliber percussion and had a 2" to 5" octagon barrel. The frame was slightly smaller than the belt model.

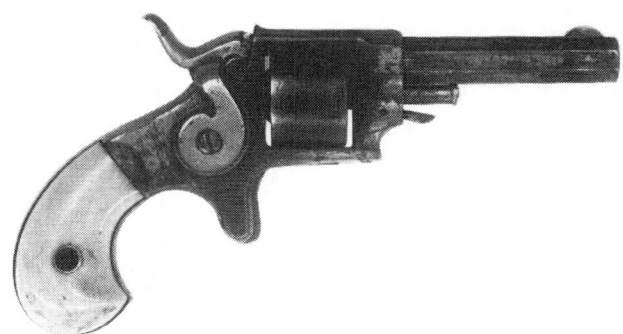

Courtesy Milwaukee Public Museum, Milwaukee, Wisconsin

NIB	Exc.	V.G.	Good	Fair	Poor

Early Production

100 manufactured.

NIB	Exc.	V.G.	Good	Fair	Poor
—	—	—	1300	725	250

Standard Production

1,000 manufactured.

NIB	Exc.	V.G.	Good	Fair	Poor
—	—	2100	975	400	225

SIDE HAMMER NAVY REVOLVER

This was a large-frame, military-type revolver that was similar to the Side Hammer Belt Model, chambered for .36 caliber percussion. It features an octagon, 5.5" to 8" barrel with a 6-shot, engraved cylinder. There was an early-production type with a friction catch on the trigger guard. There were approximately 100 manufactured between 1858 and 1861.

NIB	Exc.	V.G.	Good	Fair	Poor
—	—	—	4300	1975	575

Standard Model

1,000 manufactured.

NIB	Exc.	V.G.	Good	Fair	Poor
—	—	—	3700	1700	475

Center Hammer Army Revolver

A large, military-type, single-action revolver that was chambered for .44 caliber percussion. It had a 7.5", half-octagon barrel and a 6-shot, unfluted cylinder. The hammer was mounted in the center of the frame. The finish was blued with a case-colored hammer and trigger guard and walnut grips. The barrel was marked, "Allen & Wheelock. Worchester, Mass. U.S./Allen's Pt's. Jan. 13, 1857. Dec. 15, 1857, Sept. 7, 1858." There were approximately 700 manufactured between 1861 and 1862.

Courtesy Milwaukee Public Museum, Milwaukee, Wisconsin

NIB	Exc.	V.G.	Good	Fair	Poor
—	—	7500	4500	1875	500

Center Hammer Navy Revolver

Similar to the Army Revolver except chambered for .36 caliber percussion with a 7.5", full-octagon barrel. Examples have been noted with 5", 6", or 8" barrels. Otherwise, it was similar to the Army model.

NIB	Exc.	V.G.	Good	Fair	Poor
—	—	—	4300	1975	475

Center Hammer Percussion Revolver

A single-action revolver chambered for .36 caliber percussion. It had an octagonal, 3" or 4" barrel with a 6-shot, unfluted cylinder. The finish was blued with walnut grips. This model supposedly was made for the Providence, Rhode Island, Police Department and has become commonly referred to as the "Providence Police Model." There were approximately 700 manufactured between 1858 and 1862.

NIB	Exc.	V.G.	Good	Fair	Poor
—	—	2500	1750	750	200

LIPFIRE ARMY REVOLVER

A large, military-type, single-action revolver that was chambered for the .44 lipfire cartridge. It had a 7.5", half-octagon barrel with a 6-shot, unfluted cylinder that had notches at its rear for the cartridge lips. The finish was blued with a case-colored hammer and trigger guard and square butt walnut grips. The barrel was marked, "Allen & Wheelock, Worchester, Mass." It resembled the Center Hammer Percussion Army Revolver. There were two basic variations, with a total of 250 Lipfire Army Revolver manufactured in the early 1860s.

Early Model

Top hinged loading gate.

NIB	Exc.	V.G.	Good	Fair	Poor
—	—	—	4500	2200	600

Late Model

Bottom hinged loading gate.

NIB	Exc.	V.G.	Good	Fair	Poor
—	—	—	4000	1700	400

Lipfire Navy Revolver

Similar to the Army model, except chambered for the .36 lipfire cartridge, with an octagonal, 4", 5", 6", 7.5", or 8" barrel. There were approximately 500 manufactured in the 1860s.

NIB	Exc.	V.G.	Good	Fair	Poor
—	—	—	3300	1300	400

Lipfire Pocket Revolver

A smaller version chambered for the .32 lipfire cartridge, with an octagonal, 4", 5", or 6" barrel. There were approximately 200 manufactured in the early 1860s.

NIB	Exc.	V.G.	Good	Fair	Poor
—	—	—	2200	950	250

.32 SIDE HAMMER RIMFIRE REVOLVER

A single-action, spur-trigger, pocket revolver chambered for the .32 caliber rimfire cartridge. It had octagonal barrels from 3" to 5" in length. The finish was blued with flared-butt, walnut grips. It was marked "Allen & Wheelock Worchester, Mass." There were three variations with a total of approximately 1,000 manufactured between 1859 and 1862.

First Model
Rounded top strap.

NIB	Exc.	V.G.	Good	Fair	Poor
—	—	1125	800	450	150

Second Model
July 3, 1860 marked on frame.

NIB	Exc.	V.G.	Good	Fair	Poor
—	—	1100	795	425	150

Third Model
1858 and 1861 patent dates.

NIB	Exc.	V.G.	Good	Fair	Poor
—	—	1050	775	400	125

.22 SIDE HAMMER RIMFIRE REVOLVER

A smaller version of the .32 revolver, chambered for the .22 rimfire cartridge. It has octagonal barrels from 2.25" to 4" in length. It has a 7-shot, unfluted cylinder. There were approximately 1,500 manufactured between 1858 and 1862. There were many variations

Early Model First Issue
Access pin enters from rear.

NIB	Exc.	V.G.	Good	Fair	Poor
—	—	1300	850	475	100

Second Issue
Access pin enters from front.

NIB	Exc.	V.G.	Good	Fair	Poor
—	—	1300	850	475	100

Third Issue
Separate rear sight.

NIB	Exc.	V.G.	Good	Fair	Poor
—	—	1425	1250	600	150

Fourth to Eighth Issue
Very similar, values the same.

NIB	Exc.	V.G.	Good	Fair	Poor
—	—	900	750	300	100

SINGLE-SHOT CENTER HAMMER

A single-shot derringer-type pistol that was chambered for the .22 caliber rimfire cartridge. It had part-octagon barrels from 2" to 5.5" in length that swung to the right side for loading. Some had automatic ejectors; others did not. The frame was either brass or iron with bird's-head or squared butt walnut grips. It was marked "Allen & Wheelock" or "E. Allen & Co." There were very few manufactured in the early 1860s

Early Issue
Full-length, octagon barrel and a round, iron frame. It is rarely encountered.

NIB	Exc.	V.G.	Good	Fair	Poor
—	—	1275	1150	400	100

Standard Issue
Squared butt or bird's-head.

NIB	Exc.	V.G.	Good	Fair	Poor
—	—	1175	1050	300	100

.32 Single-Shot Center Hammer

A larger-frame pocket pistol chambered for the .32 rimfire cartridge. It has a part-octagon or full-octagon barrel of 4" or 5" in length. It swung to the right side for loading. Otherwise, this model was similar to the .22-caliber version.

NIB	Exc.	V.G.	Good	Fair	Poor
—	—	1175	1050	300	100

Vest Pocket Derringer

A small pocket pistol chambered for the .22 rimfire cartridge. It had a 2", part-octagon barrel that swung to the right-hand side for loading. The cartridges were manually extracted. It featured a brass frame with a blued or plated barrel and walnut, bird's-head grips. The barrel was marked "Allen & Co. Makers." This was an extremely small firearm, and there were approximately 200 manufactured between 1869 and 1871.

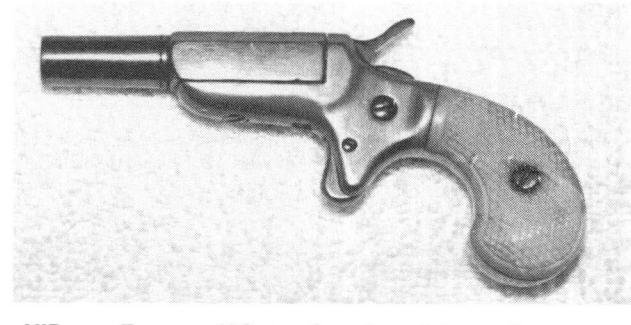

NIB	Exc.	V.G.	Good	Fair	Poor
—	—	1595	975	425	100

.32 Derringer

Similar to the Vest Pocket version, larger in size, and chambered for the .32 rimfire cartridge. It had a part-octagon barrel from 2" to 4" in length that swung to the right for loading. This version featured an automatic extractor. The barrel was marked "E. Allen & Co. Worchester, Mass." This was a very rare firearm, made between 1865 and 1871.

NIB	Exc.	V.G.	Good	Fair	Poor
—	—	1495	875	395	100

.41 Derringer

The same size and configuration as the .32 caliber model except it was chambered for the .41 rimfire cartridge with barrel lengths of 2.5" to 2.75" in length. The markings were the same. There were approximately 100 manufactured between 1865 and 1871.

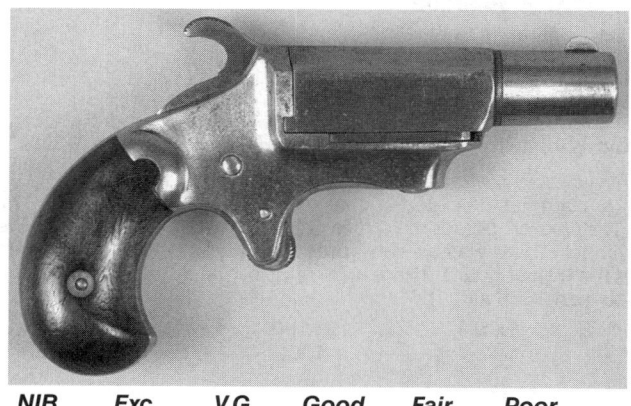

NIB	Exc.	V.G.	Good	Fair	Poor
—	—	2200	950	350	100

ALSOP, C.R.

Middletown, Connecticut

This firearms manufacturer made revolvers during 1862 and 1863. They made two basic models, the Navy and the Pocket model. Some collectors consider the Alsop to be a secondary

U.S. martial handgun, but no verifying government contracts are known to exist.

First Model Navy Revolver

A .36 cal. revolver with a 3.5", 4.5", 5.5", or 6.5" barrel length and a 5-shot cylinder. It has a blued finish, wood grips, and a peculiar hump in its backstrap. The first model has a safety device which blocks the spur trigger. This device is found on serial numbers 1-100. Markings are: "C.R. Alsop Middletown, Conn. 1860 & 1861" on the barrel. The cylinder is marked "C.R. Alsop" & "Nov. 26th, 1861" ; the side plate, "Patented Jan. 21st, 1862."

NIB	Exc.	V.G.	Good	Fair	Poor
—	—	3850	1300	500	350

Standard Model Navy Revolver

Exactly the same as the First Model without the safety device. They are serial numbered 101 to 300.

NIB	Exc.	V.G.	Good	Fair	Poor
—	—	3350	900	300	225

Pocket Model Revolver

A .31 cal. 5-shot revolver with spur trigger, 4" round barrel, blued finish, and wood grips. It is very similar in appearance to the Navy model but smaller in size. It is marked "C.R. Alsop Middletown, Conn. 1860 & 1861" on the barrel. The cylinder is marked "C.R. Alsop Nov. 26th, 1861." They are serial numbered 1-300.

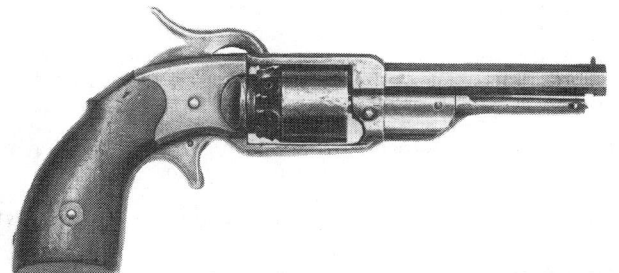

Courtesy Milwaukee Public Museum, Milwaukee, Wisconsin

NIB	Exc.	V.G.	Good	Fair	Poor
—	—	1700	700	200	125

AMAC
American Military Arms Corporation
formerly Iver Johnson
Jacksonville, Arkansas

The Iver Johnson Arms Co. was founded in 1871 in Fitchsburg, Massachusetts. It was one of the oldest and most successful of the old-line arms companies on which our modern era has taken its toll. In 1984 the company moved to Jacksonville, Arkansas; in 1987 it was purchased by the American Military Arms Corporation. This company has released some of the older designs as well as some new models. In 1993 the company went out of business. The original Iver Johnson line is listed under its own heading.

Enforcer .30 Carbine

This is a 9.5" pistol version of the M1 Carbine. It has no buttstock.

NIB	Exc.	V.G.	Good	Fair	Poor
625	500	395	300	150	100

TP-22 and TP-25

This model is a compact, double-action, pocket automatic that was styled after the Walther TP series. Chambered for either the .22 rimfire or the .25 centerfire cartridges, it has a 2.75" barrel, fixed sights and black plastic grips. The detachable magazine holds 7 shots and the finish is either blue or nickel-plated. The nickel-plated version is worth 10 percent more than the blue.

NIB	Exc.	V.G.	Good	Fair	Poor
265	195	150	100	75	50

AMAC 22 Compact or 25 Compact

This is a compact, single-action, semi-automatic pocket pistol that is chambered for the .22 rimfire or the .25 ACP cartridge. It has a 2" barrel, 5-shot magazine, plastic grips and blue or nickel finish. Add 10 percent for nickel.

NIB	Exc.	V.G.	Good	Fair	Poor
265	195	150	100	75	50

AMAC 22 Compact or 25 Compact

This is a compact, single-action, semi-automatic pocket pistol that is chambered for the .22 rimfire or the .25 ACP cartridge. It has a 2" barrel, 5-shot magazine, plastic grips and blue or nickel finish. Add 10 percent for nickel.

NIB	Exc.	V.G.	Good	Fair	Poor
265	195	150	100	75	50

AMERICAN ARMS
Garden Grove, California

Eagle .380

This pistol was a stainless steel copy of the Walther PPKS. It was a semi-auto blowback that was chambered for the .380 ACP. It was double-action and had a 3.25" barrel and a 6-shot detachable magazine. An optional feature was a black Teflon finish that would increase the value by 10 percent. This company ceased production in 1985.

NIB	Exc.	V.G.	Good	Fair	Poor
—	325	250	195	150	100

AMERICAN ARMS, INC.
North Kansas City, Missouri

Model EP-.380

A high-quality, stainless steel pocket pistol that is chambered for the .380 ACP cartridge. It is a double-action semi-automatic that holds 7 shots and has a 3.5" barrel. The grips are checkered walnut. Imported from West Germany beginning in 1988.

NIB	Exc.	V.G.	Good	Fair	Poor
425	365	325	275	225	100

Model PK-22

A domestic semi-automatic that is chambered for the .22 LR. It is a double-action with a 3.5" barrel and an 8-shot finger extension magazine. It is made of stainless steel and has black plastic grips. This model is manufactured in the U.S.A. by American Arms.

NIB	Exc.	V.G.	Good	Fair	Poor
245	200	150	125	100	75

Model CX-22

A compact version of the PK-22 with a 2.75" barrel and a 7-shot magazine. Manufacture began in 1989.

NIB	Exc.	V.G.	Good	Fair	Poor
225	200	165	125	100	75

Model TT Tokarev

The Yugoslavian version of the Soviet Tokarev chambered for 9mm Parabellum and with a safety added to make importation legal. It has a 4.5" barrel, 9-shot magazine and a blued finish with checkered plastic grips. Importation began in 1988.

NIB	Exc.	V.G.	Good	Fair	Poor
350	225	175	150	125	100

Model ZC-.380

A scaled-down version of the Tokarev that is chambered for the .380 ACP. It has a 3.5" barrel and holds 8 shots. The finish and grips are the same as on the full-sized version. Importation from Yugoslavia began in 1988.

NIB	Exc.	V.G.	Good	Fair	Poor
295	225	175	150	125	100

Aussie Model

Introduced in 1996, this is an Australian-designed semi-automatic pistol made in Spain. Chambered for the 9mm or .40 S&W cartridge it has a polymer frame with nickeled steel slide. Sold with 10-shot magazine. Barrel length is 4-3/4" and weight is 23 oz.

NIB	Exc.	V.G.	Good	Fair	Poor
400	350	300	250	200	100

Regulator

Built by Uberti this single-action revolver has a case hardened frame, polished brass trigger guard and backstrap. Barrel and cylinder are blued. One piece walnut grips. Choice of chambers in .44-40, .45 LC, or .357 Magnum. Barrel lengths from 4.75", 5.5", to 7.5". Weight is about 34 oz. with 5.75" barrel.

NIB	Exc.	V.G.	Good	Fair	Poor
395	325	275	175	—	—

Regulator Deluxe

Same as above but with steel trigger guard and backstrap. Chambered in .45 Long Colt only.

NIB	Exc.	V.G.	Good	Fair	Poor
375	300	250	150	—	—

AMERICAN ARMS CO.
Boston, Massachusetts

The history of American Arms is rather sketchy, but it appears the company was formed in 1853 as the G. H. Fox Co. and then became the American Tool & Machine Co. in 1865. In 1870 they formed a new corporation called American Arms Company with George Fox as the principle stockholder. This corporation was dissolved in 1873; a second American Arms Co. was incorporated in 1877 and a third in 1890. It is unclear if these corporations had essentially the same owners, but George H. Fox appears as a principal owner in two of the three. One could assume that financial problems forced them to bankrupt one corporation and reorganize under another. American Arms manufactured firearms in Boston, Massachusetts, from 1866 until 1893. In 1893 they moved to Bluffton, Alabama and manufactured guns until 1901.

TOP BREAK REVOLVERS

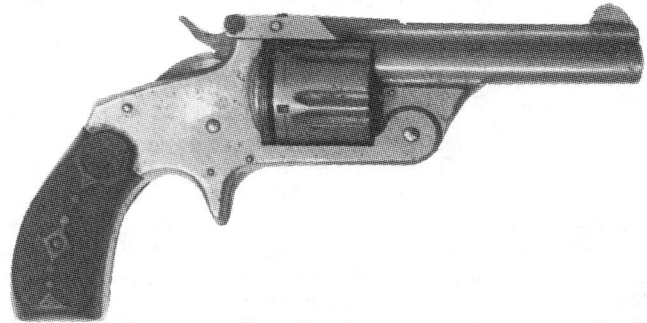

Courtesy Milwaukee Public Museum, Milwaukee, Wisconsin

Spur Trigger—Single-Action Five-Shot Revolver

These revolvers were made between 1883 and 1887 in .38 S&W only. They feature an unusual manual ring extractor and double-fluted cylinder. They are nickel plated with hard rubber grips and are marked "American Arms Company Boston Mass."

NIB	Exc.	V.G.	Good	Fair	Poor
—	550	300	100	75	25

Standard Trigger Double-Action Model 1886 Revolver

This model has a standard trigger and trigger guard, comes in .32 short and .38 S&W with a 3.5" barrel, in blue or nickel finish. The early models are equipped with the ring extractor and double fluted cylinder. Later variations have a standard star extractor and single fluted cylinder.

NIB	Exc.	V.G.	Good	Fair	Poor
—	750	300	100	75	25

Hammerless Model 1890 Double-Action

These guns were manufactured from 1890 to 1901. It has an adjustable single- or double-stage trigger pull and several unusual safety devices. It comes in .32 and .38 S&W with a 3.25" ribbed barrel, fluted cylinder, nickel finish, hard rubber grips with logo and ivory or mother of pearl grips. It is marked "American Arms Co. Boston/Pat. May 25, 1886." The top strap is marked "Pat. Pending" on early models and "Pat's May 25'86/Mar 11'89/June 17'90" on later models.

NIB	Exc.	V.G.	Good	Fair	Poor
—	750	300	100	75	25

DOUBLE-BARREL DERRINGERS

American Arms Co. manufactured a two-barrel derringer-style pocket pistol. The barrels were manually rotated to load and fire the weapon. The pistol had a nickel-plated brass frame, blued barrels, and walnut grips. The markings were: "American Arms Co. Boston, Mass." on one barrel and "Pat. Oct. 31, 1865" on the other barrel. There were approximately 2,000-3,000 produced between 1866 and 1878. Beware of fakes!

Combination .22 caliber R.F. and .32 caliber R.F.

A two-caliber combination with 3" barrel, square butt only. The most common variation.

NIB	Exc.	V.G.	Good	Fair	Poor
—	—	850	350	150	100

.32 caliber R.F., Both Barrels (3" barrel)

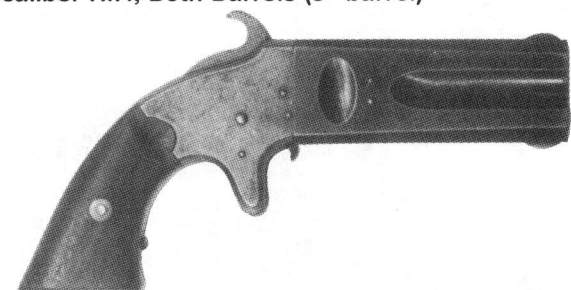

Courtesy Milwaukee Public Museum, Milwaukee, Wisconsin

3" barrel with square butt.

NIB	Exc.	V.G.	Good	Fair	Poor
—	—	1050	500	195	125

.32 caliber R.F., Both Barrels (2-5/8" barrel)
2-5/8" barrel with bird's-head grips.

NIB	Exc.	V.G.	Good	Fair	Poor
—	—	1100	550	225	150

.38 caliber R.F., Both Barrels

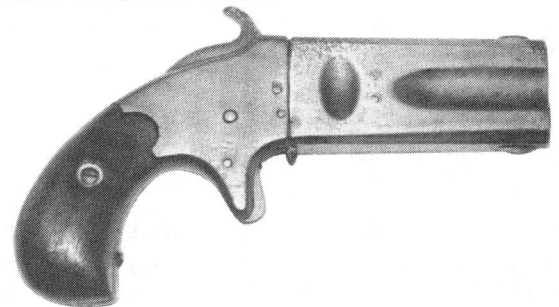

2-5/8" barrel with bird's-head grips. A rare variation.

NIB	Exc.	V.G.	Good	Fair	Poor
—	—	2500	1075	350	200

.41 caliber R.F., Both Barrels
2-5/8" barrel with square butt only.

NIB	Exc.	V.G.	Good	Fair	Poor
—	—	1850	900	200	100

AMERICAN CLASSIC
(Eagle Imports)
Wanamassa, NJ

American Classic 1911-A1

Full-size 1911-A1-style semi-auto chambered in .45 ACP. Series 70 lockwork, 8-round magazine with bumper pad, lowered ejection port, throated barrel, checkered wood grips, military-style sights, matte blue or hard chrome finish. Five-inch barrel, weight is 39 ounces. American Classic II has additional features including Novak-style sights, combat trigger and hammer, extended safety and slide stop, front slide serrations, deep blue or hard chrome finish.

NIB	Exc.	V.G.	Good	Fair	Poor
435	400	350	325	250	200

NOTE: Add $35 for Classic II, $50 for hard chrome finish.

American Classic Commander/Amigo

Same features as American Classic II except 4.25-inch barrel, weight 35-ounces. Amigo model is Officer's Model style with 3.5-inch barrel, 7-round magazine.

NIB	Exc.	V.G.	Good	Fair	Poor
460	425	360	335	260	200

NOTE: Add $50 for hard chrome finish, add $35 for Amigo model.

American Classic Trophy Model

Same features as American Classic II except 5.5-inch barrel, dovetail front fiber optic sight, Novak-style rear, ambidextrous safety, reverse plug recoil system with full-length guide rod, beveled mag well, checkered mainspring housing and hard chrome finish.

NIB	Exc.	V.G.	Good	Fair	Poor
650	600	550	500	400	300

American Classic 22 Model

Full-size, alloy-frame 1911-style pistol chambered for .22 LR. Same dimensions as American Classic with military-type sights, checkered wood grips, matte blue finish, two 10-round magazines.

NIB	Exc.	V.G.	Good	Fair	Poor
300	275	230	200	160	100

AMERICAN DERRINGER CORP.
Waco, Texas

MODEL 1 DERRINGER

Fashioned after the Remington O/U derringer this is a high quality, rugged pistol. It is built from high tensile strength stainless steel. There are over 60 different rifle and pistol calibers to choose from on special order. The upper barrel can be chambered different from the lower barrel on request. Available in a high polish finish or a satin finish. Offered with rosewood, bacote, walnut, or blackwood grips. Ivory, bonded ivory, stag, or pearl are available at extra cost. Overall length is 4.8", barrel length is 3", width across the frame is .9", width across the grip is 1.2". Typical weight is 15 oz. in .45 caliber. All guns are furnished with French fitted leatherette case. Prices are determined by caliber.

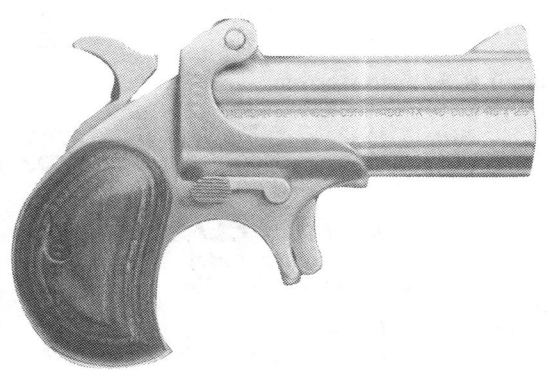

Caliber: .22 Long Rifle through .357 Mag. and .45 ACP

NIB	Exc.	V.G.	Good	Fair	Poor
450	375	300	200	100	75

Calibers: .41 Mag., .44-40, .44 Special, .44 Mag., .45 Long Colt, .410 Bore, .22 Hornet, .223 Rem., 30-30, and .45-70 Gov't.

NIB	Exc.	V.G.	Good	Fair	Poor
500	425	350	250	150	100

NOTE: Premium for rifle cartridges.

MODEL 1 LADY DERRINGER

Similar to the Model 1 but chambered for the .38 Special, .32 Magnum, .45 Colt, or .357 Magnum. Offered in two grades.

Deluxe Grade

High polished stainless steel with scrimshawed ivory grips with cameo or rose design.

NIB	Exc.	V.G.	Good	Fair	Poor
500	425	350	200	100	75

Deluxe Engraved Grade

Same as above but hand engraved in 1880s style.

NIB	Exc.	V.G.	Good	Fair	Poor
650	550	500	450	250	150

NOTE: For .45 Colt and .45/.410 add $75. For .357 magnum add $50.

Model 1 NRA 500 Series

Limited edition of 500. Also available in gold and blue finishes over stainless steel.

NIB	Exc.	V.G.	Good	Fair	Poor
425	350	250	125	100	50

MODEL 1 TEXAS COMMEMORATIVE

Built with a solid brass frame and stainless steel barrel. Dimensions are same as Model 1. Grips are stag or rosewood and offered in .45 Colt, .44-40, or .38 Special. Barrels marked "Made in the 150th Year of Texas Freedom." Limited to 500 pistols in each caliber.

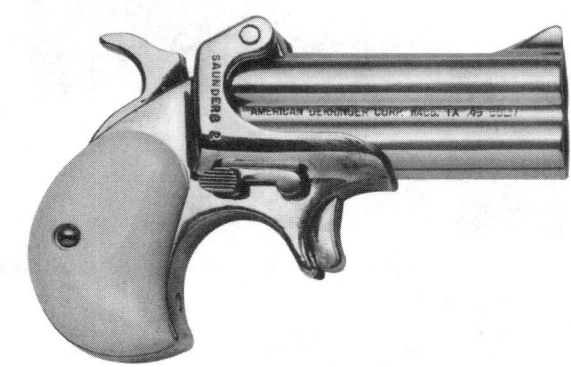

Caliber: .38 Special

NIB	Exc.	V.G.	Good	Fair	Poor
425	350	250	150	100	75

Calibers: .45 Colt and .44-40

NIB	Exc.	V.G.	Good	Fair	Poor
450	375	275	200	125	100

Deluxe Engraved

Special serial number engraved on backstrap.

NIB	Exc.	V.G.	Good	Fair	Poor
700	550	395	350	175	125

MODEL 1 125TH ANNIVERSARY COMMEMORATIVE

Built to commemorate the 125th anniversary of the derringer, 1866 to 1991. Similar to the Model 1 but marked with the patent date December 12, 1865. Brass frame and stainless steel barrel. Chambered for .440-40, .45 Colt, or .38 Special.

NIB	Exc.	V.G.	Good	Fair	Poor
425	350	250	150	100	65

Deluxe Engraved

NIB	Exc.	V.G.	Good	Fair	Poor
650	475	375	250	175	100

Model 2—Pen Pistol

Introduced in 1993 this is a legal pistol that cannot be fired from its pen position but requires that it be pulled apart and bent 80 degrees to fire. Made from stainless steel it is offered in .22 LR, .25 ACP, and .32 ACP. The length in pen form is 5.6" and in pistol form is 4.2". Barrel length is 2". Diameter varies from 1/2" to 5/8". Weight is 5 oz. No longer in production.

NIB	Exc.	V.G.	Good	Fair	Poor
600	395	300	225	100	85

Model 3

This model is a single-barrel derringer. Barrel length is 2.5" and it swings down to load. Frame and barrel are stainless steel. Offered in .38 Special or .32 Magnum. Weighs about 8 oz. Discontinued.

NIB	Exc.	V.G.	Good	Fair	Poor
200	175	115	75	65	50

Model 4

Similar in appearance to the Model 3 but fitted with a 4.1" barrel. Overall length is 6" and weight is about 16.5 oz. Chambered for 3" .410 bore, .45 Long Colt, .44 Magnum, or .357 Magnum.

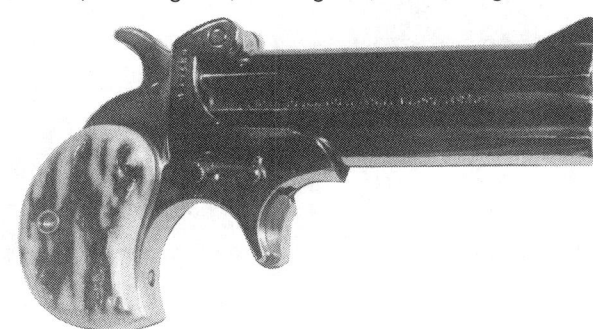

NIB	Exc.	V.G.	Good	Fair	Poor
500	425	350	250	100	75

NOTE: For .45-70 add $150. For .44 magnum add $100.

Model 4 Model 4—Engraved

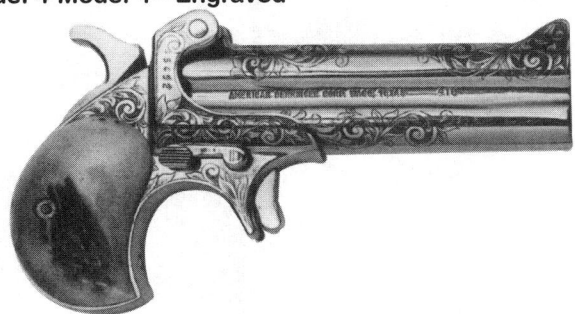

NIB	Exc.	V.G.	Good	Fair	Poor
1000	900	600	400	275	150

Model 4—Alaskan Survival Model

Similar to the Model 4 but with upper barrel chambered for .45-70 and lower barrel for .45 LC or .410. Both barrels can also be chambered for .44 Magnum or .45-70. Comes with oversized rosewood grips.

NIB	Exc.	V.G.	Good	Fair	Poor
700	625	395	250	175	100

Model 6

This double-barrel derringer is fitted with a 6" barrel chambered for the .45 LC or .410 bore. Weighs about 21 oz. Rosewood grips are standard. Optional calibers are .357 Magnum or .45 ACP. Oversize grips are optional and add about $35 to value.

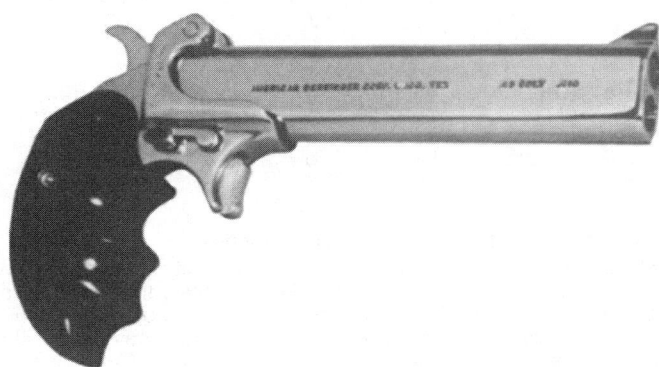

NIB	Exc.	V.G.	Good	Fair	Poor
500	450	350	300	150	100

Model 6—Engraved

NIB	Exc.	V.G.	Good	Fair	Poor
1000	900	700	450	275	150

Double-Action Derringer

High Standard-type double-barrel, double-action derringer is chambered for the .22 LR or .22 Magnum. Its barrel length is 3.5" and overall length is 5.125". Weighs approximately 11 oz. The finish is blue with black grips.

NIB	Exc.	V.G.	Good	Fair	Poor
295	245	175	100	85	75

DA 38 Double-Action Derringer

Similar to above but chambered for .38 Special, .357 Magnum, 9mm Luger, and .40 S&W. Finish is satin stainless. Grip is made from aluminum. Grips are rosewood or walnut.

NIB	Exc.	V.G.	Good	Fair	Poor
400	325	250	200	150	100

NOTE: For .40 S&W add $40.

Cop 4-Shot

Same as above but chambered for the .357 Magnum cartridge.

NIB	Exc.	V.G.	Good	Fair	Poor
1000	900	500	325	175	100

MODEL 7 DERRINGER—LIGHTWEIGHT

Manufactured as a backup gun for police officers. The frame and barrels are made of aircraft aluminum alloy; the other parts are stainless steel. This gun weighs 7.5 oz. Its appearance and function are similar to the Model 1. The finish is a gray matte with thin, matte-finished grips of rosewood or bacote. This model is chambered for and priced as listed.

Model 7 Derringer—Lightweight .32 S&W Long/.32 Magnum

NIB	Exc.	V.G.	Good	Fair	Poor
400	325	250	125	100	75

.38 S&W and .380 ACP

NIB	Exc.	V.G.	Good	Fair	Poor
400	325	250	125	100	75

.22 LR and .38 Special

NIB	Exc.	V.G.	Good	Fair	Poor
400	325	250	125	100	75

44 Special

NIB	Exc.	V.G.	Good	Fair	Poor
525	450	375	300	250	150

Model 8

This is a single-action two-shot target pistol with a manually operated hammer block safety. Safety automatically disengages when the hammer is cocked. Barrel length is 8". Chambered for the .45 Colt and .410 shotshell. Weight is 24 oz.

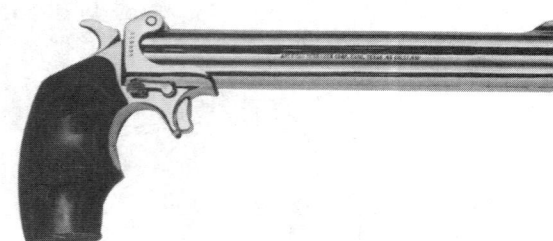

NIB	Exc.	V.G.	Good	Fair	Poor
575	500	425	350	175	100

Model 8—Engraved

NIB	Exc.	V.G.	Good	Fair	Poor
1500	1000	675	450	300	125

Model 10 Derringer

Similar to the Model 1 with a frame of aluminum alloy and all other parts, including the barrels, stainless steel. It has a gray matte finish and thin grips of rosewood or bacote. It weighs 10 oz. and is chambered for the .38 Special, .45 ACP or the .45 Colt.

NIB	Exc.	V.G.	Good	Fair	Poor
400	325	250	125	100	75

NOTE: For .45 Colt add $75.

Model 11 Derringer

A stainless steel barrel and all other parts aluminum. It weighs 11 oz. and is chambered for the .38 Special, .380 Auto, .32 Mag., .22 LR, and .22 Magnum. The grips and finish are the same as on the Model 10.

NIB	Exc.	V.G.	Good	Fair	Poor
400	325	250	125	100	75

Semmerling LM-4

The LM-4 was designed as the ultimate police backup/defense weapon. It is a manually operated, 5-shot repeater only 5.2" long, 3.7" high, and 1" wide. It is chambered for the .45 ACP and is undoubtedly the smallest 5-shot .45 ever produced. The LM-4 is made of a special tool steel and is either blued or, at extra cost, hard chrome-plated. A stainless steel version is also available. The LM-4 is not a semi-automatic, although it physically resembles one. The slide is flicked forward and back after each double-action squeeze of the trigger. This weapon is virtually hand-built and features high visibility sights and a smooth trigger.

NIB	Exc.	V.G.	Good	Fair	Poor
3000	2500	2000	1500	600	200

NOTE: Hard chrome add $200. Stainless steel add 35 percent.

LM-5

Built of stainless steel this semi-auto is chambered for the .32 or .25 Auto. The barrel length is 2.25" and the overall length is 4", height is 3". Wooden grips are standard. Offered in limited quantities. Weight is approximately 15 oz. Discontinued.

NIB	Exc.	V.G.	Good	Fair	Poor
425	350	295	150	100	50

Millennium Series 2000

This model chambered for .38 Special, .45 Colt, or .44-40. Single-action. Fitted with scrimshaw grips with a yellow rose of Texas on the left side and the Lone Star flag on the right side. Weight is about 15 oz. Supplied with red velvet box with silver inlay. Introduced in 1999.

NIB	Exc.	V.G.	Good	Fair	Poor
500	325	200	150	100	75

Gambler Millennium 2000

Similar to the Millennium Series above but fitted with rosewood grips with etched Lone Star of Texas. Supplied with brown leatherette box with copper logo inlay.

NIB	Exc.	V.G.	Good	Fair	Poor
500	325	200	150	100	75

Women of Texas Series

This model has the same features as the Millennium Series 2000. Stamped "Women of Texas Series 2000."

NIB	Exc.	V.G.	Good	Fair	Poor
500	325	200	150	100	75

Cowboy Series 2000

This model has the same features as the Gambler Millennium 2000 but with "Cowboy Series 2000" stamped on the barrel.

NIB	Exc.	V.G.	Good	Fair	Poor
500	325	200	150	100	75

AMERICAN FIRE ARMS MFG. CO., INC.
San Antonio, Texas

This company operated between 1972 and 1974, producing a .25 ACP pocket pistol and a stainless steel .38 Special derringer. A .380 auto was produced on an extremely limited basis.

American .38 Special Derringer

A well-made, stainless steel O/U derringer that was similar in appearance and function to the old Remington O/U. It had 3" barrels that pivoted upward for loading. This gun was a single-action that had an automatic selector and a spur trigger. The smooth grips were of walnut. There were approximately 3,500 manufactured between 1972 and 1974.

NIB	Exc.	V.G.	Good	Fair	Poor
—	300	225	150	125	90

American .25 Automatic

A small, blowback, semi-automatic pocket pistol that was chambered for the .25 ACP cartridge. It had a 2" barrel and was made of either stainless steel or blued carbon steel. The grips were of plain uncheckered walnut, and the detachable magazine held 7 shots. It was manufactured until 1974.

NIB	Exc.	V.G.	Good	Fair	Poor
—	275	200	125	100	75

NOTE: For stainless steel add 20 percent.

American .380 Automatic

Similar to the .25 except larger. The barrel was 3.5", and the gun was made in stainless steel only. The grips were of smooth walnut, and it held 8 shots. There were only 10 of these .380's manufactured between 1972 and 1974. They are extremely rare, but there is little collector base for this company's products, and the value is difficult to estimate.

NIB	Exc.	V.G.	Good	Fair	Poor
—	600	550	475	375	200

AMERICAN FRONTIER FIREARMS
Aguanga, California

1871-72 Open Top Standard Model

Offered in .38 or .44 caliber with non-rebated cylinder. Barrel lengths are 7.5" or 8" in round. Blued finish except silver backstrap and trigger guard. Walnut grips.

NIB	Exc.	V.G.	Good	Fair	Poor
795	625	500	400	225	100

Richards & Mason Conversion 1851 Navy Standard Model

Offered in .38 and .44 calibers with Mason ejector assembly and non-rebated cylinder with a choice of octagon barrels in 4.75", 5.5", or 7.5". Blued finish with blued backstrap and trigger guard. Walnut grips.

NIB	Exc.	V.G.	Good	Fair	Poor
795	625	500	400	225	100

1860 Richards Army Model
Chambered for .44 Colt and .38 caliber. Rebated cylinder with or without ejector assembly. Barrel length is 7.5". High polish blue finish with silver trigger guard and case hardened frame. NOTE: Guns shipped without ejector assembly will be supplied with a ramrod and plunger typical of the period.

NIB	Exc.	V.G.	Good	Fair	Poor
795	625	500	400	225	100

AMERICAN GUN CO., NEW YORK
Norwich, Connecticut
Maker—Crescent Firearms Co.

Knickerbocker Pistol (See Knickerbocker)

AMERICAN INDUSTRIES
Cleveland, Ohio
aka CALICO LIGHT WEAPONS SYSTEMS
Sparks, Nevada

Calico M-100
A semi-automatic carbine that has a 16.1" barrel with a flash suppressor. It is chambered for the .22 LR and features a folding stock, full shrouding hand guards, a 100-round capacity, helical feed, and detachable magazine. It features an ambidextrous safety, pistol grip storage compartment, and a black finished alloy frame and adjustable sights. This model was introduced in 1986.

NIB	Exc.	V.G.	Good	Fair	Poor
500	400	350	250	200	100

Calico M-100P/M-110
Similar to the M-100 .22 rimfire with a 6" barrel with muzzlebrake and no shoulder stock.

NIB	Exc.	V.G.	Good	Fair	Poor
500	400	350	250	200	75

Calico M-950 Pistol
Similar to the Model 900 rifle with a 6" barrel and no shoulder stock.

NIB	Exc.	V.G.	Good	Fair	Poor
750	575	425	350	275	100

AMERICAN WESTERN ARMS INC. (AWA)
Delray Beach, Florida

AWA Lightningbolt
Handgun version of the Lightning rifle with 12-inch barrel and variety of finishes. Chambered in .45 Colt. Values shown are for blued version.

NIB	Exc.	V.G.	Good	Fair	Poor
1000	800	675	500	400	200

AMES, N.P. PISTOLS
Springfield, Massachusetts

Overall length-11-5/8"; barrel length-6"; caliber-.54. Markings: on lockplate, forward of hammer "N.P. AMES/SPRINGFIELD/MASS," on tail, either "USN" or "USR" over date; on barrel, standard U.S. Navy inspection marks. N. P. Ames of Springfield, Massachusetts received a contract from the U.S. Navy in September 1842 for the delivery of 2,000 single-shot muzzleloading percussion pistols. All are distinguished by having a lock mechanism that lies flush with the right side of the stock. On the first 300 Ames pistols, this lock terminates in a point; the balance produced were made with locks with a rounded tail. This "boxlock" had been devised by Henry Nock in England, and was adapted to the U.S. Navy for the percussion pistols they ordered from Ames and Derringer. In addition to the 2,000 pistols for the Navy, the U.S. Revenue Cutter Service purchased 144 (distinguished by the "U S R" marks) for the forerunner of the U.S. Coast Guard. The latter commands triple the price over the "U S N" marked pistols, while the Navy pistols with pointed tails quadruple the value.

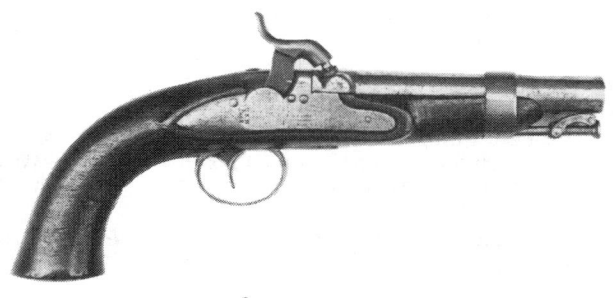

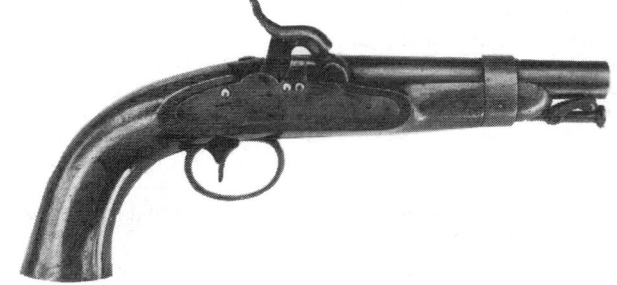

Courtesy Milwaukee Public Museum, Milwaukee, Wisconsin

NIB	Exc.	V.G.	Good	Fair	Poor
—	—	2700	1100	650	400

AMES SWORD CO.
Chicopee Falls, Massachusetts

Turbiaux Le Protector
Ames Sword Co. became one of three U.S. companies that produced this unique, French palm-squeezer pistol. The design consists of a round disk with a protruding barrel on one side and a lever on the other. The disk contains the cylinder that holds either seven 8mm rimfire or ten 6mm rimfire cartridges. The barrel protrudes between the fingers, and the lever trigger is squeezed to fire the weapon. The design was patented in 1883 and sold successfully in France into the 1890s. In 1892 Peter Finnegan bought the patents and brought them to Ames Sword. He contracted with them to produce 25,000 pistols for the Minneapolis Firearms Company. After approximately 1,500 were delivered, Finnegan declared insolvency, and after litigation, Ames secured the full patent rights. The Ames Company produced Protector Revolvers until at least 1917. (See Chicago Firearms Co. and Minneapolis Firearms Co.)

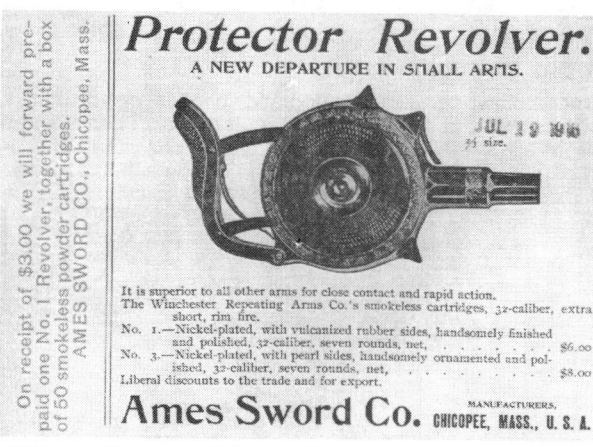

NIB	Exc.	V.G.	Good	Fair	Poor
—	—	3500	1800	900	550

AMT
formerly Arcadia Machine and Tool
Irwindale, California
See also—Galena Industries Inc.

AMT, one of several companies that succeeded Auto Mag Corp., the original manufacturer of Auto Mag pistols, operated from approx. 1984 to 1998. The prices in this section are for these earlier AMT-built guns. In 1998, Galena Ind. of Sturgis, SD purchased the rights to produce most of the AMT-developed firearms and manufactured several models from 1999 to 2001. In 2005, the rights to several AMT models were acquired by Crusader Gun Co. of Houston, parent company of High Standard Mfg. Co. Also see listing for Auto Mag.

Lightning

A single-action, semi-automatic .22 caliber pistol. Available with barrel lengths of 5" (Bull only), 6.5", 8.5", 10.5" and 12.5" (either Bull or tapered), and adjustable sights, as well as the trigger. The grips are checkered black rubber. Manufactured between 1984 and 1987.

Courtesy John J. Stimson, Jr.

NIB	Exc.	V.G.	Good	Fair	Poor
—	450	350	215	125	85

Bull's Eye Regulation Target

As above, with a 6.5" vent rib bull barrel, wooden target grips, and an extended rear sight. Manufactured in 1986 only.

NIB	Exc.	V.G.	Good	Fair	Poor
—	475	375	250	200	100

Baby Automag

Similar to the above with an 8.5" ventilated rib barrel, and Millett adjustable sights. Approximately 1,000 were manufactured.

Courtesy J.B. Wood

NIB	Exc.	V.G.	Good	Fair	Poor
—	600	450	375	225	150

Automag II

A stainless steel, semi-automatic .22 Magnum pistol. Available with 3-3/8", 4.5", and 6" barrel lengths and Millett adjustable sights, grips of black, grooved, plastic. Was first manufactured in 1987.

Courtesy J.B. Wood

NIB	Exc.	V.G.	Good	Fair	Poor
600	500	400	300	100	80

Automag III

This semi-automatic pistol is chambered for the .30 Carbine cartridge and the 9mm Winchester Magnum cartridge. Barrel length is 6.37" and overall length is 10.5". The magazine capacity is 8 rounds. Fitted with Millett adjustable rear sight and carbon fiber grips. Stainless steel finish. Pistol weighs 43 oz.

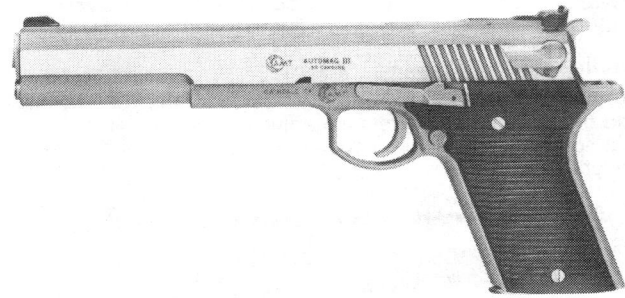

NIB	Exc.	V.G.	Good	Fair	Poor
800	695	475	275	100	80

Automag IV

Similar in appearance to the Automag III this pistol is chambered for the .45 Winchester Magnum. Magazine capacity is 7 rounds and weight is 46 oz.

NIB	Exc.	V.G.	Good	Fair	Poor
995	800	650	375	225	100

Automag V

Introduced in 1993 this model is similar in appearance to the Automag models but is chambered for the .50 caliber cartridge. A limited production run of 3000 pistols with special serial number from "1 of 3000 to 3000 of 3000." Barrel length is 6.5" and magazine capacity is 5 rounds. Weighs 46 oz. Production stopped in 1995. Add $300 each for extra conversion barrels in .45 WM or 10mm.

Courtesy J.B. Wood

NIB	Exc.	V.G.	Good	Fair	Poor
1300	800	600	500	400	150

Javelina

Produced in 1992 this pistol is chambered for the 10mm cartridge and fitted with a 7" barrel with adjustable sights. Rubber wrap-around grips. Adjustable trigger. Magazine is 8 rounds. Weight is about 47 oz.

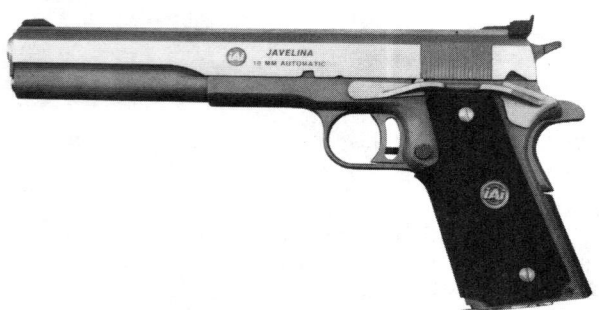

Courtesy J.B. Wood

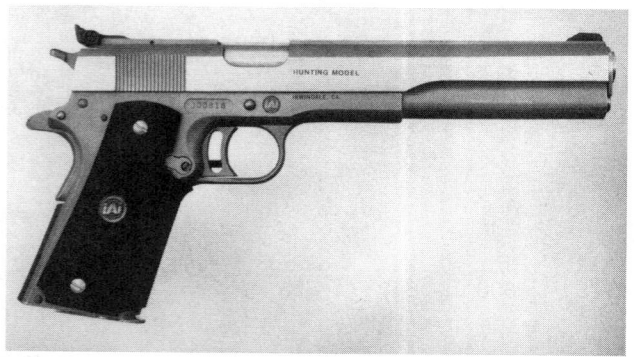

Courtesy J.B. Wood

NIB	Exc.	V.G.	Good	Fair	Poor
1150	950	675	495	—	—

Back Up Pistol

This is a small semi-automatic pocket pistol chambered for the .22 LR or the .380 ACP cartridges. This is fitted with a 2.5" barrel and is offered with either black plastic or walnut grips. The pistol weighs 18 oz. Magazine capacity is 5 rounds. Originally manufactured by TDE, then Irwindale Arms Inc., and then by AMT.

NIB	Exc.	V.G.	Good	Fair	Poor
450	325	175	125	100	85

Back Up .45 ACP, .40 S&W, 9mm

Courtesy J.B. Wood

NIB	Exc.	V.G.	Good	Fair	Poor
465	350	200	150	100	85

Back Up .38 Super, .357 SIG, .400 CorBon

NIB	Exc.	V.G.	Good	Fair	Poor
475	360	250	200	150	100

NOTE: These prices are for current production by High Standard Mfg. Co.

.380 Back Up II

Introduced in 1993 this pistol is similar to the Back Up model but with the addition of a double safety, extended finger grip on the magazine, and single-action-only. This was a special order pistol only.

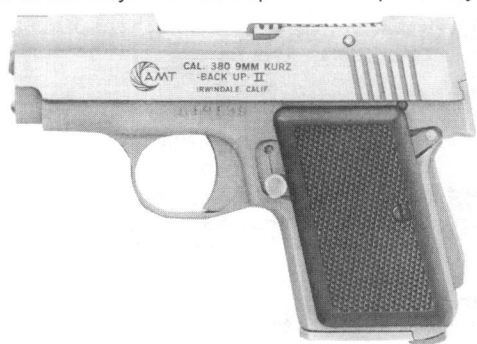

NIB	Exc.	V.G.	Good	Fair	Poor
425	300	250	200	150	100

HARDBALLER/GOVERNMENT MODEL

This model is similar to the Colt Gold Cup .45 ACP. It is offered in two versions. The first has fixed sights and rounded slide top, while the second has adjustable Millett sights and matte rib. Magazine capacity is 7 rounds. Wraparound rubber grips are standard. Long grip safety, beveled magazine well, and adjustable trigger are common to both variations. Weight is 38 oz.

Hardballer

Adjustable sights.

Courtesy J.B. Wood

NIB	Exc.	V.G.	Good	Fair	Poor
600	500	350	275	200	125

Government Model

Fixed sights.

NIB	Exc.	V.G.	Good	Fair	Poor
575	475	300	250	150	100

Hardballer Longslide

Similar to the Hardballer Model but fitted with a 7" barrel. Magazine capacity is 7 rounds. Pistol weighs 46 oz.

NIB	Exc.	V.G.	Good	Fair	Poor
750	550	395	275	200	125

.400 Accelerator

Similar to the models above but chambered for .400 CorBon cartridge and fitted with a 7" barrel. Fully adjustable sights. Introduced in 1997.

NIB	Exc.	V.G.	Good	Fair	Poor
600	500	350	275	200	125

Commando

Built on a Government model-type action and chambered for .40 S&W cartridge. Fitted with a 5" barrel and fully adjustable sights. Introduced in 1997.

NIB	Exc.	V.G.	Good	Fair	Poor
550	425	300	200	125	75

On Duty

This semi-automatic pistol features a double-action-only trigger action or double-action with decocker and is chambered for the 9mm, .40 S&W, or .45 ACP calibers. Barrel length is 4.5" and overall length is 7.75". The finish is a black anodized matte. Carbon fiber grips are standard. Furnished with 3-dot sights. Weighs 32 oz.

NIB	Exc.	V.G.	Good	Fair	Poor
450	350	250	200	150	100

Skipper

Identical to the Hardballer with a 1" shorter barrel and slide. Discontinued in 1984.

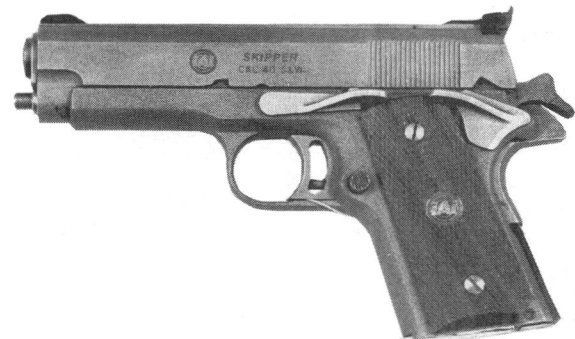

NIB	Exc.	V.G.	Good	Fair	Poor
—	450	325	275	200	125

Combat Skipper

Similar to the Colt Commander. Discontinued in 1984.

NIB	Exc.	V.G.	Good	Fair	Poor
—	425	300	250	200	125

ANCION MARX
Liege, Belgium

This company began production in the 1860s with a variety of cheaply made pinfire revolvers. They later switched to solid-frame, centerfire, "Velo-Dog" -type revolvers chambered for 5.5mm or 6.35mm. They were marketed in various countries under many different trade names. Some of the names that they will be found under are Cobalt, Extracteur, LeNovo, Lincoln, and Milady. The quality of these revolvers is quite poor; and collector interest, almost non-existent. Values do not usually vary because of trade names.

NIB	Exc.	V.G.	Good	Fair	Poor
—	—	200	135	75	45

ANDERSON
Anderson, Texas

Anderson Under Hammer Pistol

An unmarked, under hammer percussion pistol that was chambered for .45 caliber. It had a 5" half-round/half-octagonal barrel with an all steel, saw handle-shaped frame. It had a flared butt with walnut grips. The finish was blued. There is little information on this pistol.

NIB	Exc.	V.G.	Good	Fair	Poor
—	—	900	400	150	100

ANDRUS & OSBORN
Canton, Connecticut

Andrus & Osborn Under Hammer Pistol

This pistol is of the percussion type and chambered for .25 caliber. The part-round/part-octagonal barrel is 6" long and features small silver star inlays along its length. The barrel is marked "Andrus & Osborn/Canton Conn." with an eagle stamped beside it. It is marked "Cast Steel" near the breech. The grips are of walnut, and the finish is browned. Active 1863 to 1867.

NIB	Exc.	V.G.	Good	Fair	Poor
—	—	1550	625	200	100

ANSCHUTZ
Ulm, Germany

Orginally founded in 1856 by Julius and Lusie Anschutz, the company was called J.G. Anschutz, and manufactured a wide variety of firearms. In 1950, in Ulm, the new company was founded: J.G. Anschutz GmbH. Values for new guns fluctuate according to currency variations.

Model 64P

Bolt-action pistol with adjustable trigger. The action is grooved for scope mounts, and the stock is synthetic. Barrel length is 10" and is chambered for .22 LR cartridge. Weight is approximately 3 lb. 8 oz. Introduced in 1998.

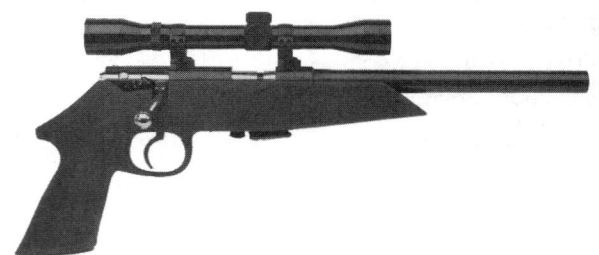

NIB	Exc.	V.G.	Good	Fair	Poor
595	500	450	250	175	75

Model 64P Mag

Same as model above but chambered for .22 WMR cartridge.

NIB	Exc.	V.G.	Good	Fair	Poor
650	525	475	275	175	75

Exemplar

A bolt-action pistol that is built on the Model 64 Match Action. It is chambered for the .22 LR cartridge and has a 10" barrel with adjustable sights and a 5-shot, detachable magazine. It features an adjustable two-stage trigger with the receiver grooved for attaching a scope. The walnut stock and forend are stippled. It was introduced in 1987.

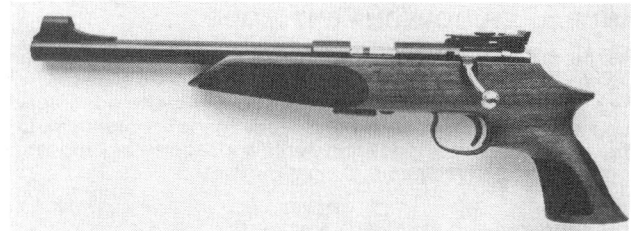

NIB	Exc.	V.G.	Good	Fair	Poor
700	600	500	225	175	100

Exemplar XIV

Similar to the standard Exemplar with a 14" barrel. It was introduced in 1988.

NIB	Exc.	V.G.	Good	Fair	Poor
800	700	600	250	200	100

ANTI GARROTTER
England

Percussion belt pistol, marked "Balls Pat. Steel." Oval is 7" long and the barrel protrudes 1-1/2"; approximately .45 caliber. A cord runs from the lock up and through the sleeve and is fired by pulling the cord. Beware of modern fakes.

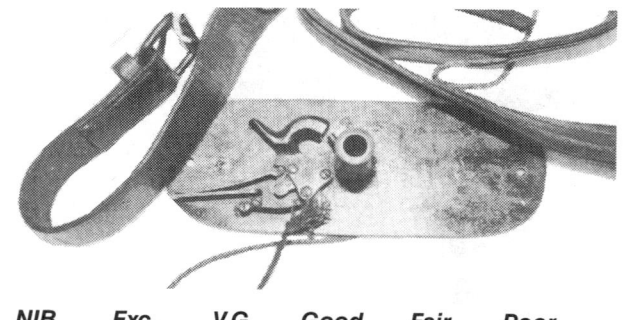

NIB	Exc.	V.G.	Good	Fair	Poor
—	—	7500	3000	800	400

APALOZO HERMANOS
Zumorraga, Spain

Spanish manufacturer from approximately 1920 to 1936. The trademark, a dove-like bird, is normally found impressed into the grips.

Apaloza

Copy of a Colt Police Positive Revolver.

NIB	Exc.	V.G.	Good	Fair	Poor
—	275	150	100	65	45

Paramount

Copy of the Model 1906 Browning chambered for 6.35mm. "Paramount" is stamped on the slide and at the top of each grip plate.

Courtesy James Rankin

NIB	Exc.	V.G.	Good	Fair	Poor
—	275	175	100	50	30

Triomphe

A copy of the Browning Model 1906 in caliber 6.35mm. The slide is inscribed "Pistolet Automatique Triomphe Acier Comprime." Cal. 6.35mm is stamped on each grip plate along with the dove logo.

Courtesy James Rankin

NIB	Exc.	V.G.	Good	Fair	Poor
—	275	175	100	50	30

ARCUS
Bulgaria

Arcus-94

Introduced in 1998 this is a semi-automatic pistol chambered for the 9mm cartridge. Fitted with an ambidextrous safety and 10-round magazine. Imported from Bulgaria.

NIB	Exc.	V.G.	Good	Fair	Poor
425	325	275	200	150	100

ARIZAGA, G.
Eibar, Spain

Spanish manufacturer prior to World War II.

Arizaga (Model 1915)

A 7.65mm semi-automatic pistol. Patterned after the Ruby-style military pistols. Magazine capacity is 9 or 12 rounds. Wood grips.

NIB	Exc.	V.G.	Good	Fair	Poor
—	275	195	100	75	45

Mondial

Similar design to the Astra pistol in the 100 series. Chambered for the 6.35mm cartridge. It has the Owl and Mondial on each grip plate.

NIB	Exc.	V.G.	Good	Fair	Poor
—	300	190	145	75	45

Pinkerton

Arizaga's standard model known to exist with a cartridge counter. Slide is marked "Pinkerton Automatic 6.35."

NIB	Exc.	V.G.	Good	Fair	Poor
—	295	175	100	75	45

Warwick

Same design as the Mondial but in caliber 7.65mm. Warwick appears on each grip plate.

NIB	Exc.	V.G.	Good	Fair	Poor
—	300	190	145	75	45

ARIZMENDI, FRANCISCO
Eibar, Spain

Originally founded in the 1890s, the company was reformed in 1914 and manufactured semi-automatic pistols.

SINGER

The Singer was manufactured in a number of different variations and in calibers 6.35mm and 7.65mm. It was earlier called the Victor. The 6.35mm models resembled the Browning 1906. The 7.65mm model resembled the Browning Model 1910.

6.35mm

Courtesy James Rankin

NIB	Exc.	V.G.	Good	Fair	Poor
—	225	195	100	50	35

7.65mm

Courtesy James Rankin

NIB	Exc.	V.G.	Good	Fair	Poor
—	175	125	75	50	35

TEUF TEUF

The Teuf Teuf was chambered in calibers 6.35mm and 7.65mm. The 7.65mm was only slightly larger than the 6.35mm model. The pistol copied its name from the Browning Model 1906 and from the Belgium Teuf Teuf. The pistol shown is a cartridge indicator model.

Courtesy James Rankin

6.35mm

NIB	Exc.	V.G.	Good	Fair	Poor
—	225	195	100	50	35

7.65mm

NIB	Exc.	V.G.	Good	Fair	Poor
—	225	195	100	50	35

WALMAN

The Walman was manufactured in a number of variations, and in calibers 6.35mm, 7.65mm, and .380. Earliest semi-automatic production was in 1908 through 1926. Certain variations were called the American Model. The model in .380 caliber had a squeeze grip safety.

6.35mm

Courtesy James Rankin

NIB	Exc.	V.G.	Good	Fair	Poor
—	225	195	100	50	35

7.65mm

Courtesy James Rankin

NIB	Exc.	V.G.	Good	Fair	Poor
—	250	200	125	60	35

.380

Courtesy James Rankin

NIB	Exc.	V.G.	Good	Fair	Poor
260	225	145	60	35	

Arizmendi

Solid-frame, folding-trigger revolver chambered for 7.65mm or .32 caliber. Normal markings are the trademark "FA" and a circled five-pointed star.

NIB	Exc.	V.G.	Good	Fair	Poor
—	200	150	80	50	25

BOLTUN—1ST VARIATION

The Bolton semi-automatic pistol was made in both calibers 6.35mm and 7.65mm. It was almost an exact copy of the Belgian Pieper. The 7.65mm model was only slightly larger than the 6.35mm model.

6.35mm

NIB	Exc.	V.G.	Good	Fair	Poor
—	250	195	125	60	35

7.65mm

NIB	Exc.	V.G.	Good	Fair	Poor
—	250	195	125	60	35

Boltun—2nd Variation

The Boltun 2nd variation is chambered for the 7.65mm cartridge and is almost an exact copy of the Browning Model 1910. It was made into the 1930s.

NIB	Exc.	V.G.	Good	Fair	Poor
—	250	195	125	60	35

ROLAND

Chambered for 6.35 and 7.65mm cartridges, this model was manufactured during the 1920s. The 7.65mm was only slightly larger than the 6.35mm model.

Courtesy James Rankin

6.35mm

NIB	Exc.	V.G.	Good	Fair	Poor
—	250	150	90	60	35

7.65mm

NIB	Exc.	V.G.	Good	Fair	Poor
—	250	150	90	60	35

Puppy

A variation of the "Velo-Dog" revolver with the barrel stamped "Puppy" and the frame bearing the "FA" trademark.

NIB	Exc.	V.G.	Good	Fair	Poor
—	250	195	125	60	35

Pistolet Automatique

Normal markings include the "FA" trademark.

NIB	Exc.	V.G.	Good	Fair	Poor
—	250	195	125	60	35

Kaba Spezial

A 6.35mm semi-automatic pistol patterned after the Browning Model 1906. The Kaba Spezial was originally made by August Menz of Suhl, Germany and sold by Karl Bauer of Berlin, Germany. The name "Kaba" was derived from the first two initials of Karl Bauer. These two pistols do not look alike.

Courtesy James Rankin

NIB	Exc.	V.G.	Good	Fair	Poor
—	275	150	100	50	35

YDEAL

The Ydeal was manufactured in four variations and in calibers 6.35mm, 7.65mm, and .380. All four variations resemble the Browning Model 1906, with the 7.65mm and .380 caliber being slightly larger.

Courtesy James Rankin

6.35mm

NIB	Exc.	V.G.	Good	Fair	Poor
—	225	175	100	60	35

7.65mm

NIB	Exc.	V.G.	Good	Fair	Poor
—	225	175	100	60	35

.380

NIB	Exc.	V.G.	Good	Fair	Poor
—	225	175	100	60	35

ARIZMENDI ZULAICA
Eibar, Spain

Cebra

A semi-automatic 7.65mm pistol patterned after the Ruby-style of Spanish automatics. The slide is marked "Pistolet Automatique

Cebra Zulaica Eibar," together with the letters "AZ" in an oval. Generally found with checkered wood grips.

Courtesy James Rankin

NIB	Exc.	V.G.	Good	Fair	Poor
—	250	150	100	50	35

Cebra Revolver

Copy of a Colt Police Positive revolver marked "Made in Spain" with the word "Cebra" cast in the grips.

NIB	Exc.	V.G.	Good	Fair	Poor
—	250	150	125	75	50

ARMALITE, INC.
Costa Mesa, California
Geneseo, Illinois (current production)

In 1995 Eagle Arms purchased the Armalite trademark and certain other assets. The new companies are organized under the Armalite name. The original company, formed in the mid 1950s, developed the AR-10, which in turn led to the development of the M-16 series of service rifles still in use today. All current models are produced at the Geneseo, Illinois, facility.

AR-24 Pistol

15-shot 9mm double-action semi-auto. Steel frame, fixed or adjustable sights. Compact version available. Introduced 2006. Pricing is for full-size pistol with adjustable sights. Deduct 15 percent for fixed sight versions.

NIB	Exc.	V.G.	Good	Fair	Poor
595	450	325	275	200	125

AR-24 Tactical Custom

Similar to above with tactical refinements including stippled front

and back straps, 3-dot luminous sights, etc. Also available in compact version (shown).

NIB	Exc.	V.G.	Good	Fair	Poor
630	475	350	300	225	150

ARMERO ESPECIALISTAS
Eibar, Spain

Alfa

"Alfa" was a trademark given a number of revolvers based upon both Colt and Smith & Wesson designs in calibers ranging from .22 to .44. Add 50 percent for S&W N-frame copies.

NIB	Exc.	V.G.	Good	Fair	Poor
—	250	200	100	75	50

Omega

A semi-automatic 6.35 or 7.65mm pistol marked "Omega" on the slide and grips.

NIB	Exc.	V.G.	Good	Fair	Poor
—	225	175	100	75	50

ARMINEX LTD.
Scottsdale, Arizona

Tri-Fire

A semi-automatic pistol chambered for 9mm, .38 Super or .45 ACP cartridges. Available with conversion units that add approximately $130 if in excellent condition. Fitted with 5", 6", or 7" stainless steel barrels. Presentation cases were available at an extra cost of $48. Approximately 250 were manufactured from 1981 to 1985.

Courtesy James Rankin

NIB	Exc.	V.G.	Good	Fair	Poor
1300	975	600	300	175	100

Target Model

As above with a 6" or 7" barrel.

Courtesy James Rankin

NIB	Exc.	V.G.	Good	Fair	Poor
1350	1000	650	350	225	100

ARMITAGE INTERNATIONAL, LTD.
Seneca, South Carolina

Scarab Skorpion

A blowback-operated, semi-automatic pistol, patterned after the Czechoslovakian Scorpion submachine gun. Chambered for the 9mm cartridge with a 4.6" barrel having military-type sights. Fitted with a 32-round, detachable box magazine. The standard finish is matte black and the grips are plastic.

NIB	Exc.	V.G.	Good	Fair	Poor
650	550	400	300	175	100

ARMSCORP OF AMERICA
Baltimore, Maryland

Hi-Power

An Argentine-made version of the Browning semi-automatic pistol chambered for 9mm with a 4.75" barrel. Matte finished with checkered synthetic grips. Introduced in 1989.

NIB	Exc.	V.G.	Good	Fair	Poor
450	350	300	250	200	100

Detective HP—Compact

As above with a 3.5" barrel.

NIB	Exc.	V.G.	Good	Fair	Poor
475	375	350	275	200	100

P22

A copy of the Colt Woodsman .22 caliber semi-automatic pistol available with either 4" or 6" barrels and a 10-shot magazine. Finish blued, grips of checkered hardwood. Introduced in 1989.

NIB	Exc.	V.G.	Good	Fair	Poor
250	150	125	100	75	50

SD9

An Israeli-made 9mm double-action semi-automatic pistol with a 3" barrel. Assembled extensively from sheet metal stampings. Loaded chamber indicator and 6-round magazine. This model is also known as the Sirkus SD9 manufactured by Sirkus Industries in Israel. Introduced in 1989.

Courtesy Jim Rankin

NIB	Exc.	V.G.	Good	Fair	Poor
300	250	200	150	100	75

Armscor/Rock Island Armory 1911A1-45 FS GI

1911-style semiauto pistol chambered in .45 ACP (8 rounds) , 9mm Parabellum, .38 Super (9 rounds). Features include checkered plastic or hardwood grips, 5-inch barrel, parkerized steel frame and slide, drift adjustable sights. MSRP: N/A.

Armscor/Rock Island Armory 1911A1-45 CS GI

1911-style Officer\qs-size semiauto pistol chambered in .45 ACP. Features plain hardwood grips, 3.5-inch barrel, parkerized steel frame and slide, drift adjustable sights. MSRP: N/A.

ARMS CORPORATION OF THE PHILIPPINES
Armscor Precision
Marikina City, Philippines

Armscor Precision is an importer of a variety of firearms made in the Philippines.

Model M100

A double-action, swing-out cylinder revolver chambered for .22, .22 Magnum, and the .38 Special cartridges. Has a 4" ventilated rib barrel. Six-shot cylinder and adjustable sights. Blued with checkered mahogany grips. No longer in production.

NIB	Exc.	V.G.	Good	Fair	Poor
200	175	150	110	80	50

Model 200P

Introduced in 1990 this 6-shot revolver is chambered for the .38 Special cartridge. It is fitted with a 4" barrel, fixed sights and wood or rubber grips. Weighs about 26 ozs.

NIB	Exc.	V.G.	Good	Fair	Poor
180	150	125	100	85	60

Model 200TC

Introduced in 1990 this model is similar to above but is fitted with adjustable sights and checkered wood grips. Weight is about 28 oz.

NIB	Exc.	V.G.	Good	Fair	Poor
200	175	150	125	100	75

Model 200DC

Similar to the Model 200P but fitted with a 2.5" barrel. Weight is about 22 oz.

NIB	Exc.	V.G.	Good	Fair	Poor
175	150	125	100	85	60

Model 201S

Similar to the Model 200P but in stainless steel.

NIB	Exc.	V.G.	Good	Fair	Poor
200	175	150	125	100	75

Model 202

Chambered for the 38 Special cartridge this 6-shot revolver is fitted with a 4" barrel and fixed sights. Blued finish. Weight is about 27 oz.

NIB	Exc.	V.G.	Good	Fair	Poor
150	120	95	75	50	25

Model 206

Similar to the Model 202 but with a 2.88" barrel. Weight is about 25 oz.

NIB	Exc.	V.G.	Good	Fair	Poor
180	140	110	75	50	25

Model 210

Same as the Model 202 but with adjustable sights. Weight is about 27 oz.

NIB	Exc.	V.G.	Good	Fair	Poor
200	150	125	75	50	25

MAP1 FS

Single/double-action 9mm semi-auto with 16+1 capacity. Fixed sights, 4.45" barrel, 40.5 oz. nickel alloy steel frame and slide. (Shorter, lighter MS model has 3.66" barrel.) Introduced 2006.

NIB	Exc.	V.G.	Good	Fair	Poor
—	350	300	200	125	75

MAPP1 FS

Single/double-action 9mm semi-auto with 16+1 capacity. Fixed sights, 4.45" barrel, 40.5 oz. polymer frame with integrated accessory rail, and nickel alloy steel slide. (Shorter, lighter MS model has 3.66" barrel.) Introduced 2006.

NIB	Exc.	V.G.	Good	Fair	Poor
—	350	300	200	175	75

Model 1911-A1

A semi-automatic pistol similar in design to the Colt Model 1911 pistol. Chambered for the .45 ACP cartridge and fitted with a 5" barrel. Blued finish. Magazine capacity is 8 rounds. Weight is about 39 oz. Also sold under the Charles Daly name.

NIB	Exc.	V.G.	Good	Fair	Poor
500	400	300	200	150	75

Model 1911-A2

Same as above but fitted with a double column magazine with a 13-round capacity. Weight is approximately 43 oz.

NIB	Exc.	V.G.	Good	Fair	Poor
600	500	375	250	195	110

NOTE: For two-tone finish add $100. For chrome finish add $130.

AROSTEGUI, EULOGIO
Eibar, Spain

Azul Royal (Model 31)

A semi-automatic or full automatic pistol in calibers 7.63 Mauser, 9mm Bergmann, or 38 ACP. Manufactured between 1935 and 1940. Fitted with a 10-round integral magazine.

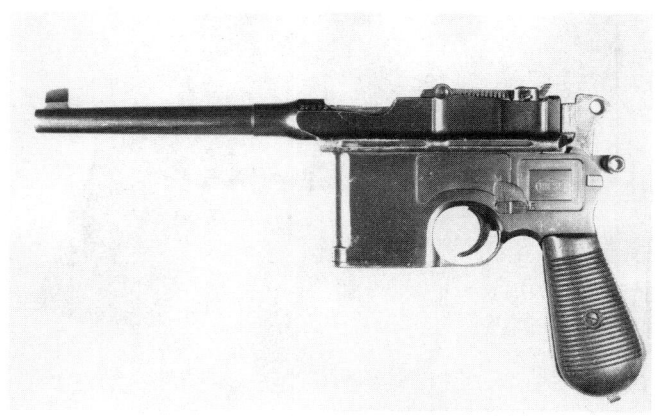

Courtesy James Rankin

NIB	Exc.	V.G.	Good	Fair	Poor
—	3000	2500	1000	500	300

NOTE: Add 300 percent for fully automatic machine pistol version.

Super Azul (M-34)

A semi-automatic or full automatic pistol in 7.63mm Mauser, 9mm Bergmann, and .38 ACP. Manufactured between 1935 and 1940. It has a removable box magazine with capacity of 10, 20, or 30 rounds. Also known as the War Model or the Standard Model.

Courtesy James Rankin

NIB	Exc.	V.G.	Good	Fair	Poor
—	3000	2500	1000	500	300

NOTE: Add 300 percent for fully automatic machine pistol version.

Azul 6.35mm

A 6.35mm semi-automatic pistol copied after the Model 1906 Browning. The frame is marked with the letters "EA" in a circle and a retriever is molded in the grips. Magazine capacity is 6 or 9 rounds.

NIB	Exc.	V.G.	Good	Fair	Poor
—	250	200	150	100	75

Azul 7.65mm

A 7.65mm semi-automatic pistol copied after the Model 1910 FN. Magazine capacity is 7 or 9 rounds.

NIB	Exc.	V.G.	Good	Fair	Poor
—	250	200	150	100	75

Velo-Dog

A folding trigger 5.5mm or 6.35mm revolver bearing the trademark "EA" on the grips.

NIB	Exc.	V.G.	Good	Fair	Poor
—	175	100	75	50	30

ARRIZABALAGA, HIJOS de C.
Eibar, Spain

Arrizabalaga

A 7.65mm semi-automatic pistol with a 9-shot magazine and a lanyard ring fitted to the butt. Checkered wood grips. ARRIZABALAGA on the slide.

Courtesy James Rankin

NIB	Exc.	V.G.	Good	Fair	Poor
—	275	175	125	75	50

Campeon

The Model 1919 6.35mm, 7.65mm, or 9mm Kurtz semi-automatic pistol with the slide marked "Campeon Patent 1919" and the plastic grips "Campeon." Supplied with 6- or 8-round magazines. "CAMPEON" appears on the slide.

Courtesy James Rankin

NIB	Exc.	V.G.	Good	Fair	Poor
—	325	275	195	75	50

NOTE: Add 25 percent for 9mm Kurtz.

Jo Lo Ar

The Model 1924 semi-automatic pistol with a tip-up barrel, cocking lever, and no trigger guard. The Jo Lo Ar was built in six calibers: 6.35mm, 7.65mm, 9mm Kurtz, 9mm Largo, and .45 ACP. Jo-Lo-Ar appears on the slide and the grips. Premium for larger calibers. Add 400 percent for .45.

Courtesy James Rankin

NIB	Exc.	V.G.	Good	Fair	Poor
—	1100	925	800	450	200

Sharpshooter

A 6.35mm, 7.65mm or 9mm Corto (short) semi-automatic pistol fitted with a cocking lever. The barrel tips up for cleaning or when using the pistol as a single-shot. "SHARPSHOOTER" appears on the slide.

Courtesy James Rankin

NIB	Exc.	V.G.	Good	Fair	Poor
—	400	300	225	150	100

ASCASO
Cataluna, Spain

Spanish Rebublican Government

A copy of the Astra Model 400 chambered for the 9mm Largo cartridge. The barrel marked "F. Ascaso Tarrassa" in an oval. Built by the Spanish government during the Spanish Civil War. Very few were made during the Spanish Civil War.

Courtesy James Rankin

NIB	Exc.	V.G.	Good	Fair	Poor
—	850	750	550	300	200

ASHTON, PETER & WILLIAM
Middletown, Connecticut

Under Hammer Pistol

A .28 to .38 caliber single-shot percussion revolver with 4" or 5" half-octagonal barrels marked "P.H. Ashton" or "W. Ashton." Blued or browned with walnut grips. Active 1850s.

NIB	Exc.	V.G.	Good	Fair	Poor
—	—	1100	500	200	100

ASTON, H./H. ASTON & CO. PISTOLS
Middleton, Connecticut

Overall length 14"; barrel length 8-1/2"; caliber .54. Markings: on lockplate, forward of hammer "U S/H. ASTON" or "U S/H. ASTON & CO.," on tail "MIDDTN/CONN/(date)" ; on barrel, standard government inspection marks. Henry Aston of Middleton, Connecticut received a contract from the U.S. War Department in February 1845 for 30,000 single-shot percussion pistols. These were delivered between 1846 and 1852, after which Ira N. Johnston continued production under a separate contract. Three thousand of these pistols were purchased for Navy usage and many of these were subsequently marked with a small anchor on the barrel near the breech. These Navy purchases will command a slight premium.

Courtesy Milwaukee Public Museum, Milwaukee, Wisconsin

NIB	Exc.	V.G.	Good	Fair	Poor
—	—	4700	4500	1750	500

ASTRA-UNCETA SA
Guernica, Spain

Astra is a brand name placed on guns built by Esperanza y Unceta and then Unceta y Cia. This Spanish company has now incorporated its trade name into its corporate name and is now know as Astra-Unceta SA. The firm under the direction of Don Pedron Unceta and Don Juan Esperanza began business in Eibar on July 17, 1908 and moved to Guernica in 1913. The Astra trademark was adopted on November 25, 1914. Esperanza began production of the Spanish Army's Campo Giro pistol in 1913. The Model 1921 was marketed commercially as the Astra 400. After the Spanish Civil War Unceta was one of only four handgun companies permitted to resume manufacturing operations. An interesting and informative side note is that pistols with 1000 to 5000 model numbers were made after 1945. Astra merged with Star before going out of business in 2006. The Astra name is planned to be resurrected as a Spanish concern.

Victoria

A 6.35mm semi-automatic pistol with a 2.5" barrel. Blued with black plastic grips. Manufactured prior to 1913.

NIB	Exc.	V.G.	Good	Fair	Poor
—	300	250	200	150	100

Astra 1911

A 6.35mm and 7.65mm semi-automatic pistol. External hammer and checkered hard rubber grips. The 7.65mm model was manufactured before the 6.35mm model.

Courtesy James Rankin

NIB	Exc.	V.G.	Good	Fair	Poor
—	375	275	175	100	75

Astra 1924

A 6.35mm semi-automatic pistol with a 2.5" barrel. The slide marked "Esperanza y Unceta Guernica Spain Astra Cal 6.35 .25." Blued with black plastic grips.

NIB	Exc.	V.G.	Good	Fair	Poor
—	300	200	125	100	75

Astra 100 (Old Model)

A semi-automatic pistol in caliber 7.65mm. Checkered hard rubber grips. Magazine capacity is 12 rounds. Introduced after WWII.

Courtesy James Rankin

NIB	Exc.	V.G.	Good	Fair	Poor
—	550	400	300	200	100

Astra 200

A 6.35mm semi-automatic pistol with a 2.5" barrel and 6-shot magazine fitted with a grip safety. Also known as the "Firecat" in the United States. Manufactured from 1920 to 1966. Add 25 percent for factory engraving.

Courtesy James Rankin

NIB	Exc.	V.G.	Good	Fair	Poor
—	300	200	125	100	75

Astra 400 or Model 1921

A 9x23 Bergman (9mm Largo)caliber semi-automatic pistol with a 6" barrel. Blued with black plastic grips. This model was adopted for use by the Spanish Army. Approximately 106,000 were made prior to 1946. Recent importation has depressed the price of these guns. Any with Nazi proofs marks are worth a 100 percent premium, but caution is advised.

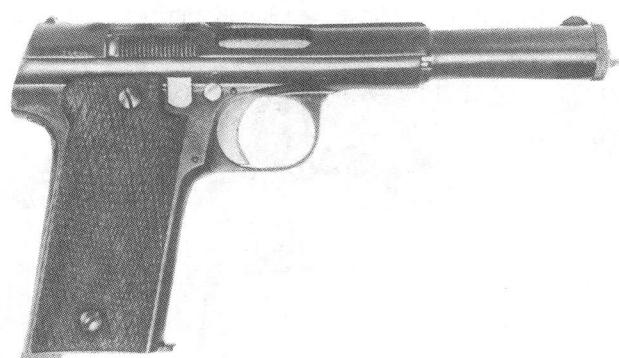

NIB	Exc.	V.G.	Good	Fair	Poor
—	475	400	250	75	40

Astra 300

As above, in 7.65mm or 9mm short. Those used during World War II by German forces bear Waffenamt marks. Approximately 171,000 were manufactured prior to 1947.

Courtesy Orvel Reichert

NIB	Exc.	V.G.	Good	Fair	Poor
—	650	475	250	150	100

NOTE: Nazi-proofed add 25 percent.

Astra 600

Similar to the Model 400, but in 9mm Parabellum. In 1943 and 1944 approximately 10,500 were manufactured. Some of these World War II guns will have Nazi proof stamp and bring a premium. A further 49,000 were made in 1946 and commercially sold.

NIB	Exc.	V.G.	Good	Fair	Poor
—	575	375	275	175	100

Astra 700

A single-action semi-automatic pistol in caliber 7.65mm. Magazine capacity is 9 rounds. Introduced in 1926.

Courtesy James Rankin

NIB	Exc.	V.G.	Good	Fair	Poor
—	500	400	300	150	100

Astra 800

Similar to the Model 600 with an external hammer and loaded chamber indicator. Blued with plastic grips having the tradename "Condor" cast in them. Approximately 11,400 were made from 1958 to 1969.

NIB	Exc.	V.G.	Good	Fair	Poor
—	1500	1200	850	500	300

Astra 900

A modified copy of the Mauser Model C96 semi-automatic pistol. Blued with walnut grips. Early examples with a small Bolo grip marked "Hope" on the chamber will bring a 20 percent premium. Serial numbers 32,788 through 33,774 were used by the German

Army in WWII and bring a 50 percent premium. Add 50 percent for matching Astra-made stock.

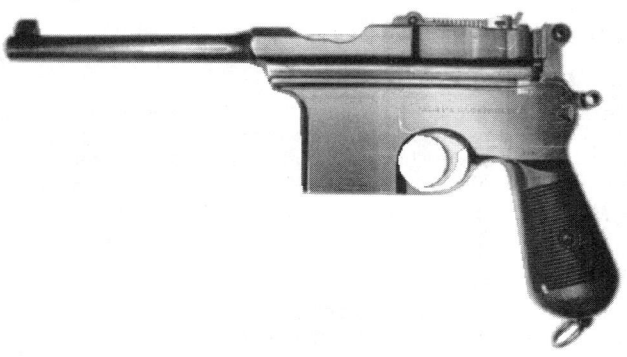

NIB	Exc.	V.G.	Good	Fair	Poor
—	2250	1750	1000	600	300

Astra 1000

A single-action semi-automatic pistol in caliber 7.65mm. Magazine capacity is 12 rounds. Introduced after WWII.

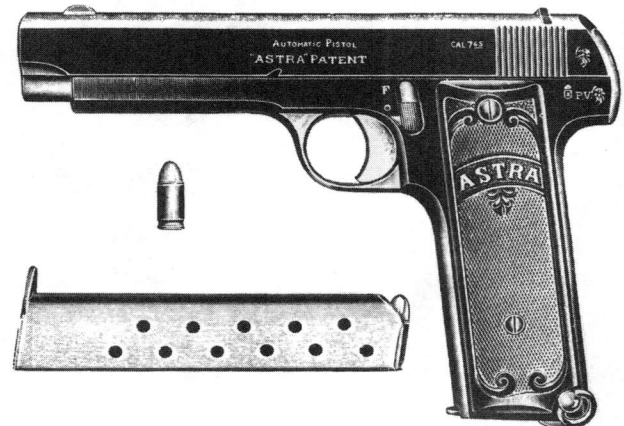

Courtesy James Rankin

NIB	Exc.	V.G.	Good	Fair	Poor
—	350	300	250	200	100

Astra 2000

As above, in .22 or 6.35mm caliber without a grip safety and with an external hammer. Blued with plastic grips.

NIB	Exc.	V.G.	Good	Fair	Poor
—	225	200	175	150	90

Astra 3000

The Model 300 in 7.65mm or 9mm short with a 6- or 7-shot magazine and loaded chamber indicator. Manufactured from 1948 to 1956.

Paul Goodwin photo

NIB	Exc.	V.G.	Good	Fair	Poor
—	600	500	325	200	100

Astra 4000 Falcon

A semi-automatic pistol that was known later as the Falcon. Calibers were .22 LR, 7.65mm, and 9mmK with magazine capacity of 10, 8, and 7 rounds. Manufactured beginning 1955.

Courtesy James Rankin

NIB	Exc.	V.G.	Good	Fair	Poor
—	575	475	325	200	100

Astra 5000 Constable

A .22, 7.65mm or 9mm short semi-automatic pistol (resembling a Walther PP Pistol) with a 3.5" barrel. Blued, chrome-plated or stainless steel with plastic grips. Also available with a 6" barrel as a sport model. Introduced in 1965. Add 15 percent for Constable Sport version with six-inch barrel and adjustable sight.

NIB	Exc.	V.G.	Good	Fair	Poor
—	395	300	250	200	100

Astra 7000

An enlarged version of the Model 2000 in .22 caliber.

NIB	Exc.	V.G.	Good	Fair	Poor
—	575	475	325	200	100

Astra A-80

A .38 Super, 9mm or .45 caliber double-action semi-automatic pistol with a 3.75" barrel and either a 9- or 15-shot magazine depending upon the caliber. Blued or chrome-plated with plastic grips. Introduced in 1982.

Courtesy James Rankin

NIB	Exc.	V.G.	Good	Fair	Poor
450	350	300	250	200	100

Astra A-90

As above, in 9mm or .45 caliber only. Introduced in 1986.

NIB	Exc.	V.G.	Good	Fair	Poor
400	350	300	250	200	100

Astra Cadix

A .22 or .38 Special double-action swing-out cylinder revolver with a 4" or 6" barrel and either 9- or 5-shot cylinder. Blued with plastic grips. Manufactured from 1960 to 1968.

NIB	Exc.	V.G.	Good	Fair	Poor
—	225	175	125	90	70

Constable A-60

A .380 caliber double-action semi-automatic pistol with a 3.5" barrel, adjustable sights and 13-shot magazine. Blued with plastic grips. Introduced in 1986.

NIB	Exc.	V.G.	Good	Fair	Poor
400	300	200	150	100	75

.357 Double-Action Revolver

Similar to Cadix but in .357 Magnum caliber with a 3", 4", 6", or 8.5" barrel, adjustable sights and 6-shot cylinder. Blued or stainless steel with walnut grips. Manufactured from 1972 to 1988.

NIB	Exc.	V.G.	Good	Fair	Poor
295	250	175	125	100	75

NOTE: Stainless steel add 10 percent.

.44/.45 Double-Action Revolver

As above, in .41 Magnum, .44 Magnum or.45 ACP caliber with 6" or 8.5" barrels and a 6-shot cylinder. Blued or stainless steel with walnut grips. Manufactured from 1980 to 1987.

NIB	Exc.	V.G.	Good	Fair	Poor
—	375	325	250	200	100

NOTE: Stainless steel add 25 percent.

Terminator

As above, in .44 Special or .44 Magnum with a 2.75" barrel, adjustable sights and 6-shot cylinder. Blued or stainless steel with rubber grips.

NIB	Exc.	V.G.	Good	Fair	Poor
—	380	330	255	200	100

NOTE: Stainless steel add 10 percent.

Convertible Revolver

Similar to the .357 D/A revolver but accompanied by a cylinder chambered for 9mm Parabellum. Barrel length 3". Blued with walnut grips. Introduced in 1986.

NIB	Exc.	V.G.	Good	Fair	Poor
—	395	325	275	150	100

RECENTLY IMPORTED PISTOLS

Model A-70

This is a lightweight semi-automatic pistol chambered for the 9mm cartridge or .40 S&W cartridge. It is fitted with 3-dot combat sights. The barrel is 3.5" long and the magazine capacity is 8 rounds for 9mm and 7 rounds for the .40 S&W. Black plastic grips and blue finish are standard. Weight is 29 oz.

NIB	Exc.	V.G.	Good	Fair	Poor
350	275	225	175	150	100

NOTE: Add $35 for nickel finish.

Model A-75

Introduced in 1993 this model features all of the standard features of the Model 70 plus selective double or single trigger action and decocking lever. Chambered for 9mm, .40 S&W, or .45 ACP. Offered in blue or nickel finish and steel or alloy frame in 9mm only. Weight for steel frame in 9mm and .40 S&W is 31 oz., for .45 ACP weight is 34.4 oz. Featherweight 9mm weight is 23.5 oz.

NIB	Exc.	V.G.	Good	Fair	Poor
375	325	250	200	150	100

NOTE: Add $35 for nickel finish.

Model A-100

This semi-automatic service pistol is chambered for the 9mm Parabellum, .40 S&W, or .45 ACP cartridges. The trigger action is double-action for the first shot, single-action for follow-up shots. Equipped with a decocking lever. The barrel is 3.8" long and the overall length is 7.5". Magazine capacity for the 9mm is 17 rounds, .40 S&W is 13 rounds, while the .45 holds 9 rounds. A blue or nickel finish is standard. Weight is approximately 34 oz. Also available in a featherweight model 9mm only at 26.5 oz.

NIB	Exc.	V.G.	Good	Fair	Poor
400	350	300	250	200	100

NOTE: Add $35 for nickel finish.

Model A-100 Carry Comp

Similar to the Model A-100 but fitted with a 4.25" barrel and 1" compensator. Blue finish only. Weight is approximately 38 oz. Magazine capacity for 9mm is 17 rounds and for the .40 S&W and .45 ACP 10 rounds.

NIB	Exc.	V.G.	Good	Fair	Poor
475	375	300	250	200	100

ATCSA
Armas de Tiro y Casa
Eibar, Spain

Colt Police Positive Copy

A .38 caliber 6-shot revolver resembling a Colt Police Positive.

NIB	Exc.	V.G.	Good	Fair	Poor
—	250	125	100	60	40

Target Pistol

A .22 caliber single-shot target pistol utilizing a revolver frame.

NIB	Exc.	V.G.	Good	Fair	Poor
—	300	175	125	100	55

AUER, B.
Louisville, Kentucky

Pocket Pistol

A .60 caliber percussion pocket pistol with a 4" octagonal barrel and a long tang extending well back along the grip. Browned, silver furniture and a checkered walnut stock. The lock is marked "B. Auer." Produced during the 1850s.

NIB	Exc.	V.G.	Good	Fair	Poor
—	—	1700	700	250	100

AUGUSTA MACHINE WORKS
Augusta, Georgia

1851 Colt Navy Copy

A .36 caliber percussion revolver with an 8" barrel and 6-shot cylinder. Unmarked except for serial numbers with either 6 or 12 stop cylinder slots. Blued with walnut grips. This is a very rare revolver.

NIB	Exc.	V.G.	Good	Fair	Poor
—	—	62500	40000	17500	5000

AUSTRALIAN AUTOMATIC ARMS LTD.
Tasmania, Australia

SAP

A 10.5" barreled pistol version of the SAR rifle. Imported from 1986 to 1989.

NIB	Exc.	V.G.	Good	Fair	Poor
1150	900	600	325	250	125

AUTAUGA ARMS INC.
Prattville, Alabama

Autauga MK II

This is a .32 ACP semi-automatic blowback pistol with a double-action trigger. Barrel length is 2.25". Fixed sights. Overall length 4.25". Weight is about 13.5 oz. Magazine capacity is 6 rounds. Introduced in 1999.

NIB	Exc.	V.G.	Good	Fair	Poor
325	275	225	195	150	100

AUTO MAG
Various Manufacturers

This popular stainless steel semi-automatic pistol was developed by the Sanford Arms Company of Pasadena, California, in the

1960s and was chambered for a special cartridge known as the .44 AMP which had a 240-grain .44 caliber bullet. Production of this arm has been carried out by a number of companies over the past 40 years. It is believed that fewer than 10,000 have been produced by the eight manufacturers involved.

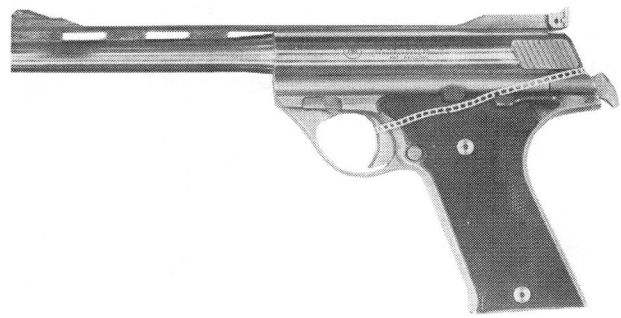

AUTO MAG CORP.
Pasadena, California

Serial number range A0000 through A3300, made with a 6.5" vent rib barrel, chambered in .44 AMP only.

44 AMP

NIB	Exc.	V.G.	Good	Fair	Poor
2700	1850	1475	995	600	300

TDE CORP. (2)
North Hollywood, California

Serial number range A3400 through A05015, made with a 6.5" vent rib barrel, chambered in .44 AMP and .357 AMP.

.44 AMP

NIB	Exc.	V.G.	Good	Fair	Poor
2150	1700	1250	850	600	300

.357 AMP

NIB	Exc.	V.G.	Good	Fair	Poor
2300	1850	1325	900	600	300

TDE CORP.
El Monte, California

Serial number range A05016 through A08300, 6.5" vent rib barrel standard. Also available in 8" and 10" barrel lengths chambered for .44 AMP and .357 AMP.

.44 AMP

NIB	Exc.	V.G.	Good	Fair	Poor
1950	1550	1000	800	600	300

.357 AMP

NIB	Exc.	V.G.	Good	Fair	Poor
1750	1300	900	700	500	300

HIGH STANDARD (2)
Hamden, Connecticut

High Standard was the national distributor for Auto Mag in 1974 and 1975. These guns were chambered for the .44 AMP and .357 AMP. HS cat. no 9346 for .44 AMP, 9347 for .357 AMP. High Standard sold 134 Auto Mags with the "H" prefix. Serial numbers are between H1 and H198, one at H1566 and three between H17219 and H17222. Of these 108 were .44 AMP and 26 were .357 AMP. High Standard also sold 911 Auto Mags between serial numbers A05278 and A07637. Of these 777 were .44 AMP and 108 were .357 AMP.

NIB	Exc.	V.G.	Good	Fair	Poor
2200	1900	1350	900	600	300

KENT LOMONT

As pistols made by this maker are essentially prototypes, it is advised that potential purchasers secure a qualified appraisal.

L. E. JURRAS CUSTOM

This custom maker produced a limited number of Auto Mag pistols in 1977. These arms are worth approximately 35-50 percent more than standard production models.

TDE CORP.
El Monte, California

Serial number range A05016 through A08300, 6.5" vent rib barrel standard. Also available in 8" and 10" barrel lengths chambered for .44 AMP and .357 AMP.

.357 AMP

NIB	Exc.	V.G.	Good	Fair	Poor
1750	1300	900	700	500	300

.44 AMP

NIB	Exc.	V.G.	Good	Fair	Poor
1950	1550	1000	800	600	300

AUTO ORDNANCE CORP.

Auto Ordnance makes reproductions of the 1911 Government Model pistol, the Thompson submachine gun (semiauto only) and the M-1 Carbine. Variations of the 1911 are marketed under both the Auto Ordnance and Thompson brand names. In 1999 the company was bought by Kahr Arms and moved from West Hurley, NY to Worcester, MA.

Auto Ordnance 1911A1

Standard model in .45 ACP with 5-inch barrel, Parkerized finish, fixed sights, plastic or checkered walnut grips. Also offered in 9mm, .38 Super, 10 mm (all discontinued in 1996), and .40 S&W (disc. 1993). Blue, satin nickel and two-tone finish were optional until 2005. In 2011 a 100th Anniversary Model was introduced with appropriate rollmarks.

NIB	Exc.	V.G.	Good	Fair	Poor
565	525	475	400	300	200

NOTE: Add $35 for nickel or two-tone finish, or for 100th Anniversary Model.

Thompson Model 1911TC

.45 ACP semi-auto with fixed sights and 7+1 capacity. Stainless frame and slide. 5" barrel, 39 oz. Laminate grips.

NIB	Exc.	V.G.	Good	Fair	Poor
650	525	395	300	200	100

Thompson Model 1911CAF

.45 ACP semi-auto with fixed sights and 7+1 capacity. Aluminum frame and stainless slide. 5" barrel, 31.5 oz. Laminate grips.

NIB	Exc.	V.G.	Good	Fair	Poor
650	525	395	300	200	100

Thompson 1911 A1—Standard

A 9mm, .38 Super or .45 caliber copy of the Colt Model 1911 A1. Pistol weighs 39 oz.

NIB	Exc.	V.G.	Good	Fair	Poor
475	325	275	200	150	100

NOTE: For 9mm and .38 Super add $20 to above prices. The 9mm and .38 Super models were discontinued in 1997.

Thompson 1911 A1—Parkerized

NIB	Exc.	V.G.	Good	Fair	Poor
475	325	275	200	150	100

Thompson 1911 A1—Deluxe

Same as above but Hi-profile 3 white dot sight system. Black textured, rubber wraparound grips.

NIB	Exc.	V.G.	Good	Fair	Poor
500	425	350	225	150	100

Thompson 1911 A1 Custom High Polish

Introduced in 1997 this model features a special high polish blued finish with numerous special options. Stocks are rosewood with medallion. Fitted with 5" barrel and chambered for .45 ACP. Weight is about 39 oz.

NIB	Exc.	V.G.	Good	Fair	Poor
575	475	—	—	—	—

Thompson 1911 A1—10mm

Same as above but chambered for the 10mm cartridge. Magazine capacity is 8 rounds. Discontinued in 1997.

NIB	Exc.	V.G.	Good	Fair	Poor
700	550	400	250	175	100

Thompson 1911 A1—Duo Tone

Chambered for the .45 ACP, the slide is blued and the frame is satin nickel. Discontinued in 1997.

NIB	Exc.	V.G.	Good	Fair	Poor
500	425	350	225	150	100

Thompson 1911 A1—Satin Nickel

Chambered for .45 ACP or .38 Super the finish is a satin nickel on both frame and slide. Blade front sight and black checkered plastic grips. Discontinued in 1997.

NIB	Exc.	V.G.	Good	Fair	Poor
500	425	350	225	150	100

Thompson 1911 A1—Competition

Chambered for .45 ACP or .38 Super the pistol is fitted with a 5" barrel with compensator and other competition features such as custom Commander hammer, flat mainspring housing, beavertail grip safety, full length recoil guide rod, extended ejector, slide stop and thumb safety. Pistol weighs 42 oz. and is 10" overall. Discontinued in 1997.

NIB	Exc.	V.G.	Good	Fair	Poor
700	625	500	350	300	150

NOTE: For .38 Super add $10 to above prices.

Thompson 1911 A1—Pit Bull

Chambered for .45 ACP and fitted with a 3-1/2" barrel this model has high profile sights and black textured rubber wraparound grips. Magazine capacity is 7 rounds and weight is 36 oz.

NIB	Exc.	V.G.	Good	Fair	Poor
500	425	350	225	150	100

ZG-51 "Pit Bull"

Same as above, with a 3.5" barrel in .45 caliber. Introduced in 1988 and renamed "PIT BULL" in 1994. Discontinued.

NIB	Exc.	V.G.	Good	Fair	Poor
500	425	350	225	150	100

Thompson 1911 A1—General

This is a Commander-size pistol with 4-1/2" barrel, high profile sights. Chambered for .45 ACP or .38 Super. Weighs 37 oz. Discontinued in 1997.

NIB	Exc.	V.G.	Good	Fair	Poor
500	425	350	225	150	100

1927 A5 Pistol/TA5

A pistol version of the Model 1927 A1 with a 13" finned barrel, aluminum alloy receiver and no shoulder stock. Reintroduced in 2008 with 10-inch barrel as Model TA5. Value of the original model is debatable, with advertised prices higher than those shown here, but few apparent sales. The TA5 version is expected to depress value of original 1927 A5s.

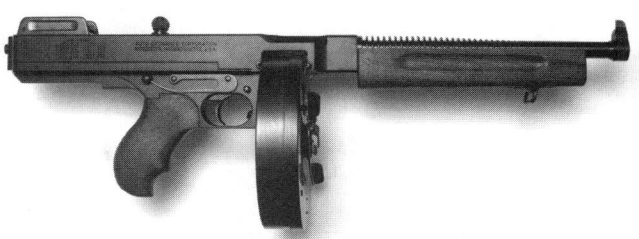

NIB	Exc.	V.G.	Good	Fair	Poor
2200	1300	1000	800	500	150

AZPIRI

Eibar, Spain

A Spanish manufacturer of pistols prior to World War II.

Avion

A 6.35mm semi-automatic pistol copied after the Model 1906 Browning. Marked "Pistolet Automatique Avion Brevete" on the slide as well as on each side of the grip plate along with an airplane logo. Manufactured from 1914 to 1918.

Courtesy James Rankin

NIB	Exc.	V.G.	Good	Fair	Poor
—	250	175	100	75	45

Colon

As above, in 6.35mm caliber, marked "Automatic Pistol Colon."

NIB	Exc.	V.G.	Good	Fair	Poor
—	250	175	100	75	45

B

B.R.F.
South Africa

B.R.F.

This is a .25 caliber semi-automatic pistol similar to the P.A.F. with a 2" barrel and 6-shot magazine. U-SA means Union of South Africa. Little is known about the manufacturer of this pistol, its origin, or dates of manufacture.

Models 682 Skeet (top), 682 Super Trap (middle) and 682 Trap (bottom)

NIB	Exc.	V.G.	Good	Fair	Poor
—	295	195	125	100	70

BACON ARMS CO.
Norwich, Connecticut

Bacon Arms operated from 1862 until 1891. They have become known primarily for the production of cheaply made, solid-frame, rimfire revolvers known as "Suicide Specials." Bacon manufactured and sold under a number of different trademarks. They were: Bacon, Bonanza, Conqueror, Express, Gem, Governor, Guardian, and Little Giant. Collector interest is low, and values for all trademarks are quite similar.

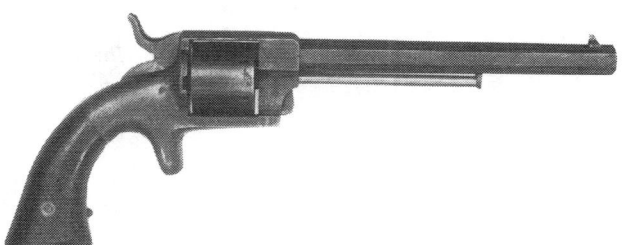

Courtesy Milwaukee Public Museum, Milwaukee, Wisconsin

NIB	Exc.	V.G.	Good	Fair	Poor
—	295	225	100	75	50

BAER CUSTOM, LES
Hillsdale, Illinois

This long-standing 1911 pistolsmith is now producing custom quality 1911 pistols on a semi-production basis.

Each pistol features a large number of custom characteristics such as forged steel frame and full slide recoil rod, double-serrated slide, beveled magazine well, checkered front strap, beavertail safety, extended magazine release button, Bo-Mar sights, and many others depending on the specific model. A representative sampling of these fine Baer pistols appears below.

COMPETITION PISTOLS

Baer 1911 Ultimate Master Combat Pistol-Compensated
Chambered for the .45 ACP and fitted with a triple port, tapered cone compensator.

NIB	Exc.	V.G.	Good	Fair	Poor
2660	1850	1000	750	600	300

Baer 1911 Ultimate Master Steel Special
Designed for steel targets and Bianchi-style competition this model is similar to above but designed for light loads. Chambered for .38 Super. Hard chrome finish.

NIB	Exc.	V.G.	Good	Fair	Poor
2900	2250	1500	950	750	350

Baer 1911 Ultimate Master Combat Pistol
Similar to the other Baer Master series pistols this model is offered in .45 ACP, .400 Cor-Bon, and .38 Super. It is fitted with a large number of special features. Offered in a 5" or 6" version. The 5" version is also offered in 9x23 caliber.

Baer 1911 Ultimate Master Combat Pistol 6" Model

NIB	Exc.	V.G.	Good	Fair	Poor
2600	1950	1350	850	650	350

Baer 1911 Ultimate Master Combat Pistol 5" Model

NIB	Exc.	V.G.	Good	Fair	Poor
2670	1920	1425	800	600	350

Baer 1911 Ultimate Master Para

Designed for IPSC competition and offered either in Unlimited version with compensator and scope or Limited version with iron sights and no compensator.

Baer 1911 Ultimate Master Para Unlimited Model

.45 ACP, .38 Super, 9x23.

NIB	Exc.	V.G.	Good	Fair	Poor
3400	2700	1750	1200	850	400

Baer 1911 Ultimate Master Para Limited Model

NIB	Exc.	V.G.	Good	Fair	Poor
2900	2000	1500	900	650	300

Baer 1911 Bullseye Wadcutter Pistol

Designed for use with wadcutter loads only. Chambered for .45 ACP.

NIB	Exc.	V.G.	Good	Fair	Poor
1650	1250	800	600	500	250

NOTE: This version is also offered with a Baer Optical mount. Add $125 for this option. For a 6" slide with LoMount BoMars sight add $200.

Baer 1911 National Match Hardball Pistol

Designed for DCM matches. Chambered for .45 ACP.

NIB	Exc.	V.G.	Good	Fair	Poor
1425	1050	700	500	400	200

Baer 1911 Target Master

Designed for NRA centerfire matches. Chambered for .45 ACP.

NIB	Exc.	V.G.	Good	Fair	Poor
1450	1150	750	550	450	250

Baer 1911 IPSC Action Pistol

Chambered for .45 ACP with blued slide and frame.

NIB	Exc.	V.G.	Good	Fair	Poor
1700	1350	850	600	450	300

Baer 1911 P.P.C. Distinguished Match

Introduced in 1999 this pistol features a 5" barrel with an adjustable Aristrocrat rear sight. Many, many special features such as double serrated slide lowered and flared ejection port extended ambi safety, checkered front strap, etc. Offered in .45 ACP, and 9mm with supported chamber. Blued finish and one magazine.

NIB	Exc.	V.G.	Good	Fair	Poor
1950	1450	900	650	475	300

NOTE: Add approximately $400 for 9mm model.

Baer 1911 P.P.C. Open Class

Similar to the model above but fitted with a 6" barrel and slide. Chambered for .45 ACP, and 9mm with supported chamber. Blued finish. Introduced in 1999.

NIB	Exc.	V.G.	Good	Fair	Poor
2150	1550	950	700	500	350

NOTE: Add approximately $400 for 9mm model.

DUTY & DEFENSE PISTOLS

Baer 1911 Premier II

Designed as a duty or defense pistol this model is chambered for the .45 ACP, .400 Cor-Bon, and 9x23 cartridges. Fitted with a 5" slide.

NIB	Exc.	V.G.	Good	Fair	Poor
1790	1350	900	600	450	250

NOTE: For stainless steel version add $150 to above prices. Add $100 for .400 Cor-Bon and $250 for 9x23.

Baer 1911 Premier II—6" barrel

Same as above but fitted with a 6" match grade barrel.

NIB	Exc.	V.G.	Good	Fair	Poor
1990	1600	1100	900	700	350

NOTE: Add $100 for .400 Cor-Bon and $300 for .38 Super. 9x23 not offered with 6" slide.

Baer 1911 Premier II—Light Weight (LW1)

Has the same features as the standard Premier II but with reduced weight aluminum frame. Furnished with low mount LCB adjustable rear sight. Offered in .45 ACP only.

NIB	Exc.	V.G.	Good	Fair	Poor
1900	1550	1100	900	700	350

Baer 1911 Premier II—Light Weight (LW2)

Same as above but with fixed combat-style rear sight.

NIB	Exc.	V.G.	Good	Fair	Poor
1900	1550	1100	900	700	350

Baer 1911 Premier II Super-Tac

Similar to the standard Premier II models but with low mount adjustable rear night sight and front sight. Special BEAR COAT finish. Offered in .45 ACP, .40 S&W, .400 Cor-Bon.

NIB	Exc.	V.G.	Good	Fair	Poor
2280	1700	1200	900	700	350

NOTE: Dual caliber .45 ACP/.400 Cor-Bon combo add $200.

Baer 1911 Prowler III

Similar to the Premier II but with a tapered cone stub weight, a full-length guide rod, and a reverse plug. Special order only.

NIB	Exc.	V.G.	Good	Fair	Poor
2580	1700	1200	950	700	350

Baer 1911 Prowler IV

Chambered for .45 ACP or .38 Super this model is built on a Para-Ordnance oversize frame. Fitted with a 5" slide. Special order only.

NIB	Exc.	V.G.	Good	Fair	Poor
2580	1900	1250	900	650	300

NOTE: For optional 6" barrel and slide add $300.

Baer 1911 Custom Carry—Commanche Length

Chambered for .45 ACP this model has several options including 4-1/2" barrel, stainless steel slide and frame, lightweight aluminum frame with blued steel slide. As of 2000 this model is furnished with night sights.

NIB	Exc.	V.G.	Good	Fair	Poor
1850	1400	950	600	450	250

NOTE: For stainless steel add $40. For lightweight frame add $130.

Baer Custom Carry—5"

Same as above but offered with 5" slide. Not offered in aluminum frame.

NIB	Exc.	V.G.	Good	Fair	Poor
2120	1700	950	600	450	250

NOTE: Add $40 for stainless steel.

NOTE: Add 10 percent for Comanche length; add 5 percent for home defense model.

Baer 1911 Thunder Ranch Special

This model features a steel frame and slide with front and rear serrations. Deluxe fixed rear sight with tritium insert. Checkered front strap. Numerous special features. Slim line grips with Thunder Ranch logo. Seven-round magazine standard. Special serial numbers with "TR" prefix. Offered in .45 ACP.

NIB	Exc.	V.G.	Good	Fair	Poor
1990	1500	950	600	450	250

Baer 1911 Thunder Ranch Special Engraved Model

As above but with engraved frame and slide.

NIB	Exc.	V.G.	Good	Fair	Poor
6600	4750	2500	1500	1150	650

Baer S.R.P. (Swift Response Pistol)

Chambered for .45 ACP and built on a Para-Ordnance frame this unit is similar to the one supplied to the FBI. Supplied with wooden presentation box.

NIB	Exc.	V.G.	Good	Fair	Poor
2590	2250	1750	1200	850	400

NOTE: For S.R.P. models built on a Baer frame or shorter 4-1/2" frame subtract $300 from NIB through Fair prices.

Baer 1911 Monolith

Introduced in 1999 this model features a 5" barrel and slide with extra long dust cover. Chambered in .45 ACP, .400 Cor-Bon, .40 S&W, 9x23, 9mm, or .38 Super all with supported chamber. Many special features such as BoMar sights, Commander-style hammer, speed trigger, etc. Blued finish with one magazine. Weight is approximately 37 oz.

NIB	Exc.	V.G.	Good	Fair	Poor
1850	1500	950	675	500	325

NOTE: For all other supported calibers add $250.

Baer 1911 Monolith Heavyweight

Introduced in 1999 this model is similar to the Monolith but with the addition of a heavier frame that adds 3.5 oz. Same calibers as available on the Monolith. Weight is approximately 40 oz.

NIB	Exc.	V.G.	Good	Fair	Poor
1930	1700	1100	775	425	250

NOTE: For all other supported calibers add $200.

Baer 1911 Monolith Tactical Illuminator

This model, introduced in 1999, has the same features as the Monolith Heavyweight above but with the addition of light mounted under the dust cover. Offered in .45 ACP and .40 S&W with supported chamber. Weight with light is approximately 44 oz.

NIB	Exc.	V.G.	Good	Fair	Poor
1850	1500	1050	795	425	250

NOTE: For all other supported calibers add $275.

Baer 1911 Monolith Commanche

Fitted with a 4.25" slide and a dust cover that covers the length of the slide. Has all the features of the standard Monolith. Comes with night sights and a deluxe fixed rear sight. Edges rounded for tactical carry. Chambered in .45 ACP only. Introduced in 2001.

NIB	Exc.	V.G.	Good	Fair	Poor
1990	1750	1100	650	400	225

Baer 1911 Monolith Commanche Heavyweight

Exactly as above but with thicker dust cover to add an additional 2 oz. of weight. Introduced in 2001.

NIB	Exc.	V.G.	Good	Fair	Poor
2150	1800	1000	600	375	200

Baer 1911 Stinger

This model features a shorter Officer's grip frame and Commanche slide and barrel. Many special features. Offered in .45 ACP. Choice of aluminum frame with blued slide, aluminum frame with stainless steel slide and stainless steel frame and slide. Weight in aluminum is about 28 oz., with stainless steel about 34 oz. Introduced in 1999.

NIB	Exc.	V.G.	Good	Fair	Poor
1890	1600	1050	750	400	225

NOTE: For aluminum frame and blued slide with supported calibers add $300. For aluminum frame with stainless slide and supported chamber add $340. For stainless frame and slide with supported chamber add $140.

Baer 1911 Stinger Stainless

Same as above but with stainless steel frame and slide. Introduced in 2001.

NIB	Exc.	V.G.	Good	Fair	Poor
1970	1670	1100	775	425	250

NEW CONCEPTS PISTOLS

This line of 1911 pistols offers custom features at a slightly lower cost. Each succeeding grade offers a few more features.

Baer 1911 Concept I

Chambered for .45 ACP and fitted with BoMar sights.

NIB	Exc.	V.G.	Good	Fair	Poor
1690	1450	975	750	550	300

Baer 1911 Concept II

Same as above but fitted with Baer adjustable sights.

NIB	Exc.	V.G.	Good	Fair	Poor
1950	1890	975	800	550	300

Baer 1911 Concept V 6"
This model is identical to the Concept V with the addition of a 6" barrel and slide. Introduced in 1999.

NIB	Exc.	V.G.	Good	Fair	Poor
1690	1450	975	750	550	300

Baer 1911 Concept III
Same as above but with stainless steel frame with blued steel slide with BoMar sights.

NIB	Exc.	V.G.	Good	Fair	Poor
2050	1990	1075	900	650	350

Baer 1911 Concept VI
Same as above but fitted with Baer adjustable sights.

NIB	Exc.	V.G.	Good	Fair	Poor
1840	1550	975	800	550	300

Baer 1911 Concept IV
Same as above but with Baer adjustable sights.

NIB	Exc.	V.G.	Good	Fair	Poor
2050	1990	1075	900	650	350

Baer 1911 Concept VI L.W.
Same as above but built on aluminum frame with supported chamber and National Match barrel.

NIB	Exc.	V.G.	Good	Fair	Poor
2050	1990	1075	900	650	350

Baer 1911 Concept VII
Features all blued 4-1/2" steel frame and slide with Baer adjustable fixed night sights.

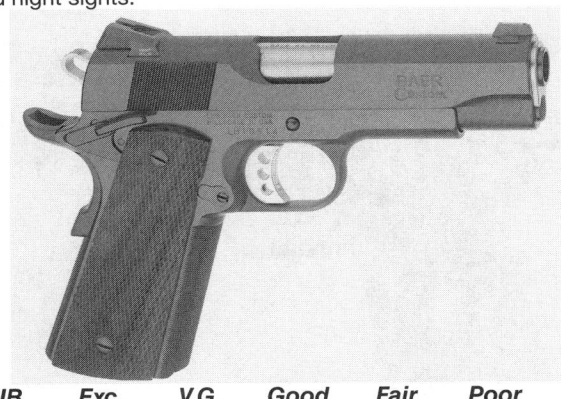

NIB	Exc.	V.G.	Good	Fair	Poor
1840	1550	975	800	550	300

Baer 1911 Concept V
This model has both stainless steel slide and frame with BoMar sights.

NIB	Exc.	V.G.	Good	Fair	Poor
2050	1990	1075	900	650	350

Baer 1911 Concept VIII
Same as above but with stainless steel slide and frame. Fixed combat night sights standard.

NIB	Exc.	V.G.	Good	Fair	Poor
2100	1850	1500	1250	700	300

Baer 1911 Concept IX

This version has a lightweight aluminum frame with 4-1/2" steel slide.

NIB	Exc.	V.G.	Good	Fair	Poor
2100	1850	1500	1250	700	300

Baer 1911 Concept X

This model features a 4-1/2" stainless steel slide with a lightweight aluminum frame.

NIB	Exc.	V.G.	Good	Fair	Poor
2100	1850	1500	1250	700	300

BAER LIGHTWEIGHT .22 CALIBER 1911 MODELS

4-1/2" Model with fixed sights

NIB	Exc.	V.G.	Good	Fair	Poor
1525	1400	950	800	550	300

5" Model with fixed sights

NIB	Exc.	V.G.	Good	Fair	Poor
1625	1400	950	800	550	300

5" Model with Bo-Mar sights

NIB	Exc.	V.G.	Good	Fair	Poor
1700	1475	1000	850	600	300

Baer Limited Edition Presentation Grade 1911

A fully hand engraved Baer 1911 with special bluing in presentation wooden box.

NIB	Exc.	V.G.	Good	Fair	Poor
6590	3995	2500	1750	1150	500

Model 1911 Twenty-Fifth Anniversary

Custom-engraved limited collector edition .45 ACP semi-auto. Built on fully functional, fully equipped Baer Premier II. Hand engraved, both sides of slide and frame. Les Baer signature. Inlaid with white gold. Ivory grips. Deep blue finish. Presentation box. Introduced 2006.

NIB	Exc.	V.G.	Good	Fair	Poor
6590	3995	2500	1750	1150	500

Ultimate Recon

Semi-auto with integral Picatinny rail, 5" barrel, .45 ACP. Blue or chrome. Comes with SureFire X-200 light. Fixed sights. 4-pound trigger. Two 8-round magazines. Cocobolo grips. Add $500 for hard chrome.

NIB	Exc.	V.G.	Good	Fair	Poor
3070	2590	1650	1100	775	450

BAFORD ARMS, INC.
Bristol, Tennessee

Thunder Derringer

A .410 bore or .44 Special single-shot pistol with 3" interchangeable barrels and a spur trigger. Additional interchangeable barrels are chambered in calibers from .22 to 9mm. Also available with a scope. Blued with a walnut grip. Introduced in 1988.

NIB	Exc.	V.G.	Good	Fair	Poor
175	110	85	70	55	35

NOTE: Add $50 for interchangeable barrel.

Fire Power Model 35

A 9mm semi-automatic pistol with a 4.75" barrel, Millett adjustable sights and 14-shot magazine. Fitted with a combat safety and hammer, and Pachmayr grips. Stainless steel. Introduced in 1988.

NIB	Exc.	V.G.	Good	Fair	Poor
550	450	365	300	250	125

BAIKAL

IZH35

This is a semi-automatic pistol chambered for the .22 LR cartridge. Fully adjustable target grip, adjustable trigger assembly, cocking indicator, detachable scope. Fitted with a 6" barrel. Introduced in 2000.

NIB	Exc.	V.G.	Good	Fair	Poor
500	400	350	200	165	95

BAKER GAS SEAL
London, England

A .577 caliber percussion revolver with a 6.5" octagonal barrel and 6-shot cylinder. When the hammer is cocked, the cylinder is forced forward tightly against the barrel breech, thus creating a gas seal. Blued, case hardened with walnut grips.

NIB	Exc.	V.G.	Good	Fair	Poor
—	2500	1900	1500	875	350

BALLARD, C. H.
Worcester, Massachusetts

Single-Shot Derringer

A .41 caliber rimfire spur trigger single-shot pistol with a 2.75" barrel marked "Ballard's." Blued with silver-plated frame and walnut grips. Manufactured during the 1870s.

NIB	Exc.	V.G.	Good	Fair	Poor
—	—	1775	1450	550	225

NOTE: Iron frame model add 20 percent.

BAR-STO PRECISION MACHINE
Burbank, California

Bar-Sto 25

A .25 caliber semi-automatic pistol with a brushed stainless steel receiver and slide. Walnut grips. Produced in 1974.

NIB	Exc.	V.G.	Good	Fair	Poor
—	325	275	175	125	100

BASCARAN, MARTIN A.
Eibar, Spain

A Spanish manufacturer of pistols prior to World War II.

Martian 6.35mm

A 6.35mm semi-automatic pistol. The slide is marked "Automatic Pistol Martian." Blued with black plastic grips having the monogram "MAB" cast in them.

NIB	Exc.	V.G.	Good	Fair	Poor
—	275	195	135	100	75

Martian 7.65mm

A semi-automatic pistol patterned after the Ruby military pistols. "Martian" is stamped on the slide with wood grips and a lanyard loop.

Courtesy James Rankin

NIB	Exc.	V.G.	Good	Fair	Poor
—	275	195	135	100	75

Thunder

A semi-automatic pistol in caliber 6.35mm. Almost a duplicate of the Martian above except for the sight placement. "Thunder" is stamped on the slide and each grip plate.

Courtesy James Rankin

NIB	Exc.	V.G.	Good	Fair	Poor
—	275	195	135	100	75

BAUER F. A. CORP.
Fraser, Michigan

Bauer 25 Automatic

A .25 caliber semi-automatic pistol made of stainless steel with a 2.5" barrel and 6-shot magazine. Walnut or imitation pearl grips. Manufactured from 1972 to 1984. After 1984 this pistol was produced under the name of Fraser for a few years. Add 15 percent for NIB.

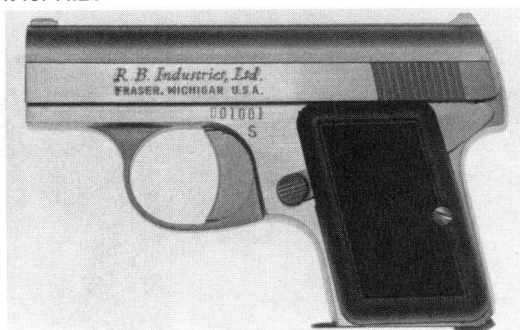

Courtesy James Rankin

NIB	Exc.	V.G.	Good	Fair	Poor
—	250	200	165	125	80

BAYONNE, MANUFACTURE D'ARMES
aka MAB
Bayonne, France

MAB Model A

Manufactured in 1921 and chambered for the 6.35mm cartridge. Patterned after the Browning Model 1906. Squeeze grip safety with a 6-round magazine.

Courtesy James Rankin

NIB	Exc.	V.G.	Good	Fair	Poor
—	295	175	115	75	50

MAB Model B

Manufactured in 1932. Chambered for 6.35mm cartridge and has an exposed hammer, no grip safety, and a 6-round magazine.

Courtesy James Rankin

NIB	Exc.	V.G.	Good	Fair	Poor
—	275	165	90	75	50

MAB Model C

Manufactured in 1933 and chambered for the 7.65mm and .380 cartridge. Patterned after the Browning Model 1910. Seven-round magazine.

Courtesy James Rankin

NIB	Exc.	V.G.	Good	Fair	Poor
—	325	225	200	125	90

MAB Model D

Manufactured in 1933. Chambered for 7.65mm and .380 cartridge. Basically a Model C with a longer barrel and a 9-round magazine.

Courtesy James Rankin

NIB	Exc.	V.G.	Good	Fair	Poor
—	400	300	250	125	100

NOTE: Add 100 percent for Nazi-marked pistols.

MAB Model E

Manufactured in 1949 and chambered for the 6.35mm cartridge. Patterned after the Model D with streamlined grips and a 10-round magazine.

NIB	Exc.	V.G.	Good	Fair	Poor
—	425	325	300	150	125

MAB Model F

Manufactured in 1950 and chambered for the .22 LR cartridge. Interchangeable barrel lengths, target grips, and a 10-round magazine.

Courtesy James Rankin

NIB	Exc.	V.G.	Good	Fair	Poor
—	425	325	200	150	125

MAB Model G

Manufactured in 1951, chambered for the .22 LR cartridge and 7.65mm cartridge. Some with Dural frames. Magazine capacity is 10 rounds for .22 LR and 8 rounds for the 7.65mm.

Courtesy James Rankin

NIB	Exc.	V.G.	Good	Fair	Poor
—	450	350	225	150	125

MAB Model GZ

Manufactured in calibers .22 LR, 6.35mm, 7.65mm, and .380. Almost identical to the Model G. Dural frames and two-tone finishes on some variations.

NIB	Exc.	V.G.	Good	Fair	Poor
—	450	350	275	150	125

MAB Model P-8 & P-15

In 1966 MAB manufactured the Model P-8 and Model P-15 in 9mm Parabellum with 8- and 15-round magazine capacity. Basically it is the same gun with different magazine capacities. The Model P-15 went to the French military as well as some commercial sales.

Courtesy James Rankin

NIB	Exc.	V.G.	Good	Fair	Poor
—	475	350	300	250	175

Model P-15 M1 Target

The MAB Model P-15 was manufactured for target shooting using the 9mm Parabellum cartridge. Most M1 Target MABs were purchased by the French military for their target teams.

Courtesy James Rankin

NIB	Exc.	V.G.	Good	Fair	Poor
—	875	750	500	350	175

MAB MODEL R

Manufactured in caliber 7.65mm Long in 1951 the Model R was similar to the Model D. Model Rs were later produced in several calibers. The .22 LR was furnished with a 10-round magazine and two different barrel lengths. The 7.65mm had a 9-round magazine while the .380 and 9mm Parabellum were fitted with 8-round magazines. Deduct 15 percent for 7.65 Long.

MAB Model R .22 Long Rifle

NIB	Exc.	V.G.	Good	Fair	Poor
—	350	250	225	150	125

7.65mm & 7.65mm Long & .380

NIB	Exc.	V.G.	Good	Fair	Poor
—	350	250	225	150	125

9mm Parabellum

NIB	Exc.	V.G.	Good	Fair	Poor
—	400	300	250	150	125

MAB Model R PARA Experimental

In the late 1950s MAB began experimenting with the Model R in caliber 9mm Parabellum. There were many of these experimental-type pistols and the 8-round, rotating barrel Model R shown led directly to the Model P-15 series.

Courtesy James Rankin

NIB	Exc.	V.G.	Good	Fair	Poor
—	1500	1250	1000	500	250

Model "Le Chasseur"

Manufactured in 1953 the Le Chasseur was a target model in .22 LR and had a 9-round magazine. It had an external hammer, target sights, and target grips.NOTE: MAB pistols that were sold in the U.S.A. were retailed by the Winfield Arms Company of Los Angeles, California, and are marked "Made in France for WAC." This does not affect value.

NIB	Exc.	V.G.	Good	Fair	Poor
—	300	200	150	125	90

BEATTIE, J.
London, England

Beattie produced a variety of revolvers during the percussion period, some of which were imported into the United States. During the period this firm was in business, it was located at these London addresses:

43 Upper Marylebone Street 1835-1838

52 Upper Marylebone Street 1838-1842

52 Upper Marylebone Street 1842-1846 & 223 Regent Street

205 Regent Street 1851-1882

104 Queen Victoria Street 1882-1894

Beattie Gas Seal Revolver

A .42 caliber single-action percussion revolver with a 6.25" octagonal barrel. When the hammer is cocked, the cylinder is forced forward against the barrel breech, thus effecting a gas seal. Blued, case hardened with walnut grips.

NIB	Exc.	V.G.	Good	Fair	Poor
—	—	5100	3500	2200	1100

BEAUMONT
Maastrict, Netherlands
1873 Dutch Service Revolver, Old Model

A 9.4mm double-action 6-shot revolver weighing 2 lbs. 12 oz.

NIB	Exc.	V.G.	Good	Fair	Poor
—	—	695	400	200	100

1873 Dutch Service Revolver, New Model

As above, with a 6-shot cylinder.

NIB	Exc.	V.G.	Good	Fair	Poor
—	—	695	400	200	100

1873 KIM, Small Model

As above, with an octagonal barrel and 5-shot cylinder.

NIB	Exc.	V.G.	Good	Fair	Poor
—	—	775	500	250	125

BECKER AND HOLLANDER
Suhl, Germany

Beholla

A semi-automatic pistol in caliber 7.65mm. Introduced in 1908 in Germany. It was manufactured by Becker & Hollander until 1920. After that date three different companies produced the Beholla under the names Stenda, Menta, and Leonhardt.

Courtesy James Rankin

NIB	Exc.	V.G.	Good	Fair	Poor
—	500	350	225	175	100

BEEMAN PRECISION ARMS, INC.
Santa Rosa, California

Although primarily known as an importer and retailer of airguns, Beeman Precision Arms, Inc. has marketed several firearms.

MP-08

A .380 caliber semi-automatic pistol, with a 3.5" barrel and 6-shot magazine, resembling the German Luger. Blued. Introduced in 1968.

NIB	Exc.	V.G.	Good	Fair	Poor
475	375	275	225	200	125

P-08

As above, in .22 caliber with an 8-shot magazine and walnut grips. Introduced in 1969.

NIB	Exc.	V.G.	Good	Fair	Poor
475	375	275	225	200	125

SP Standard

A .22 caliber single-shot target pistol with 8" to 15" barrels. Fitted with adjustable sights and walnut grips. Imported in 1985 and 1986.

NIB	Exc.	V.G.	Good	Fair	Poor
325	225	200	175	150	100

SP Deluxe

As above, with a walnut forend.

NIB	Exc.	V.G.	Good	Fair	Poor
350	250	225	200	150	100

BEERSTECHER, FREDERICK
Philadelphia, Pennsylvania (1846-1856)
Lewisburg, Pennsylvania (1857-1868)

Superposed Load Pocket Pistol

A .41 caliber superposed load percussion pistol with an average barrel length of 3", German silver mounts and walnut stock. The hammer is fitted with a moveable twin striker head so that the first charge in the barrel can be fired and then the second fired. The lock is normally marked "F. Beerstecher's/Patent 1855." Prospective purchasers are advised to secure a qualified appraisal prior to acquisition.

NIB	Exc.	V.G.	Good	Fair	Poor
—	—	6400	4800	3500	1050

Model B-76

This is an all-steel, double-action semi-automatic chambered for the 9mm Parabellum. It has a 4.25" barrel, fixed sights, and an 8-round detachable magazine.

NIB	Exc.	V.G.	Good	Fair	Poor
525	400	350	300	200	100

Model B-76S

This is the target version of the B-76. It has a 5.5" barrel, adjustable sights, and target grips.

NIB	Exc.	V.G.	Good	Fair	Poor
625	500	400	300	200	100

Model B-77

This model is similar to the B-76 except that it is chambered for the .32 ACP.

NIB	Exc.	V.G.	Good	Fair	Poor
425	300	250	200	150	100

Model B-80

This is another model similar to the B-76 except that it is chambered for the .30 Luger cartridge.

NIB	Exc.	V.G.	Good	Fair	Poor
525	395	300	200	150	100

Model B-80S

This is the target version of the B-80 with a 5.5" barrel and adjustable sights. It also features target grips.

NIB	Exc.	V.G.	Good	Fair	Poor
575	475	400	300	200	100

Model MP90S Match (World Cup)

This is a semi-automatic single-action pistol chambered for the .22 Short, .22 LR, or .32 S&W wadcutter. It is fitted with a 4-3/8" barrel with walnut match style fully adjustable grips, blade front sight and fully adjustable rear sight. Barrel has adjustable weights below. Magazine capacity is 5 rounds. Weight is about 39 oz. Previously imported by European American Armory, now imported by Benelli USA. Add 10 percent for .32 S&W.

NIB	Exc.	V.G.	Good	Fair	Poor
1200	950	700	500	300	150

Model MP95E Match (Atlanta)

Similar to the above model but with anatomically shaped grips. Choice of blue or chrome finish. Previously imported by European American Armory, now imported by Benelli U.S.A.

NIB	Exc.	V.G.	Good	Fair	Poor
750	600	450	350	225	125

NOTE: Add $60 for chrome finish.

BENTLEY, JOSEPH
Birmingham and Liverpool, England

Best known for his transitional and later patented percussion revolvers, Bentley worked at these addresses:

Birmingham11 Steelhouse Lane1829-1837

14 St. Mary's Row1840-1864

Liverpool143 Dale Street1840-1842

12 South Castle Street1842-1851

40 Lime Street & 65 Castle1852-1857

65 Castle & 37 Russell Street1857-1862

Bentley Revolver

A .44 caliber double-action percussion revolver with a 7" barrel and 5-shot cylinder. Blued, case hardened with walnut grips.

NIB	Exc.	V.G.	Good	Fair	Poor
—	—	4500	2750	2000	750

Model 1915

A 7.65mm and 9mm Glisenti caliber semi-automatic pistol with 3.5" barrel, fixed sights and 8-shot magazine. Blued with walnut grips. The 7.65mm pistol has a single-line inscription while the 9mm Glisenti has a double line. There are various styles of wood grips on this model. Manufactured between 1915 and 1922. Replaced by the Model 1915/19.

Courtesy James Rankin

NIB	Exc.	V.G.	Good	Fair	Poor
—	850	700	500	350	250

Model 1915/1917

This model is an improved version of the above pistol but chambered for the 7.65mm cartridge. It also incorporates a new barrel-mounting method and a longer cutout in the top of the slide.

Courtesy Orvel Reichert

NIB	Exc.	V.G.	Good	Fair	Poor
—	400	350	275	200	100

Model 1919

Similar to Model 1915, in 6.35mm caliber. Manufactured with minor variations and different names between 1919 and the 1940s.

Courtesy James Rankin

NIB	Exc.	V.G.	Good	Fair	Poor
—	550	450	350	300	150

Model 1923

A 9mm Glisenti caliber semi-automatic pistol with 4" barrel and 8-shot magazine. Blued with steel grips. The slide is marked, "Brev 1915-1919 Mlo 1923." Manufactured from 1923 to 1935.

Courtesy James Rankin

NIB	Exc.	V.G.	Good	Fair	Poor
—	850	600	395	265	175

Model 1931

A 7.65mm caliber semi-automatic pistol with 3.5" barrel and open-top slide. Blued with walnut grips and marked, "RM" separated by an anchor.

NIB	Exc.	V.G.	Good	Fair	Poor
—	495	425	325	250	180

MODEL 1934

As above, with 9mm short (.380 ACP)+ caliber. The slide is marked, "P. Beretta Cal. 9 Corto-Mo 1934 Brevet Gardone VT." This inscription is followed by the date of manufacture that was given numerically, followed by a Roman numeral that denoted the year of manufacture on the Fascist calendar which began in 1922. Examples are marked, "RM" (Navy), "RE" (Army), "RA" (Air Force), and "PS" (Police). Manufactured between 1934 and 1959.

NIB	Exc.	V.G.	Good	Fair	Poor
—	400	365	250	175	100

Air Force "RA" marked

NIB	Exc.	V.G.	Good	Fair	Poor
—	575	500	375	250	175

Navy "RM" marked

NIB	Exc.	V.G.	Good	Fair	Poor
—	650	575	400	275	200

Model 1934 Rumanian Contract

This model is identical to the Model 1934 except the slide is marked "9mm Scurt" instead of 9mm Corto.

NIB	Exc.	V.G.	Good	Fair	Poor
—	500	450	375	275	175

Model 1935

As above, in 7.65mm caliber. Post-war versions are known. Manufactured from 1935 to 1959.

NIB	Exc.	V.G.	Good	Fair	Poor
—	400	375	250	175	125

Model 318

An improved version of the old Model 1919 with the butt reshaped to afford a better grip. Chambered for the .25 ACP cartridge and has a 2.5" barrel. Variety of finishes with plastic grips. In the United States it is known as the "Panther." Manufactured between 1935 and 1946.

NIB	Exc.	V.G.	Good	Fair	Poor
—	350	275	250	175	125

Model 418

As above, with a rounded grip and a cocking indicator. It is known as the "Bantam" in the U.S. Introduced in 1947.

NIB	Exc.	V.G.	Good	Fair	Poor
—	275	225	175	125	90

Model 420

An engraved and chrome-plated Model 418.

NIB	Exc.	V.G.	Good	Fair	Poor
—	350	300	275	200	150

Model 421

An engraved, gold-plated Model 418 with tortoise-shell grips.

NIB	Exc.	V.G.	Good	Fair	Poor
—	475	425	325	250	150

Model 948

A .22 LR version of the Model 1934. It has either a 3.5" or 6" barrel.

NIB	Exc.	V.G.	Good	Fair	Poor
—	350	300	200	125	90

Model 949 Olympic Target

A .22 caliber semi-automatic pistol with 8.75" barrel, adjustable sights and muzzlebrake. Blued with checkered, walnut grips. Manufactured from 1959 to 1964.

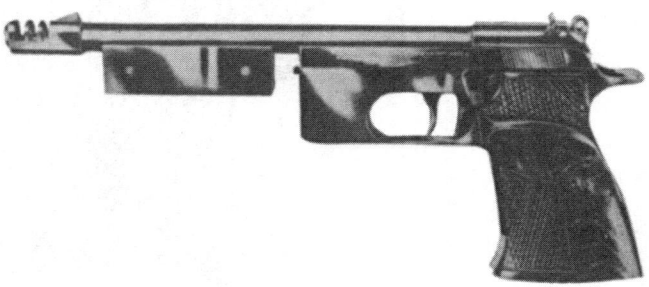

NIB	Exc.	V.G.	Good	Fair	Poor
—	750	600	500	400	200

U22 Neos 4.5/6.0

This semi-automatic .22 caliber pistol was first introduced in 2002. It is chambered for the .22 LR cartridge and fitted with a choice of 4.5" or 6" barrel with integral scope rail. Magazine capacity is 10 rounds. Weight is about 32 oz. to 36 oz. depending on barrel length.

NIB	Exc.	V.G.	Good	Fair	Poor
250	200	165	125	100	75

U22 Neos 4.5 Inox/6.0 Inox

Same as above but with special two-tone finish.

NIB	Exc.	V.G.	Good	Fair	Poor
300	250	195	150	100	75

U22 Neos 6.0/7.5 DLX

Introduced in 2003 this model features a 6" or 7.5" barrel with target sights and polymer grips with inlays. Adjustable trigger and interchangeable sights. Laser-engraved slide. Weight is about 36 oz.

NIB	Exc.	V.G.	Good	Fair	Poor
335	275	200	150	100	75

U22 Neos 6.0/7.5 Inox DLX

As above but with Inox finish.

NIB	Exc.	V.G.	Good	Fair	Poor
385	300	215	165	115	90

BERETTA 70 SERIES

These pistols began production in 1958 replacing Models 1934, 1935, 948, and 949. During the late 1960s several of these models briefly utilized a 100 series designation for the U.S. market. During the latter part of the 1970s a magazine safety was added to the 70 series and the pistols became known as the Model 70S. The 70S designation replaced model designations 70 through 75 making these older model numbers obsolete. Only the Model 76 designation continued. The 70 Series design included a cross bolt safety, sear block safety, a slide hold-open device, and a push-button magazine release. Shorty after its introduction the cross bolt safety pushbutton was replaced with a lever-type sear block safety located in the same place. **NOTE:** The above information was supplied by contributing editor John Stimson, Jr.

Model 70 (Model 100)

The Model 948 with cross bolt safety, hold-open device, and a push-button magazine release. Fixed sights. There are a number of subvariations available chambered for the .22 LR, .32 ACP, and the .380 ACP cartridges. Available with a 3.5" or 5.9" barrel and has a detachable magazine. Also known as the "Puma" when marketed in the U.S. by J.L. Galef & Sons. It was introduced in 1958 and discontinued in 1985.

NIB	Exc.	V.G.	Good	Fair	Poor
525	450	350	275	125	85

Model 70S

This is an improved Model 70. Chambered for the 7.65 (.32 ACP), 9mm Corto (.380 ACP), and the .22 LR cartridge. Magazine capacity is 7, 8, and 8 rounds respectively.

NIB	Exc.	V.G.	Good	Fair	Poor
550	475	375	295	125	85

Model 71/Jaguar (Model 101)

Similar to above model and chambered for .22 LR cartridge. Magazine capacity is 10 rounds. Frame is alloy and is fitted with a 5.9" barrel. Models imported into the U.S. prior to 1968 were fitted with 3.5" barrels.

NIB	Exc.	V.G.	Good	Fair	Poor
425	375	300	225	125	85

Model 72

This is essentially a Model 71 but sold with two sets of barrels; a 3.5" and 5.9". Fixed sights.

NIB	Exc.	V.G.	Good	Fair	Poor
450	400	325	250	150	125

Model 76 (102)

This is a .22 LR target pistol. The barrel is shrouded with an aluminum sleeve, with the rear part of the sleeve extended above the slide to hold an adjustable rear sight. Marketed in the U.S. as the Sable. Magazine capacity is 10 rounds. Briefly after 1968 imported into the U.S. as the Model 102, the New Sable.

Courtesy John J. Stimson, Jr.

NIB	Exc.	V.G.	Good	Fair	Poor
450	400	300	200	125	75

Model 950/Jetfire

A .22 caliber semi-automatic pistol with 2.25" barrel hinged at the front that could be pivoted forward for cleaning or loading, making this either a semi-auto or single-shot pistol. Blued with plastic grips. Introduced in 1955. A 4" barrel version also available. This model was known as the "Minx" in the U.S.

NIB	Exc.	V.G.	Good	Fair	Poor
325	250	215	145	95	50

Model 950B/Jetfire

As above, in .25 caliber, known as the "Jetfire" in the U.S.

NIB	Exc.	V.G.	Good	Fair	Poor
325	250	215	145	95	50

Model 950 Jetfire Inox

Same as the Model 950 Jetfire but with stainless steel finish. Introduced in 2000.

NIB	Exc.	V.G.	Good	Fair	Poor
335	250	175	135	85	50

Model 3032 Tomcat

This is a double-action semi-automatic pistol similar in appearance to the Model 950 but chambered for the .32 ACP cartridge. Barrel length is 2.45" and overall length is 5". Fixed blade front sight and drift adjustable rear sight. Plastic grips. Seven-round magazine. Blued or matte black finish. Weight is 14.5 oz.

NIB	Exc.	V.G.	Good	Fair	Poor
375	325	250	200	1350	75

NOTE: For blued finish add $30.

Model 3032 Tomcat Inox

Same as above but with stainless steel finish. Introduced in 2000.

NIB	Exc.	V.G.	Good	Fair	Poor
400	325	250	195	125	75

Model 3032 Tomcat Titanium

Same as above but with titanium finish and plastic grips. Weight is about 16 oz. Introduced in 2001.

NIB	Exc.	V.G.	Good	Fair	Poor
575	450	350	290	210	150

Alley Cat

Introduced in 2001 as a special limited run promotion pistol. Chambered for the .32 ACP cartridge this model is a Tomcat with special features such as AO Big Dot night sights. Supplied with an Alcantara inside-the-pants holster.

NIB	Exc.	V.G.	Good	Fair	Poor
575	450	350	290	210	150

Model 951

A 9mm caliber semi-automatic pistol with 4.5" barrel and fixed sights. Blued with plastic grips. It was also known as the "Brigadier" at one time. Introduced 1952.

NIB	Exc.	V.G.	Good	Fair	Poor
—	450	375	275	150	100

Model 20

A .25 ACP double-action pistol with 2.5" barrel and 9-shot magazine. Blued with either walnut or plastic grips. Discontinued in 1985.

NIB	Exc.	V.G.	Good	Fair	Poor
300	250	195	150	90	75

MODEL 21/21 BOBCAT

This small frame semi-automatic pistol, chambered for the .22 LR or .25 ACP cartridge, features a 2.4" tip-up barrel with fixed sights and a magazine capacity of 8 rounds (.25 ACP) or 7 rounds (.22 LR). Comes with either plastic or walnut grips and a deluxe version with gold line engraving. Pistol weighs about 11 to 11.8 oz. depending on caliber.

Standard Model

NIB	Exc.	V.G.	Good	Fair	Poor
325	275	250	225	175	95

Model 21EL

Gold engraved model.

NIB	Exc.	V.G.	Good	Fair	Poor
395	350	325	280	195	110

Model 21 Inox

Stainless steel.

NIB	Exc.	V.G.	Good	Fair	Poor
325	250	200	140	95	75

Model 90

A double-action, semi-automatic .32 auto pocket pistol with a 3.5" barrel and 8-round magazine. Manufactured from 1969 to 1983.

NIB	Exc.	V.G.	Good	Fair	Poor
—	395	350	295	200	125

Model 92

A 9mm caliber double-action, semi-automatic pistol with a 5" barrel, fixed sights and a 16-round, double-stack magazine. Blued with plastic grips. Introduced in 1976 and is now discontinued.

NIB	Exc.	V.G.	Good	Fair	Poor
800	600	500	400	250	200

Model 92SB-P

As above, but with a polished finish. Manufactured from 1980 to 1985.

NIB	Exc.	V.G.	Good	Fair	Poor
625	475	400	325	250	200

Model 92SB Compact

As above, with a 4.3" barrel and a shortened grip frame that holds a 14-shot magazine. Either blued or nickel-plated with wood or plastic grips. The nickel version would be worth an additional 15 percent. The wood grips would add $20 to the value. Introduced in 1980 and discontinued in 1985.

NIB	Exc.	V.G.	Good	Fair	Poor
500	425	375	325	250	200

Model 92FS

The current production Model 92 chambered for the 9mm Parabellum cartridge. Barrel length is 4.9" and rear sight is a 3-dot combat drift adjustable. The magazine capacity is 15 rounds. This semi-automatic pistol features a double- or single-action operation. The safety is manual type. The frame is a light alloy sandblasted and anodized black. The barrel slide is steel. Grips are plastic checkered with black matte finish. Equipped with spare magazine cleaning rod, and hard carrying case. Pistol weighs 34.4 oz. empty.

NIB	Exc.	V.G.	Good	Fair	Poor
550	450	350	300	200	150

Model 92FS Inox

Introduced in 2001 this pistol is chambered for the 9mm cartridge and fitted with a 4.9" barrel. The slide is black stainless steel with lightweight frame and combat-style trigger guard, reversible magazine release, and ambidextrous safety. Gray wrap-around grips. Weight is about 34 oz.

NIB	Exc.	V.G.	Good	Fair	Poor
695	575	425	350	225	175

Model 96

Identical to Model 92FS but fitted with a 10-round magazine and chambered for the .40 S&W. Introduced in 1992.

NIB	Exc.	V.G.	Good	Fair	Poor
550	450	350	300	200	150

Model 96 Combat

Introduced in 1997 this model is single-action-only with a competition tuned trigger. Developed for practical shooting competition. The barrel length is 5.9" and is supplied with a weight as standard. Rear sight is adjustable target type. Tool kit included as standard. Weight is 40 oz.

NIB	Exc.	V.G.	Good	Fair	Poor
1700	1300	950	575	350	175

Model 96 Stock

Similar to the Model 96 but in double-/single-action with a half-cock notch for cocked and locked carry. Fitted with a 4.9" barrel with fixed sights. Three interchangeable front sights are supplied as standard. Weight is 35 oz. Introduced in 1997. No longer in the U.S. product line.

NIB	Exc.	V.G.	Good	Fair	Poor
1350	950	775	500	325	150

Model 92/96FS Inox

Same as above except the barrel, slide, trigger, extractor, and other components are made of stainless steel. The frame is made of lightweight anodized aluminum alloy. The Model 96FS was discontinued in 1993.

NIB	Exc.	V.G.	Good	Fair	Poor
650	550	450	350	300	200

Model 92/96FS Centurion

Chambered for either the 9mm or .40 S&W (Model 96) this model features a 4.3" barrel, but retains a full grip to accommodate a 15-round magazine (9mm) or 10 rounds (.40 S&W). Pistol weighs approximately 33.2 oz. Introduced in 1993. Black sandblasted finish.

NIB	Exc.	V.G.	Good	Fair	Poor
550	450	400	300	200	150

Model 92FS/96 Brigadier

Same as the 92FS and 96 but with a heavier slide to reduce felt recoil. Removable front sight. Weight is about 35 oz.

NIB	Exc.	V.G.	Good	Fair	Poor
700	550	400	300	150	75

Model 92FS/96 Brigadier Inox

Same as above but with stainless steel finish. Introduced in 2000.

NIB	Exc.	V.G.	Good	Fair	Poor
750	600	475	325	175	100

Model 92G-SD/96G-SD

Introduced in 2003 this model features a decock mechanism built around a single-action/double-action trigger system. In addition, the pistol has an integral accessory rail on the frame. Fitted with a 9mm or .40 S&W 4.9" barrel with heavy slide and 3-dot tritium sights. Weight is about 35 oz.

NIB	Exc.	V.G.	Good	Fair	Poor
1000	750	500	350	195	125

Model 92F

A 9mm Parabellum caliber double-action semi-automatic pistol with a 4.9" barrel, fixed sights and a 15-shot double-stack magazine with an extended base. Matte blued finish with walnut or plastic grips. Introduced in 1984. No longer in production.

NIB	Exc.	V.G.	Good	Fair	Poor
500	400	350	300	200	150

Model 92F Compact

As above, with a 4.3" barrel and a 13-shot magazine. No longer in production.

NIB	Exc.	V.G.	Good	Fair	Poor
500	400	350	300	200	150

Model 92/96 Compact "Type M"

Essentially the same as the Model 92FS Compact but with the exception of a single column magazine that holds 8 rounds and reduces the grip thickness of the pistol. Pistol weighs 30.9 oz. Discontinued in 1993 and reintroduced in 1998. The Model 96 version (.40 S&W) was introduced in 2000.

NIB	Exc.	V.G.	Good	Fair	Poor
700	550	350	300	200	150

NOTE: Add $90 for Tritium night sights.

Model 92/96M Compact Inox

Same as above but with stainless steel slide and frame. Introduced in 2000.

NIB	Exc.	V.G.	Good	Fair	Poor
700	550	450	350	300	200

Model 92D Compact Type M

Same as above but with double-action-only trigger function.

NIB	Exc.	V.G.	Good	Fair	Poor
550	450	350	300	200	150

NOTE: Add $90 for Tritium night sights.

Model 92FS Deluxe

Identical dimensions to the full size Model 92FS with the addition of gold-plated engraved frame with gold-plated extra magazine in fitted leather presentation hard case. Grips are walnut briar with gold initial plate. Introduced in 1993.

NIB	Exc.	V.G.	Good	Fair	Poor
5500	4500	3000	2000	1500	1000

Model 92FS "470th Anniversary" Limited Edition

This model is limited to only 470 pistols worldwide. Features high polish finish with stainless steel, gold-filled engravings, walnut grips, Anniversary logo on top of slide and on the back of the chrome plated magazine. Supplied with walnut case.

NIB	Exc.	V.G.	Good	Fair	Poor
2075	1300	800	600	375	200

Model 92/96D

Same specifications as the standard Model 92 and Model 96 except that this variation has no visible hammer and is double-

action-only. This model has no manual safety. Pistol weighs 33.8 oz.

NIB	Exc.	V.G.	Good	Fair	Poor
425	375	325	275	200	150

Model 92/96DS

Same as above but with the same manual safety as found on the 92FS pistol. Introduced in 1994.

NIB	Exc.	V.G.	Good	Fair	Poor
425	375	325	275	200	150

Model 92G/96G

Designed for the French Gendarmerie, this model has now been adopted for the French Air Force as well as other government agencies. This model features a hammer drop lever that does not function as a safety when the lever is released but lowers the hammer and returns to the ready to fire position automatically. Offered to law enforcement agencies only, consumer prices N/A.

Model 92/96 Vertec

Introduced in 2002 this pistol is chambered for the 9mm or .40 S&W cartridges. Fitted with a 4.7" barrel. Double and single-action trigger. Features a new vertical grip design with a shorter trigger reach and thin grip panels. Removable front sight. and integral accessory rail on frame. Magazine capacity is 10 rounds. Weight is about 32 oz.

NIB	Exc.	V.G.	Good	Fair	Poor
700	575	425	300	225	165

Model 92 Competition Conversion Kit

The kit includes a 7.3" barrel with counterweight and elevated front sight, semi-automatic, walnut grips, and fully adjustable rear sight. Comes in special carrying case with the basic pistol.

NIB	Exc.	V.G.	Good	Fair	Poor
500	350	300	200	150	100

Model 92/96 Combo

This model features a specially designed Model 96 pistol with an extra 92FS slide and barrel assembly. Barrel lengths are 4.66". Sold with one 10-round magazine in both 9mm and .40 S&W.

NIB	Exc.	V.G.	Good	Fair	Poor
850	725	600	425	275	200

MODEL M9 LIMITED EDITION

Introduced in 1995 to commemorate the 10th anniversary of the U.S. military's official sidearm this 9mm pistol is limited to 10,000 units. Special engraving on the slide with special serial numbers. Slide stamped "u.s. 9mm M9-beretta u.s.a.-65490."

Standard Model

NIB	Exc.	V.G.	Good	Fair	Poor
825	700	450	300	200	100

Deluxe Model

Walnut grips with gold plated hammer and grip screws.

NIB	Exc.	V.G.	Good	Fair	Poor
875	750	500	350	200	100

Model 92 Billennium

Introduced in 2001 this is a limited production pistol of 2,000 units world wide. Chambered for the 9mm cartridge. Steel frame with checkered front and backstrap. Nickel alloy finish with unique engraving. Carbon fiber grips. Interchangeable sights with adjustable rear sight. Carry case standard. Single action.

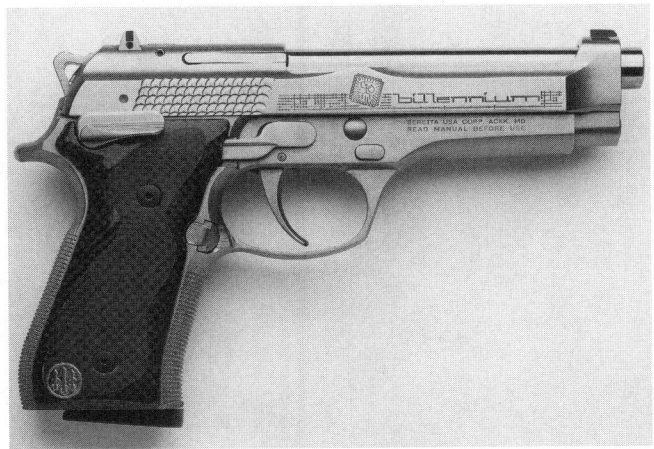

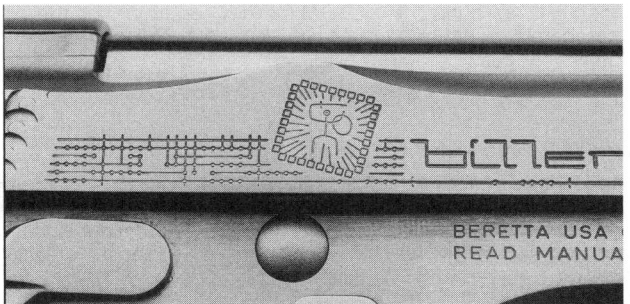

NIB	Exc.	V.G.	Good	Fair	Poor
1200	1000	800	600	475	325

92 Steel-I

Steel-frame semi-auto in 9mm or .40 S&W. Single- or single/double-action. 15+1 capacity, 4.7" barrel, 42.3 oz. IDPA certified. Fixed, 3-dot sights. Introduced 2006.

NIB	Exc.	V.G.	Good	Fair	Poor
1075	850	600	475	300	150

M9A1

Semi-auto, single/double-action in 9mm developed for U.S. Marine Corps. Capacity 10+1 or 15+1. Fixed sights. Introduced 2006.

NIB	Exc.	V.G.	Good	Fair	Poor
825	650	450	300	195	125

ELITE TEAM SERIES

In 1999 Beretta introduced a new series of pistols based on the company's M92/96 pistol. Each of these pistols has specific features for specific shooting requirements.

Model 92/96 Custom Carry

This model is fitted with a 4.3" barrel, shortened grip, and low profile control levers. Safety lever is left side only. Magazine capacity is 10 rounds. "CUSTOM CARRY" engraved on the slide. Chambered for either 9mm or .40 S&W calibers.

NIB	Exc.	V.G.	Good	Fair	Poor
625	500	400	300	200	100

Model 92/96 Border Marshall

This is the commercial version of the pistol built for the Immigration and Naturalization Service. It is fitted with a heavy-duty steel slide and short 4.7" I.N.S. style barrel. Rubber grips and night sights are standard. "BORDER MARSHALL" engraved on the slide. Offered in either 9mm or .40 S&W calibers.

NIB	Exc.	V.G.	Good	Fair	Poor
750	600	475	350	225	150

Model 92G/96G Elite

Chambered for 9mm or .40 S&W calibers this pistol is fitted with a 4.7" stainless steel barrel and heavy-duty Brigadier-style slide. The action is decock only. Slide has both front and rear serrations. Hammer is skeletonized. Beveled magazine well. Special "ELITE" engraving on the slide. Weight is about 35 oz.

NIB	Exc.	V.G.	Good	Fair	Poor
825	650	450	375	250	165

Model 92G Elite II

This version of the Elite was developed for the competition shooter. Fitted with a 4.7" barrel fitted with a heavy slide, it also has a skeletonized hammer. Beveled magazine well. Extended magazine release. Checkered front and backstrap grip. Weight is about 35 oz.

NIB	Exc.	V.G.	Good	Fair	Poor
925	725	550	395	275	150

Model 92FS Inox Tactical

This model has a satin matte finish on its stainless steel slide. The frame is anodized aluminum. Black rubber grips and night sights are standard. Offered in 9mm only.

NIB	Exc.	V.G.	Good	Fair	Poor
775	625	500	350	225	100

COUGAR SERIES

Model 8000/8040/8045 Cougar

This is a compact size pistol using a short recoil rotating barrel. It features a firing pin lock, chrome lined barrel, anodized aluminum alloy frame with Bruniton finish. Overall length is 7", barrel length is 3.6", overall height 5.5", and unloaded weight is 33.5 oz. Offered in double-/single-action as well as double-action-only. Magazine holds 10 rounds. Available in 9mm or .40 S&W. In 1998 Beretta added the .45 ACP caliber to this model.

NIB	Exc.	V.G.	Good	Fair	Poor
625	525	400	350	250	150

NOTE: Add $50 for .45 ACP models

Model 8000/8040/8045 Mini Cougar

This pistol was introduced in 1997 and is similar in design to the full size model. Offered in 9mm or .40 S&W or .45 ACP. The pistol is fitted with a 3.6" barrel (3.7" on .45 ACP). Empty weight is 27 oz. Offered in double-/single-action or double-action-only. Magazine capacity is 10 rounds for 9mm and 8 rounds for .40 S&W model. Weight is between 27 oz. and 30 oz. depending on caliber.

NIB	Exc.	V.G.	Good	Fair	Poor
500	450	350	225	125	75

NOTE: Add $50 for .45 ACP models

Model 8000F—Cougar L

Similar to the model above but fitted with a shortened grip frame. Chambered for the 9mm cartridge and fitted with a 3.6" barrel. Overall height as been reduced by .4". Weight is about 28 oz. Introduced in 2003.

NIB	Exc.	V.G.	Good	Fair	Poor
600	500	400	300	175	95

Model 9000F

Introduced in 2000 this pistol is chambered for the 9mm or .40 S&W cartridge. It is fitted with a 3.4" barrel and has a polymer frame. The "F" type has a single-action/double-action trigger. Fixed sights. Magazine capacity is 10 rounds. Weight is about 27 oz. Overall length is 6.6" and overall height is 4.8". External hammer and black finish.

NIB	Exc.	V.G.	Good	Fair	Poor
550	450	350	200	125	75

Model 9000D

Same as above but with double-action-only trigger.

NIB	Exc.	V.G.	Good	Fair	Poor
550	450	350	275	150	100

Model 9000S

This model is chambered for the 9mm or .40 S&W cartridges. Magazine capacity is 10 rounds. With optional spacer Model 92/96 magazines can also be used. Three-dot sight system. An accessory magazine bottom that extends when griped but retracts when holstered is standard. Steel alloy frame and slide. Weight is about 27 oz. Introduced in 2001.

NIB	Exc.	V.G.	Good	Fair	Poor
550	450	350	200	125	75

CHEETAH SERIES

Model 84/Cheetah

This is a small semi-automatic pistol chambered for the .380 cartridge. It has a double-column magazine that holds 13 rounds. Offered in blue or nickel finish. Grips are checkered black plastic or checkered wood.

NIB	Exc.	V.G.	Good	Fair	Poor
450	375	325	275	200	150

Model 84BB

Similar to the Model 84 but incorporates different features such as a firing pin blocking device and loaded chamber indicator. Single-column magazine holds 8 rounds of .380 shells. Discontinued in 1993.

NIB	Exc.	V.G.	Good	Fair	Poor
425	375	325	275	200	150

Model 85/Cheetah

Similar in appearance to the Model 84, but features a single-column magazine with a capacity of 8 rounds. Available in blue or nickel finish. Grips are checkered black plastic. Pistol weighs 22 oz.

NIB	Exc.	V.G.	Good	Fair	Poor
600	475	325	275	200	150

Model 86/Cheetah

This .380 ACP semi-automatic pistol has a 4.4" tip-up barrel. Magazine capacity is 8 rounds. Furnished with checkered wood grips. Pistol weighs 23 oz.

NIB	Exc.	V.G.	Good	Fair	Poor
675	500	300	250	200	150

Model 87/Cheetah

A .22 caliber double-action, semi-automatic target pistol with a 3.8" or 6" barrel, adjustable sights with a 7-shot magazine. Blued with checkered walnut grips. Introduced in 1986.

NIB	Exc.	V.G.	Good	Fair	Poor
650	525	375	250	200	150

Model 87 Target

This is a .22 caliber single-action target pistol. It features an adjustable rear sight, integral scope base, and external hammer. Anodized aluminum frame. Weight is about 41 oz. Introduced in 2000.

NIB	Exc.	V.G.	Good	Fair	Poor
700	600	395	250	200	150

Model 89/Gold Standard

A .22 caliber, semi-automatic target pistol with adjustable sights, and 10-shot, detachable magazine. Matte finish with hand-fitting walnut grips. Introduced in 1988.

NIB	Exc.	V.G.	Good	Fair	Poor
900	725	550	400	300	150

Px4 Storm Pistol

Introduced in 2005 this pistol features a single/double action trigger with decocker and is chambered for the 9mm, .45 ACP or .40 S&W cartridges. Fitted with a 4" barrel. Interchangeable grip backstraps. Reversable magazine release button. Picatinny rail. Fixed sights. Magazine capacity is 14 rounds for the .40 S&W and 17 rounds for the 9mm. Weight is about 27.5 lbs.

NIB	Exc.	V.G.	Good	Fair	Poor
500	450	375	250	195	125

Beretta Model PX4 Storm Subcompact

Similar to above but with smaller dimensions and chambered in 9mm and .40 S&W only, 10- (.40) or 13- (9mm) round capacity. Overall length 6.2". Weight: 26.1 oz.

Beretta Model PX4 Storm SD Special Duty

Similar to PX4 Storm but in .45 ACP only and with matte black slide and OD polymer frame, nine- or 10-round magazine. Overall length 8.2". Weight 28.6 oz.

NIB	Exc.	V.G.	Good	Fair	Poor
900	750	575	450	300	150

90-Two

Wrap-around polymer grip, standard or slim. Single/double-action semi-auto in 9mm (10+1, 15+1 or 17+1 capacity) or .40 S&W (10+1 or 12+1 capacity). Types D, F or G. Fixed sights. 4.9" barrel, 32.5 oz. Introduced 2006. Add 10 percent for luminous sights.

NIB	Exc.	V.G.	Good	Fair	Poor
600	475	350	290	210	150

Stampede Blue

Introduced in 2003, this single-action revolver is chambered for the choice of .45 Colt, .44-40, or .357 Magnum cartridge. Choice of 4.75", 5.5", or 7.5" barrel. Blued with Beretta case color and black polymer grips. Weight is about 2.3 lbs. depending on barrel length.

NIB	Exc.	V.G.	Good	Fair	Poor
525	400	275	195	125	75

Stampede Nickel

As above but with brushed nickel finish and walnut grips.

NIB	Exc.	V.G.	Good	Fair	Poor
500	400	295	195	125	75

Stampede Deluxe

As above but with charcoal blue finish and Beretta case color with select walnut grips.

NIB	Exc.	V.G.	Good	Fair	Poor
620	500	375	250	195	125

Stampede Bisley

Single action 6-shot Bisley replica revolver in .45 Colt or .357 Magnum. Blued with 4-3/4", 5-1/2" or 7-1/2" barrel. Introduced 2006. Add 10 percent for nickel.

NIB	Exc.	V.G.	Good	Fair	Poor
620	500	375	250	195	125

Laramie

Break-open single-action revolver reminiscent of S&W #3 chambered for.45 LC or .38 Special. Six-shot cylinder. Adjustable rear sight. 5" or 6-1/2" barrels. Introduced 2006. Add 10 percent for nickel finish. Made by Beretta subsidiary Uberti.

NIB	Exc.	V.G.	Good	Fair	Poor
1000	875	595	375	225	145

BERGER, JEAN MARIUS

St. Etienne, France
Berger

The Berger was a magazine fed repeating pistol in 7.65mm. It was a self loader and self cocker. It had all the characteristics of a semi-automatic except for the recoil operating system.

Courtesy James Rankin

NIB	Exc.	V.G.	Good	Fair	Poor
—	5900	4750	3750	3000	2000

BERGMANN, THEODOR
Gaggenau, Germany

Theodor Bergmann was a successful industrialist, designer and sometimes inventor with a deep interest in firearms based in Gaggenau, Germany. His first automatic pistol patent dates from 1892, and by 1894 he had prototype pistols, refined with the help of Louis Schmeisser, being evaluated by various governments. When his designs went into commercial production in 1896, however, they were actually manufactured by the firm of V. Charles Schilling in Suhl, the heart of German arms manufacture. Later he licensed manufacture of his "Mars" pistol to Anciens Establishment Pieper ("Bayard"), and after WWI affiliated with the Lignose firm, producing a line of .25 caliber pocket pistols, first under the Bergmann name but later marketed as Lignose. Still later several pistol designs from the August Menz firm were marketed under the "Bergmann Erben" trademark, though it's doubtful if the Bergmann firm actually had much part in their production or sale.

Model 1894 Bergmann Schmeisser

The Model 1894 was made in prototype form only, with only a few examples surviving and known serial numbers no higher than the mid teens. Most are large framed and chambered for the 8mm Bergmann-Schmeisser cartridge, though at least one was made in 7.5mm Swiss revolver for Swiss army testing and a few very compact versions, with a unique folding trigger, for 5mm Bergmann. Early Bergmann pistols had no extractor, counting on gas pressure to blow the fired (rimless-grooveless) cartridge from the chamber. Too rare to price.

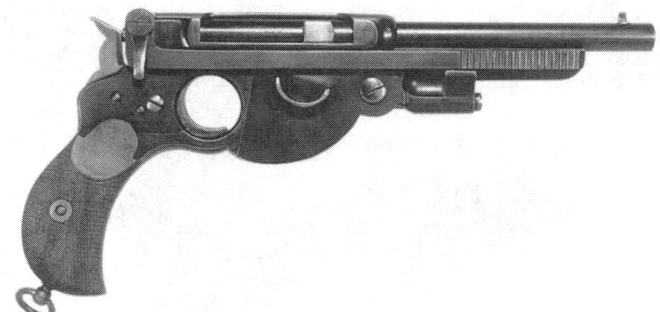

MODEL 1896, NUMBER 2

The 1896 Number 2 pistols were quite compact and chambered for the 5mm Bergmann cartridge. Early Number 2s also featured a folding trigger and no extractor, but after serial 500 or so reverted to a more conventional in-the-frame trigger and an extractor was added. About 2000 of the later model were produced. Cased sets are known, and add about 50 percent to the value.

Folding Trigger Number 2

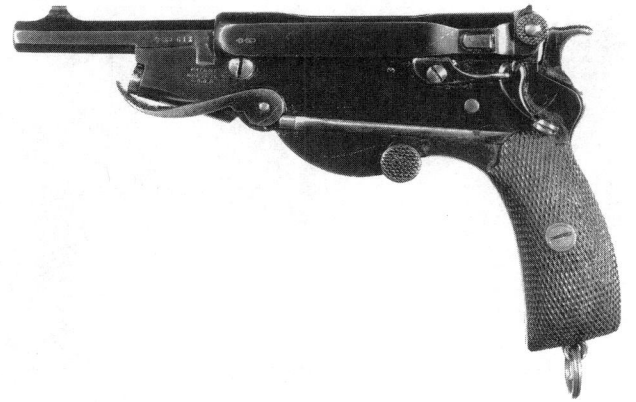

Courtesy James Rankin

NIB	Exc.	V.G.	Good	Fair	Poor
—	4700	3700	2800	1500	800

Conventional Number 2

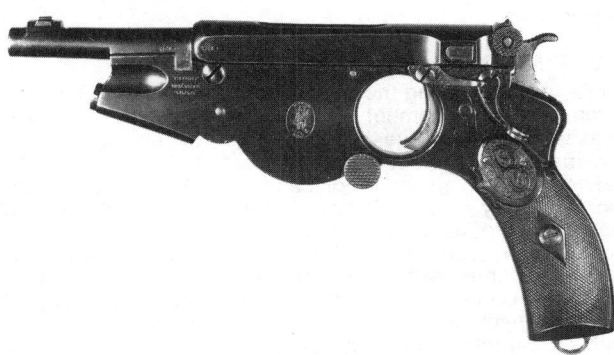

Courtesy James Rankin

NIB	Exc.	V.G.	Good	Fair	Poor
—	3700	3200	2250	1375	800

MODEL 1896 NUMBER 3

The Number 3 was a larger version of the Number 2, chambered for the 6.5mm Bergmann cartridge. Early examples had a slim gripframe and, up to about serial 800, were made without extractor like the early Number 2s. These bring about a 20 percent premium over the later examples. Number 3 serials range to a little over 4000. Add about 20 percent for dealer markings (usually English), and 50 percent for cased sets. A few target models, with long barrel, adjustable sights and set triggers are known and will bring about three times the price of a standard Number 3.

Model 1896 Number 3 First Variation

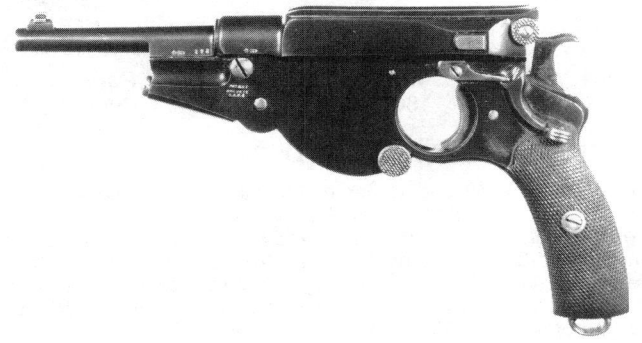

Courtesy James Rankin

NIB	Exc.	V.G.	Good	Fair	Poor
—	4050	3500	2750	1650	800

Second Variation

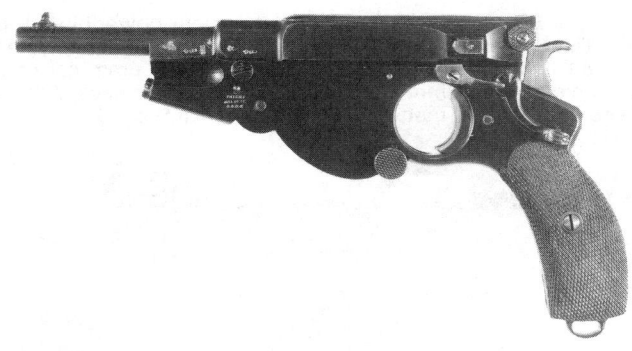

Courtesy James Rankin

NIB	Exc.	V.G.	Good	Fair	Poor
—	3500	3200	2500	1650	800

Third Variation

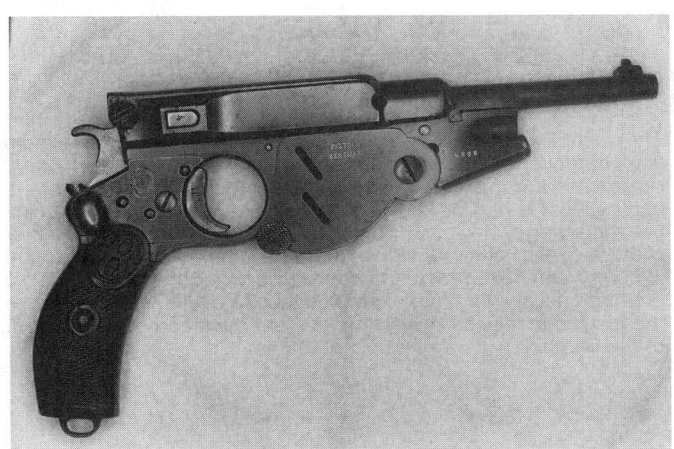

Courtesy James Rankin

NIB	Exc.	V.G.	Good	Fair	Poor
—	3700	3200	2500	1650	800

Holster and Stock Model

Courtesy James Rankin

NIB	Exc.	V.G.	Good	Fair	Poor
—	6300	5700	4950	3250	2750

Model 1896 Number 4

The Number 4 is identical to the Number 3 but chambered for a unique 8mm Bergmann cartridge and serialed in the same series with the Number 3. Both the Number 4 and its cartridge are rare; probably fewer than 200 were ever made.

NIB	Exc.	V.G.	Good	Fair	Poor
—	8000	6500	5000	3700	2900

Model 1897 Number 5

This was Bergmann's first attempt at a more powerful arm for the military market, with a unique side-moving locking system and a 10-shot removable box magazine. The 7.8mm cartridge resembled the 7.63mm Mauser, but with a longer neck. Add 60 percent for original metal framed leather holster-stock.

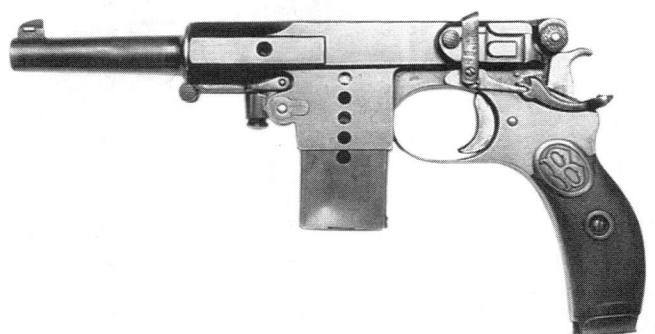

NIB	Exc.	V.G.	Good	Fair	Poor
—	8550	6900	4950	3000	2250

Bergmann Simplex

The Simplex combined some features of the 1896 pistols with improvements developed from the "Mars," resulting in a reasonable compact pocket pistol that came on the market in the early 1900s. It was chambered for the unique Bergmann-Simplex 8mm cartridge, however, and that and competition from better Browning and other designs doomed it to a short production life. Very early examples had checkered wood grips and bring a premium, as do very late examples (above serial 3000) that have the magazine release behind the magazine instead of on the front of the frame.

NIB	Exc.	V.G.	Good	Fair	Poor
—	3450	2950	2000	900	600

Bergmann "Mars"

The Mars was Bergmann's first really successful pistol aimed at the military market. Early examples, about 100 of the total 1000 or so Mars pistols made, were chambered for the 7.63mm Mauser cartridge but later Mars pistols, identified by a large "9mm" on the chamber, were chambered for the special 9mm cartridge that later became known as the 9mm Bergmann-Bayard. The Mars was adopted by the Spanish government in 1905 as their first military automatic pistol, but none were ever delivered by Bergmann. At least two Mars pistols were also made in .45 caliber for U.S. Army trials in 1906, but did not perform well and were dropped from the trials; these are too rare to price.

NIB	Exc.	V.G.	Good	Fair	Poor
—	7000	5300	3850	2500	1650

NOTE: Add 25 percent for a low serial number gun chambered for 7.63mm Mauser; add 50 percent for original Bergmann Mars holster stock.

Bergmann Bayard Model 1908

Shortly after receiving the Spanish contract for the Mars pistol, Bergmann's arrangement with Schilling to produce Bergmann pistols ended. However, he negotiated an arrangement with Anciens Establishment Pieper (Bayard) to produce the Mars and, after some minor modifications, AEP filled the Spanish contract. They also marketed the gun commercially, and later secured a production contract from the Danish army as the Model 1910. Spanish contract (proofed with a small circle divided into three segments) and very early commercial pistols have hard rubber grips that proved very fragile in service; these bring a premium as do original unmodified Danish contract guns (with a contract number and Danish letter D proof). A few Model 1908 Bergmann Bayards were equipped with leather and wood holster stocks; a complete rig is worth at least twice the price of an unslotted pistol.

Courtesy James Rankin

NIB	Exc.	V.G.	Good	Fair	Poor
—	1950	1600	1000	775	550

BERGMANN POST WAR PISTOLS

Shortly after WWI ended Bergmann came on the market with a line of .25 caliber pocket pistols; the 2 and 3 were conventional vest pocket designs with a short and long gripframe respectively; the 2a and 3a were identical except for an "Einhand" (one-hand) feature that enabled the user to cycle the slide by pulling the front of the trigger guard with his trigger finger. Soon into production (at about serial 8000) Bergmann affiliated with the Lignose firm and later Model 2 and 3 pistols were marketed under the Lignose name.

Courtesy Joe Schroeder

Model 2 and 3

NIB	Exc.	V.G.	Good	Fair	Poor
—	325	275	200	150	100

Model 2a and 3a

NIB	Exc.	V.G.	Good	Fair	Poor
—	400	375	325	275	150

Bergmann Erben Pistols

The Bergmann Erben pistols appear to be an attempt by the Bergmann family to keep the Bergmann name associated with firearms without actually investing any design or production effort. The Bergmann Erben pistols were all August Menz designs, and were undoubtedly made by Menz as well. Most noteworthy was the "Spezial" model, a very sophisticated double-action .32 pocket pistol that could be cocked for single-action fire by pulling and then releasing the trigger. Also noteworthy were several compact vest pocket .25s that also bore the Bergmann Erben name.

Bergmann Erben Spezial

NIB	Exc.	V.G.	Good	Fair	Poor
—	1650	1350	900	650	400

Bergmann Erben Model II Pistol

Courtesy James Rankin

NIB	Exc.	V.G.	Good	Fair	Poor
—	550	495	330	225	125

Bergmann Einhand

SEE—Lignose.

BERNARDELLI, VINCENZO
Brescia, Italy

Established in the 1721, this company originally manufactured military arms and only entered the commercial sporting arms market in 1928.

Vest Pocket Model

Similar to the Walther Model 9, in a 6.35mm caliber semi-automatic pistol with a 2.25" barrel, and 5-shot magazine. An extended 8-shot version was also available. Blued with plastic grips. Manufactured between 1945 and 1948.

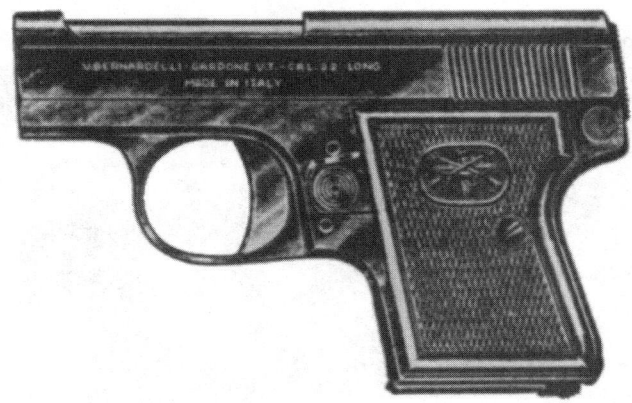

NIB	Exc.	V.G.	Good	Fair	Poor
—	350	250	180	125	100

Pocket Model

As above, in 7.65mm caliber. This model was also offered with extended barrels that protruded beyond the end of the slide. Introduced in 1947.

NIB	Exc.	V.G.	Good	Fair	Poor
—	300	225	200	150	100

Baby Model

As above, in .22 short or long rifle. Manufactured between 1949 and 1968.

NIB	Exc.	V.G.	Good	Fair	Poor
—	300	225	175	125	95

Sporter Model

A .22 caliber semi-automatic pistol with 6", 8", or 10" barrels and adjustable sights. Blued with walnut grips. Manufactured between 1949 and 1968.

NIB	Exc.	V.G.	Good	Fair	Poor
—	325	250	200	150	125

Revolvers

A .22 rimfire and .32 caliber double-action revolver with 1.5", 2", or 5" barrels. A .22 caliber, 7" barrel version with adjustable sights also available. Manufactured between 1950 and 1962.

NIB	Exc.	V.G.	Good	Fair	Poor
—	250	175	150	125	100

Model 60

A .22, .32 ACP or .380 ACP caliber semi-automatic pistol with 3.5" barrel and fixed sights. Blued with plastic grips. Manufactured since 1959.

NIB	Exc.	V.G.	Good	Fair	Poor
—	275	200	175	150	115

Model 68

A .22 rimfire caliber or .25 ACP semi-automatic pistol with a 2" barrel and 5-shot magazine. Blued with plastic grips. No longer imported into the U.S.

NIB	Exc.	V.G.	Good	Fair	Poor
—	200	175	150	100	75

Model 80

A .22 or .380 ACP caliber semi-automatic pistol with a 3.5" barrel and adjustable sights. Blued with plastic grips. Imported between 1968 and 1988.

NIB	Exc.	V.G.	Good	Fair	Poor
—	250	200	150	125	95

Model AMR

As above, with a 6" barrel.

NIB	Exc.	V.G.	Good	Fair	Poor
450	350	200	150	100	90

Model 69

A .22 caliber semi-automatic target pistol with a 6" heavy barrel, and a 10-shot magazine. Blued with checkered walnut grips.

NIB	Exc.	V.G.	Good	Fair	Poor
450	375	300	225	150	100

Model PO10

A .22 caliber, single-action, semi-automatic target pistol with a 6" barrel, adjustable target sights, barrel weights, and an adjustable trigger. Matte-black finish with stippled walnut grips. Introduced in 1989. Weight 40 oz. sold with special hard case.

NIB	Exc.	V.G.	Good	Fair	Poor
800	700	500	300	200	100

Model PO18

A 7.65mm or 9mm Parabellum caliber, double-action, semi-automatic pistol with a 4.75" barrel and a 16-shot, double stack, detachable magazine. All-steel construction. Blued with plastic grips. Walnut grips are available for an additional $40. Introduced in 1985.

NIB	Exc.	V.G.	Good	Fair	Poor
550	450	300	275	200	100

Model PO18 Compact

As above, with a 4" barrel and a shorter grip frame with a 14-shot, double-column magazine. Introduced in 1989.

NIB	Exc.	V.G.	Good	Fair	Poor
550	450	300	275	200	100

Model P. One

A full-size semi-automatic pistol chambered for the 9mm or .40 S&W calibers. Fitted with a 4.8" barrel. Can be fired double-action or single-action. Ten-shot magazine. Weight is 2.14 lbs. Available in black or chrome finish. Add $50 for chrome finish.

NIB	Exc.	V.G.	Good	Fair	Poor
625	525	400	275	200	100

Model P. One-Compact

Same as above but with 4" barrel and offered in .380 caliber as well as 9mm and .40 S&W. Weight is 1.96 lbs.

NIB	Exc.	V.G.	Good	Fair	Poor
650	550	400	275	200	100

Practical VB Target

Designed for Practical shooting this 9mm pistol has a 6" barrel with choice of 2 or 4 port compensator. It is fitted with numerous extra features. Weights is 2.2 lbs.

NIB	Exc.	V.G.	Good	Fair	Poor
1500	1200	850	600	400	200

Practical VB Custom

As above but designed for IPSC rules.

NIB	Exc.	V.G.	Good	Fair	Poor
2250	1900	1400	900	600	300

BERNARDON MARTIN
St. Etienne, France

This small firm was active between 1906 and 1912. The gun designer was Martin and the money man was Bernardon.

1907/8 Model

A 7.65mm caliber semi-automatic pistol. The left side of the slide is marked "Cal. 7.65mm St. Etienne." The trademark "BM" is molded into the grips. Sometimes found with a 32-round horseshoe magazine.Occasionally the Bernardon Martin pistol will be noted with the word "Hermetic" stamped on the slide in letters that do not match the other markings on the weapon. This was but another name for the Model 1907/8. Guns with this stamping were most likely assembled after the company ceased operations.

Courtesy James Rankin

NIB	Exc.	V.G.	Good	Fair	Poor
—	1100	875	700	450	275

NOTE: Add 50 percent for horseshoe magazine.

1908/9 Model

Introduced late in 1908 this model is similar to the Model 1907/8 with the addition of a grip safety.

NIB	Exc.	V.G.	Good	Fair	Poor
—	925	775	600	375	225

BERNEDO, VINCENZO
Eibar, Spain

B C

The B C is in caliber 6.35mm and most of the barrel is exposed. The recoil spring is housed in the rear of the receiver. The B C closely resembles the Tanque pistol.

Courtesy James Rankin

NIB	Exc.	V.G.	Good	Fair	Poor
—	325	225	200	175	150

Bernado

This model 7.65mm is in the Spanish style of the Ruby automatic pistols.

Courtesy James Rankin

NIB	Exc.	V.G.	Good	Fair	Poor
—	225	150	125	75	50

BERSA
Ramos Mejia, Argentina

Model 644

This model is a blowback pocket pistol chambered for the .22 LR. The trigger system is single-action. Barrel length is 3.5", overall length is 6.57", and empty weight is approximately 28 oz. This is the basic Bersa model from which its other models derive their design and function.

NIB	Exc.	V.G.	Good	Fair	Poor
275	175	150	125	100	75

Model 622

Similar to the Model 644 but with a slightly longer barrel.

NIB	Exc.	V.G.	Good	Fair	Poor
275	175	150	125	100	75

Model 97

This model is a slightly larger version of the Model 644 chambered for the 9mm Short.

NIB	Exc.	V.G.	Good	Fair	Poor
275	175	150	125	100	75

Model 23

A .22 rimfire caliber, double-action, semi-automatic pistol with a 3.5" barrel and 10-shot detachable magazine. Either blued or satin nickel-plated with checkered walnut grips.

NIB	Exc.	V.G.	Good	Fair	Poor
300	200	150	125	100	75

Model 223

As above, with a squared trigger guard and nylon grips. Imported after 1988.

NIB	Exc.	V.G.	Good	Fair	Poor
—	275	175	125	100	75

Model 224

As above, with a 4" barrel. Imported after 1988.

NIB	Exc.	V.G.	Good	Fair	Poor
—	275	175	125	100	75

Model 225

As above, with a 5" barrel. Discontinued in 1986.

NIB	Exc.	V.G.	Good	Fair	Poor
—	275	175	125	100	75

Model 226

As above, with a 6" barrel. Discontinued in 1988.

Courtesy John J. Stimson, Jr.

NIB	Exc.	V.G.	Good	Fair	Poor
—	275	175	125	100	75

Model 323

A .32 ACP caliber single-action semi-automatic pistol, with a 3.5" barrel, fixed sights and a 7-shot detachable magazine. Blued with molded plastic grips. Not imported after 1986.

NIB	Exc.	V.G.	Good	Fair	Poor
—	225	125	100	75	50

Model 383

As above, in .380 caliber. Discontinued in 1988.

NIB	Exc.	V.G.	Good	Fair	Poor
—	250	150	125	90	75

Model 383A

A .380 ACP caliber double-action semi-automatic pistol with a 3.5" barrel with fixed sights and 7-shot magazine. Blued with checkered walnut grips. Overall length is 6.6" and weight is about 24 oz. Available in blue or nickel finish.

NIB	Exc.	V.G.	Good	Fair	Poor
300	200	150	125	100	75

Model 83

Similar to the above model but with double-action operating system. Weighs about 26 oz. Introduced in 1988.

NIB	Exc.	V.G.	Good	Fair	Poor
300	200	150	125	100	75

Model 85

As above, with a double-column magazine. Introduced in 1988.

NIB	Exc.	V.G.	Good	Fair	Poor
350	250	200	150	100	75

Model 86

Similar to the Model 85 .380 caliber, but features a matte blue or satin nickel finish, wrap around rubber grips, and three-dot sight. Magazine capacity is 13 rounds.

NIB	Exc.	V.G.	Good	Fair	Poor
350	250	225	200	150	100

Thunder 9

Introduced in 1993 this model is a double-action 9mm pistol that features ambidextrous safety, reversible extended magazine release, ambidextrous slide release, adjustable trigger stop, combat-style hammer, three-dot sights, and matte blue finish. Magazine capacity is 15 rounds.

NIB	Exc.	V.G.	Good	Fair	Poor
350	275	250	200	150	100

Series 95/Thunder 380

This is a semi-automatic double-action pistol chambered for the .380 cartridge. Choice of matte blue or nickel finish. Barrel length is 3.5". Fixed sights. Magazine capacity is 7 rounds. Weight is about 23 oz. Add $50 for nickel.

NIB	Exc.	V.G.	Good	Fair	Poor
260	200	150	100	75	50

Thunder 380 Matte Plus

Semi-auto double-action blued pistol in .380 with 15-round magazine. Fixed sights and polymer grips. Introduced 2006.

NIB	Exc.	V.G.	Good	Fair	Poor
350	275	250	200	150	100

Thunder 9 Ultra Compact

Available blued or stainless with 10- or 13-round capacity. Double-action chambered for 9mm. 3.5" barrel, 25 oz., fixed sights and polymer grips. Introduced 2006. Add $50 for $500 stainless.

NIB	Exc.	V.G.	Good	Fair	Poor
395	300	250	200	150	100

Thunder 9/40 High Capacity Series

Double-action semi-autos available chambered for 9mm or .40 S&W and in matte blued or satin nickel-plate. Fixed sights and polymer grips. LOA 7-1/2", 4-1/4" barrel, 26 oz. Introduced 2006.

NIB	Exc.	V.G.	Good	Fair	Poor
395	300	250	200	150	100

Thunder Deluxe

This semi-automatic double-action pistol is chambered for the .380 cartridge. Blued finish. Fixed sights. Barrel length is 3.5". Weight is about 23 oz. Magazine capacity is 9 rounds.

NIB	Exc.	V.G.	Good	Fair	Poor
325	225	175	100	75	50

BERTRAND, JULES
Liege, Belgium

Le Novo

A 6.35mm caliber double-action revolver. Manufactured in the 1890s. The only identifying markings are the "JB" trademark on the grips.

NIB	Exc.	V.G.	Good	Fair	Poor
—	300	225	175	100	50

Lincoln

As above, in 7.65mm caliber.

NIB	Exc.	V.G.	Good	Fair	Poor
—	300	225	175	100	50

Le Rapide

A 6.35mm caliber, semi-automatic pistol. The Jules Bertrand logo is on the slide, as well as Le Rapide. Both are on each side of the grip plates.

Courtesy James Rankin

NIB	Exc.	V.G.	Good	Fair	Poor
—	350	275	200	125	50

BIGHORN ARMS CO.
Watertown, South Dakota

Target Pistol

A .22 caliber single-shot pistol resembling a semi-automatic. Ventilated rib barrel 6" in length. Stock of molded plastic.

NIB	Exc.	V.G.	Good	Fair	Poor
—	275	175	100	85	65

BILLINGHURST, WILLIAM
Rochester, New York

Billinghurst originally worked for James and John Miller of Rochester. After James Miller's death in 1837, Billinghurst established his own shop where he produced revolving rifles based upon Miller's 1829 patent. While these arms were originally made with percussion ignition systems (either pill or percussion cap), later examples using self-contained metallic cartridges are sometimes encountered. Billinghurst also established a well-deserved reputation for making extremely accurate percussion target pistols and rifles.

Under Hammer Pistol

This pistol is somewhat different than most of the under hammers encountered. The barrels are 12" to 18" in length and of a heavy octagonal construction. They are chambered from .30 to .38 caliber and utilize the percussion ignition system. Higher grade versions feature a part-round barrel, and it is important to note that no two pistols are alike. These pistols were furnished with detachable shoulder stocks, and a good many were cased with telescopic sights and false muzzles. This is a high quality weapon; and if encountered with the optional accessories, it would definitely warrant an individual appraisal. This firearm was manufactured in the 1850s and 1860s.

NIB	Exc.	V.G.	Good	Fair	Poor
—	—	4750	2150	800	400

NOTE: Shoulder stock add 50 percent.

BILLINGS
Location Unknown

Pocket Pistol

A .32 rimfire caliber single-shot spur trigger pistol with a 2.5" round barrel and an unusually large grip. The barrel is stamped "Billings Vest Pocket Pistol Pat. April 24, 1866." Blued with walnut grips. Manufactured between 1865 and 1868.

NIB	Exc.	V.G.	Good	Fair	Poor
—	—	3500	1500	550	195

BISMARCK
Location Unknown

Pocket Revolver

A .22 caliber spur trigger revolver with a 3" round ribbed barrel and a 7-shot, unfluted cylinder. Brass frame and the remainder was plated with rosewood grips. The barrel is marked "Bismarck." Manufactured in the 1870s.

NIB	Exc.	V.G.	Good	Fair	Poor
—	—	550	225	90	50

BITTERLICH, FRANK J.
Nashville, Tennessee

A .41 caliber single-shot percussion pistol in a variety of octagonal barrel lengths, German silver mounts, walnut stock. The barrel and locks are marked "Fr.J. Bitterlich/Nashville, Tenn." Produced between 1861 and 1867.

NIB	Exc.	V.G.	Good	Fair	Poor
—	—	5500	4900	1900	850

BITTNER, GUSTAV
Wieport, Bohemia

Bittner

A 7.7mm Bittner caliber repeating pistol with a 4.5" barrel. The bolt containing the firing pin rotates to lock the breech and is operated by the finger lever that encloses the trigger. Manufactured in mid 1890s. Fewer than 500 were made.

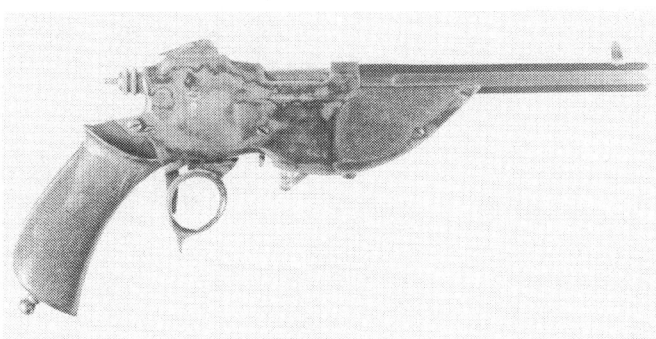

NIB	Exc.	V.G.	Good	Fair	Poor
—	15000	10500	8000	4000	2000

BLANCH, JOHN
London, England

Percussion Pistol

A .69 caliber single-shot, percussion pistol with a 5" Damascus barrel. Engraved frame and hammer with a walnut grip. Manufactured in the 1830s.

NIB	Exc.	V.G.	Good	Fair	Poor
—	—	6750	2950	1450	875

BLASER JAGDWAFFEN
Germany

Blaser HHS

This single-shot pistol has an R93 receiver and is fitted with a 14" barrel and pistol-grip fancy Turkish walnut stock. All R93 calibers are offered. Offered in both right- and left-hand models. Introduced in 2003.

NIB	Exc.	V.G.	Good	Fair	Poor
4250	3250	2000	1300	70	400

NOTE: Add $100 for left-hand models.

BLISS, F. D.
New Haven, Connecticut

Pocket Revolver

A .25 caliber spur trigger revolver with a 3.25" octagon barrel, 6-shot magazine, and a square butt. Blued with either hard rubber or walnut grips. The barrel is stamped "F.D. Bliss New Haven, Ct." There was an all-brass framed version made early in the production, and this model would be worth approximately 50 percent more than the values listed here for the standard model. Approximately 3,000 manufactured circa 1860 to 1863.

NIB	Exc.	V.G.	Good	Fair	Poor
—	—	975	525	125	75

BLISS & GOODYEAR
New Haven, Connecticut

Pocket Model Revolver

A .28 caliber percussion revolver with a 3" octagonal barrel, 6-shot magazine, unfluted cylinder and a solid frame with a removable side plate. Blued with a brass frame and walnut grips. Approximately 3,000 manufactured in 1860.

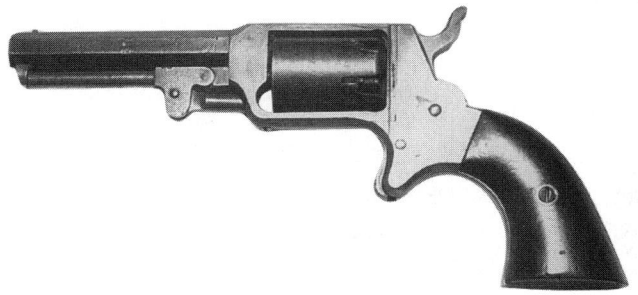

NIB	Exc.	V.G.	Good	Fair	Poor
—	—	1800	550	225	150

BLUNT & SYMS
New York, New York

UNDER HAMMER PEPPERBOX

Pepperboxes produced by Blunt & Syms are noteworthy for the fact that they incorporate a ring trigger cocking/revolving mechanism and a concealed under hammer. They were produced in a variety of calibers and the standard finish was blued. Normally these pistols are found marked simply "A-C" on the face of the barrel group. Some examples though are marked "Blunt & Syms New York." This firm was in business from approximately 1837 to 1855.

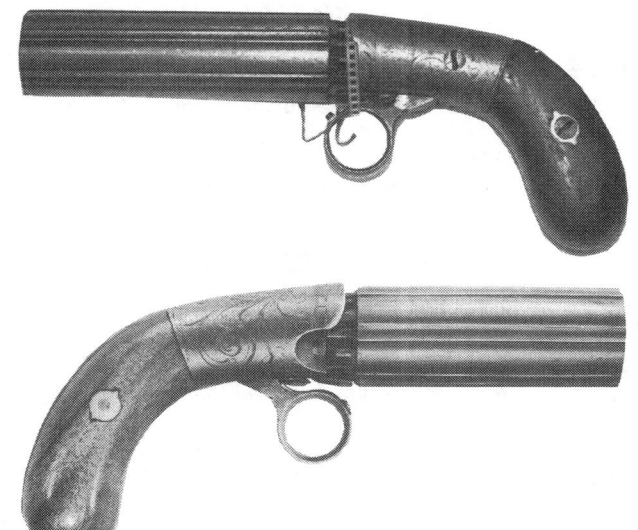

Small Frame Round Handle .25-.28 Caliber

NIB	Exc.	V.G.	Good	Fair	Poor
—	—	1800	1300	675	175

Medium Frame Round Handle .31 Caliber

NIB	Exc.	V.G.	Good	Fair	Poor
—	—	1850	1450	725	195

Round Handle Dragoon .36 Caliber

NIB	Exc.	V.G.	Good	Fair	Poor
—	—	2900	1050	900	295

Medium Frame Saw Handle .31 Caliber

NIB	Exc.	V.G.	Good	Fair	Poor
—	—	2000	750	375	175

Saw Handle Dragoon .36 Caliber

NIB	Exc.	V.G.	Good	Fair	Poor
—	—	2800	1350	750	225

Dueling Pistol

A .52 caliber percussion single-shot pistol with an octagonal barrel normally of 9" length. Steel furniture with a walnut stock. Barrel marked "B&S New York/Cast Steel."

NIB	Exc.	V.G.	Good	Fair	Poor
—	—	—	1750	725	325

Single-Shot Bar Hammer

A .36 caliber single-shot percussion pistol with a 6" half-octagonal barrel and a bar hammer. Blued or browned with walnut grips. Marked as above.

NIB	Exc.	V.G.	Good	Fair	Poor
—	—	1200	700	450	200

Side Hammer Pocket Pistol

A .31 or .35 caliber single-shot percussion pistol with a 2.5" to 6" octagonal barrel. Blued with walnut grips.

NIB	Exc.	V.G.	Good	Fair	Poor
—	—	1250	650	425	195

Side Hammer Belt Pistol

As above, in calibers ranging from .36 to .44 with barrel lengths of 4" or 6".

NIB	Exc.	V.G.	Good	Fair	Poor
—	—	1400	750	375	150

Ring Trigger Pistol

A .36 caliber percussion single-shot pistol with a 3" to 5" half-octagonal barrel and a ring trigger. Blued with walnut grips.

NIB	Exc.	V.G.	Good	Fair	Poor
—	—	1025	650	375	150

Double Barrel Pistol

A .36 to .44 caliber percussion double barrel pistol with 7.5" barrels and walnut grips. A ring trigger variation of this model is known.

NIB	Exc.	V.G.	Good	Fair	Poor
—	—	1350	650	275	125

Double Barrel Under Hammer Pistol

As above, with two under hammers and in .34 caliber with 4" barrels.

NIB	Exc.	V.G.	Good	Fair	Poor
—	—	1750	875	425	200

Derringer Style Pistol

A .50 caliber single-shot percussion pistol with a 3" barrel, German silver mounts and a walnut stock. The lock is marked "Blunt & Syms/New York."

NIB	Exc.	V.G.	Good	Fair	Poor
—	—	1800	675	395	200

BODEO

ITALIAN SERVICE REVOLVER

System Bodeo Modello 1889 (Enlisted Model)

NIB	Exc.	V.G.	Good	Fair	Poor
—	750	550	400	250	100

Modello 1889 (Officer's Model)

NIB	Exc.	V.G.	Good	Fair	Poor
—	750	550	400	250	100

BOLUMBURO, G.
Eibar, Spain

Bristol

A semi-automatic pistol in caliber 7.65mm made in the style of the Ruby military pistols. Bristol is stamped on the slide. Wood grips.

Courtesy James Rankin

NIB	Exc.	V.G.	Good	Fair	Poor
—	295	185	150	90	40

Marina 6.35mm

A semi-automatic pistol in caliber 6.35mm. Marina is stamped on each grip's plate.

NIB	Exc.	V.G.	Good	Fair	Poor
—	275	195	150	90	40

BOND ARMS INC.
Grandbury, Texas

Texas Defender

This is a stainless steel over-and-under derringer chambered for a variety of calibers such as .45 Colt/.410, .357 Magnum, 9mm, .45 ACP, and .44 Magnum. Removable triggerguard. Barrels are interchangeable. Grips are laminated black ash or rosewood. Barrel length is 3" with blade front sight and fixed rear sight. Weight is approximately 21 oz. Introduced in 1997. Add 300 percent for fully factory engraved model.

NIB	Exc.	V.G.	Good	Fair	Poor
—	400	300	200	150	100

Snake Slayer IV

Modern variation of the Remington over/under derringer. Interchangeable 4.5" barrel assemblies, rosewood grip panels, stainless finish, fixed sights. Chambered for .410-bore shotshell/.45 LC, 9mm, 10mm, .40 S&W, .45 ACP.

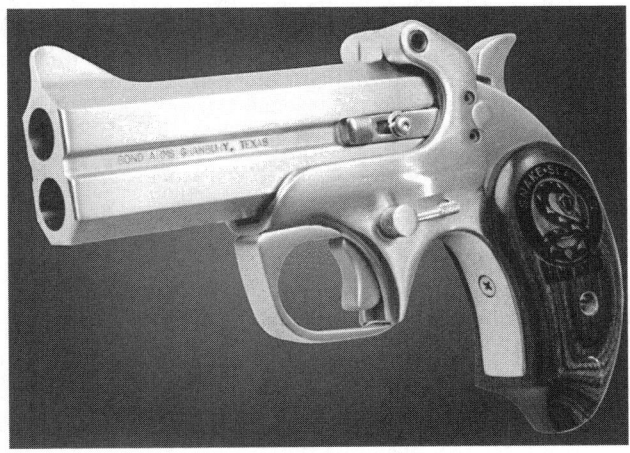

NIB	Exc.	V.G.	Good	Fair	Poor
—	400	300	200	150	100

Snake Slayer

3.5" barrels; weighs 22 oz. Interchangeable barrel assemblies, rosewood grip panels, stainless, fixed sights. Chambered for .410-bore shotshell/.45 LC, 9mm, 10mm, .40 S&W, .45 ACP).

NIB	Exc.	V.G.	Good	Fair	Poor
—	400	300	200	150	100

Courtesy James Rankin

NIB	Exc.	V.G.	Good	Fair	Poor
—	295	195	150	90	40

Marina 7.65mm

As above but in 7.65mm with Marina stamped on the slide. Wood grips and a lanyard loop.

Courtesy James Rankin

NIB	Exc.	V.G.	Good	Fair	Poor
—	275	195	150	90	40

Rex

A semi-automatic pistol in caliber 7.65mm. "Rex" is stamped on the slide with wood grips and a lanyard loop.

Courtesy James Rankin

Cowboy Defender

Derringer with 3" barrels. Weighs 19 oz. Interchangeable barrels, rosewood grip panels, stainless, fixed sights. Variety of chambering options such as .410-bore, .45 LC, .357 Mag, .38 Special, .45 ACP, .44 Special, .44-40 Win, .40 S&W, 10mm, etc. No trigger guard. Automatic extractor (except for 9mm, 10mm, .40 S&W, .45 ACP).

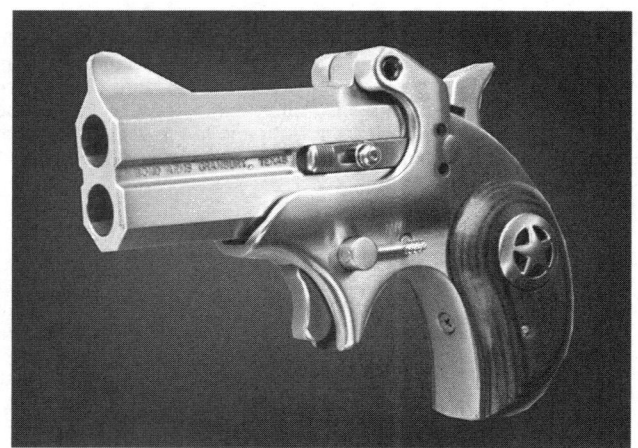

NIB	Exc.	V.G.	Good	Fair	Poor
395	350	300	225	150	75

Century 2000

Similar to Cowboy Defender but with 3.5" barrels to allow use of .410 Magnum, shotshells..357/.38 Special, .45 ACP, .44 Special, .44-40 Win, .40 S&W, 10mm, etc. Automatic extractor (except for 9mm, 10mm, .40 S&W, .45 ACP).

NIB	Exc.	V.G.	Good	Fair	Poor
425	375	300	225	150	75

BORCHARDT
Berlin, Germany
Waffenfabrik Lowe

BORCHARDT

A forerunner of the German Luger. The Borchardt was a semi-automatic pistol chambered for the 7.65mm Borchardt cartridge. It was fitted with a 6.5" barrel and the magazine held 8 rounds. The pistol was designed by Hugo Borchardt and manufactured by Ludwig Lowe of Berlin. Later models were manufactured by DWM, Deutsch Waffen Und Munitionsfabriken, Berlin. Most Borchardts come with a case which holds shoulder stock, holster, extra magazines, and numerous other accessories.

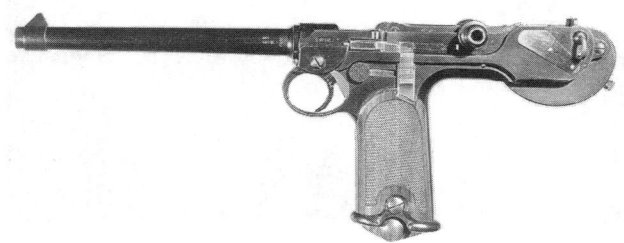

Courtesy James Rankin

Pistol Only

NIB	Exc.	V.G.	Good	Fair	Poor
—	18000	13500	—	7000	3950

Pistol with Case and Accessories

NIB	Exc.	V.G.	Good	Fair	Poor
—	23000	19000	13500	9000	5500

BORSIG
East Germany

The Borsig is the East German version of the Soviet Makarov pistol. It is a double-action, chambered for the Soviet 9x18mm cartridge. Its appearance is nearly identical to the Makarov.

NIB	Exc.	V.G.	Good	Fair	Poor
—	300	225	150	100	75

BOSWORTH, B. M.
Warren, Pennsylvania

Under Hammer Pistol

A .38 caliber single-shot percussion pistol with an under hammer and a 6" half-octagonal barrel. The frame is marked "BM Bosworth." Browned with brass grips forming part of the frame. Made circa 1850 to 1860.

NIB	Exc.	V.G.	Good	Fair	Poor
—	—	1850	800	295	125

BOWEN CLASSIC ARMS CORP.
Louisville, Tennessee

This firm was founded in 1980 by Hamilton Bowen and is a pioneer in the field of fine custom revolvers. The company offers an extensive number of modifications. Bowen Classic Arms only modifies customer's guns, it does not produce its own. Prices listed are for the modifications only on the customer-supplied revolver.For Bowen Arms not listed, pricing is whatever the market will bear. Bowen Arms are (justifiably) highly valued by their owners.

Nimrod (RS09/RS09S & RS10/RS10S)

This package is performed on the Ruger single-action revolver. It has a 5.5" tapered barrel with integral muzzle band. Baughman ramp-style blade is pinned to the express front sight base. Chambered for .41 or .44 Magnum, .45 Colt, .454 Casull, or the .50 Action Express. Includes steel ejector housing. Also offered in .475 Linebaugh or the .500 Linebaugh. Offered in blue or stainless steel.

NIB	Exc.	V.G.	Good	Fair	Poor
2500	1600	1200	800	500	300

NOTE: Add $500 for stainless steel. Add $200 for blued .475 and .500 Linebaugh, and $500 for these calibers in stainless steel.

Alpine (RD02)

This package is done on the Ruger Redhawk revolver. The action is tuned with hammer nose refitted for maximum firing pin protrusion. Barrel cut to 4". Round butt frame and reshaped factory grips. The cylinder is beveled in the Colt blackpowder style. Fitted with Ashley Emerson sights for an additional $125.

NIB	Exc.	V.G.	Good	Fair	Poor
1950	1350	875	575	325	200

NOTE: Prices listed are for 6-shot Alpines. For 5-shot Alpines add $1,250.

Colt SAA Lightweight (CS02)

This conversion is done on the Colt SAA revolver. An action reliability package is performed. A 4" barrel with dovetail front sight (no 4.75" guns). Lightened/scalloped receiver. Rebluing and recoloring and a blackpowder cylinder chamber.

NIB	Exc.	V.G.	Good	Fair	Poor
1950	1400	900	575	325	200

BRAENDLIN ARMOURY
London, England

A .450 caliber 8-barrel pistol with hinged barrels, rotating firing pin and double-action lock. Manufactured during the 1880s.

NIB	Exc.	V.G.	Good	Fair	Poor
—	—	8550	5500	3500	1850

BREN 10
Dornaus & Dixon Inc.
Huntington Beach, California

Manufactured from 1983 until 1986. Deduct 15 percent for aftermarket magazines.

Standard Bren 10

A 10mm caliber double-action semi-automatic pistol with a 5" barrel and 10-shot magazine. Stainless frame and satin-blued slide. Manufactured between 1983 and 1986. Value includes original factory magazine.

NIB	Exc.	V.G.	Good	Fair	Poor
2625	1925	1400	850	550	325

M & P Model

As above, with a matte black finish.

NIB	Exc.	V.G.	Good	Fair	Poor
2700	2100	1550	925	595	385

Special Forces Model

Chambered for 10mm cartridge and is similar to the M&P model. Offered in two models: Model D has a dark finish while Model L has a light finish. Prices listed are for Model D, add 25 percent for Model L.

NIB	Exc.	V.G.	Good	Fair	Poor
1500	1200	900	700	500	250

Dual-Master Presentation Model

As above, with a .45 caliber, extra barrel and slide and a fitted walnut case.

NIB	Exc.	V.G.	Good	Fair	Poor
6125	4375	2190	1225	875	500

Marksman Model

Similar to the Standard Model but in .45 caliber. There were 250 manufactured for the "Marksman Shop" in Chicago, Illinois.

NIB	Exc.	V.G.	Good	Fair	Poor
2450	1750	1325	700	300	275

Initial Commemorative

There were supposed to be 2,000 of these manufactured in 1986, but no one knows how many were actually produced. They are chambered for the 10mm and have a high-gloss blue finish with 22 kt. gold-plated details. The grips are laser engraved, and the whole affair is furnished in a walnut display case.

NIB	Exc.	V.G.	Good	Fair	Poor
6125	4375	3750	1750	1100	650

BRIGGS, H. A.
Norwich, Connecticut

Single-Shot Pistol

A .22 caliber single-shot spur trigger pistol with a 4" part-round/part-octagonal barrel with a downward rotating breechblock. Blued with walnut grips. Frame is marked "H.A. Briggs/Norwich, Ct." Manufactured in the 1850s and 1860s.

NIB	Exc.	V.G.	Good	Fair	Poor
—	—	2950	1250	450	200

BRILEY MANUFACTURING INC.
Houston, Texas

El Presidente Model—Unlimited

This 1911-style pistol can be built on a Caspian Arms, STI, or SVI frame. Includes scope mount, compensator, match barrel, cocking sight, lowered and flared ejection port, front and rear serrations, aluminum guide rod, and numerous other custom features. Offered in most calibers. Blued finish.

NIB	Exc.	V.G.	Good	Fair	Poor
2400	2000	1450	1000	700	350

Versatility Plus Model—Limited

Built on a 1911 frame with BoMar sight, checkered mainspring housing and checkered front strap. Many other custom features. Available in .45 ACP, .40 S&W, and 9mm.

NIB	Exc.	V.G.	Good	Fair	Poor
1950	1650	1200	800	400	225

Versatility Model—Limited

Similar to the above model but without several features such as the checkered front strap. Available in .45 ACP, .40 S&W, 9mm.

NIB	Exc.	V.G.	Good	Fair	Poor
1475	1150	800	575	265	195

Lightning Model—Action Pistol

Built on a 1911 frame this pistol features many custom components including a titanium compensator. Weight no more than 40 oz. Available in 9mm and .38 Super only.

NIB	Exc.	V.G.	Good	Fair	Poor
2450	1950	1300	850	425	200

Carry Comp Model—Defense

Built on a 1911 frame this model features a dual port cone compensator with many custom features. Barrel length is about 5". Offered in .45 ACP only.

NIB	Exc.	V.G.	Good	Fair	Poor
2450	2000	1550	1000	500	250

BRIXIA
Brescia, Italy

Model 12

A commercial version of the Model 1910 Glisenti in 9mm Glisenti caliber. The Brixia was a simplified Glisenti and was made to replace the Glisenti for the military market. The Italian military did not accept them and only a few were made for the commercial market. The only markings are the monogram eagle holding a shield cast in the grips.

Courtesy James Rankin

NIB	Exc.	V.G.	Good	Fair	Poor
—	1300	950	7850	450	325

BRNO ARMS
Uhersky Brod, Czech Republic

ZKR 551

This is a double-action or single-action revolver with a 6-round cylinder. Adjustable rear sight. Walnut grips. Fitted with 6" barrel. Chambered for .38, .32 S&W Long, and .22 LR. Weight is about 35 oz.

NIB	Exc.	V.G.	Good	Fair	Poor
1800	1350	900	700	500	275

BROLIN ARMS
La Verne, California

LEGEND SERIES—1911 AUTO PISTOL

Model L45—Standard Auto Pistol

This is the standard model with 5" barrel chambered for the .45 ACP. Fitted with throated match barrel, polished feed ramp, lowered ejection port, beveled magazine well and fixed sights. Other custom features as well. Finish is matte blue with 7-round magazine. Weight is about 36 oz.

NIB	Exc.	V.G.	Good	Fair	Poor
550	400	295	200	125	75

Model L45C—Compact Auto Pistol

Similar to the above standard model but with a 4.5" barrel. Weight is about 32 oz.

NIB	Exc.	V.G.	Good	Fair	Poor
595	550	325	225	150	100

Model L45T

This version of the L45 series was introduced in 1997 and is fitted with a compact slide on a full-size frame. Weight is 36 oz.

NIB	Exc.	V.G.	Good	Fair	Poor
595	550	325	200	125	75

NOTE: For Novak sights add $50.

PATRIOT SERIES—DPC CARRY-COMP PISTOLS

Model P45 Comp—Standard Carry Comp

This model features a 4" barrel with integral compensator cut into the slide. Other features are a custom beavertail grip safety, adjustable aluminum trigger, flat top slide, and checkered wood grips. Weight is about 37 oz.

NIB	Exc.	V.G.	Good	Fair	Poor
600	550	375	225	110	95

Model P45C Comp—Compact Carry Comp

Similar to the above model but fitted with a 3.25" barrel. Weight is about 33 oz.

NIB	Exc.	V.G.	Good	Fair	Poor
600	550	375	225	110	95

NOTE: For two-tone finish add $20.

Model P45T

This addition to the Patriot Series was introduced in 1997 and has all of the features of the Patriot pistols but is fitted with a compact slide and full size frame. Weight is about 35 oz. Also available in two-tone finish for an additional $20.

NIB	Exc.	V.G.	Good	Fair	Poor
600	550	375	225	110	95

NOTE: For Novak sights add $50.

TAC SERIES—TACTICAL 1911 PISTOLS

Model TAC-11

This series and model were introduced in 1997 and have all of the features of the L45 series with the additions of a special 5" conical match barrel, Novak Low Profile sights, black rubber contour grips, "iron claw" extractor, and optional night sights. Chambered for the .45 ACP the pistol is supplied with an 8-round magazine. Weight is approximately 37 oz.

NIB	Exc.	V.G.	Good	Fair	Poor
650	575	395	250	150	100

NOTE: For Tritium night sights add $90.

TAC SERIES—DOUBLE-ACTION PISTOLS

MS45

This is a full-size double-action pistol chambered for the .45 ACP cartridge. It is fitted with an 8-round magazine and low-profile 3-dot sights. Standard finish is matte blue.

NIB	Exc.	V.G.	Good	Fair	Poor
650	575	395	250	150	100

NOTE: Add $20 for royal blue finish.

M45

Similar to the model above but with a longer barrel. Chambered for .45 ACP and 8-round magazine.

NIB	Exc.	V.G.	Good	Fair	Poor
550	475	300	250	150	100

NOTE: Add $20 for royal blue finish.

M40

Same as M45 but chambered for .40 S&W cartridge. Magazine capacity is 10 rounds.

NIB	Exc.	V.G.	Good	Fair	Poor
500	400	275	250	150	100

NOTE: Add $20 for royal blue finish.

M90

Same as M45 model but chambered for 9mm cartridge. Magazine capacity is 10 rounds.

NIB	Exc.	V.G.	Good	Fair	Poor
500	400	300	250	150	100

NOTE: Add $20 for royal blue finish.

MC40

This is compact version of the full-size double-action models. It is fitted with a full-size frame but shorter slide. Chambered for .40 S&W cartridge. Magazine capacity is 10 rounds.

NIB	Exc.	V.G.	Good	Fair	Poor
600	500	300	250	150	100

NOTE: Add $20 for royal blue finish.

MC90

Same as above but chambered for 9mm cartridge.

NIB	Exc.	V.G.	Good	Fair	Poor
500	400	275	250	150	100

MB40

This is super-compact double-action pistol. Features a concealed hammer. Chambered for .40 S&W cartridge. Magazine capacity is 6 rounds.

NIB	Exc.	V.G.	Good	Fair	Poor
550	450	300	250	150	100

NOTE: Add $20 for royal blue finish.

MB90

Same as above but chambered for 9mm cartridge.

NIB	Exc.	V.G.	Good	Fair	Poor
550	450	300	250	150	100

PRO SERIES—COMPETITION PISTOL

Model Pro-Stock—Competition Pistol

Chambered for the .45 ACP, this pistol is designed for the competition shooter. Many special features are standard such as full-length recoil guide, front strap high relief cut, serrated flat mainspring housing, ambidextrous thumb safety and fully adjustable rear sight. Barrel length is 5" and weight is about 37 oz.

NIB	Exc.	V.G.	Good	Fair	Poor
850	675	500	350	175	100

NOTE: For two-tone finish add $20.

Model Pro-Comp—Competition Pistol

Similar to the competition model above but fitted with an integral compensator and 4" barrel. Weight is about 37 oz.

NIB	Exc.	V.G.	Good	Fair	Poor
900	700	500	375	200	100

NOTE: For two-tone finish add $20.

CUSTOM SHOP

Formula One RZ

This is a high-performance competition race gun with many special features such as supported barrel chamber, 6-port compensator, tuned trigger, extended magazine release, and many other options as standard. Chambered for .38 Super, .40 S&W cartridges. Blue finish. Add $400 for double-action.

NIB	Exc.	V.G.	Good	Fair	Poor
2500	2000	1400	1050	700	350

Formula One RS

Designed as a Limited Class competition gun with 5" barrel and chambered for .38 Super, .40 S&W, or .45 ACP calibers. Features adjustable rear sight, tuned trigger, checkered front strap and mainspring housing and other special features. Add $300 for double-action.

NIB	Exc.	V.G.	Good	Fair	Poor
2000	1600	1250	875	500	350

Formula Z

This model is a custom-built combat pistol chambered for .40 S&W, .400 Cor-Bon, or .45 ACP calibers. Fitted with a 5" or 4" barrel. Features many extra-cost features as standard.

NIB	Exc.	V.G.	Good	Fair	Poor
1300	1000	650	425	300	150

MITCHELL SINGLE-ACTION REVOLVERS

Single-Action Army Model

Offered in 4.75", 5.5", or 7.5" barrel lengths and chambered for the .45 Long Colt, .357 Magnum, or .44-40 calibers. Offered in blue finish with case hardened frame or nickel finish. Also available with dual cylinders, i.e. .45 LC/.45 ACP. Add $50 for nickel finish, and $150 for dual cylinder models.

NIB	Exc.	V.G.	Good	Fair	Poor
395	350	275	175	125	75

BROOKLYN F. A. CO.
Brooklyn, New York

Slocum Pocket Revolver

A .32 caliber spur-trigger revolver with a 3" round barrel. The frame is silver-plated brass and scroll engraved; the remainder is either blued or plated with walnut grips. The barrel is marked "B.A. Co. Patented April 14, 1863." Approximately 10,000 were manufactured in 1863 and 1864. The cylinder has five individual tubes that slide forward to open for loading and then for ejecting the spent cartridges.

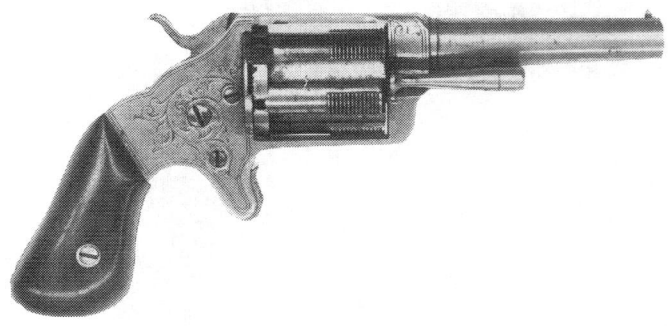

NIB	Exc.	V.G.	Good	Fair	Poor
—	—	975	325	120	75

Slocum Unfluted Cylinder Pocket Revolver

As above, but in .22 or .32 caliber with 5- or 7-shot cylinder. Approximately 250 were manufactured in .32 rimfire and 100 in .22 rimfire.

NIB	Exc.	V.G.	Good	Fair	Poor
—	—	1300	450	225	125

NOTE: .22 caliber add 25 percent.

BROWN, E.A. MANUFACTURING CO.
Alexandria, Minnesota
Brown Classic Single-Shot Pistol

This is a falling block single-shot pistol with 15" match grade barrel. Chambered for calibers from .17 Ackley to .45-70 Gov't. Walnut thumbrest grips. Handfitted. Introduced in 1998.

NIB	Exc.	V.G.	Good	Fair	Poor
1200	1000	750	600	400	200

BROWN PRODUCTS, INC., ED
Perry, Missouri

NOTE: There are a number of extra options available on Ed Brown handguns and rifles that may affect values. In August of 2010, Ed Brown announced that he would no longer be accepting orders for new rifles and, for an indefinite period of time, would be focusing on his core business of handguns. Rifle parts and limited services remain available.

Commander Bobtail

This model features a 4.25" barrel chambered for the .45 ACP, .400 Cor-Bon, .40 S&W, .38 Super, 9x23, or 9mm Luger cartridge. Modified Hogue grips from exotic wood are standard. This pistol is completely handmade and is built to the customer's specifications. Many available options. Retail prices begin at $2,400.

Classic Custom

Chambered for the .45 ACP cartridge. This is a custom built pistol with many extra features such as Videki trigger, Ed Brown wide thumb safety, stainless steel thumb safety, and extended safety, adjustable rear sight, etc. All hand-fitted parts.

NIB	Exc.	V.G.	Good	Fair	Poor
2950	2000	1500	950	450	300

Class A Limited

This is a custom-built pistol offered in a number of different calibers from .45 ACP to 9mm Luger. Fitted with a 4.25" Commander length slide. Many special features. Price listed is for the basic pistol.

NIB	Exc.	V.G.	Good	Fair	Poor
2450	1750	1300	800	500	325

Kobra Custom .45

Introduced in 2002 this pistol features a snakeskin treatment on forestrap, mainspring housing, and slide. Novak night sights and Hogue checkered wood grips standard. Many other custom features.

NIB	Exc.	V.G.	Good	Fair	Poor
1995	1400	1150	675	400	250

Kobra Carry .45

Same as above but with shorter grip frame and barrel.

NIB	Exc.	V.G.	Good	Fair	Poor
2195	1500	1200	700	425	275

Executive Target

1911 Executive Elite modified for target/range with adjustable BoMar rear sight, ambidextrous safety. 38 oz. 5" barrel chambered for .45 ACP. 7-round magazine.

NIB	Exc.	V.G.	Good	Fair	Poor
2550	2000	1500	950	450	300

Executive Elite

Government model 5" barrel, 38 oz., chambered for .45 ACP. 7-round magazine. Fixed sights. Blue/blue, stainless/blue or all-stainless.

NIB	Exc.	V.G.	Good	Fair	Poor
2300	1800	1350	900	400	275

Executive Carry

A 4.25" commander model .45 ACP with Ed Brown Bobtail. 38 oz. 7-round magazine, fixed sights. Blue/blue, stainless/blue or all-stainless.

NIB	Exc.	V.G.	Good	Fair	Poor
2400	1900	1500	950	450	300

Special Forces

Blue/blue 1911 semi-auto with 5" barrel and fixed 3-dot night sights. Chambered for .45 ACP. 38 oz.; 7-round magazine. Cocobolo grips.

NIB	Exc.	V.G.	Good	Fair	Poor
2195	1600	1150	800	550	275

BROWN MANUFACTURING CO.
Newburyport, Massachusetts

SEE—Ballard Patent Arms

SOUTHERNER DERRINGER

A .41 caliber spur-trigger single-shot pocket pistol with a pivoted 2.5" or 4" octagonal barrel marked "Southerner." Silver-plated or blued with walnut grips. This pistol was manufactured by the Merrimack Arms Co. from 1867 to 1869 and by the Brown Manufacturing Co. from 1869 to 1873.

Courtesy W. P. Hallstein III and son Chip

Brass Framed

2.5" barrel.

NIB	Exc.	V.G.	Good	Fair	Poor
—	—	875	600	325	125

Iron Frame

2.5" barrel (Brown Mfg. only).

NIB	Exc.	V.G.	Good	Fair	Poor
—	—	1025	800	500	200

Brass Frame 4" Barrel

NIB	Exc.	V.G.	Good	Fair	Poor
—	—	3700	2000	1500	500

BROWNING ARMS CO.
Morgan, Utah

EARLY SEMI-AUTOMATIC PISTOLS

In the period between 1900 and the development of the Model 1935 Hi-Power Pistol, Browning had a number of semi-automatic pistols manufactured by Fabrique Nationale of Herstal, Belgium. They were the Models 1900, 1903, 1905, 1910, 1922, the Baby, and the 1935 Model Hi-Power. These firearms will be listed in more detail with their respective values in the Fabrique Nationale section of this text.

HI-POWER MODERN PRODUCTION

This version of the FN Model 1935 is quite similar in appearance to the original described in the FN section. It is chambered for the 9mm Parabellum cartridge and has a 4.75" barrel. Models built before the passage of the crime bill have a double column, 13-round, detachable box magazine and is blued with checkered walnut grips. It has fixed sights and has been produced in its present configuration since 1954. Add a 10 percent premium for adjustable sights. A matte-nickel version, offered between 1980 and 1984, was also available and would be worth approximately 15 percent additional. This model is also avalable in .40 S&W.

Spur Hammer Version

NIB	Exc.	V.G.	Good	Fair	Poor
875	750	600	500	300	150

Round Hammer Version

NIB	Exc.	V.G.	Good	Fair	Poor
1050	900	725	600	450	200

NOTE: Add $60 for adjustable sights.

Hi-Power—.30 Luger

This version is similar to the standard Hi-Power except that it is chambered for the .30 Luger cartridge. There were approximately 1,500 imported between 1986 and 1989. The slide is marked "FN." The Browning-marked versions are quite rare and worth approximately 30 percent additional.

NIB	Exc.	V.G.	Good	Fair	Poor
—	900	725	450	300	200

Tangent Sight Model

This version is similar to the standard Hi-Power with the addition of an adjustable rear sight calibrated to 500 meters. There were approximately 7,000 imported between 1965 and 1978.

NIB	Exc.	V.G.	Good	Fair	Poor
—	1050	900	650	450	200

NOTE: If the grip frame is slotted to accept a detachable shoulder stock, add approximately 20 percent to the value; but be wary of fakes. Add an additional 10 percent for "T" series serial numbers.

RENAISSANCE HI-POWER

This is a heavily engraved version with a matte-silver finish. It features synthetic-pearl grips and a gold-plated trigger. Import on this model ended in 1979.

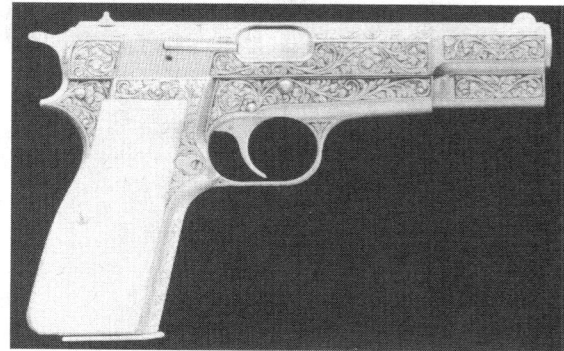

Spur Hammer Model

NIB	Exc.	V.G.	Good	Fair	Poor
2950	2600	2100	1750	1000	600

Ring Hammer Model

NIB	Exc.	V.G.	Good	Fair	Poor
3100	2850	2400	2000	1500	900

Adjustable Sight Spur Hammer Model

NIB	Exc.	V.G.	Good	Fair	Poor
3000	2650	2100	1750	1000	600

Renaissance .25 Caliber

NIB	Exc.	V.G.	Good	Fair	Poor
2400	2100	1700	1500	1000	600

Renaissance .380 Caliber

With pearl grips.

NIB	Exc.	V.G.	Good	Fair	Poor
2700	2400	2000	1600	1000	600

Renaissance .380 Caliber (Model 1971)

With wood grips and adjustable sights.

NIB	Exc.	V.G.	Good	Fair	Poor
2300	2000	1700	1500	900	500

Cased Renaissance Set

Courtesy Rock Island Auction Company

This features one example of a fully engraved and silver-finished .25 ACP "Baby," one .380 ACP pistol, and one Hi-Power. The set is furnished in a fitted walnut case or black leatherette and was imported between 1955 and 1969.

NIB	Exc.	V.G.	Good	Fair	Poor
8400	7500	5200	4000	2000	900

NOTE: For early coin finish sets add 30 percent.

Louis XVI Model

This is a heavily engraved Hi-Power pistol that features a leaf-and-scroll pattern. It is satin-finished and features checkered walnut grips. It is furnished in a fitted walnut case. To realize its true potential, this pistol must be NIB. It was imported between 1980 and 1984.

Louis XVI Model Diamond Grip Model

NIB	Exc.	V.G.	Good	Fair	Poor
3150	2500	2000	800	400	300

Louis XVI Model Medallion Grip Model

NIB	Exc.	V.G.	Good	Fair	Poor
1950	1750	1600	800	400	300

Hi-Power Centennial Model

This version is similar to the standard fixed-sight Hi-Power but is chrome-plated with the inscription, "Browning Centennial/1878-1978" engraved on the slide. It is furnished with a fitted case. There were 3,500 manufactured in 1978. As with all commemorative pistols, in order to realize its collector potential, this model should be NIB with all supplied material. Prices are for pistols built in Belgium

NIB	Exc.	V.G.	Good	Fair	Poor
1075	875	700	450	300	200

Hi-Power Capitan

This is a new version of the Hi-Power model fitted with tangent sights. Introduced in 1993. Furnished with walnut grips. Weighs about 32 oz. Assembled in Portugal.

NIB	Exc.	V.G.	Good	Fair	Poor
750	575	450	400	250	200

Hi-Power Practical

First introduced in 1993 this version is furnished with a blued slide and chrome frame. Has Pachmayr wraparound rubber grips, round-style serrated hammer, and removable front sight. Available with adjustable sights. Weighs 36 oz. Assembled in Portugal.

NIB	Exc.	V.G.	Good	Fair	Poor
845	625	500	300	200	175

Hi-Power Silver Chrome Model

Furnished in hard chrome and fitted with wraparound Pachmayr rubber grips. Weighs 36 oz. Assembled in Portugal. Add 10 percent for models with all Belgian markings. This pistol was introduced in 1981 and dropped from the Browning product line in 1984. It was reintroduced in 1991.

NIB	Exc.	V.G.	Good	Fair	Poor
750	575	500	425	225	200

Hi-Power .40 S&W

Introduced in 1994, this new version of the Hi-Power is furnished with adjustable sights, molded grips, 5" barrel and a 10-round magazine. Weighs about 35 oz.

NIB	Exc.	V.G.	Good	Fair	Poor
800	600	450	300	200	150

Hi-Power Mark III

The pistol, introduced in 1991, has a matte blued or green finish, low-profile fixed sights, and two-piece molded grips with thumb rest. Weighs 32 oz.

NIB	Exc.	V.G.	Good	Fair	Poor
900	700	500	300	200	175

Pro-9/Pro-40

This 9mm or .40 S&W double-action pistol is fitted with a 4" barrel. Stainless steel slide. Grips are composite with interchangeable backstrap inserts. Magazine capacity is 16 rounds for 9mm and 14 rounds for the .40 S&W. Weight is about 30 oz.

NIB	Exc.	V.G.	Good	Fair	Poor
725	500	375	—	—	—

BDA-380

This is a double-action, semi-automatic pistol chambered for the .380 ACP cartridge. It features a 3.75" barrel with a 14-round, double-stack, detachable magazine. The finish is either blued or nickel-plated with smooth walnut grips. This pistol was manufactured in Italy by Beretta and introduced in 1977.

NIB	Exc.	V.G.	Good	Fair	Poor
625	400	325	275	200	150

NOTE: Add 10 percent for nickel finish.

Model BDA

This is a double-action, semi-automatic pistol manufactured between 1977 and 1980 for Browning by SIG-Sauer of Germany. It is identical to the SIG-Sauer Model 220. It is chambered for 9mm Parabellum, .38 Super, and the .45 ACP cartridges. The .38 Super would be worth approximately 30 percent additional.

NIB	Exc.	V.G.	Good	Fair	Poor
—	525	425	375	300	235

Model BDM

This is a double-action, semi-automatic pistol chambered for the 9mm cartridge. The pistol is fitted with a selector switch that allows the shooter to choose between single-action model or double-action model. It features a 4.75" barrel with adjustable rear sight. The magazine capacity is 15 rounds. Weighs 31 oz. First introduced in 1991.

NIB	Exc.	V.G.	Good	Fair	Poor
560	450	350	250	200	150

Model BDM Silver Chrome

This variation of the BDM was introduced in 1997 and features a silver chrome finish on the slide and frame. The balance of the pistol is in a contrasting matte blue finish.

NIB	Exc.	V.G.	Good	Fair	Poor
560	450	350	250	200	150

Model BDM Practical

This model, also introduced in 1997, is the same as above but with the silver chrome on the frame only.

NIB	Exc.	V.G.	Good	Fair	Poor
560	450	350	250	200	150

Model BPM-D

Introduced in 1997 this new version of the BDM (Browning Pistol Model Decocker) features a double-action pistol with the first shot fired double-action and subsequent shots fired single-action. There is no manual safety. A decock lever also releases the slide.

NIB	Exc.	V.G.	Good	Fair	Poor
525	400	300	250	200	150

Model BRM-DAO

This 9mm pistol is a redesigned version of the Model BDM but the initials stand for "Browning Revolver Model Double-Action-Only." This pistol also has a finger support trigger guard for two-handed control. All other features are the same as the BPM-D pistol. Weight is approximately 31 oz.

NIB	Exc.	V.G.	Good	Fair	Poor
525	400	300	250	200	150

Nomad

This is a blowback-operated, semi-automatic pistol chambered for the .22 LR cartridge. It was offered with a 4.5" or 6.75" barrel. It has a 10-round, detachable magazine with adjustable sights and all-steel construction. The finish is blued with black plastic grips. It was manufactured between 1962 and 1974 by FN.

NIB	Exc.	V.G.	Good	Fair	Poor
500	360	275	150	75	50

Challenger

This is a more deluxe target pistol chambered for the .22 LR cartridge. It was offered with a 4.5" or 6.75" barrel and has a 10-round magazine. It is constructed entirely of steel and has adjustable sights. The finish is blued with a gold-plated trigger and checkered, wraparound, walnut grips. It was manufactured between 1962 and 1974 by FN.

Courtesy John J. Stimson, Jr.

NIB	Exc.	V.G.	Good	Fair	Poor
600	475	300	250	200	140

Renaissance Challenger

This version is fully engraved with a satin-nickel finish and furnished with a fleece-lined pouch.

NIB	Exc.	V.G.	Good	Fair	Poor
2600	2300	1600	750	500	350

Gold Line Challenger

This version is blued and has a gold-inlaid line around the outer edges of the pistol. It was cased in a fleece-lined pouch. Built in Belgium.

NIB	Exc.	V.G.	Good	Fair	Poor
2600	2300	1600	750	500	350

Challenger II

This is a blowback-operated, semi-automatic pistol chambered for the .22 LR cartridge. It has a 6.75" barrel with an alloy frame. The finish is blued with phenolic impregnated hardwood grips. This pistol was manufactured between 1976 and 1982 in Salt Lake City, Utah.

NIB	Exc.	V.G.	Good	Fair	Poor
—	450	325	175	140	100

Challenger III

This version features a 5.5" bull barrel with adjustable sights. It was manufactured between 1982 and 1984 in Salt Lake City, Utah. A 6.75", tapered-barrel version was also available and known as the Sporter.

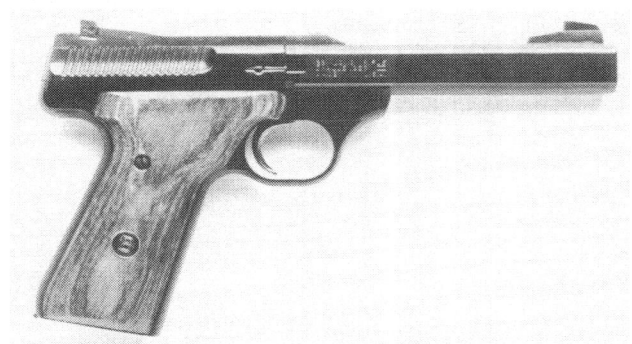

NIB	Exc.	V.G.	Good	Fair	Poor
—	400	300	150	125	90

Browning Collector's Association Edition

Fully engraved, 100 manufactured. This model was fitted with a two-piece grip.

NIB	Exc.	V.G.	Good	Fair	Poor
2950	2250	1650	1200	800	400

Medalist

This is a high-grade, semi-automatic target pistol chambered for the .22 LR cartridge. It has a 6.75", vent rib barrel with adjustable target sights. It was supplied with three barrel weights and a dry-fire-practice mechanism. The finish is blued with target type, thumbrest, walnut grips. It was manufactured between 1962 and 1974 by FN. There were four additional high-grade versions of this pistol that differed in the degree of ornamentation.

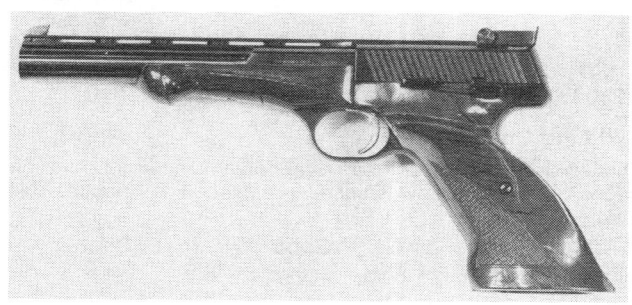

NIB	Exc.	V.G.	Good	Fair	Poor
1350	1000	800	675	375	250

International Medalist

About 700 were sold in the U.S. from 1977 to 1980. Barrels were 5-7/8" long. Built in Belgium.

Courtesy John J. Stimson, Jr.

NIB	Exc.	V.G.	Good	Fair	Poor
950	800	600	450	300	150

Second Model International Medalist

Same as above but with flat-sided barrel, dull finish, and adjustable palm rest. Built in Belgium.

Courtesy John J. Stimson, Jr.

NIB	Exc.	V.G.	Good	Fair	Poor
875	725	450	300	200	150

Gold Line Medalist

Introduced in 1962 and discontinued in 1974 with only an estimated 400 guns produced.

NIB	Exc.	V.G.	Good	Fair	Poor
2950	2750	2250	1000	750	500

Renaissance Medalist

This model was built entirely in Belgium from 1970 to 1974. Built with a one-piece grip.

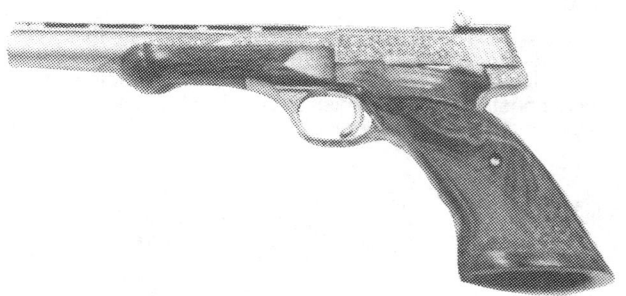

NIB	Exc.	V.G.	Good	Fair	Poor
3300	3000	2500	1200	900	700

BUCK MARK SERIES

Buck Mark

This is a blowback-operated, semi-automatic pistol chambered for the .22 LR cartridge. It has a 5.5" bull barrel with adjustable sights. It has an 11-round, detachable magazine and is matte blued with skip-line checkered synthetic grips. It was introduced in 1985. Produced in the U.S.

NIB	Exc.	V.G.	Good	Fair	Poor
350	250	175	135	110	85

NOTE: Add $25 for stainless steel version introduced in 2005.

Buck Mark Plus

This version is similar to the standard, with plain wood grips. It was introduced in 1987. Produced in the U.S.

NIB	Exc.	V.G.	Good	Fair	Poor
395	300	200	150	100	75

Buck Mark Plus Buck Mark Plus Nickel

Introduced in 1991. Add $35 to above prices.

Buck Mark Varmint

This version has a 9.75" bull barrel with a full-length ramp to allow scope mounting. It has no sights. It was introduced in 1987 and produced in the U.S.

NIB	Exc.	V.G.	Good	Fair	Poor
395	300	250	200	175	125

Buck Mark Silhouette

This version features a 9.75" bull barrel with adjustable sights. Introduced in 1987.

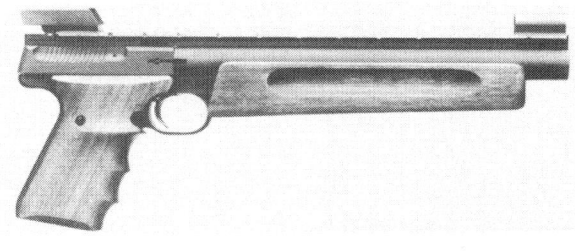

NIB	Exc.	V.G.	Good	Fair	Poor
450	350	285	220	185	140

Buck Mark 22 Micro

This version of the Buck Mark 22 is fitted with a 4" bull barrel. Available in blue, matte blue, or nickel finish. Also available in Micro Plus variation with walnut grips. Weighs 32 oz. Introduced in 1992.

NIB	Exc.	V.G.	Good	Fair	Poor
350	275	175	135	110	85

NOTE: Add $25 for stainless steel version introduced in 2005.

Buck Mark 22 Micro Micro Plus

NIB	Exc.	V.G.	Good	Fair	Poor
350	275	175	150	125	90

Buck Mark 22 Micro Micro Plus Nickel

Introduced in 1996. Add $75 to above price.

BUCK MARK 5.5

This .22 caliber pistol has a 5.5" heavy bull barrel fitted with target sights. It is offered in three separate models:

5.5 Blued Target

This version has a blued finish, contoured walnut grips, target sights. Weighs 35.5 oz. Introduced in 1990.

NIB	Exc.	V.G.	Good	Fair	Poor
475	395	250	150	100	100

5.5 Blued Target (2005)

Introduced in 2005 this model features a new target-style Cocabolo grips, a full length scope mount, and hooded target sights. Weight is 35 oz.

NIB	Exc.	V.G.	Good	Fair	Poor
525	425	300	200	150	100

5.5 Gold Target

Same as above but has a gold anodized frame and top rib. Slide is blue. Walnut grips. Introduced in 1991.

NIB	Exc.	V.G.	Good	Fair	Poor
550	425	300	200	150	125

5.5 Field

Same action and barrel as the Target Model but with adjustable field sights. Sights are hoodless. Slide and barrel is blued while the rib and frame are anodized blue. Grips are walnut. Introduced in 1991.

NIB	Exc.	V.G.	Good	Fair	Poor
450	345	225	150	100	100

5.5 Field (2005)

This model features new target style grips and full-length scope rail. Weight is about 35 oz.

NIB	Exc.	V.G.	Good	Fair	Poor
525	425	295	225	165	100

Buck Field Plus

This .22 caliber pistol has a 5.5" barrel with Truglo/Marbles' front sight. Grips are laminated rosewood. Barrel are polished blue. Weight is about 24 oz.

NIB	Exc.	V.G.	Good	Fair	Poor
425	325	225	200	150	75

Buck Mark Bullseye

Introduced in 1996 this pistol is designed for metallic silhouette competition. The fluted barrel is 7-1/4" long. Adjustable trigger pull, adjustable rear sight removable barrel are some of the features. Weight is about 36 oz. Choice of laminated wood grips or rubber grips. Add $150 for stainless.

NIB	Exc.	V.G.	Good	Fair	Poor
550	425	275	175	125	75

NOTE: For Rosewood target grips add $90.

Buck Mark Unlimited Match

This pistol is fitted with a 14" barrel with top rib. The front sight hood is slightly rearward of the muzzle for a maximum sight radius of 15". All other features are the same as the Silhouette model. Weighs 64 oz.

NIB	Exc.	V.G.	Good	Fair	Poor
700	525	375	225	175	125

Buck Mark Challenge

Introduced in 1999 this model features a lightweight 5.5" barrel with adjustable rear sight. Smaller grip diameter. Matte blue finish and 10-round magazine capacity. Weight is about 25 oz.

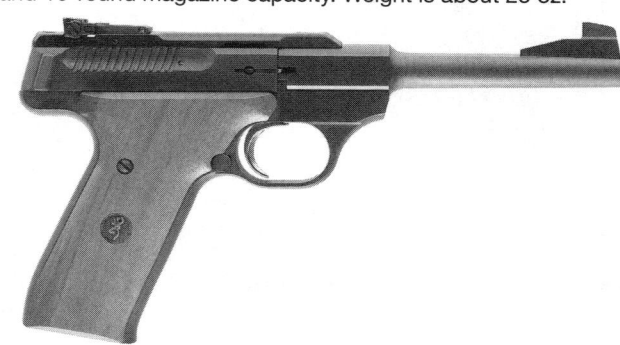

NIB	Exc.	V.G.	Good	Fair	Poor
350	250	200	175	125	100

Buck Mark Camper

This model is fitted with a heavy 5.5" barrel and has a matte blue finish. Ten-round magazine capacity. Weight is about 34 oz. Introduced in 1999.

NIB	Exc.	V.G.	Good	Fair	Poor
300	225	150	125	100	75

NOTE: Add $60 for stainless steel version.

Buck Mark Camper Cocobola UDX

Similar to above but with cocobolo Ultra DX grips and TruGlo front sight. Introduced 2008.

NIB	Exc.	V.G.	Good	Fair	Poor
375	295	245	150	100	75

Buck Mark Practical URX Fiber Optic

Matte grey finish, 5.5-inch tapered bull barrel, Ultragrip RX ambi grips, adjustable ProTarget rear sight with TruGlo fiber optic front sight. Introduced 2008.

NIB	Exc.	V.G.	Good	Fair	Poor
350	300	20	150	100	75

Buck Mark Hunter

This .22 pistol features a 7.25" heavy round barrel with Tru-glo/Marbles front sights, adjustable rear sight and integrated scope base. Grips are Cocabolo target-style. Weight is about 38 oz. Introduced in 2005.

NIB	Exc.	V.G.	Good	Fair	Poor
375	275	225	175	125	100

Buck Mark Limited Edition 25th Anniversary

This model is limited to 1,000 pistols and features a 6.75" barrel with matte blued finish and scrimshaw etched ivory grips. Pistol rug furnished as standard equipment.

NIB	Exc.	V.G.	Good	Fair	Poor
495	350	300	225	150	125

Buck Mark Bullseye Target Stainless

Blowback, single action .22 LR semi-auto. Matte blued, heavy 7.25" round and fluted stainless bull barrel. Laminated rosewood grip, adjustable sights. Introduced 2006.

NIB	Exc.	V.G.	Good	Fair	Poor
695	450	300	225	150	175

Buck Mark Bullseye Target URX

Blowback, single-action semi-auto in .22LR. Matte blued, heavy 7.25" round and fluted bull barrel. Grooved, rubberized grip, 39 oz., adjustable sights. Introduced 2006.

NIB	Exc.	V.G.	Good	Fair	Poor
475	400	325	225	150	175

Buck Mark Contour 5.5 URX

Blowback, single-action .222 semi-auto. Matte blued, contoured 5.5" barrel. Full-length scope base, 36 oz., adjustable sights. (Multiple barrel lengths and options.) Introduced 2006.

NIB	Exc.	V.G.	Good	Fair	Poor
425	365	300	250	200	100

Buck Mark Contour Lite 5.5 URX

.22 LR blowback, single-action semi-auto. Matte blued, contoured 5.5" barrel. Full-length scope base, 28 oz. Adjustable sights. (Multiple barrel lengths and options.) Introduced 2006.

NIB	Exc.	V.G.	Good	Fair	Poor
475	395	325	275	225	150

Buck Mark FLD Plus Rosewood UDX

22 LR blowback single-action semi-auto. "FLD" sculpted grip with rosewood panels. Blued, contoured 5.5" barrel, 34 oz., adjustable rear sight, fiber optic front sight. (Multiple barrel lengths and options.) Introduced 2006.

NIB	Exc.	V.G.	Good	Fair	Poor
475	395	325	275	225	150

Buck Mark Lite Splash 5.5 URX

Blowback single-action semi-auto. Matte blued finish, gold splash anodizing. Chambered for .22 LR, 5.5" barrel. Rubberized ambidextrous grip. Adjustable sights; fiber optic front sight. 28 oz. (Also available with 7.5" barrel.) Introduced 2006.

NIB	Exc.	V.G.	Good	Fair	Poor
450	375	325	275	225	150

Buck Mark Micro Standard Stainless URX

With a 4" stainless barrel, this .22 LR weighs 32 oz. Ambidextrous rubberized grip and adjustable sights. (Also available in alloy steel.) Introduced 2006.

NIB	Exc.	V.G.	Good	Fair	Poor
395	350	325	275	225	150

Buck Mark Micro Bull

4" stainless bull barrel; .22 LR; weight 33 oz. Plastic grip panels and adjustable sights. Introduced 2006.

NIB	Exc.	V.G.	Good	Fair	Poor
350	275	225	175	125	100

Buck Mark Plus Stainless Black Laminated UDX

Similar to Buck Mark Standard Stainless UDX but with ambidextrous grips. Introduced 2007.

NIB	Exc.	V.G.	Good	Fair	Poor
495	375	300	225	150	125

Buck Mark Plus UDX

Similar to Buck Mark FLD Plus but with ambidextrous walnut grips. Introduced 2007.

NIB	Exc.	V.G.	Good	Fair	Poor
425	350	300	225	150	125

Full Line Dealer Buck Mark Plus Rosewood UDX

Similar to Buck Mark Plus UDX but with ambidextrous rosewood grips. Available only to full-line and Medallion-level Browning dealers. Introduced 2007.

NIB	Exc.	V.G.	Good	Fair	Poor
425	350	300	225	150	125

Buck Mark Plus Stainless UDX

.22 LR semi-auto with finger-grooved wood grips. 5.5" barrel, 34 oz. Adjustable sights, fiber optic front sight. (Also available blued alloy steel.) Introduced 2006.

NIB	Exc.	V.G.	Good	Fair	Poor
450	350	300	225	150	125

Browning 1911-22A1

A scaled-down version of the 1911A1 chambered in .22 LR. Aluminum slide, alloy frame, blowback operated with a single-action trigger. Controls are standard 1911 including thumb and grip safeties. Other features include 10-round magazine, brown composite grips, matte blue finish. Weight is 16 ounces, barrel length is 4-1/4 inches. Compact model has 3-5/8 inch barrel. Introduced in 2011.

NIB	Exc.	V.G.	Good	Fair	Poor
500	450	400	350	300	200

BRUCE & DAVIS
Webster, Massachusetts

Double-Barreled Pistol

A .36 caliber double-barrel percussion pistol with 3" to 6" round barrels. The barrel rib marked "Bruce & Davis." Blued with walnut grips. Manufactured during the 1840s.

NIB	Exc.	V.G.	Good	Fair	Poor
—	—	925	400	175	100

BRUFF, R.P.
New York, New York

Pocket Pistol

A .41 caliber single-shot percussion pistol with 2.5" to 3" barrels. The pistol is marked "R.P. Bruff NY" in an arch and "Cast Steel." German silver with a checkered walnut stock. Manufactured between 1861 and 1870.

NIB	Exc.	V.G.	Good	Fair	Poor
—	—	1900	825	225	100

BUCO
Germany

Gas Pistol

This odd firearm looks more like a telescope than a pistol. It is chambered for a 10.55mm gas cartridge and is a single-shot. Overall it is approximately 5.5" long in its open or cocked position. The barrel is smooth bore and 3.75" in length. This pistol has no sights and no safety—one simply pulls the inner tube back much like extending a telescope, unscrews the end cap, inserts the round, and screws the cap back into place. When it is needed, a thumbnail is used to depress the sear and fire the pistol. They are marked on the end cap "Buco DRGM." No more information is available as to quantity or year of manufacture.

NIB	Exc.	V.G.	Good	Fair	Poor
—	—	650	500	350	150

BUDISCHOWSKY
Norton Armament Corp.
Mt. Clemens, Michigan

TP-70

A .22 or .25 ACP caliber semi-automatic pistol with a 2.5" barrel, fixed sights and 6-shot magazine. Stainless steel with plastic grips. Manufactured between 1973 and 1977. NOTE: The German-designed Budischowsky was originally made in Michigan by Norton Armament Corp. Michigan-made Budischowsky's are considered better quality than later examples made in Florida and Utah. Deduct 15% for non-Michigan manufacture.

.22 Rimfire Caliber

NIB	Exc.	V.G.	Good	Fair	Poor
550	425	350	300	225	150

.25 ACP Caliber

NIB	Exc.	V.G.	Good	Fair	Poor
525	400	325	275	175	125

BUL TRANSMARK LTD.
Tel-Aviv, Israel

Model M5

Introduced for the first time in the U.S. in 1996 this semi-automatic pistol bears a resemblance to the Model 1911. The frame is polymer and the slide is stainless steel. Available in 9mm, .38 Super, .40 S&W, and .45 ACP. Magazine limited to 10 rounds.

NIB	Exc.	V.G.	Good	Fair	Poor
750	600	450	350	200	100

BULLDOG SINGLE-SHOT PISTOL
Connecticut Arms & Manufacturing Co.
Naubuc, Connecticut

Bulldog

A .44 or .50 caliber single-shot spur trigger pistol with 4" or 6" barrels, and a pivoting breechblock that moves to the left for loading. Blued, case hardened and stamped "Connecticut Arms & Manf. Co. Naubuc Conn. Patented Oct. 25, 1864." There were only a few hundred manufactured, and the .50 caliber, 6" barreled versions would be worth an additional 40 percent. Produced between 1866 and 1868.

NIB	Exc.	V.G.	Good	Fair	Poor
—	—	1650	675	275	150

BURGSMULLER, K.
Krelensen, Germany

Burgo

The Rohm RG10 under another name. It is a poor quality, inexpensive .38 caliber revolver. The examples marketed by Burgsmuller are so marked. Virtually worthless.

Regent

The Regent is a .22 caliber revolver that resembles the Colt Police Positive in appearance. It is of a higher quality than the Burgo. The manufacturer is not known.

NIB	Exc.	V.G.	Good	Fair	Poor
—	165	125	75	50	5

BUSHMASTER FIREARMS INC.
Windham, Maine

Bushmaster Carbon 15 .223 Pistol

AR-style semi-auto pistol chambered in 5.56/.223. Features include a 7.5" stainless steel barrel, carbon composite receiver, shortened handguard, full-length optics rail, A2-type front sight with dual-aperture flip-up rear. 30-round magazine. Overall length 20". Weight: 2.88 lbs. Suggested retail price: N/A.

Type 97 Pistol

Similar to above but without handguard.

NIB	Exc.	V.G.	Good	Fair	Poor
1150	975	775	525	400	200

BUTLER, WM. S.
Rocky Hill, Connecticut

Single-Shot Pistol

A .36 caliber single-shot percussion pocket pistol with a 2.5" barrel and the frame and grip made in one piece. The frame marked "Wm. S. Butler's Patent/Patented Feb.3, 1857."

NIB	Exc.	V.G.	Good	Fair	Poor
—	—	975	385	150	50

BUTTERFIELD, JESSE
Philadelphia, Pennsylvania
Butterfield Army Revolver

A .41 caliber revolver with a 7" octagonal barrel, an unfluted 5-shot cylinder and features a special priming device, a disk that was loaded in front of the trigger guard. A brass frame, blued with walnut grips. The frame is stamped "Butterfield's Patent Dec. 11, 1855/Phila." Approximately 650 manufactured in 1861 and 1862.

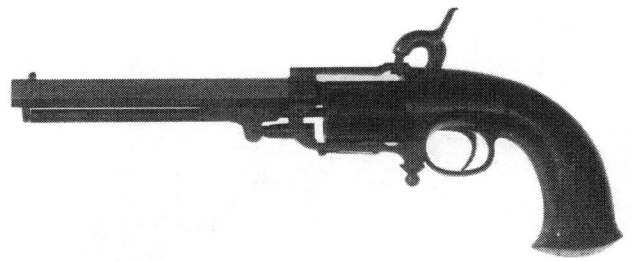

Courtesy Milwaukee Public Museum, Milwaukee, Wisconsin

NIB	Exc.	V.G.	Good	Fair	Poor
—	—	6000	2250	875	450

Butterfield Pocket Pistol

A .41 caliber single-shot percussion pistol with a 2" to 3.5" barrel. German silver with walnut stocks. The lock is marked "Butterfield's/Patent Dec 11, 1855." Extremely rare. Manufactured in the 1850s.

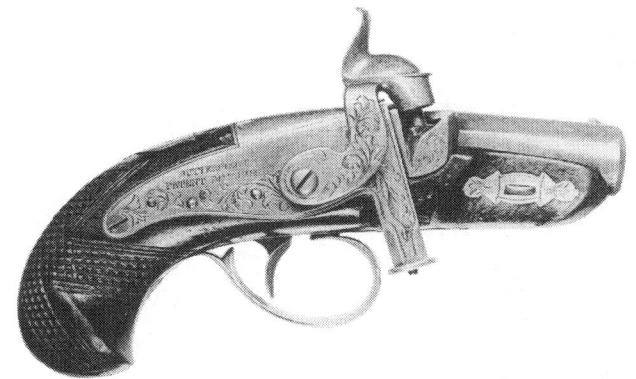

NIB	Exc.	V.G.	Good	Fair	Poor
—	—	9000	4250	1650	1000

C

CAMPO GIRO
Eibar, Spain

Esperanza y Unceta Model 1904

Designed by Lt. Col. Venancio Aguirre. This pistol was produced in limited numbers.

NIB	Exc.	V.G.	Good	Fair	Poor
—	3000	2000	1500	1000	800

Model 1910

Similar to the above, in 9mm Largo. Tested, but not adopted, by the Spanish army.

NIB	Exc.	V.G.	Good	Fair	Poor
—	2000	1500	1000	800	600

Model 1913

An improved version of the above, about 1,300 made.

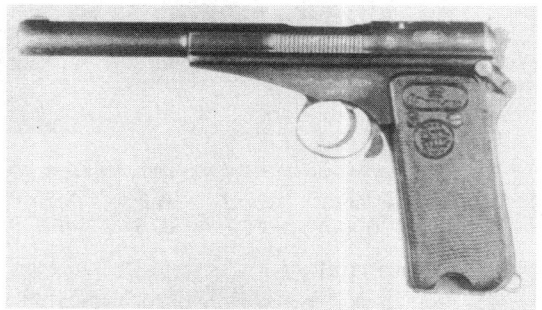

Courtesy James Rankin

NIB	Exc.	V.G.	Good	Fair	Poor
—	1500	1250	850	600	500

Model 1913/16

An improved version of the above, about 13,000 built.

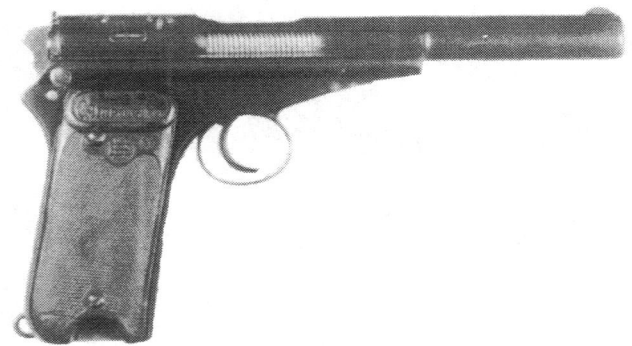

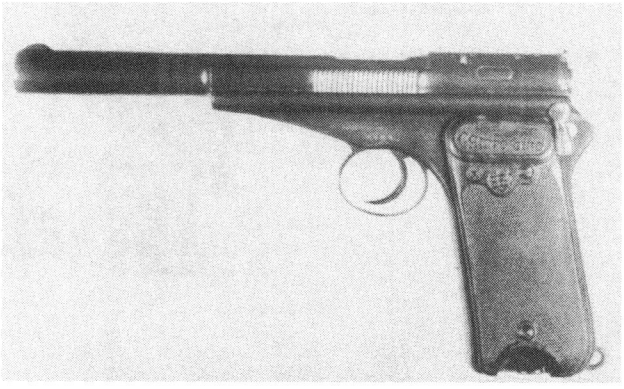

Courtesy James Rankin

NIB	Exc.	V.G.	Good	Fair	Poor
—	2000	1550	1000	600	350

CARACAL

Caracal-F

Chambered for the 9mm Parabellum, the Caracal has a DAO trigger and is striker-fired. Features include a polymer frame, steel slide, ambidextrous magazine releases and an 18-round magazine. Weight is 26.5 ounces, barrel length is 4.1-inches, finish is matte blue. Caracal-C is compact variation with 3.5-inch barrel, weighs 24.7 ounces Made in the United Arab Emirates. Introduced in 2011.

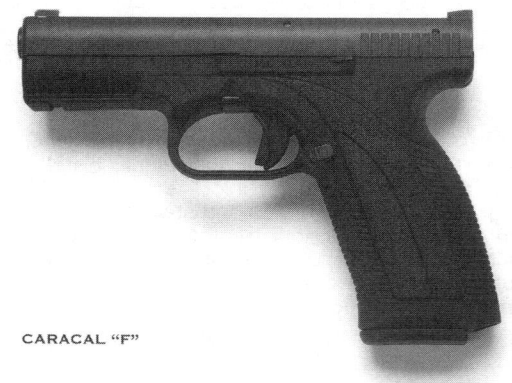

CARACAL "F"

NIB	Exc.	V.G.	Good	Fair	Poor
535	465	400	300	200	100

CARD, S. W.
Location Unknown

Under Hammer Pistol

A .34 caliber single-shot percussion pocket pistol with a 7.75" half octagonal barrel marked "S.W. Card" and "Cast Steel" . Blued with walnut grips.

NIB	Exc.	V.G.	Good	Fair	Poor
—	—	1500	450	150	50

CARLTON, M.
Haverhill, New Hampshire

Under Hammer Pistol

A .34 caliber percussion under hammer single-shot pistol with a 3.5" to 7.75" half-octagonal barrel marked "M. Carleton & Co."

Browned with walnut grips. Active 1830s and 1840s.

NIB	Exc.	V.G.	Good	Fair	Poor
—	—	1800	600	200	100

CASE WILLARD & CO.
New Hartford, Connecticut

Under Hammer Pistol

A .31 caliber single-shot percussion pistol with a 3" half-octagonal barrel marked "Case Willard & Co./New Hartford Conn." Blued, brass frame with walnut grips.

NIB	Exc.	V.G.	Good	Fair	Poor
—	—	1400	550	200	100

CASPIAN ARMS, LTD.
Hardwick, Vermont

This company is primarily a 1911 component manufacturer.

Viet Nam Commemorative

Government Model engraved by J.J. Adams and nickel-plated. The walnut grips have a branch service medallion inlaid, and gold plating was available for an additional $350. There were 1,000 manufactured in 1986.

Courtesy James Rankin

NIB	Exc.	V.G.	Good	Fair	Poor
1800	1350	950	650	475	300

CASULL ARMS, INC.
Afton, Wyoming

CA 2000

Chambered for the .22 caliber LR cartridge this stainless steel revolver has a 5-round cylinder with fold-up trigger. Double-action-only. Palm sized. The most recently-produced "Velo-Dog." Discontinued.

NIB	Exc.	V.G.	Good	Fair	Poor
550	425	350	250	200	175

CA 3800

Chambered for the .38 Casull cartridge (124 gr. 1800+fps) this pistol is fitted with a 6" match barrel and has a magazine capacity of 8 rounds. Full-length two-piece guide rod. Checkering on front strap and mainspring housing is 20 lpi. Match trigger and numerous other special features. Weight is about 40 oz. Introduced in 2000. Discontinued.

NIB	Exc.	V.G.	Good	Fair	Poor
2600	2050	1700	1200	650	300

NOTE: Add $300 for extra .45 ACP barrel.

CENTURY GUN COMPANY/ NEW CENTURY MANFACTURING
Evansville, Knightstown & Greenfield, Indiana

This revolver design was originally manufactured in 1972 by Russell Wilson, who sandcasted the bronze frame (cloned from the Colt SAA configuration) in Evansville, IN. Gene Phelps purchased the manufacturing rights for this gun and formed a partnership with Earl Keller to produce a redesigned frame, also using sandcast bronze.The original Century revolver was made in Evansville, IN beginning in 1973 (1973 was the 100th anniversary of the .45-70 Govt. cartridge — hence the term Century) and production was halted in 1976 at ser. no. 524. In late 1976, Phelps and Keller (the two original partners on the venture) dissolved their partnership and each began manufacturing their own version of the .45-70 revolver. Gene Phelps completely redesigned the gun's interior and began manufacturing the Heritage I, with an investment-cast steel frame, and without the Century's novel cross-bolt safety. Keller's Century Manufacturing, Inc. continued to produce the original Century, with some design refinements, and in 1985 the company was purchased by Dr. Paul Majors, who died in Dec. of 2001.The most recent Century revolver featured a manganese bronze frame and other components in addition to having a cross-bolt safety. They were produced in .45-70 and various other cals., in Greenfield, IN. Earl Keller died in 1986. The second series was made in Greenfield, IN with limited production resuming in 1986. Earlier handmade "Evansville" Model 100s (disc.) are currently selling for between $2,500-$3,500, depending on the region and condition. Post-Evansville guns retail from a high around $1700 (Excellent) to $9000 (Good) in .45-70; other chamberings such as .444 Marlin and .50-70 Government generally bring 10 percent to 20 percent more.In Feb., 2002, Century Mfg. was purchased by Dave Lukens & Jeff Yelton and moved to Knightstown, IN. Dave and Jeff produced approximately 500 guns. In June, 2004, Century Mfg. was purchased by Bill, Stephen, Robert, and Thomas Jordan and renamed the company to New Century Manufacturing, LLC. Production was expected to begin in late 2004.(Courtesy New Century Manufacturing)

CHAPMAN, G. & J.
Philadelphia, Pennsylvania

A .32 caliber revolver with a 4" round barrel and 7-shot cylinder. The frame is made of brass while the barrel and cylinder are of steel. The barrel is marked "G.& J. Chapman/Philada/Patent Applied For/1861." Manufactured during the1860s.

NIB	Exc.	V.G.	Good	Fair	Poor
—	—	2550	1050	550	275

CHARTER 2000, INC.
Shelton, Connecticut

Bulldog
Chambered for the .44 Special cartridge and fitted with a 2.5" barrel. Stainless steel or blued frame with 5-round cylinder. Round butt and fixed sights. Weight is 21 oz.

NIB	Exc.	V.G.	Good	Fair	Poor
320	250	175	125	—	50

NOTE: For stainless steel add $20.

Police Bulldog
This model is chambered for the .38 Special cartridge and fitted with a 4" bull or tapered barrel. Full rubber grips. Blued finish. Weight is about 24 oz. Introduced in 2002.

NIB	Exc.	V.G.	Good	Fair	Poor
320	250	175	125	75	50

Undercover
Chambered for the .38 Special cartridge and fitted with a 2" barrel. Stainless steel or blued frame with 5-round cylinder. Round butt. Weight is about 20 oz.

NIB	Exc.	V.G.	Good	Fair	Poor
280	225	175	150	—	75

NOTE: For stainless steel add $20.

Off Duty
This .38 Special revolver has an aluminum frame and 2" barrel. Combat grips. Double-action-only. Weight is about 12 oz. Introduced in 2002.

NIB	Exc.	V.G.	Good	Fair	Poor
350	250	200	150	100	75

Pathfinder
This is a stainless steel revolver chambered for the .22 caliber cartridge. Fitted with a 2" barrel and wood grips. Weight is about 17 oz. Introduced in 2002.

NIB	Exc.	V.G.	Good	Fair	Poor
265	200	165	125	75	50

Mag Pug
Chambered for the .357 Magnum cartridge and fitted with a 2.2" ported barrel. Stainless steel or blued frame. Weight is about 24 oz.

NIB	Exc.	V.G.	Good	Fair	Poor
320	250	175	125	—	50

Dixie Derringer
Stainless steel with 1.125" barrels. Chambered for the .22 LR or .22 Mag cartridges. Weight is about 8 oz. Introduced in 2002.

NIB	Exc.	V.G.	Good	Fair	Poor
190	150	125	100	50	25

NOTE: For .22 Mag. model add $10.

CHARTER ARMS CORP.
Ansonia, Connecticut/Shelton, Connecticut

Police Undercover
This model is chambered for the .38 Special or the .32 Magnum. It is fitted with a 2" barrel in blue or stainless steel finish. Offered with walnut or rubber grips. The overall length is 6.25" and weight is between 16 oz. and 19 oz. depending on grips and finish.

NIB	Exc.	V.G.	Good	Fair	Poor
350	300	175	150	100	75

Undercover Stainless Steel
As above, in stainless steel.

NIB	Exc.	V.G.	Good	Fair	Poor
390	325	225	175	—	100

Undercover Lite
Similar to Undercover but with lightweight aluminum alloy frame. Frame finishes: black/stainless, red/stainless, and red/black.

NIB	Exc.	V.G.	Good	Fair	Poor
390	325	225	175	—	100

Undercoverette
As above, with a thinner grip and in .32 S&W.

NIB	Exc.	V.G.	Good	Fair	Poor
—	350	250	125	100	75

Bulldog
Similar to the Undercover model, but in .44 Special caliber with a 2.5" or 3" barrel and 5-shot cylinder. Discontinued; replaced by Target and Pug models.

NIB	Exc.	V.G.	Good	Fair	Poor
325	275	225	175	125	100

Stainless Steel Bulldog
As above, in stainless steel.

NIB	Exc.	V.G.	Good	Fair	Poor
350	300	—	200	150	125

Target Bulldog
As above, in .357 Magnum or .44 Special with a 4" barrel fitted with adjustable rear sights. Blued with walnut grips. Manufactured from 1986 to 1988, later reintroduced.

NIB	Exc.	V.G.	Good	Fair	Poor
350	300	250	200	150	125

Pathfinder
Similar to the above, but in .22 or .22 Magnum caliber with a 2", 3", or 6" barrel with adjustable sights.

NIB	Exc.	V.G.	Good	Fair	Poor
350	300	250	200	—	125

Pathfinder Stainless Steel

As above, in stainless steel.

NIB	Exc.	V.G.	Good	Fair	Poor
360	310	260	210	160	135

Bulldog Pug

Chambered for the .44 Special cartridge it is fitted with a 2.5" barrel. Available with walnut or neoprene grips in blue or stainless steel finish with choice of spur or pocket hammer. The cylinder holds 5 rounds. Overall length is 7" and weight is between 20 oz. and 25 oz. depending on grip and finish.

NIB	Exc.	V.G.	Good	Fair	Poor
350	300	250	200	150	125

Stainless Steel Bulldog

As above, in stainless steel.

NIB	Exc.	V.G.	Good	Fair	Poor
375	325	275	225	175	125

Bulldog Tracker

As above, with a 2.5", 4", or 6" barrel in .357 Magnum only.

NIB	Exc.	V.G.	Good	Fair	Poor
375	325	275	225	175	125

Police Bulldog

As above, in .32 H&R Magnum, .38 Special or .44 Special with 3.5" or 4" barrel.

NIB	Exc.	V.G.	Good	Fair	Poor
350	300	250	200	150	125

Stainless Steel Police Bulldog

As above, in stainless steel and available also in .357 Magnum.

NIB	Exc.	V.G.	Good	Fair	Poor
350	300	250	200	150	125

Off Duty

Chambered for the .38 Special or .22 LR this revolver is fitted with a 2" barrel. Offered with either walnut or rubber grips in blue or stainless steel finish with choice of spur or pocket hammer. Weight of the .38 special version is between 17 oz. and 23 oz., depending on grip and finish. The .22 LR version weighs between 19 oz. and 22 oz. The overall length is 4.75". A nickel finish with rubber grips is also offered.

NIB	Exc.	V.G.	Good	Fair	Poor
325	275	225	175	125	100

Pit Bull

A 9mm Federal, .38 Special or .357 Magnum caliber double-action revolver with a 2.5", 3.5", or 4" barrel. Blued with rubber grips.

NIB	Exc.	V.G.	Good	Fair	Poor
400	350	250	175	125	90

The Mag Pug

A 5-shot revolver chambered for .357 Magnum. Stainless or blue. Ported 2.2" barrel. 23 oz. Fixed sights, rubber grips. Stainless or black.

NIB	Exc.	V.G.	Good	Fair	Poor
350	300	250	200	150	125

Charter Arms Southpaw

Five-shot snubnose revolver chambered in .38 Special +P. Five-shot cylinder, 2" barrel, matte black aluminum alloy frame with stainless steel cylinder. Cylinder latch and crane assembly are on right side of frame for convenience of left-hand shooters. Rubber Pachmayr-style grips. Weight: 12 oz.

NIB	Exc.	V.G.	Good	Fair	Poor
400	350	250	175	125	90

Pink Lady

Similar to Undercover Lite but with pink anodized frame. .38 Special only.

NIB	Exc.	V.G.	Good	Fair	Poor
375	325	275	225	—	125

Goldfinger

Similar to Undercover Lite but with gold anodized frame. .38 Special only.

NIB	Exc.	V.G.	Good	Fair	Poor
375	325	275	225	—	125

Patriot

Built on Bulldog frame but chambered in .327 Federal Magnum (six-shot). Rubber grips, 2.2- or 4-inch barrel. Comes with Kershaw "327" knife.

NIB	Exc.	V.G.	Good	Fair	Poor
425	300	225	175	—	100

Dixie Derringer

Stainless mini-revolver chambered for .22 LR (5 oz.) or .22 Mag (6 oz.). 5-shot, 1.175" barrel.

NIB	Exc.	V.G.	Good	Fair	Poor
175	140	100	75	50	25

Explorer II Pistol

A .22 caliber semi-automatic pistol with 6", 8", or 10" barrels. Available with a camo, black, silver, or gold finish and plastic grips. Discontinued in 1986.

NIB	Exc.	V.G.	Good	Fair	Poor
225	175	125	65	45	25

Model 40

A .22 caliber double-action semi-automatic pistol with a 3.5" barrel and 8-shot magazine. Stainless steel with plastic grips. Manufactured from 1984 to 1986.

NIB	Exc.	V.G.	Good	Fair	Poor
—	275	225	200	150	100

Model 79K

A .32 or .380 caliber double-action semi-automatic pistol with a 3.5" barrel and 7-shot magazine. Stainless steel with plastic grips. Manufactured from 1986 to 1988.

NIB	Exc.	V.G.	Good	Fair	Poor
—	350	300	250	180	125

Model 42T

A .22 caliber semi-automatic pistol with a 6" barrel and adjustable sights. Blued with walnut grips. Manufactured in 1984 and 1985.

NIB	Exc.	V.G.	Good	Fair	Poor
500	450	400	325	265	200

CHIAPPA ARMS
Dayton, Ohio

1911-22

1911-style semiauto pistol chambered in .22 LR. Features include alloy frame; steel barrel; matte blue-black or bright nickel finish, walnut-like grips, two 10-round magazines, fixed sights. Straight blowback action.

NIB	Exc.	V.G.	Good	Fair	Poor
260	225	200	150	100	75

NOTE: Add $25 for target model with adjustable sights, $25 for OD or tan finish.

Rhino14

Unique revolver chambered in .357 Magnum. Features include 2, 4-, 5- or 6-inch barrel; fixed or adjustable sights; visible hammer or hammerless design. Weight 24 to 33 oz. Walnut or synthetic grips with black frame; hexagonal-shaped cylinder. Unique design fires from bottom chamber of cylinder.

NIB	Exc.	V.G.	Good	Fair	Poor
650	600	525	475	300	200

NOTE: Add $75 for wood grips, $50 for brushed nickel finish.

CHICAGO F. A. CO.
Chicago, Illinois

Protector Palm Pistol

A .32 caliber radial cylinder revolver designed to fit in the palm of the hand and to be operated by a hinged lever mounted to the rear of the circular frame. The sideplates are marked "Chicago Firearms Co., Chicago, Ill." and "The Protector". Blued with hard rubber grip panels or nickel-plated with pearl grip panels. Manufactured by the Ames Manufacturing Company. Add 25 percent for pearl grip panels without cracks or chips.

Protector Palm Pistol Standard Model Nickel-Plated/Black Grips

NIB	Exc.	V.G.	Good	Fair	Poor
—	—	3000	2000	1000	750

NOTE: Blued finish add 50 percent. Pearl grips add 20 percent.

CHIPMUNK RIFLES/ROGUE RIFLE CO.
Lewiston, Idaho

Silhouette Pistol

A .22 caliber bolt-action pistol with a 14.5" barrel, open sights and rear pistol-grip walnut stock.

NIB	Exc.	V.G.	Good	Fair	Poor
150	125	100	80	60	40

CHYLEWSKI, WITOLD
Switzerland

A 6.35mm caliber semi-automatic pistol with a 6-round magazine, marked "Brevete Chylewski" and bears the name Neuhausen on the left side of the pistol. Approximately 1,000 were made between 1910 and 1918.This pistol was designed to be cocked with one hand.

NIB	Exc.	V.G.	Good	Fair	Poor
—	—	1250	850	550	275

CIMARRON F. A. CO.
Fredericksburg, Texas

In business since 1984 this company imports quality single-action revolvers and rifles from Uberti, Armi San Marco, and Pedersoli. **NOTE:** Cimarron also sells Uberti-manufactured blackpowder Colt reproductions, from the Patterson to the Model 1862 Pocket. For prices and specifications on these models see the Uberti section.

MODEL NO. 3 SCHOFIELD

This version of the Schofield is manufactured for Cimarron by Armi San Marco in Italy. Its parts are interchangeable with the original. It is offered in several variations and calibers. Discontinued. Beware of latch locking problems.

Civilian Model

Fitted with 7" barrel and offered in .44 Russian & .44 Special, .44 WCF, .45 Schofield, .45 Long Colt.

NIB	Exc.	V.G.	Good	Fair	Poor
875	600	525	425	300	125

Military Model

Essentially the same as the Civilian Model except for its markings.

NIB	Exc.	V.G.	Good	Fair	Poor
875	600	525	425	300	125

Wells Fargo

Similar to the Military and Civilian Model but fitted with a 5" barrel. Calibers are the same.

NIB	Exc.	V.G.	Good	Fair	Poor
875	600	525	425	300	125

NOTE: For standard nickel finish add $100 and for custom nickel finish add $150.

Model 1872 Open Top

This revolver is offered in a number of different calibers and configurations. It is chambered for the .44 SP, .44 Colt, .44 Russian, .45 Schofield, .38 Colt, .38 Special. It can be fitted with Army or Navy grips. Barrel lengths are 4.75", 5.5", or 7.5". Offered in regular blued finish, charcoal blue finish, or original finish.

NIB	Exc.	V.G.	Good	Fair	Poor
575	425	350	300	200	100

NOTE: Add $40 for charcoal finish and $50 for original finish. Add $25 for silver-plated back strap and trigger guard.

COLT SINGLE-ACTION ARMY CONFIGURATIONS

Cimarron Arms reproduction of the 1873 Colt Single-Action Army revolver comes in two basic configurations. First is the "Old Model" with the black powder frame screw-in cylinder pin retainer and circular bull's eye ejector head. Second is the "pre-war Model" style frame with spring loaded cross-pin retainer and half moon ejector head. Old Model revolvers are available in authentic old style charcoal blue finish at an extra charge. Unless otherwise stated all of these Colt reproductions are produced by Uberti of Italy. Plain walnut grips are standard unless noted.

General Custer 7th Cavalry Model

Has US military markings and is fitted with 7-1/2" barrel on an Old Model frame. Offered in .45 Long Colt only.

NIB	Exc.	V.G.	Good	Fair	Poor
650	450	350	300	200	100

Rough Rider U.S. Artillery Model

This version of the Old Model is fitted with a 5-1/2" barrel and chambered for .45 Long Colt.

NIB	Exc.	V.G.	Good	Fair	Poor
650	450	350	300	200	100

Frontier Six Shooter

This revolver is offered with a choice of 4-3/4", 5-1/2", or 7-1/2" barrel. It is chambered for .38 WCF, .357 Magnum, .44 WCF, .45 Long Colt, or .45 LC with extra .45 ACP cylinder.

NIB	Exc.	V.G.	Good	Fair	Poor
575	350	300	275	175	75

NOTE: For charcoal blue finish add $40 to NIB price. For extra .45 ACP cylinder add $30. For stainless steel add $50.

Sheriff's Model w/no ejector

Fitted with a 3" barrel and chambered in .44 WCF or .45 Long Colt. Built on an Old Model frame.

NIB	Exc.	V.G.	Good	Fair	Poor
550	350	300	275	175	75

New Sheriff's Model w/ejector

This variation is fitted with a 3-1/2" barrel with ejector and is available in .357 Magnum, .44 WCF, .44 Special, and .45 Long Colt. For checkered walnut grips add $35.

NIB	Exc.	V.G.	Good	Fair	Poor
575	400	325	275	175	75

Wyatt Earp Buntline

This is a limited edition model fitted with a 10" barrel chambered for the .45 Long Colt cartridge. Model P frame. Silver shield inlaid in grip.

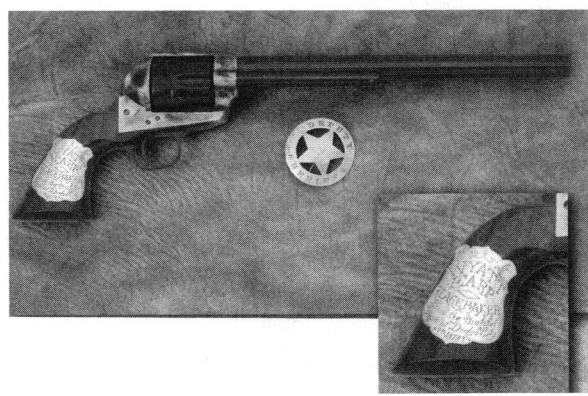

NIB	Exc.	V.G.	Good	Fair	Poor
775	600	500	425	300	125

New Thunderer

The frame is based on the Old Model fitted with a bird's-head grip with a choice of plain or checkered walnut grips. Originally offered in 3-1/2" or 4-3/4" barrel lengths; in 1997 5-1/2" barrels were offered. Chambered for .357 Magnum, .44 WCF, .44 Special, or .45 Long Colt/.45 ACP. Add $35 for checkered grips.

NIB	Exc.	V.G.	Good	Fair	Poor
575	450	325	275	175	75

Thunderer Long Tom

Same as the New Thunderer except for a barrel length of 7.5".

NIB	Exc.	V.G.	Good	Fair	Poor
550	425	350	275	175	75

Lightning

Similar to the Thunderer but with a smaller grip frame. Chambered for the .38 Special cartridge or .22 LR and fitted with 3.5", 4.75", or 5.5" barrel. Finish is blue with case hardened frame.

NIB	Exc.	V.G.	Good	Fair	Poor
475	375	315	250	150	65

Lightning .32s

This model features two cylinders chambered for the .32-20 and the .32 H&R cartridges. Choice of 3.5", 4.75", or 5.5" barrel. Introduced in 2004.

NIB	Exc.	V.G.	Good	Fair	Poor
550	400	350	275	175	75

New Model P

Offered in either Old Model or pre-war styles in a choice of 4-3/4", 5-1/2", or 7-1/2" barrel. Chambered for .32 WCF, .38 WCF, .44 WCF, .44 Special, or .45 Long Colt.

NIB	Exc.	V.G.	Good	Fair	Poor
475	400	325	275	175	75

Stainless Frontier Model P

This model is a Model P in stainless steel. Chambered for the .357 Mag or .45 Colt cartridge. Barrels are 4.75", 5.5", or 7.5". Introduced in 2004.

NIB	Exc.	V.G.	Good	Fair	Poor
550	450	400	300	200	100

A.P. Casey Model P U.S. Cavalry

Fitted with a 7-1/2" barrel and chambered for .45 Long Colt this revolver has US markings (APC) on an Old Model frame.

NIB	Exc.	V.G.	Good	Fair	Poor
550	375	325	250	150	75

Rinaldo A. Carr Model P U.S. Artillery

This is a Model P built on an Old Model frame and chambered for .45 Long Colt and fitted with a 5-1/2" barrel. US markings (RAC).

NIB	Exc.	V.G.	Good	Fair	Poor
550	425	375	275	175	100

Evil Roy Model

This model features a Model P frame with wide square-notch rear sight and wide-width front sight. Slim grips checkered or smooth. Tuned action with lightened trigger. Chambered for the .357 Mag, .45 Colt, or .44-40 cartridge. Barrel lengths are 4.75" or 5.5". Introduced in 2004.

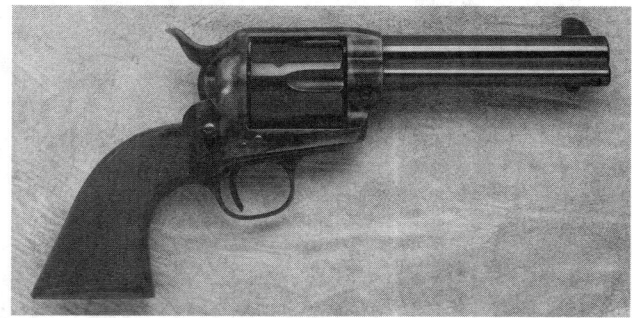

NIB	Exc.	V.G.	Good	Fair	Poor
625	550	475	375	250	125

Model P Jr.

Similar to the Model P but sized 20 percent smaller. Chambered for the .38 Special cartridge and fitted with 3.5" or 4.75" barrels. Blue with case hardened frame.

NIB	Exc.	V.G.	Good	Fair	Poor
475	400	325	250	150	75

Model P Jr. .32s

This model, introduced in 2004, features two cylinders chambered for the .32-20 and the .32 H&R cartridges. Choice of 3.5", 4.75", or 5.5" barrel.

NIB	Exc.	V.G.	Good	Fair	Poor
550	400	350	250	150	75

Cimarron 1880 Frontier Flat Top

Introduced in 1998 this model is a target version of the Colt single-action army. Rear sight is adjustable for windage and front adjustable for elevation. Offered with choice of 4.75", 5.5", or 7.5" barrels and chambered for .45 Colt, .45 Schofield, .44 WCF, and .357 Magnum. Choice of model P frame or pre-war frame.

NIB	Exc.	V.G.	Good	Fair	Poor
550	450	325	225	150	100

Cimarron Bisley

Exact copy of the Colt Bisley with case hardened frame. Choice of 4.75", 5.5", or 7.5" barrels and calibers from .45 Colt, .45 Schofield, .44 WCF, to .357 Magnum. Introduced in 1998.

NIB	Exc.	V.G.	Good	Fair	Poor
550	450	325	225	150	100

Cimarron Bisley Flat Top

Offered in the same barrel lengths and caliber as the standard Bisley with the addition of a windage adjustable rear sight and elevation adjustable front sight. Introduced in 1998.

NIB	Exc.	V.G.	Good	Fair	Poor
550	450	325	225	150	100

El Pistolero

This budget-priced revolver was introduced in 1997 and features a brass backstrap and trigger guard with plain walnut grips. Offered in 4-3/4", 5-1/2", and 7-1/2" barrel lengths. Chambered for .45 Long Colt or .357 Magnum.

NIB	Exc.	V.G.	Good	Fair	Poor
350	250	200	125	75	50

Doc Holliday Thunderer

This nickel-plated SAA in .45 Colt has a 3.5-inch barrel, Cimarron Tru Ivory grips, and comes with a matching numbered dagger and a shoulder holster designed to carry both items.

NIB	Exc.	V.G.	Good	Fair	Poor
1150	1000	800	650	450	300

Rooster Shooter SAA

Replica of SAA used by John Wayne in many movies. Chambered in .357 Mag., .44-40 or .45 Colt with antique grey finish, artificial ivory grips. Introduced in 2010.

NIB	Exc.	V.G.	Good	Fair	Poor
700	625	525	400	300	250

Man With No Name SAA

Replica of gun used by Clint Eastwood in several "Spaghetti Westerns" in .45 Colt with 4.75 or 5.5-inch barrel, cased-colored finish, wood grips with rattlesnake inlay. Introduced in 2010.

NIB	Exc.	V.G.	Good	Fair	Poor
750	650	550	425	300	250

RICHARDS CONVERSIONS

Model 1851

Chambered for .38 Special, .38 Colt, and .44 Colt. Fitted with 5" or 7" barrels.

NIB	Exc.	V.G.	Good	Fair	Poor
550	450	325	225	150	100

Model 1861

Chambered for .38 Special, .38 Colt, and .44 Colt. Fitted with 5" or 7" barrels.

NIB	Exc.	V.G.	Good	Fair	Poor
550	450	325	225	150	100

Model 1860

Chambered for .38 Special, .38 Colt, and .44 Colt. Fitted with 5" or 7.5" barrels.

NIB	Exc.	V.G.	Good	Fair	Poor
550	450	325	225	150	100

Relic Finish

Offered by Cimarron as an extra cost item on its revolvers. This finish duplicates the old worn antique finish seen on many used historical Colts. Add $40 to the NIB price for any Cimarron revolver with this finish.

CLARK, F. H.
Memphis, Tennessee

Pocket Pistol

A .41 caliber single-shot percussion pistol with a 3.5" to 5" barrel, German silver mounts and end cap, and the barrel is stamped "F.H. Clark & Co./Memphis." Manufactured in the 1850s and 1860s.

NIB	Exc.	V.G.	Good	Fair	Poor
—	—	5350	1900	550	200

CLEMENT, CHAS.
Liege, Belgium

Model 1903

A 5.5mm Glisenti caliber semi-automatic pistol. Barrel raises at the muzzle to begin the loading procedure.

Courtesy James Rankin

NIB	Exc.	V.G.	Good	Fair	Poor
—	575	475	350	220	110

Model 1907

As above, but in 6.35mm and 7.65mm caliber.

Courtesy Orvel Reichert

NIB	Exc.	V.G.	Good	Fair	Poor
—	475	395	325	200	100

Model 1908

Similar to the Model 1907 but with the magazine release at the bottom of the frame. Fitted with a larger grip.

Courtesy J.B. Wood

NIB	Exc.	V.G.	Good	Fair	Poor
—	575	450	295	200	125

Model 1909

A semi-automatic pistol in 6.35mm and 7.65mm calibers. Similar to the Model 1908 but with barrel and chamber housing in one piece.

Courtesy James Rankin

NIB	Exc.	V.G.	Good	Fair	Poor
—	575	450	300	225	100

Model 1910

Redesigned version of the above with the barrel and housing all one piece. This unit is held in position by the trigger guard.

Courtesy Orvel Reichert

NIB	Exc.	V.G.	Good	Fair	Poor
—	575	475	395	350	275

Model 1912

A 6.35mm caliber semi-automatic pistol marked "Clement's Patent"; others, "Model 1912 Brevet 243839." This model is quite different from earlier Clement models.

Courtesy James Rankin

NIB	Exc.	V.G.	Good	Fair	Poor
—	425	295	250	195	100

American Model

Revolver copy of the Colt Police Positive. It was chambered for .38 caliber.

NIB	Exc.	V.G.	Good	Fair	Poor
—	425	295	250	150	90

COBRA ENTERPRISES, INC.
Salt Lake City, Utah

DERRINGERS

Long Bore Series

This series is chambered for the .22 WMR, .38 Special, or the 9mm cartridge. Fitted with a 3.5" barrel. Black synthetic, laminate oak, or laminate rosewood grips. Chrome or black finish. Weight is about 16 oz.

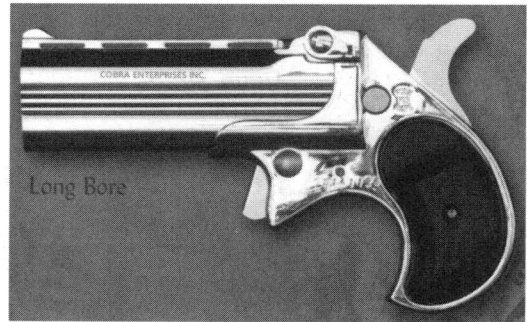

NIB	Exc.	V.G.	Good	Fair	Poor
250	200	160	125	100	75

Big Bore Series

Chambered for the .22 WMR, .32 H&R Mag., and the .38 Special. Barrel length is 2.75". Choice of black synthetic, laminate oak, or laminate rosewood grips. Chrome or black finish. Weight is about 14 oz.

NIB	Exc.	V.G.	Good	Fair	Poor
250	200	160	125	100	75

SEMI-AUTO PISTOLS

C-32/C-380

Chambered for the .32 ACP or .380 cartridges. Fitted with a 2.8" barrel. Chrome or black finish. Magazine capacity is 5 rounds for the .380 and 6 rounds for the .32 ACP. Weight is about 22 oz.

NIB	Exc.	V.G.	Good	Fair	Poor
175	125	80	60	40	25

C-9mm

This is a double-action-only pistol chambered for the 9mm cartridge. Fitted with a 3.3" barrel. Magazine capacity is 10 rounds. Load indicator. Polymer grips. Weight is about 21 oz.

NIB	Exc.	V.G.	Good	Fair	Poor
275	215	150	115	75	45

Patriot .45

This is double-action-only pistol chambered for the .45 ACP cartridge. Barrel length is 3". Frame is black polymer. Slide is stainless steel. Magazine capacity is 6 rounds. Weight is about 20 oz.

NIB	Exc.	V.G.	Good	Fair	Poor
350	225	150	115	75	45

COBRAY INDUSTRIES
S.W.D., Inc.
Atlanta, Georgia

M-11 Pistol

A 9mm caliber semi-automatic pistol. It fires from the closed bolt and is made of steel stampings with a parkerized finish. It is patterned after, though a good deal smaller than, the Ingram Mac 10.

NIB	Exc.	V.G.	Good	Fair	Poor
—	375	295	150	100	75

NOTE: Add $70 for stainless steel. Add $150 for pre-ban models.

M-12

Same as above but chambered for the .380 ACP cartridge.

NIB	Exc.	V.G.	Good	Fair	Poor
—	375	295	150	100	75

NOTE: Add $150 for pre-ban models.

COCHRAN TURRET
C. B. Allen
Springfield, Massachusetts

Pistol

Action similar to the company's under-hammer percussion turret rifle with 4" to 7" barrels.

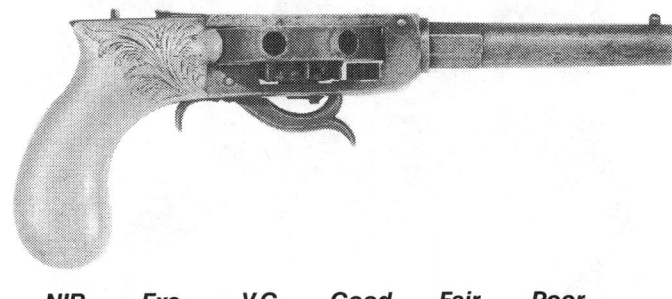

NIB	Exc.	V.G.	Good	Fair	Poor
—	—	26500	21000	9700	3000

COFER, T. W.
Portsmouth, Virginia

Cofer Navy Revolver

A .36 caliber spur trigger percussion revolver with a 7.5" octagonal barrel and 6-shot cylinder. The top strap is marked "T.W. Cofer's/Patent." and the barrel "Portsmouth, Va." This revolver was manufactured in limited quantities during the Civil War.

NIB	Exc.	V.G.	Good	Fair	Poor
—	—	120000	43500	6500	1500

COGSWELL
London, England

Cogswell Pepperbox Pistol

A .47 caliber 6-shot percussion pepperbox with case hardened barrels, German silver frame and walnut grips. Normally marked "B. Cogswell, 224 Strand, London" and "Improved Revolving Pistol."

NIB	Exc.	V.G.	Good	Fair	Poor
—	—	4400	1950	975	550

COLT'S PATENT FIRE ARMS MANUFACTURING COMPANY

Hartford, Connecticut

COLT PATERSON MODELS

Pocket or Baby Paterson Model No. 1

The Paterson was the first production revolver manufactured by Colt. It was first made in 1837. The Model 1 or Pocket Model is the most diminutive of the Paterson line. The revolver is serial numbered in its own range, #1 through #500. The numbers are not visible without dismantling the revolver. The barrel lengths run from 1.75" to 4.75". The standard model has no attached loading lever. The chambering is .28 caliber percussion and it holds five shots. The finish is all blued, and the grips are varnished walnut. It has a roll-engraved cylinder scene, and the barrel is stamped "Patent Arms Mfg. Co. Paterson N.J. Colt's Pt." Cased examples in Very Good or better condition can bring upwards of $200,000.

NIB	Exc.	V.G.	Good	Fair	Poor
—	—	125000	50000	19500	5000

Belt Model Paterson No. 2

The Belt Model Paterson is a larger revolver with a straight-grip and an octagonal barrel that is 2.5" to 5.5" in length. It is chambered for .31 caliber percussion and holds five shots. The finish is all blued, with varnished walnut grips and no attached loading lever. It has a roll-engraved cylinder scene, and the barrel is stamped "Patent Arms Mfg. Co. Paterson N.J. Colt's Pt." The serial number range is #1-#850 and is shared with the #3 Belt Model. It was made from 1837-1840. An excellent cased example was auctioned by Rock Island Auction in 2007 for $414,000.

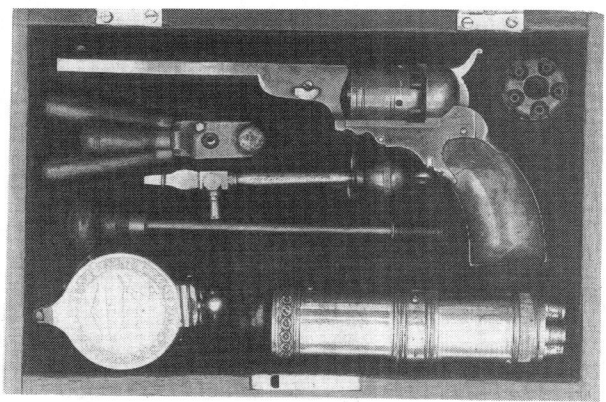

Courtesy Buffalo Bill Historical Center, Cody, Wyoming

NIB	Exc.	V.G.	Good	Fair	Poor
—	400000	225000	75000	28500	7500

Belt Model Paterson No. 3

This revolver is quite similar to the Model #2 except that the grips are curved outward at the bottom to form a more handfilling configuration. They are serial numbered in the same #1-#850 range. Some attached loading levers have been noted on this model, but they are extremely rare and would add approximately 35 percent to the value.

NIB	Exc.	V.G.	Good	Fair	Poor
—	—	—	95000	40000	10000

Ehlers Model Pocket Paterson

John Ehlers was a major stockholder and treasurer of the Patent Arms Mfg. Co. when it went bankrupt. He seized the assets and inventory. These revolvers were Pocket Model Patersons that were not finished at the time. Ehlers had them finished and marketed them. They had an attached loading lever, and the abbreviation "Mfg Co." was deleted from the barrel stamping. There were 500 revolvers involved in the Ehlers variation totally, and they were produced from 1840-1843.

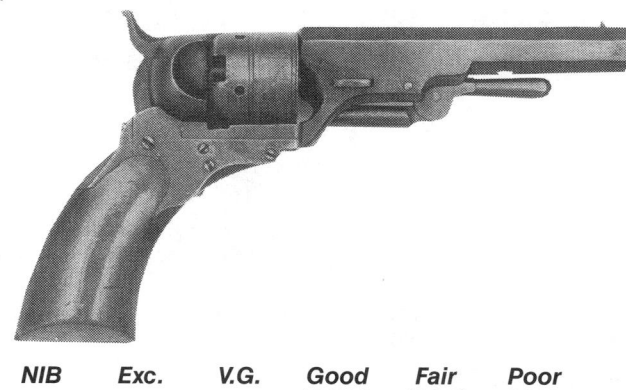

NIB	Exc.	V.G.	Good	Fair	Poor
—	—	—	75000	30000	8000

Ehlers Belt Model Paterson

The same specifications apply to this larger revolver as they do to the Ehlers Pocket Model. It falls within the same 500 revolver involvement and is rare.

NIB	Exc.	V.G.	Good	Fair	Poor
—	—	—	75000	30000	8000

Texas Paterson Model No. 5

This is the largest and most sought after of the Paterson models. It is also known as the Holster Model. It has been verified as actually seeing use by both the military and civilians on the American frontier. It is chambered for .36 caliber percussion, holds five shots, and has an octagonal barrel that ranges from 4" to 12" in length. It has been observed with and without the attached loading lever, but those with it are rare. The finish is blued, with a case-colored hammer. The grips are varnished walnut. The cylinder is roll-engraved; and the barrel is stamped "Patent Arms Mfg. Co. Paterson, N.J. Colts Pt." Most Texas Patersons are well used and have a worn appearance. One in excellent or V.G. condition would be highly prized. A verified military model would be worth a great deal more than standard, so qualified appraisal would be essential. The serial number range is #1-#1000, and they were manufactured from 1838-1840. The attached loading lever brings approximately a 25 percent premium.

NIB	Exc.	V.G.	Good	Fair	Poor
—	—	—	150000	60000	17500

COLT WALKER-DRAGOON MODELS

Walker Model Revolver

The Walker is a massive revolver. It weighs 4 lbs., 9 oz. and has a 9" part-round/part-octagonal barrel. The cylinder holds six shots and is chambered for .44 caliber percussion. There were 1,000 Walker Colts manufactured in 1847, and nearly all of them saw extremely hard use. Originally this model had a roll-engraved cylinder, military inspection marks, and barrel stamping that read "Address Saml. Colt-New York City." Practically all examples noted have had these markings worn or rusted beyond recognition. Because the Walker is perhaps the most desirable and sought-after Colt from a collector's standpoint and because of the extremely high value of a Walker in any condition, qualified appraisal is definitely recommended. These revolvers were serial numbered A, B, C, and D Company 1-220, and E Company 1-120. An Excellent example was auctioned by James D. Julia in 2008 for $920,000.

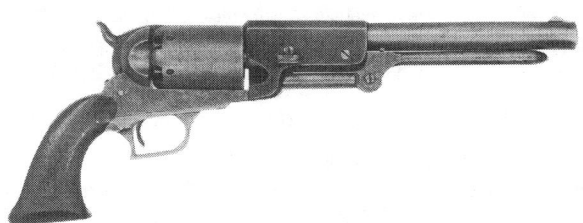

Courtesy Buffalo Bill Historical Center, Cody, Wyoming

NIB	Exc.	V.G.	Good	Fair	Poor
—	900000	675000	400000	200000	59500

Civilian Walker Revolver

This model is identical to the military model but has no martial markings. They are found serial numbered 1001 through 1100.

NIB	Exc.	V.G.	Good	Fair	Poor
—	—	500000	395000	195000	58000

Whitneyville Hartford Dragoon

This is a large, 6-shot, .44 caliber percussion revolver. It has a 7.5" part-round/part-octagonal barrel. The frame, hammer, and loading lever are case colored. The remainder is blued, with a brass trigger guard and varnished walnut grips. There were only 240 made in late 1847. The serial numbers run from 1100-1340. This model is often referred to as a Transitional Walker. Some of the parts used in its manufacture were left over from the Walker production run. This model has a roll-engraved cylinder scene, and the barrel is stamped "Address Saml. Colt New York-City." This is an extremely rare model.

NIB	Exc.	V.G.	Good	Fair	Poor
—	—	140000	100000	55000	28500

Walker Replacement Dragoon

This extremely rare Colt (300 produced) is sometimes referred to as the "Fluck" in memory of the gentleman who first identified it as a distinct and separate model. They were produced by Colt as replacements to the military for Walkers that were no longer fit for service due to mechanical failures. They were large, 6-shot, .44 caliber percussion revolvers with 7.5" part-round/part-octagonal barrels. Serial numbers ran from 2216 to 2515. The frame, hammer, and loading lever are case-colored; the remainder, blued. The grips, which are longer than other Dragoons and similar to the Walkers, are of varnished walnut and bear the inspectors mark "WAT" inside an oval cartouche on one side and the letters "JH" on the other. The frame is stamped "Colt's/Patent/U.S." The letter "P" appears on various parts of the gun.

NIB	Exc.	V.G.	Good	Fair	Poor
—	—	75000	55000	25000	6000

FIRST MODEL DRAGOON

Another large, 6-shot, .44 caliber percussion revolver. It has a 7.5" part-round/part-octagonal barrel. The frame, hammer, and loading lever are case colored; the remainder, blued with a brass grip frame and square backed trigger guard. The trigger guard is silver-plated on the Civilian Model only. Another distinguishing feature on the First Model is the oval cylinder stop notches. The serial number range is 1341-8000. There were approximately 5,000 made. The cylinder is roll-engraved; and the barrel stampings read "Address Saml. Colt, New York City." "Colt's Patent" appears on the frame. On Military Models the letters "U.S." also appear on the frame.

Military Model

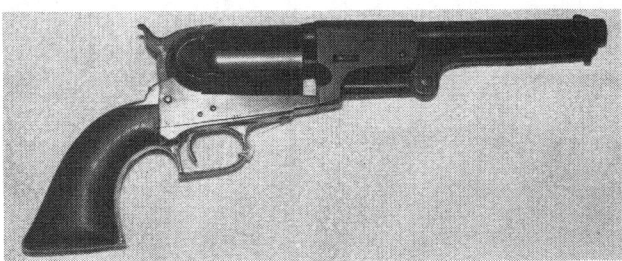

NIB	Exc.	V.G.	Good	Fair	Poor
—	—	65000	40000	20000	3500

Civilian Model

NIB	Exc.	V.G.	Good	Fair	Poor
—	—	55000	35000	18000	3000

SECOND MODEL DRAGOON

Most of the improvements that distinguish this model from the First Model are internal and not readily apparent. The most obvious external change is the rectangular cylinder-stop notches. This model is serial numbered from 8000-10700, for a total production of approximately 2,700 revolvers manufactured in 1850 and 1851. There is a Civilian Model, a Military Model, and an extremely rare variation that was issued to the militias of New Hampshire and Massachusetts (marked "MS."").

Civilian Model

NIB	Exc.	V.G.	Good	Fair	Poor
—	—	55000	35000	25000	3500

Military Model

NIB	Exc.	V.G.	Good	Fair	Poor
—	—	62500	40000	30000	3000

Militia Model

NIB	Exc.	V.G.	Good	Fair	Poor
—	—	75000	45000	30000	3000

THIRD MODEL DRAGOON

This is the most common of all the large Colt percussion revolvers. Approximately 10,500 were manufactured from 1851 through 1861. It is quite similar in appearance to the Second Model, and the most obvious external difference is the round trigger guard. The Third Model Dragoon was the first Colt revolver available with a detachable shoulder stock. There are three basic types of stocks, and all are quite rare as only 1,250 were produced. There are two other major variations we will note—the "C.L." Dragoon, which was a militia-issued model and is rare, and the late-issue model with an 8" barrel. These are found over serial number 18000, and only 50 were produced.

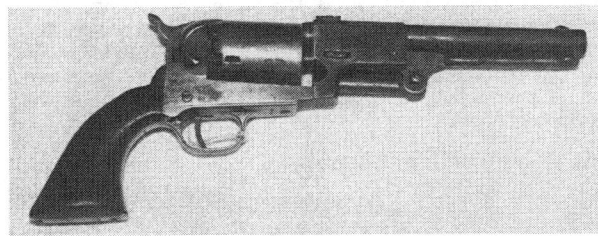

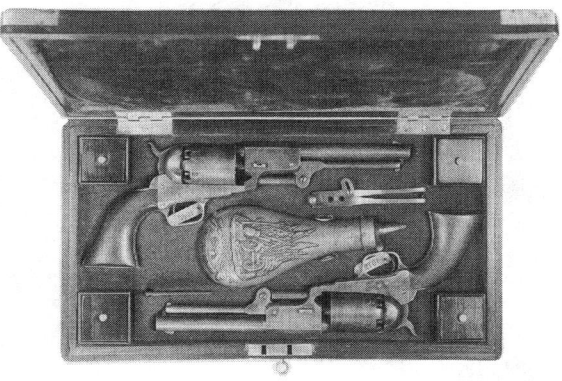

Courtesy Buffalo Bill Historical Center, Cody, Wyoming

Civilian Model

NIB	Exc.	V.G.	Good	Fair	Poor
—	—	27500	15000	2500	1000

Military Model

NIB	Exc.	V.G.	Good	Fair	Poor
—	—	47000	30000	17500	3000

Shoulder Stock Cut Revolvers

NIB	Exc.	V.G.	Good	Fair	Poor
—	—	51000	35000	20000	3000

Shoulder Stocks

NIB	Exc.	V.G.	Good	Fair	Poor
—	—	15000	8000	4000	2000

C.L. Dragoon

Hand engraved, not stamped.

NIB	Exc.	V.G.	Good	Fair	Poor
—	—	60000	57500	17500	3000

8" Barrel Late Issue

NIB	Exc.	V.G.	Good	Fair	Poor
—	—	55000	42500	25000	3000

Hartford English Dragoon

This is a variation of the Third Model Dragoon. The only notable differences are the British proofmarks and the distinct #1-#700 serial number range. Other than these two features, the description given for the Third Model would apply. These revolvers were manufactured in Hartford but were finished at Colt's London factory from 1853-1857. Some bear the hand-engraved barrel marking "Col. Colt London." Many of the English Dragoons were elaborately engraved, and individual appraisal would be a must. Two hundred revolvers came back to America in 1861 to be used in the Civil War.

NIB	Exc.	V.G.	Good	Fair	Poor
—	—	35000	25000	12000	3000

MODEL 1848 BABY DRAGOON

This is a small, 5-shot, .31 caliber percussion revolver. It has an octagonal barrel in lengths of 3", 4", 5", and 6". Most were made without an attached loading lever, although some with loading levers have been noted. The frame, hammer, and loading lever (when present) are case colored; the barrel and cylinder, blued. The grip frame and trigger guard are silver-plated brass. There were approximately 15,500 manufactured between 1847 and 1850. The serial range is between 1-5500. The barrels are stamped "Address Saml. Colt/New York City." Some have been noted with the barrel address inside brackets. The frame is marked "Colt's/Patent." The first 10,000 revolvers have the Texas Ranger/Indian roll-engraved cylinder scene; the later guns the stagecoach holdup scene. This is a popular model, and many fakes have been noted.

Texas Ranger/Indian Scene

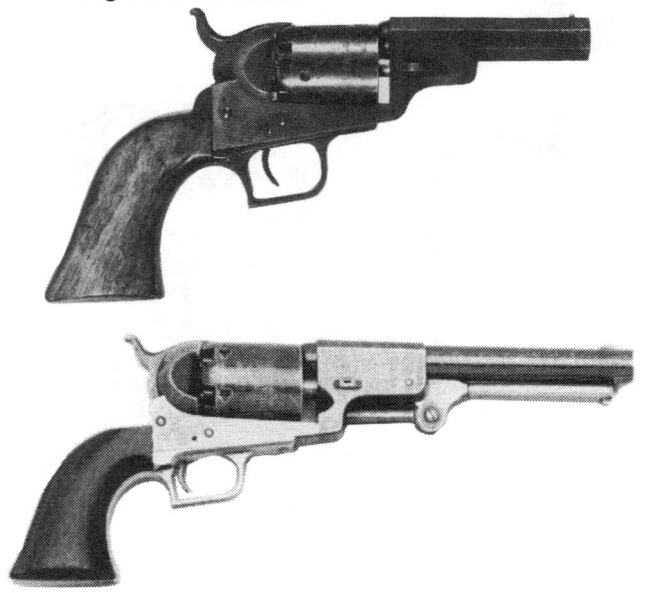

NIB	Exc.	V.G.	Good	Fair	Poor
—	—	19500	12000	6500	2000

NOTE: Attached loading lever add 15 percent.

Stagecoach Holdup Scene

NIB	Exc.	V.G.	Good	Fair	Poor
—	—	20500	13000	7000	2000

Model 1849 Pocket Revolver

This is a small, either 5- or 6-shot, .31 caliber percussion revolver. It has an octagonal barrel 3", 4", 5", or 6" in length. Most had loading gates, but some did not. The frame, hammer, and loading lever are case colored; the cylinder and barrel are blued. The grip frame and round trigger guard are made of brass and are silver plated. There are both large and small trigger guard variations noted. This is the most plentiful of all the Colt percussion revolvers, with approximately 325,000 manufactured over a 23-year period, 1850-1873. There are over 200 variations of this model, and one should consult an expert for individual appraisals. There are many fine publications specializing in the field of Colt percussion revolvers that would be helpful in the identification of the variations. The values represented here are for the standard model.

NIB	Exc.	V.G.	Good	Fair	Poor
—	—	3400	2950	1200	300

London Model 1849 Pocket Revolver

Identical in configuration to the standard 1849 Pocket Revolver, the London-made models have a higher quality finish and their own serial number range, 1-11000. They were manufactured from 1853 through 1857. They feature a roll-engraved cylinder scene, and the barrels are stamped "Address Col. Colt/London." The first 265 revolvers, known as early models, have brass grip frames and small round trigger guards. They are quite rare and worth approximately 50 percent more than the standard model that has a steel grip frame and large oval trigger guard.

NIB	Exc.	V.G.	Good	Fair	Poor
—	—	3400	2950	1200	300

MODEL 1851 NAVY REVOLVER

This is undoubtedly the most popular revolver Colt produced in the medium size and power range. It is a 6-shot, .36-caliber percussion revolver with a 7.5" octagonal barrel. It has an attached loading lever. The basic model has a case colored frame hammer, and loading lever, with silver-plated brass grip frame and trigger guard. The grips are varnished walnut. Colt manufactured approximately 215,000 of these fine revolvers between 1850 and 1873. The basic Navy features a roll-engraved cylinder scene of a battle between the navies of Texas and Mexico. There are three distinct barrel stampings—serial number 1-74000, "Address Saml. Colt New York City"; serial number 74001-101000 "Address Saml. Colt. Hartford, Ct."; and serial number 101001-215000 "Address Saml. Colt New York U.S. America." The left side of the frame is stamped "Colt's/Patent" on all variations. This model is also available with a detached shoulder stock, and values for the stocks today are nearly as high as for the revolver itself. Careful appraisal should be secured before purchase. The number of variations within the 1851 Navy model designation makes it necessary to read specialized text available on the subject.

Square Back Trigger Guard, 1st Model, Serial #1-1000

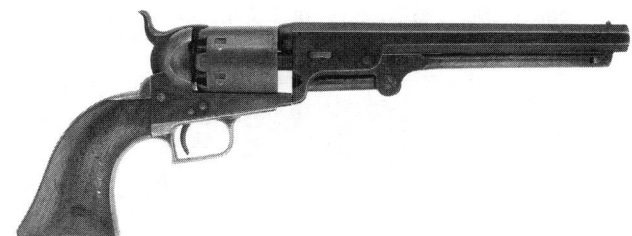

Courtesy Rock Island Auction Company

NIB	Exc.	V.G.	Good	Fair	Poor
—	—	50000	42500	27000	5500

Square Back Trigger Guard, 2nd Model, Serial #1001-4200

NIB	Exc.	V.G.	Good	Fair	Poor
—	—	37500	30000	10000	2500

Small Round Trigger Guard, Serial #4201-85000

Courtesy Milwaukee Public Museum, Milwaukee, Wisconsin

NIB	Exc.	V.G.	Good	Fair	Poor
—	—	9500	8000	2500	500

Large Round Trigger Guard, Serial #85001-215000

NIB	Exc.	V.G.	Good	Fair	Poor
—	—	9500	8000	2500	500

Martial Model

"U.S." stamped on the left side of frame; inspector's marks and cartouche on the grips.

NIB	Exc.	V.G.	Good	Fair	Poor
—	—	42000	20000	7000	1000

Shoulder Stock Variations

1st and 2nd Model Revolver cut for stock only. An expert appraisal is recommended prior to a purchase of these very rare variations.

NIB	Exc.	V.G.	Good	Fair	Poor

Shoulder Stock Variations Stock Only

NIB	Exc.	V.G.	Good	Fair	Poor
—	—	22000	17000	7000	1250

Shoulder Stock Variations 3rd Model Cut For Stock

Revolver only.

NIB	Exc.	V.G.	Good	Fair	Poor
—	—	17500	11500	4000	1250

Shoulder Stock Variations Stock Only

NIB	Exc.	V.G.	Good	Fair	Poor
—	—	12500	9000	3750	1000

LONDON MODEL 1851 NAVY REVOLVER

These revolvers are physically similar to the U.S.-made model with the exception of the barrel address, which reads "Address Col. Colt. London." There are also British proofmarks stamped on the barrel and cylinder. There were 42,000 made between 1853 and 1857. They have their own serial number range, #1-#42,000. There are two major variations of the London Navy, and again a serious purchaser would be well advised to seek qualified appraisal as fakes have been noted.

Navy Revolver 1st Model

Serial #1-#2,000 with a small round brass trigger guard and grip frame. Squareback guard worth a 40 percent premium.

NIB	Exc.	V.G.	Good	Fair	Poor
—	—	16500	8000	2150	700

Navy Revolver 2nd Model

Serial #2,001-#42,000, steel grip frame, and large round trigger guard.

NIB	Exc.	V.G.	Good	Fair	Poor
—	—	15000	7500	1800	600

Navy Revolver Hartford Manufactured Variation

Serial numbers in the 42,000 range.

NIB	Exc.	V.G.	Good	Fair	Poor
—	—	15000	7500	1800	600

COLT SIDE HAMMER MODELS

MODEL 1855 SIDE HAMMER "ROOT" POCKET REVOLVER

The "Root," as it is popularly known, was the only solid-frame revolver Colt ever made. It has a spur trigger and walnut grips, and the hammer is mounted on the right side of the frame. The standard finish is a case colored frame, hammer, and loading lever, with the barrel and cylinder blued. It is chambered for both .28 caliber and .31 caliber percussion. Each caliber has its own serial number range—1-30000 for the .28 caliber and 1-14000 for the .31 caliber. The model consists of seven basic variations, and the serious student should avail himself of the fine publications dealing with this model in depth. Colt produced the Side Hammer Root from 1855-1870.

Models 1 and 1A Serial #1-384

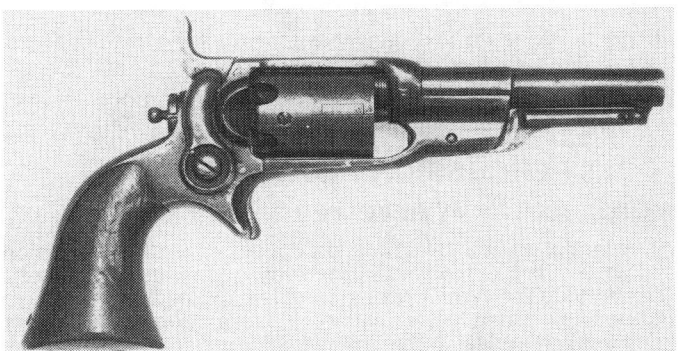

Courtesy Milwaukee Public Museum, Milwaukee, Wisconsin

3.5" octagonal barrel, .28 caliber, roll-engraved cylinder, Hartford barrel address without pointing hand.

NIB	Exc.	V.G.	Good	Fair	Poor
—	—	12000	6000	3500	1200

Model 2 Serial #476-25000

Same as Model 1 with pointing hand barrel address.

NIB	Exc.	V.G.	Good	Fair	Poor
—	—	7500	3500	1900	500

Model 3 Serial #25001-30000

Same as the Model 2 with a full fluted cylinder.

NIB	Exc.	V.G.	Good	Fair	Poor
—	—	7500	3500	1900	500

Model 3A and 4 Serial #1-2400

.31 caliber, 3.5" barrel, Hartford address, full fluted cylinder.

NIB	Exc.	V.G.	Good	Fair	Poor
—	—	7250	3250	1800	500

Model 5 Serial #2401-8000

.31 caliber, 3.5" round barrel, address "Col. Colt New York."

NIB	Exc.	V.G.	Good	Fair	Poor
—	—	6500	2900	1300	300

Model 5A Serial #2401-8000

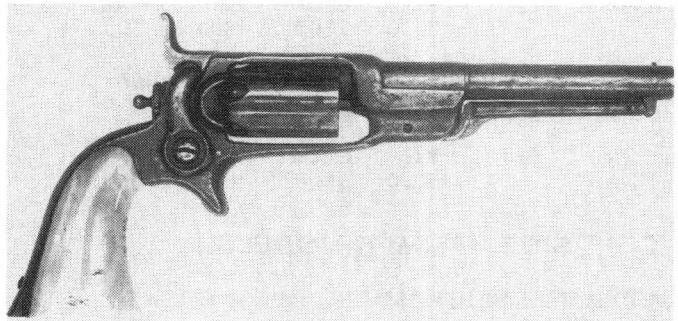

Courtesy Milwaukee Public Museum, Milwaukee, Wisconsin

Same as Model 5 with a 4.5" barrel.

NIB	Exc.	V.G.	Good	Fair	Poor
—	—	6500	2900	1300	300

Models 6 and 6A Serial #8001-11074

Same as Model 5 and 5A with roll-engraved cylinder scene.

NIB	Exc.	V.G.	Good	Fair	Poor
—	—	6750	2995	1350	300

Models 7 and 7A Serial #11075-14000

Same as Models 6 and 6A with a screw holding in the cylinder pin.

NIB	Exc.	V.G.	Good	Fair	Poor
—	—	6750	2995	1350	300

COLT PERCUSSION REVOLVERS

MODEL 1860 ARMY REVOLVER

This model was the third most produced of the Colt percussion handguns. It was the primary revolver used by the Union Army during the Civil War. Colt delivered 127,156 of these revolvers to be used during those hostilities. This is a 6-shot .44 caliber percussion revolver. It has either a 7.5" or 8" round barrel with an attached loading lever. The frame, hammer, and loading lever are case colored; the barrel and cylinder are blued. The trigger guard and front strap are brass, and the backstrap is blued steel. The grips are one-piece walnut. The early models have the barrels stamped "Address Saml. Colt Hartford Ct." Later models are stamped "Address Col. Saml. Colt New-York U.S. America." "Colt's/Patent" is stamped on the left side of the frame; ".44 Cal.," on the trigger guard. The cylinder is roll engraved with the naval battle scene. There were a total of 200,500 1860 Army Revolvers manufactured between 1860 and 1873.

Martial Marked Model

NIB	Exc.	V.G.	Good	Fair	Poor
—	—	8500	7500	3500	900

Civilian Model

This model is found in either 3- or 4-screw variations and it may or may not be cut for a shoulder stock. Civilian models are usually better finished.

Courtesy Milwaukee Public Museum, Milwaukee, Wisconsin

NIB	Exc.	V.G.	Good	Fair	Poor
—	—	7500	6000	3000	800

Full Fluted Cylinder Model

Approximately 4,000 Army's were made with full fluted cylinders. They appear in the first 8,000 serial numbers.

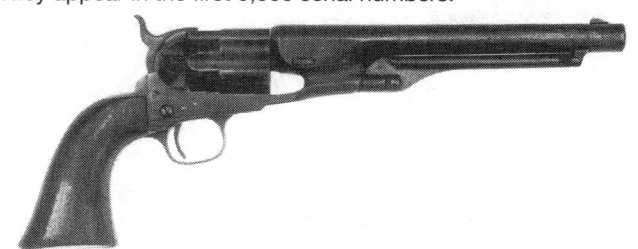

Courtesy Milwaukee Public Museum, Milwaukee, Wisconsin

NIB	Exc.	V.G.	Good	Fair	Poor
—	—	16500	15000	7000	2000

Full Fluted Cylinder Model Shoulder Stock 2nd Type

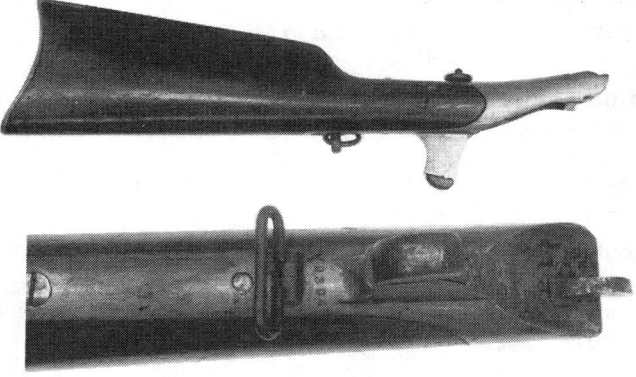

Courtesy Milwaukee Public Museum, Milwaukee, Wisconsin

MODEL 1861 NAVY REVOLVER

This model is a 6-shot, 7.5" round-barreled, .36 caliber percussion revolver. The frame, hammer, and attached loading lever are case colored. The barrel and cylinder are blued. The grip frame and trigger guard are silver-plated brass. The grips are of one-piece walnut. The cylinder has the roll-engraved naval battle scene, and the barrel stamping is "Address Col. Saml. Colt New-York U.S. America." The frame is stamped "Colts/Patent" with "36 Cal." on the trigger guard. There are not many variations within the 1861 Navy model designation, as less than 39,000 were made between 1861 and 1873.

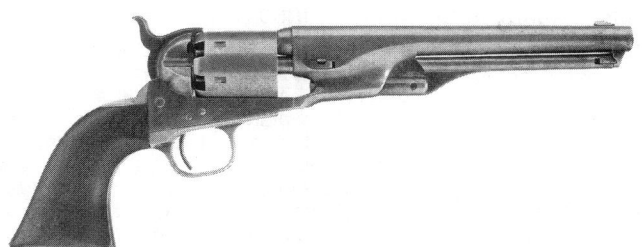

Courtesy Rock Island Auction Company

Civilian Model

NIB	Exc.	V.G.	Good	Fair	Poor
—	—	12500	7500	3500	900

Military Model

Marked "U.S." on frame, inspector's cartouche on grip. 650 were marked "U.S.N." on the butt.

NIB	Exc.	V.G.	Good	Fair	Poor
—	—	22000	18000	5500	1800

Shoulder Stock Model

Only 100 3rd-type stocks were made. They appear between serial #11000-#14000. These are very rare revolvers.

Revolver

NIB	Exc.	V.G.	Good	Fair	Poor
—	—	—	—	5000	1500

Stock

NIB	Exc.	V.G.	Good	Fair	Poor
—	—	—	10000	4250	1000

Fluted Cylinder Model

Approximately the first 100 were made with full fluted cylinders.

NIB	Exc.	V.G.	Good	Fair	Poor
—	—	50000	30000	7500	2000

MODEL 1862 POCKET NAVY REVOLVER

This is a smaller, 5-shot, .36 caliber percussion revolver that resembles the configuration of the 1851 Navy. It has a 4.5", 5.5", or 6.5" octagonal barrel with an attached loading lever. The frame, hammer, and loading lever are case colored; the barrel and cylinder, blued. The grip frame and trigger guard are silver-plated brass; and the one-piece grips, of varnished walnut. The stagecoach holdup scene is roll-engraved on the cylinder. The frame is stamped "Colt's/Patent" ; and the barrel, "Address Col. Saml. Colt New-York U.S. America." There were approximately 19,000 manufactured between 1861 and 1873. They are serial numbered in the same range as the Model 1862 Police. Because a great many were used for metallic cartridge conversions, they are quite scarce today.The London Address Model with blued steel grip frame would be worth more than the standard model. Add 50 percent.

NOTE: Longer barrels will bring a premium over the 4.5" length.

Standard Production Model

NIB	Exc.	V.G.	Good	Fair	Poor
—	—	6000	3750	1200	500

MODEL 1862 POLICE REVOLVER

This is a slim, attractively designed revolver that some consider to be the most aesthetically pleasing of all the Colt percussion designs. It has a 5-shot, half-fluted cylinder chambered for .36 caliber. It is offered with a 3.5", 4.5", 5.5", or 6.5" round barrel. The frame, hammer, and loading lever are case colored; the barrel and cylinder, blued. The grip frame is silver-plated brass; and the one-piece grips, varnished walnut. The barrel is stamped "Address Col. Saml Colt New-York U.S. America" ; the frame has "Colt's/Patent" on the left side. One of the cylinder flutes is marked "Pat Sept. 10th 1850." There were approximately 28,000 of these manufactured between 1861 and 1873. Many were converted to metallic cartridge use, so they are

quite scarce on today's market.The London Address Model would be worth approximately twice the value of the standard model.

Courtesy Milwaukee Public Museum, Milwaukee, Wisconsin

NOTE: Longer barrels will bring a premium over the 3.5" or 4.5" length.

Standard Production Model

NIB	Exc.	V.G.	Good	Fair	Poor
—	—	6000	2950	1000	400

COLT METALLIC CARTRIDGE CONVERSIONS

THUER CONVERSION REVOLVER

Although quite simplistic and not commercially successful, the Thuer Conversion was the first attempt by Colt to convert the percussion revolvers to the new metallic cartridge system. This conversion was designed around the tapered Thuer cartridge and consists of a ring that replaced the back part of the cylinder, which had been milled off. This ring is stamped "Pat. Sep. / 15. 1868." The ejection position is marked with the letter "E." These conversions have rebounding firing pins and are milled to allow loading from the front of the revolver. This conversion was undertaken on the six different models listed; and all other specifications, finishes, markings, etc., not directly affected by the conversion would be the same as previously described. From a collectible and investment standpoint, the Thuer Conversion is very desirable. Competent appraisal should be secured if acquisition is contemplated.

Model 1849 Pocket Conversion

NIB	Exc.	V.G.	Good	Fair	Poor
—	—	—	15500	4000	2000

Model 1851 Navy Conversion

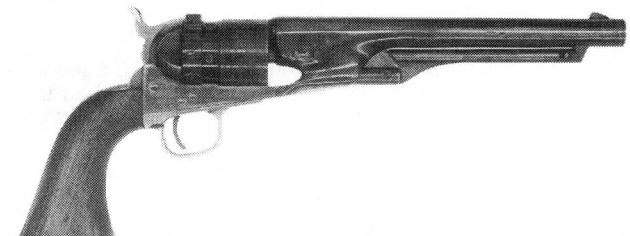

Courtesy Milwaukee Public Museum, Milwaukee, Wisconsin

NIB	Exc.	V.G.	Good	Fair	Poor
—	—	—	18000	5000	2000

Model 1860 Army Conversion

NIB	Exc.	V.G.	Good	Fair	Poor
—	—	—	19500	6000	2000

Model 1861 Navy Conversion

NIB	Exc.	V.G.	Good	Fair	Poor
—	—	—	19500	6000	2000

Model 1862 Police Conversion

NIB	Exc.	V.G.	Good	Fair	Poor
—	—	—	13500	3500	1500

NOTE: Blued models will bring higher prices than nickel models in the same condition.

Model 1862 Pocket Navy Conversion

NIB	Exc.	V.G.	Good	Fair	Poor
—	—	—	13500	3500	1500

RICHARDS CONVERSION, 1860 ARMY REVOLVER

This was Colt's second attempt at metallic cartridge conversion, and it met with quite a bit more success than the first. The Richards Conversion was designed for the .44 Colt cartridge and has a 6-shot cylinder and an integral ejector rod to replace the loading lever that had been removed. The other specifications pertaining to the 1860 Army Revolver remain as previously described if they are not directly altered by the conversion. The Richards Conversion adds a breechplate with a firing pin and its own rear sight. There were approximately 9,000 of these Conversions manufactured between 1873 and 1878.

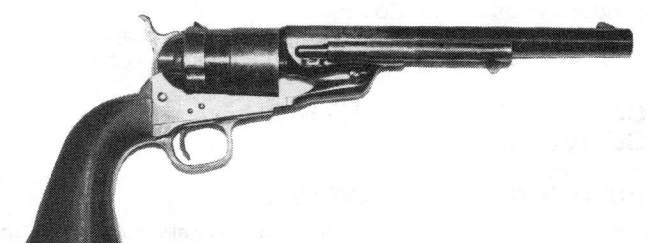

Civilian Model

NIB	Exc.	V.G.	Good	Fair	Poor
—	—	10000	3950	2000	600

NOTE: Blued models will bring higher prices than nickel models in the same condition.

Martially Marked Variation

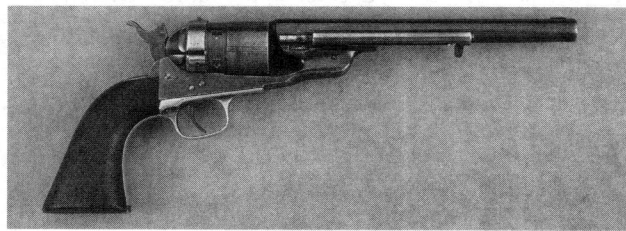

Courtesy Little John's Auction Service, Inc., Paul Goodwin photo

This variation is found with mixed serial numbers and a second set of conversion serial numbers. The "U.S." is stamped on the left side of the barrel lug, and inspector's cartouche appears on the grip. This is a very rare Colt revolver.

NIB	Exc.	V.G.	Good	Fair	Poor
—	—	18000	15000	8000	2000

Transition Richards Model

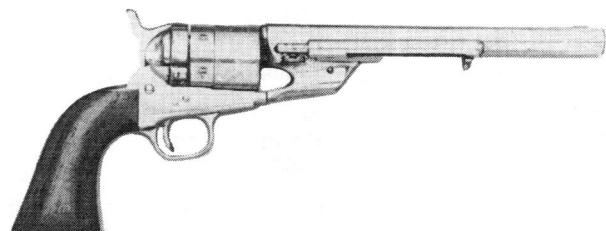

Courtesy Bonhams & Butterfields, San Francisco, California

This variation is marked by the presence of a firing pin hammer.

NIB	Exc.	V.G.	Good	Fair	Poor
—	—	9500	7000	3000	1200

Richards-Mason Conversion, 1860 Army Revolver

This conversion is different from the Richards Conversion in a number of readily apparent aspects. The barrel was manufactured with a small lug much different in appearance than seen on the standard 1860 Army. The breechplate does not have its own rear sight, and there is a milled area to allow the hammer to contact the base of the cartridge. These Conversions were also chambered for the .44 Colt cartridge, and the cylinder holds 6 shots. There is an integral ejector rod in place of the loading lever. The barrels on some are stamped either "Address Col. Saml. Colt New-York U.S. America" or "Colt's Pt. F.A. Mfg. Co. Hartford, Ct." The patent dates 1871 and 1872 are stamped on the left side of the frame. The finish of these revolvers, as well as the grips, were for the most part the same as on the unconverted Armies; but for the first time, nickel-plated guns are found. There were approximately 2,100 of these Conversions produced in 1877 and 1878.

NIB	Exc.	V.G.	Good	Fair	Poor
—	—	13500	7000	2500	800

RICHARDS-MASON CONVERSIONS 1851 NAVY REVOLVER

These revolvers were converted in the same way as the 1860 Army previously described, the major difference being the caliber .38, either rimfire or centerfire. Finishes are mostly the same as on unconverted revolvers, but nickel-plated guns are not rare.

Production Model Serial #1-3800

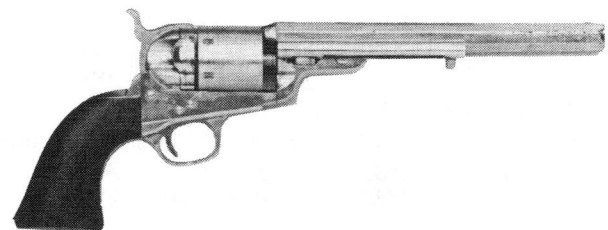

Courtesy Bonhams & Butterfields, San Francisco, California

NIB	Exc.	V.G.	Good	Fair	Poor
—	—	11000	5500	2000	800

NOTE: Blued models will bring higher prices than nickel models in the same condition.

U.S. Navy Model Serial #41000-91000

"USN" stamped on butt; steel grip frame.

NIB	Exc.	V.G.	Good	Fair	Poor
—	—	16000	9500	3000	1000

RICHARDS-MASON CONVERSION 1861 NAVY REVOLVER

The specifications for this model are the same as for the 1851 Navy Conversion described above, with the base revolver being different. There were 2,200 manufactured in the 1870s.

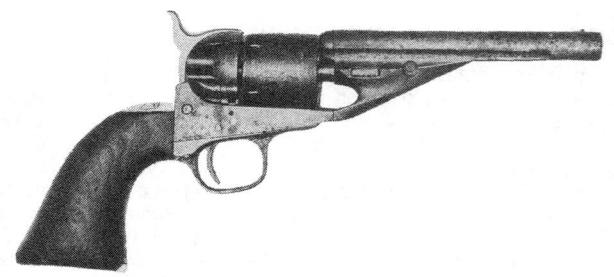

Courtesy Wallis & Wallis, Lewes, Sussex, England

Standard Production Model Serial #100-3300

NIB	Exc.	V.G.	Good	Fair	Poor
—	—	11500	6250	1500	500

NOTE: Blued models will bring higher prices than nickel models in the same condition.

U.S. Navy Model Serial #1000-9999

NIB	Exc.	V.G.	Good	Fair	Poor
—	—	15000	7500	3500	1000

MODEL 1862 POLICE AND POCKET NAVY CONVERSIONS

The conversion of these two revolver models is the most difficult to catalog of all the Colt variations. There were approximately 24,000 of these produced between 1873 and 1880. There are five basic variations with a number of sub-variations. The confusion is usually caused by the different ways in which these were marked. Depending upon what parts were utilized, caliber markings could be particularly confusing. One must also consider the fact that many of these conversion revolvers found their way into secondary markets, such as Mexico and Central and South America, where they were either destroyed or received sufficient abuse to obliterate most identifying markings. The five basic variations are all chambered for either the .38 rimfire or the .38 centerfire cartridge. All held 5 shots, and most were found with the round roll-engraved stagecoach holdup scene. The half-fluted cylinder from the 1862 Police is quite rare on the conversion revolver and not found at all on some of the variations. The finishes on these guns were pretty much the same as they were before conversion, but it is not unusual to find nickel-plated specimens. Blued models will bring a premium over nickel in the same condition. The basic variations are listed.

Round Barrel Pocket Navy with Ejector

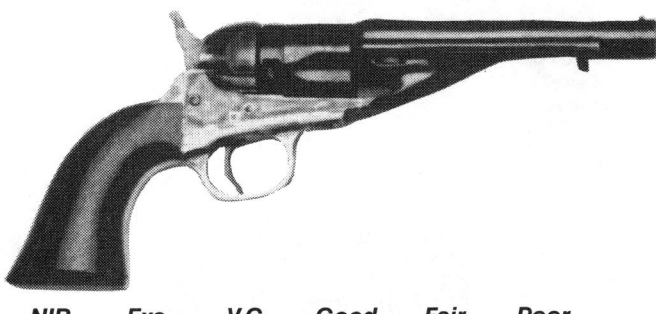

NIB	Exc.	V.G.	Good	Fair	Poor
—	—	7500	3500	1600	800

3.5" Round Barrel Without Ejector

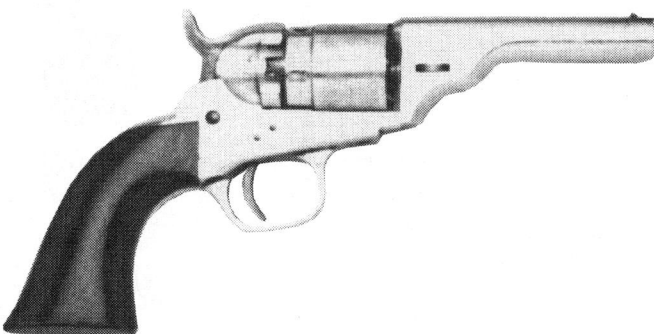

NIB	Exc.	V.G.	Good	Fair	Poor
—	—	5500	2500	1000	300

NOTE: Blued models will bring higher prices than nickel models in the same condition.

4.5" Octagonal Barrel Without Ejector

NIB	Exc.	V.G.	Good	Fair	Poor
—	—	6500	3500	1200	400

Model 1862 Pocket Navy Octagon Barrel with Ejector

NOTE: Half-fluted cylinder add 20 percent.

NIB	Exc.	V.G.	Good	Fair	Poor
—	—	7500	3850	1500	600

NOTE: Blued models will bring higher prices than nickel models in the same condition.

Model 1862 Police Round Barrel with Ejector

NIB	Exc.	V.G.	Good	Fair	Poor
—	—	7500	3850	1500	600

MODEL 1871-1872 OPEN TOP REVOLVER

This model was the first revolver Colt manufactured especially for a metallic cartridge. It was not a conversion. The frame, 7.5" or 8" round barrel, and the 6-shot cylinder were produced for the .44 rimfire metallic cartridge. The grip frame and some internal parts were taken from the 1860 Army and the 1851 Navy. Although this model was not commercially successful and was not accepted by the U.S. Ordnance Department, it did pave the way for the Single-Action Army that came out shortly thereafter and was an immediate success. This model is all blued, with a case colored hammer. There are some with silver-plated brass grip frames, but most are blued steel. The one-piece grips are of varnished walnut. The cylinder is roll-engraved with the naval battle scene. The barrel is stamped "Address Col. Saml. Colt New-York U.S. America." The later production revolvers are barrel stamped "Colt's Pt. F.A. Mfg. Co. Hartford, Ct. U.S.A." The first 1,000 revolvers were stamped "Colt's/Patent." After that, 1871 and 1872 patent dates appeared on the frame. There were 7,000 of these revolvers manufactured in 1872 and 1873.

1860 Army Grip Frame

NIB	Exc.	V.G.	Good	Fair	Poor
—	—	27500	15000	4500	800

NOTE: Blued models will bring higher prices than nickel models in the same condition.

1851 Navy Grip Frame

NIB	Exc.	V.G.	Good	Fair	Poor
—	—	29000	17500	4000	1200

COLT DERRINGERS AND POCKET REVOLVER

First Model Derringer

This is a small all-metal single-shot. It is chambered for the .41 rimfire cartridge. The 2.5" barrel pivots to the left and downward for loading. This model is engraved with a scroll pattern and has been noted blued, silver, or nickel-plated. The barrel is stamped "Colt's Pt. F.A. Mfg. Co./Hartford Ct. U.S.A/ No.1." ".41 Cal." is stamped on the frame under the release catch. There were approximately 6,500 of this model manufactured from 1870-1890. It was the first single-shot pistol Colt produced.

Courtesy Rock Island Auction Company

NIB	Exc.	V.G.	Good	Fair	Poor
—	—	3750	2500	1200	400

Second Model Derringer

Although this model has the same odd shape as the First Model, it is readily identifiable by the checkered varnished walnut grips and the "No 2" on the barrel after the address. It is also .41 rimfire and has a 2.5" barrel that pivots in the same manner as the First Model. There were approximately 9,000 of these manufactured between 1870 and 1890.

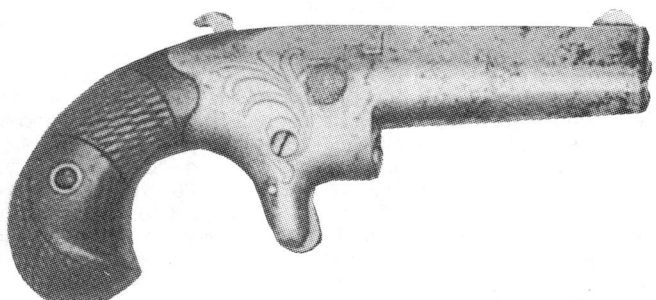

Courtesy Wallis & Wallis, Lewes, Sussex, England

NIB	Exc.	V.G.	Good	Fair	Poor
—	—	3200	2000	900	400

THIRD MODEL DERRINGER

This model was designed by Alexander Thuer who was also responsible for Colt's first metallic cartridge conversion. It is often referred to as the "Thuer Model" for this reason. It is also chambered for the .41 rimfire cartridge and has a 2.5" barrel that pivots to the right (but not down) for loading. The Third Model has a more balanced appearance than its predecessors, and its commercial success (45,000 produced between 1875 and 1910) reflects this. The barrel on this model is stamped "Colt" in small block letters on the first 2,000 guns. The remainder of the production features the "COLT" in large italicized print. The ".41 Cal." is stamped on the left side of the frame. This model will be found with the barrel blued or plated in either silver or nickel and the bronze frame plated. The grips are varnished walnut.

First Variation, Early Production

This has a raised area ("pregnant frame") on the underside of the frame through which the barrel screw passes, and the spur is not angled. Small block "Colt" lettering on barrel.

NIB	Exc.	V.G.	Good	Fair	Poor
—	—	8000	6500	2200	1000

First Variation, Late Production

This is similar to early production but has large italicized "COLT" on barrel.

NIB	Exc.	V.G.	Good	Fair	Poor
—	—	2350	3250	1500	600

NOTE: Blued models will bring a premium over nickel in the same condition.

Production Model

NIB	Exc.	V.G.	Good	Fair	Poor
—	—	1800	800	400	200

HOUSE MODEL REVOLVER

There are two basic versions of this model. They are both chambered for the .41 rimfire cartridge. The 4-shot version is known as the "Cloverleaf" due to the shape of the cylinder when viewed from the front. Approximately 7,500 of the nearly 10,000 House revolvers were of this 4-shot configuration. They are offered with a 1.5" or 3" barrel. The 1.5" length is quite rare, and some octagonal barrels in this length have been noted. The 5-shot round-cylinder version accounts for the rest of the production. It is found with serial numbers over 6100 and is offered with a 2-7/8" length barrel only. This model is stamped on the top strap "Pat. Sept. 19, 1871." This model has brass frames that are sometimes nickel-plated. The barrels are found either blued or plated. The grips are varnished walnut or rosewood. There were slightly fewer than 10,000 of both variations manufactured from 1871-1876.

NOTE: Blued models will bring a premium over nickel in the same condition.

Cloverleaf with 1.5" Round Barrel

NIB	Exc.	V.G.	Good	Fair	Poor
—	—	3750	3000	1250	400

Cloverleaf with 3" Barrel

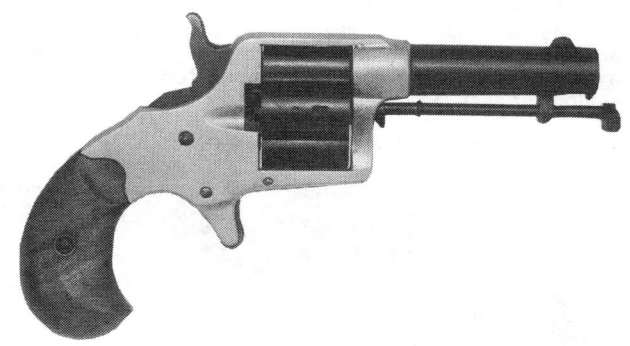

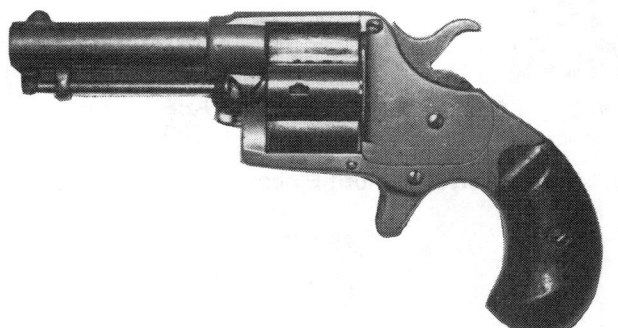

Courtesy Buffalo Bill Historical Center, Cody, Wyoming

NIB	Exc.	V.G.	Good	Fair	Poor
—	—	1750	1500	500	200

House Pistol with 5-Shot Round Cylinder

NIB	Exc.	V.G.	Good	Fair	Poor
—	—	1550	1300	500	200

OPEN TOP POCKET REVOLVER

This is a .22-caliber rimfire, 7-shot revolver that was offered with either a 2-3/8" or a 2-7/8" barrel. The model was a commercial success, with over 114,000 manufactured between 1871 and 1877. There would undoubtedly have been a great deal more sold had not the cheap copies begun to flood the market at that time, forcing Colt to drop this model from the line. This revolver has a silver or nickel-plated brass frame and a nickel-plated or blued barrel and cylinder. The grips are varnished walnut. The cylinder bolt slots are found toward the front on this model. "Colt's Pt. F.A. Mfg. Co./Hartford, Ct. U.S.A." is stamped on the barrel and ".22 Cal." on the left side of the frame.

Early Model with Ejector Rod

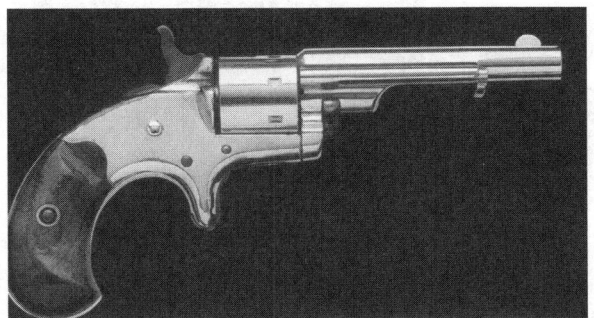

Courtesy Bonhams & Butterfields

NIB	Exc.	V.G.	Good	Fair	Poor
—	—	2000	1750	800	400

NOTE: Blued models will bring a premium over nickel in the same condition.

Production Model without Ejector Rod

NIB	Exc.	V.G.	Good	Fair	Poor
—	—	1250	600	300	150

NEW LINE REVOLVER .22

This was the smallest framed version of the five distinct New Line Revolvers. It has a 7-shot cylinder and a 2.25" octagonal barrel. The frame is nickel-plated, and the balance of the revolver is either nickel-plated or blued. The grips are of rosewood. There were approximately 55,000 of these made from 1873-1877. Colt also stopped production of the New Lines rather than try to compete with the "Suicide Specials." "Colt New .22" is found on the barrel; and ".22 Cal.," on the frame. The barrel is also stamped "Colt's Pt. F.A. Mfg.Co./Hartford, Ct. U.S.A."

1st Model

Short cylinder flutes.

NIB	Exc.	V.G.	Good	Fair	Poor
—	—	1300	600	300	150

NOTE: Blued models will bring higher prices than nickel models in the same condition.

2nd Model

Courtesy Bonhams & Butterfields, San Francisco, California

Long cylinder flutes.

NIB	Exc.	V.G.	Good	Fair	Poor
—	—	750	500	250	125

NOTE: Prices above are for nickel finish. Blued models will bring a premium of 100 percent.

New Line Revolver .30

This is a larger version of the .22 New Line. The basic difference is the size, caliber, caliber markings, and the offering of a blued version with case colored frame. There were approximately 11,000 manufactured from 1874-1876.

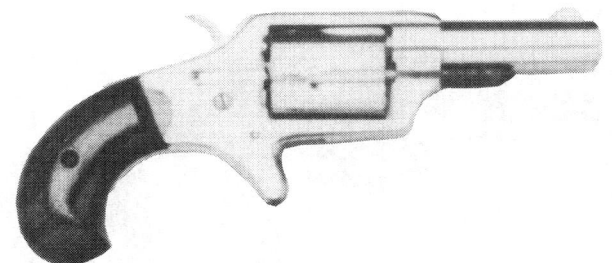

Courtesy Wallis & Wallis, Lewes, Sussex, England

NIB	Exc.	V.G.	Good	Fair	Poor
—	—	1000	750	300	150

New Line Revolver .32

This is the same basic revolver as the .30 caliber except that it is chambered for the .32-caliber rimfire and .32-caliber centerfire and is so marked. There were 22,000 of this model manufactured from 1873-1884. This model was offered with the rare 4" barrel, and this variation would be worth nearly twice the value of a standard model.

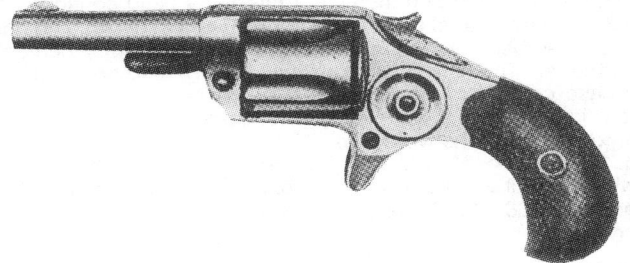

Courtesy Bonhams & Butterfields, San Francisco, California

NIB	Exc.	V.G.	Good	Fair	Poor
—	—	1550	850	300	150

NOTE: Blued models will bring a premium over nickel in the same condition.

New Line Revolver .38

There were approximately 5,500 of this model manufactured between 1874 and 1880. It is chambered for either the .38 rimfire or .38 centerfire caliber and is so marked. This model in a 4" barrel would also bring twice the value.

Courtesy Rock Island Auction Company

NIB	Exc.	V.G.	Good	Fair	Poor
—	—	1500	800	400	200

NOTE: Prices above are for nickel finish. Blued models will bring a premium of 100 percent.

New Line Revolver .41

This is the "Big Colt," as it was sometimes known in advertising of its era. It is chambered for the .41 rimfire and the .41 centerfire and is so marked. The large caliber of this variation makes this the most desirable of the New Lines to collectors. There were approximately 7,000 of this model manufactured from 1874-1879. A 4"-barreled version would again be worth a 100 percent premium.

NIB	Exc.	V.G.	Good	Fair	Poor
—	—	2000	1375	650	300

New House Model Revolver

This revolver is similar to the other New Lines except that it features a square-butt instead of the bird's-head configuration, a 2.25" round barrel without ejector rod, and a thin loading gate. It is chambered for the .32 (rare), .38, and the .41 centerfire cartridges. The finish was either full nickel-plated or blued, with a case colored frame. The grips are walnut, rosewood or (for the first time on a Colt revolver) checkered hard rubber, with an oval around the word "Colt." The barrel address is the same as on the other New Lines. The frame is marked "New House," with the caliber. There were approximately 4,000 manufactured between 1880-1886. .32 caliber model would bring a 10 percent premium.

Courtesy Milwaukee Public Museum, Milwaukee, Wisconsin

NIB	Exc.	V.G.	Good	Fair	Poor
—	—	1495	1000	450	250

NEW POLICE REVOLVER

This was the final revolver in the New Line series. It is chambered for .32, .38, and .41 centerfire caliber. The .32 and .41 are quite rare. It is offered in barrel lengths of 2.25", 4.5", 5.5", and 6.5". An ejector rod is found on all but the 2.5" barrel. The finish is either nickel or blued and case colored. The grips are hard rubber with a scene of a policeman arresting a criminal embossed on them; thusly the model became known to collectors as the "Cop and Thug" model. The barrel stamping is as the other New Lines, and the frame is stamped "New Police .38." There were approximately 4,000 of these manufactured between 1882-1886.

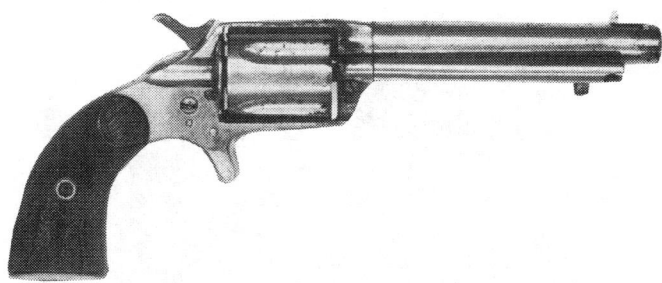

Courtesy Milwaukee Public Museum, Milwaukee, Wisconsin

Long Barrel Model with Ejector

NIB	Exc.	V.G.	Good	Fair	Poor
—	—	—	3250	1400	700

NOTE: The .32 and .41 caliber versions of this model will bring a 40-50 percent premium. Blued models and models with 5.5" or 6.5" barrels will bring a premium. Short barrel model will bring about 50 percent of the listed prices.

COLT'S SINGLE-ACTION ARMY REVOLVER

NOTE: As a rule of thumb nickel guns will bring a deduction of 20-30 percent. For revolvers with 4.75" barrels add 10-15 percent. For checkered grips add 20 percent.

The Colt Single-Action Army, or Peacemaker as it is sometimes referred to, is one of the most widely collected and recognized firearms in the world. With few interruptions or changes in design, it has been manufactured from 1873 until the present. It is still available on a limited production basis from the Colt Custom Shop. The variations in this model are myriad. It has been produced in 30 different calibers and barrel lengths from 2.5" to 16", with 4.75", 5.5", and 7.5" standard. The standard finish is blued, with a case colored frame. Many are nickel-plated. Examples have been found silver- and gold-plated, with combinations thereof. The finest engravers in the world have used the SAA as a canvas to display their artistry. The standard grips from 1873-1883 were walnut, either oil-stained or varnished. From 1883 to approximately 1897, the standard grips were hard rubber with eagle and shield. After this date, at serial number 165000, the hard rubber grips featured the Rampant Colt. Many special-order grips were available, notably pearl and ivory, which were often checkered or carved in ornate fashion. The variables involved in establishing values on this model are extreme. Added to this, one must also consider historical significance, since the SAA played a big part in the formative years of the American West. Fortunately for those among us interested in the SAA, there are a number of fine publications available dealing exclusively with this model. It is my strongest recommendation that they be acquired and studied thoroughly to prevent extremely expensive mistakes. The Colt factory records are nearly complete for this model, and research should be done before acquisition of rare or valuable specimens. For our purposes we will break down the Single-Action Army production as follows: Antique or Black Powder, 1873-1898, serial number 1-175000 The cylinder axis pin is retained by a screw in the front of the frame. Pre-war, 1899-1940, serial number 175001-357859 The cylinder axis pin is retained by a spring-loaded button through the side of the frame. This method is utilized on the following models, as well. Post-war 2nd Generation, 1956-1978, serial number 0001SA-99999SA 3rd Generation, 1978-Present, serial #SA1001. A breakdown of production by caliber will follow the chapter. It is important to note that the rarer calibers and the larger calibers bring higher values in this variation.

COLT ANTIQUE SINGLE-ACTION ARMY REVOLVER

1st Year Production "Pinched Frame" 1873 Only

It is necessary to categorize this variation on its own. This is one of the rarest and most interesting of all the SAAs—not to mention that it is the first. On this model the top strap is pinched or constricted approximately one-half inch up from the hammer to form the rear sight. The highest surviving serial number having this feature is #156, the lowest #1. From these numbers, it is safe to assume that the first run of SAAs were all pinched-frame models; but there is no way to tell how many there were, since Colt did not serial number the frames in the order that they were manufactured. An educated guess would be that there were between 50 and 150 pinched frame guns in all and that they were all made before mid-July 1873. The reason for the change came about on the recommendation of Capt. J.R. Edie, a government inspector who thought that the full fluted top strap would be a big improvement in the sighting capabilities of the weapon. The barrel length of the first model is 7.5"; the standard caliber, .45 Colt; and the proper grips were of walnut. The front sight blade is German silver. Needless to say, this model will rarely be encountered; and if it is, it should never be purchased without competent appraisal.

NIB	Exc.	V.G.	Good	Fair	Poor
—	—	275000	175000	30000	10000

NOTE: Certain 3-digit and 4-digit serial numbers will command a substantial premium. Seek an expert appraisal prior to sale.

Early Military Model 1873-1877

The serial number range on this first run of military contract revolvers extends to #24000. The barrel address is in the early script style with the # symbol preceding and following. The frame bears the martial marking "US," and the walnut grips have the inspector's cartouche stamped on them. The front sight is steel as on all military models; the barrel length, 7.5". The caliber is .45 Colt, and the ejector rod head is the bull's-eye or donut style with a hole in the center of it. The finish features the military polish and case colored frame, with the remainder blued. Authenticate any potential purchase; many spurious examples have been noted.

NIB	Exc.	V.G.	Good	Fair	Poor
—	90000	75000	28000	18000	5000

NOTE: Certain 3-digit and 4-digit serial numbers will command a substantial premium. Seek an expert appraisal prior to sale.

Early Civilian Model 1873-1877

This model is identical to the Early Military Model but has no military acceptance markings or cartouches. Some could have the German silver front sight blade. The early bull's-eye ejector rod head is used on this model. The Civilian Model has a higher degree of polish than is found on the military models, and the finish on these early models could be plated or blued with a case colored frame. This model also has a script barrel address. The grips are standard one-piece walnut. Ivory-grip models are worth a premium.

NIB	Exc.	V.G.	Good	Fair	Poor
—	45000	34000	20000	9000	6000

NOTE: Revolvers produced from 1878 to 1885 will command a premium. Seek an expert appraisal prior to sale.

Late Military Model 1878-1891

The later Military Models are serial numbered to approximately #136000. They bear the block-style barrel address without the #

prefix and suffix. The frames are marked "US," and the grips have the inspector's cartouche. The finish is the military-style polish, case colored frame; and the remainder, blued. Grips are oil-stained walnut. On the military marked Colts, it is imperative that potential purchases be authenticated as many fakes have been noted.

NIB	Exc.	V.G.	Good	Fair	Poor
—	68000	39500	14000	10000	6000

Artillery Model 1895-1903

A number of "US" marked SAAs were returned either to the Colt factory or to the Springfield Armory, where they were altered and refinished. These revolvers have 5.5" barrels and any combination of mixed serial numbers. They were remarked by the inspectors of the era and have a case colored frame and a blued cylinder and barrel. Some have been noted all blued within this variation. This model, as with the other military marked Colts, should definitely be authenticated before purchase. Some of these revolvers fall outside the 1898 antique cutoff date that has been established by the government and, in our experience, are not quite as desirable to investors. They are generally worth approximately 20 percent less.

NIB	Exc.	V.G.	Good	Fair	Poor
—	18000	12500	8000	4000	3000

London Model

These SAAs were manufactured to be sold through Colt's London Agency. The barrel is stamped "Colt's Pt. F.A. Mfg. Co. Hartford, Ct. U.S.A. Depot 14 Pall Mall London." This model is available in various barrel lengths. It is generally chambered for .45 Colt, .450 Boxer, .450 Eley, .455 Eley, and rarely .476 Eley, the largest of the SAA chamberings. A good many of these London Models were cased and embellished, and they should be individually appraised. This model should be authenticated as many spurious examples have been noted.

NIB	Exc.	V.G.	Good	Fair	Poor
—	22000	15000	10000	4500	2000

Frontier Six-Shooter 1878-1882

Several thousand SAAs were made with the legend "Colt's Frontier Six Shooter" acid-etched into the left side of the barrel instead of being stamped. This etching is not deep, and today collectors will become ecstatic if they discover a specimen with mere vestiges of the etched panel remaining. These acid-etched SAAs are serial numbered #45000-#65000. They have various barrel lengths and finishes, but all are chambered for the .44-40 caliber.

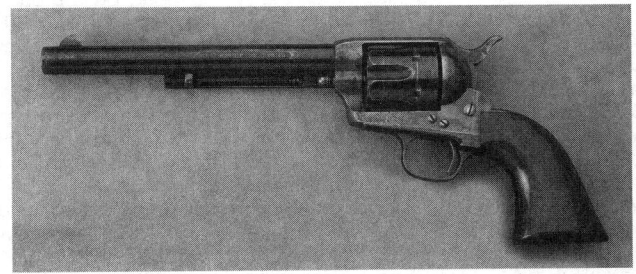

Courtesy Little John's Auction Service, Inc., Paul Goodwin photo

NIB	Exc.	V.G.	Good	Fair	Poor
—	40000	20000	14000	7000	5000

Sheriff's or Storekeeper's Model 1882-1898

This model was manufactured with a short barrel (2.5"-4.75"). Most have 4" barrels. It features no ejector rod or housing, and the frame is made without the hole in the right forward section to accommodate the ejector assembly. The Sheriff's or Storekeeper's Model is numbered above serial #73000. It was manufactured with various finishes and chambered for numerous calibers. This model continued after 1898 into the smokeless or modern era. Examples manufactured in the pre-war years are worth approximately 20 percent less. Although faking this model is quite difficult, it has been successfully attempted.

Courtesy Little John's Auction Service, Inc., Paul Goodwin photo

NIB	Exc.	V.G.	Good	Fair	Poor
—	50000	35000	22000	9000	5000

NOTE: Nickel models will command a premium.

Flattop Target Model 1888-1896

This model is highly regarded and sought after by collectors. It is not only rare (only 925 manufactured) but is an extremely attractive and well-finished variation. It is chambered for 22 different calibers from .22 rimfire to .476 Eley. The .22 rimfire, .38 Colt, .41, and .45 Colt are the most predominant chamberings. The 7.5" barrel length is the most commonly encountered.The serial number range is between #127000-#162000. Some have been noted in higher ranges. The finish is all blued, with a case colored hammer. The checkered grips are either hard rubber or walnut. The most readily identifying feature of the flattop is the lack of a groove in the top strap and the sight blade dovetailed into the flattop. The front sight has a removable blade insert. The values given are for a standard production model chambered for the calibers previously mentioned as being the most common. It is important to have other calibers individually appraised as variance in values can be quite extreme.

NIB	Exc.	V.G.	Good	Fair	Poor
—	35000	25000	15000	8000	4000

Bisley Model 1894-1915

This model was named for the target range in Great Britain, where their National Target Matches were held since the nineteenth century. The model was designed as a target revolver with an odd humped-back grip that was supposed to better fill the hand while target shooting. It is also easily identified by the wide low profile hammer spur, wide trigger, and the name "Bisley" stamped on the barrel. The Bisley production fell within the serial number range #165000-#331916. There were 44,350 made.It was offered in 16 different chamberings from .32 Colt to .455 Eley. The most common calibers were .32-20, .38-40, .41, .44-40, and .45 Colt. The barrel lengths are 4.75", 5.5", and 7.5". The frame and hammer are case-colored; the remainder, blued. Smokeless powder models produced after 1899 utilized the push-button cylinder pin retainer. The grips are checkered hard rubber. This model was actually designed with English sales in mind; and though it did sell well over there, American sales accounted for most of the Bisley production. The values we provide here cover the standard calibers and barrel lengths. Rare calibers and/or other notable variations can bring greatly fluctuating values.

NIB	Exc.	V.G.	Good	Fair	Poor
—	9000	6500	4500	2500	1200

NOTE: Nickel models will command a premium.

Bisley Model Flattop Target 1894-1913

This model is quite similar to the Standard Bisley Model, with the flattop frame and dovetailed rear sight feature. It also has the removable front sight insert. It has an all-blued finish with case-colored hammer only and is available with a 7.5" barrel. Smokeless powder models produced after 1899 utilized the push-button cylinder pin retainer. The calibers are the same as the standard Bisley. Colt manufactured 976 of these revolvers. The advice regarding appraisal would also apply.

NIB	Exc.	V.G.	Good	Fair	Poor
—	25000	16000	9500	3500	1800

NOTE: Nickel models will command a premium.

Standard Civilian Production Models 1876-1898

This final designated category for the black powder or antique SAAs includes all the revolvers not previously categorized. They have barrel lengths from 4.75", 5.5", and 7.5" and are chambered for any one of 30 different calibers. The finishes could be blued, blued and case colored, or plated in nickel, silver, gold, or combinations thereof. Grips could be walnut, hard rubber, ivory, pearl, stag, or bone. The possibilities are endless. The values given here are for the basic model, and we again strongly advise securing qualified appraisal when not completely sure of any model variation.

NOTE: For Standard Civilian Production Models with screw-in frame, serial number to 163,000 add a 25-100 percent premium depending on year built. Seek an expert appraisal prior to sale.

NIB	Exc.	V.G.	Good	Fair	Poor
—	30000	18000	12000	8000	3000

COLT PRE-WAR SINGLE-ACTION ARMY REVOLVER 1899-1940

Standard Production Pre-war Models

The 1899 cutoff has been thoroughly discussed, but it is interesting to note that the actual beginning production date for smokeless models was 1900. The pre-war Colts are, all in all, quite similar to the antiques—the finishes, barrel lengths, grips, etc. Calibers are also similar, with the exception of the obsolete ones being dropped and new discoveries added. The most apparent physical difference between the smokeless powder and black powder models is the previously discussed method of retaining the cylinder axis pin. The pre-war Colts utilized the spring-loaded button through the side of the frame. The black powder models utilized a screw in the front of the frame. The values we furnish for this model designation are for these standard models only. The serial number range on the pre-war SAAs is 175001-357859. Note that any variation can have marked effects on value fluctuations, and qualified appraisal should be secured. Note: Scarce chamberings command 30 percent to 100 percent premium.

NIB	Exc.	V.G.	Good	Fair	Poor
—	12500	8000	3500	2500	1500

Long Fluted Cylinder Model 1913-1915

Strange as it may seem, the Colt Company has an apparent credo they followed to never throw anything away. That credo was never more evident than with this model. These Long Flute Cylinders were actually left over from the model 1878 Double-Action Army Revolvers. Someone in the hierarchy at Colt had an inspiration that drove the gunsmiths on the payroll slightly mad: to make these cylinders fit the SAA frames. There were 1,478 of these Long Flutes manufactured. They are chambered for the .45 Colt, .38-40, .32-20, .41 Colt, and the .44 Smith & Wesson Special. They were offered in the three standard barrel lengths and were especially well-polished, having what has been described as Colt's "Fire Blue" on the barrel and cylinder. The frame and hammer are case colored. They are fitted with checkered hard rubber grips and are particularly fine examples of Colt's craft. Rare.

NIB	Exc.	V.G.	Good	Fair	Poor
—	17500	1000	6000	3250	2000

COLT POST-WAR SINGLE-ACTION ARMY REVOLVER (AKA SECOND GENERATION)

STANDARD POST-WAR MODEL 1956-1975

In 1956 the shooting and gun-collecting fraternity succeeded in convincing Colt that there was a market for a re-introduced SAA. The revolver was brought back in the same external configuration. The only changes were internal. The basic specifications as to barrel length and finish availability were the same. The calibers available were .38 Special, .357 Magnum, .44 Special, and .45 Colt. The serial number range of the re-introduced 2nd Generation, as it is sometimes known, Colt is #000ISA-73000SA. Values for the standard post-war Colts are established by four basic factors: caliber (popularity and scarcity), barrel length, finish, and condition. Shorter barrel lengths are more desirable than the 7.5". The .38 Special is the rarest caliber, but the .45 Colt and .44 Special are more sought after than the .357 Magnum. Special feature revolvers, such as the 350 factory-engraved guns produced during this period, must be individually appraised. The ivory situation in the world today has become quite a factor, as ivory grips are found on many SAAs. We will attempt to take these factors into consideration and evaluate this variation as accurately and clearly as possible. Remember as always, when in doubt secure a qualified appraisal. NOTE: 4.75" barrel add 25 percent. 5.5" barrel add 15 percent. Nickel finish add 75-100 percent. Ivory grips add $250.

7.5" Barrel Model.38 Special

NIB	Exc.	V.G.	Good	Fair	Poor
4000	3500	1700	900	700	600

.357 Magnum

NIB	Exc.	V.G.	Good	Fair	Poor
3000	1950	900	750	700	650

.44 Special

NIB	Exc.	V.G.	Good	Fair	Poor
3750	2950	1500	1100	1000	750

.45 Colt

NIB	Exc.	V.G.	Good	Fair	Poor
2600	1850	1600	1000	900	750

Sheriff's Model 1960-1975

Between 1960 and 1975, there were approximately 500 Sheriff's Models manufactured. The first of these were marketed by Centennial Arms. They have 3" barrels and no ejector rod assemblies. The frames were made without the hole for the ejector rod to pass through. They were blued, with case colored frames; 25 revolvers were nickel-plated and would bring a sizable premium if authenticated. The barrels are marked "Colt Sheriff's Model." The serial number has an "SM" suffix. They are chambered for the .45 Colt cartridge.

NIB	Exc.	V.G.	Good	Fair	Poor
3000	2200	1800	1200	850	600

NOTE: Nickel finish add 20 percent.

Buntline Special 1957-1975

The "Buntline Special" was named after a dime novelist named Ned Buntline, who supposedly gave this special long barrel revolver to Wyatt Earp. The story is suspected to be purely legend as no Colt records exist to lend it credence. Be that as it may, the Colt factory decided to take advantage of the market and produced the 12" barreled SAA from 1957-1974. There were approximately 3,900 manufactured. They are chambered for the .45 Colt cartridge and are offered in the blued and case colored finish. Only 65 Buntlines are nickel-plated, making this an extremely rare variation that definitely should be authenticated before purchase. Walnut grips are the most commonly noted, but they are also offered with the checkered hard rubber grips. The barrels are marked on the left side "Colt Buntline Special .45."

NIB	Exc.	V.G.	Good	Fair	Poor
3100	2250	1250	850	600	500

NOTE: Nickel finish add 60 percent.

New Frontier 1961-1975

The New Frontier is readily identified by its flattop frame and adjustable sight. It also has a high front sight. Colt manufactured approximately 4,200 of them. They are chambered for the .357 Magnum, .45 Colt, .44 Special (255 produced), and rarely (only 49 produced) in .38 Special. A few were chambered for the .44-40 cartridge. The 7.5" barrel length is by far the most common, but the 4.75" and 5.5" barrels are also offered. The standard finish is case colored and blued. Nickel-plating and full blue are offered but are rarely encountered. Standard grips are walnut. The barrel is stamped on the left side "Colt New Frontier S.A.A." The serial has the "NF" suffix.

NIB	Exc.	V.G.	Good	Fair	Poor
2500	1850	1200	800	600	500

NOTE: 4.75" barrel add 25 percent. 5.5" barrel add 20 percent. Full Blue add 50 percent. .38 Special add 50 percent. .44 Special add 30 percent. 44-40 add 30 percent

New Frontier Buntline Special 1962-1967

This model is rare, as Colt only manufactured 70 during this five-year period. They are similar to the standard Buntline, with a 12" barrel. They are chambered for .45 Colt only.

NIB	Exc.	V.G.	Good	Fair	Poor
5500	3750	2000	1500	1000	700

COLT THIRD GENERATION SINGLE-ACTION ARMY 1976-1981

In 1976 Colt made some internal changes in the SAA. The external configuration was not altered. The serial number range began in 1976 with #80000SA, and in 1978 #99999SA was reached. At this time the suffix became a prefix, and the new serial range began with #SA01001. This model's value is determined in much the same manner as was described in the section on the 2nd Generation SAAs. Caliber, barrel length, finish, and condition are once again the four main determining factors. The prevalence of special-order guns was greater during this period, and many more factory-engraved SAAs were produced. Colt's Custom Shop was quite active during this period. Custom guns are valued according to the prevailing market.

7.5" BARREL.357 MAGNUM

NIB	Exc.	V.G.	Good	Fair	Poor
1500	1100	895	750	600	500

.44-40

NIB	Exc.	V.G.	Good	Fair	Poor
1950	1550	900	750	600	500

.44 Special

NIB	Exc.	V.G.	Good	Fair	Poor
2000	1200	900	700	550	500

.45 Colt

NIB	Exc.	V.G.	Good	Fair	Poor
1750	1300	900	750	600	500

NOTE: 4.75" barrel add 25 percent. 5.5" barrel add 10 percent. Nickel plated add 10 percent. Ivory grips add $250.

Sheriff's Model 3rd Generation

This model is similar to the 2nd Generation Sheriff's Model. The serial number and the fact that this model is also chambered for the .44-40 are the only external differences. Colt offered this model with interchangeable cylinders—.45 Colt/.45 ACP or .44-40/.44 Special—available in 3" barrel, blued and case colored finish standard.

NIB	Exc.	V.G.	Good	Fair	Poor
1500	1275	950	600	450	400

NOTE: Interchangeable cylinders add 30 percent. Nickel finish add 10 percent. Ivory grips add $250.

Buntline Special 3rd Generation

This is the same basic configuration as the 2nd Generation with the 12" barrel. Standard finish blued and case-colored, it is chambered for .45 Colt and has checkered hard rubber grips.

NIB	Exc.	V.G.	Good	Fair	Poor
1500	1275	950	600	450	400

NOTE: Nickel finish add 20 percent.

New Frontier 3rd Generation

This model is similar in appearance to the 2nd Generation guns. The 3rd Generation New Frontiers have five-digit serial numbers; the 2nd Generation guns, four-digit numbers. That and the calibers offered are basically the only differences. The 3rd Generations are chambered for the .44 Special and .45 Colt and are rarely found in .44-40. Barrel lengths are 7.5" standard, with the 4.75" and 5.5" rarely encountered.

NIB	Exc.	V.G.	Good	Fair	Poor
1650	1225	750	550	500	400

NOTE: .44-40 add 20 percent. 4.75" barrel add 35 percent. 5.5" barrel add 25 percent.

COLT RECENT PRODUCTION SINGLE-ACTION ARMY 1982-PRESENT

Standard Single-Action Army–Optional Features

Nickel finish add $125. Royal blue finish add $200. Mirror brite finish add $225. Gold plate add $365. Silver plate add $365. Class A engraving add $875. Class B engraving add $1,200. Class C engraving add $1,500. Class D engraving add $1,750. Buntline engraving add 15 percent.

NIB	Exc.	V.G.	Good	Fair	Poor
1400	1100	850	650	500	300

Colt Cowboy (CB1850)

Introduced in 1998 this model is a replica of the Single-Action Army that features a modern transfer bar safety system. Made in USA using some Canadian-built parts. Offered with 5.5" barrel and chambered for .45 Colt. Sights are fixed with walnut grips. Blued barrel with case colored frame. Discontinued in 2003.

NIB	Exc.	V.G.	Good	Fair	Poor
850	650	500	400	300	200

Colt Single-Action Army "Legend Rodeo"

A limited-edition revolver built to commemorate Colt's official PRCA sponsorship. Limited to 1,000. Chambered for .45 Long Colt fitted with a 5-1/2" barrel. Nickel finish Buffalo horn grips with gold medallions. Machine engraved and washed in gold. Discontinued 1998.

NIB	Exc.	V.G.	Good	Fair	Poor
2750	2250	—	—	—	—

Frontier Six Shooter (2008)

New reintroduction of classic .44-40 Peacemaker. Black powder-style frame and 4-3/4-, 5-1/2- and 7-1/2-inch barrel lengths. Blued finish with color casehardened frame or nickel. Discontinued 2010.

NIB	Exc.	V.G.	Good	Fair	Poor
1550	1100	750	600	400	200

Sheriff's and Storekeeper's Model (2008)

New reintroduction of classic Sheriff's (4-inch barrel) and Storekeeper's Model (3-inch barrel) without ejector assembly. Black powder-style frame. Blued finish with color casehardened frame or nickel. .45 Colt or .44-40. Discontinued 2010.

NIB	Exc.	V.G.	Good	Fair	Poor
1550	1100	750	600	400	200

175th Anniversary SAA Limited Edition

From the Colt Custom Shop to celebrate the 175th anniversary of the Colt Company, this model was introduced in 2011 with production limited to 175 units in each of the three standard barrel lengths of 4.75, 5.5 and 7.5-inches. In .45 Colt only, features include a black powder frame, Royal Blue finish, 24 karat Gold plated scroll on the frame, cylinder and barrel depicting the Rampant Colt icon, Colt Dome, Serpentine Colt, Sam Colt signature and a banner with the text "1836 — 175th Anniversary — 2011."

NIB	Exc.	V.G.	Good	Fair	Poor
1425	1350	1000	—	—	—

New Frontier Third Generation

Reintroduction of the adjustable-sighted, flattop-frame version of the Single Action Army that was last made in 1975. Chambered in .357 Magnum, .44 Special or .45 Colt and in all three standard barrel lengths. The rear sight is adjustable for windage and elevation, and there is a ramp style front sight. Finish is Colt's Royal Blue on both the barrel and cylinder with a color case hardened frame. Two-piece walnut grips are decorated with a gold medallion. Introduced in 2011.

NIB	Exc.	V.G.	Good	Fair	Poor
1300	1225	900	—	—	—

COLT SCOUT MODEL

NOTE: A surprising number of Colt pistols are still found in their original boxes, even older models. This can add 100 percent to the value of the pistol. My thanks to Bruce Buckner, Jr., for his suggestions for and corrections to this section. Anyone wishing to procure a factory letter authenticating a Single-Action Army should do so by writing to: COLT HISTORIAN, P.O. BOX 1868, HARTFORD, CT 06101. There is a charge of $50 per serial number for this service. If Colt cannot provide the desired information, $10 will be refunded. Enclose the Colt model name, serial number, and your name and address, along with the check.

Frontier Scout 1957-1971

This is a scaled-down version of the SAA that is chambered for the .22 LR with an interchangeable .22 Magnum cylinder. It is offered with a 4.75", or a 9.5" barrel. The frame is alloy. First year production frame were duotone with frame left in the white and the balance of the revolver blued. All blue models and wood grips became available in 1958. In 1961 the duotone model was dropped from production. All the Q series guns were offered in duotone finish; F series guns were made in duotone and full blue. A .22 Magnum model was first offered in 1959. In 1964 dual cylinders were introduced. These revolvers have "Q" or "F" serial number suffixes. In 1960 the "K" series Scout was introduced and featured a heavier frame, nickel plating, and wood grips. The majority of commemorative revolvers are of this type. This series was discontinued in 1970. Prices are about 15 percent higher than for the "Q" and "F" series guns.

NIB	Exc.	V.G.	Good	Fair	Poor
450	325	200	175	125	90

NOTE: 9.5" Buntline add 50 percent. Extra cylinder add 10 percent.

Peacemaker & New Frontier .22

This model is similar to the Frontier Scout, with a steel case-colored or blued frame. Fitted with old style black plastic eagle grips. Peacemaker 22 and New Frontier 22 revolvers were initially offered with 4.75, 6 and 7.5 inch barrels (Buntline). After about one year of production the 4.75 inch barrel was discontinued and a 4.4 inch barrel was offered in each model. It also has an interchangeable .22 Magnum cylinder. The Peacemaker 22 was only available with a steel receiver with a color-casehardened finish. The grip frames were alloy. The same is true of the New Frontier 22 revolvers except that (as noted in the book), the New Frontier 22 GS series was available with color-casehardened or blue receivers. Both Peacemaker 22 and New Frontier 22 revolvers were available in the single caliber

(.22 LR only) and dual caliber (.22 LR and .22 Magnum) models. The factory had separate model numbers for these variations. Also, the factory offered "P" series or "\q62" model Frontier Scouts and Buntline Scouts. This was a significant model variation. Most of these revolvers had a "G" suffix although some built in 1974 had a "L" suffix. In 1982 through 1986 a New Frontier model with cross-bolt safety was offered. This model is often referred to as the "GS" series. This revolver was offered with adjustable sights only. No Peacemakers were offered in this series.

NIB	Exc.	V.G.	Good	Fair	Poor
550	475	300	200	150	100

Scout Model SAA 1962-1971

This is basically a scaled-down version of the SAA chambered for the .22 LR cartridge. This model is offered with a 4.75", 6", or 7" barrel. The earlier production has case-colored frames with the remainder blued; later production is all blued. Grips are checkered hard rubber. This model was discontinued in 1986.

NIB	Exc.	V.G.	Good	Fair	Poor
400	275	200	150	100	75

COLT DOUBLE-ACTION REVOLVERS

MODEL 1877 "LIGHTNING" AND "THUNDERER"

The Model 1877 was Colt's first attempt at manufacturing a double-action revolver. It shows a striking resemblance to the Single-Action Army. Sales on this model were brisk, with over 166,000 produced between 1877 and 1909. Chambered for two different cartridges, the .38 Colt, known as the "Lightning," and .41 Colt, as the "Thunderer." The standard finishes are blued, with case-colored frame and nickel plate. The bird's-head grips are of checkered rosewood on the early guns and hard rubber on the majority of the production run. The barrel lengths most often encountered are 2.5" and 3.5" without an ejector rod, and 4.5" and 6" with the rod. Other barrel lengths from 1.5" through 10" were offered. The Model 1877 holds 6 shots in either caliber. There were quite a few different variations found within this model designation. Values furnished are for the standard variations. Antiques made before 1898 would be more desirable from an investment standpoint. Note that these revolvers have a reputation as "watchmaker's nightmares" and non-functioning examples command substantially reduced prices.

Without Ejector, 2.5" and 3.5" Barrel

NIB	Exc.	V.G.	Good	Fair	Poor
—	3000	2000	800	500	350

With Ejector, 4.5" and 6" Barrel

NIB	Exc.	V.G.	Good	Fair	Poor
—	3000	1800	800	750	450

NOTE: Premium for blued guns add 25 percent. Premium for shorter than 2-1/2" add 50 percent. .41 Caliber "Thunderer" add 10 percent. Over 6" barrel add 50 percent. London barrel address add 20 percent. .32 caliber add 50 percent. Rosewood grips add 10 percent.

MODEL 1878 "FRONTIER"

This model is a large and somewhat ungainly looking revolver. It has a solid frame with a removable trigger guard. The cylinder does not swing out, and there is a thin loading gate. It has bird's-head grips made of checkered hard rubber; walnut would be found on the early models. The finish is either blued and case-colored or nickel-plated. The Model 1878 holds 6 shots, and the standard barrel lengths are 4.75", 5.5", and 7.5" with an ejector assembly and 3", 3.5", and 4" without. The standard chamberings for the Model 1878 are .32-20, .38-40, .41 Colt, .44-40, and .45 Colt. This model was fairly well received because it is chambered for the large calibers that were popular in that era. Colt manufactured 51,210 between 1878 and 1905. Antique models made before 1898 would be more desirable from an investment standpoint.

Standard

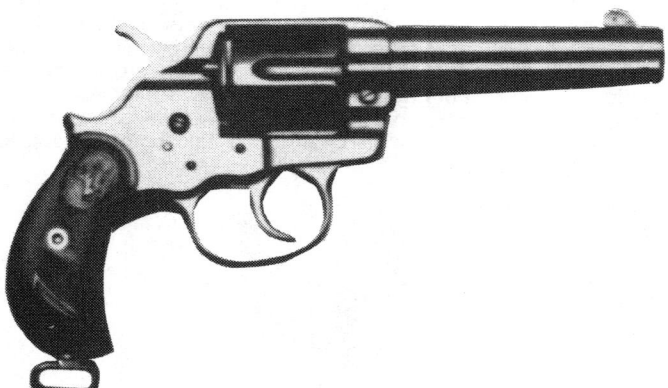

Courtesy Bonhams & Butterfields, San Francisco, California

NIB	Exc.	V.G.	Good	Fair	Poor
—	4200	3000	1200	800	400

NOTE: Add a 15 percent premium for blued revolvers. Add 10-50 percent premium for calibers other than .44-40 or .45.

Omnipotent

This is a special order version of the model above with the name "Omnipotent" stamped on the barrel.

NIB	Exc.	V.G.	Good	Fair	Poor
—	16000	10000	6000	3000	1000

Sheriff's Model

Chambered for .44-40 or .45 Colt with barrels lengths of 3.5" or 4".

NIB	Exc.	V.G.	Good	Fair	Poor
—	6000	4000	2000	1000	800

Model 1902 (Philippine or Alaskan Model)

This is a U.S. Ordnance contract Model 1878. It has a 6" barrel and is chambered for .45 Colt. The finish is blued, and there is a lanyard swivel on the butt. This model bears the U.S. inspector's marks. It is sometimes referred to as the Philippine or the Alaskan model. The trigger guard is quite a bit larger than standard.

Courtesy Bonhams & Butterfields

NIB	Exc.	V.G.	Good	Fair	Poor
—	5500	3500	1800	1000	600

Model 1889 Navy—Civilian Model

The 1889 Navy is an important model from a historical standpoint as it was the first double-action revolver Colt manufactured with a swing-out cylinder. They produced 31,000 of them between 1889 and 1894. The Model 1889 is chambered for the .38 Colt and the .41 Colt cartridges. The cylinder holds 6 shots. It is offered with a 3", 4.5", or 6" barrel; and the finish was either blued or nickel-plated. The grips are checkered hard rubber with the "Rampant Colt" in an oval molded into them. The patent dates 1884 and 1888 appear in the barrel marking, and the serial numbers are stamped on the butt.

NIB	Exc.	V.G.	Good	Fair	Poor
—	3000	1500	1000	600	300

NOTE: Add premium for blued models. For 3" barrel add 20 percent.

Model 1889 U.S. Navy—Martial Model

This variation has a 6" barrel, is chambered for .38 Colt, and is offered in blued finish only. "U.S.N." is stamped on the butt. Most of the Navy models were altered at the Colt factory to add the Model 1895 improvements. An original unaltered specimen would be worth as much as 50 percent premium over the altered values listed.

Courtesy Bonhams & Butterfields, San Francisco, California

NIB	Exc.	V.G.	Good	Fair	Poor
—	9000	5000	2500	1000	500

MODEL 1892 "NEW ARMY AND NAVY" —CIVILIAN MODEL

This model is similar in appearance to the 1889 Navy. The main differences are improvements to the lockwork function. It has double bolt stop notches, a double cylinder locking bolt, and shorter flutes on the cylinder. The .38 Smith & Wesson and the .32-20 were added to the .38 Colt and .41 Colt chamberings. The checkered hard rubber grips are standard, with plain walnut grips found on some contract series guns. Barrel lengths and finishes are the same as described for the Model 1889. The patent dates 1895 and 1901 appear stamped on later models. Colt manufactured 291,000 of these revolvers between 1892 and 1907. Antiques before 1898 are more desirable from an investment standpoint.

NIB	Exc.	V.G.	Good	Fair	Poor
—	2000	800	500	200	100

NOTE: For 3" barrel add 20 percent.

Model 1892 U.S. Navy—Martial Model

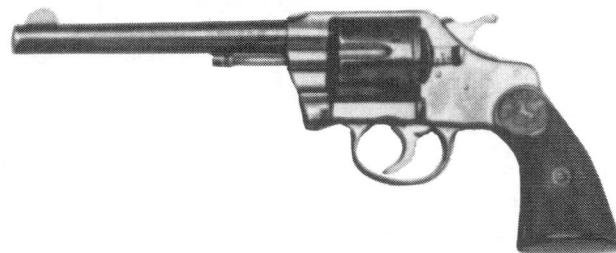

Courtesy Bonhams & Butterfields, San Francisco, California

NIB	Exc.	V.G.	Good	Fair	Poor
—	3500	2000	800	600	400

Model 1892 U.S. Army—Martial Model

NIB	Exc.	V.G.	Good	Fair	Poor
—	3500	2000	800	600	400

Model 1896/1896 Army

NIB	Exc.	V.G.	Good	Fair	Poor
—	3500	2000	800	600	400

Model 1905 Marine Corps

This model is a variation of the New Army and Navy Model. It was derived from the late production with its own serial range #10001-10926. With only 926 produced between 1905 and 1909, it is quite rare on today's market and is eagerly sought after by Colt Double-Action collectors. This model is chambered for the .38 Colt and the .38 Smith & Wesson Special cartridges. It holds 6 shots, has a 6" barrel, and is offered in a blued finish only. The grips are checkered walnut and are quite different than those found on previous models. "U.S.M.C." is stamped on the butt; patent dates of 1884, 1888, and 1895 are stamped on the barrel. One hundred twenty-five of these revolvers were earmarked for civilian sales and do not have the Marine Corps markings; these will generally be found in better condition. Values are similar.

Courtesy Faintich Auction Services, Inc., Paul Goodwin photo

NIB	Exc.	V.G.	Good	Fair	Poor
—	4500	3500	2000	1500	750

NEW SERVICE MODEL

This model was in continual production from 1898 through 1944. It is chambered for 11 different calibers: .38 Special, .357 Magnum, .38-40, .44 Russian, .44 Special, .44-40, .45 ACP, .45 Colt, .450 Eley, .455 Eley, and .476 Eley. It is offered in barrel lengths from 2" to 7.5", either blued or nickel-plated. Checkered hard rubber grips were standard until 1928, and then checkered walnut grips were used with an inletted Colt medallion. This was the largest swing-out cylinder double-action revolver that Colt ever produced, and approximately 356,000 were manufactured over the 46 years they were made. There are many different variations of this revolver, and one should consult a book dealing strictly with Colt for a thorough breakdown and description.

Courtesy Cherry's Collector Firearms Auction, Paul Goodwin photo

Early Model, #1-21000

NIB	Exc.	V.G.	Good	Fair	Poor
—	1200	850	450	200	125

Early Model Target, #6000-15000

Courtesy Faintich Auction Services, Inc., Paul Goodwin photo

Checkered walnut grips, flattop frame, 7.5" barrel.

NIB	Exc.	V.G.	Good	Fair	Poor
—	3000	1500	550	300	200

Improved Model, #21000-325000

Courtesy Faintich Auction Services, Inc., Paul Goodwin photo

Has internal locking improvements.

NIB	Exc.	V.G.	Good	Fair	Poor
—	1150	850	450	175	150

Improved Target Model, #21000-325000

Courtesy Faintich Auction Services, Inc., Paul Goodwin photo

NIB	Exc.	V.G.	Good	Fair	Poor
—	2250	1500	550	300	200

U.S. Army Model 1909, #30000-50000

5.5" barrel, .45 Colt, walnut grips, "U.S. Army Model 1909" on butt.

NIB	Exc.	V.G.	Good	Fair	Poor
—	1750	900	550	300	200

U.S. Navy Model 1909, #50000-52000

Same as above with "U.S.N." on butt.

NIB	Exc.	V.G.	Good	Fair	Poor
—	2600	1800	1000	350	250

U.S. Marine Corps Model 1909, #21000-23000

Checkered walnut grips, "U.S.M.C." on butt.

NIB	Exc.	V.G.	Good	Fair	Poor
—	3000	2000	1200	650	450

U.S. Army Model 1917, #150000-301000

Courtesy Faintich Auction Services, Inc., Paul Goodwin photo

Smooth walnut grips, 5.5" barrel, .45 ACP. Model designation stamped on butt.

NIB	Exc.	V.G.	Good	Fair	Poor
—	1300	900	600	300	225

Model 1917 Civilian, #335000-336000

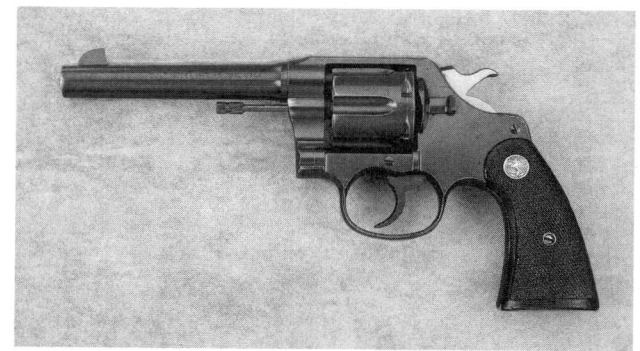

Approximately 1,000 made in .45 ACP only from Army parts overrun. No military markings.

NIB	Exc.	V.G.	Good	Fair	Poor
—	1500	950	600	250	200

Late Model New Service, #325000-356000

Checkered walnut grips and internal improvements.

NIB	Exc.	V.G.	Good	Fair	Poor
—	1550	975	650	300	225

Shooting Master, #333000-350000

Round-butt, checkered walnut grips with Colt medallion, 6" barrel, "Colt Shooting Master" on barrel, flattop frame with target sights. Chambered for the .38 Special cartridge.

Courtesy Faintich Auction Services, Inc., Paul Goodwin photo

NIB	Exc.	V.G.	Good	Fair	Poor
—	1950	1200	850	400	300

NOTE: Add 100 percent premium for .44 Special, .45 ACP, and .45 Colt.

Shooting Master, #333000-350000 Magnum Model New Service, Over #340000

Chambered for .357 Magnum, .38 Special.

NIB	Exc.	V.G.	Good	Fair	Poor
—	2400	2000	1000	500	200

New Pocket Model

This was the first swing-out cylinder, double-action pocket revolver made by Colt. It is chambered for .32 Colt and .32 Smith & Wesson. It holds 6 shots and is offered with barrel lengths of 2.5", 3.5", 5", and 6". The finish is blued or nickel-plated, and the grips are checkered hard rubber with the oval Colt molded into them. "Colt's New Pocket" is stamped on the frame. 1884 and 1888 patent dates are stamped on the barrel of later-production guns. There were approximately 30,000 of these manufactured between 1893 and 1905. Antiques made before 1898 are more desirable.

NIB	Exc.	V.G.	Good	Fair	Poor
—	750	450	300	250	150

NOTE: Early production without patent dates add 25 percent. 5" barrel add 10 percent.

Pocket Positive

Externally this is the same revolver as the New Pocket, but it has the positive lock feature. It was manufactured between 1905 and 1940.

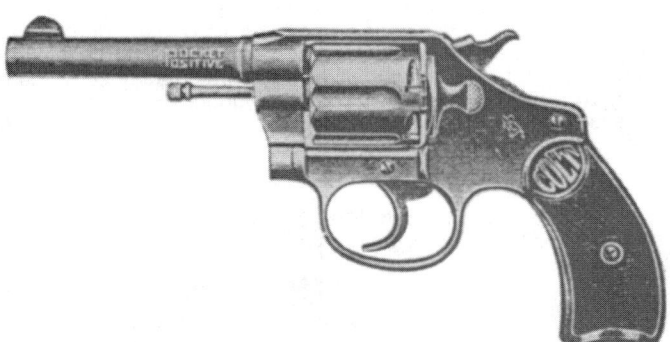

NIB	Exc.	V.G.	Good	Fair	Poor
—	700	475	325	225	125

Army Special Model

This is a heavier-framed improved version of the New Army and Navy revolver. It is chambered for the .32-20, .38 Colt, .38 Smith & Wesson, and .41 Colt. It is offered with a 4", 4.5", 5", and 6" barrel. The finish is blued or nickel-plated, and the grips are checkered hard rubber. The serial number range is #291000-#540000, and they were manufactured between 1908-1927.

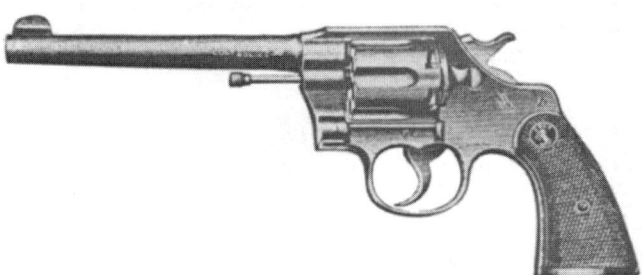

NIB	Exc.	V.G.	Good	Fair	Poor
—	650	475	250	200	150

New Police Model

This model appears similar to the New Pocket Model. The frame is stamped "New Police." It is chambered for the .32 Colt, .32 Colt New Police, and .32 Smith & Wesson cartridges. The barrel lengths are 2.5", 4", and 6". The finishes are blued or nickel-plated. Colt manufactured 49,500 of this model from 1896-1907. The New York City Police Department purchased 4,500 of these revolvers, and the backstraps are so marked. There was also a target model of this revolver, which features a 6" barrel with a flattop frame and target sights, of which 5,000 were produced.

NIB	Exc.	V.G.	Good	Fair	Poor
—	600	350	225	150	100

NOTE: New York Police marked add 30 percent. Target model add 20 percent.

Police Positive

This is externally the same as the New Police with the addition of the positive lock feature and two new chamberings—the .38 New Police and the .38 Smith & Wesson. They were manufactured from 1905-1947.

NIB	Exc.	V.G.	Good	Fair	Poor
—	700	475	250	200	150

Police Positive Target

This is basically the same as the New Police Target with the positive lock feature. It is chambered in .22 LR, the .22 WRF, as well as the other cartridges offered in the earlier model. Deduct 20 percent for WRF.NOTE: A .22 caliber Police Positive chambered for the .22 Short and Long cartridge may be seen with British proofs. Several such revolvers were sold to London Armory in this configuration during the late 1920s. A NIB example recently sold for $1,200.

NIB	Exc.	V.G.	Good	Fair	Poor
—	725	500	300	175	100

Police Positive Special

This model is similar to the Police Positive but has a slightly larger frame to accept the longer cylinder needed to chamber more powerful cartridges such as the .38 Special, in addition to the original chamberings. They were manufactured from 1907-1973.

NIB	Exc.	V.G.	Good	Fair	Poor
—	600	450	250	150	100

Police Positive Special Mark V

Introduced in 1994 this is an updated version of the Police Positive Special. This model features an underlug 4" barrel with rubber grips and fixed sights. The butt is rounded. The revolver is rated to fire .38 caliber +P rounds. Overall length is 9" and weighs approximately 30 oz.

NIB	Exc.	V.G.	Good	Fair	Poor
550	400	300	150	100	85

Officer's Model Target 1st Issue

This revolver is chambered for the .38 Special cartridge. It has a 6" barrel and is blued. It has a flattop frame with adjustable target sights. Colt manufactured this model from 1904-1908.

NIB	Exc.	V.G.	Good	Fair	Poor
—	1000	750	350	300	200

Officer's Model Target 2nd Issue

This model is similar to the 1st Issue but is offered in .22 LR and .32 Police Positive caliber, as well as in .38 Special. It also is furnished with a 4", 4.5", 5", 6", and 7.5" barrel in .38 Special only. It has checkered walnut grips. Colt manufactured this model between 1908 and 1940.

Courtesy Faintich Auction Services, Inc., Paul Goodwin photo

NIB	Exc.	V.G.	Good	Fair	Poor
—	700	550	300	250	150

Camp Perry Single-Shot

This model was created by modifying an Officer's Model frame to accept a special flat single-shot "cylinder." This flat chamber pivots to the left side and downward for loading. The pistol is chambered for .22 LR and is offered with an 8" (early production) or 10" (late production) barrel. The finish is blued, with checkered walnut grips. The name "Camp Perry Model" is stamped on the left side of the chamber; the caliber is on

the barrel. Colt named this model after the site of the U.S. Target Competition held annually at Camp Perry, Ohio. They manufactured 2,525 of these between 1920 and 1941. **NOTE**: This gun serial numbered 101-2525 with 2488 produced from 1926-1941. In 1934 standard barrel length was reduced from 10" to 8" at approximately serial number 2150.

NIB	Exc.	V.G.	Good	Fair	Poor
—	2500	1750	950	600	400

NOTE: Add 100 percent premium for 10" barrel. Add 50 percent premium for original box.

Officer's Model Match

Introduced in 1953 this model is similar to the Officer's Model Target and chambered for either the .22 caliber cartridge or the .38 Special with 6" barrel. The revolver is fitted with a heavy tapered barrel and wide hammer spur with adjustable rear sight and ramp front sight. It was sold with checkered walnut target grips. Blued finish is standard. Discontinued in 1970. The standard of long action could be fired both double- or single-action. The .22 caliber version prices are listed. Officer's Model Match in .38 caliber will bring approximately 20 percent less. **NOTE:** This model was also produced in .22 Magnum. This is rather a rare gun in this caliber with approximately 800 produced.

NIB	Exc.	V.G.	Good	Fair	Poor
—	750	600	450	350	250

Officer's Model Match .22 Caliber in Short Action—Single-Action-Only

NIB	Exc.	V.G.	Good	Fair	Poor
—	1000	750	600	500	350

Official Police

This was a popular revolver in the Colt line for many years. It was manufactured from 1927 to 1969. It is chambered for .32-20 and .41 Colt. These calibers were discontinued in 1942 and 1930, respectively. The .38 Special was chambered throughout the entire production run, and .22 LR was added in 1930. This model holds 6 shots, has a square-butt, and is offered with 2", 4", 5", and 6" barrel lengths. The grips are checkered walnut. The finish is either blued or nickel-plated.

NIB	Exc.	V.G.	Good	Fair	Poor
—	600	425	350	200	150

NOTE: Nickel-plated add 10 percent. .22 LR add 20 percent.

Commando Model

This model, for all intents and purposes, is an Official Police chambered for .38 Special, with a 2", 4", or 6" barrel. This model is Parkerized and stamped "Colt Commando" on the barrel. There were approximately 50,000 manufactured between 1942-1945 for use in World War II.

Courtesy Richard M. Kumor, Sr.

NIB	Exc.	V.G.	Good	Fair	Poor
—	750	550	375	150	100

NOTE: Add 30 percent for 2" barrel.

Marshall Model

This is an Official Police that is marked "Colt Marshall" on the barrel and has an "M" suffix in the serial number. It has a 2" or 4" barrel and a round butt. The finish is blued. There were approximately 2,500 manufactured between 1954 and 1956.

NIB	Exc.	V.G.	Good	Fair	Poor
—	1000	700	500	250	150

Colt .38 SF-VI

Introduced in 1995 this model is essentially a Detective Special in stainless steel with a new internal mechanism. Has a transfer bar safety mechanism. Fitted with a 2" barrel and cylinder holds 6 rounds of .38 Special. A 4" barrel in bright stainless steel is also available. Weight is 21 oz. and overall length is 7".

NIB	Exc.	V.G.	Good	Fair	Poor
650	475	350	225	150	100

Colt .38 SF-VI Special Lady

Introduced in 1996 this 2" barrel version is similar to the above model with the addition of a bright finish and bobbed hammer. Weight is 21 oz.

NIB	Exc.	V.G.	Good	Fair	Poor
650	450	300	200	150	100

Detective Special 1st Issue / 2nd Issue

This model is actually a Police Positive Special with a 2" barrel. It was originally chambered for .32 New Police, .38 New Police, (which were discontinued) and .38 Special, which continued until the end of the production run. The finish is blued or nickel and it is offered with wood or plastic grips. There were over 400,000 manufactured between 1926 and 1972. A few 2nd issue (post WWII) units came with 3" barrels.

NIB	Exc.	V.G.	Good	Fair	Poor
—	850	650	525	200	100

NOTE: For pre-war 1st issue (serial number 331000 - 490000) add 50 percent. For nickel finish add 25 percent. For 3" barrel add 30 percent.

Detective Special 3rd Issue

This is basically a modernized, streamlined version with a 2" or 3" barrel with a shrouded ejector rod, wraparound checkered walnut grips and is chambered for .38 Special. It was finished in blue or nickel plate. Made from 1973 to 1986 and 1993 to 1995.

NIB	Exc.	V.G.	Good	Fair	Poor
650	475	300	250	—	—

Banker's Special

The Bankers Special is a 2" barreled, easily concealed revolver. It was designed with bank employees in mind. It is chambered for .38 Special and was offered in blued finish. The revolver was also offered in .22 caliber. The grips are rounded but full-sized, and Colt utilized this feature in advertising this model. The U.S. Postal Service equipped its railway mail clerks with this model. There were approximately 35,000 manufactured between 1926 and 1943.

NIB	Exc.	V.G.	Good	Fair	Poor
—	1500	975	500	250	150

NOTE: Nickel models will command a premium. A Banker's Special in .22 caliber will command a premium.

Cobra 1st Issue

The Cobra is simply an alloy-framed lightweight version of the Detective Special. It weighs only 15 oz. The Cobra is chambered for .32, .38 Special, and .22 LR. This model is available in either a round-butt or square-butt version with a 4" barrel only. They were manufactured between 1950 and 1973.

NIB	Exc.	V.G.	Good	Fair	Poor
750	600	500	350	200	100

NOTE: Add $50 for nickel finish.

NIB	Exc.	V.G.	Good	Fair	Poor
—	850	650	525	200	100

Cobra 2nd Issue

The same as the 1st Issue in .38 Special only, this is streamlined with wraparound walnut grips and shrouded ejector rod.

Detective Special II (DS-II)

Introduced in 1997 this version of the Detective special features new internal lock work and a transfer bar safety mechanism. It is fitted with a 2" barrel, has a capacity of six rounds, and is chambered for the .38 Special. In 1998 this model was offered chambered for .357 Magnum cartridge as well. Rubber combat style grips are standard. Weight is approximately 21 oz. Stainless steel finish.

NIB	Exc.	V.G.	Good	Fair	Poor
650	475	300	225	—	—

Colt Magnum Carry

Introduced in 1999, this model is essentially a renamed Detective Special II. Stainless steel finish. Weight is 21 oz.

NIB	Exc.	V.G.	Good	Fair	Poor
—	525	375	250	150	100

NOTE: For nickel add 30 percent.

Agent 1st Issue

This revolver is basically the same as the 1st Issue Cobra with a shortened grip frame. This was done to make the Agent more concealable. Colt manufactured the Agent 1st Issue from 1955-1973.

NIB	Exc.	V.G.	Good	Fair	Poor
—	650	400	225	150	100

Border Patrol

This model is quite rare, as Colt manufactured only 400 of them in 1952. It is basically a Police Special with a heavy 4" barrel. It is chambered for the .38 Special and was built to be strong. The finish is blued and serial numbered in the 610000 range.

NIB	Exc.	V.G.	Good	Fair	Poor
—	5000	3000	2000	1000	500

Agent L.W. 2nd Issue

This is a streamlined version with the shrouded ejector rod. In the last four years of its production, it was matte finished. Colt manufactured this model between 1973 and 1986.

NIB	Exc.	V.G.	Good	Fair	Poor
—	550	400	275	175	150

Aircrewman Special

This model was especially fabricated for the Air Force to be carried by their pilots for protection. It is extremely lightweight at 11 oz. The frame and the cylinder are made of aluminum alloy. It has a 2" barrel and is chambered for the .38 Special. The finish was blued, with checkered walnut grips. There were approximately 1,200 manufactured in 1951, and they are marked "U.S." or "A.F."

NIB	Exc.	V.G.	Good	Fair	Poor
—	4500	2500	1500	800	250

Courier

This is another version of the Cobra. It features a shorter grip frame and a 3" barrel. This model is chambered for .32 and .22 rimfire. There were approximately 3,000 manufactured in 1955 and 1956.

NIB	Exc.	V.G.	Good	Fair	Poor
1300	750	600	500	350	150

NOTE: .22 Rimfire add 20 percent.

Trooper

This model was designed specifically by Colt to fill the need for a large, heavy-duty, powerful revolver that was accurate. The Trooper filled that need. It was offered with a 4" or 6" barrel and blued or nickel finishes with checkered walnut grips. The Trooper is chambered for the .38 Special, .357 Magnum, and there is a .22 rimfire version for the target shooters. This model was manufactured between 1953 and 1969. Add 10 percent for .357 or .22.

NIB	Exc.	V.G.	Good	Fair	Poor
—	600	475	300	150	100

Colt .357 Magnum

This is a deluxe version of the Trooper. It is offered with a special target wide hammer and large target-type grips. The sights are the same as Accro target model. It features a 4" or 6" barrel and a blued finish and was manufactured between 1953 and 1961. There were fewer than 15,000 produced.

NIB	Exc.	V.G.	Good	Fair	Poor
—	675	495	300	200	150

Diamondback

This model is a medium-frame, duty-type weapon suitable for target work. It has the short frame of the Detective Special with the ventilated rib 2.5", 4", or 6" barrel. It is chambered for .38 Special and .22 rimfire for the target shooters. The finish is blued or nickel-plated, with checkered walnut grips. The Diamondback features adjustable target sights, wide target hammer, and a steel frame. It was manufactured between 1966 and 1986.

NIB	Exc.	V.G.	Good	Fair	Poor
1300	800	500	300	250	150

NOTE: Premium for 2.5" barrel or nickel finish.

Viper

This is an alloy-framed revolver chambered for the .38 Special. It has a 4" barrel and was manufactured between 1977 and 1984. The Viper is essentially a lightweight version of the Police Positive.

NIB	Exc.	V.G.	Good	Fair	Poor
800	595	425	200	125	100

PYTHON

The Python was often described as the Cadillac of the Colt double-action revolve line. It was originally designed to be a large-frame .38 Special target revolver but shortly before the Python was introduced in 1955, Colt management decided to chamber it for the .357 Magnum. (A .38 Special 8-inch barrel variation was made in the early 1980s. See separate listing.) The Python was offered in barrel lengths of 2.5, 3 (very rare), 4, 6 and 8-inches. Features included a ventilated rib, full lug barrel and an adjustable rear sight. Finish choices were Royal Blue, nickel plated, matte stainless and high polished "Ultimate" stainless. The Python remained in the catalog as a regular production item until 1996. The following year the Colt Custom Shop started making the Python on a special-order-only basis. Known as the Python Elite, it was produced by the Custom Shop until 2006. The early (pre-1970) production guns in very good to excellent condition can command premiums from 10 to 25 percent and those with 3-inch barrels up to 50 percent. Nickel-plated, 3-inch barreled Pythons should be confirmed with a Colt factory letter and can command premiums of 400 to 500 percent.

NIB	Exc.	V.G.	Good	Fair	Poor
1500	1050	700	500	400	225

Matte Stainless Steel

NIB	Exc.	V.G.	Good	Fair	Poor
1550	1100	775	600	500	275

"The Ultimate" Bright Stainless

NIB	Exc.	V.G.	Good	Fair	Poor
1600	1150	850	600	500	300

Elite

This Custom Shop model features a stainless steel satin finish or blued finish. Adjustable red ramp front sight. Custom wood grips and choice of 4" or 6" barrel.

NIB	Exc.	V.G.	Good	Fair	Poor
1900	1300	900	675	400	300

.38 Special

This is an 8" barreled Python chambered for the .38 Special only. It was a limited-production venture that was not a success. It was offered in blue only.

NIB	Exc.	V.G.	Good	Fair	Poor
—	950	700	475	300	225

Hunter

The Hunter was a special 8" .357 Magnum Python with an extended eye relief Leupold 2X scope. The grips are neoprene with gold Colt medallions. The revolver, with mounted scope and accessories, was fitted into a Haliburton extruded aluminum case. The Hunter was manufactured in 1981 only.

NIB	Exc.	V.G.	Good	Fair	Poor
2000	1650	1000	500	400	300

Metropolitan MK III

This revolver is basically a heavier-duty version of the Official Police. It is chambered for .38 Special and fitted with a 4" heavy barrel. It is finished in blue only and was manufactured from 1969-1972.

NIB	Exc.	V.G.	Good	Fair	Poor
750	525	350	250	100	75

Lawman MK III

This model is offered chambered for the .357 Magnum with a 2" or 4" barrel. It has checkered walnut grips and is either blued or nickel-plated. Colt manufactured the Lawman between 1969 and 1983.

NIB	Exc.	V.G.	Good	Fair	Poor
—	550	400	300	200	100

Lawman MK V

This is an improved version of the MK III. It entailed a redesigned grip, a shorter lock time, and an improved double-action. It was manufactured 1982-1985.

NIB	Exc.	V.G.	Good	Fair	Poor
525	375	300	200	150	100

Trooper MK III

This revolver was intended to be the target-grade version of the MK III series. It is offered with a 4", 6", or 8" vent-rib barrel with a shrouded ejector rod similar in appearance to the Python. It is chambered for the .22 LR and the .22 Magnum, as well as .357 Magnum. It features adjustable target sights, checkered walnut target grips, and is either blued or nickel-plated. This model was manufactured between 1969 and 1983.

NIB	Exc.	V.G.	Good	Fair	Poor
750	400	325	200	150	100

Trooper MK V

This improved version of the MK III was manufactured between 1982 and 1985.

NIB	Exc.	V.G.	Good	Fair	Poor
825	550	375	200	150	100

Boa

This is basically a deluxe version of the Trooper MK V. It has all the same features plus the high polished blue found on the Python. Colt manufactured 1,200 of these revolvers in 1985, and the entire production was purchased and marketed by Lew Horton Distributing Company in Southboro, Massachusetts.

NIB	Exc.	V.G.	Good	Fair	Poor
1200	850	475	325	250	150

Peacekeeper

This model was designed as a duty-type weapon with target capabilities. It is offered with a 4" or 6" barrel chambered for .357 Magnum. It features adjustable sights and neoprene combat-style grips and has a matte blued finish. This model was manufactured between 1985 and 1987.

NIB	Exc.	V.G.	Good	Fair	Poor
650	475	375	200	150	100

KING COBRA

The King Cobra has a forged steel frame and barrel and a full length ejector rod housing. The barrel is fitted with a solid rib. This model is equipped with an adjustable, white outline rear sight and a red insert front sight. Colt black neoprene combat style grips are standard. Discontinued.NOTE: In 1998 all King Cobras were drilled and tapped for scope mounts.

Blued

NIB	Exc.	V.G.	Good	Fair	Poor
875	650	375	250	200	100

Stainless Steel

Offered in 4" or 6" barrel lengths. In 1997 this model was introduced with optional barrel porting. No longer in production.

NIB	Exc.	V.G.	Good	Fair	Poor
975	725	400	275	200	125

High Polish Stainless Steel

NIB	Exc.	V.G.	Good	Fair	Poor
975	725	400	275	200	125

ANACONDA

This double-action .44 Magnum revolver was introduced in 1990. It is offered with 4", 6", or 8" barrel lengths. The 4" model weighs 47 oz., the 6" model weighs 63 oz., and the 8" model weighs 59 oz. The Anaconda holds 6 rounds and is available with a matte stainless steel finish. For 1993 a new chambering in .45 Colt was offered for the Anaconda. This model was offered with a 6" or 8" barrel in a matte stainless steel finish revolver chambered for the .44 Remington Magnum cartridge. It is currently offered with a 6" or 8" barrel and adjustable red-insert front and white-outline rear sights. It is constructed of matte-finished stainless steel and has black neoprene fingergroove grips with gold Colt medallions. In 1996 the Realtree model was offered with 8" barrel. Chambered for the .44 Magnum cartridge. Furnished with either adjustable rear sight and ramp front sights or special scope mount. No longer in production. Reintroduced in 2001 In .44 Magnum with 4", 6", or 8" barrel. Once again, discontinued. **NOTE:** In 1998 the Anaconda was drilled and tapped for scope mounts and buyers had the option of barrel porting.

.44 Magnum

NIB	Exc.	V.G.	Good	Fair	Poor
1300	950	650	495	300	200

.45 Colt

NIB	Exc.	V.G.	Good	Fair	Poor
1200	850	600	450	300	200

Realtree Camo Model—Adjustable Sights

NIB	Exc.	V.G.	Good	Fair	Poor
1600	1100	750	575	350	250

Realtree Camo Model—Scope Mounts

NIB	Exc.	V.G.	Good	Fair	Poor
1600	1100	750	575	350	250

COLT SEMI-AUTOMATIC PISTOLS

The Colt Firearms Co. was the first of the American gun manufacturers to take the advent of the semi-automatic pistol seriously. This pistol design was becoming popular among European gun makers in the late 1880s and early 1900s. In the United States, however, the revolver was firmly ensconced as the accepted design. Colt realized that if the semi-auto could be made to function reliably, it would soon catch on. The powers that be at Colt were able to negotiate with some of the noted inventors of the day, including Browning, and to secure or lease the rights to manufacture their designs. Colt also encouraged the creativity of their employees with bonuses and incentives and, through this innovative thinking, soon became the leader in semi-auto pistol sales—a position that they have never really relinquished to any other American gun maker. The Colt semi-automatic pistols represent an interesting field for the collector of Colt handguns. There were many variations with high enough production to make it worthwhile to seek them out. There are a number of fine books on the Colt semi-automatics, and anyone wishing to do so will be able to learn a great deal about them. Collector interest is high in this field, and values are definitely on the rise.

MODEL 1900

This was the first of the Colt automatic pistols. It was actually a developmental model with only 3,500 being produced. The Model 1900 was not really a successful design. It was quite clumsy and out of balance in the hand; however it was reliable in function during Army trials. This model is chambered for the .38 Rimless smokeless cartridge. It has a detachable magazine that holds seven cartridges. The barrel is 6" in length. The finish is blued, with a case-colored hammer and safety/sight combination. The grips are either plain walnut, checkered walnut, or hard rubber. This pistol is a Browning design, and the left side of the slide is stamped "Browning's Patent" with the 1897 patent date. Colt sold 200 pistols to the Navy and 200 to the Army for field trials and evaluation. The remaining 3,300 were sold on the civilian market. This model was manufactured from 1900-1903. **NOTE:** Many of the original 1900 pistols had the original sight/safety converted to Model 1902 configuration. These are worth about 50 percent less than unconverted pistols.

Standard Civilian Production

NIB	Exc.	V.G.	Good	Fair	Poor
—	10000	7500	3500	1250	750

U.S. Navy Military Model

NIB	Exc.	V.G.	Good	Fair	Poor
—	17500	12000	7500	2500	1000

U.S. Army Military Model—1st Contract

NIB	Exc.	V.G.	Good	Fair	Poor
—	20000	15000	10000	4000	2000

U.S. Army Military Model—2nd Contract

NIB	Exc.	V.G.	Good	Fair	Poor
—	16000	10000	6300	2000	1500

Model 1902 Sporting Pistol

This model is chambered for the .38 ACP cartridge. It has a 7-round detachable magazine and a 6" barrel and is blued, with checkered hard rubber grips featuring the "Rampant Colt" molded into them. The most notable features of the 1902 Sporting Model are the rounded butt, rounded hammer spur, dovetailed rear sight, and the 1897-1902 patent dates. Colt manufactured approximately 7,500 of these pistols between 1903 and 1908.

Paul Goodwin photo

NIB	Exc.	V.G.	Good	Fair	Poor
—	3500	2000	1250	750	450

Model 1902 Military Pistol Early Model with Front of Slide Serrated

NIB	Exc.	V.G.	Good	Fair	Poor
—	4000	2400	1500	750	450

Model 1902 Military Pistol Standard Model with Rear of Slide Serrated

NIB	Exc.	V.G.	Good	Fair	Poor
—	2500	1750	1000	500	400

Model 1902 Military Pistol U.S. Army Marked, #15001-15200 with Front Serrations

NIB	Exc.	V.G.	Good	Fair	Poor
—	6000	5000	2500	1250	600

Model 1903 Pocket Hammer Pistol

This was the first automatic pocket pistol Colt produced. It is essentially identical to the 1902 Sporting Model with a shorter slide. The barrel length is 4.5", and it is chambered for the .38 ACP cartridge. It is blued, with a case-colored hammer, with checkered hard rubber grips that have the "Rampant Colt" molded into them. The detachable magazine holds 7 rounds. There were approximately 26,000 manufactured between 1903 and 1929.

Paul Goodwin photo

NIB	Exc.	V.G.	Good	Fair	Poor
—	2000	1500	800	350	200

Model 1903 Hammerless, .32 Pocket Pistol (Model M)

This was the second pocket automatic Colt manufactured. It was another of John Browning's designs, and it developed into one of Colt's most successful pistols. This pistol is chambered for the .32 ACP cartridge. Initially the barrel length was 4"; this was shortened to 3.75". The detachable magazine holds 8 rounds. The standard finish is blue, with quite a few nickel plated. The early model grips are checkered hard rubber with the "Rampant Colt" molded into them. Many of the nickel plated pistols had pearl grips. In 1924 the grips were changed to checkered walnut with the Colt medallions. The name of this model can be misleading as it is not a true hammerless but a concealed hammer design. It features a slide stop and a grip safety. Colt manufactured 572,215 civilian versions of this pistol and approximately 200,000 more for military contracts. This model was manufactured between 1903 and 1945.

Courtesy Richard M. Kumor, Sr.

NIB	Exc.	V.G.	Good	Fair	Poor
—	750	500	450	300	200

NOTE: Early Model 1897 patent date add 40 percent. Nickel-plated with pearl grips add $100. 4" barrel to #72,000 add 20 percent.

Model 1903 Hammerless, .32 Pocket Pistol U.S. Military Model

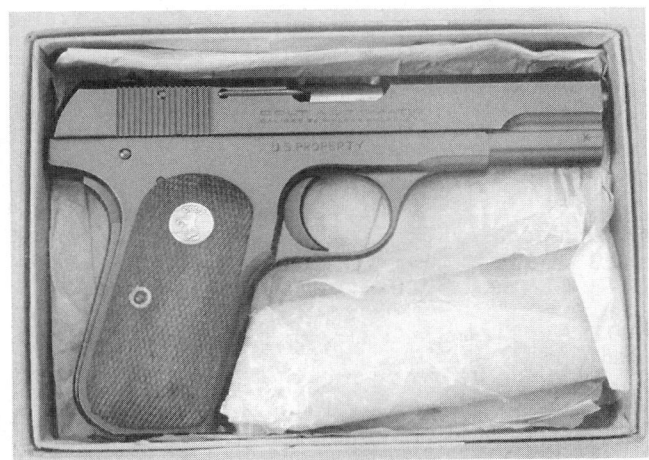

Serial prefix M, marked "U.S. Property" on frame, Parkerized finish.

NIB	Exc.	V.G.	Good	Fair	Poor
—	1400	850	400	300	250

NOTE: Pistols issued to General Officers will command a premium of 50 percent.

MODEL 1908 HAMMERLESS .380 POCKET PISTOL

This model is essentially the same as the .32 Pocket Pistol, chambered for the more potent .380 ACP, also known as the 9mm Browning short. Other specifications are the same. Colt manufactured approximately 138,000 in this caliber for civilian sales. An unknown number were sold to the military.

Standard Civilian Model

NIB	Exc.	V.G.	Good	Fair	Poor
—	1200	850	600	350	250

NOTE: Nickel with pearl grips add $100.

Military Model

Serial prefix M, marked "U.S. Property" on frame, blue finish. General Officer's pistol add 50 percent.

NIB	Exc.	V.G.	Good	Fair	Poor
—	1800	1350	950	500	300

MODEL 1908 HAMMERLESS .25 VEST POCKET MODEL

This was the smallest automatic Colt made. It is chambered for the .25 ACP cartridge, has a 2" barrel, and is 4.5" long overall. It weighs a mere 13 oz. This is a true pocket pistol. The detachable magazine holds 6 shots. This model was offered in blue or nickel-plate, with grips of checkered hard rubber and checkered walnut on later versions. This model has a grip safety, slide lock, and a magazine disconnector safety. This was another Browning design, and Fabrique Nationale manufactured this pistol in Belgium before Colt picked up the rights to make it in the U.S. This was a commercial success by Colt's standards, with approximately 409,000 manufactured between 1908 and 1941.

Courtesy Orvel Reichert

Civilian Model

NIB	Exc.	V.G.	Good	Fair	Poor
—	750	500	300	200	100

NOTE: Add 30 percent for nickel finish, 50 percent for factory pearl grips.

Military Model

"U.S. Property" marked on right frame. Very rare.

NIB	Exc.	V.G.	Good	Fair	Poor
—	3500	2500	1350	450	300

MODEL 1905 .45 AUTOMATIC PISTOL

The Spanish American War and the experiences with the Moros in the Philippine campaign taught a lesson about stopping power or the lack of it. The United States Army was convinced that they needed a more powerful handgun cartridge. This led Colt to the development of a .45 caliber cartridge suitable for the semi-automatic pistol. The Model 1905 and the .45 Rimless round were the result. In actuality, this cartridge was not nearly powerful enough to satisfy the need, but it led to the development of the .45 ACP. Colt believed that this pistol/cartridge combination would be a success and was geared up for mass production. The Army actually bought only 200 of them, and the total production was approximately 6,300 from 1905 to 1911. The pistol has a 5" barrel and detachable 7-shot magazine and is blued, with a case-colored hammer. The grips are checkered walnut. The hammer was rounded on the first 3,600 pistols and was changed to a spur hammer on the later models. The right side of the slide is stamped "Automatic Colt / Caliber 45 Rimless Smokeless." This model was not a commercial success for Colt—possibly because it has no safety whatsoever except for the floating inertia firing pin. The 200 military models have grip safeties only. A small number (believed to be less than 500) of these pistols were grooved to accept a shoulder stock. The stocks were made of leather and steel and made to double as a holster. These pistols have been classified "Curios and Relics" under the provisions of the Gun Control Act of 1968.

Civilian Model

NIB	Exc.	V.G.	Good	Fair	Poor
—	5000	3500	1750	950	400

Military Model, Serial #1-201

NIB	Exc.	V.G.	Good	Fair	Poor
—	8500	6500	4500	1500	500

COLT 1911/1911A1

EARLY COLT "1911 COMMERCIAL GOVERNMENT MODEL"

Serial numbers through about C4500, high polish on all parts and fire-blue finish on the trigger, slide stop, thumb safety, hammer pins, ejector, and stock screws. Pistols in the latter part of the serial range did not have fire blued stock screws. Pistols through about serial C350 had the dimpled magazine catch. The main spring housing pin was rounded on both ends in the pistols through about serial C2000. Keyhole (punch and sawcut) magazines were shipped on pistols through serial C3500.

Courtesy Karl Karash

NIB	Exc.	V.G.	Good	Fair	Poor
—	10000	6500	3000	1400	900

NOTE: Three-digit serial number add 20 percent. Two-digit serial number add 40 percent. For finish 99-100 percent add 30-50 percent.

Standard with Un-numbered Slide

Above about serial # C4500 with un-numbered slide to about serial #C127300. No fire blue. Polished finished but not mirror finish. Loop magazine until about C90000. A number of variations exist within this wide serial range such as slide nomenclature and position of the "Rampant Colt," but none currently receives any particular premium.

NIB	Exc.	V.G.	Good	Fair	Poor
—	3500	2100	1500	900	700

NOTE: Finish 99-100 percent add 20-50 percent.

Standard with Numbered Slide

Colt started to number the slide with the receiver's serial number at about serial #C127300. This practice continued for commercial production through WWII, and all 1911 commercial pistols after about serial C127300 to about serial C136000 (when 1911A1 production had taken over). The first numbered slide pistols (in the C127xxx range) had the slide numbered on the bottom of the slide rail. This only lasted a short time and the numbering was moved to behind the firing pin stop plate by serial C128000. Subtract 20 percent for a mismatched slide number. The changes between the 1911 Commercial Government Model and the 1911A1 Commercial Government were phased in during this period.

NIB	Exc.	V.G.	Good	Fair	Poor
—	3500	2100	1400	900	650

NOTE: Finish 99-100 percent add 20-50 percent.

FOREIGN CONTRACTS

Argentine Contracts

Multiple contracts were awarded by Argentina between 1914 and 1948 to supply .45 caliber pistols to their armed forces, police, and government agencies. these contracts totaled 21,616 pistols of which 2,151 were the 1911 model. Pistols differ from the Standard Government Model in that they are usually marked with an Argentine crest as well as the normal Colt commercial markings including the C prefix serial number. Colt also supplied Argentina the 1911A1 model "modelo 1927" that had its own serial number range of #1 to #10000 with no C prefix. Most of these pistols are well used, reblued, had mixed parts, and have import markings. Prices listed are for completely original pistols. Reblue=Fair/Poor.

NIB	Exc.	V.G.	Good	Fair	Poor
—	1500	1100	750	500	400

NOTE: Finish 99-100 percent add 20-100 percent.

Russian Order

This variation is chambered for .45 ACP and has the Russian version of "Anglo Zakazivat" stamped on the frame. There were about 51,000 of these blued pistols manufactured in 1915-1916. They are found between serial numbers C21000 and C89000. This variation is rarely encountered today, but a few have recently been imported and advertised. One should be extremely cautious and verify the authenticity if contemplating a purchase, as fakes have been noted. Despite market uncertainties demand for original pistols is high. (Reblue=Fair/Poor)

NIB	Exc.	V.G.	Good	Fair	Poor
—	5500	3900	2350	1600	1000

NOTE: Finish 99-100 percent add 30-100 percent.

Canadian Contract

This group of 5099 pistols serial numbered between about C3077 and C13500 were purchased by the Canadian Government in 1914. Most observed pistols appear to be unmarked and can be identified only by a Colt factory letter. Others have been observed with the Canadian Broad Arrow property mark as well as unit markings. Often these unit markings are applied in a very rudimentary manner that detracts considerably from the appearance. (Any applied markings done crudely, deduct 10-50 percent.) Due to the nature of these markings, a Colt factory letter is probably a requirement to authenticate these pistols. Refinish=Fair/Poor.

NIB	Exc.	V.G.	Good	Fair	Poor
—	3100	2200	1450	950	650

NOTE: Finish. 99-100 percent add 20-50 percent.

British Contract

This series is chambered for the British .455 cartridge and is so marked on the right side of the slide. The British "Broad Arrow" proofmark will often be found. These pistols were made in 1915-1919 and follow the same numeric serial number sequence as the normal Government models, except that the "C" prefix was replaced with a "W." They are commercial series pistols. The magazine well of these .455 pistols is slightly larger than a standard Cal. .45 Auto pistol and will accept a Cal.45 magazine, but a standard Cal. 45 will not accept a Cal. .455 magazine. All pistols in the W19001 to W19200 range as well as some in the W29000 range are believed to be JJ marked above the left trigger guard bow. Add 25 percent for JJ marked. Some pistols in the C101000 to about C109000 range have RAF marks as well as a welded ring in the lanyard loop. Most RAF pistols have been refinished and many have been converted to .45 cal. by changing the barrels. Refinish=Fair/Poor.

NIB	Exc.	V.G.	Good	Fair	Poor
—	3200	2000	1250	850	650

NOTE: Finish. 99-100 percent add 20-50 percent. Add 25 percent for RAF. Wrong barrel less 35 percent.

Norwegian Kongsberg Vapenfabrikk Pistol Model 1912

Serial number 1-96.

NIB	Exc.	V.G.	Good	Fair	Poor
—	5000	3200	2200	1600	1200

NOTE: These pistols are so rare that almost any price would not be out of order for an original pistol. Finish 99-100 percent add 20-30 percent.

Norwegian Kongsberg Vapenfabrikk Pistol Model 1914

Serial number 97-32854.

NIB	Exc.	V.G.	Good	Fair	Poor
—	1350	1050	900	770	600

NOTE: Finish 99-100 percent add 20-50 percent.

Kongsberg Vapenfabrikk Model 1914 (Norwegian) Copy

Serial number 29615 to 30535. Waffenamt marked on slide and barrel. CAUTION: Fakes have been reported. Any Waffenamt-marked pistol outside this serial range is probably counterfeit.

NIB	Exc.	V.G.	Good	Fair	Poor
—	4500	2700	2000	1200	900

NOTE: Finish 99-100 percent add 20-30 percent.

PRE-WWII COLT "1911A1 COMMERCIAL GOVERNMENT MODEL"

NOTE: For a complete listing of Colt 1911 military pistols with photos, technical data, and prices see the Standard Catalog of Military Firearms.The commercial "Government Models" made by Colt between the wars may be the best pistols that Colt ever produced. The civilian configurations of the 1911 and 1911A1 were known as "Government Models." They were identical to the military models, with the exception of the fit, finish, and markings. However, commercial production of the 1911A1 pistols was stopped when WWII started. Therefore, production changes of the 1911A1 pistols were not carried over to the contemporary commercial pistols because there was no contemporary commercial production. The "C" serial number prefix designated the commercial series until 1950, when it was changed to a "C" suffix. The "Government Model" pistols were polished and blued until about serial number C230,000, when the top, bottom, and rear were matte finished. The words "Government Model" as well as the usual "Verified Proof" mark were stamped on all but about the first 500 pistols when post-war production commenced at C220,000. Some of these first 500 also lacked the verified proof mark. These first post-war pistols used some leftover military parts such as triggers and stocks. Pre-war pistols all had checkered walnut grips. Post-war pistols generally had plastic grips until the "midrange" serial when the wood grips returned. There were a number of different commercial models manufactured. They are individually listed. Manufactured by Colt from 1925-1942 from about serial number C136000 to about serial number C215000. Only a few pistols from serial #C202000 to C215000 were shipped domestically, as most were shipped to Brazil or renumbered into military models. See Model 1911A1 commercial to military conversions.

Domestic Sales

These pistols have numbered slides, no foreign markings, no Swartz safeties and no additions whatsoever.

NIB	Exc.	V.G.	Good	Fair	Poor
—	3900	2700	1500	750	500

NOTE: Finish 99-100 percent add 30-60 percent.

Export Sales

Usually with foreign crest or foreign inscription of a county such as Argentina or Brazil. This pistol has a numbered slide. Some variations with the foreign markings are more rare than the standard domestic pistols and have a developed local followings who have raised their prices considerably. The Argentine pistols do not have the collector interest that the others or the "Standard" domestic pistols have. Four factors have reduced collector interest in the Argentine Colt pistols compared to the rest:1.Most of the Argentine-marked pistols have been recently imported and have the legally required important markings.2.Many of the Argentine-marked pistols have been advertised and sold in the wholesale trade publications at utility prices.3.Most of the recent import pistols from Argentina have been refinished or are in "well used" condition.4.Most of the recent import pistols from Argentina have had some parts changed or swapped with other pistols and are not in original condition.The few Argentine pistols that remain in original and excellent or better condition usually sell for less than their "plain Jane" counterparts, and they sell for much less than the rarer Brazilian and Mexican pistols.

Argentine Colt-made 1911A1 model pistols without Swartz safeties

NIB	Exc.	V.G.	Good	Fair	Poor
—	1100	800	650	550	450

NOTE: Finish 99-100 percent add 20-30 percent.

Brazilian, Mexican, and other South American (except Argentina)

Colt-made "1911A1 Commercial Government Model" pistols.

NIB	Exc.	V.G.	Good	Fair	Poor
—	6500	4500	2800	1700	1000

NOTE: Finish 99-100 percent add 20-100 percent.

COLT NATIONAL MATCH CALIBER .45, PRE-WWII, .45 (WITHOUT SWARTZ SAFETIES)

The National Match Commercial pistol was introduced by Colt at the 1930 National Matches at Camp Perry. Production began in 1932. The right side of the slide was marked "NATIONAL MATCH" and the mainspring housing had no lanyard loop. The National Match modifications to the standard pistol, as described in Colt literature included: "A tighter barrel, better sights, and a hand polished action." The "tighter barrel" probably amounted to a tighter fit between the barrel bushing and barrel. The hand polishing of the action probably produced a greatly improved trigger pull, but overall, the barrel slide lockup was probably only superficially improved. Colt also advertised a "Selected Match Grade" barrel. Colt advertising indicated that scores using the National Match pistols improved greatly and they probably did to a degree, but most of the improvement was probably due to the improved (wider) sights and improved trigger pull. The very first pistols had fixed sights, but by about SN C177,000 the "Stevens Adjustable Rear Target Sight" was available. Both fixed and adjustable sights were available thereafter throughout production. The total number of National Match pistols with each type of sight is not known, but one author (Kevin Williams, Collecting Colt's National Match Pistols) estimates that the percentage of adjustable sight equipped National Match pistols may have been only 20 percent. Note that the Colt National Match pistol is not referred to here as a "1911A1" because this pistol lacks the military lanyard loop that is present in all Standard Government Models. This is simply a matter of personal preference. Also note that "Colt National Match" Pre-war pistols are also "Government models" as the receiver was marked as such throughout production.

With Adjustable Sights

NIB	Exc.	V.G.	Good	Fair	Poor
—	4800	2900	1700	1050	900

NOTE: Finish 99-100 percent add 30-60 percent.

Fixed Sights

NIB	Exc.	V.G.	Good	Fair	Poor
—	3700	2500	1400	900	750

SWARTZ SAFETIES, PRE-WWII, FIRING PIN AND HAMMER/SEAR

The "Swartz Safeties" are a pair of devices that Colt installed in 1911A1 Commercial Government Models" and 1911A1 Commercial National Match pistols in the late 1930s and early 1940s. The first device, a firing pin block that was actuated by the grip safety, prevented the firing pin from moving forward unless the grip safety was squeezed. The second Swartz safety device, the Hammer/Sear safety prevented a possible unsafe half cock position. The Swartz firing pin block safety can be observed by pulling the slide back all the way and looking at the top of the frame. A Swartz-safety-equipped 1911A1 pistol will have a second pin protruding up, next to the conventional disconnector pin. This second pin pushes a spring loaded piston in the rear part of the slide that is visible when the slide is pulled back and the slide is viewed from underneath. This piston, in turn, blocks the firing pin when relaxed. A second Swartz safety (the Swartz Sear Safety), is usually built into pistols equipped with the Swartz firing pin block safety. The sear safety can sometimes be detected by the drag marks of the notched sear on the round portion of the hammer where the sear rides on. Pulling the hammer all the way back will expose these drag marks if they are visible. Presence of the drag marks, however, does not ensure that the Swartz-modified sear safety parts are all present. Disassembly may be required to verify the correct parts are all present. The Swartz Safeties are referred to in Colt Factory letters as the "NSD" (New Safety Device).(From SN C162,000 to C215,000 about 3,000 total National Match pistols were made with and without Swartz safeties.) The number of National Match pistols having the Swartz safeties is unknown. However only a few pistols below serial C190000 had the safeties installed and of the pistols made after C190000, most were Standard Models shipped to Brazil and Argentina. The Brazilian pistols were without the safeties or the cutouts. The Argentine pistols were shipped in two batches of 250 pistols each. Both of these Argentine batches appear to have had the safeties installed as a number of them have recently been imported into the U.S.A. Probably much less than half of the total Colt made National Match pistols had the Swartz safeties. The total number of pistols (both Standard Government Model and National Match) shipped with Swartz safeties is probably much less than 3,000. And probably much less than half of the total Colt made National Match pistols had the Swartz safeties. Swartz safeties were also installed in late Super .38 and Super Match .38 pistols.

Standard Colt 1911A1 Commercial "GOVERNMENT MODEL" Marked Pistol with Numbered Slide

"Swartz safeties," no foreign markings. Fixed sights only, no additions whatsoever. Rare, seldom seen.

NIB	Exc.	V.G.	Good	Fair	Poor
—	3750	2500	1900	1150	850

NOTE: Finish 99-100 percent add 20-50 percent.

COLT NATIONAL MATCH CALIBER PRE-WWII, .45. PRE-WWII (WITH "SWARTZ SAFETIES")

Serial number C186,000-C215,000 probably less than 1,500 pistols. Colt would rework fixed sights equipped pistols on a repair order with Stevens adjustable sight. Therefore, a Colt letter showing that the pistol was originally shipped with adjustable sights is in order for any adjustable sight-equipped pistol.

Stevens Adjustable Sights

NIB	Exc.	V.G.	Good	Fair	Poor
—	6200	3550	2400	1350	1000

Fixed Sights

NIB	Exc.	V.G.	Good	Fair	Poor
—	4700	2750	1700	1050	800

NOTE: Finish 99-100 percent add 30-60 percent.

Standard 1911A1 Pre-WWII, "GOVERNMENT MODEL" Export Sales

With "Swartz Safeties" and usually a foreign crest or foreign inscription mainly from Argentina. The vast majority of Swartz equipped foreign contract pistols were shipped to Argentina, but Argentine pistols do not have the collector interest that the others or the plain domestic pistols have. Four factors reduce collector interest in the Colt made Argentine pistols compared to the rest:1.Most of the Argentine-marked pistols have been recently imported and have the legally required Import Markings.2.Many of the Argentine-marked pistols have been advertised and sold in the wholesale trade publications at utility prices.3.Most of the recent import Argentine pistols have been refinished or are in "well used" condition.4.Most of the recent import pistols from Argentina have had some parts changed or swapped with other pistols and are not in original condition. The few of these Argentine Swartz equipped pistols that remain in original and excellent or better condition usually sell for less than their "plain Jane" domestic counterparts, and they sell for much less than the much rarer Brazilian and Mexican pistols. Perhaps these depressed prices represent a bargain for collectors with an eye to the future when the supply of these extremely rare pistols dries up. 100 percent reblue = Fair/Poor.

NIB	Exc.	V.G.	Good	Fair	Poor
—	1400	1050	900	650	550

NOTE: Finish 99-100 percent add 20-30 percent.

Normal Brazilian and Mexican Pistols (w/Swartz Safeties)

These pistols do not normally have Swartz safeties, but if any were found, they would be expected to sell for at least the amount listed.

NIB	Exc.	V.G.	Good	Fair	Poor
—	9500	7000	4000	2500	1200

NOTE: Finish 99-100 percent add 20-30 percent.

Argentine Contract Pistols "Modelo Argentino 1927, Calibre .45"

These pistols were delivered to Argentina in 1927. The right side of the slide is marked with the two-line inscription "Ejercito Argentino Colt Cal .45 Mod. 1927." There is also the Argentine National Seal and the "Rampant Colt." SN 1-10,000. Verified proof, Assembler's mark, and Final inspectors mark under left stock by upper bushing. None had Swartz Safeties. Most of these pistols were reblued. Reblued = Fair/Poor.

NIB	Exc.	V.G.	Good	Fair	Poor
—	1400	1050	850	600	400

NOTE: The abundance of these and other refinished Argentine pistols has depressed the prices of all original finish Argentine pistols. Finish 99-100 percent add 20-50 percent.

"Military to Commercial Conversions"

Some 1911 Military pistols that were brought home by GIs were subsequently returned to the Colt factory by their owners, for repair or refinishing. If the repair included a new barrel, the pistol would have been proof fired and a normal Verified proof mark affixed to the trigger guard bow in the normal commercial practice. If the pistol was refinished between about 1920 and 1942, the slide would probably be numbered to the frame again in the normal commercial practice. These pistols are really remanufactured Colt pistols of limited production and should be valued at least that of a contemporary 1911A1 commercial pistol. Only pistols marked with identifiable Colt markings should be included in this category. Very seldom seen.

NIB	Exc.	V.G.	Good	Fair	Poor
—	1900	1300	975	550	425

NOTE: Finish 99-100 percent add 30 percent.

REWORKS OF COLT 1911 AND 1911A1 COMMERCIAL "GOVERNMENT MODEL" PISTOLS

Since Colt rework records are lost, reworked and refinished pistols without identifiable Colt applied markings are probably not verifiable as Colt reworks, and should be considered refinished pistols of unknown pedigree. The standard rule of thumb is that the value of a reworked/refinished pistol is equivalent to a similar original pistol in "Poor" condition. Many beginning collectors start by buying a pistol with either no original finish or it has been refinished. The first thing they ask is where can I get it refinished, and second is how much will it cost? A quality restoration will often cost $1,000, and that added to an initial cost of $600 will produce a pistol that might sell for $1,000 to $1,200. The lesson is that the cost to rework and refinish will seldom be recovered when the pistol is sold. Since these pistols are not original pistols, their prices are much closer to a utility shooter and depend a lot on the overall appearance of the pistol. A professionally restored example might sell for as high as $1,100 but a poorly refinished example would probably rank with the import-marked refinished pistols ($300).

COLT 1911A1 POST WWII COMMERCIAL PRODUCED, DOMESTIC SALES, 1946-1969

SN C220,000 to about C220,500

No "GOVERNMENT MODEL" marking, a few have no verified proof. Many parts are leftover military.

NIB	Exc.	V.G.	Good	Fair	Poor
—	2300	1650	1150	950	750

NOTE: Finish 99-100 percent add 20-50 percent.

SN C220,500 to about C249,000 verified proof and "GOVERNMENT MODEL" marking

Many parts are leftover military in the first few thousand pistols. No foreign markings.

NIB	Exc.	V.G.	Good	Fair	Poor
—	1450	950	650	535	450

NOTE: Finish 99-100 percent add 20-30 percent. Less 30 percent for foreign markings.

SN 255,000-C to about 258,000-C Slide Factory Roll Marked "PROPERTY OF THE STATE OF NEW YORK," verified proof, and "GOVERNMENT MODEL" marking (250 pistols total)

A few leftover military parts are still used. A few pairs of pistols remain as consecutive pairs.

Courtesy Karl Karash

NIB	Exc.	V.G.	Good	Fair	Poor
—	1600	900	600	550	450

NOTE: Finish 99-100 percent add 20-50 percent. Add 10 percent for consecutive pairs.

SN 249,500-C to about 335,000-C, verified proof and "GOVERNMENT MODEL" marking

No foreign markings.

NIB	Exc.	V.G.	Good	Fair	Poor
—	1400	900	625	500	400

NOTE: Finish 99-100 percent add 20-30 percent. Less 30 percent for foreign markings.

SN 334,500-C to about 336,169-C, BB (Barrel Bushing) marked

About 1000 pistols. Verified proof and "GOVERNMENT MODEL" marking.

NIB	Exc.	V.G.	Good	Fair	Poor
—	1375	900	700	575	450

NOTE: Finish 99-100 percent add 20-50 percent.

COLT 1911A1 POST WWII COMMERCIAL PRODUCED, DOMESTIC SALES, 1946-1969

Super .38 1929 Model, Pre-WWII

This pistol is identical in outward physical configuration to the .45 ACP Colt Commercial. It is chambered for the .38 Super cartridge and has a magazine that holds 9 rounds. The right side of the slide is marked "Colt Super .38 Automatic" in two lines, followed by the "Rampant Colt." The last few thousand pre-war Super .38 pistols made had the Swartz Safety parts installed, but some pistols were assembled post-war with leftover parts. These post-war-assembled pistols did not have the Swartz safeties installed but most (possibly all) had the cutouts. In 1945, 400 pistols were purchased by the U.S. Government. These 400 pistols bear the G.H.D. acceptance mark as well as the Ordnance crossed cannons. (G.H.D. and Ordnance marked add 30-50 percent. A factory letter is probably necessary here.) Some collectors feel that post-war assembly and post-war chemical tank blueing adds a premium, others feel that it requires a deduction. Post-war assembly may add 15 percent or it may deduct 15 percent.)

NIB	Exc.	V.G.	Good	Fair	Poor
—	3600	2400	1400	1100	800

NOTE: Finish 99-100 percent add 33 percent. Swartz Safeties add 20 percent.

COLT 1911A1 POST WWII COMMERCIAL PRODUCED, DOMESTIC SALES, 1946-1969

SUPER MATCH .38 1935 MODEL, PRE-WWII

Only 5,000 of these specially fit and finished target-grade pistols were manufactured. They have fixed sights or the Stevens adjustable sights, and the top surfaces are matte-finished to reduce glare. Twelve hundred of these pistols were purchased and sent to Britain in 1939, at the then-costly rate of $50 per unit. The last few thousand pre-war Super .38 pistols made had the Swartz safety parts installed, but some pistols were assembled post-war with leftover parts. These post-war-assembled pistols did not have the Swartz safeties installed but most (possibly all) had the cutouts. In 1945, 400 pistols were purchased by the U.S. Government. These 400 pistols bear the G.H.D. acceptance mark as well as the Ordnance crossed cannons. G.H.D. and Ordnance marked add 30-50 percent. A factory letter is probably necessary here. Swartz Safeties add 20 percent. Some collectors feel that post-war assembly and post-war chemical tank bluing adds a premium, others feel that it requires a deduction. Post-war assembly may add 15 percent or it may deduct 15 percent.

Adjustable Sights

NIB	Exc.	V.G.	Good	Fair	Poor
—	7500	4200	3000	1800	1200

Fixed Sights

NIB	Exc.	V.G.	Good	Fair	Poor
—	6000	3850	2850	1600	1150

NOTE: Finish 99-100 percent add 20-75 percent for both models.

ACE AND SERVICE MODEL ACE

Rebuilt from service pistols at Springfield Armory between 1955 and about 1967 and at Rock Island in 1968. These pistols were built and rebuilt each year with a portion being sold to competitors by the NRA. Each year improvements were added to the rebuild program. Four articles in the "National Rifleman" document these pistols well: August 1959, April 1963, June 1966, and July 1966. Many parts for these pistols have been available and many "Look Alike" pistols have been built by basement armorers. Pistols generally came with a numbered box and shipping papers. Prices listed are for pistols with numbered box or papers. Less box and papers deduct 30 percent. When well-worn, these pistols will offer little over a standard pistol. Early pistols are much less commonly seen, but seem to be less sought after since they look largely like normal issue pistols.

Ace Model .22 Pistol

Starting on June 21, 1913, the U.S. Military along with "Springfield Armory" and "Colt Patented Firearms Manufacturing Co." attempted to develop a .22 cal rimfire pistol that could be used for training purposes. By 1927, the military became convinced that a pistol identical to the standard "Service Pistol" but in .22 cal rimfire was impractical and dropped the idea. In 1930 Colt purchased advertising that, in effect, requested the shooting public to let the company know if they would be interested in a .22 rimfire pistol built similar to the Government Model. The response must have been positive because in 1931 the Colt Ace appeared on the market. The Ace uses the same frame as the Government Model with a highly modified slide and a heavy barrel. It is chambered for .22 LR cartridge only. The size is the same as the larger-caliber version, and the weight is 36 oz. The operation is straight blowback. The Ace has a 10-round detachable magazine and features the "Improved Ace Adjustable Target Sight." The markings on the left side of the slide are the same as on the Government Model; the right side reads "Colt Ace 22 Long Rifle." At first the Army purchased a few pistols (totaling 206) through 1936. The Army concluded that the function of the Ace was less than perfect, as they concluded the .22 rimfire lacked the power to consistently and reliably operate the slide. Approximately 11,000 Ace pistols were manufactured, and in 1941 they were discontinued. Many owners today find that although the ACE is somewhat selective to ammunition, with full power loads, it is a highly reliable pistol when properly cleaned and maintained.

NIB	Exc.	V.G.	Good	Fair	Poor
—	2500	1750	1100	1000	900

NOTE: Finish 99-100 percent add 33 percent.

PRE-1945 SERVICE MODEL ACE .22 R. F. PISTOL

In 1937 Colt introduced this improved version of the Ace Pistol. It utilizes a floating chamber invented by David "Carbine" Williams, the firearm's designer who invented the "Short Stroke Gas Piston" that is the basis of the MI carbine while serving time on a Southern chain gang. Colt's advertised that this pistol with its floating chamber would give the Service Model Ace the reliability and "feel" of a .45 Auto. Today, owners of the Service Model ACE pistols find that they require regular maintenance and cleaning in order to keep the close-fitting floating chamber from binding. Furthermore, fouling appears to be much worse with some brands and types of ammunition. Most owners feel that although the perceived recoil of the Service Model ACE is noticeably greater than that of the ACE, it falls far short of a .45 Auto's recoil. The serial number is prefixed by the letters "SM." The external configuration is the same as the Ace, and the slide is marked "Colt Service Model Ace .22 Long Rifle." Most were sold to the Army and some on a commercial basis. There were a total of 13,803 manufactured before production ceased in 1945.

Blued pistols (before about SN SM 3840)

NIB	Exc.	V.G.	Good	Fair	Poor
—	3900	2300	1700	1150	1000

Parkerized pistols (after about SN SM 3840)

NIB	Exc.	V.G.	Good	Fair	Poor
—	2800	1850	1300	950	700

NOTE: Finish 99-100 percent add 20-30 percent for both models. Add 20 percent for "US Property" marking.

Service Model Ace-Post-War

Introduced in 1978 this model is similar to the pre-war model. Production ceased in 1982.

NIB	Exc.	V.G.	Good	Fair	Poor
—	1100	950	875	800	600

NOTE: Finish 99-100 percent add 20-30 percent.

CONVERSION UNITS .22-.45, .45-.22

In 1938 Colt released a .22-caliber conversion unit. With this kit, one who already owned a Government Model could simply switch the top half and fire inexpensive .22 rimfire ammunition. The unit consists of a slide marked "Service Model Ace," barrel with floating chamber, ejector, slide lock, bushing, recoil spring, 10-shot magazine, and box. The Conversion Units feature the Stevens adjustable rear sight. Later that same year, a kit to convert the Service Model Ace to .45 ACP was offered. In 1942 production of these units ceased. The .22 kit was reintroduced in 1947; the .45 kit was not brought back. (Finish 99-100 percent add 20-30 percent.) Subtract 20 percent if box is missing. Be alert, as sometimes a conversion unit is found on a Service Model ACE receiver and a Service model Ace upper is sold as a "Conversion Unit." Conversion Units are ALWAYS marked "Conversion Unit." Service Model ACE" pistols lack the "Conversion Unit" marking.

Pre-war and Post-war "U" numbered Service Model Ace Conversion Unit, .22-.45 (to convert .45 cal. to .22 cal.)

The pre-war conversion units were serial numbered U1-U2000.

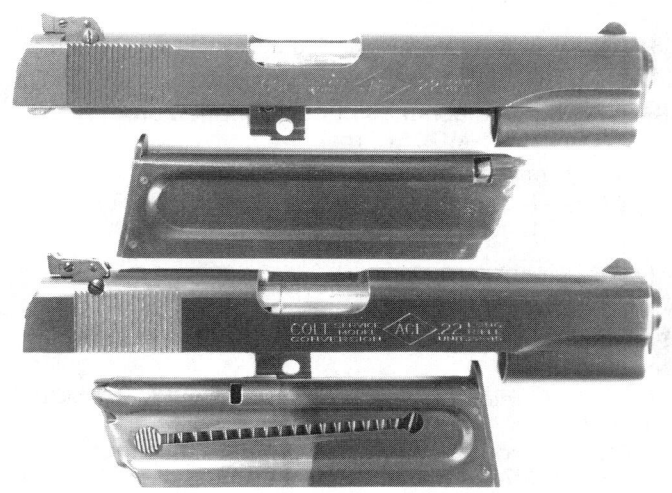

Courtesy Karl Karash

NIB	Exc.	V.G.	Good	Fair	Poor
—	1200	950	550	500	450

NOTE: Finish 99-100 percent add 20-30 percent.

.45-.22 Post-war .22 Post-war Conversion Units

These were serial numbered U2001-U2670.

NIB	Exc.	V.G.	Good	Fair	Poor
—	650	550	500	450	425

NOTE: Finish 99-100 percent add 20-30 percent.

.45-.22 Post-war .22 Conversion Unit Unnumbered

30 percent premium for Stevens adjustable sights, 1946 only.

NIB	Exc.	V.G.	Good	Fair	Poor
—	400	350	250	225	175

NOTE: Finish 99-100 percent add 20-30 percent.

MILITARY NATIONAL MATCH .45 PISTOLS

Paul Goodwin photo

NIB	Exc.	V.G.	Good	Fair	Poor
—	1500	1075	775	600	475

NOTE: Finish 99-100 percent add 20-30 percent.

Military National Match Pistols (Drake Slide)

In 1964, Springfield Armory used some of these specially machined and hardened slides to build the Military National Match pistols that year. This year's pistol is perhaps the most identifiable NM pistol due to the unique slide marking. However, Drake was only the supplier of the slides that year. Colt supplied the slides in the following year (1965).

Courtesy Karl Karash

NIB	Exc.	V.G.	Good	Fair	Poor
—	1550	1100	790	610	485

NOTE: Finish 99-100 percent add 20-30 percent.

Gold Cup National Match (pre-Series 70)

This model is chambered for the .45 ACP, features the flat mainspring housing of the 1911, and has a match-grade barrel and bushing. The parts were hand fitted, and the slide has an enlarged ejection port. The trigger is the long version with an adjustable trigger stop, and the sights are adjustable target type. The finish is blued, with checkered walnut grips and gold medallions. The slide is marked "Gold Cup National Match," and the serial number is prefixed by the letters "NM." This pistol was manufactured from 1957 to 1970.

NIB	Exc.	V.G.	Good	Fair	Poor
—	1100	850	625	500	400

NOTE: Finish 99-100 percent add 20-30 percent.

Gold Cup MKIII National Match

This pistol is identical to the Gold Cup .45 except that it is chambered for the .38 Mid-Range Wad Cutter round. It was manufactured from 1961 until 1974.

Courtesy John J. Stimpson

NIB	Exc.	V.G.	Good	Fair	Poor
—	1050	875	600	450	350

NOTE: Finish 99-100 percent add 20-30 percent.

Colt 1911A1 AMU (Army Marksmanship Unit)

NIB	Exc.	V.G.	Good	Fair	Poor
—	2700	2250	1450	900	400

NOTE: For Army modified pistols deduct 70 percent.

COLT LICENSED AND UNLICENSED FOREIGN-MADE 1911A1 AND VARIATIONS

Argentine D.G.F.M.

Direccion General de Fabricaciones Militares made at the F.M.A.P. (Fabrica Militar de Arms Portatiles [Military Factory of Small Arms]). Licensed copies SN 24,000 to 112,494. Parts are generally interchangeable with Colt-made 1911A1 type pistols. Most pistols were marked "D.G.F.M. - (F.M.A.P.)." Late pistols were marked FM within a cartouche on the right side of the slide. These pistols are found both with and without import markings, often in excellent condition, currently more often in refinished condition, and with a seemingly endless variety of slide markings. None of these variations have yet achieved any particular collector status or distinction, unless new in box. A new in the box DGFM recently sold at auction for $1,200. In fact many of these fine pistols have and continue to be used as the platforms for the highly customized competition and target pistols that are currently popular. Refinished=Fair/Poor.

Courtesy Karl Karash

NIB	Exc.	V.G.	Good	Fair	Poor
—	575	475	400	350	300

NOTE: Finish 99-100 percent-NIB add 10-30 percent)

NOTE: Finish 99-100 percent-NIB add 10-30 percent.

Argentine-Made Ballester Molina

Un-licensed, Argentine redesigned versions. (Parts are NOT interchangeable with Colt except for the barrel and magazine.) These pistols are found both with and without import markings. Pistols without import markings usually have a B prefix number stamped on the left rear part of the mainspring housing and are often in excellent to new original condition. The vast majority of currently available pistols are found in excellent but refinished condition. Only the pistols with no import markings that are in excellent-to-new original condition have achieved any particular collector status. Most of these pistols that are being sold today are being carried and shot rather than being collected. Refinished = Fair/Poor.

Courtesy Karl Karash

NIB	Exc.	V.G.	Good	Fair	Poor
—	600	375	300	215	190

Brazilian Models 1911A1

Made by "Fabrica de Itajuba" in Itajuba, Brazil, and the Imbel Model 973, made by "Industriade Material Belico do Brazil" in Sao Paulo, Brazil. The Itajuba is a true copy of the Colt 1911A1, and the Imbel is also believed to be a true copy. However, an Imbel has yet to be examined by the author. Too rarely seen in the U.S.A. to establish a meaningful price.

MODEL 1911A1 AUTOMATIC PISTOL MILITARY MODEL

NOTE: For Colt military Model 1911A1 pistols see a complete listing with photos, prices, technical data, and history in the Standard Catalog of Military Firearms, 2nd Edition.

COLT MODEL 1911A1 1970 - CURRENT

The Model 1911A1 was manufactured by Colt until 1971 when the Series 70 Government Model superseded it. The modifications in the new model were a slightly heavier slide and a slotted collet barrel bushing. In 1983 Colt introduced the Series 80 models which had an additional passive firing pin safety lock. The half-cock notch was also redesigned. At the beginning of 1992 another change was made to the Model 1911A1 model in the form of an enhanced pistol. Included were the Government models, the Commander, the Officer's model, the Gold Cup, and the Combat Elite. These modifications are the result of Colt's desire to meet the shooters demand for a more "customized" pistol. Colt chose some of the most popular modifications to perform on their new enhanced models. They include beavertail safety grip, a slotted Commander-style hammer, a relief cut under the trigger guard, a beveled magazine well, a slightly longer trigger, a flat top rib, and angled slide serrations. The Model 1911A1 may be the most modified handgun in the world.

MKIV Series 70 Government Model

This model is essentially a newer version of the 1911A1. It has the prefix "70G" from 1970-1976, "G70" from 1976-1980, and "70B" from 1980-1983, when production ceased. This model is offered in blue or nickel plate and has checkered walnut grips with the Colt medallion. It is chambered for .45 ACP, .38 Super, 9mm, and 9mm Steyr (foreign export only).

NIB	Exc.	V.G.	Good	Fair	Poor
950	775	600	400	250	200

MKIV Series 70 Gold Cup National Match

This is the newer version of the 1957 National Match. It features a slightly heavier slide and Colt Elliason sights. The chambering is .45 ACP only. The Accurizer barrel and bushing was introduced on this model. It was manufactured from 1970-1983.

NIB	Exc.	V.G.	Good	Fair	Poor
1200	900	750	550	500	400

Series 70 Gunsite Pistol

This model features a 5" barrel, thin rosewood grips, Gold Cup serrations, Heinie front sight and Novak rear sight, and several other special features. Available in blue of stainless steel. Introduced in 2004.

NIB	Exc.	V.G.	Good	Fair	Poor
1200	1050	825	600	400	200

Series 70 Gunsite Pistol Commander

As above but with 4.25" barrel.

NIB	Exc.	V.G.	Good	Fair	Poor
1200	1050	825	600	400	200

COLT ENHANCED GOVERNMENT MODELS

There are three different and distinct manufacturing cycles that not only affect the value of these rifles but also the legal consequences of their modifications.Pre-Ban Colt AR-15 rifles (Pre-1989): Fitted with bayonet lug, flash hider, and stamped AR-15 on lower receiver. Rifles that are NIB have a green label. It is legal to modify this rifle with any AR-15 upper receiver. These are the most desirable models because of their pre-ban features.Colt Sporters (Post-1989-pre-September 1994): This transition model has no bayonet lug, but it does have a flash hider. There is no AR-15 designation stamped on the lower receiver. Rifles that are NIB have a blue label. It is legal to modify this rifle with upper receivers made after 1989, i.e. no bayonet lug. These are less desirable than pre-ban AR-15s.Colt Sporters (Post-September 1994): This rifle has no bayonet lug, no flash hider, and does not have the AR-15 designation stamped on the lower receiver. Rifles that are NIB have a blue label. It is legal to modify this rifle only with upper receivers manufactured after September 1994. These rifles are the least desirable of the three manufacturing periods because of their lack of pre-ban military features and current manufacture status.

Commander

This is a shortened version of the Government model. It has a 4.25" barrel, a lightweight alloy frame, and a rounded spur hammer. The total weight of the Commander is 27.5 oz. The serial number has the suffix "LW." The Commander is chambered for the .45 ACP, 9mm, and .38 Super. The latter two have been discontinued. Some were chambered for 7.65 Parabellum for export only. The Commander was introduced in 1949. No longer in production.

NIB	Exc.	V.G.	Good	Fair	Poor
800	625	450	350	300	200

Combat Commander

The Combat Commander was produced in response to complaints from some quarters about the excessive recoil and rapid wear of the alloy-framed Commander. This model is simply a Commander with a steel frame. The Combat Commander weighs 32 oz. and is offered in blue or satin nickel with walnut grips. No longer in production.

NIB	Exc.	V.G.	Good	Fair	Poor
850	550	475	375	300	200

MK IV SERIES 80 GOVERNMENT MODEL

This model was introduced in 1983. It is, for all purposes, the same externally as the Series 70. The basic difference is the addition of the new firing pin safety on this model. No longer in production.NOTE: In 1997 Colt offered this model with fixed white dot sights.

Blued

NIB	Exc.	V.G.	Good	Fair	Poor
850	725	550	400	300	250

Nickel Plated

NIB	Exc.	V.G.	Good	Fair	Poor
825	700	525	375	300	250

Stainless Steel

NIB	Exc.	V.G.	Good	Fair	Poor
875	725	550	400	300	250

Polished Stainless Steel

NIB	Exc.	V.G.	Good	Fair	Poor
875	725	550	400	300	250

Colt 1991A1

Introduced in 1992 this Colt Government Model is designed to resemble the original GI service issue Government Model. Offered in .45 ACP, a 5" barrel, 7-round magazine, black composition grips, and a special parkerized finish. In 1996 this model was also chambered for the 9x23 cartridge. No longer in production.

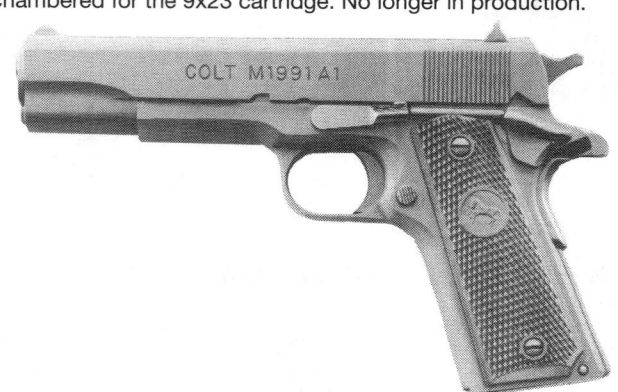

NIB	Exc.	V.G.	Good	Fair	Poor
700	600	425	300	150	125

NOTE: This pistol was offered in stainless steel in 1996. Add $50 to the above prices.

M1991A1 Commander

Chambered for the .45 ACP this model has all of the same features as the standard M1991A1 with a slightly shorter 4.25" barrel. Reintroduced in 2004.

NIB	Exc.	V.G.	Good	Fair	Poor
300875	550	400	300	225	125

NOTE: In 1997 Colt offered this model in stainless steel with fixed white dot sights. Add $100 to NIB price.

M1991A1 Compact

Chambered for the .45 ACP this model has a 3.25" barrel. It is 1.5" shorter than the standard M1991A1 model and .375" shorter in height. Its magazine holds 6 rounds. No longer in production.

NIB	Exc.	V.G.	Good	Fair	Poor
900	600	425	300	150	125

NOTE: In 1997 Colt offered this model in stainless steel with fixed white dot sights. Add $50 to NIB price.

MK IV SERIES 80 GOLD CUP NATIONAL MATCH

Externally the same as the Series 70 Gold Cup with the new firing pin safety. No longer in production.

Blued

NIB	Exc.	V.G.	Good	Fair	Poor
1200	900	675	500	350	250

Stainless Steel

NIB	Exc.	V.G.	Good	Fair	Poor
1200	900	675	500	350	250

Polished Stainless Steel

NIB	Exc.	V.G.	Good	Fair	Poor
1200	900	675	500	350	250

OFFICER'S ACP

This is a shortened version of the Government Model. It has a 3.5" barrel and weighs 37 oz. It is chambered for the .45 ACP only and has checkered walnut grips. The Officer's ACP was introduced in 1985. No longer in production.

Blued

NIB	Exc.	V.G.	Good	Fair	Poor
1000	700	525	325	250	200

Matte Blued

NIB	Exc.	V.G.	Good	Fair	Poor
1000	700	525	325	250	200

Satin Nickel

Discontinued 1985.

NIB	Exc.	V.G.	Good	Fair	Poor
1050	750	575	375	295	200

Stainless Steel

NIB	Exc.	V.G.	Good	Fair	Poor
1100	800	625	425	345	200

Lightweight Officer's ACP

This is an alloy-framed version that weighs 24 oz. It was introduced in 1986. No longer in production.

NIB	Exc.	V.G.	Good	Fair	Poor
1000	700	525	325	250	200

Concealed Carry Officer's Model

This model features a lightweight aluminum frame with stainless steel Commander slide. Barrel length is 4.25" and it is chambered for .45 ACP cartridge. Fitted with lightweight trigger, combat style hammer, and Hogue grips. Weight is approximately 34 oz. Introduced in 1998. No longer in production.

NIB	Exc.	V.G.	Good	Fair	Poor
1000	700	525	325	250	200

Delta Gold Cup

Introduced in 1992 the Delta Gold Cup is chambered for the 10mm, features a 5" barrel, stainless steel finish, adjustable Accro sights, special trigger, and black rubber wraparound grips. Features all of the new "Enhanced" model features. No longer in production.

NIB	Exc.	V.G.	Good	Fair	Poor
1050	875	700	600	400	200

DELTA ELITE

This model is chambered for the 10mm Norma cartridge. It is offered in blue or stainless steel. The grips are black neoprene with the Delta medallion. It features a high-profile three-dot combat sight system. The Delta Elite was introduced in 1987. No longer in production.

Blued

NIB	Exc.	V.G.	Good	Fair	Poor
1200	925	650	425	300	250

Stainless Steel

NIB	Exc.	V.G.	Good	Fair	Poor
1250	950	675	400	300	250

Polished Stainless Steel

NIB	Exc.	V.G.	Good	Fair	Poor
1250	950	675	400	300	250

Combat Elite

This is a specialized Government model that has a 5" barrel and adjustable Accro sights. It is chambered either in .45 ACP or .38 Super. It weighs 38 oz. and has an 8-round magazine for the .45 ACP and a 9-round magazine for the .38 Super. Finish can be either blue or matte stainless steel. No longer in production. (Colt issued a recall notice for the safety on this model in June 2009. Pistols with serial numbers from CG10000E to CG11293E should be sent to the factory for parts replacement.)

NIB	Exc.	V.G.	Good	Fair	Poor
1050	875	700	600	400	200

Combat Target Model

Introduced in 1996 this 5" barrel 1911 model features a fitted barrel, Gold Cup-style trigger, tuned action, flat top slide, relieved ejection port, skeletonized hammer, wide grip safety, high cut trigger guard, beveled magazine well, and adjustable sights. Weight is 39 oz. Offered in both blue and stainless steel. In 1996 this model was also chambered for the new 9x23 cartridge as well as the .45 ACP and the .38 Super. No longer in production.NOTE: In 1997 Colt expanded this Target Model to include a number of different variations. They are listed.

NIB	Exc.	V.G.	Good	Fair	Poor
1050	875	700	600	400	200

NOTE: Add $50 for stainless steel version.

Combat Target Model Combat Target Combat Commander

Barrel length is 4-1/4". Chambered for .45 ACP. Stainless steel finish. Weight is 36 oz. Has all other Combat Target features. No longer in production.

NIB	Exc.	V.G.	Good	Fair	Poor
1050	875	700	600	400	200

Combat Target Model Combat Target Officer's ACP

Fitted with a 3-1/2" barrel and chambered for .45 ACP. Stainless steel finish. Weight is about 34 oz. Has all other Combat Target features. No longer in production.

NIB	Exc.	V.G.	Good	Fair	Poor
1050	875	700	600	400	200

Special Combat Government

This pistol features a 5" barrel, double diamond rosewood grips, extended ambidextrous thumb safety, and steel checkered mainspring housing with extended magazine well. Chambered for the .45 ACP or .38 Super cartridges. Adjustable Bomar rear sight. Magazine capacity is 8 rounds. Choice of hard chrome or blue/satin nickel finish.

NIB	Exc.	V.G.	Good	Fair	Poor
2000	1500	—	—	—	—

Colt Special Combat Government Carry Model

1911-style semi-auto pistol chambered in .45 ACP (8+1) or .38 Super (9+1). Semi-custom features include Novak front and rear night sights, skeletonized three-hole trigger, slotted hammer, black/silver synthetic grips, Smith & Alexander upswept beavertail grip palm swell safety and extended magazine well, Wilson tactical ambidextrous safety. Five-inch barrel. Available in blued, hard chrome, or blue/satin nickel finish, depending on chambering.

NIB	Exc.	V.G.	Good	Fair	Poor
1450	1100	—	—	—	—

XSE SERIES MODEL O PISTOLS

Introduced in 1999, these models are an enhanced version of the Colt 1911 and features front slide serrations, checkered, double diamond rosewood grips, adjustable McCormick trigger, three-dot dovetail rear sights, ambidextrous safety, enhanced tolerances, aluminum frame, and stainless steel slide. Chambered for .45 ACP cartridge.

Colt O-Model Government (01070XS)

Fitted with a 5" barrel and 8-round magazine.

NIB	Exc.	V.G.	Good	Fair	Poor
1200	775	595	475	350	200

Colt O-Model Concealed Carry Officer's (09850XS)

Fitted with a 4.25" barrel and 7-round magazine.

NIB	Exc.	V.G.	Good	Fair	Poor
1250	800	625	475	350	200

Colt O-Model Commander (04012XS)

Fitted with a 4.25" barrel and 8-round magazine.

NIB	Exc.	V.G.	Good	Fair	Poor
1200	775	595	475	350	200

Colt O-Model Lightweight Commander (04860XS)

Fitted with a 4.25" barrel and 8-round magazine. Weight is about 26 oz.

NIB	Exc.	V.G.	Good	Fair	Poor
1200	775	595	475	350	200

1991 SERIES MODEL O PISTOLS

This series of pistol was introduced in 1991 and is to replace the standard Colt 1911 series pistols. These pistols feature checkered rubber composite grips, smooth trigger, fixed sights, beveled magazine well and standard thumb safety and service style grip safety. Chambered for .45 ACP cartridge and 7-round magazines.

Colt O-Model Government Matte (01991)

Fitted with a 5" barrel, black matte finish, carbon steel frame and slide.

NIB	Exc.	V.G.	Good	Fair	Poor
800	650	495	350	295	200

Colt O-Model Government Stainless (01091)

Fitted with a 5" barrel, mattel stainless finish on stainless steel frame and slide.

NIB	Exc.	V.G.	Good	Fair	Poor
920	700	550	400	300	200

Colt O-Model Commander Stainless (04091U)

Fitted with a 4.25" barrel and matte stainless finish with stainless steel frame and slide.

NIB	Exc.	V.G.	Good	Fair	Poor
920	700	550	400	300	200

Colt O-Model Commander (04691)

Fitted with a 4.25" barrel and black matte finish with carbon steel frame and slide.

NIB	Exc.	V.G.	Good	Fair	Poor
870	650	—	—	—	—

Colt O-Model Gold Cup

This model has the same features as the O-Model Commander with the addition of a 5" barrel with a stainless steel frame and slide. Slide top is rounded. Magazine capacity is 8 rounds. Weight is about 39 oz. Introduced in 1999.

NIB	Exc.	V.G.	Good	Fair	Poor
1400	1050	800	575	300	200

Colt Defender

This single-action pistol was introduced in 1998. This model features a lightweight aluminum alloy frame and stainless steel slide. It is chambered for the .45 ACP or .40 S&W cartridge and is fitted with a 3" barrel. Magazine capacity is 7 rounds. Rubber wraparound grips. Weight is approximately 23 oz. and overall length is 6.75".

NIB	Exc.	V.G.	Good	Fair	Poor
850	650	475	300	250	200

Colt Defender Model O (07000D)

This model takes the place of Defender and was introduced in 2000. It has a brushed stainless finish with a 3" barrel. Skeletonized composite trigger, beveled magazine well, extended thumb safety and upswept beavertail with palm swell. Chambered for .45 ACP only. (Colt issued a recall notice for the guide pad on this model in June 2009. Pistols with serial numbers from DR33036 o DR35948 should be sent to the factory for parts replacement.)

NIB	Exc.	V.G.	Good	Fair	Poor
950	700	525	350	200	145

1911 – WWI Replica

Single-action semi-auto chambered in .45 ACP. Faithful external reproduction of the WWI-era service pistol with original-style rollmarks, grips, sights, carbonia blue finish, etc. Series 70 lockwork. Made from 2003 - 2009.

NIB	Exc.	V.G.	Good	Fair	Poor
1025	850	625	575	400	200

1911 - WWI 1918 Replica

Based on the military model made in 1918. Black finish and World War I rollmarks. This model was also offered in a Presentation Grade with blue or nickel finish and Colt Custom Shop "A" engraving. In excellent or new condition, this could add a premium of 100 percent. Made in 2008 and 2009. (Colt issued a recall notice for the safety on this model in June of 2009. Pistols with serial numbers from 1001WWI to 3431WWI should be sent to the factory for parts replacement.)

NIB	Exc.	V.G.	Good	Fair	Poor
900	800	600	500	400	200

1911A1 - WWII Replica

Replica of U.S. Military sidearm of World War II. Parkerized finish, WWII-ear rollmarks, lanyard loop, original style composite grips and packaging. Made in .45 ACP only by the Colt Custom Shop from 2001 to 2004. Series 70 lockwork. (Colt issued a recall notice for the safety on this model in June 2009. Pistols with serial numbers from 4597WMK to 5414WMK should be sent to the factory for parts replacement.)

NIB	Exc.	V.G.	Good	Fair	Poor
1075	950	700	575	400	200

Colt New Agent Double Action Only

Similar to New Agent single action except has double-action-only operating system. Spur-less hammer design with second-strike capability and no manual safety. Double-diamond slim fit grips, snag free trench sighting system, 7-shot magazine. In .45 ACP only. (Colt issued a recall notice for the safety and guide pad on this model in June of 2009. Pistols with serial numbers from GT01001 to GT04505 should be sent to the factory for parts replacement.)

NIB	Exc.	V.G.	Good	Fair	Poor
850	750	600	500	400	200

Colt Model 1991 DAO

Double-action-only version of the Lightweight Government Model. Spur-less hammer design with second-strike capability and no manual safety. Double-diamond slim fit grips, 7-shot magazine. In .45 ACP only. Introduced in 2011.

NIB	Exc.	V.G.	Good	Fair	Poor
950	800	700	550	400	250

Colt Model 1911 100th Anniversary Series

These two limited edition Model 1911s were introduced in 2011 to commemorate the 100th anniversary of the legendary pistol. Model 1911ANVIII is based on the 1918 configuration with custom rollmarks on the receiver relating to the 100th anniversary. Orders on this model were to be taken only until November 30, 2011. The higher grade version, Model 1911ANVII, features scroll engraving and historic Colt symbols highlighted in 24 karat gold, and comes in a glass-topped walnut display case. Production for this model was to be limited to 750 units. Higher grade variants limited to 100 units with A, B, C or D levels of engraving were also scheduled for 2011 at prices ranging from $2640 to $6528.

1911ANVII

NIB	Exc.	V.G.	Good	Fair	Poor
2150	1800	1500	—	—	—

1911ANVIII

NIB	Exc.	V.G.	Good	Fair	Poor
1075	900	750	—	—	—

Colt Government Model 1911 .22 LR Series

A licensed reproduction of the 1911A1 in .22 Long Rifle manufactured by Umarex USA. Blow-back action with 12-shot magazine and other standard 1911 specifications including 5-inch barrel, thumb and grip safeties, diamond checkered wood grips, blue finish and drift-adjustable rear sight. (Gold Cup has fully adjustable sight.) Weight is approximately 33 ounces. Offered in three variants: standard model, Rail Gun, and Gold Cup. Introduced in 2011. Prices below are for standard model.

NIB	Exc.	V.G.	Good	Fair	Poor
350	300	275	225	175	100

Colt Concealed Carry

Chopped, lightweight 1911-style semi-auto chambered in .45 ACP. Weighs 25 oz. unloaded; overall length 6.75"; 7+1 capacity; Series 80 lockwork; black anodized aluminum frame with double-diamond wood grips. Introduced 2007.

NIB	Exc.	V.G.	Good	Fair	Poor
950	700	525	350	200	150

New Agent

7+1 .45 ACP semi-auto with aluminum frame, fized sights, Series 80 action, slim-fit grips and 6.75-inch overall length. Introduced 2007.

NIB	Exc.	V.G.	Good	Fair	Poor
950	700	525	350	200	150

Colt Rail Gun

1911-style semi-auto pistol chambered in .45 ACP. Stainless steel frame and slide, front and rear slide serrations, skeletonized trigger, integral; accessory rail, Smith & Alexander upswept beavertail grip palm swell safety, white dot front sight and Novak rear. Rosewood double diamond grips, tactical thumb safety, National Match barrel. Capacity 8+1.

NIB	Exc.	V.G.	Good	Fair	Poor
950	700	525	350	200	150

Double Eagle

This is a double-action semi-automatic pistol chambered for the 10mm Auto and the .45 ACP cartridges. It has a 5" barrel and an 8-round detachable box magazine. It is constructed of stainless steel and has checkered black synthetic grips. The sights are fixed and utilize the three-dot system. No longer in production.

NIB	Exc.	V.G.	Good	Fair	Poor
1200	775	595	475	350	200

Double Eagle Officer's Model

This is a compact version of the double-action Double Eagle pistol chambered for .45 ACP only. No longer in production.

NIB	Exc.	V.G.	Good	Fair	Poor
1025	850	625	575	400	200

Double Eagle Combat Commander

Based on the standard Double Eagle design but with a slightly shorter 4.25" barrel, the Double Eagle Combat Commander fits between the standard model and the smaller Officer's Model. Available in .45 ACP and .40 S&W (1993) this model weighs about 36 oz., holds 8 rounds, has white dot sights, and checkered Xenoy grips. The finish is matte stainless steel. No longer in production.

NIB	Exc.	V.G.	Good	Fair	Poor
1025	850	625	575	350	200

Double Eagle First Edition

This version of the double-action Double Eagle pistol is chambered for the 10mm Auto and is furnished with a Cordura holster, double-magazine pouch, and three magazines, as well as a zippered black Cordura case.

NIB	Exc.	V.G.	Good	Fair	Poor
1100	875	650	500	375	300

.38 Super (2006)

1911-style single-action semi-auto chambered in .38 Super. Nine-shot magazine, double-diamond walnut or checkered hard rubber stocks, fixed 3-dot sights, 5" barrel. Stainless, bright stainless or blued finish.

NIB	Exc.	V.G.	Good	Fair	Poor
1100	875	650	500	375	300

Pocket Nine

This double-action semi-automatic pistol is chambered for the 9mm cartridge. The frame is aluminum alloy and the slide is stainless steel. Barrel length is 2.75". Magazine capacity is 6 rounds. Wraparound rubber grips standard. Overall length is 5.5". Weight is approximately 17 oz. No longer in production.

NIB	Exc.	V.G.	Good	Fair	Poor
950	700	525	350	250	175

Tac Nine

Introduced in 1999, this double-action-only semi-automatic pistol is chambered for the 9mm cartridge. It has a 2.75" barrel with an aluminum alloy frame and stainless steel slide. Tritium night sights. Wraparound rubber grips are standard. The finish is black oxide. Enhanced tolerances. Weight is about 17 oz. No longer in production.

NIB	Exc.	V.G.	Good	Fair	Poor
975	725	550	375	250	175

NOTE: Nickel finish add 10 percent. Stainless steel add 10 percent.

Mustang

This is a more compact version of the .380 Government Model. It has a 2.75" barrel and a 5-round detachable magazine. No longer in production.

NIB	Exc.	V.G.	Good	Fair	Poor
850	650	475	300	250	200

Mustang Pocketlite

A lightweight version of the Mustang that features an aluminum alloy receiver. The finish is blued only, and it has synthetic grips. It was introduced in 1987. No longer in production.

NIB	Exc.	V.G.	Good	Fair	Poor
850	650	475	300	250	200

Government Pocketlite LW

Similar to the Mustang but fitted with a 3.25" barrel and a 7-round magazine. This model has an aluminum frame and stainless steel slide. Fixed sights. Black composition grips. Weight is approximately 15 oz. No longer in production.

NIB	Exc.	V.G.	Good	Fair	Poor
850	650	475	300	250	200

NOTE: Stainless steel add 10 percent.

Mustang Plus II

This version of the Mustang pistol features the 2.75" barrel with the longer grip frame that accommodates a 7-round magazine. It was introduced in 1988 and is offered in blue, as well as stainless steel. No longer in production.

NIB	Exc.	V.G.	Good	Fair	Poor
850	650	475	300	250	200

Colt Pony

Introduced in 1997 this semi-automatic pistol is chambered for the .380 ACP. It is fitted with a 2-3/4" barrel and a bobbed hammer. It is double-action-only. The grips are black composition. Sights are a ramp front with fixed rear. Finish is Teflon and stainless steel. Magazine capacity is 6 rounds. Overall length is 5-1/2". Weight is 19 oz. No longer in production.

NIB	Exc.	V.G.	Good	Fair	Poor
850	650	475	300	250	200

Colt Pony PocketLite

Same as above but with aluminum and stainless steel frame. Weight is approximately 13 oz. No longer in production.

NIB	Exc.	V.G.	Good	Fair	Poor
850	650	475	300	250	200

NOTE: Nickel finish add 10 percent. Stainless steel add 10 percent.

.380 Series 80 Government Model

This is a single-action, blowback-operated semi-automatic pistol chambered for the .380 ACP cartridge. It has a 3.25" barrel and a 7-round magazine. The sights are fixed. It is available either blued, nickel plated, or stainless steel. It has synthetic grips and was introduced in 1985. No longer in production.

NIB	Exc.	V.G.	Good	Fair	Poor
875	675	500	325	275	200

Colt CZ40

Introduced in 1998 this double-action .40 S&W pistol was built for Colt by CZ in the Czech Republic. It is fitted with a 4" barrel and has black polymer grips. The frame is alloy with a carbon steel slide with blue finish. Magazine capacity is 10 rounds. Weight is approximately 34 oz. No longer in production.

NIB	Exc.	V.G.	Good	Fair	Poor
900	750	600	500	400	225

COLT WOODSMAN

Text and photos by Bob RayburnThe original Colt .22 Target Model was designed by John Moses Browning and improved by engineers at Colt Firearms prior to the start of production in 1915, and major design updates were made in 1947 and again in 1955. Those three designs constitute what collectors call the three series of Woodsman pistols. First Series refers to all those built on the frame used prior to and during World War II. Second Series includes all versions built on the second frame design from 1947 until 1955, and Third Series means the third frame design as used from 1955 to the end of production in 1977.Each series had a Target Model, a Sport Model, and a Match Target Model. All models are very similar: the Sport Model, for example, is merely the Target Model with a short barrel, and in some cases different sights or grips. The Match Target is nearly the same as the Sport or Target Model, but with a heavier, slab-sided barrel, a squared-off frame at the front of the receiver to mate with the heavy barrel, and improved sights. In the post-war years only there were also three very similar economy models: First the Challenger, then the Huntsman, and finally the Targetsman. The actions of the economy models are identical to the higher-end models of the same period internally; they lack only some of the refinements.These guns were not assembled in strict numerical sequence. Furthermore, even when changes were made, old parts were used up at the same time new parts were being introduced. As a result, there is no hard and fast serial number dividing line for any particular feature, and serial number overlaps of several thousand are common. All models of the Woodsman line, in all three series, are discussed here, but there are numerous variations in details that are primarily of interest to specialized collectors. For more details see Bob Rayburn's Colt Woodsman Pocket Guide, a 96-page pocket-sized guide to the Colt Woodsman line, available for $10 (including shipping) from:

Bob Rayburn
PO Box 97104
Lakewood, WA 98497
or online at http://www.colt22.com
or http://www.coltwoodsman.com

Values listed here are for the pistol only, without extras, for guns in the middle of each condition range. These are guidelines to the prevailing retail values for the collector or shooter who is buying it as the end user, not what one might expect to receive from a gun dealer who is buying it to resell. Furthermore, within the Excellent and Very Good condition categories, there is a considerable spread in value, especially for the older and more collectible versions. Excellent, for example, means 98 percent or more original blue, but a very nice pre-Woodsman with 100 percent of the original blue would likely be worth twice as much to a serious collector as one with only 98 percent. At the other end of the condition scale, in the Fair and Poor categories, the individual values of component parts become significant, and effectively set a floor value. A poor condition, rusty, pitted pre-Woodsman or First Series Match Target would still have good value if it included the original magazine and grips in nice condition, for example. In addition, there are sometimes rare variations within the broad categories that can significantly enhance the value. Include the original crisp condition box, instructions, and tools, and the value goes up more, especially for high condition early guns. On the other hand, rust, pitting (even very minor), rebluing, or other non-factory modifications will significantly reduce the values from those listed in the Very Good category or better.

FIRST SERIES

In 1915 the intended market was the target shooter, and there was only one model: the Colt .22 LR Automatic Target Pistol. That model, however, proved to be very popular not only with target shooters, but also with hunters, trappers, campers, and other outdoorsmen. Management at Colt noticed this, of course, and decided to give the pistol a new name that more closely reflected its widespread use. THE WOODSMAN was the name chosen, and that roll mark was added to the side of the receiver in 1927, at approximately serial number 54000. To further satisfy the broader market, Colt introduced the Sport Model in 1933, and the Match Target Model in 1938. The compact and beautifully balanced Sport Model was a near perfect "kit gun" for the outdoorsman, and the Match Target was designed for the special needs of the serious target shooters. Approximately 54,000 pre-Woodsmans (all with 6-5/8 inch barrels) and a combined total of approximately 110,000 Woodsman marked Sport and Target Models were produced in the first series. The Sport Model and Target Model were serial numbered together after the Sport Model was added to the line in 1933, so it is not possible to easily determine how many of each were manufactured. It is safe to say that the Target Model far outnumbered the Sport Model. During the war years of 1942-45 the Match Target was the only Woodsman model built, and virtually the entire production was for the US military.

Pre-Woodsman

This model was made from 1915-1927. It has a 10-round magazine capacity, blue finish, checkered walnut grips, and 6-5/8" barrel. It was designed for .22 LR standard velocity ammunition. The rear sight is adjustable for windage, the front sight for elevation. Up until approximately serial number 31000 the barrel was a very thin, so-called "pencil barrel." The barrel weight and diameter were increased slightly in 1922 to what collectors now call the "medium weight barrel." There were also numerous small changes in the grips, magazines, and markings over the years. Approximately 54,000 were made in all variations.

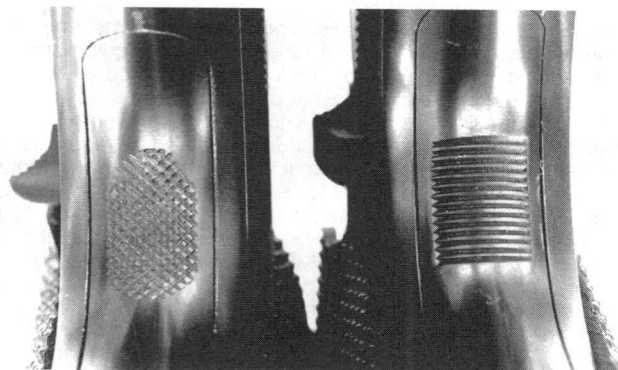

An early pre-Woodsman

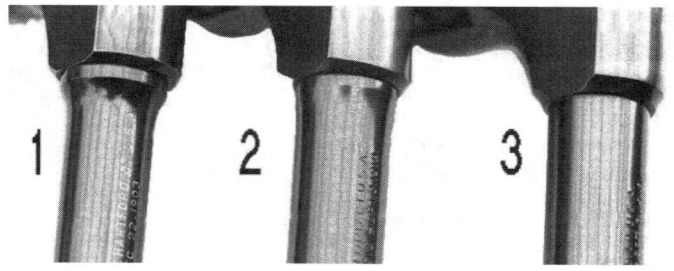

A checkered pattern in an oval on the mainspring housing (left) indicates a pre-Woodsman or First Series Woodsman Target model that was designed for standard velocity .22 Long Rifle ammunition only. A series of horizontal parallel lines in a rectangular pattern (right) indicates one that was designed for high-velocity .22 Long Rifle ammunition. All guns in the series made after 1932 were designed for high-velocity ammunition, and that includes all Sport, Match Target, Challenger, Huntsman, and Targetsman models. The post-WWII guns have no pattern on the mainspring housing but they were all made for high-velocity ammunition.

NIB	Exc.	V.G.	Good	Fair	Poor
—	1600	1000	500	250	200

Woodsman Target

Initially this was exactly the same as the late pre-Woodsman, with the exception of THE WOODSMAN marking on the side of the receiver. Later there were small changes in the sights, trigger, and markings. In 1934 the barrel profile was again modified to a larger diameter, heavier barrel. This third and final pre-WWII barrel profile lacked the fillet, or step-down, as was present on the earlier pencil barrel and medium barrel, and is therefore commonly called the "straight taper" barrel. A significant modification occurred in 1932 when a new heat-treated mainspring housing and stiffer recoil spring were phased in to allow the use of the increasingly popular high velocity .22 LR ammunition. While this change has been widely reported to have taken place at serial number 83790, it was actually phased in over a period of time and a range of serial numbers, spanning at least 81000-86000, within which range both standard and high speed versions can be found. Fortunately Colt changed the marking on the back of the mainspring housing (see photo) to allow visual differentiation. Colt also sold a conversion kit to modify the older guns for use with high velocity ammunition. The kit consisted of a new style mainspring housing, a stiffer recoil spring, and a coil type magazine spring for use in the very early guns that had a Z type magazine spring.

NIB	Exc.	V.G.	Good	Fair	Poor
—	1300	850	500	250	200

Woodsman Sport

With the Woodsman proving to be increasingly popular with outdoorsmen of all types, Colt decided to market a Woodsman better suited for a "take along" gun for hiking, camping, etc. This was accomplished in 1933 by merely shortening the barrel from 6-5/8 inches to 4-1/2 inches, and announcing the new Sport Model. Other than barrel length, the only difference between the Target Model and the Sport Model was an adjustable front sight on the Target Model and a fixed front sight on the Sport Model. Later a front sight adjustable for elevation would be an available option for the Sport Model. Colt called this arrangement "Target Sights," and indeed it was the same front sight used on the Target Model. A First Series Sport Model with an adjustable front sight will command a premium of approximately 25 percent over the values listed.

NIB	Exc.	V.G.	Good	Fair	Poor
—	1600	1100	600	250	200

Woodsman Match Target

Colt introduced the Match Target Woodsman in 1938, with its own serial number series beginning at MT1, and continuing until 1944 with serial number MT16611. The new features included larger grips, a heavier barrel (6-5/8"), and a rear sight fully adjustable for both windage and elevation. To signify its intended market a Bullseye Target pattern was placed on the side of the barrel. That led to its nickname of "Bullseye Match Target." The elongated, one-piece wraparound walnut grips also picked up a nickname, due to their unusual shape. Unfortunately, the so-called "Elephant Ear" grips are somewhat fragile and are often broken. In addition, many of the serious target shooters of the day replaced them with custom grips with thumb rest and palm swell, and the original grips were set aside and eventually lost or discarded. For those reasons the original grips are often missing, and that severely affects the value. Values listed assume original one-piece walnut wraparound Elephant Ear grips with no cracks, repairs, or modifications, and a correct Match Target marked magazine. The values listed for Fair and Poor condition are primarily salvage value, and reflect the high value of original "Elephant Ear" grips and Match Target marked magazines for spare parts. Approximately 11,000 were produced for the civilian market from 1938-1942.

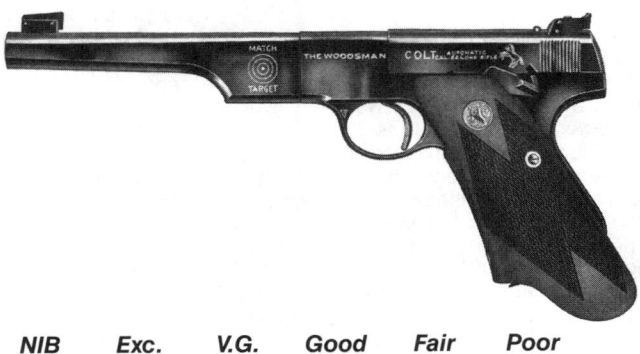

NIB	Exc.	V.G.	Good	Fair	Poor
—	3200	1700	850	650	550

Military Woodsman Match Target

After the United States entered World War II at the end of 1941,

civilian production at Colt was stopped and the total effort was devoted to the U.S. military. Slightly more than 4000 First Series Match Target Woodsmans were delivered on U.S. Government contract from 1942-1944. Most of them, but not all, had serial numbers above MT12000. With possible rare exceptions they all had U.S. Property or U.S. military markings, standard blue finish, 6-5/8" barrel, and extended length plastic stocks. The plastic stocks are sometimes erroneously called elephant ear stocks. The military plastic stocks are still relatively easy to find and inexpensive and, since they will fit any First Series Colt Woodsman, they are often used as replacement grips on non-military guns. Since the military guns had plastic grips, rather than the costly and desirable "Elephant Ear" grips, the salvage value in the Fair and Poor condition range is less than that for the civilian model.

NIB	Exc.	V.G.	Good	Fair	Poor
—	3400	1900	950	550	350

SECOND SERIES

After World War II Colt entered a lengthy period of clearing up government contracts and retooling for the civilian market. The Woodsman line was extensively revised and modernized. The second series guns began appearing near the end of 1947, although no appreciable numbers were shipped until 1948. The Second Series Woodsman had essentially the same action and many of the same internals as the first series guns, but were larger and heavier, with a longer grip frame. New features included a magazine safety, automatic slide stop when the magazine was emptied, fully adjustable rear sight, heavier barrels, and a 6-inch barrel length on the Target and Match Target Models, rather than 6-5/8 inches, as on the first series. Other new features included a push button magazine release just aft of the trigger guard, like that on the large frame Government Model semi-automatics, a lanyard ring concealed in the butt, and a provision for attaching a plastic grip adapter to the backstrap, thereby accommodating different sized hands. Elevation adjustment was incorporated into the rear sight of all Woodsman models, and the adjustable front sight was replaced with a fixed blade. Serial numbers were restarted at 1-S, and are intermixed for all three models. Approximately 146,000 of the three models were produced.In 1950 Colt added the Challenger to the line of second series pistols, the first of the economy models. Internally the Challenger is nearly identical to the Woodsman pistols of the same era, but externally it lacks most of the refinements introduced with the Second Series Woodsman. It has no magazine safety, automatic slide stop, adjustable sights, push button magazine release, lanyard ring, or grip adapters. It was available with either a 6-inch or 4-1/2 inch barrel, and had its own serial number series beginning with 1-C. Approximately 77,000 were produced.

Woodsman Target 6 inch barrel

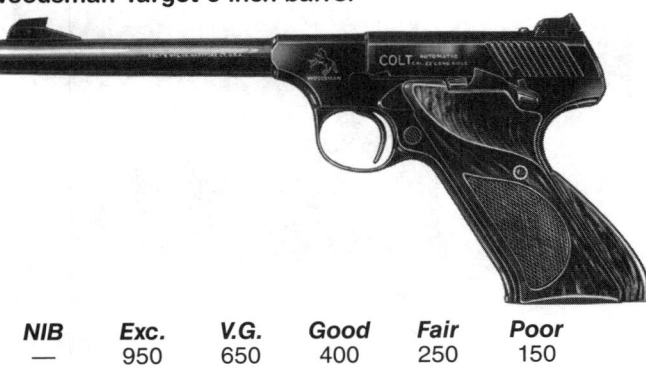

NIB	Exc.	V.G.	Good	Fair	Poor
—	950	650	400	250	150

Woodsman Sport 4-1/2 inch barrel

NIB	Exc.	V.G.	Good	Fair	Poor
—	975	600	450	250	150

Woodsman Match Target 6 inch barrel

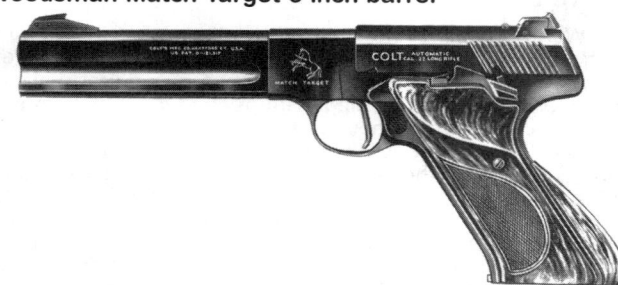

NIB	Exc.	V.G.	Good	Fair	Poor
—	1200	750	550	350	150

Woodsman Match Target 4-1/2 inch barrel

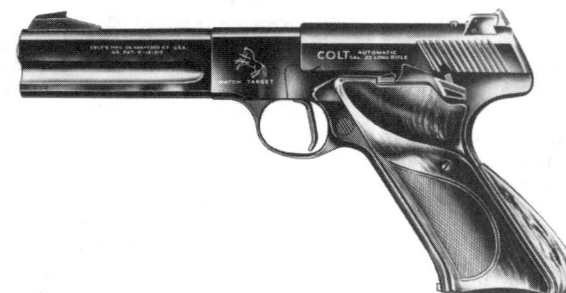

Second Series Match Target Model with 4-1/2 inch barrel.

Introduced in 1950.

NIB	Exc.	V.G.	Good	Fair	Poor
—	1400	850	600	350	150

Challenger 4-1/2 inch barrel

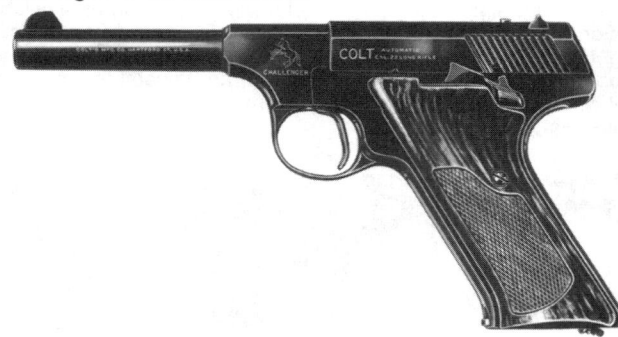

NIB	Exc.	V.G.	Good	Fair	Poor
—	650	450	325	200	150

Challenger 6 inch barrel

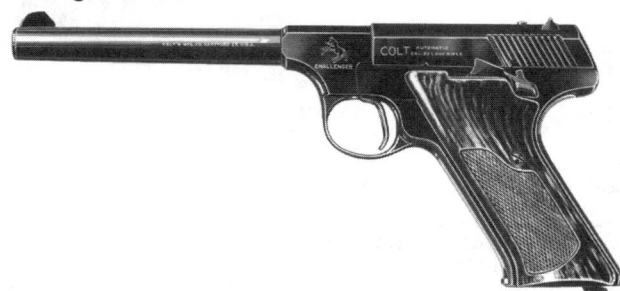

NIB	Exc.	V.G.	Good	Fair	Poor
—	650	425	350	200	150

THIRD SERIES

In 1955 Colt again redesigned the Woodsman line. The most obvious change was in the location of the magazine release, which was again placed at the heel of the butt, just as on the first series guns. Other changes were made over time in the markings, grips, sights, and trigger. The Sport, Target, and Match Target models continued. The Challenger was replaced by the very similar Huntsman, with either a 4-1/2 inch or 6 inch barrel. In 1959 the Targetsman was added to the line. The Targetsman differs from the Huntsman only in having an adjustable rear sight and a thumbrest on the left grip panel, and was available with a 6-inch barrel only. All Third Series models had black plastic grips until 1960, and checkered walnut grips thereafter. The Huntsman has no thumbrest on the grips. All other Third Series models have a thumbrest on the left grip panel. It is difficult to impossible to determine how many of each model were produced in the third series, due to a very complex serial numbering scheme. Approximately 1000 Third Series Sport, Target, and Match Target Models were numbered at the end of the second series serial number range, from 146138-S to 147138-S. Numbers were then restarted at 160001-S, so there are no post-WWII Woodsmans with numbers in the 148xxx-S to 159xxx-S range. The Challenger serial numbers, meantime, had reached approximately 77143-C prior to the Challenger being replaced by the Huntsman (note the C suffix, for Challenger). The Huntsman initially continued in the Challenger serial number series, although numbers skipped forward to 90000-C before restarting. The Targetsman, when added to the line early in 1959, joined the Huntsman in using the -C suffix serial numbers, which were by then up to 129300-C. Then in 1969, when Woodsman serial numbers had reached 241811-S and the -C numbers had reached 194040-C, Colt decided to integrate the serial numbers for all versions of the Woodsman, Huntsman, and Targetsman and restart numbering again. This time they started with 001001S. That worked fine until numbers reached 099999S, and rolled over to 100000S. Numbers used in

1951-52 were then being inadvertently duplicated, with one small exception: the earlier guns had a -S suffix while the later ones had only an S (no hyphen before the S). Apparently that was not enough of a distinction to satisfy federal regulations, so when Colt discovered the error after approximately 1,330 had already been numbered, the existing "double headers" were hand stamped with an S prefix, in addition to the S suffix, in order to salvage them. Serial numbers were then restarted yet again, this time at 300000S, and continued to 317736S, when production ended.

Woodsman Target 6 inch barrel

NIB	Exc.	V.G.	Good	Fair	Poor
—	850	550	400	250	150

Woodsman Sport 4-1/2 inch barrel

NIB	Exc.	V.G.	Good	Fair	Poor
—	900	600	400	250	150

Woodsman Match Target 6 inch barrel

NIB	Exc.	V.G.	Good	Fair	Poor
—	1000	750	525	350	150

Woodsman Match Target 4-1/2 inch barrel

With the introduction of the Third Series guns, Colt moved the magazine catch back to the heel of the butt, where it had been on the first series.

Added to the line in 1950.

NIB	Exc.	V.G.	Good	Fair	Poor
—	1200	850	600	350	150

Huntsman 644-1/2 or 6 inch barrel

NIB	Exc.	V.G.	Good	Fair	Poor
—	650	450	325	200	150

Targetsman 6-1/2 inch barrel, 4-1/2 inch (rare)

NIB	Exc.	V.G.	Good	Fair	Poor
—	675	475	350	200	150

Junior Pocket Model

This diminutive unit is only 4.5" long overall and weighs 12 oz. Colt did not manufacture this pistol, but rather had it made for them by Astra in Spain. The pistol was introduced in 1958 chambered for .25 ACP. One year later a .22 Short version appeared. Both had external hammers and detachable 6-round magazines. The passage of the 1968 Gun Control Act made import of a weapon of this size illegal, so Colt discontinued its relationship with Astra. The pistol was re-introduced in 1970 as an American-made product and was produced for two more years. Production ceased in 1972. Astra also made this pistol and called it the Cub.

NIB	Exc.	V.G.	Good	Fair	Poor
525	375	250	175	125	75

NOTE: .22 Short add 25 percent.

Cadet / Colt .22

Introduced in 1994 this .22 caliber semi-automatic pistol is offered with a 4-1/2" barrel and stainless steel finish. The model was renamed Colt .22 in 1995. The sights are fixed and magazine capacity is 11 rounds. Overall length is 8-5/8" and weight is approximately 33 oz.

NIB	Exc.	V.G.	Good	Fair	Poor
350	300	265	225	125	50

Colt .22 Target

Introduced in 1995 this model features a 6" bull barrel with removable front sight and adjustable rear sight. Black composite monogrip stock. Stainless steel finish. Weight is 40.5 oz.

NIB	Exc.	V.G.	Good	Fair	Poor
475	325	300	250	150	75

COLT CUSTOM SHOP

The Colt Custom Shop has developed several models over the years that are available to the public. The basis of these offerings are standard Colt Models upgraded to perform special functions.

Special Combat Government Model (Competition)

This is a competition ready model. Chambered for the .45 ACP it comes fitted with a skeletonized trigger, upswept grip safety, custom tuned action, polished feed ramp, throated barrel, flared ejection port, cutout commander hammer, two 8-round magazines, hard chromed slide and receiver, extended thumb safety, Bomar rear sight, Clark dovetail front sight, and flared magazine funnel. The pistol has been accurized and is shipped with a certified target.

NIB	Exc.	V.G.	Good	Fair	Poor
1750	1200	800	500	300	200

Special Combat Government Model (Carry)

This model has all of the same features as the competition model except that it has a royal blue finish, special bar-dot night sights, ambidextrous safety. It has also been accurized and shipped with a certified target.

NIB	Exc.	V.G.	Good	Fair	Poor
1550	1000	700	400	300	200

Gold Cup Commander

Chambered for the .45 ACP and has these features: heavy-duty adjustable target sights, beveled magazine well, serrated front strap, checkered mainspring housing, wide grip safety, Palo Alto wood grips, and stainless steel or royal blue finish.

NIB	Exc.	V.G.	Good	Fair	Poor
1400	875	650	600	500	375

U.S. Shooting Team Gold Cup

This is a limited edition Gold Cup .45 ACP with special blue, sights, grips. The U.S. Shooting Team logo is rolled on the slide. Limited to 500 pistols and built for Lew Horton..

NIB	Exc.	V.G.	Good	Fair	Poor
1400	875	650	600	500	375

Gold Cup Trophy

Introduced in 1997 this model features .45 ACP 5" barrel 1911 with a choice of stainless steel or blue finish. Several custom features such as skeletonized hammer and trigger. Adjustable rear sight and wraparound rubber grips are standard. The pistol has been accurized and is shipped with a target. Magazine capacity is 7 or 8 rounds. Weight is approximately 39 oz.

NIB	Exc.	V.G.	Good	Fair	Poor
1000	900	675	625	525	400

McCormick Commander

This is a limited edition pistol made for Lew Horton in 1995 and limited to 100 pistols. It has many special features. The slide is engraved and there is a gold rampant colt on the slide.

NIB	Exc.	V.G.	Good	Fair	Poor
1600	1000	750	600	500	375

McCormick Officer

This Lew Horton exclusive pistol has factory installed McCormick parts and a hard chrome finish. A total of 500 guns were built in 1995.

NIB	Exc.	V.G.	Good	Fair	Poor
1500	875	650	600	500	375

McCormick Factory Racer

This is a limited edition pistol from Lew Horton. It is a full size government model with hard chrome finish, special barrel, trigger safety, and other custom features. Each gun is rollmarked "McCormick Factory Racer" on the slide. Special serial numbers from MFR001 to MFR500.

NIB	Exc.	V.G.	Good	Fair	Poor
1300	775	650	600	500	375

Colt Classic .45 Special Edition

This Lew Horton model is limited to 400 pistols and features a royal blue polish with special "Classic .45" gold etched on the slide. Pearlite grips.

NIB	Exc.	V.G.	Good	Fair	Poor
1300	775	650	600	500	375

125th Anniversary Edition Peacemaker

Introduced in 1998 this model features a V-shaped rear sight with two-line patent date. Barrel is 4.75" and is chambered for .45 Colt cartridge. The cylinder is the second generation type and the hammer is knurled. Frame and hammer are case colored with blue barrel. Grips are two piece walnut with oil finish. Special serial number range SA74000 to SA75999.

NIB	Exc.	V.G.	Good	Fair	Poor
1950	1350	950	600	500	375

Custom Anaconda

Custom-tuned action, Magnaported barrel, with Elliason rear sight. The contoured trigger is polished smooth. Comes with Pachmayr grips and brushed stainless steel finish.

NIB	Exc.	V.G.	Good	Fair	Poor
1950	1275	800	600	300	200

Ultimate Python

Custom tuned action with both Elliason and Accro sighting systems. Both rubber and walnut grips are included. Bright stainless steel or royal blue finish. Available only with 6" barrel.

NIB	Exc.	V.G.	Good	Fair	Poor
1800	1275	800	600	300	200

Python Elite

This model has a hand-tuned .357 Magnum action with a choice of 4" or 6" barrel with adjustable rear sight and red ramp front sight. On the 4" barrel models grips are rubber service, while on the 6" models they are rubber target style. Finish is stainless steel or royal blue. Weight is about 38 oz. with 4" barrel and 43 oz. with 6" barrel.

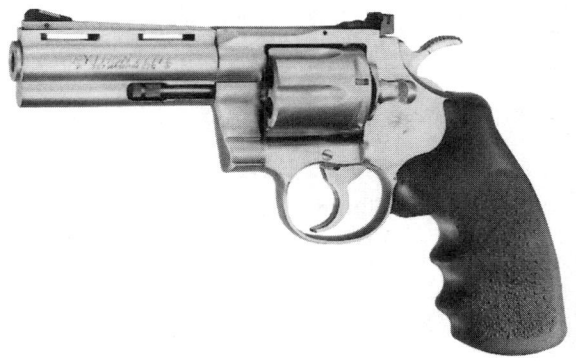

NIB	Exc.	V.G.	Good	Fair	Poor
1900	1300	900	675	400	300

Anaconda Hunter

Comes with a Leupold 2X scope, heavy-duty mounts, cleaning accessories, both walnut and rubber grips, in a hard case. Furnished only with an 8" barrel.

NIB	Exc.	V.G.	Good	Fair	Poor
1800	1275	800	600	300	200

Bobbed Detective Special

First offered in 1994 this model features a bobbed hammer, a front sight with night sight, and honed action. Available in either chrome or blue finish.

NIB	Exc.	V.G.	Good	Fair	Poor
775	600	450	300	150	100

Limited Class .45 ACP

1911 auto. Designed for tactical competition. Supplied with a parkerized matte finish, lightweight composite trigger, extended ambidextrous safety, upswept grip safety, beveled magazine well, accurized, and shipped with a signed target. Introduced in 1993.

NIB	Exc.	V.G.	Good	Fair	Poor
1450	1050	650	450	300	200

Compensated Model .45 ACP

This competition pistol has a hard chrome receiver, bumper on magazine, extended ambidextrous safety, blue slide with full profile BAT compensator, Bomar rear sight, and flared funnel magazine well. Introduced in 1993.

NIB	Exc.	V.G.	Good	Fair	Poor
1450	1050	650	450	300	200

Compensated .45 ACP Commander

Introduced in 1998 and limited to 500 pistols. This model is fitted with a full-length guide rod, extended beavertail safety, skeletonized hammer, Novak-style sights, and checkered walnut double-diamond grips.

NIB	Exc.	V.G.	Good	Fair	Poor
1350	975	575	400	300	200

Nite Lite .380

Supplied with a bar-dot night sight, special foil mark on barrel slide, Teflon-coated alloy receiver, stainless slide, high-capacity grip-extension magazine, and a standard magazine. Shipped with a soft carrying case. Introduced in 1993.

NIB	Exc.	V.G.	Good	Fair	Poor
1350	975	575	400	300	200

Standard Tactical Model

Built for 20th Anniversary of IPSC competition shooting in 1996. Built on the Colt Government model with round top slide and chamber for .45 ACP. Many special features special serial numbers. Limited to 1,500 pistols.

NIB	Exc.	V.G.	Good	Fair	Poor
1450	875	600	450	300	200

Superior Tactical Model

Same as above but built on an enhanced frame with many custom features. Special serial numbers limited to 500 pistols.

NIB	Exc.	V.G.	Good	Fair	Poor
1550	975	700	550	400	200

Deluxe Tactical Model

Same as above but with added features. Limited to 250 pistols.

NIB	Exc.	V.G.	Good	Fair	Poor
1650	1075	800	650	500	300

COLT REPRODUCTION PERCUSSION REVOLVERS

NOTE: The revolvers listed were manufactured in a variety of styles (cylinder form, stainless steel, etc.) that affect prices. Factory engraved examples command a considerable premium over the prices listed. Imported from Italy.

Walker

Made from 1979 to 1981; serial numbers 1200-4120 and 32256 to 32500.

NIB	Exc.	V.G.	Good	Fair	Poor
950	750	500	—	—	—

Walker Heritage Model

NIB	Exc.	V.G.	Good	Fair	Poor
1000	—	—	—	—	—

First Model Dragoon

Made from 1980 to 1982; serial numbers 24100-34500.

NIB	Exc.	V.G.	Good	Fair	Poor
595	400	300	—	—	—

Second Model Dragoon

Made from 1980 to 1982; serial numbers as above.

NIB	Exc.	V.G.	Good	Fair	Poor
595	400	300	—	—	—

Third Model Dragoon

Made from 1980 to 1982; serial numbers as above.

NIB	Exc.	V.G.	Good	Fair	Poor
595	400	300	—	—	—

Model 1848 Pocket Pistol

Made in 1981; serial numbers 16000-17851.

NIB	Exc.	V.G.	Good	Fair	Poor
600	425	325	—	—	—

Model 1851 Navy Revolver

Made from 1971 to 1978; serial numbers 4201-25100 and 24900-29150.

NIB	Exc.	V.G.	Good	Fair	Poor
595	400	300	—	—	—

Model 1860 Army Revolver

Made from 1978 to 1982; serial numbers 201000-212835.

NIB	Exc.	V.G.	Good	Fair	Poor
595	400	300	—	—	—

Model 1861 Navy Revolver

Made during 1980 and 1981; serial numbers 40000-43165.

NIB	Exc.	V.G.	Good	Fair	Poor
595	400	300	—	—	—

Model 1862 Pocket Pistol

Made from 1979 to 1984; serial numbers 8000-58850.

NIB	Exc.	V.G.	Good	Fair	Poor
595	400	300	—	—	—

Model 1862 Police Revolver

Made from 1979 to 1984; serial numbers in above range.

NIB	Exc.	V.G.	Good	Fair	Poor
595	400	300	—	—	—

COLT BLACKPOWDER ARMS
Brooklyn, New York

These blackpowder revolvers and rifles were made under license from Colt. Imported from Italy. No longer in business.

1842 Paterson Colt No. 5 Holster Model

This model is a copy of the No. 5 Holster model and is chambered for the .36 caliber ball. Fitted with a 7.5" octagon barrel. Hand engraved. This is a special order revolver.

NIB	Exc.	V.G.	Good	Fair	Poor
1900	1200	900	600	450	200

Walker

This .44 caliber large-frame revolver is fitted with a 9" barrel.

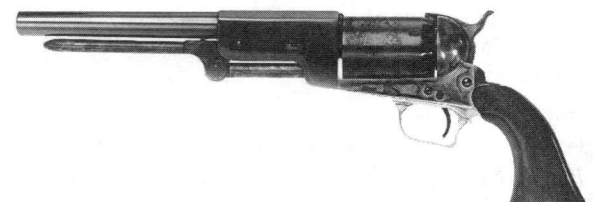

NIB	Exc.	V.G.	Good	Fair	Poor
975	600	350	300	200	150

Walker 150th Anniversary Model

Marked "A Company No. 1" in gold. Introduced 1997.

NIB	Exc.	V.G.	Good	Fair	Poor
975	600	350	300	200	150

Whitneyville Hartford Dragoon

Similar in appearance to the Walker colt this revolver is fitted with a 7-1/2" barrel and a silver plated iron backstrap and trigger guard. This is a limited edition with a total of 2,400 guns built with serial numbers between 1100 through 1340.

NIB	Exc.	V.G.	Good	Fair	Poor
1075	700	450	32	225	200

Marine Dragoon

Special limited edition presentation grade in honor of U.S. Marine Corps.

NIB	Exc.	V.G.	Good	Fair	Poor
1100	725	450	32	225	200

3rd Model Dragoon

Another large-frame revolver with 7-1/2" barrel with a brass backstrap, 3-screw frame, and unfluted cylinder.

NIB	Exc.	V.G.	Good	Fair	Poor
675	500	350	300	200	150

3rd Model Dragoon Steel Backstrap

NIB	Exc.	V.G.	Good	Fair	Poor
600	425	375	325	200	150

3rd Model Dragoon Fluted Cylinder

NIB	Exc.	V.G.	Good	Fair	Poor
610	435	375	325	200	150

Cochise Dragoon

This is a commemorative issue Third Model with gold inlay frame and barrel with special grips.

NIB	Exc.	V.G.	Good	Fair	Poor
975	600	350	300	200	150

Colt 1849 Model Pocket

A small-frame revolver chambered in .31 caliber with a 4" barrel. Fitted with one-piece walnut grips.

NIB	Exc.	V.G.	Good	Fair	Poor
575	475	325	275	200	150

Colt 1851 Model Navy

This is medium-frame revolver chambered in .36 caliber with 7-1/2" barrel. Walnut grips and case color frame.

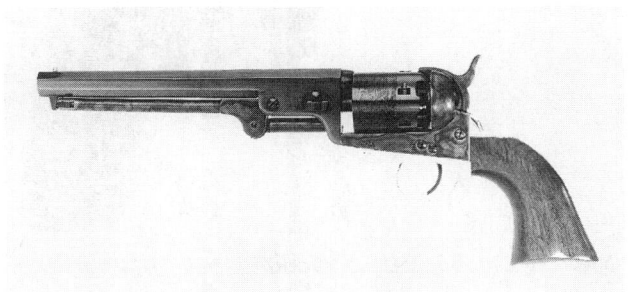

NIB	Exc.	V.G.	Good	Fair	Poor
635	575	400	300	200	125

Colt 1851 Model Navy Dual Cylinder

NIB	Exc.	V.G.	Good	Fair	Poor
675	595	400	300	200	125

Colt Model 1860 Army

This model is chamber in .44 caliber with roll engraved cylinder and one piece walnut grips. Barrel length is 8".

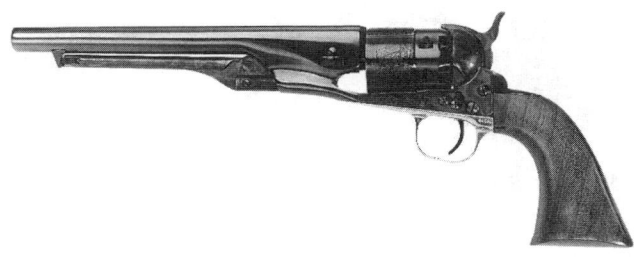

NIB	Exc.	V.G.	Good	Fair	Poor
675	575	400	300	200	125

Colt Model 1860 Army Dual Cylinder

NIB	Exc.	V.G.	Good	Fair	Poor
700	600	450	350	225	150

Colt Model 1860 Army Fluted Cylinder

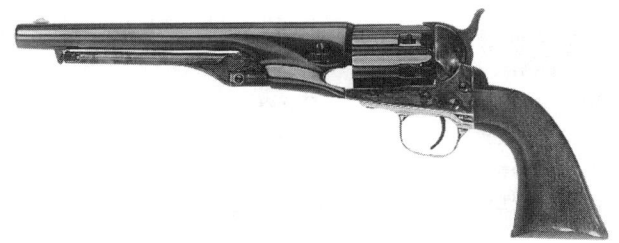

NIB	Exc.	V.G.	Good	Fair	Poor
675	575	400	300	200	125

Colt 1860 Officer's Model

This is a deluxe version of the standard 1860 with a special blued finish and gold crossed sabres. This is a 4-screw frame with 8" barrel and 6-shot rebated cylinder.

NIB	Exc.	V.G.	Good	Fair	Poor
675	575	450	375	250	150

Colt Model 1860 Army Gold U.S. Cavalry

Features a gold engraved cylinder and gold barrel bands.

NIB	Exc.	V.G.	Good	Fair	Poor
650	575	450	375	250	150

Colt Model 1860 Army Gold U.S. Cavalry Stainless Steel

NIB	Exc.	V.G.	Good	Fair	Poor
575	400	350	300	200	150

Colt 1860 Heirloom Edition

This is an elaborately engraved revolver done in the Tiffany-style and fitted with Tiffany-style grips.

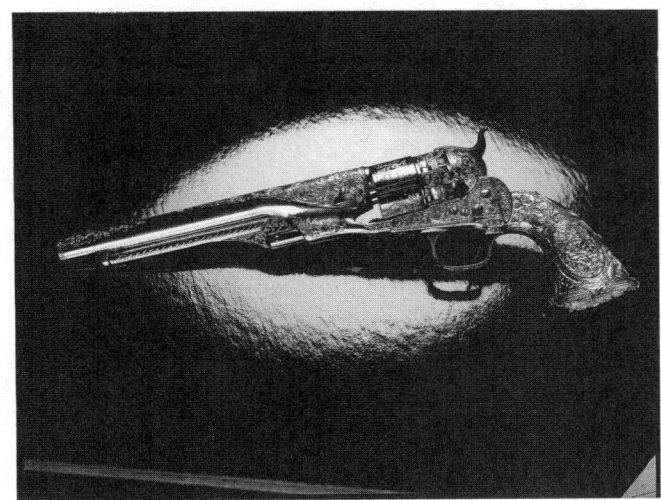

NIB	Exc.	V.G.	Good	Fair	Poor
4100	3000	2175	1400	850	450

Colt Model 1861 Navy

This .36 caliber revolver features a 7-1/2" barrel with engraved cylinder, case colored frame and one piece walnut grips.

NIB	Exc.	V.G.	Good	Fair	Poor
700	550	350	300	200	150

Colt Model 1861 Navy General Custer

Same as above but with engraved frame and cylinder.

NIB	Exc.	V.G.	Good	Fair	Poor
975	850	700	500	300	200

Colt Model 1862 Pocket Navy

This small-frame revolver is fitted with a round engraved cylinder with a 5" octagon barrel with hinged loading lever. Chambered for .36 caliber.

NIB	Exc.	V.G.	Good	Fair	Poor
550	475	325	275	200	150

Colt Model 1862 Trapper-Pocket Police

This small-frame revolver is fitted with a 3-1/2" barrel, silver backstrap, and trigger guard. The cylinder is semi-fluted and chambered in .36 caliber.

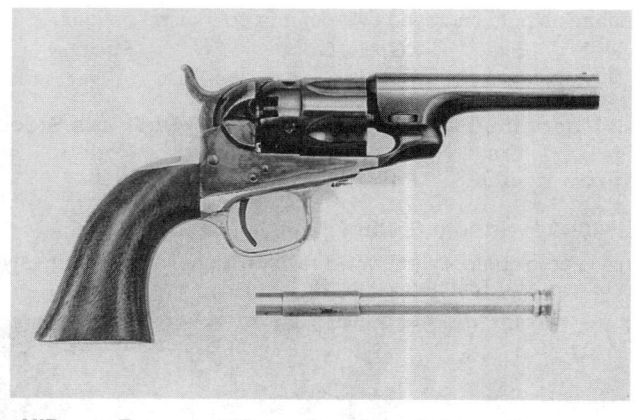

NIB	Exc.	V.G.	Good	Fair	Poor
600	475	325	275	200	150

COLUMBIA ARMORY
Columbia, Tennessee

A trade name applied to a variety of solid frame cartridge revolvers made by John T. Smith Company of Rock Falls, Connecticut. They were marked "SAFETY HAMMERLESS REVOLVER." This model was made under several trade names.

NIB	Exc.	V.G.	Good	Fair	Poor
—	—	225	110	75	50

COLUMBUS F. A. MFG. CO.
Columbus, Georgia

Columbus Revolver

A .36-caliber double-action percussion revolver with a 6-shot, unfluted cylinder and a 7.5" octagonal barrel. Similar in appearance to the 1851 Colt Navy. The pistol is browned steel, with brass gripstraps and walnut grips. The barrel is marked "Columbus Fire Arms Manuf. Co/Columbus Ga." 100 revolvers were manufactured in 1863 and 1864.

NIB	Exc.	V.G.	Good	Fair	Poor
—	—	115000	55000	35000	12500

COMANCHE (also see FIRESTORM)
Buenos Aires, Argentina

Comanche I

Single-/double-action revolver chambered in .22 LR. Nine-shot cylinder, 6" barrel, adjustable sights, blued or stainless steel construction with rubber grips.

NIB	Exc.	V.G.	Good	Fair	Poor
225	150	100	65	35	15

Comanche II

Similar to above but in .38 Special with 2", 3" or 4" barrel.

NIB	Exc.	V.G.	Good	Fair	Poor
225	150	100	65	35	15

Comanche III

Similar to above but in .357 Magnum and additional 6" barrel option.

NIB	Exc.	V.G.	Good	Fair	Poor
250	150	100	65	35	15

Super Comanche

Single-shot break-action pistol chambered in .410/.45 Colt. Matte black finish, rubber grips.

NIB	Exc.	V.G.	Good	Fair	Poor
195	150	125	85	50	25

COMPETITOR CORP.
New Ipswich, New Hampshire

Competitor Single-Shot

This single-shot pistol is chambered for calibers from .22 LR to .50 Action Express. Choice of barrels lengths from 10.5", 14", and 16". Ramp front sight. Adjustable single stage trigger. Interchangeable barrels. Matte blue finish. Weight is approximately 59 oz. depending on barrel length. Introduced in 1988.

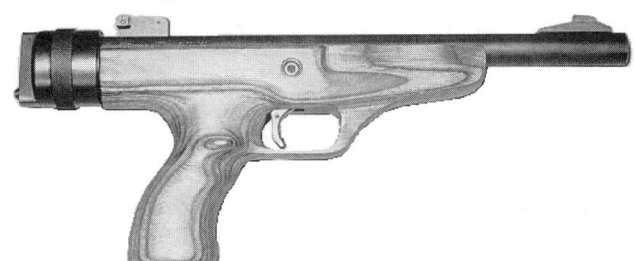

NIB	Exc.	V.G.	Good	Fair	Poor
465	325	275	225	175	125

CONNECTICUT ARMS CO.
Norfolk, Connecticut

Pocket Revolver

A .28 caliber spur trigger revolver with 3" octagonal barrel, 6-shot unfluted cylinder, using a cup-primed cartridge and loads from the front of the cylinder. There is a hinged hook on the side of the frame under the cylinder that acts as the extractor. Silver-plated brass, blued with walnut grips. The barrel is marked "Conn. Arms Co. Norfolk, Conn." Approximately 2,700 manufactured in the 1860s.

NIB	Exc.	V.G.	Good	Fair	Poor
—	—	950	750	300	100

CONNECTICUT VALLEY ARMS CO.
Norcross, Georgia

Siber

A .45 caliber percussion pistol patterned after the Swiss Siber.

NIB	Exc.	V.G.	Good	Fair	Poor
450	325	275	225	150	100

Kentucky

A .45 caliber single-shot percussion pistol with a 10" barrel and walnut stock.

NIB	Exc.	V.G.	Good	Fair	Poor
140	125	100	80	60	40

Philadelphia Derringer

A .45 caliber single-shot percussion pistol with a 3.25" barrel and walnut stock.

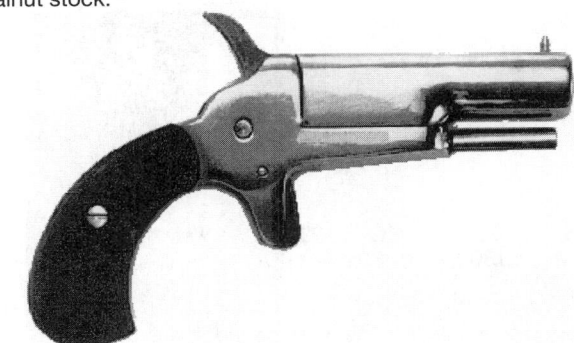

NIB	Exc.	V.G.	Good	Fair	Poor
125	95	50	40	30	20

Sheriff's Model

A .36 caliber percussion revolver, nickel-plated with walnut grips.

NIB	Exc.	V.G.	Good	Fair	Poor
225	200	175	150	125	100

3rd Model Dragoon

NIB	Exc.	V.G.	Good	Fair	Poor
225	200	175	150	125	100

Colt Walker Replica

NIB	Exc.	V.G.	Good	Fair	Poor
425	295	225	200	175	150

Remington Bison

NIB	Exc.	V.G.	Good	Fair	Poor
250	225	200	175	150	125

Pocket Police

NIB	Exc.	V.G.	Good	Fair	Poor
135	110	100	85	65	45

Pocket Revolver

Chambered for .31 caliber. Fitted with 4" octagon barrel. Cylinder holds five bullets. Solid brass frame. Weighs about 15 oz.

NIB	Exc.	V.G.	Good	Fair	Poor
225	150	85	75	60	50

Wells Fargo

NIB	Exc.	V.G.	Good	Fair	Poor
225	150	85	75	60	50

1851 Navy

NIB	Exc.	V.G.	Good	Fair	Poor
250	225	200	175	150	125

1861 Navy

NIB	Exc.	V.G.	Good	Fair	Poor
250	225	200	175	150	125

1860 Army

NIB	Exc.	V.G.	Good	Fair	Poor
250	225	200	175	150	125

1858 Remington

NIB	Exc.	V.G.	Good	Fair	Poor
275	225	125	100	75	50

1858 Remington Target

As above, but fitted with adjustable sights.

NIB	Exc.	V.G.	Good	Fair	Poor
275	225	125	100	75	50

Bison

A 6-shot .44 caliber revolver with 10-1/4" octagonal barrel. Solid brass frame. Weighs about 48 oz.

NIB	Exc.	V.G.	Good	Fair	Poor
275	225	125	100	75	50

Hawken Pistol

This is a .50 caliber percussion pistol with 9-3/4" octagon barrel. The stock is hardwood. Weighs about 50 oz.

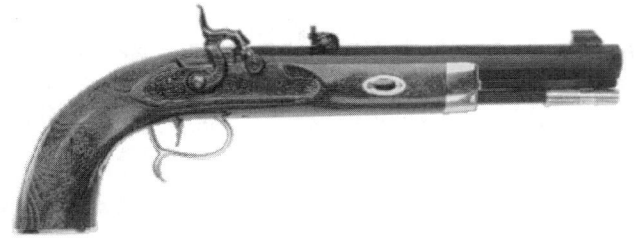

NIB	Exc.	V.G.	Good	Fair	Poor
250	180	115	75	65	50

CONSTABLE, R.
Philadelphia, Pennsylvania

Pocket Pistol

A single-shot percussion pistol with a 3" round or octagonal barrel. German-silver mounts and walnut stock. These pistols are marked "R. Constable Philadelphia" and were manufactured during the late 1840s and 1850s.

NIB	Exc.	V.G.	Good	Fair	Poor
—	—	2200	1100	550	200

CONTINENTAL
RWM
Cologne, Germany

Pocket Pistol (6.35mm)

A 6.35mm caliber semi-automatic pistol with a 2" barrel, internal hammer, and a 7-shot detachable magazine. Blued with plastic grips, and the slide is marked "Continental Kal. 6.35." Produced during the 1920s.NOTE: This pistol may have been manufactured in Spain and carried German proof marks, because it was sold by RWM in Germany.

NIB	Exc.	V.G.	Good	Fair	Poor
—	300	150	125	100	75

Pocket Pistol (7.65mm)

This is a German-made pistol chambered for the 7.65mm cartridhe. It is fitted with a 3.9" barrel. Rear sight is a U-notch in the slide. Magazine capacity is 8 rounds. Weight is about 20 oz. Made prior to 1914.

NIB	Exc.	V.G.	Good	Fair	Poor
—	500	300	225	150	100

CONTINENTAL ARMS CO.
Norwich, Connecticut

Pepperbox

A .22 caliber 5-barrel pepperbox with a spur trigger and 2.5" barrels marked "Continental Arms Co. Norwich Ct. Patented Aug. 28, 1866." Some examples of this pistol are to be found marked "Ladies Companion."

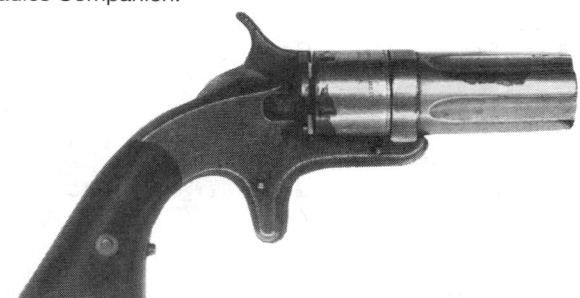

Courtesy Milwaukee Public Museum, Milwaukee, Wisconsin

NIB	Exc.	V.G.	Good	Fair	Poor
—	—	2250	1000	350	250

COONAN ARMS CO.
Maplewood, Minnesota

Model A

A .357 Magnum semi-automatic pistol with a 5" barrel, a 7-shot, detachable magazine, and fixed sights. Stainless steel with walnut grips. Introduced in 1981 and discontinued in 1984.

NIB	Exc.	V.G.	Good	Fair	Poor
1500	1150	875	500	350	275

Model B

An improved version of the above with a linkless barrel system, extended grip safety, enclosed trigger bar, and a more contoured grip. A 6" barrel is available, as are adjustable sights, as extra cost options. A .38 Special conversion is also available. Introduced in 1985. A number of other options are also available that will affect value.

NIB	Exc.	V.G.	Good	Fair	Poor
1550	1175	925	675	500	300

NOTE: For 6" barrel add $40, Bomar adjustable sights add $130, .38 Special Conversion add $40, checkered walnut grips add $40, with Teflon slide add $100, with Teflon frame add $100.

Comp I

As above, with 6" barrel and attached compensator and a stippled front grip strap. Introduced in 1989.

NIB	Exc.	V.G.	Good	Fair	Poor
1600	1250	1000	700	550	350

NOTE: For 6" barrel add $40; Bomar adjustable sights add $130; .38 Special conversion add $40; checkered walnut grips add $40; with Teflon slide add $100; with Teflon frame add $100.

Comp I Deluxe

As above, with a blued stainless steel slide, checkered grip straps, and a finer finishing.

NIB	Exc.	V.G.	Good	Fair	Poor
1650	1300	1050	750	600	400

Classic

This model features an integrated compensator with 5" barrel. Pistol is supplied with checkered walnut grips, Millett adjustable rear sight, and two-tone Teflon finish. Magazine capacity is 7 rounds, weight is 42 oz., and overall length is 8.3".

NIB	Exc.	V.G.	Good	Fair	Poor
1700	1300	1050	600	—	—

Cadet

Chambered for the .357 magnum cartridge this model has a 3.9" barrel with smooth walnut grips, and fixed rear sight. Magazine capacity is 6 rounds; weight is about 39 oz., and overall length is

7.8". Height of the pistol is 5.3". Coonan Arms refers to this model as the "Short Grip."

NIB	Exc.	V.G.	Good	Fair	Poor
1150	875	675	500	400	400

NOTE: For 6" barrel add $40, Bomar adjustable sights add $130, .38 Special Conversion add $40, checkered walnut grips add $40, with Teflon slide add $100, with Teflon frame add $100.

Cadet II

Same as above but with a standard grip. Magazine capacity of this model is 7 rounds.

NIB	Exc.	V.G.	Good	Fair	Poor
1150	875	675	500	400	200

NOTE: For 6" barrel add $40; Bomar adjustable sights add $130; .38 Special conversion add $40; checkered walnut grips add $40; with Teflon slide add $100; with Teflon frame add $100.

.41 Magnum Model

Introduced in 1997 this model is chambered for the .41 Magnum cartridge and fitted with a 5" barrel with smooth walnut grips and fixed sights.

NIB	Exc.	V.G.	Good	Fair	Poor
1700	1250	975	800	550	350

NOTE: For 6" barrel add $40; Bomar adjustable sights add $130; .38 Special conversion add $40; checkered walnut grips add $40; with Teflon slide add $100; with Teflon frame add $100.

COOPER, J. M. & CO.
Philadelphia, Pennsylvania

Pocket Revolver

A .31 caliber percussion double-action revolver with 4", 5", or 6" octagonal barrel, and a 6-shot unfluted cylinder. Blued with walnut grips. During the first two years of production they were made in Pittsburgh, Pennsylvania, and were so marked. Approximately 15,000 were manufactured between 1864 and 1869.

Courtesy Milwaukee Public Museum, Milwaukee, Wisconsin

NIB	Exc.	V.G.	Good	Fair	Poor
—	—	1850	775	200	100

NOTE: Pittsburgh-marked models add 20 percent.

COOPERATIVA OBRERA
Eibar, Spain

Longines

A 7.65mm caliber semi-automatic pistol. The slide is marked "Cal. 7.65 Automatic Pistol Longines."

NIB	Exc.	V.G.	Good	Fair	Poor
—	275	175	150	110	85

COPELAND, FRANK
Worcester, Massachusetts

Pocket Revolver .22

A .22 cartridge spur trigger revolver with a 2.5" barrel, 7-shot magazine, an unfluted cylinder and lock notches on the front. Frame is brass, blued walnut, or rosewood grips. The barrel marked "F. Copeland, Worcester, Mass." Manufactured in the 1860s.

NIB	Exc.	V.G.	Good	Fair	Poor
—	—	700	300	125	100

.32 Revolver

A .32 caliber spur trigger revolver with a 5-shot fluted cylinder and an iron frame. Nickel-plated. The barrel marked "F. Copeland, Sterling, Mass." Manufactured in the 1860s.

NIB	Exc.	V.G.	Good	Fair	Poor
—	—	700	300	150	75

COWLES & SON
Chicopee, Massachusetts

Single-Shot

A .22 or .30 caliber single-shot spur trigger pistol with a 3.25" round barrel. Silver-plated brass frame, blued with walnut grip. Approximately 200 manufactured in 1865.

Courtesy Richard M. Kumor Sr.

NIB	Exc.	V.G.	Good	Fair	Poor
—	—	1500	775	250	100

CRESCENT F. A. CO.
Norwich, Connecticut
Revolver

A typical S&W copy made by Crescent in Norwich, Connecticut. It was a top-break, double-action, that was found either blued or nickel-plated with checkered, black hard rubber grips. The cylinder held 5 shots and was chambered for the .32 S&W cartridge.

NIB	Exc.	V.G.	Good	Fair	Poor
—	250	150	125	85	40

CRISPIN, SILAS
New York, New York
Revolver

A .32 Crispin caliber 5- or 6-shot revolver produced in limited quantities. Some are marked "Smith Arms Co., New York City. Crispin's Pat. Oct. 3, 1865." The most noteworthy feature of these revolvers is that the cylinder is constructed in two pieces so that the belted Crispin cartridge can be used. It is believed that these revolvers were only made on an experimental basis, between 1865 and 1867.

NIB	Exc.	V.G.	Good	Fair	Poor
—	—	19000	7500	2500	1000

CRUCELEGUI, HERMANOS
Eibar, Spain

A 5mm, 6.35mm, 7.65mm, and 8mm caliber double-action revolver. The trade names used were; Puppy, Velo-Mith, Le-Brong, Bron-Sport, C.H., and Brong-Petit.

NIB	Exc.	V.G.	Good	Fair	Poor
—	250	150	80	60	35

CUMMINGS & WHEELER
Lowell, Massachusetts
Pocket Revolver

Similar to the Cummings Pocket Revolver with subtle differences such as the length of the flutes on the cylinder and the size and shape of the grip. The barrel is slightly longer and is marked "Cummings & Wheeler, Lowell, Mass."

NIB	Exc.	V.G.	Good	Fair	Poor
—	—	750	350	150	100

CUMMINGS, O. S.
Lowell, Massachusetts
Pocket Revolver

A .22 caliber spur trigger revolver with a 3.5" ribbed round barrel, and a 7-shot fluted cylinder. Nickel-plated with rosewood grip. The barrel is stamped "O.S. Cummings Lowell, Mass." Approximately 1,000 manufactured in the 1870s.

NIB	Exc.	V.G.	Good	Fair	Poor
—	—	675	300	150	100

CZ
(Ceska Zbrojovka)
Uhersky Brod, Czech Republic

Established by Karel Bubla and Alois Tomiska in 1919. This company later merged with Hubertus Engineering Company. In 1949 the company was nationalized. CZ regularly exports 90 percent of its production to over 80 countries.

NOTE: As of 1998, CZ firearms have been imported exclusively by CZ-USA, a wholly-owned distribution subsidiary of Ceska Zbrojovka a.s. Uhersky Brod, (CZUB) of the Czech Republic.

Fox

A 6.35mm caliber semi-automatic pistol with a 2-1/8" barrel, tubular slide, a folding trigger and no trigger guard. Fox and CZ are inscribed on the slide. The CZ logo is on each grip plate. Blued with plastic grips. Manufactured between 1919 and 1936.

Courtesy James Rankin

NIB	Exc.	V.G.	Good	Fair	Poor
—	900	750	600	400	200

CZ 1921 Praga

A semi-automatic pistol in 7.65mm caliber. The first service pistol manufactured in Czechoslovakia. Production began in 1920. Praga is stamped on the slide and on each grip plate for commercial models. The service models were fitted with wood grips.

Courtesy James Rankin

NIB	Exc.	V.G.	Good	Fair	Poor
—	650	550	475	350	200

Army Pistol 1922 (Nickl-Pistole)

Designed by Josef Nickl of Mauser. First approved by the Army in 1921, this pistol was chambered for the .380 ACP (9mmKurtz/9x17mm) cartridge. Plagued by design problems, it was produced only in 1922 and 1923. Fewer than 22,000 were built.

NIB	Exc.	V.G.	Good	Fair	Poor
—	650	500	350	200	150

CZ 1922

A semi-automatic pistol in caliber 6.35mm. Very similar to the Fox above. It has no sights but is fitted with a conventional trigger guard. CZ is stamped on the slide and the CZ logo on each grip plate. Grips are plastic or wood. Manufactured between 1922 and 1936.

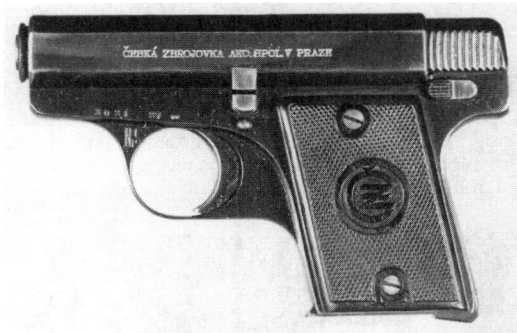

Courtesy James Rankin

NIB	Exc.	V.G.	Good	Fair	Poor
—	550	450	350	300	200

CZ 1924

The first large-production military pistol produced by CZ. Chambered for the 9mmK cartridge. It is the first of the CZ models with wraparound grips of both wood and plastic. CZ logo is seen on plastic grips. A lanyard loop is attached to the base of the butt. Manufactured from 1925 to 1932.

Courtesy James Rankin

NIB	Exc.	V.G.	Good	Fair	Poor
—	650	500	400	300	200

CZ 1927

A semi-automatic pistol chambered for the 7.65mm cartridge, marked the same as the CZ 1924, but the cocking grooves on the slide are cut vertically instead of sloped as on the earlier model. This model was blued with checkered, wrap-around, plastic grips. These early guns were beautifully made and marked, "Ceska Zbrojovka AS v Praze." After the war, these pistols continued in production until 1951. There were more than 500,000 manufactured. **NOTE:** Some of these pistols were made with an extended barrel for the use of a silencer. This variation brings a large premium. Fewer than 10 CZ27s were made in .22 caliber. An expert opinion is suggested if a sale is contemplated.

NIB	Exc.	V.G.	Good	Fair	Poor
—	650	475	300	200	165

NOTE: Nazi-proofed add 50 percent.

CZ 1936

A 6.35mm caliber semi-automatic pistol with 2.5" barrel, and double-action-only lockwork. It has plastic wraparound grips with the CZ logo on each side. It replaced the Model 1922 in 1936. Discontinued in 1940 because of wartime production.

Courtesy James Rankin

NIB	Exc.	V.G.	Good	Fair	Poor
—	450	350	300	200	100

CZ 1938

A semi-automatic double-action pistol in caliber 9mmK. Manufactured for the Czechoslovakian military from 1938 to 1940. Barrel length is 4.7". Weight is about 32 oz. Magazine capacity is 8 rounds. Wraparound plastic grips with the CZ logo on each side.

Courtesy James Rankin

NIB	Exc.	V.G.	Good	Fair	Poor
—	550	500	400	300	200

CZ 1945

This model is a small .25 caliber (6.35mm) pocket pistol that is double-action-only. It was produced and sold after World War II. It is a modified version of the CZ 1936. Approximately 60,000 were built between 1945 and 1949.

Courtesy James Rankin

NIB	Exc.	V.G.	Good	Fair	Poor
—	350	300	250	175	125

CZ 1950

This is a blowback-operated, semi-automatic, double-action pistol chambered for the 7.65mm cartridge. It is patterned after the Walther Model PP with a few differences. The safety catch is located on the frame instead of the slide; and the trigger guard is not hinged, as on the Walther. It is dismantled by means of a catch on the side of the frame. Although intended to be a military pistol designed by the Kratochvil brothers, it proved to be underpowered and was adopted by the police. There were few released on the commercial market.

Courtesy James Rankin

NIB	Exc.	V.G.	Good	Fair	Poor
—	250	150	125	100	50

CZ 1952

This Czech army sidearm is a semi-automatic pistol chambered for the 7.62mm cartridge and fitted with a 4.7" barrel. It has a very complex locking system using two rollers inside the frame. Magazine capacity is 8 rounds. Weight is about 34 oz. Production ended in 1956.

NIB	Exc.	V.G.	Good	Fair	Poor
—	300	275	225	125	75

CURRENTLY IMPORTED PISTOLS

All currently imported CZ pistols can be ordered with tritium night sights with the exception of models CZ 97B and CZ 100. Add $80 for this option.

NOTE: Substantial premium for factory-engraved examples.

CZ 75

Designed by the Koucky brothers in 1975, this model bears little resemblance to previous CZ pistols. Considered by many, including the late Jeff Cooper, to be the best pistol ever to come from the Czech Republic and one of the finest semi-autos in the world. Chambered for the 9mm Parabellum cartridge it is copied in many countries. This pistol has a breechlock system utilizing a Browning-style cam. The slide rides on the inside of the slide rails. Magazine capacity is 15 rounds, barrel length is 4.72", overall length is 8", and the empty pistol weighs 34.5 oz. Offered in black paint, matte or polished blue finish.

NIB	Exc.	V.G.	Good	Fair	Poor
500	450	425	400	325	250

CZ 75 30th Anniversary

Introduced in 2005 this model features special 30th anniversary engraving, gold inlays, gold plated controls, high gloss blue finish, engraved blonde finished birch grips. Magazine capacity is 15 rounds. Limited to 1,000 pistols.

NIB	Exc.	V.G.	Good	Fair	Poor
850	675	500	400	300	200

CZ 75 B

Introduced in 1994 this CZ model is an updated version of the original CZ 75. It features a pinned front sight, a commander hammer, non-glare ribbed barrel, and a squared trigger guard. Also offered in .40 S&W chamber.

NIB	Exc.	V.G.	Good	Fair	Poor
510	400	300	250	175	125

NOTE: For .40 S&W add $30. For glossy blue add $20, for dual tone finish $25, and for nickel add $25. For tritium night sights add $80.

CZ 75 Compact

Introduced in 1992, this is a compact version of the CZ 75. The barrel length is 3.9", the overall length is 7.3", and the weight is about 32 oz. Offered in black paint, matte or polished blue finish. Traditional single-action double-action.

NIB	Exc.	V.G.	Good	Fair	Poor
475	425	300	250	175	125

NOTE: For .40 S&W add $30. For glossy blue add $20, for dual tone finish $25, and for nickel add $25. For tritium night sights add $80.NOTE: In 2005 this model was offered with accessory rail and ambidextrous manual safety. Add $50 to above prices.

CZ 75 Compact D

Essentially the same as the CZ 75 Compact but with a decocking double-action system and lightweight alloy frame. Weight approximately 25 oz.

NIB	Exc.	V.G.	Good	Fair	Poor
555	450	300	225	150	100

NOTE: Only 20 of these pistols were imported into the U.S. No longer in production. Expert appraisal suggested prior to sale.

CZ 75 B Tactical

Chambered for the 9mm Luger cartridge and fitted with a 4.7" barrel. This pistol has a single-action/double-action trigger. Fixed sights. Rubber grips. Slide is black polycoat and the frame is a military green finish. Weight is about 35 oz. Add 10 percent for night sights.

NIB	Exc.	V.G.	Good	Fair	Poor
475	400	325	250	175	125

CZ 75 BD

Has all the same features as the Model 75 B but with the addition of a decocking double-action. Black polycoat finish.

NIB	Exc.	V.G.	Good	Fair	Poor
450	400	300	225	150	100

CZ BD Compact

Introduced in 2001 this model features a 3.9" barrel with decocking lever. Chambered for the .40 S&W cartridge. Blued finish. Magazine capacity is 10 rounds. Weight is about 32 oz. All other features same as CZ 75 B Compact.

NIB	Exc.	V.G.	Good	Fair	Poor
400	350	300	225	150	100

CZ BD Compact Carry

Same as the model above but with rounded edges including trigger guard.

NIB	Exc.	V.G.	Good	Fair	Poor
425	375	300	225	150	100

CZ 75 B SA

This model was introduced in 2000 and features a single-action trigger designed for competitive shooting that can be carried in condition one. Fitted with a straight trigger, manual safety, and chambered for the 9mm cartridge. Weight is about 35 oz.

NIB	Exc.	V.G.	Good	Fair	Poor
520	400	325	225	150	100

CZ 75 Semi-Compact

This model was introduced in 1994 and has the same barrel length as the Compact (3.9") but has the same full-size grip as the CZ 75. Magazine capacity is 15 rounds of 9mm. Overall length is 7.3".

NIB	Exc.	V.G.	Good	Fair	Poor
495	350	300	250	175	100

CZ 75 D PCR Compact

Introduced in 2000 this pistol is chambered for the 9mm cartridge and features a light alloy frame and 3.9" barrel. Trigger is both single and double-action with decocking lever. Low profile sights. Serrated front and rear backstrap. Designed for the Czech national police force. Magazine capacity is 10 rounds. Weight is about 27 oz.

NIB	Exc.	V.G.	Good	Fair	Poor
525	425	350	225	150	100

CZ 75 Champion

This model is chambered for the .40 S&W, 9mm, and 9x21 cartridges. Single-action-only trigger with straight trigger. Fitted with a 4.5" barrel with low profile adjustable sights and three port compensator. Furnished with blue slide and nickel frame. Hand fitted. Weight is about 36 oz.

NIB	Exc.	V.G.	Good	Fair	Poor
1475	1150	975	675	500	300

CZ 75 DAO

This model is similar to the CZ 75 but with a double-action-only trigger, no safety lever and a spurless hammer. Offered in 9mm and .40 S&W. Barrel length is 4.7". Weight is about 35 oz. Introduced in 2000.

NIB	Exc.	V.G.	Good	Fair	Poor
695	525	450	350	250	175

CZ P-01

Introduced in 2002 this pistol replaced the CZ 75 with the Czech National Police. It features a forged aluminum alloy frame and 3.8" barrel. Decocker single-action/double-action. Fixed sights. Fitted with M3 accessory rail. Rubber grips. Ten-round magazine. Black polycoat finish. Weight is about 29 oz.

NIB	Exc.	V.G.	Good	Fair	Poor
600	525	450	350	250	175

CZ 75 Standard IPSC (ST)

Designed and built for IPSC competition. Chambered for .40 S&W and fitted with a 5.4" barrel. Single-action-only trigger. Special high-profile sights. Weight is about 45 oz.

NIB	Exc.	V.G.	Good	Fair	Poor
1000	850	775	625	500	300

CZ 75 M IPSC

Similar to the CZ 75 Standard IPSC with the addition of a two-port compensator with blast shield to protect frame-mounted optics. Slide racker standard. Red Dot optics. Barrel length is 3.9". Weight is about 45 oz. Introduced in 2001.

NIB	Exc.	V.G.	Good	Fair	Poor
1350	1200	1050	675	550	325

CZ 75 Silver Anniversary Model

This model commemorates the 25th anniversary of the CZ Model 75 pistol. It features a high polish nickel finish with walnut grips. The number "25" is inlaid in the grips. A total of 1000 pistols will be produced with about 500 allocated for the U.S. market.

NIB	Exc.	V.G.	Good	Fair	Poor
850	700	600	500	400	225

CZ 75 Stainless

All steel construction, double-stack magazines, 3-dot fixed sights and chambered for 9mm. 16+1 or 10+1 capacity with 4.72" barrel. The first stainless from CZ. Introduced 2006.

NIB	Exc.	V.G.	Good	Fair	Poor
675	550	425	350	275	150

CZ 75 SP-01 Shadow

Chambered 9mm for IPSC "Production" Division competition. 19+1 capacity, 4.72" barrel. 41 oz., wood grip. Introduced 2006.

NIB	Exc.	V.G.	Good	Fair	Poor
650	600	500	400	300	175

CZ 75 SP-01 Shadow Custom

Chambered in 9mm Parabellum. Steel slide and frame, CZ Custom Shop trigger job. Cold hammer-forged barrel, fiber-optic front sight, aluminum grips and 19-round magazine. Weight 36 ounces, 4.7-inch barrel and dual-tone finish. Customized for IPSC Production division. Introduced in 2011.

NIB	Exc.	V.G.	Good	Fair	Poor
1000	900	750	650	450	300

CZ 75 TS Czechmate

Comes with all parts necessary to compete in IPSC Open or Limited divisions. Chambered in 9mm Parabellum. Steel slide and frame, single-action grips, comes with compensator and C-More red dot sight installed and ambidextrous slide racker. Includes front-sight adapter that replaces compensator, rear sight, ambidextrous safeties, aluminum grips, magazine well, one 26-round and three 20-round magazines. Weight 48 ounces, 5.4-inch barrel, matte blue finish. Introduced in 2011.

NIB	Exc.	V.G.	Good	Fair	Poor
2900	2500	2000	1500	800	350

CZ 75 Tactical Sport

Single-action for IPSC competition. Chambered in 9mm and .40 S&W. Dual tone (nickel/blued). Capacity 20+1 (9mm) or 16+1 (.40 S&W). 5.4" barrel; 45 oz. Introduced 2006.

NIB	Exc.	V.G.	Good	Fair	Poor
1100	900	675	500	400	200

CZ 85 B

This model is similar in appearance to the CZ 75 but offers some new features such as ambidextrous safety and slide stop levers, squared trigger guard, adjustable sight, and ribbed slide. Caliber, magazine capacity, and weight are same as CZ 75.

NIB	Exc.	V.G.	Good	Fair	Poor
525	475	425	300	250	175

NOTE: For .40 S&W add $30. For glossy blue add $20, for dual tone finish $25, and for nickel add $25.

CZ 85 Combat

Similar to the CZ 85 but with the addition of adjustable sights, walnut grips, round hammer, and free dropping magazine.

NIB	Exc.	V.G.	Good	Fair	Poor
500	450	325	250	175	125

NOTE: For .40 S&W add $30. For glossy blue add $20, for dual tone finish $25, and for nickel add $25.

CZ 40B

Introduced in 2002 this model is similar to the CZ 75 but features an alloy frame similar in shape to the Colt Model 1911. It is a single-action/double-action design. Barrel length is 4.7". Magazine capacity is 10 rounds. Chambered for the .40 S&W cartridge. Weight is about 35 oz.

NIB	Exc.	V.G.	Good	Fair	Poor
625	500	400	300	200	125

CZ Kadet

Chambered for the .22 LR cartridge and fitted with a 4.7" barrel. This model is a fixed barrel blowback semi-automatic pistol. Adjustable sights and blue finish. Weight is about 36 oz.

NIB	Exc.	V.G.	Good	Fair	Poor
510	400	300	225	175	100

CZ 75 Kadet Conversion

This is a separate conversion kit for the CZ 75/85 series. It converts these pistols to .22 LR. Adjustable rear sight. Supplied with 10-round magazine.

NIB	Exc.	V.G.	Good	Fair	Poor
300	225	200	150	100	50

CZ 2075 RAMI

Introduced in 2004 this 9mm or .40 S&W pistol is fitted with a 3" barrel. It has a single-action/double-action trigger. The design is based on the CZ Model 75. Magazine capacity is 10 rounds for the 9mm and 8 rounds for the .40 S&W. Weight is about 25 oz.

NIB	Exc.	V.G.	Good	Fair	Poor
450	400	350	300	250	175

CZ 83

This is a fixed-barrel .380 caliber pistol. It features an ambidextrous safety and magazine catch behind the trigger guard. The pistol is stripped by means of a hinged trigger guard. Barrel length is 3.8", overall length is 6.8", and weight is about 23 oz.

NIB	Exc.	V.G.	Good	Fair	Poor
475	325	200	175	150	125

NOTE: For nickel finish add $5. In 1993 Special Editions of the above pistols were introduced. These Special Editions consist of special finishes for the then-currently imported CZ pistols. They are high polish blue, nickel, chrome, gold, and a combination of the above finishes. These Special Edition finishes may affect price; they add between $100 and $250 to the cost of the pistol when new.

CZ 97 B

This pistol was planned for production in the summer of 1997. It is chambered for the .45 ACP cartridge. It is fitted with a 4.8" barrel and has a single-action/double-action mode. Magazine capacity is 10 rounds. Wood grips with blue finish. Weight is approximately 40 oz.

NIB	Exc.	V.G.	Good	Fair	Poor
665	525	400	300	175	100

CZ 100

This is a semi-automatic pistol, introduced in 1996, chambered for the 9mm or .40 S&W cartridge. It has a plastic frame and steel slide. Barrel length is 3.75". Weight is approximately 24 oz. U.S. magazine capacity is 10 rounds.

NIB	Exc.	V.G.	Good	Fair	Poor
525	450	325	2000	150	100

CZ
Strakonice, Czech Republic

This firm is a separate company from the one located in Uhershy Brod. Prior to the collapse of the Soviet Union both companies were owned and operated by the state.

Model TT 40/45/9

This is semi-automatic pistol chambered for the .40 S&W, .45 ACP, or 9mm cartridges. Fitted with a 3.8" barrel. Trigger is single-action/double-action or double-action-only. Magazine capacity is 10 rounds. Weight is about 26 oz.

NIB	Exc.	V.G.	Good	Fair	Poor
575	425	300	200	125	100

D

DAEWOO
Pusan, Korea

DH-40

This semi-automatic pistol is chambered for the .40 S&W cartridge. It has a 4.13" barrel and a magazine capacity of 11 rounds. Weight is approximately 32 oz.

NIB	Exc.	V.G.	Good	Fair	Poor
495	375	300	250	175	100

DP-51B

This semi-automatic pistol is chambered for the 9mm cartridge and is fitted with a 4.13" barrel. Magazine capacity is 13 rounds. Overall length is 7.5" and weight is approximately 28 oz.

NIB	Exc.	V.G.	Good	Fair	Poor
400	325	275	225	175	100

DP-51SB

This is a more compact design with 3.6" barrel and 10-round magazine. Weight is 27 oz. Stainless steel finish.

NIB	Exc.	V.G.	Good	Fair	Poor
450	395	275	225	175	100

DP-51CB

Same as above but fitted with a 3.6" barrel. Magazine capacity is 10 rounds. Weight is about 26 oz.

NIB	Exc.	V.G.	Good	Fair	Poor
450	375	300	250	175	100

DP-52

This semi-automatic pistol is chambered for the .22 LR cartridge. It has a 3.82" barrel length and a magazine capacity of 10 rounds. It operates in double-action and single-action modes. Overall length is 6.7" and weight is approximately 23 oz.

NIB	Exc.	V.G.	Good	Fair	Poor
395	325	250	200	150	100

DH380

Introduced in 1996 this semi-automatic pistol is chambered for the .380 ACP cartridge. It is fitted with a 3.8" barrel and has a magazine capacity of 8 rounds. The firing model is double- or single-action. Weight is approximately 24 oz.

NIB	Exc.	V.G.	Good	Fair	Poor
425	375	275	225	150	100

Daly ZDA

Introduced in 2005 this pistol is chambered for the 9mm or .40 S&W cartridge. Fitted with a 4.5" ramped barrel. Ambidextrous slide release/dececker/lock as well as magazine release. Loaded chamber indicator. Magazine capacity is 15 rounds for 9mm and 12 rounds for the .40 S&W.

NIB	Exc.	V.G.	Good	Fair	Poor
590	450	375	300	175	100

Field 1911-A1 FS/MS/CS

Chambered for .45 ACP with a choice of 5" (FS), 4" (MS), or 3.5" (CS) barrel and various special features such as front and rear slide serrations, extended beavertail safety, and lightweight trigger. Magazine capacity is 8 rounds. Overall length is 8.75".

NIB	Exc.	V.G.	Good	Fair	Poor
575	400	300	200	175	115

Superior 1911-A1 EFS/EMS/ECS

Same as the Field Grade described above but with a blued frame and stainless steel slide. Introduced in 1999.

NIB	Exc.	V.G.	Good	Fair	Poor
550	450	350	200	175	115

Empire 1911-A1 EFS

Same as the Field Grade but in full stainless with both stainless steel slide and frame. Introduced in 1999.

NIB	Exc.	V.G.	Good	Fair	Poor
630	475	350	225	195	125

Field 1911-A2P

Same as above but with 10-round magazine.

NIB	Exc.	V.G.	Good	Fair	Poor
570	450	350	225	195	125

.22 Caliber Conversion Kit

Offered with adjustable sights for models with 5" barrel only. First offered in 1999.

NIB	Exc.	V.G.	Good	Fair	Poor
200	150	100	65	45	25

Field 1911-A1 PC

This model is fitted with a 4" barrel and slide. It also has a polymer frame. Produced under license from STI. Introduced in 1999.

NIB	Exc.	V.G.	Good	Fair	Poor
575	400	300	200	175	115

Superior 1911-A1 PC

Same as the model above but with stainless steel slide and black polymer frame. Introduced in 1999.

NIB	Exc.	V.G.	Good	Fair	Poor
595	425	325	225	195	125

Field 1911 Target EFST

Fitted with a 5" barrel and chambered for the .45 ACP cartridge. Eight-round magazine. Blued finish. Fully adjustable rear sight with dovetail front sight. Weight is about 40 oz.

NIB	Exc.	V.G.	Good	Fair	Poor
620	475	350	240	195	125

Empire 1911 Target EFST

As above but with stainless steel finish.

NIB	Exc.	V.G.	Good	Fair	Poor
790	600	475	350	240	125

Empire Custom Match Target

Same as Empire target but with hand polished stainless steel finish with 20 lpi checkered front strap.

NIB	Exc.	V.G.	Good	Fair	Poor
800	600	500	375	255	135

Daly HP

Introduced in 2003 this U.S.-made 9mm pistol is similar to the famous Browning Hi-Power. Fitted with a 5" barrel. XS sighting system. Weight is about 35 oz.

NIB	Exc.	V.G.	Good	Fair	Poor
550	400	350	225	195	125

Daly M-5 Government

This is a polymer frame pistol chambered for the 9mm, .40 S&W, or the .45 ACP cartridge. Fitted with a 5" barrel, high rise beavertail and ambidextrous safety. Low profile sights. Weight is around 34 oz. Made in Israel by BUL. Introduced in 2003.

NIB	Exc.	V.G.	Good	Fair	Poor
720	575	400	275	225	100

Daly M-5 Commander

Same as above but fitted with a 4.375" barrel. Weight is about 30 oz.

NIB	Exc.	V.G.	Good	Fair	Poor
720	575	400	275	225	100

Daly M-5 Ultra-X

This is an ultra compact model.

NIB	Exc.	V.G.	Good	Fair	Poor
720	575	400	275	225	100

Daly M-5 IPCS

This model has a 5" barrel and is fitted with a stainless steel slide with adjustable sights. Flared and lowered ejection port and extended mag release. Weight is about 34 oz.

NIB	Exc.	V.G.	Good	Fair	Poor
1500	1150	725	600	325	125

Daly Classic 1873 Single Action

Chambered for the .45 Colt or the .357 Mag., this revolver is offered with 4.75", 5.5", or 7.5" barrel. Choice of walnut or simulated Ivory grips. Stainless steel, blue or case colored finish. Introduced in 2005.

NIB	Exc.	V.G.	Good	Fair	Poor
450	350	285	250	195	150

NOTE: Add $30 for steel backstrap and trigger guard. Add $200 for stainless steel.

J.H., G.P., and D.E. Dance began production of percussion revolvers for the Confederate States of America in Columbia, Texas, in mid-1862, moving to Anderson, Texas, in early 1864. Based on surviving serial numbers, the combined output at both places did not exceed 350 pistols. Most of these were in the "Army" (.44 caliber) size but a limited number of "Navy" (.36 caliber) were also manufactured. Nearly all are distinguished by the absence of a "recoil shield" on the frame behind the cylinders. As Colt M1851 "Navy" revolvers closely resemble the Dance Navy revolvers, great care must be exercised in examining revolvers purported to be Dance Navies.

.36 Caliber

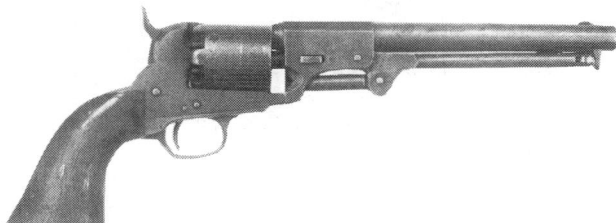

Courtesy Milwaukee Public Museum, Milwaukee, Wisconsin

NIB	Exc.	V.G.	Good	Fair	Poor
—	—	85000	67500	20000	7000

.44 Caliber

NIB	Exc.	V.G.	Good	Fair	Poor
—	—	90000	68000	20000	5500

DANSK REKYLRIFFEL SYNDIKAT
Copenhagen, Denmark

This firm was founded in 1896. In 1936 it became known as Madsen, makers of the famous Madsen light machine gun. The Schouboe pistols were designed by Jens Schouboe, the chief engineer for Dansk. They were developed in 1900-1902. The first year of manufacture was in 1902.

Schouboe Model 1902

A 7.65mm caliber semi-automatic pistol with a conventional blowback design. Production began in 1903 and ended in 1908, with fewer than 1,000 manufactured.

Courtesy James Rankin

NIB	Exc.	V.G.	Good	Fair	Poor
—	15500	12000	8200	5000	3000

Schouboe Model 1904

A semi-automatic pistol in caliber 11.35mm. The Model 1904 was an enlarged Model 1902. The name Dansk Rekylriffel is stamped on the slide.

Courtesy James Rankin

NIB	Exc.	V.G.	Good	Fair	Poor
—	24500	20500	16500	11000	5000

Schouboe Model 1907

An 11.35mm caliber semi-automatic pistol designed to fire a 55-grain, copper-aluminum-and-wood projectile at a velocity of 1625 fps. The pistol has the name Dansk Rekylriffel and Schouboe stamped on the slide. Some of these pistols had grip frames slotted for stocks. Five hundred were manufactured before production stopped in 1917.

Courtesy James Rankin

NIB	Exc.	V.G.	Good	Fair	Poor
—	24000	20000	16000	10500	5000

NOTE: Combination holster/shoulder stocks were made for this model, but are extremely rare. If present with a pistol, they would add approximately $5,000 to the value.

Schouboe Model 1907 9mm

As above but chambered for the 9mm cartridge. Very few of these pistols were built.

Courtesy James Rankin

NIB	Exc.	V.G.	Good	Fair	Poor
—	14000	11000	8250	5500	3000

Schouboe Model 1910/12

This model is chambered for the 11.35mm cartridge, and was involved in U.S. military tests in 1912.

Courtesy James Rankin

NIB	Exc.	V.G.	Good	Fair	Poor
—	24500	21500	16500	11000	5000

Schouboe Model 1916

This model is also chambered for the 11.35mm cartridge. It is fitted with a very large slide release and safety lever on the left side of the pistol. The name of the manufacturer is stamped on the slide.

Courtesy James Rankin

NIB	Exc.	V.G.	Good	Fair	Poor
—	24000	21050	16500	11000	5000

DARDICK CORP.
Hamden, Connecticut

Perhaps one of the most unusual firearms to have been designed and marketed in the United States during the 20th century. It utilizes a "tround," which is a triangular plastic case enclosing a cartridge. The action of these arms consists of a revolving carrier that brings the trounds from the magazine into line with the barrel. Discontinued in 1962. Values below are for boxed examples with supply of tround ammunition. Deduct 50 to 75 percent for unboxed, loose examples without ammunition.

Series 110

3" barrel. Chambered in .38 Dardick only.

NIB	Exc.	V.G.	Good	Fair	Poor
—	2500	1650	1500	1100	500

Series 1500

A carbine conversion kit consisting of a long barrel and shoulder stock was available and would bring a premium of $750 to $1400 depending on the condition.

NIB	Exc.	V.G.	Good	Fair	Poor
—	5000	3000	1750	1500	900

DARLING, B. & B. M.
Belingham, Massachusetts

Darling Pepperbox Pistol

A .30 caliber percussion 6-shot pepperbox with 3.25" length barrels. Blued with walnut grips. This is one of the rarest American pepperboxes and copies are known to have been made. Consequently, prospective purchasers are advised to secure a qualified appraisal prior to acquisition. Manufactured during the late 1830s.

NIB	Exc.	V.G.	Good	Fair	Poor
—	—	4950	1950	600	600

DAVIS, A. JR.
Stafford, Connecticut

Under Hammer Pistol

A .31 caliber single-shot under hammer percussion pistol with a 7.5" half octagonal barrel and brass frame. The grips are of maple and formed with a bottom tip. The top strap marked "A. Davis Jr./Stafford Conn."

NIB	Exc.	V.G.	Good	Fair	Poor
—	—	1250	775	350	100

DAVIS INDUSTRIES
Mira Loma, California

This company was founded in 1987 by Jim Davis in Chino, California. The company ceased operations in 2001. Remaining stocks and production machinery purchased by Cobra Enterprises, 1960 S. Milestone Drive, Suite F, Salt Lake City, UT 84104.

D-Series Deringer

A .22 LR, .22 WMR, .25 ACP and .32 ACP caliber double-barrel Over/Under derringer with 2.4" barrels. Black Teflon or chrome-plated finish with laminated wood grips. Weighs approximately 9.5 oz.

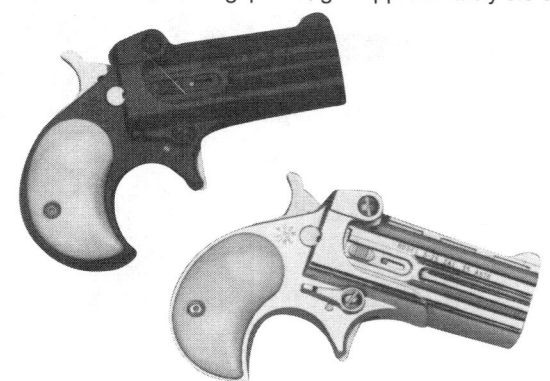

NIB	Exc.	V.G.	Good	Fair	Poor
150	75	40	30	25	20

Big Bore D-Series

Similar to the above model but chambered for the .38 Special and .32 H&R Magnum. Barrel length is 2.75". Weighs about 11.5 oz.

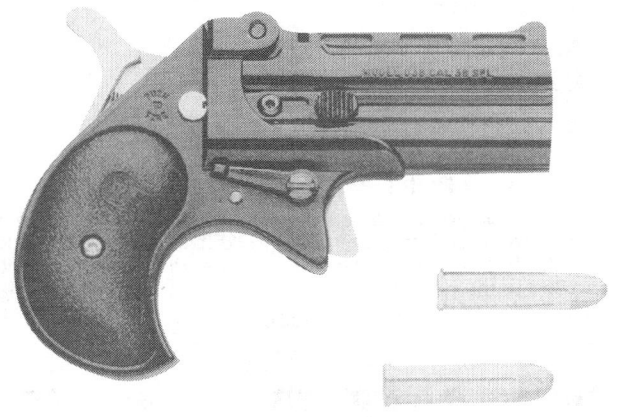

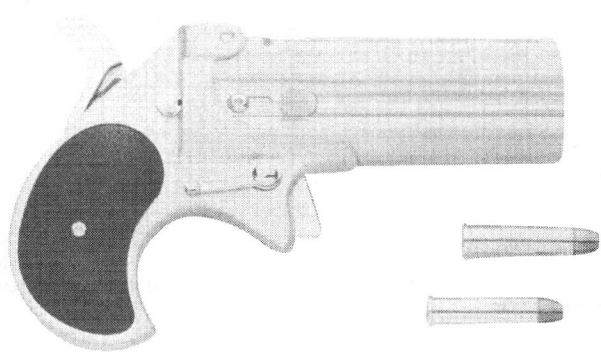

NIB	Exc.	V.G.	Good	Fair	Poor
150	75	40	30	25	20

Long Bore D-Series

Introduced in 1994 this two-shot pistol is chambered for the .22 LR , .22 WMR, .32 ACP, .32 H&R Mag., .380 ACP, 9mm, and .38 Special cartridges. Barrel length is 3.75", overall length is 5.65" and weight is approximately 13 oz.

NIB	Exc.	V.G.	Good	Fair	Poor
150	75	40	30	25	20

P-32

A .32 caliber semi-automatic pistol with a 2.8" barrel and 6-shot magazine. Black Teflon or chrome-plated finish with laminated wood grips. Overall length is 5.4". Weighs approximately 22 oz.

NIB	Exc.	V.G.	Good	Fair	Poor
150	75	40	30	25	20

P-380

As above, in .380 caliber.

NIB	Exc.	V.G.	Good	Fair	Poor
175	85	65	50	40	30

DAVIS-WARNER ARMS CORPORATION
Norwich, Connecticut

Established in 1917, when N.R. Davis & Sons purchased the Warner Arms Company. Manufactured shotguns, as well as revolvers and semi-automatic pistols. Ceased operations in 1930. The Crescent Arms Company purchased the proprietary rights to the name and briefly assembled shotguns under the name (probably from parts acquired in the purchase) until Crescent was in turn purchased by J.C. Stevens.Initially, the Davis-Warner shotguns were identical to those made by Davis (page 360), but they subsequently made a Davis Grade B.S. Hammerless, Davis-Warner Expert and Davis Grade D.S. The pistols made by the company included .32 caliber revolvers and two Browning Patent semi-automatics made in Belgium for the company.

Davis-Warner Swing Out Revolver

Double-action .32 caliber revolver with a 5" or 6" barrel.

NIB	Exc.	V.G.	Good	Fair	Poor
—	200	150	120	75	50

Davis-Warner Semi-Automatic Pistols

Browning Patent .25 ACP, .32 ACP or .380 caliber pistols.

NIB	Exc.	V.G.	Good	Fair	Poor
—	350	275	175	125	75

Warner Infallible Semi-Automatic Pistol

Fyrberg Patent .32 ACP. Not a particularly robust design.

Courtesy J.B. Wood

NIB	Exc.	V.G.	Good	Fair	Poor
—	350	275	175	125	75

DAW, G. H.
London, England

Revolver

A .38 caliber double-action percussion revolver with a 5.5" barrel marked "George H. Daw, 57 Threadneedle St. London, Patent No. 112." Blued, with walnut grips. Manufactured in the 1860s.

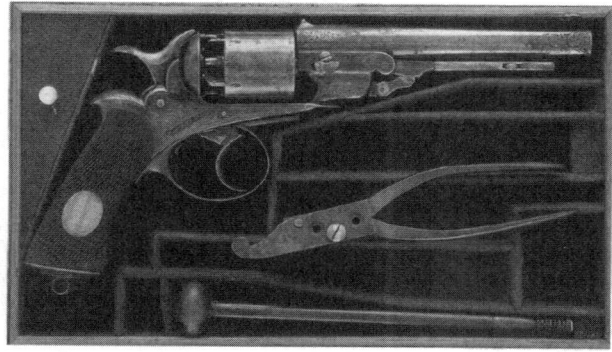

NIB	Exc.	V.G.	Good	Fair	Poor
—	—	5750	3500	1975	1000

DEANE-HARDING
London, England

Revolver

A .44 caliber percussion revolver with a 5.25" barrel and 5-shot cylinder. Blued, case hardened with walnut grips. Manufactured during the late 1850s.

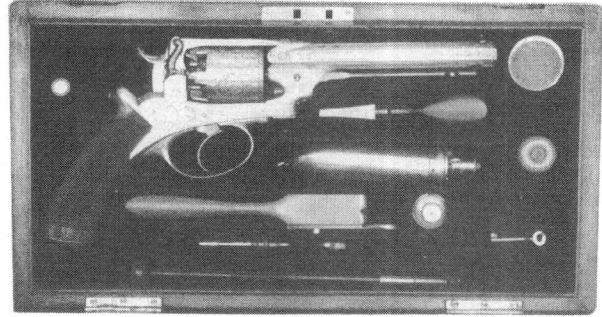

Courtesy Bonhams & Butterfields, San Francisco, California

NIB	Exc.	V.G.	Good	Fair	Poor
—	—	8500	2750	1475	850

DECKER, WILHELM
Zella St. Blasii, Germany

Revolver

A 6.35mm double-action revolver with a 6-shot cylinder and concealed hammer. Unusual bar-type trigger design. Blued with plastic grips. Manufactured prior to 1914. Very few of these revolvers were produced.

NIB	Exc.	V.G.	Good	Fair	Poor
—	2100	1500	750	325	100

DEMIRETT, J.
Montpelier, Vermont

Under Hammer Pistol

A .27 caliber single-shot percussion pistol with 3" to 8" barrels and an under hammer. The barrel marked "J. Demerrit / Montpelier / Vermont." Blued with maple, walnut or stag horn grips. Active from 1866 to the mid-1880s.

NIB	Exc.	V.G.	Good	Fair	Poor
—	—	2700	825	350	200

DERINGER REVOLVER AND PISTOL CO.
Philadelphia, Pennsylvania

After Henry Deringer's death, his name was used by I.J. Clark who manufactured rimfire revolvers on Charles Foehl's patents between 1870 and 1879.

Deringer Model I

A .22 caliber spur trigger revolver with a hinged octagonal barrel and 7-shot cylinder. Manufactured circa 1873.

NIB	Exc.	V.G.	Good	Fair	Poor
—	—	—	650	275	150

Deringer Model II

As above, with a round barrel and also available in .32 caliber.

NIB	Exc.	V.G.	Good	Fair	Poor
—	—	—	425	200	100

Centennial 1876

A .22, .32, or .38 caliber solid frame revolver.

NIB	Exc.	V.G.	Good	Fair	Poor
—	—	—	900	450	200

DERINGER RIFLES AND PISTOLS, HENRY
Philadelphia, Pennsylvania

Henry Deringer Sr. and his son, Henry Jr., were well established in Philadelphia by the close of the War of 1812, having made both sporting and military rifles at that place since the turn of the century. Henry Jr. continued in the gun trade until the outbreak of the American Civil War, primarily producing flintlock and percussion military rifles, at least 2,500 "Northwest guns" and 1,200 rifles for the Indian trade, a few percussion martial pistols, but most importantly the percussion pocket pistols that became so popular that they took on his misspelled name as a generic term, the "derringers."

Deringer U.S. Navy Contract "Boxlock" Pistols

Overall length 11-5/8"; barrel length 6"; caliber .54. Markings: on lockplate, "US/DERINGER/ PHILADELIA" or merely "DERINGER/ PHILADEL\qA" in center, the tail either plain or marked "U.S.N./(date)" ; barrels sometimes marked with U.S. Navy inspection marks. Deringer was granted a contract with the U.S. Navy in 1845 for 1,200 of the new "boxlock" percussion pistols also made by Ames. All of these appear to have been delivered. From the extra parts, Deringer is thought to have assembled several hundred extra pistols, some of which he rifled. The latter bring a premium, even though quantities remain enigmatic.

NIB	Exc.	V.G.	Good	Fair	Poor
—	—	4050	1550	1225	750

Deringer Percussion Pocket Pistols

The most famous of Henry Deringer's products, an estimated 15,000 were produced between the Mexican War through the Civil War, usually in pairs. The popularity of the pistol is attested in the large number of imitations and the nickname "Derringer" applied to them, even when clearly not Deringer's products. Prices can fluctuate widely based on agent marks occasionally found on barrel. Care is advised in purchasing purported "true" derringers. Beware of fakes!

Courtesy Milwaukee Public Museum, Milwaukee, Wisconsin

NIB	Exc.	V.G.	Good	Fair	Poor
—	—	7000	2250	1600	800

Principal Makers of Deringer-Style Pocket Pistols

William AFFLERBACH, Philadelphia, PA
Balthaser AUER, Louisville, KY
Frederick BEERSTECHER, Philadelphia and Lewisburg, PA
Franz J. BITTERLICH, Nashville, TN
BLUNT & SYMS, New York, NY
Richard P. BRUFF, New York, NY
Jesse S. BUTTERFIELD, Philadelphia, PA
Daniel CLARK, Philadelphia, PA
Richard CONSTABLE, Philadelphia, PADELONG & SON, Chattanooga, TN
MOSES DICKSON, Louisville, KY
Horace E. DIMICK, St. Louis, MO
Gustau ERICHSON, Houston, TX
B.J. EUSTACE & Company, St. Louis, MO
James E. EVANS, Philadelphia, PA
W.S. EVANS, Philadelphia, PA
FIELD, LANGSTROTH & Company, Philadelphia, PA
Daniel FISH, New York, NY
FOLSOM BROTHERS & Company, New Orleans, LA
August G. GENEZ, New York, NY
George D. H. GILLESPIE, New York, NY
Frederick G. GLASSICK, Memphis, TN
James GOLCHER, Philadelphia, PA
Joseph GRUBB & Company, Philadelphia, PA
John H. HAPPOLDT, Charlestown, SC
John M. HAPPOLDT, Columbus, George, and Charlestown, SCHAWS & WAGGONER, Columbia, SC
HODGKINS & SONS, Macon, GA
Louis HOFFMAN, Vicksburg, MSHYDE & GOODRICH, New Orleans, LA
Joseph JACOB, Philadelphia, PAWilliam W. KAYE, Philadelphia, PA
Benjamin KITTERIDGE, Cincinnati, OH
Peter W. KRAFT, Columbia, SC
John KRIDER, Philadelphia, PA
Jacob KUNTZ, Philadelphia, PA
Martille La FITTE, Natchitoches, LA
A. Frederichk LINS, Philadelphia, PA
C. LOHNER, Philadelphia, PA
John P. LOWER, Denver, CO
A.R. MENDENHALL, Des Arc, AK

John MEUNIER, Milwaukee, WI
William D. MILLER, New York, NY
MURPHY & O'CONNELL, New York, NY
— NEWCOMB, Natchez, MS
Charles A. OBERTEUFFER, Philadelphia, PA
Stephen O'DELL, Natchez, MS
Henry C. PALMER, St. Louis, MO
R. PATRICK, New York, NY
REID & TRACY, New York, NY
William ROBERTSON, Philadelphia, PA
ROBINSON & KRIDER, Philadelphia, PA
Ernst SCHMIDT & Company, Houston, TX
SCHNEIDER & GLASSICK, Memphis, TN
W.A. SEAVER, New York, NY
Paul J. SIMPSON, New York, NY
SLOTTER & Company, Philadelphia, PA
Patrick SMITH, Buffalo, NY
SPRANG & WALLACE, Philadelphia, PA
Adam W. SPIES, New York, NY
Casper SUTER, Selma, AL
Jacob F. TRUMPLER, Little Rock, AK
Edward TRYON, Jr., Philadelphia, PA
George K. TRYON, Philadelphia, PA
TUFTS & COLLEY, New York, NY
WOLF, DASH & FISHER, New York, NY
Alfred WOODHAM, New York, NY
Andrew WURFFLEIN, Philadelphia, PA
John WURFFLEIN, Philadelphia, PA

Deringer Percussion Pocket Pistols Agent Names Found On Deringer Pocket Pistols

W.C. ALLEN, San Francisco, CA
W.H. CALHOUN, Nashville, TN
CANFIELD & BROTHERS, Baltimore, MD
F. H. CLARK & CO., Memphis, TN
COLEMAN & DUKE, Cahaba, AL
M.W. GALT & BROTHER, Washington, DC
J.B. GILMORE, Shreveport, LA
A.B. GRISWOLD & CO., New Orleans, LA
HYDE & GOODRICH, New Orleans, LA
LULLMAN & VIENNA, Memphis, TN
A.J. MILLSPAUGH, Shreveport, LA
H.G. NEWCOMB, Natchez, MSA.J. PLATE, San Francisco, CA
J.A. SCHAFER, Vicksburg, MSS.L. SWETT, Vicksburg, MSA. J. TAYLOR, San Francisco, CAWOLF & DURRINGER, Louisville, KY

DESERT EAGLE/ISRAELI MILITARY INDUSTRIES

The Desert Eagle is a semi-automatic gas-operated pistol chambered for the .357 Magnum, .41 Magnum, .44 Magnum, and .50 Action Express. It is produced by Israel Military Industries. The pistols are furnished with a standard 6" barrel but 10" and 14" interchangeable barrels are offered as options. Also available are these interchangeable barrels that are Mag-Na-Ported. The standard material used for frame is steel, but stainless and aluminum are also available. The standard finish for these pistols is black oxide but custom finishes are available on special order. These special finishes are: gold, stainless steel, satin nickel, bright nickel, polished blue, camo, matte chrome, polished chrome, brushed chrome, and matte chrome with gold. All of these special order finishes as well as the optional barrels will affect the prices of the pistols. Prices listed here will reflect standard pistols only.

Desert Eagle .357 Magnum

Standard with 6" barrel and black oxide finish. Magazine capacity is 9 rounds. Standard weight is 58 oz.

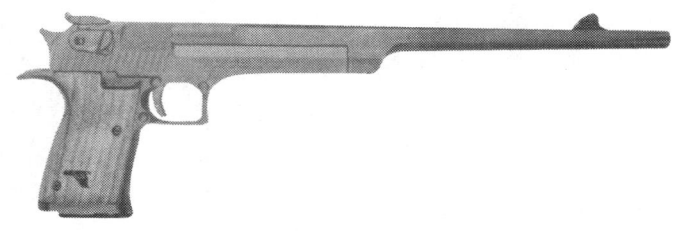

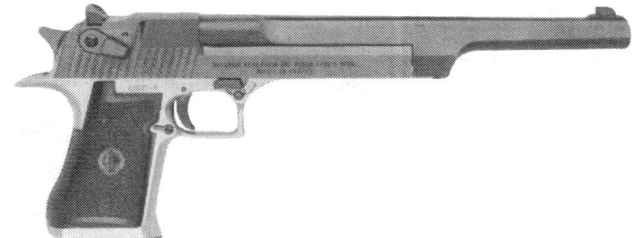

NIB	Exc.	V.G.	Good	Fair	Poor
1250	900	700	500	400	250

Desert Eagle .41 Magnum/.44 Magnum

Standard barrel length is 6" with black oxide finish. Magazine capacity is 8 rounds. Weight for standard pistol is 63 oz. Add 10 percent for .41.

NIB	Exc.	V.G.	Good	Fair	Poor
1350	900	700	500	400	250

Desert Eagle .50 Action Express

Standard barrel length is 10" with black oxide finish. Magazine capacity is 7 rounds. Standard weight is 72 oz.

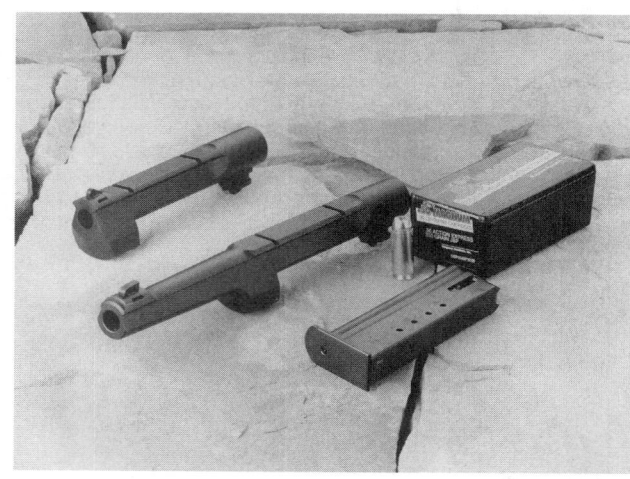

Interchangeable barrels make the Desert Eagle a truly versatile handgun. The .50 AE shown here will handle the biggest game in North America.

NIB	Exc.	V.G.	Good	Fair	Poor
1450	900	700	500	400	250

DESERT EAGLE MARK XIX

Introduced in 1996 this new design is manufactured in the U.S. and allows the interchangeability of barrels to switch calibers between the same receiver. A single receiver can be turned into six different pistols in three Magnum calibers. Available are the .50 A.E., .44 Mag., and .357 Mag. in barrel lengths of 6" or 10". Separate magazines are also required. Eight different finishes are offered as well. A separate bolt assembly is necessary to convert the .44/.50 calibers to the .357. There are so many different possibilities with this design that only the basic pistol prices are given. Extra barrel assemblies are an additional cost. Prices range from $280 to $160 depending on caliber and length.

.50A.E. w/6" Barrel

NIB	Exc.	V.G.	Good	Fair	Poor
1450	900	700	500	300	200

.50A.E. w/10" Barrel

NIB	Exc.	V.G.	Good	Fair	Poor
1350	1000	750	500	300	200

.44 Mag. w/6" Barrel

NIB	Exc.	V.G.	Good	Fair	Poor
1250	900	700	450	300	200

.44 Mag. w/10" Barrel

NIB	Exc.	V.G.	Good	Fair	Poor
1350	1000	750	500	300	200

.357 Mag. w/6" Barrel

NIB	Exc.	V.G.	Good	Fair	Poor
1250	900	700	450	300	200

.357 Mag. w/10" Barrel

NIB	Exc.	V.G.	Good	Fair	Poor
1350	1000	750	500	300	200

.440 Cor-Bon w/6" Barrel (1999)

NIB	Exc.	V.G.	Good	Fair	Poor
1200	950	700	600	500	300

.440 Cor-Bon w/10" Barrel (1999)

NIB	Exc.	V.G.	Good	Fair	Poor
1300	1000	750	650	550	325

Bolt Assembly—.44/.50 or .357

NIB	Exc.	V.G.	Good	Fair	Poor
220	175	150	100	75	50

MARK XIX COMPONENT SYSTEM

Introduced in 2000 this system features a Mark XIX frame with a .44 magnum 6" and 10" barrels; .50AE with 6" and 10" barrel; and .357 magnum with 6" and 10" barrel. Supplied with ICC aluminum case. Also offered with 6" only barrel components or 10" only barrel components.

6" & 10" Component System

NIB	Exc.	V.G.	Good	Fair	Poor
3990	2990	2500	1875	1150	500

6" Component System

NIB	Exc.	V.G.	Good	Fair	Poor
2575	1900	1500	1200	700	350

10" Component System

NIB	Exc.	V.G.	Good	Fair	Poor
2815	2100	1600	1325	725	400

BABY EAGLE

The Baby Eagle is a smaller version of the Desert Eagle. It is an all-steel construction, extra long slide rail, nylon grips, combat style trigger guard, ambidextrous thumb safety, decocking safety. It is a double-action design and available in 9mm, .40 S&W, .41 Action Express. Standard finish is black oxide but matte chrome and brushed are offered as optional finishes. Fixed sights are standard. Fixed night sights and adjustable night sights are options.

.40 S&W (Standard)

Supplied with 4.5" barrel and black oxide finish, it has a magazine capacity of 10 rounds. Empty weight is 38 oz.

NIB	Exc.	V.G.	Good	Fair	Poor
500	400	350	300	250	200

9mm (Standard)

Fitted with a 4.5" barrel and black oxide finish, this model has a magazine capacity of 16 rounds. Empty weight is 38 oz.

NIB	Exc.	V.G.	Good	Fair	Poor
500	400	350	300	250	200

.41 Action Express

This model also has a 4.7" barrel and black oxide finish. Magazine capacity is 11 rounds. Empty weight is 38 oz.

NIB	Exc.	V.G.	Good	Fair	Poor
500	400	350	300	250	200

Short Barrel (Semi-Compact)

This 9mm, 40 S&W, or .45 ACP model features a 3.6" barrel with frame-mounted safety. Weight is about 36 oz. Magazine holds 10 rounds.

NIB	Exc.	V.G.	Good	Fair	Poor
500	400	350	300	250	200

Short Barrel/Short Grip (Compact)

This 9mm or .40 S&W version has a 3.6" barrel and shorter grip (3.25") than standard. Magazine capacity is still 10 rounds. Weight is about 38 oz. Frame-mounted safety.

NIB	Exc.	V.G.	Good	Fair	Poor
500	400	350	300	250	200

Semi-Compact Polymer

This pistol has a polymer frame and a 3.9" barrel chambered for the 9mm or .40 S&W cartridge. Weight is about 29 oz.

NIB	Exc.	V.G.	Good	Fair	Poor
500	400	325	285	225	175

Compact Polymer

As above but with 3.6" barrel and short grip. Weight is about 27 oz.

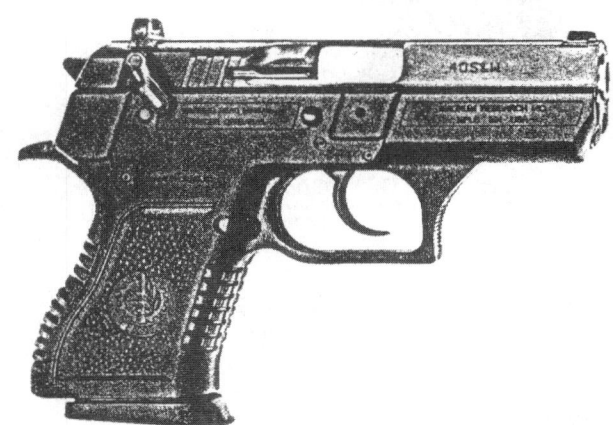

NIB	Exc.	V.G.	Good	Fair	Poor
500	400	325	285	225	175

NOTE: These custom shop finishes for Desert Eagle pistols are available: Satin nickel, bright nickel, polished and deep blued, matte hard chrome, polished hard chrome, brushed hard chrome, 24K gold. All finishes except gold add $195 to price of pistol. For gold finish add $500. For gold appointments add $195.

Lone Eagle

This is a single-shot rotating breech pistol designed to fire centerfire cartridges. The standard finish is a black oxide blue luster. The barrel is drilled and tapped for scope mounts. Standard barrel length is 14". Fixed, adjustable, or silhouette sights are offered as options. Stock assembly is made from Lexan. The handgun is offered in these calibers: .22-250, .223, .22 Hornet, .243, .30-30, .30-06, .308, .357 Mag., .358 Win., .35 Rem., .44 Mag., .444 Marlin, 7mm-08, 7mm Bench Rest. Weighs between 4 lbs. 3 oz. to 4 lbs. 7 oz. depending on caliber.

NIB	Exc.	V.G.	Good	Fair	Poor
400	300	275	250	200	125

Desert Eagle Micro Desert Eagle Pistol

Small-frame DAO pocket pistol chambered in .380 ACP. Features include a 2.22" barrel, fixed low-profile sights, steel slide, aluminum alloy frame, nickel-teflon finish, six-round capacity. Overall length 4.52". Weight: 14 oz. Suggested retail price: To be announced.

NIB	Exc.	V.G.	Good	Fair	Poor
450	350	250	200	150	100

DETONICS
Middlestadt, Illinois

Current manufacturer of Detonics 1911-style pistols.

Combat Master

The latest version of the very first compact 1911 developed in the 1970s by the original Detonics company. In .45 ACP with a 3.5-inch octagonal barrel, two-tone finish, aluminum/Dymondwood grips, 6+1 capacity, stainless steel frame and slide, weight 30 oz. Introduced in 2010.

NIB	Exc.	V.G.	Good	Fair	Poor
850	775	700	550	—	—

Nemesis HT

Full-size with 5-inch barrel, chambered in .40 S&W, weight 38 oz., capacity 9+1. Other features same as above. Introduced in 2011.

NIB	Exc.	V.G.	Good	Fair	Poor
1950	1800	1500	1100	—	—

DTX

A polymer-frame, double-action-only pistol chambered in 9mm or .40 S&W, Barrel is 4.25-inches, weight 25 oz., capacity 16+1 (9mm), 14+1 (.40). Introduced in 2011.

NIB	Exc.	V.G.	Good	Fair	Poor
975	900	775	625	450	250

DETONICS FIREARMS INDUSTRIES / NEW DETONICS

This series of compact 1911-type pistols was first manufactured by Detonics Firearms Industries in Bellvue, WA from 1976 to 1988. That firm was sold to New Detonics Mfg. Corp. of Phoenix, AZ, which operated from 1989 to 1992. In 2004 the brand was resurrected and returned to production by Detonics USA in Pendergrass, GA. Then in 2007 Detonics USA and all if its predecessors was sold to a group of investors who established the current company, known only as Detonics, in Middlestadt, IL.

Mark I

A .45 caliber semi-automatic pistol with a 3.25" barrel and 6-shot magazine. Matte blued with walnut grips. Discontinued in 1981.

NIB	Exc.	V.G.	Good	Fair	Poor
—	550	450	400	300	200

Mark II

As above, with satin nickel-plated finish. Discontinued in 1979.

NIB	Exc.	V.G.	Good	Fair	Poor
—	550	450	400	300	200

Mark III

As above, with hard chrome plating. Discontinued in 1979.

NIB	Exc.	V.G.	Good	Fair	Poor
—	600	500	450	350	250

Mark IV

As above, with polished blue finish. Discontinued in 1981.

NIB	Exc.	V.G.	Good	Fair	Poor
—	550	450	400	300	200

Combat Master

The Mark I in 9mm, .38 Super, or .45 caliber.

NIB	Exc.	V.G.	Good	Fair	Poor
975	800	600	500	400	250

Combat Master Mark V

As above, in stainless steel with a matte finish. Discontinued in 1985.

NIB	Exc.	V.G.	Good	Fair	Poor
975	800	600	500	400	250

Combat Master Mark VI

As above, with adjustable sights and the sides of the slide polished. 1,000 were made in .451 Detonics Magnum caliber.

NIB	Exc.	V.G.	Good	Fair	Poor
900	750	600	500	400	250

NOTE: .451 Detonics Magnum add 40 percent.

Combat Master Mark VII

As above, without sights.

NIB	Exc.	V.G.	Good	Fair	Poor
900	750	600	500	400	250

NOTE: .451 Detonics Magnum add 40 percent.

Military Combat MC2

As above, in 9mm, .38 Super or .45 caliber with fixed sights, dull finish and Pachmayr grips. Discontinued in 1984.

NIB	Exc.	V.G.	Good	Fair	Poor
675	600	500	425	300	200

Scoremaster

As above, in .45 or .451 Detonics Magnum with a 5" or 6" barrel, Millet sights and a grip safety.

NIB	Exc.	V.G.	Good	Fair	Poor
1250	1000	800	600	400	250

Janus Competition Scoremaster

As above, in .45 caliber with a compensated barrel. Introduced in 1988.

NIB	Exc.	V.G.	Good	Fair	Poor
1750	1450	1250	850	650	300

Servicemaster

As above, with a 4.25" barrel, interchangeable sights and matte finish. Discontinued in 1986.

NIB	Exc.	V.G.	Good	Fair	Poor
—	1000	800	600	400	200

Pocket 9

A 9mm double-action semi-automatic pistol with a 3" barrel and 6-shot magazine. Matte finish stainless steel. Discontinued in 1986.

NIB	Exc.	V.G.	Good	Fair	Poor
—	400	350	275	225	175

Combat Master

Fitted with a 3.5-inch barrel chambered for the .45 ACP, .40 S&W, .357 SIG, .38 Super, or the 9mm Para cartridges. Checkered rosewood grips. Low profile fixed sights. Magazine capacity is 6-rounds. Height of pistol is 4.75-inches. Overall length is 7-inches. Weight is about 34 oz. All stainless steel including springs. Introduced in 2005.

NIB	Exc.	V.G.	Good	Fair	Poor
1300	1050	650	425	300	175

Street Master

Chambered for the .45 ACP cartridge and fitted with a 5-inch barrel. Checkered rosewood grips. All stainless steel including springs. Height is 4.75-inches. Overall length is 8.5-inches. Weight is about 39 oz. Magazine capacity is 6-rounds. Fixed sights. Introduced in 2005.

NIB	Exc.	V.G.	Good	Fair	Poor
1200	950	675	450	325	195

Model 9-11-01

This model, introduced in 2005, is chambered for the .45 ACP cartridge and fitted with a 5-inch barrel. All stainless steel construction. Checkered rosewood grips. Height is about 5.5-inches. Overall length is 8.625-inches. Weight is about 43 oz. Magazine capacity is 7-rounds. Fixed sights.

NIB	Exc.	V.G.	Good	Fair	Poor
1200	950	675	450	325	195

DEUTSCHE WERKE
Erfurt, Germany

Ortgies

A semi-automatic pistol in 6.35mm and 7.65mm. The 6.35mm pistol was manufactured in 1921 and the 7.65mm model in 1922 by the Ortgies Company. The pistols had the "HO" logo for Heinrich Ortgies on each grip. Later the Ortgies Company was bought by Deutsche Werke. The grip logo was "D." Over the period the Ortgies were manufactured with four different slide legends.

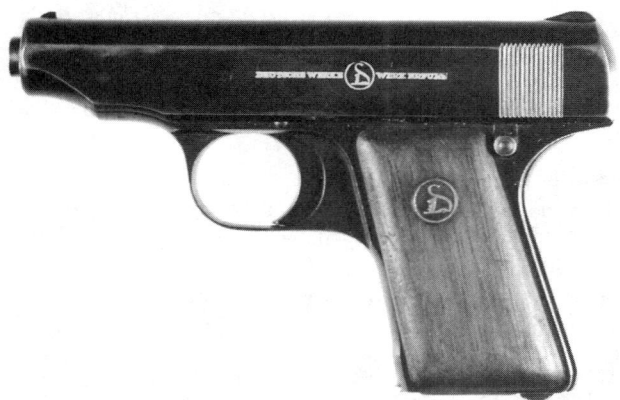

Courtesy James Rankin

NIB	Exc.	V.G.	Good	Fair	Poor
—	450	325	275	200	100

Ortgies 9mm

As above but with the addition of a hold-open button on the left side of the slide. Caliber is 9mmk, aka .380 ACP.

Courtesy James Rankin

NIB	Exc.	V.G.	Good	Fair	Poor
—	450	375	250	175	100

DEVISME, F. P.
Paris, France

One of the more popular French gunsmiths of the mid-19th century, F.P. Devisme manufactured a wide variety of firearms including single-shot percussion pistols, double-barrel percussion rifles and shotguns, percussion revolvers and cane guns. After 1858 this maker manufactured cartridge weapons of the same style as his percussion arms. The quality of all of his products is uniformly high and it is impossible to provide generalized price guide.

DICKINSON, E. L. & J.
Springfield, Massachusetts

Ranger

A .32 caliber spur trigger revolver with a 6-shot cylinder.

NIB	Exc.	V.G.	Good	Fair	Poor
—	—	525	450	200	100

Single-Shot

A .32 caliber single-shot pistol with a 3.75" hinged barrel, silver plated brass frame, blued barrel and walnut grips.

NIB	Exc.	V.G.	Good	Fair	Poor
—	—	775	650	250	100

DIMICK, H.E.
St. Louis, Missouri

While this maker is primarily known for half stock Plains Rifles, he also manufactured a limited number of percussion pistols. These vary in length, caliber, stock form and type of furniture. The values listed should only be used as a rough guide. Prospective purchasers should secure a qualified appraisal prior to acquisition. Active 1849 to 1873.

NIB	Exc.	V.G.	Good	Fair	Poor
—	—	—	7500	2750	900

DOMINO
Brescia, Italy

Model OP 601 Match Pistol

A .22 caliber short semi-automatic pistol with a 5.6" vented barrel, target sights, adjustable and removable trigger. Blued with adjustable walnut grips.

NIB	Exc.	V.G.	Good	Fair	Poor
1700	1200	800	550	300	175

Model SP 602 Match Pistol

As above, in .22 LR caliber.

Courtesy John J. Stimsom, Jr.

NIB	Exc.	V.G.	Good	Fair	Poor
1700	1200	800	550	300	175

DORNHEIM, G.C.
Suhl, Germany

Gecado Model 11

A 6.35mm semi-automatic pistol bearing the name "Gecado" on the slide. Fitted with a 2.2" barrel. Magazine capacity is 6 rounds. Weight is about 15 oz. Marketed by G.C. Dornheim. Copy of the FN Browning Model 1906.

Courtesy James Rankin

NIB	Exc.	V.G.	Good	Fair	Poor
—	300	225	125	75	50

Gecado 7.65mm

A 7.65mm semi-automatic pistol bearing the name "Gecado" on the slide. Fitted with a 2.6" barrel. Magazine capacity is 7 rounds. Weight is about 21 oz. Marketed by G.C. Dornheim.

NIB	Exc.	V.G.	Good	Fair	Poor
—	275	150	125	75	50

DOUBLESTAR, CORP.
Winchester, Kentucky

1911 Combat Pistol

Full-size Government Model .45 ACP with 5-inch barrel, stainless slide, forged frame, black finish. Novak white-dot LoMount sights, Picatinny rail, 8-shot magazine, checkered wood grips. Introduced 2010.

NIB	Exc.	V.G.	Good	Fair	Poor
1150	1000	875	700	400	300

DOUG TURNBULL RESTORATION, INC.
Bloomfield, New York

This company began operation in 1983 as a one-man shop. Today the company numbers 14 people and does finish work for most major firearms manufacturers. The company also installs Miller single triggers. The models listed are a series of special run firearms produced by Turnbull.

DT COLT

This model is a current Colt SAA reworked to look like the pre-1920 SAA. Assigned serial numbers beginning with 001DT these revolvers are offered in .45 Colt, .44-40, and .38-40 calibers. Barrel lengths are 4.75", 5.5", and 7.5". The standard DT has color case hardened frame and the rest of the gun charcoal blue. Cylinder flutes are enlarged and the front of the cylinder is beveled. Many special options offered which will affect cost. Prices listed are for standard revolvers. Valuues for these very special guns is strictly what the market will bear.

ear Offered—1998

NIB	Exc.	V.G.	Good	Fair	Poor
1795	—	—	—	—	—

Year Offered—1999

NIB	Exc.	V.G.	Good	Fair	Poor
2250	—	—	—	—	—

Year Offered—2000

NIB	Exc.	V.G.	Good	Fair	Poor
2500	—	—	—	—	—

EHBM Colt

This is a Colt SAA current production revolver limited to 50 guns chambered of the .45 Colt and fitted with a 5.5" barrel. Special features. Serial numbers EHBM01 to EHBM50. First offered in 2000.

NIB	Exc.	V.G.	Good	Fair	Poor
2650	2300	1600	1250	700	500

Smith & Wesson No. 3 Schofield

Introduced in 2002 this is a special new production S&W Schofield with special serial numbers with a "DTR" prefix starting with serial number 0001. The frame, barrel, and cylinder are charcoal blued while the trigger, trigger guard, and barrel latch are bone color case hardened. Factory wood grips are standard. Engraving is optional.

NIB	Exc.	V.G.	Good	Fair	Poor
2300	2450	1900	1550	875	500

Colt/Winchester Cased Set

A cased set with a Colt Model 1873 engraved revolver and a Winchester Model 1894. Colt is chambered for the .45 Colt cartridge and fitted with a 7.5" barrel. Engraving is "B" coverage. Model 1894 is chambered for the .45 Colt cartridge and is in the saddle ring configuration. Engraving pattern is #9 with deer. Checkered walnut stock. Limited to five sets total. Serial numbers 160DT to 164DT.

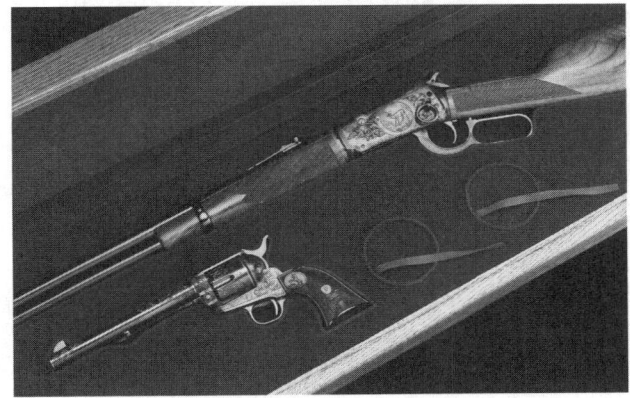

NIB	Exc.	V.G.	Good	Fair	Poor
5750	4300	3750	2500	1500	600

General Patton Colt

This limited run of engraved Colt Model 1873 single-action army revolvers is fitted with ivory grips and full-coverage engraving. Chambered for the .45 Colt cartridge and fitted with a 4.75" barrel. Helfricht-style engraving. Silver-plated finish. Limited to 10 revolvers total. Serial numbers GP01 to GP10.

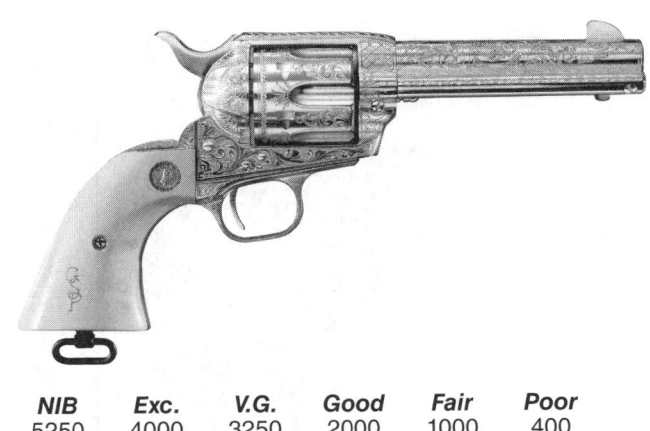

NIB	Exc.	V.G.	Good	Fair	Poor
5250	4000	3250	2000	1000	400

Theodore Roosevelt Colt

This Colt single-action army revolver features carved ivory grips, full coverage engraving with gold cylinder, hammer and ejector rod. Chambered for the .44-40 cartridge and fitted with a 7.5" barrel. Nimschke-style engraving. Balance of gun is silver plated. Supplied with fitted case. Limited to 25 revolvers total. Serial numbers TR01 to TR25.

NIB	Exc.	V.G.	Good	Fair	Poor
7750	6000	5000	4000	3000	600

Classic Cowboy

Custom-tuned and authentically-finished USFA 1873-style single action revolver. Chambered in virtually all historically-correct centerfire cartridges. Barrel: 4.75, 5.5 and 7.5 inches. Black hard rubber grips standard. Bone charcoal case-hardened and charcoal blue finish. Introduced 2006.

NIB	Exc.	V.G.	Good	Fair	Poor
1650	1300	950	675	400	300

DOWNSIZER CORPORATION
Santee, California

Model WSP

Introduced in 1998, this is billed as the world's smallest pistol by the manufacturer. It is a single-shot, double-action-only pistol with tip-up barrel. It is chambered for .22 Mag., .32 Mag., .357 Mag., 9mm, .40 S&W, and .45 ACP cartridges. Barrel length is 2.1". Overall length is 3.25". Height is 2.25", thickness is .9". Weight is approximately 11 oz. Built from stainless steel.

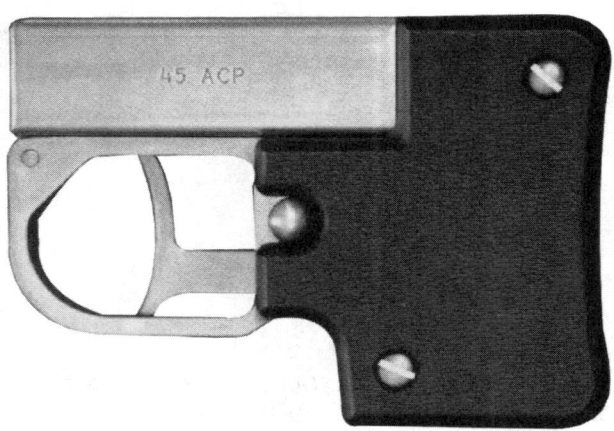

NIB	Exc.	V.G.	Good	Fair	Poor
400	325	275	225	175	125

DPMS
St. Cloud, Minnesota

Panther A-15 Pump Pistol

Same as the company's AR-15 pump rifle but fitted with a 10.5" barrel. Weight is about 5 lbs.

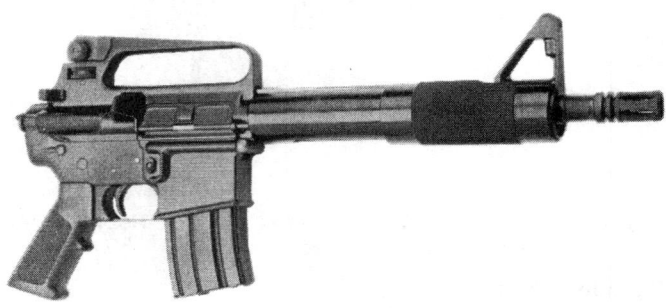

NIB	Exc.	V.G.	Good	Fair	Poor
1450	1100	750	575	450	300

DRISCOLL, J.B.
Springfield, Massachusetts

Single-Shot Pocket Pistol

A small pistol chambered for .22 rimfire. It has a 3.5" octagonal barrel that pivots downward for loading after a trigger-like hook under the breech is pulled. It has a spur trigger, silver-plated brass frame, and a blued barrel. The square butt is flared at the bottom, and the grips are walnut. There were approximately 200 manufactured in the late 1860s.

NIB	Exc.	V.G.	Good	Fair	Poor
—	—	1000	375	100	50

DRULOV
Czech Republic

This company was part of the national co-operative under communist rule when the Czech Republic was part of Czechoslovakia. The company was formed in 1948. The company specialized in low-cost but well made rimfire target pistols.

Drulov Model 70 Standard

This model is a bolt-action single-shot pistol chambered for the .22 Long Rifle. A knob at the rear of the frame opened the bolt. When the bolt is closed the firing pin is cocked. The barrel is 9.75" long with an adjustable front sight for windage. The rear sight is adjustable for elevation. Wooden wraparound grips with thumb rest are standard. Weighs about 44 oz.

NIB	Exc.	V.G.	Good	Fair	Poor
—	300	200	175	100	75

Drulov Model 70 Special

Same as above but with the addition of a set trigger.

NIB	Exc.	V.G.	Good	Fair	Poor
—	350	250	200	150	100

Drulov Model 75

This model features a set trigger, better sights, and grip. The rear sight is fully adjustable.

NIB	Exc.	V.G.	Good	Fair	Poor
—	400	300	250	200	150

Pav

This target pistol was introduced between World War I and World War II. It is an inexpensive pistol with a fixed front sight and a notch for the rear sight. Like the other models above it is also a single-shot chambered for the .22 Long Rifle cartridge. The barrel is 10.25" and weighs about 35 oz.

Courtesy Orvel Reichert

NIB	Exc.	V.G.	Good	Fair	Poor
—	175	150	100	75	50

B&T TP9 Tactical Pistol

Swiss made recoil-operated, rotating-bolt semi-auto chambered in 9mm Parabellum. Semi-auto, civilian-legal version of B&T TP9SF select-fire submachine gun. Planned to be imported in 2007.

NIB	Exc.	V.G.	Good	Fair	Poor
1100	950	775	600	475	350

DUSEK, F.
Opocno, Czech Republic

Dusek commenced business in the mid-1920s and continued to make firearms through WWII. They manufactured pistols for Nazi Germany under the contract code "aek." After the war the communists took over, and Dusek's designs were relegated to the CZ factory.

Perla

This 6.35mm pistol has a fixed barrel and open-topped slide. It resembles a Walther design and is striker-fired. The slide is marked "Automat Pistole Perla 6.35mm" ; the grips, "Perla 6.35." Dusek made this model from the early 1930s until WWII.

NIB	Exc.	V.G.	Good	Fair	Poor
—	335	225	165	100	80

Duo

DAK-5Replace with DAK-6-7

Courtesy J.B. Wood

NIB	Exc.	V.G.	Good	Fair	Poor
—	375	250	195	100	80

NOTE: Nazi-marked examples will bring a 25 percent premium.

D. W. M.
Berlin, Germany

SEE—Luger & Borchardt

Model 22

A 7.65mm caliber semi-automatic pistol with 3.5" barrel. Blued with walnut grips; later changed to plastic grips. Approximately 40,000 manufactured between 1921 and 1931.

NIB	Exc.	V.G.	Good	Fair	Poor
—	950	775	500	400	250

ECHAVE & ARIZMENDI
Eibar, Spain

Founded in 1911, this company produced the usual poor quality, early Spanish semi-automatic pistols. They did improve their quality later on and were permitted to return to gun manufacturing after the Spanish civil war. They were one of the few pistol makers to survive this period. They imported many models, and their products are not particularly of interest to collectors.

Basque, Echasa, Dickson, or Dickson Special Agent

These four pistols are the same semi-automatic pistols but chambered in .22 LR, 6.35mm, 7.65mm, and 9mmK respectively. Their magazine capacities are 10, 9, 7, and 6 rounds. They are manufactured with alloy frames and various finish combinations. The specific model names are stamped on the slides and grip plates.

Courtesy James Rankin

NIB	Exc.	V.G.	Good	Fair	Poor
—	295	185	125	90	50

Bronco Model 1913

A semi-automatic pistol in caliber 6.35mm. Patterned after the Browning Model 1906 with a squeeze grip safety. Bronco is stamped on the slide and on each side of the grip plate.

Courtesy James Rankin

NIB	Exc.	V.G.	Good	Fair	Poor
—	295	185	125	90	50

Bronco Model 1918

A semi-automatic pistol chambered for both 6.35mm or 7.65mm. Both are patterned after the Browning Model 1906 with a squeeze grip safety. The 7.65mm pistol is approximately 1/2" longer and higher than the 6.35mm. It has a magazine capacity of 7 rounds. The 6.35mm pistol has a magazine capacity of 6 rounds.

Courtesy James Rankin

NIB	Exc.	V.G.	Good	Fair	Poor
—	295	185	125	90	50

Echasa

Similar to the 6.35mm Bronco, without a grip safety. It is marked "Model 1916."

NIB	Exc.	V.G.	Good	Fair	Poor
—	295	185	125	90	50

Lightning

A renamed version of the Bronco in 6.35mm.

NIB	Exc.	V.G.	Good	Fair	Poor
—	295	185	125	90	50

Pathfinder

A semi-automatic pistol similar to the Bronco above but in caliber 6.35mm and 7.65mm. Sold in the U.S. by Stoeger. The 7.65mm Pathfinder holds 12 rounds. The values listed are for both pistol models.

NIB	Exc.	V.G.	Good	Fair	Poor
—	295	185	125	90	50

Protector Model 1915 and 1918

A semi-automatic pistol in caliber 6.35mm. Similar to the Echasa model. "Protector" is stamped on the slide while the grip plates have various logos of the firms that marketed the pistol.

Courtesy James Rankin

NIB	Exc.	V.G.	Good	Fair	Poor
—	275	185	100	70	40

Selecta Model 1918

A semi-automatic pistol chambered for 7.65mm cartridge. Patterned after the Protector but chambered for the 7.65mm. "Selecta" is stamped on the slide and Echave Arizmendi logo is on each of the grip plates.

Courtesy James Rankin

NIB	Exc.	V.G.	Good	Fair	Poor
—	295	185	125	90	50

ECHEVERRIA
(STAR)

Megastar

This is a double-action semi-automatic pistol chambered for the 10mm or .45 ACP cartridge. It features a three-position ambidextrous selective decocking lever, rubber grips, combat-style trigger guard, slotted hammer, and checkered mainspring housing. Barrel length is 4.6" and the magazine capacity is 12 rounds. Available in either blue or starvel (brushed chrome). The pistol weighs 47.6 oz.

NIB	Exc.	V.G.	Good	Fair	Poor
500	450	350	250	200	100

Firestar-M/43, M/40, and M45

This is a compact large caliber semi-automatic pistol offered in 9mm, the M43, .40 S&W, the M40, and the .45 ACP, the M45. It features an ambidextrous safety, steel frame and slide, checkered rubber grips. The barrel is 3.4" on the M43 and M40 and 3.6" on the M45. Choice of finish is blue or starvel (brushed chrome). A finger rest magazine is optional. Weight for the M43 and M40 is 30 oz. while the M56 weighs 35 oz. Introduced in 1990.

NIB	Exc.	V.G.	Good	Fair	Poor
400	300	250	200	150	100

Firestar Plus

This is a lightweight version of the Firestar Series with the addition of a double column magazine. Offered in the 9mm caliber in either blue or starvel finish this pistol has a magazine capacity of 10 rounds and weighs 24 oz. Introduced in 1992.

NIB	Exc.	V.G.	Good	Fair	Poor
450	350	—	250	175	125

Starfire Model 31P

This model evolved from the Models 28 and 30. It is chambered for either the 9mm Parabellum or .40 S&W. The trigger action is double-action/single-action. Barrel length is 3.9". It is fitted with a two position safety/decocking lever. The magazine capacity for the 9mm is 15 rounds while the .40 S&W holds 11 rounds. The pistol weighs 39 oz.

NIB	Exc.	V.G.	Good	Fair	Poor
425	350	300	250	200	100

Starfire Model 31PK

Similar to the Model 31P but built on an alloy frame. Chambered for 9mm only with a 15-round magazine capacity. Weight is 30 oz.

NIB	Exc.	V.G.	Good	Fair	Poor
400	325	275	225	200	100

Ultrastar

Introduced in 1994 this compact 9mm or .40 S&W semi-automatic pistol with a polymer frame features a 3.57" barrel, a 9-round magazine, a blued finish and an overall length of 7". It weighs about 26 oz. It has a double-action operating system, a windage adjustable rear sight, and an ambidextrous two-position safety.

NIB	Exc.	V.G.	Good	Fair	Poor
400	365	305	275	200	100

ECHEVERRIA, STAR-BONIFACIO SA (STAR)
Eibar, Spain

An old-line Spanish company that survived the Spanish civil war. It was founded in 1908 by Jean Echeverria, but the early records of the company were lost during the civil war. The early pistols the company produced were patterned after the Mannlicher designs, and the trade name Star was the closest thing to Steyr that could be used. After the close of WWI, the company began production of the open-topped slide Star for which they have become known. They also produced a large 1911-type pistol that was successful. During the civil war, the plant was damaged and the company records destroyed; but after the cessation of hostilities, they were one of only three gun companies that were allowed to remain in business. The company is now defunct.

Star Model 1908

The first pistol produced under the Star banner. It is a Mannlicher copy that is chambered for 6.35mm. It has a 3" fixed barrel and an open-topped slide. The detachable magazine holds 8 shots. The finish is blued, and the grips are checkered plastic. The slide is marked "Automatic Pistol Star Patent."

Courtesy James Rankin

NIB	Exc.	V.G.	Good	Fair	Poor
—	350	275	200	150	100

Star Model 1914

Similar to the Model 1908, with a 5" barrel and larger grips that have the Star name molded into them. This model was the first to have the six-pointed star surrounded by rays of light (that became the Star trademark) stamped on its slide.

Courtesy James Rankin

NIB	Exc.	V.G.	Good	Fair	Poor
—	350	275	200	150	100

Star Model 1919

Also a copy of a Mannlicher design and differs from its predecessors chiefly in the way the pistol is disassembled. This model has a spring catch at the top of the trigger guard. This model also has a small spur on the hammer, and the magazine release was relocated to a button behind the trigger guard instead of a catch at the bottom of the butt. This model was chambered for 6.35mm, 7.65mm and 9mm short, with various barrel lengths offered. The maker's name, as well as the Star trademark, is stamped into the slide. This model was produced until 1929.

Courtesy James Rankin

NIB	Exc.	V.G.	Good	Fair	Poor
—	350	275	200	150	100

Star Model 1919 New Variation

Same as above but with full spur hammer.

Courtesy James Rankin

NIB	Exc.	V.G.	Good	Fair	Poor
—	350	275	200	150	100

Modelo Militar

Represents the first pistol Star produced that was not a Mannlicher design copy. This model was copied from the Colt 1911. It was chambered initially for the 9mm Largo in hopes of securing a military contract. When this contract was awarded to Astra, Star chambered the Model 1919 for the .38 Super and the .45 ACP and put it on the commercial market. This model is like the Colt 1911—it has a Browning-type swinging link and the same type of lock up. However there is no grip safety, and the thumb safety functions differently. Add 30 percent for marked .38 Super.

NIB	Exc.	V.G.	Good	Fair	Poor
—	425	325	245	175	125

Star Model A

A modification of the Model 1919, chambered for the 7.65mm, 7.63mm Mauser, 9mm Largo, and the .45 ACP cartridge. The slide is similar in appearance to the 1911 Colt, and the spur hammer has a small hole in it. Early models had no grip safety, but later production added this feature. Some models are slotted for addition of a shoulder stock.

Courtesy James Rankin

NIB	Exc.	V.G.	Good	Fair	Poor
—	425	325	245	175	125

Star Model B

Similar to the Model A except that it is almost an exact copy of the Colt 1911. It is chambered for 9mm Parabellum and has a spur hammer with no hole. This model was introduced in 1928.

Courtesy Orvel Reichert

NIB	Exc.	V.G.	Good	Fair	Poor
—	425	325	245	175	125

Star Model C

The Model B chambered for the 9mm Browning long cartridge. It was manufactured in the 1920s.

NIB	Exc.	V.G.	Good	Fair	Poor
—	350	265	175	125	90

Star Model CO

A pocket pistol similar to the early open-topped Star pistols. It is chambered for the 6.35mm cartridge, and the finish is blued with checkered plastic grips that bear the Star name and logo. This model was manufactured between 1930 and 1957.

Courtesy James Rankin

NIB	Exc.	V.G.	Good	Fair	Poor
—	275	195	125	100	75

Star Model D

A medium-sized pistol that is similar in appearance to a smaller Model A. It is chambered for the 9mm short cartridge and was called the "Police and Pocket Model" after it was adopted by the Spanish police. It was manufactured between 1930 and 1941.

NIB	Exc.	V.G.	Good	Fair	Poor
—	300	195	175	110	80

Star Model E

A pocket pistol chambered for the 6.35mm cartridge. It has a 2.5" barrel and an external hammer. The detachable magazine holds 5 rounds, and the finish is blued with checkered plastic grips. This model was manufactured between 1932 and 1941.

NIB	Exc.	V.G.	Good	Fair	Poor
—	250	195	165	110	80

Star Model F

The first of the .22 caliber Star pistols. It has a 4" barrel, a 10-shot magazine, and fixed sights. The finish is blued, and the plastic grips are checkered. This model was manufactured between 1942 and 1967.

NIB	Exc.	V.G.	Good	Fair	Poor
—	300	265	200	110	75

Star Model F Target

Similar to the Model F, with a 6" barrel.

NIB	Exc.	V.G.	Good	Fair	Poor
—	325	275	210	125	100

Star Model F Sport

Has a 5" barrel and was also manufactured between 1962 and 1967.

NIB	Exc.	V.G.	Good	Fair	Poor
—	325	275	210	125	100

Star Model F Olympic

Has a 6" barrel and adjustable sights. It is furnished with a muzzlebrake and barrel weights. It was manufactured between 1942 and 1967.

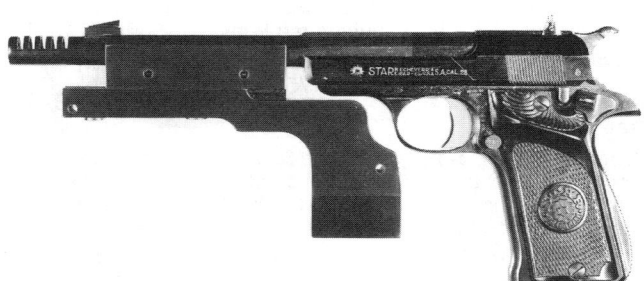

Courtesy James Rankin

NIB	Exc.	V.G.	Good	Fair	Poor
—	350	265	175	125	90

Star Model F Olympic Rapid Fire

Similar to the Olympic but is chambered for .22 Short only.

NIB	Exc.	V.G.	Good	Fair	Poor
—	375	295	185	150	125

Star Model FR

Has an adjustable sight and a slide stop. The 4" barrel is heavier, with flattened sides. It was manufactured between 1967 and 1972.

NIB	Exc.	V.G.	Good	Fair	Poor
—	325	275	210	125	100

Star Model FRS

Similar to the Model FR, with a 6" barrel. It is also available chrome-plated with white checkered plastic grips. It was introduced in 1967.

NIB	Exc.	V.G.	Good	Fair	Poor
—	295	225	175	125	100

Star Model FM

A heavier-framed version of the Model FRS. It has a 4.5" barrel and is available in blue or chrome-plated. It was introduced in 1972.

NIB	Exc.	V.G.	Good	Fair	Poor
—	325	275	210	125	100

Star Model H

Similar to the old Model CO—only larger in size. It is chambered for the 7.65mm cartridge and was manufactured between 1932 and 1941.

NIB	Exc.	V.G.	Good	Fair	Poor
—	250	195	150	125	100

Star Model HK

A pocket-sized version of the Model F chambered for .22 Short. It has a 2.5" barrel and is quite scarce on today's market.

NIB	Exc.	V.G.	Good	Fair	Poor
—	325	275	210	125	100

Star Model HN

Simply the Model H chambered for the 9mm Short cartridge. It was manufactured and discontinued at the same time as the Model H was.

NIB	Exc.	V.G.	Good	Fair	Poor
—	275	202	165	125	100

Star Model I

An improved version of the Model H with a 4" barrel and a recontoured grip. It was chambered for 7.65mm and was produced until 1941. After the war it was resumed and survived until the mid-1950s, when it was replaced by the modernized Model IR that would be valued approximately the same.

NIB	Exc.	V.G.	Good	Fair	Poor
—	250	195	150	125	100

Star Model M

Similar to the Model B, chambered for the .38 Auto (NOT .38 Super) cartridge.

NIB	Exc.	V.G.	Good	Fair	Poor
—	375	295	185	150	125

Star Model P

The post-war version of the Model B, fitted with a 5" barrel and chambered for the .45 ACP cartridge. Checkered walnut grips and blued finish.

NIB	Exc.	V.G.	Good	Fair	Poor
—	400	350	265	195	125

Star Model CU "Starlet"

Similar to the Model CO, with an alloy frame that was anodized in black, blue, gray, green, or gold. It has a steel slide that is blued or chrome-plated. It has checkered, white plastic grips and is chambered for the .25 ACP cartridge. It has a 2.5" barrel, fixed sights, and a 5-shot magazine. This model was introduced in 1975 and was not imported after 1986.

NIB	Exc.	V.G.	Good	Fair	Poor
—	250	175	145	100	75

Star Model 1941 S

Add 100 percent to prices listed for pistols issued to Spanish Air Force with box, cleaning rod, instruction sheet, and two numbered magazines.

Courtesy Richard M. Kumor Sr.

NIB	Exc.	V.G.	Good	Fair	Poor
—	250	210	175	125	75

Star Model BKS "Starlight"

The smallest locked-breech automatic chambered for the 9mm cartridge at the time. It has an alloy frame and a 4.25" barrel. It is similar in appearance to a scaled-down Colt 1911 without a grip safety. It has an 8-shot magazine and is either blued or chrome-plated, with checkered plastic grips. This model was manufactured between 1970 and 1981.

NIB	Exc.	V.G.	Good	Fair	Poor
—	325	275	210	125	100

Star Model PD

Chambered for the .45 ACP cartridge and has a 4" barrel. It has an alloy frame and a 6-shot magazine and adjustable sights and is blued with checkered walnut grips. It was introduced in 1975.

NIB	Exc.	V.G.	Good	Fair	Poor
400	325	275	225	175	125

Star Model BM

A steel-framed 9mm that is styled after the Colt 1911. It has an 8-shot magazine and a 4" barrel. It is available either blued or chrome-plated.

NIB	Exc.	V.G.	Good	Fair	Poor
350	300	250	200	150	125

Star Model BKM

Similar to the BM, with an alloy frame.

NIB	Exc.	V.G.	Good	Fair	Poor
375	325	275	225	175	125

Star Model 28

The first of Star's Super 9s. It is a double-action semi-automatic chambered for the 9mm Parabellum cartridge. It has a 4.25" barrel and a steel frame. The magazine holds 15 shots. The construction of this pistol was totally modular, and it has no screws in its design. It is blued with checkered synthetic grips and was manufactured in 1983 and 1984.

NIB	Exc.	V.G.	Good	Fair	Poor
425	365	295	200	150	100

Star Model 30M

An improved version of the Model 28, that is quite similar in appearance. It was introduced in 1985.

NIB	Exc.	V.G.	Good	Fair	Poor
450	350	300	250	200	125

Star Model 30/PK

Similar to the Models 28 and 30M, with a lightweight alloy frame.

NIB	Exc.	V.G.	Good	Fair	Poor
450	350	300	250	200	125

ECLIPSE
Enterprise Gun Works
Pittsburgh, Pennsylvania

Single-Shot Derringer

This pocket pistol was made by the firm of James Bown & Son, doing business as the Enterprise Gun Works. It is chambered for .22 or .32-caliber rimfire cartridges. A few in .25 rimfire have been noted and would add approximately 25 percent to the values listed. The barrel is 2.5" in length and is part-round/part-octagonal. It pivots sideways for loading. It has a spur trigger and a bird's-head grip. The barrel is stamped "Eclipse." It is made of nickel-plated iron, with walnut grips. There were approximately 10,000 manufactured between 1870 and 1890.

NIB	Exc.	V.G.	Good	Fair	Poor
—	—	650	250	100	75

ELGIN CUTLASS
Springfield, Massachusetts

Manufactured by two companies—C.B. Allen of Springfield, Massachusetts, and Morill, Mosman and Blair of Amherst, Massachusetts. It is a unique pistol that has an integral knife attachment affixed to the gun barrel. It was designed and patented by George Elgin and simultaneously produced by the two companies. The inspiration for this weapon was supposedly Jim Bowie, who at that time had made a name as a knife fighter with his large "Bowie" knife. The blades for these pistols were supplied by N.P. Ames of the famed Ames Sword Co. These pistols are much sought after, and one must exercise caution as fraudulent examples have been noted.

C. B. ALLEN-MADE PISTOLS
U.S. Navy Elgin Cutlass Pistol

Chambered for .54 caliber percussion and has a 5" octagonal smooth-bore barrel. The Bowie-style blade is 11" long by 2" wide and is forged together with the trigger guard and the knuckle guard that protects the grip. The handle is walnut. This pistol was issued to the U.S. Navy's Wilkes-South Sea Exploration Expedition, and the markings are "C.B. Allen / Springfield / Mass." "Elgin's Patent" and the letters "CB", "CBA" along with the date 1837. If the sheath that was issued with this knife pistol is included and in sound condition, it would add approximately $700 to the value. There were 150 manufactured for the U.S. Navy in 1838.

NIB	Exc.	V.G.	Good	Fair	Poor
—	—	35500	14000	7500	4750

Civilian Model

Chambered for .35 or .41 caliber percussion and has a 4" octagonal barrel with a 7.5"-10" knife blade. It has a round trigger guard but does not have the knuckle bow across the grip, as found on the military model. They are marked "C.B. Allen Springfield, Mass." Blades marked "N.P. Ames" have been noted. There were approximately 100 manufactured in 1837.

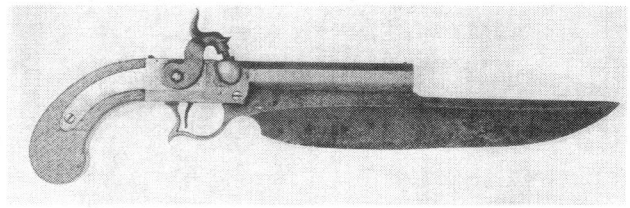

NIB	Exc.	V.G.	Good	Fair	Poor
—	—	33500	13000	6250	3250

MORILL, MOSMAN AND BLAIR-MADE PISTOLS
Small Model

The main difference in the pistols of the two makers is that this model has a round barrel and a square-back trigger guard that comes to a point at the rear. This version is chambered for .32 caliber percussion and has a 2.75" barrel. The knife blade is 7.5" in length and is screwed to the frame. This model is unmarked except for a serial number. The number produced is unknown, and they were manufactured in 1837.

NIB	Exc.	V.G.	Good	Fair	Poor
—	—	33500	13000	6250	3250

Large Model

Chambered for .36 caliber percussion and has a 4" round barrel and a 9" knife blade. The pistol is usually marked "Cast Steel" and serial numbered. The blade is etched with an American eagle, stars, and an urn with flowers. "Elgin Patent" is etched in the center. This model was also manufactured in 1837.

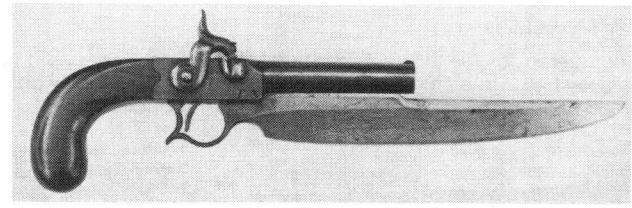

Courtesy Milwaukee Public Museum, Milwaukee, Wisconsin

NIB	Exc.	V.G.	Good	Fair	Poor
—	—	37000	14500	7000	3900

ELLS, JOSIAH
Pittsburgh, Pennsylvania

POCKET REVOLVER

Three distinct variations of this percussion revolver. They are chambered for .28 and .31 caliber and have 6-shot unfluted cylinders. They have been noted with 2.5", 3", and 3.75" octagonal barrels.

Model 1

The first model has an open-topped frame and is chambered for .28 caliber. The cylinder holds 5 or 6 shots, and the hammer is of the bar type. It was offered with a 2.5" or 3" barrel. The markings are "J. Ells; Patent; 1854." There were approximately 625 manufactured between 1857 and 1859.

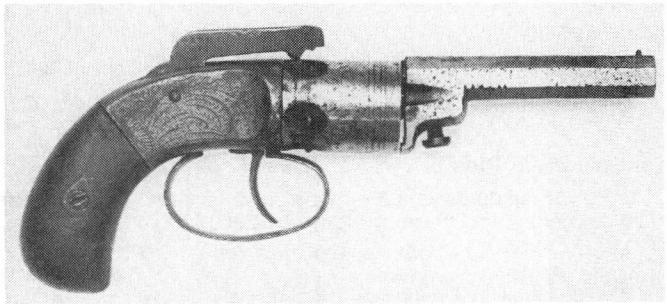

Courtesy Milwaukee Public Museum, Milwaukee, Wisconsin

NIB	Exc.	V.G.	Good	Fair	Poor
—	—	1700	875	375	200

Model 2

The second model is similar to the first, with a solid-topped frame. They have 5-shot cylinders and 3.75" long barrels. There were approximately 550 manufactured.

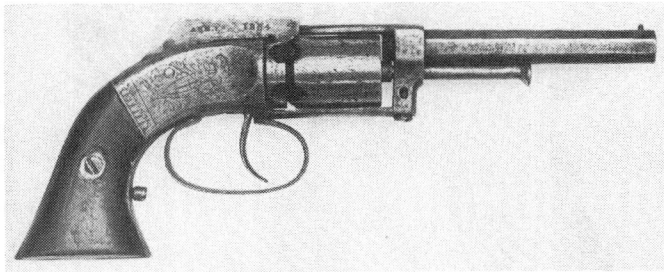

Courtesy Milwaukee Public Museum, Milwaukee, Wisconsin

NIB	Exc.	V.G.	Good	Fair	Poor
—	—	1750	750	365	200

Model 3

The third model is radically different from its forerunners. It has a closed-top frame and a conventional spur-type hammer that strikes from the right side. It functions either as a double- or single-action. It is chambered for .28 caliber and has a 5-shot cylinder and a 3.75" barrel. There were only about 200 manufactured between 1857 and 1859.

NIB	Exc.	V.G.	Good	Fair	Poor
—	—	1850	995	425	200

E.M.F. CO., INC.
Santa Ana, California
SEE—Uberti, Aldo

An importer and a distributor of quality Italian-made reproduction firearms. Most of its offerings are listed in the section dealing with Aldo Uberti firearms.

Hartford Bisley

This single-action revolver is fitted with a Colt Bisley grip. Chambered for .45 Long Colt as well as .32-20, .357 Magnum, .38-40, and .44-40 calibers. Barrel lengths are 4-3/4", 5-1/2", and 7-1/2". Plain walnut grips.

NIB	Exc.	V.G.	Good	Fair	Poor
525	425	300	225	145	105

Hartford Express

A single Colt SAA frame and barrel with a Colt Lightning-style grip. Chambered for .45 Long Colt in 4-3/4", 5-1/2", or 7-1/2" barrel lengths.

NIB	Exc.	V.G.	Good	Fair	Poor
525	425	300	225	145	105

Hartford Pinkerton

This model features a 4" barrel with ejector and a bird's-head grip. Chambered for 45 Long Colt, .32-20, .357 Magnum, .38-40, .44-40, and .44 Special.

NIB	Exc.	V.G.	Good	Fair	Poor
525	425	300	225	145	105

ENFIELD AMERICAN, INC.
Atlanta, Georgia

MP-45

A blowback-operated, semi-automatic assault pistol chambered for the .45 ACP cartridge. It was offered with a barrel length of 4.5" through 18.5". The long barrel features a shroud. The finish is

Parkerized, and there were four different magazines available in 10, 20, 30, and 50-round capacities. This firearm was manufactured in 1985 only.

NIB	Exc.	V.G.	Good	Fair	Poor
—	575	475	295	175	125

ENTREPRISE ARMS, INC.
Irwindale, California

ELITE SERIES

This is the basic model with stainless steel barrels, fixed sights, squared trigger guard, adjustable match trigger, checkered slide release, high ride grip safety, flat mainspring housing, and a number of other special features. Magazine capacity is 10 rounds.

Elite P500

Chambered for .45 ACP and fitted with a 5" barrel. Weight is about 40 oz.

NIB	Exc.	V.G.	Good	Fair	Poor
750	600	495	350	200	100

Elite P425

This model has a 4.25" barrel. Weight is approximately 38 oz.

NIB	Exc.	V.G.	Good	Fair	Poor
750	600	495	350	200	100

Elite 325

This model has a 3.25" barrel with a weight of 36 oz.

NIB	Exc.	V.G.	Good	Fair	Poor
750	600	495	350	200	100

TACTICAL SERIES

This model has an ambidextrous thumb lock with lightweight match hammer with matching sear. National match barrel with match extractor, full length one-piece guide rod, Novak sights, dovetail front sight, matte black finish, and a host of other features. Magazine capacity is 10 rounds.

Tactical P500

This model is chambered for the .45 ACP cartridge and has a 5" barrel and a weight of approximately 40 oz.

NIB	Exc.	V.G.	Good	Fair	Poor
995	795	600	495	350	100

Tactical P425

This model is fitted with a 4.25" barrel and weighs about 38 oz.

NIB	Exc.	V.G.	Good	Fair	Poor
995	795	600	495	350	100

Tactical P325

This model is fitted with a 3.25" barrel and has a weight of 36 oz.

NIB	Exc.	V.G.	Good	Fair	Poor
995	795	600	495	350	100

Tactical P325 Plus

This model features a 3.25" barrel and is fitted to a full size Government model frame. Weight is about 37 oz.

NIB	Exc.	V.G.	Good	Fair	Poor
1050	800	615	500	365	105

TITLEIST NATIONAL MATCH SERIES

This model is chambered for either the .45 ACP or .40 S&W cartridge. It has all the features of the Elite Series with an adjustable rear sight and dovetail Patridge front sight. Many other special features.

Titleist P500

This model is fitted with a 5" barrel. Weight is about 40 oz.

NIB	Exc.	V.G.	Good	Fair	Poor
995	795	600	495	350	100

NOTE: Add $20 for .40 S&W chambering.

Boxer Model

Chambered for the .45 ACP cartridge and fitted with a 5" barrel this model features a ramped bull barrel, wide ambi safety and high-mass chiseled slide. Weight is approximately 44 oz.

NIB	Exc.	V.G.	Good	Fair	Poor
1200	975	750	600	375	125

TOURNAMENT SERIES

These are the top-of-the-line models that feature all of the Elite Series features plus oversized magazine release button, checkered front strap, and flared extended magazine well.

TSM I

This is a limited class competition pistol. All these model are hand crafted. Fitted with a 5" barrel and choice of calibers. Weight is about 40 oz.

NIB	Exc.	V.G.	Good	Fair	Poor
2300	1750	1375	900	675	300

TSM II

This is a long slide model with cocking serrations on front and rear of slide. Barrel is 6". Weight is about 44 oz.

NIB	Exc.	V.G.	Good	Fair	Poor
2300	1750	1375	900	675	300

TSM III

This is an open class pistol designed for scope mount. Barrel is 5.5" long. Fitted with 7 port compensator. Many other custom features.Weight is about 44 oz.

NIB	Exc.	V.G.	Good	Fair	Poor
2700	2000	1525	1050	700	310

ERICHSON, G.
Houston, Texas

Pocket Pistol

A close copy of the Philadelphia-style Henry Deringer. It is chambered for .45-caliber percussion and has a 3.25" barrel. The mountings are German silver and not engraved; the stock is walnut. The hammer is deeply fluted; and the forend, carved. The barrel is marked "G. Erichson / Houston, Texas." The number produced is unknown, but examples are scarce. They were manufactured in the 1850s and 1860s.

NIB	Exc.	V.G.	Good	Fair	Poor
—	—	6500	3000	1000	400

ERMA WERKE WAFFENFABRIK
Erfurt, Germany
Post-war
Dachau, Germany

Known primarily as a manufacturer of submachine guns, but they are also in the handgun and rifle business. In 1933 they answered the German army's need for an inexpensive practice weapon by producing a .22 rimfire conversion unit for the Luger pistol. This was marketed commercially and was available for many years. The success of this unit led the company to produce other inexpensive target and plinking pistols. After the war they were reorganized in the western sector and resumed submachine gun production. In 1964 they returned to the sporting firearms business with the introduction of their .22 rimfire Luger-lookalike pistol. Since then, they have produced many like-quality firearms. They were imported by Excam of Hialeah, Florida. This association is now terminated, and they are currently imported by Beeman Precision in Santa Rosa, California, and Mandell Shooting Supplies in Scottsdale, Arizona.

Erma .22 Luger Conversion Unit

Produced for the German army in 1933 and then became a successful commercial item. It would turn a standard 9mm or 7.65mm Luger into an inexpensive-to-shoot .22 rimfire. The unit consists of a barrel insert, a breech block, and toggle unit with its own lightened recoil spring, and a .22 magazine. This unit was furnished with a wooden box. There were many different sized units to fit various caliber and barrel-length Lugers, but

all used the same parts and concept. These units have become desirable to Luger collectors.

NIB	Exc.	V.G.	Good	Fair	Poor
—	500	425	350	275	200

.22 Target Pistol (Old Model)

A semi-automatic target pistol in caliber .22 LR. This model was offered with 4", 6", or 8" barrels. The frame is made from a cast zinc alloy, and there is an external hammer. There are adjustable sights, and balance weights were available. Magazine capacity is 10 rounds. Weight is about 35 oz. This pistol was manufactured in 1936 and 1937.

Courtesy James Rankin

NIB	Exc.	V.G.	Good	Fair	Poor
—	800	725	500	350	100

.22 Target Pistol (New Model) Master Model

An improved version of the old model that features a new grip angle and a magazine and takedown device like that of the Luger. There were interchangeable barrels and three basic models — the "Sport," "Hunter," and the "Master." The difference was the length of the barrels — 4", 8", and 12", respectively. Magazine capacity is 10 rounds. Weight is about 39 oz. These pistols were manufactured between 1937 and 1940, when they were discontinued due to Erma's involvement in the war effort.

Courtesy James Rankin

NIB	Exc.	V.G.	Good	Fair	Poor
—	850	700	500	400	125

KGP-SERIES

Made to resemble the Luger quite closely. They utilized the mechanical features of the .22 conversion unit and developed a pistol around it. There are many different versions of this pistol chambered for .22 rimfire, .32 ACP, and .380 ACP. The original designation was the KGP-68; but the Gun Control Act of 1968 required that a magazine safety be added, and the model was redesignated the KGP-68A. The last designations for the three calibers are KGP-22, KGP-32, and KGP-38. These pistols were manufactured between 1964 and 1986, and their values are listed.

KGP-68

A 4" barrel and is chambered for the .32 ACP and the .380 ACP cartridges. It has a 6-shot magazine and an anodized alloy receiver. Weight is about 23 oz. This model is also known as the Beeman MP-08.

Courtesy James Rankin

NIB	Exc.	V.G.	Good	Fair	Poor
—	450	400	300	200	100

KGP-69

A .22 rimfire version of this series, with an 8-shot magazine capacity. Weight is about 30 oz. It is also known as the Beeman P-08.

NIB	Exc.	V.G.	Good	Fair	Poor
—	300	200	150	100	75

ET-22 "Navy Luger" Long-Barreled Pistol

A rare firearm. According to some estimates only 375 were produced. It features a 11.75" barrel and is chambered for the .22 rimfire cartridge. It has an artillery Luger-type rear sight and checkered walnut grips, with a smooth walnut forend. The pistol was furnished with a red-felt-lined, black leatherette case.

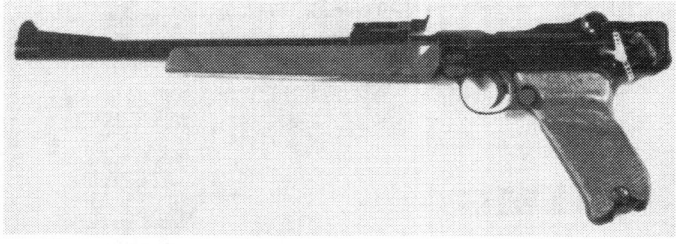

NIB	Exc.	V.G.	Good	Fair	Poor
—	900	675	400	250	150

KGP-32 & KGP-38

These two designations are the later versions of the KGP-68 and 68A.

NIB	Exc.	V.G.	Good	Fair	Poor
—	350	300	250	200	125

ESP 85A

A high quality target pistol imported by Mandall Shooting Supply. It features an interchangeable barrel system that converts the chambering from .22 rimfire to .32 S&W long wad cutter. The barrels are both 6" in length, and there are adjustable and interchangeable sights and a 5- or 8-shot detachable magazine. Weight is about 41 oz. The finish is blued, and the grips are stippled target types. The gun is furnished in a padded hard case with two extra magazines and takedown tools. This unit was introduced in 1989.

NIB	Exc.	V.G.	Good	Fair	Poor
1100	1000	850	700	550	450

EP-25

A semi-automatic pistol in caliber 6.35mm. Fitted with 2.75" barrel. Weight is about 18 oz. Mostly marketed outside of Germany. It has a polished blue finish and wood grips. Erma is stamped on the slide and on each of the grip's plates.

Courtesy James Rankin

NIB	Exc.	V.G.	Good	Fair	Poor
—	275	195	150	100	75

RX-22 and PX-22

A semi-automatic .22 rimfire copy of the Walther PPK. It has a 7-round magazine. Assembled in the U.S. with parts from Germany by various companies that marketed the pistol in the U.S. It has a black plastic wraparound grips with the Erma logo on each side.

Courtesy James Rankin

NIB	Exc.	V.G.	Good	Fair	Poor
—	240	175	150	100	75

ER-772 Match

A target revolver chambered for the .22 rimfire and has a 6" shrouded barrel with a solid rib. The swing-out cylinder holds

6 shots, and the sights are adjustable. The finish is blued, with stippled target grips. This model was introduced in 1989.

NIB	Exc.	V.G.	Good	Fair	Poor
700	500	450	350	250	200

ER-773 Match

Similar to the ER-772 except that it is chambered for the .32 S&W long cartridge.

NIB	Exc.	V.G.	Good	Fair	Poor
725	550	475	375	250	200

ER-777

Basically a similar revolver to the ER-773 except that it has a 4.5" or 5" barrel and is chambered for the .357 Magnum cartridge. The revolver is larger and has standard sport grips. This model was introduced in 1989.

NIB	Exc.	V.G.	Good	Fair	Poor
700	500	450	350	250	200

ERQUIAGA
Eibar, Spain

Another Spanish company that commenced business during WWI as a subcontractor on the French "Ruby" contract. They manufactured the usual poor quality, 7.65mm Eibar-type pistol.

Fiel

The trade name found on the Ruby subcontract pistol described above. It is marked "Erquiaga y Cia Eibar Cal. 7.65 Fiel."

Courtesy James Rankin

NIB	Exc.	V.G.	Good	Fair	Poor
—	200	150	125	100	75

Fiel 6.35

After the end of WWI, a 1906 Browning copy was made. It is chambered for the 6.35mm cartridge. The markings are "Automatic Pistol 6.35 Fiel No. 1." Later models had "EMC" molded into the grip.

NIB	Exc.	V.G.	Good	Fair	Poor
—	195	135	100	75	50

Marte

Another poor-quality "Eibar" -type pistol that is chambered for the 6.35mm and that was made in the early 1920s.

NIB	Exc.	V.G.	Good	Fair	Poor
—	195	135	100	75	50

ERRASTI, A.
Eibar, Spain

Errasti manufactured a variety of inexpensive yet serviceable pistols from the early 1900s until the Spanish Civil War.

Velo-Dog

Usual cheap solid-frame folding-trigger revolvers one associates with the model designation. They were chambered in 5.5mm and 6.35mm and were made in the early 1900s.

NIB	Exc.	V.G.	Good	Fair	Poor
—	195	135	100	75	50

M1889

In 1915-1916 Errasti produced the 10.4mm Italian army service revolver. The quality was reasonably good. They were marked "Errasti Eiber" on the right side of the frame.

NIB	Exc.	V.G.	Good	Fair	Poor
—	400	295	200	125	75

Errasti

Two "Eibar" type Browning copies were made under this trade name. One was chambered for the 6.35mm, the other the 7.65mm. They were both marked "Automatic Pistol Errasti."

Courtesy James Rankin

NIB	Exc.	V.G.	Good	Fair	Poor
—	195	135	110	75	50

Errasti Oscillante

Manufactured in the 1920s, these revolvers were copied from the Smith & Wesson Military & Police design. They were chambered for the .32, .38, and .44 calibers with the .38 being the most frequently encountered. Add 30 percent for .44.

NIB	Exc.	V.G.	Good	Fair	Poor
—	250	195	125	95	50

Dreadnaught, Goliath, and Smith Americano

These three trade names were found on a group of poor quality nickel-plated revolvers. They were made from 1905 through 1920 and were obvious copies of the Iver Johnson design. They had break-open actions, ribbed barrel, and were chambered for .32,

.38, and .44 calibers. They are scarce today, as most have long since fallen apart. Add 30 percent for .44.

NIB	Exc.	V.G.	Good	Fair	Poor
—	225	175	100	75	50

ESCODIN, M.
Eibar, Spain

This company made a Smith & Wesson revolver copy from 1924 through 1931. It is chambered for the .32 and the .38 Special. The only marking is a coat of arms stamped on the left side of the frame.

NIB	Exc.	V.G.	Good	Fair	Poor
—	175	125	100	75	50

ESPIRIN, HERMANOS
Eibar, Spain

Euskaro

This poor-quality, often unsafe revolver was manufactured from 1906 until WWI. They are copies of the Iver Johnson design break-open actions, chambered for .32. .38, and .44. This product epitomizes the worst Eibar had to offer during the pre-Civil War era. Add 30 percent for .44.

NIB	Exc.	V.G.	Good	Fair	Poor
—	200	125	75	50	25

EUROARMS OF AMERICA
Winchester, Virginia

An importer of blackpowder muzzle-loading firearms, primarily replicas of early American weapons.

1851 Navy

A replica of the Colt revolver chambered for .36 or .44 caliber percussion. It has a squareback, silver-plated trigger guard and a 7.5" barrel.

NIB	Exc.	V.G.	Good	Fair	Poor
275	225	170	110	75	45

1851 Navy Police Model

Chambered for .36 caliber with a 5-shot, fluted cylinder and a 5.5" barrel.

NIB	Exc.	V.G.	Good	Fair	Poor
275	225	170	110	75	45

1851 Navy Sheriff's Model

A 5" barrelled version of the Navy Model.

NIB	Exc.	V.G.	Good	Fair	Poor
275	225	170	110	75	45

1851 "Schneider & Glassick" Navy

A replica of the Confederate revolver chambered for .36 or .44 caliber percussion.

NIB	Exc.	V.G.	Good	Fair	Poor
150	100	80	60	50	35

1851 "Griswold & Gunnison" Navy

A replica of this Confederate revolver chambered for .36 or .44 caliber percussion.

NIB	Exc.	V.G.	Good	Fair	Poor
285	235	170	110	75	45

1862 Police

A replica of the Colt Model 1862 chambered for .36 caliber percussion, with a 7.5" barrel and a steel frame.

NIB	Exc.	V.G.	Good	Fair	Poor
275	225	170	110	75	45

1860 Army

A replica of the Colt revolver chambered for .44 caliber percussion. It was offered with a 5" or 8" barrel.

NIB	Exc.	V.G.	Good	Fair	Poor
275	225	170	110	75	45

1861 Navy

A replica of the Colt revolver chambered for .36 caliber percussion.

NIB	Exc.	V.G.	Good	Fair	Poor
275	225	170	110	75	45

1858 Remington Army or Navy

Replicas of the Remington percussion revolvers chambered for .36 or .44 caliber.

NIB	Exc.	V.G.	Good	Fair	Poor
275	225	170	110	75	45

EUROPEAN AMERICAN ARMORY CORP.
EAA Witness P-Series Full Size

Introduced in 1998 this is a full size polymer frame pistol chambered for 9mm, .40 S&W, .45 ACP, .38 Super, and 10mm cartridges. Barrel length is 4.55". Overall length is 8.5" with an empty weight of 31 oz. Rear sight is adjustable for windage. Magazine capacity for 9mm is 28 rounds and .40 S&W is 15 rounds while the .45 ACP model holds 10 rounds. For the 10mm model magazine capacity is 15 rounds.

NIB	Exc.	V.G.	Good	Fair	Poor
525	425	325	225	180	100

NOTE: Add $30 for ported barrel.

EAA Witness P-Series Carry-Comp

This model is fitted with a 4.25" ported barrel. Chambered for .45 ACP.

NIB	Exc.	V.G.	Good	Fair	Poor
470	375	275	200	150	100

EAA Witness P-Series Compact

Similar to the above model but with a barrel length of 3.55". Weight is about 26 oz.

NIB	Exc.	V.G.	Good	Fair	Poor
450	350	250	200	150	100

NOTE: Add $30 for ported barrel.

EAA Witness P-S Series

Built on a different frame size from the P-Series pistols. This model is chambered for the .22 LR, 9mm, or .40 S&W cartridges. Barrel length is 4.55". Weight is about 31 oz.

NIB	Exc.	V.G.	Good	Fair	Poor
400	325	275	200	150	100

EAA WITNESS CARRY COMP

This model is offered in 9mm, .41 AE, .40 S&W, and .45 ACP. It features a 1" steel compensator. The barrel is 4.1" long. Overall length is the same as the standard model as is magazine capacity. Offered in blue or blue chrome finish. Weighs 34 oz.

Old Configuration

NIB	Exc.	V.G.	Good	Fair	Poor
425	350	300	250	200	175

NOTE: For .45 ACP add 15 percent to above prices.

New Configuration

NIB	Exc.	V.G.	Good	Fair	Poor
500	450	375	325	250	175

EAA WITNESS STANDARD

Available in 9mm, .41 AE, .40 S&W, and .45 ACP with 4.5" barrel. Magazine capacity: 9mm-16 rounds, .41 AE-11 rounds, .40 S&W-12 rounds, .45 ACP-10 rounds. Offered in blue, chrome, two-tone, and stainless steel. Weighs approximately 33 oz.

Old Configuration

NIB	Exc.	V.G.	Good	Fair	Poor
385	325	275	225	175	125

New Configuration

NIB	Exc.	V.G.	Good	Fair	Poor
500	375	295	225	175	125

NOTE: For chrome, two-tone, and stainless steel add 5 percent to above prices.

EAA WITNESS SUBCOMPACT

Offered in the same calibers as the standard model but fitted with a 3.66" barrel and shorter grip. Magazine capacity: 9mm-13 rounds, .41 AE-9 rounds, .40 S&W 9 rounds, .45 ACP-8 rounds. Weighs about 30 oz. Offered in blue, chrome, two-tone, and stainless steel.

Old Configuration

NIB	Exc.	V.G.	Good	Fair	Poor
425	350	295	235	175	125

New Configuration

NIB	Exc.	V.G.	Good	Fair	Poor
460	350	275	225	175	125

NOTE: For chrome, two-tone, and stainless steel add 5 percent to above prices.

EAA WITNESS SPORT L/S

This model features a longer slide for its 4.75" barrel. Offered in 9mm, .41 AE, .40 S&W, and .45 ACP. Magazine capacity: 9mm-19 rounds, .41 AE-13 rounds, .40 S&W 14 rounds, and .45 ACP-11 rounds. This model is also fitted with adjustable rear sight and extended safety. Available in two-tone finish. Weighs about 34.5 oz. A ported barrel is offered as an option.

Old Configuration

NIB	Exc.	V.G.	Good	Fair	Poor
625	550	500	400	300	200

New Configuration

NIB	Exc.	V.G.	Good	Fair	Poor
625	550	500	400	300	200

NOTE: For .45 ACP add 10 percent to prices.

EAA Witness Combo 9/40

This model offers a 9mm conversion kit, and a .40 S&W conversion kit. These kits consist of a slide, barrel, recoil spring and guide, and magazine. Available in standard or subcompact size in blue, chrome, or two-tone finish.

NIB	Exc.	V.G.	Good	Fair	Poor
595	495	425	350	275	175

NOTE: For chrome or two-tone finish add 5 percent to above prices.

EAA Witness Silver Team Match

This is designed as a competition pistol. It is fitted with a 5.25" barrel. It has these features: dual chamber compensator, single-action trigger, extended safety, competition hammer, paddle magazine release, checkered walnut grips, and adjustable rear sight or drilled and tapped for scope mount. Offered in 9mm-19 rounds, .40 S&W 14 rounds, .41 AE-13 rounds, .45 ACP-11 rounds, and 9 x 21. Finish is blue and weight is approximately 34 oz.

NIB	Exc.	V.G.	Good	Fair	Poor
900	800	700	600	450	300

EAA WITNESS SPORT

This model is built on the standard Witness frame with the addition of an adjustable rear sight and extended safety. Offered in 9mm, .41 AE, .40 S&W, .45 ACP in standard model magazine capacity. Weighs 33 oz. Available in two-tone finish.

Old Configuration

NIB	Exc.	V.G.	Good	Fair	Poor
550	475	400	300	200	150

New Configuration

NIB	Exc.	V.G.	Good	Fair	Poor
550	475	400	300	200	150

NOTE: For .45 ACP add 10 percent to above prices.

EAA Witness Hunter

This model features a camo finish with a 6" barrel. Chambered for the .45 ACP or 10mm cartridge. Drilled and tapped for scope mount and adjustable sights. Magazine capacity is 10 rounds. Weight is about 41 oz. Also available with blued finish.

NIB	Exc.	V.G.	Good	Fair	Poor
975	800	575	395	250	150

EAA Witness Gold Team Match

This is a full race competition pistol with triple chamber compensator, beaver tail grip safety, beveled magazine well, adjustable rear sight or drilled and tapped for scope mount, extended safety and magazine release, competition hammer, square trigger guard, checkered front and backstrap, competition grips, and hard chrome finish. Same barrel length, magazine capacity, and calibers as the Silver Team Match. Weighs 38 oz.

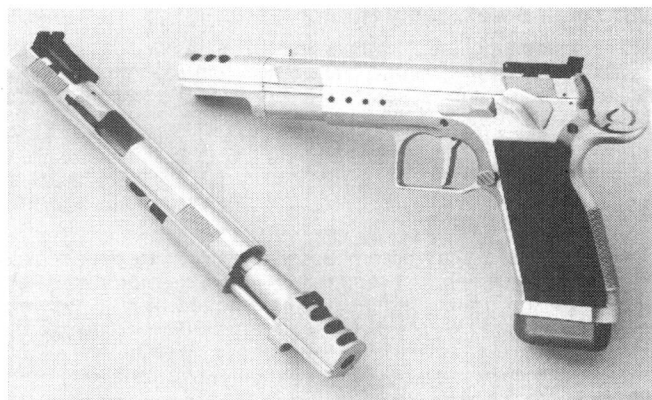

NIB	Exc.	V.G.	Good	Fair	Poor
1700	1250	900	750	600	400

EAA Witness Limited Class Pistol

This model is built on the Witness Match frame with competition grips, high capacity magazine, extended safety and magazine release, single-action trigger, long slide with adjustable rear sight, and match grade barrel. Offered in 9mm, .40 S&W, .38 Super, and .45 ACP with blue finish.

NIB	Exc.	V.G.	Good	Fair	Poor
1200	975	725	550	400	300

EAA Stock

Introduced in 2005 this pistol features a 4.5" tapered cone barrel chambered for the 9mm, .40S&W, .45ACP, or .10mm cartridge.

Hard chrome finish, extended safety, wood checkered grips, and fully adjustable sights. Weight is about 33 oz.

NIB	Exc.	V.G.	Good	Fair	Poor
825	695	595	400	200	100

EAA Witness Multi Class Pistol Package

This package consists of one Witness Limited Class pistol with a complete unlimited class top half. The top half is made up of a standard length slide with super sight, recoil guide and spring, match grade competition barrel (threaded for compensator), and a dual chamber compensator. Available in 9mm, .40 S&W, 9 x 21, .45 ACP, 9 x 23, and .38 Super. Finish is blue.

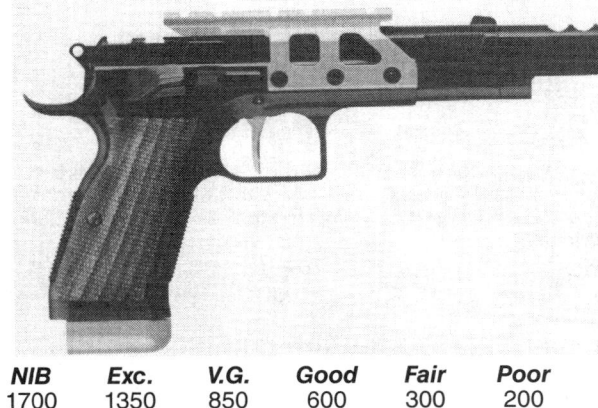

NIB	Exc.	V.G.	Good	Fair	Poor
1700	1350	850	600	300	200

Witness Elite Match

Single action semi-auto featuring 4.5" polygonal rifled steel barrel, adjustable rear sights, rubber grips. Two-tone finish. Chambered for 9 mm (18+1), 10 mm (15+1), 38 Super (15+1), .40 S&W (15+1) and .45 ACP (10+1). 33 oz. Introduced 2006.

NIB	Exc.	V.G.	Good	Fair	Poor
725	600	450	300	200	100

Zastava EZ Pistol

CZ75 clone. Single-/double-action pistol with four-inch (Full Size) or 3.5-inch (Compact) barrel, polymer frame. Chambered in 9mm, .40 S&W or .45 ACP. Magazine capacity varies from 7 rounds (.45 ACP) to 15 (9mm).

NIB	Exc.	V.G.	Good	Fair	Poor
375	300	265	225	165	100

Thor

This is a single shot pistol chambered for the .223 Rem., .270 Win., .30-06, .300 Win., .375 Win., .44 Mag., .45-70, .50 S&W, .7mm-08, or the .7mm Rem. Mag. Fitted with a 14" barrel, the receiver has an integral top rail for scope mount. Weight is about 5 lbs.

NIB	Exc.	V.G.	Good	Fair	Poor
1150	850	675	500	355	145

OTHER EAA IMPORTED FIREARMS

BUL 1911 SERIES

BUL Government

Chambered for the .45 ACP cartridge and fitted with 4.8" barrel. Polymer frame. Tactical rear sight with dovetail front sight. Fully checkered grip. Black or stainless steel slide. Weight is about 24 oz. Magazine capacity is 10 rounds. Introduced in 2002.

NIB	Exc.	V.G.	Good	Fair	Poor
550	450	300	200	125	75

NOTE: Add $50 for stainless steel slide.

BUL Commander

Same as above but fitted with 3.8" barrel.

NIB	Exc.	V.G.	Good	Fair	Poor
550	450	300	200	125	75

NOTE: Add $50 for stainless steel slide.

BUL Stinger

This model has a 3" barrel.

NIB	Exc.	V.G.	Good	Fair	Poor
550	450	300	200	125	75

NOTE: Add $50 for stainless steel slide.

EAA Big Bore Bounty Hunter

This model is a single-action revolver made in Germany. It features three-position hammer, forged barrel, and walnut grips. Offered in .357 Mag., .45 Long Colt, and .44 Mag. in 4.5", 5.5", or 7.5" barrel lengths. Choice of finish includes blue or case-colored frame, chrome, gold, or blue and gold.

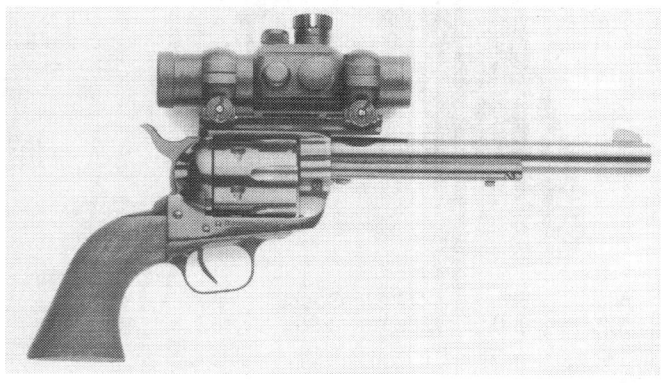

NIB	Exc.	V.G.	Good	Fair	Poor
400	300	225	175	150	125

NOTE: For chrome, gold, or blue and gold finish add 20 percent.

EAA Small Bore Bounty Hunter

This is a single-action .22 caliber revolver. It has wood grips and is available in blue or blue and brass finish. Barrel lengths are 4.75", 6", and 9". It is chambered for .22 LR or .22 Winchester Rimfire Magnum.

NIB	Exc.	V.G.	Good	Fair	Poor
275	200	145	125	75	60

EAA F.A.B. 92 Pistol

This model is a semi-automatic pistol similar to the Witness, but fitted with a hammer drop safety and slide mounted safety, that is both a double-action or single-action. It is available in either a full size (33 oz.) or compact size (30 oz.). The full size version has a 4.5" barrel while the compact is fitted with a 3.66" barrel. Offered in 9mm or .40 S&W in blue, two-tone, or chrome finish.

NIB	Exc.	V.G.	Good	Fair	Poor
395	300	225	175	125	100

EAA European Standard Pistol

This is a single-action semi-automatic pistol with external hammer, slide grip serrations, wood grips, and single column magazine. The barrels length is 3.2" and overall length is 6.5". Chambered for .22 LR, 380 ACP, and .32 ACP. The magazine capacity is 10 rounds for the .22 LR, 7 rounds for .380, and 7 rounds for .32. Offered in blue, blue/chrome, chrome, blue/gold. Weighs 26 oz.

NIB	Exc.	V.G.	Good	Fair	Poor
195	155	110	95	75	50

EAA European Target Pistol

This model features adjustable rear sight, external hammer, single-action trigger, walnut target grips, and adjustable weight system. Chambered for .22 LR. Offered in blue finish and weighs 40 oz.

NIB	Exc.	V.G.	Good	Fair	Poor
355	295	225	175	150	100

EAA Windicator Standard Grade

This German-built model is a double-action revolver chambered for the .22 LR, .22 Winchester Rimfire Magnum, .32 H&R, and .38 Special. It is offered in 2", 4", and 6" barrel lengths. The cylinder capacity for the .22 LR/.22 WRM is 8 rounds, .32 H&R is 7 rounds, and the .38 Special is 6 rounds. The cylinder is unfluted. Finish is blue.

NIB	Exc.	V.G.	Good	Fair	Poor
275	165	135	110	75	60

EAA Windicator Basic Grade

This model is chambered for the .38 Special or the .357 Magnum with 2" barrel. The fluted cylinder holds 6 rounds. Finish is blue.

NIB	Exc.	V.G.	Good	Fair	Poor
275	165	135	110	75	60

EAA WINDICATOR TACTICAL GRADE

This model is similar in appearance to the standard grade but is chambered for the .38 Special with 2" or 4" barrel. The 4" barrel has an integral compensator. Finish is blue.

2" Barrel

NIB	Exc.	V.G.	Good	Fair	Poor
190	150	125	100	80	60

4" Barrel

NIB	Exc.	V.G.	Good	Fair	Poor
250	200	150	125	100	75

EAA Windicator Target Grade

This model has these special features: adjustable trigger pull, walnut grips, adjustable rear sight, drilled and tapped for scope mount, target hammer, adjustable trigger stop. Fitted with 6" target barrel. Chambered for .22 LR, .38 Special, .357 Mag. Blue finish.

NIB	Exc.	V.G.	Good	Fair	Poor
350	275	225	200	150	100

EAA Benelli Silhouette Pistol

This is a specialized competition pistol with a semi-automatic action. The stocks are match type walnut with stippling. The palm shelf is adjustable. The barrel is 4.3" long. Fully adjustable sights. It is chambered for the .22 LR, .22 Short, and the .32 WC. Supplied with loading tool and cleaning rod. The .22 Caliber version weighs 38.5 oz. Overall length is 11.7".

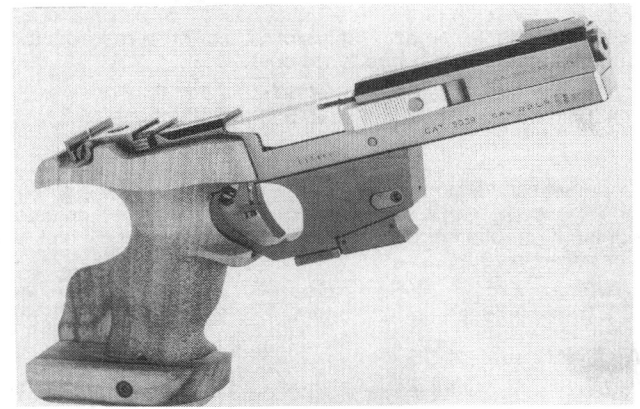

NIB	Exc.	V.G.	Good	Fair	Poor
2000	1350	995	750	600	400

EAA Astra Pistol SEE—Astra

EVANS, J. E.
Philadelphia, Pennsylvania

Pocket Pistol

A copy of the Philadelphia-made Henry Deringer pistol and is chambered for .41 caliber. It utilizes the percussion ignition system and has barrels from 2.5" to 3" in length. The stock is of walnut with a checkered grip, and the mountings are scroll engraved German silver. The barrel is marked "J.E. Evans Philada." These pistols were manufactured in the 1850s.

NIB	Exc.	V.G.	Good	Fair	Poor
—	—	1250	1850	775	350

EXCAM
Hialeah, Florida

An importer of firearms, not a manufacturer. The Erma and Uberti products imported by this company are under their own heading in this book. The other products that they imported are listed here. They are no longer in business.

TA 76

Patterned after the Colt Single Action Army and is chambered for the .22 rimfire cartridge. It has a 4.75", 6", or 9" barrel and blue finish with wood grips. It is offered with brass trigger guard and backstrap and also offered chrome-plated. A combo model with an extra .22 Magnum cylinder is available and would add 10 percent to the listed values.

NIB	Exc.	V.G.	Good	Fair	Poor
—	100	75	65	40	25

TA 38 Over-and-Under Derringer

A two-shot derringer patterned after the Remington derringer. It is chambered for the .38 Special cartridge, has 3" barrels that pivot upward for loading, and is blued with checkered nylon grips. This model was discontinued in 1985.

NIB	Exc.	V.G.	Good	Fair	Poor
—	100	75	65	40	25

TA 90

A double-action, semi-automatic copy of the CZ-75 that some experts rate as the finest combat handgun in the world. It is chambered for the 9mm Parabellum and has a 4.75" barrel. It is constructed of steel and is finished with a matte blue or chrome with checkered wood or rubber grips. The detachable magazine holds 15 rounds.

NIB	Exc.	V.G.	Good	Fair	Poor
425	375	325	275	200	150

BTA-90B

A compact version of the TA 90, that has a 3.5" barrel and a 12-round detachable magazine. It is similar in all other respects to the standard model, with rubber grips only.

NIB	Exc.	V.G.	Good	Fair	Poor
425	375	325	275	200	150

TA 90 SS

A competition version of the TA 90, that is similar to the standard model except that it is compensated and features adjustable sights. It is offered either blued or chrome-plated and was introduced in 1989.

NIB	Exc.	V.G.	Good	Fair	Poor
650	575	500	400	325	225

TA 41, 41C, and 41 SS

This series of pistols is identical to the TA 90 series except that they are chambered for the .41 Action Express cartridge. Their values are about 10 percent higher than the 9mm versions. They were introduced in 1989.

Warrior Model W 722

A double-action revolver chambered for the .22 rimfire and the .22 rimfire Magnum with an interchangeable cylinder. It has a 6" barrel, adjustable sights, and an 8-shot cylinder capacity. It is blued, with checkered plastic grips. This model was not imported after 1986.

NIB	Exc.	V.G.	Good	Fair	Poor
—	100	75	50	35	20

Model W384

A double-action revolver chambered for the .38 Special cartridge, with a 4" or 6" vent rib barrel, blued finish, and plastic grips. It was discontinued in 1986.

NIB	Exc.	V.G.	Good	Fair	Poor
—	175	125	100	75	50

Model W357

Similar to the W384 except that it is chambered for the .357 Magnum cartridge. It was discontinued in 1986.

NIB	Exc.	V.G.	Good	Fair	Poor
—	200	150	125	100	75

Targa GT 26

A blowback-operated, semi-automatic pistol chambered for the .25 ACP cartridge. It has a 2.5" barrel and a 6-shot detachable magazine. It is finished in blue or matte chrome, with a choice of alloy or steel frame. The grips are wood.

Targa GT 26 Steel Frame Version

NIB	Exc.	V.G.	Good	Fair	Poor
125	90	75	50	40	30

Targa GT 26 Alloy Frame Version

NIB	Exc.	V.G.	Good	Fair	Poor
100	75	50	35	30	25

GT 22

A semi-automatic pistol chambered for the .22 LR cartridge. It has a 4" barrel, fixed sights, and a 10-round magazine. Available either blued or matte chrome-plated and has wooden grips.

NIB	Exc.	V.G.	Good	Fair	Poor
200	175	150	125	90	70

GT 22T

Similar to the GT 22, with a 6" barrel and adjustable target-type sights.

NIB	Exc.	V.G.	Good	Fair	Poor
225	200	175	150	100	75

GT 32

A blowback-operated semi-automatic pistol chambered for the .32 ACP cartridge. It has a 7-round magazine and is either blued or matte chrome-plated with wood grips.

NIB	Exc.	V.G.	Good	Fair	Poor
200	175	150	125	90	75

GT 380

Similar to the GT 32 except that it is chambered for the .380 ACP cartridge.

NIB	Exc.	V.G.	Good	Fair	Poor
225	175	150	125	100	75

GT 380XE

Similar to the GT 380, with an 11-shot, high-capacity, detachable magazine.

NIB	Exc.	V.G.	Good	Fair	Poor
225	200	175	150	125	100

EXCEL INDUSTRIES
Chino, California

Accelerator Pistol

This is a semi-automatic pistol available in .22 WMR or .17 HMR. Barrel length is 8.5" with a .875" diameter. Stainless steel with polymer grip. The barrel is fitted with an aluminum rib with target sights and a Weaver base. Magazine capacity is 9 rounds. Weight is about 54 oz. Introduced in 2004.

NIB	Exc.	V.G.	Good	Fair	Poor
425	320	250	165	125	75

FABRIQUE NATIONALE
Herstal, Belgium

In 1889 Fabrique Nationale (or FN) was founded by a group of Belgian investors for the purpose of manufacturing Mauser rifles for the Belgian army. This was to be accomplished under license from Mauser, with the technical assistance of Ludwig Loewe of Berlin. A few years later, in the late 1890s, John Browning arrived in Europe seeking a manufacturer for his semi-automatic shotgun. He had severed his ties with Winchester after a disagreement. This led to a long association that worked out extremely well for both parties. Later Browning became associated with Colt, and the world market was divided—with the Eastern Hemisphere going to FN and the Western Hemisphere to Colt. In this section, we list arms that bear the FN banner. The FN-manufactured firearms produced under the Browning banner are listed in the Browning section of this book.

Model 1900

A blowback-operated semi-automatic pistol chambered for the 7.65mm cartridge. It has a 4" barrel and fixed sights and is blued with molded plastic grips. It was manufactured between 1899 and 1910. This model is referred to as the "Old Model."

NIB	Exc.	V.G.	Good	Fair	Poor
—	550	375	310	200	150

Model 1903

A considerable improvement over the Model 1900. It is also a blowback-operated semi-automatic; but the recoil spring is located under the barrel, and the firing pin travels through the slide after being struck by a hidden hammer. The barrel is held in place by five locking lugs that fit into five grooves in the frame. This pistol is chambered for the 9mm Browning long cartridge and has a 5" barrel. The finish is blued with molded plastic grips, and the detachable magazine holds 7 rounds. There is a detachable shoulder stock/holster along with a 10-round magazine that was

available for this model. These accessories are extremely rare and if present would make the package worth approximately five times that of the pistol alone. There were approximately 58,000 manufactured between 1903 and 1939.

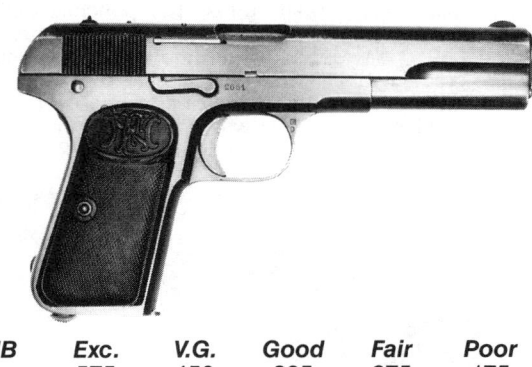

NIB	Exc.	V.G.	Good	Fair	Poor
—	575	450	395	275	175

MODEL 1906

A smaller version of the Model 1903, designed to be a pocket pistol and chambered for the 6.35mm cartridge. It became known as the "Vest Pocket" model and was also the basis for many Eibar copies. It has a 2.5" barrel and was produced in two distinct variations. The first variation had no safety lever or slide lock and relied on the grip safety. The second variation, that occurred at approximately serial number 100000, added this safety lever and slide lock, which helped simplify dismantling of the pistol. This model was available either blued or nickel-plated. The plated models would bring a 10 percent premium. There were approximately 1,086,100 manufactured between 1906 and 1959.

Under Serial Number 100000

NIB	Exc.	V.G.	Good	Fair	Poor
—	500	395	275	200	125

Over Serial Number 100000

NIB	Exc.	V.G.	Good	Fair	Poor
—	475	350	250	175	100

Model 1910 "New Model"

Chambered for 7.65mm and 9mm short. It has a 3.5" barrel, is blued, and has molded plastic grips. The principal difference between this model and its predecessors is that the recoil spring on the Model 1910 is wrapped around the barrel. This gives the slide a more graceful tubular appearance instead of the old slab-sided look. This model has the triple safety features of the 1906 Model 2nd variation. This model was adopted by police forces around the world. It was manufactured between 1912 and 1954.

Courtesy Orvel Reichert

NIB	Exc.	V.G.	Good	Fair	Poor
—	425	300	250	175	125

NOTE: Add 75 percent if Nazi marked with original magazine.

Model 1922

NIB	Exc.	V.G.	Good	Fair	Poor
—	350	225	175	125	100

"Baby" Model

A smaller and lighter version of the Model 1906. It is chambered for the 6.35mm cartridge and has a 2" barrel. There is no grip safety or slide lock on this model, and it appears to be more square in shape than the Model 1906. This model was offered in blue, with molded plastic grips. Early models have the word "Baby" molded into the grips; post-1945 versions do not. There is also a nickel-plated version with pearl grips. There were over 500,000 of these manufactured between 1931 and 1983. Late-production specimens command a slight premium.

NIB	Exc.	V.G.	Good	Fair	Poor
—	575	400	300	225	150

MODEL 1935/HI-POWER/GP

The last design from John Browning and was developed between 1925 and 1935. This pistol is known as the Model 1935, the P-35, Hi-Power or HP, and also as the GP (which stood for "Grand Puissance") and was referred to by all those names at one time or another. The HP is essentially an improved version of the Colt 1911 design. The swinging link was replaced with a fixed cam, which was less prone to wear. It is chambered for the 9mm Parabellum and has a 13-round detachable magazine. The only drawback to the design is that the trigger pull is not as fine as that of the 1911, as there is a transfer bar instead of a stirrup arrangement. This is necessary due to the increased magazine capacity resulting in a thicker grip. The barrel is 4.75" in length. It has an external hammer with a manual and a magazine safety and was available with various finishes and sight options and was furnished with a shoulder stock. The Model 1935 was used by many countries as their service pistol as such there are many variations. We list these versions and their approximate values.

PRE-WAR COMMERCIAL MODEL

Found with either a fixed sight or a sliding tangent rear sight and is slotted for a detachable shoulder stock. It was manufactured from 1935 until 1940.

Fixed Sight Version

NIB	Exc.	V.G.	Good	Fair	Poor
—	725	600	475	375	275

Tangent Sight Version

NIB	Exc.	V.G.	Good	Fair	Poor
—	1200	850	675	550	400

NOTE: Wood holster stock add 50 percent.

PRE-WAR MILITARY CONTRACT

The Model 1935 was adopted by many countries as a service pistol, and they are listed.

Belgium

NIB	Exc.	V.G.	Good	Fair	Poor
—	1200	1050	900	600	375

Canada and China (See John Inglis & Company)Denmark

NIB	Exc.	V.G.	Good	Fair	Poor
—	1250	1100	950	650	400

Great Britain

NIB	Exc.	V.G.	Good	Fair	Poor
—	1150	1000	850	550	325

Estonia

NIB	Exc.	V.G.	Good	Fair	Poor
—	1200	1050	900	600	375

Holland

NIB	Exc.	V.G.	Good	Fair	Poor
—	1250	1100	950	650	400

Latvia

NIB	Exc.	V.G.	Good	Fair	Poor
—	1500	1350	1050	775	500

Lithuania

NIB	Exc.	V.G.	Good	Fair	Poor
—	1250	1100	950	650	400

Romania

NIB	Exc.	V.G.	Good	Fair	Poor
—	1500	1350	1050	775	500

PRE-WAR MILITARY CONTRACT GERMAN MILITARY PISTOLE MODELL 640(B)

In 1940 Germany occupied Belgium and took over the FN plant. The production of the Model 1935 continued, with Germany taking the output. The FN plant was assigned the production code "ch," and many thousands were produced. The finish on these Nazi guns runs from as fine as the Pre-war Commercial series to downright crude, and it is possible to see how the war was progressing for Germany by the finish on their weapons. One must be cautious with some of these guns as there have been fakes noted with their backstraps cut for shoulder stocks, producing what would appear to be a more expensive variation. Individual appraisal should be secured if any doubt exists.

Fixed Sight Model

NIB	Exc.	V.G.	Good	Fair	Poor
—	600	450	400	300	250

Tangent Sight Model

Courtesy Orvel Reichert

50,000 manufactured.

NIB	Exc.	V.G.	Good	Fair	Poor
—	900	750	700	550	400

Captured Pre-war Commercial Model

These pistols were taken over when the plant was occupied. They are slotted for stocks and have tangent sights. There were few produced between serial number 48,000 and 52,000. All noted have the WA613 Nazi proof mark. Beware of fakes!

NIB	Exc.	V.G.	Good	Fair	Poor
—	1700	1400	1150	750	500

POST-WAR MILITARY CONTRACT

Manufactured from 1946, and they embody some design changes—such as improved heat treating and barrel locking. Pistols produced after 1950 do not have barrels that can interchange with the earlier model pistols. The earliest models have an "A" prefix on the serial number and do not have the magazine safety. These pistols were produced for many countries, and there were many thousands manufactured.

Fixed Sight

NIB	Exc.	V.G.	Good	Fair	Poor
—	525	425	375	300	250

Tangent Sight

NIB	Exc.	V.G.	Good	Fair	Poor
—	800	675	575	400	300

Slotted and Tangent Sight

NIB	Exc.	V.G.	Good	Fair	Poor
—	1300	1050	750	500	400

POST-WAR COMMERCIAL MODEL

Introduced in 1950 and in 1954. Those imported into the U.S.A. are marked Browning Arms Co. These pistols have the commercial polished finish.

Fixed Sight

NIB	Exc.	V.G.	Good	Fair	Poor
—	550	425	350	300	250

Tangent Sight

NIB	Exc.	V.G.	Good	Fair	Poor
—	850	650	500	400	350

Slotted and Tangent Sight

NIB	Exc.	V.G.	Good	Fair	Poor
—	1350	1100	800	550	450

FAIRBANKS, A. B.
Boston, Massachusetts

All Metal Pistol

This odd pistol was produced of all metal, with a one-piece cast brass frame and handle and an iron barrel and lock system. It is chambered for .33 caliber and utilizes the percussion ignition system. The barrel lengths noted are of 3" to 10". The barrels are marked "Fairbanks Boston. Cast Steel." They were manufactured between 1838 and 1841.

NIB	Exc.	V.G.	Good	Fair	Poor
—	—	1050	350	150	75

FALCON FIREARMS
Northridge, California

Portsider

A copy of the Colt 1911 built for a left-handed individual. It is constructed of stainless steel and is similar in all other respects to the Colt. It was introduced in 1986. A scarce 1911.

NIB	Exc.	V.G.	Good	Fair	Poor
700	575	450	375	300	225

Portsider Set

A matching serial numbered pair consisting of a left-handed and a right-handed version of this model. It was cased, and there were only 100 manufactured in 1986 and 1987.

NIB	Exc.	V.G.	Good	Fair	Poor
1400	1250	1000	750	600	475

Gold Falcon

The frame was machined from solid 17-karat gold. The slide is stainless steel, and the sights have diamond inlays. It was engraved to the customer's order, and there were only 50 manufactured.

NIB	Exc.	V.G.	Good	Fair	Poor
50000	30000	25000	15000	7500	700

F.A.S.
Italy

Model 601

A high-grade, competition target pistol chambered for the .22 Short cartridge. It is a semi-automatic, with a 5.5" barrel and adjustable target sights. The detachable magazine holds 5 rounds, and the finish is blued with wraparound target grips. This model was discontinued in 1988.

NIB	Exc.	V.G.	Good	Fair	Poor
—	1450	1150	775	550	300

Model 602

Similar to the Model 601 except that it is chambered for the .22 LR. It was discontinued in 1987.

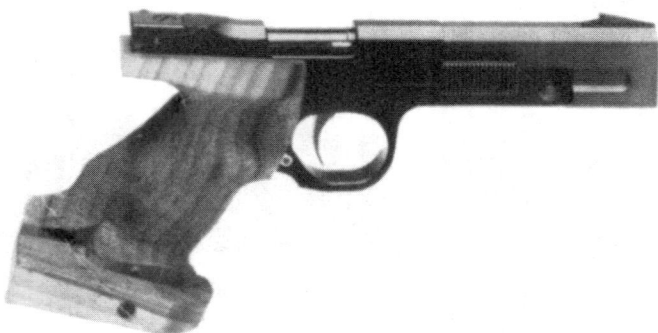

NIB	Exc.	V.G.	Good	Fair	Poor
—	1250	10500	725	500	250

Model 603

Chambered for the .32 S&W wadcutter cartridge and features adjustable grips. It was discontinued in 1987.

NIB	Exc.	V.G.	Good	Fair	Poor
—	1350	1075	775	500	250

FAYETTEVILLE ARMORY PISTOLS AND RIFLES
Fayetteville, North Carolina

In 1861, the U.S. Arsenal at Fayetteville, North Carolina, was seized by the officials of that state and later turned over to the government of the Confederate States of America. While still controlled by the state of North Carolina, a number of inferior flintlock arms were altered at the arsenal from flint to percussion, including a number of U.S. M1836 pistols and U.S. M1819 Hall rifles (the latter also shortened and remodeled into cavalry carbines). In accordance with an agreement between the governors of Virginia and North Carolina, the rifle machinery seized at the former U.S. Armory at Harpers Ferry, Virginia, was also sent to Fayetteville, where in 1862 the Confederacy began the construction of rifles modeled after the U.S. M1855 rifle. Production continued until 1865 when the advance of Sherman's armies necessitated the evacuation of the armory.

Fayetteville Armory Percussion Pistols (U.S. M1836 Pistols, Altered)

Overall length 13-1/4"; barrel length 8-1/2"; caliber .54. Markings: same as U.S. M1836 contact pistols, i.e. the locks either marked with eagle head over "A. WATERS/MILBURY MS./(date)" or "US/R. JOHNSON/MIDDN CONN./(date)" and various barrel proofmarks; also occasionally marked "N. CAROLINA." The Fayetteville Armory altered approximately 900 U.S. M1836 pistols from flintlock to percussion. These arms were altered by enlarging the flint touchhole and screwing in a cylindrical drum in place of the pan and frizzen. The distinguishing feature of the Fayetteville alteration is the clean-out screw at the face of the cylinder and the "S" shaped hammer, not unlike that used on post-1862 dated rifles.

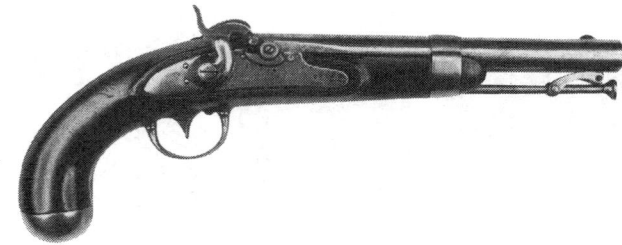

Courtesy Milwaukee Public Museum, Milwaukee, Wisconsin

NIB	Exc.	V.G.	Good	Fair	Poor
—	—	3250	1350	950	400

FEATHER INDUSTRIES, INC.
Trinidad, Colorado

Mini-AT

A blowback-operated semi-automatic pistol chambered for the .22 LR cartridge. It is a 5.5"-barreled version of the AT-22 rifleand has a 20-round magazine. This model was manufactured between 1986 and 1989.

NIB	Exc.	V.G.	Good	Fair	Poor
375	250	175	150	125	100

Guardian Angel

A two-shot, Over/Under, derringer-style pistol. It is chambered for the 9mm Parabellum and can be converted to fire the .38 Super cartridge. It is constructed of stainless steel and has an internal hammer and fully enclosed trigger. It was introduced in 1988.

NIB	Exc.	V.G.	Good	Fair	Poor
225	125	100	75	50	40

FEDERAL ORDNANCE, INC.
South El Monte, California

An importer as well as a manufacturer that basically fabricates new and custom firearms out of existing older military parts. The firearms they import are military surplus weapons. The firearms covered here are of Federal Ordnance manufacture.

Model 714 Broomhandle Mauser

A remanufactured C96-type pistol chambered for 7.63mm or 9mm Parabellum. It utilizes a new manufactured frame and surplus parts. It features a 10-round detachable magazine, adjustable sights, and walnut grips. Manufactured 1986 to 1991. A Bolo Model with a smaller grip was produced in 1988 only.

NIB	Exc.	V.G.	Good	Fair	Poor
650	500	400	300	250	100

Standard Broomhandle

A refurbished surplus C-96 Mauser pistol with a new 7.63mm or 9mm barrel. All springs are replaced, and the entire gun is refinished. It is furnished with a shoulder stock/holster of Chinese manufacture.

NIB	Exc.	V.G.	Good	Fair	Poor
800	650	525	450	350	275

Ranger 1911A1

Federal Ordnance's version of the 1911A1 Colt service pistol. It is made of all steel, is chambered for .45 ACP, and has checkered walnut grips and phiosphate-style finish. It was introduced in 1988.

NIB	Exc.	V.G.	Good	Fair	Poor
500	375	325	275	225	150

FEG (FEGYVER ES GAZKESZULEKGYAR)
Budapest, Hungary

Rudolf Frommer was a first-class engineer who became associated with Fegyvergyar in 1896. In 1900 he became the manager and held that position until his retirement in 1935. He died one year later in 1936. His designs were successful and prolific. They were used militarily and sold on the commercial market as well.

Model 1901

An odd pistol that was not successful at all. It was chambered for an 8mm cartridge that was the forerunner of the 8mm Roth Steyr. It has a long, slender barrel, which was actually a collar with the barrel within. It has a rotary bolt and external hammer and is recoil-operated. There is a 10-round integral magazine, and it is loaded from the top via a stripper clip. This pistol was manufactured from 1903 to 1905.

Courtesy James Rankin

NIB	Exc.	V.G.	Good	Fair	Poor
—	2450	1795	1000	700	350

Model 1906

An improved version of the 1901, chambered for the 7.65mm Roth-Sauer cartridge. It is, for all intents and purposes, the same action; but on later models a detachable 10-round magazine was adopted. It was manufactured between 1906 and 1910 in small quantity.

NIB	Exc.	V.G.	Good	Fair	Poor
—	2300	1750	1000	700	350

Model 1910

The final version in this series of pistols and is similar with the addition of a grip safety. Chambered for 7.65mm Browning.

NIB	Exc.	V.G.	Good	Fair	Poor
—	2600	1950	1100	700	350

Frommer Stop Model 1912

A semi-automatic pistol in caliber 7.65mm or 9mmK. It is unusual in that it operates on a long recoil system. Frommer is stamped on the slide as well as the Frommer Stop logo on each side of the wood or plastic grip plates.

Courtesy James Rankin

NIB	Exc.	V.G.	Good	Fair	Poor
—	450	300	225	150	50

Frommer Baby Model

A smaller version of the Stop that was designed as a pocket pistol with a 2" barrel and chambered for the same calibers. It was manufactured at the same time as the Stop Model.

Courtesy James Rankin

NIB	Exc.	V.G.	Good	Fair	Poor
—	375	250	200	125	75

Frommer Lilliput

This pocket pistol is chambered for 6.35mm and outwardly resembles the Baby. It is actually a simple, blowback-operated, semi-automatic pistol and was a good deal less complex to produce. This model was introduced in 1921.

Courtesy James Rankin

NIB	Exc.	V.G.	Good	Fair	Poor
—	350	225	175	125	75

Model 1929

A semi-automatic pistol in 9mmK. It is based on the Browning designed blowback-action. This pistol replaced the earlier models. A few of these pistols were made in .22 Long Rifle.

Courtesy James Rankin

NIB	Exc.	V.G.	Good	Fair	Poor
—	450	350	225	175	100

Model 1929 .22 Caliber

NIB	Exc.	V.G.	Good	Fair	Poor
—	975	825	725	450	250

Model 1937

A semi-automatic pistol in caliber 7.65mm or 9mmK. This pistol was designed by Frommer and manufactured by Femaru. It is also known as the Model 1937.

Courtesy James Rankin

Nazi Proofed 7.65mm Version

NIB	Exc.	V.G.	Good	Fair	Poor
—	450	350	225	175	100

9mm Short Hungarian Military Version

NIB	Exc.	V.G.	Good	Fair	Poor
—	425	325	200	175	100

Model R-9

A copy of the Browning Hi-Power semi-automatic pistol. It is chambered for 9mm Parabellum and has a 4.75" barrel. The frame is steel, and the finish is blued with checkered wood grips. The detachable magazine holds 13 shots, and the sights are fixed. This model was imported in 1986 and 1987 only.

NIB	Exc.	V.G.	Good	Fair	Poor
—	375	250	225	175	100

Model AP-9

This pistol has been manufactured in Hungary under a number of different names. It is known as the AP-9, Walam 48, AP-66, and the Attila. It is a semi-automatic pistol in calibers 7.65mm and 9mmK. It is similar to the Walther Model PP. It has a 7-round magazine and alloy frame. There are various styles of grip plates.

Courtesy James Rankin

NIB	Exc.	V.G.	Good	Fair	Poor
—	325	200	150	100	50

Model PPH

A copy of the Walther PP, chambered for the .380 ACP cartridge. It is a double-action semi-automatic with a 3" barrel, alloy frame, and a blued finish, with thumb rest checkered plastic grips. It was imported in 1986 and 1987 only.

NIB	Exc.	V.G.	Good	Fair	Poor
—	350	200	175	100	75

Model B9R

This semi-automatic pistol is chambered for the .380 ACP cartridge and fitted with a 4" barrel, it features double or single-action trigger operation. The frame is alloy and weighs about 25 oz. Magazine capacity is 15 rounds.

NIB	Exc.	V.G.	Good	Fair	Poor
375	225	200	175	125	75

Model PA-63

Same as above but chambered for the 9mm Makarov (9x18mm) cartridge.

NIB	Exc.	V.G.	Good	Fair	Poor
—	275	175	125	100	50

Model FP-9

This model is a copy of the Browning Hi-Power pistol. Chambered for the 9mm Luger cartridge. It features a walnut checkered grip with blue finish. Barrel is 5" and overall length is 8". The top of the slide features a full-length ventilated rib with fixed sights. Weighs 35 oz. Magazine capacity is 14 rounds.

NIB	Exc.	V.G.	Good	Fair	Poor
300	175	150	125	90	70

MODEL P9R

This is similar to the model above and follows the Browning Hi-Power lines with the exception of the ventilated rib. Barrel length is 4.66" and the pistol is offered in blue or chrome finish. Magazine capacity is 15 rounds.

Blue

NIB	Exc.	V.G.	Good	Fair	Poor
325	200	150	125	90	70

Chrome

NIB	Exc.	V.G.	Good	Fair	Poor
350	225	175	150	120	80

Model P9RK

Similar to model above but fitted with 4.12" barrel and 7.5" overall length. Finger grooves on front strap and backstrap is serrated. Weighs about 34 oz.

NIB	Exc.	V.G.	Good	Fair	Poor
300	200	150	125	90	70

FEMARU
Budapest, Hungary

Hungary became a communist satellite in the mid-1950s. At this time the Femaru company was designated to replace the firm of Fegyvergyar as the official Hungarian arms manufacturer. The products are of good quality.

Model 37

This semi-automatic pistol was built in both 7.65mm and 9mm Short calibers. It is well designed pistol of quality construction. It is fitted with a grip safety and exposed hammer. The Hungarian military adopted the pistol in 1937. It was produced until the late 1940s. Early guns were marked "Femaru Fegyver es Gepgyar RT Budapest" but during the war the Nazi code for these guns was "jhv." The 9mm models have a 7-round magazine while the

7.65 models have an 8-round magazine. During World War II the Germans designed this pistol the "Pistol Mod 37 Kal 7.65 (Ung.)." Add 75 percent for Nazi proofed examples.

Courtesy Richard M. Kumor, Sr.

NIB	Exc.	V.G.	Good	Fair	Poor
—	350	275	225	150	100

Hege

A complete copy of the Walther PP. It is chambered for the 7.65mm and manufactured to be sold by Hegewaffen of Germany. The slide is so marked, along with a Pegasus in a circle. The designation "AP 66 Cal.7.65" also appears. The pistol was intended for export sales in the U.S. and other western countries.

NIB	Exc.	V.G.	Good	Fair	Poor
—	350	225	175	125	100

Tokagypt

15,000 of these pistols were built in 1958, under contract for the Egyptian army. It is a modified version of the Soviet TT-33 Tokarev chambered for the 9mm Parabellum with a safety added. The balance were sold commercially, some under the trademark "Firebird."

NIB	Exc.	V.G.	Good	Fair	Poor
—	475	350	275	200	125

Walam

Another Walther PP copy of excellent quality chambered for the 9mm short or .380 ACP. The pistols were sold on the commercial market—some designated Model 48.

NIB	Exc.	V.G.	Good	Fair	Poor
—	350	225	175	125	100

FERRY, ANDREWS & CO.
Stafford, Connecticut

Under Hammer Pistol

This boot pistol is chambered for .36 caliber percussion and has a 3" part-round, part-octagonal barrel. They are similar to the other under hammer pistols that were produced in Connecticut and Massachusetts. The top strap was marked "Andrews Ferry & Co." The number manufactured is unknown. They were produced in the 1850s.

NIB	Exc.	V.G.	Good	Fair	Poor
—	—	1550	700	395	125

FIALA ARMS COMPANY
New Haven, Connecticut

FIALA REPEATING TARGET PISTOL

A different type of pistol than what is commonly encountered. Outwardly it resembles a semi-automatic Colt Woodsman; in actuality it is a manually operated firearm that must be cycled by hand after every shot. It was chambered for the .22 rimfire and was offered with interchangeable barrels in lengths of 3", 7.5", and 20". Also offered was a detachable buttstock. The finish is blued, and the grips are found in both smooth and ribbed walnut. The rear sight is a square-notched blade that tips up into an elevation-adjustable peep sight. They are marked "Fiala Arms and Equipment Co. Inc. / New Haven Conn. / Patents Pending" on the right side of the frame behind the grip and Model 1920/Made in U.S.A. on the right side of the frame above the trigger guard. The left side of the frame was marked "FIALA ARMS" above the image of the polar bear with the "TRADE MARK" below the polar bear in the area above the trigger guard. This pistol was also furnished in one of three variations of cases that were optionally available: a canvas case, a black leatherette case, velvet-lined and fitted with a lock and key, and a tan leather version of the leatherette case. A fixed 7.5" barrel variation was also produced. A 7.5" smoothbore barrel was catalogued as a silencer. Some 20" smoothbore barrels were produced. Some pistols bear the names "Columbia Arms Company," and "Botwinik Brothers." The government has classified this pistol with its stock as a "Curio or Relic" and in its complete state is a very desirable collectible.NOTE: See also Schall & Co.

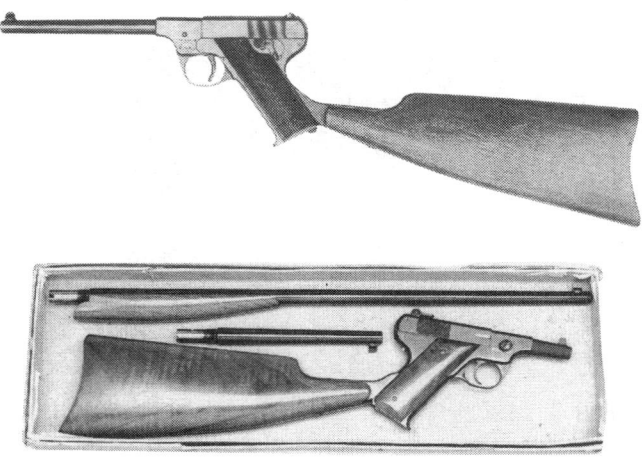

Courtesy Butterfield & Butterfield, San Francisco, California

Fiala Repeating Target Pistol Complete, Three Barrels, Stock, Tools, and Case

NIB	Exc.	V.G.	Good	Fair	Poor
—	2500	2100	1250	675	550

Fiala Repeating Target Pistol Gun Only

Courtesy Dr. Jon Miller

NIB	Exc.	V.G.	Good	Fair	Poor
—	800	700	450	275	175

F.I.E.
Hialeah, Florida

Firearms Import and Export was engaged in the business of importing the Franchi shotgun (which is listed under its own heading) and the Arminius revolver (which is made in Germany). They were also distributors for the Titan semi-automatic pistols, which are manufactured in the U.S.A. They were also importing a series of 9mm pistols from Italy that are produced by Tanfoglio and known as the TZ series. F.I.E. was no longer in business as of 1990.

TZ 75

A copy of the CZ 75 Czechoslovakian combat pistol produced by Tanfoglio in Italy. It is a 9mm, double-action semi-automatic with a 4.75" barrel, all-steel construction, fixed sights, and a 15-shot magazine. It is offered either blued or matte chrome plated, with wood or rubber grips.

NIB	Exc.	V.G.	Good	Fair	Poor
450	350	300	250	200	150

TZ 75 Series 88

An improved version that is also chambered for the .41 Action Express cartridge. It has a firing pin safety and can be carried cocked and locked. There are a few other minor changes. It was introduced in 1988.

NIB	Exc.	V.G.	Good	Fair	Poor
500	375	325	250	200	150

KG-99

A blowback-operated, semi-automatic assault pistol chambered for the 9mm Parabellum cartridge. It has a 36-round magazine. It was discontinued in 1984.

NIB	Exc.	V.G.	Good	Fair	Poor
550	450	350	250	200	150

Spectre Assault Pistol

An assault-type semi-automatic pistol chambered for the 9mm Parabellum. It has a 30- or 50-round magazine available. It was introduced in 1989.

NIB	Exc.	V.G.	Good	Fair	Poor
800	675	575	400	300	200

Titan II .22

A semi-automatic pistol chambered for the .22 LR. It has a 10-shot magazine and a blued finish with walnut grips. It is made in the U.S.A.

NIB	Exc.	V.G.	Good	Fair	Poor
275	150	100	75	50	25

Titan E32

A single-action, blowback-operated, semi-automatic pistol that was chambered for the .32 ACP and is now chambered for the .380 ACP cartridge. The finish is blue or chrome-plated, and the grips are walnut.

NIB	Exc.	V.G.	Good	Fair	Poor
300	175	150	125	100	75

Super Titan 11

Similar to the Titan except that it has a 12-round, high-capacity magazine.

NIB	Exc.	V.G.	Good	Fair	Poor
325	200	175	150	100	75

Titan 25

A smaller version of the Titan Series chambered for the .25 ACP cartridge. It is blued or chrome-plated.

NIB	Exc.	V.G.	Good	Fair	Poor
200	75	50	40	30	20

Titan Tigress

Similar to the Titan 25 except that it is gold-plated and cased.

NIB	Exc.	V.G.	Good	Fair	Poor
225	115	90	75	50	30

D38 Derringer

A two-shot, Over/Under, Remington-style derringer chambered for the .38 Special cartridge. It is chrome-plated and was dropped from the line in 1985.

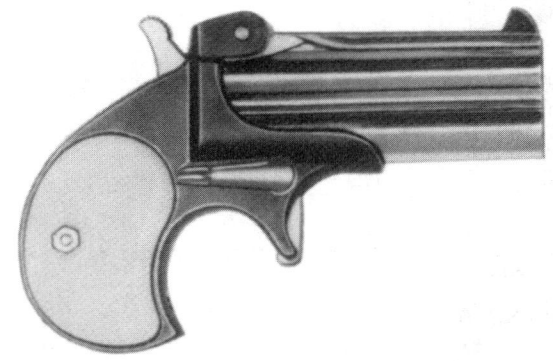

NIB	Exc.	V.G.	Good	Fair	Poor
145	75	45	35	25	20

D86 Derringer

A single-shot derringer with a 3" barrel. It is chambered for the .38 Special cartridge and is chrome-plated. There is an ammunition storage compartment in the butt and a transfer bar safety that makes it safer to carry. This model was introduced in 1986.

NIB	Exc.	V.G.	Good	Fair	Poor
150	80	65	50	35	20

SINGLE-ACTION ARMY REPLICA REVOLVERS

There is a series of single-action, .22 caliber revolvers that were patterned after the Colt Single-Action Army. They were manufactured in the U.S.A. or Brescia, Italy. They are inexpensive and of fair quality. The differences between these models are basically barrel lengths, type of sights, and finish. They all are chambered for the .22 LR and have interchangeable .22 Magnum cylinders. We list them for reference purposes.

Cowboy

NIB	Exc.	V.G.	Good	Fair	Poor
250	125	100	80	75	50

Gold Rush

NIB	Exc.	V.G.	Good	Fair	Poor
250	125	100	80	75	50

Texas Ranger

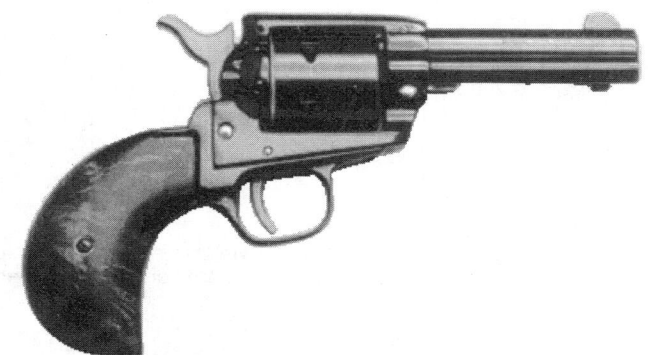

NIB	Exc.	V.G.	Good	Fair	Poor
200	85	75	50	35	20

Buffalo Scout

NIB	Exc.	V.G.	Good	Fair	Poor
175	80	70	50	35	20

NOTE: Add 50 percent for faux "gold"-plated Yellow Rose of Texas variant.

Legend S.A.A.

NIB	Exc.	V.G.	Good	Fair	Poor
250	125	100	80	75	50

Hombre (Arminius)

A single-action made in Germany by Arminius. It is patterned after the Colt Single-Action Army revolver. The Hombre is chambered for the .357 Magnum, .44 Magnum, and .45 Colt cartridges. It is offered with a 5.5", 6", or 7.5" barrel, case-colored frame, and blued barrel and cylinder, with smooth walnut grips. The backstrap and trigger guard are offered in brass and will bring a 10 percent premium.

NIB	Exc.	V.G.	Good	Fair	Poor
325	225	175	125	100	75

ARMINIUS REVOLVERS

Model 522TB

A swing-out cylinder, double-action revolver chambered for the .22 rimfire cartridge. It has a 4" barrel and is blued with wood grips.

NIB	Exc.	V.G.	Good	Fair	Poor
250	125	100	75	50	30

722

Similar to the 522, with an 8-shot cylinder and a 6" barrel. It is available with a chrome finish.

NIB	Exc.	V.G.	Good	Fair	Poor
250	125	100	75	50	30

532TB

A 7-shot, double-action revolver chambered for the .32 S&W cartridge. It has a 4" barrel and adjustable sights and is finished in either blue or chrome.

NIB	Exc.	V.G.	Good	Fair	Poor
250	130	110	80	60	40

732B

Similar to the 532TB, with a 6" barrel and fixed sights. It was discontinued in 1988.

NIB	Exc.	V.G.	Good	Fair	Poor
225	100	80	65	50	35

Standard Revolver

A double-action, swing-out cylinder revolver chambered for .32 Magnum or .38 Special. It has a 4" or 6" barrel and fixed sights and is blued with wood grips. This model is made in the U.S.A. and was introduced in 1989.

NIB	Exc.	V.G.	Good	Fair	Poor
225	100	75	50	35	20

Models 384TB and 386TB

These two models are double-action chambered for the .38 Special cartridge. The 384 has a 4" barrel; and the 386, a 6" barrel. They are available in blue or chrome plate and were discontinued in 1985.

NIB	Exc.	V.G.	Good	Fair	Poor
250	125	100	85	65	50

Model 357TB

Similar to the 384TB except that it is chambered for the .357 Magnum cartridge and is offered with a 3", 4", or 6" barrel.

NIB	Exc.	V.G.	Good	Fair	Poor
250	125	100	85	65	50

222, 232, and 382TB

These models are double-action swing-out cylinder revolvers chambered for .22 rimfire, .32 S&W, and .38 Special. They are 2"-barreled snub-nosed revolvers, with either blued or chrome-plated finishes. They were discontinued in 1985.

NIB	Exc.	V.G.	Good	Fair	Poor
200	100	75	50	40	25

Model 3572

A similar revolver to the 382TB except that it is chambered for the .357 Magnum cartridge. It was discontinued in 1984.

NIB	Exc.	V.G.	Good	Fair	Poor
250	125	100	85	65	50

FIRESTORM
Argentina

Firestorm .22 LR

A semi-automatic pistol chambered for the .22 Long Rifle cartridge. Ten-round magazine capacity. Matte blue finish or duotone.

NIB	Exc.	V.G.	Good	Fair	Poor
250	185	135	100	75	45

Firestorm .32

Double-action semi-auto chambered for .32 with 10+1 capacity. Blued, 3.5" barrel, 23 oz. Fixed sights and rubber grips. Introduced 2006.

NIB	Exc.	V.G.	Good	Fair	Poor
275	215	155	125	95	50

Firestorm .380

This semi-auto double-action pistol is chambered for the .380 ACP cartridge and fitted with a 3.5" barrel. Fixed three-dot combat sights. Matte blue or duotone finish. Magazine capacity is 7 rounds. Weight is about 23 oz.

NIB	Exc.	V.G.	Good	Fair	Poor
295	225	195	150	95	50

Mini Firestorm 9mm

This 9mm semi-auto double-action pistol is fitted with a 3.5" barrel. White outline drift adjustable target sights. Matte blue finish. Polymer grips. Magazine capacity is 10 rounds. Weight is about 25 oz.

NIB	Exc.	V.G.	Good	Fair	Poor
350	275	215	165	115	75

Mini Firestorm .40 S&W

As above but chambered for the .40 S&W cartridge.

NIB	Exc.	V.G.	Good	Fair	Poor
350	275	215	165	115	75

Firestorm .45 Government

This is a single-action semi-automatic pistol chambered for the .45 ACP cartridge. Fitted with a 5.125" barrel and 3 dot fixed combat sights. Magazine capacity is 7 rounds. Black rubber grips. Matte blue, nickel, or duotone finish. Weight is about 36 oz.

NIB	Exc.	V.G.	Good	Fair	Poor
350	275	215	165	115	75

Compact Firestorm .45 Government

As above but with 4.25" barrel. Weight is about 34 oz.

NIB	Exc.	V.G.	Good	Fair	Poor
350	275	215	165	115	75

Mini Firestorm .45 Government

As above but with 3.14" barrel. Black polymer grips and magazine capacity of 10 rounds. Weight is about 31 oz.

NIB	Exc.	V.G.	Good	Fair	Poor
350	275	215	165	115	75

1911 Mil-Spec Standard Government

1911A1-style single-action semi-auto chambered in .45 ACP; 5.125" barrel, steel frame, 7- or 8-round magazine, steel frame, plastic or wood grips, matte blue or deluxe polished blue finish.

NIB	Exc.	V.G.	Good	Fair	Poor
350	275	215	165	115	75

FNH USA, INC.
McLean, Virginia

This company is a subsidary of FN Herstal in Belgium. It is essentially the sales and marketing arm for FN in the U.S. market.

Model Forty-Nine

This pistol is built by FN Manufacturing, Inc. in Columbia, S.C. It has a polymer frame and stainless steel slide. Chambered for 9mm or .40 S&W cartridge. Barrel length is 4.25". Magazine capacity is 16 rounds for law enforcement and 10 rounds for commercial sales. It features a repeatable secure striker trigger system. Offered in stainless steel slide or black coated slide. Weight is about 26 oz. Offered primarily for sale to law enforcement agencies. Introduced in 2000.

NIB	Exc.	V.G.	Good	Fair	Poor
470	375	300	250	225	135

Model FNP-9/FNP-40

Introduced in 2003, this pistol is chambered for the 9mm or .40 S&W cartridge. Fitted with a 4" barrel and featuring a polymer frame. The action is a double-action/single-action design with an ambidextrous manual decocking lever. Fixed sights. Ten-round magazine capacity. Weight is about 33 oz.

NIB	Exc.	V.G.	Good	Fair	Poor
550	425	375	300	250	125

FNP-45

A longer-frame version of the FNP-9 chambered for .45 ACP. Barrel length is 4.5 inches and weight is 33.3 ounces. Ambidextrous mag release and decocker/safety, forward slide serrations. Magazine capacity: 10 or 15 rounds. Black or Flat Dark Earth finish. Interchangeable backstrap inserts.

NIB	Exc.	V.G.	Good	Fair	Poor
700	625	500	375	250	150

FNP-45 Tactical

Developed for the U.S. Joint Combat Pistol Program, this .45 ACP tactical model has a 5.3-inch threaded barrel for a suppressor or other accessories, high-profile combat sights, two mounting bases for optional red dot sights, MIL-STD 1913 rail. Black or Flat Dark Earth finish. Weight: 33.6 oz.

NIB	Exc.	V.G.	Good	Fair	Poor
1250	1050	850	625	350	250

FNP-45 Competition

Designed as a major caliber competition pistol. Same overall features as FNP-45 plus fiber optic front sight and Picatinny rail. Introduced in 2011.

NIB	Exc.	V.G.	Good	Fair	Poor
1050	850	700	500	300	250

FNX-9, FNX-40

Chambered in 9mm or .40 S&W. Magazine capacity: 17 (9mm), 14 (.40). Weight 22 to 24 ounces. Stainless steel slide has front and rear cocking serrations. Other features include ambidextrous operating controls. Four interchangeable back-strap inserts.

NIB	Exc.	V.G.	Good	Fair	Poor
600	535	450	325	250	150

FNH Five-seveN

Single-action design chambered for 5.7x28mm round. Magazine capacity: 10 or 20 rounds. Matte black, olive drab green or Flat Dark Earth finish. Ambidextrous safety and accessory mounting rail. Barrel length, four inches, weight 21 ounces. Three-dot combat sights, adjustable rear.

NIB	Exc.	V.G.	Good	Fair	Poor
1100	975	800	575	250	150

Model HP-SA

This is the famous John Browning design Hi-Power pistol. Chambered for the 9mm or .40 S&W cartridge. Barrel length is 4.6". Magazine capacity is 10 rounds. Weight is around 32 oz. Blued finish.

NIB	Exc.	V.G.	Good	Fair	Poor
900	750	595	400	200	125

Model HP-SA-SFS

Introduced in 2003 this variant of the Hi-Power pistol features a single-action double-action mechanism that allows cocked-and-locked carry with the hammer and slide locked. When the safety is pushed off the hammer is set in the cocked position and is fired single action.

NIB	Exc.	V.G.	Good	Fair	Poor
900	750	595	400	200	125

Model HP-DA/HP-DAO

This model is offered in two different configurations. The first is with double-action/single-action trigger while the second is double-action-only. Chambered for the 9mm cartridge, the pistol is fitted with fixed sights. Magazine capacity is 15 rounds for law enforcement and 10 rounds for commerical sales. Weight is about 31 oz. Intended primarly for law enforcement sales. Introduced in 2000.

NIB	Exc.	V.G.	Good	Fair	Poor
900	750	595	400	200	125

Model HP-DA/HP-DAO Compact

As above but in a smaller and lighter package.

NIB	Exc.	V.G.	Good	Fair	Poor
900	750	595	400	200	125

Model BDA/BDAO Compact

This is a short recoil compact pistol chambered for the 9mm Parabellum cartridge. Fitted with a double-action/single-action trigger or double-action-only trigger. Each configuration has a 10-round magazine capacity. Weight is about 28 oz. Corrosion-resistant finish. Fixed sights.

NIB	Exc.	V.G.	Good	Fair	Poor
800	650	500	395	200	125

FOEHL & WEEKS
Philadelphia, Pennsylvania

Columbian

A .32 or .38 caliber revolver marked with the patent date "20 January 1891."

NIB	Exc.	V.G.	Good	Fair	Poor
—	—	350	150	75	50

Columbian Automatic

A .38 caliber revolver with a hinged barrel and cylinder assembly.

NIB	Exc.	V.G.	Good	Fair	Poor
—	—	400	200	100	75

Perfect

As above, with a concealed hammer and also in .32 caliber.

NIB	Exc.	V.G.	Good	Fair	Poor
—	—	400	200	100	75

FOEHL, C.
Philadelphia, Pennsylvania

Derringer

A .41 caliber percussion single-shot pistol with a 2" barrel, German silver mounts and a walnut stock. The lock marked "C. Foehl."

NIB	Exc.	V.G.	Good	Fair	Poor
—	—	1950	750	300	110

FOLSOM, H.
St. Louis, Missouri

Derringer

A .41 caliber single-shot percussion pocket pistol with a 2.5" barrel, German silver mounts and a walnut stock. The barrel marked "H. Folsom."

NIB	Exc.	V.G.	Good	Fair	Poor
—	—	1150	800	350	275

FOREHAND & WADSWORTH
Worcester, Massachusetts

Established in 1871 and operated under the above name until 1890 when it became the Forehand Arms Company. Hopkins & Allen purchased the company in 1902.

Single-Shot Derringer

A .22 caliber single-shot pocket pistol with a 2" half-octagonal pivoted barrel, spur trigger and nickel- or silver-plated frame. Walnut grips. The barrel marked "Forehand & Wadsworth Worcester."

NIB	Exc.	V.G.	Good	Fair	Poor
—	—	1450	600	250	100

Single-Shot .41 Derringer

As above in .41 caliber with a 2.5" round barrel.

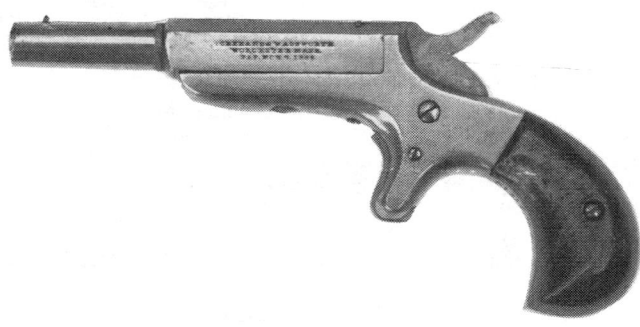

Courtesy Milwaukee Public Museum, Milwaukee, Wisconsin

NIB	Exc.	V.G.	Good	Fair	Poor
—	—	1000	850	450	200

Side Hammer .22

A .22 caliber spur trigger revolver with a 2.25" to 4" octagonal barrel and 7-shot cylinder. Blued or nickel-plated with walnut grips.

NIB	Exc.	V.G.	Good	Fair	Poor
—	—	675	475	200	100

Center Hammer

A .32 caliber spur trigger revolver with a 3.5" octagonal barrel and 6-shot cylinder. Blued or nickel-plated with rosewood or walnut grips. The top strap commonly found marked "Terror."

Courtesy Milwaukee Public Museum, Milwaukee, Wisconsin

NIB	Exc.	V.G.	Good	Fair	Poor
—	—	400	300	200	100

Old Model Army Single-Action Revolver

A .44 Russian caliber revolver with a 7.5" round barrel and 6-shot cylinder. The barrel marked "Forehand & Wadsworth, Worchester, Mass. U.S. Patd. Oct. 22, '61, June 27, '71 Oct. 28, '73." Blued with walnut grips. Approximately 250 were manufactured between 1872 and 1878.

NIB	Exc.	V.G.	Good	Fair	Poor
—	—	4000	3250	2000	500

New Model Army Single-Action Revolver

Similar to the above, with a 6.5" barrel and half-cock notch on the hammer. Approximately 250 were made between 1878 and 1882. Intersting note: In 2008, United States Fire Arms announced plans to remanufacture this model.

NIB	Exc.	V.G.	Good	Fair	Poor
—	—	3750	3000	2250	500

Double-Action Revolver

A .32 or .38 centerfire or rimfire caliber double-action revolver with a 3.5" barrel and 6- or 7-shot cylinder. The .32 caliber version marked "Forehand & Wadsworth Double-Action," and the .38 caliber "American Bulldog." Manufactured from 1871 to 1890.

NIB	Exc.	V.G.	Good	Fair	Poor
—	400	300	200	100	35

British Bulldog

A .32 or .38 centerfire solid frame double-action revolver resembling the Webley Bulldog.

NIB	Exc.	V.G.	Good	Fair	Poor
—	—	395	300	150	75

British Bulldog .44

As above in .44 Webley caliber with a 5" barrel and 5-shot cylinder.

NIB	Exc.	V.G.	Good	Fair	Poor
—	—	450	325	175	100

Swamp Angel

A .41 caliber single-action revolver with a 3" barrel and 5-shot cylinder. The top strap marked "Swamp Angel."

NIB	Exc.	V.G.	Good	Fair	Poor
—	—	425	275	100	50

Forehand Arms Co.
1898-1902

Perfection Automatic

A .32 or .38 caliber double-action revolver with a hinged barrel and cylinder assembly. Varying barrel lengths. Blued or nickel-plated with hard rubber grips.

NIB	Exc.	V.G.	Good	Fair	Poor
—	275	250	100	75	50

FOWLER, B. JR.
Hartford, Connecticut

Percussion Pistol

A .38 caliber single-shot percussion pistol with a 4" half octagonal barrel, iron frame and maple grips. The barrel marked "B. Fowler, Jr." Manufactured between 1835 and 1838.

NIB	Exc.	V.G.	Good	Fair	Poor
—	—	995	550	325	150

FRASER F. A. CORP.
Fraser, Michigan

Fraser .25 cal.

A .25 ACP caliber semi-automatic pistol with a 2.25" barrel and 6-round magazine. Stainless steel with black nylon grips. There is a 24 kt. gold-plated model that is worth approximately $100 additional. Later made under Fraser name by different company in 1990.

NIB	Exc.	V.G.	Good	Fair	Poor
250	175	125	100	50	35

FREEDOM ARMS
Freedom, Wyoming

"Percussion" Mini-Revolver

A .22 caliber spur trigger revolver with 1", 1.75", or 3" barrel lengths, 5-shot cylinder and a bird's-head grip. Stainless steel. A belt buckle is available that houses the pistol for an additional $40.

NIB	Exc.	V.G.	Good	Fair	Poor
300	250	195	125	100	75

Bostonian (aka Boot Gun)

As above, with a 3" barrel, in .22 Magnum. Discontinued 1992.

NIB	Exc.	V.G.	Good	Fair	Poor
375	300	225	150	80	60

Patriot (aka Boot Gun)

As above, in .22 LR caliber. Discontinued 1992.

NIB	Exc.	V.G.	Good	Fair	Poor
375	300	225	150	80	60

Minuteman

As above, with a 3" barrel. Discontinued in 1988.

NIB	Exc.	V.G.	Good	Fair	Poor
375	300	225	150	80	60

Ironsides

As above, in .22 Magnum with a 1" or a 1.75" barrel.

NIB	Exc.	V.G.	Good	Fair	Poor
375	300	225	150	80	60

Celebrity

As above, with the belt buckle mount for either .22 or .22 Magnum revolvers.

NIB	Exc.	V.G.	Good	Fair	Poor
400	325	275	225	150	100

NOTE: .22 Magnum Model add $25.

PREMIER AND FIELD GRADE REVOLVERS

Both grades use the same materials and machining tolerances. The difference is in the finish, standard components, and warranty.The Premier Grade has a bright brushed finish, screw adjustable rear sight, laminated hardwood grips, and a limited lifetime warranty.The Field Grade has a matte finish, adjustable rear sight for elevation only, Pachmayr rubber grips, and a one year warranty.

Casull Field Grade Model 83

A .454 Casull Magnum revolver with a 4.75", 6", 7.5", and a 10" barrel and standard fixed sights. Fires a 225-grain bullet. Also offered in .50 AE, .475 Linebaugh, .44 Rem. Mag., .41 Magnum, and .357 Magnum. Adjustable sights available as a $75 option. Matte stainless steel with black rubber Pachmayr grips. Introduced in 1988.

NIB	Exc.	V.G.	Good	Fair	Poor
1825	1400	800	550	—	—

NOTE: Add $75 for .454 Casull, .475 Linebaugh, or .50 AE calibers.

Casull Premier Grade Model 83

A .454 Mag., .44 Rem. Mag., .45 Win. Mag., .475 Linebaugh, and .50 AE, with replaceable forcing and walnut grips. The finish is a brush stainless steel. The adjustable sights are an extra cost option on this model as well. Offered in barrel lengths of 4.75", 6", 7.5", and 10" except for .475 Casull. .55 Wyoming Express added 2006.

NIB	Exc.	V.G.	Good	Fair	Poor
2150	1800	1250	850	500	350

NOTE: Extra cylinders are available for these models in .45 Colt, .45 Win. Mag., and .45 ACP. Add $250 to the price of the gun for each cylinder. Add $75 for .454 Casull, .475 Linebaugh, or .50 AE calibers.

Model 97

This revolver is chambered for either the .357 Magnum, .45 Colt, .44 Special, and .22 Long Rifle cartridges. Available in Field or Premier grades. Available with a choice of 4.25", 5.5" or 7.5" barrel. Optional .45 ACP cylinder of .45 Colt and optional .38 Special cylinder for .357 Magnum model.In 2004 this model was also offered in .17 HMR and .32 H&R Magnum calibers.

NIB	Exc.	V.G.	Good	Fair	Poor
1800	1350	1000	600	400	300

NOTE: There are a number of extra-cost options that will affect the price. Some of these options are sights, grips, Mag-Na-Port barrels, slings and trigger overtravel screws. Add $265 for extra .38 Special, .45 ACP cylinder or .22 WMR cylinder. Add $475 for extra fitted .22 Long Rifle match grade cylinder. Add $215 for match grade chambered instead of .22 Long Rifle sport chamber.

MODEL 353

Chambered for .357 Magnum cartridge with choice of 4.75", 6", 7.5", or 9" barrel length. Adjustable sights. This model designation no longer used; see Model 97.

Field Grade
NIB	Exc.	V.G.	Good	Fair	Poor
1650	1300	950	550	350	250

Premier Grade
NIB	Exc.	V.G.	Good	Fair	Poor
2150	1800	1250	700	500	300

Signature Edition

As above, with a highly polished finish, rosewood grips, 7.5" barrel only and a fitted case. The serial numbers are DC1-DC2000. (The DC represents Dick Casull, the designer of the firearm.) A total of 2,000 were made.

NIB	Exc.	V.G.	Good	Fair	Poor
2500	1950	1300	750	550	350

MODEL 252

This is a stainless steel version of the large frame revolver chambered for the .22 Long Rifle cartridge. Available in 5.12", 7.5", or 10" barrel lengths. Matte finish. This designation no longer used, see Model 97.

Silhouette Class

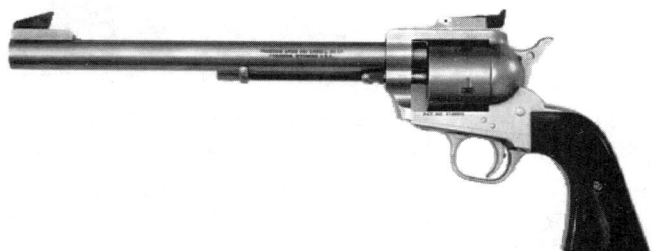

10" barrel.
NIB	Exc.	V.G.	Good	Fair	Poor
1700	1150	850	600	450	250

NOTE: Optional .22 magnum cylinder available for $250.

Varmint Class

5.12" or 7.5" barrel.
NIB	Exc.	V.G.	Good	Fair	Poor
1700	1150	850	600	450	250

MODEL 757

Introduced in 1999, this five-shot revolver is chambered for the .475 Linebaugh cartridge. Fitted with adjustable sights and offered in both Field and Premier grades. Choice of 4.75", 6", or 7.5" barrel. This designation no longer used; see Model 83.

Field Grade
NIB	Exc.	V.G.	Good	Fair	Poor
1400	1100	750	500	400	300

Premier Grade
NIB	Exc.	V.G.	Good	Fair	Poor
1800	1450	1100	750	500	400

MODEL 654

This five-shot revolver is chambered for the .41 Magnum cartridge. Adjustable sights. Introduced in 1999. This designation no longer used; see Model 97.

Field Grade
NIB	Exc.	V.G.	Good	Fair	Poor
1325	1050	750	500	400	300

Premier Grade
NIB	Exc.	V.G.	Good	Fair	Poor
1750	1400	1100	750	500	400

Model 83 .500 Wyoming Express

Similar to Model 83 but chambered in .500 Wyoming Express. Introduced 2007.

NIB	Exc.	V.G.	Good	Fair	Poor
2150	1800	1250	700	500	300

FREEMAN, AUSTIN T.
Hoard's Armory
Watertown, New York

Army Model Revolver

A .44 caliber percussion revolver with a 7.5" round barrel and a 6-shot unfluted cylinder with recessed nipples. Blued, casehardened rammer and hammer, and walnut grips. The frame is marked "Freeman's Pat. Dec. 9, 1862/Hoard's Armory, Watertown, N.Y." Several thousand were manufactured in 1863 and 1864.

NIB	Exc.	V.G.	Good	Fair	Poor
—	—	5800	2200	550	200

FYRBERG, ANDREW
Worcester and Hopkinton, Massachusetts

Revolvers

A 3"-barreled .32 caliber and a 3.5" .38 caliber revolver with round ribbed barrels and round butts. The grips bear the trademark, "AFCo." This model was most likely made by Iver Johnson for Andrew Fyrberg.

NIB	Exc.	V.G.	Good	Fair	Poor
—	250	145	100	75	50

GABBET-FAIRFAX, H.
Birmingham, England

Mars

Designed by Hugh Gabbet-Fairfax, this semi-automatic pistol was first produced on an experimental basis by Webley & Scott Revolvers in the 1890s. After Webley gave up on the idea an extremely limited number were built by the Mars Automatic Pistol Syndicate, Ltd., 1897 to 1905. The pistol was produced in four calibers; the 8.5mm Mars, 9mm Mars, .45 Mars Short Case, and .45 Mars Long Case. This was the most powerful handgun cartridge of its time and remained so until well after World War II. It is estimated that only about 80 of these pistols were ever produced.

Courtesy James Rankin

NIB	Exc.	V.G.	Good	Fair	Poor
—	45000	30500	19500	9200	6000

NOTE: Webley examples are worth a premium.

GABILONDO Y URRESTI
Guernica, Spain
Elgoibar, Spain
SEE—Llama

This Spanish firm was founded in 1904 to produce inexpensive revolvers of the Velo-Dog type. Sometime around 1909 the firm began to manufacture the Radium revolver. In 1914 the company produced a semi-automatic pistol distributed as the Ruby. This pistol soon became the mainstay of the company with orders of 30,000 pistols a month for the French army. With the end of WWI Gabilondo Y Urresti moved to Elgoeibar, Spain. The company produced a Browning 1910 replica pistol until the early 1930s. It was at this point that Gabilondo began to manufacture a Colt Model 1911 copy that became known as the Llama. For information of specific Llama models see the Llama section. The pistols listed reflect the pre-Llama period and are so marked with the trade name of that particular model. The monogram "GC" frequently appears on the grips but not on the slide.

Velo-Dog Revolver

A 6.35mm double-action revolver with a 1.5" barrel, folding trigger and concealed hammer. Blued with walnut grips. Manufactured from 1904 to 1914.

NIB	Exc.	V.G.	Good	Fair	Poor
—	295	195	125	75	50

Radium

A semi-automatic pistol in caliber 7.65mm. Produced both for the commercial and military market in the Ruby style. "Radium" is stamped on the slide as well as the top of each grip plate.

Courtesy James Rankin

NIB	Exc.	V.G.	Good	Fair	Poor
—	295	195	125	100	70

Ruby

A 7.65mm caliber semi-automatic pistol. Discontinued in 1930.

NIB	Exc.	V.G.	Good	Fair	Poor
—	250	175	150	100	75

Bufalo 6.35mm

A semi-automatic pistol in caliber 6.35mm. A copy of the Browning Model 1906 with a squeeze grip safety. Has "Bufalo" stamped on the slide and the Gabilondo logo along with a buffalo's head on each side of the grip plates. Manufactured between 1918 and 1925.NOTE: The spelling of "Bufalo" is as it appears on the pistol.

Courtesy James Rankin

NIB	Exc.	V.G.	Good	Fair	Poor
—	275	175	150	100	75

Bufalo 7.65mm

A semi-automatic pistol in caliber 7.65mm. Patterned after the Browning Model 1910 with a squeeze grip safety. There were two models, with either a 7-round or a 9-round magazine. The model with the 9-round magazine usually is fitted with wood grips and a lanyard ring. A buffalo's head is inset in each grip plate. Manufactured between 1918 and 1925.

Courtesy James Rankin

NIB	Exc.	V.G.	Good	Fair	Poor
—	275	175	125	100	75

Bufalo 9mmK

A semi-automatic pistol in caliber 9mmK. Nearly the same pistol as the 7.65mm model but fitted with a grip safety. "Bufalo" is stamped on the slide and the Gabilondo logo and buffalo's head are on each grip plate. Manufactured between 1918 and 1925.

Courtesy James Rankin

NIB	Exc.	V.G.	Good	Fair	Poor
—	295	205	145	105	70

Danton 6.35mm

A semi-automatic pistol in caliber 6.35mm. Patterned after the Browning Model 1906 with a grip safety. "Danton" appears on the slide as well as the grips. The Gabilondo logo is on each grip plate. Manufactured between 1925 and 1931.

Courtesy James Rankin

NIB	Exc.	V.G.	Good	Fair	Poor
—	275	175	125	100	75

DANTON WAR MODEL

A semi-automatic pistol in caliber 7.65mm. Similar to the Bufalo above and it was made with and without a grip safety. It came in two models with 9- and 20-round magazines. Fitted with a lanyard ring. "Danton" stamped on the slide and the grips. The Gabilondo log is on each side of the grip plates. Manufactured between 1925 and 1931.

Courtesy James Rankin

Nine-Round Magazine

NIB	Exc.	V.G.	Good	Fair	Poor
—	275	175	125	100	75

Twenty-Round Magazine

NIB	Exc.	V.G.	Good	Fair	Poor
—	550	325	250	200	100

Perfect

This semi-automatic pistol was chambered for the 6.35mm and 7.65mm cartridges. It was a cheap, low-priced pistol marketed by Mugica. These pistols usually have the word "Perfect" on the grips. The slide may be stamped with the name MUGICA but many are not.

NIB	Exc.	V.G.	Good	Fair	Poor
—	275	175	125	100	75

Plus Ultra

This pistol is chambered for the 7.65mm cartridge and was built from 1925 to 1933. It had a 20-round magazine that gave the pistol an unusual appearance. "Plus Ultra" appears on the slide and the grips. A Gabilondo logo is on each grip plate. Equipped with a lanyard ring.

Courtesy James Rankin

NIB	Exc.	V.G.	Good	Fair	Poor
—	1200	875	650	425	250

GALAND, C.F.
Liege, Belgium

Galand, Galand & Sommerville, Galand Perrin (Galand M1872)

A 7mm, 9mm, and 12mm caliber double-action revolver with a 6-shot cylinder, open frame, a unique ejection system that, by means of rotating a lever downward from the trigger guard, causes the barrel and cylinder to slide forward, leaving the ejector and the spent cases behind. Circa 1872.

Courtesy Bonhams & Butterfields

NIB	Exc.	V.G.	Good	Fair	Poor
—	—	1350	875	550	150

Velo-Dog

A 5.5mm Velo-Dog caliber fixed trigger and guard double-action revolver with open-top design. Later models (.22 and 6.35mm caliber) feature folding triggers and no trigger guards.

NIB	Exc.	V.G.	Good	Fair	Poor
—	250	165	125	75	50

Le Novo

As above, with a concealed hammer and in 6.35mm caliber.

NIB	Exc.	V.G.	Good	Fair	Poor
—	250	165	125	75	50

Tue-Tue

A .22 short, 5.5mm Velo-Dog, and 6.35mm caliber double-action revolver with a concealed hammer, folding trigger, and a swing-out cylinder with central extractor. Introduced in 1894.

NIB	Exc.	V.G.	Good	Fair	Poor
—	250	165	125	75	50

GALENA INDUSTRIES INC.
Sturgis, South Dakota

In 1998 Galena Industries purchased the rights to use the AMT trademark and manufacturing rights to many, but not all, AMT designs. For AMT models made by AMT see that section. This company's designs have been acquired by Crusader/High Standard of Houston, Texas.

AMT Backup

This model features a double-action-only trigger system and is offered in both stainless steel and matte black finish. The small frame .380 Backup weighs 18 oz. with its 2.5" barrel. The large frame Backups are fitted with a 3" barrel and are offered in 9mm, .38 Super, .357 Sig., .40 S&W, .400 CorBon, and .45 ACP. Weights are approximately 23 oz. and magazine capacity is 5 to 6 rounds, depending on caliber.

Galena .380 DAO Backup

NIB	Exc.	V.G.	Good	Fair	Poor
525	375	275	200	125	100

NOTE: Add $50 for .38 Super, .357 Sig, and .400 CorBon.

Automag II

This semi-automatic pistol is chambered for the .22 WMR cartridge. Offered in 3.38", 4.5", or 6" barrel lengths. Magazine capacity is 9 rounds except for the 3.38" model where capacity is 7 rounds. Weight is about 32 oz.

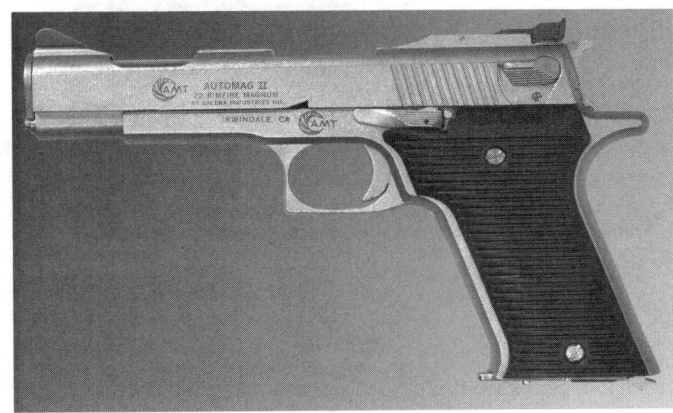

NIB	Exc.	V.G.	Good	Fair	Poor
695	550	325	225	125	100

Automag III

This pistol is chambered for the .30 Carbine cartridge. Barrel length is 6.38" and weight is about 43 oz. Stainless steel finish.

NIB	Exc.	V.G.	Good	Fair	Poor
800	675	375	250	150	100

Automag IV

This model is chambered for the .45 Winchester Magnum cartridge. It is fitted with a 6.5" barrel and has a magazine capacity of 7 rounds. Weight is approximately 46 oz.

NIB	Exc.	V.G.	Good	Fair	Poor
800	675	375	250	150	100

Automag .440 CorBon

This semi-automatic pistol is chambered for the .440 CorBon cartridge and fitted with a 7.5" barrel. Magazine capacity is 5 rounds. Finish is matte black. Weight is about 46 oz. Checkered walnut grips. Introduced in 2000. Special order only.

NIB	Exc.	V.G.	Good	Fair	Poor
1000	900	750	575	400	175

Galena Accelerator

This model has a 7" barrel built on a 1911 frame and is chambered for the .400 CorBon. Magazine capacity is 7 rounds. Weight is about 46 oz. Finish is stainless steel.

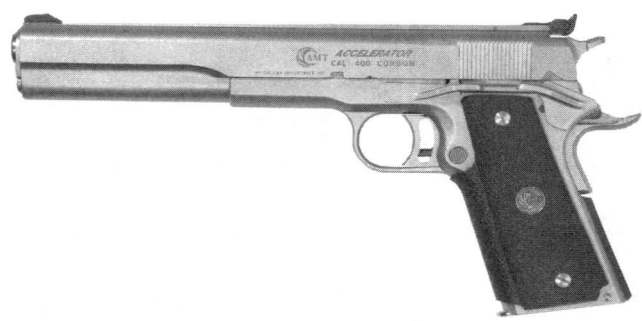

NIB	Exc.	V.G.	Good	Fair	Poor
850	725	550	400	300	100

Galena Hardballer

This pistol is based on the Colt Model 1911 design and is chambered for the .45 ACP cartridge. It is fitted with a 5" barrel and has a magazine capacity of 7 rounds. Finish is stainless steel. Adjustable trigger and beveled magazine well. Also offered chambered for the .40 S&W and .400 CorBon cartridges. Weight is about 38 oz.

NIB	Exc.	V.G.	Good	Fair	Poor
1000	900	750	575	400	175

Galena Longslide

This model is chambered for the .45 ACP cartridge and fitted with a 7" barrel. Magazine capacity is 7 rounds with weight about 46 oz. Finish is stainless steel.

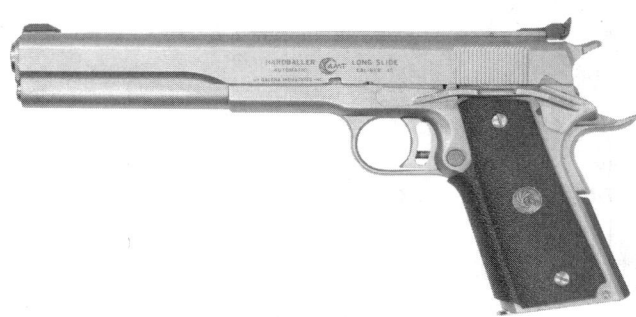

NIB	Exc.	V.G.	Good	Fair	Poor
850	725	550	400	300	10

Galena Commando

The Commando is chambered for the .40 S&W cartridge and fitted with a 4" barrel. Magazine capacity is 8 rounds. Weight is about 38 oz. Finish is stainless steel.

NIB	Exc.	V.G.	Good	Fair	Poor
550	400	295	225	175	100

GALESI, INDUSTRIA ARMI
Brescia, Italy

Rino Galesi Armi, Collebeato, Italy, manufactured shotguns, revolvers, and automatic pistols. The firm's name changed from Rino Galesi Armi to Industria Armi Galesi, to Rigarmi di Rino

Galesi. Their semi-automatic pistols were designated by model year, model number, and a 500 Series. Most models named in the 500 Series came after the firm changed its name to Industria Armi Galesi.

Model 1923

A 6.35mm and 7.65mm caliber semi-automatic pistol. Has a squeeze grip safety and wood grip plates with crest. Model 1923 is stamped on the slide.

Courtesy James Rankin

NIB	Exc.	V.G.	Good	Fair	Poor
—	275	195	145	75	50

Model 1930

A 6.35mm and 7.65mm caliber semi-automatic pistol. A very few were made in 1946 in 9mm Parabellum. Based on the 1910 Browning design. Blued with plastic grips. The slide marked "Brevetto Mod. 1930."

Courtesy James Rankin

NIB	Exc.	V.G.	Good	Fair	Poor
—	275	195	145	75	50

Model 1930 9mm Parabellum

NIB	Exc.	V.G.	Good	Fair	Poor
—	600	500	400	300	100

Model 6

Updated Model 1930. Manufactured approximately 1938 to 1948 in calibers; 22 Short, .22 Long, .22 Long Rifle, 6.35mm, 7.65mm, and 9mm Short.

Courtesy James Rankin

NIB	Exc.	V.G.	Good	Fair	Poor
—	350	175	100	75	50

Model 9

Manufactured from approximately 1947 to 1956 in calibers .22 Short, .22 Long, .22 Long Rifle, 6.35mm, 7.65mm, and 9mm Short. Also, listed under the 500 Series. The .22 versions were marketed as "the smallest .22 pistols ever built."

Courtesy James Rankin

NIB	Exc.	V.G.	Good	Fair	Poor
—	295	175	100	75	50

GAMBA, RENATO
Gardone V. T., Italy

SAB G90

A 7.65 Parabellum or 9mm caliber double-action semi-automatic pistol with a 4.75" barrel, and 15-shot magazine. Blued or chrome-plated with walnut grips.

NIB	Exc.	V.G.	Good	Fair	Poor
575	450	350	300	250	175

SAB G91 Compact

As above, with a 3.5" barrel and a 12-shot magazine.

NIB	Exc.	V.G.	Good	Fair	Poor
550	400	325	275	225	150

Trident Fast Action

A .32 S&W or .38 Special caliber double-action revolver with a 2.5" or 3" barrel and 6-shot cylinder. Blued, with walnut grips.

NIB	Exc.	V.G.	Good	Fair	Poor
500	400	300	250	200	150

Trident Super

As above, with a 4" ventilated-rib barrel.

NIB	Exc.	V.G.	Good	Fair	Poor
550	400	325	275	225	150

Trident Match 900

As above, with 6" heavy barrel, adjustable sights and target type, walnut grips.

NIB	Exc.	V.G.	Good	Fair	Poor
850	700	550	400	350	200

GARATE, HERMANOS
Ermua, Spain

Cantabria

A 6.35mm caliber folding-trigger double-action revolver with a concealed hammer, cocking spur and a short barrel resembling the slide on a semi-automatic. The name "Cantabria" is stamped on the left side.

NIB	Exc.	V.G.	Good	Fair	Poor
—	300	175	125	100	75

Velo-Stark

A double-action folding-trigger revolver with concealed hammer.

NIB	Exc.	V.G.	Good	Fair	Poor
—	250	150	100	75	50

GARRET, J. & F. CO.
Greensboro, North Carolina

Garrett Single-Shot Pistol

A .54 caliber single-shot percussion pistol with an 8.5" round barrel, swivel ramrod, walnut stock and brass mounts. Marked on

the barrel breech "G.W." or "S.R." Approximately 500 were made in 1862 and 1863.

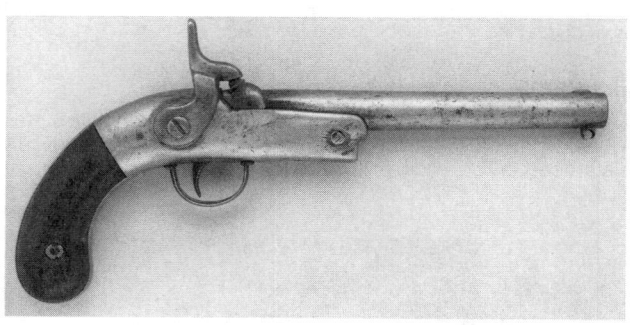

Courtesy Bonhams & Butterfields

NIB	Exc.	V.G.	Good	Fair	Poor
—	—	4550	165	1000	500

GASSER, LEOPOLD
Ottakring, Austria

M1870

An 11mm caliber double-action revolver with a 14.75" or 9.3" barrel, and 6-shot cylinder. Marked "Gasser Patent, Guss Stahl." It also bears an Austrian eagle and an apple pierced by an arrow, with the words "Schutz Mark."

NIB	Exc.	V.G.	Good	Fair	Poor
—	650	425	230	175	125

M1870/74

As above, with a steel frame.

NIB	Exc.	V.G.	Good	Fair	Poor
—	650	425	350	175	125

Gasser-Kropatschek M1876

An M1870/74 weighing 1 lb., 11 oz. and 9mm caliber.

NIB	Exc.	V.G.	Good	Fair	Poor
—	600	400	300	150	100

Montenegrin Gasser

A 10.7mm caliber double-action revolver with 5" or 6" barrels, and 5-shot cylinder. Engraved, silver and gold inlay, and ivory or bone grips. Values given are for the plain, unadorned model. Embellished models will need individual appraisal.

NIB	Exc.	V.G.	Good	Fair	Poor
—	650	425	350	200	150

Rast & Gasser M1898

A 8mm caliber double-action revolver with 4.75" barrel, 8-shot cylinder, solid-frame revolver with loading gate and an integral ejector rod.

NIB	Exc.	V.G.	Good	Fair	Poor
—	650	425	350	175	125

GATLING ARMS CO.
Birmingham, England

Established in 1888, this company remained in operation until approximately 1890. Although primarily involved with the marketing of Gatling Guns, it did market the one revolver listed.

Kynoch-Dimancea

A .38 or .45 caliber double-action hammerless revolver with a 6-shot cylinder. The loading system is rather unusual—a spur that resembles a hammer is pulled down, allowing the barrel and cylinder to pivot and to be pulled forward. During this motion the empty cases are ejected and new ones could be inserted. Marked "The Gatling Arms and Ammunition Co. Birmingham" ; some are also marked "Dimancea Patent."

NIB	Exc.	V.G.	Good	Fair	Poor
—	—	2400	1275	750	350

GAUCHER
France

GN 1

This is a single-shot, bolt-action pistol chambered for the .22 Long Rifle. It is fitted with a 10" barrel with blade front sight and adjustable rear sight. Adjustable trigger. Hardwood target grips. Weight is approximately 38 oz. Introduced in 1990.

NIB	Exc.	V.G.	Good	Fair	Poor
525	425	350	225	145	100

GAVAGE, A.
Liege, Belgium

A 7.65mm caliber semi-automatic pistol with a fixed barrel and a concealed hammer. Similar in appearance to the Clement. Markings with "AG" molded into the grips. Some have been found bearing German Waffenamts. Manufactured from 1930s to 1940s.

Courtesy James Rankin

NIB	Exc.	V.G.	Good	Fair	Poor
—	450	325	250	150	100

GAZANAGA, ISIDRO
Eibar, Spain

Destroyer M1913

A 6.35mm or 7.65mm caliber semi-automatic pistol. The 6.35mm model is copied after the 1906 Browning. "Destroyer" is stamped on the slide with the Isidro logo on each side of the grip plate. Produced through WWI.

Courtesy James Rankin

NIB	Exc.	V.G.	Good	Fair	Poor
—	295	195	145	75	50

Destroyer M1916

A 7.65mm caliber semi-automatic pistol with a 7- or 9-shot magazine. A Ruby style pistol manufactured by the Spanish during World War I. "Destroyer" stamped on the slide. Wood grips.

Courtesy James Rankin

NIB	Exc.	V.G.	Good	Fair	Poor
—	325	225	125	75	50

Destroyer Revolver

A good quality .38 caliber copy of the Colt Police Positive.

NIB	Exc.	V.G.	Good	Fair	Poor
—	295	165	155	100	75

Super Destroyer

A 7.65mm caliber copy of the Walther PP. The slide is stamped "Pistola Automatica 7.65 Super Destroyer."

NIB	Exc.	V.G.	Good	Fair	Poor
—	325	195	175	100	75

Surete

As above in 7.65mm caliber. Marked "Cal. 7.65 Pistolet Automatique Surete" with "IG" stamped on the frame.

NIB	Exc.	V.G.	Good	Fair	Poor
—	295	165	155	100	75

GEM

Bacon Arms Company
Norwich, Connecticut

SEE—Bacon Arms Company

Pocket Revolver

A .22 caliber spur trigger revolver with a 1.25" octagonal barrel. The frame is iron, engraved, nickel-plated, with walnut or ivory grips. The barrel marked "Gem." Manufactured between 1878 and 1883.

NIB	Exc.	V.G.	Good	Fair	Poor
—	—	1950	700	300	145

GENEZ, A. G.

New York, New York

Located at 9 Chambers Street, Genez made a wide variety of firearms during his working life (ca. 1850 to 1875). The most commonly encountered of his arms today are single-shot percussion pistols and percussion double-barrel shotguns. More rarely seen are single-shot percussion target rifles. A number of the arms he made were decorated by Louis D. Nimschke. Genez products signed by Nimschke command considerable premiums over the values for the standard firearms listed.

Pocket Pistol

A .41 caliber single-shot percussion pistol with a 3" barrel, German silver mountings and a walnut stock. Manufactured in the 1850s and 1860s.

NIB	Exc.	V.G.	Good	Fair	Poor
—	—	3950	1850	500	175

GENSCHOW, G.

Hamburg, Germany

Geco

A 6.35mm, 7.65mm, .32 Long, and 8mm Lebel caliber folding trigger double-action revolver.

NIB	Exc.	V.G.	Good	Fair	Poor
—	275	175	100	75	50

German Bulldog

A .32, .38, and .45 caliber folding trigger double-action revolver with solid frames, integral ejector rods, and loading gates. The proofmarks indicate Belgian manufacture.

NIB	Exc.	V.G.	Good	Fair	Poor
—	275	175	110	75	50

GERING, H. M. & CO.

Arnstadt, Germany

Leonhardt

A semi-automatic pistol in caliber 7.65mm. Almost identical to the Beholla pistol made by Becker. Leonhardt is stamped on the slide along with the Gering logo on each of the grip plates.

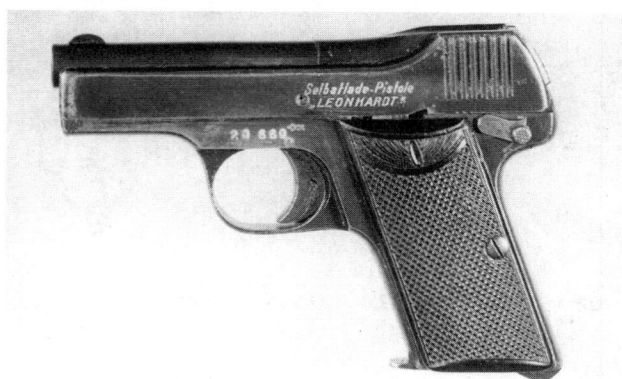

Courtesy James Rankin

NIB	Exc.	V.G.	Good	Fair	Poor
—	425	325	250	200	100

GERSTENBERGER & EBERWEIN

Gussenstadt, Germany

Em-Ge, G.& E., Omega & Pic

A series of poor-quality revolvers sold in the U.S.A. before 1968. .22 and .32 calibers with 2.25" barrels, and 6-shot cylinder. The editor does not consider these safe to shoot, even if new in the box. Worthless

GIBBS

New York, New York

Pistol

A caliber percussion pistol made by Hull & Thomas of Ilion, New York, in 1855 or 1856.

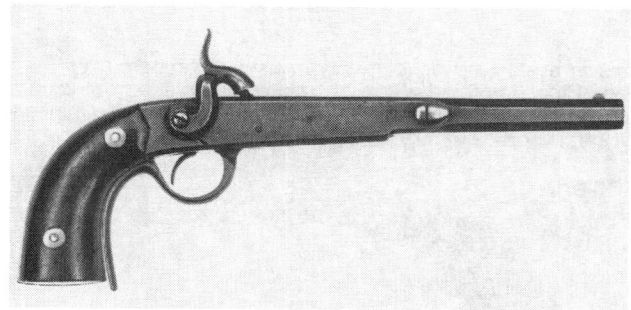

Courtesy Milwaukee Public Museum, Milwaukee, Wisconsin

NIB	Exc.	V.G.	Good	Fair	Poor
—	—	3600	2750	1250	400

GIBBS TIFFANY & CO.

Sturbridge, Massachusetts

Under Hammer Pistol

A .28 caliber single-shot percussion pistol with 3" to 8" barrels. A browned iron frame, walnut or maple pointed handle trimmed with brass. The top strap is marked "Gibbs Tiffany & Co." Active 1820 to 1838.

NIB	Exc.	V.G.	Good	Fair	Poor
—	—	1250	650	250	100

GILLESPIE
New York, New York
Derringer Type Pocket Pistol

A .41 caliber single-shot percussion pistol with a 2.5" barrel and a walnut stock. Manufactured from 1848 to 1870.

NIB	Exc.	V.G.	Good	Fair	Poor
—	—	2950	1350	500	200

GLOCK
Deutsch-Wagram, Austria
Smyrna, Georgia

First imported into the U.S.A. in 1985. Completely manufactured in Austria until 2004 when Glock opened its plant in Georgia to produce the polymer frames. Offered in many models but main differences are caliber, sighting systems, barrel and slide length and grip length/magazine capacity. In 2010 the Gen4 (fourth generation) of Glock pistols was introduced. Gen4 features include three interchangeable back-straps, reversible magazine release button, improved recoil spring assembly and rough-textured frame (RTF) to enhance grip traction. As of 2011, all new-production units of the following models had the Gen4 features: M17, M19, M22, M23, M26, M27, M31, M35.

Glock 17

This model is chambered for the 9mm Parabellum cartridge. It is a double-action-only semi-automatic that has a 4.49" barrel and a 17-shot detachable magazine. The empty weight of this pistol is 21.91 oz.

NIB	Exc.	V.G.	Good	Fair	Poor
520	425	325	300	275	175

NOTE: Add $70.00 if equipped with Meprolight night sights. Add $90 if equipped with Trijicon night sights. Add $30 if equipped with adjustable sights. Add 10 percent for Gen4 if NIB.

Glock 17C

Similar to the Model 17 but with the additional feature of an integral ported barrel. Specifications are the same except for weight: 17C weighs 21.9 oz. Also available with OD green frame.

NIB	Exc.	V.G.	Good	Fair	Poor
525	475	350	300	275	175

NOTE: Add $70.00 if equipped with Meprolight night sights. Add $90 if equipped with Trijicon night sights. Add $30 if equipped with adjustable sights.

Glock 17CC

Introduced in 1998 this is a compensated competition version of the C variation. It is fitted with an extended slide stop lever, extended magazine release, adjustable sights and a target trigger pull. This is special order item only.

NIB	Exc.	V.G.	Good	Fair	Poor
700	600	500	400	300	200

Glock 17L Competition Model

This version features a 6" compensated barrel and adjustable sights. The trigger is fine-tuned to provide between 5 to 8 lbs. trigger pull. This model was introduced in 1988. In 1990 this pistol won the I.P.S.C. World Stock Gun Championship. This pistol has limited availablity in the U.S. Also available with OD green frame.

NIB	Exc.	V.G.	Good	Fair	Poor
730	600	475	350	300	225

Glock 19

This is similar in appearance to the Model 17 but is a compact version with a 4" barrel and a smaller grip that will accept either a 15-round or the standard 17-round magazine that protrudes a bit. Weight for this model is 20.99 oz. empty. The grip straps on this model are serrated as they are on the other Glock models. It was introduced in 1988 and is currently in production. Also available with OD green frame.

NIB	Exc.	V.G.	Good	Fair	Poor
525	475	350	300	275	175

NOTE: Add $70.00 if equipped with Meprolight night sights. Add $90 if equipped with Trijicon night sights. Add $30 if equipped with adjustable sights. Add 10 percent for Gen4 if NIB.

Glock 19C

Same as above but with integral ported barrel. Weight is 20.7 oz. Also available with OD green frame.

NIB	Exc.	V.G.	Good	Fair	Poor
550	475	350	300	275	175

NOTE: Add $70.00 if equipped with Meprolight night sights. Add $90 if equipped with Trijicon night sights. Add $30 if equipped with adjustable sights.

Glock 19CC

Introduced in 1998 this is a compensated competition version of the C variation. It is fitted with an extended slide stop lever, extended magazine release, adjustable sights and a target trigger pull. This is special order item only.

NIB	Exc.	V.G.	Good	Fair	Poor
700	600	500	350	300	275

Glock 22

Almost identical in appearance to the Model 17, the Model 22 is chambered for the .40 S&W cartridge. It comes standard with a 15-round clip. It has a slightly larger and heavier slide. Weight is 22.36 oz. Also available with OD green frame.

NIB	Exc.	V.G.	Good	Fair	Poor
525	475	350	300	275	175

NOTE: Add $70.00 if equipped with Meprolight night sights. Add $90 if equipped with Trijicon night sights. Add $30 if equipped with adjustable sights. Add 10 percent for Gen4 if NIB.

Glock 22C

Same as the Glock 22 model but with the addition of an integral ported barrel. Weight is 22.5 oz. Also available with OD green frame.

NIB	Exc.	V.G.	Good	Fair	Poor
550	475	350	300	275	175

NOTE: Add $70.00 if equipped with Meprolight night sights. Add $90 if equipped with Trijicon night sights. Add $30 if equipped with adjustable sights.

Glock 22CC

Introduced in 1998 this is a compensated competition version of the C variation. It is fitted with an extended slide stop lever, extended magazine release, adjustable sights and a target trigger pull. This is special order item only.

NIB	Exc.	V.G.	Good	Fair	Poor
700	600	500	350	300	275

Glock 23

Model 23 is chambered for the .40 S&W cartridge. Its slide is slightly heavier and larger than the Model 19. Weight is 21.67 oz. The Glock 23 magazine holds 13 rounds. Also available with OD green frame.

NIB	Exc.	V.G.	Good	Fair	Poor
525	475	350	300	275	175

NOTE: Add $70.00 if equipped with Meprolight night sights. Add $90 if equipped with Trijicon night sights. Add $30 if equipped with adjustable sights. Add 10 percent for Gen4 if NIB.

Glock 23C

Same as above but with integral ported barrel. Weight is 20.9 oz. Also available with OD green frame.

NIB	Exc.	V.G.	Good	Fair	Poor
550	475	350	300	275	175

NOTE: Add $70.00 if equipped with Meprolight night sights. Add $90 if equipped with Trijicon night sights. Add $30 if equipped with adjustable sights.

Glock 23CC

Introduced in 1998 this is a compensated competition version of the C variation. It is fitted with an extended slide stop lever, extended magazine release, adjustable sights and a target trigger pull. This is special order item only.

NIB	Exc.	V.G.	Good	Fair	Poor
700	600	500	350	300	275

Glock 24

Chambered for the .40 S&W cartridge, it is fitted with a 6" barrel. Weight is 26.5 oz.

NIB	Exc.	V.G.	Good	Fair	Poor
675	550	400	350	300	175

NOTE: Add $70.00 if equipped with Meprolight night sights. Add $90 if equipped with Trijicon night sights. Add $30 if equipped with adjustable sights.

Glock 24C

Same as above but with a ported barrel.

NIB	Exc.	V.G.	Good	Fair	Poor
700	525	400	300	250	200

NOTE: Add $70.00 if equipped with Meprolight night sights. Add $90 if equipped with Trijicon night sights. Add $30 if equipped with adjustable sights.

Glock 24CC

Introduced in 1998 this is a compensated competition version of the C variation. It is fitted with an extended slide stop lever, extended magazine release, adjustable sights and a target trigger pull. This is special order item only.

NIB	Exc.	V.G.	Good	Fair	Poor
700	600	500	350	300	275

Glock 20 and Glock 21

Both of these models are identical in physical appearance except for the caliber: the Model 20 is chambered for the 10mm cartridge while the Model 21 is chambered for the .45 ACP. Both have a barrel length of 4.60". The Model 20 has a 15-round clip and weighs 26.35 oz. while the Model 21 has a 13-round magazine and weighs 25.22 oz. Also available with OD green frame.

NIB	Exc.	V.G.	Good	Fair	Poor
550	425	350	300	250	200

NOTE: Add $70.00 if equipped with Meprolight night sights. Add $90 if equipped with Trijicon night sights. Add $30 if equipped with adjustable sights.

Glock 20 SF Short Frame Pistol

DAO semi-auto similar to Glock Model 20 but with short-frame design. Chambered in 10mm Auto. Features include 4.61" barrel with hexagonal rifling, fixed sights, extended sight radius. Overall length 8.07". Weight: 27.51 oz.

NIB	Exc.	V.G.	Good	Fair	Poor
550	475	350	300	275	175

Glock 21 SF

Slenderized version of Model 21 with slimmer frame and ambidextrous magazine catch. Introduced 2007. Photo courtesy Ken Lunde.

Courtesy Ken Lunde

NIB	Exc.	V.G.	Good	Fair	Poor
550	475	350	300	275	175

Glock 20C and 21C

Same as Models 20 and 21 but with integral ported barrel. Also available with OD green frame.

NIB	Exc.	V.G.	Good	Fair	Poor
600	475	400	325	250	200

NOTE: Add $70.00 if equipped with Meprolight night sights. Add $90 if equipped with Trijicon night sights. Add $30 if equipped with adjustable sights.

Glock 20CC/21CC

Introduced in 1998 this is a compensated competition version of the C variation. It is fitted with an extended slide stop lever, extended magazine release, adjustable sights and a target trigger pull. This is special order item only.

NIB	Exc.	V.G.	Good	Fair	Poor
700	600	500	350	300	275

Glock 26 and Model 27

Both of these models are identical except for caliber. Introduced in 1995 these are subcompact versions of the full-size Glocks. The Model 26 is chambered for the 9mm cartridge, while the Model 27 is chambered for the .40 S&W cartridge. The 9mm version magazine capacity is 10 rounds and the 40 caliber version holds 9 rounds. The overall length is 6-1/4" with a barrel length of 3-1/2". The height is 4-3/16" and the width is 1-1/4". Weight for both models is about 20 oz. Standard are a dot front sight and white outline rear adjustable sight. Also available with OD green frame.

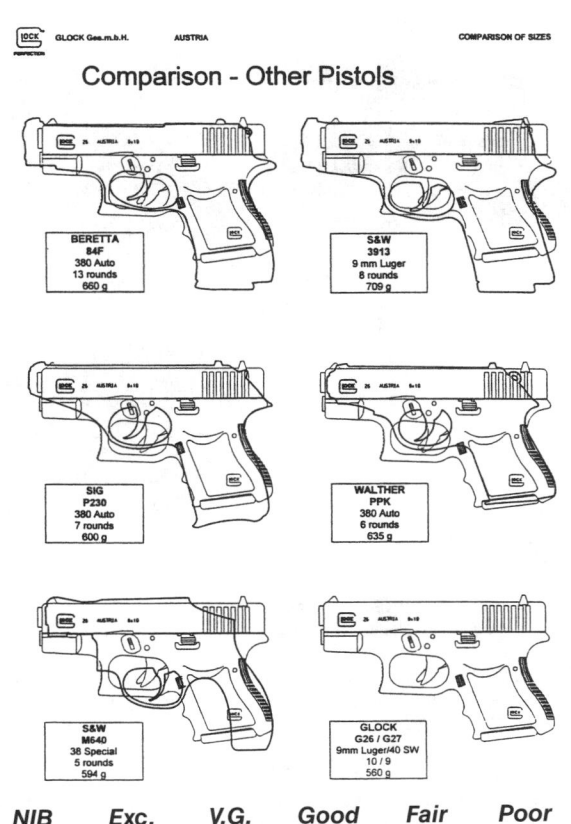

NIB	Exc.	V.G.	Good	Fair	Poor
550	475	350	300	275	175

NOTE: Add $70.00 if equipped with Meprolight night sights. Add $90 if equipped with Trijicon night sights. Add $30 if equipped with adjustable sights. Add 10 percent for Gen4 if NIB.

Glock 29 and Glock 30

These two pistols were introduced in 1997. The Model 29 is chambered for the 10mm cartridge while the Model 30 is chambered for the .45 ACP cartridge. Barrel length is 3.78". Weight is about 24 oz. Overall length is 6.77". The Model 29 has a magazine capacity of 10 rounds while the Model 30 has a standard capacity of 10 rounds with a optional capacity of 9 rounds. With the 10-round magazine in place the Model 30 magazine protrudes slightly below the grip. With the 9-round magazine in place the magazine fits flush with the bottom of the grip. Also available with OD green frame.

Model 29

Model 30

NIB	Exc.	V.G.	Good	Fair	Poor
550	475	350	300	275	175

NOTE: Add $70.00 if equipped with Meprolight night sights. Add $90 if equipped with Trijicon night sights. Add $30 if equipped with adjustable sights.

Glock Model 29 SF Short Frame Pistol

DAO semi-auto similar to Glock Model 29 but with short-frame design. Chambered in 10mm Auto. Features include 3.78" barrel with hexagonal rifling, fixed sights, extended sight radius. Overall length 6.97". Weight: 24.52 oz.

NIB	Exc.	V.G.	Good	Fair	Poor
575	495	350	300	275	175.

Glock 31

Chambered for the .357 SIG cartridge this pistol is fitted with a 4.5" barrel and a magazine capacity of 10 rounds (15 rounds law enforcement). Overall length is 7.3" and the height is 5.4". Weight is about 23.3 oz. Introduced in 1998. Also available with OD green frame.

NIB	Exc.	V.G.	Good	Fair	Poor
550	475	350	300	275	175

NOTE: Add $70.00 if equipped with Meprolight night sights. Add $90 if equipped with Trijicon night sights. Add $30 if equipped with adjustable sights. Add 10 percent for Gen4 if NIB.

Glock 31C

Same as the Model 31 but with an integral compensator. Also available with OD green frame.

NIB	Exc.	V.G.	Good	Fair	Poor
575	495	350	300	275	175

NOTE: Add $70.00 if equipped with Meprolight night sights. Add $90 if equipped with Trijicon night sights. Add $30 if equipped with adjustable sights.

Glock 31CC

Introduced in 1998 this is a compensated competition version of the C variation. It is fitted with an extended slide stop lever, extended magazine release, adjustable sights and a target trigger pull. This is special order item only.

NIB	Exc.	V.G.	Good	Fair	Poor
700	600	500	350	300	275

Glock 32

Similar to the Glock 31 except fitted with a 4" barrel. Overall length is 6.85" and height is 5". Magazine capacity is 10 rounds (13 rounds law enforcement). Weight is approximately 21.5 oz. Introduced in 1998. Also available with OD green frame.

NIB	Exc.	V.G.	Good	Fair	Poor
575	495	350	300	275	175

NOTE: Add $70.00 if equipped with Meprolight night sights. Add $90 if equipped with Trijicon night sights. Add $30 if equipped with adjustable sights.

Glock 32C

Same as above but fitted with integral ported barrel and slide. Also available with OD green frame.

NIB	Exc.	V.G.	Good	Fair	Poor
700	600	500	350	300	275

Glock 32CC

Introduced in 1998 this is a compensated competition version of the C variation. It is fitted with an extended slide stop lever, extended magazine release, adjustable sights and a target trigger pull. This is special order item only.

NIB	Exc.	V.G.	Good	Fair	Poor
700	600	500	350	300	275

Glock 33

This .357 SIG model has a 3.5" barrel and an overall length of 6.3". Height is 4.2" and weight is about 17.7 oz. Introduced in 1998. Also available with OD green frame.

NIB	Exc.	V.G.	Good	Fair	Poor
575	495	350	300	275	175.

NOTE: Add $70.00 if equipped with Meprolight night sights. Add $90 if equipped with Trijicon night sights. Add $30 if equipped with adjustable sights.

Glock 34

This model is chambered for the 9x19 cartridge and has a 5.3" barrel, overall length of 8.2", and a magazine capacity of 10 rounds. Empty weight is approximately 23 oz. Also available with OD green frame.

NIB	Exc.	V.G.	Good	Fair	Poor
575	495	350	300	275	175.

NOTE: Add $70.00 if equipped with Meprolight night sights. Add $90 if equipped with Trijicon night sights. Add $30 if equipped with adjustable sights.

Glock 35

The Glock 35 is chambered for the .40 S&W cartridge. It has the same dimensions as the Glock 34 except for weight, which is 24.5 oz. Also available with OD green frame.

NIB	Exc.	V.G.	Good	Fair	Poor
700	600	500	350	300	275

NOTE: Add $70.00 if equipped with Meprolight night sights. Add $90 if equipped with Trijicon night sights. Add $30 if equipped with adjustable sights. Add 10 percent for Gen4 if NIB.

Glock 36

Introduced in 1999, this model is similar to the Model 30 but fitted with a single-column magazine with a capacity of 6 rounds. The width of the pistol is .14" less than the Model 30. Barrel length is 3.78". Weight is 20 oz. Also available with OD green frame.

NIB	Exc.	V.G.	Good	Fair	Poor
575	495	350	300	275	175.

NOTE: Add $70.00 if equipped with Meprolight night sights. Add $90 if equipped with Trijicon night sights. Add $30 if equipped with adjustable sights.

Glock 37

This semi-automatic pistol is chambered for the .45 G.A.P. cartridge, which is slightly shorter than the .45 ACP cartridge. This cartridge has a muzzle speed of 951 fps and muzzle energy of 405 ft. lbs. Fitted with a 4.49" barrel. Height is 5.5". Overall length is 7.3". Weight is about 26 oz. Also available with OD green frame.

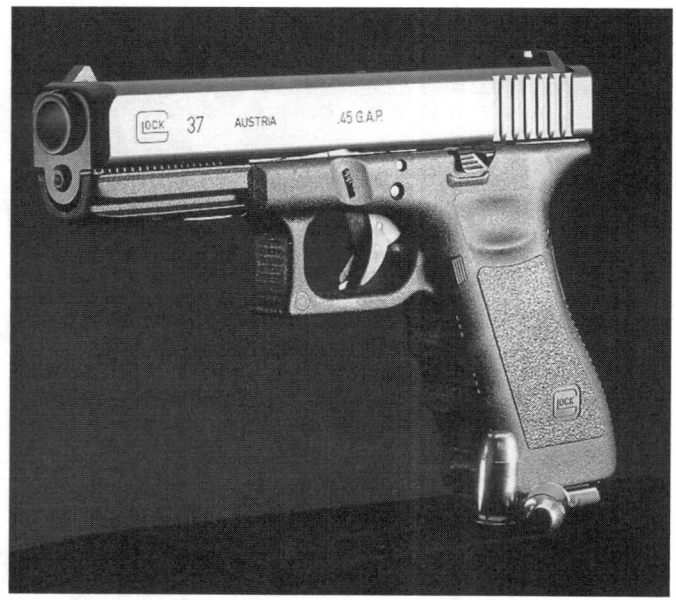

NIB	Exc.	V.G.	Good	Fair	Poor
575	495	350	300	275	175

Glock 38

This .45 G.A.P. pistol is fitted with a 4" barrel. Height is 5" and overall length is 6.85". Magazine capacity is 8 rounds. Weight is about 24 oz. Introduced in 2005. Also available with OD green frame.

NIB	Exc.	V.G.	Good	Fair	Poor
575	495	350	300	275	175

NOTE: Add $70.00 if equipped with Meprolight night sights. Add $90 if equipped with Trijicon night sights. Add $30 if equipped with adjustable sights.

Glock 39

Introduced in 2005 this sub-compact .45 G.A.P. pistol has a 3.46" barrel. Height is 4.17" and overall length is 6.3". Magazine capacity is 8 rounds. Weight is about 19.3 oz. Also available with OD green frame.

NIB	Exc.	V.G.	Good	Fair	Poor
575	495	350	300	275	175

NOTE: Add $70.00 if equipped with Meprolight night sights. Add $90 if equipped with Trijicon night sights. Add $30 if equipped with adjustable sights.

Glock Model G17/G22/G19/G23 RTF2

Similar to Models G17, G22, G19 and G23 but with rough textured frame. MSRP: N/A.

Glock 22 Gen4

Similar to Model G22 but with multiple backstrap system allowing three options: a short frame version, medium frame or large frame; reversible, enlarged magazine release catch; dual recoil spring assembly; new Rough Textured Frame (RTF) surface designed to enhance grip traction. MSRP: N/A.

GONCZ CO.
Hollywood, California

GA Pistol

The GC Carbine with a 9.5" shrouded barrel and a 16- or 18-shot magazine. Black with a one-piece grip. Manufactured between 1985 and 1987.

NIB	Exc.	V.G.	Good	Fair	Poor
525	400	295	200	150	100

GAT-9 Pistol

As above, in a 9mm caliber with an adjustable trigger and hand-honed action.

NIB	Exc.	V.G.	Good	Fair	Poor
600	475	375	300	225	150

GA Collector's Edition

A hand-polished stainless steel limited production of the above.

NIB	Exc.	V.G.	Good	Fair	Poor
825	675	600	500	400	300

GS Pistol

The Model GA with a plain 5" barrel. In 1987 pistols were made in stainless steel.

NIB	Exc.	V.G.	Good	Fair	Poor
350	275	225	175	125	75

GS Collector's Edition

A hand-polished, limited-production, stainless steel version of the GS.

NIB	Exc.	V.G.	Good	Fair	Poor
775	625	550	475	350	250

GOUDRY, J.F.
Paris, France

Double-action 10-shot turret pistol. Marked on barrel rib J.F. Goudry Paris and Systeme A. Norl. By raising the gate on the left side the turret can be removed and reloaded or another preloaded turret inserted.

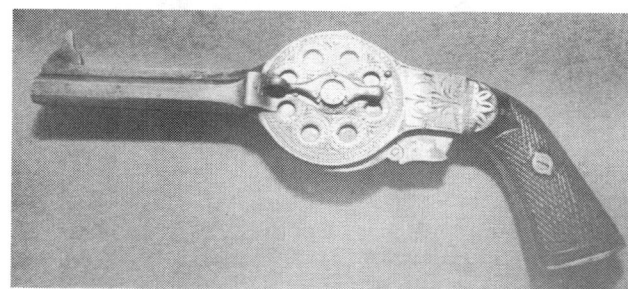

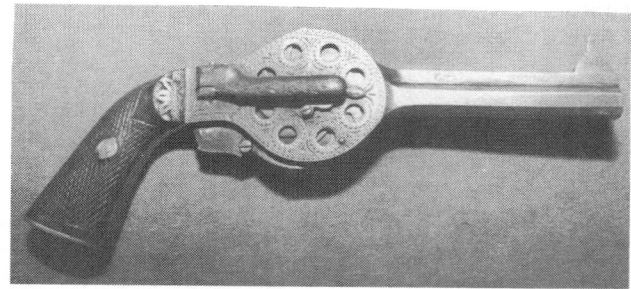

NIB	Exc.	V.G.	Good	Fair	Poor
—	—	6500	2000	1000	500

GOVERNOR
Norwich, Connecticut

Pocket Revolver

A .22 caliber spur trigger revolver with a 3" barrel and 7-shot cylinder. These revolvers were made from modified Bacon pepperboxes. The top strap marked "Governor." Manufactured from approximately 1868 to 1874.

NIB	Exc.	V.G.	Good	Fair	Poor
—	—	725	650	250	100

GRAND PRECISION, FABRIQUE D'ARMES DE
Eibar, Spain

Bulwark Model 1913

This model is chambered for the 6.35mm cartridge and is an exact copy of the Browning Model 1906 complete with squeeze grip safety. Marketed by Beistegui Hermanos. Bulwark is stamped on the slide and B.H. stamped on the grip plate.

Courtesy James Rankin

NIB	Exc.	V.G.	Good	Fair	Poor
—	295	195	150	75	40

Bulwark Model 1914

Chambered for the 7.65mm cartridge and in the style of the Ruby military pistols of WWI. Magazine capacity is 9 rounds.

Courtesy James Rankin

NIB	Exc.	V.G.	Good	Fair	Poor
—	275	225	150	75	40

Bulwark 6.35mm

A semi-automatic pistol in caliber 6.35mm patterned after the Browning Model 1906, and marketed by Beistegue Hermanos.

Courtesy James Rankin

NIB	Exc.	V.G.	Good	Fair	Poor
—	250	175	115	75	40

Libia 6.35mm

This model is also patterned after the Browning Model 1906 with squeeze safety. Libia is stamped on the slide and each grip plate. Marketed by Beistegui Hermanos.

Courtesy James Rankin

NIB	Exc.	V.G.	Good	Fair	Poor
—	275	225	150	750	40

Libia 7.65mm

Similar to the model above but chambered for the 7.65mm cartridge.

Courtesy James Rankin

NIB	Exc.	V.G.	Good	Fair	Poor
—	275	225	150	75	40

GREAT WESTERN ARMS COMPANY

During the 10 years that Great Western was in business the quality of its firearms was inconsistent due to uncertain management and finances. This left the company's reputation damaged and allowed Colt and Ruger to dominate the single-action market. By 1961 Great Western Arms Company was no longer able to compete. Despite, or perhaps because of, the company's unstable history there is considerable collector interest in these firearms. Approximately 22,000 single-action revolvers were built and fewer than 3,500 derringers were manufactured from 1953 to 1961. Standard barrel lengths were: 4-3/4, 5-1/2, and 7-1/2 inches. Standard calibers were: .38 Special, .357 Magnum, .357 Atomic, .44 Special, .44-40, .44 Magnum, .45 Long Colt, and .22 Long Rifle. Standard finishes were: Case hardened frame and blued barrel and cylinder, or all blue finish. **NOTE:** For guns to be in NIB condition they must have original boxes and paper work. Factory engraved guns must be supported by some type of invoice, letter, or other provenance to realize full value. Great Westerns were also available in kit form. Assembled kit guns are not as valuable as factory-built guns. Deduct 25-40 percent for kit guns unless in disassembled form. **NOTE:** The market for Great Western factory-built guns is extremely volatile because of their increasing scarcity and historical significance.

Centerfire Single-Action

Courtesy John C. Dougan

NIB	Exc.	V.G.	Good	Fair	Poor
695	550	425	350	250	200

.22 Long Rifle Single-Action

NIB	Exc.	V.G.	Good	Fair	Poor
450	335	295	250	200	150

Fast Draw Model

Brass backstrap and trigger guard.

NIB	Exc.	V.G.	Good	Fair	Poor
700	550	475	400	300	225

Deputy Model

4-inch barrel with full length sight rib.

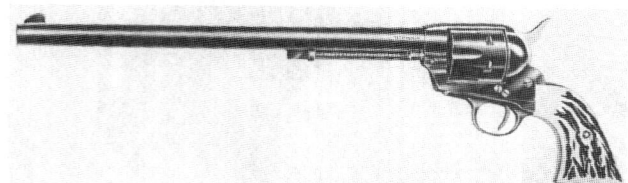

Courtesy John C. Dougan

NIB	Exc.	V.G.	Good	Fair	Poor
900	750	600	425	250	—

NOTE: For calibers other than standard such as .22 Hornet, .32-20, .45 ACP, .22 Magnum, .30 Carbine or .357 Atomic add 10 percent premium. For factory plated pistols add 10 percent. For factory cased pistols add 20 percent. For Sheriff's Model or Buntline Special add 15 percent. For factory ivory grips add $175; for stag grips add $95, and for pearl grips add $150. Factory-engraved guns will add $750 to $3,500 to above prices depending on coverage.

Derringer Model—.22 Magnum RF

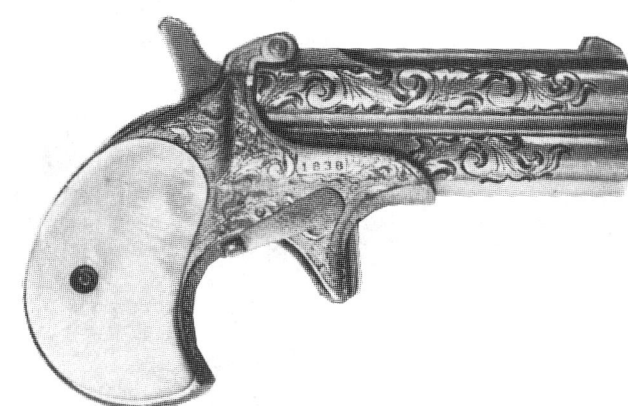

Courtesy John C. Dougan

NIB	Exc.	V.G.	Good	Fair	Poor
—	500	375	250	200	150

NOTE: Factory-engraved Derringers add $350 to $500.

Target Model

Flattop with micro sights.

NIB	Exc.	V.G.	Good	Fair	Poor
—	550	475	400	300	225

Derringer Model .38 Special & .38 S&W

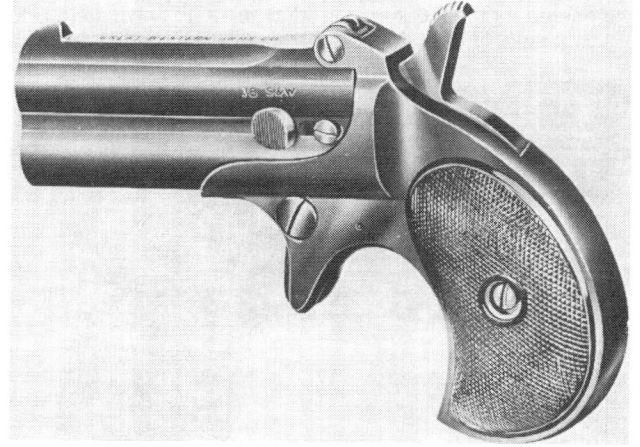

Courtesy John C. Dougan

NIB	Exc.	V.G.	Good	Fair	Poor
—	625	475	275	175	100

Unassembled Kit Gun—In the White

NIB	Exc.	V.G.	Good	Fair	Poor
350	300	—	—	—	—

GREEN, E.
Cheltenham, England

Green

A .450 and .455 caliber double-action revolver, popular with its military users in the late 1800s.

NIB	Exc.	V.G.	Good	Fair	Poor
—	—	2000	875	550	300

GRENDEL, INC.
Rockledge, Florida

P-10 Pistol

A .380 caliber semi-automatic pistol with a 3" barrel, 11-shot magazine, matte black finish with black plastic grips. The pistol has a plastic frame with plastic magazine. It is offered in electroless nickel-plate, as well as a green Teflon finish for a slightly higher price.

NIB	Exc.	V.G.	Good	Fair	Poor
295	250	195	150	125	75

NOTE: Green finish add $5. Electroless nickel add $15.

P-12

This semi-automatic double-action pistol is chambered for the .380 ACP cartridge. Fitted with a 3" barrel, checkered polymer grips, and blued finish. Magazine capacity is 10 rounds. Weight is about 13 oz. Introduced in 1992.

NIB	Exc.	V.G.	Good	Fair	Poor
295	250	195	150	125	75

P-30

Introduced in 1990 this is a double-action semi-automatic pistol chambered for the .22 WMR cartridge. Fitted with a 5" barrel or 8" barrel. Fixed sights. Magazine capacity is 30 rounds. Weight is about 21 oz. Discontinued in 1994.

NIB	Exc.	V.G.	Good	Fair	Poor
450	350	275	125	85	75

P-30L

Same as above model but in 8" barrel only. Also discontinued in 1994.

NIB	Exc.	V.G.	Good	Fair	Poor
450	350	275	125	85	75

P-30M

Similar to the P-30 but fitted with a removable muzzlebrake.

NIB	Exc.	V.G.	Good	Fair	Poor
450	350	275	125	85	75

P-31

This is a semi-automatic pistol chambered for .22 WMR cartridge. Fitted with an 11" barrel, muzzlebrake. Black matte finish. Weight is approximately 48 oz. Introduced in 1991 but no longer in production.

NIB	Exc.	V.G.	Good	Fair	Poor
450	350	275	125	85	75

GRIFFON
South Africa

Griffon 1911 A1 Combat

This semi-automatic single-action pistol is chambered for the .45 ACP cartridge and fitted with a 4" ported barrel. Aluminum trigger and high-profile sights are standard. Frame is chrome and slide is blued. Magazine capacity is 7 rounds.

NIB	Exc.	V.G.	Good	Fair	Poor
600	500	400	295	200	125

GRISWOLD & GUNNISON
Griswoldville, Georgia

1851 Navy Type

A .36 caliber percussion revolver with a 7.5" barrel and 6-shot cylinder. The frame and grip straps made of brass and the barrel as well as cylinder made of iron. Approximately 3,700 were made between 1862 and 1864, for the Confederate government. NOTE: This revolver is sometimes referred to as the Griswold and Grier.

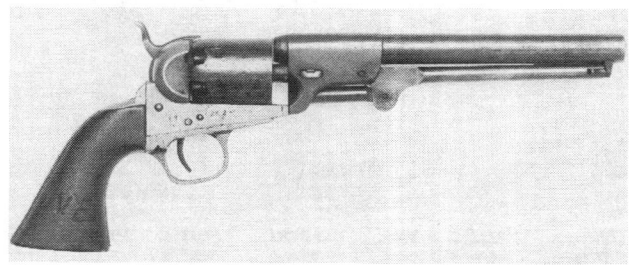

Courtesy Milwaukee Public Museum, Milwaukee, Wisconsin

NIB	Exc.	V.G.	Good	Fair	Poor
—	—	38500	14000	2750	1350

GROSS ARMS CO.
Tiffin, Ohio

Pocket Revolver

A .25 and .30 caliber spur trigger revolver with a 6" octagonal barrel, a 7-shot cylinder and marked "Gross Arms Co., Tiffin, Ohio." Blued, with walnut grips. Only a few hundred were manufactured between 1864 and 1866.

NIB	Exc.	V.G.	Good	Fair	Poor
—	—	1700	600	300	150

GRUBB, J. C. & CO.
Philadelphia, Pennsylvania

Pocket Pistol

A .41 caliber single-shot percussion pistol with various barrel lengths. German silver, walnut stock and engraved lock and trigger guard. The lock is marked "J.C. Grubb." Several hundred were manufactured between 1860 and 1870.

NIB	Exc.	V.G.	Good	Fair	Poor
—	—	1550	800	650	170

GUION, T. F.
New Orleans, Louisiana

Pocket Pistol

A .41 caliber single-shot percussion pistol with a 2.5" barrel, German silver mountings, and a walnut stock. Manufactured in the 1850s.

NIB	Exc.	V.G.	Good	Fair	Poor
—	—	2150	1850	550	275

GUNWORKS LTD.
Buffalo, New York

Model 9 Derringer

An Over/Under derringer chambered in 9mm, .38 Special, .38 Super, and .357 Magnum caliber with 2.5" barrels, with a spur trigger and Millet sights. Nickel-plate, with walnut grips. Manufacturing ceased in 1986.

NIB	Exc.	V.G.	Good	Fair	Poor
—	175	125	90	75	50

H.J.S. INDUSTRIES, INC.
Brownsville, Texas
Frontier Four Derringer

A .22 caliber four-barreled pocket pistol with 2.5" sliding barrels, stainless steel frame and barrel grip and walnut grips. Recalled due to risk of unintentional discharge.

NIB	Exc.	V.G.	Good	Fair	Poor
—	450	400	275	150	50

Lone Star Derringer

A .38 Special caliber single-shot spur trigger pistol with a 2.5" barrel. Stainless steel with wood grips.

NIB	Exc.	V.G.	Good	Fair	Poor
—	300	250	175	125	50

H-S PRECISION, INC.
Rapid City, South Dakota
Varmint Pistol

Bolt-action single-shot pistol chambered for a wide variety of calibers from .17 Rem. to 7mm BR. Fitted with a heavy contour fluted stainless steel match barrel. Synthetic stock with center grip. Matte black finish. Weight is about 5.25 to 5.5 lbs.

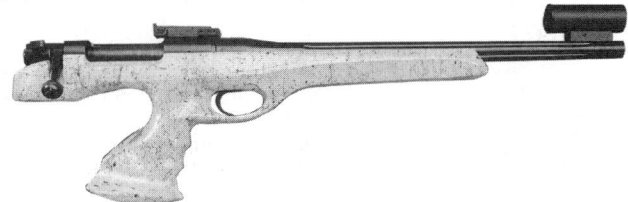

NIB	Exc.	V.G.	Good	Fair	Poor
1500	1200	950	600	400	225

Silhouette Pistol

Same as above but with sporter contoured barrel. Weight is about 4.5 lbs.

NIB	Exc.	V.G.	Good	Fair	Poor
1500	1200	950	600	400	225

HAENEL, C. G.
Suhl, Germany

Established in 1840, this company began to manufacture semi-automatic pistols after Hugo Schmeisser joined the firm in 1921 as its chief engineer.

Model 1

A 6.35mm caliber semi-automatic pistol with a 2.48" barrel, striker-fired, a 6-shot magazine. Weight is approximately 13.5 oz. The left side of the slide is stamped "C.G. Haenel Suhl-Schmeisser Patent." Each grip panel is marked "HS" in an oval.

NIB	Exc.	V.G.	Good	Fair	Poor
—	500	400	295	200	125

Model 2

As above, but shorter (2" barrel) and lighter in weight (12 oz.). "Schmeisser" is molded into the grips.

NIB	Exc.	V.G.	Good	Fair	Poor
—	550	425	350	225	150

HAFDASA
Buenos Aires, Argentina
Ballester-Molina

A copy of the Colt Model 1911 semi-automatic pistol differing only in the absence of a grip safety, smaller grip and the finger grooves on the slide. The slide stamped "Pistola Automatica Cal. .45 Fabricado por HAFDASA Patentes Internacional Ballester Molina Industria Argentina" on the slide. Introduced in 1941.

Courtesy James Rankin

NIB	Exc.	V.G.	Good	Fair	Poor
—	475	400	300	225	100

Criolla

A .22 caliber automatic pistol, similar to the Ballester-Molina. Some were sold commercially under the trademark "La Criolla."

NIB	Exc.	V.G.	Good	Fair	Poor
—	1000	800	650	500	250

Hafdasa

A .22 caliber semi-automatic pistol with a tubular receiver. A true hammerless, striker-fired, with an angled grip. Markings are "HA" on the butt.

NIB	Exc.	V.G.	Good	Fair	Poor
—	400	325	275	200	100

Zonda

As above, but marked "Zonda."

NIB	Exc.	V.G.	Good	Fair	Poor
—	400	325	275	200	100

Rigaud

A semi-automatic copy of the Colt Model 1911 with no grip safety. Caliber is .45 ACP and later .22 LR. Barrel length is 5". Magazine capacity is 7 rounds. The .22 caliber was introduced in 1940.

Courtesy James Rankin

NIB	Exc.	V.G.	Good	Fair	Poor
—	475	400	300	225	100

Campeon

The same as the Ballester-Molina but with a floating chamber to accommodate the .22 LR cartridge. There were three variations of the target model: Sights, trigger, and barrel lengths. The pistol was first introduced in 1941 and produced until 1953.

Courtesy James Rankin

NIB	Exc.	V.G.	Good	Fair	Poor
—	750	550	400	300	200

HAHN, WILLIAM
New York, New York

Pocket Pistol

A .41 caliber single-shot percussion pistol with a 2.5" round barrel, German silver mountings, and a walnut stock. Manufactured in the 1860s and 1870s.

NIB	Exc.	V.G.	Good	Fair	Poor
—	—	1950	1050	475	250

HALE, H. J.
Bristol, Connecticut

Under Hammer Pistol

A .31 caliber single-shot, under hammer percussion pistol with a 5" or 6" part-round, part-octagonal barrel and an iron frame with either a pointed or a round walnut butt. Markings read "H.J.Hale/Warranted/Cast Steel." Manufactured during the 1850s.

NIB	Exc.	V.G.	Good	Fair	Poor
—	—	995	375	245	125

HALE & TULLER
Hartford, Connecticut

Under Hammer Pistol

A .44 caliber single-shot under hammer percussion pistol with a 6" tapered round barrel and a pointed walnut grip. Manufactured at the Connecticut State Prison between 1837 and 1840.

NIB	Exc.	V.G.	Good	Fair	Poor
—	—	975	450	200	125

Model 100 Free Pistol

A .22 caliber single-shot Martini-action target pistol with an 11.5" octagonal barrel, adjustable sights, single set trigger and walnut stocks. Manufactured from 1933 to 1949.

NIB	Exc.	V.G.	Good	Fair	Poor
—	1000	825	700	550	325

Model 101

As above, with a heavy round barrel and more sophisticated target sights. A matte-blued finish and was manufactured between 1956 and 1960.

NIB	Exc.	V.G.	Good	Fair	Poor
—	1000	825	700	550	325

Model 102

As above, with highly polished blue finish. Manufactured between 1956 and 1960.

NIB	Exc.	V.G.	Good	Fair	Poor
—	1000	825	700	550	325

Model 103

Similar to the Model 101, with a lighter-weight octagonal barrel, high-polished blued finish. Manufactured between 1956 and 1960.

NIB	Exc.	V.G.	Good	Fair	Poor
—	1100	925	825	650	425

Model 104

As above, with a lightweight round barrel. Manufactured between 1961 and 1965.

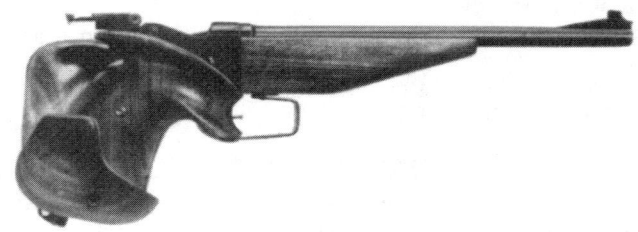

NIB	Exc.	V.G.	Good	Fair	Poor
—	950	625	550	450	300

Model 105

As above, with a redesigned stock and an improved action. Manufactured between 1962 and 1965.

NIB	Exc.	V.G.	Good	Fair	Poor
—	950	625	550	450	300

Model 106

As above, with an improved trigger.

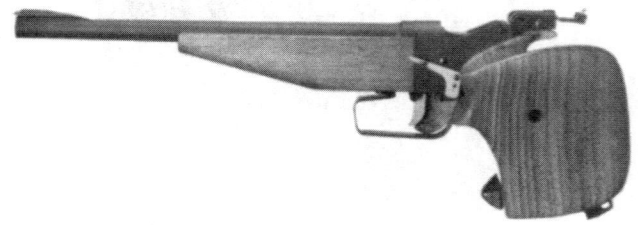

NIB	Exc.	V.G.	Good	Fair	Poor
—	950	625	550	450	300

Model 107

This variation is fitted with a five-level set trigger. Introduced in 1965 and discontinued in 1971.

NIB	Exc.	V.G.	Good	Fair	Poor
—	950	625	550	450	300

Model 107 Deluxe

As above, but engraved and with a carved stock.

NIB	Exc.	V.G.	Good	Fair	Poor
—	1500	1250	900	800	500

Model 120-1 Free Pistol

A bolt-action, single-shot pistol in .22 LR caliber with a a 9.9" barrel, adjustable target sights, activated for loading and cocking by an alloy lever on the side of the bolt. Blued, with checkered walnut grips.

NIB	Exc.	V.G.	Good	Fair	Poor
—	1200	975	600	425	250

Model 120-2

As above with contoured grips.

NIB	Exc.	V.G.	Good	Fair	Poor
—	1200	975	600	425	250

Model 120 Heavy Barrel

As above, with a 5.7" heavy barrel.

NIB	Exc.	V.G.	Good	Fair	Poor
—	1200	975	600	425	250

Model 150

A single-shot, Martini-action .22 caliber pistol with an 11.25" barrel, adjustable sights, contoured grips and a single-set trigger. Blued with walnut stocks.

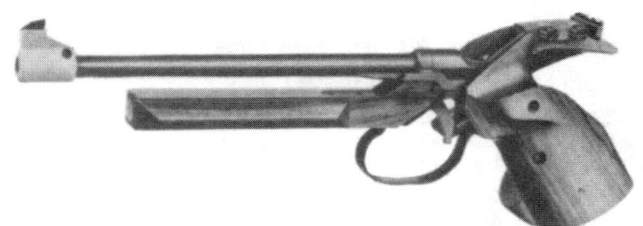

NIB	Exc.	V.G.	Good	Fair	Poor
—	1500	1100	775	500	350

Model 152

As above, with an 11.25" barrel, and an electronic release trigger.

NIB	Exc.	V.G.	Good	Fair	Poor
—	1800	1300	1050	600	450

International Model 206

A .22 caliber semi-automatic pistol with a 7.5" barrel, an integral muzzlebrake, adjustable sights, and walnut grips. Manufactured between 1962 and 1969.

NIB	Exc.	V.G.	Good	Fair	Poor
—	825	700	575	425	300

International Model 207

As above, with adjustable grips.

NIB	Exc.	V.G.	Good	Fair	Poor
—	850	725	600	450	325

International Model 208

A .22 caliber semi-automatic pistol with a 6" barrel, adjustable sights and an 8-shot magazine, adjustable trigger, and target grips. The barrel is drilled and tapped for the addition of barrel weights. Manufactured between 1966 and 1988.

NIB	Exc.	V.G.	Good	Fair	Poor
—	1850	1550	1250	1000	750

International Model 208 Deluxe

As above, with an engraved receiver, and carved grips. Discontinued in 1988.

NIB	Exc.	V.G.	Good	Fair	Poor
—	3250	2750	2500	2000	1500

International Model 209

A .22 Short caliber semi-automatic pistol with a 4.75" barrel, a muzzlebrake, adjustable target sights, and 5-shot magazine. Blued, with walnut grips. Manufactured between 1966 and 1970.

NIB	Exc.	V.G.	Good	Fair	Poor
—	1200	975	600	425	250

International Model 210

As above, with adjustable grips.

NIB	Exc.	V.G.	Good	Fair	Poor
—	1225	1000	625	450	275

International Model 211

As above, with non-adjustable thumb rest grips.

NIB	Exc.	V.G.	Good	Fair	Poor
—	1300	1075	700	475	300

Model 212

A .22 caliber semi-automatic pistol with a 5" barrel, and adjustable sights. Blued with walnut grips.

NIB	Exc.	V.G.	Good	Fair	Poor
—	1300	1075	700	475	300

Model 230

A .22 Short caliber semi-automatic pistol with a 6.3" barrel, a 5-shot magazine, adjustable sights and walnut grip. Manufactured between 1970 and 1983.

NIB	Exc.	V.G.	Good	Fair	Poor
—	1350	1125	750	525	325

Model 232

A .22 short caliber semi-automatic pistol with a 5" barrel, adjustable sights, and a 6-shot magazine. Contoured walnut grips. Introduced in 1984.

NIB	Exc.	V.G.	Good	Fair	Poor
—	1300	1075	700	475	300

Model 280

This is the new state-of-the-art target pistol from Hammerli. It features a modular design and has a frame of carbon fiber material. It has a 4.6" barrel with adjustable sights, trigger, and grips. It is chambered for .22 LR or .32 wadcutter. The magazine holds 5 rounds, and the pistol was introduced in 1988.

NIB	Exc.	V.G.	Good	Fair	Poor
—	1800	1500	1350	1000	600

Model SP 20

Introduced in 1998, this pistol has a very low sight line and features a wide variety of special items such as adjustable buffer system, anatomically shaped trigger in various sizes, various receiver colors, change over caliber system from .22 LR to .32 S&W.

NIB	Exc.	V.G.	Good	Fair	Poor
1750	1325	900	800	500	—

DAKOTA

A single-action revolver based on the Colt SAA design. It has a solid frame and is loaded through a gate. It is chambered for .22 LR, .357 Magnum, .44-40, and .45 Colt and was offered with barrel lengths of 5", 6", and 7.5". It has a 6-shot cylinder and is blued, with a brass trigger guard and walnut grips.

Rimfire Calibers

NIB	Exc.	V.G.	Good	Fair	Poor
—	450	350	200	100	50

Centerfire Calibers

NIB	Exc.	V.G.	Good	Fair	Poor
—	650	475	325	150	100

Super Dakota

Similar to the Dakota but is chambered for .41 and .44 Magnum, with adjustable sights.

NIB	Exc.	V.G.	Good	Fair	Poor
—	650	475	325	150	100

Virginian

Basically a more deluxe version of the Dakota. It is chambered for the .357 and .45 Colt cartridge. The trigger guard and back strap are chrome plated, with the frame case colored and the remainder blued. This model features the "Swissafe" safety system that allows the cylinder axis pin to be locked back to prevent the hammer from falling.

NIB	Exc.	V.G.	Good	Fair	Poor
—	750	575	400	200	125

HAMMERLI-WALTHER
Lenzburg, Switzerland

These target pistols were produced by Hammerli under license from Walther after WWII. This project continued until approximately 1963, when production was ceased.

Olympia Model 200 Type 1952

A .22 caliber semi-automatic pistol with a 7.5" barrel, a 10-shot magazine, adjustable target sights, and a blued with walnut grips. Manufactured between 1952 and 1958.

NIB	Exc.	V.G.	Good	Fair	Poor
—	900	775	575	475	350

Model 200 Type 1958

As above with an integral muzzlebrake. Manufactured between 1958 and 1963.

NIB	Exc.	V.G.	Good	Fair	Poor
—	950	725	625	495	350

Model 201

A Model 200 Type 1952 with a 9.5" barrel. Manufactured between 1955 and 1957.

NIB	Exc.	V.G.	Good	Fair	Poor
—	950	725	625	495	350

Model 202

Similar to the Model 201, with adjustable walnut grips. Manufactured between 1955 and 1957.

NIB	Exc.	V.G.	Good	Fair	Poor
—	950	725	625	495	350

Model 203

Similar to the Model 200, with the adjustable grips, available with or without a muzzlebrake.

NIB	Exc.	V.G.	Good	Fair	Poor
—	950	725	625	495	350

Model 204

A .22 caliber semi-automatic pistol with a 7.5" barrel, a muzzlebrake, and barrel weights. Manufactured between 1956 and 1963.

NIB	Exc.	V.G.	Good	Fair	Poor
—	975	750	650	525	375

Model 205

As above, with adjustable target grips. Manufactured between 1956 and 1963.

NIB	Exc.	V.G.	Good	Fair	Poor
—	1000	775	675	575	450

HAMMOND BULLDOG
Connecticut Arms & Mfg. Co.
Naubuc, Connecticut

Hammond Bulldog

A .44 rimfire single-shot spur trigger pistol with a 4" octagonal barrel that pivots to open. Blued with checkered walnut grips. Manufactured from 1864 to approximately 1867.

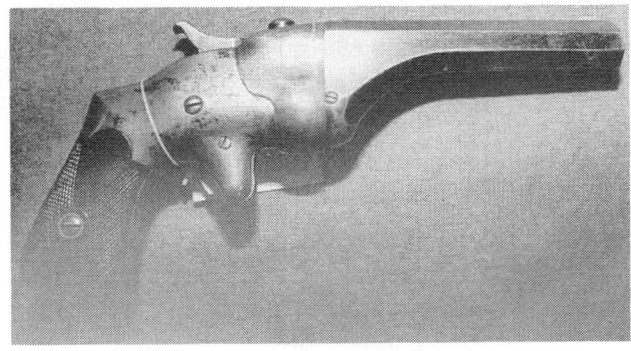

NIB	Exc.	V.G.	Good	Fair	Poor
—	775	550	375	250	100

HAMMOND MFG. CO., GRANT
New Haven, Connecticut

Military Automatic Pistol

A .45 ACP caliber semi-automatic pistol with a 6.75" barrel and an 8-shot magazine. Blued, with checkered walnut grips. Marked on the right of the slide "Grant Hammond Mfg. Corp. New Haven, Conn." The left side shows the patent dates. Manufactured in 1917. As all the known specimens of this pistol exhibit differences, it is believed that they were only made as prototypes. The highest serial number known is under 20. Too rare to price.

Courtesy Horst Held

Grant Hammond 7.65mm Pistol

A semi-automatic pistol in 7.65mm caliber. Has a blow-forward action and a spur hammer. Too rare to price.

Courtesy James Rankin

HANKINS, WILLIAM
Philadelphia, Pennsylvania

Pocket Revolver

A .26 caliber spur trigger percussion revolver with a 3" octagonal barrel, and a 5-shot unfluted cylinder. Blued with walnut grips. Approximately 650 were manufactured in 1860 and 1861.

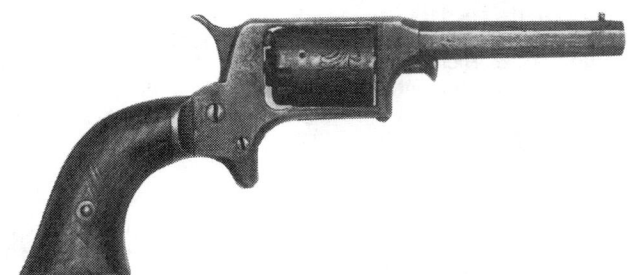

Courtesy Milwaukee Public Museum, Milwaukee, Wisconsin

NIB	Exc.	V.G.	Good	Fair	Poor
—	—	3250	1700	600	200

HARRINGTON & RICHARDSON, INC.
Madison, North Carolina

Established in 1877 by G.H. Harrington and W.A. Richardson. The arms originally produced by this company were marketed under the trade name Aetna. In November 2000 the Marlin Firearms Company purchased the assets of Harrington & Richardson. In 2008 it was announced that H&R/NEF/Marlin had been acquired by Remington Arms, and that H&R's Gardner, Mass., plant would be closed and absorbed into Remington's existing production facilities.

Model No. 1

A .32 or .38 caliber spur-trigger single-action revolver with a 3" octagonal barrel, solid frame, a 7-shot or a 5-shot cylinder, depending on the caliber. Nickel-plated with checkered rubber bird's-head grips. Barrel marked "Harrington & Richardson Worcester, Mass." Approximately 3,000 were manufactured in 1877 and 1878.

NIB	Exc.	V.G.	Good	Fair	Poor
—	300	250	200	125	75

Model No. 1-1/2

A .32 caliber spur-trigger, single-action revolver with a 2.5" octagonal barrel and a 5-shot cylinder. Nickel-plated, round-butt rubber grips with an "H&R" emblem molded in. Approximately 10,000 were manufactured between 1878 and 1883.

NIB	Exc.	V.G.	Good	Fair	Poor
—	175	150	125	75	50

Model No. 2-1/2

As above, with a 3.25" barrel and a 7-shot cylinder. Approximately 5,000 were manufactured between 1878 and 1883.

NIB	Exc.	V.G.	Good	Fair	Poor
—	175	150	125	75	50

Model No. 3-1/2

Similar to the Model 2-1/2 except in .38 rimfire caliber with a 3.5" barrel and a 5-shot cylinder. Approximately 2,500 were manufactured.

NIB	Exc.	V.G.	Good	Fair	Poor
—	200	175	150	100	75

Model No. 4-1/2

A .41 rimfire caliber spur trigger revolver with a 2.5" barrel and 5-shot cylinder. Approximately 1,000 were manufactured.

NIB	Exc.	V.G.	Good	Fair	Poor
—	250	200	175	125	90

Model 1880

A .32 or .38 S&W centerfire caliber double-action revolver with a 3" round barrel, a solid frame, and a 5- or 6-shot cylinder, depending on the caliber. Nickel-plated with hard rubber grips. Marked "Harrington & Richardson Worchester, Mass." Approximately 4,000 were manufactured between 1880 and 1883.

NIB	Exc.	V.G.	Good	Fair	Poor
—	250	200	175	125	90

The American Double-Action

A .32, .28, or .44 centerfire caliber double-action revolver with a 2.5", 4.5", or 6" round or octagonal barrel, a 5- or 6-shot fluted cylinder, depending on the caliber, and solid frame, nickel-plated, with some blue models noted. The grips are hard rubber. Marked "The American Double Action." Some noted are marked "H&R Bulldog." Approximately 850,000 were manufactured between 1883 and 1940. Add 150 percent for .44.

NIB	Exc.	V.G.	Good	Fair	Poor
—	250	125	100	85	65

The Young America Double-Action

A .22 rimfire or .32 S&W centerfire caliber, double-action revolver, with 2", 4.5", or 6" round or octagonal barrels, solid frame, and a 5- or 7-shot cylinder, depending on the caliber. Blued or nickel-plated, with hard rubber grips. Marked "Young America Double Action" or "Young America Bulldog." Approximately 1,500,000 were manufactured between 1884 and 1941.

NIB	Exc.	V.G.	Good	Fair	Poor
—	200	125	100	85	65

Hunter

A .22 caliber double-action revolver with a 10" octagonal barrel and a 9-shot fluted cylinder. Blued, with checkered walnut grips.

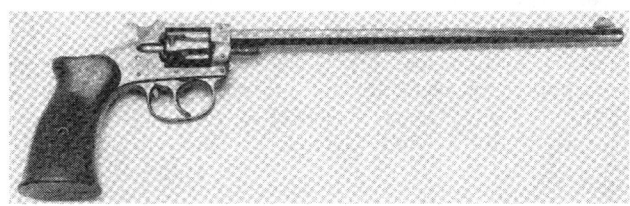

Courtesy Mike Stuckslager

NIB	Exc.	V.G.	Good	Fair	Poor
—	400	300	200	150	100

Trapper

As above, with a 6" octagonal barrel and a 7-shot cylinder. Otherwise it is similar to the Hunter.

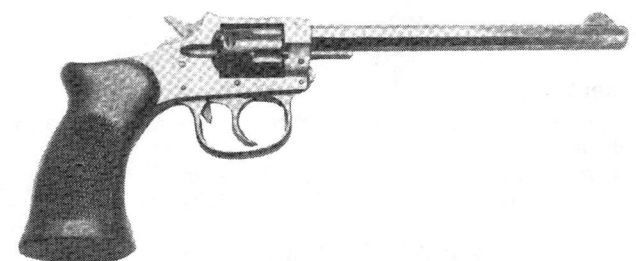

Courtesy Mike Stuckslager

NIB	Exc.	V.G.	Good	Fair	Poor
—	200	150	125	100	75

Self-Loader

A 6.35mm or 7.65mm semi-automatic pistol with a 2" or 3.5" barrel, a 6- or 8-shot magazine. Similar in ouutline to the Webley. The larger 7.65 model has a grip safety. Blued or nickel-plated with checkered, hard rubber grips that bear the H&R monogram. The slide is marked, "H&R Self-Loading" with 1907 or 1909 patent dates. Approximately 16,500 were manufactured in 6.35mm between 1912 and 1916 and 34,500 in 7.65mm manufactured between 1916 and 1924. Add 10 percent for .32.

Courtesy Orvel Reichert

NIB	Exc.	V.G.	Good	Fair	Poor
—	500	400	275	200	125

First Model Hand Ejector

A .32 or .38 centerfire caliber double-action revolver with a 3.25" ribbed round barrel. This version does not feature the automatic ejection found on later models. Nickel-plated, with hard rubber grips. The company name is marked on the barrel. Approximately 6,000 were manufactured between 1886 and 1888.

NIB	Exc.	V.G.	Good	Fair	Poor
—	200	150	125	90	65

Model 1 Double-Action Revolver

A .32, .32 Long, and the .38 S&W caliber double-action revolver with a 3.25" ribbed round barrel, and a 5- or 6-shot cylinder, depending on the caliber. Nickel-plated, with hard rubber grips. Approximately 5,000 were manufactured between 1887 and 1889.

NIB	Exc.	V.G.	Good	Fair	Poor
—	175	145	110	80	50

Model 2

Similar to the Model 1, with 2.5", 3.25", 4", 5", or 6" barrels. The grips feature the H&R target logo. There were approximately 1,300,000 manufactured between 1889 and 1940.

NIB	Exc.	V.G.	Good	Fair	Poor
—	125	100	80	65	40

Knife Model

The Model 2 with a 4" ribbed round barrel having a folding 2.25" double-edged knife mounted under the barrel. Blued or nickel-plated. Approximately 2,000 were manufactured between 1901 and 1917.

NIB	Exc.	V.G.	Good	Fair	Poor
—	650	495	375	250	150

Model 922 First Issue

A .22 caliber double-action revolver with a 2.5", 4", or 6" barrel. Blued, with checkered walnut grips.

NIB	Exc.	V.G.	Good	Fair	Poor
—	150	125	100	75	50

Target Model

A .22 LR or .22 rimfire Magnum caliber double-action revolver with 7-shot cylinder, a break-open frame and a 6" barrel with fixed sights. Blued, with checkered walnut grips.

NIB	Exc.	V.G.	Good	Fair	Poor
—	150	125	100	75	50

.22 Special

A .22 LR or the .22 rimfire Magnum double-action, break-open revolver with a 6" barrel and a 7-shot cylinder. Blued, with checkered walnut grips.

NIB	Exc.	V.G.	Good	Fair	Poor
—	175	150	125	90	65

Expert

As above, with a 10" barrel.

NIB	Exc.	V.G.	Good	Fair	Poor
—	150	125	100	75	50

No. 199 Sportsman

A .22 caliber single-action, break-open revolver with a 6" barrel, adjustable target sights and a 9-shot cylinder. Blued, with checkered walnut grips.

NIB	Exc.	V.G.	Good	Fair	Poor
—	275	200	150	100	75

Defender

A .38 S&W caliber double-action, break-open revolver with a 4" or 6" barrel and fixed sights. Blued, with plastic grips.

NIB	Exc.	V.G.	Good	Fair	Poor
—	275	200	145	75	50

New Defender

A .22 caliber double-action, break-open revolver with a 2" barrel and a 9-shot cylinder. Blued with checkered, walnut round-butt grips.

NIB	Exc.	V.G.	Good	Fair	Poor
—	225	200	175	125	90

.22 U.S.R.A./MODEL 195 SINGLE-SHOT MATCH TARGET PISTOL

Also called the Model 195, this pistol underwent nearly constant modifications from its inception in 1928 until production ceased in 1941. Its development was greatly influenced by the United States Revolver Association (USRA), which established certain rules for target pistol shooting. The lack of any H&R-published model chronology for the estimated 3,500 guns manufactured makes model determination by examination complicated; a further difficulty is that H&R supplied newly designed parts to owners of older variations, who would then retrofit their pistols with newer triggers, hammers, sights, and trigger guards. Extracted from the available literature, the parts represent approximately: 14 different stocks and virtually endless custom variations by Walter F. Roper; 5 different trigger guards; 3 different triggers; 2 different hammers; 2 different extractors; 3 barrel lengths (7", 8", 10"); and 3 barrel rib styles. From this array of potential characteristics, at least four distinct variations can be identified.

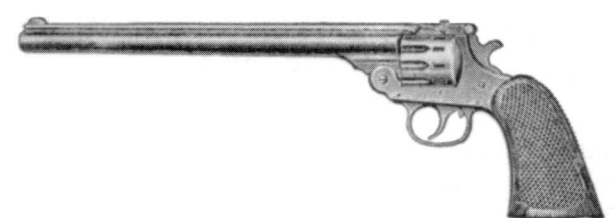

Variations 1 to 3

NIB	Exc.	V.G.	Good	Fair	Poor
—	600	450	325	275	200

.22 U.S.R.A./Model 195 Pistol, Variation 4

NIB	Exc.	V.G.	Good	Fair	Poor
—	650	500	350	325	250

Variation 1, pre-U.S.R.A., 1928-30: Not marked U.S.R.A., and known as the "H&R Single-Shot Pistol." There is no finger rest between the trigger guard and front grip strap; it was advertised with "sawhandle" shape grip copied from the Model 1 or 2 smooth bore H&R Handy-Gun, manufactured with a 10" "hourglass" barrel with a deeply undercut rib. These are the first 500 pistols. Variation 2, U.S.R.A. Keyhole Barrel, 1930-31: This is the standard "early" model marked U.S.R.A., has a finger rest, and non-sawhandle grips; however, several grip shapes were offered as options. The grip screw goes from rear of grip into threaded hold in back grip strap. Variation 3, Modified Keyhole Barrel, 1931: Modification of Variation 2 to improve rear sight, barrel catch changed, reduced spent cartridge force by replacing cylindrical extractor with less powerful hinged type, and the hammer cocking spur and finger rest were made wider. The 8" barrel was offered as an option to standard 10" length, and the number of different grip shapes was increased. This is a transition model between "early" Variation 2 and "final" Variation 4 designs. Variation 4, Tapered Slabside Barrel, 1931-41: New "truncated teardrop" barrel cross section shape; new standard barrel length of 7", with 10" optional; adjustable trigger; new sear; grip screw location was changed to front of grip; and front sight was adjustable for elevation. The trigger design was changed from curved to straight beveled type with relocated cocking surfaces, and the number of grip shapes increased further to 13 types. A front sight protector was supplied as standard equipment, and luggage style case offered as an option. It appears that Variation 4 was introduced around 1931; the 1932 advertisements describe the fully redesigned gun, but picture Variation 2, indicating H&R probably did not re-photograph the new design. The final variation has a special, tight bore .217" in diameter, with bullet seating .03125" (1/32") into rifling, and is among the most accurate of single-shot .22 caliber pistols. The Model 195/U.S.R.A. was relatively expensive, costing approximately $30 in 1932, and increased to slightly more than $36 by the time production ended in 1941, yet was the least expensive of all single-shot .22 target pistols of quality.

Model 504

A .32 H&R Magnum caliber double-action, swing-out cylinder revolver with a 4" or 6" heavy barrel, adjustable sights, and 5-shot cylinder. Blued, with either black plastic or walnut grips. Smaller version manufactured with a 3" or 4" barrel and a round butt.

NIB	Exc.	V.G.	Good	Fair	Poor
—	350	275	150	90	65

Model 532

As above, but with a cylinder that has to be removed for loading. Manufactured in 1984 and 1985.

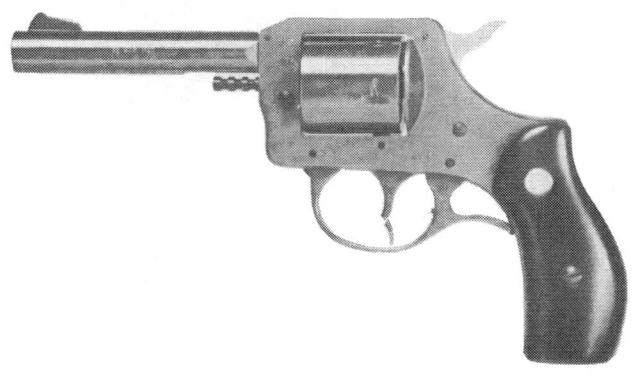

NIB	Exc.	V.G.	Good	Fair	Poor
—	275	175	125	75	50

Model 586

A .32 H&R Magnum caliber double-action revolver with a 4.5", 5.5", 7.5", or 10" barrel, adjustable sights and a 5-shot cylinder. Blued, with either black plastic or walnut grips.

NIB	Exc.	V.G.	Good	Fair	Poor
—	325	275	175	150	100

Model 603

A .22 rimfire Magnum caliber double-action revolver with a 6" flat-sided barrel and swing-out 6-shot cylinder. Blued, with smooth walnut grips.

NIB	Exc.	V.G.	Good	Fair	Poor
—	225	165	140	110	85

Model 604

As above, with a 6", ribbed, heavy barrel.

NIB	Exc.	V.G.	Good	Fair	Poor
—	295	215	175	125	100

Model 622

A .22 caliber solid-frame double-action revolver with a 2.5" or 4" barrel. Blued, with round-butt plastic grips.

NIB	Exc.	V.G.	Good	Fair	Poor
—	150	100	65	50	25

Model 623

As above, but nickel-plated.

NIB	Exc.	V.G.	Good	Fair	Poor
—	165	110	80	60	40

Model 649

The Model 622, with a 5.5" or 7.5" barrel.

NIB	Exc.	V.G.	Good	Fair	Poor
—	150	125	100	75	50

Model 650

As above, but nickel-plated.

NIB	Exc.	V.G.	Good	Fair	Poor
—	175	150	125	75	50

Model 660

A .22 caliber solid-frame, Western-style revolver with a 5.5" barrel and is a double-action. Blued, with walnut grips. It is also known as the "Gunfighter."

NIB	Exc.	V.G.	Good	Fair	Poor
—	150	125	100	50	25

Model 666

A .22 or .22 rimfire Magnum caliber double-action revolver with a 6" barrel and a 6-shot cylinder. Blued, with plastic grips. Manufactured between 1976 and 1982.

NIB	Exc.	V.G.	Good	Fair	Poor
—	150	125	100	50	25

Model 676

Similar to the Model 660. Blued, with a case colored frame. It has walnut grips. Manufactured between 1976 and 1982.

NIB	Exc.	V.G.	Good	Fair	Poor
—	175	150	100	75	50

Model 686

Similar to the Model 660 "Gunfighter" with a 4.5", 5.5", 7.5", 10", or 12" barrel.

NIB	Exc.	V.G.	Good	Fair	Poor
—	175	150	125	100	75

Model 732

A .32 caliber double-action, solid-frame revolver with a swingout cylinder, a 2.5" or 4" barrel and a 6-shot cylinder. Blued, with black plastic grips. Also known as the "Guardsman."

NIB	Exc.	V.G.	Good	Fair	Poor
—	150	125	90	65	45

Model 733

As above, but nickel-plated and a 2.5" barrel.

NIB	Exc.	V.G.	Good	Fair	Poor
—	175	150	100	75	50

Model 900

A .22 caliber solid-frame revolver with a removable cylinder, a 2.5", 4", or 6" barrel and a 9-shot cylinder. Blued, with black plastic grips. Manufactured between 1962 and 1973.

NIB	Exc.	V.G.	Good	Fair	Poor
—	150	125	90	60	40

Model 901

As above, but chrome-plated with white plastic grips. Manufactured in 1962 and 1963 only.

NIB	Exc.	V.G.	Good	Fair	Poor
—	150	125	90	60	40

Model 903

As above, with a swing-out cylinder, a flat-sided, 6" barrel, and a 9-shot cylinder. Blued, with walnut grips.

NIB	Exc.	V.G.	Good	Fair	Poor
—	150	125	90	75	50

Model 904

As above, with a ribbed heavy barrel.

NIB	Exc.	V.G.	Good	Fair	Poor
—	175	150	125	100	50

Model 905

As above, but nickel-plated.

NIB	Exc.	V.G.	Good	Fair	Poor
—	200	175	150	80	65

Model 922 Second Issue

A .22 rimfire caliber solid-frame revolver with a 2.5", 4", or 6" barrel. Blued, with black plastic grips. Manufactured between 1950 and 1982.

NIB	Exc.	V.G.	Good	Fair	Poor
—	150	90	80	60	40

Model 923

As above, but nickel-plated.

NIB	Exc.	V.G.	Good	Fair	Poor
—	160	90	80	60	40

Model 925

A .38 S&W caliber double-action, break-open, hand ejector revolver with a 2.5" barrel, adjustable sights and a 5-shot cylinder. Blued, with a one-piece wraparound grip. Manufactured between 1964 and 1984.

NIB	Exc.	V.G.	Good	Fair	Poor
—	250	175	125	75	50

Model 935

As above, but nickel-plated.

NIB	Exc.	V.G.	Good	Fair	Poor
—	260	200	150	100	50

Model 929

A .22 rimfire solid-frame, swing-out revolver with a 2.5", 4", or 6" barrel and a 9-shot cylinder. Blued, with plastic grips. It is also known as the "Sidekick." Manufactured between 1956 and 1985.

NIB	Exc.	V.G.	Good	Fair	Poor
—	225	150	125	65	45

Model 929 Sidekick—New Model

Reintroduced in 1996 this single- and double-action revolver chambered for the .22 short, long, or LR cartridges. Cylinder holds 9 rounds. Sold with a lockable storage case, nylon holster, and gun oil and gun grease samples. Weighs about 30 oz. Discontinued. Made from 1996 - 1999.

NIB	Exc.	V.G.	Good	Fair	Poor
250	175	150	100	75	50

Model 929 Sidekick Trapper Edition

Same as above but with grey laminate grips and special "NTA" Trapper Edition roll stamp on barrel. Made in 1996.

NIB	Exc.	V.G.	Good	Fair	Poor
275	175	150	100	75	50

Model 930

As above, but nickel-plated and not available with a 6" barrel.

NIB	Exc.	V.G.	Good	Fair	Poor
—	250	150	125	65	45

Model 939 Ultra Sidekick

As above, with a ventilated rib, flat sided 6" barrel, adjustable sights, thumb rest grips and features a safety device whereby the pistol could not be fired unless it was unlocked by a furnished key. Manufactured between 1958 and 1982.

NIB	Exc.	V.G.	Good	Fair	Poor
—	225	200	150	75	50

Model 939 Premier

Similar to the above models but fitted with a 6" barrel with sighting rib, adjustable rear sight, hard wood grips, high polished blued finish. Weighs about 36 oz. Made from 1995 - 1999.

NIB	Exc.	V.G.	Good	Fair	Poor
250	225	200	125	75	50

Model 940

A round-barreled version of the above.

NIB	Exc.	V.G.	Good	Fair	Poor
—	225	200	125	75	50

Model 949

A .22 caliber double-action, Western-type revolver with a 5.5" barrel with an ejector rod, 9-shot, gate-loaded cylinder and adjustable sights. Blued, with walnut grips. Manufactured between 1960 and 1985.

NIB	Exc.	V.G.	Good	Fair	Poor
—	200	175	150	75	50

Model 949 Western

Similar to the above model this revolver is offered with a choice of 5.5" or 7.5" barrel. Adjustable rear sight, walnut grips, and case colored frame and backstrap with blued cylinder and barrel. Weight is about 36 oz.

NIB	Exc.	V.G.	Good	Fair	Poor
250	200	150	100	75	50

Model 950

As above, but nickel-plated.

NIB	Exc.	V.G.	Good	Fair	Poor
—	250	175	125	75	50

Model 976

As above, with a case-hardened frame.

NIB	Exc.	V.G.	Good	Fair	Poor
—	200	150	100	75	50

Model 999 Sportsman

A .22 rimfire caliber double-action, break-open, self ejecting revolver with a 6" or 4" barrel ventilated rib barrel and windage adjustable sights. Blued, with walnut grips. Weighs about 30 oz. with 4" barrel and 34 oz. with 6" barrel.

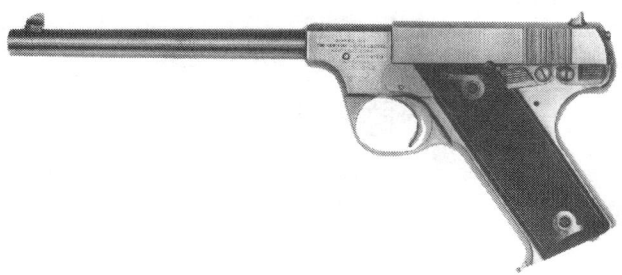

Courtesy John J. Stimson, Jr.

NIB	Exc.	V.G.	Good	Fair	Poor
—	600	475	365	225	175

NIB	Exc.	V.G.	Good	Fair	Poor
500	425	350	295	175	100

Engraved Model 999

As above, but engraved.

NIB	Exc.	V.G.	Good	Fair	Poor
550	450	375	300	200	125

Amtec 2000

This is a German-designed (Erma) and American-built double-action revolver introduced in 1996. Offered in 2" or 3" barrel and chambered for .38 Special cartridge. Pachmayr composition grips. Cylinder holds 5 rounds. Weight is approximately 25 oz. Discontinued.

NIB	Exc.	V.G.	Good	Fair	Poor
250	200	200	150	75	50

HARTFORD ARMS & EQUIPMENT CO.
Hartford, Connecticut

Established in 1925, this firm was purchased by the High Standard Company in 1932.

Single-Shot Target

A .22 caliber single-shot pistol with a 6.75" round barrel, fixed sights and either walnut or composition grips. The frame marked "Manfd. by the/ Hartford Arms and Equip. Co./ Hartford, Conn./ Patented .22 cal./ l.r." on the left side in front of ther breach. Although this pistol resembles a semi-automatic, it is in fact a single-shot manually operated pistol. NOTE: Add $150 premium for guns in original Hartford Arms box numbered to the gun. Add $250 premium for guns in original High Standard box numbered to the gun.

Courtesy John J. Stimson, Jr.

NIB	Exc.	V.G.	Good	Fair	Poor
—	595	450	325	250	150

Model 1925

Semi-automatic pistol chambered for .22 caliber with 6.75" round barrel, checkered hard black rubber grips or ribbed walnut grips. Magazine capacity is 10 rounds. The frame is marked, "manfd. by/ the hartford arms and equip. co./ hartford, conn./ .22 cal/long rifle" on the left side in front of the breach. Approximately 5,000 were produced from 1925 to 1932.

NOTE: Add $150 premium for guns in original Hartford Arms box numbered to the gun.

HAVILAND & GUNN
Ilion, New York

Gallery Pistol

A .17 caliber rimfire single-shot pistol with a 5" barrel. The barrel and frame made of one piece of iron and nickel plated. There are no markings on these pistols whatsoever. Believed to have been made during the 1870s.

NIB	Exc.	V.G.	Good	Fair	Poor
—	—	1150	550	175	100

HAWES & WAGGONER
Philadelphia, Pennsylvania

Pocket Pistol

A .41 caliber single-shot percussion pistol with a 3" barrel, German silver mountings, and a walnut stock. Manufactured in the 1850s.

NIB	Exc.	V.G.	Good	Fair	Poor
—	—	2250	925	475	275

HAWES
Los Angeles, California

An importer of handguns primarily made in Europe.

Courier

A .25 caliber, blowback, semi-automatic pocket pistol manufactured by Galesi.

NIB	Exc.	V.G.	Good	Fair	Poor
—	125	100	75	50	25

Diplomat

A .380 ACP pistol with an external hammer.

NIB	Exc.	V.G.	Good	Fair	Poor
—	150	125	100	75	50

Trophy

A J.P. Sauer & Sohn, manufactured revolver with a swing-out cylinder and a 6" barrel. Chambered for the .22 LR and the .38 Special. Has adjustable sights.

NIB	Exc.	V.G.	Good	Fair	Poor
—	250	200	175	125	90

Medalion

As above, with a 3", 4", or 6" barrel and fixed sights.

NIB	Exc.	V.G.	Good	Fair	Poor
—	200	175	125	100	75

MARSHAL SINGLE-ACTION ARMY REVOLVERS

J. P. Sauer made a Western-styled series for Hawes based in appearance on the Colt Single-Action Army.

Silver City Marshal

A .22 LR or .22 rimfire Magnum caliber single-action revolver with a 5.5" barrel, 6-shot cylinder, and fixed sights.

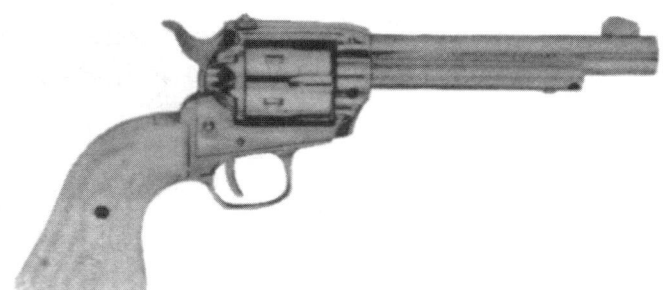

NIB	Exc.	V.G.	Good	Fair	Poor
—	150	125	95	50	25

Western Marshal

A .357 Magnum, .44 Magnum, .45 Colt, .45 ACP, .44-40, 9mm, .22 LR, and .22 rimfire Magnum single-action revolver with fixed sights. Blued.

NIB	Exc.	V.G.	Good	Fair	Poor
—	350	275	195	100	75

Texas Marshal

As above, but nickel-plated.

NIB	Exc.	V.G.	Good	Fair	Poor
—	350	275	195	100	75

Montana Marshal

The Western Marshal with a brass backstrap and trigger guard.

NIB	Exc.	V.G.	Good	Fair	Poor
—	350	275	195	100	75

Deputy Marshal

A .22 LR and .22 rimfire Magnum single-action revolver with a 5.5" barrel, and 6-shot cylinder.

NIB	Exc.	V.G.	Good	Fair	Poor
—	150	125	95	50	25

Tip-Up Target Pistol

Replica of the Stevens Model 35 .22 LR single-shot. Globe front sight, adjustable rear.

NIB	Exc.	V.G.	Good	Fair	Poor
—	275	200	135	75	35

Chief Marshal

A .357 Magnum, .44 Magnum, and the .45 Colt caliber revolver with a 6.5" barrel, and 6-shot cylinder and adjustable sights. Blued.

NIB	Exc.	V.G.	Good	Fair	Poor
—	350	275	195	100	75

Federal Marshal

A 6-shot single-action revolver in .357 Magnum, .44 Magnum, and the .45 Colt caliber.

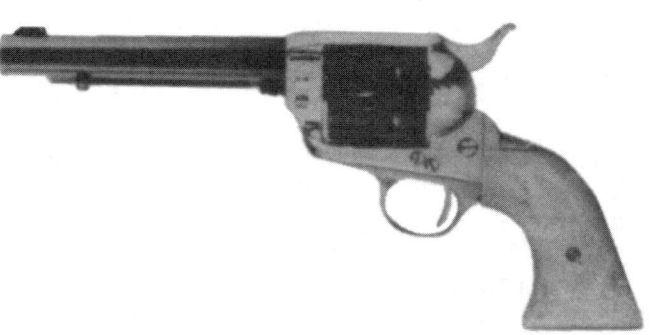

NIB	Exc.	V.G.	Good	Fair	Poor
—	350	275	195	100	75

HDH, SA.
Henrion, Dassy & Heuschen
Liege, Belgium

Cobold

A 9.4mm Dutch, 10.6mm German, .38, and .45 caliber double-action five-shot revolver with solid frame, octagonal barrel, and an odd safety catch that locks the cylinder.

NIB	Exc.	V.G.	Good	Fair	Poor
—	500	325	275	150	100

Puppy

A 5.5mm to 7.65mm caliber folding trigger, double-action revolver. Most are "Velo-Dogs."

NIB	Exc.	V.G.	Good	Fair	Poor
—	200	150	100	75	50

Lincoln

A .22 caliber folding trigger, double-action revolver with a solid frame, imitation pearl or ivory grips, and engraving.

NIB	Exc.	V.G.	Good	Fair	Poor
—	200	150	100	75	50

Lincoln-Bossu

A 5.5mm or 6.35mm caliber folding trigger double-action revolver ("Velo-Dog" type) with solid-frame and hammerless.

NIB	Exc.	V.G.	Good	Fair	Poor
—	200	150	100	75	50

Left Wheeler

A Colt Police Positive copy in .32 or .38 caliber. The last revolver HDH manufactured.

NIB	Exc.	V.G.	Good	Fair	Poor
—	200	150	125	100	75

HECKLER & KOCH
Oberndorf/Neckar, Germany

At the end of WWII, the French dismantled the Mauser factory as part of their reparations; and the buildings remained idle until 1949, when firearms production was again allowed in Germany. Heckler & Koch was formed as a machine tool enterprise and occupied the vacant Mauser plant. In the early 1950s Edmund Heckler and Theodor Koch began to produce the G3 automatic rifle based on the Spanish CETME design and progressed to machine guns and sub-machine guns and eventually to the production of commercial civilian rifles and pistols. In 1990 the company got into financial difficulties because of a failed contract bid. In December 1990 the French state consortium GIAT announced the purchase of Heckler and Koch, but a little more than a year later the contract was canceled. Later in 1991 the company was purchased by Royal Ordnance of Britain. In 2002 the company was sold to a combined group of European investors and long-time company managers.

HK4

This is a blowback-operated semi-automatic pistol based on the Mauser HSc design. It is chambered for .22 LR, .25 ACP, .32 ACP, and .380. These calibers were easily converted by switching the barrels, recoil springs and magazines. The rimfire model could be changed by rotating the breechface. The conversion kits were available for all calibers. The barrel is 3" long; and the finish is blued, with molded plastic thumb rest grips. This pistol was sold from 1968-1973 as the Harrington & Richardson HK4 and is so marked. It was discontinued in 1984.

.22 Caliber or .380 Caliber

NIB	Exc.	V.G.	Good	Fair	Poor
—	475	350	250	200	100

.25 Caliber or .32 Caliber

NIB	Exc.	V.G.	Good	Fair	Poor
—	350	300	250	200	100

Conversion Units

NIB	Exc.	V.G.	Good	Fair	Poor
—	150	125	90	60	30

P9

This is a single-action, delayed-blowback semi-automatic pistol chambered for 9mm or 7.65mm Parabellum. The action is based on the G-3 rifle mechanism. The barrel is 4" in length, and the pistol has an internal hammer and a thumb-operated hammer drop and decocking lever. There is also a manual safety and a loaded-chamber indicator. The finish is Parkerized, and the grips are molded plastic and well contoured. It has fixed sights. This model was manufactured between 1977 and 1984. This model is rarer than the P9S model.

NIB	Exc.	V.G.	Good	Fair	Poor
800	650	500	400	300	200

P9S

This model is similar to the Model P9 except that the action features a double-action capability and it is chambered for the .45 ACP and the 9mm Parabellum with a 5.5" barrel. This model was also manufactured between 1977 and 1984.

NIB	Exc.	V.G.	Good	Fair	Poor
800	650	500	400	300	200

P9S Target Model

This version is similar to the Model P9S chambered for the 9mm or .45 ACP cartridges, with adjustable sights, and an adjustable trigger. It was discontinued in 1984.

NIB	Exc.	V.G.	Good	Fair	Poor
1400	1100	900	600	500	300

P9S Competition

Similar to the P9S target but with the addition of barrel weights and special competition grips.

NIB	Exc.	V.G.	Good	Fair	Poor
2000	1500	1200	750	500	275

VP 70Z

This is a blowback-operated semi-automatic chambered for the 9mm Parabellum cartridge. It is striker-fired and double-action-only. The barrel is 4.5" long, and the double-column magazine holds 18 rounds. The finish is blued, and the receiver and grip are molded from plastic. This model was discontinued in 1984.

NIB	Exc.	V.G.	Good	Fair	Poor
550	450	350	300	250	200

P7 PSP

This was the first of the squeeze-cocked H&K pistols. It is a single-action semi-automatic that is placed in the firing position by pressure on the front of the grip strap. This moves the striker into battery; and firing is then accomplished by a single action pressure on the trigger, releasing the grip strap cocking device and decocking the mechanism. This particular model does not have the extended finger guard on the trigger and also does not have an ambidextrous safety. It was discontinued in 1984.

NIB	Exc.	V.G.	Good	Fair	Poor
1100	900	700	600	500	400

P7 K3

This is the "Squeeze Cocker" chambered for either the .380 or .22 LR caliber. It has a recoil buffer that is oil-filled and a 3.8" barrel. The magazine holds 8 rounds. This model was introduced in 1988.

NIB	Exc.	V.G.	Good	Fair	Poor
1800	1600	1350	900	500	300

P7 K3 .22 Caliber Conversion Kit

This unit will convert the P7 K3 to fire the .22 LR cartridge.

NIB	Exc.	V.G.	Good	Fair	Poor
900	800	650	300	150	75

P7 K3 .32 ACP Caliber Conversion Kit

NIB	Exc.	V.G.	Good	Fair	Poor
700	500	400	100	75	50

P7 M8

This is the 8-shot newer version of the "squeeze cocker." It has the heat-shield finger guard and the ambidextrous safety. It has a 4" barrel and a 3-dot sight system. The finish is matte blue or nickel with stippled black plastic grips. This model is no longer in production.

NIB	Exc.	V.G.	Good	Fair	Poor
1500	1200	900	700	500	300

NOTE: For night sights, introduced in 1993, add $100.

P7 M10

A new addition to the P7 series in 1993, this variation is chambered for the .40 S&W cartridge. Magazine holds 10 rounds and the finish is available in either blue or nickel. Pistol weighs 2.69 lbs.

NIB	Exc.	V.G.	Good	Fair	Poor
2000	1600	1000	650	500	300

NOTE: For night sights add $100.

P7 M13

This version is similar to the P7 M8 except that it has a double column 13-shot magazine.

NIB	Exc.	V.G.	Good	Fair	Poor
2200	1750	1200	650	500	300

NOTE: For night sights add $100.

SP89

Introduced in the early 1990s, this is a large frame semi-automatic pistol chambered for the 9mm cartridge. It features a 15-round magazine and a square notch rear sight with a hooded front sight. The pistol has a 4.5" barrel and is 13" overall. It weighs 4.4 lbs. In August 1993 this model was no longer imported due to a ban on assault pistols.

NIB	Exc.	V.G.	Good	Fair	Poor
4000	3600	3200	2500	1800	1000

USP SERIES

NOTE: Late in 1999 H&K began shipping its USPs and Mark 23s with an internal locking system. This lock-out is installed in the grip and blocks the movement of the hammer, trigger, and slide. It is operated with a two pronged key, supplied with the pistol. This system is in addition to the traditional trigger lock that is sold with each H&K firearm. In 2001 the stainless steel version of these pistols was discontinued.In 2005 H&K offered a limited edition run of color frame variations for the USP line. These colors are Desert tan, green and gray. Gray: USP 45 and USP 40 CompactGreen: USP 45, USP 40, USP 40 Compact, and USP 45 TacticalDesert Tan: USP 45, USP 40, USP 40 Compact, and USP 45 Tactical and Mark 23Retail prices are the same for these color variations as the standard black frame pistols

USP 40

Introduced in 1993 this new semi-automatic H&K pistol features a new design that incorporates a short recoil modified Browning action. Chambered for the .40 S&W cartridge this model has a 4.13" barrel and a magazine capacity of 13 rounds. Stainless steel model introduced in 1996. It weighs 1.74 lbs. Available in seven different variations from traditional double-action to double-action-only and various safety locations and styles. These variants numbered by H&K are listed. 1.DA/SA with safe position and control lever on left side of frame.2.DA/SA with safe position and control lever on right side of frame.3.DA/SA without safe position and decocking lever on left side of frame.4.DA/SA without safe position and decocking lever on left side of frame.5.DA only with safe position and safety lever on left side of frame.6.DA only with safe position and safety lever on right side of frame.7.DA only without control lever.9.DA/SA with safe position and safety lever on left side of frame.10.DA/SA with safety lever on the right side of frame.

NIB	Exc.	V.G.	Good	Fair	Poor
975	825	675	325	275	150

USP 40 Compact

Same as 9mm Compact model but chambered for .40 S&W cartridge. Weight is about 27 oz. All other dimensions are the same.

NIB	Exc.	V.G.	Good	Fair	Poor
900	800	650	300	250	125

USP 45

Introduced in 1995 this version is slightly larger than the 9mm and .40 S&W models. Barrel length is 4.41" and overall length is 7.87". Weight is 1.9 lbs. The USP 45 is available in the same variants as the other USP models. Magazine capacity is 12 rounds.

From top to bottom is the USP 45, the USP 40, and the

H&K Stainless Steel Model

USP 40 Compact

NIB	Exc.	V.G.	Good	Fair	Poor
900	800	650	300	250	125

NOTE: For stainless steel model add $45.

USP 9

Same as the USP 40 but chambered for the 9mm cartridge. Magazine holds 16 rounds and pistol weighs 1.66 lbs. This model also has the choice of seven variations as listed above for the USP 40. New for 1993.

NIB	Exc.	V.G.	Good	Fair	Poor
900	800	650	300	250	125

NOTE: For stainless steel model add $45.

USP 9SD

This variation of the USP 9 is fitted with target sights to see over an optional sound suppressor. The barrel is threaded left-hand and does not have an O-ring and does not require a thread cap. Introduced in 2004.

NIB	Exc.	V.G.	Good	Fair	Poor
1100	950	775	500	350	200

NOTE: For stainless steel model add $45.

USP 9 Compact

Introduced in 1997 this 9mm model is a smaller version of the full size USP 9. There are some internal differences due to size. Barrel length is 3.58". Overall length is 6.81". Magazine capacity is 10 rounds. Weight is approximately 26 oz. Also available with stainless steel slide. Add $45 to NIB price.

NIB	Exc.	V.G.	Good	Fair	Poor
800	600	450	300	200	150

USP Compact LEM (Law Enforcement Modification)

This model, introduced in 2002, is identical to the USP Compact .40 S&W Variant 7, but with a double-action-only trigger with a special trigger mechanism. The mechanism improves the double-action trigger performance and reduces the weight of pull to between 7.5 and 8.5 lbs. Offered in blued finish.

NIB	Exc.	V.G.	Good	Fair	Poor
1150	1000	750	500	300	150

USP 45 Match

Introduced in 1997 this model is a match grade variation of the USP. It is chambered for the .45 ACP cartridge. Fitted with a 6.02" barrel with barrel weight assembly. Adjustable rear sight and target front sight. Adjustable trigger stop. Blued finish. Weight is approximately 38 oz. Also available in a stainless steel version.

NIB	Exc.	V.G.	Good	Fair	Poor
1500	1300	1050	800	475	275

NOTE: Add $60 for stainless steel.

USP 45 Compact

Introduced in 1997 this pistol is chambered for the .45 ACP cartridge. It has a 3.8" barrel and an overall length of 7.1". It weighs approximately 28 oz. Magazine capacity is 8 rounds.

NIB	Exc.	V.G.	Good	Fair	Poor
1100	950	775	500	350	200

USP 45 Compact Tactical

Blued semi-auto .45 ACP. Double-action with 4.46" barrel, 8-round capacity. 27.5 oz. Polymer grip.

NIB	Exc.	V.G.	Good	Fair	Poor
1100	950	775	500	350	200

USP .357 Compact

Introduced in mid-1998 this pistol is built on the same frame as the .40 S&W Compact but chambered for the .357 SIG cartridge. Magazine capacity is 10 rounds. Weight is about 28 oz.

NIB	Exc.	V.G.	Good	Fair	Poor
1000	850	4675	375	250	150

USP 45 Expert

Introduced in the fall of 1998, this .45 ACP pistol is fitted with a 5.2" barrel and slide and 10-round magazine. Overall length is 8.7" and height is 1.87". Weight is approximately 30 oz. Adjustable low-profile sights. Limited availability of between 1,000 and 2,500 pistols. In 2003 this model was also offered chambered for the 9mm and the .40 S&W cartridge.

NIB	Exc.	V.G.	Good	Fair	Poor
1355	1200	900	600	300	150

NOTE: H&K price reduction in 2005.

USP 45 Tactical

This pistol was introduced in 1998. It is an enhanced version of the USP 45. It is fitted with a 4.9" threaded barrel with adjustable high profile target sights. Overall length is 8.6" and weight is approximately 36 oz. Magazine capacity is 10 rounds. Availability limited to between 1,000 and 2,500 pistols.

NIB	Exc.	V.G.	Good	Fair	Poor
1100	850	625	425	300	175

USP Elite

Introduced in 2003 this model features a 6.2" barrel chambered for the 9mm or .45 ACP cartridge. Fitted with a match trigger, adjustable trigger stop, adjustable micrometer rear target sights, extended floorplate and loaded chamber indicator. Weight is about 30 oz. empty. Magazine capacity is 10 rounds.

NIB	Exc.	V.G.	Good	Fair	Poor
1400	1150	800	575	250	135

NOTE: H&K price reduction in 2005.

USP 45 50th Anniversary Commemorative

Limited to 1,000 pistols this pistol features a high polish blue with 50th anniversary logo engraved in gold and silver. Supplied with custom-made wooden box with commemorative coin. Introduced in 2000.

NIB	Exc.	V.G.	Good	Fair	Poor
1100	850	625	425	300	175

P2000 GPM

Introduced in 2003 this model is similar to the USP compact LEM pistol but with several modular features, such as interchangeable back straps, ambidextrous slide release, and short trigger reset distance. Chambered for the 9mm or .40 S&W cartridge and fitted with a 3.62" barrel. Fixed sights. Magazine capacity is 12 rounds for the .40S&W and .357 SIG, and 13 rounds for the 9mm. Weight is about 22 oz.

NIB	Exc.	V.G.	Good	Fair	Poor
875	700	500	350	250	125

NOTE: Add $30 for magazine disconnect.

P2000 SK

This semi-auto double-action pistol is a subcompact version of the P2000. It is chambered for the 9mm or .40 S&W cartridge as well as the .357 SIG .It has a 2.5" barrel with an overall length of 6.4". Magazine capacity is 10 rounds for 9mm, 12 rounds for the .357 SIG, and 9 rounds for the .40 S&W. Weight is about 21 oz. Introduced in 2004.

NIB	Exc.	V.G.	Good	Fair	Poor
1100	850	625	425	300	175

Mark 23

Very similar to the H&K's US government contract pistol developed for special Operation Units. Chambered for the .45 ACP and fitted with a 5.87" barrel, this pistol has a polymer frame with steel slide. Magazine capacity is 10 rounds on civilian models and 12 rounds on law enforcement models. Barrel is threaded for noise suppressor. Weight is about 42 oz.

NIB	Exc.	V.G.	Good	Fair	Poor
2200	1850	1200	875	500	250

HK45

Full-size autoloader chambered in .45 ACP. Features include polygonal bore, front and rear slide serrations, integrated picatinny rail, ambi mag release levers, interchangeable backstrap panels, polymer frame, modular action design allowing for double action, single action or double action-only operation. Measures 7.52 inches overall length. 10+1 capacity.

NIB	Exc.	V.G.	Good	Fair	Poor
1100	850	625	425	300	175

HK45 Compact

Similar to above but with 8-round capacity; overall length 7.2 inches.

NIB	Exc.	V.G.	Good	Fair	Poor
1100	850	625	425	300	175

P30

Polymer-frame 9mm autoloader. Features include loaded chamber indicator, integral picatinny rail, oversized trigger guard, double or single action fiurting mode with decocker, "Hostile Environment" black finish, ambidextrous, oversized controls. Add 10 percent for longslide variant.

NIB	Exc.	V.G.	Good	Fair	Poor
850	675	575	450	250	150

HEINZELMANN, C.E.
Plochipnam Neckar, Germany

Heim

A 6.35mm semi-automatic pistol with a 2" barrel. Detachable magazine holds 6 rounds. Weight is approximately 11 oz. Manufactured during the 1930s and marked on the frame "C.E. Heinzelmann Plochingen A.N. Patent Heim-6.35."

NIB	Exc.	V.G.	Good	Fair	Poor
—	800	675	550	400	200

HELFRICHT
Zella-Mehlis, Germany

Model 3 Pocket Pistol

A 6.35mm semi-automatic pistol with a 2" barrel and 6-shot magazine. Weight is about 11 oz. Blued with checkererd black plastic grips having the monogram "KH" cast in them. These pistols have no external sights.

Courtesy James Rankin

NIB	Exc.	V.G.	Good	Fair	Poor
—	500	400	300	200	100

Model 4 Pocket Pistol

A semi-automatic pistol in caliber 6.35mm. It has checkered black plastic grips with the "KH" logo on each grip.

Courtesy James Rankin

NIB	Exc.	V.G.	Good	Fair	Poor
—	400	300	200	150	100

HENRION & DASSY
Liege, Belgium

Semi-Automatic

A 6.35mm semi-automatic pistol with a 2.5" barrel and 5-shot magazine. Blued with black plastic grips. Marked "H&D."

NIB	Exc.	V.G.	Good	Fair	Poor
—	600	500	450	375	275

HERITAGE MANUFACTURING, INC.
Opa Locka, Florida

Stealth

This is a 9mm semi-automatic pistol. It has a black polymer frame with stainless steel slide. Barrel length is 3.9" with overall length at 6.3". Magazine capacity is 10 rounds. Weight is approximately 20 oz. A .40 S&W version is scheduled to be introduced in the summer of 1996. Offered with a black finish, two-tone black chrome with stainless steel side panels, or black chrome.

NIB	Exc.	V.G.	Good	Fair	Poor
275	225	175	150	125	100

Model H25S

A semi-automatic pistol chambered for the .25 ACP cartridge. Barrel length is 2.25" and overall length is 4.58". Weight is about 13.5 oz. Frame mounted safety. Single-action-only. Available in blue or nickel.

NIB	Exc.	V.G.	Good	Fair	Poor
150	125	100	85	65	50

Sentry

This is a double-action revolver chambered for the .38 Special. Cylinder holds 6 rounds. Barrel length is 2". Weight is about 23 oz. Blue or nickel finish.

NIB	Exc.	V.G.	Good	Fair	Poor
130	100	85	65	50	30

ROUGH RIDER

Single-action revolver chambered for the .22 caliber cartridges. Barrel lengths are 4.75", 6.5", and 9". Cylinder holds 6 rounds. Weight is about 34 oz. Available in blue or nickel finish.

NIB	Exc.	V.G.	Good	Fair	Poor
165	125	100	75	50	30

Combination Cylinder—.22 Mag.

NIB	Exc.	V.G.	Good	Fair	Poor
190	150	120	75	50	30

Bird's-Head Grip & Combo Cylinder

NIB	Exc.	V.G.	Good	Fair	Poor
190	150	120	75	50	30

Rough Rider .17 HMR

Introduced in 2004.

NIB	Exc.	V.G.	Good	Fair	Poor
190	150	120	75	50	30

Rough Rider .32

Six-shot revolver chambered for .32 H&R Magnum centerfire (interchangeably .32 S&W, .32 S&W Long). Black satin finish. Offered with 3.5", 4.75" or 6.5" barrels. 35 oz. (6.5" bbl.). 11.785" LOA.) Fixed sights. Bird's head grip available.

NIB	Exc.	V.G.	Good	Fair	Poor
240	190	140	95	75	50

Rough Rider Big-Bore Series

Six-shot, steel-frame revolver chambered for .357, .44-40 or .45 Long Colt. Barrel lengths 4.75", 5.5" or 7.5". 36 oz. Fixed sights. Add 10 percent for chrome finish.

NIB	Exc.	V.G.	Good	Fair	Poor
350	275	200	150	100	50

HERTER'S
Waseca, Minnesota

An importer and retailer of European-made firearms. Active until approximately 1980.

Guide

A .22 caliber double-action swing-out cylinder revolver with a 6" barrel and 6-shot cylinder. Blued with walnut grips.

NIB	Exc.	V.G.	Good	Fair	Poor
—	125	95	70	45	30

Power-Mag Revolver

A .357 Magnum, .401 Herter Power Mag, and .44 Magnum caliber single-action revolver with a 4" or 6" barrel and 6-shot cylinder. Blued, with walnut grips. Add 10 percent for .401.

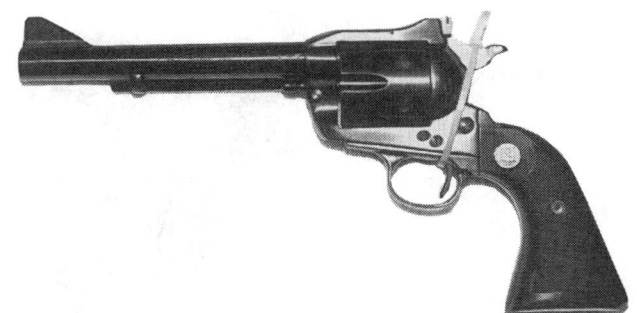

NIB	Exc.	V.G.	Good	Fair	Poor
—	400	325	200	125	75

Western

As above, in .22 caliber.

NIB	Exc.	V.G.	Good	Fair	Poor
—	200	150	125	75	50

HESSE ARMS
Inver Grove Heights, Minnesota

HI-POINT FIREARMS
MKS Supply
Dayton, Ohio

Model C

This is a 9mm single-action compact semi-automatic pistol with a 3.5" barrel. Magazine capacity is 8 rounds. Black or chrome finish. Weight is 32 oz.

NIB	Exc.	V.G.	Good	Fair	Poor
125	100	85	75	65	50

Model C Polymer

Same as above but with polymer frame. Weight is 28 oz.

NIB	Exc.	V.G.	Good	Fair	Poor
140	110	85	75	65	50

Model C Comp

Introduced in 1998 this 9mm model features a 4" barrel with compensator, adjustable sights and 10-round magazine.

NIB	Exc.	V.G.	Good	Fair	Poor
170	130	100	90	75	50

Model JH

All steel construction chambered for .45 ACP with 4.5" barrel. Magazine capacity is 7 rounds. Weight is 39 oz.

NIB	Exc.	V.G.	Good	Fair	Poor
180	135	100	85	75	50

Model 40SW

Same as above but chambered for .40 S&W cartridge. Eight-round magazine capacity. Weight is 39 oz.

NIB	Exc.	V.G.	Good	Fair	Poor
180	135	100	85	75	50

Model .45 Polymer

This model has a polymer frame and 4.5" barrel chambered for the .45 ACP cartridge. Magazine capacity is 9 rounds. Weight is about 32 oz.

NIB	Exc.	V.G.	Good	Fair	Poor
180	135	100	85	75	50

Model .40 Polymer

As above but chambered for the .40 S&W cartridge with a magazine capacity of 10 rounds. Weight is about 32 oz.

NIB	Exc.	V.G.	Good	Fair	Poor
180	135	100	85	75	50

Model CF

This pistol is chambered for the .380 ACP cartridge and is fitted with a polymer frame. Magazine capacity is 8 rounds. Barrel length is 3.5". Weight is 29 oz.

NIB	Exc.	V.G.	Good	Fair	Poor
120	95	65	40	30	25

NOTE: Add $25 for compensator model.

.380 ACP Compensated

Semi-auto with fully-adjustable 3-dot sights, muzzle compensator, 4" barrel, 31 oz, polymer frame. Two magazines: one 10-round, one 8-round. Add 50 percent for laser sight.

NIB	Exc.	V.G.	Good	Fair	Poor
150	125	100	85	75	50

HIGH STANDARD
New Haven, Connecticut 1932-1945
Hamden, Connecticut 1946-1977
East Hartford, Connecticut 1977-1984

NOTE: See High Standard Manufacturing Co., Houston, TX at the end of this semi-auto pistol section.

LETTER MODELS

Model B

A .22 LR caliber semi-automatic pistol with either a 4.5" or a 6.75" round barrel and a 10-shot magazine. Blued; came with checkered hard rubber grips (later production versions have checkered grips impressed with the High Standard monogram). Introduced 1932, with serial numbers beginning at 5000. Early production utilized Hartford parts. Approximately 65,000 made. Add $75 premium for Type-I-B takedown. Add a $75 premium for early models with Hartford Arms front sight, safety, and takedown levers. Box with papers add premium of 15 percent. C&R eligible. Most guns are found in serial number ranges from 5,000 to about 95,894 and 148198 to about 151021.

NIB	Exc.	V.G.	Good	Fair	Poor
—	600	475	215	125	90

Model B-US

A version of the Model B with slight contour modifications to the back of the frame. Approximately 14,000 were made for the U.S. government in 1942-1943. Most are marked "PROPERTY OF U.S." on the top of the barrel and on the right side of the frame. Monogrammed hard rubber grips. Most guns are found in serial number range 92344 to about 111631.

NIB	Exc.	V.G.	Good	Fair	Poor
—	800	520	375	175	125

NOTE: Box with papers add premium of 20 percent.

Model C

Like the Model B except in .22 Short. Introduced 1936; approximately 4,700 made. Both plain and monogrammed hard rubber grips. Available with either a 4.5" or a 6.75" round barrel.

NIB	Exc.	V.G.	Good	Fair	Poor
—	725	450	300	225	150

NOTE: Add $75 premium for I-A takedown. Add $175 premuim for I-B takedown. Box with papers add premium of 15 percent.

Model A

Similar to the Model B but with checkered walnut grips over an extended grip and an adjustable sight. Introduced 1938; approximately 7,300 made. Available with either a 4.5" or a 6.75" round barrel. The same light barrel as the Model B.

NIB	Exc.	V.G.	Good	Fair	Poor
—	975	750	400	175	125

NOTE: Add $175 premium for I-B takedown. Box with papers add premium of 15 percent.

Model D

Similar to a Model A but with a heavier weight barrel. (The middle weight barrel.) Available with either a 4.5" or a 6.75" barrel and optional checkered walnut grips. Introduced 1938; approximately 2,500 made.

NIB	Exc.	V.G.	Good	Fair	Poor
—	835	490	310	200	130

NOTE: Add $175 premium for I-B takedown. Box with papers add premium of 15 percent.

Model E

Like the Model D but with a still heavier weight barrel (the heavy weight barrel). Available with either a 4.5" or a 6.75" barrel. Checkered walnut grips with thumb rest. Introduced 1938; approximately 2,600 made.

NIB	Exc.	V.G.	Good	Fair	Poor
—	1500	925	650	250	140

NOTE: Add $175 for I-B takedown. Box with papers add premium of 18 percent.

Model S

Not a production model. Like the model B but with a smooth bore. Nine registered as Model S. Additional five with Model C slides are registered, Model C/S. Note ivory bead front sight. Others may exist but only 14 are registered with BATF. Manufactured in 1939 and 1940. Values for both variations are equal. 6.75" barrels.
NOTE: Serial numbers for registered samples.

NIB	Exc.	V.G.	Good	Fair	Poor
—	5250	3950	3000	—	—

Hammer Letter Models

Second models made. Like the letter models with external hammers.

MODEL H-B, TYPE 1 PRE-WAR

Like the Model B but with exposed hammer. Introduced 1940; approximately 2,100 made.

NIB	Exc.	V.G.	Good	Fair	Poor
—	725	425	275	175	125

NOTE: Box with papers add premium of 15 percent.

Model H-B, Type 2 Post-War

Post-war variation has an external safety. Approximately 25,000 made.

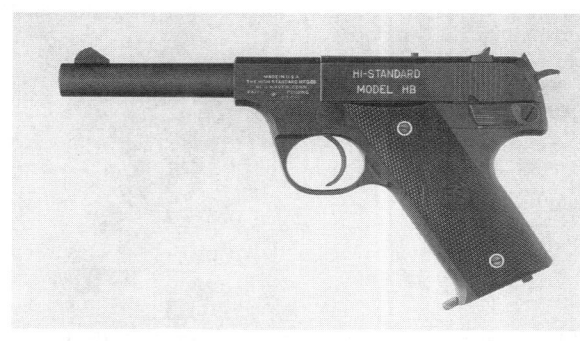

NIB	Exc.	V.G.	Good	Fair	Poor
—	550	375	225	150	100

NOTE: Box with papers add premium of 15 percent.

Model H-A

Like the Model A but with exposed hammer. Introduced 1940; approximately 1,040 made.

NIB	Exc.	V.G.	Good	Fair	Poor
—	1600	1100	750	500	300

NOTE: Box with papers add premium of 15 percent.

Model H-D

Like the Model D but with exposed hammer. Introduced 1940; approximately 6,900 made.

NIB	Exc.	V.G.	Good	Fair	Poor
—	1500	1000	650	400	250

NOTE: Box with papers add premium of 15 percent.

Model H-E

Like the Model E but with exposed hammer. Introduced 1940; approximately 2,100 made.

NIB	Exc.	V.G.	Good	Fair	Poor
—	1800	950	700	275	150

NOTE: Box with papers add premium of 15 percent.

Model USA—Model HD

Similar to the Model HD but 4.5" barrel only. Had fixed sights, checkered black hard rubber grips and an external safety. Early models blued; later model Parkerized. Introduced 1943; approximately 44,000 produced for the U.S. government.

NIB	Exc.	V.G.	Good	Fair	Poor
—	800	625	450	225	125

NOTE: Box with papers add premium of 20 percent.

Model USA—Model HD-MS

A silenced variation of the USA Model HD. Approximately 2,000 produced for the OSS during 1944 and 1945. 6.75" shrouded barrel. Early models blued; later model Parkerized. Only a few registered with BATF for civilian ownership.

NIB	Exc.	V.G.	Good	Fair	Poor
—	6600	5500	—	—	—

Model H-D Military

Similar to the HD but with external safety. Early production had checkered plastic grips; later production changed to checkered walnut. Introduced 1945; approximately 150,000 produced.

NIB	Exc.	V.G.	Good	Fair	Poor
—	600	450	275	200	125

NOTE: Box with papers add premium of 15 percent.

LEVER LETTER MODELS

Third design models which incorporate interchangeable barrels with a lever takedown.

G-.380

A .380 caliber semi-automatic pistol with a 5" barrel and 6-shot magazine. Blues with checkered plastic grips. Fixed sights. Introduced 1947, discontinued 1950; approximately 7,400 made. High Standard's only production centerfire pistol.

NIB	Exc.	V.G.	Good	Fair	Poor
—	750	550	375	150	115

NOTE: Box with papers add premium of 10 percent.

G-B

Similar characteristics with the Model B but with interchangeable 4.5" or 6.75" barrels. Sold with either barrel or as a combination with both barrels. Fixed sights. Blued with monogrammed plastic grips. Last short frame model produced. Introduced 1949, discontinued 1950; approximately 4,900 produced.

NIB	Exc.	V.G.	Good	Fair	Poor
—	575	350	250	135	100

NOTE: Box with papers add premium of 15 percent. Add $225 premium for factory combination.

G-D

Similar characteristics with the Model D but with interchangeable 4.5" or 6.75" barrels. Sold with either barrel or as a combination with both barrels. Adjustable sights. Blued with checkered walnut grips. Optional checkered thumb rest walnut grips. Introduced 1949, discontinued 1950; approximately 3,300 produced.

NIB	Exc.	V.G.	Good	Fair	Poor
—	975	750	450	195	125

NOTE: Add $325 premium for factory combination, $50 premium for factory target grips. Box with papers add premium of 15 percent.

G-E

Similar characteristics with the Model E but with interchangeable 4.5" or 6.75" barrels. Sold with either barrel or as a combination with both barrels. Adjustable sights. Blued with checkered thumb rest walnut grips. Introduced 1949, discontinued 1950; approximately 2,900 produced.

NIB	Exc.	V.G.	Good	Fair	Poor
—	1275	800	450	225	135

NOTE: Add $375 premium for factory combination. Box with papers add premium of 15 percent.

Olympic (commonly called "G-O")

New gun design for competitive shooting in .22 Short caliber. 4.5" or 6.75" barrels. Sold with either barrel or as a combination with both barrels. Grooved front and back straps on frame. Adjustable sights. Blued with checkered thumb rest walnut grips. Introduced 1949, discontinued 1950; approximately 1,200 produced. This model uses a special curved magazine. A few guns will utilize a straight-back magazine. The majority of these Olympics use the curved magazine with a humped back.

NIB	Exc.	V.G.	Good	Fair	Poor
—	1500	875	550	225	125

NOTE: Add $375 premium for factory combination. Box with papers add premium of 15 percent. Add $300 for the straight magazine variation.

LEVER NAME MODELS

Fourth design models evolving from the lever letter series designs with slight changes.

Supermatic

.22 LR caliber pistol with 10-shot magazine. Heavy round barrel, blued finish; adjustable sights and brown plastic thumb rest grips. Grooved front and back straps on frame. Available with 4.5" or 6.75" barrels or combination with both barrels. Ribbed barrels and provisions for weights. A 2 oz. and a 3 oz. weight were provided with this model, as was a filler strip for when the weights were not used.

NIB	Exc.	V.G.	Good	Fair	Poor
—	750	550	400	275	135

NOTE: Add $250 for factory combination. Box with papers add premium of 15 percent.

Olympic

.22 Short caliber pistol with 10-shot magazine. Heavy round barrel, blued finish, adjustable sights and brown plastic thumb rest grips. Grooved front and back straps on frame. Available with 4.5" or 6.75" barrels or combination with both barrels. Ribbed barrels and provisions for weights. Weights of 2 oz. and 3 oz. were provided with this model, as was a filler strip for when the weights were not used.

NIB	Exc.	V.G.	Good	Fair	Poor
—	1000	750	575	275	150

NOTE: Add $250 for factory combination. Box with papers add premium of 15 percent.

Field King

.22 LR caliber pistol with 10-shot magazine. Heavy round barrel, blued finish, adjustable sights and brown plastic thumb rest grips. Available with 4.5" or 6.75" barrels or combination with both barrels. No rib on barrels or provisions for weights.

NIB	Exc.	V.G.	Good	Fair	Poor
—	575	380	250	150	125

NOTE: Add $225 premium for factory combination. Box with papers add premium of 15 percent.

Sport King

.22 caliber pistol with 10-shot magazine. Lightweight round barrel, blued finish, fixed sights and brown plastic thumb rest grips. Available with 4.5" or 6.75" barrels or combination with both barrels. Early models did not have a slide holdback when the magazine was empty. Early variation without holdback was produced in about twice the quantity as the later models incorporating this feature.

NIB	Exc.	V.G.	Good	Fair	Poor
—	425	300	225	155	110

NOTE: Add $200 premium for factory combination. Box with papers add premium of 15 percent. Add a $25 premium for guns with holdback feature.

100 SERIES MODELS

Fifth design models evolving from the lever name series designs. This series introduced the small pushbutton barrel release takedown and deletes the shrouded breach.

Supermatic S-100

Like the lever takedown Supermatic but with new takedown. Available with 4.5", 6.75", or a combination with both barrel lengths. Grooved front and back straps on frame. This model produced briefly in 1954. Weights of 2 oz. and 3 oz. were provided with this model, as was a filler strip for when the weights were not used.

NIB	Exc.	V.G.	Good	Fair	Poor
—	825	600	400	175	125

NOTE: Add $250 for factory combination. Box with papers add premium of 15 percent.

Olympic O-100

Like the lever takedown Olympic but with new takedown. Available with 4.5", 6.75", or a combination with both barrel lengths. Grooved front and back straps on frame. This model produced briefly in 1954. Weights of 2 oz. and 3 oz. were provided with this model, as was a filler strip for when the weights were not used.

NIB	Exc.	V.G.	Good	Fair	Poor
—	1250	700	475	250	135

NOTE: Add $250 for factory combination. Box with papers add premium of 15 percent.

Field King FK-100

Like the lever takedown Field King but with new takedown. Available with 4.5", 6.75", or a combination with both barrel lengths. This model produced briefly in 1954.

NIB	Exc.	V.G.	Good	Fair	Poor
—	750	495	385	175	125

NOTE: Add $225 premium for factory combination. Box with papers add premium of 15 percent.

Sport King SK-100

Like the lever takedown Sport King but with new takedown. Available with 4.5", 6.75", or a combination with both barrel lengths. This model produced 1954 to 1957. In late 1958 Col. Rex Applegate imported about 300 of these pistols into Mexico. These guns are marked with his compay's name "ARMAMEX." Marked "ARMAMEX, MEXICO" on the right side of the barrel and "SPORT KING/CAL .22 L.R." on the left side of the barrel. Serial numbers around 870,084-870,383. Note that the Applegate guns were made after the 102 series was in production. Armamex catalog number 1910.

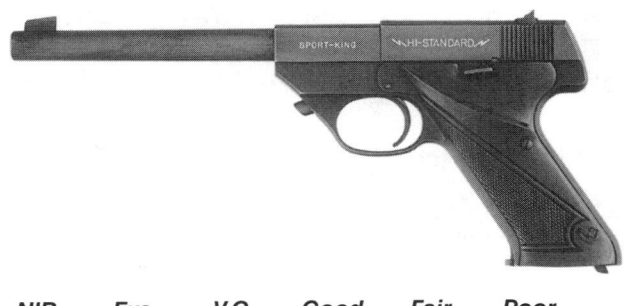

NIB	Exc.	V.G.	Good	Fair	Poor
—	425	250	200	135	100

NOTE: Add $200 premium for factory combination. Add $250 premium for Armamex version. Box with papers add premium of 10 percent.

Sport King Lightweight SK-100

Aluminum frame like Flite King LW-100 but in .22 LR caliber. Produced 1956 to 1964. Also available nickel plated 1957 to 1960.

NIB	Exc.	V.G.	Good	Fair	Poor
—	525	325	200	140	100

NOTE: Add $150 premium for nickel finish, $200 premium for factory combination. Box with papers add premium of 12 percent.

Flite King LW-100

.22 Short caliber semi-automatic pistol with 10-shot magazine. Blued finish with black anodized aluminum frame and slide. Brown plastic checkered thumb rest grips. Fixed sights. Available with 4.5", 6.75", or a combination with both barrel lengths. This model produced 1954 to 1957.

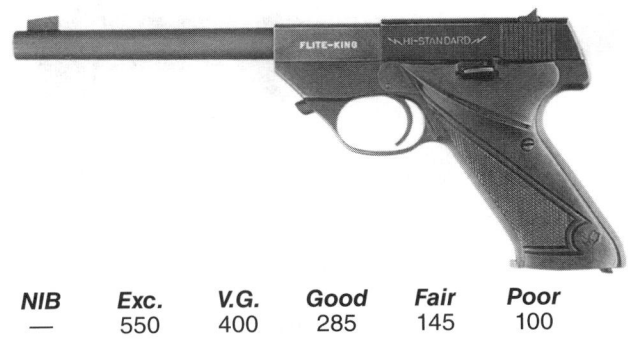

NIB	Exc.	V.G.	Good	Fair	Poor
—	550	400	285	145	100

NOTE: Add $200 for factory combination. Box with papers add premium of 12 percent.

Dura-Matic M-100

.22 LR caliber semi-automatic pistol with 10-shot magazine. Striker-fired, fixed sights, blued finish, brown checkered plastic one-piece grip. Takedown by thumb nut. Available with 4.5", 6.5", or a combination with both barrel lengths. This model produced briefly in 1954.

NIB	Exc.	V.G.	Good	Fair	Poor
—	350	225	165	150	95

NOTE: Add $150 premium for factory combination. Box with papers add premium of 12 percent.

101 SERIES MODELS

Sixth design models evolving from the 100 series. This series continued the small pushbutton barrel release takedown.

Olympic O-101

A .22 Short caliber semi-automatic pistol with a 10-shot magazine. Heavy round barrel, blued finish, adjustable sights and brown plastic thumb rest grips. Grooved front and back straps on frame. Available with 4.5", 6.75", or a combination with both barrel lengths. The 6.75" barrel incorporates a muzzlebrake with one slot on either side of the front sight.

NIB	Exc.	V.G.	Good	Fair	Poor
—	950	600	450	200	175

NOTE: Add $250 premium for factory combination. Box with papers add premium of 13 percent.

Supermatic S-101

A .22 LR caliber semi-automatic pistol with a 10-shot magazine. Heavy round barrel, blued finish, adjustable sights and brown plastic thumb rest grips. Grooved front and back straps on frame. Available with 4.5", 6.75", or a combination with both barrel lengths. The 6.75" barrel incorporates a muzzlebrake with one slot on either side of the front sight. Also produced with U.S. marking for the military.

NIB	Exc.	V.G.	Good	Fair	Poor
—	775	475	360	190	130

NOTE: Add $250 premium for factory combination. Box with papers add premium of 13 percent.

Field King FK-101

A .22 LR caliber semi-automatic pistol with a 10-shot magazine. Heavy round barrel, blued finish, adjustable sights and brown plastic thumb rest grips. Available with 4.5", 6.75", or a combination with both barrel lengths.

NIB	Exc.	V.G.	Good	Fair	Poor
—	625	475	360	175	125

NOTE: Add $225 premium for factory combination. Box with papers add premium of 15 percent.

Dura-Matic M-101

Like the Dura-matic M-100 with slightly different locking method for thumb nut takedown. Produced 1954 to 1970. Later appeared renamed "Plinker" M-101 in 1971 to 1973. Plinker not available with both barrel combinations. A slightly modified version was sold by Sears Roebuck & Co. as the J. C. Higgins M-80.

NIB	Exc.	V.G.	Good	Fair	Poor
—	350	225	140	110	80

NOTE: Add $150 premium for factory combination. Box with papers add premium of 10 percent.

Conversion Kits

These kits convert .22 LR to .22 Short and include a barrel, an aluminum slide, and magazine for .22 Short to .22 LR in which case the slide is steel. Prices are for the kit in original factory boxes.
NOTE: First advertised for 101 Series guns. Later, versions were produced for lever takedown guns. Catalog numbers unknown for conversion kits for lever takedown guns.

NIB	Exc.	V.G.	Good	Fair	Poor
—	600	475	—	—	—

102 & 103 SERIES MODELS

The 102 Series was a major design change incorporating a new frame with a large pushbutton takedown release. Also new was a superb adjustable sight. There is little difference between the two series.

Supermatic Trophy

A .22 LR caliber semi-automatic pistol with a 10-shot magazine. A tapered barrel with an enlarged register at the muzzle end to hold a removable muzzlebrake. Super polished blue finish; adjustable sights; 2 and 3 oz. adjustable weights and checkered walnut thumb rest grips. Grooved front and back straps on frame. Available with 6.75", 8" or 10" barrels. Occasionally sold as a combination including two barrels. Premiums for 10" barrels and combinations in original boxes. 5.5" bull barrel available in 103s after April 1962, 7.25" fluted barrels available in 103s after April 1963.

NIB	Exc.	V.G.	Good	Fair	Poor
—	1100	775	525	200	120

NOTE: Add $125 premium for 8" barrel and $225 premium for 10" barrel. Box with papers add premium of 12 percent. Occasionally found with the optional light oak ca

Supermatic Citation

Like the Supermatic Trophy with checkered plastic grips. Blued finish without the trophy's super polished finish. Grooved front and back straps on frame. 5.5" bull barrel available in 103s after April 1962. Also produced with U.S. marking for the military.

NIB	Exc.	V.G.	Good	Fair	Poor
—	725	495	375	165	120

NOTE: Add $100 premium for 8" barrel and $200 premium for 10" barrel. Box with papers add premium of 12 percent. Occasionally found with optional light oak case, which will command a premium of about 18 percent.

Supermatic Tournament

A .22 LR caliber semi-automatic pistol with a 10-shot magazine. Barrels are round and tapered. Blued finish, adjustable sights and checkered plastic grips. Available with 4.5", 6.75", or a combination with both barrels. Combinations available in 102 Series only. 5.5" bull barrel replaced the 4.5" barrel in early 1962. Also produced with U.S. marking for the military.

NIB	Exc.	V.G.	Good	Fair	Poor
—	640	475	275	155	110

NOTE: Add $200 premium for factory combination. Box with papers add premium of 12 percent.

Olympic

A .22 Short caliber version of the Supermatic Citation. Early models marked "Olympic Citation," changed to "Olympic" only in 1960. Grooved front and back straps on frame. 6.75", 8" and 10" barrels produced. 5.5" bull barrel available on later 103 production.

NIB	Exc.	V.G.	Good	Fair	Poor
—	1150	600	375	175	120

NOTE: Add $125 premium for 8" barrel and $225 premium for 10" barrel and $150 premium for "Olympic Citation" marked guns. Box with papers add premium of 12 percent.

Olympic ISU

Like an Olympic but only available with a 6.75" barrel with integral muzzlebrake. Grooved front and back straps on frame.

NIB	Exc.	V.G.	Good	Fair	Poor
—	1150	675	360	165	120

NOTE: Box with papers add premium of 12 percent.

Olympic Trophy ISU

An Olympic ISU with a Supermatic Trophy finish. Grooved front and back straps on frame. Produced in the 103 Series only. Fewer than 500 produced.

NIB	Exc.	V.G.	Good	Fair	Poor
—	2400	775	375	165	135

NOTE: Box with papers add premium of 10 percent.

Sport King

A .22 LR caliber semi-automatic pistol with a 10-shot magazine. Barrels are lightweight, round, and tapered. Blued finish; fixed sights and checkered plastic grips. Available with 4.5", 6.75", or a combination with both barrel lengths. Produced 1957 to 1970 and 1974 to 1977. Also available 1974 to 1977 with nickel finish. $100 premium for nickel finish and $200 premium for factory combination. **NOTE:** Box with papers add premium of 10 percent.

Flite King

A .22 Short caliber version of the Sport King Models 102 and 103. Note these models have steel frames.

NIB	Exc.	V.G.	Good	Fair	Poor
—	475	360	265	150	100

NOTE: Add $200 premium for factory combination. Box with papers add premium of 12 percent.

Sharpshooter

A .22 LR caliber semi-automatic pistol with a 10-shot magazine. 5.5" bull barrel, blued finish, adjustable sights, checkered plastic grips. Some produced with Model 103-marked slides. Although the 103-marked guns have 1969 and later serial numbers they were shipped after the introduction of the Sharpshooter in 1971 and were probably converted from unsold Sport Kings. No premium for 103-marked. Variation without series marked on slide is the most plentiful. Produced 1971 to 1977.

NIB	Exc.	V.G.	Good	Fair	Poor
—	500	325	265	154	110

NOTE: Box with papers add premium of 15 percent.

Conversion Kits

These kits convert .22 LR to .22 Short and include a barrel, an aluminum slide, and magazine. Prices are for kits in original boxes.

NIB	Exc.	V.G.	Good	Fair	Poor
—	900-700	575	—	—	—

104 SERIES MODELS

The last of the slant grip gun designs. The early production marked "Model 104." Later production is unmarked.

Olympic

Like the 103 Series 8" barrel models.

NIB	Exc.	V.G.	Good	Fair	Poor
—	1200	650	375	175	110

NOTE: Box with papers add premium of 12 percent.

Olympic ISU

Like the 103 model. 6.75" barrel with integral brake. 5.5" version introduced in 1964. Catalogs and price list refer to the 9295 as both Olympic and Olympic ISU. It met the ISU regulations and included a removable muzzlebrake and weights.

NIB	Exc.	V.G.	Good	Fair	Poor
—	1100	625	360	175	110

NOTE: Box with papers add premium of 12 percent.

Victor

A .22 LR caliber semi-automatic pistol with a 10-shot magazine. 4.5" and 5.5" slab-sided barrels with either ventilated or solid ribs. The adjustable sights are integral with the rib. Blue finish, barrel tapped for weight, checkered walnut thumb rest grips. Grooved front and back straps on frame. Probably fewer than 600 of these slant grip Victors in all configurations. Probably fewer than 40 each of the 4.5" guns. Trigger is adjustable for both pull and over-travel. Most guns in serial number range above 2401xxx with a few in the ML serial number series. Note the early vent rib barrels were steel and later ones aluminum without a change in catalog numbers. BEWARE—fakes exist.

NIB	Exc.	V.G.	Good	Fair	Poor
—	2750	1500	600	425	250

NOTE: Add $75 premium for steel rib, $200 premium for solid rib, and $200 premium for 4.5" barrel. Box with papers add premium of 15 percent.

106 SERIES MODELS

Referred to as military models, this series was designed to provide the same grip angles and feel of the Colt military model 1911. This design was introduced in 1965 and continued through most of 1968.

Supermatic Trophy

Like the 104 Series Supermatic Trophy with the new military frame. Stippled front and back straps on frame.

NIB	Exc.	V.G.	Good	Fair	Poor
—	1000	600	425	190	120

NOTE: Add $100 premium for high polish blue finish, $200 premium for guns with boxes and accessories if factory records verify model numbers. Box with papers add premium of 12 percent.

Supermatic Citation

Like the 104 Series Supermatic Citation with the new military frame. Stippled front and back straps on frame.

NIB	Exc.	V.G.	Good	Fair	Poor
—	675	475	300	200	120

NOTE: Add $150 premium for guns with boxes and accessories if factory records verify model numbers. Box with papers add premium of 12 percent.

Supermatic Tournament

Like the 104 Series Supermatic Tournament with the new military frame. Stippled front and back straps on frame.

NIB	Exc.	V.G.	Good	Fair	Poor
—	600	375	250	165	120

NOTE: Add $125 premium for guns with boxes and accessories if factory records verify model numbers. Box with papers add premium of 12 percent.

Olympic

Listed in catalog but not in shipping records. Catalog number 9235 for 5.5" barrel. WARNING: There is no evidence that this model was actually produced.

Olympic ISU

Like the 104 Series Olympic ISU with the new military frame. Stippled front and back straps on frame.

NIB	Exc.	V.G.	Good	Fair	Poor
—	1050	650	385	200	120

NOTE: Add $200 premium for guns with boxes and accessories if factory records verify model numbers. Box with papers add premium of 12 percent.

107 SERIES MODELS

The evolutionary successor to the 106 Series. This series had the frame redesigned to eliminate the plugging of the spring hole produced with the old tooling. During the time of this series production, the MILITARY marking on the frame was removed and then later reappeared near the end of the end of the traditional serial number series. The MILITARY marking is absent from the guns with the ML prefixed serial numbers. There is no premium associated with these variations.

Olympic ISU

Like the 106 Series Olympic ISU.

NIB	Exc.	V.G.	Good	Fair	Poor
—	1100	675	525	225	110

NOTE: Box with papers add premium of 12 percent.

Olympic ISU 1980 Commemorative

A limited edition of the 107 Olympic ISU with 1,000 produced. "USA" prefix on serial numbers from 0001 to 1000. Engraved, right side of slide has the five gold ring Olympic logo. Offered with lined presentation case.

NIB	Exc.	V.G.	Good	Fair	Poor
—	1500	850	525	300	175

NOTE: Prices are for guns with box, papers, and presentation case; otherwise deduct $250 for guns in excellent condition.

Supermatic Trophy

Like the 106 Series Supermatic Trophy.

NIB	Exc.	V.G.	Good	Fair	Poor
—	925	550	360	200	120

NOTE: Box with papers add premium of 12 percent.

Supermatic Trophy 1972 Commemorative

A limited edition of the 107 Supermatic Trophy with 1000 planned. "T" prefix on serial numbers from 0000 to 999. Engraved, right side of slide has the five gold ring Olympic logo. Offered with lined presentation case. Only 107 guns listed in the shipping records, plus one frame. A couple of prototypes believed to exist in the regular serial number series. Prices are for guns in original presentation cases. **NOTE:** One fully engraved gun is known.

NIB	Exc.	V.G.	Good	Fair	Poor
6250	4500	—	—	—	—

Supermatic Citation

Like the 106 Series Supermatic Citation.

NIB	Exc.	V.G.	Good	Fair	Poor
—	625	425	300	225	110

NOTE: Box with papers add premium of 12 percent.

Supermatic Tournament

Like the 106 Series Supermatic Tournament. Smooth front and back straps on frame.

NIB	Exc.	V.G.	Good	Fair	Poor
—	550	360	300	175	110

NOTE: Box with papers add premium of 12 percent.

Sport King

Like the 103 Series Sport King with the military frame.

NIB	Exc.	V.G.	Good	Fair	Poor
—	345	225	195	155	100

NOTE: Box with papers add premium of 12 percent.

Sharpshooter

Like the 103 Series Sharpshooter with the military frame.

NIB	Exc.	V.G.	Good	Fair	Poor
—	450	300	225	175	110

NOTE: Box with papers add premium of 12 percent.

Survival Kit

An electroless nickel Sharpshooter with 5.5" barrel in a canvas carrying case with an extra electroless nickel magazine.

NIB	Exc.	V.G.	Good	Fair	Poor
—	750	500	300	175	110

NOTE: Deduct $100 for guns without the case and $65 for guns without the extra magazine for guns in excellent condition.

Victor

A .22 LR caliber semi-automatic pistol with a 10-shot magazine. 4.5" and 5.5" slab-sided barrels with either ventilated or solid ribs. The adjustable sights are integral with the rib. Blue finish, barrel tapped for weight, checkered walnut thumb rest grips. Stippled front and back straps on frame. Early ventilated ribs were steel; aluminum replaced the steel on later ventilated ribs. Still later a clearance groove was added for spent shell ejection behind the barrel. Early models marked THE VICTOR on the left side of the barrel; later guns marked simply VICTOR on the left side of the frame. A few transition guns marked in both locations.

NIB	Exc.	V.G.	Good	Fair	Poor
—	775	500	350	200	120

NOTE: Add $125 premium for steel ribs, $125 premium for solid rib guns, premium for 4.5" barreled guns, $140 premium for Hamden guns (7-digit serial numbers and ML prefix serial numbers below ML 25,000). Box with papers add premium of 12 percent.

10-X

A .22 LR caliber semi-automatic pistol with a 10-shot magazine. Matte blue finish, adjustable sights, checkered walnut thumb rest grips painted black. Stippled front and back straps on frame.

Available with 5.5" bull barrel. Assembled by a master gunsmith. Gunsmith's initials stamped in frame under left grip panel. Produced in 1981.

NIB	Exc.	V.G.	Good	Fair	Poor
—	2750	1550	900	350	125

NOTE: Prices are for guns with box and papers including test target. Otherwise deduct $175.

SH SERIES MODELS

The final design produced by High Standard. A change in takedown from the large pushbutton introduced with the 102 Series and continuing through the 107 Series, to a hex socket head cap screw takedown.

Supermatic Trophy

Like the 107 Supermatic Trophy with a new takedown.

NIB	Exc.	V.G.	Good	Fair	Poor
—	600	375	275	165	120

NOTE: Box with papers add premium of 10 percent.

Supermatic Citation

Like the 107 Supermatic Citation with a new takedown.

NIB	Exc.	V.G.	Good	Fair	Poor
—	525	350	250	175	120

NOTE: Box with papers add premium of 10 percent.

Citation II

A new gun like the Supermatic Citation but with the barrel slabbed on the sides like the Victor and smooth front and back straps on frame. 5.5" and 7.25" barrels available. Blued finish, adjustable sights. Electroless nickel version utilized in some survival kits.

NIB	Exc.	V.G.	Good	Fair	Poor
—	475	350	250	155	110

NOTE: Box with papers add premium of 10 percent.

Sport King

Like the 107 Sport King with a new takedown. Electroless nickel finish also available.

NIB	Exc.	V.G.	Good	Fair	Poor
—	300	225	165	140	90

NOTE: Box with papers add premium of 10 percent.

Victor

Like the 107 Victor with a new takedown. Only available with 5.5" barrel.

NIB	Exc.	V.G.	Good	Fair	Poor
—	550	330	250	175	110

NOTE: Box with papers add premium of 10 percent.

Sharpshooter

Like the 107 Sharpshooter with a new takedown. Electroless nickel version utilized in some survival kits.

NIB	Exc.	V.G.	Good	Fair	Poor
—	375	250	200	155	110

NOTE: Box with papers add premium of 10 percent.

10-X

Like the 107 10-X with a new takedown. Also available with 7.25" fluted barrel and a 5.5" ribbed barrel like a Victor.

NIB	Exc.	V.G.	Good	Fair	Poor
—	2350	1450	825	350	125

NOTE: Prices are for guns with box and papers including test target. Otherwise deduct $150. Add $500 premium for 7.25" barrel, $1,000 for ribbed barrel like Victor.

Survival Kit

Either an electroless nickel Sharpshooter or electroless nickel Citation II with 5.5" barrel in a canvas carrying case with an extra electroless nickel magazine. Two different fabrics utilized during production.

NIB	Exc.	V.G.	Good	Fair	Poor
—	700	475	275	200	110

NOTE: Deduct $100 for guns without the case and $65 for guns without the extra magazine for guns in excellent condition.

Conversion Kits for Military Frame Guns

These kits convert .22 LR to .22 Short and include a barrel, an aluminum slide, and 2 magazines.

NIB	Exc.	V.G.	Good	Fair	Poor
—	625	390	—	—	—

NOTE: Prices are for kits in original boxes.

HIGH STANDARD MANUFACTURING CO. HOUSTON, TEXAS

This company was established in 1993. Among its employees are several who worked for the High Standard Company that closed its doors in Connecticut in 1984. The remaining semi-auto pistols in this section were made in Houston. This firm expanded in 2004 by purchasing the assets of AMT-Auto Mag and Interarms.

RECENTLY MANUFACTURED HOUSTON MODELS

Supermatic Citation

Chambered for the .22 LR and fitted with a 5.5" barrel. Matte blue or Parkerized finish. Weight is about 44 oz. Discontinued.

NIB	Exc.	V.G.	Good	Fair	Poor
425	325	275	225	175	100

Supermatic Citation MS

Designed for metallic silhouette shooting and introduced in 1996. Fitted with a 10" barrel. Weight is approximately 49 oz. Discontinued.

NIB	Exc.	V.G.	Good	Fair	Poor
675	575	425	350	250	125

Supermatic Tournament

Chambered for .22 LR and fitted with a 5.5" barrel. Matte blue finish. Weight is approximately 44 oz.

NIB	Exc.	V.G.	Good	Fair	Poor
600	450	350	250	175	100

Supermatic Trophy

Offered with 5.5" or 7.25" barrels and chambered for .22 LR. Adjustable trigger, barrel weights, gold-plated trigger, safety, slide stop and magazine catch. Matte blue or Parkerized finish. Weight is about 45 oz. Add 10 percent for 7.25" barrel.

NIB	Exc.	V.G.	Good	Fair	Poor
600	450	350	250	150	100

Olympic Model

Chambered for .22 Short and fitted with a 5.5" bull barrel. Blued finish. Weight is approximately 44 oz.

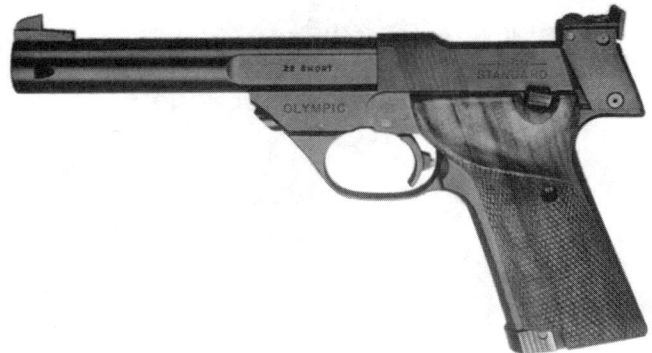

NIB	Exc.	V.G.	Good	Fair	Poor
625	425	300	250	200	100

Olympic ISU

Similar to the previous model but fitted with a 6.75" barrel with internal stabilizer. Magazine capacity is 5 rounds. Checkered walnut grips. Weight is approximately 45 oz. This model was discontinued in 1995.

NIB	Exc.	V.G.	Good	Fair	Poor
600	500	350	300	200	150

Olympic Rapid Fire

Introduced in 1996. Chambered for the .22 Short cartridge with a 4" barrel, integral muzzlebrake and forward mounted compensator. Special grips. Weight is about 46 oz. Discontinued.

NIB	Exc.	V.G.	Good	Fair	Poor
1995	1550	1200	900	600	—

Sport King

Chambered for .22 LR and fitted with a 4.5" or 6.75" barrel. Adjustable rear sight. Weight is about 44 oz. Limited edition.

NIB	Exc.	V.G.	Good	Fair	Poor
650	400	225	150	100	80

Victor

With 4.5" barrel and blue or Parkerized finish.

NIB	Exc.	V.G.	Good	Fair	Poor
625	525	350	300	200	125

10-X

Fitted with 5.5" barrel. Weight is about 44 oz. From HS Custom Shop.

NIB	Exc.	V.G.	Good	Fair	Poor
850	700	550	450	350	200

10-X—Shea Model

Fitted with a 4.5" or 5.5" barrel. Limited to 150 pistols per year. Add 10 percent for 5.5 barrel.

NIB	Exc.	V.G.	Good	Fair	Poor
1100	850	700	500	350	200

Olympic Trophy Space Gun

Semi-auto pistol chambered in .22 LR. Recreation of famed competition "Space Gun" from 1960s. Features include 8- or 10-inch barrel; 10-round magazine; adjustable sights; barrel weight; adjustable muzzle brake; blue-black finish with gold highlights.

NIB	Exc.	V.G.	Good	Fair	Poor
950	850	725	550	400	200

DERRINGERS

A .22 caliber or .22 Magnum caliber Over/Under double-action-only derringer with 3.50" barrels. They are found with three different types of markings:Type 1 Markings are found on early models which are marked "HI-STANDARD" / "DERRINGER" and have the EAGLE logo on the left side of the barrel. These models were marked "D-100" for the .22 caliber and "DM-101" for the .22 Magnum on the left side of the barrel. Date range 1962 to about 1967.Type 2 Markings are found on later models were marked "HI- STANDARD" / "DERRINGER" and had the TRIGGER logo. The early .22 caliber models were marked D-100 and the later .22 caliber models beginning about 1969 were marked D-101 on the left side of the barrel. The .22 Magnum models were marked DM-101on the left side of the barrel. Date range 1967 to about 1970.Type 3 Markings are found on the latest models were marked simply "DERRINGER" without HI STANDARD, or either logo. These models were also marked D-101 for the .22 caliber and DM-101 for the .22 Magnum on the left side of the barrel. Date Blue, white or black grips

Blued finish, white or black grips, 1962-1984

NIB	Exc.	V.G.	Good	Fair	Poor
—	250	185	140	80	65

Nickel Finish black grips, introduced 1970

NIB	Exc.	V.G.	Good	Fair	Poor
—	250	185	140	80	65

Electroless Nickel Finish with checkered walnut grips

NIB	Exc.	V.G.	Good	Fair	Poor
—	275	190	145	80	65

Silver-Plated Derringer

A .22 Magnum derringer with a presentation case. Faux black mother of pearl grips. 501 made. Serial numbers SP 0 through SP 500. Produced in 1981.

NIB	Exc.	V.G.	Good	Fair	Poor
—	500	275	175	90	75

Gold-Plated Derringers

NIB	Exc.	V.G.	Good	Fair	Poor
—	450	300	200	100	80

NOTE: Prices are for GP serial number guns with presentation case. $100 premium for DM prefix guns in Exc. condition with presentation case. $150 premium for 1960s gold guns in Exc. condition with presentation cases.

REVOLVERS

Police-Style Revolvers

The revolvers begin with the R-100 design series and continue through the R-109 design series. Later steel-framed Sentinels carry no design series markings. The changes of design series designations indicate design changes to the guns. The only R-105 known to date is a private label gun made for Sears. The design series designations and the associated catalog numbers listed are the best estimates at the time of publication.Earliest Sentinels in 1955 were in a seperate serial number series from 1 through approximately 45000. Then they were included in serial number series common to all handguns. In 1974 they were again put in a separate serial number series with an S prefix: S101 through S79946. Many of the later guns had a V suffix which indicated the gun was visually imperfect but guaranteed to work properly.

SENTINEL ALUMINUM FRAMES

A 9-shot single-action or double-action revolver with swing-out cylinder for .22 Short, Long, or LR cartridges. Fixed sights. The Sentinel snub 2.375" barrel model had a bobbed hammer from its introduction until 1960. Beginning in 1961 this changed to a standard spur hammer with no change in the catalog number. Beginning with R-102 series the ejector had a spring return. Available in configurations listed.High Standard private-labeled the aluminum-framed Sentinels for both Sears and Western Auto. From 1957 through 1962 High Standard offered the 2.375" snub-barreled Sentinel in three different color anodized frames. These guns had nickel-plated cylinders, triggers, and hammers. The grips were round-butt ivory-colored plastic.

NIB	Exc.	V.G.	Good	Fair	Poor
—	300	200	125	95	

NOTE: Add $20 premium for nickel. Deduct $15 for early models without spring return ejector.

aluminum frames Gold

NIB	Exc.	V.G.	Good	Fair	Poor
—	500	275	185	80	55

NOTE: Add $20 for R-102 marked guns.

aluminum frames Turquoise

NIB	Exc.	V.G.	Good	Fair	Poor
—	575	300	185	80	55

NOTE: Add $20 for R-102 marked guns.

aluminum frames Pink

NIB	Exc.	V.G.	Good	Fair	Poor
—	575	270	185	80	55

NOTE: Add $20 for R-102 marked guns.

Sentinel Imperial

Has two-piece walnut square-butt grips, ramp front and adjustable rear sights.

NIB	Exc.	V.G.	Good	Fair	Poor
—	300	200	125	95	70

NOTE: Add $15 premium for nickel.

Sentinel Deluxe

Has two-piece walnut square-butt grips and fixed sights.

NIB	Exc.	V.G.	Good	Fair	Poor
—	300	200	125	95	70

NOTE: Add $20 premium for nickel.

Sentinel Snub

Has a 2.375" barrel with round-butt grips.

NIB	Exc.	V.G.	Good	Fair	Poor
—	300	200	125	95	70

NOTE: Add $20 premium for nickel.

Sentinel Steel Frames

This model is like the Mark I Sentinels without the Mark I markings. Offered as a combination with cylinders for .22 LR and .22 Win. Mag. Prices are for guns with both cylinders.

NIB	Exc.	V.G.	Good	Fair	Poor
—	350	295	250	115	55

NOTE: Add $25 premium for adjustable sights. Deduct $50 for guns with only one cylinder.

Kit Gun

A 9-shot single-action or double-action revolver with swing-out cylinder for .22 Short, Long, or LR cartridges. Blue finish, aluminum frame, 4.0" barrel, and adjustable sights. Wood round-butt grips.

NIB	Exc.	V.G.	Good	Fair	Poor
—	275	195	125	80	55

Camp Gun

A nine-shot single-action or double-action revolver with swing-out cylinder for .22 Short, Long, or LR cartridges or for.22 mag. Also available as a combination with both cylinders. Blue finished steel frame, adjustable sights.

NIB	Exc.	V.G.	Good	Fair	Poor
—	275	195	120	80	55

NOTE: Add $50 premium for combination with both cylinders.

Sentinel Mark I

A 9-shot single-action or double-action revolver with swing-out cylinder for .22 Short, Long, or LR cartridges. Steel frame, and fixed sights. Available with blue and nickel finishes in 2", 3", and 4" barrels. Adjustable sights available on 3" and 4" barreled guns only. Wood square-butt grips.

NIB	Exc.	V.G.	Good	Fair	Poor
—	255	180	135	80	55

NOTE: Add $25 premium for adjustable sights. Add $25 for nickel.

Sentinel Mark IV

Like the Mark I above except in .22 Magnum.

NIB	Exc.	V.G.	Good	Fair	Poor
—	275	200	145	80	55

NOTE: Add $25 premium for nickel. $25 premium for adjustable sights.

Sentinel Mark II

A .357 Magnum single-action or double-action 6-shot revolver with swing-out cylinder. Blue finish, steel frame, fixed sights. Produced by Dan Wesson for High Standard Sold 1974 through 1975.

NIB	Exc.	V.G.	Good	Fair	Poor
—	325	265	175	90	60

Sentinel Mark III

Like the Mark II above except with adjustable sights. Sold 1974 through 1975.

NIB	Exc.	V.G.	Good	Fair	Poor
—	350	290	200	90	60

Power Plus

A five-shot single-action or double-action revolver with swing-out cylinder for .38 Special cartridges. Blue finished steel frame. Only 177 guns produced. Serial numbers between PG 1010 and PG 1273.

NIB	Exc.	V.G.	Good	Fair	Poor
—	575	400	275	110	70

Crusader

A .44 Magnum or .45 Colt caliber double-action swing-out cylinder revolver with a unique geared action. Adjustable sights. 6-shot cylinder. The first 51 guns had the long barrels, special engraving, a gold crusader figure on the side plate, and an aniversary rollmark to commemorate High Standard's 50th anniversary.

Crusader .45 Colt

NIB	Exc.	V.G.	Good	Fair	Poor
—	1000	750	500	350	200

NOTE: Prices for serial numbers 0 through 50 with the 8.375" barrels.

Crusader .44 Magnum

NIB	Exc.	V.G.	Good	Fair	Poor
—	1200	800	550	375	225

NOTE: Prices for serial numbers 51 through 500 with the 6.5" barrels.

WESTERN-STYLE REVOLVERS

The Western-style revolvers begin with the W-100 design series and continue through the W-106 design series. Later steel-framed Sentinels carry no design series markings. The changes of design series designations indicate design changes to the guns. The design series designations and the associated catalog numbers which are listed are the best estimates at the time of publication. High Standard private labeled the aluminum-framed Western-style revolvers for both Sears and Western Auto.

Double Nine with Aluminum Frame

A 9-shot single-action or double-action revolver for .22 Short, Long, or LR cartridges for all aluminum frame guns. One model has grip straps and trigger guard with gold plating contrasting with the blue frame.

NIB	Exc.	V.G.	Good	Fair	Poor
—	325	250	195	100	55

NOTE: Add Add $25 premium for nickel.

Double Nines with Steel Frame

Available as .22 S / L / LR, .22 mag, or a combination with both cylinders.

NIB	Exc.	V.G.	Good	Fair	Poor
—	325	250	195	100	55

NOTE: Add $45 premium for combination models $20 premium for nickel.

Longhorn

A 9-shot single-action or double-action revolver for .22 Short, Long, or LR cartridges for all aluminum frame guns. Blue finish, fixed sights, and square-butt grips. One model has grip straps and trigger guard with gold plating contrasting with the blue frame. A Sears version exists.

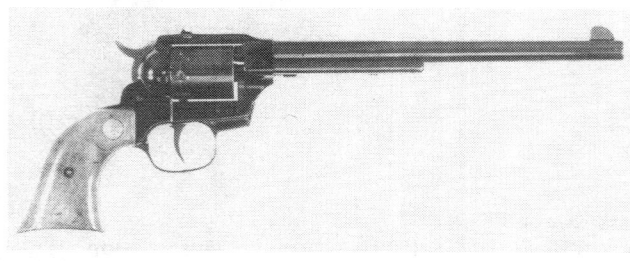

NIB	Exc.	V.G.	Good	Fair	Poor
—	375	300	250	200	100

Longhorns with Steel Frame

Guns available as .22 S / L / LR, .22 mag., or a combination with both cylinders.

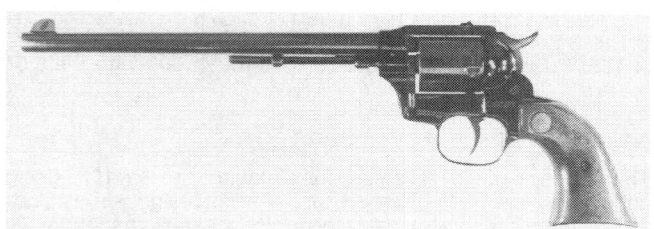

NIB	Exc.	V.G.	Good	Fair	Poor
—	375	300	250	200	100

NOTE: Add $45 premium for combination models, and a $25 premium for adjustable sights.

Marshall

A nine-shot single-action or double-action revolver for .22 Short, Long, or LR cartridges. Blue finish. Aluminum frame, 5.5" barrel, fixed sights and square-butt stag style plastic grips. Offered in a special promotion package with a holster, trigger lock and spray can of G-96 gun scrubber. Price is for gun only. Add $40 premium if box, papers and accessories are present and in excellent condition.

NIB	Exc.	V.G.	Good	Fair	Poor
—	350	250	125	80	55

Posse

A nine-shot single-action or double-action revolver for .22 Short, Long, or LR cartridges. Blue finish with brass colored grip straps and trigger guard. Aluminum frame, 3.5" barrel, fixed sights and square-butt walnut grips.

NIB	Exc.	V.G.	Good	Fair	Poor
—	400	275	135	90	55

Natchez

A 9-shot single-action or double-action revolver for .22 Short, Long, or LR cartridges. Aluminum frame, 4.5" barrel, fixed sights and bird's-head-style ivory-colored plastic grips.

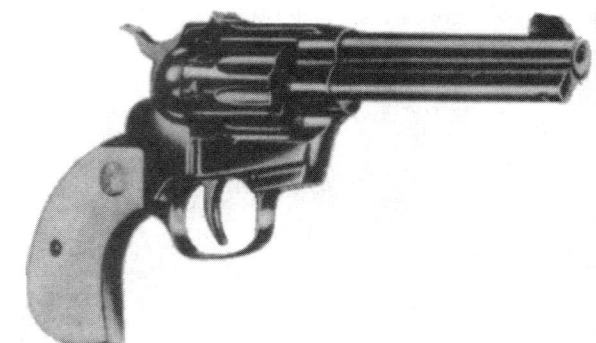

NIB	Exc.	V.G.	Good	Fair	Poor
—	450	325	225	125	60

Hombre

A nine shot single-action or double-action revolver for .22 Short, Long, or LR cartridges. Blue or nickel finish. Aluminum frame, 4" barrel, fixed sights and square-butt walnut grips.

NIB	Exc.	V.G.	Good	Fair	Poor
—	375	300	250	200	100

NOTE: Add $20 premium for nickel.

Durango

A nine-shot single- or double-action revolver for .22 Short, Long, or LR cartridges. Blue or nickel finish. Aluminum or steel frame, 4.5" or 5.5" barrel, fixed or adjustable sights and square-butt walnut grips. Two models have their grip straps and trigger guard with contrasting plating to the blue frame.

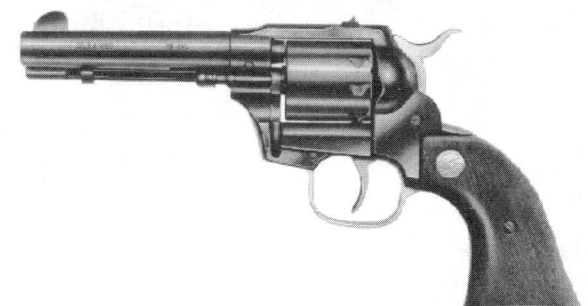

NIB	Exc.	V.G.	Good	Fair	Poor
—	375	300	250	200	100

NOTE: Add $20 premium for nickel. Add $25 premium for steel frame and $25 premium for adjustable sights.

BLACKPOWDER REVOLVERS

These guns were a series of .36 caliber cap-and-ball revolvers that began production in 1974 and ran through 1976. These are reproductions of the Confederate copies of the Colt Model 1851 Navy. Note most Confederate copies of the Colt had round barrels, not octagonal as found on Colts. The frames were made by High Standard and the balance of the parts by Uberti. The guns were assembled and finished by High Standard.

Griswold & Gunnison

Blued finish with a brass frame. Six-shot single-action. Commemorative gun came wtih a pine presentation case and a brass belt plate depicting the Georgia state seal.

NIB	Exc.	V.G.	Good	Fair	Poor
—	325	—	175	—	—

NOTE: Price is for gun in case with accessories. Deduct $100 for gun only in Exc. condition.

Leech & Rigdon

Blued finish with a steel frame. Six-shot single-action. Commemorative gun came with a presentation case and a reproduction of a Civil War belt buckle.

NIB	Exc.	V.G.	Good	Fair	Poor
—	325	235	175	—	—

NOTE: Price is for gun in case with accessories. Deduct $100 for gun only in Exc. condition.

Schneider & Glassick

Blued finish with a steel frame. Six-shot single-action. Commemorative gun came with a presentation case and a modern version of a Confederate "D" guard Bowie knife.

NIB	Exc.	V.G.	Good	Fair	Poor
—	450	235	175	—	—

Bicentennial 1776-1976

Blued finish with a steel frame. Six-shot single-action. Guns came with two versions of presentation case. One case is pine, marked High Standard and the trigger logo is on the lid with a powder flask and silver dollar-sized medallion inside. The other is a brown leatherette covered case with American Bicentennial 1776-1976 and contains a pewter Bicentennial belt buckle.

NIB	Exc.	V.G.	Good	Fair	Poor
—	450	235	175	—	—

Special Presentation Bicentennial

100 guns were available in presentation cases with "US" serial number prefixes. Serial numbers US 11 through US 50 are in walnut presentation cases with purple fitted lining and a pewter Bicentennial belt buckle. The top of the case is marked "Limited Edition / American Bicentennial / 1776 – 1976." The guns are engraved on the frame, cylinder barrel, loading lever, and hammer. Catalog number 9339 has a steel frame with a round barrel and catalog number 9340 has a brass frame with an octagonal barrel.

NIB	Exc.	V.G.	Good	Fair	Poor
—	675	500	350	—	—

HILL, W.J.
Birmingham, England
Hill's Self-Extracting Revolver

A .32 caliber double-action folding trigger revolver with a 3.75" barrel and 6-shot cylinder. Marked "Hill's Patent Self Extractor." Blued with walnut grips.

NIB	Exc.	V.G.	Good	Fair	Poor
—	—	1025	495	295	150

HILLIARD, D. H.
Cornish, New Hampshire
Under Hammer Pistol

A .34 caliber under hammer percussion pistol with varying barrel lengths. Blued with walnut grips. Active 1842 to 1877.

NIB	Exc.	V.G.	Good	Fair	Poor
—	—	950	475	200	100

HINO-KOMURA
Tokyo, Japan

A 7.65mm or 8mm Nambu semi-automatic pistol manufactured in limited quantities between 1905 and 1912. The operation of this pistol involves pulling the muzzle forward until the slide engages a catch on the trigger assembly. Pulling the trigger at this point allows the barrel to move back and engage the cartridge nose into the chamber. Squeezing the grip safety then allows the barrel to slam back into the fixed firing pin on the breechblock. Prospective purchasers are advised to secure a qualified appraisal prior to acquisition.

NIB	Exc.	V.G.	Good	Fair	Poor
—	3850	3600	3000	2250	1000

HOFFMAN, LOUIS
Vicksburg, Mississippi
Pocket Pistol

A .41 caliber percussion pocket pistol with a 3" barrel, German silver mounts and walnut stock. Active 1857 to 1886.

NIB	Exc.	V.G.	Good	Fair	Poor
—	—	900	525	200	100

HOLMES FIREARMS
Wheeler, Arkansas
MP-22

A .22 caliber semi-automatic pistol with a 6" barrel and alloy receiver. Anodized black finish with a walnut grip. Manufactured in 1985.

NIB	Exc.	V.G.	Good	Fair	Poor
425	325	250	200	150	100

MP-83

Similar to the above, but in 9mm or .45 caliber. Manufactured in 1985.

NIB	Exc.	V.G.	Good	Fair	Poor
550	425	325	250	200	125

NOTE: Several of the Holmes pistols have been declared machine guns by the BATF because of their easy conversion to full automatic. Make sure before purchase that a Class III license is not required.

HOOD F. A. CO.
Norwich, Connecticut

A manufacturer of spur trigger .22 or .32 caliber revolvers with varying length barrels and finishes. Many of these revolvers are found stamped only with trade names. This type of handgun is often referred to as a suicide special to denote its poor quality and lack of reliability.

NIB	Exc.	V.G.	Good	Fair	Poor
—	—	250	145	75	50

HOPKINS & ALLEN
Norwich, Connecticut

SEE—Bacon Arms Co. & Merwin Hulbert & Co.

Established in 1868, this company produced a variety of spur trigger revolvers in .22, .32, .38, or .41 caliber often marked with trade names such as: Acme, Blue Jacket, Captain Jack, Chichester, Defender, Dictator, Hopkins & Allen, Imperial Arms Co., Monarch, Mountain Eagle, Ranger, Tower's Police Safety, Universal and XL.Some of these revolvers are hinged-frame, double-action break-opens with round-ribbed barrels of various lengths. Blued or nickel-plated, with checkered plastic grips.

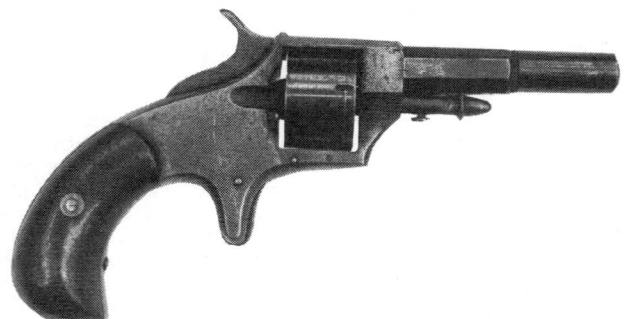

Courtesy Milwaukee Public Museum, Milwaukee, Wisconsin

NIB	Exc.	V.G.	Good	Fair	Poor
—	—	550	275	125	75

Dictator

A .36 caliber percussion or .38 rimfire single-action revolver with a 4" barrel and 5-shot cylinder. Blued with walnut grips. The barrel marked "Dictator." Approximately 6,000 percussion revolvers were made and 5,000 rimfire.

NIB	Exc.	V.G.	Good	Fair	Poor
—	—	1000	725	400	125

Navy Revolver

A .38 caliber rimfire single-action revolver with a 6.5" barrel marked, "Hopkins & Allen Mfg. Co., Pat. Mar. 28, 71, Apr. 27, 75" and a 6-shot cylinder. The top strap marked "XL Navy." Blued or nickel-plated with walnut grips. Several hundred were made between 1878 and 1882.

NIB	Exc.	V.G.	Good	Fair	Poor
—	—	1950	1650	675	175

Army Revolver

As above, in .44 rimfire with a 4.5", 6", or 7.5" barrel. The top strap marked "XL No. 8." Several hundred were manufactured between 1878 and 1882.

NIB	Exc.	V.G.	Good	Fair	Poor
—	—	2800	2500	925	350

Derringer

A .22 caliber single-shot pistol with a hinged 1.75" barrel that pivots downwards for loading. Blued or nickel-plated with walnut, ivory, or pearl grips. The frame marked, "Hopkins & Allen Arms Co., Norwich, Conn. U.S.A." Several hundred were manufactured in the 1880s and 1890s.

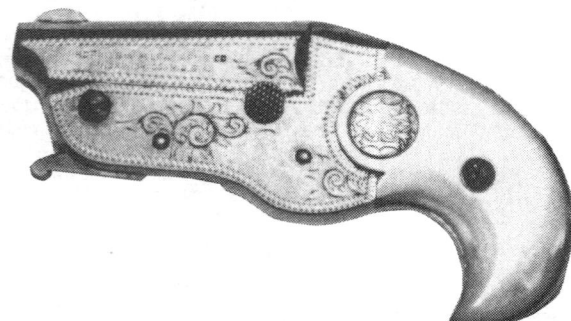

NIB	Exc.	V.G.	Good	Fair	Poor
—	—	2750	950	330	150

HUSQVARNA
Husqvarna, Sweden

HUSQVARNA
Husqvarna, Sweden

Model 1907

This pistol is a copy of the FN Browning Model 1903 made for the Swedish Army. It is identical in every way to the FN model. Many were converted to the .380 caliber and imported into the U.S.

Courtesy Orvel Reichert

NIB	Exc.	V.G.	Good	Fair	Poor
—	400	325	225	150	100

NOTE: If converted to .380 caliber reduce values by 50 percent.

Chicago Cub

A .22 caliber folding trigger double-action revolver with a 2" barrel and 6-shot cylinder.

NIB	Exc.	V.G.	Good	Fair	Poor
—	50	40	30	25	20

Detective

A .22 or .22 WMR caliber double-action revolver with a 2.5" barrel and 6-shot cylinder. Blued with plastic grips.

NIB	Exc.	V.G.	Good	Fair	Poor
—	65	50	40	30	25

Frontier Six Shooter

A .22 or .22 WMR caliber single-action revolver with a 6-shot cylinder.

NIB	Exc.	V.G.	Good	Fair	Poor
—	125	95	50	40	30

Frontier Six Shooter

As above, in .357 Magnum, .44 Magnum or .45 Colt.

NIB	Exc.	V.G.	Good	Fair	Poor
—	225	195	175	100	50

Lahti

A 9mm caliber semi-automatic pistol with a 5.5" barrel and 8-shot magazine. Designed by Aino Lahti and adopted as the standard Swedish sidearm in 1940. Add 75 percent for complete military rig with holsters and magazines.

NIB	Exc.	V.G.	Good	Fair	Poor
—	800	675	475	225	150

Maxim

A .25 caliber semi-automatic pistol with a 2" barrel and 5-shot magazine.

NIB	Exc.	V.G.	Good	Fair	Poor
—	75	65	50	40	30

Military

A .22, .32 or .380 caliber double-action semi-automatic pistol with a 4" barrel and 6-shot magazine.

NIB	Exc.	V.G.	Good	Fair	Poor
—	100	80	60	50	40

Stingray

A .25 caliber semi-automatic pistol with a 2.5" barrel and 5-shot magazine.

NIB	Exc.	V.G.	Good	Fair	Poor
—	75	65	50	40	30

Panzer

A .22 caliber semi-automatic pistol with a 4" barrel and 7-shot magazine.

NIB	Exc.	V.G.	Good	Fair	Poor
—	75	65	50	40	30

Stuka

Similar to the above.

NIB	Exc.	V.G.	Good	Fair	Poor
—	75	65	50	40	30

Automatic Derringer

A .22 caliber over-and-under pocket pistol patterned after the Remington Double Derringer.

NIB	Exc.	V.G.	Good	Fair	Poor
—	50	40	30	25	20

Accurate Ace

A .22 caliber Flobert-action pistol.

NIB	Exc.	V.G.	Good	Fair	Poor
—	50	40	30	25	20

Favorite

A .22 or .22 WMR caliber copy of the Steven's single-shot pistol with a 6" barrel and nickel-plated frame.

NIB	Exc.	V.G.	Good	Fair	Poor
—	100	80	70	50	25

Gold Rush Derringer

A .22 caliber spur trigger single-shot pistol with a 2.5" barrel.

NIB	Exc.	V.G.	Good	Fair	Poor
—	100	80	70	50	25

Target Model

A .22 or .22 WMR bolt-action single-shot pistol with a 10" barrel, adjustable sights and walnut grip.

NIB	Exc.	V.G.	Good	Fair	Poor
—	50	40	30	25	20

HYDE & SHATTUCK
Hatfield, Massachusetts

Queen Derringer

A .22 caliber spur trigger single-shot pistol with a 2.5" half octagonal barrel. Blued or nickel-plated with walnut grips. The barrel normally marked "Queen," but sometimes "Hyde & Shattuck." Manufactured between 1876 and 1879.

NIB	Exc.	V.G.	Good	Fair	Poor
—	—	650	400	300	150

HYPER
Jenks, Oklahoma

I

I.G.I.
Itaiguns International
Zingone de Tressano, Italy

Domino SP602

A .22 caliber semi-automatic target pistol with a 6" barrel and 5-shot magazine (that is inserted into the action from the top), adjustable trigger and customized grips.

NIB	Exc.	V.G.	Good	Fair	Poor
—	950	725	625	450	250

Domino OP601

As above, but in .22 short caliber.

NIB	Exc.	V.G.	Good	Fair	Poor
—	950	725	625	450	250

IAI-AMERICAN LEGENDS
Houston, Texas

M-2000

This is a Government model .45 ACP pistol fitted with a 5" barrel and 7-round magazine. Fixed sights. Wood grips. Parkerized finish. Weight is about 38 oz.

NIB	Exc.	V.G.	Good	Fair	Poor
475	375	325	250	175	100

M-999

Similar to the above model but with rubber-style combat grips, extended slide stop, safety, and magazine release. Fixed sights. Offered with stainless steel slide and blued frame or all stainless steel. Supplied with 7-round magazine. Weight is about 38 oz.

NIB	Exc.	V.G.	Good	Fair	Poor
475	350	275	200	125	75

NOTE: Add $25 for stainless steel frame.

M-777

Same as M-999 but fitted with 4.25" barrel. Weight is about 36 oz.

NIB	Exc.	V.G.	Good	Fair	Poor
475	350	275	200	125	75

NOTE: Add $25 for stainless steel frame.

M-6000

This .45 ACP pistol is fitted with a 5" barrel, plastic grips, extended slide stop, safety, and magazine release. Safety is ambidextrous. Magazine capacity is 8 rounds. Fixed sights. Weight is about 38 oz.

NIB	Exc.	V.G.	Good	Fair	Poor
475	375	325	250	175	100

M-5000

This model is similar to the M-6000 but fitted with a 4.25" barrel. Weight is about 36 oz.

NIB	Exc.	V.G.	Good	Fair	Poor
475	375	325	250	175	100

INDIAN ARMS CORP.
Detroit, Michigan

Indian Arms .380

A .380 caliber semi-automatic pistol with a 3.25" barrel and 6-shot magazine. Made of stainless steel and finished either in the white or blued with walnut grips. Manufactured from 1975 to 1977.

NIB	Exc.	V.G.	Good	Fair	Poor
—	350	250	200	150	100

INGRAM
Military Armament Corp.
Atlanta, Georgia

MAC 10

A 9mm or .45 caliber open-bolt semi-automatic pistol with a 5.75" barrel and 32-shot magazine. Anodized with plastic grips. Discontinued.

NIB	Exc.	V.G.	Good	Fair	Poor
750	500	375	250	175	100

NOTE: Accessory kit (barrel extension and extra magazine) add 20 percent.

MAC 10AI

As above, but firing from a closed bolt. Add 300 percent for earlier open-bolt model.

NIB	Exc.	V.G.	Good	Fair	Poor
750	600	250	200	150	100

NOTE: Accessory kit add 20 percent.

MAC 11

As above in a smaller version and chambered for the 9mm cartridge. Add 300 percent for earlier open-bolt model.

NIB	Exc.	V.G.	Good	Fair	Poor
800	650	350	150	100	50

NOTE: Accessory kit add 20 percent.

INTERARMS
Alexandria, Virginia

An importer of arms made by Howa Machine, Star and Walther. This firm is no longer in business.

HANDGUNS

Helwan Brigadier

A 9mm semi-automatic pistol with a 4.5" barrel, fixed sights, and 8-shot magazine. Blued with plastic grips. Introduced in 1988.

NIB	Exc.	V.G.	Good	Fair	Poor
375	275	200	175	125	100

FEG R-9

A 9mm semi-automatic pistol patterned after the Browning 35 with a 13-shot magazine. Blued with walnut grips. Manufactured in 1986 and 1987.

NIB	Exc.	V.G.	Good	Fair	Poor
—	350	250	185	145	100

FEG PPH

A .380 caliber double-action semi-automatic pistol with a 3.5" barrel and 6-shot magazine. Blued with plastic grips.

NIB	Exc.	V.G.	Good	Fair	Poor
—	300	175	150	125	100

Mark II AP

A copy of the Walther PP. Chambered for the .380 ACP or .22 LR cartridge.

NIB	Exc.	V.G.	Good	Fair	Poor
300	175	125	100	75	50

Mark II APK

A copy of the Walther PPK. Chambered for the .380 ACP cartridge only.

NIB	Exc.	V.G.	Good	Fair	Poor
300	175	125	100	75	50

Mauser Parabellum Karabiner

A 9mm caliber semi-automatic carbine with an 11.75" barrel and detachable shoulder stock. Fitted in a leather case.NOTE: Only 100 were imported into the United States and this arm is subject to BATF registration.

NIB	Exc.	V.G.	Good	Fair	Poor
6500	5750	5000	4000	3000	2250

Mauser Parabellum Cartridge Counter

A reproduction of the cartridge counter Luger. Fitted in a leather case with only 100 units imported into the United States.

NIB	Exc.	V.G.	Good	Fair	Poor
4000	3000	2500	2000	1500	1000

Virginian Dragoon

A .44 Magnum single-action revolver with a 6", 7.5", 8.75", or 12" barrel, adjustable sights and 6-shot cylinder. Originally made in Switzerland and then in the U.S.A. Discontinued in 1984. Add 20 percent for Swiss manufacture.

NIB	Exc.	V.G.	Good	Fair	Poor
—	325	275	200	150	100

Stainless Dragoon

As above, in stainless steel.

NIB	Exc.	V.G.	Good	Fair	Poor
—	375	300	245	175	105

Virginian .22 Convertible

As above, in .22 caliber with a 5.5" barrel.

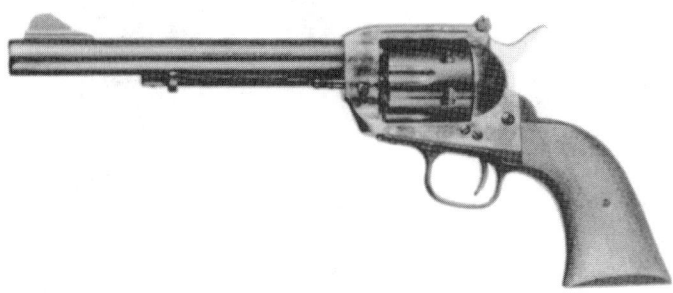

NIB	Exc.	V.G.	Good	Fair	Poor
—	275	200	125	100	75

Virginian Stainless .22 Convertible

As above, in stainless steel.

NIB	Exc.	V.G.	Good	Fair	Poor
—	295	225	165	100	80

INTERDYNAMICS OF AMERICA
Miami, Florida

KG-9

A 9mm caliber semi-automatic pistol with a 3" barrel and 36-shot magazine. Manufactured from 1981 and 1983. Note that earliest models fire from open bolt and are valued at approximately 150 percent of the values shown here.

NIB	Exc.	V.G.	Good	Fair	Poor
—	800	650	575	500	300

KG-99

As above, with a barrel shroud. Manufactured from 1981 and 1984.

NIB	Exc.	V.G.	Good	Fair	Poor
—	800	650	575	500	300

KG-99 Stainless

As above, in stainless steel. Manufactured in 1984.

NIB	Exc.	V.G.	Good	Fair	Poor
—	800	650	575	500	300

KG-99M

A more compact version of the above. Manufactured in 1984.

NIB	Exc.	V.G.	Good	Fair	Poor
—	800	650	575	500	300

INTRATEC USA, INC.
Miami, Florida

TEC-9

A 9mm caliber semi-automatic pistol with a 5" shrouded barrel and 36-shot magazine. Introduced in 1985.

NIB	Exc.	V.G.	Good	Fair	Poor
450	350	295	200	15	100

TEC-9M

As above, with a 3" barrel and 20-shot magazine. Also made in stainless steel.

NIB	Exc.	V.G.	Good	Fair	Poor
450	350	295	200	15	100

TEC-22 "Scorpion"

Similar to the above, but in .22 caliber with a 4" barrel and 30-shot magazine.

NIB	Exc.	V.G.	Good	Fair	Poor
325	225	175	100	75	50

TEC-38

A .38 caliber over-and-under double-action derringer with 3" barrels. Manufactured between 1986 and 1988.

NIB	Exc.	V.G.	Good	Fair	Poor
—	195	125	90	65	45

IRVING, W.
New York, New York

Single-Shot Derringer

A .22 caliber spur trigger single-shot pistol with a 2.75" half octagonal barrel. Silver plated brass frame, blued barrel and rosewood grips. The barrel marked "W. Irving." Manufactured in the 1860s. The .32 caliber variation has a 3" barrel and is worth approximately 40 percent more than the values listed.

NIB	Exc.	V.G.	Good	Fair	Poor
—	—	1050	475	195	125

POCKET REVOLVER
1st Model

A .31 caliber spur trigger percussion revolver with a 3" octagonal barrel, 6-shot cylinder and brass frame. The barrel marked "W. Irving." Approximately 50 were made between 1858 and 1862.

NIB	Exc.	V.G.	Good	Fair	Poor
—	—	2500	925	275	175

2nd Model

A .31 caliber percussion revolver with a 4.5" round barrel, loading lever and either brass or iron frame. The barrel marked "Address W. Irving. 20 Cliff St. N.Y." Approximately 600 manufactured with a brass frame and 1,500 with a frame of iron. The brass-frame version will bring a premium of about 35 percent.

NIB	Exc.	V.G.	Good	Fair	Poor
—	—	1450	495	200	100

ITHACA GUN CO.
Ithaca, New York

This material was supplied by Walter C. Snyder and is copyrighted in his name. Used with the author's permission. The Ithaca Gun Company was founded by William Henry Baker, John VanNatta, and Dwight McIntyre. Gun production started during the latter half of 1883 at an industrial site located on Fall Creek, Ithaca, New York. Leroy Smith joined the company by 1885 and George Livermore joined the firm in 1887. By 1894 the company was under the exclusive control of Leroy Smith and George Livermore. Many of the company's assets were purchased by the Ithaca Acquisition Corporation in 1987 and moved to King Ferry, New York, where it operated until May, 1996. Now dba Ithaca Gun Company of Upper Sandusky, Ohio.

X-Caliber

A .22 to .44 Magnum caliber single-shot pistol with 10" or 15" barrels featuring a dual firing pin system so that interchangeable barrels could be used. The Model 20 is blued; the Model 30 is Teflon coated. Introduced in 1988. Made by Sterling Arms. Add 20 percent premium for .44.

NIB	Exc.	V.G.	Good	Fair	Poor
600	475	300	225	175	125

Model 1911

The first 1911 made by Ithaca since WWII. Chambered in .45 ACP with hand-lapped carbon steel frame and slide, checkered front strap, skeletonized hammer and trigger, checkered cocobolo grips, and choice of adjustable Novak Combat or Bomar Target sights. Other features include a stainless steel Match grade barrel and bushing, and a full-length, two-piece guide rod. Optional lockable canvas case. Introduced in 2011.

NIB	Exc.	V.G.	Good	Fair	Poor
1440	1225	1000	750	—	—

NOTE: Add $100 for case.

IVER JOHNSON ARMS, INC.
Middlesex, New Jersey
SEE—AMAC

Established in 1883 in Fitchburg, Massachusetts, this company has produced a wide variety of firearms during its existence.

Trade Name Revolvers

A series of spur trigger revolvers were made by Iver Johnson bearing only the trade names such as Encore, Eclipse, Favorite, Tycoon, and Eagle. In general, the value for these revolvers are listed.

NIB	Exc.	V.G.	Good	Fair	Poor
—	250	170	120	95	65

Safety Automatic Double-Action

A .22, .32 CF, or .38 CF caliber double-action revolver produced in a variety of barrel lengths with or without exposed hammers. Manufactured between 1893 and 1950.

NIB	Exc.	V.G.	Good	Fair	Poor
—	250	170	120	95	65

Model 1900

A .22 to .38 caliber double-action revolver with a 2.5", 4.5", or 6" barrel. Blued or nickel-plated with rubber grips and no cartridge ejecting system. Manufactured between 1900 and 1947.

NIB	Exc.	V.G.	Good	Fair	Poor
—	250	170	120	95	65

Safety Cycle Automatic

Similar to the Safety Automatic with a 2" barrel.

NIB	Exc.	V.G.	Good	Fair	Poor
—	250	170	120	95	65

Petite

A .22 Short caliber double-action folding trigger revolver with a 1" barrel and 7-shot cylinder. Nickel-plated with rubber grips. Introduced in 1909.

NIB	Exc.	V.G.	Good	Fair	Poor
—	350	250	200	150	100

Supershot Sealed 8

A .22 caliber double-action revolver with a 6" barrel and counterbored 8-shot cylinder. Blued with rubber grips. Manufactured from 1919 to 1957.

NIB	Exc.	V.G.	Good	Fair	Poor
—	250	170	120	95	65

Protector Sealed 8

As above, with a 2.5" barrel.

NIB	Exc.	V.G.	Good	Fair	Poor
—	250	170	120	95	65

Supershot 9

Similar to the Supershot Sealed 8 with a 9-shot uncounterbored cylinder. Manufactured between 1929 and 1949.

NIB	Exc.	V.G.	Good	Fair	Poor
—	250	170	120	95	65

Trigger Cocker Single-Action

A .22 caliber single-action revolver with a 6" barrel and 8-shot counterbored cylinder. Blued with walnut grips. Manufactured between 1940 and 1947.

NIB	Exc.	V.G.	Good	Fair	Poor
—	200	125	100	50	25

Model 844

A .22 caliber double-action revolver with a 4.5" or 6" barrel, adjustable sights, and an 8-shot cylinder. Manufactured in the 1950s.

NIB	Exc.	V.G.	Good	Fair	Poor
—	225	140	100	80	40

Model 855

As above, but single-action with a 6" barrel. Manufactured in the 1950s.

NIB	Exc.	V.G.	Good	Fair	Poor
—	225	140	100	80	40

Model 55A Sportsmen Target

A .22 caliber single-action revolver with a 4.75" or 6" barrel, fixed sights and 8-shot cylinder. Blued with walnut grips.

NIB	Exc.	V.G.	Good	Fair	Poor
—	200	125	100	75	35

Model 55S-A Cadet

A .22 to .38 caliber single-action revolver with a 2.5" barrel and fixed sights. Blued with plastic grips. Introduced in 1955.

NIB	Exc.	V.G.	Good	Fair	Poor
—	250	170	120	95	65

Model 57A Target

As above, with a 4.5" or 6" barrel and adjustable sights. Manufactured between 1955 and 1975.

NIB	Exc.	V.G.	Good	Fair	Poor
—	175	110	85	60	35

Model 66 Trailsman

A .22 caliber double-action revolver with a 6" barrel, adjustable sights, and 8-shot cylinder. Blued with walnut grips. Manufactured between 1958 and 1975.

NIB	Exc.	V.G.	Good	Fair	Poor
—	125	75	65	50	25

Model 67 Viking

As above, with a safety hammer.

NIB	Exc.	V.G.	Good	Fair	Poor
—	125	75	65	50	25

Model 67S Viking Snub

Same as above but fitted with 2" barrel.

NIB	Exc.	V.G.	Good	Fair	Poor
—	125	75	65	50	25

Model 50

A .22 or .22 Magnum single-action revolver with a 4.75" or 6" barrel, 8-shot cylinder and either fixed or adjustable sights. Also known as the Sidewinder. Manufactured between 1961 and 1975.

NIB	Exc.	V.G.	Good	Fair	Poor
—	125	75	65	50	25

American Bulldog

A .22 to .38 caliber double-action revolver with a 2.5" or 4" barrel and adjustable sights. Blued or nickel-plated with plastic grips. Manufactured between 1974 and 1976.

NIB	Exc.	V.G.	Good	Fair	Poor
—	175	100	75	50	25

Rookie

A .38 caliber revolver with a 4" barrel and 5-shot cylinder. Blued or nickel-plated with plastic grips.

NIB	Exc.	V.G.	Good	Fair	Poor
—	175	100	75	50	25

Cattleman Series

Manufactured by Aldo Uberti and listed under that name in this book.

Model X300 Pony

A .380 semi-automatic pistol with a 3" barrel and 6-shot magazine. Blued with plastic grips. Introduced in 1975.

NIB	Exc.	V.G.	Good	Fair	Poor
—	275	195	165	135	85

Trailsman

A .22 caliber semi-automatic pistol with a 4.5" or 6" barrel and 10-shot magazine. Blued with plastic or walnut grips.

NIB	Exc.	V.G.	Good	Fair	Poor
—	275	195	165	135	85

TP22/TP25 Pistol

A .22 or .25 ACP caliber double-action semi-automatic pistol with a 2.8" barrel and 7-shot magazine. Blued or nickel-plated with plastic grips.

NIB	Exc.	V.G.	Good	Fair	Poor
—	275	195	165	135	85

THE "NEW" IVER-JOHNSON BRAND (2006)

The Iver Johnson name resurfaced in 2006 in connection with a line of firearms based in Rockledge, Florida.

Frontier Four Derringer

Four-barrel, stainless .22 LR single-action derringer with unique rotating firing pin. Based on old Sharps derringer. 5.5 oz. Introduced 2006.

NIB	Exc.	V.G.	Good	Fair	Poor
195	150	100	75	50	—

EAGLE TARGET SERIES

1911 .45

All-steel 7+1 capacity 1911 .45 ACP with 5" Government or 4.5" Commander barrel. Adjustable white outline rear sight. Adjustable trigger. Polished blue. Introduced 2006.

NIB	Exc.	V.G.	Good	Fair	Poor
650	550	425	315	250	150

1911 .22 LR

Aluminum slide and frame, 15+1 capacity 1911 .22 LR with 5" Government or 4.5" Commander barrel. 19 oz. Adjustable white outline rear sight. Adjustable trigger. Blued or stainless. Introduced 2006.

NIB	Exc.	V.G.	Good	Fair	Poor
600	500	400	300	200	100

RAVEN SERIES

1911 .45

All-steel 7+1 capacity 1911 .45 ACP with 5" Government or 4.5" Commander barrel. Fixed sights. Matte blue, Parkerized or two-tone. Introduced 2006.

NIB	Exc.	V.G.	Good	Fair	Poor
550	425	315	250	150	100

1911 .22 LR

Aluminum slide and frame, 15+1 capacity 1911 in .22 LR with 5" Government or 4.5" Commander barrel. 19 oz. Fixed sights. Matte blued or stainless two-tone finish. Introduced 2006.

NIB	Exc.	V.G.	Good	Fair	Poor
550	425	315	250	150	100

IXL
New York, New York

Pocket Revolver

A .31 caliber double-action percussion revolver with a 4" octagonal barrel and 6-shot cylinder. Blued with walnut grips. The barrel marked "IXL N.York." Approximately 750 were made without hammer spurs and 150 with side mounted hammers during the 1850s.

NIB	Exc.	V.G.	Good	Fair	Poor
—	—	—	1250	600	300

Navy Revolver

As above in .36 caliber. Approximately 100 were made with both center and side mounted hammers during the 1850s.

NIB	Exc.	V.G.	Good	Fair	Poor
—	—	—	3250	1400	500

J

JACQUESMART, JULES
Liege, Belgium

Le Monobloc

A 6.35mm semi-automatic pistol with a 2" barrel and 6-shot magazine. The slide marked "Le Monobloc/Pistolet Automatique/ Brevefte." Blued with composition grips. Production ceased in 1914.

Courtesy James Rankin

NIB	Exc.	V.G.	Good	Fair	Poor
—	550	450	350	200	100

JAGER WAFFENFABIK
Suhl, Germany

Jager Semi-Automatic Pistol

A 7.65mm caliber semi-automatic pistol with a 3" barrel and 7-shot magazine. Largely made from steel stampings. Weight is approximately 23 oz. Blued with plastic grips. The slide marked "Jager-Pistole DRP Angem." Approximately 5,500 were made prior to 1914.

Courtesy Richard M. Kumor, Sr.

NIB	Exc.	V.G.	Good	Fair	Poor
—	500	375	325	175	100

NOTE: Add 50 percent for Imperial proofed examples.

JENISON, J. & CO.
Southbridge, Connecticut

Under Hammer Pistol

A .28 caliber single-shot under hammer percussion pistol with a 4" half-octagonal barrel marked "J.Jenison & Co./Southbridge, Mass." Blued with a maple or oak grip. Manufactured during the 1850s.

NIB	Exc.	V.G.	Good	Fair	Poor
—	—	1550	850	400	200

JENNINGS F. A., INC.
Carson City, Nevada

Distributors of arms manufactured by Calwestco in Chino, California, and Bryco Firearms in Carson City, Nevada.

J-22

A .22 caliber semi-automatic pistol with a 2.5" barrel and 6-shot magazine. Aluminum, finished in bright chrome, Teflon, or satin nickel with plastic or wood grips.

NIB	Exc.	V.G.	Good	Fair	Poor
150	90	75	65	50	35

Bryco Model 25

A .25 caliber semi-automatic pistol with a 2.5" barrel and 6-shot magazine. Constructed and finished as above.

NIB	Exc.	V.G.	Good	Fair	Poor
150	90	75	65	50	35

Bryco Model 38

A .22, .32, or .380 semi-automatic pistol with a 2.8" barrel and 6-shot magazine. Constructed and finished as above.

NIB	Exc.	V.G.	Good	Fair	Poor
150	90	75	65	50	35

Bryco Model 48

Similar to the above, with a redesigned trigger guard with a squared forward section. Introduced in 1988.

NIB	Exc.	V.G.	Good	Fair	Poor
150	90	75	65	50	35

JERICHO
Israeli Military Industries, Israel

Jericho

A 9mmv or .41 Action Express double-action semi-automatic pistol with a 4.72" barrel, polygonal rifling, ambidextrous safety and fixed sights. Blued with plastic grips.

NIB	Exc.	V.G.	Good	Fair	Poor
575	500	400	350	300	200

JOHNSON, STAN, BYE & CO.
Worcester, Massachusetts

Established in 1871 by Martin Bye and Iver Johnson. This company primarily manufactured inexpensive pistols. In 1883 Johnson assumed full control of the company and renamed it the Iver Johnson Arms Company.

Defender, Eagle, Encore, Eureka, Favorite, Lion, Smoker, and Tycoon

A .22, .32, .38, or .44 caliber spur trigger revolver manufactured with various barrel lengths and normally nickel-plated. The barrel marked with one of the above trade names.

NIB	Exc.	V.G.	Good	Fair	Poor
—	—	500	200	75	25

Eclipse

A .22 caliber spur trigger single-shot pistol with a 1.5" barrel. Blued with walnut grips.

NIB	Exc.	V.G.	Good	Fair	Poor
—	—	250	100	50	25

American Bulldog

A .22, .32, or .38 caliber double-action revolver with a 3" barrel. Blued or nickel-plated with walnut or composition grips.

NIB	Exc.	V.G.	Good	Fair	Poor
—	—	250	100	50	25

JOSLYN FIREARMS COMPANY
Stonington, Connecticut

ARMY MODEL REVOLVER

A .44 caliber side hammer percussion revolver with an 8" octagonal barrel and 5-shot cylinder. Blued, case hardened with walnut grips. The barrel marked "B. F. Joslyn/Patd. May 4, 1858." Martially marked examples are worth a premium of approximately 25 percent over the values listed.

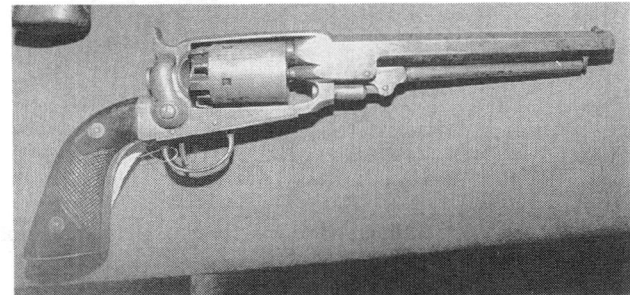

First Model

With a brass trigger guard and iron butt cap. Approximately 500 made in 1861.

NIB	Exc.	V.G.	Good	Fair	Poor
—	—	6000	4750	2000	650

Second Model

Fitted with an iron trigger guard and without a butt cap. Approximately 2,500 were made in 1861 and 1862.

NIB	Exc.	V.G.	Good	Fair	Poor
—	—	5500	4250	1600	500

JURRAS, LEE
Prescott, Arizona
SEE—Auto Mag

While Jurras is best known for manufacturing the last model of the Auto Mag, he also produced the pistol listed sold by J. & G. Sales in Prescott, Arizona.

Howdah Pistol

A .375, .416, .460, .475, .500, and .577 caliber single-shot pistol with a 12" barrel, adjustable sights and Nitex finish, built on a Thompson/Center Contender frame. Supposedly approximately 100 produced.

NIB	Exc.	V.G.	Good	Fair	Poor
—	1750	1100	800	650	500

KAHR ARMS
Blauvelt, New York

K9

This is a semi-automatic pistol chambered for the 9mm cartridge. It is a ultra-compact size. The barrel length is 3.5" and the overall length is 6". The width at the slide is .9". The magazine capacity is 7 rounds. Available in blue or electroless nickel finish. Weight is 25 oz.

NIB	Exc.	V.G.	Good	Fair	Poor
550	425	325	250	150	75

NOTE: Add $30 for blackened stainless steel slide; $130 for night sights.

Lady K9

Same as above but with lightened recoil spring.

NIB	Exc.	V.G.	Good	Fair	Poor
500	375	300	225	125	50

K9 Elite

Introduced in 2003 this 9mm model features a 3.5" barrel and polished stainless steel slide. Magazine capacity is 7 rounds. Weight is about 25 oz.

NIB	Exc.	V.G.	Good	Fair	Poor
575	425	350	275	150	100

NOTE: Add $110 for night sights.

MK9 Elite

Introduced in 2003 this 9mm model features a 3" barrel and polished stainless steel slide. Magazine capacity is 7 rounds. Weight is about 24 oz.

NIB	Exc.	V.G.	Good	Fair	Poor
725	595	450	300	175	100

NOTE: Add 15 percent for laser grips or night sights.

P9 Compact Polymer

Introduced in 1999 this 9mm model features a 3.5" barrel with double-action-only trigger. Black polymer frame with stainless steel slide. Overall length is 6", height is 4.5". Weight is about 18 oz. Magazine capacity is 7 rounds.

NIB	Exc.	V.G.	Good	Fair	Poor
625	550	475	325	250	100

K9 Compact Polymer Covert

Same as the model above but with 1/2" shorter grip frame. Weight is about 17 oz. Magazine capacity is 6 rounds. Introduced in 1999.

NIB	Exc.	V.G.	Good	Fair	Poor
625	550	475	325	250	100

TP9

Introduced in 2004 this 9mm model features a black polymer frame with matte stainless steel slide. Fitted with a 4" barrel. Weight is about 20 oz.

NIB	Exc.	V.G.	Good	Fair	Poor
625	550	475	325	250	100

NOTE: Add 15 percent for Novak night sights.

TP40

Double-action-only semi-auto pistol chambered in .40 S&W. Black polymer frame, matte stainless slide, 4" barrel, textured polymer grips, 6- or 7-round capacity depending on magazine. Drift-adjustable white bar-dot sights or Novak two-dot tritium sights. Introduced 2006.

NIB	Exc.	V.G.	Good	Fair	Poor
625	550	475	325	250	100

PM9

This 9mm model is fitted with a 3" barrel with blackened stainless steel slide and black polymer frame. Magazine capacity is 6 rounds. Weight is about 16 oz. Introduced in 2004.

NIB	Exc.	V.G.	Good	Fair	Poor
850	700	475	325	250	100

NOTE: Add 15 percent for night sights.

PM9 Micro

Fitted with a 3" barrel and chambered for the 9mm cartridge this pistol weighs about 16 oz. Polymer frame and stainless steel slide. Introduced in 2002.

NIB	Exc.	V.G.	Good	Fair	Poor
700	600	400	300	200	100

K40

This model is similar to the K9 but is chambered for the .40 S&W cartridge. Magazine capacity is 6 rounds. Weight is 26 oz.

NIB	Exc.	V.G.	Good	Fair	Poor
750	650	450	350	250	150

NOTE: Add 15 percent for night sights.

K40 Elite

Introduced in 2003 this .40 S&W model features a 3.5" barrel and polished stainless steel slide. Magazine capacity is 6 rounds, beveled magazine well. Weight is about 26 oz.

NIB	Exc.	V.G.	Good	Fair	Poor
800	700	575	400	300	175

NOTE: For night sights add 15 percent. For nickel finish add 10 percent. For black titanium finish add $15 percent. For the K40 stainless steel version add 5 percent.

K40 Covert

Similar to the K40 with a 1/2" shorter grip frame and flush fitting 5-round magazine. Barrel length is 3.5". Weight is about 25 oz. Finish is matte stainless steel.

NIB	Exc.	V.G.	Good	Fair	Poor
575	425	350	275	150	100

MK40

This .40 S&W model is fitted with a 3" barrel. Its overall length is 5.4" and height is 4". Finish is matte stainless steel. Magazine capacity is 5 rounds. Uses same magazines as K40 Covert. Introduced in 1999.

NIB	Exc.	V.G.	Good	Fair	Poor
700	600	400	300	200	100

MK40 Elite

Introduced in 2003 this .40 S&W model features a 3" barrel and polished stainless steel slide. Magazine capacity is 5 rounds, beveled magazine well. Weight is about 25 oz.

NIB	Exc.	V.G.	Good	Fair	Poor
750	625	525	425	225	150

NOTE: Add 10 percent for night sights.

P40

Similar to the P9 but chambered for the .40 S&W cartridge. Fitted with a 3.5" match grade barrel and matte stainless steel slide and black polymer frame. Supplied with two 6-round stainless steel magazines. Weight is approximately 19 oz. Introduced in 2001.

NIB	Exc.	V.G.	Good	Fair	Poor
550	425	325	250	150	75

NOTE: Night sights.

P45

Introduced in 2005 this polymer frame stainless steel slide model is chambered for the .45 ACP cartridge. Barrel length is 3.5". Fixed sights. Magazine capacity is 6 rounds. Height of pistol is 4.8". Overall length is 6.3". Slide width is 1". Weight is about 18.5 oz.

NIB	Exc.	V.G.	Good	Fair	Poor
675	550	375	275	170	125

NOTE: Add 15 percent for night sights.

MK9

This is a 9mm model with double-action-only trigger. Barrel length is 3". Overall length is 5.5" and height is 4". Weight is approximately 22 oz. One 6-round magazine and one 7-round magazine with grip extension standard. This model is fitted with a specially designed trigger for shorter trigger stroke.

NIB	Exc.	V.G.	Good	Fair	Poor
700	600	400	300	200	100

NOTE: Add 15 percent for night sights or laser grips.

CW9

This 9mm model, introduced in 2005, features a 3.5" barrel, polymer frame, and stainless steel slide. Magazine capacity is 7 rounds. Height of pistol is 4.5". Overall length is 6". Slide width is .9".

NIB	Exc.	V.G.	Good	Fair	Poor
475	375	250	200	150	100

CW40

Semi-auto with textured polymer grip chambered for .40 S&W and 6+1 capacity. Double-action with 3.6" barrel, 16.8 oz. Adjustable rear sights. Introduced 2006.

NIB	Exc.	V.G.	Good	Fair	Poor
500	375	300	225	125	50

Wilson Combat Kahr Pistols

Offered in both the K9 and K40 models this is a customized pistol by Wilson's Gun Shop. It features hard chrome frame, black slide, 30 lpi checkering on front strap, beveled magazine well and several other special features. Initial production for the K40 is 50 pistols and for the K9 25 pistols.

NIB	Exc.	V.G.	Good	Fair	Poor
1300	1050	800	550	325	200

Model 1911PKZ

This model uses the Auto-Ordnance 1911 pistols re-engineered by Kahr Arms. This model includes a Parkerized finish, lanyard loop and U.S. Army roll mark of the slide. Seven-round magazine standard. Introduced in 2001.

NIB	Exc.	V.G.	Good	Fair	Poor
475	375	250	—	—	—

Model 1911 Standard

This model features a blued finish, plastic grips with Thompson medallion and bullet logo on the slide. Seven-round magazine. Introduced in 2001.

NIB	Exc.	V.G.	Good	Fair	Poor
450	325	250	200	150	100

Model 1911C

Similar to the Standard Model but with a 4.25" barrel.

NIB	Exc.	V.G.	Good	Fair	Poor
500	400	250	200	150	100

Model 1911WGS Deluxe

This model has a blued finish, rubber wrap-around grips with Thompson medallion, high profile white dot sights, and Thompson bullet logo on the slide. Seven-round magazine. Introduced in 2001.

NIB	Exc.	V.G.	Good	Fair	Poor
575	475	425	300	225	125

P380 .380 ACP Pistol

NOTE: Add 15 percent for night sights.

NIB	Exc.	V.G.	Good	Fair	Poor
625	500	400	295	175	75

KBI, INC.
Harrisburg, Pennsylvania

PSP-25

A .25 caliber semi-automatic pistol with a 2" barrel manufactured in Charlottesville, Virginia, under license from Fabrique Nationale. Introduced in 1989.

NIB	Exc.	V.G.	Good	Fair	Poor
275	200	175	150	100	—

KEL-TEC CNC INDUSTRIES
Cocoa, Florida

Kel-Tec PMR-30

Caliber: .22 WMR, steel barrel and slide, glass reinforced Zytel grip frame and slide cover, 30-round magazine, single-action trigger, ambidextrous manual safety, fiber optic sights and accessory rail. Weight: 13.6 ounces, 4.3-inch fluted barrel with matte black finish. New 2011.

NIB	Exc.	V.G.	Good	Fair	Poor
360	310	250	200	150	75

P-11

This is a semi-automatic pistol chambered for the 9mm cartridge. It is double-action-only with a barrel length of 3.1". Overall length is 5.6". Weight is 14 oz. Magazine capacity is 10 rounds. Standard model has blued slide with black grip. Stainless steel and Parkerized finish are offered as well.

NIB	Exc.	V.G.	Good	Fair	Poor
320	225	175	125	100	100

NOTE: Add $100 for stainless steel and $40 for Parkerized finish. Add $60 for hard chrome.

P-32

This .32 caliber semi-automatic pistol is fitted with a 2.68" barrel. The action is double-action-only. Overall length is 5", overall height is 3.5". Magazine capacity is 7 rounds. Weight is about 6.6 oz. Blued slide and frame.

NIB	Exc.	V.G.	Good	Fair	Poor
305	225	175	125	100	100

NOTE: Add $40 for Parkerized finish. Add $60 for hard chrome.

P-3AT

This model is chambered for the .380 cartridge and fitted with a 2.75" barrel. Blued finish. Magazine capacity is 6 rounds. Weight is about 7.3 oz.

NIB	Exc.	V.G.	Good	Fair	Poor
310	225	175	125	100	100

NOTE: Add $40 for Parkerized finish and $60 for hard chrome finish.

P-40

This model is similar to the P-11 but chambered for the .40 S&W cartridge. Barrel length is 3.3". Magazine capacity is 9 rounds. Weight is approximately 16 oz. Blued finish.

NIB	Exc.	V.G.	Good	Fair	Poor
320	225	175	125	100	100

NOTE: Add $40 for Parkerized finish. Add $60 for hard chrome.

PLR-16

A 5.56 mm NATO gas-operated, semi-automatic AR-15-style long-range pistol. Windage-adjustable rear sight. Picatinny rail. Muzzle threaded for muzzle-brake. 9.2" barrel, 51 oz. 10-round or M-16 magazine. Blued finish, polymer construction. Introduced 2006.

NIB	Exc.	V.G.	Good	Fair	Poor
650	550	425	325	200	100

KENDALL, NICANOR
Windsor, Vermont

Under Hammer Pistol

A .31 to .41 caliber under hammer percussion pistol with 4" to 10" octagonal/round barrels marked "N.Kendall/Windsor,Vt." Browned or blued with brass mounts and maple grips. Manufactured in the 1850s.

NIB	Exc.	V.G.	Good	Fair	Poor
—	—	1950	600	200	125

KENO
Unknown

Derringer

A .22 caliber single-shot spur trigger pistol with a 2.5" barrel, brass frame, and walnut grips. The barrel blued or nickel-plated and marked "Keno."

NIB	Exc.	V.G.	Good	Fair	Poor
—	—	750	500	175	100

KERR
London, England

Kerr Revolver

A .44 caliber double-action percussion revolver with a 5.5" barrel and 6-shot cylinder. Blued with walnut grips. The frame marked "Kerr's Patent 648" ; and "London Armoury Bermondsey."

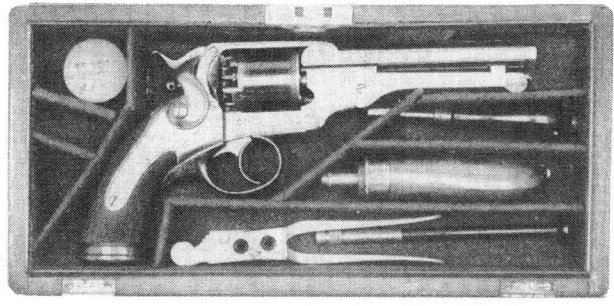

Courtesy Bonhams & Butterfields, San Francisco, California

NIB	Exc.	V.G.	Good	Fair	Poor
—	—	4250	2000	800	300

KIMBALL ARMS COMPANY
Detroit, Michigan

Semi-Automatic Pistol

A .30 carbine caliber semi-automatic pistol with a 3.5" or 5" barrel. Blued with plastic grips. Also believed to have been made in .22 Hornet and .357 Magnum, though few legitimate examples have been seen. Manufactured from 1955 to 1958. Approximately 238 were made.

NIB	Exc.	V.G.	Good	Fair	Poor
—	3000	2000	1500	1000	450

KIMBER MFG., INC.
Yonkers, New York

Kimber of Oregon was established in April 1979 by Greg and Jack Warne. The company produced high quality rimfire and centerfire rifles until going out of business in early 1991. Kimber produced approximately 60,000 rifles during its operation. In April 1993, Greg Warne opened Kimber of America in Clackamas, Oregon. This new company presently manufactures the same high-quality rifles built on an improved Model 82 Sporter action and stock, but in rimfire only. In 1995 the company expanded its product line to include centerfire rifles as well as a 1911 .45 ACP semi-automatic pistol line. In 1997 manufacturing operations were consolidated in the New York pistol factory and the two factories in Oregon were closed.

CUSTOM SERIES

First introduced in 1996 this is a quality built American-made 1911 designed by Chip McCormick for Kimber. **NOTE:** In 2001 Kimber phased in a new safety system on its pistols: the Kimber firing pin safety. Models with this new firing pin safety will bear the designation "II" as part of their model name.

Custom

Barrel length is 5" with black oxide finish fixed sights. Black synthetic grips. Magazine capacity is 8 rounds. Weight is about 38 oz.

NIB	Exc.	V.G.	Good	Fair	Poor
1000	800	650	475	300	150

NOTE: For Walnut grips add $10.00. For night sights add $100.

Custom II

NIB	Exc.	V.G.	Good	Fair	Poor
825	675	500	375	250	125

NOTE: For Walnut grips add $10.00. For night sights add $100.

Custom Heritage Edition

Chambered for .45 ACP cartridge and fitted with a 5" barrel. Magazine capacity is 7 rounds. Checkered front strap, ambidextrous thumb safety, aluminum trigger, hand checkered rosewood grips, special edition markings on slide. Sights are low-profile fixed. Weight is about 38 oz. Introduced in 2000.

NIB	Exc.	V.G.	Good	Fair	Poor
1150	950	700	495	300	150

Custom Stainless

Similar to Custom but in stainless steel.

NIB	Exc.	V.G.	Good	Fair	Poor
1000	800	650	475	300	150

NOTE: For night sights add $100.

Stainless Limited Edition

Similar to the Custom Stainless except for black thumb release, black grip safety, black magazine release button, and black barrel bushing. Limited to approximately 1,200 pistols.

NIB	Exc.	V.G.	Good	Fair	Poor
1200	950	775	575	350	150

Custom Target

The Custom Target has the same features as the Custom with the addition of an adjustable rear sight.

NIB	Exc.	V.G.	Good	Fair	Poor
825	675	500	375	250	125

Custom TLE II (Tactical Law Enforcement)

Introduced in 2003 this model features Meprolight three-dot night sights and 30 lpi checkering on the front strap. Magazine capacity is 7 rounds. Weight is about 38 oz.

NIB	Exc.	V.G.	Good	Fair	Poor
900	700	500	375	250	125

NOTE: In 2004 a stainless steel version was offered. Add $135 for this model.

Custom TLE/RL II

This model is similar ot the TLE with the addition of an integral tactical rail. Weight is about 39 oz. Introduced in 2004.

NIB	Exc.	V.G.	Good	Fair	Poor
1050	825	675	450	295	150

Stainless II

Chambered for the .45 ACP or .40 S&W cartridge and fitted with a 5" barrel with fixed low profile sights. Both frame and slide are satin stainless steel. Magazine capacity for the .45 ACP is 7 rounds and 8 rounds for the .40 S&W. Weight is about 38 oz.

NIB	Exc.	V.G.	Good	Fair	Poor
865	650	450	275	150	100

Stainless II (polished)

As above but chambererd for the .38 Super cartridge. Frame and slide are polished stainless steel. Magazine capacity is 9 rounds. Weight is about 38 oz. Introduced in 2005.

NIB	Exc.	V.G.	Good	Fair	Poor
1150	950	700	495	300	150

Kimber Stainless Ultra TLE II

1911-syle semiauto pistol chambered in .45 ACP. Features include 7-round magazine; full length guide rod; aluminum frame with stainless slide; satin silver finish; checkered frontstrap; 3-inch barrel; tactical gray double diamond grips; tritium 3-dot night sights. MSRP: $1210.

Stainless Target II

Chambered for the .45 ACP or .38 Super cartridge with a slide and frame machined from stainless steel. Weight is 38 oz.

NIB	Exc.	V.G.	Good	Fair	Poor
980	750	600	400	250	125

Stainless Target II 9mm/10mm

As above but chambered for the 9mm or 10mm cartridge. The 9mm pistol has a magazine capacity of 9 rounds and the 10mm has a magazine capacity of 8 rounds. Both of these pistols are produced on a one-run basis only with production in the low hundreds. Introduced in 2003.

NIB	Exc.	V.G.	Good	Fair	Poor
1150	950	700	495	300	150

Stainless Target II (polished)

As above but chambered for the .38 Super cartridge. Frame and slide are polished stainless steel. Magazine capacity is 9 rounds. Weight is about 38 oz. Introduced in 2005.

NIB	Exc.	V.G.	Good	Fair	Poor
1200	950	775	575	350	150

Stainless Target Limited Edition

Similar to the Stainless Target but with black thumb safety, black grip safety, black slide release, and black barrel bushing. This model is limited to approximately 700 pistols. Introduced in 1998.

NIB	Exc.	V.G.	Good	Fair	Poor
900	700	500	375	250	125

Custom Royal

This has all the features of the Custom plus a high polish blue finish, hand checkered walnut grips, and long guide rod.

NIB	Exc.	V.G.	Good	Fair	Poor
900	700	500	375	250	125

Custom Royal II

NIB	Exc.	V.G.	Good	Fair	Poor
950	750	500	375	250	125

Custom TLE/RL II Special Edition

This .45 ACP pistol is fitted with a 5" barrel with fixed night sights. Steel frame and slide with tactical accessory rail on frame. Black rubber grips. Black matte finish. Magazine capacity is 7 rounds. Weight is about 38 oz. Introduced in 2003.

NIB	Exc.	V.G.	Good	Fair	Poor
1150	950	700	495	300	150

Warrior

This model, introduced in 2005, is chambered for the .45 ACP cartridge and fitted with a 5" barrel with night sights. Grips are Kimber G-10 Tactical with lanyard loop. Accessory rail on frame. KimPro finish. Magazine capacity is 7 rounds. Weight is about 39 oz.

NIB	Exc.	V.G.	Good	Fair	Poor
1200	950	775	575	350	150

Desert Warrior

This model is similar to the Warrior but with a desert tan finish and lighter tan G10 tactical grips.

NIB	Exc.	V.G.	Good	Fair	Poor
1200	950	775	575	350	150

25TH ANNIVERSARY LIMITED EDITIONS

Anniversary Custom

Introduced in 2004 this is a limited edition of 1,911 pistol. Chambered for the .45 ACP cartridge. Select walnut grips. Serial numbered: KAPC0001-KAPC1911.

NIB	Exc.	V.G.	Good	Fair	Poor
850	650	450	275	150	100

Anniversary Gold Match

This .45 ACP pistol is limited to 500 pistols. Serial numbered KAPG0001-KAPG0500.

NIB	Exc.	V.G.	Good	Fair	Poor
1200	950	775	575	350	150

Anniversary Match Pair Custom

This is a matched pair of Custom pistols in .45 ACP. Matching serial numbers and presentation case. Limited to 250 pairs.

NIB	Exc.	V.G.	Good	Fair	Poor
2750	2100	—	—	—	—

GOLD MATCH SERIES

Gold Match

All of the features of the Custom Royal plus BoMar adjustable sights, fancy checkered diamond grips.

NIB	Exc.	V.G.	Good	Fair	Poor
1200	950	775	575	350	150

Gold Match II

NIB	Exc.	V.G.	Good	Fair	Poor
1500	1200	950	575	400	150

Stainless Gold Match

Similar to the Gold Match except slide and frame are stainless steel. Introduced in 1998.

NIB	Exc.	V.G.	Good	Fair	Poor
1200	950	775	575	350	150

Gold Team Match II

Introduced in 2003 this .45 ACP 5" barrel model features a stainless steel slide and frame along with a Kimber Tactical Extractor with loaded chamber indicator. Front strap is checkered 30 lpi and the grips are red, white, and blue USA Shooting Team logo. Weight is about 38 oz.

NIB	Exc.	V.G.	Good	Fair	Poor
1550	1225	950	575	400	150

Team Match II .38 Super

As above but without external extractor. Limited production run. Introduced in 2003.

NIB	Exc.	V.G.	Good	Fair	Poor
1500	1200	950	575	400	150

TEN II SERIES

In 2002 the Polymer series pistols were upgraded to the Ten II series with the addition of a firing pin block safety, a Kimber-made frame of improved dimensions, and an external extractor. The orginial Polymer pistol magazines of 10 and 14 rounds will interchange with the newer Ten II Series pistols.

Polymer

This model features a polymer frame with a matte black oxide slide. Sights are McCormick low profile. Barrel length is 5" and overall length is 8.75". Weight is about 34 oz. Magazine is 14 rounds. One 14-round magazine is supplied with gun when new.

NIB	Exc.	V.G.	Good	Fair	Poor
850	675	550	395	200	100

Polymer Stainless

Similar to the Polymer model but with a stainless steel slide. Weight is the same as the Polymer model; 34 oz.

NIB	Exc.	V.G.	Good	Fair	Poor
925	750	600	425	225	125

Polymer Target

Introduced in 1998 this pistol has a matte black oxide slide with adjustable sights. Magazine is 14 rounds. Weight is about 34 oz.

NIB	Exc.	V.G.	Good	Fair	Poor
950	775	625	450	245	150

Polymer Stainless Target

Same as above but with stainless steel slide. Introduced in 1998.

NIB	Exc.	V.G.	Good	Fair	Poor
950	775	625	450	245	150

Polymer Pro Carry Stainless

Chambered for the .45 ACP cartridge with a 4" barrel. McCormick Low Profile sights. Stainless steel slide with black polymer frame. Weight is about 32 oz. Magazine capacity is 14 rounds. Introduced in 1999.

NIB	Exc.	V.G.	Good	Fair	Poor
850	675	550	395	200	100

Polymer Stainless Gold Match

This model is similar to the Polymer Gold Match with the addition of a stainless steel slide. This model is also chambered for several calibers: .45 ACP, .40 S&W, 9mm, and .38 Super. Weight is about 34 oz.

NIB	Exc.	V.G.	Good	Fair	Poor
1200	950	775	575	350	150

Pro Carry Ten II

This .45 ACP model features a 4" bull barrel with no barrel bushing. Stainess steel slide. Weight is about 28 oz.

NIB	Exc.	V.G.	Good	Fair	Poor
850	675	550	395	200	100

Ultra Ten II

Introduced in 2001 this pistol is chambered for the .45 ACP cartridge and fitted with a 3" barrel. Stainless steel slide and black Polymer frame. Supplied with 10-round magazine. McCormick low-profile sights. Weight is about 24 oz.

NIB	Exc.	V.G.	Good	Fair	Poor
850	675	550	395	200	100

Ultra Ten CDP II

Introduced in 2003 this model features night sights and rounded edges. Fitted with a 3" bull barrel. Chambered for the .45 ACP. Weight is about 24 oz.

NIB	Exc.	V.G.	Good	Fair	Poor
1200	950	775	575	350	150

Gold Match Ten II

This .45 ACP 5" barrel model has all of the standard features of the Gold Match with a black Polymer frame and blued steel slide. Magazine capacity is 14 rounds. Weight is approximately 34 oz.

NIB	Exc.	V.G.	Good	Fair	Poor
1200	950	775	575	350	150

BP Ten II

This .45 ACP pistol has a 5" barrel and a 10-round magazine capacity. Steel slide with polymer frame. Fixed sights. Black matte finish. Weight is about 30 oz. Introduced in 2003.

NIB	Exc.	V.G.	Good	Fair	Poor
850	675	550	395	200	100

Pro BP Ten II

As above but with 4" barrel. Weight is about 31 oz. Introduced in 2003.

NIB	Exc.	V.G.	Good	Fair	Poor
850	675	550	395	200	100

COMPACT SERIES

Compact

These steel frame and slide pistols are fitted with a 4" bull barrel and shortened grip (.4" shorter than full size). Offered in .45 ACP. Finish is matte black oxide. Grips are black synthetic. Overall length is 7.7". Weight is about 43 oz. Introduced in 1998.

NIB	Exc.	V.G.	Good	Fair	Poor
675	550	400	300	200	100

Compact Aluminum

This model has the same appearance as the Compact but with an aluminum frame. Matte black finish. Weight is approximately 28 oz. Introduced in 1998.

NIB	Exc.	V.G.	Good	Fair	Poor
675	550	400	300	200	100

Compact Stainless

Same as the Compact model but with a stainless steel slide and frame. Offered in both .45 ACP and .40 S&W. Introduced in 1998.

NIB	Exc.	V.G.	Good	Fair	Poor
850	675	550	395	200	10

Pro Carry Stainless Night Sights

As above but fitted with night sights.

NIB	Exc.	V.G.	Good	Fair	Poor
950	750	625	450	275	175

Pro TLE/RL II

Introduced in 2005 this model features a 45 ACP with 4" barrel with night sights. Slide and frame are steel with a steel finish. Accessory rail on frame. Magazine capacity is 7 rounds. Weight is about 36 oz.

NIB	Exc.	V.G.	Good	Fair	Poor
850	675	550	395	200	100

Compact Stainless II

NIB	Exc.	V.G.	Good	Fair	Poor
900	675	500	375	250	125

Compact Stainless Aluminum

Offered in both .45 ACP and .40 S&W this model features a 4" barrel with stainless steel slide and aluminum frame. Weight is about 28 oz.

NIB	Exc.	V.G.	Good	Fair	Poor
750	600	475	300	200	100

NOTE: Add $25 for .40 S&W models.

PRO CARRY

Pro Carry II

Introduced in 1998 this .45 ACP or .40 S&W model features a full-size aluminum frame and 4" slide and bull barrel. Other features are match grade trigger, beveled magazine well, full-length guide rod, low-profile combat sights, and 7-round magazine. Finish is matte black oxide. Weight is approximately 28 oz. In 2005 this model was offered in 9mm.

NIB	Exc.	V.G.	Good	Fair	Poor
1150	950	700	495	300	150

Stainless Pro TLE/RL II

As above but with stainless steel frame and slide. Introduced in 2005.

NIB	Exc.	V.G.	Good	Fair	Poor
1250	925	750	525	350	175

Kimber Super Carry Pro

1911-style semi-auto pistol chambered in .45 ACP. Features include 8-round magazine; ambidextrous thumb safety; carry melt profiling; full length guide rod; aluminum frame with stainless slide; satin silver finish; super carry serrations; 4-inch barrel; micarta laminated grips; tritium night sights.

NIB	Exc.	V.G.	Good	Fair	Poor
1300	1125	950	500	300	200

SUPER CARRY SERIES

Kimber Super Carry Custom HD

The .45 Carry Pro pistols feature a stainless steel slide and frame, match-grade barrel and bushing, ambidextrous thumb safety, beaver-tail tang, and directional serrations on the slide, mainspring housing and front strap. Other features include night sights, an 8-round magazine, rounded heel and "melt" treatment for easy carrying. Weight: 38 ounces, 5-inch barrel and Kim-Pro

NIB	Exc.	V.G.	Good	Fair	Poor
850	675	550	395	200	100

Pro Carry II Night Sights

As above but fitted with night sights.

NIB	Exc.	V.G.	Good	Fair	Poor
900	725	600	425	250	150

Pro Carry Stainless

Same as Pro Carrybut with stainless steel slide.

finish. Super Carry Pro has 4-inch barred, Ultra has 3-inch and 6-round magazine. Introduced in 2011.

NIB	Exc.	V.G.	Good	Fair	Poor
1400	1200	1000	750	300	200

Kimber Super Carry Ultra Plus

Combines the full-size, round-heel frame of the Carry Pro with the short slide and 3-inch barrel of the Carry Ultra. Lightweight alloy frame reduces weight to 25 ounces with 8-round magazine. Introduced in 2011.

NIB	Exc.	V.G.	Good	Fair	Poor
650	535	450	400	300	200

CLASSIC .45 PISTOLS

ULTRA CARRY II SERIES
Ultra Carry

This model is chambered for the .45 ACP or .40 S&W cartridge. It is fitted with a 3" barrel with McCormick low profile sights. Grips are black synthetic. Magazine capacity is 7 rounds. Weight is about 25 oz. Black oxide finish. Introduced in 1999.

NIB	Exc.	V.G.	Good	Fair	Poor
1350	1150	965	725	300	200

Kimber Solo Carry

A micro compact pistol designed for concealed carry, this is a single-action, striker-fired 9mm with stainless steel slide, alloy frame, 6-round magazine, ambidextrous thumb safety and magazine release. Weight is 17 ounces, barrel length 2.7-inches. Width is 1.2-inches and overall length 5.5-inches. Finish is Kim Pro or bright stainless. Introduced in 2011.

NIB	Exc.	V.G.	Good	Fair	Poor
765	600	475	350	200	100

NOTE: Add $100 for night sights.

Ultra Carry II

NIB	Exc.	V.G.	Good	Fair	Poor
800	625	500	375	225	125

Ultra Carry Stainless

Same as above but with stainless steel slide.

NIB	Exc.	V.G.	Good	Fair	Poor
850	650	525	395	245	135

NOTE: Add $25 for .40 S&W model. Add $100 for night sights.

Ultra Carry Stainless II

NIB	Exc.	V.G.	Good	Fair	Poor
875	675	550	425	260	150

CUSTOM SHOP PISTOLS

Centennial Edition 1911

Highly artistic 1911-style semiauto pistol chambered in .45 ACP. Features include color case-hardened steel frame; extended thumb safety; charcoal-blue finished steel slide; 5-inch match grade barrel; special serial number; solid smooth ivory grips; nitre blue pins; adjustable sights; presentation case. Edition limited to 250 units. Finished by Doug Turnbull Restoration. MSRP: $4352.

Royal Carry

This is a limited edition of 600 pistols. Chambered for .45 ACP and fitted with a 4" barrel with night sights. Hand checkered rosewood grips. Steel slide and aluminum frame. High polish blue finish. Magazine capacity is 7 rounds. Weight is approximately 28 oz. Introduced in 1998.

NIB	Exc.	V.G.	Good	Fair	Poor
1000	800	650	475	300	150

Elite Carry

Introduced in 1998 this custom shop pistol is limited to 1,200 pistols. Chambered for .45 ACP with a 4" barrel with night sights. Frame is aluminum with black oxide finish. Slide is steel with stainless steel finish. Ambidextrous extended thumb safety, checkered front strap, match trigger, and hand checkered rosewood grips. Magazine capacity is 7 rounds. Weight is about 28 oz.

NIB	Exc.	V.G.	Good	Fair	Poor
1000	800	650	475	300	150

Gold Guardian

This limited edition custom shop pistol is limited to 300 pistols. Chambered for .45 ACP and fitted with a 5" barrel with fixed night sights. Stainless steel slide and frame. Ambidextrous extended thumb safety, match grade barrel, extended magazine well, match trigger, and special markings and serial number. Magazine capacity is 8 rounds and weight is about 38 oz. Introduced in 1998.

NIB	Exc.	V.G.	Good	Fair	Poor
1500	1200	950	575	400	150

Combat Carry

This 4" barrel pistol is chambered for the .45 ACP or .40 S&W cartridge. Many custom features. Special markings. Stainless steel slide and blued frame. Night sights standard. Weight is approximately 28 oz. Introduced in 1999.

NIB	Exc.	V.G.	Good	Fair	Poor
1050	850	675	500	325	165

Gold Combat

This full-size pistol is chambered for the .45 ACP cartridge. Many custom features. Night sights standard. Special markings. Weight is about 38 oz. Blued slide and frame. Introduced in 1999.

NIB	Exc.	V.G.	Good	Fair	Poor
1680	1250	925	700	350	175

Gold Combat II

NIB	Exc.	V.G.	Good	Fair	Poor
1730	1300	925	750	425	200

Gold Combat Stainless

Same as the model above but with stainless steel slide.

NIB	Exc.	V.G.	Good	Fair	Poor
1725	1300	925	750	425	200

Gold Combat Stainless II

NIB	Exc.	V.G.	Good	Fair	Poor
1680	1250	925	700	350	175

Super Match

This is Kimber's most accurate .45 ACP pistol. Fitted with a 5" barrel and many special features. Adjustable sights. Weight is about 38 oz. Stainless steel slide and frame with two-tone finish. Introduced in 1999.

NIB	Exc.	V.G.	Good	Fair	Poor
1925	1500	900	600	350	175

Super Match II

NIB	Exc.	V.G.	Good	Fair	Poor
1985	1550	900	600	350	175

LTP II

Designed for limited pistol competition. Fitted with external extractor, flat top serrated slide with adjustable sights, and extended and beveled magazine well. Fitted with a 5" barrel with tungsten guide rod. Ten-round magazine. Front strap has 20 lpi checkering. Weight is about 38 oz.

NIB	Exc.	V.G.	Good	Fair	Poor
2100	1575	925	625	375	200

Raptor II

Introduced in 2005 this .45 ACP model features a 5" barrel with night sights. Blued finished. This model also has scale serrations on front strap and slide along with scaled zebra wood grips. Magazine capacity is 8 rounds. Weight is about 38 oz.

NIB	Exc.	V.G.	Good	Fair	Poor
1215	925	750	525	350	175

Pro Raptor II

Similar to the Raptor II except for a 4" barrel. Weight is about 35 oz. Introduced in 2005.

NIB	Exc.	V.G.	Good	Fair	Poor
1100	825	700	500	300	125

Grand Raptor

This is a .45 ACP pistol with 5" match grade stainless steel barrel with adjustable night sights, black aluminum trigger, and rosewood grips. The slide serrations are lizard scale. Stainless steel frame. The slide is matte black and engraved with the Custom Shop logo.

NIB	Exc.	V.G.	Good	Fair	Poor
1500	1200	950	575	400	150

Ultra Raptor II

This .45 ACP model features a 3" ramped match grade bushingless bull barrel. Fixed night sights. Ambidextrous thumb safety. Lizard scale slide serrations. Introduced in 2005.

NIB	Exc.	V.G.	Good	Fair	Poor
1250	925	750	525	350	175

Ultra RCP II

Introduced in 2003 this pistol features a 3" barrel, aluminum frame, sight rail, and a 26 oz. weight. Chambered for the .45 ACP cartridge. Magazine capacity is 7 rounds. No longer in production.

NIB	Exc.	V.G.	Good	Fair	Poor
1300	975	795	550	370	195

Gold Combat RL II

Similar to the above model but with premium trigger, KimPro finish, and rosewood grips. Magazine capacity is 8 rounds. Weight is about 38 oz. Introduced in 2003.

Gold Combat RL II

NIB	Exc.	V.G.	Good	Fair	Poor
1775	1325	1100	700	425	245

Target Match

A limited edition of 1,000 pistols chambered for the .45 ACP cartridge. Matte black frame with adjustable sights. Match grade barrel and chamber. Solid aluminum trigger. Checkered front strap and underside of trigger guard. Special serial numbers: KTM0001-KTM1000. Introduced in 2005.

NIB	Exc.	V.G.	Good	Fair	Poor
1400	1050	875	650	395	175

SuperAmerica

Billed as Kimber's ultimate top-of-the-line custom 1911. Polished/matte blue finish, scroll engraving, mammoth ivory grips, presentation case with matching sheath knife. Introduced 2007.

NIB	Exc.	V.G.	Good	Fair	Poor
3000	2250	1700	1000	600	225

CDP SERIES (CUSTOM DEFENSE PACKAGE)

Ultra CDP

This custom shop model features a 3" barrel, night sights, hand checkered rosewood grips, numerous custom features. Finish is stainless steel slide and matte black frame. Chambered for .45 ACP cartridge. Magazine capacity is 6 rounds. Weight is about 25 oz. Introduced in 2000.

NIB	Exc.	V.G.	Good	Fair	Poor
1100	825	700	500	300	125

Ultra CDP II

Compact 1911-syle semiauto pistol chambered in .45 ACP. Features include 7-round magazine; ambidextrous thumb safety; carry melt profiling; full length guide rod; aluminum frame with stainless slide; satin silver finish; checkered frontstrap; 3-inch barrel; rosewood double diamond Crimson Trace lasergrips grips; tritium 3-dot night sights.

NIB	Exc.	V.G.	Good	Fair	Poor
1550	1350	850	525	350	175

Compact CDP

This model, introduced in 2000, features a 4" bull barrel, night sights, hand checkered rosewood grips, and other custom features. Stainless steel slide and matte black frame. Chambered for .45 ACP cartridge. Magazine capacity is 6 rounds. Weight is about 28 oz.

NIB	Exc.	V.G.	Good	Fair	Poor
1200	950	775	575	350	150

Compact CDP II

NIB	Exc.	V.G.	Good	Fair	Poor
1250	995	795	595	350	150

Pro CDP

This model is similar to the Compact CDP but with a full length grip. Magazine capacity is 7 rounds and weight is about 28 oz. Introduced in 2000.

NIB	Exc.	V.G.	Good	Fair	Poor
1100	825	700	500	300	125

Pro CDP II

NIB	Exc.	V.G.	Good	Fair	Poor
1175	900	775	550	350	150

Custom CDP

This .45 ACP full-size pistol is fitted with a 5" match grade barrel and stainless steel slide with front and rear beveled serrations. Matte black steel frame with checkered rosewood grips. Night sights standard. Introduced in 2001.

NIB	Exc.	V.G.	Good	Fair	Poor
1200	950	775	575	350	150

Custom CDP II

NIB	Exc.	V.G.	Good	Fair	Poor
1250	1000	800	600	375	165

ECLIPSE II SERIES

Eclipse Custom II

Chambered for the .45 ACP cartridge and fitted with a 5" barrel with match-grade bushing. Fixed night sights. Magazine capacity is 8 rounds. Weight is about 38 oz. Introduced in 2002. In 2005 this model was offered in 10mm.

NIB	Exc.	V.G.	Good	Fair	Poor
1175	900	775	550	350	150

NOTE: Add $110 for 10mm model.

Eclipse Target II

Similar to the Eclipse Custom II with the addition of adjustable night sights. Introduced in 2002.

NIB	Exc.	V.G.	Good	Fair	Poor
1200	950	775	575	350	150

Eclipse Ultra II

This .45 ACP pistol with a 3" barrel has a slide machined from a stainless steel forging. Frontstrap checkering. Fixed night sights. Magazine capacity is 7 rounds. Weight is about 34 oz. Introduced in 2002.

NIB	Exc.	V.G.	Good	Fair	Poor
1100	825	700	500	300	125

Eclipse Pro II

This model is similar to the Eclipse Ultra II but features a full-length grip frame and a 4" barrel. Fixed night sights. Introduced in 2002.

NIB	Exc.	V.G.	Good	Fair	Poor
1100	825	700	500	300	125

Eclipse Pro Target II

Similar to the Eclipse Pro but fitted with adjustable night sights. Introduced in 2002.

NIB	Exc.	V.G.	Good	Fair	Poor
1190	950	725	525	325	150

TACTICAL SERIES

This series of pistols was introduced in 2003. Each pistol has 30 lpi checkering on the front strap and under the trigger guard, Meprolight three dot night sights, an extended and beveled magazine well, magazines with extended bumper pads, laminated grips, and match grade barrel and chamber.

Tactical Custom II

Chambered for the .45 ACP cartridge and fitted with a 5" barrel. Magazine capacity is 7 rounds. Weight is about 31 oz.

NIB	Exc.	V.G.	Good	Fair	Poor
1250	1000	800	600	375	165

Tactical Pro II

This model is fitted with a 4" barrel. Weight is about 28 oz.

NIB	Exc.	V.G.	Good	Fair	Poor
1250	1000	800	600	375	165

Tactical Ultra II

This model is fitted with a 3" barrel. Weight is about 25 oz.

NIB	Exc.	V.G.	Good	Fair	Poor
1250	1000	800	600	375	165

COVERT SERIES

Custom Covert II

1911-style semi-auto carry gun chambered in .45 ACP. Aluminum frame, steel slide. Frame finished in Desert Tan; slide finished in matte black. Five-inch barrel with 3-dot sights. Introduced in 2007.

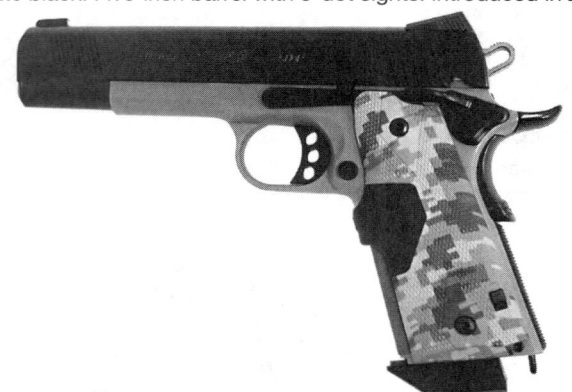

NIB	Exc.	V.G.	Good	Fair	Poor
1500	1200	950	575	400	150

Pro Covert II

Similar to Custom Covert II but with four-inch barrel. Introduced in 2007.

NIB	Exc.	V.G.	Good	Fair	Poor
1500	1200	950	575	400	150

Ultra Covert II

Similar to Pro Covert II but with three-inch barrel. Introduced 2007.

NIB	Exc.	V.G.	Good	Fair	Poor
1300	975	795	550	370	195

KPD 40

Kimber Pro Defense double-action .40 S&W semi-auto. Comes with two 12-round magazines for 12+1 capacity. 4.1" barrel, 25 oz. Fixed white dot sights. Introduced 2006.

NIB	Exc.	V.G.	Good	Fair	Poor
550	425	300	195	125	100

AEGIS SERIES

Pro Aegis II

1911-style semi-auto carry gun chambered in 9mm Parabellum. Aluminum frame, steel slide. Frame finished in matte aluminum; slide finished in matte black. Four-inch bull barrel with 3-dot sights. Introduced in 2007.

NIB	Exc.	V.G.	Good	Fair	Poor
1000	800	650	475	300	150

Custom Aegis II

Full-size 1911-style semi-auto carry gun chambered in 9mm Parabellum. Aluminum frame, steel slide. Frame finished in matte aluminum; slide finished in matte black. Five-inch bull barrel with 3-dot sights. Introduced in 2007.

NIB	Exc.	V.G.	Good	Fair	Poor
1100	825	700	500	300	125

Ultra Aegis II

Similar to Pro Aegis II but with four-inch barrel. Introduced in 2007.

NIB	Exc.	V.G.	Good	Fair	Poor
1100	825	700	500	300	125

RIMFIRE SERIES

Rimfire Custom

Introduced in 2003 this .22 caliber pistol features a 5" barrel with fixed sights and 10-round magazine. Matte black or silver anodized finish. Weight is about 23 oz.

NIB	Exc.	V.G.	Good	Fair	Poor
750	525	365	225	150	100

Rimfire Target

As above but fitted with adjustable sights. In 2004 this model was also available in .17 Mach 2 caliber.

NIB	Exc.	V.G.	Good	Fair	Poor
800	575	400	275	200	125

Rimfire Super

This model was introduced in 2004 and features a serrated flat top slide with flutes in the upper corners, an ambidextrous thumb safety, an alimunum trigger, and two-tone finish. Weight is about 23 oz.

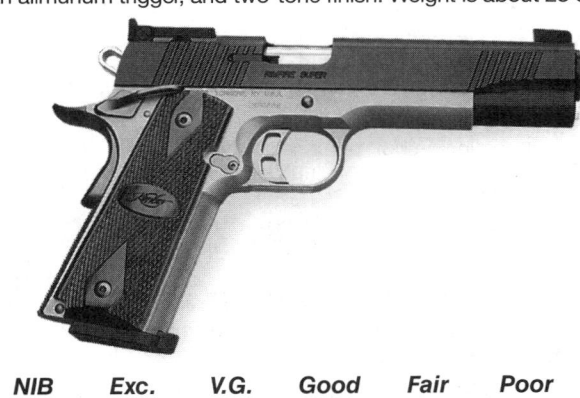

NIB	Exc.	V.G.	Good	Fair	Poor
1100	825	700	500	300	125

.22 LR Conversion Kit

Introduced in 1998 this Kimber kit features a complete upper assembly: slide, barrel, guide rod, shock buffer, and 10-round magazine. Finish is satin silver or satin blue. Will fit all Kimber 1911 .45 ACP models. In 2005 this kit was also offered for the .17 Mach 2 cartridge conversion.

NIB	Exc.	V.G.	Good	Fair	Poor
300	250	200	125	75	25

KING PIN
Unknown

Derringer

A .22 caliber spur trigger brass constructed single-shot pistol with a 2.5" barrel and walnut grips. Believed to have been made during the 1880s.

NIB	Exc.	V.G.	Good	Fair	Poor
—	—	675	200	100	50

KIRRIKALE, ENDUSTRISI
Ankara, Turkey

Kirrikale Pistol

A 7.65 or 9mm short caliber semi-automatic pistol with a 3.5" barrel and 6-shot magazine. Blued with plastic grips. The slide marked "MKE" ; and "Kirrikale Tufek Fb Cal.—." Imported by Firearms Center in Victoria, Texas, and also by Mandall Shooting Supplies. This was an unauthorized copy of the Walther PP that was imported into the U.S. briefly.

NIB	Exc.	V.G.	Good	Fair	Poor
450	350	275	225	150	100

KLIPZIG & COMPANY
San Francisco, California

Pocket Pistol

A .41 caliber single-shot percussion pistol with a 2.5" barrel, German silver mounts and walnut stocks. Manufactured during the 1850s and early 1860s.

NIB	Exc.	V.G.	Good	Fair	Poor
—	—	1950	975	400	200

KNICKERBOCKER
Made by Crescent Fire Arms Co.

Knickerbocker Pistol nfa

The Knickerbocker is a 14" double-barreled 20 gauge smooth bore pistol manufactured by Crescent Fire Arms Co. of Norwich, Connecticut. On the basis of its hammerless design and the dates of production of similarly designed firearms by Crescent, the Knickerbocker was probably manufactured sometime during the early 1900s. The receiver is case hardened, and the barrels are nickel-plated. The right side of the receiver is stamped AMERICAN GUN CO./ NEW YORK U S A; the left side is stamped KNICKERBOCKER. It probably was intended for law enforcement and/or defensive purposes, and manufactured using the same techniques used to produce the Ithaca Auto & Burglar Gun. The receiver is fitted with a checkered pistol grip resembling that of the Model 1 and Model 2 smooth bore H&R Handy-Gun. The only known specimen of the Knickerbocker bears serial number 200114. The Knickerbocker was classified as an "any other weapon" under the NFA in 1934 because it was originally designed as "a so-called shotgun with a pistol grip" and because it is concealable (see Treasury Department ruling S.T. 772, dated August 6, 1934). Its rarity precludes being able to reliably estimate its value at this time.

KNIGHT RIFLES
Centerville, Iowa

This company was started in 1985 by Tony Knight. The company produces in-line blackpowder muzzleloading rifles and a complete line of accessories

HK-94 Hawkeye Pistol

This is a .50 caliber pistol fitted with a 12" barrel and an overall length of 20" and a weight of 52 oz. Offered in stainless steel or blued finish. First offered in 1993 and discontinued in 1998.

NIB	Exc.	V.G.	Good	Fair	Poor
400	300	250	200	150	100

NOTE: Add $70 for stainless steel.

KOHOUT & SPOLECNOST
Kdyne, Czechoslovakia

Mars

A 6.35 or 7.65mm caliber semi-automatic pistol, the larger caliber having a grip safety. Blued with plastic grips impressed with the word "Mars." The slide marked "Mars 7.65 (or 6.35) Kohout & Spol. Kdyne." Manufactured between 1928 and 1945.

NIB	Exc.	V.G.	Good	Fair	Poor
—	350	250	200	150	100

Niva, PZK

Similar to the above in 6.35mm caliber.

NIB	Exc.	V.G.	Good	Fair	Poor
—	350	250	200	150	100

KOLB, HENRY M.
Philadelphia, Pennsylvania

The revolvers listed were manufactured by Henry Kolb and Charles Foehl until 1912 when R.F. Sedgely replaced Foehl. Manufacture continued until approximately 1938.

Baby Hammerless

A .22 caliber folding-trigger double-action revolver with an enclosed hammer and 5-shot cylinder.

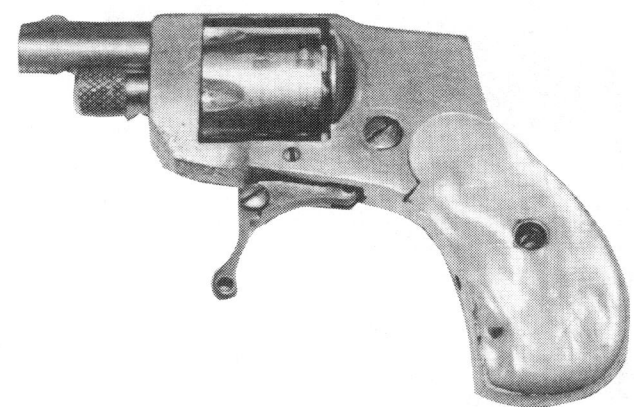

NIB	Exc.	V.G.	Good	Fair	Poor
—	300	200	150	100	50

New Baby Hammerless

Similar to the above, with a hinged barrel to facilitate loading.

NIB	Exc.	V.G.	Good	Fair	Poor
—	300	200	150	100	50

KOLIBRI/Frederich Pfannl
Rehberg, Austria

2.7mm

A 2.7mm semi-automatic pistol with a 7-round magazine. F.P. trademark are on the grips as well as the Kolibri name at the bottom of the grips. A single cartridge may be worth as much as $75!

Courtesy James Rankin

NIB	Exc.	V.G.	Good	Fair	Poor
—	2500	1550	850	600	400

3mm

A 3mm semi-automatic pistol with a 6-round magazine. The 3mm version is the rarer of the two Kolibri pistols. The F.P. trademark is on the grips.

Courtesy James Rankin

NIB	Exc.	V.G.	Good	Fair	Poor
—	2800	2000	1500	1000	600

KOMMER, THEODOR WAFFENFABRIK
Zella Mehlis, Germany

Model 1

A 6.35mm semi-automatic pistol with an 8-shot magazine. Blued with plastic grips. Kommer name is both on the slide and the frame with T.K. trademark on the grips. Manufactured during the 1920s.

Courtesy James Rankin

NIB	Exc.	V.G.	Good	Fair	Poor
—	300	250	200	150	90

Model 2

A 6.35mm semi-automatic pistol with a 6-round magazine similar to the Model 1906 Browning. Barrel length is 2". Weight is about 13 oz. The Kommer name is on the slide. The late TH.K. trademark is on the grips. Manufactured in the 1930s.

Courtesy James Rankin

NIB	Exc.	V.G.	Good	Fair	Poor
—	300	250	200	150	90

Model 3

A 6.35mm semi-automatic pistol with a 9-round magazine. The Kommer name is on the slide and the TH.K. trademark is on the grips. Same as the Model 2 with extended grips straps for longer magazine.

Courtesy James Rankin

NIB	Exc.	V.G.	Good	Fair	Poor
—	300	250	200	150	90

Model 4

A 7.65mm caliber semi-automatic pistol with a 7-shot magazine and without a grip safety. Similar to the FN Model 1901. Barrel length is 3". Weight is about 20 oz. The slide marked "Waffenfabrik Kommer Zella Mehlis Kal. 7.65." Manufactured between 1936 and 1940.

NIB	Exc.	V.G.	Good	Fair	Poor
—	375	325	275	175	100

KORRIPHILA
Germany

HSP

A 7.65mm Luger, .38 Special, 9mm Police, 9mm Luger, 9mm Steyr, 10mm ACP, and the .45 ACP caliber double-action semi-automatic pistol with a 4" barrel made of stainless steel.

NIB	Exc.	V.G.	Good	Fair	Poor
7500	6000	5000	2500	1250	550

HSP HSP—Single-Action Only

NIB	Exc.	V.G.	Good	Fair	Poor
7500	6000	5000	2500	1250	550

Odin's Eye

Essentially the same model as above in the same calibers with choice of barrel lengths of 4" or 5". Frame and slide are made of Damascus steel.

NIB	Exc.	V.G.	Good	Fair	Poor
14000	10000	7500	4000	1500	500

KORTH
Germany

Korth started business in Ratzegurg, Germany, in 1954.

Semi-Automatic Pistol

A 9mm caliber double-action semi-automatic pistol with a 4" barrel, adjustable sights and 13-shot magazine. Other calibers are offered such as .40 S&W, .357 SIG, and 9x21. Optional 5" barrel is also offered. Weight is about 44 oz. Matte or polished blue with walnut grips. Introduced in 1985.

NIB	Exc.	V.G.	Good	Fair	Poor
7000	5000	3750	2750	1300	650

Combat Revolver

A .22 LR, .22 Magnum, .357 Magnum, and 9mm caliber revolver with a 3", 4", 5.25", or 6" barrel and 6-shot cylinder. The barrels and cylinders are interchangeable, matte or polished blue with walnut grips.

NIB	Exc.	V.G.	Good	Fair	Poor
5000	3900	3000	1750	1150	700

Match Revolver

Built in the same calibers as the Combat revolver with a choice of 5.25" or 6" barrel. Adjustable rear sight with adjustable sight notch widths. Machined trigger shoe. Grips are adjustable match grips with oiled walnut and matte finish.

NIB	Exc.	V.G.	Good	Fair	Poor
6250	5000	4000	2250	1500	1000

KRAUSER, ALFRED
Zella Mehlis, Germany

Helfricht or Helkra

A 6.35mm semi-automatic pistol with a 2" barrel. Produced in four models, the fourth with an enclosed barrel. Blued with composition grips. Manufactured from 1921 to 1929.

NIB	Exc.	V.G.	Good	Fair	Poor
—	475	400	350	250	150

KRIDER, J. H.
Philadelphia, Pennsylvania

Pocket Pistol

A .41 caliber percussion pocket pistol with a 3" barrel, German silver furniture and walnut stock. The barrel marked "Krider Phila." Manufactured during the 1850s and 1860s.

NIB	Exc.	V.G.	Good	Fair	Poor
—	—	1750	700	300	150

KSN INDUSTRIES
Israel

Golan

A semi-automatic pistol, introduced in 1996, chambered for the 9mm or .40 S&W cartridge. Double-action trigger with ambidextrous controls. Barrel length is 3.9" and magazine capacity is 10 rounds in U.S. In rest of the world 15 rounds for 9mm and 11 rounds for the .40 S&W. Weight is 29 oz.

NIB	Exc.	V.G.	Good	Fair	Poor
650	525	400	325	200	100

Kareen MK II

This single-action semi-automatic pistol is chambered for the 9mm cartridge. The barrel length is 4.5". Ambidextrous safety and rubber grips. Steel slide and frame. Weight is about 34 oz.

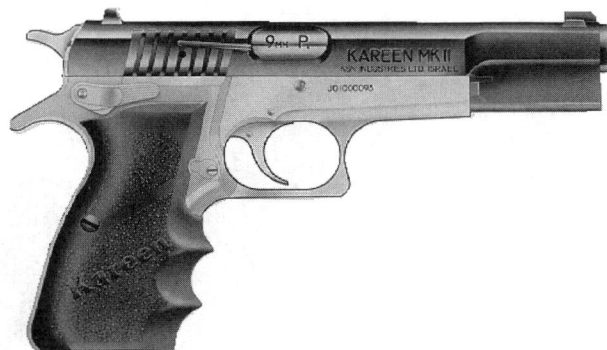

NIB	Exc.	V.G.	Good	Fair	Poor
500	395	250	200	150	100

Kareen MK II—Compact

Same as above but fitted with a 3.9" barrel. Weight is about 32 oz.

NIB	Exc.	V.G.	Good	Fair	Poor
575	425	325	250	200	150

GAL

Same as the full size Kareen but chambered for the .45 ACP cartridge.

NIB	Exc.	V.G.	Good	Fair	Poor
575	425	325	250	200	150

KUFAHL, G. L.
Sommerda, Germany

Kufahl Needle-Fire Revolver

Designed and patented in Britain in 1852 by G.L. Kufahl, who tried unsuccessfully to interest a British company in producing it. He then went to the firm of Rheinmettal Dreyse, where a needle-fire gun was produced in 1838. This company manufactured his design. This revolver was chambered for a unique, totally consumed .30 caliber "cartridge." A lead projectile had the ignition percussion cap affixed to its base, with the propellant powder in the rear. The firing pin had to be long enough to penetrate the powder charge and hit the percussion cap. This does not sound efficient, but realize that these were the days before cartridges. This revolver has a 3.2" barrel and an unfluted cylinder that holds six shots. It is not bored all the way through but is loaded from the front. The finish is blued, with a modicum of simple engraving and checkered wood grips that protrude all the way over the trigger. The markings are "Fv.V. Dreyse Sommerda."

NIB	Exc.	V.G.	Good	Fair	Poor
—	—	2950	1600	650	400

KYNOCH GUN FACTORY
Birmingham, England

Established by George Kynoch in approximately 1886, this company ceased operation in 1890.

Early Double Trigger Revolver

A .45 caliber double trigger revolver with a 6" barrel, 6-shot cylinder and enclosed hammer. Blued with walnut grips. Manufactured in 1885.

NIB	Exc.	V.G.	Good	Fair	Poor
—	—	1600	950	575	350

Late Double Trigger Revolver

Similar to the above, but in .32, .38, or .45 caliber with the cocking trigger enclosed within the trigger guard. Approximately 600 of these revolvers were made between 1896 and 1890.

NIB	Exc.	V.G.	Good	Fair	Poor
—	—	2100	1575	900	575

L

LAGRESE
Paris, France

Lagrese Revolver

A large ornate revolver chambered for the .43 rimfire cartridge. It has a 6.25" barrel and a 6-shot fluted cylinder. This revolver has no top strap; and the frame, as well as the grip straps, are cast in one piece with the barrel screwed into the frame. It is loaded through a gate and has double-action lockwork. The outstanding feature about this well-made revolver is its extremely ornate appearance. There are more sweeps and curves than could be imagined and in general outline somewhat resmbles the leMat, though with a sisngle barrel. It is engraved and blued, with well-figured curved walnut grips. It is marked "Lagrese Bte a Paris" and was manufactured in the late 1860s.

NIB	Exc.	V.G.	Good	Fair	Poor
—	—	3500	2750	1300	875

LAHTI
Finland
SEE—Husqvarna

Lahti

This is a commercial version of the Finnish L-35 9mm pistol. These late pistols have the barrel and trigger guard design of the L-35 but the barrel extension of the Swedish M40. Produced in the late 1950s.

Courtesy J.B. Wood

Late Commercial Lahti with "Valmet" stamped on top.

NIB	Exc.	V.G.	Good	Fair	Poor
—	1250	1000	800	550	300

LANCASTER, CHARLES
London, England

4 Barreled Pistol

A unique pistol for several reasons. It is chambered for the .476 rimfire cartridge and has four 6.25" barrels. The bore has a slightly twisted oval pattern that imparts a spin to the bullet. The barrels are hinged at the bottom and break downward for loading. It is a double-action type lockwork with a long, difficult trigger pull. The pistol is well made; and the caliber, suitably heavy to insure stopping power. The primary goal was military; and it was successful, seeing action in the Sudan campaigns of 1882 and 1885. This powerful weapon was also popular with big game hunters as a backup sidearm. The finish is blued, with checkered walnut grips. It is marked "Charles Lancaster (Patent) 151 New Bond St. London." This model was introduced in 1881. There are smaller-caliber versions of this pistol with shorter barrels. They are not as well known as the large-caliber version, and the values would be similar as their rarity would be balanced by the desirability of the large bore models.

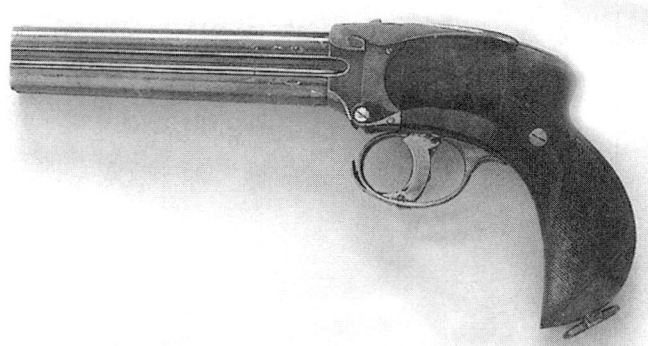

NIB	Exc.	V.G.	Good	Fair	Poor
—	—	8000	5750	2500	1500

2 Barreled Pistol

Similar to the 4 barreled version, with only two superposed barrels chambered for a variety of calibers from .320 to .577. It was also chambered for the 20 gauge and .410 bore shotshell. The advantage to the 2 barreled pistol is that it is lighter and better balanced. The 2 barrel is less common than the 4 barrel version.

Courtesy James Rankin

NIB	Exc.	V.G.	Good	Fair	Poor
—	—	6000	3750	1750	1000

LANG, J.
London, England

Percussion Pistol

Chambered for .60 caliber percussion. It is a single-barreled, muzzle-loading pistol with a 3.25" barrel. This is essentially a defensive weapon that was well made, with Damascus barrels and an ornate engraved hammer and frame.

NIB	Exc.	V.G.	Good	Fair	Poor
—	—	4510	3000	1100	600

Gas Seal Revolver

Chambered for the .42 caliber percussion and has a 4.75" barrel. The unfluted cylinder holds 6 shots and is spring-loaded to be forced into the barrel when cocked, in order to obtain the "Gas Seal" feature desired. This revolver was well made and finished. It is lightly engraved, with a case-colored cylinder and a blued barrel and frame. The grips are finely checkered walnut, and the markings are "J.Lang 22 Cockspur St. London." This type of firearm was the forerunner of later designs such as the Russian Nagant. This revolver was manufactured in the 1850s.

NIB	Exc.	V.G.	Good	Fair	Poor
—	—	3000	1500	1000	550

LANGENHAN, FRIEDRICH
Zella Mehlis, Germany

Langenhan Army Model

A blowback-operated semi-automatic pistol chambered for the 7.65mm Auto Pistol cartridge. It has a 4" barrel and a detachable magazine that holds 8 rounds. Weight is about 24 oz. The pistol was made with a separate breechblock that is held into the slide by a screw. This feature doomed this pistol to eventual failure as when this screw became worn, it could loosen when firing and allow the breechblock to pivot upwards—and the slide would then be propelled rearward and into the face of the shooter. This pistol was produced with wood grips.

NIB	Exc.	V.G.	Good	Fair	Poor
—	375	300	250	175	100

Langenhan Open Model

A semi-automatic pistol that is similar to the Army Model with some minor variations, and an open window in the frame. Checkered hard rubber grips with "FL" logo on each side.

Courtesy James Rankin

NIB	Exc.	V.G.	Good	Fair	Poor
—	400	325	275	200	100

Langenhan Closed Model

Similar to the Open Model with closed frame and other minor variations.

Courtesy James Rankin

NIB	Exc.	V.G.	Good	Fair	Poor
—	400	325	275	200	100

Model 2

A blowback-operated semi-automatic pistol chambered for the 6.35mm cartridge. It has a 3" barrel and an 8-round detachable magazine. Weight is about 18 oz. The pistol fires by means of a concealed hammer, and the breechblock is separate from the rest of the slide and is held in place by a heavy crossbolt. The finish is blued, and the grips are molded checkered black plastic with the monogram "F.L." at the top. The slide is marked "Langenhan 6.35." This model was manufactured between 1921 and 1936.

Courtesy James Rankin

NIB	Exc.	V.G.	Good	Fair	Poor
—	375	300	250	200	100

Model 3

Similar to the Model 2 except that it is somewhat smaller. The barrel is 2.25" in length, and the butt is only large enough to house a 5-round detachable magazine. Weight is about 17 oz. The markings are the same with the addition of "Model 111" on the slide. This model was also manufactured until 1936.

NIB	Exc.	V.G.	Good	Fair	Poor
—	325	275	250	200	150

LAR MFG. CO.
West Jordan, Utah

Grizzly Mark I

A .357 Magnum, .45 ACP, 10mm, or .45 Winchester Magnum semi-automatic pistol with a 5.4", 6.5", 8", or 10" barrel, Millett sights, ambidextrous safety and 7-shot magazine. Parkerized, blued, or hard-chrome plated with rubber grips. Available with cartridge conversion units, telescope mounts, or a compensator. Weight is approximately 48 oz. Introduced in 1984.

NIB	Exc.	V.G.	Good	Fair	Poor
1400	150	950	700	400	200

Grizzly Mark II

As above, with fixed sights and without the ambidextrous safety. Manufactured in 1986.

NIB	Exc.	V.G.	Good	Fair	Poor
—	1300	1050	775	475	300

Grizzly Mark IV

Similar to the Mark I but chambered for the .44 Magnum cartridge. Barrel length is 5.4" or 6.5". Choice of blue or Parkerized finish.

NIB	Exc.	V.G.	Good	Fair	Poor
1500	1100	775	500	400	200

Grizzly Mark V

Same as above model but chambered for .50 AE cartridge. Empty weight is 56 oz. Add $200 for nickel finish.

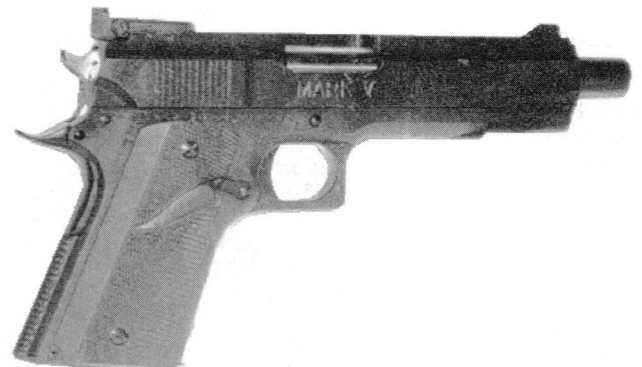

NIB	Exc.	V.G.	Good	Fair	Poor
1950	1350	1000	650	425	200

Grizzly State Pistol

This is a limited edition of 50 Grizzly pistols with serial numbers that match the order in which each state was admitted into the union. Each pistol features the state outline, the state seal, and the name of the state engraved in gold. Supplied with a cherry wood fitted case with glass top. Chambered for .45 Win. Mag cartridge.

NIB	Exc.	V.G.	Good	Fair	Poor
3000	—	—	—	—	—

LASERAIM ARMS
Little Rock, Arkansas

Series I

Offered in 10mm or .45 ACP this single-action semi-automatic pistol is fitted with a 6" barrel with compensator. Adjustable rear sight. Stainless steel frame and barrel with matte black Teflon finish. Introduced in 1993. Magazine capacity for 10mm is 8 rounds and 7 rounds for .45 ACP. Weight is about 46 oz.

NIB	Exc.	V.G.	Good	Fair	Poor
650	550	400	300	200	100

Series II

This is similar to the Series I except this model has no compensator. It is fitted with a 5" barrel and stainless steel finish. A compact version has a 3-3/8" barrel. Introduced in 1993. Weight is 43 oz. for 5" barrel and 37 oz. for compact version.

NIB	Exc.	V.G.	Good	Fair	Poor
625	525	375	275	175	100

Series III

This model is similar to the Series II except it is offered with 5" barrel only with a dual port compensator. Introduced in 1994. Weight is about 43 oz.

NIB	Exc.	V.G.	Good	Fair	Poor
650	550	400	300	200	100

LE FRANCAIS
St. Etienne, France

Francais D'Armes et Cycles de St. Etienne

SEE—Manufrance

Gaulois

An 8mm palm pistol designed by Brun-Latrige and manufactured by Le Francais. Furnished with a 5-round magazine.

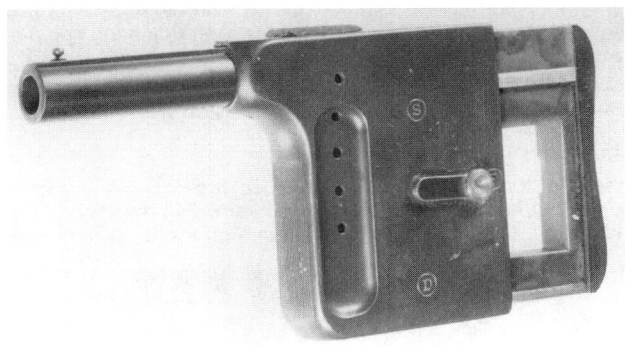

Courtesy James Rankin

NIB	Exc.	V.G.	Good	Fair	Poor
—	—	950	550	400	300

Le Francais Model 28 (Type Armee)

A unique pistol chambered for the 9mm Browning cartridge. It is a large pistol, with a 5" barrel that was hinged with a tip-up breech. This is a blowback-operated semi-automatic pistol that has no extractor. The empty cases are blown out of the breech by gas pressure. The one feature about this pistol that is desirable is that it is possible to tip the barrel breech forward like a shotgun and load cartridges singly, while holding the contents of the magazine in reserve. This weapon has fixed sights and a blued finish, with checkered walnut grips. It was manufactured in 1928.

Courtesy James Rankin

NIB	Exc.	V.G.	Good	Fair	Poor
—	1250	950	750	500	200

Police Model (Type Policeman)

A blowback-operated, double-action semi-automatic that is chambered for the .25 ACP cartridge. It has a 3.5" barrel and a 7-round magazine. It has the same hinged barrel feature of the Model 28 and is blued, with fixed sights and Ebonite grips. This model was manufactured 1913 to 1914.

Courtesy James Rankin

NIB	Exc.	V.G.	Good	Fair	Poor
—	800	650	450	300	150

Officer's Model (Pocket Model)

May also be referred to a "Staff Model." Also a blowback-operated semi-automatic chambered for the .25 ACP cartridge. It has a 2.5" barrel and a concealed hammer. It has fixed sights and the finish is blued. The grips are Ebonite. This model was manufactured between 1914 and 1938 in two variations: early and second type.

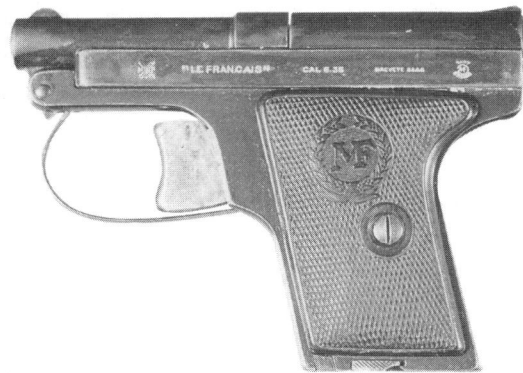

Courtesy James Rankin

Early variation Pocket

NIB	Exc.	V.G.	Good	Fair	Poor
—	300	250	200	150	100

Target Model (Type Champion)

Chambered for 6.35mm cartridge and fitted with a 6" barrel. Extended magazine base is for grip purchase, not additional cartridges.

Courtesy James Rankin

NIB	Exc.	V.G.	Good	Fair	Poor
—	900	700	550	400	275

LE MAT
Paris, France

LeMat

Has a somewhat unique background that makes it a bit controversial among collectors. It is a foreign-made firearm manufactured in Paris, France, as well as in Birmingham, England. It was designed and patented by an American, Jean Alexander Le Mat of New Orleans, Louisiana; and it was purchased for use by the Confederate States of America and used in the Civil War. This is a curious firearm as it is a huge weapon that has two barrels. The top 6.5" barrel is chambered for .42 caliber percussion and is supplied by a 9-shot unfluted cylinder that revolves on a 5", .63 caliber, smoothbore barrel that doubles as the cylinder axis pin. These two barrels are held together by a front and a rear ring. The rear sight is a notch in the nose of the hammer, and there is an attached ramrod on the side of the top barrel. The weapon is marked "Lemat and Girards Patent, London." The finish is blued, with checkered walnut grips. There were fewer than 3,000 manufactured, of which approximately one-half were purchased by the Confederate States of America. They were made between 1856 and 1865.

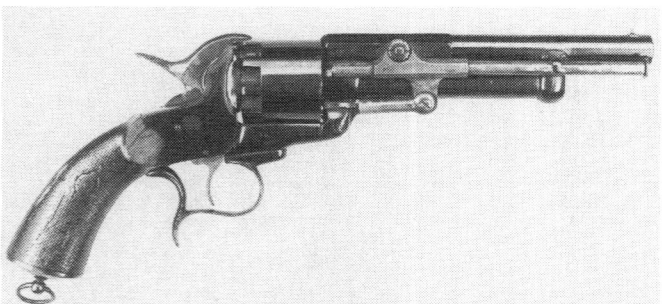

Courtesy Milwaukee Public Museum, Milwaukee, Wisconsin

NIB	Exc.	V.G.	Good	Fair	Poor
—	—	30000	25000	7500	1750

Baby LeMat

Similar in appearance (though a good deal smaller in size) to the standard model pistol. It is chambered for .32 caliber percussion and has a 4.25" top barrel and a .41 caliber smoothbore lower barrel. The cylinder is unfluted and holds 9 shots. The barrel is marked "Systeme Le Mat Bte s.g.d.g. Paris." It has British proofmarks and is blued, with checkered walnut grips. This is the scarcest model Le Mat, as there were only an estimated 100 manufactured and used by the Confederate States of America in the Civil War.

NIB	Exc.	V.G.	Good	Fair	Poor
—	—	28500	22000	1100	3300

LE PAGE SA.
Liege, Belgium

Pinfire Revolver

This company was in the business of revolver manufacture in the 1850s, producing a .40 caliber pinfire revolver that was similar to the Lefauchaux and other pinfires of the day. The barrel lengths vary, and the unfluted cylinder holds 6 shots. These pistols are double-action and are sometimes found with ornate, but somewhat crude engraving. The finish is blued, with wood grips. The quality of these weapons is fair. They were serviceable; but the ammunition created somewhat of a problem, as it is rather fragile and difficult to handle with the protruding primer pin to contend with.

NIB	Exc.	V.G.	Good	Fair	Poor
—	—	775	325	200	125

Semi-Automatic Pistol

A semi-automatic pistol with an open top slide, and exposed hammer. It is chambered for the 6.35mm, 7.65mm, 9mm Short, and 9mm Long cartridges. It has a large grip with finger grooves.

Courtesy James Rankin

NIB	Exc.	V.G.	Good	Fair	Poor
—	875	675	525	300	200

Pocket Pistol

A semi-automatic pistol in caliber 6.35mm. Checkered hard rubber grips with crossed sword and pistol logo of Le Page on each side of the grip.

Courtesy James Rankin

NIB	Exc.	V.G.	Good	Fair	Poor
—	325	275	225	175	75

LEECH & RIGDON
Greensboro, Georgia

Leech & Rigdon Revolver

This Confederate revolver was patterned after the 1851 Colt Navy. It is chambered for .36 caliber percussion and has a 6-shot unfluted cylinder. The 7.5" barrel is part-octagonal and has a loading lever beneath it. The frame is open-topped; and the finish is blued, with brass grip straps and walnut one-piece grips. The barrel is marked "Leech & Rigdon CSA." There were approximately 1,500 revolvers manufactured in 1863 and 1864. These were all contracted for by the Confederacy and are considered to be a prime acquisition for collectors. Beware of fakes!

Courtesy Jim and Caroline Cerny

NIB	Exc.	V.G.	Good	Fair	Poor
—	—	42000	27500	11000	2750

LEFAUCHAUX, CASIMER & EUGENE
Paris, France

Pinfire Revolver

The pinfire ignition system was invented by Casimir Lefauchaux in 1828 but was not widely used until the 1850s. It consists of a smooth rimless case that contains the powder charge and a percussion cap. A pin protrudes from the side of this case at the rear and when struck by the hammer is driven into the cap, thereby igniting the charge and firing the weapon. The pistols for this cartridge are slotted at the end of the cylinder to allow the pins to protrude and be struck by the downward blow of the hammer. This particular revolver is chambered for .43 caliber and has a 5.25" barrel. The cylinder holds 6 shots; and the finish is blued, with checkered walnut grips. This revolver was manufactured after 1865 and was selected for service by the French military.

NIB	Exc.	V.G.	Good	Fair	Poor
—	—	—	575	250	125

LEONARD, G.
Charlestown, Massachusetts

Pepperbox

A .31-caliber, four-barreled pepperbox with a concealed hammer. The barrels are 3.25" in length. There is a ring trigger used to cock the weapon, while a smaller trigger located outside the ring is used to fire the weapon. The barrels on this pistol do not revolve. There is a revolving striker inside the frame that turns to fire each chamber. The barrels must be removed for loading and capping purposes. The frame is iron and blued, with engraving. The rounded grips are walnut. The barrel is stamped "G. Leonard Jr. Charlestown." There were fewer than 200 manufactured in 1849 and 1850.

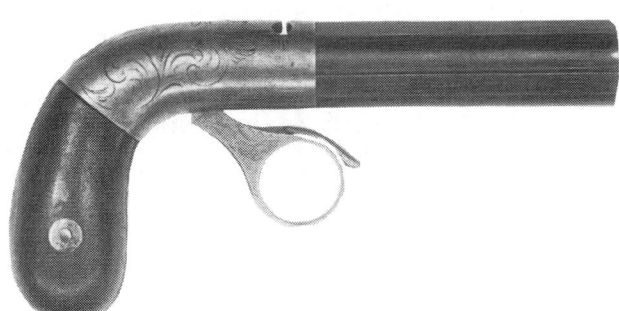

NIB	Exc.	V.G.	Good	Fair	Poor
—	—	1850	725	300	150

LES, INC.
Skokie, Illinois

Rogak P-18

A 9mm caliber double-action semi-automatic pistol with a 5.5" barrel and 18-shot magazine. Stainless steel. Discontinued.

NIB	Exc.	V.G.	Good	Fair	Poor
—	380	350	295	200	150

LIDDLE & KAEDING
San Francisco, California

Pocket Revolver

Manufactured by Forehand and Wadsworth and stamped with the above name. This company was a dealer in California and had nothing whatever to do with the production of this revolver. It is chambered for the .32 rimfire cartridge and has a 3.25" octagonal barrel and a 5-shot fluted cylinder. The frame is iron; and the finish is blued, with walnut grips. There were a few hundred manufactured between 1880 and 1886. The dealer's name is marked on the top strap.

NIB	Exc.	V.G.	Good	Fair	Poor
—	—	575	450	200	75

LIEGEOISE D ARMES
Liege, Belgium

Liegeoise Pistol

A semi-automatic pistol in 6.35mm caliber.

Courtesy James Rankin

NIB	Exc.	V.G.	Good	Fair	Poor
—	250	200	175	125	75

LIGNOSE
Suhl, Germany

In 1921, Bergmann Industriewerke was incorporated into Aktiengesellschaft Lignose, Berlin, with a manufacturing division in Suhl.

Liliput Model I

Manufactured in caliber 6.35mm during the 1920s.

NIB	Exc.	V.G.	Good	Fair	Poor
—	400	300	200	150	100

Lignose Model 2

The Pocket Model in 6.35mm caliber.

Courtesy James Rankin

NIB	Exc.	V.G.	Good	Fair	Poor
—	450	400	350	250	150

Lignose Model 3

The same as the Model 2 but with a 9-round magazine capacity.

NIB	Exc.	V.G.	Good	Fair	Poor
—	750	650	500	400	250

Einhand Model 2A

This unique design resembled the Swiss Chylewski. It allows the shooter to cock and fire this blowback-operated semi-automatic pistol with one hand (Einhand). It is chambered for the 6.35mm cartridge and has a 2" barrel. The magazine holds 6 shots, and the finish is blued, with molded horn grips marked "Lignose." The trigger guard on this pistol has a reverse curve that fits the finger, and it moves backward to cock the slide. The short-grip model without the Einhand feature was the Model 2; the long grip model without the Einhand was the Model 3. The first 9,000 to 10,000 examples (all four variations serial numbered in the same series) were marketed under the Bergmann name; only later Lignose. It was manufactured in the early 1920s by the Bergman Company, but the firm was merged with Lignose under whose name it was produced.

Courtesy James Rankin

NIB	Exc.	V.G.	Good	Fair	Poor
—	750	650	500	400	250

Einhand Model 3A

Similar to the Model 2A, with a longer grip that houses a 9-shot magazine. All other specifications are the same as the Model 2A.

Courtesy Orvel Reichert

NIB	Exc.	V.G.	Good	Fair	Poor
—	850	700	650	500	300

LINDE A.
Memphis, Tennessee

Pocket Pistol

This company manufactured a small, concealable firearm patterned after the Henry Deringer Philadelphia-type pistol. It is chambered for .41 caliber percussion and has a 2.5" barrel, German silver mountings, and a walnut stock. It was manufactured in the 1850s.

NIB	Exc.	V.G.	Good	Fair	Poor
—	—	2150	875	300	150

LINDSAY, JOHN P.
Naugatuck, Connecticut
Union Knife Company

The Union Knife Company manufactured the Lindsay 2-shot pistols for the inventor, John P. Lindsay. There are three separate and distinct models listed.

2 Shot Belt Pistol

An oddity. It is a single-barreled, .41 caliber percussion pistol with a double chamber that contains two powder charges and projectiles that are simultaneously fired by two separate hammers. The hammers are released by a single trigger that allows them to fall in the proper sequence. The 5.5" octagonal barrel is contoured into a radical stepped-down shape, and there is a spur trigger. The frame is brass and has scroll engraving. The barrel is blued and is marked "Lindsay's Young America." There were estimated to be fewer than 100 manufactured between 1860 and 1862.

NIB	Exc.	V.G.	Good	Fair	Poor
—	—	4400	1500	700	300

2 Shot Pocket Pistol

A smaller version of the Belt Pistol. It is chambered for the same caliber but has a 4" barrel. There were approximately 200 manufactured between 1860 and 1862.

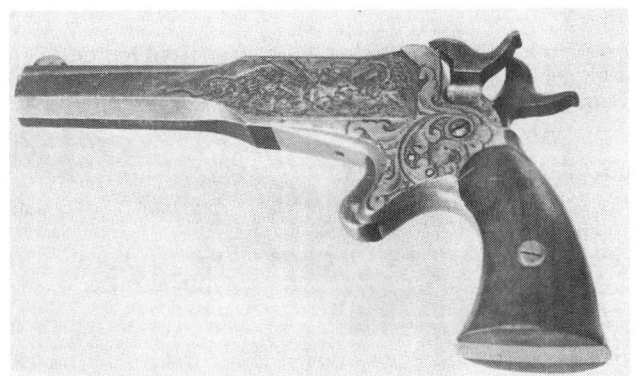

NIB	Exc.	V.G.	Good	Fair	Poor
—	—	3500	3000	1100	400

2 Shot Martial Pistol

A large version of the Lindsay design. It is chambered for .45 caliber smoothbore and has an 8.5" part-round, part-octagonal barrel. In other respects it is similar to the smaller models. The inventor tried to sell this pistol to the government but was unsuccessful. It was estimated that there were 100 manufactured between 1860 and 1862.

NIB	Exc.	V.G.	Good	Fair	Poor
—	—	—	5400	2200	700

LINS, A. F.
Philadelphia, Pennsylvania

Pocket Pistol

Chambered for .41 caliber percussion and a copy of the Henry Deringer pistol. It has a 3" barrel and a walnut stock and is marked "A. Fred. Lins. Philada." This pistol was manufactured between 1855 and 1860.

NIB	Exc.	V.G.	Good	Fair	Poor
—	—	2100	1075	350	200

LLAMA
Manufactured by

Gabilondo y Cia

Vitoria, Spain

This is the same firm that was founded in 1904 and produced several inexpensive revolvers and pistols prior to 1931. In 1931 the company began to produce a semi-automatic pistol based on the Colt Model 1911. They were of high quality and have been sold around the world. After the Spanish civil war the company moved its facilities to Vitoria, Spain, where it continued to build handguns under the Llama trade name. In the 1980s the firm introduced a new line of pistols that were more modern in design and function. The Llama pistol is still produced today.

For Llama pistols built prior to 1936 the slide marking reads: "GABILONDO Y CIA ELOEIBAR (ESPANA) CAL 9MM/.380IN LLAMA." For pistols built after 1936 the slide marking reads: "LLAMA GABILONDO Y CIA ELOEIBAR (ESPANA) CAL 9MM .380." Current production Llama pistols will show a slide marking with either "LLAMA CAL..." or "GABILONDO Y CIA VITORIA (ESPANA)" and the Llama logo. "Llama" is now a trade name for handguns manufactured by Bersa of Argentina.

LLAMA SEMI-AUTOMATICS

Model I-A

This is a 7.65mm blowback design introduced in 1933. Magazine capacity is 7 rounds. The barrel was 3.62", overall length 6.3", and weight about 19 oz.

NIB	Exc.	V.G.	Good	Fair	Poor
—	275	225	125	100	75

Model II

Chambered for the 9mm Short introduced in the same year. Identical to the Model I. Discontinued in 1936.

NIB	Exc.	V.G.	Good	Fair	Poor
—	265	200	150	125	100

Model III

An improved version of the Model II. Introduced in 1936 and discontinued in 1954.

NIB	Exc.	V.G.	Good	Fair	Poor
—	275	225	175	125	100

Model III-A

Similar to the Model III, chambered for the .380 ACP, but with the addition of the Colt-type grip safety. Introduced in 1955. Weight is about 23 oz.

NIB	Exc.	V.G.	Good	Fair	Poor
—	300	250	195	125	100

Model IV

Chambered for the 9mm Largo or .380 ACP. Is not fitted with a grip safety. Introduced in 1931, it is the first of the Llama designs.

NIB	Exc.	V.G.	Good	Fair	Poor
—	275	225	175	125	100

Model V

The same as the Model IV but was intended for export to the United States and is stamped "made in Spain" on the slide.

NIB	Exc.	V.G.	Good	Fair	Poor
—	275	225	175	125	100

Model VI

Chambered for the 9mm Short and without a grip safety.

NIB	Exc.	V.G.	Good	Fair	Poor
—	275	225	175	125	100

Model VII

Introduced in 1932 and manufactured until 1954. Chambered for the .38 Auto cartridge. It does not have a grip safety.

NIB	Exc.	V.G.	Good	Fair	Poor
—	400	300	225	150	100

Model VIII

This model was introduced in 1955 and is chambered for the .45 ACP, .38 Auto, or 9mm Largo. It is fitted with a grip safety. Barrel length is 5", overall length is 8.5", and weight is about 38 oz. Magazine capacity is 7 rounds.

NIB	Exc.	V.G.	Good	Fair	Poor
—	400	300	225	150	100

NOTE: Many of these pistols are marked ".38." It is unclear whether these pistols were intended for use with the .38 Super cartridge or with the milder .38 Auto. We do not recommend full-house Super loadings in these pistols.

Model IX

Chambered for the 7.65mm Para, 9mm Largo, or .45 ACP, this model has a locked breech with no grip safety. Built from 1936 to 1954.

NIB	Exc.	V.G.	Good	Fair	Poor
—	400	300	200	150	100

Model IX-A

This version of the Model IX is fitted with a grip safety. Current production models are chambered for the .45 ACP only. Weighs about 30 oz. with 5" barrel.

NIB	Exc.	V.G.	Good	Fair	Poor
—	400	300	200	150	100

Model IX-B

This version of the Model IX series is chambered in .45 ACP. It is fitted with an extended slide release, black plastic grips, and target-type hammer. Offered in blue or satin chrome finish.

NIB	Exc.	V.G.	Good	Fair	Poor
400	300	250	175	125	100

Model IX-C

This is the last large-frame version of the Model IX. It is chambered for the .45 ACP and is fitted with a 5.125" barrel. Blade front sight with adjustable rear sight. Magazine capacity is 10 rounds. Weight is approximately 41 oz.

NIB	Exc.	V.G.	Good	Fair	Poor
400	300	250	200	150	100

Model IX-D

This model is a compact frame version with a 4.25" barrel and chambered for the .45 ACP cartridge. Stocks are black rubber. Fixed front sight with adjustable rear. Introduced in 1995. Magazine capacity is 10 rounds. Weight is about 39 oz.

NIB	Exc.	V.G.	Good	Fair	Poor
450	350	250	200	150	100

Model X

First produced in 1935, this model is chambered for the 7.65mm cartridge. It has no grip safety.

NIB	Exc.	V.G.	Good	Fair	Poor
—	295	225	150	100	75

Model X-A

This version is similar to the Model X but with a grip safety. Produced from 1954 to the present.

NIB	Exc.	V.G.	Good	Fair	Poor
—	300	225	150	100	75

Model XI

Chambered for the 9mm Parabellum cartridge this model is different from previous models with a longer curved butt, ring hammer, and vertically grooved walnut grips. Magazine capacity is 9 rounds. Barrel length is 5". Discontinued in 1954.

NIB	Exc.	V.G.	Good	Fair	Poor
—	350	300	250	175	125

Model XI-B

Similar to the Model XI but with a spur hammer and shorter barrel.

NIB	Exc.	V.G.	Good	Fair	Poor
400	375	275	150	100	75

Model XII-B

This model is chambered for the .40 S&W cartridge. It has a compact frame.

NIB	Exc.	V.G.	Good	Fair	Poor
400	375	275	150	100	75

Model XV

Chambered for the .22 Long Rifle this model is marked "Especial." It is fitted with a grip safety and comes in several finishes and with different grip styles. The barrel length is 3.6", the overall length is 6.5", and the weight is about 17 oz.

NIB	Exc.	V.G.	Good	Fair	Poor
—	325	275	195	125	100

Model XVI

This is a deluxe version of the Model XV with engraving, ventilated rib, and adjustable sights.

NIB	Exc.	V.G.	Good	Fair	Poor
—	350	275	200	150	100

Model XVII "Especial"

This vest pocket-sized model is chambered for the .22 Short. It is small version of the Model XV with a finger-contoured grip.

NIB	Exc.	V.G.	Good	Fair	Poor
—	275	225	175	125	100

Model XVIII

Introduced in 1998 this model is chambered for the .25 ACP cartridge and offered with gold or chrome finish and stag grips.

NIB	Exc.	V.G.	Good	Fair	Poor
—	300	225	175	150	125

Model Omni

This pistol is chambered for the .45 ACP or 9mm cartridge and fitted with a 4.25" barrel. Blued finish. Adjustable rear sight. Magazine capacity is 7 rounds for the .45 ACP and 13 rounds for the 9mm. Weight is approximately 40 oz. Produced between 1984 and 1986.

Courtesy J.B. Wood

NIB	Exc.	V.G.	Good	Fair	Poor
475	350	250	150	125	100

Model Max-I

Introduced in 1995 this 1911 design single-action model features a choice of 9mm or .45 ACP chambers with a 4.25" barrel or a 5.125" barrel. Black rubber grips with blade front sight and adjustable rear sight. Weight is 34 oz. for compact model and 36 oz. for Government model.

NIB	Exc.	V.G.	Good	Fair	Poor
400	350	250	175	150	100

NOTE: For compact model add $25. For duo-tone model add $25.

Model Mini-Max

This version is chambered for the 9mm, .40 S&W, or .45 ACP. Furnished with a 6-round magazine. Barrel length is 3.5". Checkered rubber grips. Introduced in 1996. Weight is about 35 oz. Choice of blue, duo-tone, satin chrome, or stainless steel.

NIB	Exc.	V.G.	Good	Fair	Poor
400	375	275	150	100	75

NOTE: Add $40 for satin chrome finish. Add $60 for stainless. Add $20 for duo-tone finish.

Mini-Max Sub Compact

This semi-automatic is chambered for the 9mm, .40 S&W, or .45 ACP cartridge. It is fitted with a 3.14" barrel with an overall length of 6.5" and a height of 4.5". Skeletonized combat-style hammer. Grips are black polymer. Weight is about 31 oz. Introduced in 1999.

NIB	Exc.	V.G.	Good	Fair	Poor
400	375	275	150	100	75

NOTE: Add $40 for satin chrome finish. Add $60 for stainless. Add $20 for duo-tone finish.

Mini-Max Sub Compact

Chambered for the .45 ACP cartridge, this is a single-action pistol. Fitted with a 3.14" barrel with steel frame and black polymer grips. Magazine capacity is 10 rounds. Overall length is 6.5" and overall height is 4.5". Weight is about 31 oz. Matte blue, chrome or duo-tone finish.

NIB	Exc.	V.G.	Good	Fair	Poor
400	375	275	150	100	75

NOTE: Add $15 for chrome finish and $10 for duo-tone finish.

Model Max-I with Compensator

Similar to the Max-I with the addition of a compensator. This model introduced in 1996. Weight is about 42 oz.

NIB	Exc.	V.G.	Good	Fair	Poor
450	400	300	175	125	95

Micro-Max

This pistol is chambered for the .32 ACP or .380 cartridge. It operates on a straight blowback system with a single-action trigger. Black polymer grips. Barrel length is 3.6". Overall length is 6.5" and height is 4.37". Weight is approximately 23 oz. Introduced in 1999.

NIB	Exc.	V.G.	Good	Fair	Poor
400	375	275	150	100	75

NOTE: Add $20 for satin chrome finish.

Model 82

This is a large-frame double-action semi-automatic pistol. It features plastic grips, ambidextrous safety, 3-dot sights. The barrel length is 4.25" and overall length is 8". Weight is approximately 39 oz. Choice of blue or satin chrome finish.

NIB	Exc.	V.G.	Good	Fair	Poor
650	500	350	250	150	100

Model 87 Competition

Chambered for the 9mm cartridge and fitted with a integral muzzle compensator. Has a number of competition features such as beveled magazine well and oversize safety and magazine release. Magazine capacity is 14 rounds. Offered between 1989 and 1993.

NIB	Exc.	V.G.	Good	Fair	Poor
1200	925	650	525	300	150

Llama Compact Frame Semi-Automatic

A 9mm or the .45 ACP caliber semi-automatic pistol with a 4.25" barrel and either a 7- or 9-shot detachable magazine. Blued. Introduced in 1986.

NIB	Exc.	V.G.	Good	Fair	Poor
350	300	225	150	100	75

Llama Small Frame Semi-Automatic

A .22, .32 ACP, and the .380 ACP caliber semi-automatic pistol with a 3-11/16" barrel and 7-shot detachable magazine. Either blued or satin chrome finished.

NIB	Exc.	V.G.	Good	Fair	Poor
350	300	225	150	100	75

NOTE: Add $75 for satin chrome finish.

Llama Large Frame Semi-Automatic

A 9mm, .38 Super or .45 ACP caliber semi-automatic pistol with a 5.25" barrel and either a 7- or 9-shot detachable magazine, depending on the caliber. Blued or satin chrome.

NIB	Exc.	V.G.	Good	Fair	Poor
450	400	300	175	125	100

NOTE: Add $125 for satin chrome finish.

Mugica

Eibar gun dealer Jose Mugica sold Llama pistols under his private trade name. They are marked "mugica-ebir-spain" on the slide. These pistols do not seem to have any additional value over and above their respective Llama models. For the sake of clarification the Mugica models are listed with their Llama counterparts:

Mugica Model 101	Llama Model X
Mugica Model 101-G	Llama Model X-A
Mugica Model 105	Llama Model III

Mugica Model 105-G   Llama Model III-A
Mugica Model 110   Llama Model VII
Mugica Model 110-G   Llama Model VIII
Mugica Model 120   Llama Model XI

Tauler

In an arrangement similar to Mugica a gun dealer in Madrid sold Llama pistols under his own brand name. Most of these pistols were sold in the early 1930s to police and other government officials. The most common Llama models were Models I to VIII. Slide inscriptions were in English and had the name Tauler in them. No additional value is attached to this private trademark.

REVOLVERS

Ruby Extra Models

These revolvers were produced in the 1950s and were copies of Smith & Wessons. They were marked "RUBY EXTRA" on the left side of the frame. At the top of the grips was a Ruby medallion. The barrel address is stamped: gabilondo y cia elgoeibar espana. The Ruby Extra Models represent the company's attempts to produce and sell a low-cost revolver.

Model XII

This model is chambered for the .38 Long cartridge and is fitted with a 5" barrel and a squared butt.

NIB	Exc.	V.G.	Good	Fair	Poor
—	200	150	125	100	75

Model XIII

Chambered for the .38 Special, this revolver has a round butt with 4" or 6" ventilated rib barrel. The 6" barreled gun was fitted with adjustable sights and target grips.

NIB	Exc.	V.G.	Good	Fair	Poor
—	225	175	150	125	100

Model XIV

Offered in .22 LR or .32 caliber, this model was available in a wide choice of barrel lengths and sights.

NIB	Exc.	V.G.	Good	Fair	Poor
—	200	150	125	100	75

Model XXII Olimpico

This model was designed as a .38 Special target revolver. It features an adjustable anatomic grip, adjustable rear sight, ventilated rib barrel, and a web that joins the barrel to the ejector shroud.

NIB	Exc.	V.G.	Good	Fair	Poor
—	275	225	150	125	100

Model XXIX Olimpico

This is the Model XXI I chambered for the .22 LR.

NIB	Exc.	V.G.	Good	Fair	Poor
—	250	200	150	125	100

Model XXVI

Chambered for the .22 LR, it features traditional grips and shrouded ejector rod.

NIB	Exc.	V.G.	Good	Fair	Poor
—	175	150	125	100	75

Model XXVII

Similar to the model above but fitted with a 2" barrel and chambered for the .32 Long cartridge.

NIB	Exc.	V.G.	Good	Fair	Poor
—	175	150	125	100	75

Model XXVIII

This model is chambered for the .22 LR and is fitted with a 6" barrel. It has a ramp front sight and adjustable rear sight.

NIB	Exc.	V.G.	Good	Fair	Poor
—	200	175	150	100	75

Model XXXII Olimpico

This model is a .32 target revolver with an unusual cylinder and frame design.

NIB	Exc.	V.G.	Good	Fair	Poor
—	400	300	250	200	150

Llama Martial

A .22 or the .38 Special caliber double-action revolver with a 6-round swingout cylinder, a 4" or 6" barrel and adjustable sights. Blued, with checkered hardwood grips. Manufactured between 1969 and 1976.

NIB	Exc.	V.G.	Good	Fair	Poor
—	275	225	200	150	125

NOTE: Add $25 for engraved chrome, $50 for engraved blue, and 600 percent for gold model.

Llama Comanche I

This .22 caliber revolver is fitted with a 6" barrel and has a 9 shot cylinder. Rubber grips with adjustable sights. Choice of blue or stainless steel. Weight is about 39 oz.

NIB	Exc.	V.G.	Good	Fair	Poor
240	175	125	100	75	50

Llama Comanche II

As above, in .38 Special caliber with 6 shot cylinder. Choice of 3" or 4" barrel. Rubber grips and adjustable sights. Blue or stainless steel. Weight is about 30 oz.

NIB	Exc.	V.G.	Good	Fair	Poor
225	175	125	100	75	50

Llama Comanche III

As above, in .357 Magnum with a 3", 4", 6", barrel and adjustable sights. Rubber grips. Blue or stainless steel. Weight is about 30 oz. for 3" or 4" barrel guns and 39 oz. for 6" gun. Introduced in 1975.

NIB	Exc.	V.G.	Good	Fair	Poor
275	225	175	125	100	75

NOTE: Add 20 percent for satin chrome finish.

Llama Super Comanche

As above, in .357 or .44 Magnum with a 10" ventilated rib barrel and adjustable sights. Blued, with walnut grips. Weight is about 47 oz.

NIB	Exc.	V.G.	Good	Fair	Poor
325	250	200	150	100	75

LOEWE, LUDWIG & CO.
Berlin, Germany
SEE—Borchardt

During the 1870s and 1880s this firm manufactured a close copy of the Smith & Wesson Russian Model for the Russian government. They are marked "Ludwig Loewe Berlin" on the top of the barrel.

Loewe Smith & Wesson Russian Revolver

NIB	Exc.	V.G.	Good	Fair	Poor
—	—	1250	600	325	125

LOHNER, C.
Philadelphia, Pennsylvania

Pocket Pistol

A .44 caliber single-shot percussion pistol with a 5" barrel, German silver mounts and walnut grip. The barrel marked "C. Lohner." Manufactured during the 1850s.

NIB	Exc.	V.G.	Good	Fair	Poor
—	—	1600	675	250	125

LOMBARD, H. C. & CO.
Springfield, Massachusetts

Pocket Pistol

A .22 caliber single-shot spur trigger pistol with a 3.5" octagonal barrel. The frame is silver plated, barrel blued and grips are of walnut. Barrel marked "H.C. Lombard & Co. Springfield, Mass."

NIB	Exc.	V.G.	Good	Fair	Poor
—	—	500	225	150	100

LORCIN ENGINEERING CO., INC.
Mira Loma, California

NOTE: This company was in business from 1989 to 1999.

Model L-25

A .25 caliber semi-automatic pistol with a 2.5" barrel and 7-shot magazine. Weight is 14.5 oz. Overall length is 4.8". Introduced in 1989.

NIB	Exc.	V.G.	Good	Fair	Poor
125	100	75	40	30	20

Model LT-25

Same as above but with aluminum alloy frame. Introduced in 1989.

NIB	Exc.	V.G.	Good	Fair	Poor
125	100	75	40	30	20

Model L-22

Chambered for the .22 LR cartridge with a 2.5" barrel. Magazine capacity is 9 rounds. Introduced in 1989. Weight is 16 oz.

NIB	Exc.	V.G.	Good	Fair	Poor
125	100	75	40	30	20

Model L-380

This semi-automatic pistol is chambered for the .380 ACP cartridge. Barrel length is 3.5" with a magazine capacity of 7 rounds. Introduced in 1992. Weight is about 23 oz.

NIB	Exc.	V.G.	Good	Fair	Poor
125	100	75	40	30	20

Model I-380 10th Anniversary

Same as above but frame and slide are plated in 24 karat gold. Limited edition model.

NIB	Exc.	V.G.	Good	Fair	Poor
125	100	75	40	30	20

Model L-32

Same as above but chambered for the .32 ACP cartridge. Introduced in 1992

NIB	Exc.	V.G.	Good	Fair	Poor
125	100	75	40	30	20

Model LH-380

This semi-automatic pistol is chambered for the .380 ACP cartridge. The barrel length is 4.5" and the magazine capacity is 10 rounds. Offered in black, satin or bright chrome finishes.

NIB	Exc.	V.G.	Good	Fair	Poor
150	125	100	75	60	50

Model L-9mm

Same as above but chambered for 9mm cartridge. Weight is 36 oz.

NIB	Exc.	V.G.	Good	Fair	Poor
150	125	100	75	60	50

Derringer

This over-and-under pistol is chambered for the .38 Special, .357 Magnum, and .45 ACP. Barrel length is 3.5". Overall length is 6.5".

NIB	Exc.	V.G.	Good	Fair	Poor
140	120	95	65	50	40

LUGERS
Various Manufacturers

Just before the turn of the 20th century, Georg Luger redesigned the Borchardt semi-automatic pistol so that its mainspring was housed in the rear of the grip. The resulting pistol was to prove extremely successful and his name has become synonymous with the pistol despite the fact his name never appeared on it.These companies manufactured Luger pattern pistols at various times.

1. DWM - Deutsch Waffen und Munitions - Karlsruhe, Germany
2. The Royal Arsenal of Erfurt Germany
3. Simson & Company - Suhl, Germany
4. Mauser - Oberndorf, Germany
5. Vickers Ltd. - England
6. Waffenfabrik Bern - Bern, Switzerland
7. Heinrich Krieghoff - Suhl, Germany

Those interested in these pistols are advised to read the various books written about the marque which are listed in the bibliography at the close of this book.

DEUTSCH WAFFEN UND MUNITIONS

1899/1900 Swiss Test Model

4.75" barrel, 7.65mm caliber. The Swiss Cross in Sunburst is stamped over the chamber. The serial range runs to three digits. With fewer than 100 manufactured and only one known to exist, it is one of the rarest of the Lugers and the first true Luger that was produced. This model is far too rare to estimate an accurate value.

1900 Swiss Contract

4.75" barrel, 7.65mm caliber. The Swiss Cross in Sunburst is stamped over the chamber. The military serial number range is 2001-5000; the commercial range, 01-21250. There were approximately 2,000 commercial and 3,000 military models manufactured.

NIB	Exc.	V.G.	Good	Fair	Poor
—	8000	6750	4000	1500	1000

NOTE: Wide trigger add 20 percent.

1900 Commercial

4.75" barrel, 7.65mm caliber. The area above the chamber is blank. The serial range is 01-19000, and there were approximately 5,500 manufactured for commercial sale in Germany or other countries. Some have "Germany" stamped on the frame. These pistols were imported into the U.S., and some were even stamped after blueing.

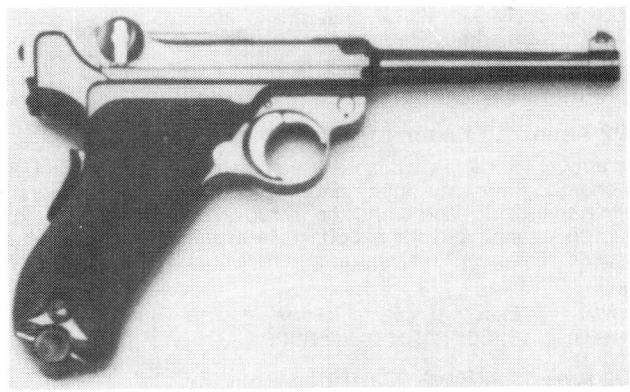

Courtesy Gale Morgan

NIB	Exc.	V.G.	Good	Fair	Poor
—	8500	7250	3000	1000	650

1900 American Eagle

4.75" barrel, 7.65mm caliber. The American Eagle crest is stamped over the chamber. The serial range is between 2000-200000, and there were approximately 11,000-12,000 commercial models marked "Germany" and 1,000 military test models without the commercial import stamp. The serial numbers of this military lot have been estimated at between 6100-7100.

NIB	Exc.	V.G.	Good	Fair	Poor
—	6000	4200	1500	850	600

1900 Bulgarian Contract

An old model, 1900 Type, with no stock lug. It has a 4.75" barrel and is chambered for the 7.65mm cartridge. The Bulgarian crest is stamped over the chamber, and the safety is marked in Bulgarian letters. The serial range is 20000-21000, with 1,000 manufactured. This is a military test model and is quite rare as most were rebarreled to 9mm during the time they were used. Even with the 9mm versions, approximately 10 are known to exist. It was the only variation to feature a marked safety before 1904.

Courtesy Gale Morgan

NIB	Exc.	V.G.	Good	Fair	Poor
—	12500	8500	4000	2500	1800

1902 Prototype

6" barrel, 7.65mm caliber. The serial numbers are in the 10000 range with a capital B, and the chamber is blank. The 6" barrel is of a heavy contour, and there were less than 10 manufactured. The rarity of this variation precludes estimating value.

1902 Commercial—"Fat Barrel"

Thick 4" barrel, 9mm caliber. The area above the chamber is blank. It is chambered for the 9mm cartridge, and the serial numbers fall within the 22300-22400 and the 22900-23500 range. There were approximately 600 manufactured, and the greater part of those noted were marked "Germany" for export purposes.

NIB	Exc.	V.G.	Good	Fair	Poor
—	12500	9500	6000	4000	1500

1902 American Eagle

As above, with an American Eagle stamped over the chamber. It is chambered for the 9mm cartridge, and the serial numbers fall within the 22100-22300 and the 22450-22900 range. This model was solely intended for export sales in the U.S.A., and all are marked "Germany" on the frame. There were approximately 700 manufactured.

NIB	Exc.	V.G.	Good	Fair	Poor
—	15500	12500	5500	3750	1300

1902 American Eagle Cartridge Counter

As above, with a "Powell Indicating Device" added to the left grip. A slotted magazine with a numbered window that allows visual access to the number of cartridges remaining. There were 50 Lugers altered in this way at the request of the U.S. Board of Ordnance, for U.S. Army evaluation. The serial numbers are 22401-22450. Be especially wary of fakes!

NIB	Exc.	V.G.	Good	Fair	Poor
—	30500	25500	16000	6000	3500

1903 Commercial

4" barrel, 7.65mm caliber. The chamber area is blank. There were approximately 50 manufactured for export to France, serial numbered 25000-25050. The extractor on this model is marked "CHARGE."

NIB	Exc.	V.G.	Good	Fair	Poor
—	20500	14500	5000	3200	2500

1904 Navy

6" thick barrel, 9mm caliber. The chamber area is blank, and the extractor is marked "Geladen." The safety is marked "Gesichert." There were approximately 1,500 manufactured in the one- to four-digit serial range, for military sales to the German Navy. The toggle has a "lock" comparable to 1900 types.

NIB	Exc.	V.G.	Good	Fair	Poor
—	40500	30500	16000	6000	4500

1906 Navy Commercial

This is a new model, 1906 Type, with stock lug. It has a 6" barrel and is chambered for the 9mm cartridge. The chamber is blank, and the extractor is marked "Geladen." The safety is marked "Gesichert," and some have the "Germany" export stamp. The proper magazine has a wood bottom with concentric circles on the sides. There were approximately 2,500 manufactured in the 25050-65000 serial range. They were produced for commercial sales in and outside of Germany.

NIB	Exc.	V.G.	Good	Fair	Poor
—	8000	5800	2700	1500	1000

1906 Commercial

4" barrel, 9mm caliber. The extractor is marked "Geladen," and the area of the frame under the safety in its lower position is polished and not blued. The chamber is blank. There were approximately 4,000 manufactured for commercial sales. Some have the "Germany" export stamp. The serial range is 26500-68000.

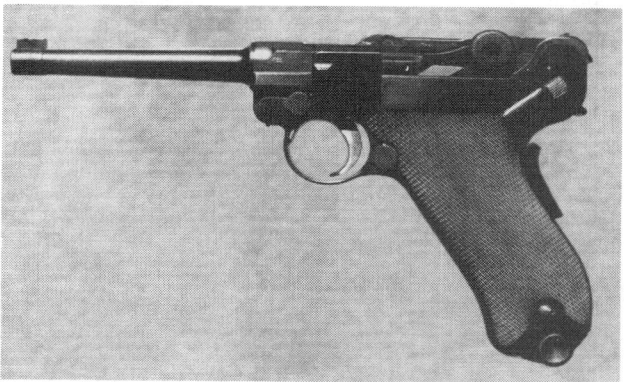

Courtesy Orvel Reichert

NIB	Exc.	V.G.	Good	Fair	Poor
—	5000	4000	1600	800	600

1906 Commercial (Marked Safety)

As above, with the area of the frame under the safety in its lowest position is marked "Gesichert" and the barrel is 4.75" in length and chambered for the 7.65mm cartridge. There were approximately 750 manufactured, serial numbered 25050-26800.

NIB	Exc.	V.G.	Good	Fair	Poor
—	5500	4500	2000	800	600

1906 American Eagle

4" barrel, 9mm caliber. The chamber area has the American Eagle stamped upon it. The extractor is marked "Loaded," and the frame under the safety at its lowest point is polished and not blued. This model has no stock lug. There were approximately 3,000 manufactured for commercial sale in the U.S.A. in the serial range 25800-69000.

NIB	Exc.	V.G.	Good	Fair	Poor
—	4450	3000	1200	700	500

NOTE: Add 10 percent premium for "cal. 9mm" mag.

1906 American Eagle (Marked Safety)

4.75" barrel, 7.65mm caliber. The frame under the safety at its lowest point is marked "Gesichert." There were approximately 750 manufactured in the 25100-26500 serial number range.

Courtesy Gale Morgan

NIB	Exc.	V.G.	Good	Fair	Poor
—	5000	4000	1500	1200	800

1906 American Eagle 4.75" Barrel

As above but with polished bright safety area. Approximately 8,000 manufactured in the 26500-69000 serial range.

NIB	Exc.	V.G.	Good	Fair	Poor
—	5000	3500	1100	700	450

1906 U.S. Army Test Luger .45 Caliber

5" barrel, .45 ACP caliber. Sent to the United States for testing in 1907. The chamber is blank; the extractor is marked "Loaded," and the frame is polished under the safety lever. The trigger on this model has an odd hook at the bottom. Only five of these pistols were manufactured. Buyer Caution: Perfect copies of this pistol are currently being produced.

1906 Swiss Commercial

4.75" barrel, 7.65mm caliber. The Swiss Cross in Sunburst appears over the chamber. The extractor is marked "Geladen," and the frame under the safety is polished. There is no stock lug, and the proofmarks are commercial. There were approximately 1,000 manufactured in the 35000-55000 serial number range.

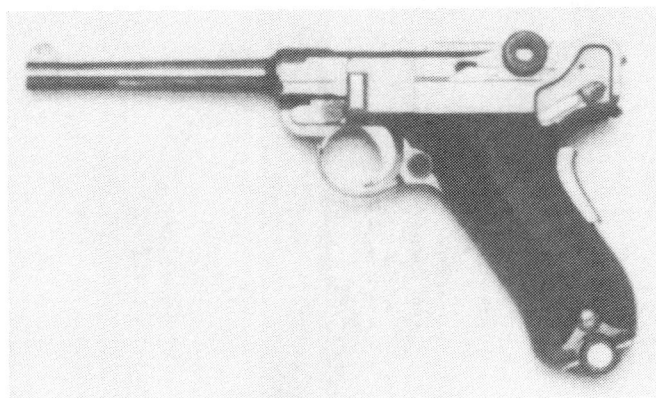

Courtesy Bonhams & Butterfields, San Francisco, California

NIB	Exc.	V.G.	Good	Fair	Poor
—	5800	4700	2500	1400	800

1906 Swiss Military

As the Swiss Commercial, except with military proofmarks.

NIB	Exc.	V.G.	Good	Fair	Poor
—	5500	3800	2200	900	700

1906 Swiss Police Cross in Shield

As above, with a shield replacing the sunburst on the chamber marking. There were 10,215 of both models combined. They are in the 5000-15215 serial number range.

Courtesy Gale Morgan

NIB	Exc.	V.G.	Good	Fair	Poor
—	5200	4200	2000	1000	700

1906 Dutch Contract

4" barrel, 9mm caliber. It has no stock lug, and the chamber is blank. The extractor is marked "Geleden" on both sides, and the safety is marked "RUST" with a curved upward pointing arrow. This pistol was manufactured for military sales to the Netherlands, and a date will be found on the barrel of most examples encountered. The Dutch refinished their pistols on a regular basis and marked the date on the barrels. There were approximately 4,000 manufactured, serial numbered between 1 and 4000.

Courtesy Gale Morgan

NIB	Exc.	V.G.	Good	Fair	Poor
—	7000	4250	1500	800	600

1906 Royal Portuguese Navy

4" barrel, 9mm caliber, and has no stock lug. The Royal Portuguese Naval crest, an anchor under a crown, is stamped above the chamber. The extractor is marked "CARREGADA" on the left side. The frame under the safety is polished. There were approximately 1,000 manufactured with one- to four-digit serial numbers.

NIB	Exc.	V.G.	Good	Fair	Poor
—	12500	9500	6500	4000	2500

1906 Royal Portuguese Army (M2)

4.75" barrel, 7.65mm caliber. It has no stock lug. The chamber area has the Royal Portuguese crest of Mannuel II stamped upon it. The extractor is marked "CARREGADA." There were approximately 5,000 manufactured, with one- to four-digit serial numbers.

NIB	Exc.	V.G.	Good	Fair	Poor
—	4000	3200	1200	600	500

1906 Republic of Portugal Navy

4" barrel, 9mm caliber. It has no stock lug, and the extractor was marked "CARREGADA." This model was made after 1910, when Portugal had become a republic. The anchor on the chamber is under the letters "R.P." There were approximately 1,000 manufactured, with one- to four-digit serial numbers.

NIB	Exc.	V.G.	Good	Fair	Poor
—	11500	9500	5500	2500	1500

1906 Brazilian Contract

4.75" barrel, 7.65mm caliber. It has no stock lug, and chamber area is blank. The extractor is marked "CARREGADA," and the frame under the safety is polished. There were approximately 5,000 manufactured for military sales to Brazil.

NIB	Exc.	V.G.	Good	Fair	Poor
—	3750	2900	1100	750	450

1906 Bulgarian Contract

4.75" barrel, 7.65mm caliber. It has no stock lug, and the extractor and safety are marked in cyrillic letters. The Bulgarian crest is stamped above the chamber. Nearly all of the examples located have the barrels replaced with 4" 9mm units. This was done after the later 1908 model was adopted. Some were refurbished during the Nazi era, and these pistols bear Waffenamts and usually mismatched parts. There were approximately 1,500 manufactured, with serial numbers of one- to four-digits.

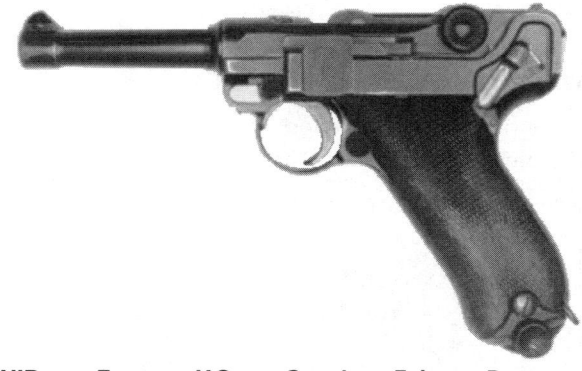

NIB	Exc.	V.G.	Good	Fair	Poor
—	10000	7500	5000	3500	1500

1906 Russian Contract

4" barrel, 9mm caliber. It has no stock lug, and the extractor and safety are marked with cyrillic letters. Crossed Nagant rifles are stamped over the chamber. There were approximately 1,000 manufactured, with one- to four-digit serial numbers; but few survive. This is an extremely rare variation, and caution should be exercised if purchase is contemplated.

Courtesy Gale Morgan

NIB	Exc.	V.G.	Good	Fair	Poor
—	14500	12500	6500	4000	2500

1906 Navy 1st Issue

6" barrel, 9mm caliber. The safety and extractor are both marked in German, and the chamber area is blank. There is a stock lug, and the unique two-position sliding Navy sight is mounted on the rear toggle link. There were approximately 12,000 manufactured for the German Navy, with serial numbers of one- to five-digits. The wooden magazine bottom features concentric rings.

Courtesy Gale Morgan

NIB	Exc.	V.G.	Good	Fair	Poor
—	8500	6500	4000	1500	950

NOTE: Many of these pistols had their safety changed so that they were "safe" in the lower position. Known as "1st issue altered." Value at approximately 20 percent less.

1906 Navy 2nd Issue

As above, but manufactured to be safe in the lower position. Approximately 11,000 2nd Issue Navies manufactured, with one- to five-digit serial numbers—some with an "a" or "b" suffix. They were produced for sale to the German Navy.

Courtesy Gale Morgan

NIB	Exc.	V.G.	Good	Fair	Poor
—	7000	4500	2500	1200	700

1908 Commercial

4" barrel, 9mm caliber. It has no stock lug, and the chamber area is blank. The extractor and the safety are both marked in German, and many examples are marked with the "Germany" export stamp. There were approximately 9,000 manufactured in the 39000-71500 serial number range.

NIB	Exc.	V.G.	Good	Fair	Poor
—	5000	3500	750	600	450

1908 Navy Commercial

6" barrel, 9mm caliber. It has a stock lug, no grip safety, and the characteristic two-position sliding sight mounted on the rear toggle link. The chamber area is blank, and the safety and extractor are both marked. The "Germany" export stamp appears on some examples. There were approximately 1,500 manufactured, in the 44000-50000 serial number range.

NIB	Exc.	V.G.	Good	Fair	Poor
—	6100	5200	2500	1750	1250

1908 Navy

As above, with the "Crown M" military proof. They may or may not have the concentric rings on the magazine bottom. There were approximately 40,000 manufactured, with one- to five-digit serial numbers with an "a" or "b" suffix. These Lugers are quite scarce as many were destroyed during and after WWI.

NIB	Exc.	V.G.	Good	Fair	Poor
—	5150	3700	2000	1100	800

1914 Navy

Similar to the above, but stamped with the dates from 1914-1918 above the chamber. Most noted are dated 1916-1918. There were approximately 30,000 manufactured, with one- to five-digit serial numbers with an "a" or "b" suffix. They are scarce as many were destroyed as a result of WWI.Buyer Caution: Many counterfeit pistols reported.

NIB	Exc.	V.G.	Good	Fair	Poor
—	5500	3500	1580	950	700

1908 Military 1st Issue

4" barrel, 9mm caliber. It has no stock lug, and the extractor and safety are both marked in German. The chamber is blank. There were approximately 20,000 manufactured, with one- to five-digit serial numbers—some with an "a" suffix.

NIB	Exc.	V.G.	Good	Fair	Poor
—	2500	1500	600	500	350

1908 Military Dated Chamber (1910-1913)

As above, with the date of manufacture stamped on the chamber.

NIB	Exc.	V.G.	Good	Fair	Poor
—	1700	1100	600	500	350

1913 Commercial

As above, with a grip safety. Approximately 1,000 manufactured, with serial numbers 71000-72000; but few have been noted, and it is considered to be quite rare.

NIB	Exc.	V.G.	Good	Fair	Poor
—	3200	2200	1300	850	600

1914 Military

As above, with a stock lug.

NIB	Exc.	V.G.	Good	Fair	Poor
—	2500	1700	600	500	350

NOTE: Add 50 percent to a 1914 dated chamber without a stock lug.

1914 Artillery

8" barrel, 9mm caliber. It features a nine-position adjustable sight that has a base that is an integral part of the barrel. This model has a stock lug and was furnished with a military-style flat board stock and holster rig (see Accessories). The chamber is dated from 1914-1918, and the safety and extractor are both marked. This model was developed for artillery and machine gun crews; and many thousands were manufactured, with one- to five-digit serial numbers—some have letter suffixes. This model is quite desirable from a collector's standpoint and is rarer than its production figures would indicate. After the war many were destroyed as the allies deemed them more insidious than other models, for some reason.

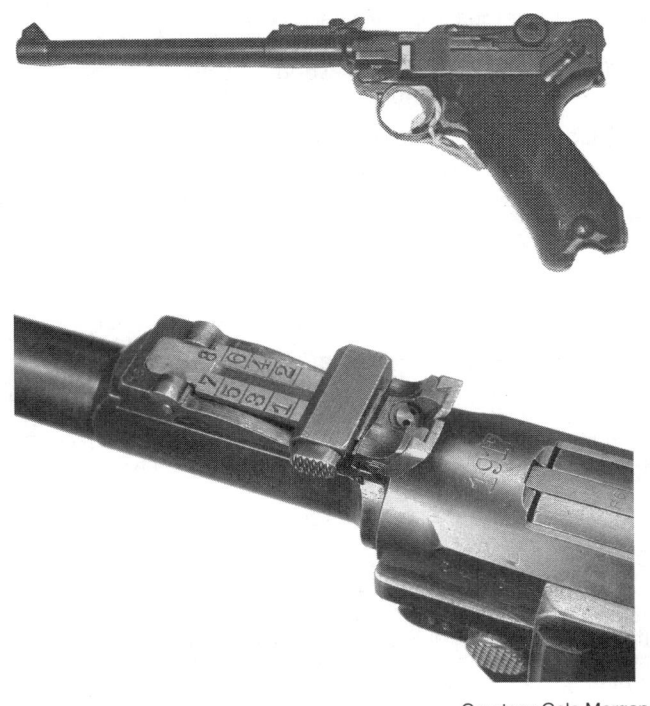

Courtesy Gale Morgan

NIB	Exc.	V.G.	Good	Fair	Poor
—	13500	8000	4300	1900	900

NOTE: For models stamped with 1914 date add 75 percent.

DWM Double Dated

4" barrel, 9mm cartridge. The date 1920 or 1921 is stamped over the original chamber date of 1910-1918, creating the double-date nomenclature. These are arsenal-reworked WWI military pistols and were then issued to the German military and/or police units within the provisions of the Treaty of Versailles. Many thousands of these Lugers were produced.

NIB	Exc.	V.G.	Good	Fair	Poor
—	1800	1000	550	400	300

1920 Police Rework

As above, except that the original manufacture date was removed before the rework date was stamped. There were many thousands of these produced.

NIB	Exc.	V.G.	Good	Fair	Poor
—	900	750	500	350	300

1920 Commercial

Similar to the above, with 3.5" to 6" barrels in 7.65mm or 9mm and marked "Germany" or "Made in Germany" for export. Others are unmarked and were produced for commercial sale inside Germany. Some of these pistols are military reworks with the markings and the proofmarks removed; others were newly manufactured. The extractors and safety are both marked, and the chamber is blank. The serial number range is one to five digits, and letter suffixes often appear.

NIB	Exc.	V.G.	Good	Fair	Poor
—	2200	1400	950	450	350

NOTE: Add 15 percent for 9mm.

1920 Commercial Navy

6" barrel, 9mm caliber. Some have a stock lug; others have been noted without. The chamber area is generally blank, but some have been found with 1914-1918 dates stamped upon them. These were reworked by DWM from Military Navy Lugers after WWI for commercial sales. They are marked "Germany" or "Made in Germany" and were sold by Stoeger Arms, among others. The extractor and safety are both marked, and the unique Navy sight is on the rear toggle link. No one knows exactly how many were produced, but they are quite scarce.

NIB	Exc.	V.G.	Good	Fair	Poor
—	7000	3500	2100	1100	850

1920 Commercial Artillery

8" barrel, 9mm caliber. Erfurt-manufactured pistols, as well as DWM-manufactured pistols, were reworked in this manner. The export markings "Germany" or "Made in Germany" are found on most examples. The number produced is not known, but examples are quite scarce.

NIB	Exc.	V.G.	Good	Fair	Poor
—	5000	3000	1100	700	450

1920 Long Barrel Commercial

10" to 24" barrels, 7.65mm or 9mm caliber. The extractor and safety are both marked, and an artillery model rear sight is used. This model was often built to a customer's specifications. They are rare, and the number manufactured is not known.

NIB	Exc.	V.G.	Good	Fair	Poor
—	5000	3450	1500	1000	800

1920 Carbine

11.75" barrel, 7.65mm caliber. The chamber is blank, and the extractor is marked either "Geleden" or "Loaded." The safety is not-marked. The carbine has a checkered walnut forearm and stock, and most have the "Germany" or "Made in Germany" export stamp. There were few of these carbines manufactured for commercial sales in and outside of Germany.

NIB	Exc.	V.G.	Good	Fair	Poor
—	18500	10500	5000	2500	1500

NOTE: With stock add 25 percent.

1920 Navy Carbine

Assembled from surplus Navy parts with the distinctive two position, sliding navy sight on the rear toggle link. Most are marked with the export stamp and have the naval military proofmarks still in evidence. The safety and extractor are marked, and rarely one is found chambered for the 9mm cartridge. Few were manufactured.

NIB	Exc.	V.G.	Good	Fair	Poor
—	19500	11000	5250	3000	1700

1920 Swiss Commercial

3.5"-6" barrels, 7.65mm or 9mm caliber. The Swiss Cross in Sunburst is stamped over the chamber, and the extractor is marked "Geladen." The frame under the safety is polished. There were a few thousand produced, with serial numbers in the one- to five-digit range, sometimes with a letter suffix.

NIB	Exc.	V.G.	Good	Fair	Poor
—	5000	3500	1600	1000	800

1923 Stoeger Commercial

3.5" to 24" barrels, 7.65mm or 9mm caliber. There is a stock lug. The chamber area is either blank or has the American Eagle stamped on it. The export stamp and "A.F.Stoeger Inc. New York" is found on the right side of the receiver. The extractor and safety are marked in German or English. This was the model that Stoeger registered with the U.S. Patent office to secure the Luger name, and some examples will be so marked. There were less than 1,000 manufactured, with one- to five-digit serial numbers without a letter suffix. Individual appraisal must be secured on barrel lengths above 6". Be wary as fakes have been noted. The values given here are for the shorter barreled models.

Courtesy Gale Morgan

NIB	Exc.	V.G.	Good	Fair	Poor
—	5500	4500	1800	1000	700

NOTE: For barrel lengths over 8" add 25 percent.

Abercrombie & Fitch Commercial 100

Swiss Lugers were made for commercial sale in the United States by "Abercrombie & Fitch Co. New York. Made in Switzerland." — in either one or two lines—is stamped on the top of the barrel. The barrel is 4.75" in length, and there were 49 chambered for 9mm and 51 chambered for the 7.65mm cartridge. This pistol has a grip safety and no stock lug. The Swiss Cross in Sunburst is stamped over the chamber. The extractor is marked, but the safety area is polished. The serial range is four digits—some with a letter suffix. This is a rare and desirable Luger. Be careful of fakes on models of this type and rarity.

NIB	Exc.	V.G.	Good	Fair	Poor
—	12500	9500	5000	3000	2000

1923 Commercial

7-1/2" barrel, 7.65mm caliber. It has a stock lug, and the chamber area is blank. The extractor and safety are both marked in German. These pistols were manufactured for commercial sales in and outside of Germany. There were approximately 18,000 produced, with serial numbers in the 73500-96000 range.

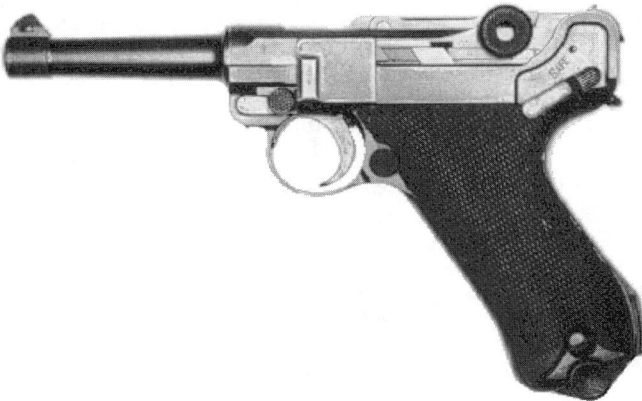

NIB	Exc.	V.G.	Good	Fair	Poor
—	1900	1400	800	600	450

1923 Commercial Safe & Loaded

As above, except that the extractor and safety are marked in English "Safe" & "Loaded." There were approximately 7,000 manufactured in the 73500-96000 serial number range.

Courtesy Gale Morgan

NIB	Exc.	V.G.	Good	Fair	Poor
—	3200	2200	1000	800	500

1923 Dutch Commercial & Military

4" barrel, 9mm caliber. It has a stock lug, and the chamber area is blank. The extractor is marked in German, and the safety is marked "RUST" with a downward pointing arrow. This model was sold commercially and to the military in the Netherlands. There were approximately 1,000 manufactured in the one- to three-digit serial range, with no letter suffix.

NIB	Exc.	V.G.	Good	Fair	Poor
—	4000	2800	1000	850	550

Royal Dutch Air Force

4" barrel, 9mm caliber. Marked with the Mauser Oberndorf proofmark and serial numbered in the 10000 to 14000 range. The safety marked "RUST."

NIB	Exc.	V.G.	Good	Fair	Poor
—	4500	2900	1000	800	550

VICKERS LTD.

NOTE: Vickers was not a manufacturer but an intermediary marketer.

1906 Vickers Dutch

4" barrel, 9mm caliber. There is no stock lug, and it uses a grip safety. The chamber is blank, and the extractor is marked "Geleden." "Vickers Ltd." is stamped on the front toggle link. The safety is marked "RUST" with an upward pointing arrow. Examples have been found with an additional date as late as 1933 stamped on the barrel. These dates indicate arsenal refinishing and in no way detract from the value of this variation. Arsenal reworks are matte-finished, and the originals are a higher-polished rust blue. There were approximately 10,000 manufactured in the 1-10100 serial-number range.

NIB	Exc.	V.G.	Good	Fair	Poor
—	3800	3000	1800	1200	750

ERFURT ROYAL ARSENAL

1908 Erfurt

4" barrel, 9mm caliber. It has no stock lug; and the year of manufacture, from 1910-1913, is stamped above the chamber. The extractor and safety are both marked in German, and "ERFURT" under a crown is stamped on the front toggle link. There were many thousands produced as Germany was involved in WWI. They are found in the one- to five-digit serial range, sometimes with a letter suffix.

NIB	Exc.	V.G.	Good	Fair	Poor
—	2100	1350	600	400	350

1914 Erfurt Military

4" barrel, 9mm caliber. It has a stock lug and the date of manufacture over the chamber, 1914-1918. The extractor and safety are both marked in German, and the front link is marked "ERFURT" under a crown. The finish on this model is rough; and as the war progressed in 1917 and 1918, the finish got worse. There were many thousands produced with one- to five-digit serial numbers, some with letter suffixes.

NIB	Exc.	V.G.	Good	Fair	Poor
—	1300	950	600	400	350

1914 Erfurt Artillery

8" barrel, 9mm caliber. It has a stock lug and was issued with a flat board-type stock and other accessories which will be covered in the section of this book dealing with same. The sight is a nine-position adjustable model. The chamber is dated 1914-1918, and the extractor and safety are both marked in German. "ERFURT" under a crown is stamped on the front toggle link. There were a great many manufactured with one- to five-digit serial numbers, some with a letter suffix. This model is similar to the DWM Artillery except that the finish is not as fine.

NIB	Exc.	V.G.	Good	Fair	Poor
—	3400	2200	1100	800	600

NOTE: Add 50 percent for 1914 dated chamber.

Double Date Erfurt

4" barrel, 9mm caliber. The area above the chamber has two dates: the original 1910-1918, and the date of rework, 1920 or 1921. The extractor and safety are both marked in German, and this model can be found with or without a stock lug. "ERFURT" under a crown is stamped on the front toggle link. Police or military unit markings are found on the front of the grip straps more often than not. There were thousands of these produced by DWM as well as Erfurt.

NIB	Exc.	V.G.	Good	Fair	Poor
—	950	700	500	400	350

SIMSON & CO. SUHL, GERMANY

Note: Simson was the official rework firm for the German army. Thanks to Edward Tinker for his contributions to this section.

Simson & Co. Rework

4" barrels, 9mm caliber. The chamber is blank, but some examples are dated 1917 or 1918. The forward toggle link is stamped "SIMSON & CO. Suhl." The extractor and safety are marked in German. Most examples have stock lugs; some have been noted without them. The only difference between military models and commercial models is the proofmarks.

NIB	Exc.	V.G.	Good	Fair	Poor
—	2500	1650	900	600	500

Simson Grip Safety Rework

4" barrel, 9mm caliber and a grip safety was added. There is a stock lug. The chamber area is blank; the extractor is marked but the safety is not. There were only a few of these commercial reworks manufactured, and caution should be taken to avoid fakes.

NIB	Exc.	V.G.	Good	Fair	Poor
—	3700	2600	1500	850	550

Simson Dated Military

4" barrel, 9mm caliber. There is a stock lug, and the year of manufacture from 1925-1926 is stamped above the chamber (below serial number 700). The extractor and the safety are both marked in German. The checkered walnut grips of Simson-made Lugers are noticeably thicker than others. This is an extremely rare variation. Approximately 2,000 were manufactured with one- to three-digit serial numbers, and few seem to have survived.

NIB	Exc.	V.G.	Good	Fair	Poor
—	3600	2600	1800	900	650

Simson S Code

4" barrel, 9mm caliber. The forward toggle link is stamped with a Gothic S, possibly for "Simson." It has a stock lug, and the area above the chamber is blank. The extractor and the safety are both marked. The grips are also thicker. There were fewer than 12,000 manufactured with one- to five-digit serial numbers—some with the letter "a" suffix. This pistol is quite rare on today's market.

NIB	Exc.	V.G.	Good	Fair	Poor
—	4200	3000	1500	1000	750

EARLY NAZI ERA MAUSER REWORKS

Produced between 1930 and 1933, and normally marked with Waffenamt markings.

Deaths Head Rework

4" barrel, 9mm caliber. It has a stock lug; and a skull and crossbones are stamped, in addition to the date of manufacture, on the chamber area. This date was from 1914-1918. The extractor and safety are both marked. The Waffenamt proof is present. It is thought that this variation was produced for the 1930-1933 era "SS" division of the Nazi Party. Mixed serial numbers are

encountered on this model and do not lower the value. This is a rare Luger on today's market.

NIB	Exc.	V.G.	Good	Fair	Poor
—	2900	1900	950	600	450

Kadetten Institute Rework

4" barrel, 9mm caliber. It has a stock lug, and the chamber area is stamped "K.I." above the date 1933. This stood for Cadets Institute, an early "SA" and "SS" officers' training school. The extractor and safety are both marked, and the Waffenamt is present. There were only a few hundred reworked, and the variation is quite scarce. Be wary of fakes.

NIB	Exc.	V.G.	Good	Fair	Poor
—	3700	2900	1100	800	600

Mauser Unmarked Rework

4" barrel, 9mm caliber. The entire weapon is void of identifying markings. There is extensive refurbishing, removal of all markings, rebarreling, etc. The stock lug is present, and the extractor and safety are marked. The Waffenamt proofmark is on the right side of the receiver. The number manufactured is not known.

NIB	Exc.	V.G.	Good	Fair	Poor
—	2100	1350	850	600	450

MAUSER MANUFACTURED LUGERS

1930-1942 DWM

Mauser Oberndorf

4" barrel, 9mm caliber. It has a stock lug, blank chamber area and a marked extractor and safety. This is an early example of Mauser Luger, and the front toggle link is still marked DWM as leftover parts were intermixed with new Mauser parts in the production of this pistol. This is one of the first Lugers to be finished with the "Salt" blue process. There were approximately 500 manufactured with one- to four-digit serial numbers with the letter "v" suffix. This is a rare variation.

NIB	Exc.	V.G.	Good	Fair	Poor
—	7000	6100	2000	1500	900

1934/06 Swiss Commercial Mauser

4.75" barrel, 7.65mm caliber. There is no stock lug, but it has a grip safety. The Swiss Cross in Sunburst is stamped above the chamber. The extractor and safety are marked in German. The front toggle link is marked with the Mauser banner. There were approximately 200 manufactured for commercial sale in Switzerland. This variation is very well finished, and the serial numbers are all four digits with a "v" suffix.

NIB	Exc.	V.G.	Good	Fair	Poor
—	8000	6000	4000	1800	1000

1935/06 Portuguese "GNR"

4.75" barrel, 7.65mm caliber. It has no stock lug but has a grip safety. The chamber is marked "GNR," representing the Republic National Guard. The extractor is marked "Carregada" ; and the safety, "Seguranca." The Mauser banner is stamped on the front toggle link. There were exactly 564 manufactured according to the original contract records that the Portuguese government made public. They all have four-digit serial numbers with a "v" suffix.

NIB	Exc.	V.G.	Good	Fair	Poor
—	4500	3300	1800	900	750

1934 Mauser Commercial

4" barrel, 7.65mm or 9mm caliber. It has a stock lug, and the chamber area is blank. The extractor and the safety are marked. The Mauser banner is stamped on the front toggle link. The finish on this pistol was very good, and the grips are either checkered walnut or black plastic on the later models. There were a few thousand manufactured for commercial sales in and outside of Germany.

NIB	Exc.	V.G.	Good	Fair	Poor
—	4000	3500	1650	1100	700

S/42 K Date

4" barrel, 9mm caliber. It has a stock lug, and the extractor and safety are marked. This was the first Luger that utilized codes to represent maker and date of manufacture. The front toggle link is marked S/42 in either Gothic or script; this was the code for Mauser. The chamber area is stamped with the letter "K," the code for 1934, the year of manufacture. Approximately 10,500 were manufactured with one- to five-digit serial numbers—some with letter suffixes.

NIB	Exc.	V.G.	Good	Fair	Poor
—	8000	5500	2200	1200	1000

S/42 G Date

As above, with the chamber stamped "G," the code for the year 1935. The Gothic lettering was eliminated, and there were many thousands of this model produced.

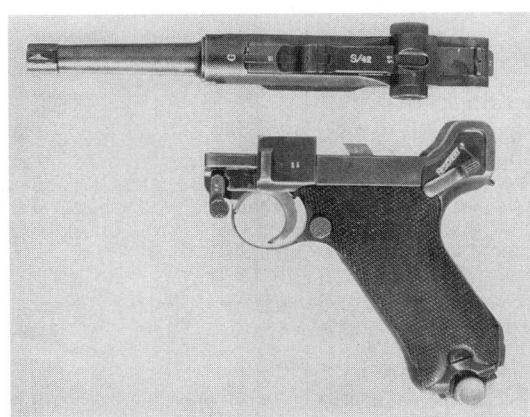

Courtesy Orvel Reichert

NIB	Exc.	V.G.	Good	Fair	Poor
—	3100	2300	1000	650	450

Dated Chamber S/42

4" barrel, 9mm caliber. The chamber area is dated 1936-1940, and there is a stock lug. The extractor and safety are marked. In 1937 the rust blue process was eliminated entirely, and all subsequent pistols were salt blued. There were many thousands manufactured with one- to five-digit serial numbers—some with the letter suffix.

NIB	Exc.	V.G.	Good	Fair	Poor
—	2100	1400	750	500	400

NOTE: Rarest variation is early 1937 with rust blued and strawed parts, add 20 percent.

S/42 Commercial Contract

4" barrel, 9mm caliber. It has a stock lug, and the chamber area is dated. It has a marked extractor and safety. The unusual feature is that, although this was a commercial pistol, the front toggle link is stamped S/42, which was the military code for Mauser. There were only a few hundred manufactured, so perhaps the toggles were left over from previous military production runs. The serial number range is four digits with the letter "v."

NIB	Exc.	V.G.	Good	Fair	Poor
—	3100	2300	1000	750	450

Code 42 Dated Chamber

4" barrel, 9mm caliber. The new German code for Mauser, the number 42, is stamped on the front toggle link. There is a stock lug. The chamber area is dated 1939 or 1940. There were at least 50,000 manufactured with one- to five-digit serial numbers; some have letter suffixes.

NIB	Exc.	V.G.	Good	Fair	Poor
—	1800	1050	650	400	350

41/42 Code

As above, except that the date of manufacture is represented by the final two digits (e.g. 41 for 1941). There were approximately 20,000 manufactured with the one- to five-digit serial number range.

NIB	Exc.	V.G.	Good	Fair	Poor
—	1900	1550	900	700	500

byf Code

As above, with the "byf" code stamp on the toggle link. The year of manufacture, either 41 or 42, is stamped on the chamber. This model was also made with black plastic, as well as walnut grips. There were many thousands produced with the one- to five-digit serial numbers—some with a letter suffix.

NIB	Exc.	V.G.	Good	Fair	Poor
—	3250	1800	950	450	350

Persian Contract 4"

4" barrel, 9mm caliber. It has a stock lug, and the Persian crest is stamped over the chamber. All identifying markings on this variation—including extractor, safety and toggle—are marked in Farsi, the Persian alphabet. There were 1,000 manufactured. The serial numbers are also in Farsi.

NIB	Exc.	V.G.	Good	Fair	Poor
—	7000	5500	3500	2500	2000

Persian Contract Artillery

As above, with an 8" barrel and nine-position adjustable sight on the barrel. This model is supplied with a flat board stock. There were 1,000 manufactured and sold to Persia.

NIB	Exc.	V.G.	Good	Fair	Poor
—	1000	7500	3500	1750	1000

1934/06 Dated Commercial

4.75" barrel, 7.65mm caliber. It has a grip safety but no stock lug. The year of manufacture, from 1937-1942, is stamped above the chamber, and the Mauser banner is stamped on the front link. The extractor is marked, but the safety is not. There were approximately 1,000 manufactured with one- to three-digit serial numbers—some with the letter suffix.

NIB	Exc.	V.G.	Good	Fair	Poor
—	3500	2600	1400	900	500

1934 Mauser Dutch Contract

4" barrel, 9mm caliber. The year of manufacture, 1936-1940, is stamped above the chamber. The extractor is marked "Geladen," and the safety is marked "RUST" with a downward pointing arrow. The Mauser banner is stamped on the front toggle link. This was a military contract sale, and approximately 1,000 were manufactured with four-digit serial numbers with a letter "v" suffix.

NIB	Exc.	V.G.	Good	Fair	Poor
—	4500	3650	2000	1100	850

1934 Mauser Swedish Contract

4.75" barrel, 9mm or 7.65mm caliber. The chamber is dated 1938 or 1939. The extractor and safety are both marked in German, and there is a stock lug. The front toggle link is stamped with the Mauser banner. There were only 275 dated 1938 and 25 dated 1939 in 9mm. There were only 30 chambered for 7.65mm dated 1939. The serial number range is four digits with the letter "v" suffix.

NIB	Exc.	V.G.	Good	Fair	Poor
—	5200	3800	2000	1500	700

1934 Mauser Swedish Commercial

4" barrel, 7.65mm caliber. 1940 is stamped over the chamber; "Kal. 7.65" is stamped on the left side of the barrel. The extractor and safety are both marked, and the Mauser banner is stamped on the front toggle link. There is a stock lug. This model is rare as there were only a few hundred manufactured with four digit serial numbers with the letter "w" suffix.

NIB	Exc.	V.G.	Good	Fair	Poor
—	4500	2950	1200	850	600

1934 Mauser German Contract

4" barrel, 9mm caliber. The chamber is dated 1939-1942, and the front toggle link is stamped with the Mauser banner. There is a stock lug, and the extractor and safety are both marked. The grips are either walnut or black plastic. There were several thousand manufactured with one- to five-digit serial numbers—some with letter suffixes. They were purchased for issue to police or paramilitary units.

NIB	Exc.	V.G.	Good	Fair	Poor
—	3500	3200	1500	800	550

Austrian Bundes Heer (Federal Army)

4" barrel, 9mm caliber. The chamber is blank, and there is a stock lug. The extractor and safety are marked in German, and the Austrian Federal Army Proof is stamped on the left side of the frame above the trigger guard. There were approximately 200 manufactured with four-digit serial numbers and no letter suffix.

NIB	Exc.	V.G.	Good	Fair	Poor
—	3400	2350	1200	700	500

Mauser 2 Digit Date

4" barrel, 9mm caliber. The last two digits of the year of manufacture—41 or 42—are stamped over the chamber. There is a stock lug, and the Mauser banner is on the front toggle link. The extractor and safety are both marked, and the proofmarks were commercial. Grips are either walnut or black plastic. There were approximately 2,000 manufactured for sale to Nazi political groups. They have one- to five-digit serial numbers; some have the letter suffix.

NIB	Exc.	V.G.	Good	Fair	Poor
—	3500	2600	1500	900	650

Ku Luger (Prefix or suffix)

A 4" barrel, 9mm Luger probably manufactured by Mauser for the German Luftwaffe in the early 1940s. The serial number (on the left side receiver area) has a "Ku" prefix or suffix. Total production is estimated at 5000 pieces.

Courtesy Gale Morgan

NIB	Exc.	V.G.	Good	Fair	Poor
—	3900	2400	1200	900	550

KRIEGHOFF MANUFACTURED LUGERS

1923 DWM/Krieghoff Commercial

4" barrel, 7.65mm or 9mm caliber. The chamber is dated 1921 or left blank. There is a stock lug. The front toggle is marked DWM, as they manufactured this Luger to be sold by Krieghoff. "Krieghoff Suhl" is stamped on the back above the lanyard loop. The second "F" in Krieghoff was defective, and all specimens have this distinctive die strike. The safety and extractor are marked in German. There were only a few hundred manufactured with four-digit serial numbers with the letter "i" suffix.

NIB	Exc.	V.G.	Good	Fair	Poor
—	4000	2200	950	650	500

DWM/Krieghoff Commercial

As above, but marked "Heinrich Krieghoff Waffenfabrik Suhl" on the right side of the frame. Some examples have the "Germany" export stamp. There were several hundred manufactured with four-digit serial numbers with a letter suffix.

NIB	Exc.	V.G.	Good	Fair	Poor
—	3800	3650	2000	950	800

Krieghoff Commercial Inscribed Side Frame

4" or 6" barrel, 7.65mm or 9mm caliber. 1,000 were marked "Heinrich Krieghoff Waffenfabrik Suhl" on the right side of the frame, and 500 were devoid of this marking. All have the dagger and anchor trademark over "H.K. Krieghoff Suhl" on the front toggle link. The extractor and the safety are both marked. There is a stock lug, and the grips are of brown checkered plastic. There were approximately 1,500 manufactured with one- to four-digit serial numbers with a "P" prefix.

NIB	Exc.	V.G.	Good	Fair	Poor
—	8500	6400	3000	2000	1000

S Code Krieghoff

4" barrel, 9mm caliber. The Krieghoff trademark is stamped on the front toggle link, and the letter "S" is stamped over the chamber. There is a stock lug, and the extractor and safety are both marked. The grips are wood on early manufactured pistols and brown checkered plastic on later examples. There were approximately 4,500 manufactured for the Luftwaffe with one- to four-digit serial numbers.

NIB	Exc.	V.G.	Good	Fair	Poor
—	7750	5500	2000	950	750

Grip Safety Krieghoff

4" barrel, 9mm caliber. The chamber area is blank, and the front toggle link is stamped with the Krieghoff trademark. There is a stock lug and a grip safety. The extractor is marked "Geleden," and the safety is marked "FEUER" (fire) in the lower position. The grips are checkered brown plastic. This is a rare Luger, and the number produced is not known.

NIB	Exc.	V.G.	Good	Fair	Poor
—	8500	5900	3400	1700	900

36 Date Krieghoff

4" barrel, 9mm caliber. It has a stock lug and the Krieghoff trademark on the front toggle link. The safety and extractor are marked, and the grips are brown plastic. The two-digit year of manufacture, 36, is stamped over the chamber. There were approximately 700 produced in the 3800-4500 serial number range.

NIB	Exc.	V.G.	Good	Fair	Poor
—	8200	5250	2600	1200	950

4 Digit Dated Krieghoff

As above, with the date of production, 1936-1945, stamped above the chamber. There were approximately 9,000 manufactured within the 4500-14000 serial number range.

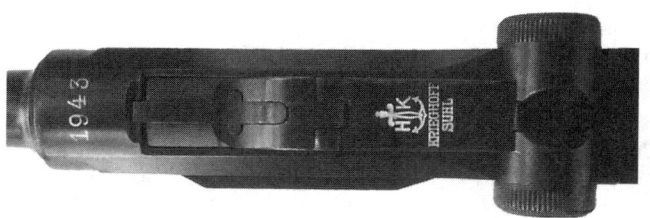

Courtesy Gale Morgan

NIB	Exc.	V.G.	Good	Fair	Poor
—	4500	3400	1850	950	750

NOTE: Later years add 20-35 percent premium.

2nd Series Krieghoff Commercial

4" barrel, 9mm caliber. There is a stock lug, and the Krieghoff trademark is stamped on the front link. The chamber area is blank, and the extractor and safety are marked. There were approximately 500 manufactured for commercial sales inside Germany. The date of manufacture is estimated at 1939-1940, as this variation has the dark finish that results from blueing without polishing the surface, which was done during these years. The grips are coarsely checkered black plastic. The serial number range is one to three digits with a "P" prefix.

NIB	Exc.	V.G.	Good	Fair	Poor
—	6000	4200	2200	1300	800

Post-war Krieghoff

4" barrel, 9mm caliber. There is a stock lug, and the chamber area is blank. The extractor and safety are marked, and the serial numbers in the one- to three-digit range are unusually large—about 3/16ths of an inch. There were 300 of these post-war Lugers produced for the occupation forces. They were assembled from leftover parts, and only 150 have the Krieghoff trademark on the front toggle link—the second 150 have blank links.

NIB	Exc.	V.G.	Good	Fair	Poor
—	6000	3500	2000	750	650

Krieghoff Post-war Commercial

As above, in 7.65mm caliber and the extractor not marked. Approximately 200 manufactured with standard-sized two- or three-digit serial numbers. They were supposedly sold to the occupation forces in the PX stores.

NIB	Exc.	V.G.	Good	Fair	Poor
—	6500	3500	2200	700	550

LUGER ACCESSORIES

Detachable Carbine Stocks

Approximately 13" in length, with a sling swivel and horn buttplate.

NIB	Exc.	V.G.	Good	Fair	Poor
—	5500	3500	1500	700	500

Artillery Stock with Holster

The artillery stock is of a flat board style approximately 13.75" in length. There is a holster and magazine pouches with straps attached. This is a desirable addition to the Artillery Luger.

NIB	Exc.	V.G.	Good	Fair	Poor
—	2750	1600	500	400	300

Navy Stock without Holster

As above, but 12.75" in length with a metal disc inlaid on the left side.

NIB	Exc.	V.G.	Good	Fair	Poor
—	3950	2000	1000	500	400

NOTE: With holster add 100 percent.

Ideal Stock/Holster with Grips

A telescoping metal tube stock with an attached leather holster. It is used in conjunction with a metal-backed set of plain grips that correspond to the metal hooks on the stock and allow attachment. This Ideal Stock is U.S. patented and is so marked.

NIB	Exc.	V.G.	Good	Fair	Poor
—	2000	1400	1000	700	450

Drum Magazine 1st Issue

A 32-round, snail-like affair that is used with the Artillery Luger. It is also used with an adapter in the German 9mm submachine gun. The 1st Issue has a telescoping tube that is used to wind the spring. There is a dust cover that protects the interior from dirt.

NIB	Exc.	V.G.	Good	Fair	Poor
—	2000	1700	1000	550	300

Drum Magazine 2nd Issue

As above, with a folding spring winding lever.

NIB	Exc.	V.G.	Good	Fair	Poor
—	2000	1700	1000	550	300

Drum Magazine Loading Tool

This tool is slipped over the magazine and allows the spring to be compressed so that cartridges could be inserted.

NIB	Exc.	V.G.	Good	Fair	Poor
—	800	550	500	300	200

Drum Carrying Case

The same caveat as above applies.

NIB	Exc.	V.G.	Good	Fair	Poor
—	250	200	125	100	50

Holsters

Produced in a wide variety of styles.
Up to $800, depending on condition and scarcity.

LATE PRODUCTION MAUSER LUGERS MANUFACTURED DURING THE 1970S

P.08 Interarms

4" or 6" barrel, 7.65mm or 9mm caliber.

NIB	Exc.	V.G.	Good	Fair	Poor
1750	1000	550	400	350	300

Swiss Eagle Interarms

Swiss-style straight front grip strap and the American Eagle crest over the chamber. It is chambered for 7.65mm or 9mm and is offered with a 4" or 6" barrel.

NIB	Exc.	V.G.	Good	Fair	Poor
1200	950	650	350	325	300

Cartridge Counter

Chambered for 9mm cartridge and fitted with a slotted grip to show cartridge count in magazine.

NIB	Exc.	V.G.	Good	Fair	Poor
2000	1600	1100	750	500	350

Commemorative Bulgarian

The Bulgarian crest is stamped over the chamber. There were only 100 produced.

NIB	Exc.	V.G.	Good	Fair	Poor
2000	1600	1100	750	500	350

Commemorative Russian

Crossed Nagant rifles are stamped over the chamber. There were 100 produced.

NIB	Exc.	V.G.	Good	Fair	Poor
2000	1600	1100	750	500	350

JOHN MARTZ CUSTOM LUGERS

.45 ACP or .357 SIG

6" barrel, .45 ACP caliber. Assembled from two Luger pistols that were split and welded together. 85 manufactured.

Baby Luger 9mm & 7.65mm

A compact Luger pistol. Approximately 205 were produced.

Courtesy Gale Morgan

Baby Luger .380 ACP

As above, in .380 caliber. Approximately 7 were manufactured.

Courtesy Gale Morgan

LUNA
Zella-Mehlis, Germany

Model 200 Free Pistol

A .22 caliber Martini action single-shot pistol with an 11" barrel, adjustable sights, and walnut grips. Manufactured prior to WWII.

NIB	Exc.	V.G.	Good	Fair	Poor
—	1850	1250	800	500	300

Model 300 Free Pistol

This model is a single-shot target pistol chambered for .22 Short cartridge. Fitted with an 11" barrel, set trigger, walnut stocks and forearm with adjustable palm rest. Built from about 1929 to 1939.

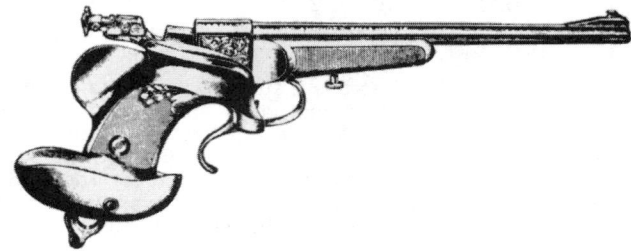

NIB	Exc.	V.G.	Good	Fair	Poor
—	1950	1250	800	500	300

LYMAN
Middletown, Connecticut

Plains Pistol

Available in .50 or .54 caliber percussion.

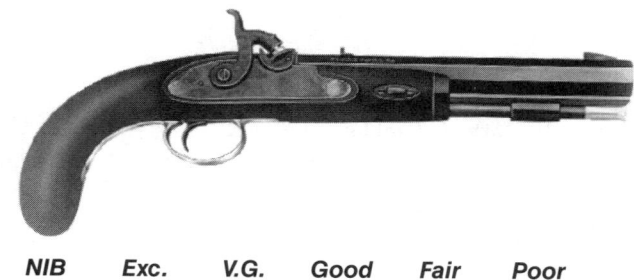

NIB	Exc.	V.G.	Good	Fair	Poor
375	250	200	125	75	50

M

M. B. ASSOCIATES-GYROJET
San Ramon, California

Established in 1960 by R. Maynard and Art Biehl, M. B. Associates produced the Gyrojet pistols and carbines from 1962 to 1970. Basically a hand held rocket launcher, shooting a 12mm or 13mm spin stablized rocket cartridge, composed of four-part solid rocket fuel. The nose of the round was forced rearward onto a stationary firing pin, igniting the fuel, expelling the round and recocking for the next shot. These were not very accurate and led to MBA's demise. Ammunition typically sells for $35 per round or more. Intoduction provided by Dave Rachwal.

Mark I Model A

13mm pistol, cased with a Goddard commemorative medal and 10 dummy rounds, black anodized finish, with walnut grips.

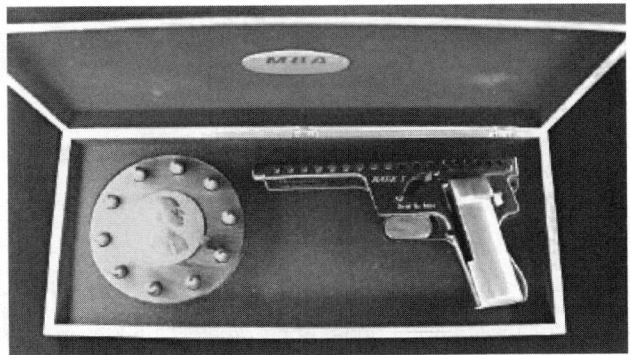

NIB	Exc.	V.G.	Good	Fair	Poor
—	2195	1500	1200	900	500

Mark I Model B

13mm pistol, cased with the commemorative Goddard medal and 10 dummy rounds, black with walnut grips or antique nickel with pearlite grips.

NIB	Exc.	V.G.	Good	Fair	Poor
—	1895	1695	1000	600	300

Mark I Model B

13mm pistol, cardboard box, black anodized with walnut grips usually. This model was produced in many variations and finishes.

NIB	Exc.	V.G.	Good	Fair	Poor
—	995	800	650	400	200

Mark II Model C

12mm pistol, black anodized with walnut grips. This was manufactured for the 12mm round to conform with the 1968 gun control act, because 13mm is 51 cal. and 12mm is 49 cal.

NIB	Exc.	V.G.	Good	Fair	Poor
—	995	800	650	400	200

M.O.A. CORP.
Dayton, Ohio

Maximum

A single-shot pistol manufactured in a variety of calibers from .22 rimfire to .454 Casull with an 8.5", 10", or 14" barrel, adjustable sights, stainless steel receiver blued barrel and walnut grip. Introduced in 1986.

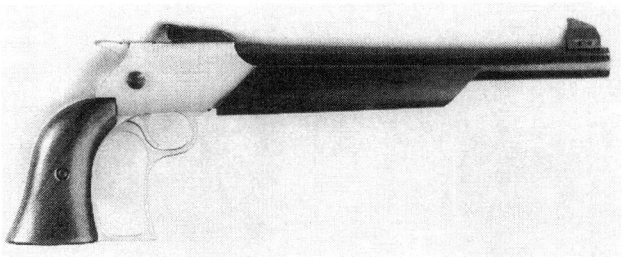

NIB	Exc.	V.G.	Good	Fair	Poor
800	600	475	325	250	125

NOTE: Add 100 percent for stainless steel barrel.

MAGNUM RESEARCH, INC.
Minneapolis, Minnesota

SEE ALSO—Desert Eagle

BFR (Long Cylinder)

This is a single-action revolver with a long cylinder chambered for .22 Hrnet, .30-30, .475/.480, .444, .45-70, .460 S&W, and .45 LC/.410 with 7.5" or 10" barrel and .444 Marlin with 10" barrel. Also chambered for .500 S&W Magnum. Fitted with adjustable sights and stainless steel finish. Weight is about 4 lbs. with 7.5" barrel. Introduced in 1998.

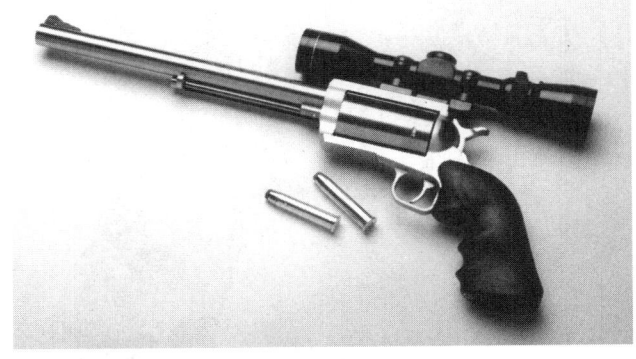

NIB	Exc.	V.G.	Good	Fair	Poor
900	775	500	350	200	100

BFR Little Max (Short Cylinder)

This single-action revolver has a standard cylinder chambered for the .454 Casull (6.5", 7.5", or 10" barrel), .45 Long Colt (6.5" or 7.5" barrel), .22 Hornet (7.5" barrel), or .50 A.E (7.5" barrel). Weight is about 3.5 lbs. with 7.5" barrel. Introduced in 1998. Discontinued.

NIB	Exc.	V.G.	Good	Fair	Poor
800	675	500	350	200	100

Magnum Research Micro Desert Eagle Pistol

Double action only semiauto pistol chambered in .380. Features include steel slide, aluminum allow frame, black polymer grips, nickel silver or blue anodized frame, 6-round capacity, fixed sights, 2.2-inch barrel. Weight less than 14 oz. Price: $535.

Magnum Research Desert Eagle Magnum Pistol

Enormous gas-operated semiauto pistol chambered in .50 AE, .44 Magnum, .357 Magnum. Features include 6- or 10-inch barrel, adjustable sights, variety of finishes. Now made in the USA. Price: $1650 to $2156.

IMI SP-21

This is semi-automatic double-action pistol chambered for the 9mm, .40 S&W, or .45 ACP cartridge. Barrel length is 3.9". Magazine capacity is 10 rounds for all calibers. Polymer frame with steel slide and barrel. Weight is about 26 oz. Made in Israel by Israel Military Industries. Discontinued.

NIB	Exc.	V.G.	Good	Fair	Poor
550	400	300	200	150	100

Baby Eagle

Single/double action semi-auto pistol chambered in 9mm, .40 S&W and .45 ACP. Steelor polymer frame, black finish. Decocker. Made in Israel.

NIB	Exc.	V.G.	Good	Fair	Poor
550	425	295	200	150	125

Picuda Pistol

Pistol version of the MLR-1722 with a 10-inch barrel. Chambered in .22 LR or .17 Mach-2. Laminated stock.

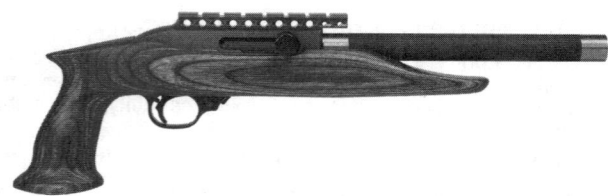

NIB	Exc.	V.G.	Good	Fair	Poor
700	575	400	275	150	100

MALTBY, HENLEY AND CO.
New York, New York
Spencer Safety Hammerless Revolver

A .32 caliber double-action revolver with a 3" barrel and 5-shot cylinder. The frame and barrel made of brass and the cylinder of steel. The barrel marked "Spencer Safety Hammerless Pat. Jan. 24, 1888 & Oct. 29, 1889." Several thousand were manufactured during in the 1890s.

Courtesy Mike Stuckslager

NIB	Exc.	V.G.	Good	Fair	Poor
—	—	325	225	125	75

MANHATTAN FIREARMS COMPANY
Norwich, Connecticut

Newark, New Jersey
Bar Hammer Pistol

A .31, .34, or .36 caliber single-shot percussion pistol with a 2" or 4" barrel. The hammer marked "Manhattan F.A. Mfg. Co. New York." Blued with walnut grips. Approximately 1,500 were made during the 1850s.

NIB	Exc.	V.G.	Good	Fair	Poor
—	—	1050	750	300	150

Shotgun Hammer Pistol

A .36 caliber bar hammer single-shot percussion pistol with a 5.5" half octagonal barrel marked as above. Blued with walnut grips. Approximately 500 were made.

NIB	Exc.	V.G.	Good	Fair	Poor
—	—	1050	750	300	150

PEPPERBOX

A .28 or .31 caliber double-action percussion pepperbox with 3", 4", or 5" barrels and 5- or 6-shot barrel groups. Blued, case hardened with walnut grips. Marked as above and also "Cast Steel." The major variations of this pistol are as follows:

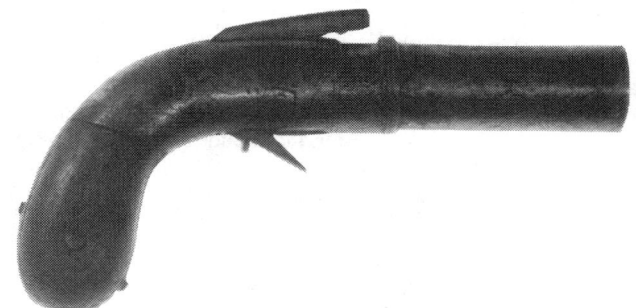

Courtesy Milwaukee Public Museum, Milwaukee, Wisconsin

Three-shot with 3" Barrel

Manually rotated barrels.

NIB	Exc.	V.G.	Good	Fair	Poor
—	—	950	550	250	125

Five-shot with 3", 4", 5" Barrel

Automatically rotated barrels.

NIB	Exc.	V.G.	Good	Fair	Poor
—	—	1100	650	450	250

Six-shot with 3" or 4" Barrel

Automatic rotation.

NIB	Exc.	V.G.	Good	Fair	Poor
—	—	1100	650	450	250

Six-shot with 5" Barrel

Automatic rotation.

NIB	Exc.	V.G.	Good	Fair	Poor
—	—	1600	1200	550	350

POCKET REVOLVER

A .31 caliber percussion revolver with a 4", 5", or 6" barrel and either 5-shot or 6-shot cylinder. Blued, case hardened with walnut grips. The barrel marked, "Manhattan Firearms/Manufg. Co. New York" on the 5-shot model, serial numbers from 1 to approximately 1,000, and "Manhattan Firearms Mfg. Co. New York" on the 6-shot model. The frame marked "December 27, 1859."

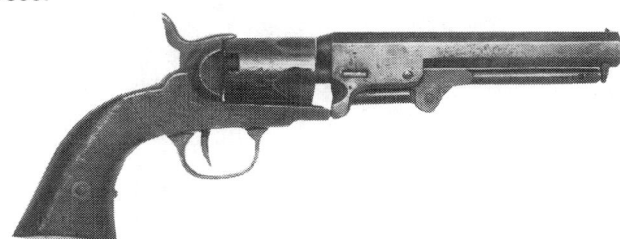

Courtesy Milwaukee Public Museum, Milwaukee, Wisconsin

First Model—Five-Shot

NIB	Exc.	V.G.	Good	Fair	Poor
—	—	1200	600	450	150

Second Model—Six-Shot

NIB	Exc.	V.G.	Good	Fair	Poor
—	—	1200	600	450	150

London Pistol Company

As above, but marked "London Pistol Company." Approximately 200 manufactured between 1859 and 1861.

NIB	Exc.	V.G.	Good	Fair	Poor
—	—	1400	750	450	150

.36 CALIBER PERCUSSION REVOLVER

A .36 caliber percussion revolver with a 4", 5", or 6.5" octagonal barrel and 5- or 6-shot cylinder. Blued, case hardened with walnut grips. Approximately 78,000 were made between 1859 and 1868. There were five variations.

Courtesy Milwaukee Public Museum, Milwaukee, Wisconsin

Automatic rotation.

Model I

A 5-shot cylinder marked "Manhattan Firearms Mfg. Co. New York." The serial numbers from 1 through 4200.

NIB	Exc.	V.G.	Good	Fair	Poor
—	—	1500	1050	550	150

NOTE: The 6" barreled version would be worth a 15 percent premium.

Model II

As above with the 1859 patent date marked on the barrel. The serial range is 4200 to 14500.

NIB	Exc.	V.G.	Good	Fair	Poor
—	—	1650	1350	550	150

Model III

A 5-shot cylinder and marked, "Manhattan Firearms Co. Newark NJ," together with the 1859 patent date. The serial numbers are from 14500 to 45200.

NIB	Exc.	V.G.	Good	Fair	Poor
—	—	1575	1200	500	150

Model IV

As above, with a modified recoil shield and the patent date March 8, 1864, added to the barrel inscription. Serial numbers from 45200 to 69200.

NIB	Exc.	V.G.	Good	Fair	Poor
—	—	1600	1250	450	150

Model V

NIB	Exc.	V.G.	Good	Fair	Poor
—	—	1700	1350	550	200

.22 Caliber Pocket Revolver

A .22 caliber spur trigger revolver with a 3" barrel and 7-shot cylinder. Blued, silver plated with walnut or rosewood grips. Approximately 17,000 were made during the 1860s. A fairly close copy of the S&W No. 1.

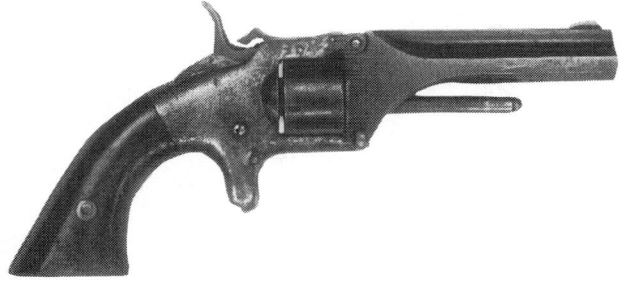

Courtesy Milwaukee Public Museum, Milwaukee, Wisconsin

NIB	Exc.	V.G.	Good	Fair	Poor
—	—	550	300	250	100

MANHATTAN-AMERICAN STANDARD HERO

A .34 caliber single-shot percussion pistol with a 2" or 3" round barrel that unscrews for loading. Blued, brass frame with walnut grips. Marked "A.S.T. Co./HERO." Made by the American Standard Tool Company, Manhattan's successor. Approximately 30,000 manufactured between 1868 and 1873.

Manhattan Manufactured

Marked, "HERO/M.F.A.Co." Approximately 5,000 were produced.

NIB	Exc.	V.G.	Good	Fair	Poor
—	—	625	550	250	100

American Standard Manufactured

Approximately 25,000 were produced.

NIB	Exc.	V.G.	Good	Fair	Poor
—	—	625	500	225	100

MANN, FRITZ
Suhl, Germany

6.35mm Pocket Pistol

A 6.35mm caliber semi-automatic pistol with a 1.65" barrel and 5-shot magazine. Blued with plastic grips having the name "Mann" cast in them. This pistol, which weighs only 9 oz., is one of the smallest semi-automatic pistols ever manufactured. Made between 1920 and 1922.

NIB	Exc.	V.G.	Good	Fair	Poor
—	395	295	200	150	100

7.65mm Pocket Pistol

A 7.65mm or 9mm short semi-automatic pistol with a 2.35" barrel and 5-shot magazine. Blued with plastic grips that have the name "Mann" cast in them. Manufactured between 1924 and 1929.

NIB	Exc.	V.G.	Good	Fair	Poor
—	375	275	200	150	100

MANUFRANCE
St. Etienne, France
SEE—Le Francais

Auto Stand

A .22 caliber semi-automatic pistol manufactured by Pyrenees and sold by Manufrance under the trade name Auto Stand.

NIB	Exc.	V.G.	Good	Fair	Poor
—	250	225	200	150	100

Buffalo Stand

A .22 caliber bolt-action pistol with a 12" barrel and adjustable sights. Blued with a walnut stock. Manufactured prior to 1914.

NIB	Exc.	V.G.	Good	Fair	Poor
—	250	225	200	150	100

Le Agent

An 8mm caliber double-action revolver with a 5" barrel. Blued with walnut grips.

NIB	Exc.	V.G.	Good	Fair	Poor
—	200	100	175	150	75

Le Colonial

As above, with an enclosed hammer.

NIB	Exc.	V.G.	Good	Fair	Poor
—	200	175	150	100	75

LeFrancais

A semi-automatic pistol chambered for the 7.65mm cartridge. Built on the blowback design. The 7.65mm pistols were first built in 1950 and production stopped in 1959. Very few of these pistols are in the U.S.

Courtesy J.B. Wood

NIB	Exc.	V.G.	Good	Fair	Poor
—	525	425	300	200	100

MANURHIN
Saint-Bonnet-le-Chateau, France

This company manufactured the Walther PP and PPK models under license and these are marked "Manufacture de Machines du Haut-Rhin" on the left front of the slide and "Lic Excl. Walther" on the left rear. These arms were imported into the U.S.A. in the early 1950s by Thalson Import Company of San Francisco, California, and later by Interarms. The latter are marked "Mark 11" and "Made in France." Note: For all models, add 15 percent for police markings.

NEW PRODUCTION

Manurhin is now owned by Chapuis Armes.

Model PP

Similar to the Walther Model PP, with a revised safety. Discontinued.

NIB	Exc.	V.G.	Good	Fair	Poor
—	400	350	300	225	150

Model PPK/S

Similar to the Walther Model PPK/S, with a revised safety. Discontinued.

NIB	Exc.	V.G.	Good	Fair	Poor
—	400	350	300	225	150

Model PP Sports

This is a target version of the PP chambered for the .22 caliber shell. Available in various barrel lengths. Discontinued.

NIB	Exc.	V.G.	Good	Fair	Poor
—	400	350	300	225	150

Model 73 Defense Revolver

A .38 Special or .357 Magnum caliber double-action swing-out cylinder revolver with a 2.5", 3", or 4" barrel having fixed sights. Blued with walnut grips.

NIB	Exc.	V.G.	Good	Fair	Poor
1150	1000	850	750	500	350

Model 73 Gendarmerie

As above, with a 5.5", 6", or 8" long barrel and adjustable sights.

NIB	Exc.	V.G.	Good	Fair	Poor
1250	1100	900	800	550	400

Model 73 Sport

Similar to the above, with a shortened lock time and target-style adjustable sights.

NIB	Exc.	V.G.	Good	Fair	Poor
1250	1100	900	800	550	400

Model 73 Convertible

As above, with interchangeable .22, .32, or .38 caliber barrels and cylinders.

NIB	Exc.	V.G.	Good	Fair	Poor
2250	1850	1600	1400	950	750

Model 73 Silhouette

Similar to the Model 73 Sport, but in .22 to .357 Magnum caliber with a 10" or 10.75" shrouded barrel and formfitting walnut grips.

NIB	Exc.	V.G.	Good	Fair	Poor
1200	1050	850	750	500	350

MARATHON PRODUCTS, INC.
Santa Barbara, California

.22 Hot Shot Pistol

A .22 caliber bolt-action pistol with a 14.5" barrel. Blued with a walnut stock. Manufactured in 1986 and 1987.

NIB	Exc.	V.G.	Good	Fair	Poor
—	100	55	45	30	25

MARBLE'S ARMS & MFG. CO.
Gladstone, Michigan

Marble's Game Getter Gun (NFA, curio or relic)

Marble's suspended sales of the Game Getter in the United States after the Treasury Department ruled it was a "firearm" under the NFA, but continued sales abroad. Its retail price in 1934 was about $24 (12" or 15" barrels) to $26 (18" barrels). The Bureau of Internal Revenue removed the 18" barrel variation from the NFA in a Letter Ruling dated March 1, 1939. Today, the 12" and 15" barrel variations are controlled under the NFA in the "any other weapon" category. If the shoulder stock is removed from a 12", 15", or 18" barreled Game Getter, however, ATF has ruled it to be an NFA "firearm" subject to a $200 transfer tax.

Model 1908

Serial numbered from A to M; then 001 to 10000.

NIB	Exc.	V.G.	Good	Fair	Poor
—	1800	1200	750	550	425

Model 1921

RIGHT SIDE:

Calibers 22 & 44 Patent Allowed	Calibers 22 & 44 Patent Allowed

Each of the markings on the right side is enclosed within an elongated circle.

OTHER CHARACTERISTICS:

Separate flat buttplate attached with two screws up to approximately serial number 1200; afterwards, a flattened buttplate was integrally formed from the same round steel used to form the skeleton stock. Early stocks have drop adjustment with a knurled collar 3/8" diameter by 13/16" long; at approximately serial number 2500, the collar was changed to 1/2" by 5/8" long. The hammer spur is curved down up to approximately serial number 2,000, then the curve at hammer is up. The Model 1908 was originally designed for .22 short, long or LR and .44 shot and ball ammunition, but the most satisfactory load was the long-cased .44-40 that held the shot in place with a disk and mouth crimp. The 1915 Marble's catalog stated the Model 1908 was available for use with the 2" .410 shotgun shell; chambering is slightly different from that of the .44-40, but is seldom encountered. Production of the Model 1908 was not resumed because of World War I. To meet the continuing demand for this extremely popular firearm, Marble's produced an entirely new gun in 1921. The grip, folding stock (made from cold-rolled sheet metal and nickel-plated), and other features were redesigned. The serial number range for the Model 1921 is 10001 (shipped in October 1921) to 20076. Most production of the Model 1921 apparently ended around the time of World War II; however, factory records disclose that Marble's was exporting 15" barrel Model 1921s into Canada in 1955, where their registration was not required at that time. Marble's also assembled approximately 200 Model 1921s from parts circa 1960-61, and sold them (without the holster) for $200 each. The Model 1921 was originally designed from the 2" .410 shotgun shell, but Marble's changed the extractor marking on some guns to 2-1/2" or 2 1/2" to indicate factory rechambering for the 2.5" shell, which has been reported to have started in 1924. However, the change to a 2-1/2" chamber may not have been uniform, because both 2" and 2-1/2" marked guns have been observed in low (14000) and high (19000) serial number ranges. The lowest serial number with 2" marking observed so far is 14601. The range from approximately 14500 to 17000 have plastic rather than walnut grips, a single-bladed rear sight rather than multiple-blade, and blued rather than case-hardened hammer. Outside this range, only 19288 has the 2" marking; and number 19692 is marked 2-1/2". No Model 1921 Game Getters are known to have been factory chambered for the 3" .410 shell. The markings on the Model 1921 are:

LEFT SIDE:

Marble'S Game Getter Gun Gladstone, Mich.U.S.A.	Marble Arms & Mfg.Co.

RIGHT SIDE:

UPPER BARREL 22 S.L. LR.&N.R.A
LOWER BARREL .44GG & .410 2"OTHER

CHARACTERISTICS:

Other barrel markings for the Model 1921 in .410 are .410 2-1/2" and .410 2-1/2"; the latter appears in the serial number range from approximately 15000 to 16600, and in the low

19000 range. Plastic grips were used in the serial range from approximately 14600 to 17000.The Model 1921 was originally designed for the 2" .410 shotgun shell, but Marble's changed the extractor marking on some guns to 2-1/2" or 2-1/2" to indicate factory rechambering for the 2.5" shell, apparently on a random or special-order basis (both 2" and 2-1/2" marked guns have been observed in low (14000) and high (19000) serial number ranges). The lowest serial number with 2?" marking observed so far is 14601. The range from approximately 14500 to 17000 have plastic rather than walnut grips, single-bladed rear sight rather than multiple-blades, and blued rather than case hardened hammer. Outside this range, only 19288 has the 2?" marking; number 19692 is marked 2-1/2". No Model 1921 Game Getters are known to have been factory chambered for the 3" .410 shell.

NIB	Exc.	V.G.	Good	Fair	Poor
—	1800	1200	750	550	425

NOTE: Boxed guns (wooden box, Model 1908; cardboard box, Model 1921) with accessories, or 18" barrel variations, nonstandard calibers (.25-20, .32-20, .38-40, etc.) command premiums of 50 to 200 percent or more; an original holster is $75 to $150. Two new-in-box Model 1908 with 15" and 18" barrels sold for $2,700 and $3,600, respectively, in 1994. An original wooden Model 1908 box alone may sell for $500 to $900. All 18" barrel variations are rare.

Marble's Game Getter Pistol and other special-order or experimental Game Getters NFA, curio or relic

Contemporary articles and advertisements in Hunter-Trader-Trapper, and some early Marble's catalogs, state that a small number of Model 1908 Game Getters were originally manufactured (with rifled barrels) for .25-20, .32-20, and.38-40 cartridges. An illustrated advertisement in a 1910 issue of Hunter-Trapper-Trader states that 12", 15" and 18" barrel Game Getters were available for delivery in .25-20, .32-20 and .38-40, and that these firearms were designed as over-and-under rifles with rifled barrels. An article in the October 1913 issue of Outdoor Life states that Marble's was manufacturing a Game Getter pistol, with 10" barrels, and that any barrel length could be ordered.Original factory records have confirmed the manufacture of the foregoing Game Getters, and clarified their designs. All original guns are thus correctly classified as experimental or special-order guns, and all are extremely rare. Factory records disclose that about 20 each of the Model 1908 were manufactured with .22/25-20 and .22/.32-20 over-and-under rifled barrels, but the barrel lengths are not specified. No .22/.38-40 Model 1908 Game Getters are listed in the factory records, but that may not have precluded a later factory alteration to that configuration. It is important to note that any Model 1908 Game Getter with over-and-under rifled barrels less than 18" in length is currently subject to registration under the NFA as a short barreled rifle, with a $200 transfer tax. Under current law, if these firearms are not registered they are contraband and cannot be legally owned unless ATF administratively removes them from the NFA as collector's items.Factory records disclose that eight Model 1908 Game Getter pistols were manufactured, and all were shipped to a Minneapolis hardware store. Two specimens have been located: serial number 3810, with a 8" .22/.44 smooth bore barrel, and serial number 3837, with a 10" .22/.44 smooth bore barrel. Inspection of serial numbers 3810 and 3837 (including removal of the grips) reveal they were never fitted with shoulder stocks, because the portion of the frame which would have accommodated the stock was never machined out to receive one. Under current law, an original Marble's Game Getter pistol is subject to registration under the NFA as an "Any Other Weapon" with a $5 transfer tax. According to very incomplete factory records, a relatively small number—about a dozen—Model 1921 Game Getters were manufactured with .22/.38-40 rifled barrels, but the barrel lengths are not specified. It is possible that other factory-original configurations exist, such as .22/.25-20 and others.

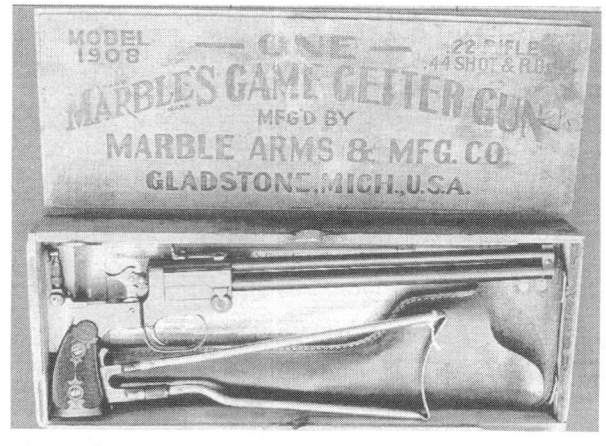

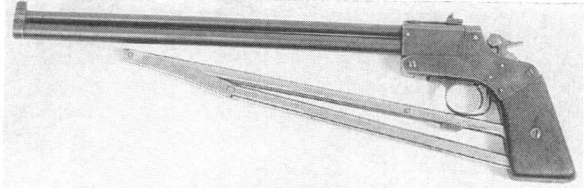

MARGOLIN
Tula, Soviet State Arsenal
Model MT Sports

This is a semi-automatic .22 caliber pistol with no barrel weights and is not threaded for a compensator. Barrel length is 7.5". Furnished with a black plastic case with spare magazine and repair parts. Discontinued.

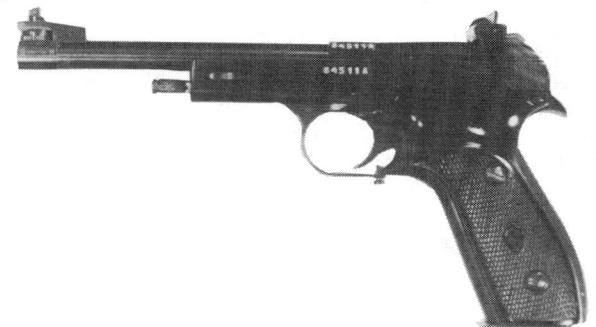

Courtesy Orvel Reichert

NIB	Exc.	V.G.	Good	Fair	Poor
—	600	500	400	300	200

Model MTS-1

A .22 short semi-automatic pistol with a 5.9" barrel having an integral muzzle brake (7.4" overall), adjustable walnut grips and a 6-shot magazine. Normally, accompanied by a wooden case with cleaning accessories. Discontinued.

Courtesy Orvel Reichert

NIB	Exc.	V.G.	Good	Fair	Poor
—	1300	1025	800	450	350

Model MTS-2

As above, in .22 LR with a 5.9" barrel. Discontinued.

Courtesy Orvel Reichert

An unusual Margolin .22 caliber Olympic Model with wrap around square barrel weights and wooden case.

NIB	Exc.	V.G.	Good	Fair	Poor
—	1200	900	600	400	350

MARIETTE BREVETTE
Liege, Belgium

A number of European manufacturers produced percussion pepperbox pistols based upon a patent issued to Mariette during the 1840s and 1850s. These pistols have detachable barrels that are loaded at the breech, double-action ring triggers, and internally mounted hammers. They are normally blued and foliate engraved.

6 Barrel Pepperbox

NIB	Exc.	V.G.	Good	Fair	Poor
—	—	2250	900	400	—

4 Barrel Pepperbox

NIB	Exc.	V.G.	Good	Fair	Poor
—	—	2250	900	400	—

MARLIN FIREARMS CO.
Madison, North Carolina

NOTE: Marlin, along with its subsidiaries Harrington & Richardson/NEF, is now owned by Remington Arms.

1st Model Derringer

This was the first handgun produced by Marlin. The barrel is 2-1/16" long and pivots to the side for loading. There is a plunger under the frame that is depressed to free the barrel. This device is a Ballard patent. This pistol is chambered for the .22 rimfire cartridge, and there is no extractor. The frame is brass and usually nickel-plated. It has two grooves milled beneath the blued barrel. The grips are of rosewood. The barrel is stamped "J.M. Marlin, New Haven, Ct." There were approximately 2,000 manufactured between 1863 and 1867. They are quite scarce on today's market.

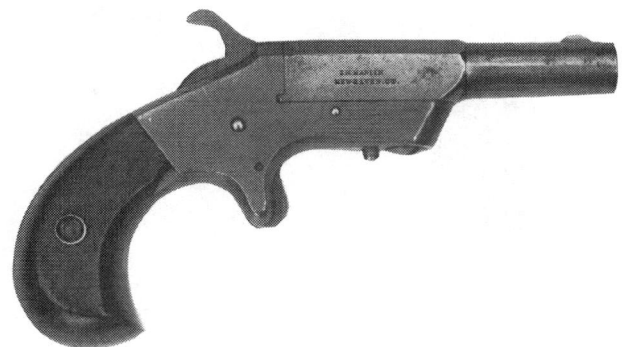

Courtesy Milwaukee Public Museum, Milwaukee, Wisconsin

NIB	Exc.	V.G.	Good	Fair	Poor
—	—	1350	750	300	100

Victor Model Derringer

This model is similar in appearance to the "O.K." Model but is larger in size and is chambered for the .38-caliber rimfire cartridge. The barrel is 2-11/16" long; and there was, for the first time, an extractor. The finish and function were unchanged. The right side of the barrel is stamped "J.M. Marlin/New Haven, Ct./Pat. April 5.1870." "Victor" is stamped on the top of the barrel. There were approximately 4,000 manufactured between 1870 and 1881.

NIB	Exc.	V.G.	Good	Fair	Poor
—	—	1600	1250	500	150

O.K. Model Derringer

The O.K. Model is chambered for .22, .30, and .32 rimfire cartridges. The barrel is 2-1/8" or 3-1/8" on the .32. There is no extractor, and it functions as the 1st Model. The frame is plated brass with flat sides, and the barrel is found either blued or nickel-plated. The grips are rosewood. The markings are the same as on the 1st Model but are located on the right side of the barrel. The top of the barrel is marked "O.K." There were approximately 5,000 manufactured between 1863 and 1870.

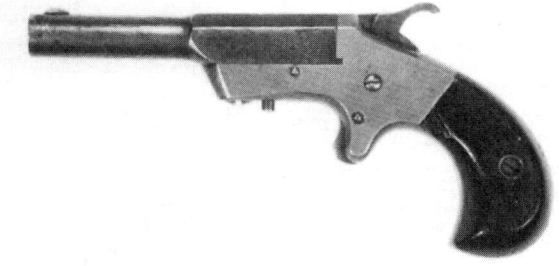

Photo by Lt. Col. William S. Brophy from Marlin Firearms with permission

NIB	Exc.	V.G.	Good	Fair	Poor
—	—	1350	750	300	100

NEVERMISS MODEL DERRINGER

This model was made in three different sizes chambered for the .22, .32, and .41 rimfire cartridges. The barrel is 2.5" long and swings sideways for loading. The frame is plated brass, and the barrels are either blued or nickel-plated. The grips are rosewood. The frame is grooved under the barrels as on the 1st model. There is an extractor on this model. The barrel markings are the same as on the "Victor," with the top of the barrel marked "Nevermiss." There were approximately 5,000 manufactured between 1870 and 1881.

.22 Caliber Model

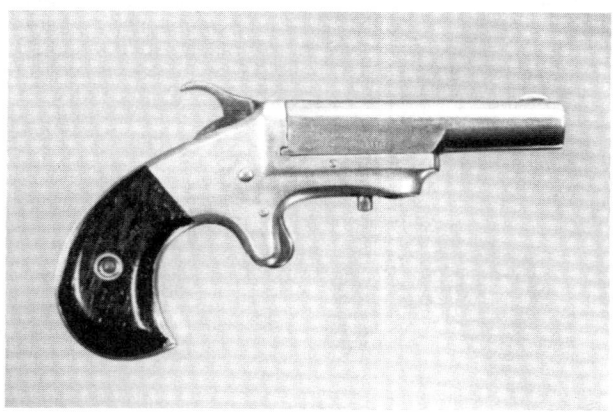

Photo by Lt. Col. William S. Brophy from Marlin Firearms with permission

NIB	Exc.	V.G.	Good	Fair	Poor
—	—	1500	1150	500	100

.32 Caliber Model

Photo by Lt. Col. William S. Brophy from Marlin Firearms with permission

NIB	Exc.	V.G.	Good	Fair	Poor
—	—	1200	750	350	100

.41 Caliber Model

Photo by Lt. Col. William S. Brophy from Marlin Firearms with permission

NIB	Exc.	V.G.	Good	Fair	Poor
—	—	3750	2500	1000	400

Stonewall Model Derringer

This model is identical to the .41-caliber "Nevermiss," but the top of the barrel is marked "Stonewall." It is rarely encountered.

Photo by Lt. Col. William S. Brophy from Marlin Firearms with permission

NIB	Exc.	V.G.	Good	Fair	Poor
—	—	6000	4250	2000	750

O.K. Pocket Revolver

This is a solid-frame, spur-trigger, single-action revolver chambered for the .22 rimfire short. The round barrel is 2.25", and the 7-shot cylinder is unfluted. The frame is nickel-plated brass with a blue or nickel-plated barrel, and the bird's-head grips are rosewood. The cylinder pin is removable and is used to knock the empty cases out of the cylinder. The top of the barrel is marked "O.K." and "J.M. Marlin. New Haven, Conn. U.S.A." There were approximately 1,500 manufactured between 1870 and 1875.

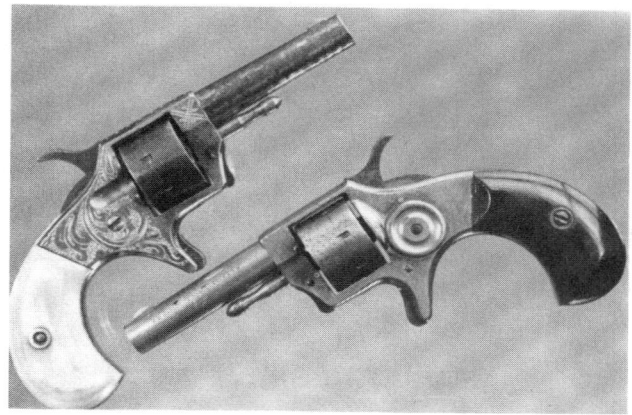

Photo by Lt. Col. William S. Brophy from Marlin Firearms with permission

NIB	Exc.	V.G.	Good	Fair	Poor
—	—	700	500	200	75

Little Joker Revolver

This model is similar in appearance to the "O.K." model; some are reported to have engraving and ivory or pearl grips. There were approximately 500 manufactured between 1871 and 1873.

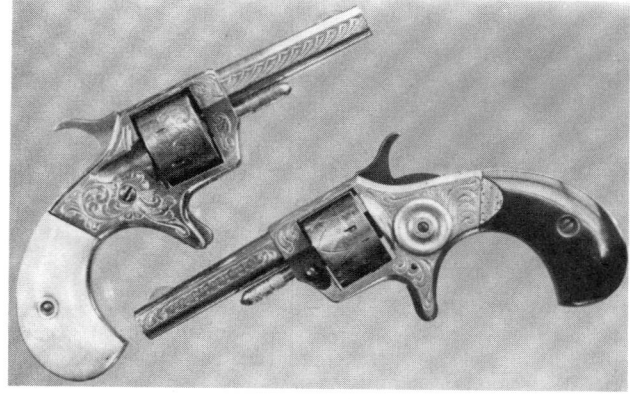

Photo by Lt. Col. William S. Brophy from Marlin Firearms with permission

NIB	Exc.	V.G.	Good	Fair	Poor
—	—	500	500	350	125

J. M. MARLIN STANDARD POCKET REVOLVERS

In 1872 Marlin began production of its Smith & Wesson look-alike. The Manhattan Firearms Company had developed a copy of the Model 1 S&W .22 cartridge revolver. In 1868 the company ceased business, and the revolvers were produced by the American Standard Tool Company until their dissolution in 1873. In 1872 Marlin had entered into an agreement with this company to manufacture these revolvers, which were no longer protected by the Rollin White patent after 1869. The Marlin revolvers are similar to those made by American Standard, the only real difference being that Marlin grips are of the bird's-head round configuration. A contoured grip frame and a patented pawl spring mechanism is utilized on the Marlin revolvers.

MARLIN XXX STANDARD 1872 POCKET REVOLVER

This is the first in the series of four Standard model revolvers. It is chambered for the .30 caliber rimfire. The earlier model has an octagonal 3-1/8" barrel; and the later, a round 3" barrel. There are round and octagonal barrel variations (with unfluted cylinder) and round barrel variations (with short and long fluted cylinders). All of the barrels are ribbed and tip up for loading. They have plated brass frames, and the barrels are nickel-plated. The bird's-head grips are of rosewood or hard rubber, bearing the monogram "M.F.A. Co." inside a star. There is a spur trigger. The markings "J.M. Marlin-New Haven Ct." appear on the earlier octagonal barreled models. "U.S.A. Pat. July 1. 1873" was added to the later round barreled models. All barrels are marked "XXX Standard 1872." There were approximately 5,000 of all types manufactured between 1872 and 1887.

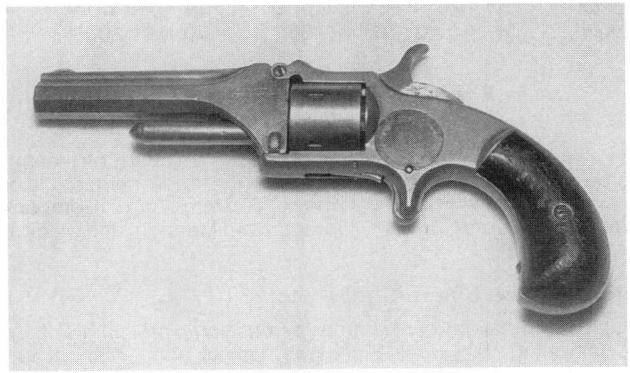

Octagon Barrel—Early Variation

NIB	Exc.	V.G.	Good	Fair	Poor
—	—	900	500	300	75

Round Barrel—Non-Fluted Cylinder

NIB	Exc.	V.G.	Good	Fair	Poor
—	—	800	400	275	75

Round Barrel—Short Fluted Cylinder

NIB	Exc.	V.G.	Good	Fair	Poor
—	—	750	350	200	75

Round Barrel—Long Fluted Cylinder

NIB	Exc.	V.G.	Good	Fair	Poor
—	—	750	450	150	75

MARLIN XX STANDARD 1873 POCKET REVOLVER

This model is similar in appearance to the XXX 1872 model except that it is chambered for the .22 long rimfire and is marked "XX Standard 1873." There are three basic variations: the early octagonal barrel model with non-fluted cylinder, the round barrel model with non-fluted cylinder, and the round barrel with fluted cylinder. Function and features are the same as described for the "XXX Standard 1872" model. There were approximately 5,000 manufactured between 1873 and 1887.

Early Octagon Barrel Model

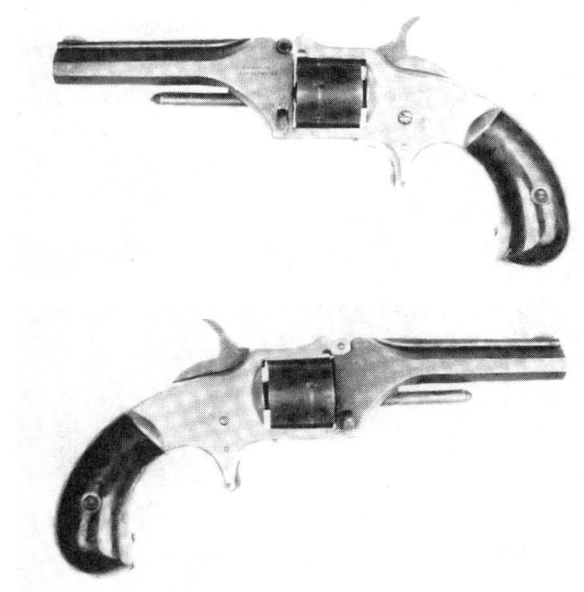

Photo by Lt. Col. William S. Brophy from Marlin Firearms with permission

NIB	Exc.	V.G.	Good	Fair	Poor
—	—	900	600	200	100

Round Barrel—Fluted Cylinder

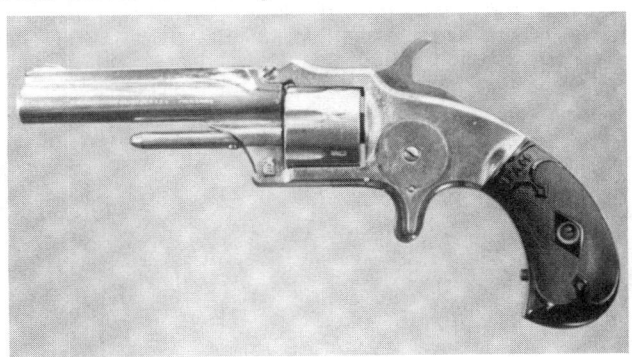

Photo by Lt. Col. William S. Brophy from Marlin Firearms with permission

NIB	Exc.	V.G.	Good	Fair	Poor
—	—	750	500	200	75

Round Barrel—Non-Fluted Cylinder

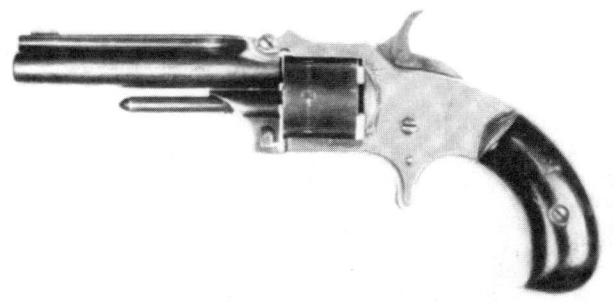

Photo by Lt. Col. William S. Brophy from Marlin Firearms with permission

NIB	Exc.	V.G.	Good	Fair	Poor
—	—	875	650	400	100

Marlin No. 32 Standard 1875 Pocket Revolver

This model is also similar in appearance to the "XXX Standard 1872" model except that it is chambered for the .32 rimfire cartridge. The 3" barrel is round with a rib, and the 5-shot cylinder is fluted and is in two different lengths to accommodate either the .32 Short or Long cartridge. The finish, function, and most markings are the same as on previous models with the exception of the barrel top marking "No. 32 Standard 1875." There were approximately 8,000 manufactured between 1875 and 1887.

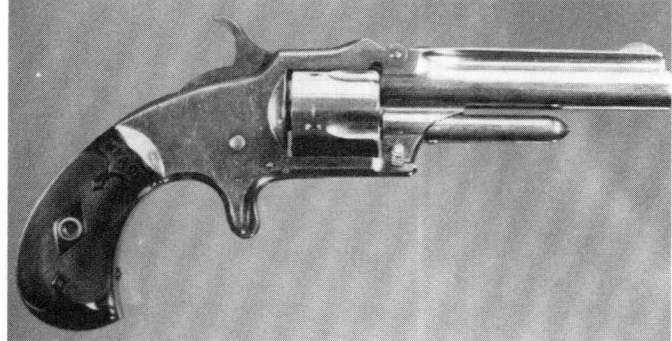

Photo by Lt. Col. William S. Brophy from Marlin Firearms with permission

NIB	Exc.	V.G.	Good	Fair	Poor
—	—	675	450	200	75

Marlin 38 Standard 1878 Pocket Revolver

This model is different than its predecessors in that it features a steel frame and flat bottom butt, with hard rubber monogram grips. There was still a spur trigger, and the 3.25" ribbed round barrel still tipped up for loading. This model is chambered for the .38 centerfire cartridge. The finish is full nickel plate, and the top of the barrel is marked "38 Standard 1878." There were approximately 9,000 manufactured between 1878 and 1887.

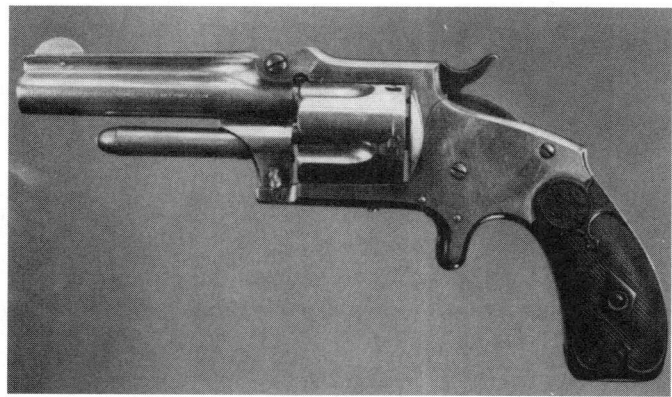

Photo by Lt. Col. William S. Brophy from Marlin Firearms with permission

NIB	Exc.	V.G.	Good	Fair	Poor
—	—	900	600	250	75

Marlin 1887 Double-Action Revolver

This is the last handgun that Marlin produced and the only double-action. It is chambered for the .32 or the .38 caliber centerfire cartridges and is of the break-open auto-ejector type. The fluted cylinder holds 6 shots in .32 and 5 shots in .38 caliber. The round ribbed barrel is 3.25" in length, and the frame is made of steel. The standard finish is nickel-plated with a blued trigger guard. Many full-blued examples have been noted. The round butt grips are hard rubber, and the top of the barrel is marked "Marlin Firearms Co. New Haven Conn. U.S.A./Patented Aug. 9 1887." There were approximately 15,000 manufactured between 1887 and 1899.

Photo by Lt. Col. William S. Brophy from Marlin Firearms with permission

NIB	Exc.	V.G.	Good	Fair	Poor
—	—	800	500	200	75

MARSTON, S.W.
New York, New York

Double-Action Pepperbox

A .31 caliber double-action percussion pepperbox with a 5" barrel group and ring trigger. Blued with walnut grips. Manufactured between 1850 and 1855.

NIB	Exc.	V.G.	Good	Fair	Poor
—	—	2000	1125	600	250

2 Barrel Pistol

A .31 or .36 revolving barrel 2-shot pistol with a ring trigger. The barrel marked "J.Cohn & S.W.Marston-New York." Blued, brass frame with walnut grips. Manufactured during the 1850s.

NIB	Exc.	V.G.	Good	Fair	Poor
—	—	2700	1250	450	200

MARSTON, W. W. & CO.
New York, New York

W.W. Marston & Company manufactured a variety of firearms some of which are marked only with the trade names: Union Arms Company, Phoenix Armory, Western Arms Company, Washington Arms Company, Sprague and Marston, and Marston and Knox.

Double-Action Single-Shot Pistol

A .31 or .36 caliber bar hammer percussion pistol with a 2.5" or 5" half octagonal barrel. Blued with walnut grips. Manufactured during the 1850s.

NIB	Exc.	V.G.	Good	Fair	Poor
—	—	650	325	150	100

Pocket Revolver

A .31 caliber percussion revolver with a 3.25" to 7.5" barrel and 6-shot cylinder. Blued with walnut grips. Approximately 13,000 were manufactured between 1857 and 1862.

NIB	Exc.	V.G.	Good	Fair	Poor
—	—	1250	550	200	125

Navy Revolver

A .36 caliber percussion revolver with a 7.5" or 8.5" octagonal barrel and 6-shot cylinder. Blued with walnut grips. Manufactured between 1857 and 1862.

NIB	Exc.	V.G.	Good	Fair	Poor
—	—	3100	1400	600	200

Single-Action Pistol

A .31 or .36 caliber percussion pistol with a 4" or 6" barrel. Blued with walnut grips. Manufactured during the 1860s.

NIB	Exc.	V.G.	Good	Fair	Poor
—	—	675	580	250	100

BREECH LOADING PISTOL

A .36 caliber breech loading percussion pistol with a 4" to 8.5" half octagonal barrel and either a brass or iron frame. Blued, case hardened with walnut grips. Approximately 1,000 were manufactured in the 1850s.

Courtesy Milwaukee Public Museum, Milwaukee, Wisconsin

Brass Frame

NIB	Exc.	V.G.	Good	Fair	Poor
—	—	4400	3600	1650	500

Iron Frame

NIB	Exc.	V.G.	Good	Fair	Poor
—	—	3900	3000	1100	300

Double-Action Pepperbox

A .31 caliber double-action 6-shot percussion pepperbox with 4" or 5" barrel groups and a bar hammer. Blued, case hardened with walnut grips. Manufactured during the 1850s.

Courtesy Milwaukee Public Museum, Milwaukee, Wisconsin

NIB	Exc.	V.G.	Good	Fair	Poor
—	—	3200	2500	1150	300

3 BARRELED DERRINGER

A .22 caliber 3-barreled spur-trigger pocket pistol with a sliding knife blade mounted on the left side of the 3" barrel group. Blued, silver-plated with walnut grips. The barrel marked "Wm. W. Marston/New York City." Approximately 1,500 were manufactured between 1858 and 1864.

Knife Bladed Model

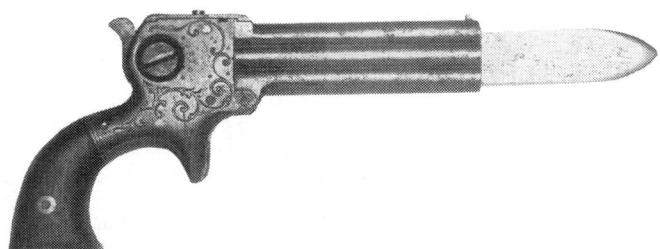

Courtesy Milwaukee Public Museum, Milwaukee, Wisconsin

NIB	Exc.	V.G.	Good	Fair	Poor
—	—	5575	4100	1650	400

Model Without Knife

Courtesy Milwaukee Public Museum, Milwaukee, Wisconsin

NIB	Exc.	V.G.	Good	Fair	Poor
—	—	2550	2000	775	200

.32 Caliber 3 Barrel Derringer

Similar to the above, but in .32 caliber with either 3" or 4" barrels and not fitted with a knife blade. Approximately 3,000 were manufactured between 1864 and 1872.

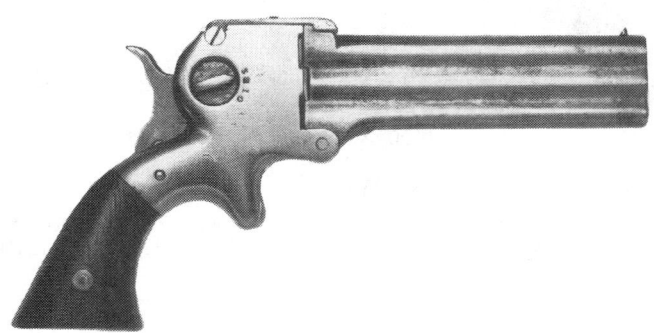

Courtesy Milwaukee Public Museum, Milwaukee, Wisconsin

NIB	Exc.	V.G.	Good	Fair	Poor
—	—	3750	3000	825	200

MASSACHUSETTS ARMS CO.
Chicopee Falls, Massachusetts

WESSON & LEAVITT DRAGOON

A .40 caliber percussion revolver with a 7" round barrel, 6-shot cylinder and side-mounted hammer. Blued, case hardened with walnut grips. Approximately 800 were manufactured in 1850 and 1851.

Early Model with 6" Barrel

Approximately 30 made.

NIB	Exc.	V.G.	Good	Fair	Poor
—	—	8500	6600	275	750

Fully Marked 7" Barrel Standard Model

NIB	Exc.	V.G.	Good	Fair	Poor
—	—	8000	6050	2200	650

Wesson & Leavitt Belt Revolver

A .31 caliber percussion revolver with a 3" to 7" round barrel and 6-shot cylinder. Similar in appearance to the above. Approximately 1,000 were manufactured in 1850 and 1851.

Courtesy Milwaukee Public Museum, Milwaukee, Wisconsin

NIB	Exc.	V.G.	Good	Fair	Poor
—	—	3000	1900	775	250

Maynard Primed Belt Revolver

Similar to the above, with a Maynard tape primer. Approximately 1,000 were manufactured between 1851 and 1857.

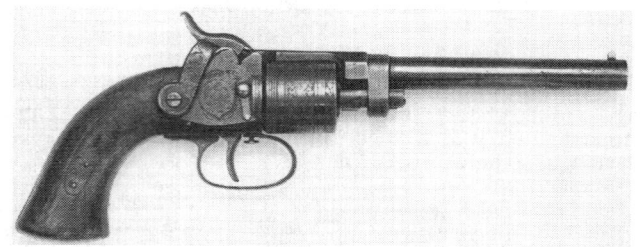

Courtesy Milwaukee Public Museum, Milwaukee, Wisconsin

NIB	Exc.	V.G.	Good	Fair	Poor
—	—	3700	2750	880	250

Maynard Primed Pocket Revolver

Similar to the above, but in .28 or .30 caliber with 2.5" to 3.5" octagonal or round barrels. Approximately 3,000 were made between 1851 and 1860.

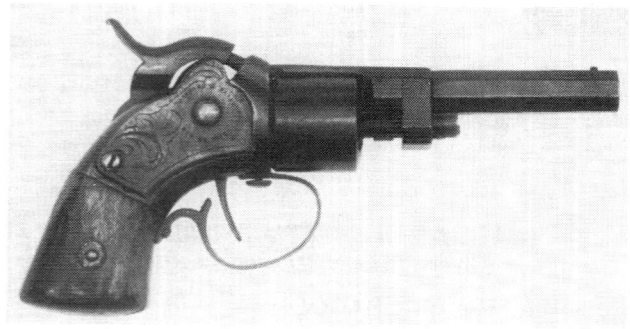

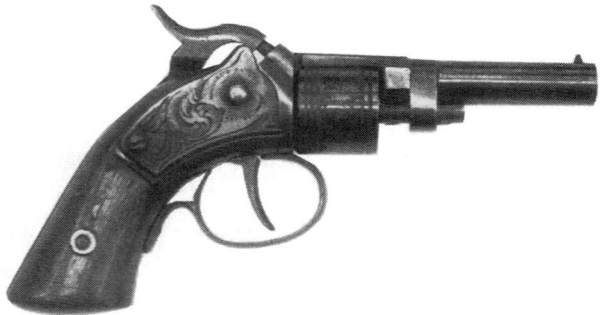

Courtesy Milwaukee Public Museum, Milwaukee, Wisconsin

NIB	Exc.	V.G.	Good	Fair	Poor
—	—	1950	1400	625	200

Adams Patent Navy Revolver

As above, in .36 caliber with a 6" octagonal barrel. Approximately 600 of the 1,000 made were purchased by the U.S. government.

Courtesy Milwaukee Public Museum, Milwaukee, Wisconsin

NIB	Exc.	V.G.	Good	Fair	Poor
—	—	3750	2500	825	300

NOTE: Those bearing inspection marks will bring approximately a 20 percent premium over the values listed.

Single-Shot Pocket Pistol

A .31 caliber single-shot percussion pistol with a 2.5" to 3.5" half octagonal barrel and a Maynard tape primer. The barrel marked "Mass. Arms Co/Chicopee Falls" and the primer door "Maynard's Patent Sept. 22, 1845." Blued, case hardened with walnut grips. Manufactured in the 1850s.

NIB	Exc.	V.G.	Good	Fair	Poor
—	—	4000	2750	925	300

MATEBA ARMS
Italy

AutoRevolver

Introduced in 2000, this revolver is chambered for the .357 Magnum or .44 Magnum with 4", 6", or 8" barrel. The gun features a single-action trigger that has a reciprocating cylinder that fires from the bottom chamber rather than the top. The firing of the gun cocks the hammer and cycles the action for the next round. Available with or without compensator. Offered in blue or nickel finish. Extra barrels available. Distributed in USA by American Western Arms (AWA).

NIB	Exc.	V.G.	Good	Fair	Poor
1600	1100	900	600	400	200

NOTE: Guns without compensator deduct $80. For nickel finish add $50. For extra barrel add $140.

MAUSER WERKE
Oberndorf-am-Neckar, Germany

Established in 1869 by Peter and Wilhelm Mauser, this company came under the effective control of Ludwig Loewe and Company of Berlin in 1887. In 1896 the latter company was reorganized under the name *Deutsches Waffen und Munition* or as it is betterknown, DWM.

MODEL 1896 "BROOMHANDLE MAUSER PISTOL"

Manufactured from 1896 to 1939, the Model 1896 Pistol was produced in a wide variety of styles as listed. It is recommended that those considering the purchase of any of the models listed should consult Breathed & Schroeder's *System Mauser* (Chicago 1967) as it provides detailed descriptions and photographs of the various models.

PRICING NOTE: Prices listed are for the pistol only. A correct, matching stock/holster will add approximately 40 percentto value of each category. non-matching stock/holster will add between $350 to $600 to prices.

Courtesy Gale Morgan

Large Ring Cutaway

"BUYER BEWARE" ALERT by Gale Morgan: I have personallly seen English Crest, the U.S. Great Seal, unheard-of European dealers, aristocratic Coats-of-Arms, and Middle East Medallions beautifully photo-etched into the magazine wells and rear panels of some really common wartime commercials with price tags that have been elevated to $2,500 plus. They are quite eye-catching and if they are sold as customized/modified Mausers, the seller can price the piece at whatever the market will bear. However, if sold as a factory original—BUYER BEWARE.

Six-Shot Step-Barrel Cone Hammer

A 7.63mm semi-automatic pistol with a 5.5" barrel, fixed rear sight and checkered walnut grips. Marked "Ruecklauf Pistole System Mauser, Oberndorf am/Neckar 1896." Very few were manufactured. Too rare to price.

Twenty-Shot Step-Barrel Cone Hammer

As above, with a 20-shot extended magazine and tangent rear sight. Engraved "system mauser" on top of chamber. Too rare to price.

System Mauser 10-Shot Cone Hammer

As above, with either fixed or tangent rear sight. Step barrel (pictured) is very rare as is tapered barrel. Magazine capacity 10 rounds.

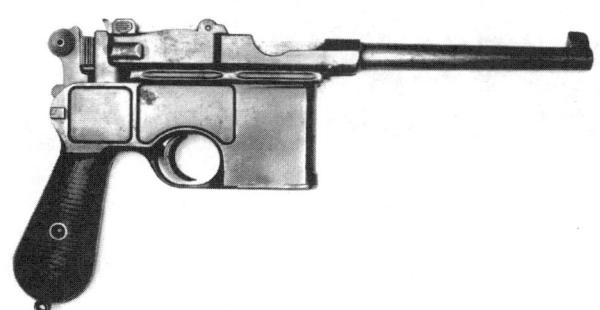

Courtesy Joe Schroeder

NIB	Exc.	V.G.	Good	Fair	Poor
—	17000	13000	10000	8000	7000

Six-Shot Standard Cone Hammer

Similar to the above but with no step in the barrel, 6-shot magazine and marked "Waffenfabrik Mauser, Oberndorf A/N" over the chamber. May have fixed or, rarely, tangent rear sight.

NIB	Exc.	V.G.	Good	Fair	Poor
—	12000	9000	6750	4500	3000

Twenty-Shot Cone Hammer

As above, with an extended magazine holding 20 cartridges. May have panels or flat sides.

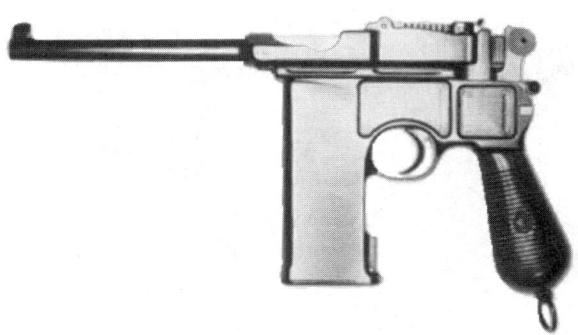

Courtesy Joe Schroeder

NIB	Exc.	V.G.	Good	Fair	Poor
—	30000	25000	15000	10000	7000

Standard Cone Hammer

As above, with a 10-shot magazine and 23-groove grips.

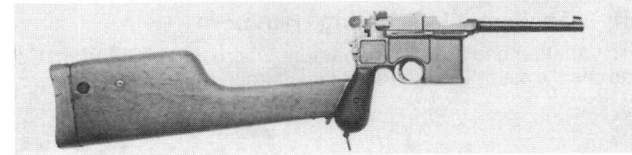

Courtesy Rock Island Auction Company

NIB	Exc.	V.G.	Good	Fair	Poor
—	4500	3500	2250	1400	800

Fixed Sight Cone Hammer

Similar to the standard Cone Hammer except that a fixed, integral sight is machined into the barrel extension.

Courtesy Joe Schroeder

NIB	Exc.	V.G.	Good	Fair	Poor
—	5500	3500	2500	1500	1000

Turkish Contract Cone Hammer

As above, but sight marked in Farsi and bearing the crest of Sultan Abdul-Hamid II on the frame. Approximately 1,000 were made.

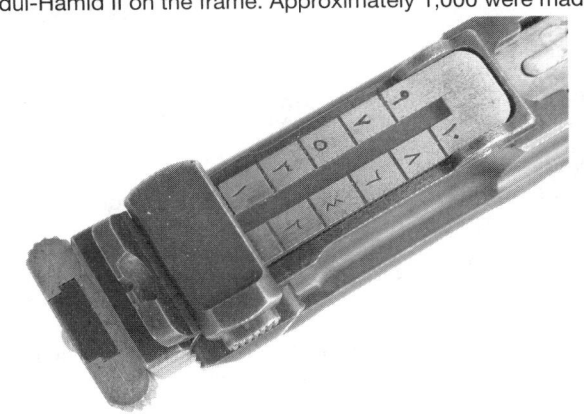

Courtesy Gale Morgan

NIB	Exc.	V.G.	Good	Fair	Poor
—	12000	8000	6500	3000	2000

Early Transitional Large Ring Hammer

This variation has the same characteristics of the "Standard Cone Hammer" except the hammer has a larger, open ring.

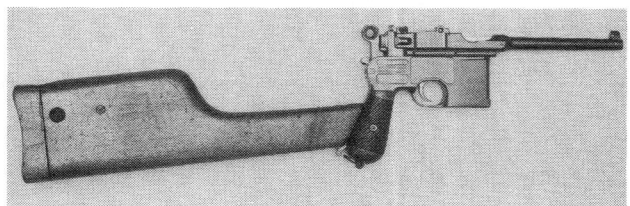

Courtesy Wallis & Wallis, Lewes, Sussex, England

NIB	Exc.	V.G.	Good	Fair	Poor
—	3500	2800	2500	1150	800

Model 1899 Flat Side—Italian Contract

Similar to the above, with a 5.5" barrel, adjustable rear sight and the frame sides milled flat. Left flat of chamber marked with "DV" proof. Approximately 5,000 were manufactured in 1899.

Courtesy Joe Schroeder

NIB	Exc.	V.G.	Good	Fair	Poor
—	4500	3500	2000	1200	900

Early Flat Side

Similar to the above, except with "pinned" rear sight and without the Italian markings.

NIB	Exc.	V.G.	Good	Fair	Poor
—	3000	2700	1500	1000	750

Late Flat Side

Similar to the above, with an integral pin mounted adjustable rear sight and often marked with dealer's names such as "Von Lengerke & Detmold, New York."

NIB	Exc.	V.G.	Good	Fair	Poor
—	2700	2200	1500	1000	750

Flat Side Bolo

Similar to the above, but with a 3.9" barrel, fixed sights, and checkered walnut grips. Very rare.

NIB	Exc.	V.G.	Good	Fair	Poor
—	7500	6000	4000	3000	2000

Early Large Ring Hammer Bolo

As above, with a milled frame, adjustable rear sight, and grooved wood or hard rubber grips cast with a floral pattern. 10-shot magazine.

NIB	Exc.	V.G.	Good	Fair	Poor
—	4700	3700	2000	1500	1000

Shallow-Milled Panel Model

Full size. Similar to the above, with a 5.5" barrel and either 23-groove walnut or checkered hard rubber grips. Shallow frame panels.

NIB	Exc.	V.G.	Good	Fair	Poor
—	3800	2700	1000	750	500

Deep-Milled Panel Model

As above, with deeper milled panels on the sides of the receiver.

NIB	Exc.	V.G.	Good	Fair	Poor
—	3500	2000	1500	1000	750

Late Large Ring Hammer Bolo

Similar to the Early Large Ring Hammer Bolo, but with the late style adjustable rear sight.

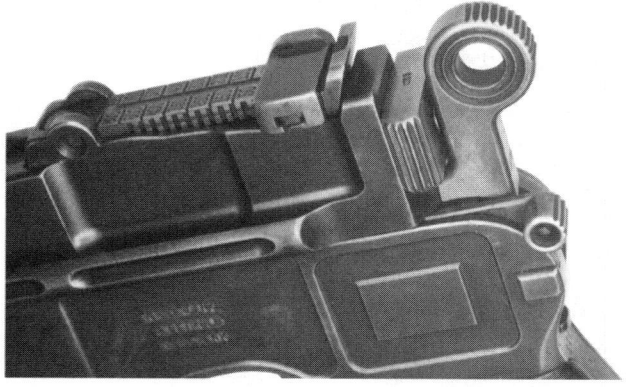

Courtesy Joe Schroeder

NIB	Exc.	V.G.	Good	Fair	Poor
—	3000	2500	1500	1000	750

Six-Shot Large Ring Bolo

Similar to the above Large Ring Bolo but with six-shot magazine. This model may be equipped with either fixed or tangent sights.

Courtesy James Rankin

NIB	Exc.	V.G.	Good	Fair	Poor
—	8700	6500	5000	3000	1800

Early Small Ring Hammer Model, Transitional

The Model 96 with an early long extractor, a hammer with a small-diameter hole, and a 5.5" barrel. The grips have 34 grooves.

Courtesy Joe Schroeder

NIB	Exc.	V.G.	Good	Fair	Poor
—	3200	2000	1500	1000	500

CURRENT MAUSER PRODUCTION PISTOLS
Model 80 SA

This single-action semi-automatic pistol is based on the Browning Hi-Power design. Chambered for the 9mm Parabellum cartridge it has a barrel length of 4.66" and a magazine capacity of 14 rounds. Weighs approximately 35 oz.

NIB	Exc.	V.G.	Good	Fair	Poor
550	475	295	175	125	100

Early Small Ring Hammer Bolo Model

As above, with a 3.9" barrel and wood or hard rubber grips cast with a floral pattern. Serial numbers in the 40,000 range.

NIB	Exc.	V.G.	Good	Fair	Poor
—	4000	3000	2000	1500	600

CURRENT MAUSER PRODUCTION PISTOLS
Model Compact DA

Same as above but double-action trigger and shorter barrel: 4.13". Weighs approximately 33 oz.

NIB	Exc.	V.G.	Good	Fair	Poor
340	320	250	175	125	100

Model 90 DA

Similar to the Model 80 but with a double-action trigger.

NIB	Exc.	V.G.	Good	Fair	Poor
550	475	295	175	125	100

Six-Shot Small Ring Hammer Model

As above, with 27-groove walnut grips.

NIB	Exc.	V.G.	Good	Fair	Poor
—	7200	5000	3000	1800	1000

Model M2 (Imported by SIGARMS)

Introduced in 2000 this pistol is chambered for the .45 ACP, .40 S&W, or .357 SIG cartridges. It has an aluminum alloy frame and steel slide. The action is an enclosed hammerless striker-fired design. Barrel length is 3.5". Fixed sights. Weight is about 29 oz. Magazine capacity for .45 ACP is 8 rounds, for .40 S&W and .357 SIG capacity is 10 rounds.

NIB	Exc.	V.G.	Good	Fair	Poor
475	400	300	200	150	100

Standard Pre-war Commercial

A Model 96 with a 5.5" barrel, late-style adjustable rear sight and either 34-groove walnut grips or checkered hard rubber grips. Often found with dealers markings such as "Von Lengerke & Detmold."

Courtesy Joe Schroeder

NIB	Exc.	V.G.	Good	Fair	Poor
—	2500	1800	1200	650	300

9mm Export Model

As above, in 9mm Mauser with 34-groove walnut grips.

NIB	Exc.	V.G.	Good	Fair	Poor
—	3250	2250	1500	1000	700

Mauser Banner Model

Standard pre-war features except chamber stamped with the Mauser Banner trademark and 32-groove walnut grips. Approximately 10,000 were manufactured.

Courtesy Joe Schroeder

NIB	Exc.	V.G.	Good	Fair	Poor
—	4000	3200	2300	1100	600

Persian Contract

Persian rampant lion on left rear panel. Prospective purchasers should secure a qualified appraisal prior to acquisition. Serial numbers in the 154000 range.

NIB	Exc.	V.G.	Good	Fair	Poor
—	4200	3500	2250	1400	1000

Standard Wartime Commercial

Identical to the pre-war Commercial Model 96, except that it has 30 groove walnut grips and the rear of the hammer is stamped "NS" for new safety. Many also bear German or Austrian military acceptance proofs.

Courtesy Gale Morgan

NIB	Exc.	V.G.	Good	Fair	Poor
—	1700	1100	800	500	350

9mm Parabellum Military Contract

As above, in 9mm Parabellum caliber with 24 groove grips, stamped with a large "9" filled with red paint.

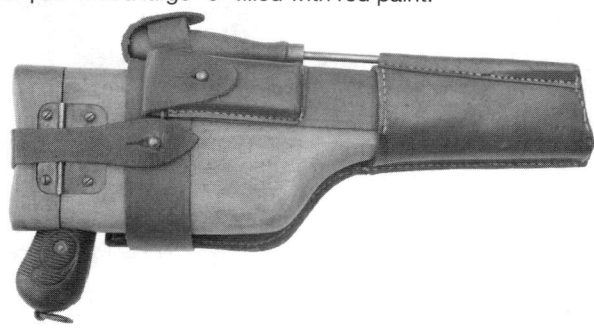

NIB	Exc.	V.G.	Good	Fair	Poor
—	3200	2000	1000	700	450

1920 Rework

A Model 96 modified to a barrel length of 3.9" and in 7.63mm Mauser or 9mm Parabellum caliber. Often encountered with police markings.

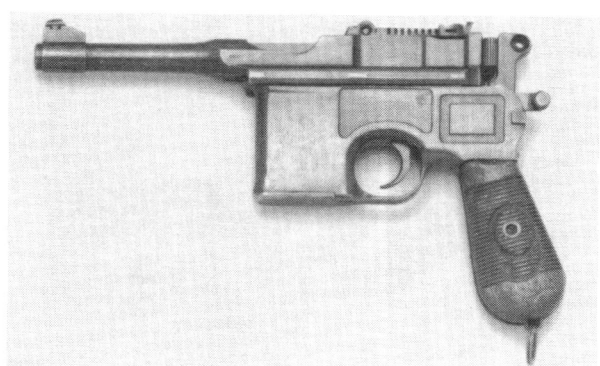

Courtesy Bonhams & Butterfields, San Francisco, California

NIB	Exc.	V.G.	Good	Fair	Poor
—	1500	1000	500	400	350

Luger Barreled 1920 Rework

Similar to the above, but fitted with a Luger barrel of 4" in length. 23 groove walnut grips and of 9mm caliber.

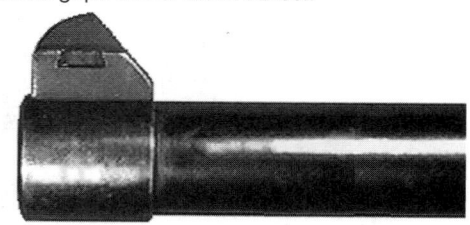

Courtesy Gale Morgan

NIB	Exc.	V.G.	Good	Fair	Poor
—	2000	1200	700	500	450

Early Post-war Bolo Model

A Model 96 in 7.63mm caliber with a 3.9" barrel, adjustable rear sight and 22-groove walnut grips.

NIB	Exc.	V.G.	Good	Fair	Poor
—	2400	1300	600	400	200

Late Post-war Bolo Model

As above, with the Mauser Banner trademark stamped on the left rear panel.

Courtesy Gale Morgan

NIB	Exc.	V.G.	Good	Fair	Poor
—	2200	1200	700	400	200

French Gendarme Model

A standard Model 96 fitted with a 3.9" barrel and checkered hard rubber grips. Although reputed to have been made under a French contract, no record of that has been found to date.

Courtesy James Rankin

NIB	Exc.	V.G.	Good	Fair	Poor
—	3700	2500	1000	600	350

Early Model 1930

A 7.63mm caliber Model 96 with a 5.2" stepped barrel, grooved side rails, 12-groove walnut grips and late-style safety.

Courtesy Gale Morgan

NIB	Exc.	V.G.	Good	Fair	Poor
—	2600	1900	1200	800	500

Late Model 1930

Similar to the above, except for solid receiver rails.

NIB	Exc.	V.G.	Good	Fair	Poor
—	2800	2100	1200	800	400

MODEL 1896 "BROOMHANDLE MAUSER PISTOL"

Model 1930 Removable Magazine

Similar to the above, but with a detachable magazine. Prospective purchasers should secure a qualified appraisal prior to acquisition. Too rare to price.

CHINESE COPIES

Chinese Marked, Handmade Copies

Crude copies of the Model 96 and unsafe to fire.

NIB	Exc.	V.G.	Good	Fair	Poor
—	500	400	350	250	175

Taku-Naval Dockyard Model

Approximately 6,000 copies of the Model 96 were made at the Taku-Naval Dockyard in several variations, both flat and paneled sides.

NIB	Exc.	V.G.	Good	Fair	Poor
—	3500	1500	1000	600	400

Shansei Arsenal Model

Approximately 8,000 Model 96 pistols were manufactured in .45 ACP caliber.Copies of the Model 96 were made by Unceta (Astra) and Zulaica y Cia (Royal) and marketed by the firm of Beistegui

Hermanos. These copies are covered in their own sections of this text. **NOTE:** Within the past several years, a large quantity of Model 96 pistols exported to or made in China have been imported into the United States. It has been reported that some newly made copies of the Shansei .45 were recently exported from China. Proceed with caution.

Shansei Panel Marking

Courtesy Gale Morgan

NIB	Exc.	V.G.	Good	Fair	Poor
—	5000	3500	2250	1500	1300

MAUSER POCKET PISTOLS

Model 1910

A 6.35mm (.25 ACP) caliber pistol with a 3" barrel, 9-shot magazine and either a checkered walnut or (scarce) hard rubber wraparound grip. Early examples (below serial 60,000 or so) have a pivoting takedown latch above the trigger guard and are identified as "Sidelatch" models by collectors. Later production Models 1910s are often identified as the Model 1910/14. Manufactured from 1910 to 1934.

Model 1910 Sidelatch Model

NIB	Exc.	V.G.	Good	Fair	Poor
—	1200	900	600	300	300

Model 1910 Later Production (Model 1910/14)

NIB	Exc.	V.G.	Good	Fair	Poor
—	450	275	200	150	100

MODEL 1914

A larger version of the Model 1910, chambered for 7.65mm Browning (.32 ACP) with a 3.5" or (rarely) 4.5" barrel. Very early examples up to serial 2500 or so had a contoured hump on the slide and are called "Humpbacks" by collectors; these bring a considerable premium. Model 1914s with police or military markings bring a small premium. Manufactured between 1914 and 1934.

Model 1914 "Humpback"

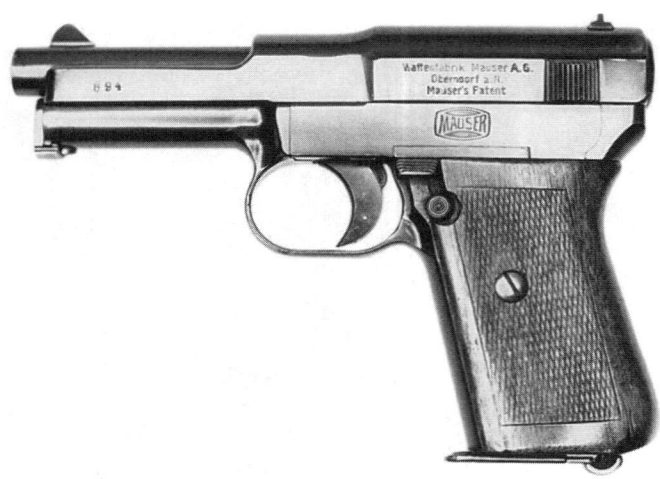

NIB	Exc.	V.G.	Good	Fair	Poor
—	4000	3000	1750	800	400

Model 1914 (later)

NIB	Exc.	V.G.	Good	Fair	Poor
—	475	300	200	150	100

Model 1912/14

While Mauser's pocket pistols were very successful on the commercial market, Mauser was also trying to develop a larger caliber pistol for military use. The most successful of these was the Model 1912/14, though only about 200 were ever made. A few of these did reach the commercial market, and it's likely the pistol would have continued in production had WWI not broken out. Higher serial numbered guns were slotted for a Model 1896-style holster stock, and a few of these also had tangent sights.

NIB	Exc.	V.G.	Good	Fair	Poor
—	29000	17000	11000	8000	4000

NOTE: Add 25 percent for shoulder stock.

Model WTP I

This was Mauser's first post-WWI new design and first vest pocket pistol, with a 2.5" barrel and 6-shot magazine capacity. Grips were plastic wraparound, with one, two or three grip screws depending on production period. Production ended in the late 1930s, when the WTP II was introduced.

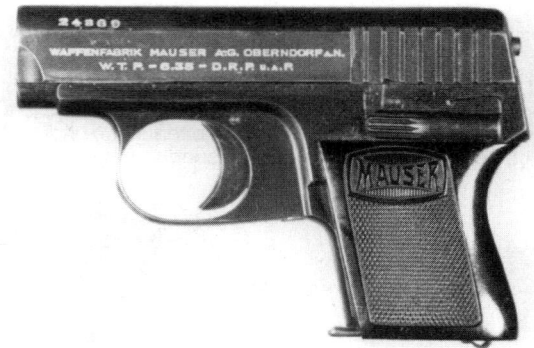

NIB	Exc.	V.G.	Good	Fair	Poor
—	600	300	250	175	125

Model WTP II

The WTP II was a much more compact design that its predecessor, with a 2" barrel and separate grip panels instead of Mauser's usual wraparound grip. Production was limited by the outbreak of WWII, so the WTP II is much scarcer than the WTP I. Under French occupation at least several hundred WTP IIs were assembled and sold; these can be identified by their very low electric penciled serial numbers and lack of German proofing, and bring a slight premium over the pre-war German manufactured pistols.

Courtesy Gale Morgan

NIB	Exc.	V.G.	Good	Fair	Poor
—	650	450	325	250	175

MODEL 1934

In response to competition from Walther and others, in 1934 Mauser spruced up its aging 1910/14 and 1914 pistols with a new high-polish finish and form-fitting swept back grips. Nickel finish was also offered, but is very rare (50 percent premium, but beware of renickeled blued guns). The 7.65mm pistols became popular with both the military and police, but those so marked can bring a considerable premium.

GALLERY OF HANDGUNS

Custom features and a light, compact aluminum frame make Kimber's Ultra TLE II a spectacular choice for both self defense and speed-shoot handgun games.

The DA-only BODYGUARDs—a .380 ACP pistol and a .38 Special +P revolver—from Smith & Wesson could be everything a person ever wanted in a concealed handgun. Flat and subtly designed—even the revolver!—both guns get the benefit of an ambidextrously activated INSIGHT laser.

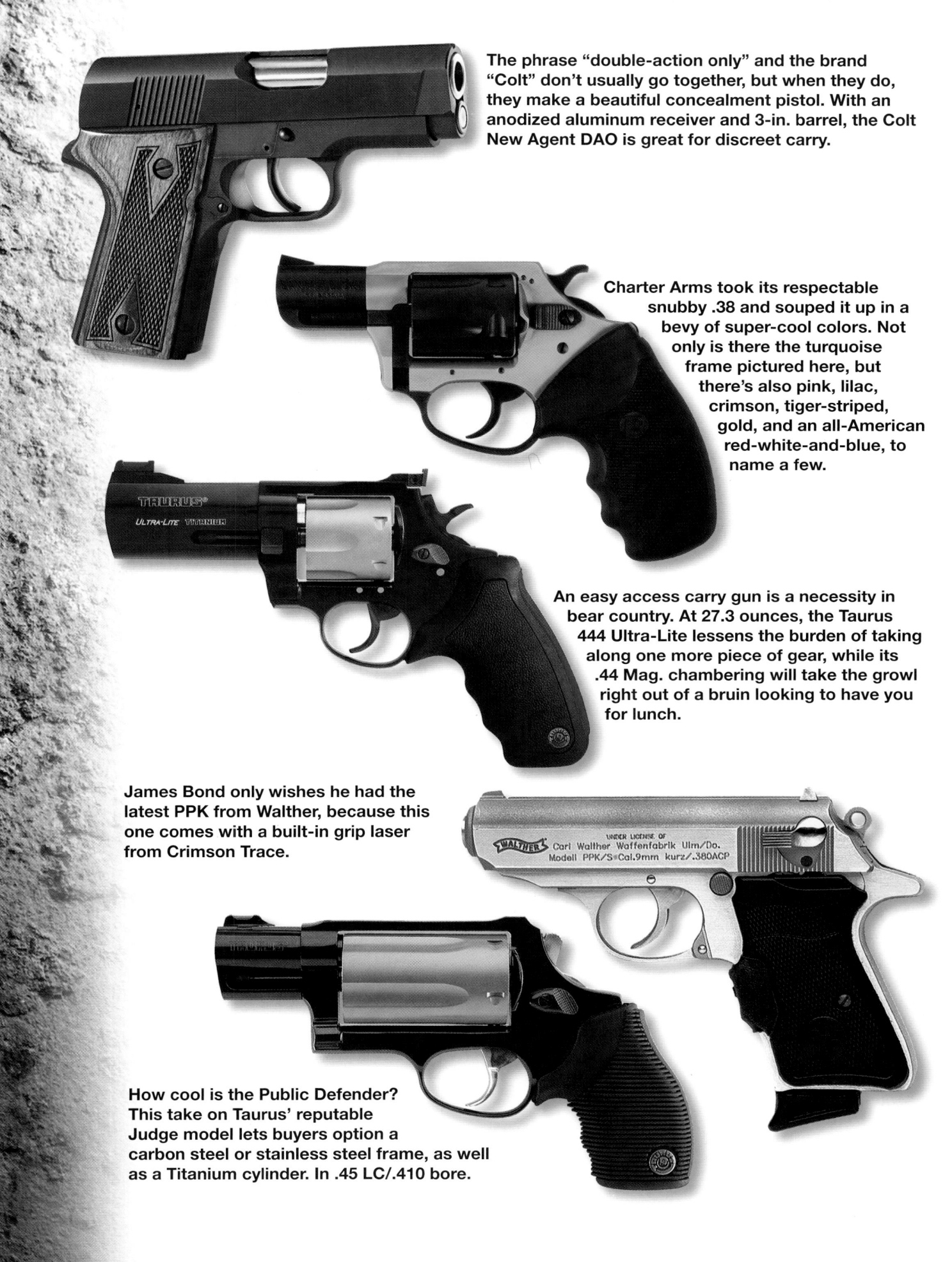

The phrase "double-action only" and the brand "Colt" don't usually go together, but when they do, they make a beautiful concealment pistol. With an anodized aluminum receiver and 3-in. barrel, the Colt New Agent DAO is great for discreet carry.

Charter Arms took its respectable snubby .38 and souped it up in a bevy of super-cool colors. Not only is there the turquoise frame pictured here, but there's also pink, lilac, crimson, tiger-striped, gold, and an all-American red-white-and-blue, to name a few.

An easy access carry gun is a necessity in bear country. At 27.3 ounces, the Taurus 444 Ultra-Lite lessens the burden of taking along one more piece of gear, while its .44 Mag. chambering will take the growl right out of a bruin looking to have you for lunch.

James Bond only wishes he had the latest PPK from Walther, because this one comes with a built-in grip laser from Crimson Trace.

How cool is the Public Defender? This take on Taurus' reputable Judge model lets buyers option a carbon steel or stainless steel frame, as well as a Titanium cylinder. In .45 LC/.410 bore.

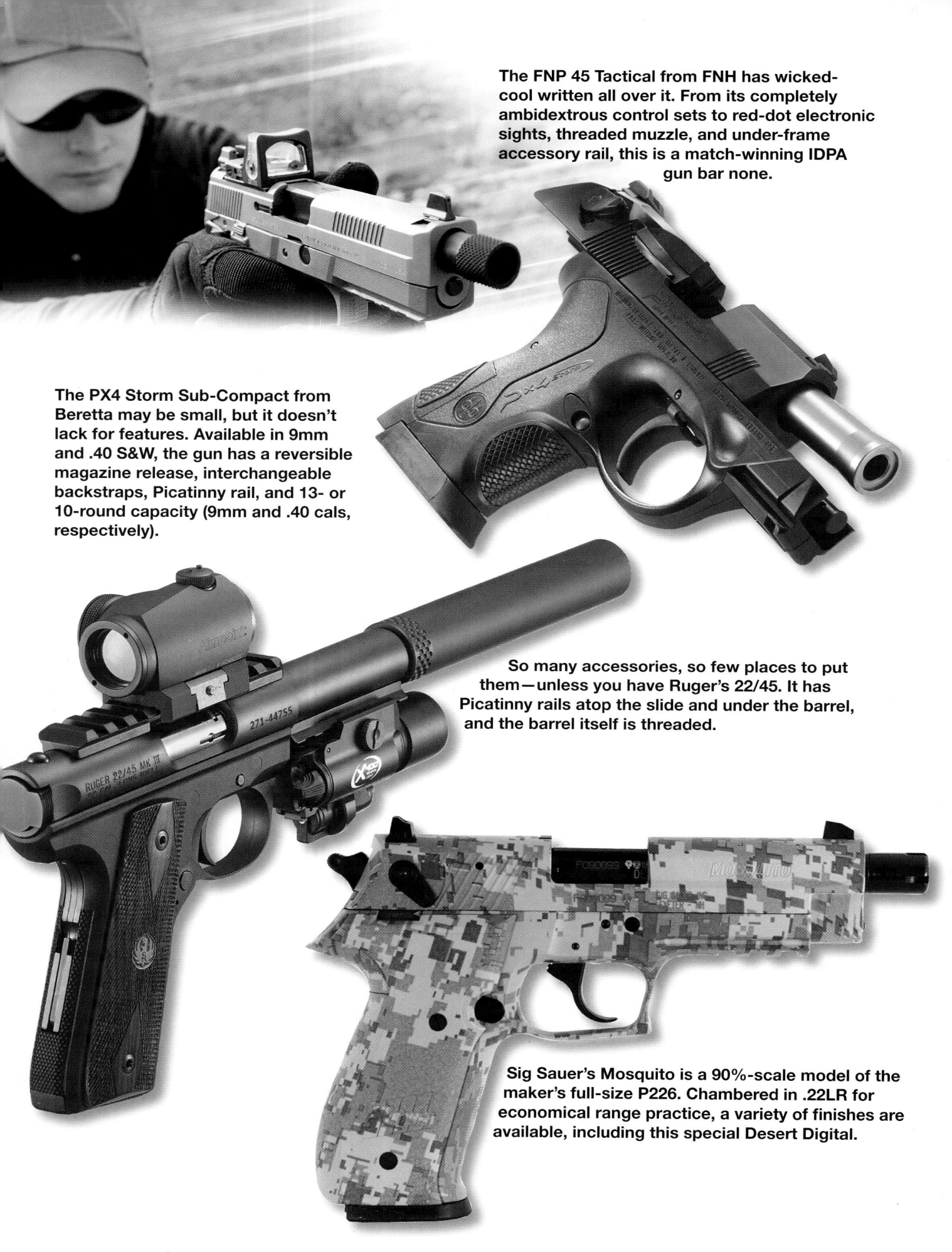

The FNP 45 Tactical from FNH has wicked-cool written all over it. From its completely ambidextrous control sets to red-dot electronic sights, threaded muzzle, and under-frame accessory rail, this is a match-winning IDPA gun bar none.

The PX4 Storm Sub-Compact from Beretta may be small, but it doesn't lack for features. Available in 9mm and .40 S&W, the gun has a reversible magazine release, interchangeable backstraps, Picatinny rail, and 13- or 10-round capacity (9mm and .40 cals, respectively).

So many accessories, so few places to put them—unless you have Ruger's 22/45. It has Picatinny rails atop the slide and under the barrel, and the barrel itself is threaded.

Sig Sauer's Mosquito is a 90%-scale model of the maker's full-size P226. Chambered in .22LR for economical range practice, a variety of finishes are available, including this special Desert Digital.

Want to make the cut in speed competition? Then Kimber's Team Match II is the way to go. Designed for the USA Shooting rapid fire team, this gun has it all, from accuracy and strap checkering to a match-grade 4-lb. trigger and full-length guide rod.

You've seen stainless, you've seen blued, you've seen gold, but tiger stripes? One thing's for sure, if this Desert Eagle Mark XIX is yours, you're going to get a LOT of attention!

The Walther P22 is a super choice for youth shooters new to handguns. The .22LR pistol has a DA-only 11-lb. trigger, multiple safeties, and ambidextrous controls—and a variety of cool colors like lime green and hot pink that are sure to get new young shooters excited.

John Browning died before he could complete his design of the Browning Hi Power, and so it was finished by Fabrique Nationale gunsmith Dieudonné Saive. In French, Hi-Power is translated to "Grande Puissance," or GP, instead of our HP abbreviation.

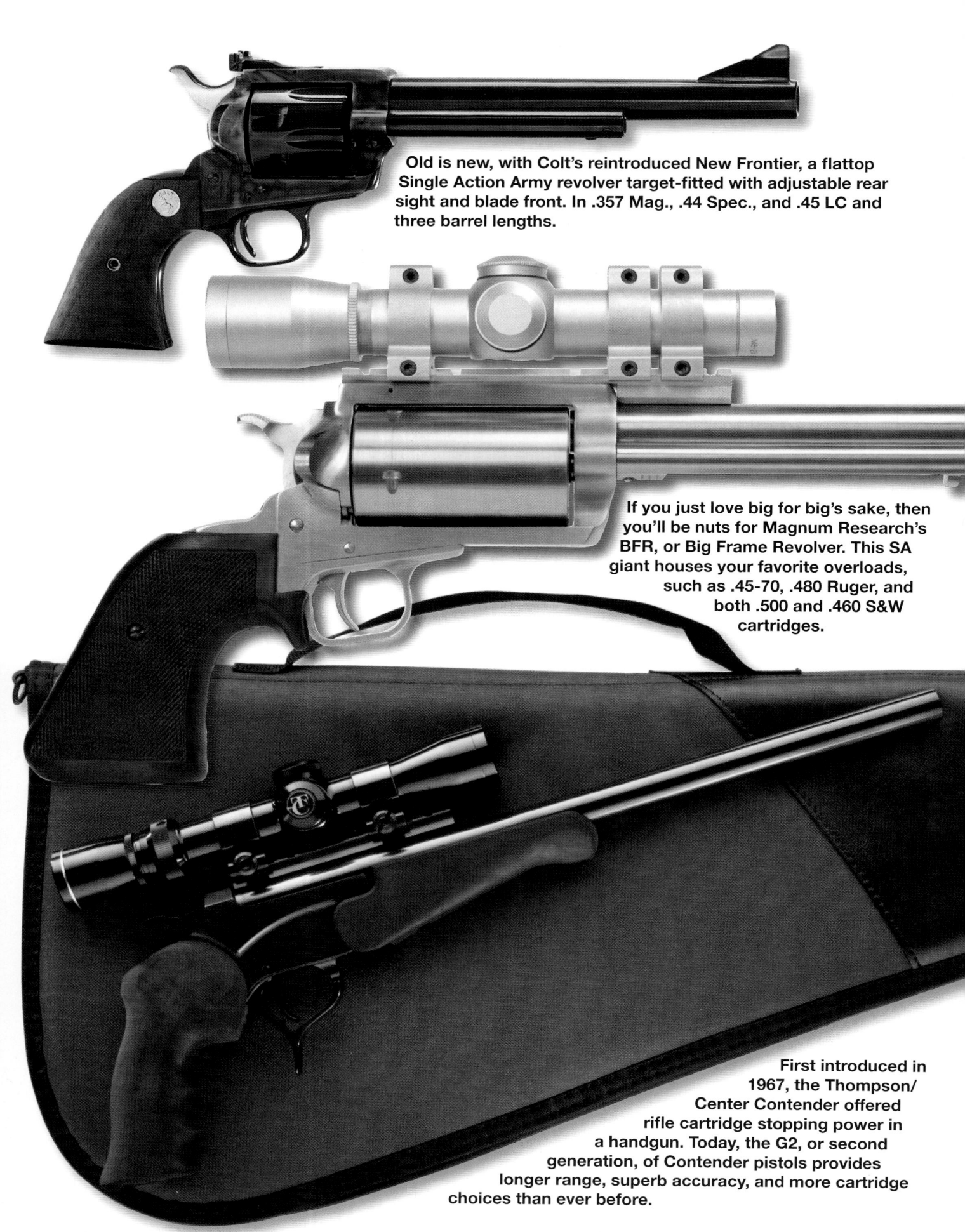

Old is new, with Colt's reintroduced New Frontier, a flattop Single Action Army revolver target-fitted with adjustable rear sight and blade front. In .357 Mag., .44 Spec., and .45 LC and three barrel lengths.

If you just love big for big's sake, then you'll be nuts for Magnum Research's BFR, or Big Frame Revolver. This SA giant houses your favorite overloads, such as .45-70, .480 Ruger, and both .500 and .460 S&W cartridges.

First introduced in 1967, the Thompson/Center Contender offered rifle cartridge stopping power in a handgun. Today, the G2, or second generation, of Contender pistols provides longer range, superb accuracy, and more cartridge choices than ever before.

Owning a gun with a Colt logo is owning a small piece of history, but never more so than when you add a true collectible to your gun vault. Today's Modern Masters Single Action Army revolvers are limited edition works of art, with refined hand engraving that's ink-baked to add depth and character.

There's all sorts of plinking fun to be had with Ruger's Single-Ten. The traditionally designed single-action revolver houses a .22-cal.10-round cylinder, and that means less time reloading and more time shooting.

Nah, you can't get this in the full-auto version, but the Thompson TA5-1 semi-auto .45 ACP is just about as much fun, especially when you latch on the 50-round drum magazine. Talk about target shredding!

Bad things more often happen at night, but Kimber's Ultra Covert II won't leave you in the dark. With laser grips and Tactical Wedge night sights, wear this gun with anything khaki and the bad guys will never see you coming.

Most compact .45s have limited 6 or 7+1 capacities. If you want more, or even if you just have a bigger hand that feels better with a thicker grip, then Para Ordnance's 14+1 Warthog is your carry gun.

Get out of the 1911 rut and into a comp pistol that gives a definitive speed edge. Springfield Armory's XD(M) 5.25 Comp polymer frame 9mm features, .40 S&W, or .45 ACP a top slide lightning cut to reduce gun mass and increase cycling speed, as well as a Minimal—that's what the (M) is for—reset trigger that helps keep you on the target for faster shot-to-shot delivery.

Courtesy Orvel Reichert

6.35mm

NIB	Exc.	V.G.	Good	Fair	Poor
—	525	325	250	200	125

7.65mm Commercial

NIB	Exc.	V.G.	Good	Fair	Poor
—	450	325	250	200	125

7.65mm Eagle L proofed

NIB	Exc.	V.G.	Good	Fair	Poor
—	675	450	300	250	150

7.56mm Large Eagle over M (Navy)

NIB	Exc.	V.G.	Good	Fair	Poor
—	1200	750	450	300	200

MODEL HSC

NOTE: Add 20 percent for Waffenamt markings, and 50 percent for Navy marked front straps.

Courtesy Orvel Reichert

Low Grip Screw Model

As above, with screws that attach the grip located near the bottom of the grip. Highly-polished blue, checkered walnut grips and the early address without the lines and has the Eagle N proof. Some have been observed with Nazi Kreigsmarine markings. Approximately 2,000 were manufactured.

NIB	Exc.	V.G.	Good	Fair	Poor
—	6000	4500	1800	750	650

Early Commercial Model

A highly polished blued finish, checkered walnut grips, the standard Mauser address on the slide, and the Eagle N proofmark. The floorplate of the magazine stamped with the Mauser Banner.

NIB	Exc.	V.G.	Good	Fair	Poor
—	650	500	350	175	125

Transition Model

As above, but not as highly finished.

NIB	Exc.	V.G.	Good	Fair	Poor
—	525	400	300	150	100

Early Nazi Army Model

Courtesy Orvel Reichert

NIB	Exc.	V.G.	Good	Fair	Poor
—	650	550	400	200	125

Late Nazi Army Model

NIB	Exc.	V.G.	Good	Fair	Poor
—	450	375	250	150	100

Early Nazi Navy Model

NIB	Exc.	V.G.	Good	Fair	Poor
—	1000	800	550	400	300

Wartime Nazi Navy Model

NIB	Exc.	V.G.	Good	Fair	Poor
—	800	600	500	400	200

Early Nazi Police Model

NIB	Exc.	V.G.	Good	Fair	Poor
—	600	500	425	250	175

Wartime Nazi Police Model

NIB	Exc.	V.G.	Good	Fair	Poor
—	500	400	350	250	175

Wartime Commercial Model

As above, without acceptance markings on the trigger guard.

NIB	Exc.	V.G.	Good	Fair	Poor
—	425	350	300	200	125

French Manufactured Model

Blued or Parkerized with walnut or plastic grips and the trigger guard marked on the left side with the monogram "MR."

NIB	Exc.	V.G.	Good	Fair	Poor
—	375	275	225	150	100

MODEL HSC POST-WAR PRODUCTION

In the late 1960s Mauser resumed production of the HSc in both 7.65mm and 9mm Browning short (.380). Five thousand post-war HSc pistols were specially marked with an American eagle, and bring a slight premium over standard marked pistols. In the 1980s Mauser licensed HSc production to Gamba in Italy, which produced an enlarged frame version of the HSc with a double-column magazine. In both German and Italian production, .380s bring about a 20 percent premium over .32s.

Mauser Production (.32)

NIB	Exc.	V.G.	Good	Fair	Poor
—	525	450	300	175	125

Gamba Production

NIB	Exc.	V.G.	Good	Fair	Poor
—	600	475	325	200	100

NOTE: In February 1999 SIGARMS announced the acquisition of the Mauser line of small arms. With the acquisition, SIG assumes the rights to the Mauser name and will integrate the Mauser product line into SIGARMS' line of small arms.

MEAD & ADRIANCE
St. Louis, Missouri

This company retailed a variety of single-shot percussion pistols most of which were manufactured by Ethan Allen of Grafton, Massachusetts. In general, the value for pistols marked "Mead & Adriance" are listed.

NIB	Exc.	V.G.	Good	Fair	Poor
—	—	2500	1650	550	250

MENZ, AUGUST
Suhl, Germany

Established prior to WWI to manufacture Beholla pistols, this company was purchased by Lignose in 1937.

Menta

Identical to the Beholla, which is listed separately.

NIB	Exc.	V.G.	Good	Fair	Poor
—	350	250	200	150	100

Liliput

A 4.25mm caliber semi-automatic pistol with a 2" barrel and 6-shot magazine. Overall length 3.5", weight 10 oz. The slide marked "Liliput Kal. 4.25." Also manufactured in 6.35mm caliber. These pistols have an overall length of 4". Blued with composition grips.

NIB	Exc.	V.G.	Good	Fair	Poor
—	800	600	450	300	200

Menz Model II

As above in 7.65mm caliber.

NIB	Exc.	V.G.	Good	Fair	Poor
—	400	300	250	200	125

Menz VP Model

Similar to the Model 2, but in 6.35mm caliber with a 2.35" barrel, 6-shot magazine and fitted with a cocking indicator.

NIB	Exc.	V.G.	Good	Fair	Poor
—	400	300	250	200	125

Model III

A total redesign. It has a closed-top slide, and the quality is much better than the previous Menz pistols. It has a fixed barrel and is similar to the Model 1910 Browning with an exposed hammer. This model was produced until 1937.

NIB	Exc.	V.G.	Good	Fair	Poor
—	450	350	300	250	150

MERIDEN FIREARMS CO.
Meriden, Connecticut

Pocket Pistol

A .32 or .38 caliber double-action revolver manufactured in a variety of barrel lengths and with either an exposed or enclosed hammer. Nickel-plated with rubber grips. The barrel marked "Meriden Firearms Co. Meriden, Conn. USA." Manufactured between 1895 and 1915.

NIB	Exc.	V.G.	Good	Fair	Poor
—	—	375	200	75	50

MERRILL
Fullerton, California

Sportsman

A single-shot pistol manufactured in a variety of calibers with either a 9" or 12" octagonal barrel having a wide ventilated rib, adjustable sights, and integral telescope mounts. Blued with walnut grips.

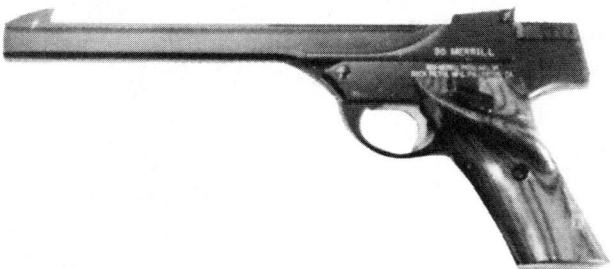

NIB	Exc.	V.G.	Good	Fair	Poor
—	700	575	325	175	125

NOTE: Interchangeable barrels add $100. Wrist support add $25.

MERWIN & BRAY
Worcester, Massachusetts

This company marketed a number of firearms produced by various manufacturers under their own name.

Merwin & Bray Pocket Pistol

A .32 caliber spur trigger single-shot pistol with a 3.5" barrel. Blued, silver-plated with walnut grips. The barrel marked "Merwin & Bray New York."

NIB	Exc.	V.G.	Good	Fair	Poor
—	—	—	300	150	75

MERWIN HULBERT & CO.
New York, New York

Merwin Hulbert & Co., New York City. Founder Joseph Merwin had previously been involved in Merwin & Bray. Merwin Hulbert & Co. or its principals were also involved in Phoenix Rifle, Evans Rifle Company, American Cartridge Company, and Hopkins & Allen of Norwich, CT. Most Merwin Hulbert revolvers will be marked with the Hopkins & Allen name, in addition to Merwin Hulbert. They were made for a fairly brief period, with most production apparently taking place during the 1870s & early 1880s. There has been some confusion over a classification system for MH revolvers. The system adopted here is based on the distinctions listed in Art Phelps' book, The Story of Merwin Hulbert & Co. Firearms. We believe this is the first time the Phelps system has been adapted to a list format.

LARGE-FRAME MERWIN HULBERT SIXGUNS

There has been a marked increase in interest in Merwin Hulbert & Co. over the past decade, with many coming to recognize them as one of the pre-eminent makers of large-frame revolvers used in the American West. Total production of large-frame revolvers has been estimated at a few thousand by some sources. However, the frequency with which they are encountered suggests possibly greater production. MH used a unique system of opening, loading & unloading their revolvers which was supposed to allow selective ejection of spent shells, leaving remaining cartridges in place. A latch on the bottom of the frame is pushed toward the rear of the gun, and the barrel and cylinder are rotated to the right (clockwise, as viewed from the rear of the revolver) 90 degrees. The barrel and cylinder are then pulled forward, far enough to allow empty brass to fall free. This system required exceptional quality machining, and some modern authorities are on record as considering the Merwin Hulbert to have the finest workmanship of all revolvers of the era. All are .44 caliber 6-shot large-frame revolvers. Beyond that, to fully identify a large-frame Merwin Hulbert, you must specify the following: 1. MODEL DESIGNATION — First Model has an open top and scoop flutes, round barrel, and two small screws above the trigger guard. Second Model is similar to the first, except with only one screw above the trigger guard. Third Model has a top-strap with standard flutes and a round barrel. Fourth Model is similar to the third, except that it has a ribbed barrel. The open-top 1st and 2nd Models seem to be more sought after. The 4th Model is rare, and will bring a premium from a serious Merwin collector. 2. FRONTIER ARMY or POCKET ARMY — Frontier Army models have a square butt, and were made in 1st through 4th models. Pocket Army models have a bird's-head butt with a pointed extension with lanyard hole, and are found in 2nd or 3rd Model configuration. Generally, the Frontier Army will bring more than the Pocket Army. 3. SINGLE-ACTION or DOUBLE-ACTION — The topstrap models, 3rd and 4th, were manufactured in both single-action and double-action. The single-action models tend to bring more. 4. BARREL LENGTH — Standard barrel length on the Frontier Army 1st, 2nd, & 3rd Models is 7", with a 5-1/2" barrel common on the 4th Model. Standard barrel length on the Pocket Army was a more "pocket-sized" 3-1/2". However, somewhat ironically, bird's-head butt models marked "Pocket Army" were also produced with full length 7" barrels. Generally, these longer barrels will bring a bit more than the shorter ones. 5. CALIBER — Most common is .44-40 (designated "Winchester Calibre 1873"). Merwins were also chambered for .44 Merwin Hulbert (somewhat similar to the S&W .44 American cartridge), and .44 Russian. The less common calibers may bring a small premium from serious Merwin collectors. 6. FOREIGN COPIES — The Merwin Hulbert design was relatively widely copied during the period of use, particularly in Spain. It seems that much of this production may have gone to Mexico, and some found their way to the U.S. Although these Spanish copies may bear markings such as "System Merwin Hulbert" or other usage of the words "Merwin Hulbert," they generally will not be found with the Hopkins & Allen marking. Spanish firms making Merwin copies included Orbea Hermanos and Anitua y Charola. These Spanish copies may bring half or less of what an original Merwin will bring, and it can sometimes take a fairly experienced eye to tell the difference. 7. ENGRAVING — Special order engraving was available, and it was usually executed in a distinctive and colorful "punch dot" style, which has come to be associated with Merwins (although it is occasionally encountered on other makes of firearms). For a long time, this style was somewhat dismissed as a bit crude and lacking in artistry. However, a new appreciation of Merwin engraving has emerged, and factory engraved pieces will bring a significant premium. Often, a panel scene depicts an animal, object, or landmark. These panel scenes have an almost "folk art" quality to them, and will enhance the value further. Engraved Merwins are sometimes encountered with the engraving filled with colored enamel, quite rare, and, if original, this will bring a further premium. 8. FINISH — The vast majority were nickel plated. Original blued guns will bring a premium.

First Model Frontier Army, .44 open top

Two screws, square butt, 7" barrel.

NIB	Exc.	V.G.	Good	Fair	Poor
—	—	5500	3000	1500	500

Second Model Frontier Army, .44 open top

One screw, square butt, 7" barrel.

NIB	Exc.	V.G.	Good	Fair	Poor
—	—	4500	2750	1000	500

Second Model Pocket Army, .44 open top

Bird's-head butt. 3-1/2" barrel standard, 7" will bring a premium.

NIB	Exc.	V.G.	Good	Fair	Poor
—	—	3500	2000	700	400

Third Model Frontier Army, Single-Action, .44, topstrap

Square butt, 7" barrel.

NIB	Exc.	V.G.	Good	Fair	Poor
—	—	3750	2250	800	450

Third Model Frontier Army, Double-Action, .44, topstrap

Square butt, 7" barrel.

NIB	Exc.	V.G.	Good	Fair	Poor
—	—	3250	1750	700	400

Third Model Pocket Army, Single-Action, .44 topstrap

Bird's-head butt. 3-1/2" barrel standard, 7" will bring a premium.

NIB	Exc.	V.G.	Good	Fair	Poor
—	—	3250	1750	700	400

Third Model Pocket Army, Double-Action, .44, topstrap

Bird's-head butt. 3-1/2" barrel standard, 7" will bring a premium.

NIB	Exc.	V.G.	Good	Fair	Poor
—	—	3000	1600	650	400

Fourth Model Frontier Army, Single-Action, .44, topstrap

Ribbed barrel, scarce. 5-1/2" barrel seems to be most common, also offered in 7" and 3-1/2".

NIB	Exc.	V.G.	Good	Fair	Poor
—	—	5000	2750	800	550

Fourth Model Frontier Army, Double-Action, .44, topstrap

Ribbed barrel. Barrel lengths as above.

NIB	Exc.	V.G.	Good	Fair	Poor
—	—	4750	2500	750	550

SMALL FRAME MERWIN HULBERT POCKET REVOLVERS

The .32 & .38 centerfire revolvers were manufactured with the unique Merwin Hulbert twist-open system, like the large frame revolvers. They were often advertised as chambered for the .32 MH & Co. or .38 MH & Co. cartridges, but it appears as if these cartridges may have been essentially the same as the .32 S&W and .38 S&W rounds. Of course, the Merwin Hulbert revolvers were manufactured for the original lower pressure black-powder loadings of these cartridges. Saw-handled grip frames were standard, although some were manufactured with the distinctive Pocket Army type pointed "skullcrusher" bird's-head grip frames, and these will generally bring a premium. Most common barrel length for most models is 3-1/2", with 5-1/2" barrels somewhat scarcer in most models, and 2-3/4" barrels quite scarce and worth a premium. A number of police departments purchased small frame Merwin Hulbert revolvers in the late 19th century. Department marked guns will bring a premium. Terminology alert—note that the .44 caliber "Pocket Army" model is a large-frame, and is listed in the section above. The .22 Merwin Hulbert revolver is the only one not to use the MH twist-open system. It is, instead, a tip-up revolver closely resembling the S&W Model One.

First Pocket Model Single-Action

Spur-trigger, cylinder pin exposed at front of frame, round loading aperture in recoil shield (no loading gate), five-shot .38, scarce.

NIB	Exc.	V.G.	Good	Fair	Poor
—	—	1250	800	300	175

Second Pocket Model Single-Action

Spur-trigger, cylinder pin exposed, sliding loading gate, five-shot .38.

NIB	Exc.	V.G.	Good	Fair	Poor
—	—	1000	650	285	150

Third Pocket Model Single-Action Spur-Trigger

Enclosed cylinder pin, sliding loading gate, five-shot .38.

NIB	Exc.	V.G.	Good	Fair	Poor
—	—	950	600	225	125

Third Pocket Model Single-Action w/Trigger Guard

Five-shot .38.

NIB	Exc.	V.G.	Good	Fair	Poor
—	—	1000	675	285	150

Double-Action Pocket Model, medium frame

Usually .38 five shot. Scarce .32 seven shot will bring a 25 percent to 50 percent premium. Patent marked folding hammer spur will bring a small premium.

NIB	Exc.	V.G.	Good	Fair	Poor
—	—	900	900	225	150

Double-Action Pocket Model, small frame

.32 cal. five shot. Patent marked folding hammer spur will bring a small premium.

NIB	Exc.	V.G.	Good	Fair	Poor
—	—	800	550	185	125

Tip-up .22 Spur-Trigger

.22 rimfire, a S&W patent infringement, looks similar to S&W Mod. One Third Issue. Scarce. "Made by Merwin Hulbert & Co. for Smith & Wesson" marking will bring a small premium.

NIB	Exc.	V.G.	Good	Fair	Poor
—	—	1000	650	275	175

METROPOLITAN ARMS CO.
New York, New York

Established in February 1864, this company manufactured copies of the Colt Model 1851 and 1861 Navy Revolvers, as well as copies of the Colt Model 1862 Police Revolver. Two of the firm's principle officers were Samuel and William Syms (formerly of Blunt & Syms) and it is believed that they were responsible for production. Curiously, although most Metropolitan pistols were produced during the 1864 to 1866 period, the company itself was not dissolved until 1920.

1851 NAVY REVOLVER

A .36 caliber percussion revolver with a 7.5" octagonal barrel and 6-shot cylinder. Blued, case hardened with walnut grips. The barrel marked "Metropolitan Arms Co. New York." Approximately 6,000 of these revolvers were made during the 1860s. Those bearing H.E. Dimick markings are worth considerably more than the standard marked examples.

Standard Navy Model

NIB	Exc.	V.G.	Good	Fair	Poor
—	—	—	4100	1400	500

H.E. Dimick Navy Model

NIB	Exc.	V.G.	Good	Fair	Poor
—	—	—	8000	3000	850

1861 Navy Revolver

A .36 caliber percussion revolver with a 7.5" round barrel and 6-shot cylinder. The loading lever of the rack-and-pinion type. Blued, case hardened with walnut grips. The barrel marked "Metropolitan Arms Co. New York." Approximately 50 were made in 1864 and 1865.

NIB	Exc.	V.G.	Good	Fair	Poor
—	—	—	8000	3300	950

Police Revolver

A .36 caliber percussion revolver with either 4.5", 5.5" or 6.5" round barrels and a fluted 5-shot cylinder. Blued, case hardened with walnut grips. The barrel normally marked "Metropolitan Arms Co. New York," although examples have been noted without any markings. Approximately 2,750 were made between 1864 and 1866.

NIB	Exc.	V.G.	Good	Fair	Poor
—	—	2400	1650	650	250

MINNEAPOLIS F. A. CO.
Minneapolis, Minnesota

Palm Pistol

A .32 caliber radial cylinder pistol with a 1.75" barrel manufactured by the Ames Manufacturing Company (see the Ames entry). Nickel-plated with hard rubber grips. The sideplates marked "Minneapolis Firearms Co." and "The Protector." Several thousand were sold during the 1890s.

NIB	Exc.	V.G.	Good	Fair	Poor
—	—	2250	1850	950	300

Trophy II

A semi-automatic pistol chambered for the .22 LR cartridge. Offered in either 7-1/4" fluted or 5-1/2" bull barrel. Barrels are interchangeable. Trigger is adjustable for weight and pull. Walnut grips with thumb rest are standard.

NIB	Exc.	V.G.	Good	Fair	Poor
400	325	275	200	150	100

Citation II

Similar to the Trophy II but with a matte satin finish.

NIB	Exc.	V.G.	Good	Fair	Poor
375	300	250	200	150	100

Sharpshooter II

This is a stainless steel target pistol with 5-1/2" bull barrel to which barrel weights can be added. Fully adjustable rear sight and checkered walnut grips are standard.

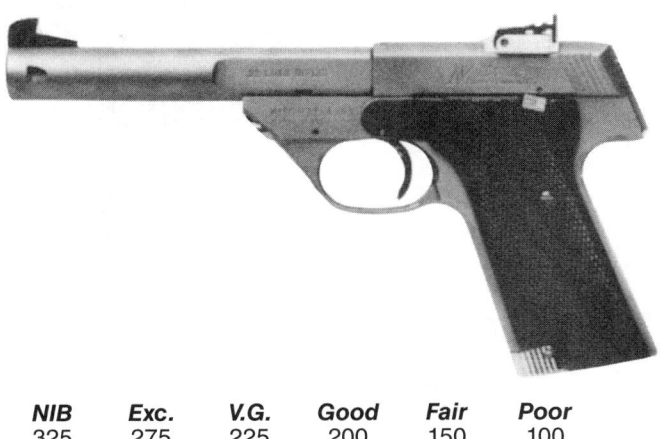

NIB	Exc.	V.G.	Good	Fair	Poor
325	275	225	200	150	100

Olympic I.S.U.

This competition pistol features a 6-3/4" barrel with integral stabilizer. Rear sight is adjustable as is the trigger. Barrel weights are adjustable as well as removable.

NIB	Exc.	V.G.	Good	Fair	Poor
525	475	400	300	200	100

Victor II

This .22 caliber pistol is built from stainless steel and has interchangeable barrels in 4-1/2" or 5-1/2" lengths. Barrels have full length ventilated ribs, checkered walnut grips with thumb rest. Gold plated trigger is adjustable.

NIB	Exc.	V.G.	Good	Fair	Poor
450	375	325	250	175	125

Victor II with Weaver Rib

NIB	Exc.	V.G.	Good	Fair	Poor
525	450	375	275	175	125

HIGH STANDARD COLLECTORS' ASSOCIATION SPECIAL EDITIONS

Limited run of Mitchell's version of the High Standard pistol with special roll marking on the slide "High Standard / Collectors Association / Special Edition" and a special serial number series with a HSCA prefix. Manufactured by Pastucek Industries, Fort Worth, Texas.

Trophy II

5.5" barrel. See standard Mitchell guns for rest of description.

NIB	Exc.	V.G.	Good	Fair	Poor
420	325	—	—	—	—

Victor II

4.5" barrel. See standard Mitchell guns for rest of description.

NIB	Exc.	V.G.	Good	Fair	Poor
450	325	—	—	—	—

Citation II

7.25" barrel. See standard Mitchell guns for rest of description.

NIB	Exc.	V.G.	Good	Fair	Poor
400	300	—	—	—	—

Three Gun Set

Includes Trophy II, Olympic ISU, and Victor II. Eleven sets manufactured.

NIB	Exc.	V.G.	Good	Fair	Poor
1400	1100	—	—	—	—

Six Gun Set

Includes 5.5" Trophy II, 6.75" Olympic II, and 4.5" Victor II, Sharpshooter II, Citation II, and 4.5" Sport King II. Nineteen sets manufactured.

NIB	Exc.	V.G.	Good	Fair	Poor
2450	1975	—	—	—	—

Skorpion

A .32 caliber semi-automatic pistol with a 4.75" barrel and either 20- or 30-shot magazine. Blued with plastic grips. Imported from Yugoslavia in 1987 and 1988 only.

NIB	Exc.	V.G.	Good	Fair	Poor
—	600	500	425	350	175

Spectre

A 9mm caliber semi-automatic pistol with an 8" shrouded barrel and either 30- or 50-shot magazine. Blued with plastic grips. Also produced with an 18" barrel and folding buttstock. Imported from Yugoslavia in 1987 and 1988.

NIB	Exc.	V.G.	Good	Fair	Poor
—	600	500	425	350	175

MITCHELL'S MAUSERS
Fountain Valley, California

Centurion Revolver

This is a double-action revolver with either a 4" or 6" barrel. Chambered for the .357 Magnum cartridge. Blued or stainless steel.

NIB	Exc.	V.G.	Good	Fair	Poor
695	550	400	300	200	100

Valkyrie Revolver

This revolver is chambered for the .44 Magnum cartridge and has a choice of 4" or 6" barrel. Blued or stainless steel.

NIB	Exc.	V.G.	Good	Fair	Poor
895	700	500	400	300	200

Gold Series '03 Pistol

Chambered for the 9mm, .40 S&W, or .45 ACP cartridge. Built on the Model 1911 Government Model. Blued or stainless steel.

NIB	Exc.	V.G.	Good	Fair	Poor
795	600	450	325	250	150

MKE
Ankara, Turkey

Kirrikale

A 7.65 or 9mm short semi-automatic pistol with a 4" barrel and 7-shot magazine. It is an unauthorized copy of the Walther PP. Blued with plastic grips.

NIB	Exc.	V.G.	Good	Fair	Poor
450	375	275	225	150	100

MODESTO SANTOS CIA.
Eibar, Spain

Action, Corrientes, and M.S.

A 6.35mm or 7.65mm caliber semi-automatic pistol of low quality marked on the slide "Pistolet Automatique Model 1920." Blued with composition grips having the monogram "M.S." cast in them. Manufactured between 1920 and 1935.

NIB	Exc.	V.G.	Good	Fair	Poor
—	275	175	125	75	50

MOORE'S PATENT FIREARMS CO.
Brooklyn, New York

In 1866 this company became known as the National Arms Company.

NO. 1 DERRINGER

A .41 caliber spur trigger all metal pistol with a 2.5" barrel. Blued or silver-plated. Approximately 10,000 were manufactured between 1860 and 1865. This model was also marketed as the No. 1 Derringer by the Colt Company after they purchased the National Arms Company in 1870.

Courtesy Milwaukee Public Museum, Milwaukee, Wisconsin

1st Variation Marked "Patent Applied For"

NIB	Exc.	V.G.	Good	Fair	Poor
—	—	3200	2500	1100	400

2nd Variation Marked "D. Moore Patented Feb. 19 1861"

NIB	Exc.	V.G.	Good	Fair	Poor
—	—	2200	1500	700	250

Standard Model Marked "Moore's Pat F.A. Co."

NIB	Exc.	V.G.	Good	Fair	Poor
—	—	1200	850	350	150

National Arms Co. Production

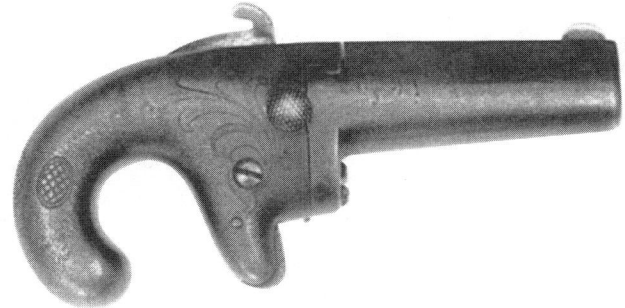

Courtesy Milwaukee Public Museum, Milwaukee, Wisconsin

NIB	Exc.	V.G.	Good	Fair	Poor
—	—	1250	875	385	150

No. 1 Derringer Iron Model

NIB	Exc.	V.G.	Good	Fair	Poor
—	—	1300	1100	550	250

Pocket Revolver

A .32 teat fire caliber spur trigger revolver with a round 3.25" barrel and 6-shot cylinder. Blued or silver plated with walnut grips. Approximately 30,000 were manufactured between 1864 and 1870.

NIB	Exc.	V.G.	Good	Fair	Poor
—	—	800	550	275	100

Belt Revolver

A .32 rimfire caliber revolver with a 4", 5", or 6" octagonal barrel and 7-shot cylinder. The barrel and cylinder blued, the brass frame sometimes silver-plated with walnut grips. The barrel marked "D. Moore Patent Sept. 18, 1860." Several thousand were manufactured between 1861 and 1863.

Courtesy Milwaukee Public Museum, Milwaukee, Wisconsin

Belt Revolver and Holster belonging to Capt. Henry Kellogg, Illinois 33rd during American Civil War

NIB	Exc.	V.G.	Good	Fair	Poor
—	—	1450	950	350	150

MORGAN & CLAPP
New Haven, Connecticut

Single-Shot Pocket Pistol

A .22 or .23 caliber spur trigger single-shot pistol with a 3.5" octagonal barrel. Blued, silver-plated frame with walnut grips. The barrel marked "Morgan & Clapp New Haven." Active 1864 to 1867.

NIB	Exc.	V.G.	Good	Fair	Poor
—	—	1150	650	250	100

MORINI
Italy

C-80 Standard

A .22 caliber single-shot pistol with a free floating 10" barrel, match sights, adjustable frame, and adjustable grips. Discontinued in 1989.

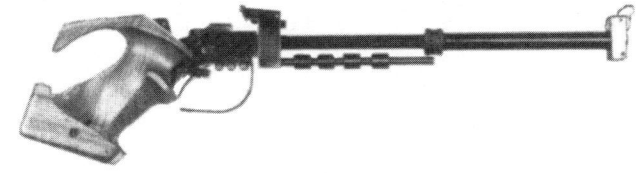

NIB	Exc.	V.G.	Good	Fair	Poor
—	1100	800	675	550	250

CM-80 Super Competition

As above, with a trigger adjustable from 5 to 120 grams pressure, Plexiglass front sight and a polished finish. Discontinued in 1989.

NIB	Exc.	V.G.	Good	Fair	Poor
—	1200	900	750	650	300

Model 84E Free Pistol

Introduced in 1995 this competition pistol features an 11.4" barrel chambered for the .22 LR. It is a single-shot. Adjustable sights with adjustable electronic trigger. Weight is about 44 oz.

NIB	Exc.	V.G.	Good	Fair	Poor
1650	1150	900	700	500	200

MOSSBERG, O. F. & SONS, INC.
North Haven, Connecticut

Founded by Oscar F. Mossberg in 1892 at Fitchburg, Massachusetts, this company for a time was located at Chicopee Falls, Massachusetts, and since 1919 has been in North Haven, Connecticut. It is the oldest family-owned firearms manufacturer in America.

Brownie

A .22 caliber four-barreled pocket pistol with a revolving firing pin. This pistol resembles a semi-automatic. Manufactured from 1906 to approximately 1940. Premium for in box with papers.

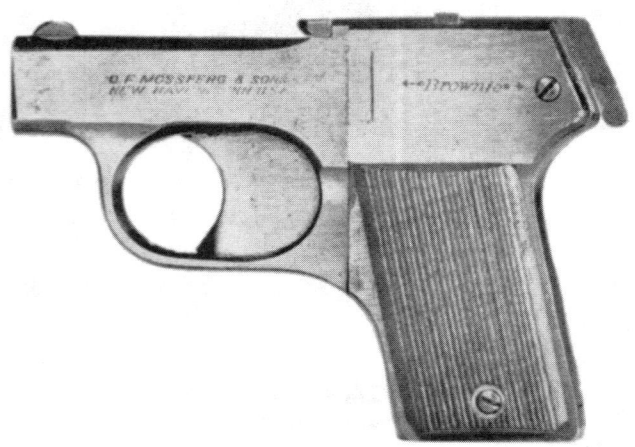

NIB	Exc.	V.G.	Good	Fair	Poor
—	450	325	300	225	150

Mossberg International Models 702 and 802 Plinkster Pistols

Semiauto (702) or bolt action (802) pistols chambered in .22 LR. Features include black synthetic or laminated wood stock, 10-inch blued barrel, ergonomic grips, 10-shot detachable box magazine. Introduced 2010. Price: N/A.

MURPHY & O'CONNEL
New York, New York

Pocket Pistol

A .41 caliber single-shot percussion pocket pistol with a 3" barrel, German silver mounts and a walnut stock. Manufactured during the 1850s.

NIB	Exc.	V.G.	Good	Fair	Poor
—	—	3500	2950	1100	450

N

NATIONAL ARMS CO.
Brooklyn, New York
SEE—Moore's Patent Firearms Co.

The successor to the Moore's Patent Firearms Company in 1865. Purchased by the Colt Company in 1870.

Large Frame Teat-Fire Revolver

A .45 teat fire caliber revolver with a 7.5" barrel and 6-shot cylinder. Blued or silver-plated with walnut grips. The barrel marked "National Arms Co. Brooklyn." The exact number of these revolvers made is unknown, but it is estimated to be fewer than 30.

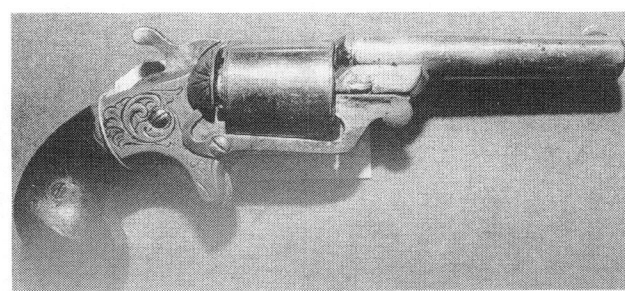

NIB	Exc.	V.G.	Good	Fair	Poor
—	—	24500	19000	6050	850

No. 2 Derringer

A .41 caliber spur trigger pocket pistol with a 2.5" barrel. Blued or silver-plated with walnut grips. Later manufactured by the Colt Company as their No. 2 Derringer.

Courtesy Rock Island Auction Company

NIB	Exc.	V.G.	Good	Fair	Poor
—	—	1750	1300	550	150

NAVY ARMS COMPANY
Martinsburg, West Virginia

Not a manufacturer but an importer. Founded in 1957 by Val Forgett to enhance the shooting of blackpowder firearms without destroying the originals. The first replica was the Colt 1851 Navy. Thus, the name of the new company, "Navy Arms." In the early 1980s Navy Arms began importing surplus firearms from European countries. Navy Arms continues to offer both blackpowder replicas and foreign imports. For a short period of time the company imported double-barrel shotguns. This was discontinued in 1990. Most if not all of the guns listed below are also to be found under the manufacturers' names as well as those of other importers.

Le Page Pistol

This .44 caliber percussion pistol has a 10.25" tapered octagon barrel, adjustable single set trigger. The lock, trigger guard, and buttcap are engraved. The walnut stocks are hand checkered. Weighs 36 oz.

NIB	Exc.	V.G.	Good	Fair	Poor
450	375	300	250	200	100

Le Page Pistol Single Cased Set

NIB	Exc.	V.G.	Good	Fair	Poor
580	530	475	400	300	150

Le Page Pistol Double Cased Set

NIB	Exc.	V.G.	Good	Fair	Poor
995	875	750	600	400	200

Le Page Flintlock

Same as above but with flintlock ignition. Weighs 41 oz.

NIB	Exc.	V.G.	Good	Fair	Poor
470	425	350	250	150	100

Le Page Smoothbore Flintlock Pistol

Same as above but with a smooth bore.

NIB	Exc.	V.G.	Good	Fair	Poor
470	425	350	250	150	100

Le Page Smoothbore Flintlock Pistol Single Cased Set

NIB	Exc.	V.G.	Good	Fair	Poor
800	700	600	400	300	150

Le Page Smoothbore Flintlock Pistol Double Cased Set

NIB	Exc.	V.G.	Good	Fair	Poor
1395	1275	1050	600	400	200

Kentucky Pistol

A percussion replica of a pistol developed in the 1840s. It has a 10.125" blued barrel, case colored lock, brass furniture and trigger guard with walnut stock. Weighs 32 oz.

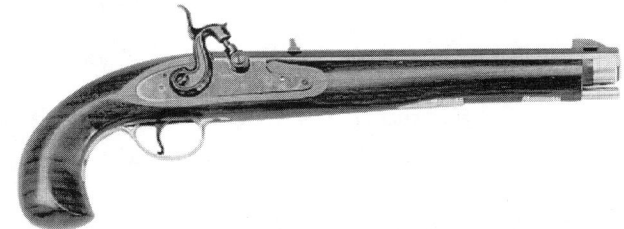

NIB	Exc.	V.G.	Good	Fair	Poor
295	225	200	125	85	60

Kentucky Pistol Single Cased Set

NIB	Exc.	V.G.	Good	Fair	Poor
350	275	225	175	125	75

Kentucky Pistol Double Cased Set

NIB	Exc.	V.G.	Good	Fair	Poor
550	450	350	250	150	100

Kentucky Flintlock Pistol

Same as above but with flintlock ignition.

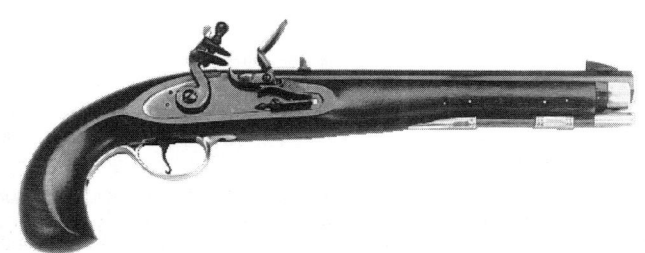

NIB	Exc.	V.G.	Good	Fair	Poor
225	175	150	100	75	60

Kentucky Flintlock Pistol Single Cased Set
NIB	Exc.	V.G.	Good	Fair	Poor
350	275	225	175	125	75

Kentucky Flintlock Pistol Double Cased Set
NIB	Exc.	V.G.	Good	Fair	Poor
550	450	350	275	175	100

Harpers Ferry Pistol

This pistol has a .58 caliber rifled 10" barrel. Case hardened lock and walnut stock. Weight is approximately 39 oz.

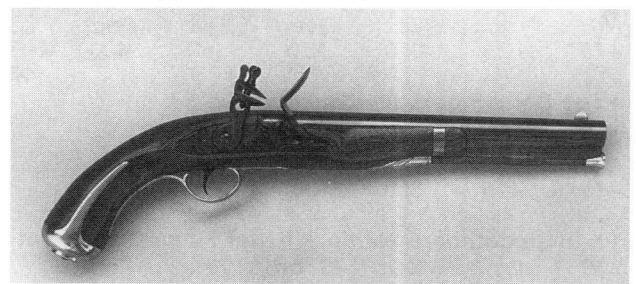

NIB	Exc.	V.G.	Good	Fair	Poor
300	250	200	150	100	75

Harpers Ferry Pistol Single Cased Set
NIB	Exc.	V.G.	Good	Fair	Poor
350	275	225	175	125	100

18th Georgia Le Mat Pistol

This 9-shot .44 caliber percussion revolver has a 7.625" blued barrel and engraved cylinder. An engraved banner on the left side of the frame reads "DEO VINDICE." Hammer and trigger are case colored. Stocks are checkered walnut. Comes with Le Mat mould and velvet draped French fitted case. Weighs 55 oz.

NIB	Exc.	V.G.	Good	Fair	Poor
795	625	500	400	300	150

Beauregard Le Mat Pistol

This is a replica of the Cavalry model. Comes cased.

NIB	Exc.	V.G.	Good	Fair	Poor
1000	800	650	550	350	200

Navy Le Mat

This model features a knurled pin barrel release and spur barrel selector.

NIB	Exc.	V.G.	Good	Fair	Poor
795	625	500	400	300	150

Army Le Mat

This model features a knurled pin barrel release and cross pin barrel selector.

NIB	Exc.	V.G.	Good	Fair	Poor
795	625	500	400	300	150

Cavalry Le Mat

This model features a lanyard ring, spur trigger, lever type barrel release, and cross pin barrel selector.

NIB	Exc.	V.G.	Good	Fair	Poor
795	625	500	400	300	150

Starr Double-Action Model 1858 Army

This model is a double-action revolver chambered for .44 caliber. Fitted with a 6" barrel. Blued finish. Weight is about 48 oz.

NIB	Exc.	V.G.	Good	Fair	Poor
350	250	200	150	100	75

Starr Single-Action Model 1863 Army

This model is fitted with an 8" barrel and is chambered for .44 caliber. Blued finish and walnut stock. Weight is about 48 oz.

NIB	Exc.	V.G.	Good	Fair	Poor
350	250	200	150	100	75

1862 New Model Police

This replica is based on the Colt .36 caliber pocket pistol of the same name. It features a half fluted and re-dated cylinder, case colored frame and loading gate, and a polished brass trigger guard and backstrap. Barrel length is 5.5" and pistol weigh 26 oz.

NIB	Exc.	V.G.	Good	Fair	Poor
300	250	175	150	100	75

1862 New Model Book-Style Cased Set
NIB	Exc.	V.G.	Good	Fair	Poor
350	250	200	150	100	75

Paterson Revolver

This replica is the five-shot .36 caliber. The cylinder is scroll engraved with a stagecoach scene. The hidden trigger drops down when the hammer is cocked. Barrel is 9" and the pistol weighs 43 oz.

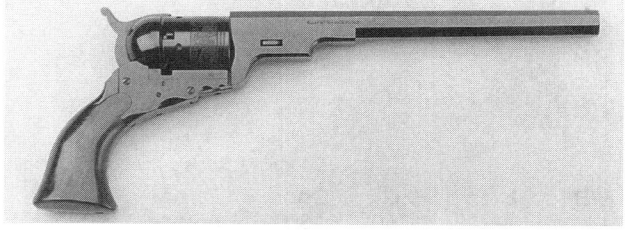

NIB	Exc.	V.G.	Good	Fair	Poor
475	425	350	250	150	100

Engraved Paterson Revolver

This model features hand engraving with silver inlays.

NIB	Exc.	V.G.	Good	Fair	Poor
575	475	350	250	200	100

1851 Navy

This Colt replica is offered in either .36 or .44 caliber. A naval battle scene is engraved in the cylinder. The octagon barrel length is 7.5". The trigger guard and backstrap are polished brass. The walnut grips are hand rubbed. Weighs 32 oz.

NIB	Exc.	V.G.	Good	Fair	Poor
350	250	200	150	100	75

1851 Navy Single Cased Set

NIB	Exc.	V.G.	Good	Fair	Poor
375	275	225	150	100	75

1851 Navy Double Cased Set

NIB	Exc.	V.G.	Good	Fair	Poor
550	450	375	275	200	100

NOTE: Optional shoulder stock add $100.

1851 Navy Conversion

This is a replica of the Colt 1851 Navy cartridge conversion. Offered in 38 Special or .38 Long Colt with choice of 5.5" or 7.5" barrels. Weight is about 40 oz.

NIB	Exc.	V.G.	Good	Fair	Poor
475	425	350	250	150	100

Augusta 1851 Navy Pistol

Available with either 5" or 7.5" barrel. Engraved with "A" coverage.

NIB	Exc.	V.G.	Good	Fair	Poor
350	250	200	150	100	75

Model 1851 Navy Frontiersman

Introduced in 2003 this revolver features a 5" .36 caliber barrel. The receiver, loading lever and hammer are case colored while the barrel and cylinder are charcoal blued. Fitted with a German silver backstrap and walnut grips.

NIB	Exc.	V.G.	Good	Fair	Poor
350	250	200	150	100	75

Reb Model 1860 Pistol

This is a replica of the Confederate Griswold and Gunnison revolver. It features a blued round 7.5" barrel, brass frame, trigger guard and backstrap. Offered in .36 or .44 caliber. Weighs 44 oz.

NIB	Exc.	V.G.	Good	Fair	Poor
165	150	125	90	75	35

Reb 1860 Sheriff's Model

Same as above but fitted with a 5" barrel. Weighs 40 oz.

NIB	Exc.	V.G.	Good	Fair	Poor
165	150	125	90	75	35

1847 Walker Dragoon

This is a replica of the rare Colt .44 caliber revolver. The barrel and cylinder are blued while the frame and loading lever are case colored. Barrel length is 9" and pistol weighs 75 oz.

NIB	Exc.	V.G.	Good	Fair	Poor
400	325	275	250	200	100

1847 Walker Dragoon Single Cased Set

NIB	Exc.	V.G.	Good	Fair	Poor
450	375	325	250	200	100

1847 Walker Dragoon Single Deluxe Cased Set

NIB	Exc.	V.G.	Good	Fair	Poor
525	425	350	300	200	100

1860 Army Pistol

This .44 caliber model features a case colored frame and loading lever with blued barrel, cylinder, and backstrap. The trigger guard is brass. The cylinder is engraved with a battle scene. Barrel is 8" and pistol weighs 41 oz.

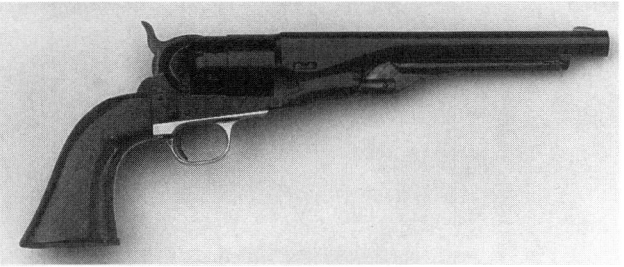

NIB	Exc.	V.G.	Good	Fair	Poor
350	250	200	150	100	75

1860 Army Pistol Single Cased Set

NIB	Exc.	V.G.	Good	Fair	Poor
375	275	225	150	100	75

1860 Army Pistol Double Cased Set

NIB	Exc.	V.G.	Good	Fair	Poor
550	450	375	275	200	100

1860 Army Conversion

Chambered for the .38 Special or .38 Long Colt this model is fitted with either a 5.5" or 7.5" barrel. Blued finish. Walnut grips. Weight is about 40 oz.

NIB	Exc.	V.G.	Good	Fair	Poor
475	425	350	250	150	100

1858 New Model Remington-Style Pistol

This replica has a solid frame, as did the original. The frame and 8" barrel are blued, while the trigger guard is brass. Walnut grips are standard. Weighs 40 oz.

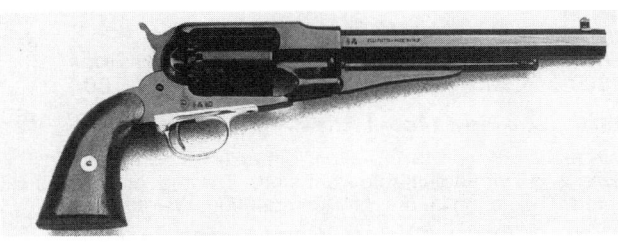

NIB	Exc.	V.G.	Good	Fair	Poor
350	250	200	150	100	75

1858 New Model Remington-Style Pistol Single Cased Set

NIB	Exc.	V.G.	Good	Fair	Poor
375	275	225	150	100	75

1858 New Model Remington-Style Pistol Double Cased Set

NIB	Exc.	V.G.	Good	Fair	Poor
550	450	375	275	200	100

Stainless Steel 1858 New Model Army

Same as above but in stainless steel. Weighs 40 oz.

NIB	Exc.	V.G.	Good	Fair	Poor
375	275	225	150	100	75

Stainless Steel 1858 New Model Army Single Cased Set

NIB	Exc.	V.G.	Good	Fair	Poor
375	275	225	150	100	75

Stainless Steel 1858 New Model Army Double Cased Set

NIB	Exc.	V.G.	Good	Fair	Poor
550	450	375	275	200	10

Brass Framed 1858 New Model Army

This version features a highly polished brass frame. Barrel length is 7.75".

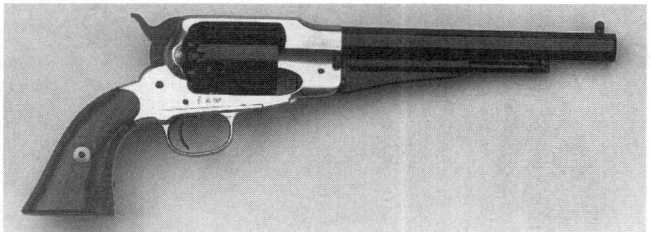

NIB	Exc.	V.G.	Good	Fair	Poor
165	150	125	90	75	35

Brass Framed 1858 New Model Army Single Cased Set

NIB	Exc.	V.G.	Good	Fair	Poor
250	200	150	100	75	60

Brass Framed 1858 New Model Army Double Cased Set

NIB	Exc.	V.G.	Good	Fair	Poor
395	325	300	250	200	100

1858 Target Model

Same as above but features a patridge front sight and an adjustable rear sight. Barrel length is 8".

NIB	Exc.	V.G.	Good	Fair	Poor
300	225	175	125	75	50

Deluxe 1858 New Model Army

This replica is built to the exact dimensions as the original. The barrel is 8" with adjustable front sight. The trigger guard is silver plated. The action is tuned for competition. Weighs 46 oz.

NIB	Exc.	V.G.	Good	Fair	Poor
400	325	250	200	150	100

Spiller and Burr Pistol

This is a .36 caliber pistol with 7" blued octagon barrel. The frame is brass with walnut grips. Weighs 40 oz.

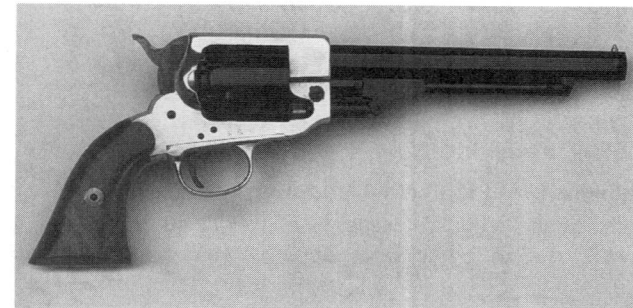

NIB	Exc.	V.G.	Good	Fair	Poor
350	250	200	150	100	75

Spiller and Burr Pistol Single Cased Set

NIB	Exc.	V.G.	Good	Fair	Poor
375	275	225	150	100	75

Spiller and Burr Pistol Double Cased Set

NIB	Exc.	V.G.	Good	Fair	Poor
550	450	375	275	200	100

Rogers and Spencer

This model features a 7.5" barrel with blued frame and barrel. Offered in .44 caliber. Walnut grips. Weighs 48 oz.

NIB	Exc.	V.G.	Good	Fair	Poor
375	275	225	150	100	75

"London Gray" Rogers and Spencer Pistol

Same as above but with a burnished satin chrome finish.

NIB	Exc.	V.G.	Good	Fair	Poor
375	275	225	150	100	75

Rogers and Spencer Target Model

Same as standard model but fitted with adjustable target sights.

NIB	Exc.	V.G.	Good	Fair	Poor
375	275	225	150	100	75

1861 Navy Conversion

Replica of the cartridge conversion of the 1861 Navy. Chambered for .38 Special or .38 Long Colt. Fitted with either a 5.5" or 7.5" barrel. Weight is about 40 oz.

NIB	Exc.	V.G.	Good	Fair	Poor
475	425	350	250	150	100

1872 Colt Open Top

This model features a 5.5" or 7.5" barrel with case hardened frame, blued barrel and cylinder, and silver-plated brass trigger guard and backstrap. Walnut grips. Chambered for .38 caliber cartridge. Weight is about 40 oz.

NIB	Exc.	V.G.	Good	Fair	Poor
500	375	225	175	150	125

1873 Colt-Style Single-Action Army

This replica features a case colored frame and hammer with blued round barrel in 3", 4.75", 5.5", or 7.5" lengths. Trigger guard and cylinder are blued. Offered in .44-40, .45 Long Colt, .357 Magnum, and .32-20.

NIB	Exc.	V.G.	Good	Fair	Poor
500	375	225	175	150	125

Model 1873 SAA Stainless Gunfighter

Introduced in 2003 this model is the same as the standard 1873, but features all stainless steel construction. Offered in .45 Colt and .357 Magnum caliber with choice of 4.75", 5.5", or 7.5" barrel. Weight is about 45 oz. depending on barrel length.

NIB	Exc.	V.G.	Good	Fair	Poor
525	400	250	195	150	125

Model 1873 SAA Stainless Gunfighter Economy Model 1873 S.A.A.

NIB	Exc.	V.G.	Good	Fair	Poor
325	250	200	150	125	100

Model 1873 SAA Stainless Gunfighter Nickel 1873 S.A.A.

NIB	Exc.	V.G.	Good	Fair	Poor
525	400	250	195	150	125

1873 U.S. Cavalry Model

This .45 Long Colt model features U.S. arsenal stampings, case colored frame, and walnut grips. Barrel length is 7.5" and pistol weighs 45 oz.

NIB	Exc.	V.G.	Good	Fair	Poor
500	375	225	175	150	125

1873 Pinched Frame Model

This is a replica of the "pinched" frame 1873 with "U" shape rear sight notch. Chambered for .45 Colt with 7.5" barrel.

NIB	Exc.	V.G.	Good	Fair	Poor
500	375	225	175	150	125

1873 Flat Top Target

This model features a windage adjustable rear sight on a flat top frame and a spring loaded front sight. Barrel length is 7.5". Offered in .45 Colt. Weight is about 40 oz. Introduced in 1998.

NIB	Exc.	V.G.	Good	Fair	Poor
500	375	225	175	150	125

Deputy Single-Action Army

Similar to the Model 1873 but with a bird's-head grip. Barrel lengths are 3", 3.5", 4", and 4.75". Chambered for .44-40 and .45 Colt.

NIB	Exc.	V.G.	Good	Fair	Poor
400	325	250	200	150	100

Shootist Model S.A.A.

This model is a reproduction of the Colt 1873. Parts are interchangeable with the originals. Blued barrel, cylinder, trigger guard, and backstrap. Case hardened frame and hammer. Walnut grips. Offered in 4.75", 5.5", and 7.5" barrel lengths. Chambered for .357 Magnum, .44-40, or .45 Colt.

NIB	Exc.	V.G.	Good	Fair	Poor
500	375	225	175	150	125

Scout Small Frame Revolver

This model is identical to the Colt 1873 SAA but with smaller dimensions. Offered in .38 Special with choice of 4.75" or 5.5" barrel. Weight is about 30 oz. Introduced in 2003.

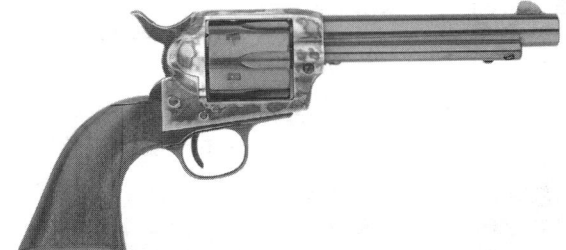

NIB	Exc.	V.G.	Good	Fair	Poor
400	325	250	200	150	100

Deluxe 1873 Colt Revolver

This model is chambered for the .32-20 cartridge and features bright charcoal blue with case colored frame and hammer. Walnut grips. Fitted with a 5.5" barrel. Limited production. Weight is about 41 oz.

NIB	Exc.	V.G.	Good	Fair	Poor
500	375	225	175	150	125

Bisley Model

This model features the famous Bisley grip. Barrel length is 4.75", 5.5", and 7.5". Chambered for .44-40 or .45 Colt.

NIB	Exc.	V.G.	Good	Fair	Poor
500	375	225	175	150	125

Bisley Flat Top Target

Similar to the Bisley but with 7.5" barrel with flat top frame with adjustable front sight and windage adjustable rear sight. Chambered for .44-40 or .45 Colt. Weight is about 40 oz.

NIB	Exc.	V.G.	Good	Fair	Poor
525	400	250	195	150	125

1875 Remington-Style Revolver

The frame is case colored while all other parts are blued except for brass trigger guard. Available in .44-40 or .45 Long Colt. Furnished with walnut grips. Barrel length is 7.5". Weighs 41 oz.

NIB	Exc.	V.G.	Good	Fair	Poor
500	375	225	175	150	125

1890 Remington-Style Revolver

This is a modified version of the 1875 model that is also offered in .44-40 or .45 Long Colt. The web under the barrel has been eliminated. It has blued 5.5" steel barrel and frame. Lanyard loop is on bottom of walnut grips. Weighs 39 oz.

Same as above but with brass trigger guard and backstrap.

NIB	Exc.	V.G.	Good	Fair	Poor
500	375	225	175	150	125

TOP BREAK REVOLVERS
Model 1875 Schofield—Wells Fargo 5" barrel

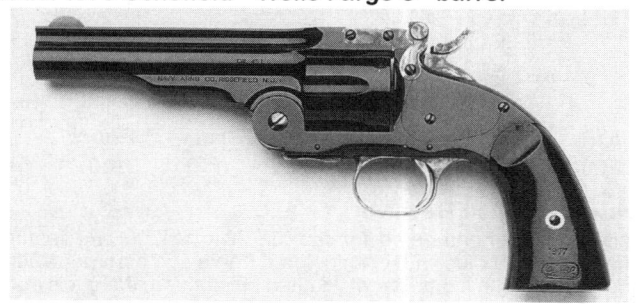

NIB	Exc.	V.G.	Good	Fair	Poor
750	650	525	450	350	125

Model 1875 Schofield—Cavalry 7" barrel
A reproduction of the S&W Model 3 top break revolver in either .44-40 or .45 Long Colt. The Cavalry model has a 7" barrel while the Wells Fargo model has a 5" barrel. Weight is about 39 oz.

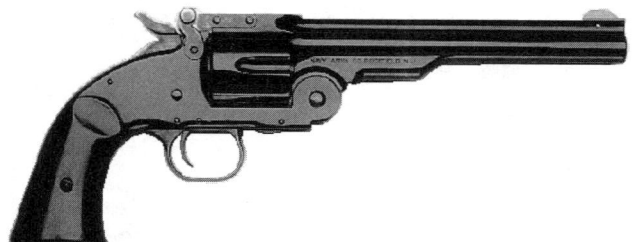

NIB	Exc.	V.G.	Good	Fair	Poor
750	650	525	450	350	125

Model 1875 Schofield—Deluxe
This model has a charcoal blue finish with gold inlays and "A" style hand engraving. Available in either the Cavalry or Wells Fargo model. Special order only.

NIB	Exc.	V.G.	Good	Fair	Poor
1000	800	675	550	425	200

Model 1875 Schofield—B Engraved
Available In Cavalry or Wells Fargo Model. This grade is "B" style engraved with 35 percent coverage. Special order only.

NIB	Exc.	V.G.	Good	Fair	Poor
1100	900	775	650	525	250

Model 1875 Schofield—C Engraved
This model is available in Cavalry or Wells Fargo with "C" style engraving with 50 percent coverage. Special order only.

NIB	Exc.	V.G.	Good	Fair	Poor
1150	950	800	675	55	275

Model 1875 Schofield Founder's Model
Introduced in 2003 to honor Val Forgett, Sr. and Aldo Uberti. This revolver features a charcoal blued barrel and cylinder with color case hardened receiver, backstrap, trigger guard and trigger. Grip are white ivory polymer. Limited production with special serial number prefix of "VF."

NIB	Exc.	V.G.	Good	Fair	Poor
750	650	525	450	350	125

Model 1875 Schofield—Hideout
This is a short-barrel variation of the Schofield. It is fitted with a 3.5" barrel and chambered for the .44-40 or .45 Colt cartridge. Weight is about 38 oz.

NIB	Exc.	V.G.	Good	Fair	Poor
750	650	525	450	350	125

New Model Russian
Built around the single-action Smith & Wesson Model 3, this revolver is chambered for the .44 Russian cartridge. It is fitted with a 6.5" barrel. Case colored spur trigger guard, latch and hammer. Blued frame, barrel and cylinder. Walnut grips. Weight is about 40 oz. Introduced in 1999.

NIB	Exc.	V.G.	Good	Fair	Poor
750	650	525	450	350	125

MILITARY SURPLUS ARMS
TT-Olympia Pistol
This is a reproduction of the Walther target pistol. Chambered for .22 LR. Barrel length is 4.625" and pistol weighs 27 oz.

NIB	Exc.	V.G.	Good	Fair	Poor
275	200	150	125	100	50

TU-90 Pistol
This model is based on the Tokagypt pistol. It features a wraparound grip with thumb rest. Barrel length is 4.5" and pistol weighs 30 oz.

NIB	Exc.	V.G.	Good	Fair	Poor
250	190	115	75	50	40

Luger
A .22 caliber semi-automatic pistol with a 4", 6", or 8" barrel, fixed sights, and 10-shot magazine. Blued with walnut grips. Manufactured in the U.S.A. in 1986 and 1987.

NIB	Exc.	V.G.	Good	Fair	Poor
—	325	275	225	175	125

Grand Prix Silhouette Pistol
A .30-30, .44 Magnum, 7mm Special, and .45-70 caliber single-shot pistol with a 13.75" barrel, adjustable sights, and an aluminum, heat-disbursing rib. Matte-blued, walnut grips and forearm. Manufactured in 1985.

NIB	Exc.	V.G.	Good	Fair	Poor
—	450	375	295	225	150

NEAL, W.
Bangor, Maine

Under Hammer Pistol

A .31 caliber under hammer percussion pistol with 5" to 8" barrels, iron frame and walnut grip. The barrel marked "Wm. Neal/Bangor, Me."

NIB	Exc.	V.G.	Good	Fair	Poor
—	—	1350	1000	450	150

NEPPERHAN FIREARMS CO.
Yonkers, New York

Pocket Revolver

A .31 caliber percussion revolver with 3.5" to 6" barrels and a 5-shot cylinder. Blued, case hardened with walnut grips. The barrel marked "Nepperhan/Fire Arms Co" and on some additionally "Yonkers New York." The latter are worth a slight premium over the values listed. Approximately 5,000 were made during the 1860s.

NIB	Exc.	V.G.	Good	Fair	Poor
—	—	1400	1000	385	200

NEW ENGLAND FIREARMS CO.
Gardner, Massachusetts

New England Firearms Company is owned by Marlin.

Model R22

.22 Magnum or .32 H&R Magnum double-action revolver with a 2.5", 4", or 6" barrel and either a 6- or 9-shot cylinder. Blued or nickel-plated with walnut grips. Introduced in 1988.

NIB	Exc.	V.G.	Good	Fair	Poor
150	100	80	70	60	40

NEWBURY ARMS CO.
Catskill, New York
Albany, New York

Pocket Pistol

A .25 caliber spur trigger pocket pistol with a 4" octagonal barrel. Blued, silver-plated with walnut grips.

NIB	Exc.	V.G.	Good	Fair	Poor
—	—	2400	2050	875	200

Pocket Revolver

A .26 caliber double-action percussion revolver with a 5" barrel and C-shaped exposed trigger. Blued with an iron or brass frame and walnut grips. The barrel marked "Newbury Arms Co. Albany." Produced in limited numbers between 1855 and 1860.

NIB	Exc.	V.G.	Good	Fair	Poor
—	—	7800	6900	3000	750

NEWCOMB, H. G.
Natchez, Mississippi

Pocket Pistol

A .41 caliber percussion pocket pistol with a 2.5" barrel, German silver mounts and a walnut stock. Manufactured in the 1850s.

NIB	Exc.	V.G.	Good	Fair	Poor
—	—	2400	1850	700	250

NICHOLS & CHILDS
Conway, Massachusetts

Percussion Belt Revolver

A .34 caliber percussion revolver with a 6" round barrel and 6-shot cylinder. Blued or browned with walnut grips. It is estimated that fewer than 25 were made in 1838.

NIB	Exc.	V.G.	Good	Fair	Poor
—	—	1450	1175	4900	1250

NIGHTHAWK CUSTOM
Berryville, Arkansas

Custom Talon/Talon II

1911-style semi-auto with 5" (Talon) or 4.25" (Talon II) barrel and fixed or adjustable sights. Several other barrel lengths/finishes available.

NIB	Exc.	V.G.	Good	Fair	Poor
2400	1950	1550	1200	700	300

Custom Predator

1911-style semi-auto with 5" barrel or 4.25" and fixed or adjustable sights. Several other barrel lengths/finishes available.

NIB	Exc.	V.G.	Good	Fair	Poor
2800	2350	1850	1400	750	300

GRP

Global Response Pistol. 1911-style semi-auto with 5" or 4.25" barrel and fixed or adjustable sights. Several other barrel lengths/finishes available.

NIB	Exc.	V.G.	Good	Fair	Poor
2400	1950	1550	1200	700	300

NORINCO
Peoples Republic of China
China North Industries Corp.

Norinco is a state-owned conglomerate in China that exported firearms to the United States from 1988 to 1995. Importation of Norinco firearms was banned in conjunction with the 1994 Crime Bill and various trade sanctions against China, with the exception of several shotguns that were marketed between 1999 and 2002.

Type 54-1 Tokarev

A 7.62x25mm caliber semi-automatic pistol with a 4.6" barrel, fixed sights, and 8-shot magazine. Blued with plastic grips. Imported in 1989.

NIB	Exc.	V.G.	Good	Fair	Poor
—	300	250	200	100	80

1911 A1

Steel-framed clone of the 1911 .45 A1 semi-auto. Very popular with competition shooters as a platform for custom guns. No longer imported.

NIB	Exc.	V.G.	Good	Fair	Poor
—	400	350	200	100	80

Model 213 Pistol

A copy of the Browning P-35 semi-automatic pistol. Sold in 1988 only.

NIB	Exc.	V.G.	Good	Fair	Poor
—	250	200	150	100	75

Type 59 Makarov

A .380 or 9mm Makarov caliber double-action semi-automatic pistol with a 3.5" barrel and 8-shot magazine. Blued with plastic grips.

NIB	Exc.	V.G.	Good	Fair	Poor
—	275	250	225	175	125

NORTH & COUCH
New York, New York

ANIMAL TRAP GUN

A .28 or .30 caliber percussion pepperbox with either a 1.75" or 2.12" barrel group and a hammer made with or without a spur. Marked "North & Couch, Middletown, Conn." or "North & Couch New York." Manufactured during the 1860s.

Disk Hammer Model

NIB	Exc.	V.G.	Good	Fair	Poor
—	—	2200	1850	700	300

Spur Hammer Model

NIB	Exc.	V.G.	Good	Fair	Poor
—	—	3000	2750	900	350

NORTH AMERICAN ARMS
Provo, Utah

MINI-REVOLVER

A .22 or .22 Magnum caliber spur trigger revolver with a 1" or 2.5" barrel and 5-shot cylinder. Stainless steel with plastic or laminated rosewood grips. Introduced in 1975 and made in the styles listed.

Standard Rimfire Version

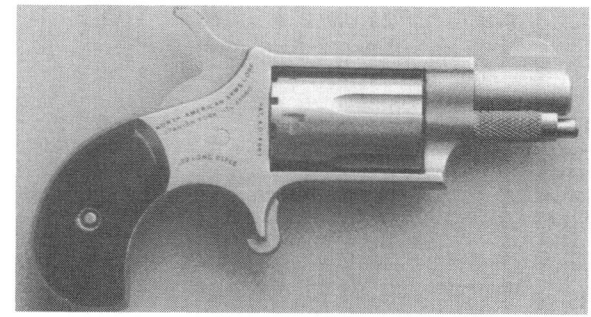

NIB	Exc.	V.G.	Good	Fair	Poor
225	175	150	—	125	100

2 Cylinder Magnum Convertible Version

NIB	Exc.	V.G.	Good	Fair	Poor
275	200	175	—	145	125

Viper Belt Buckle Version

NIB	Exc.	V.G.	Good	Fair	Poor
225	175	150	—	125	100

Magnum Version

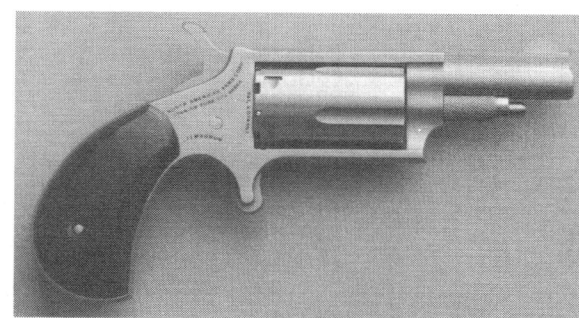

NIB	Exc.	V.G.	Good	Fair	Poor
250	200	175	—	150	100

Standard 3 Gun Set

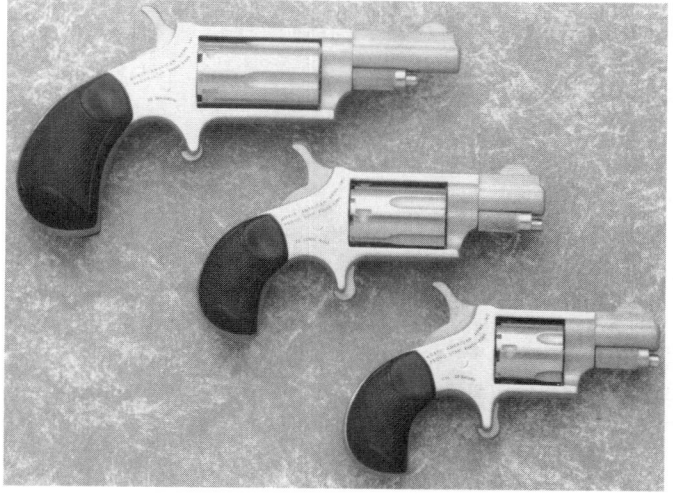

NIB	Exc.	V.G.	Good	Fair	Poor
725	575	400	—	300	225

Deluxe 3 Gun Set

NIB	Exc.	V.G.	Good	Fair	Poor
800	650	475	—	375	275

Cased .22 Magnum

NIB	Exc.	V.G.	Good	Fair	Poor
350	250	200	—	150	125

Companion

This is a .22 caliber cap-and-ball mini revolver. It has a 1.125" barrel. Overall length is 4.6" and weight is about 5 oz.a

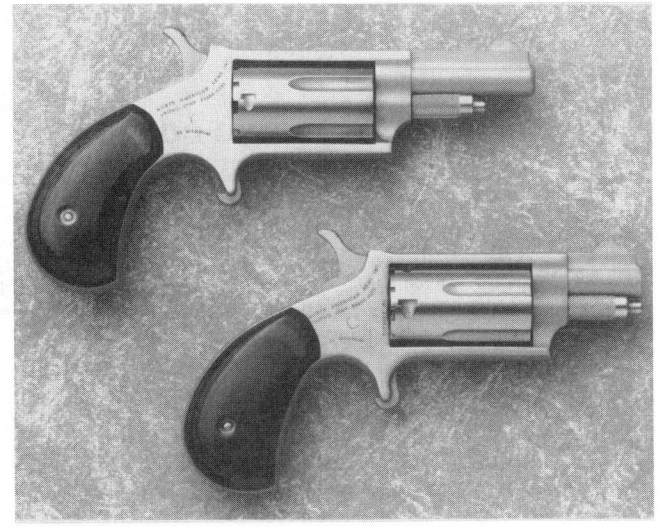

NIB	Exc.	V.G.	Good	Fair	Poor
200	165	150	125	100	75

Super Companion

Same as above but with longer cylinder. It has a 1.62" barrel and weighs about 7 oz.

NIB	Exc.	V.G.	Good	Fair	Poor
200	165	150	125	100	75

Black Widow

This is a five-shot fixed-sight revolver with oversize black rubber grips with a 2" or 4" barrel. Chambered for .22 LR or .22 Win. Mag. Stainless steel. Weight is approximately 8.8 oz.

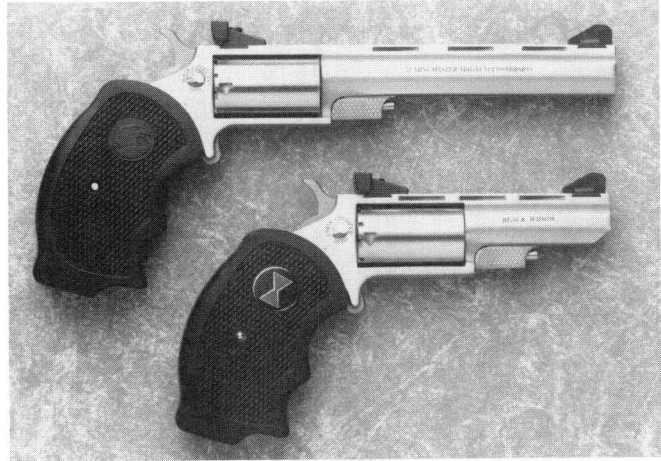

NIB	Exc.	V.G.	Good	Fair	Poor
280	225	175	125	100	75

NOTE: Add $20 for adjustable sights.

Mini-Master

This model is similar to the Black Widow with a 2" or 4" barrel. This model also gives a choice of either .22 LR or .22 Win. Mag. Stainless steel. Weight is approximately 10.7 oz.

NIB	Exc.	V.G.	Good	Fair	Poor
280	225	175	125	100	75

NOTE: Add $20 for adjustable sights.

"THE EARL" SINGLE-ACTION REVOLVER

Single-action mini-revolver patterned after 1858-style Remington percussion revolver. Chambered in .22 Magnum with .22 Long Rifle accessory cylinder. Features include a 4" octagonal barrel, spur trigger, five-shot cylinder, faux loading lever that serves as cylinder pin release, wood grips, fixed notch rear sight and barleycorn front sight. Overall length 7-3/4". Weight: 6.8 oz.

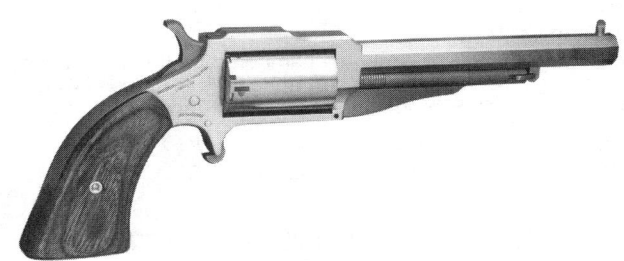

.22 Magnum only

NIB	Exc.	V.G.	Good	Fair	Poor
290	225	175	125	100	75

.22 convertible

NIB	Exc.	V.G.	Good	Fair	Poor
325	275	200	150	125	100

Single-Action Revolver

A polished stainless steel single-action revolver chambered for the .45 Winchester Magnum and the .450 Magnum Express cartridge. It has a 7.5" barrel and a 5-shot cylinder. There is a transfer bar safety, and the grips are walnut. This model was discontinued in 1988. Available with two cylinders.

NIB	Exc.	V.G.	Good	Fair	Poor
—	1200	950	700	400	250

NOTE: Add $200 for extra cylinder.

Guardian

This is a semi-automatic double-action-only pocket pistol chambered in .32 ACP, .32 NAA or .25 NAA. Magazine capacity is 6 rounds and the barrel length is 2.2". Overall length of the pistol is 4.4" and weight empty is 13.5 oz. Introduced in 1998. Add 25 percent for Crimson Trace laser grips.

NIB	Exc.	V.G.	Good	Fair	Poor
400	300	225	175	150	125

Guardian .380

Similar to the above model but chambered for the .380 cartridge. Barrel length is 2.5". Magazine capacity is 6 rounds. Weight is about 19 oz. Add $25 percent for Crimson Trace lasergrips.

NIB	Exc.	V.G.	Good	Fair	Poor
450	350	250	195	175	150

NORTH AMERICAN ARMS CORP.
Toronto, Canada

Brigadier

A .45 ACP caliber semi-automatic pistol with a 5" barrel, 8-shot magazine and alloy frame. Weight 4.5 lbs. Produced in limited quantity between 1948 and 1951. Rarely if ever seen; value should be in excess of $5000 in Excellent or better condition.

NORTON ARMAMENT CORPORATION
Mt. Clemens, Michigan
SEE—Budischowsky

This firm manufactured Budischowsky Model TP-70 semi-automatic pistols prior to 1979. After that date, these arms were made by the American Arms and Ammunition Company. Values below are for early Michigan production. Deduct 15 percent for later Florida and Utah production.

NIB	Exc.	V.G.	Good	Fair	Poor
—	500	375	250	125	100

NORWICH PISTOL CO.
Norwich, Connecticut

Established in 1875 by the New York retailer Maltby, Curtis & Company, this firm manufactured a wide variety of inexpensive spur trigger revolvers that were sold under these trade names: America, Bulldozer, Challenge, Chieftain, Crescent, Defiance, Hartford Arms, Maltby Henley, Metropolitan Police, Nonpariel, Norwich Arms, Parole, Patriot, Pinafore, Prairie King, Protector, Spy, True Blue, U.M.C. Winfield Arms.The company ceased operations in 1881. The value for any of its arms listed is approximate.

NIB	Exc.	V.G.	Good	Fair	Poor
—	—	300	200	75	50

NOWLIN MANUFACTURING COMPANY
Claremore, Oklahoma

Match Classic

This 1911 pistol has a wide range of features. It can be chambered in 9mm, .38 Super, 9x23, .40 S&W, and .45 ACP. It has a 5" barrel, adjustable trigger, checkered main spring housing, hardwood grips, front and rear cocking serrations. The price listed is for the basic pistols. Options will greatly affect price.

NIB	Exc.	V.G.	Good	Fair	Poor
1600	1250	800	600	400	250

Compact Carry

This pistol is similar to the Match Classic with the exception of a 4" barrel on a full-size frame. Again options will greatly affect price.

NIB	Exc.	V.G.	Good	Fair	Poor
1495	1100	700	500	300	200

Match Master

These hand-built pistols offered a choice of S.T.I., Caspian Hi-Cap, or Nowlin STD Gov't frames. Available in 9mm, 9x23, .38 Super, .40 S&W, and .45 ACP. Many special features are included in standard pistol and many extra cost options are available.

NIB	Exc.	V.G.	Good	Fair	Poor
2400	1750	1200	800	600	300

NOTE: Add $140 for hard chrome finish.

O.D.I.
Midland Park, New Jersey

Viking

A .45 caliber double-action semi-automatic pistol with a 5" barrel and 7-shot magazine. Stainless steel with teak grips. Manufactured in 1981 and 1982.

NIB	Exc.	V.G.	Good	Fair	Poor
700	625	375	300	200	100

Viking Combat

As above, with a 4.25" barrel.

NIB	Exc.	V.G.	Good	Fair	Poor
700	625	375	300	200	100

O'CONNELL, DAVID
New York, New York

Pocket Pistol

A .41 caliber percussion pocket pistol with a 2.5" barrel, German silver mounts, and walnut stock. Manufactured during the 1850s.

NIB	Exc.	V.G.	Good	Fair	Poor
—	—	3650	3000	1025	300

O'DELL, STEPHEN
Natchez, Mississippi

Pocket Pistol

A .34 to .44 caliber percussion pocket pistol with a 2" to 4" barrel, German silver mounts and walnut stock. Manufactured during the 1850s.

NIB	Exc.	V.G.	Good	Fair	Poor
—	—	6750	6000	2500	950

OBREGON
Mexico City, Mexico

This is a .45 caliber semi-automatic pistol with a 5" barrel. Similar to the Colt M1911A1 but with a combination side and safety latch on the left side of the frame. The breech is locked by rotating the barrel, instead of the Browning swinging link. This unusual locking system results in a tubular front end appearance to the pistol. Originally designed for the Mexican military it was not adopted as such and only about 1,000 pistols were produced and sold commercially. The pistol is 8.5" overall and weighs about 40 ozs. The magazine holds seven cartridges. This is a rare pistol; an independent appraisal is suggested prior to sale.

NIB	Exc.	V.G.	Good	Fair	Poor
—	3750	2300	1850	1550	800

OJANGUREN Y VIDOSA
Eibar, Spain

This typical Eibar company produced mediocre firearms from the early 1920s and was forced out of business during the Spanish Civil War.

Apache (Model 1920)

A typical Eibar Browning copy that is chambered for the 6.35mm cartridge. It is of the typical low quality associated with most Spanish arms of this era. The slide is marked "Pistole Browning Automatica Cal. 6.35 Apache." The finish is blued, and the plastic grips have a head with a beret and the word "Apache" molded into them.

NIB	Exc.	V.G.	Good	Fair	Poor
—	250	175	125	75	50

Apache (Model 1920)

As above but chambered for the 7.65mm cartridge.

Courtesy James Rankin

NIB	Exc.	V.G.	Good	Fair	Poor
—	275	225	190	100	75

Ojanguren

The trade name this company used to cover the line of revolvers they produced in the 1930s. They produced two in .32 caliber and two chambered for the .38 Special cartridge. They are similar in appearance and have barrel lengths of either 3" or 6". The finishes are blued, and they have plastic grips. One of the .38 caliber models—the "Legitimo Tanque"—is a reasonably well-made gun that was popular with the Spanish target shooters.

These guns have little collector value, little practical value and are all priced alike.

NIB	Exc.	V.G.	Good	Fair	Poor
—	175	125	100	75	50

Tanque

A blowback-operated semi-automatic chambered for the 6.35mm cartridge. It has a 1.5" barrel and is actually an original design, which was rarely found on Eibar guns of this period. It has an oddly shaped slide, and the barrel is retained by means of a screw in the front of the frame. It has a 6-shot magazine, and the slide is marked "6.35 Tanque Patent." The plastic grips have a tank molded into them and the word "Tanque," as well as the letters "O&V."

NIB	Exc.	V.G.	Good	Fair	Poor
—	175	125	100	75	50

OLYMPIC ARMS, INC.
Olympia, Washington

Black Widow

A .45 caliber semi-automatic pistol with a 3.9" barrel and 6-shot magazine. Nickel-plated with ivory Micarta grips with a spider engraved on them.

NIB	Exc.	V.G.	Good	Fair	Poor
700	575	450	350	300	200

Enforcer

A .45 caliber semi-automatic pistol with a 3.8" barrel and 6-shot magazine. Parkerized, anodized or nickel-plated with rubber grips. Weight is approximately 36 oz.

NIB	Exc.	V.G.	Good	Fair	Poor
650	500	400	350	300	200

Match Master

As above, with a 5" barrel and 7-shot magazine. Weight is about 40 oz.

NIB	Exc.	V.G.	Good	Fair	Poor
650	500	400	350	300	200

Match Master 6"

Same as above but with 6" barrel and slide. Weight is approximately 44 oz.

NIB	Exc.	V.G.	Good	Fair	Poor
675	550	400	350	300	200

Cohort

Fitted with a 4" bull barrel with a full size frame. Magazine capacity is 7 rounds. Weight is about 38 oz.

NIB	Exc.	V.G.	Good	Fair	Poor
675	550	400	350	300	200

Safari G.I.

This model is built on a Match Master frame with 5" barrel with fixed sights. Finish is flat black Parkerized. Checkered walnut grips.

NIB	Exc.	V.G.	Good	Fair	Poor
600	450	400	350	300	200

Schuetzen Pistol Works Big Deuce

This model is made in the Olympic Arms specialty shop called Schuetzen Pistol Works. Marked "Schuetzen Pistol Works" on the slide and "Safari Arms" on the frame. Introduced in 1995. This semi-automatic pistol is chambered for the .45 ACP cartridge and fitted with a 6" barrel, smooth walnut grips, and a number of other custom features. Magazine capacity is 7 rounds. Weight is approximately 40 oz. Black slide with stainless steel frame.

NIB	Exc.	V.G.	Good	Fair	Poor
950	800	700	500	275	150

Schuetzen Pistol Works Crest

Similar to the above model with the same markings. This version features a .45 ACP pistol with 4.5", 5", or 5.5" barrel. Checkered walnut grips. Offered in both right- and left-hand configurations. Stainless steel finish. Introduced in 1993. Weight is about 39 oz. depending on barrel length.

NIB	Exc.	V.G.	Good	Fair	Poor
800	650	500	400	275	150

NOTE: Left-hand model will bring a small premium.

Schuetzen Pistol Works Griffon

Similar to the above specialty models. This version is fitted with a 5" barrel and smooth walnut grips. Magazine capacity is 10 rounds. Stainless steel finish. Numerous custom features. Introduced in 1995.

NIB	Exc.	V.G.	Good	Fair	Poor
1300	1150	975	650	400	200

Schuetzen Pistol Works Carrier

Special built model along the lines of the Detonics Score Master with adjustable sights.

NIB	Exc.	V.G.	Good	Fair	Poor
700	600	500	400	250	150

Black-Tac

Semi-auto .45 ACP pistol treated with "black-tac" process – advantages of hard chrome without its drawbacks such as embrittlement.

NIB	Exc.	V.G.	Good	Fair	Poor
800	650	500	400	275	150

Constable

Semi-auto pistol chambered for .45 ACP with 4" barrel, 5.75" sight radius, 7+1 capacity, 35 oz. Introduced 2006.

NIB	Exc.	V.G.	Good	Fair	Poor
950	800	700	500	275	150

Custom Street Deuce

Semi-auto chambered for .45 ACP with 5.2" bull barrel, 7" sight radius, 7+1 capacity, 38 oz. Many options. Introduced 2006.

NIB	Exc.	V.G.	Good	Fair	Poor
1300	1150	975	650	400	200

Custom Journeyman

Semi-auto chambered for .45 ACP with 4" bull barrel, 6" sight radius, 6+1 capacity, 35 oz. Many options. Introduced 2006.

NIB	Exc.	V.G.	Good	Fair	Poor
1100	800	675	500	300	150

Trail Boss

Semi-auto pistol in the Westerner line chambered for .45 ACP. 6" barrel, 8" sight radius, 7+1 capacity, 43 oz. Introduced 2006.

NIB	Exc.	V.G.	Good	Fair	Poor
950	800	700	500	275	150

Westerner

Semi-auto pistol chambered for .45 ACP with 5" barrel, 7" sight radius, 7+1 capacity, 39 oz. Introduced 2006.

NIB	Exc.	V.G.	Good	Fair	Poor
950	800	700	500	275	150

Wolverine

Polymer-frame, vent-rib replica of the old "ray gun" .22 Whitney Wolverine semi-auto pistol. Cool, baby!

NIB	Exc.	V.G.	Good	Fair	Poor
300	265	250	200	150	100

Model OA-96

This model has a 6" barrel with pistol grip only, no buttstock. The 30-round magazine is pinned and cannot be detached. Break-open-action allows loading with stripper clips. Overall length is 15.75". Weight is about 4.2 lbs. BATF approved.

NIB	Exc.	V.G.	Good	Fair	Poor
1100	800	675	500	300	150

Model OA-98

Similar to the OA-93 but with lightening holes on the grip, mount, magazine. Fitted with a 6" barrel with no vertical grip. Weight is about 3 lbs. No buttstock.

NIB	Exc.	V.G.	Good	Fair	Poor
1100	800	675	500	300	150

OMEGA
Geneseo, Illinois
Springfield Armory

Omega Pistol

A high-grade target-type pistol that is patterned after the Colt Model 1911 pistol, with marked improvements. It is chambered for the .38 Super, 10mm, and the .45 ACP cartridges. The barrel is either 5" or 6" in length and has polygonal rifling. The barrels are furnished either ported or plain and feature a lockup system that eliminates the barrel link and bushing associated with the normal Browning design. This pistol has a dual extractor system, adjustable sights, and Pachmayr grips. It was introduced in 1987.

NIB	Exc.	V.G.	Good	Fair	Poor
900	725	575	450	350	150

ORBEA & CIA
Eibar, Spain

Pocket Pistol

A 6.35mm semi-automatic pistol with a 2.5" barrel. Blued with plastic grips. The slide marked "Orbea y Cia Eibar Espana Pistola Automatica Cal. 6.35." Manufactured from approximately 1918 to 1936.

NIB	Exc.	V.G.	Good	Fair	Poor
—	250	175	125	75	50

ORTGIES, HEINRICH & CO.
Erfurt, Germany

Ortgies Pistol

A 6.35mm or 7.65mm semi-automatic pistol with a 2.75" or 3.25" barrel. Blued with walnut grips. The slide marked "Ortgies & Co. Erfurt." After 1921, these pistols were manufactured by Deutsche Werke. Deduct $100 for 6.35mm.

NIB	Exc.	V.G.	Good	Fair	Poor
—	550	300	175	125	85

OSBORN, S.
Canton, Connecticut

Under Hammer Pistol

A .34 caliber under hammer percussion pistol with a 7" half octagonal barrel, brass mounts and a walnut grip. The barrel marked "S. Osborn/Canton, Conn."

NIB	Exc.	V.G.	Good	Fair	Poor
—	—	800	550	250	125

OSGOOD GUN WORKS
Norwich, Connecticut

Duplex Revolver

A .22 caliber spur trigger revolver with two super-imposed barrels, the upper most of .22 caliber and the lower a .32 caliber. The cylinder with eight .22 chambers. The hammer fitted with a moveable firing pin so that the pistol can be used either as a revolver or as a single shot with a .32 caliber barrel. Blued or nickel-plated with hard rubber grips. The barrel marked "Osgood Gun Works-Norwich Conn." and "Duplex." An unknown quantity were manufactured during the 1880s.

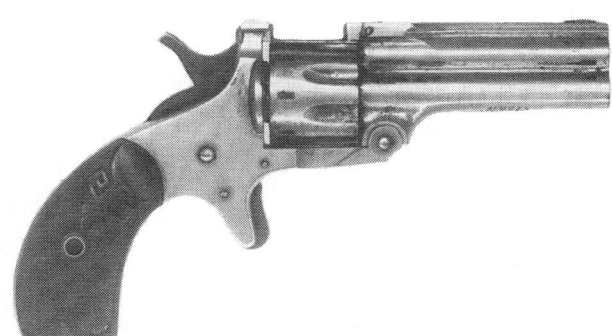

Courtesy Milwaukee Public Museum, Milwaukee, Wisconsin

NIB	Exc.	V.G.	Good	Fair	Poor
—	—	1600	875	350	100

OWA
Osterreiche Werke Anstalt
Vienna, Austria

OWA Pocket Pistol

A 6.35mm semi-automatic pistol with a 2" barrel. "OWA" logo cast in the grips. Blued with plastic grips. Manufactured between 1920 and 1925.

Courtesy Orvel Reichert

NIB	Exc.	V.G.	Good	Fair	Poor
—	400	325	200	150	1000

P.38
WALTHER COMMERCIAL

The Commercial version of the P.38 is identified by commercial proofmarks of a crown over N or an eagle over N. Production started at around serial number 1000 and went through serial number 26659. This was the first of the commercial pistols and was a high-quality, well made gun with a complete inscription on the left slide. A few of these early pistols were equipped with checkered wooden grips. The quality decreased as the war progressed. There are many variations of these commercial models and values can range up to more than $30,000. It is suggested that these pistols be appraised and evaluated by an expert. For post-war Walther P.38 pistols see the Walther section. A few of the Walther Commercial Model variations are listed.

MOD HP
H Prefix w/rectangular firing pin

NIB	Exc.	V.G.	Good	Fair	Poor
—	3200	2000	950	750	450

Early w/High Gloss Blue

NIB	Exc.	V.G.	Good	Fair	Poor
—	3000	1750	750	600	400

.30 caliber, extremely rare

NIB	Exc.	V.G.	Good	Fair	Poor
—	28000	—	—	—	—

Early w/High Gloss Blue & Alloy Frame

NIB	Exc.	V.G.	Good	Fair	Poor
—	10000	6500	3500	2000	1000

Croatian contract, 100 built, 6 known

NIB	Exc.	V.G.	Good	Fair	Poor
—	10000	—	—	—	—

Late w/Military Blue Finish

NIB	Exc.	V.G.	Good	Fair	Poor
—	2000	1400	750	550	350

NOTE: Add $500 for "Eagle/359" on right side.

MOD P38—Late with Military Blue

NIB	Exc.	V.G.	Good	Fair	Poor
—	2700	1750	750	600	400

"ac45" Zero Series

1200 made.

NIB	Exc.	V.G.	Good	Fair	Poor
—	2800	1750	750	600	400

WALTHER MILITARY

ZERO SERIES
First Issue

NIB	Exc.	V.G.	Good	Fair	Poor
—	8500	5500	3500	2500	1500

Second Issue

NIB	Exc.	V.G.	Good	Fair	Poor
—	7000	4500	3250	2000	1000

Third Issue

NIB	Exc.	V.G.	Good	Fair	Poor
—	3500	2200	1250	800	500

480 CODE

NIB	Exc.	V.G.	Good	Fair	Poor
—	8500	5500	3000	1750	1000

"AC" CODES

This variation follows the 480 code.

"ac" (no date)

NIB	Exc.	V.G.	Good	Fair	Poor
—	9500	6000	4250	2800	2000

"AC40"
Added

NIB	Exc.	V.G.	Good	Fair	Poor
—	3800	2500	1750	1000	600

Standard

NIB	Exc.	V.G.	Good	Fair	Poor
—	2500	1200	950	700	500

"AC41"
1st Variation

NIB	Exc.	V.G.	Good	Fair	Poor
—	2200	1100	700	500	350

2nd Variation

NIB	Exc.	V.G.	Good	Fair	Poor
—	1500	750	600	450	300

3rd Variation

NIB	Exc.	V.G.	Good	Fair	Poor
—	1300	600	475	400	300

"AC42"
1st Variation

NIB	Exc.	V.G.	Good	Fair	Poor
—	1300	550	400	350	275

2nd Variation

NIB	Exc.	V.G.	Good	Fair	Poor
—	1100	500	400	300	250

"AC43"
1st Variation

NIB	Exc.	V.G.	Good	Fair	Poor
—	900	450	300	250	200

2nd Variation

NIB	Exc.	V.G.	Good	Fair	Poor
—	550	350	300	250	200

Single Line Slide

NIB	Exc.	V.G.	Good	Fair	Poor
—	1200	550	450	350	250

"AC44"

NIB	Exc.	V.G.	Good	Fair	Poor
—	800	450	300	250	200

NOTE: Add $300 for FN frame (Eagle/140).

"AC45"

1st Variation

NIB	Exc.	V.G.	Good	Fair	Poor
—	800	450	300	250	200

2nd Variation

NIB	Exc.	V.G.	Good	Fair	Poor
—	950	500	325	300	250

3rd Variation

NIB	Exc.	V.G.	Good	Fair	Poor
—	750	400	300	250	200

NOTE: Add $200 for pistols with Czech barrels; barrel code "fnh."

MAUSER MILITARY

"byf42"

NIB	Exc.	V.G.	Good	Fair	Poor
—	2200	1200	700	500	300

"byf43"

NIB	Exc.	V.G.	Good	Fair	Poor
—	950	550	300	250	200

"byf44"

NIB	Exc.	V.G.	Good	Fair	Poor
—	950	550	300	250	200

NOTE: Add $100 for dual tone finish that is a combination of blue and gray components.

AC43/44—FN slide

NIB	Exc.	V.G.	Good	Fair	Poor
—	2200	1200	725	550	400

"SVW45"

"German Proofed

NIB	Exc.	V.G.	Good	Fair	Poor
—	2200	1200	725	550	400

French Proofed

NIB	Exc.	V.G.	Good	Fair	Poor
—	650	400	300	250	200

"svw46" —French Proofed

NIB	Exc.	V.G.	Good	Fair	Poor
—	800	500	400	350	300

MAUSER "POLICE" P.38

"byf/43"

NIB	Exc.	V.G.	Good	Fair	Poor
—	2500	1700	1200	800	500

"byf/44"

NIB	Exc.	V.G.	Good	Fair	Poor
—	2500	1700	1200	800	500

"ac/43"

NIB	Exc.	V.G.	Good	Fair	Poor
—	5000	3500	2000	1250	800

"ac/44"

NIB	Exc.	V.G.	Good	Fair	Poor
—	5000	3500	2000	1250	800

"svw/45"

NIB	Exc.	V.G.	Good	Fair	Poor
—	6000	4500	2500	1600	1000

SPREEWERKE MILITARY

"CYQ"

Eagle /211 on frame

2 known.

NIB	Exc.	V.G.	Good	Fair	Poor
—	5000	—	—	—	—

1st Variation

NIB	Exc.	V.G.	Good	Fair	Poor
—	1400	1000	750	600	500

Standard Variation

NIB	Exc.	V.G.	Good	Fair	Poor
—	800	400	275	250	200

NOTE: If "A" or "B" prefix add $250.

Zero Series

NIB	Exc.	V.G.	Good	Fair	Poor
—	1250	550	400	350	275

NOTE: Add $250 for AC43 or AC44 marked "FN" slide.

POST-WAR PISTOLS

Standard Slides

NIB	Exc.	V.G.	Good	Fair	Poor
—	400	250	200	175	150

Single Line Code (Rare)

NIB	Exc.	V.G.	Good	Fair	Poor
—	1000	550	350	250	200

Manurhin

NIB	Exc.	V.G.	Good	Fair	Poor
—	400	300	200	175	150

P.A.F.
Pretoria Small Arms Factory
Pretoria, South Africa

P.A.F. Junior

A .22 or .25 caliber semi-automatic pistol with a 2" barrel and 6-shot magazine. Blued with plastic grips. Slide marked "Junior Verwaardig in Suid Afrika Made in South Africa." Manufactured during the 1950s.

NIB	Exc.	V.G.	Good	Fair	Poor
—	350	250	125	100	70

PARA USA (PARA-ORDNANCE)
Pineville, North Carolina

Previously known as Para-Ordnance of Scarborough, Ontario, Canada. In 2009 the company relocated to Pineville, North Carolina.

Para 1911 100th Anniversary

Classic 1911 styling to commemorate the centennial of the design. Caliber .45 ACP, military-style thumb and grip safeties, solid muzzle bushing and hammer, and three-dot sights. Weight 39 ounces, 5-inch barrel, Covert Black finish. Smooth cocobolo grips. Comes with one 7- and one 8-round magazine.

NIB	Exc.	V.G.	Good	Fair	Poor
925	775	665	500	350	200

Model P14.45

Similar in appearance to the Colt Government model this .45 ACP semi-automatic pistol features a 5" barrel, flared ejection port, combat style hammer beveled magazine well and a 13-round magazine capacity. Overall length is 8.5" and weight is 40 oz. for steel and stainless steel version and 31 oz. for alloy frame model. Finish is black except for stainless steel model.

NIB	Exc.	V.G.	Good	Fair	Poor
700	550	500	400	300	200

NOTE: Add $50 for steel frame, $45 for stainless steel, and $30 for duo-tone.

Model P14.45 Limited

Similar to the above model but with extra features such as full length recoil guide, beavertail grip safety, adjustable rear sight, competition hammer, lowered ejection port, front and rear slide serrations, and trigger overtravel stop. Match grade barrel. Choice of black carbon steel or stainless steel finish. Weight is about 40 oz.

NIB	Exc.	V.G.	Good	Fair	Poor
1200	900	725	575	400	200

Model P14.45 LDA/P14.45 LDA Stainless

This model is essentially the same as the P14.45 but with a double-action trigger. Offered in black carbon steel only. Weight is about 40 oz. First introduced in 1999.

NIB	Exc.	V.G.	Good	Fair	Poor
800	600	400	350	225	150

NOTE: Add $50 for stainless steel.

Model P16.40

This is essentially the same as the Model 14.45 except that it is chambered for the .40 S&W cartridge. The magazine capacity is 15 rounds.

NIB	Exc.	V.G.	Good	Fair	Poor
800	600	400	350	225	150

NOTE: Add $50 for steel frame, $45 for stainless steel, and $30 for duo-tone.

Model P16.40 Limited

Similar to the above model but with extra features such as full length recoil guide, beavertail grip safety, adjustable rear sight, competition hammer, lowered ejection port, front and rear slide serrations, and trigger overtravel stop. Match grade barrel. Black carbon steel finish.

NIB	Exc.	V.G.	Good	Fair	Poor
1200	900	725	575	400	200

Model P16.40 LDA

This model is a double-action version of the P16.40 in black carbon steel only. First offered in 1999.

NIB	Exc.	V.G.	Good	Fair	Poor
800	600	400	350	225	150

Model P13.45

Introduced in 1994 this .45 ACP model features a 4-1/4" barrel with a 13-round magazine. The grip is 1/4" longer than the 12.45 model. Offered in light alloy, carbon, or stainless steel. Overall length is 7-3/4" and the height is 5-1/4". Weight is about 36 oz. in steel version and 28 oz. in alloy version.

NIB	Exc.	V.G.	Good	Fair	Poor
600	450	350	300	200	100

NOTE: Add $50 for steel frame, $45 for stainless steel, and $30 for duo-tone.

Model P13.45/P12.45 Limited

Similar to the above model but with extra features such as full length recoil guide, beavertail grip safety, adjustable rear sight, competition hammer, lowered ejection port, front and rear slide serrations, and trigger overtravel stop. Match grade barrel. Black carbon steel finish.

P13.45

NIB	Exc.	V.G.	Good	Fair	Poor
800	600	400	350	225	150

Model P12.45 LDA/P12.45 LDA

This model is fitted with a 3.5" barrel and has a magazine capacity of 12 rounds. It features a double-action trigger. Finish is black. Weight is about 34 oz. Introduced in 2000.

NIB	Exc.	V.G.	Good	Fair	Poor
750	600	450	300	200	100

NOTE: Add $50 for stainless steel.

Model P12.45/P12.40

Similar to the Model P14 but in a smaller package. Introduced in 1993. Has all the same features as the Model P14 but has a magazine capacity of 11 rounds. Also available in alloy, steel, or stainless steel this model weighs 24 oz. in alloy model and 33 oz. in steel models. The P12.40 is the same model but chambered for .40 S&W cartridge.

NIB	Exc.	V.G.	Good	Fair	Poor
800	600	400	350	225	150

NOTE: Add $50 for steel frame, $45 for stainless steel, and $30 for duo-tone.

Model P10.45/P10.40/P10.9

Introduced in 1996 this model is the smallest semi-auto .45 ACP in production. Overall length is 6.5" with height of 4.5". Magazine capacity is 10 rounds. Barrel length is 3.5". Offered in stainless steel, duo-tone, or black alloy finish. Also offered chambered for .40 S&W cartridge and the 9mm cartridge. Weight is about 31 oz. for stainless and 24 oz. for alloy model.

NIB	Exc.	V.G.	Good	Fair	Poor
600	450	350	300	00	100

NOTE: Add $50 for steel frame, $45 for stainless steel, and $30 for duo-tone.

Model P10.45 Limited

Similar to the above model but with extra features such as full length recoil guide, beavertail grip safety, adjustable rear sight, competition hammer, lowered ejection port, front and rear slide serrations, and trigger overtravel stop. Match grade barrel. Black carbon steel finish.

NIB	Exc.	V.G.	Good	Fair	Poor
650	500	400	300	200	100

Model P18.9

This pistol is chambered for the 9mm cartridge and is fitted with a 5" barrel. Finish is stainless steel. Rear sight is adjustable; dovetail front sight. Magazine capacity is 18 rounds (10 rounds for US and Canada). Weight is approximately 40 oz.

NIB	Exc.	V.G.	Good	Fair	Poor
775	625	500	350	200	125

Model P18.9 LDA

This is a double-action version of the P18-9. Offered in black carbon steel only. Introduced in 1999.

NIB	Exc.	V.G.	Good	Fair	Poor
775	625	500	350	200	125

Model C7.45 LDA (Para Companion)

This .45 ACP pistol is fitted with a 3.5" barrel. Stainless steel slide and frame. Low profile fixed sights. Magazine is 7 rounds. Weight is about 32 oz.

NIB	Exc.	V.G.	Good	Fair	Poor
700	550	400	300	200	100

Model C6.45 LDA (Para Carry)

Similar to the model above but with 3" barrel and 6-round magazine. Weight is about 30 oz.

NIB	Exc.	V.G.	Good	Fair	Poor
750	575	550	375	200	100

Model Stealth Carry

This model, introduced in 2005, is chambered for the .45 ACP cartridge and fitted with a 3" barrel with Novak adjustable sights. LDA trigger. Black slide and frame with black polymer grips. Magazine capacity is 6 rounds. Weight is about 30 oz.

NIB	Exc.	V.G.	Good	Fair	Poor
850	675	550	425	300	150

Model Para CCW

Introduced in 2003 this .45 ACP model features a 4.25" barrel with stainless steel receiver and frame. Magazine capacity is 7 rounds. Fitted with the LDA trigger system. Weight is about 34 oz.

NIB	Exc.	V.G.	Good	Fair	Poor
900	800	650	500	350	125

Model Para Companion Carry Option

This model is similar to the CCW above but it is fitted with a 3.5" barrel. Weight is about 32 oz. Introduced in 2003.

NIB	Exc.	V.G.	Good	Fair	Poor
775	575	400	300	200	100

Model Tac-Four

This .45 ACP model features the LDA trigger system. It is fitted with a 4.25" barrel and has a stainless steel slide and frame. Early models shipped with two pre-ban 13-round magazines. Later models will ship with two 10-round magazines. Weight is about 36 oz. Introduced in 2003.

NIB	Exc.	V.G.	Good	Fair	Poor
900	800	650	500	350	125

Model Tac-Four LE

Same as above but shipped with two 13-round magazines to certified law enforcement only, back in the ban days.

NIB	Exc.	V.G.	Good	Fair	Poor
900	800	650	500	350	125

PARA PXT SERIES PISTOLS

NOTE: In 2004 the company introduced a new extractor called the Power Extractor (PXT). The company also added a number of new finishes and features for its PXT line. All Para pistols have integral ramp barrels that are of match grade quality. All pistols have full-length guide rod, match trigger, flared ejection port, extended slide lock safety, beavertail grip safety, cocobolo stocks with gold medallion and high-visibility, low-mount, dovetail, three-dot sights.Para has introduced five finishes:1.Sterling—All stainless steel, black slide with polished sides.2.Stealth—Black slide, black frame with black fire controls.3.Black Watch—Black slide, green frame with green fire controls on hi-cap models, and black controls on single- stack models.4.Regal—Black slide, black frame with stainless steel fire controls.5.Spec Ops—Green slide, green frame with black fire controls.

SINGLE ACTION, SINGLE STACK MODELS

Model LTC

This .45 ACP pistol has a 4.25" ramped match barrel with steel receiver and Regal finish. Fixed 3-dot sights. Cocobolo wood grips with gold medallion. Magazine capacity is 7 rounds. Weight is about 37 oz.

NIB	Exc.	V.G.	Good	Fair	Poor
775	575	400	300	200	100

Model LTC Alloy

As above but with alloy frame. Weight is about 28 oz.

NIB	Exc.	V.G.	Good	Fair	Poor
775	575	400	300	200	100

Model LTC Stainless

Same as the Model LTC but with stainless steel frame and slide. Weight is about 35 oz. Introduced in 2005.

NIB	Exc.	V.G.	Good	Fair	Poor
800	625	500	400	150	125

Model Hawg 9

Chambered for the 9mm cartridge and fitted with a 3" ramped barrel. Alloy receiver and steel slide. Fixed 3-dot sights. Black polymer stocks with black slide, black frame and stainless steel fire controls. Weight is about 24 oz. 12-shot magazine. Introduced in 2005.

NIB	Exc.	V.G.	Good	Fair	Poor
800	625	500	400	150	125

Hawg 7

Caliber .45 ACP, single-action trigger, stainless steel slide, alloy frame with Griptor grooves, extended thumb and grip safeties, fiber optic front and 2-dot rear sights, 7-round magazine. Weight 32 ounces, 3.5-inch barrel with Covert Black finish. Introduced in 2011.

NIB	Exc.	V.G.	Good	Fair	Poor
800	675	550	400	300	200

Model OPS

This .45 ACP pistol is fitted with a 3.5" barrel. It has a stainless steel frame and slide. Low mount fixed sights. Cocobolo grips. Magazine capacity is 7 rounds. Weight is about 32 oz. Introduced in 2005.

NIB	Exc.	V.G.	Good	Fair	Poor
850	675	550	425	300	150

Model 1911

This .45 ACP model has a 5" barrel with steel receiver and Regal finish. Magazine capacity is 7 rounds. Weight is about 39 oz.

NIB	Exc.	V.G.	Good	Fair	Poor
775	575	400	300	200	100

1911 SSP

7+1 capacity .45 ACP 1911-style semi-auto with 5" barrel. 39 oz. Competition triggers and hammers. Fixed sights. Cocobolo grip panels.

NIB	Exc.	V.G.	Good	Fair	Poor
925	800	675	500	400	175

GI Expert LTC

Caliber .45 ACP, single-action trigger, Commander-length stainless slide on alloy frame, extended grip safety, competition trigger, fiber optic front and 2-dot rear sights. Weight 28 ounces, 4.25-inch barrel with Covert Black finish. Magazine capacity 8-rounds.

NIB	Exc.	V.G.	Good	Fair	Poor
750	635	500	400	300	200

1911 Wild Bunch

Designed for SASS Traditional and Modern "Wild Bunch" shooting matches. Class 1911 features. Caliber .45 ACP, traditional thumb and grip safeties, hammer, solid trigger, recoil system, 7-round magazine, plain sights and barrel without integral ramp. Weight 39 ounces, 5-inch barrel with Covert Black finish. Introduced in 2011.

NIB	Exc.	V.G.	Good	Fair	Poor
685	585	475	400	300	200

Slim Hawg

A .45 ACP pistol with 6+1 capacity. Single-stack, single-action 1911. Barrel 3", 30 oz. Stainless construction, checkered wood grips. Fixed, 3-dot sights. Introduced 2006.

NIB	Exc.	V.G.	Good	Fair	Poor
850	675	550	425	300	150

HIGH CAPACITY, SINGLE ACTION MODELS

Warthog

Introduced in 2004 this .45 ACP pistol is fitted with a 3" barrel. The receiver is alloy. Black slide and frame with stainless steel fire controls. Overall length is 6.5". Height is 4.5". Magazine capacity is 10 rounds. Weight is about 24 oz. In 2005 this model was also chambered for the 9mm cartridge.

NIB	Exc.	V.G.	Good	Fair	Poor
925	800	675	500	400	175

Stainless Warthog

Stainless .45 ACP with 10+1 capacity. Single-stack, single-action 1911. Barrel 3", 31 oz. Fixed, 3-dot sights and plastic grips. Introduced 2006.

NIB	Exc.	V.G.	Good	Fair	Poor
875	675	575	400	300	150

Stealth Warthog

Chambered for the .45 ACP cartridge and fitted with a 3" ramped barrel. Black alloy slide with black frame and black fire controls. Tritium night sights. Extended slide lock, beavertail grip and firing pin. Weight is about 24 oz. Introduced in 2004.

NIB	Exc.	V.G.	Good	Fair	Poor
850	675	550	425	300	150

Stainless Warthog

Stainless .45 ACP with 10+1 capacity. Single-stack, single-action 1911. Barrel 3", 31 oz. Fixed, 3-dot sights and plastic grips. Introduced 2006.

NIB	Exc.	V.G.	Good	Fair	Poor
925	800	675	500	400	175

Lite Hawg 9

Double-stack, 12+1 single-action 9mm in non-reflective black finish. Barrel 3", 31.5 oz and capacity. Fixed, 3-dot sights. Introduced 2006.

NIB	Exc.	V.G.	Good	Fair	Poor
850	675	550	425	300	150

P12.45

This .45 ACP model is fitted with a 3.5" barrel and has a stainless steel receiver with stainless finish. Magazine capacity is 10 (12) rounds. Weight is about 34 oz.

NIB	Exc.	V.G.	Good	Fair	Poor
800	625	500	400	150	125

P13.45

This .45 ACP pistol has a 4.25" barrel with stainless steel receiver and Spec Ops finish. Magazine capacity is 10 (13) rounds. Weight is about 36 oz.

NIB	Exc.	V.G.	Good	Fair	Poor
750	575	550	375	200	100

Midnight Blue P14-45

Double-stack, 14+1 single-action 45 ACP in non-reflective black. 5" barrel, fixed, 3-dot sights and black plastic grips. Introduced 2006.

NIB	Exc.	V.G.	Good	Fair	Poor
750	575	550	375	200	100

Hi-Cap LTC

Introduced in 2005 this model is chambered for the .45 ACP cartridge and fitted with a 4.25" barrel with low mount fixed sights. Green frame, green slide with black fire controls. Black polymer grips. Magazine capacity is 14 rounds. Weight is about 37 oz.

NIB	Exc.	V.G.	Good	Fair	Poor
850	675	550	425	300	150

Stealth P14.45

This .45 ACP model is fitted with a 5" barrel and has a steel receiver with Stealth finish. Magazine capacity is 10 (14) rounds. Weight is about 40 oz.

NIB	Exc.	V.G.	Good	Fair	Poor
850	675	550	425	300	150

14.45 Tactical

Based upon the classic Para-Ordnance 14.45 high-capacity 1911 design in .45 ACP. Stainless steel slide and frame with 14-round, double-stack magazine. Custom features include Ed Brown National Match barrel, bushing, slide stop and checkered mainspring housing; Dawson Precision mag well; ambidextrous thumb safeties; extended grip tang and accessory rail. Sights are adjustable rear and fiber optic front. Covert Black finish. Weight is 42 ounces, barrel length 5-inches. PXT Tactical model is same except for single-stack frame, 8-round magazine, 4.25-inch barrel and weight of 36 ounces.

NIB	Exc.	V.G.	Good	Fair	Poor
1350	1150	875	650	350	200

P14.45

As above but with stainless steel receiver and finish.

NIB	Exc.	V.G.	Good	Fair	Poor
925	800	675	500	400	175

P18.45

This model is chambered for the 9mm Parabellum cartridge and fitted with a 5" barrel. The receiver is stainless steel with stainless steel finish. Magazine is 10 (18) rounds. Weight is about 40 oz.

NIB	Exc.	V.G.	Good	Fair	Poor
850	675	525	375	200	125

HIGH CAPACITY, SINGLE ACTION, LIMITED MODELS

S12.45 Limited

This .45 ACP pistol has a 3.5" barrel with stainless steel receiver and Sterling finish. Magazine capacity is 10 (12) rounds. Weight is about 34 oz. Introduced in 2005.

NIB	Exc.	V.G.	Good	Fair	Poor
925	800	675	500	400	175

S13.45 Limited

A .45 ACP pistol with 4.25" barrel. Stainless steel receiver and Sterling finish. Spurless hammer. Magazine capacity is 10 (13) rounds. Weight is about 36 oz.

NIB	Exc.	V.G.	Good	Fair	Poor
925	800	675	500	400	175

Stealth S14.45 Limited

This .45 ACP pistol is fitted with a 5" barrel and has a steel receiver with Stealth finish. Magazine capacity is 10 (14) rounds. Weight is about 40 oz.

NIB	Exc.	V.G.	Good	Fair	Poor
925	800	675	500	400	175

S14.45 Limited

As above but with stainless steel receiver and Sterling finish.

NIB	Exc.	V.G.	Good	Fair	Poor
1000	795	600	450	275	225

Long Slide Limited

Lengthened barrel and slide for competition or hunting. Caliber .435 ACP. Weight is 41 ounces, barrel length is 6-inches. Front and rear slide serrations, ambidextrous thumb safeties, extended grip safety, adjustable rear and fiber optic front sight, 14-round magazine and stainless finish. Introduced in 2011.

NIB	Exc.	V.G.	Good	Fair	Poor
1200	1025	825	650	450	300

Stealth S16.40 Limited

This pistol is chambered for the .40 S&W cartridge and fitted with a 5" barrel. Receiver is steel with Stealth finish. Magazine capacity is 10 (16) rounds. Weight is about 40 oz.

NIB	Exc.	V.G.	Good	Fair	Poor
925	800	675	500	400	175

S16.40 Limited

As above but with stainless steel receiver and Sterling finish.

NIB	Exc.	V.G.	Good	Fair	Poor
925	800	675	500	400	175

18.9 Limited

Chambered for the 9mm Parabellum, features include stainless steel slide and frame with dual grasping grooves, 18-round magazine, adjustable rear and fiber optic front sight, ambidextrous thumb safeties, extended grip tang and competition trigger. Weight is 40 ounces, barrel length is 5-inches, finish is bright stainless.

NIB	Exc.	V.G.	Good	Fair	Poor
1100	875	750	575	350	200

Todd Jarrett .40 USPSA P-16

A limited edition 16+1 (or 10+1) .40 S&W custom competition pistol with adjustable rear sight and fiber optic front sight. 5" barrel, 40 oz., covert non-reflective black or sterling.

NIB	Exc.	V.G.	Good	Fair	Poor
1500	1250	900	675	450	200

Todd Jarrett .45 USPSA

Limited edition 8+1 .45 ACP caliber custom competition pistol with adjustable rear sight and fiber optic front sight. 5" barrel, 39 oz.; covert non-reflective black or stainless finish.

NIB	Exc.	V.G.	Good	Fair	Poor
1500	1250	900	675	450	200

LDA, DOUBLE ACTION, SINGLE STACK, CARRY OPTION

Companion II

Caliber .45 ACP, Light Double Action (LDA) trigger, Commander-length stainless slide on full-size stainless frame, extended grip safety, fiber optic front sight and 8-round magazine. Weight 35 ounces, 4.25-inch barrel with Covert Black finish. Introduced in 2011.

NIB	Exc.	V.G.	Good	Fair	Poor
775	650	550	400	300	200

Carry Model

This .45 ACP model has a 3" barrel and stainless steel receiver with stainless finish. Magazine capacity is 6 rounds. Weight is about 30 oz.

NIB	Exc.	V.G.	Good	Fair	Poor
925	800	675	500	400	175

Stealth Carry

Similar to the model above but with Stealth finish and Novak adjustable sights.

NIB	Exc.	V.G.	Good	Fair	Poor
925	800	675	500	400	175

CCO (Companion Carry Option)

This .45 ACP model is fitted with a 3.5" barrel. The receiver is stainless steel with a stainless finish. Magazine capacity is 7 rounds. Weight is about 32 oz.

NIB	Exc.	V.G.	Good	Fair	Poor
850	700	575	400	300	125

CCW

Similar to the model above but fitted with a 4.45" barrel. Weight is about 34 oz.

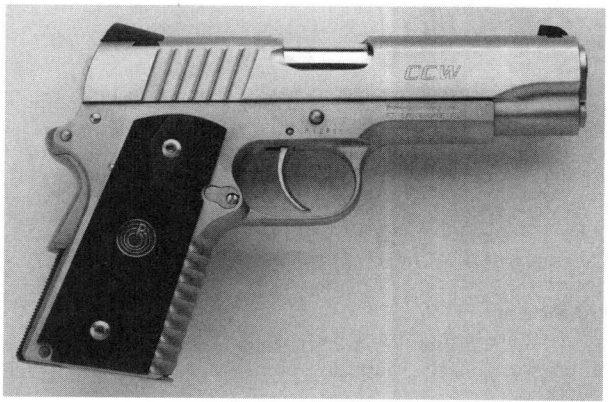

NIB	Exc.	V.G.	Good	Fair	Poor
850	700	575	400	300	125

DOUBLE ACTION ONLY, SINGLE STACK MODELS

Black Watch Companion

This .45 ACP pistol is fitted with a 3.5" barrel. Receiver is stainless steel with black watch finish. Magazine capacity is 7 rounds. Weight is about 32 oz.

NIB	Exc.	V.G.	Good	Fair	Poor
850	675	525	375	200	125

TAC-S

Chambered for the .45 ACP cartridge with a 4.45" barrel. Steel receiver and Spec Ops finish. Magazine capacity is 7 rounds. Weight is about 35 oz.

NIB	Exc.	V.G.	Good	Fair	Poor
750	575	550	375	200	100

Black Watch SSP

This .45 ACP pistol has a 5" barrel with steel receiver and Black Watch finish. Fixed 3-dot sights. Match trigger. Cocobolo wood grip with gold medallion. Magazine capacity is 7 rounds. Weight is about 39 oz.

NIB	Exc.	V.G.	Good	Fair	Poor
750	575	550	375	200	100

SSP

Similar to the model above but with stainless steel reciever and stainless finish.

NIB	Exc.	V.G.	Good	Fair	Poor
800	625	500	400	150	125

LDA, DOUBLE ACTION, SINGLE STACK, LIMITED MODELS

Stealth Limited

This .45 ACP pistol has a 5" barrel with adjustable sights. Receiver is steel with Stealth finish. Magazine capacity is 7 rounds. Weight is about 40 oz.

NIB	Exc.	V.G.	Good	Fair	Poor
850	700	575	400	300	125

Limited

This .45 ACP model has a 5" barrel and stainless steel receiver with Sterling finish. Magazine capacity is 7 rounds. Weight is about 40 oz. Adjustable sights.

NIB	Exc.	V.G.	Good	Fair	Poor
925	800	675	500	400	175

LDA, DOUBLE ACTION, HIGH CAPACITY, CARRY OPTION SERIES

Carry 12

This is a 45 ACP pistol with a 3.5" barrel fitted with night sights. Receiver is stainless steel with a stainless finish. Magazine capacity is 10 (12) rounds. Weight is about 34 oz.

NIB	Exc.	V.G.	Good	Fair	Poor
850	700	575	400	300	125

Tac-Four

This .45 ACP model is fitted with a 4.35" barrel. Stainless steel receiver with Spec Ops finish. Magazine capacity is 10 (13) rounds. Sight are 3-dot. Weight is about 36 oz.

NIB	Exc.	V.G.	Good	Fair	Poor
850	700	575	400	300	125

Tac-Five

Light double-action 9mm with 18+1 capacity. 5" barrel, 37.5 oz., stainless finish, adjustable rear sight, plastic grips.

NIB	Exc.	V.G.	Good	Fair	Poor
850	700	575	400	300	125

LDA, DOUBLE ACTION, HIGH CAPACITY MODELS

Stealth Hi-Cap .45

This .45 ACP pistol has a 5" barrel with steel receiver and Stealth finish. Spurless hammer. sights are 3-dot. Magazine capacity is 10 (14) rounds. Weight is about 40 oz.

NIB	Exc.	V.G.	Good	Fair	Poor
800	625	500	400	150	125

Hi-Cap .45

Similar to the model above but with stainless steel receiver and stainless finish.

NIB	Exc.	V.G.	Good	Fair	Poor
800	625	500	400	150	125

Colonel

This .45 ACP pistol is fitted with a 4.25" barrel with low mount fixed sights. The slide and frame are green with black fire controls. Black polymer grips. Magazine capacity is 14 rounds. Weight is about 37 oz. Introduced in 2005.

NIB	Exc.	V.G.	Good	Fair	Poor
800	625	500	400	150	125

Hi-Cap .40

This model is chambered for the .40 S&W cartridge and fitted with a 5" barrel with 3-dot sights. Stainless steel receiver with stainless finish. Magazine capacity is 10 (16) rounds. Weight is about 40 oz.

NIB	Exc.	V.G.	Good	Fair	Poor
800	625	500	400	150	125

Stealth Hi-Cap 9

This 9mm pistol is fitted with a 5" barrel with 3-dot sights and steel receiver with Stealth finish. Magazine capacity is 10 (18) rounds. Weight is about 40 oz.

NIB	Exc.	V.G.	Good	Fair	Poor
800	625	500	400	150	125

Hi-Cap 9

Similar to the model above but for stainless steel receiver and stainless finish.

NIB	Exc.	V.G.	Good	Fair	Poor
850	700	575	400	300	125

Covert Black Nite-Tac

Introduced in 2005 this .45 ACP pistol is fitted with a 5" barrel with covert black finish. Low mount fixed sights. Magazine capacity is 14 rounds. Weight is about 40 oz.

NIB	Exc.	V.G.	Good	Fair	Poor
850	700	575	400	300	125

Nite-Tac

As above but with stainless steel frame and slide. Introduced in 2005.

NIB	Exc.	V.G.	Good	Fair	Poor
800	625	500	400	150	125

Nite-Tac .40

A .40 S&W 16+1 capacity double-action duty pistol with fixed sights. 5" barrel, 40 oz., stainless finish.

NIB	Exc.	V.G.	Good	Fair	Poor
800	625	500	400	150	125

Nite-Tac 9

A 9mm 18+1 double-action duty pistol with fixed sights. 5" barrel, 40 oz., stainless finish.

NIB	Exc.	V.G.	Good	Fair	Poor
800	625	500	400	150	125

This .40 S&W pistol has a 5" barrel with 3-dot sights and a stainless steel receiver with Sterling finish. Magazine capacity is 16 rounds. Weight is about 40 oz.

NIB	Exc.	V.G.	Good	Fair	Poor
1000	875	725	575	400	200

Stealth Hi-Cap Limited 9

This model is chambered for the 9mm cartridge and fitted with a 5" barrel with 3-dot sights. The receiver is steel with Stealth finish. Magazine capacity is 18 rounds. Weight is about 40 oz.

NIB	Exc.	V.G.	Good	Fair	Poor
1000	875	725	575	400	200

Hi-Cap Limited 9

As above but with stainless steel receiver and Sterling finish.

NIB	Exc.	V.G.	Good	Fair	Poor
1200	975	825	650	450	225

Stealth Hi-Cap Ltd .45

This .45 ACP pistol has a 5" barrel with 3-dot sights and spurless hammer. Receiver is steel with Stealth finish. Magazine capacity is 10 (14) rounds. Weight is about 40 oz.

NIB	Exc.	V.G.	Good	Fair	Poor
1000	875	725	575	400	200

Hi-Cap Limited .45

This model is similar to the one above but with stainless steel receiver and Sterling finish.

NIB	Exc.	V.G.	Good	Fair	Poor
1200	975	825	650	450	225

PARDINI
Italy

Standard Target Pistol

A .22 caliber semi-automatic pistol with a 4.7" barrel, adjustable rear sight and adjustable trigger. Blued with two sizes of walnut grips, one suitable for use by ladies. Introduced in 1986.

NIB	Exc.	V.G.	Good	Fair	Poor
1450	1200	975	800	600	350

Rapidfire Pistol

Similar to the above, in .22 short with an alloy bolt, 4.6" barrel and enclosed grip. Weight is about 43 oz. Introduced in 1995.

NIB	Exc.	V.G.	Good	Fair	Poor
1450	1200	975	800	600	350

Centerfire Pistol

Similar to the standard model, but in .32 Smith & Wesson caliber. Introduced in 1986.

NIB	Exc.	V.G.	Good	Fair	Poor
1450	1200	975	800	600	350

Free Pistol

A .22 caliber single-shot pistol with a 9.8" barrel, adjustable sights and adjustable grip. Furnished with barrel weights. Weight is about 35 oz. Introduced in 1995.

NIB	Exc.	V.G.	Good	Fair	Poor
1550	1300	1050	900	700	450

PARKER
Springfield, Massachusetts

4-Shot Pistol

A .33 caliber percussion pistol with a 4" half-octagonal barrel and a 4-shot sliding chamber. Marked "Albert Parker/Patent Secured/ Springfield, Mass." Original finish unknown with walnut grips. Prospective purchasers are advised to secure a qualified appraisal prior to acquisition.

NIB	Exc.	V.G.	Good	Fair	Poor
—	—	1500	13500	6000	2000

PARKER FIELD & SONS
London, England

Gas Seal Revolver

A .42 caliber percussion revolver with a 6" barrel and 6-shot cylinder. Blued, case hardened with walnut grips. Manufactured during the 1860s.

NIB	Exc.	V.G.	Good	Fair	Poor
—	—	2500	1950	900	450

PARKER-HALE LTD.
Birmingham, England

S&W Victory Conversion

A .22 caliber double-action revolver with a 4" barrel and 6-shot cylinder. Blued with walnut grips. An alteration of the Smith & Wesson Victor model.

NIB	Exc.	V.G.	Good	Fair	Poor
—	295	200	150	100	75

PEAVY, A. J.
South Montville, Maine

Knife-Pistol

A .22 caliber single-shot knife pistol constructed of steel and brass with a folding trigger. The sideplates marked "A.J. Peavy Pat. Sept. 5, \xd4 65 & Mar. 27, \xd4 66." Produced between 1866 and 1870.

NIB	Exc.	V.G.	Good	Fair	Poor
—	—	6000	4700	1900	500

PECARE & SMITH
New York, New York

Pepperbox

A .28 caliber 4-shot or 1-shot percussion pepperbox with a folding trigger and 4" barrel group. The barrel group enclosed within an iron casing. Blued, silver-plated frame with walnut grips. The barrel casing marked "Pecare & Smith." Manufactured during the 1840s and early 1850s.

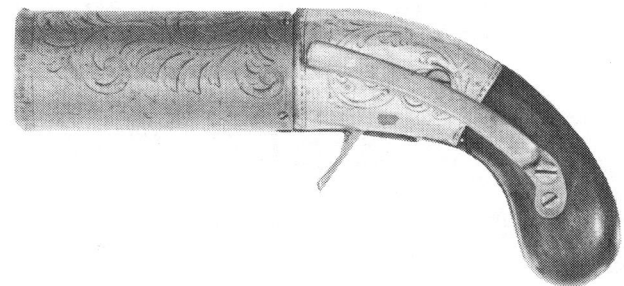

NIB	Exc.	V.G.	Good	Fair	Poor
—	—	4800	3000	1300	350

Ten-Shot Pepperbox (rare)

NIB	Exc.	V.G.	Good	Fair	Poor
—	—	9500	6600	2750	600

PEDERSOLI, DAVIDE
Brescia, Italy

Davide Pedersoli & C. was founded in 1957 by the late Davide Pedersoli. In the nearly half-century since, Pedersoli has established itself as a manufacturer of extremely high-quality replica and modern firearms. Pedersoli products are frequently marked with the importer's or retailer's name (e.g., Dixie Gun Works or Cabela's) rather than the Pedersoli brand, usually at widely varying discounts. Many muzzleloading rifles and pistols are available in kit form at reduced prices. NOTE: Rapidly-fluctuating currency markets can result in values for newly-imported Pedersoli guns being 10-15 percent higher than the values listed below.

Mang In Graz Pistol

Recreation of single-shot percussion pistol made c. 1850 by Martin Mang. .38 or .44 caliber. Add 10 percent for target model, 20 percent for deluxe.

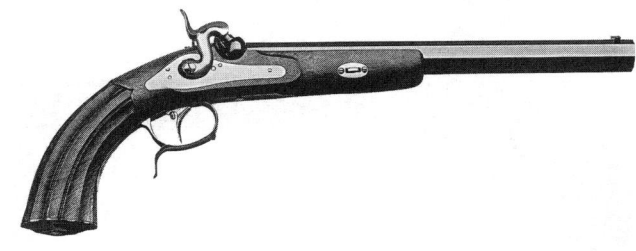

NIB	Exc.	V.G.	Good	Fair	Poor
1100	750	500	400	300	150

Kuchenreuter Pistol

Recreation of single-shot percussion pistol made c. 1854 by Bartholomaus Kuchenreuter of Steinweg, Germany. .38 or .44 caliber. Add 20 percent for deluxe.

NIB	Exc.	V.G.	Good	Fair	Poor
1350	900	600	500	400	200

Mortimer Pistol

Recreation of single-shot pistol first made c. 1810 by H. W Mortimer & Son of London. .44 caliber, smooth or rifled barrel.

Percussion and flint versions available. Add 10 percent for Match model, 20 percent for deluxe.

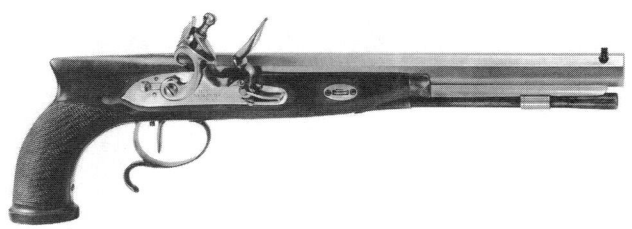

NIB	Exc.	V.G.	Good	Fair	Poor
895	755	525	375	250	100

LePage Dueller

Recreation of single-shot duelling pistol made by Henry LePage c. 1840. Percussion and flint versions available. .31, .36 or .44 caliber. Add 20 percent fordeluxe.

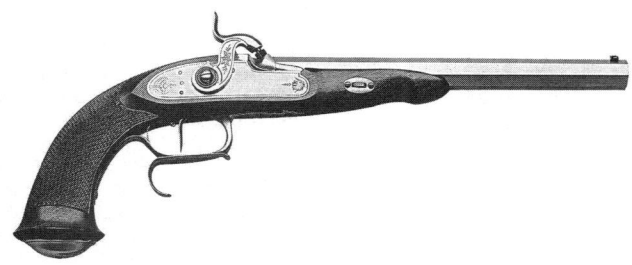

NIB	Exc.	V.G.	Good	Fair	Poor
895	755	525	375	250	100

Charles Moore Duelling Pistol

Recreation of single-shot duelling pistol made by Charles Moore of London c. 1800. Percussion and flint versions available. .36 or .44 caliber. Add 10 percent for target model.

NIB	Exc.	V.G.	Good	Fair	Poor
600	450	300	200	100	50

Carleton Underhammer Pistol

Recreation of saw-handled underhammer percussion pistol c. 1850. .36 caliber.

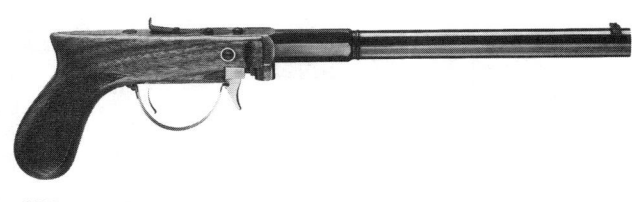

NIB	Exc.	V.G.	Good	Fair	Poor
750	600	450	300	150	75

Remington Pattern Target Revolver

Replica of Remington "1858-style" .44-caliber percussion revolver.

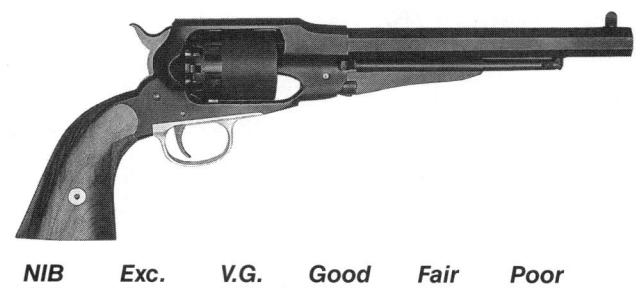

NIB	Exc.	V.G.	Good	Fair	Poor
450	350	250	100	75	50

Rogers & Spencer Target Percussion Target Revolver

Replica of the .44-caliber Rogers and Spencer revolver that didn't quite make it in time for the Civil War.

NIB	Exc.	V.G.	Good	Fair	Poor
425	325	250	100	75	50

Kentucky Pistol

Recreation of single-shot pistol of American colonial era. Flint and percussion versions available. .45, .50 and .54 caliber. Add 50 percent for "Silver Star" models.

NIB	Exc.	V.G.	Good	Fair	Poor
300	250	225	150	100	50

Bounty Pistol

Similar to Kentucky Pistol standard version but with 16" barrel. .45 or .50 caliber only.

NIB	Exc.	V.G.	Good	Fair	Poor
300	250	225	150	100	50

Navy Moll Pistol

Similar to Kentucky pistol but with brass trim. Flint and percussion versions available. .45 caliber.

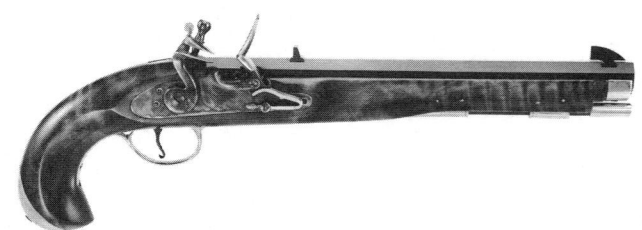

NIB	Exc.	V.G.	Good	Fair	Poor
425	325	250	100	75	50

Harper's Ferry Pistol

Recreation of .58-caliber flintlock pistol procured for the U. S. Navy in 1806.

NIB	Exc.	V.G.	Good	Fair	Poor
425	325	250	100	75	50

Queen Anne Pistol

Recreation of English 17th-century cannon-barrel flintlock pistol. .50-caliber smoothbore barrel. Steel or brass construction.

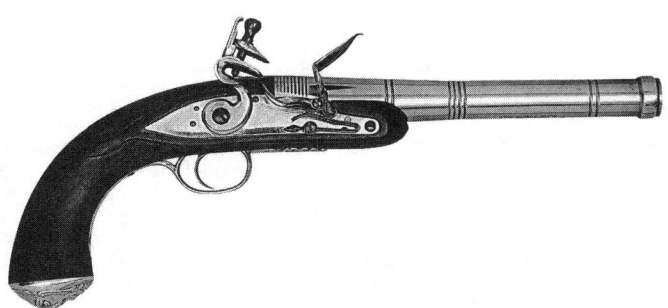

NIB	Exc.	V.G.	Good	Fair	Poor
375	295	225	75	50	25

An IX Pistol

Recreation of .69-caliber Napoleonic flintlock cavalry pistol of 1803. Brass trim.

NIB	Exc.	V.G.	Good	Fair	Poor
500	400	300	200	100	50

An XIII Pistol

Simplified 1806 version of the An IX pistol.

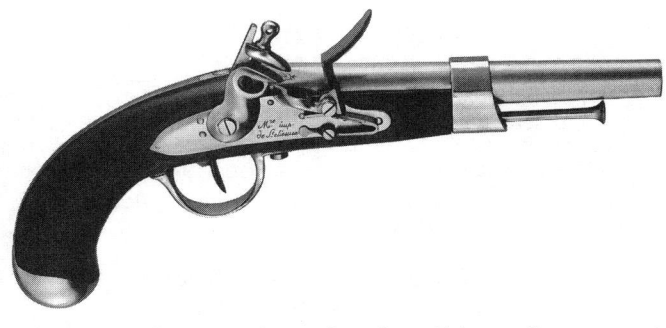

NIB	Exc.	V.G.	Good	Fair	Poor
500	400	300	200	100	50

Remington Rider Derringer

Recreation of Remington Rider single-shot .177 percussion parlor pistol. Available in the white or with casehardened, gold-toned or engraved/silvered finish. Pricing for basic model.

NIB	Exc.	V.G.	Good	Fair	Poor
175	150	100	75	50	25

Derringer Liegi

Recreation of c. 1850 screw-barrel percussion pocket pistol with folding trigger and bag grip. .44 caliber. Add 10 percent for engraved model.

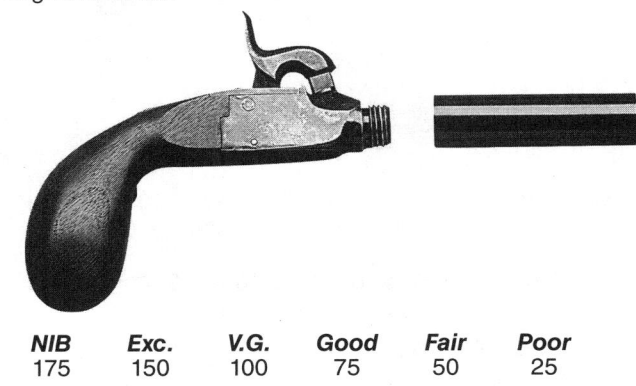

NIB	Exc.	V.G.	Good	Fair	Poor
175	150	100	75	50	25

Zimmer Pistol

Recreation of c. 1850 single-shot percussion parlor pistol. .177 caliber; fluted grip with butt cap. Discontinued.

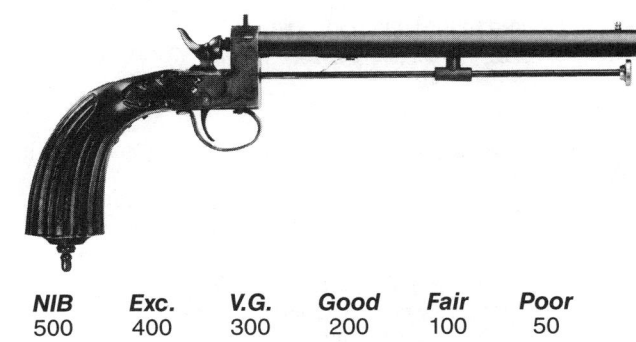

NIB	Exc.	V.G.	Good	Fair	Poor
500	400	300	200	100	50

Saloon Pistol

Recreation of c. 1850 single-shot percussion parlor pistol. .36 or .177 caliber. Discontinued.

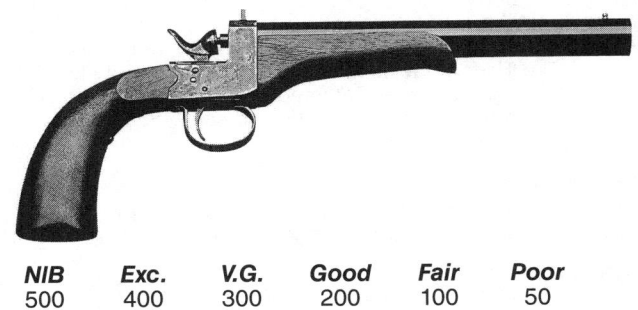

NIB	Exc.	V.G.	Good	Fair	Poor
500	400	300	200	100	50

PERRY & GODDARD
Renwick Arms Co.
New York, New York

Derringer

A .44 caliber single-shot spur trigger pistol with a 2" octagonal barrel. Blued or silver-plated with walnut or gutta-percha grips. The barrel may be swiveled so that either end can serve as the chamber and is marked "Double Header/ E.S. Renwick." Produced in limited quantities during the 1860s.

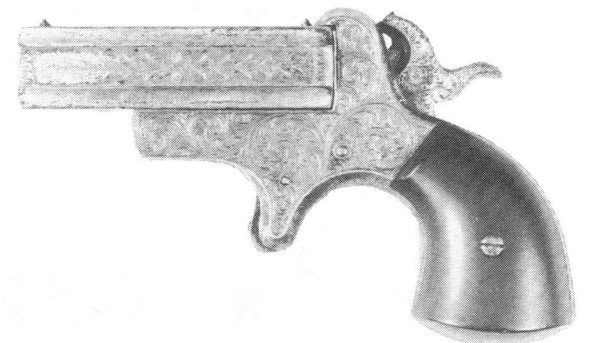

NIB	Exc.	V.G.	Good	Fair	Poor
—	—	21000	9400	1500	500

PERRY PATENT FIREARMS CO.
Newark, New Jersey

SINGLE-SHOT PISTOL

A .52 caliber breech-loading percussion pistol with a 6" round barrel. Blued with walnut grips. The barrel marked "Perry Patent Firearms Co./Newark, N.J." Approximately 200 were made between 1854 and 1856 in two styles.

1st Type

Long, contoured trigger guard, opening lever.

NIB	Exc.	V.G.	Good	Fair	Poor
—	—	4950	1900	500	200

2nd Type

S curved shorter trigger guard and an automatic primer feed that protrudes from the butt.

NIB	Exc.	V.G.	Good	Fair	Poor
—	—	4700	1650	500	200

PETTINGILL C. S.
New Haven, Connecticut
Rogers, Spencer & Co.
Willowvale, New York

POCKET REVOLVER

A hammerless, double-action .31 caliber percussion revolver having a 4" octagonal barrel. The frame of brass or iron. Blued barrel, the grips of oil finished walnut. The First and Second Models are marked "Pettingill's Patent 1856" as well as "T.K. Austin." The Third Model is marked "Pettengill Patent 1856," and "Raymond and Robitaille Patented 1858." Approximately 400 were manufactured in the late 1850s and early 1860s.

1st Model

Brass frame.

NIB	Exc.	V.G.	Good	Fair	Poor
—	—	2750	2000	1100	400

2nd Model

Iron frame.

NIB	Exc.	V.G.	Good	Fair	Poor
—	—	1650	1000	660	200

3rd Model

NIB	Exc.	V.G.	Good	Fair	Poor
—	—	1400	800	450	200

Navy Revolver

As above but in .34 caliber with a 4.5" barrel and a 6-shot cylinder. The frame of iron, blued overall, and the grips of walnut. This model is marked "Pettengill's Patent 1856" and "Raymond & Robitaille Patented 1858." Approximately 900 were manufactured in the late 1850s and early 1860s.

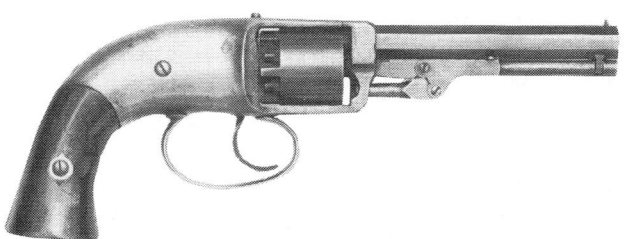

Courtesy Milwaukee Public Museum, Milwaukee, Wisconsin

NIB	Exc.	V.G.	Good	Fair	Poor
—	—	3500	1900	775	250

Army Model Revolver

As above but of .44 caliber and fitted with a 7.5" barrel. The frame of iron that is case hardened, the octagonal barrel blued, the grips of oil finished walnut. Early production models are marked as the Navy models, while later production examples are marked "Petingill's Patent 1856, pat'd July 22, 1856 and July 27, 1858." Some examples will be found with government inspector's marks and are worth approximately 25 percent more. It is believed that 3,400 were made in the 1860s.

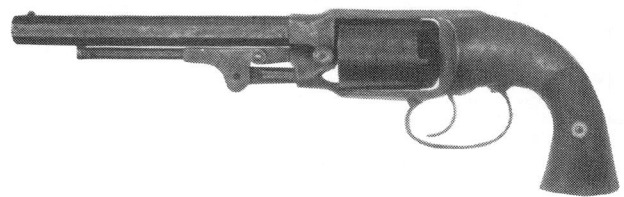

Courtesy Milwaukee Public Museum, Milwaukee, Wisconsin

NIB	Exc.	V.G.	Good	Fair	Poor
—	—	4950	2250	1650	500

PFANNL, FRANCOIS
Krems, Austria

Erika

A 4.25mm semi-automatic pistol with a hinged barrel assembly. The barrel either 1.5" or 2.25" in length. The grips are marked "Erika." Approximately 3,500 made between 1912 and 1926.

NIB	Exc.	V.G.	Good	Fair	Poor
—	3000	2500	1750	900	500

PHILLIPS & RODGERS INC.
Huntsville, Texas

Medusa Model 47

Introduced in 1996 this unique multi-caliber revolver is designed to chamber, fire, and extract almost any cartridge using 9mm, .357, or .38 cartridges—a total of about 25 different calibers. The barrel lengths are 2.5", 3", 4", 5", or 6". Rubber grips and interchangeable front sights. Finish is matte blue. Rarely if ever encountered. Disccontinued.

NIB	Exc.	V.G.	Good	Fair	Poor
1100	850	550	450	275	150

Ruger 50 Conversion

This conversion, executed on a new revolver, converts a .44 Magnum Ruger into a .50 Action Express. Stainless steel or blue with 5-shot cylinder. Barrel length is 6.5".

NIB	Exc.	V.G.	Good	Fair	Poor
1000	800	550	450	275	150

PHOENIX
Lowell, Massachusetts

Pocket Pistol

A rare .25 ACP semi-automatic pistol with a 2.25" barrel and 6-round magazine. Receiver and slide are blued, the grips are of hard rubber. Manufactured during the 1920s.

NIB	Exc.	V.G.	Good	Fair	Poor
—	950	700	350	200	100

PHOENIX ARMS
Ontario, California

HP22

A pocket-size semi-automatic pistol chambered for the .22 Long Rifle cartridge. Barrel length is 3". Magazine capacity is 11 rounds. Offered in bright chrome or polished blue finish with black checkered grips. Top of gun is fitted with vent rib. Overall length is 4.1" and weight is about 20 oz.

NIB	Exc.	V.G.	Good	Fair	Poor
175	125	90	65	40	25

HP25

This model is the same as above but chambered for the .25 ACP cartridge. Magazine capacity is 10 rounds.

NIB	Exc.	V.G.	Good	Fair	Poor
175	125	90	65	40	25

HP22/HP25 Target

A conversion kit to convert the HP22/HP25 into a target pistol. Kit includes extended vent rib barrel and a convertible 10-round magazine. Finish is either blue or nickel.

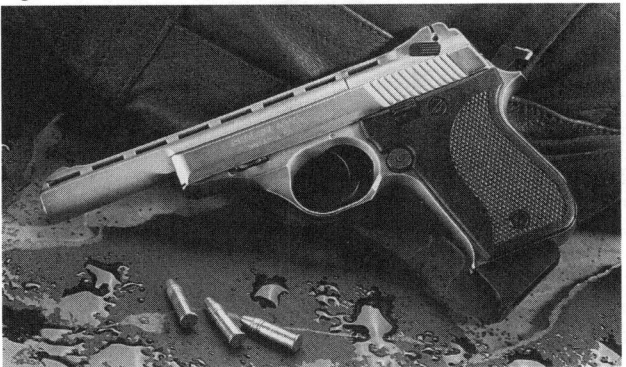

NIB	Exc.	V.G.	Good	Fair	Poor
100	75	60	40	30	25

Raven

A small pocket-size semi-automatic pistol chambered for the .25 ACP cartridge. Magazine capacity is 6 rounds. Barrel length is 2.4" with fixed sights. Offered in 3 finishes: bright chrome, satin nickel, or polished blue. Grips are either ivory, pink pearl, or black. Overall length is 4.8" and weight is approximately 15 oz.

NIB	Exc.	V.G.	Good	Fair	Poor
175	125	90	65	40	25

PICKERT, FRIEDRICH
Arminius Waffenfabrik
Zella-Mehlis, Germany

This firm produced revolvers bearing the trade name "Arminius." The revolvers manufactured by Pickert of the double-action type, with or without exposed hammers. Some models are fitted with ejectors, while others have removable cylinders. Calibers and barrel lengths vary. After WWII, the trade name was acquired by Hermann Wiehauch.

Arminius 7.65mm

A five-shot concealed hammer revolver in 7.65mm caliber. The Arminius head is on the grips.

Courtesy James Rankin

NIB	Exc.	V.G.	Good	Fair	Poor
—	350	225	175	125	90

Arminius Single-Shot Target Pistol

A single-shot target pistol chambered for the 22 caliber cartridge. Some of these were built under the name PICKERT. The Arminius name is seen on the frame.

Courtesy James Rankin

NIB	Exc.	V.G.	Good	Fair	Poor
—	900	700	600	400	300

Pickert Revolver

Similar to the Arminius revolver but with a half-round, half-octagon barrel. Chambered for the 7.54mm cartridge.

Courtesy James Rankin

NIB	Exc.	V.G.	Good	Fair	Poor
—	275	225	175	150	100

PIEPER, HENRI & NICOLAS
Liege, Belgium

Originally founded by Henri Pieper in 1859, the company was reorganized in 1898 when his son, Nicolas, assumed control. The firm is perhaps best known for a series of semi-automatic pistols that are listed below, but Pieper also manufactured a bewildering variety of drillings, combination guns, cape guns, rook rifles, salon rifles and even volley guns. These guns must be evaluated on their own merits, and their value is strictly a function of what the market will bear.

Pieper Model 1907

A 6.35 or 7.65mm semi-automatic pistol featuring a hinged barrel assembly 2.5" in length. Receiver and barrel are blued, the grips are of hard rubber with the firm's trademark cast in them. The Model 1907 variation does not have a hinged barrel assembly. The Model 1908 is also known as the "Basculant," and the Model 1918 as the "Demontant."

Courtesy Orvel Reichert

NIB	Exc.	V.G.	Good	Fair	Poor
—	250	150	125	100	75

Model 1908/Basculant

This is a tipping barrel pistol chambered for the 6.35mm Auto cartridge. Similar in appearance to the Model 1907 this model had several improvements. The front end of the barrel was retained by a pivot bolt and the recoil spring rod had a hook that engaged the lug on the slide.

Courtesy Orvel Reichert

NIB	Exc.	V.G.	Good	Fair	Poor
—	275	175	150	125	100

Pieper Bayard Revolver

In competition with the Nagant gas seal revolver, Henri Pieper developed a superior design. Revolvers of this type have 5" barrels and are chambered for 8mm cartridges. The first model of this revolver had an automatic ejection system, while the second version utilized a swing-out cylinder. Standard finish is blued, with checkered hard rubber grips.

NIB	Exc.	V.G.	Good	Fair	Poor
—	1000	750	500	250	100

Legia

This model was patterned after that of the Browning, and is chambered for the 6.35mm cartridge. The standard magazine holds 6 cartridges but a 10-round magazine was also available.

NIB	Exc.	V.G.	Good	Fair	Poor
—	250	150	125	100	75

Bayard

A 6.35, 7.65 or 9mm short semi-automatic pistol with a 2.5" barrel. Standard magazine capacity 6 rounds. The slide is stamped "Anciens Etablissement Pieper Liege, Belgium."

NIB	Exc.	V.G.	Good	Fair	Poor
—	250	150	125	100	75

PILSEN, ZBROVKA
Pilsen, Czechoslovakia

Pocket Pistol

Essentially a Model 1910 Browning semi-automatic pistol without a grip safety, this pistol was of 7.65mm caliber and had a 3.5" barrel with a 6-round magazine. The slide is marked "Akciova Spolecnost drive Skodovny zavody Zbrovka Plzen." Standard finish is blued, the grips of hard rubber. Manufactured during the 1920s.

NIB	Exc.	V.G.	Good	Fair	Poor
—	300	200	150	125	100

PLAINFIELD ORDNANCE CO.
Middlesex, New Jersey

MODEL 71

A stainless steel .22 caliber semi-automatic pistol with a 10-shot magazine and 1" barrel. Also available in .25 ACP and conversion kits were available.

Conversion Kit

NIB	Exc.	V.G.	Good	Fair	Poor
—	50	40	30	25	20

.22 or .25 Caliber Pistol

NIB	Exc.	V.G.	Good	Fair	Poor
—	175	125	100	75	50

Model 72

As above except with an alloy frame.

NIB	Exc.	V.G.	Good	Fair	Poor
—	175	125	100	75	50

PLANT'S MANUFACTURING CO.
New Haven, Connecticut

ARMY MODEL REVOLVER

A large single-action revolver chambered for a .42 caliber cup-primed cartridge that loads from the front of the cylinder. Barrel length 6" and of octagonal form with a rib. The frame is made of either brass or iron. Finish is blued, with walnut or rosewood grips. Interchangeable percussion cylinders also were made for these revolvers. If present, the values would be increased approximately 30 percent. This revolver was marketed by Merwin & Bray, and there were approximately 1,500 of the 1st and 2nd Models manufactured and 10,000 of the 3rd Model in the 1860s.

1st Model Brass Frame

Marked "Plant's Mfg. Co. New Haven, Ct." on the barrel, "M & B" on the side of the frame, and "Patented July 12, 1859" on the cylinder. Approximately 100 manufactured.

NIB	Exc.	V.G.	Good	Fair	Poor
—	—	2750	1025	700	150

1st Model Iron Frame

As above with an iron frame. Approximately 500 made.

NIB	Exc.	V.G.	Good	Fair	Poor
—	—	2750	1025	700	300

2nd Model Rounded Brass Frame

This model is distinguished by the markings "Merwin & Bray, New York" on the frame and the patent date "July 21, 1863". Approximately 300 made.

NIB	Exc.	V.G.	Good	Fair	Poor
—	—	3600	1400	700	300

2nd Model Iron Frame

As above with an iron frame.

NIB	Exc.	V.G.	Good	Fair	Poor
—	—	2500	825	500	300

3rd Model

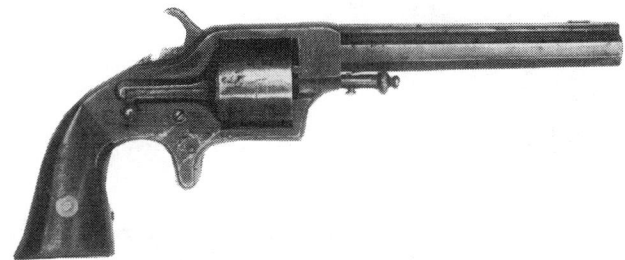

Courtesy Milwaukee Public Museum, Milwaukee, Wisconsin

As above with a flat brass frame.

NIB	Exc.	V.G.	Good	Fair	Poor
—	—	1900	1300	450	150

Pocket Revolver

Similar to the Army model described above except chambered for .30 caliber cartridges. Barrel length 3.5", five-shot cylinder. The frame normally silver plated, barrel and cylinder blued and the grips of rosewood or walnut. This model is encountered with a variety of retailer's markings: Eagle Arms Co., New York, "Reynolds, Plant & Hotchkiss, New Haven, Ct.," and Merwin & Bray Firearms Co., N.Y." Approximately 20,000 were made.

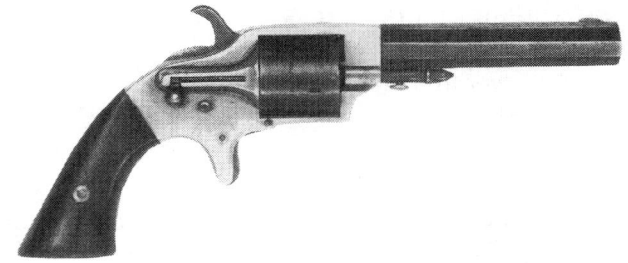

Courtesy Milwaukee Public Museum, Milwaukee, Wisconsin

NIB	Exc.	V.G.	Good	Fair	Poor
—	—	1100	600	250	100

POINTER
Hopkins & Allen
Norwich, Connecticut

Single-Shot Derringer

An unmarked Hopkins & Allen single-shot pistol stamped "Pointer" on the barrel. Barrel length 2.75", caliber .22, frame of nickel-plated brass. The barrel swings sideways for loading. Bird's-head walnut grips. It is believed that about 2,500 were made between 1870 and 1890.

NIB	Exc.	V.G.	Good	Fair	Poor
—	—	450	375	250	100

POND, LUCIUS, W.
Worchester, Massachusetts

POCKET REVOLVER

A single-action, spur trigger .32 caliber revolver with octagonal barrels of 4", 5", or 6" length. The barrel top strap and cylinder pivot upwards for loading. Made with either brass or iron frames. A screwdriver is fitted in the butt. As these revolvers were an infringement of Rollin White's patent, they were discontinued. Some revolvers are to be found with the inscription "Manuf'd. for

Smith & Wesson Pat'd. April 5, 1855." These examples are worth approximately 20 percent more than the values listed.

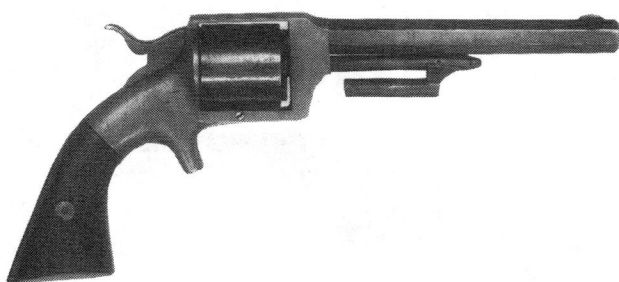

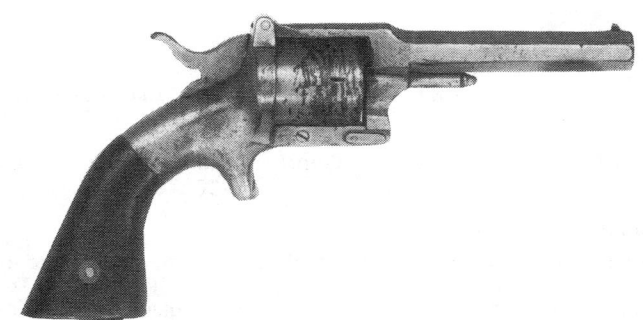

Courtesy Milwaukee Public Museum, Milwaukee, Wisconsin

Pocket Revolver Brass Framed Revolver

As above with a flat brass frame.

NIB	Exc.	V.G.	Good	Fair	Poor
—	—	1100	875	350	100

Pocket Revolver Iron Framed Revolver

NIB	Exc.	V.G.	Good	Fair	Poor
—	—	1000	775	300	75

SEPARATE CHAMBER REVOLVER

To avoid the Rollin White patent, this revolver is chambered for .22 or .32 caliber rimfire cartridges that fit into separate steel chamber inserts that can be removed from the front of the cylinder for loading. The .22 caliber version has a 3.5" octagonal barrel with a 7-round unfluted cylinder; the .32 caliber version has a 4", 5", or 6" octagonal barrel and 6-shot unfluted cylinder. Frames are of silver-plated brass; and the barrels and cylinders are blued. Grips of walnut. Standard markings include "L.W. Pond, Worcester, Mass." and patent dates. Approximately 2,000 manufactured in .22 caliber and 5,000 in .32 caliber between 1863 and 1870.

As above with a flat brass frame.

.22 Caliber Version

NIB	Exc.	V.G.	Good	Fair	Poor
—	—	1750	1400	550	150

.32 Caliber Version

As above with a flat brass frame.

NIB	Exc.	V.G.	Good	Fair	Poor
—	—	1750	1400	550	150

PORTER, P. W.
New York, New York

Turret Revolver

An extremely rare 9-shot vertical cylinder .41 caliber percussion revolver with a 5.25" round barrel. The trigger guard is also a lever that turns the cylinder and cocks the hammer. An automatic primer system is also fitted to this revolver. Manufactured during the 1850s in an unknown quantity.

NIB	Exc.	V.G.	Good	Fair	Poor
—	—	23500	19500	8800	100

PRAHA ZBROJOVKA
Prague, Czechoslovakia

Established in 1918 by A. Novotny, this company ceased operations in 1926.

VZ2L

A 7.65mm semi-automatic pistol patterned after the Model 1910 Browning, but without a grip safety. Barrel length 3.5", magazine capacity 6 rounds, grips of wood. The slide is marked "Zbrojowka Praga Praha."

NIB	Exc.	V.G.	Good	Fair	Poor
—	400	250	200	150	100

Praga 1921

A 6.35mm semi-automatic pistol with a slide of stamped steel cut with a finger groove at the front. Folding trigger. The barrel 2" in length. The slide is marked "Zbrojowka Praga Praha Patent Cal 6.35." The grips of molded plastic, with the name "Praga" cast in them. A dangerous feature of this pistol is that it is striker-fired with no hammer and is intended to be carried fully loaded and cocked in the pocket with absolutely no safety of any kind. I do not recommend this. The folding trigger does not spring out until the slide is drawn back slightly by using the finger groove in the front of it.

NIB	Exc.	V.G.	Good	Fair	Poor
—	375	225	200	150	100

PRATT, H.
Roxbury, Massachusetts

Under Hammer Pistol

A .31 caliber percussion single-shot pistol with an 8.5" octagonal barrel. The frame marked "H. Pratt's/ Patent." Manufactured during the 1850s.

NIB	Exc.	V.G.	Good	Fair	Poor
—	—	1700	1350	650	200

PRECISION SMALL ARMS
Beverly Hills, California

PSA-25

This is a semi-automatic pistol chambered for the .25 ACP. The barrel length is 2.13". Magazine capacity is 6 rounds. The frame and slide is steel alloy. Weight is 9.5 oz. Overall length is 4.11". Grips are black polymer. Standard finish is black oxide. Modeled after the Browning Baby.

NIB	Exc.	V.G.	Good	Fair	Poor
525	400	300	225	150	75

NOTE: For brushed chrome finish add $50 and for stainless steel add $75.

Featherweight Model

Same as above, but with aluminum frame and chrome slide with gold-plated trigger.

NIB	Exc.	V.G.	Good	Fair	Poor
1000	850	700	475	250	100

Diplomat Model

Black oxide with gold highlights and ivory grips.

NIB	Exc.	V.G.	Good	Fair	Poor
1900	1550	1100	800	500	100

Montreaux Model

Gold plated with ivory grips.

NIB	Exc.	V.G.	Good	Fair	Poor
2550	2000	1500	1050	800	100

Renaissance Model

Same as above but with hand engraved steel frame and slide. Antique stain chrome finish.

NIB	Exc.	V.G.	Good	Fair	Poor
3950	3200	2500	2000	1200	100

Imperiale

Inlaid gold filigree over blue with scrimshawed ivory grips.

NIB	Exc.	V.G.	Good	Fair	Poor
6500	5800	5000	4000	2100	100

PRESCOTT, E. A.
Worcester, Massachusetts

Percussion Pocket Revolver

A .31 caliber percussion spur trigger revolver with either 4" or 4.25" octagonal barrel and a 6-shot cylinder. The frame of brass, and the grips of walnut. It is believed that approximately 100 were manufactured during 1860 and 1861.

NIB	Exc.	V.G.	Good	Fair	Poor
—	—	3700	2500	1125	200

Pocket Revolver

A .22 or .32 spur trigger revolver with a barrel of either 3" or 4" length. The .22 caliber version has a 7-shot cylinder and the .32 caliber version a 6-shot cylinder. The standard markings are "E.A. Prescott Worchester Mass. Pat. Oct. 2, 1860." Approximately 1,000 were manufactured between 1862 and 1867.

NIB	Exc.	V.G.	Good	Fair	Poor
—	—	1050	825	350	100

Navy Revolver

A single-action revolver fitted with a conventional trigger, chambered for .38 rimfire cartridges with a 7.25" octagonal barrel. The unfluted cylinder holds 6 shots. The frame is of either silver-plated brass or blued iron; and the barrel and the cylinder are blued, with walnut grips. The barrel marked "E.A. Prescott, Worcester, Mass. Pat. Oct. 2, 1860." It is believed that several hundred were manufactured between 1861 and 1863. The iron frame model will bring a small premium.

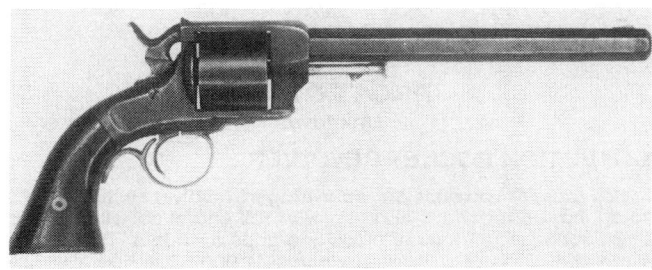

Courtesy Milwaukee Public Museum, Milwaukee, Wisconsin

NIB	Exc.	V.G.	Good	Fair	Poor
—	—	1850	1400	550	200

Army Revolver

Similar in appearance to the Navy model but with a larger frame. Chambered for .44 caliber rimfire cartridge. Fitted with a 9" octagon barrel with extractor rod and loading gate on right side of frame. Very rare.

NIB	Exc.	V.G.	Good	Fair	Poor
—	—	24500	19500	8800	600

Belt Revolver

Although similar in appearance to early Smith & Wesson revolvers, the Prescott has a solid frame. Available in either .22 or .32 caliber, the .22 caliber model has a 3" barrel and the .32 caliber a 5.75" barrel. Markings are identical found on the Pocket Revolver. Approximately 300 were manufactured between 1861 and 1863.

NIB	Exc.	V.G.	Good	Fair	Poor
—	—	1150	825	325	100

PROFESSIONAL ORDNANCE, INC.
Ontario, California

NOTE: This company has been purchased by Bushmaster.

Carbon-15 Pistol—Type 97

Introduced in 1996 this semi-automatic pistol is built on a carbon fiber upper and lower receiver. Chambered for the 5.56 cartridge it has a 7.25" fluted stainless steel barrel. Ghost ring sights are standard. Magazine is AR-15 compatible. Quick detach compensator. Furnished with a 10-round magazine. Weight is approximately 46 oz. **NOTE:** This pistol has several options which will affect value.

NIB	Exc.	V.G.	Good	Fair	Poor
925	700	550	425	300	150

Carbon-15 Pistol—Type 21

Introduced in 1999 this model features a light profile stainless steel 7.25" barrel. Ghost ring sights are standard. Optional recoil compensator. A 30-round magazine is standard until supplies are exhausted. Weight is about 40 oz.

NIB	Exc.	V.G.	Good	Fair	Poor
925	700	550	425	300	150

PROTECTION
Unknown

PROTECTION POCKET REVOLVER

A .28 caliber percussion spur-trigger revolver with a 3.25" octagonal barrel and 6-shot cylinder roll engraved with a police arrest scene. The frame of brass and grips of walnut. The cylinder is marked "Protection." Approximately 1,000 were manufactured during the late 1850s and early 1860s.

1st Model

Roll engraved cylinder.

NIB	Exc.	V.G.	Good	Fair	Poor
—	—	1500	1150	450	100

2nd Model

Plain cylinder above serial no. 650.

NIB	Exc.	V.G.	Good	Fair	Poor
—	—	1300	950	350	100

PYRENEES
Hendaye, France

Founded in 1923, this company has produced a variety of models. The most popular of which was the "Unique" series. Prior to 1939, a variety of trade names were marked on their products such as these: Superior, Capitan, Cesar, Chantecler, Chimere Renoir, Colonial, Prima, Rapid Maxima, Reina, Demon, Demon-marine, Ebac, Elite, Gallia, Ixor, Le Majestic, St. Hubert, Selecta, Sympathique, Touriste, Le Sanspariel, Le Tout Acier, Mars, Perfect, Triomphe Francais, Unis & Vindex. Following 1939 this company's products are simply stamped "Unique."

Model 10 Unique

A 6.35mm semi-automatic pistol similar to the Model 1906 Browning. The slide is marked "Le Veritable Pistolet Francais Unique." Introduced in 1923.

NIB	Exc.	V.G.	Good	Fair	Poor
—	295	195	165	100	75

Model 11

As above with a grip safety and loaded chamber indicator.

NIB	Exc.	V.G.	Good	Fair	Poor
—	325	225	195	150	100

Model 12

As above but without the loaded chamber indicator.

NIB	Exc.	V.G.	Good	Fair	Poor
—	295	195	165	100	75

Model 13

As above with a 7-shot magazine.

NIB	Exc.	V.G.	Good	Fair	Poor
—	295	195	165	100	75

Model 14

As above with a 9-shot magazine.

NIB	Exc.	V.G.	Good	Fair	Poor
—	295	195	165	100	75

Model 15

As above but in 7.65mm caliber. Introduced in 1923.

NIB	Exc.	V.G.	Good	Fair	Poor
—	295	195	165	100	75

Model 16

As above with a 7-shot magazine.

Courtesy Orvel Reichert

NIB	Exc.	V.G.	Good	Fair	Poor
—	295	195	165	100	75

Model 17

As above with a 9-shot magazine.

Courtesy Orvel Reichert

NIB	Exc.	V.G.	Good	Fair	Poor
—	325	225	195	150	100

Model 18

A 7.65mm caliber semi-automatic pistol patterned after the Model 1920 Browning but without a grip safety.

NIB	Exc.	V.G.	Good	Fair	Poor
—	295	195	165	100	75

Model 19

As above with a 7-shot magazine.

NIB	Exc.	V.G.	Good	Fair	Poor
—	295	195	165	100	75

Model 20

As above but with a 9-shot magazine.

NIB	Exc.	V.G.	Good	Fair	Poor
—	325	225	195	150	100

Model 21

As above except chambered for the 9mm short cartridge.

NIB	Exc.	V.G.	Good	Fair	Poor
—	325	225	195	150	100

NOTE: During World War II production at this company was taken over by the Nazis. Consequently, the various models listed above will be found with German inspection marks. These arms are worth approximately 25 percent more than the values listed.

POST-WAR UNIQUE

Model BCF66

A 9mm short semi-automatic pistol with a 3.5" barrel, open top slide and external hammer. The slide marked "Armes Unique Hendaye BP France." Blued finish blued, plastic grips.

NIB	Exc.	V.G.	Good	Fair	Poor
—	295	195	165	100	75

Model C

Virtually identical to the Model 17 listed above. The slide marked "7.65 Court 9 coups Unique." Blued finish, plastic grips with the trademark "PF" in a circle cast into them.

NIB	Exc.	V.G.	Good	Fair	Poor
—	250	175	150	125	75

Model F

Identical to the Model C except chambered for 9mm Short cartridges. Magazine capacity 8 rounds.

NIB	Exc.	V.G.	Good	Fair	Poor
—	295	195	165	100	75

Model D

A .22 caliber semi-automatic pistol with barrels ranging from 4" to 7.5" in length. The 7.5" barreled version is fitted with a muzzlebrake. Magazine capacity 10 rounds. Finish blued, plastic grips.

NIB	Exc.	V.G.	Good	Fair	Poor
—	275	225	200	150	125

Model DES/VO

Identical to the Model D but chambered for .22 Short cartridges.

NIB	Exc.	V.G.	Good	Fair	Poor
—	275	225	200	150	125

Model L

Similar to the Model D except chambered for .22, .32 ACP, and 9mm Short cartridges. Available with either a steel or alloy frame.

NIB	Exc.	V.G.	Good	Fair	Poor
—	295	195	165	100	75

Model DES 69

As above with better quality sights, special trigger and improved grips.

NIB	Exc.	V.G.	Good	Fair	Poor
—	325	225	195	150	100

Model 2000

Courtesy John J. Stimson, Jr.

NIB	Exc.	V.G.	Good	Fair	Poor
1250	950	775	500	350	150

QUINABAUG MFG. CO.
Southridge, Massachusetts

Under Hammer Pistol

A .31 caliber percussion under hammer pistol with barrels from 3" to 8" in length. Frame of blued iron, the grips of walnut or maple. The top of the frame is marked "Quinabaug Rifle M'g Co. Southbridge, Mass." The barrels are normally marked "E. Hutchings & Co. Agents." Manufactured during the 1850s.

NIB	Exc.	V.G.	Good	Fair	Poor
—	—	1900	1400	600	200

R

R. G. INDUSTRIES
Miami, Florida
Rohm Gmbh
Sontheim/Brenz, Germany

An importer of inexpensive handguns of dubious quality that ceased operations in 1986. Just about as crummy as it gets.

RG-25
A .25 caliber semi-automatic pistol available with either a blued or chrome-plated finish.

NIB	Exc.	V.G.	Good	Fair	Poor
—	75	65	50	25	0

RG-16
A double-barrel .22 caliber chrome-plated derringer.

NIB	Exc.	V.G.	Good	Fair	Poor
—	75	65	50	20	0

RG-17
As above except chambered for. 38 Special cartridge.

NIB	Exc.	V.G.	Good	Fair	Poor
—	75	70	60	25	0

RG-14
A .22 caliber double-action revolver with a 4" barrel and 6-shot cylinder. Blued finish, plastic grips.

NIB	Exc.	V.G.	Good	Fair	Poor
—	75	70	60	25	0

RG-30
A .22 LR or Magnum double-action revolver. Blued finish, plastic grips.

NIB	Exc.	V.G.	Good	Fair	Poor
—	75	65	50	25	0

RG-40
A .38 Special double-action revolver with swing-out cylinder. Blued finish, plastic grips.

NIB	Exc.	V.G.	Good	Fair	Poor
—	75	70	60	25	0

RG-57
A .357 or .44 Magnum double-action revolver with 6-shot cylinder. Blued finish, checkered wood grips.

NIB	Exc.	V.G.	Good	Fair	Poor
—	75	70	60	25	0

RG-63
A .22 caliber double-action revolver resembling a Colt Model 1873.

NIB	Exc.	V.G.	Good	Fair	Poor
—	75	70	60	25	0

RG-66
A .22 or .22 Magnum single-action revolver patterned after the Colt Model 1873.

NIB	Exc.	V.G.	Good	Fair	Poor
—	90	70	50	25	0

RG-66T
As above with adjustable sights.

NIB	Exc.	V.G.	Good	Fair	Poor
—	90	70	50	25	0

RG-74
A .22 caliber double-action revolver with swing-out cylinder.

NIB	Exc.	V.G.	Good	Fair	Poor
—	75	65	55	25	0

RG-88
A .357 Magnum double-action revolver with swing-out cylinder.

NIB	Exc.	V.G.	Good	Fair	Poor
—	75	65	55	25	0

R.E.
Valencia, Spain

The initials "R.E." stand for "Republica Espana." This copy of the Spanish Army Model 1921, also known as the Astra 400, was produced between 1936 and 1939 during the Spanish Civil War by the Republican forces. This variation can be identified by the "RE" monogram on the butt and the absence of any manufacturer's stampings.

NIB	Exc.	V.G.	Good	Fair	Poor
—	475	325	250	175	100

RADOM
Radom, Poland

NOTE: For history, technical data, descriptions, photos, and prices see the Standard Catalog of Military Firearms.

VIS-35 Reissue
This is an exact copy of the original VIS-35 pistol. Limited to 100 pistols with fewer than that number imported into the U.S. The importer, "Dalvar of USA" is stamped on the barrel. Subtract 50 percent for "non-eagle" version.

NIB	Exc.	V.G.	Good	Fair	Poor
2300	2000	1500	1100	600	300

RANDALL FIREARMS CO.
Sun Valley, California

NOTE: Randall prototypes can be identified by a "T" prefix. Add 50 percent to the price for this variety. For serial numbers under 2000 add $100 to $150.

Model A111

Caliber is .45 Auto, barrel length 5", round-slide top, right-hand with fixed sights. Total production: 3,431.

Randall matched set, serial-number RFOO010C. Made for the TV series "Magnum PI." (Photo by Steve Comus)

NIB	Exc.	V.G.	Good	Fair	Poor
1050	950	650	400	350	200

NOTE: For original box add a premium of $100 for Exc. through Good prices.

Model A121

Caliber is .45 Auto, barrel length 5", flat-slide top, right-hand with fixed sights. Total production: 1,067.

NIB	Exc.	V.G.	Good	Fair	Poor
1150	1000	800	425	375	200

NOTE: For original box add a premium of $100 for Exc. through Good prices.

Model A131

Caliber is .45 Auto, barrel length 5", flat-slide top, right-hand with Millet sights. Total production: 2,083.

Randall A131/SO in .451 Detonics Magnum with Randall memorabilia. (Photo by Larry Gray)

NIB	Exc.	V.G.	Good	Fair	Poor
1300	1050	875	550	400	200

NOTE: For original box add a premium of $100 for Exc. through Good prices.

Model A112

Caliber is 9mm, barrel length 5", round-slide top, right-hand with fixed sights. Total production: 301.

NIB	Exc.	V.G.	Good	Fair	Poor
1350	950	900	575	425	200

NOTE: For original box add a premium of $100 for Exc. through Good prices.

Model A122

Caliber 9mm. barrel length 5", flat-slide top, right-hand with fixed sights. Total production: 18.

NIB	Exc.	V.G.	Good	Fair	Poor
1900	1600	1350	800	540	300

NOTE: For original box add a premium of $100 for Exc. through Good prices.

Model A211

Caliber .45 Auto, barrel length 4-1/4", round-slide top, right-hand with fixed sights. Total production: 922.

NIB	Exc.	V.G.	Good	Fair	Poor
1150	1000	800	425	375	200

NOTE: For original box add a premium of $100 for Exc. through Good prices.

Model A231

Caliber .45 Auto, barrel length 4-1/4", flat-slide top, right-hand with Millet sights. Total production: 574.

NIB	Exc.	V.G.	Good	Fair	Poor
1350	950	900	575	425	200

NOTE: For original box add a premium of $100 for Exc. through Good prices.

Model A212

Caliber 9mm, barrel length 4-1/4", round-slide top, right-hand with fixed sights. Total production: 76.

NIB	Exc.	V.G.	Good	Fair	Poor
1450	1050	925	650	500	300

NOTE: For original box add a premium of $100 for Exc. through Good prices.

Model A232

Caliber 9mm. barrel length 4-1/4", flat-slide top, right-hand with Millet sights. Total production: 5.

NIB	Exc.	V.G.	Good	Fair	Poor
2400	1900	1565	—	—	—

NOTE: For original box add a premium of $100 for Exc. through Good prices.

Model A311

Caliber .45 Auto, barrel length 4-1/4", round-slide top, right-hand with fixed sights. Total production: 361.

A311B black oxide LeMay special order by "Soldier of Fortune" magazine for field testing in El Salvador. (Photo by Steve Comus)

NIB	Exc.	V.G.	Good	Fair	Poor
1700	1375	1150	900	700	300

NOTE: For original box add a premium of $100 for Exc. through Good prices.

Model A331 Curtis LeMay

Caliber .45 Auto, barrel length 4-1/4", flat-slide top, right-hand with Millet sights. Total production: 293.

NIB	Exc.	V.G.	Good	Fair	Poor
1800	1475	1250	950	735	300

Model A312

Caliber 9mm. barrel length 4-1/4", round-slide top, right-hand with fixed sights. Total production: 2.

NIB	Exc.	V.G.	Good	Fair	Poor
3750	3300	2575	—	—	—

NOTE: For original box add a premium of $100 for Exc. through Good prices.

Model A332

Caliber 9mm. barrel length 4-1/4", flat-slide top, right-hand with Millet sights. Total production: 9.

NIB	Exc.	V.G.	Good	Fair	Poor
2250	1775	1450	1000	750	300

NOTE: For original box add a premium of $100 for Exc. through Good prices.

Model B111

Caliber .45 Auto, barrel length 5", round-slide top, left-hand with fixed sights. Total production: 297.

NIB	Exc.	V.G.	Good	Fair	Poor
1900	1550	1200	975	700	300

NOTE: For original box add a premium of $100 for Exc. through Good prices.

Model B121

Caliber .45 Auto, barrel length 5", flat-slide top, left-hand with fixed sights. Total production: 110.

NIB	Exc.	V.G.	Good	Fair	Poor
2250	1775	1450	1000	750	300

NOTE: For original box add a premium of $100 for Exc. through Good prices.

Model B122

Caliber 9mm. barrel length 5", flat-slide top, left-hand with fixed sights. Total production: 2.

NIB	Exc.	V.G.	Good	Fair	Poor
4000	3500	2675	—	—	—

Model B123

Caliber .38 Super, barrel length 5", flat-slide top, left-hand with fixed sights. Total production: 2.

NIB	Exc.	V.G.	Good	Fair	Poor
4000	3500	2675	—	—	—

Model B131

Caliber .45 Auto, barrel length 5", flat-slide top, left-hand with Millet sights. Total production: 225.

B131/SO left-habd service model with custom Chuck Stapel knife. (Photo by Steve Comus)

NIB	Exc.	V.G.	Good	Fair	Poor
2075	1700	1400	875	700	300

NOTE: For original box add a premium of $100 for Exc. through Good prices.

Model B311

Caliber .45 Auto, barrel length 4-1/4", round-slide top, left-hand with fixed sights. Total production: 52.

Randall left-hand B311 with original box. Few left-hand Randalls were shipped in boxes. Most were shipped in Randall pistol rugs. (Photo by Steve Comus)

NIB	Exc.	V.G.	Good	Fair	Poor
2250	1775	1450	1000	750	300

NOTE: For original box add a premium of $100 for Exc. through Good prices.

Model B312

Caliber 9mm. barrel length 4-1/4", round-slide top, left-hand with fixed sights. Total production: 9.

Randall B312 left-hand 9mm LeMay, one of the most sought-after of the B-series guns. Only nine were manufactured. (Photo by Steve Comus)

Randall B312 left-hand 9mm LeMay, one of the most sought-after of the B-series guns. Only nine were manufactured. (Photo by Steve Comus)

NIB	Exc.	V.G.	Good	Fair	Poor
3750	3300	2575	—	—	—

NOTE: For original box add a premium of $100 for Exc. through Good prices.

Model B331

Caliber .45 Auto, barrel length 4-1/4", flat-slide top, left-hand with Millet sights. Total production: 45.

NIB	Exc.	V.G.	Good	Fair	Poor
2500	2050	1675	1100	600	300

NOTE: For original box add a premium of $100 for Exc. through Good prices.

Model C311

Caliber .45 Auto, barrel length 4-1/4", round-slide top, right-hand with fixed sights. Total production: 1.

NIB	Exc.	V.G.	Good	Fair	Poor
4250	—	—	—	—	—

Model C332

Caliber 9mm. barrel length 4-1/4", flat-slide top, right-hand with Millet sights. Total production: 4.

NIB	Exc.	V.G.	Good	Fair	Poor
1900	1550	1200	975	700	300

Model B321 SET

Serial number REK I.

NIB	Exc.	V.G.	Good	Fair	Poor
24500	—	—	—	—	—

Model A111/111 Matched Set

Serial numbers RFOOOOOC, RFOO001C, RFOO010-C, RFOO024C.

NIB	Exc.	V.G.	Good	Fair	Poor
9200	—	—	—	—	—

Austrian Randall

Total production: 5.

Close-up view of Austrian proof marks. (Photo by Christopher Todd)

NIB	Exc.	V.G.	Good	Fair	Poor
32500	—	—	—	—	—

NOTE: Prototypes with "T" serial numbers add 50 percent. For serial numbers under 2000 add $200 to $300. With factory box add $100 for A111, A121, and A131. Add $200 for all other right-hand models and $300 for all left-hand models.

RANDALL MAGAZINES

.45 LeMay—Right-Hand
NIB	Exc.	V.G.	Good	Fair	Poor
100	90	80	80	—	—

.45 LeMay—Dogleg Right-Hand
NIB	Exc.	V.G.	Good	Fair	Poor
80	70	70	70	—	—

.45 LeMay—Left-Hand
NIB	Exc.	V.G.	Good	Fair	Poor
150	130	125	125	—	—

.45 LeMay—Dogleg Left-Hand
NIB	Exc.	V.G.	Good	Fair	Poor
140	130	120	120	—	—

.45 Service—Right-Hand
NIB	Exc.	V.G.	Good	Fair	Poor
60	45	40	40	—	—

.45 Service—Left-Hand
NIB	Exc.	V.G.	Good	Fair	Poor
125	115	100	100	—	—

9mm Service—Right-Hand
NIB	Exc.	V.G.	Good	Fair	Poor
125	115	100	100	—	—

9mm Service—Left-Hand
NIB	Exc.	V.G.	Good	Fair	Poor
200	175	150	150	—	—

RAVEN ARMS
Industry, California

P-25

A .25 caliber semi-automatic pistol with a 2.75" barrel and 6-round magazine. Available with a blued, chrome or nickel-plated finish and walnut grips. Manufacture ceased in 1984.

NIB	Exc.	V.G.	Good	Fair	Poor
—	100	75	50	35	25

MP-25
As above with a die-cast frame and imitation ivory grips.
NIB	Exc.	V.G.	Good	Fair	Poor
110	80	55	45	35	25

RECORD-MATCH ANSCHUTZ
Zelia-Mehlis, Germany

Model 210 Free Pistol

A single-shot .22 caliber target pistol using a Martini falling block action. Barrel length 11", set trigger, and adjustable sights. Blued finish with checkered walnut grips and forend. Manufactured during the 1930s.

NIB	Exc.	V.G.	Good	Fair	Poor
—	1500	1200	1000	825	400

Model 210A
As above with a lightweight alloy frame.
NIB	Exc.	V.G.	Good	Fair	Poor
—	1425	1125	975	775	350

Model 200 Free Pistol
As above without a set trigger.

NIB	Exc.	V.G.	Good	Fair	Poor
—	1125	1050	875	550	300

REEDER, GARY CUSTOM GUNS
Flagstaff, Arizona

This company offers complete guns as listed below. It also offers custom options built on customer guns as well. An extensive number of custom options is available on any of these models. Prices listed below reflect the standard for that particular model. Retail prices only are listed below due to lack of active secondary market for these limited edition guns. Reeder is a custom manufacturer, or restylist, working primarily with Ruger frames. Only a representative sampling of his works is presented here, and the values are estimates ony. Since many of Reeder's guns are made to custom specs, their value is largely a matter of finding the right buyer.

Arizona Ranger Classic
Built on a Ruger Vaquero this model is chambered for the .45 Long Colt cartridge and fitted with a choice of a 4.5", 5.5", or 7.5" barrel. Blue or stainless steel finish. Special engraving with Stag grips.
NIB	Exc.	V.G.	Good	Fair	Poor
1400	1225	975	—	—	—

Badlands Classic
Built on a Ruger Vaquero and chambered for the .45 Long Colt cartridge with an extra .45 ACP cylinder. Fitted with a 4.5" barrel. Special engraving. Pearl grips.
NIB	Exc.	V.G.	Good	Fair	Poor
1400	1225	975	—	—	—

Black Widow
Chambered for the .44 Magnum cartridge and fitted with a 4.625" barrel with black Chromex finish. Round butt with black Cape Buffalo horn grips. Engraved with Black Widow on each side of the cylinder. Built on a Ruger Super Blackhawk.

NIB	Exc.	V.G.	Good	Fair	Poor
1300	1075	850	—	—	—

Black Widow II

Similar to the Black Widow but chambered for the .45 Long Colt cartridge. Barrel length is 4.5".

NIB	Exc.	V.G.	Good	Fair	Poor
1350	1125	900	—	—	—

Cowboy Classic

Built on a Ruger Vaquero and chambered for the .45 Long Colt with a 6.75" barrel. Stainless steel or black Chromix finish. Ivory polymer or pearlite grips. Special engraving.

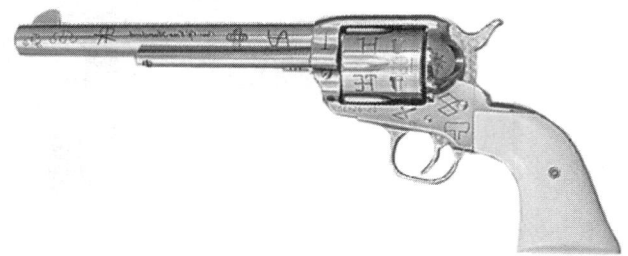

NIB	Exc.	V.G.	Good	Fair	Poor
1350	1125	900	—	—	—

Cowtown Classic

Built on a Ruger Vaquero and chambered for the .45 Long Colt with 7.5" barrel. Special engraving. Walnut grips.

NIB	Exc.	V.G.	Good	Fair	Poor
1350	1125	900	—	—	—

Gamblers Classic

Built on a Ruger Vaquero and chambered for the .45 Long Colt with a 2.5" barrel. Stainless steel or black Chromix finish. Choice of black or white pearl grips. No ejector rod. Special engraving.

NIB	Exc.	V.G.	Good	Fair	Poor
1350	1125	900	—	—	—

Lone Star Classic

Built on a Ruger Vaquero and chambered for the .45 Long Colt cartridge with 7.5" barrel. Stainless steel finish. Special engraving and walnut grips with five notches.

NIB	Exc.	V.G.	Good	Fair	Poor
1350	1125	900	—	—	—

Long Rider Classic

Built on a Ruger Vaquero and chambered for the .45 Long Colt cartridge with 4.5", 5.5", or 7.5" barrel. Special engraving with black Chromix finish. Gunfighter grip with simulated pearl or ivory.

NIB	Exc.	V.G.	Good	Fair	Poor
1350	1125	900	—	—	—

Texas Ranger Classic

Built on a Ruger Vaquero frame and chambered for the .45 Long Colt cartridge with 4.5", 5.5", or 7.5" barrel. Stainless steel finish. Special engraving. Simulated pearl gunfighter grips.

NIB	Exc.	V.G.	Good	Fair	Poor
1350	1125	900	—	—	—

Trail Rider Classic

Built on a Ruger Vaquero frame and chambered for the .45 Long Colt cartridge with 7.5" barrel. Black Chromix finish. Special engraving. Simulated pearl grips.

NIB	Exc.	V.G.	Good	Fair	Poor
1350	1125	900	—	—	—

Tombstone Classic

Built on a Ruger Vaquero frame and chambered for the .45 Long Colt cartridge with 3.5" barrel. Black Chromix finish. Special engraving. Simulated pearl or ivory bird's-head grips.

NIB	Exc.	V.G.	Good	Fair	Poor
1350	1125	900	—	—	—

Doc Holliday Classic

Built on a Ruger Vaquero frame and chambered for the .45 Long Colt cartridge with 3.5" barrel. Stainless steel or black Chromix finish. Special engraving. Simulated pearl gambler grips.

NIB	Exc.	V.G.	Good	Fair	Poor
1350	1125	900	—	—	—

Night Rider

Built on a Ruger Vaquero frame and chambered for the .44-40 cartridge with 7.5" barrel. Black Chromix finish. Special engraving. Stag grips.

NIB	Exc.	V.G.	Good	Fair	Poor
1350	1125	900	—	—	—

Ultimate Vaquero

Built on a Ruger Vaquero frame and chambered for the .45 Long Colt cartridge with 4" barrel. Stainless steel or black Chromix finish. Special engraving. Simulated pearl gambler grips.

NIB	Exc.	V.G.	Good	Fair	Poor
1350	1125	900	—	—	—

Ultimate Bisley

Built on a Ruger Vaquero frame and chambered for the .45 Long Colt or .44 magnum cartridge with 4.5", 5.5", 6.5", or 7.5" barrel. Black Chromix finish. Special engraving. Simulated pearl or ivory Bisley grips.

NIB	Exc.	V.G.	Good	Fair	Poor
1350	1125	900	—	—	—

Long Colt Hunter

Built on a Ruger Blackhawk frame and chambered for the .45 Long Colt cartridge with 5.5" or 7.5" barrel. Stainless steel finish. Adjustable rear sight with gold bead front sight. Special engraving. Ebony grips.

NIB	Exc.	V.G.	Good	Fair	Poor
1350	1125	900	—	—	—

Long Colt Hunter II

Built on a Ruger Redhawk frame and chambered for the .45 Long Colt or .44 Magnum cartridge with 5" barrel. Stainless steel finish. Special engraving. Wooden gunfighter grips.

NIB	Exc.	V.G.	Good	Fair	Poor
1350	1125	900	—	—	—

African Hunter

Built on a Ruger Bisley or Super Blackhawk frame and chambered for the .475 or .500 Linebaugh cartridge with 6" barrel. Available with or without muzzlebrake. Adjustable rear sight and interchangeable front sights. Stainless steel or black Chromix finish. Special engraving. Ebony grips.

NIB	Exc.	V.G.	Good	Fair	Poor
1350	1125	900	—	—	—

Ultimate 41

Built on a Ruger Blackhawk frame and chambered for the .41 magnum or .41 GNR cartridge with 4.5", 5.5", or 7.5" barrel. Unfluted cylinder. Stainless steel finish. Adjustable rear sights. Special engraving. Ebony grips.

NIB	Exc.	V.G.	Good	Fair	Poor
1500	1295	950	—	—	—

Coyote Classic

Built on a Ruger frame and chambered for the .22 Hornet, .22 K Hornet, .218 Bee, .218 Mashburn Bee, .17 Ackley Bee, .17 Ackley Hornet, .256 Winchester, and .25-20 with 8" barrel. Adjustable rear sight and drilled and tapped for scope mount. Black Chromix or stainless steel finish. Special engraving. Laminated cherry grips.

NIB	Exc.	V.G.	Good	Fair	Poor
1350	1125	900	—	—	—

Classic Hunter

Built on a Ruger Vaquero frame and chambered for the .475 Linebaugh cartridge with heavy 6" barrel. Black Chromix finish. Special engraving. Laminated ironwood, cherry, or walnut gunfighter grips.

NIB	Exc.	V.G.	Good	Fair	Poor
1500	1295	950	—	—	—

Alaskan Grizzly

Built on a Ruger Vaquero frame and chambered for the .475 or .500 Linebaugh cartridge with customer's choice of barrel. Black Chromix or stainless steel finish. Special engraving. Horn or black laminated gunfighter grips.

NIB	Exc.	V.G.	Good	Fair	Poor
1350	1125	900	—	—	—

Ultimate Back Up 2

Built on a Ruger Blackhawk or Super Blackhawk frame and chambered for the .475 or .500 Linebaugh cartridge with 3.5" ported barrel. Stainless steel finish. Special engraving. Laminated wood or Buffalo horn grips.

NIB	Exc.	V.G.	Good	Fair	Poor
1500	1295	950	—	—	—

Montana Hunter

Built on a Ruger Blackhawk or Super Blackhawk frame and chambered for the .45 Long Colt or .44 Magnum cartridge with customer's choice of barrel. Stainless steel finish. Special engraving. Laminated gunfighter grips.

NIB	Exc.	V.G.	Good	Fair	Poor
1350	1125	900	—	—	—

Alaskan Survivalist

Built on a Ruger Redhawk frame and chambered for the .45 Long Colt or .44 Magnum cartridge with 3" barrel. Adjustable rear sight. Stainless steel finish. Special engraving. Ebony round butt grips.

NIB	Exc.	V.G.	Good	Fair	Poor
1350	1125	900	—	—	—

Kodiak Hunter

Built on a Contender frame and chambered for the .50 Action Express or .454 Casull cartridge. Barrel length is 10". Black Chromix finish. Adjustable rear sight with barrel band front sight. Special engraving. Walnut grips.

NIB	Exc.	V.G.	Good	Fair	Poor
1350	1125	900	—	—	—

Ultimate Encore

Built on a Thompson/Center frame and chambered for a variety of big bore cartridges. Fitted with a 15" barrel with muzzle-brake. Black Chromix finish. Ghost ring rear sight. Special engraving.

NIB	Exc.	V.G.	Good	Fair	Poor
1350	1125	900	—	—	—

Ultimate 44

Built on the customer's Ruger Hunter this model features an extra long five-shot cylinder, Bisley hammer and trigger, special grip frame with laminated cherry grips, Magna-Ported barrel, sling swivels, and action job. Game scene engraving.

NIB	Exc.	V.G.	Good	Fair	Poor
1500	1295	950	—	—	—

Southern Comfort

Built on the customer's Blackhawk or Super Blackhawk Ruger this revolver features a five-shot cylinder chambered for the .454 Casull cartridge, tear drop hammer, special set back trigger, special grip frame, and light engraving. Barrel length to the customer's choice.

NIB	Exc.	V.G.	Good	Fair	Poor
1500	1295	950	—	—	—

Professional Hunter

This model features a number of special features from an extended frame to a five-shot cylinder. Choice of calibers from .224 GNR to .500 Maximum. Fitted with a 8" barrel with heavy taper. Limited production.

NIB	Exc.	V.G.	Good	Fair	Poor
2750	2295	1650	—	—	—

Ultimate 480

This model is built on the customer's Ruger Blackhawk or Super Blackhawk and is chambered for the .480 cartridge. Cylinder has five rounds, heavy barrel to customer's length, special grip. Blued or stainless steel.

NIB	Exc.	V.G.	Good	Fair	Poor
1400	1195	875	—	—	—

Ultimate 500

This model is chambered for the .500 S&W cartridge. Fitted with a heavy five-shot cylinder and barrel length of customer's choice. Black or ivory Micarta grips. Engraved games scenes and other special features.

NIB	Exc.	V.G.	Good	Fair	Poor
2750	2295	1650	—	—	—

Classic 45

This model is chambered for the .45 Colt, .45 ACP, or .45 Schofield cartridge without full moon clips. It is fitted with a six-shot unfluted cylinder. Special set back trigger, Bisley hammer, Super Blackhawk or Blackhawk stainless steel frame, and other special features.

NIB	Exc.	V.G.	Good	Fair	Poor
1350	1125	900	—	—	—

The BMF

This model features a 4" barrel chambered for the .500 Maximum cartridge and Magna-Ported. Bisley grip. Satin stainless steel finish with black Micarta grips. Game scene engraved.

NIB	Exc.	V.G.	Good	Fair	Poor
2750	2295	1650	—	—	—

Double Duce

This Ruger Single Six revolver is fitted with an eight-shot cylinder and 8" barrel for the .22 WMR cartridge. Longer grip frame with red cherry grips. Game scene engraved.

NIB	Exc.	V.G.	Good	Fair	Poor
1350	1125	900	—	—	—

Ultimate Black Widow

This model, built on the customer's Blackhawk, Bisley, or Super Blackhawk Ruger, is chambered for the .475 or .500 Linebaugh. Heavy duty five-shot cylinder. Barrel length to customer's choice. Bisley grip with black Micarta grips. Black Chromix finish.

NIB	Exc.	V.G.	Good	Fair	Poor
1350	1125	900	—	—	—

REFORM
Suhl, Germany
August Schuler

Reform Pistol

A 6.35 or .25 ACP four barreled double-action pistol constructed so that the barrel unit rises upward when the trigger is pulled. It superficially resembles a semi-automatic pistol. Blued with hard rubber grips. Manufactured between 1906 and about 1913.

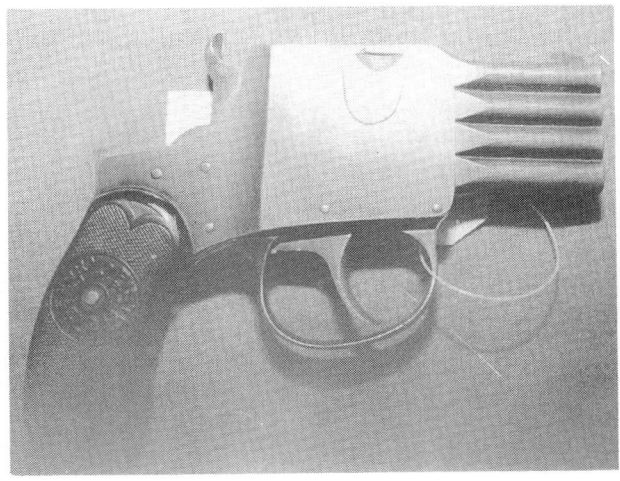

NIB	Exc.	V.G.	Good	Fair	Poor
—	1750	1200	950	600	375

REID, JAMES
New York, New York

Model 1 Revolver

A spur trigger .22 caliber revolver with a 3.5" octagonal barrel and 7-shot unfluted cylinder. Blued with walnut grips. The barrel marked "J. Reid, New York." Approximately 500 were manufactured between 1862 and 1865.

NIB	Exc.	V.G.	Good	Fair	Poor
—	—	1175	950	375	100

Model 2 Revolver

As above but in .32 caliber, the barrel marked "Address W.P. Irving, 20 Cliff Street. N.Y." or "James P. Fitch. N.Y." Approximately 1,300 were manufactured between 1862 and 1865.

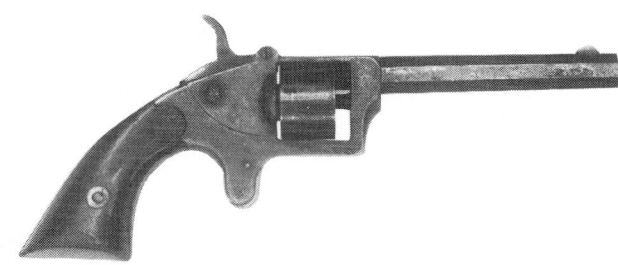

NIB	Exc.	V.G.	Good	Fair	Poor
—	—	1175	950	385	100

Model 3 Revolver

Similar to the above, but with the grip angle sharpened. Chambered for the .32 rimfire cartridge with a 4.75" barrel. The cylinder chambers are threaded so that percussion nipples can be inserted. The barrel is marked "J. Reid N.Y. City." Approximately 300 were made between 1862 and 1865.

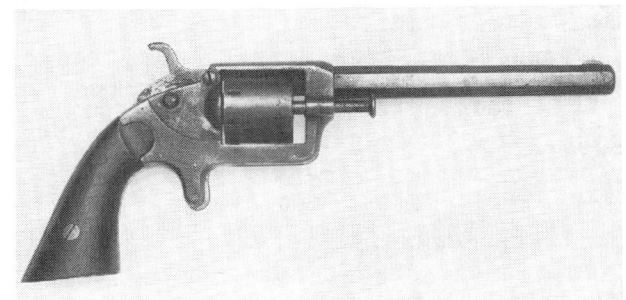

NIB	Exc.	V.G.	Good	Fair	Poor
—	—	1550	1375	550	200

Model 4 Revolver

As above with barrel lengths varying from 3.75" to 8". Approximately 1,600 were manufactured between 1862 and 1865.

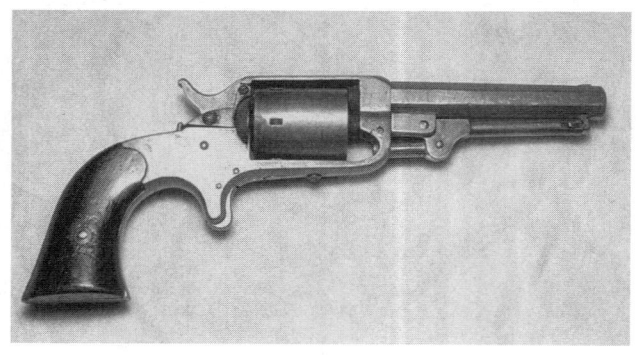

NIB	Exc.	V.G.	Good	Fair	Poor
—	—	1550	1375	550	200

"MY FRIEND" KNUCKLE DUSTER

A 7-shot .22 caliber revolver constructed entirely of metal and without a barrel. The frame of silver-plated brass or blued iron and marked "My Friend Patd. Dec. 26, 1865." The grip is formed with a finger hole so that the pistol can be used as a set of brass knuckles.

Courtesy W.P. Hallstein III and son Chip

Brass Frame

NIB	Exc.	V.G.	Good	Fair	Poor
—	1550	1200	800	500	200

Iron Frame

NIB	Exc.	V.G.	Good	Fair	Poor
—	2800	2250	800	500	250

.32 CALIBER KNUCKLE DUSTER

As above but .32 caliber. Approximately 3,400 were manufactured between 1869 and 1884.

Brass Frame

NIB	Exc.	V.G.	Good	Fair	Poor
—	1800	1500	800	600	200

Iron Frame

NIB	Exc.	V.G.	Good	Fair	Poor
—	2800	2250	1300	800	250

.41 Caliber Knuckle Duster

As above but .41 caliber and marked "J. Reid's Derringer." Approximately 300 were manufactured between 1875 and 1878.

NIB	Exc.	V.G.	Good	Fair	Poor
—	18500	15000	9000	6500	1500

Model No. 1 Knuckle Duster

As above with a 3" barrel. Approximately 350 were made between 1875 and 1880.

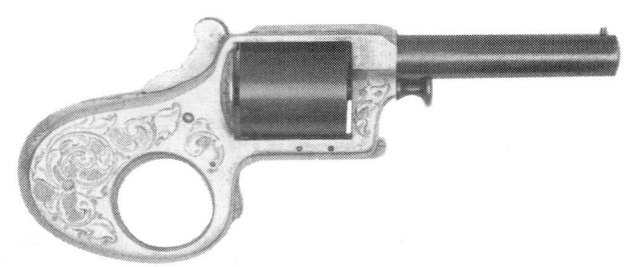

Courtesy W.P. Hallstein III and son Chip

NIB	Exc.	V.G.	Good	Fair	Poor
—	3350	2750	1300	850	250

Model No. 2 Knuckle Duster

As above with a 1.75" barrel. Approximately 150 were made between 1875 and 1880.

NIB	Exc.	V.G.	Good	Fair	Poor
—	3950	3000	1700	1250	500

Model No. 3 Derringer

A .41 caliber revolver with a 3" octagonal barrel and 5-shot fluted cylinder. The frame silver-plated and the barrel as well as cylinder blued. Approximately 75 were made between 1880 and 1884.

NIB	Exc.	V.G.	Good	Fair	Poor
—	2900	2500	1200	950	350

Model No. 4 Derringer

As above but with a brass frame and walnut grips and marked "Reid's Extra." Approximately 200 were made during 1883 and 1884.

NIB	Exc.	V.G.	Good	Fair	Poor
—	1800	1500	1000	700	250

New Model Knuckle Duster

Similar to the Model 2 with a 2" barrel and 5-shot cylinder. The barrel marked "Reid's New Model .32 My Friend." Approximately 150 were made in 1884.

NIB	Exc.	V.G.	Good	Fair	Poor
—	1800	1500	1050	650	250

REISING ARMS CO.
Hartford, Connecticut

Standard Model

A .22 caliber semi-automatic pistol with a hinged 6.5" barrel and 10-round magazine. Standard finish is blued, however, nickel-plated versions are known. The slide marked with the company's name and patent dates. Bakelite grips impressed with a bear's head and the motto "Reising, It's A Bear." Manufactured in both New York City and Hartford, during the 1920s. CAUTION: High-velocity ammunition should not be used in these pistols.

Courtesy John J. Stimson, Jr.

Standard Model New York Manufacture

NIB	Exc.	V.G.	Good	Fair	Poor
—	500	400	300	200	100

Standard Model Hartford Manufacture

NIB	Exc.	V.G.	Good	Fair	Poor
—	450	350	275	175	100

REMINGTON ARMS COMPANY, INC.
Madison, North Carolina

Founded in 1816 by Eliphalet Remington, this company has the distinction of being the oldest firearms manufacturing firm in the United States. Since 1856 it has been known by four different names: between 1856 and 1888, E. Remington & Sons; 1888-1910, Remington Arms Company; 1910-1925, Remington Arms U.M.C. Company (Union Metallic Cartridge Company); and 1925 to the present, Remington Arms Company.

1st Model Remington-Beals Revolver

A .31 caliber 5-shot percussion revolver with a 3" octagonal barrel. The cylinder turning mechanism is mounted on the left outside frame. Blued, case hardened, silver-plated, brass trigger guard and gutta-percha grips. The barrel marked, "F. Beal's Patent, June 24, '56 & May 26, '57" and the frame, "Remington's Ilion, N.Y." Approximately 5,000 were manufactured in 1857 and 1858.

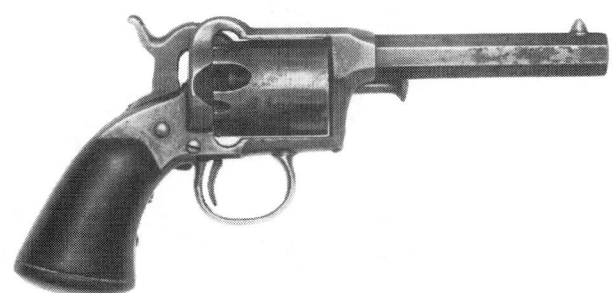

Courtesy Milwaukee Public Museum, Milwaukee, Wisconsin

NIB	Exc.	V.G.	Good	Fair	Poor
—	—	2100	900	500	300

2nd Model Remington-Beals Revolver

A spur trigger .31 caliber 5-shot percussion revolver with a 3" octagonal barrel. Blued, case hardened with a squared gutta-percha grip. The barrel marked, "Beals Patent 1856 & 57, Manufactured by Remingtons Ilion, N.Y." Approximately 1,000 were manufactured between 1858 and 1860.

NIB	Exc.	V.G.	Good	Fair	Poor
—	—	8800	4500	2500	1000

3rd Model Remington-Beals Revolver

A .31 caliber 5-shot percussion revolver with a 4" octagonal barrel. A loading lever mounted beneath the barrel. Blued, case hardened with gutta-percha grips. The barrel marked, "Beals Pat. 1856, 57, 58 and also "Manufactured by Remingtons, Ilion, N.Y." Approximately 1,500 were manufactured in 1859 and 1860.

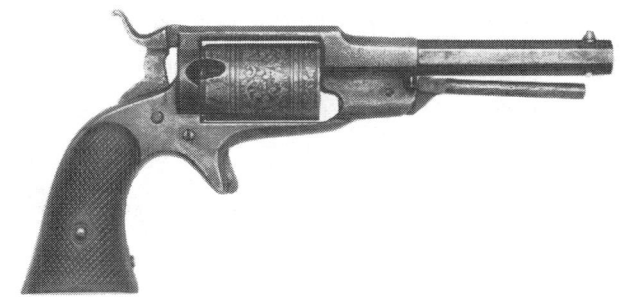

Courtesy Milwaukee Public Museum, Milwaukee, Wisconsin

NIB	Exc.	V.G.	Good	Fair	Poor
—	—	5000	3350	1150	500

Remington-Rider Revolver

A double-action .31 caliber percussion revolver with a 3" barrel and 5-shot cylinder. Most of these revolvers were blued but a few were nickel-plated, case hardened with gutta-percha grips. This model is also encountered altered to .32 rimfire. The barrel marked, "Manufactured by Remingtons, Ilion, N.Y., Riders Pt. Aug. 17, 1858, May 3, 1859." Approximately 20,000 were manufactured between 1860 and 1873.

NIB	Exc.	V.G.	Good	Fair	Poor
—	—	1400	1100	675	300

NOTE: The cartridge variation is worth approximately 20 percent less than the original percussion version.

Remington-Beals Army Revolver

A .44 caliber percussion revolver with an 8" barrel and 6-shot cylinder. Blued, case hardened with walnut grips. The barrel marked "Beals Patent Sept. 14, 1858 Manufactured by Remington's Ilion, New York." Approximately 2,500 were manufactured between 1860 and 1862.

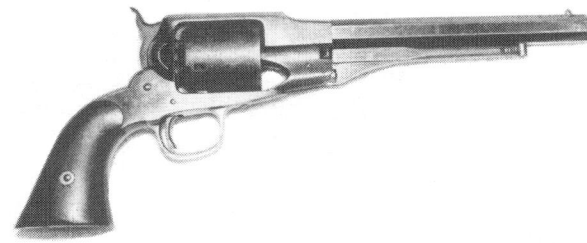

NIB	Exc.	V.G.	Good	Fair	Poor
—	—	4750	2500	1500	500

NOTE: A martially marked example is extremely rare and would be worth approximately 35 percent additional.

Remington-Beals Navy Revolver

Similar in appearance to Remington-Beals Army Revolver, but in .36 caliber with a 7.5" octagonal barrel. The first examples of this model were fitted with a loading lever that would not allow the cylinder pin to be completely removed. These examples are worth approximately 80 percent more than the standard model. Approximately 1,000 of these revolvers were purchased by the United States government and martially marked examples are worth approximately 40 percent more than the values listed below. Manufactured from 1860 to 1862 with a total production of approximately 15,000.

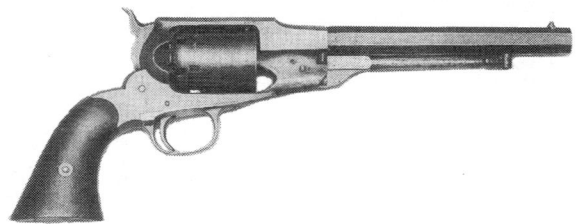

Courtesy Wallis & Wallis, Lewes, Sussex, England

NIB	Exc.	V.G.	Good	Fair	Poor
—	—	3750	2500	1500	500

1861 Army Revolver

A .44 caliber percussion revolver with an 8" octagonal barrel and 6-shot cylinder. The loading lever is cut with a slot so that the cylinder pin can be drawn forward without the lever being lowered. Blued, case hardened with walnut grips. The barrel marked "Patented Dec. 17, 1861 Manufactured by Remington's, Ilion, N.Y." Some examples were converted to .46 caliber rimfire cartridge, and would be worth approximately 25 percent more than the original, martially marked, standard percussion model. Approximately 12,000 were manufactured in 1862. This model is also known as the "Old Army Model."

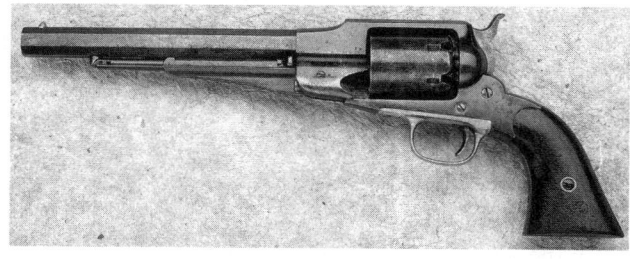

Paul Goodwin photo

NIB	Exc.	V.G.	Good	Fair	Poor
—	—	4750	2000	1000	500

1861 Navy Revolver

As above, but .36 caliber with a 7.25" octagonal barrel. Blued, case hardened with walnut grips. This model is also found altered to .38 metallic cartridge. Cartridge examples are worth approximately 35 percent less than the percussion versions. Approximately 8,000 were manufactured in 1862.

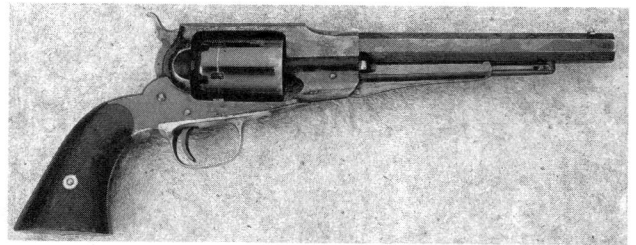

Paul Goodwin photo

NIB	Exc.	V.G.	Good	Fair	Poor
—	—	5000	2500	1500	500

NOTE: Add 25 percent for martial.

NEW MODEL ARMY REVOLVER

A .44 caliber 6-shot percussion revolver with an 8" octagonal barrel. Blued, case hardened with walnut grips. The barrel marked "Patented Sept. 14, 1858 E. Remington & Sons, Ilion, New York, U.S.A. New Model." Approximately 132,000 were made between 1863 and 1873.

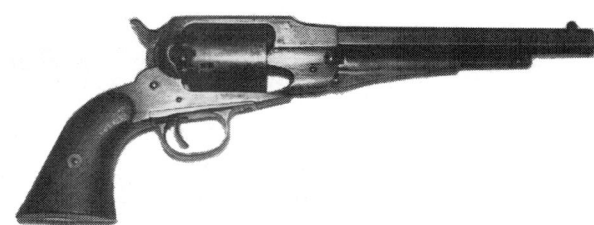

Standard Model—Military Version

NIB	Exc.	V.G.	Good	Fair	Poor
—	—	3750	1750	1100	400

Civilian Model—No Government Inspector's Markings

NIB	Exc.	V.G.	Good	Fair	Poor
—	—	3200	1400	875	400

.44 or .46 Cartridge Conversion

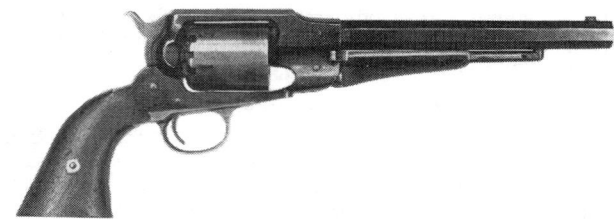

Courtesy Milwaukee Public Museum, Milwaukee, Wisconsin

NIB	Exc.	V.G.	Good	Fair	Poor
—	—	3000	1400	875	400

NEW MODEL NAVY REVOLVER

As above, but .36 caliber with a 7.23" octagonal barrel. Approximately 22,000 were made between 1863 and 1875.

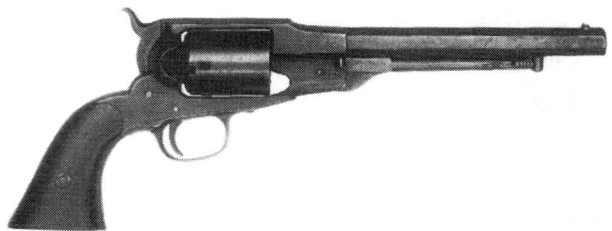

Courtesy Milwaukee Public Museum, Milwaukee, Wisconsin

Military Version

NIB	Exc.	V.G.	Good	Fair	Poor
—	4200	3000	1100	850	400

Civilian Version

NIB	Exc.	V.G.	Good	Fair	Poor
—	3600	2200	900	600	400

.38 Cartridge Conversion—1873 to 1888

NIB	Exc.	V.G.	Good	Fair	Poor
—	3200	2000	875	450	300

New Model Single-Action Belt Revolver

As above, but with a 6.5" barrel. Blued or nickel-plated, case hardened with walnut grips. This model is sometimes encountered altered to .38 cartridge. Cartridge examples are worth approximately 25 percent less than the values listed below. Approximately 3,000 were made between 1863 and 1873.

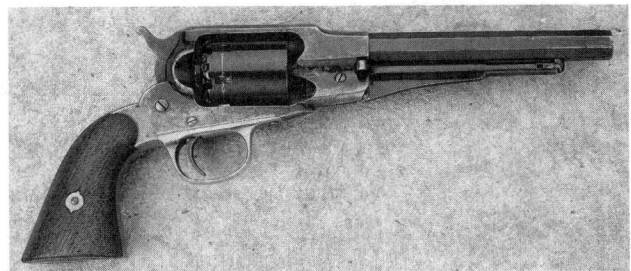

Paul Goodwin photo

NIB	Exc.	V.G.	Good	Fair	Poor
—	—	3000	1500	1000	500

NOTE: Blued models will command a premium.

Remington-Rider Double-Action Belt Revolver

A double-action .36 caliber percussion revolver with a 6.5" octagonal barrel marked, "Manufactured by Remington's, Ilion, N.Y. Rider's Pt. Aug. 17, 1858, May 3, 1859." Blued or nickel-plated, case hardened with walnut grips. This model is also found altered to cartridge and such examples would be worth approximately 20 percent less than the values listed below. Several hundred of this model were made with fluted cylinders and are worth a premium of about 25 percent. Approximately 5,000 were made between 1863 and 1873.

Courtesy Milwaukee Public Museum, Milwaukee, Wisconsin

NIB	Exc.	V.G.	Good	Fair	Poor
—	—	2750	1500	900	400

New Model Police Revolver

A .36 caliber percussion revolver with octagonal barrels ranging from 3.5" to 6.5" and with a 5-shot cylinder. Blued or nickel-plated, case hardened with walnut grips. This model is also found altered to cartridge and such examples would be worth approximately 20 percent less than the values listed below. Approximately 18,000 were manufactured between 1863 and 1873.

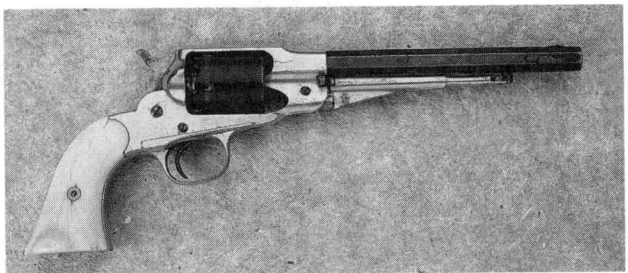

Paul Goodwin photo

NIB	Exc.	V.G.	Good	Fair	Poor
—	—	2500	1200	600	300

NOTE: Blued models will command a premium.

NEW MODEL POCKET REVOLVER

A .31 caliber spur trigger percussion revolver with octagonal barrels ranging from 3" to 4.5" in length and a 5-shot cylinder. Blued or nickel-plated, case hardened, walnut grips. The barrel marked, "Patented Sept. 14, 1858, March 17, 1863 E. Remington & Sons, Ilion, New York U.S.A. New Model." Approximately 25,000 were manufactured between 1863 and 1873.

1st Version

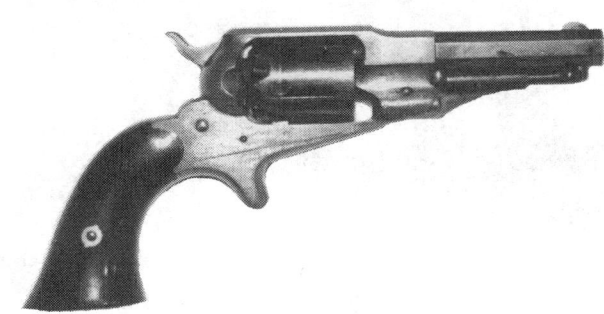

Brass frame and trigger.

NIB	Exc.	V.G.	Good	Fair	Poor
—	—	3200	1800	1300	300

2nd Version

Iron frame, brass trigger.

NIB	Exc.	V.G.	Good	Fair	Poor
—	—	2750	1400	900	300

3rd Version

Iron frame, iron trigger.

NIB	Exc.	V.G.	Good	Fair	Poor
—	—	2400	1200	800	300

.32 Cartridge Conversion

NIB	Exc.	V.G.	Good	Fair	Poor
—	—	2200	1000	600	300

NOTE: Add 15 percent for blued models.

Remington-Rider Derringer

A small, silver-plated brass single-shot .17 caliber percussion pistol with a 3" round barrel. The barrel marked, "Rider's Pt. Sept. 13, 1859." Approximately 1,000 were manufactured between 1860 and 1863. Beware of fakes.

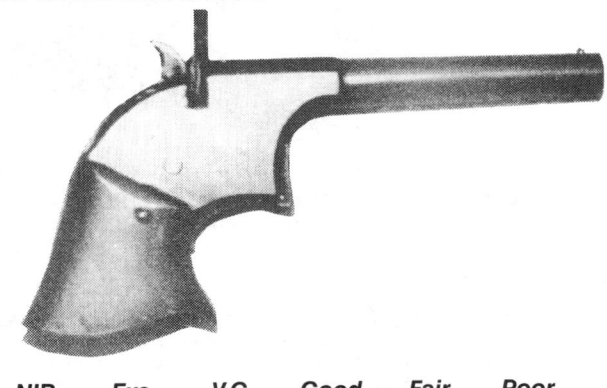

NIB	Exc.	V.G.	Good	Fair	Poor
—	—	6900	3300	975	300

Zig-Zag Derringer

A 6-shot .22 caliber revolving barrel pocket pistol with barrels 3.25" in length. The barrels are cut with zigzag grooves, which are part of the revolving mechanism. The trigger is formed as a ring that when moved forward and rearward turns the barrels and cocks the internal hammer. The barrel group marked "Elliot's Patent Aug. 17, 1858 May 29, 1860" as well as "Manufactured by Remington's Ilion, N.Y." Approximately 1,000 were manufactured in 1861 and 1862.

Paul Goodwin photo

NIB	Exc.	V.G.	Good	Fair	Poor
—	—	3600	1650	650	300

REMINGTON-ELLIOT DERRINGER

A 5-shot .22 or 4-shot .32 caliber pepperbox pistol with a revolving firing pin. Blued or nickel-plated with hard rubber grips. The barrel group marked "Manufactured by E. Remington & Sons, Ilion, N.Y. Elliot's Patents May 19, 1860 - Oct.1, 1861." Approximately 25,000 were manufactured between 1863 and 1888.

5-shot .22 caliber

NIB	Exc.	V.G.	Good	Fair	Poor
—	—	2000	1300	750	200

4-shot .32 caliber

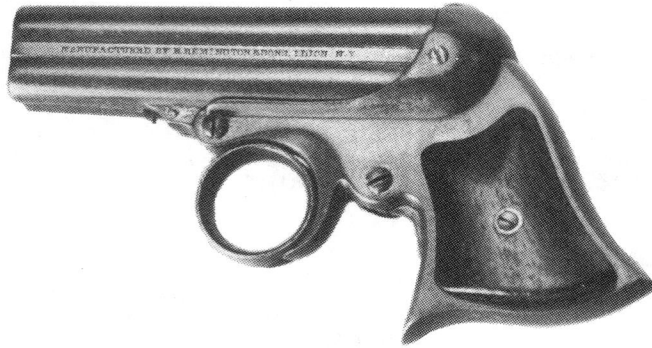

Courtesy W.P. Hallstein III and son Chip

NIB	Exc.	V.G.	Good	Fair	Poor
—	—	2000	1300	750	200

Vest Pocket Pistol

A .22 caliber single-shot pistol with a 3.25" barrel. Blued or nickel-plated with walnut grips. The barrel marked "Remington's Ilion, N.Y. Patent Oct. 1, 1861." Early examples have been noted without any barrel markings. Approximately 25,000 were manufactured from 1865 to 1888.

Paul Goodwin photo

NIB	Exc.	V.G.	Good	Fair	Poor
—	—	1500	750	400	200

NOTE: Add a 35 percent premium for blued models.

Large-Bore Vest Pocket Pistol

As above, but in .30, .32, or .41 caliber with barrel lengths of either 3.5" or 4". Blued or nickel-plated with walnut or rosewood grips. The barrel markings as above except for the addition of the patent date, November 15, 1864. The smaller caliber versions are worth approximately 20 percent more than the .41 caliber. Approximately 10,000 were made from 1865 to 1888.

NIB	Exc.	V.G.	Good	Fair	Poor
—	1750	1500	675	350	150

NOTE: Add a 35 percent premium for blued models.

Remington-Elliot Single-Shot Derringer

A .41 caliber single-shot pistol with a 2.5" round barrel. Blued or nickel-plated with walnut, ivory, or pearl grips. The barrel marked "Remingtons, Ilion, N.Y. Elliot Pat. Aug. 27, 1867." Approximately 10,000 were manufactured between 1867 and 1888.

NIB	Exc.	V.G.	Good	Fair	Poor
—	—	1850	850	400	125

NOTE: Add a 35 percent premium for blued models.

REMINGTON OVER-AND-UNDER DERRINGER

A double-barrel .41 caliber pocket pistol with 3" round barrels that pivot upward for loading. There is a lock bar to release the barrels on the right side of the frame. The firing pin raises and lowers automatically to fire each respective barrel. It has a spur trigger and bird's-head grip. The finish is either blued or nickel-plated; and it is featured with walnut, rosewood, or checkered hard rubber grips. Examples with factory pearl or ivory grips would be worth a small premium. Approximately 150,000 were manufactured between 1866 and 1935.

NOTE: For all variations of the Remington Over-Under Derringer below, examine closely for broken or cracked barrel hinge and subtract from value accordingly.

Early Type I

Manufactured without an extractor, this type is marked "E. Remington & Sons, Ilion, N.Y." on one side and "Elliot's Patent Dec. 12, 1865" on the other side of the barrel rib. Only a few hundred were manufactured in 1866.

NIB	Exc.	V.G.	Good	Fair	Poor
—	5000	4500	3000	2000	1000

NOTE: Add a 25 percent premium for blued models.

Type I Mid-Production

As above, but fitted with an extractor. Manufactured in the late 1860s.

NIB	Exc.	V.G.	Good	Fair	Poor
—	3500	2750	1100	550	250

NOTE: Add a 25 percent premium for blued models.

Type I Late Production

Fitted with an automatic extractor and marked on the top of the barrel rib. Manufactured from the late 1860s to 1888.

NIB	Exc.	V.G.	Good	Fair	Poor
—	3400	2600	1000	450	200

NOTE: Add a 25 percent premium for blued models.

Type II

Marked "Remington Arms Co., Ilion, N.Y." on the barrel rib. Manufactured between 1888 and 1911.

NIB	Exc.	V.G.	Good	Fair	Poor
—	—	1900	875	450	200

NOTE: Add a 25 percent premium for blued models.

Type III

Marked "Remington Arms - U.M.C. Co., Ilion, N.Y." on the barrel rib. Manufactured between 1912 and 1935.

NIB	Exc.	V.G.	Good	Fair	Poor
—	—	1750	875	450	200

NOTE: For Type III models, blue or nickel prices are the same.

Remington-Rider Magazine Pistol

A 5-shot .32 caliber magazine pistol with a spur trigger and 3" octagonal barrel. The magazine is located beneath the barrel and can be loaded from the front. Blued, nickel-plated or case hardened with walnut, pearl, or ivory grips. The barrel marked "E. Remington & Sons, Ilion, N.Y. Riders Pat. Aug. 15, 1871." Approximately 10,000 were manufactured between 1871 and 1888.

Courtesy William F. Krause

NIB	Exc.	V.G.	Good	Fair	Poor
—	—	1950	825	350	150

NOTE: For blued finish add a 50 percent premium.

Model 1865 Navy Rolling Block Pistol

A spur trigger single-shot rolling block .50 caliber rimfire cartridge pistol with an 8.5" round barrel. Blued, case hardened with walnut grips and forend. The barrel marked "Remingtons, Ilion N.Y. U.S.A. Pat. May 3d Nov. 15th, 1864 April 17th, 1866." Examples bearing military inspection marks are worth approximately 25 percent more than the values listed below. Examples are also to be found altered to centerfire cartridge and these are worth approximately 10 percent less than the values listed below. Approximately 6,500 were manufactured between 1866 and 1870.

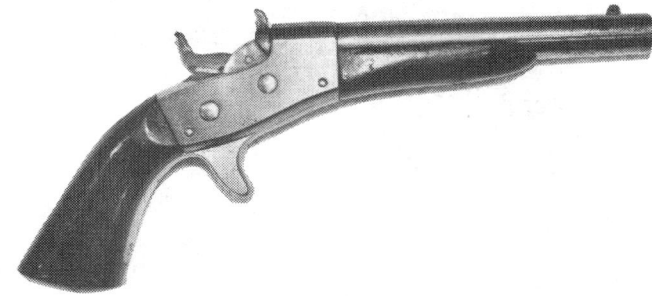

NIB	Exc.	V.G.	Good	Fair	Poor
—	—	3500	2500	1000	400

Model 1867 Navy Rolling Block Pistol

A .50 caliber single-shot rolling block pistol with a 7" round barrel. Blued, case hardened with walnut grips and forend. The majority of these pistols were purchased by the United States government and civilian examples without inspection marks are worth approximately 30 percent more than the values listed.

NIB	Exc.	V.G.	Good	Fair	Poor
—	—	2100	1650	875	200

Model 1871 Army Rolling Block Pistol

A .50 caliber rolling block single-shot pistol with an 8" round barrel. Blued, case hardened with walnut grips and forend. The distinguishing feature of this model is that it has a rearward extension at the top of the grip and a squared butt. Approximately 6,000 were made between 1872 and 1888. Engraved ivory-stocked versions, as pictured below, will bring considerable premiums.

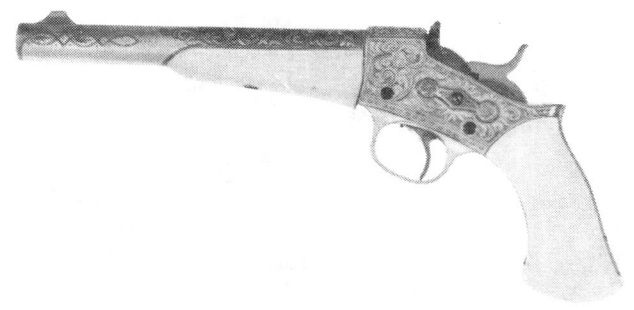

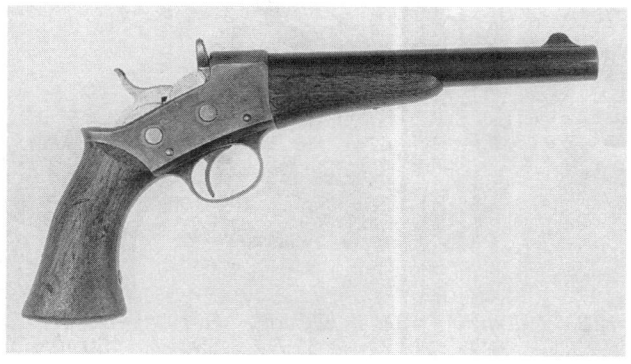

NIB	Exc.	V.G.	Good	Fair	Poor
—	—	2350	1800	875	400

Remington-Smoot No. 1 Revolver

A .30 caliber spur trigger revolver with a 2.75" octagonal barrel and 5-shot fluted cylinder. Blued or nickel-plated with walnut or hard rubber grips. The barrel rib is marked, "E. Remington & Sons, Ilion, N.Y. Pat. W. S. Smoot Oct. 21, 1873." Examples dating from the beginning of production are found with a revolving recoil shield. Such examples would command approximately a 300 percent premium over the values listed.

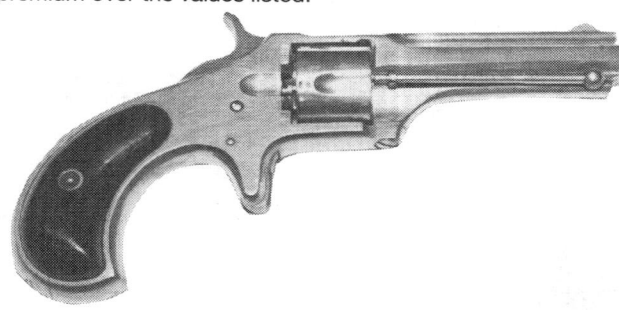

NIB	Exc.	V.G.	Good	Fair	Poor
—	—	1650	1100	675	250

NOTE: For blued finish add a 50 percent premium.

Remington-Smoot No. 2 Revolver

As above, except in .32 caliber; approximately 20,000 were made between 1878 and 1888.

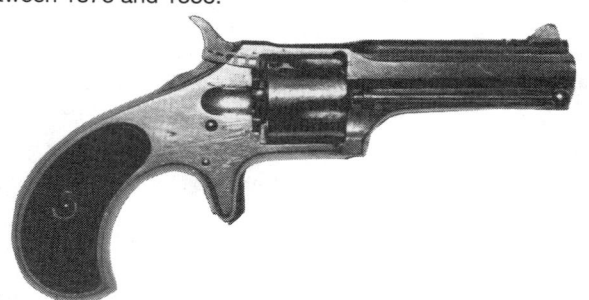

NIB	Exc.	V.G.	Good	Fair	Poor
—	—	875	600	275	100

NOTE: For blued finish add a 50 percent premium.

Remington-Smoot No. 3 Revolver

Two variations of this spur trigger .38 caliber revolver exist. One with a rounded grip and no barrel rib, the other with a squared back, squared butt grip with a barrel rib. Centerfire versions are also known and they are worth approximately 10 percent more than the values listed below. Blued or nickel-plated with hard rubber grips. Approximately 25,000 were made between 1878 and 1888.

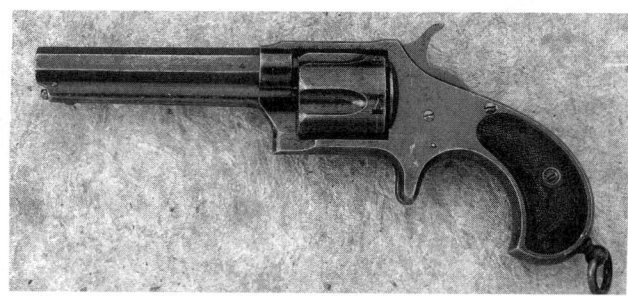

Paul Goodwin photo

NIB	Exc.	V.G.	Good	Fair	Poor
—	—	650	550	325	100

NOTE: For blued finish add a 50 percent premium.

New No. 4 Revolver

A .38 or .41 caliber spur trigger revolver with a 2.5" barrel and no ejector rod. Blued or nickel-plated with hard rubber grips. The barrel marked "E. Remington & Sons, Ilion, N.Y." Approximately 10,000 were manufactured between 1877 and 1888.

Paul Goodwin photo

NIB	Exc.	V.G.	Good	Fair	Poor
—	1250	775	475	225	100

NOTE: For blued finish add a 50 percent premium.

Remington Iroquois Revolver

A .22 caliber spur trigger revolver with a 2.25" barrel and 7-shot cylinder. Blued or nickel-plated with hard rubber grips. The barrel marked "Remington, Ilion, N.Y." and "Iroquois." Some examples of this model will be found without the Remington markings. Approximately 10,000 were manufactured between 1878 and 1888.

NIB	Exc.	V.G.	Good	Fair	Poor
—	—	975	825	385	150

NOTE: For blued finish add a 50 percent premium.

Model 1875 Single-Action Army

A .44 Remington or .44-40 or .45 caliber single-action revolver with a 7.5" barrel. Blued or nickel-plated, case hardened with walnut grips. Some examples are to be found fitted with a lanyard ring at the butt. The barrel marked "E. Remington & Sons Ilion, N.Y. U.S.A." Approximately 25,000 were manufactured between 1875 and 1889.

Courtesy Milwaukee Public Museum, Milwaukee, Wisconsin

NIB	Exc.	V.G.	Good	Fair	Poor
—	—	4800	3200	1900	600

NOTE: Blued version add 40 percent.

Model 1890 Single-Action Army

A .44-40 caliber single-action revolver with a 5.5" or 7.5" barrel and 6-shot cylinder. Blued or nickel-plated with hard rubber grips bearing the monogram "RA" at the top. The barrel marked "Remington Arms Co., Ilion, N.Y." Approximately 2,000 were made between 1891 and 1894. Beware of fakes.

Paul Goodwin photo

NIB	Exc.	V.G.	Good	Fair	Poor
—	—	4950	3600	2250	750

NOTE: Blued version add 40 percent.

Model 1891 Target Rolling Block Pistol

A .22, .25 Stevens, or .32 S&W caliber single-shot rolling block pistol with a 10" half octagonal barrel fitted with target sights. Blued, case hardened with walnut grips and forend. The barrel marked "Remington Arms Co. Ilion, N.Y.," and the frame "Remingtons Ilion N.Y. U.S.A. Pat. May 3 Nov. 15, 1864 April 17, 1866 P S." This is an extremely rare pistol, with slightly more than 100 manufactured between 1892 and 1898. Prospective purchasers are advised to secure a qualified appraisal prior to acquisition.

Paul Goodwin photo

NIB	Exc.	V.G.	Good	Fair	Poor
—	—	3700	2750	1200	500

Mark III Signal Pistol

A 10 gauge spur trigger flare pistol with a 9" round barrel. The frame of brass and the barrel of iron finished matte black with walnut grips. The barrel marked "The Remington Arms - Union Metallic Cartridge Co., Inc. Mark III, Remington Bridgeport Works Bridgeport, Connecticut U.S.A." Approximately 25,000 were manufactured between 1915 and 1918.

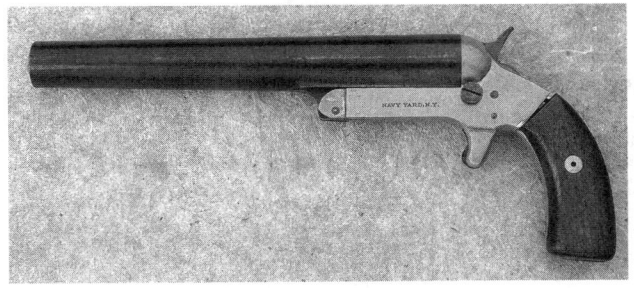

Paul Goodwin photo

NIB	Exc.	V.G.	Good	Fair	Poor
—	—	725	375	110	55

Model 51

A .32 or .380 caliber semi-automatic pistol with a 3.5" barrel and magazines capable of holding either 7 or 8 cartridges depending on the caliber. Blued with hard rubber grips having the legend "Remington UMC" in a circle at the top. The slide marked "The Remington Arms - Union Metallic Cartridge Co., Inc. Remington Ilion Wks. Ilion, N.Y. U.S.A. Pedersen's Patents Pending." Later versions carried a 1920 and a 1921 patent date. The early examples have nine grooves on the slide; later models have 15 grooves with the frame marked "Remington Trademark." Early variations are worth approximately 10 percent more than the values listed below and .32 caliber examples are worth approximately 25 percent additional. Approximately 65,000 were manufactured between 1918 and 1934.

Courtesy Orvel Reichert

NIB	Exc.	V.G.	Good	Fair	Poor
—	750	575	350	125	75

Model 53

Built in 1917 in .45 ACP for the U.S. government test. Similar to the Model 51 except for size and an external hammer. Tested by the US Army and Navy. Overall length is 8.25", weight is about 35 oz., and magazine capacity is 7 rounds. Too rare to price.

Courtesy James Rankin

Model XP-100

A .221 Remington Fireball or .223 Remington caliber bolt-action single-shot pistol with a 14.5" ventilated rib barrel and adjustable sights. Blued with a nylon stock. Introduced in 1963. Discontinued.

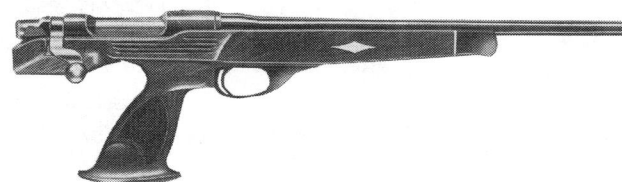

NIB	Exc.	V.G.	Good	Fair	Poor
800	600	375	300	225	175

Model XP-100 Silhouette

As above, chambered for either the 7mm Remington or .35 Remington cartridges and fitted with a 15" barrel drilled and tapped for a telescope. Discontinued.

NIB	Exc.	V.G.	Good	Fair	Poor
725	525	325	250	200	125

Model XP-100 Custom

A custom-made version of the above with a 15" barrel and either a nylon or walnut stock. Available in .223 Remington, .250 Savage, 6mm Benchrest, 7mm Benchrest, 7mm-08, or .35 Remington calibers. Introduced in 1986. Discontinued.

NIB	Exc.	V.G.	Good	Fair	Poor
950	800	650	550	425	300

Model XP-100 Hunter

This model features a laminated wood stock, 14.5" drilled and tapped barrel, and no sights. It is offered in these calibers:

.223 Rem., 7mm BR Rem., 7mm-08 Rem., and .35 Rem. Discontinued.

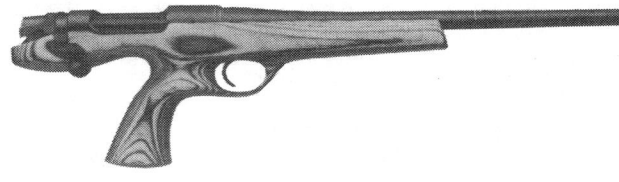

NIB	Exc.	V.G.	Good	Fair	Poor
800	675	375	300	250	175

Model XP-100R Repeater

Introduced in 1998, this model is chambered for the 9.22-250, .223, .260, and .35 Rem. cartridges. It is fitted with a 14.5" barrel that is drilled and tapped for sights. The receiver is drilled and tapped for scope mounts. Fiberglass stock. Weight is approximately 4.5 lbs. Manufacturered 1998. Discontinued.

NIB	Exc.	V.G.	Good	Fair	Poor
750	600	400	325	225	200

REMINGTON 1911R1 SERIES

Model 1911R1

Combines traditional 1911 features with modern touches. Caliber .45 ACP, carbon steel slide and frame, traditionally styled trigger, hammer, recoil system, walnut grips, 7-round magazine, thumb and grip safeties. Dovetailed front and rear sights with white dots, lowered and flared ejection port. Weight 38.5 ounces, 5-inch barrel and Satin Black Oxide finish. Model 1911 Enhanced model has match-grade barrel and bushing, front cocking serrations, extended thumb safety and beavertail tang, textured grips, adjustable rear and fiber optic front sights and lightweight trigger and hammer. Introduced 2010.

NIB	Exc.	V.G.	Good	Fair	Poor
600	525	435	350	200	150

NOTE: Add 15 percent for Enhanced model.

Model 1911R1 Centennial

Same features as 1911R1 but with special Centennial engravings on the slide, a Centennial serial number range, dovetailed brass-bead front and black serrated rear sight, and custom grips with Remington medallions.

NIB	Exc.	V.G.	Good	Fair	Poor
1100	925	800	600	—	—

Model 1911R1 Centennial Limited Edition

Same features as above with uniquely engraved slide with gold banner, custom charcoal blued finish, 24-karat gold front sight, smooth exhibition grade walnut grips. Each Limited Edition model is hand assembled and comes in a custom wood presentation case. Introduced in 2011 with production scheduled for only 300 units.

NIB	Exc.	V.G.	Good	Fair	Poor
2000	1900	1800	—	—	—

REPUBLIC ARMS, INC.
Chino, California

This company was in business from 1997 to 2001. The Republic Patriot pistol may still be available from Cobra Enterpises.

RAP 440

This pistol is chambered for the .40 S&W or 9mm cartridges. It is double-action/single-action operation. Fitted with a 3-3/4" barrel, it has a magazine capacity of 7 rounds. Grips are two-piece black plastic. Weight is approximately 32 oz. Sights are three dot with fixed ramp front and windage adjustable rear. Introduced in 1998. Imported by TSF of Fairfax, Virginia.

NIB	Exc.	V.G.	Good	Fair	Poor
550	450	300	200	150	100

Republic Patriot

This is a double-action-only .45 ACP caliber pistol with a 3" barrel and fixed sights. Black polymer frame with checkered grips and stainless steel slide. Magazine capacity is 6 rounds. Weight is about 20 oz. Introduced in 1997.

NIB	Exc.	V.G.	Good	Fair	Poor
325	250	200	150	100	75

RETOLAZA HERMANOS
Eibar, Spain

Brompetier

A folding trigger 6.35mm or 7.65mm caliber double-action revolver with a 2.5" barrel and a safety mounted on the left side of the frame. Manufactured until 1915.

NIB	Exc.	V.G.	Good	Fair	Poor
—	250	125	85	70	45

Gallus or Titan

A 6.35mm semi-automatic pistol normally marked "Gallus" or "Titan." Blued with plastic grips.

NIB	Exc.	V.G.	Good	Fair	Poor
—	275	150	100	75	50

Liberty, Military, Retolaza, or Paramount

A 6.35mm or 7.65mm semi-automatic pistol with a 3" barrel and 8-shot magazine. The slide marked with any of the trade names listed above.

NIB	Exc.	V.G.	Good	Fair	Poor
—	275	150	100	75	50

Puppy

A folding trigger .22 caliber double-action revolver with a 5-shot cylinder. The trade name "Puppy" stamped on the barrel.

NIB	Exc.	V.G.	Good	Fair	Poor
—	175	125	75	50	25

Stosel

A 6.35mm semi-automatic pistol marked on the slide "Automatic Pistol Stosel No. 1 Patent." Blued with plastic grips.

NIB	Exc.	V.G.	Good	Fair	Poor
—	275	150	100	75	50

Titanic

A 6.35mm semi-automatic pistol with a 2.5" barrel, the slide marked "1913 Model Automatic Pistol Titanic Eibar." Blued with plastic grips.

Exc.	V.G.	Good	Fair	Poor
275	150	100	75	50

REUNIES
Liege, Belgium

Dictator

A 6.35mm semi-automatic pistol with a 1.5" barrel, 5-shot magazine and the name "Dictator" together with the company's details stamped on the slide. This pistol features a bolt of tubular form, the front end of which is hollow and encloses the barrel breech. Manufactured from 1909 to approximately 1925.

NIB	Exc.	V.G.	Good	Fair	Poor
—	275	150	100	75	50

Texas Ranger or Cowboy Ranger

Patterned after the Colt Model 1873 revolver. This pistol is of .38 Special caliber and has a 5.5" barrel. The barrel is marked with the company's details and either the legend "Cowboy Ranger" or "Texas Ranger." Manufactured from 1922 to 1931.

NIB	Exc.	V.G.	Good	Fair	Poor
—	350	200	100	75	50

REXIO DE ARMAS (COMANCHE)
Argentina

RS 22

A 9-shot revolver chambered for the .22 LR cartridge. Choice of blued or stainless steel frame. Fixed or adjustable sights. Barrel lengths are 4" or 6". Fitted with rubber grips.

NIB	Exc.	V.G.	Good	Fair	Poor
235	175	150	125	75	50

NOTE: Add $30 for stainless steel.

RS 22M

Same as above but chambered for the .22 Win. mag cartridge.

NIB	Exc.	V.G.	Good	Fair	Poor
235	175	150	125	75	50

NOTE: Add $30 for stainless steel.

RJ 22

This revolver is chambered for the .22 LR cartridge and fitted with a 3", 4", or 6" barrel. Checkered walnut grips or synthetic grips. Adjustable rear sight. Blued finish.

NIB	Exc.	V.G.	Good	Fair	Poor
175	125	95	75	50	25

RJ 38

Same as above but chambered for .38 Special cartridge.

NIB	Exc.	V.G.	Good	Fair	Poor
175	125	95	75	50	25

RS 357

Same as above but chambered for the .357 mMagnum cartridge and offered with 3", 4", or 6" barrels.

NIB	Exc.	V.G.	Good	Fair	Poor
235	175	125	95	75	50

NOTE: Add $30 for stainless steel.

Outfitter Single-Shot

This is a break down single pistol chambered for the .45 Colt/.410 .22 LR or .22 Win. mag. Blued 10" barrel with synthetic grip. Weight is about 43 oz.

NIB	Exc.	V.G.	Good	Fair	Poor
200	150	—	—	—	—

Outfitter Single-Shot Compact

Same as above but with 6" barrel in .22 Win. Mag or .45 Colt/.410.

NIB	Exc.	V.G.	Good	Fair	Poor
200	150	125	95	75	50

RHEINMETALL
Sommerda, Germany

Dreyse 6.35mm Model 1907

A 6.35mm semi-automatic pistol with a 2" barrel, manual safety and 6-shot magazine. Weight is about 14 oz. The slide marked "Dreyse." Blued with hard rubber grips having the trademark "RFM" molded in them. The patent for this design was issued in 1909 to Louis Schmeisser.

Courtesy James Rankin

NIB	Exc.	V.G.	Good	Fair	Poor
—	400	250	200	150	100

Dreyse 7.65mm Model 1907

As above, but chambered for the 7.65mm cartridge, with a 3.6" barrel and a 7-shot magazine. Weight is about 25 oz. Blued with horn grips.

Courtesy Orvel Reichert

NIB	Exc.	V.G.	Good	Fair	Poor
—	300	200	150	125	75

Dreyse 9mm

As above, but chambered for the 9mm cartridge with a 5" barrel and an 8-shot magazine. Weight is about 37 oz. The slide marked "Rheinische Metallwaaren Und Maschinenfabrik, Sommerda." Blued with hard rubber grips. Manufactured prior to 1916 and in small numbers.

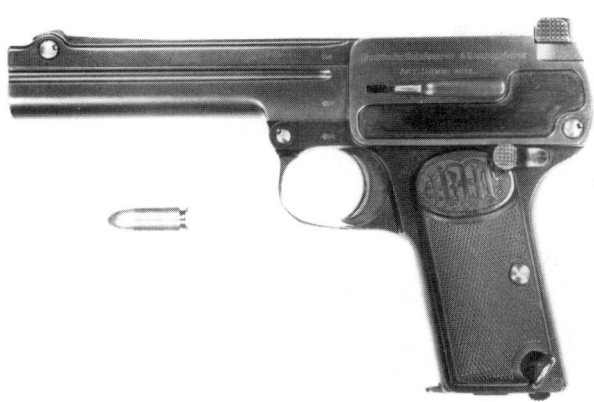

Courtesy James Rankin

NIB	Exc.	V.G.	Good	Fair	Poor
—	4500	3750	2500	1500	750

Rheinmetall 32

A 7.65mm semi-automatic pistol with a 3.65" barrel and an 8-shot magazine. The slide marked "Rheinmetall ABT. Sommerda." Blued with walnut grips. Overall length is 6.5" and weight is about 23.5 oz. Production of this pistol began in 1920.

Courtesy James Rankin

NIB	Exc.	V.G.	Good	Fair	Poor
—	350	225	175	125	90

Rheinmetall 9mm

This is a 9mm version of the Rheinmetall and was built in 1935 to compete with the 9mm Parabellum German military pistols of that time. It was unsuccessful. Too Rare To Price

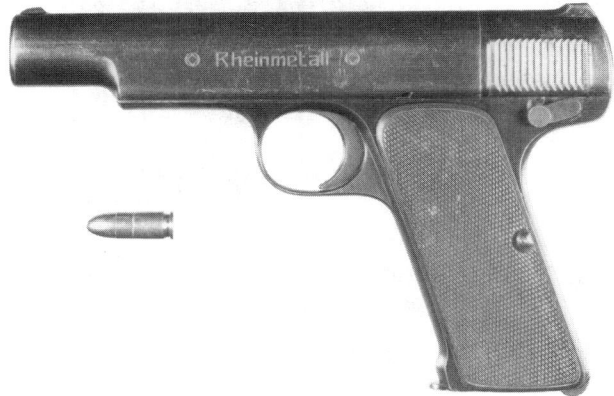

Courtesy James Rankin

RIGDON, ANSLEY & CO.
Augusta, Georgia

1851 COLT NAVY TYPE

A .36 caliber percussion revolver with a 7.5" barrel and 6-shot cylinder. Blued with walnut grips. Initial production examples marked "Augusta, GA. C.S.A." and later models "C.S.A." Approximately 1,000 were manufactured in 1864 and 1865.

Courtesy Milwaukee Public Museum, Milwaukee, Wisconsin

Early Production Model

NIB	Exc.	V.G.	Good	Fair	Poor
—	—	70000	61000	27500	2000

Standard Production Model

NIB	Exc.	V.G.	Good	Fair	Poor
—	—	63500	4950	1925	1500

ROBAR AND de KIRKHAVE
Liege, Belgium

Model 1909-1910

A 6.35mm or 7.65mm caliber semi-automatic pistol with a 3" barrel. The barrel is located under the recoil spring housing. The slide is marked "Pistolet Automatique Jieffeco Depose Brevete SGDG." Blued with plastic grips. Manufactured from 1910 to 1914. Copy of Browning Model 1900.

Courtesy James Rankin

NIB	Exc.	V.G.	Good	Fair	Poor
—	500	400	300	200	100

Model 1911

A semi-automatic pistol in caliber 6.35mm. Same as the Model 1909-1910. Slide serrations have been added at the muzzle.

Courtesy James Rankin

NIB	Exc.	V.G.	Good	Fair	Poor
—	500	400	300	200	100

Model 1912

A semi-automatic pistol in caliber 7.65mm. Similar to the Model 1909-1910. Slide serrations have been added at the muzzle.

Courtesy James Rankin

NIB	Exc.	V.G.	Good	Fair	Poor
—	500	400	300	200	100

Melior Model 1907

A semi-automatic pistol in calibers 6.35mm and 7.65mm. Barrel is located under the recoil spring housing.

Courtesy James Rankin

NIB	Exc.	V.G.	Good	Fair	Poor
—	500	400	300	200	100

Melior Model 1913-1914

A semi-automatic pistol in caliber 6.35mm and 7.65mm. Same as the Model 1907 but with slide serrations at the muzzle.

NIB	Exc.	V.G.	Good	Fair	Poor
—	500	400	300	200	100

Melior Pocket Model

A semi-automatic pistol in 6.35mm caliber. It is nearly identical to the Jieffeco's made by the same company, Robar. It was manufactured in the 1920s and imported into the U.S. by Phoenix Arms Company, Mass. The Phoenix name appears on the pistol. The model resembles the FN Browning Model 1910.

Courtesy James Rankin

NIB	Exc.	V.G.	Good	Fair	Poor
—	350	250	175	125	75

Melior Vest Pocket Model

A semi-automatic pistol in caliber 6.35mm with open-top slide. Blue finish with black checkered rubber grips with Robar logo "ROC" on each grip.

Courtesy James Rankin

NIB	Exc.	V.G.	Good	Fair	Poor
—	300	250	200	150	100

Melior Model .22 Long Rifle

A semi-automatic pistol chambered for the .22 LR cartridge. Very similar in appearance to the Pocket Model, but with no squeeze grip safety.

Courtesy James Rankin

NIB	Exc.	V.G.	Good	Fair	Poor
—	500	400	300	200	100

Melior Model .22 Target

A semi-automatic in .22 LR caliber. Barrel is detachable so that various lengths may be used. A knurled nut at the front of the slide allows for barrel changes.

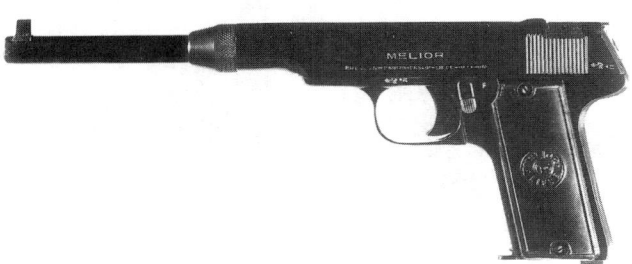

Courtesy James Rankin

NIB	Exc.	V.G.	Good	Fair	Poor
—	500	400	300	200	100

New Model Jieffeco (7.65mm)

In the 1920s Robar and de Kirkhave introduced a New Model Jieffeco, similar to the FN Browning Model 1910. As this time the right to import the Jieffeco into the U.S. was arranged with Davis Warner Arms Corp., New York, whose company name was used on the pistol. The model is a semi-automatic pistol in caliber 7.65mm. On the slide is "Pistolet Automatique Jieffeco Repose."

Courtesy James Rankin

NIB	Exc.	V.G.	Good	Fair	Poor
—	350	250	175	125	75

New Model Jieffeco (6.35mm)

Courtesy James Rankin

NIB	Exc.	V.G.	Good	Fair	Poor
—	350	250	175	125	75

Mercury

As above, in .22 caliber and imported by Tradewinds of Tacoma, Washington. The slide marked "Mercury Made in Belgium." Blue or nickel-plated. Manufactured from 1946 to 1958.

NIB	Exc.	V.G.	Good	Fair	Poor
—	200	150	125	100	75

ROBBINS & LAWRENCE
Windsor, Vermont

Pepperbox

A .28 or .31 caliber percussion 5 barrel pistol with the barrel groups measuring 3.5" or 4.5" in length. Ring trigger, blued iron frame with simple scroll engraving and browned barrels, which are marked "Robbins & Lawrence Co. Windsor, VT. Patent. 1849." The barrel groups for this pistol were made in two types: fluted in both calibers, and ribbed in .31 caliber only. Approximately 7,000 were made between 1851 and 1854.

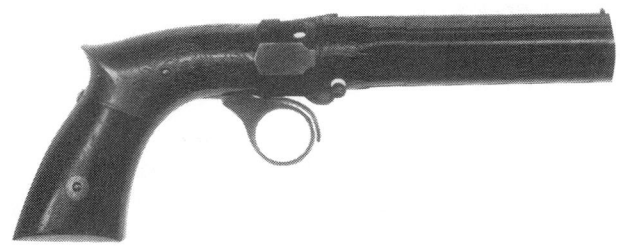

NIB	Exc.	V.G.	Good	Fair	Poor
—	—	2700	2200	650	200

ROBERTSON
Philadelphia, Pennsylvania

Pocket Pistol

A .41 caliber single-shot percussion derringer with barrels ranging in length from 3" to 4.5". The barrel marked "Robertson, Phila."

NIB	Exc.	V.G.	Good	Fair	Poor
—	—	2000	1650	500	200

ROCK RIVER ARMS, INC.
Colona, Illinois

Elite Commando

Built on a National Match frame with 4" National Match slide with double serrations and lowered ejection port (5" barrel optional). Front strap is 30 lpi. Night sights standard. Aluminum trigger and many more customs features. Checkered cocobolo grips.

Guaranteed 2.5" groups at 50 yards. Chambered for the .45 ACP cartridge.

NIB	Exc.	V.G.	Good	Fair	Poor
1725	1300	950	775	500	300

Standard Match

Many of the same features as the above model without the night sights. Also chambered for the .45 ACP cartridge.

NIB	Exc.	V.G.	Good	Fair	Poor
1025	750	600	450	300	200

National Match Hardball

Similar features as above models but with adjustable rear Bomar sight with dovetail front sight. Chambered for .45 ACP cartridge.

NIB	Exc.	V.G.	Good	Fair	Poor
1500	1100	825	675	500	300

Bullseye Wadcutter

This model features Rock River slide scope mount. Guaranteed to shoot 1.5" groups at 50 yards. Chambered for .45 ACP.

NIB	Exc.	V.G.	Good	Fair	Poor
1650	1250	925	750	525	325

Basic Limited Match

Similar to the Bullseye Wadcutter but with Bomar adjustable rear sight and dovetail front sights. Chambered for the .45 ACP.

NIB	Exc.	V.G.	Good	Fair	Poor
1700	1300	950	750	525	325

Limited Match

This match pistol comes standard with many custom features. Guaranteed to shoot 1.5" groups at 50 yards. Chambered for the .45 ACP.

NIB	Exc.	V.G.	Good	Fair	Poor
2050	1550	1150	800	575	350

Hi-Cap Basic Limited

This model gives the customer the choice of STI, SVI, Para-Ordnance, or Entrèprise frames. Many special features. Chambered for the .45 ACP.

NIB	Exc.	V.G.	Good	Fair	Poor
1895	1500	1200	800	575	300

NOTE: Add $200 for Para-Ordnance or Entrèprise frames.

Ultimate Match Achiever

This is an IPSC-style pistol with scope and three port muzzle compensator with many special features. Chambered for the .38 Super cartridge.

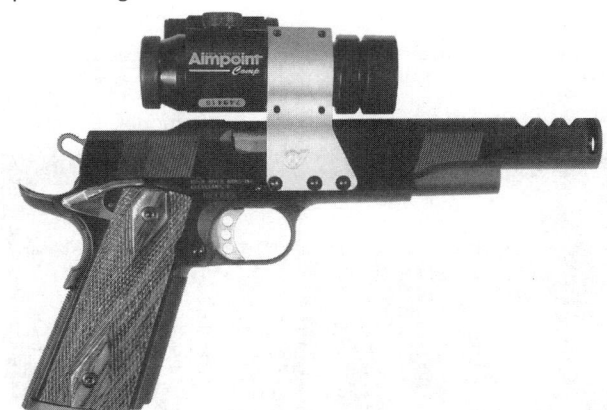

NIB	Exc.	V.G.	Good	Fair	Poor
2250	1750	1150	800	575	350

Match Master Steel

This is a Bianchi-style pistol with scope and three port muzzle-brake. Chambered fo the .38 Super Cartridge.

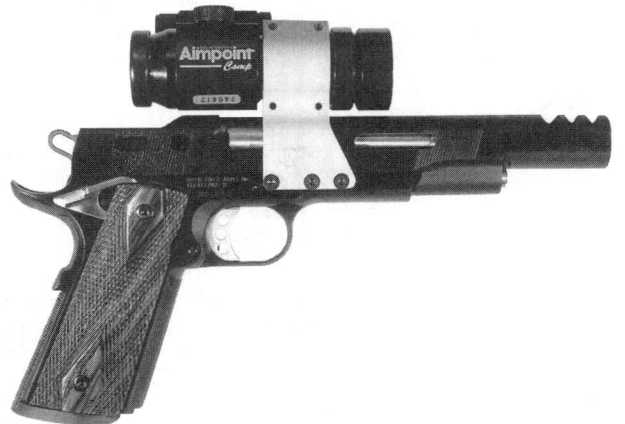

NIB	Exc.	V.G.	Good	Fair	Poor
2350	1850	1200	850	600	375

Basic Carry

Introduced in 2005 this .45 ACP model features a 5" match barrel. Checkered front strap, lowered and flared ejection port, Novak rear sight, dehorned for carry, and rosewood grips. Many other special features.

NIB	Exc.	V.G.	Good	Fair	Poor
1525	1150	825	675	500	300

Pro Carry

Similar to Basic Carry but with 4.25", 5" or 6" barrel and choice of Heinie or Novak tritium sights and polished finish; guaranteed to shoot 2.5" group at 50 yards with select ammunition. Other options available.

NIB	Exc.	V.G.	Good	Fair	Poor
1795	1400	1100	675	500	250

Tactical Pistol

This .45 ACP pistol is fitted with a 5" slide with front serrations and match grade barrel. Heine or Novak rear sight, checkerd front strap, tactical mag catch and safety. Dehorned for carry. Rosewood grips. Introduced in 2005.

NIB	Exc.	V.G.	Good	Fair	Poor
1925	1450	1200	800	575	300

NOTE: Add $200 for Black "T" finish.

Limited Police Competition 9mm

This 9mm model features a 5" slide with double serrations. Three position rear sight with dovetail front sight. Checkered front strap. Deluxe blued finish. Deluxe grips. Many other special features. Introduced in 2005.

NIB	Exc.	V.G.	Good	Fair	Poor
2310	1750	1150	800	575	350

NOTE: Add $200 for Black "T" finish.

Unlimited Police Competition 9mm

Similar to the above but with additional special features such as a 6" slide. Introduced in 2005.

NIB	Exc.	V.G.	Good	Fair	Poor
2310	1750	1150	800	575	350

NOTE: Add $200 for Black "T" finish.

ROGERS & SPENCER
Utica, New York

Army Revolver

A .44 caliber 6-shot percussion revolver with a 7.5" octagonal barrel. The barrel marked "Rogers & Spencer/Utica, N.Y." Blued, case hardened hammer with walnut grips bearing the inspector's mark "RPB." Approximately 5,800 were made between 1863 and 1865.

Courtesy Milwaukee Public Museum, Milwaukee, Wisconsin

NIB	Exc.	V.G.	Good	Fair	Poor
—	—	3500	2500	1000	550

ROHM GMBH
Sonthein/Brenz, Germany

This firm produced a variety of revolvers marked with various trade names that were imported into the United States prior to 1968. Essentially, they are of three types: 1) solid-frame, gateloading models; 2) solid-frame, swingout-cylinder revolvers; and 3) solid-frame, swingout-cylinder revolvers. They are of low quality and little collector interest. Junk, with virtually no value.

ROHRBAUGH
Bayport, New York

R9/R9S

Introduced in 2004 this is a very small 9mm pistol. Offered with or without sights. Magazine capacity is 6 rounds. Barrel length is 2.9". Height is 3.7", length is 5.2", slide width is .812", and weight is about 12.8 oz. Values shown are for basic model.

Courtesy John J. Stimson, Jr.

NIB	Exc.	V.G.	Good	Fair	Poor
1200	950	775	600	400	200

380/380S

NIB	Exc.	V.G.	Good	Fair	Poor
—	950	775	600	400	200

ROMERWERKE
Suhl, Germany

Romer

A .22 caliber semi-automatic pistol with a 2.5" or 6.5" barrel and 7-shot magazine. The barrels are interchangeable and marked "Kal. .22 Long Rifle," the slide marked "Romerwerke Suhl." Blued, with plastic grips. Manufactured between 1924 and 1926.

NIB	Exc.	V.G.	Good	Fair	Poor
—	625	500	450	325	225

RONGE, J. B.
Liege, Belgium

Bulldog

A .32, .380, or .45 caliber double-action revolver with a 3" barrel. Unmarked except for the monogram "RF" on the grips. Various trade names have been noted on these revolvers and are believed to have been applied by retailers. Manufactured from 1880 to 1910.

NIB	Exc.	V.G.	Good	Fair	Poor
—	250	150	100	75	50

ROSSI, AMADEO
São Leopoldo, Brazil

NOTE: Rossi handguns are manufactured under license by Taurus.

HANDGUNS

Model 51

A .22 caliber double-action revolver with a 6" barrel, adjustable sights and a 6-shot cylinder. Blued with walnut grips. Imported prior to 1986.

NIB	Exc.	V.G.	Good	Fair	Poor
—	150	100	75	50	40

Model 511 Sportsman

As above, with a 4" barrel and made of stainless steel with walnut grips. Introduced in 1986.

NIB	Exc.	V.G.	Good	Fair	Poor
225	200	150	125	100	75

Model 461

This is a 6-round revolver chambered for the .357 Magnum cartridge. Fitted with a 2" barrel. Rubber grips and blued finish. Weight is about 26 oz.

NIB	Exc.	V.G.	Good	Fair	Poor
300	225	195	150	125	75

Model 462

Same as above but with stainless steel finish.

NIB	Exc.	V.G.	Good	Fair	Poor
350	275	225	165	140	90

Model 68S

This new version was introduced in 1993 and features a shrouded ejector rod and fixed sights. Chambered for the .38 Special cartridge, it is offered with either 2" or 3" barrel. Grips wood or rubber. Finish is blue or nickel. Weighs about 23 oz.

NIB	Exc.	V.G.	Good	Fair	Poor
175	150	125	100	75	60

Model 69

As above, in .32 Smith & Wesson caliber with a 3" barrel and 6-shot cylinder. Imported prior to 1986.

NIB	Exc.	V.G.	Good	Fair	Poor
—	125	100	75	50	40

Model 70

As above, in .22 caliber with a 3" barrel and 6-shot cylinder. Imported prior to 1986.

NIB	Exc.	V.G.	Good	Fair	Poor
—	125	100	75	50	40

Model 84

A stainless steel, .38 Special caliber double-action revolver with ribbed 3" or 4" barrel. Blued with walnut grips. Imported in 1985 and 1986.

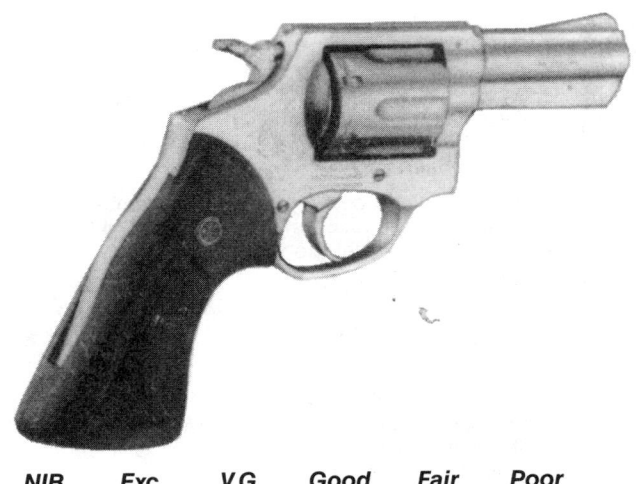

NIB	Exc.	V.G.	Good	Fair	Poor
—	175	150	125	100	75

Model 851

As above, with either a 3" or 4" ventilated rib barrel and adjustable sights.

NIB	Exc.	V.G.	Good	Fair	Poor
200	175	150	125	100	75

Model 68

A .38 Special double-action revolver with a 2" or 3" barrel and 5-shot cylinder. Blued or nickel-plated with walnut grips.

NIB	Exc.	V.G.	Good	Fair	Poor
225	175	150	125	100	75

Model 31

A .38 Special caliber double-action revolver with a 4" barrel and 5-shot cylinder. Blued or nickel-plated with walnut grips. Imported prior to 1986.

NIB	Exc.	V.G.	Good	Fair	Poor
225	175	150	125	100	75

Model 677

This model was first introduced in 1997 and is chambered for the .357 Magnum cartridge. It has a matte blue finish with 2" barrel and black rubber grips. Weight is about 26 oz.

NIB	Exc.	V.G.	Good	Fair	Poor
300	250	200	150	125	100

Model 88S

Introduced in 1993 this improved model has the same features of the Model 68 with the addition of a stainless finish. It is chambered for the .38 Special cartridge and is fitted with either a 2" or 3" barrel. Available with either wood or rubber grips. Cylinder holds 5 cartridges. Weighs approximately 22 oz.

NIB	Exc.	V.G.	Good	Fair	Poor
325	275	225	165	140	100

Model 351

This revolver is chambered for the .38 Special +P cartridge. Fitted with a 2" barrel and rubber grips. 5 round cylinder. Blued finish. Weight is about 24 oz.

NIB	Exc.	V.G.	Good	Fair	Poor
300	250	200	150	125	100

Model 352

Same as above but with stainless steel finish.

NIB	Exc.	V.G.	Good	Fair	Poor
325	275	225	165	140	100

Model 951

A .38 Special caliber double-action revolver with a 3" or 4" ventilated rib barrel and 6-shot cylinder. Blued with walnut grips. Introduced in 1985.

NIB	Exc.	V.G.	Good	Fair	Poor
300	250	200	150	125	100

Model 971

As above, in .357 Magnum caliber with a solid ribbed 4" barrel and enclosed ejector rod. Adjustable sights. Blued with walnut grips. Introduced in 1988.

NIB	Exc.	V.G.	Good	Fair	Poor
300	250	200	150	125	100

Model 971 Comp

Introduced in 1993. Similar to the Model 971 with the addition of a compensator on a 3.25" barrel. Overall length is 9" and weight is 32 oz. Chambered for .357 Magnum cartridge.

NIB	Exc.	V.G.	Good	Fair	Poor
335	265	200	150	125	100

Model 971 Stainless

As above, but constructed of stainless steel with checkered black rubber grips. Introduced in 1989.

NIB	Exc.	V.G.	Good	Fair	Poor
350	275	225	150	125	100

Model 972

Revolver; 6-shot polished stainless double-action .357 Magnum. Adjustable rear sight and red insert on front sight. 6" barrel, rubber grip, 35 oz. Uses Taurus security system. Introduced 2006.

NIB	Exc.	V.G.	Good	Fair	Poor
375	295	250	150	125	100

Model 877

Introduced in 1996 this 6-shot revolver is chambered for the .357 magnum cartridge. It is fitted with a 2" heavy barrel. Stainless steel with black rubber grips. Weight is about 26 oz.

NIB	Exc.	V.G.	Good	Fair	Poor
350	275	225	150	125	100

Model 89

As above, in .32 Smith & Wesson caliber with a 3" barrel.

NIB	Exc.	V.G.	Good	Fair	Poor
325	275	225	165	140	100

Model 971 VRC (vented rib compensator)

Introduced in 1996 this variation features a choice of a 6", 4", or 2.5" vent rib barrel with integral compensator. Stainless steel with black rubber grips. Weight is from 30 oz. to 39 oz. depending on barrel length.

NIB	Exc.	V.G.	Good	Fair	Poor
375	295	250	150	125	100

Model 988 Cyclops

Introduced in 1997 this model is chambered for the .357 Magnum cartridge and is fitted with four recessed compensator ports on each side of the muzzle. Offered in 8" or 6" barrel lengths this six-shot double-action revolver weighs about 44 ozs. for the 6" model and 51 ozs. for the 8" model. Stainless steel finish.

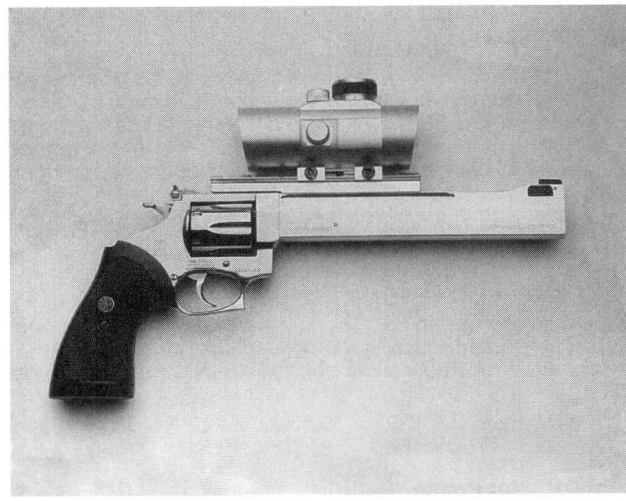

Cyclops with scope mounted

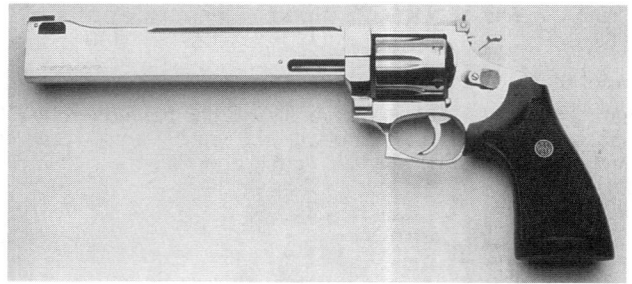

NIB	Exc.	V.G.	Good	Fair	Poor
525	475	350	275	200	150

Model 720

This double-action revolver is chambered for the .44 Special and features a five-round cylinder and 3" barrel. Overall length is 8" and weight is about 27.5 oz. Finish is stainless steel.

NIB	Exc.	V.G.	Good	Fair	Poor
525	475	350	275	200	150

RUBY ARMS COMPANY
Guernica, Spain

Ruby

A 6.35mm or 7.35mm caliber semi-automatic pistol with a 3.5" barrel and 6-shot magazine. The slide marked "Ruby." Blued with plastic grips.

NIB	Exc.	V.G.	Good	Fair	Poor
—	275	175	125	75	50

RUPERTUS, JACOB
Philadelphia, Pennsylvania

Navy Revolver

This model is equally as rare as the Army model. It is chambered for .36 caliber percussion. Otherwise it is quite similar in appearance to the Army model. There were approximately 12 manufactured in 1859. Both of these revolvers were manufactured for test purposes and were not well-received by the military, so further production was not accomplished.

NIB	Exc.	V.G.	Good	Fair	Poor
—	—	15000	11750	5500	1250

Pocket Model Revolver

This is a smaller version of the Army and Navy model, chambered for .25 caliber percussion. It has no loading lever and has a 3-1/8" octagonal barrel. There were approximately 12 manufactured in 1859.

NIB	Exc.	V.G.	Good	Fair	Poor
—	—	11000	8250	3600	950

Double-Barrel Pocket Pistol

A .22 caliber double-barrel pistol with 3" round barrels and a spur trigger. The hammer fitted with a sliding firing pin. Blued with walnut grips.

NIB	Exc.	V.G.	Good	Fair	Poor
—	—	2400	1900	850	200

Army Revolver

This is an extremely rare revolver chambered for .44 caliber percussion. It has a 7.25" octagon barrel with an integral loading lever that pivots to the side instead of downward. The hammer is mounted on the side, and there is a pellet priming device located on the backstrap. There is only one nipple on the breech that lines up with the top of the cylinder. The cylinder is unfluted and holds 6-shots. The finish is blued, with walnut grips; and the frame is marked "Patented April 19, 1859." There were less than 12 manufactured in 1859. It would behoove one to secure a qualified independent appraisal if a transaction were contemplated.

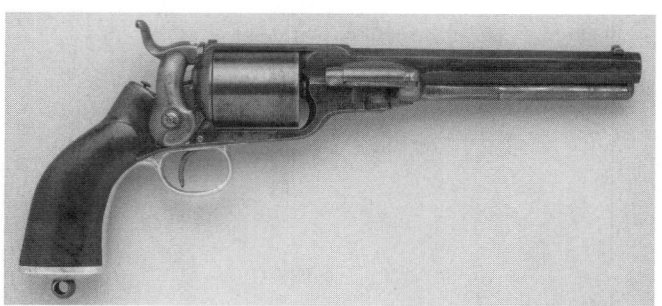

Courtesy Greg Martin Auctions

NIB	Exc.	V.G.	Good	Fair	Poor
—	—	28500	12000	5500	1500

Single-Shot Pocket Pistol

A .22, .32, .38, or .41 rimfire single-shot pistol with half-octagonal barrels, ranging in length from 3" to 5". The barrel marked "Rupertus Pat'd. Pistol Mfg. Co. Philadelphia." Blued with walnut grips. Approximately 3,000 were made from 1870 to 1885.

NIB	Exc.	V.G.	Good	Fair	Poor
—	—	900	650	225	75

NOTE: The .41 caliber variety is worth approximately 200 percent more than the values listed.

Spur Trigger Revolver

A .22 caliber spur trigger revolver with a 2.75" round barrel and unfluted cylinder. The top strap marked "Empire Pat. Nov. 21, 71." Blued or nickel-plated with walnut grips. A .41 caliber spur trigger revolver with a 2-7/8" round barrel and a 5-shot fluted cylinder. Blued or nickel-plated with walnut grips. The top strap marked "Empire 41" and the barrel "J. Rupertus Phila. Pa." Manufactured during the 1870s and 1880s.

NIB	Exc.	V.G.	Good	Fair	Poor
—	—	450	150	75	100

NOTE: The .41 caliber variety is worth approximately 25 percent more than the values listed.

S

S.E.A.M.
Eibar, Spain

This retailer sold a number of pistols produced by the firm of Urizar prior to 1935.

Praga

A 7.65 caliber semi-automatic pistol marked "Praga Cal 7.65" on the slide. Blued with plastic grips impressed with the trademark S.E.A.M.

NIB	Exc.	V.G.	Good	Fair	Poor
—	275	175	125	90	65

S.E.A.M.

A 6.35mm semi-automatic pistol with a 2" barrel. The slide marked "Fabrica de Armas SEAM." Blued with black plastic grips, having the trademark "SEAM" cast into them.

NIB	Exc.	V.G.	Good	Fair	Poor
—	250	175	125	90	65

Silesia

As above, but of 7.65mm caliber with a 3" barrel and having the word "Silesia" stamped on the slide.

NIB	Exc.	V.G.	Good	Fair	Poor
—	250	175	125	90	65

S.W.D., INC.
Atlanta, Georgia

Cobray M-11

A 9mm semi-automatic pistol with a 32-round magazine. Parkerized finish.

NIB	Exc.	V.G.	Good	Fair	Poor
—	550	495	400	275	100

SACKET, D. D.
Westfield, Massachusetts

Under Hammer Pistol

A .34 or .36 single-shot percussion pistol with a half octagonal 3" or 4" barrel marked "D. D. Sacket/Westfield/Cast Steel." Manufactured during the 1850s.

NIB	Exc.	V.G.	Good	Fair	Poor
—	—	1550	1200	550	165

SAFARI ARMS
Phoenix, Arizona

In operation from 1978 to 1987, this company was purchased by Olympic Arms of Olympia, Washington, in 1987 and the models listed are currently produced by that company under different trade names.

Enforcer

A .45 caliber semi-automatic pistol with a 3.9" barrel and 5-shot magazine. Patterned after the Colt Model 1911. Blued, Armaloy, electroless nickel-plate or Parkerized finish with checkered walnut or neoprene grips.

NIB	Exc.	V.G.	Good	Fair	Poor
700	600	500	400	350	150

Match Master

As above, with a 5" barrel.

NIB	Exc.	V.G.	Good	Fair	Poor
700	600	500	400	350	150

Black Widow

As above, with ivory Micarta grips etched with a black widow.

NIB	Exc.	V.G.	Good	Fair	Poor
700	600	500	400	350	150

Model 81

As above, without the grip etching. Also offered in .38 caliber.

NIB	Exc.	V.G.	Good	Fair	Poor
800	700	600	500	400	200

Model 81L

As above, with a 6" barrel.

NIB	Exc.	V.G.	Good	Fair	Poor
850	750	650	550	450	200

Ultimate Unlimited

A bolt-action single-shot pistol with a 15" barrel chambered for variety of cartridges. Blued with a laminated stock.

NIB	Exc.	V.G.	Good	Fair	Poor
850	750	650	550	450	200

Survivor I Conversion Unit

A conversion unit lifted to the Model 1911 frame that alters that pistol to a bolt-action carbine. Barrel length 16.25", caliber .223, folding stock.

NIB	Exc.	V.G.	Good	Fair	Poor
300	275	250	200	150	100

SARDIUS
Israel

SD-9

A 9mm double-action semi-automatic pistol with a 3" barrel and 6-shot magazine. Matte black finish with composition grips. Imported since 1988.

NIB	Exc.	V.G.	Good	Fair	Poor
425	300	250	200	150	100

SARSILMAZ
Mercan/Istanbul, Turkey

Professional

CZ-75-style compensated semi-auto in white chrome finish chambered for 9mm. Single-action with adjustable trigger, laser engraving. 16 or 18 round capacity. 42.3 oz.; 5.1" barrel. MSRP: $437.

K2

CZ-75-style double-action semi-auto in white chrome or blued. Chambered for 9mm. 16 or 18 round capacity. 35.3 oz.; 4.6" barrel. Plastic grips.

NIB	Exc.	V.G.	Good	Fair	Poor
—	300	225	175	125	50

Kama Sport

CZ-75-style semi-auto 9mm in white chrome or blued. Double-action with 3.9" compensated barrel, laser engraving. 15+1 or 17+1 capacity. 35.4 oz. Plastic grips.

NIB	Exc.	V.G.	Good	Fair	Poor
—	325	250	195	135	50

Kama

CZ-75-style semi-auto 9mm in white chrome or blued. Double-action with 4.3" compensated barrel, laser engraving. 15+1 or 17+1 capacity. 35.4 oz.; 7.7". Plastic grips.

NIB	Exc.	V.G.	Good	Fair	Poor
—	300	225	175	125	50

Kilinc 2000 Mega

CZ-75-style semi-auto 9mm in white chrome or blued. Double-action with 4.7" barrel. 16 or 18 capacity. 35 oz. Fixed sights.

NIB	Exc.	V.G.	Good	Fair	Poor
—	300	225	175	125	50

Kilinc 2000 Light

CZ-75-style semi-auto 9mm in white chrome, blued or camo. Double-action with 4.7" barrel, laser engraving. 15+1 or 17+1 capacity. 35.4 oz. Plastic grips.

NIB	Exc.	V.G.	Good	Fair	Poor
—	300	225	175	125	50

Hancer 2000/2000 Light

CZ-75-style semi-auto 9mm in white chrome or blued. Double-action with 3.9" barrel, laser engraving. 13+1 capacity. 33.5 oz. (25.4 oz. Light model). Plastic grips.

NIB	Exc.	V.G.	Good	Fair	Poor
—	300	225	175	125	50

Bernardelli

CZ-75-style double-action semi-auto in 9mm. Black/white or blued finish. The 15+1 model has a 4.7" barrel, 27 oz., Plastic grips. The 13+1 model has a 3.9" barrel; 26.7 oz. Plastic grips, fixed sights.

NIB	Exc.	V.G.	Good	Fair	Poor
—	300	225	175	125	50

SAUER & SON, J. P.
Suhl and Eckernfoerde, Germany

This is the oldest firearms manufacturing firm in Germany. It was founded in 1751 in Suhl. During this period the company produced high quality handguns and long guns. In 1938 it introduced a new double-action semi-automatic pistol, the Sauer 38H. This pistol had the first decocking lever ever used on a mass produced pistol. In 1951 the company relocated to Eckernfoerde where it continued to produced high quality forearms.NOTE: The Model 90 Supreme and Model 202 are currently imported by SIGARMS Inc.

PISTOLS

Written and compiled by our very good friend Jim Cate.

Bär Pistol

Invented by Burkard Behr and made by Sauer. This was Sauer's first modern small pistol. It has stacked barrels (over/under configuration) that allow the shooter to fire two shots, rotate the barrel, and then fire two more shots before loading. It was first patented in Germany in 1897 and in the USA in 1899. It shoots the 7mm B\x8a r cartridge only. (DO NOT ATTEMPT TO FIRE THE .25 ACP/6.35mm CARTRIDGE IN THIS PISTOL.) It was made from 1897 to 1911 or 1912. Some pistols have Bakelite grips; some have diamond-pattern checkered wood grips. A case extractor rod screws into the bottom of the frame. No trigger guard. Add $150 for original box and instructions.

NIB	Exc.	V.G.	Good	Fair	Poor
—	1250	800	450	275	–

Roth-Sauer Model

The very first automatic pistol produced by J.P. Sauer & Son and designed by Karl Krinka for George Roth. It is available only in 7.65 Roth-Sauer caliber. It is a locked breech design, beautifully finished and extremely well made. Later this design was modified and became the Roth-Steyr military pistol which was adopted by Austria in 1907. A difficult-to-find pistol.

NIB	Exc.	V.G.	Good	Fair	Poor
—	2500	1800	900	500	300

SAUER MODEL 1913

FIRST SERIES

Incorporates an extra safety button on the left side of the frame near the trigger and the rear sight is simply a milled recess in the cocking knob itself. The serial number range runs from 1 to approximately 4750 and this first series is found only in 7.65mm caliber. All were for commercial sales as far as can be determined. Some were tested by various militaries, no doubt. A. European variation—all slide legends are in the German language B. English Export variation—slide legends are marked, J.P. Sauer & Son, Suhl - Prussia, "Sauer's Patent" Pat'd May 20 1912 Both were sold in thick paper cartons or boxes with the color being a reddish purple with gold colored letters, etc. Examples of the very early European variation are found with the English language brochure or manual as well as an extra magazine, cleaning brush and grease container. These were shipped to England or the U.S. prior to Sauer producing the English Export variation.

A. European variation:

NIB	Exc.	V.G.	Good	Fair	Poor
—	1500	900	650	400	250

B. English Export variation:

NIB	Exc.	V.G.	Good	Fair	Poor
—	1800	1200	800	500	300

ORIGINAL BOX WITH ACCESSORIES AND MANUAL: Add $500 if complete and in very good to excellent condition.

SECOND SERIES

Extra safety button eliminated, rear sight acts as cocking knob retainer.

COMMERCIAL VARIATIONS

Normal European/German slide markings are normally found; however it has been called to my attention that there are English Export pistols in this SECOND SERIES which have the English markings on the slide which are similar to those found on the FIRST SERIES of the Model 1913. This is applicable to both the 7.65mm and 6.35mm model 1919 pistols. These are exceptional scarce pistols and should command at least a 50 percent premium, perhaps more due to their rarity. This commercial variation had factory manuals printed in English, Spanish and German which came with the cardboard boxed pistols. With the original Sauer box accessories and manual: Add $300 if in very good to excellent condition.

Caliber 7.65mm variation

NIB	Exc.	V.G.	Good	Fair	Poor
—	450	375	300	250	100

Caliber 7.65 variation with all words in English (i.e Son, Prussia, etc.)

NIB	Exc.	V.G.	Good	Fair	Poor
—	800	575	450	300	200

POLICE VARIATIONS

These will be of the standard German Commercial configuration but nearly always having the Zusatzsicherung (additional safety) added to the pistol. This safety is found between the regular safety lever and the top of the left grip. Police used both calibers, 7.65mm and 6.35mm but the 7.65 was predominant. After the early part of the 1930s the 6.35 was not available to police departments. Thus the 6.35mm police marked Sauer is rather scarce in relation to the 7.65mm caliber. A few in 7.65mm are dated 1920 on the left side of the frame and were used by auxiliary policemen in Bavaria. Normal police property markings are on the front or rear gripstraps. Most were originally issued with at least two magazines and a police accepted holster. The mags were usually numbered and the holsters are found with and without pistol numbers.

Caliber 6.35mm police marked without Zusatzsicherung

NIB	Exc.	V.G.	Good	Fair	Poor
—	500	350	275	200	75

Caliber 6.35mm police marked with Zusatzsicherung

NIB	Exc.	V.G.	Good	Fair	Poor
—	550	375	275	200	75

Caliber 7.65mm police marked without Zusatzsicherung

NIB	Exc.	V.G.	Good	Fair	Poor
—	575	325	275	175	125

Caliber 7.65mm police marked with Zusatzsicherung

NIB	Exc.	V.G.	Good	Fair	Poor
—	500	350	275	175	125

NOTE: Add 10 percent for one correctly numbered magazine, or 20 percent if found with both correctly numbered magazines. Add 30 percent if found with correct holster and magazines.

R.F.V. (REICH FINANZ VERWALTUNG)

This Sauer variation is rarely found in any condition. The R.F.V. markings and property number could be 1 to 4 digits. This variation is found in both calibers and were used by the Reich's Customs and Finance department personnel.

Caliber 6.35mm R.F.V. marked pistols

NIB	Exc.	V.G.	Good	Fair	Poor
—	1000	750	500	350	250

Caliber 7.65mm R.F.V. marked pistols

NIB	Exc.	V.G.	Good	Fair	Poor
—	750	600	400	300	200

IMPERIAL MILITARY VARIATIONS

These were normal German commercial variations of the time period having either the Imperial Eagle acceptance marking applied on the front of the trigger guard and having the small Imperial Army inspector's acceptance marking (crown over a scriptic letter) on the right side of the frame close to the Nitro proof; or having just the Imperial Army inspector's marking alone. Usually these pistols are found in the 40000 to 85000 range. However, the quantity actually Imperial Military accepted is quite low even though thousands were privately purchased by the officer corps. There are examples in 6.35mm which are Imperial Military accepted but these are very scarce.

Caliber 7.65mm Imperial Military accepted pistols

NIB	Exc.	V.G.	Good	Fair	Poor
—	700	500	350	275	150

NOTE: Add 30 percent for 6.35mm .

Paramilitary marked Sauer pistols of the 1925-35 period

A very few of the Model 1913 pistols will have been marked by paramilitary groups or organizations of this period. Usually this marking is no more than a series of numbers above another series of numbers, such as 23 over 12. These are found usually on the left side of the frame next to the left grip. Most of these numbers are indicative of property numbers assigned to a particular pistols belonging to a particular SA Group, Stahlhelm, or a rightwing organization such as the Red Front (early communist). Any pistol of this type should be examined by an expert to determine if it is an original example.

NIB	Exc.	V.G.	Good	Fair	Poor
—	450	375	275	200	100

Norwegian police usage, post World War II

After the war was over many surplus German weapons were put back into use by the government of Norway. The Germans had occupied this country and large numbers of weapons remained when the fighting ended. This included a large number of surplus Sauer pistols being utilized by the police (POLITI) forces. Most of the Sauers that were used by the Politi which have been imported into the U.S. have been the Model 1913; however there were a number of the Model 1930 pistols which reached our country as well. All examples, regardless of the model, have the word POLITI stamped on the slide as well as a rampant lion on a shield under a crown marking. Following this is the property number and this number is also stamped into the left side of the frame. Most saw much usage during the post-war period. All are in 7.65mm caliber.

NIB	Exc.	V.G.	Good	Fair	Poor
—	350	300	200	150	100

MODEL 1913/19 IN 6.35MM

This particular pistol must be divided into three (3) subvariations. This variation appears to be in a serial number range of its own. The first subvariation appears to run from 1 to 40000. It is highly doubtful if this quantity was manufactured. The second subvariation incorporates a Zusatzsicherung or Additional Safety which can be seen between the normal safety lever and the top of the left grip. It locked the trigger bar when in use. This second range appears to run from approximately serial number 40000 to 51000 which probably was continuous in the number produced. Lastly, the third subvariation examples were manufactured during or after 1926. The trigger guard has a different shape; the slide has a greater area of vertical milled finger grooves; the added Additional safety (Zusatzsicherung) now acts as the hold open device as well. These are found up to approximately 57000. Then a few examples of the first subvariation are found from 57000 up to about 62500. This was, no doubt, usage of remaining parts.

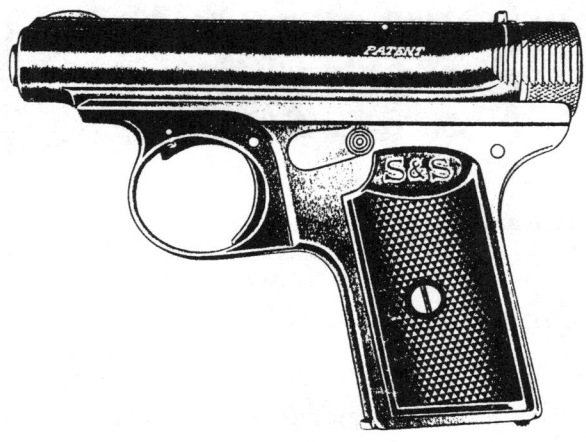

Caliber 6.35mm first subvariation

NIB	Exc.	V.G.	Good	Fair	Poor
—	450	375	250	150	75

Caliber 6.35mm second subvariation

NIB	Exc.	V.G.	Good	Fair	Poor
—	475	375	250	150	75

Caliber 6.35mm third subvariation

NIB	Exc.	V.G.	Good	Fair	Poor
—	650	500	500	200	100

Caliber 6.35mm English export variation

(all words in English; i.e. Son, Prussia, etc.); very rare, only one example known.

NIB	Exc.	V.G.	Good	Fair	Poor
—	1000	700	500	300	200

NOTE: Any commercial pistol could be special ordered with a factory nickel finish, special grip material (pearl, wood, etc.) as well as different types of engraving. It would be in your best interest to have these pistols examined by an expert.

1926 EXPORT MODEL

This variation's name comes from actual Sauer factory records found in the Suhl Archive. It is an interim pistol produced during the 1926 to early 1929 period. It is found only in the 7.65mm caliber. This was an advancement of the normal 1913 design which included changes in (1) the safety lever's design that became a slide hold open device as well, (2) shape of the frame was altered in that the trigger guard became more streamlined and the rear of the frame was shortened, and serrations were added to the slide as well as the cocking knob. These are found in the 162000 to 169000 range in relatively small clusters. Two to four thousand are presumed to have been manufactured. A scarce Sauer pistol! To date, none have been seen in nickel.

NIB	Exc.	V.G.	Good	Fair	Poor
—	825	700	500	300	150

W.T.M.-Westentaschen Model—Vest Pocket Model

Several variations of vest pocket pistols were manufactured. The first was called a Model 1920 by the Sauer firm. We usually refer to it as the Model 1924. This pistol, as well as all other W.T.M. examples, were designed to carry in your pocket. They are quite small in size and are found only in the 6.35mm or .25 ACP caliber. Later on in 1928 an updated version became available and was referred to a the Model 1928. These differed in internal parts design, slide configuration and the bottom of the grip was marked, "Cal.6.35.28." The last version appeared in 1933 and still utilized the same grips but the trigger and some other small parts differed. All three were available in blue or nickel finish, as well as engraving and fancy grip material. A very few of the Model 1933 had stainless steel (NIROSTA marked) barrels.

Model 1920

Serrations on the front and rear of the slide.

NIB	Exc.	V.G.	Good	Fair	Poor
—	550	450	300	200	75

Model 1928

"Cal. 6.35.28" on the black Bakelite grips.

NIB	Exc.	V.G.	Good	Fair	Poor
—	500	450	300	185	75

Model 1933

Different type of trigger and found in the 253000 to early 254000 serial number range.

NIB	Exc.	V.G.	Good	Fair	Poor
—	700	575	400	275	150

NOTE: Add $200 for factory nickel, $250 for factory engraving, $250 for exotic grip material, $500 for factory paper box with cleaning brush, extra magazine and brochure, $750 in original factory imitation leather covered metal presentation case with accessories, $500 for NIROSTA marked stainless barrel.

MODEL 1930 VARIATIONS

DUTCH MODELS

These different types of Dutch pistols will have JOH MUNTS - AMSTERDAM on the left side of the slide. The grips are usually a mottled gray color. Sauer manufactured different pistols for the Dutch police, Navy, Army, Department of Finance, S.M.N. (Steam Ships Netherlands) and possibly other agencies.

Dutch Police

First variation manufactured w/o adjustable front sight and w/o lanyard loop.

NIB	Exc.	V.G.	Good	Fair	Poor
—	650	450	350	250	125

Amsterdam Police

Manufactured w/o adjustable sight but having a lanyard loop.

NIB	Exc.	V.G.	Good	Fair	Poor
—	700	500	350	250	125

Navy

Made without adjustable sight and having the Anchor & Crown marked on the rear gripstrap.

NIB	Exc.	V.G.	Good	Fair	Poor
—	1000	750	400	250	125

S.M.N.

Found with and w/o adjustable front sights, no lanyard loop, S.M.N. marked horizontally near bottom of rear gripstrap.

NIB	Exc.	V.G.	Good	Fair	Poor
—	1000	700	375	225	100

Department of Finance

Found with and w/o adjustable front sight, no lanyard loop, DF over date-1933-on rear grip strap

NIB	Exc.	V.G.	Good	Fair	Poor
—	850	700	385	250	150

NOTE: Accessories: cleaning rod, brush, aluminum oil bottle and manuals, add accordingly.

1930 COMMERCIAL MODEL

These pistols were for sale in Germany and other countries through normal commercial outlets. A very few are factory nickeled, engraved or both; some are with the NIROSTA marked barrels and a very few were made in Duralumin or Dural. The standard caliber was 7.65mm hut a very limited number were made in .22 LR (.22 Long). Standard grip material is black Bakelite. Most of the regular pistols were purchased by military officers, some went to paramilitary groups, such as the SA.

Standard Commercial

NIB	Exc.	V.G.	Good	Fair	Poor
—	600	450	300	200	125

Standard Commercial with NIROSTA marked barrel, 7.65mm

NIB	Exc.	V.G.	Good	Fair	Poor
—	900	600	350	275	150

Standard Commercial in .22 LR (.22 Long)

NIB	Exc.	V.G.	Good	Fair	Poor
—	2500	1800	1200	500	300

Duralumin (Dural) Variation, 7.65mm

NIB	Exc.	V.G.	Good	Fair	Poor
—	3500	2750	2000	1200	450

NOTE: For any variation listed add $100 for nickel finish; $500 for engraving; $600 for both nickel and engraving; with nickel, engraving, and with a fancy grip material (pearl or ebony, etc.) $750.

BEHORDEN MODEL

The Behorden (Authority) Model is different from the Model 1930 in that it has a trigger safety and a loaded indicator provided.

Behorden Commercial

These are normally found with a high polished blued finish. It was available with a nickel finish, engraving, or both, as well as fancy grip material and a NIROSTA marked barrel. The regular caliber is 7.65mm, but a very few are know in .22 LR that are probably prototype pistols.

NIB	Exc.	V.G.	Good	Fair	Poor
—	675	550	400	350	200

NOTE: Add $100 for nickel finish, $250 for engraving, $350 for both, $500 with nickel, engraving, and a fancy grip material; $500 for NIROSTA marked stainless barrel. Add 300 percent for .22 caliber.

Late Behorden Commercial

These are actually Model 1930 pistols found in the 220000 to 223000 serial number range which do not have the trigger safety and/or the indicator pin.

NIB	Exc.	V.G.	Good	Fair	Poor
—	600	450	300	200	125

DURALUMIN MODEL (DURAL)

The frame and slide are made of the Duralumin material. These are rare pistols!

Blue Anodized Variation

Found with and w/o NIROSTA marked barrels.

NIB	Exc.	V.G.	Good	Fair	Poor
—	4000	3500	2500	1500	850

NOTE: Add $250 for the stainless barrel.

Nonanodized Variation

Found with and w/o NIROSTA marked barrels.

NIB	Exc.	V.G.	Good	Fair	Poor
—	4000	3500	2500	1500	850

NOTE: Add $250 for the stainless barrel.

Presentation Examples of Anodized and Nonanodized Variations

Please consult an expert for pricing.

POLICE MODELS

Examples will be found with police acceptance on the left side of the trigger guard and in a few cases on the front or rear grip straps. Black Bakelite grips are standard.

Sunburst K Police Acceptance

Nonadjustable front sight (a round blade).

NIB	Exc.	V.G.	Good	Fair	Poor
—	600	500	350	275	200

Sunburst K Police Acceptance

Adjustable front sight.

NIB	Exc.	V.G.	Good	Fair	Poor
—	750	625	450	300	225

Diamond in Sunburst Police Acceptance

All known are with the adjustable front sight.

NIB	Exc.	V.G.	Good	Fair	Poor
—	875	700	500	300	225

Grip Strap Marked Variations

(Having abbreviations of a city and the property number of the pistol on the grip strap.) Very few of these are known. Examples are S.Mg. 52, Sch. 78, etc.

NIB	Exc.	V.G.	Good	Fair	Poor
—	750	550	375	250	150

MODEL 36/37

These very few pistols are all prototype Sauer pistols which preceded the Model 38. They are in the 210,000 range. Please consult an expert to determine value! EXTREMELY RARE.

MODEL 38 AND 38-H (H MODEL) VARIATIONS

MODEL 38

This pistol started at 260000. It is Crown N Nitro proofed, has a cocking/decocking lever, and a loaded indicator pin, and is double-action. It has a high polish blue; is in 7.65m/m (the standard production pistol); is found without the thumbsafety on the slide; with a pinned mag release. VERY RARE.

One Line Slide Legend Variation (pinned magazine release button - no screw)

Crown N proofs. Approximately 250 produced. Extremely rare!

NIB	Exc.	V.G.	Good	Fair	Poor
—	3800	3000	2000	600	300

Two Line Slide Legend Variation (pinned magazine release button - no screw)

C/N proofs, blued, with pinned magazine release (about 850 produced) VERY RARE.

NIB	Exc.	V.G.	Good	Fair	Poor
—	2600	2000	1500	500	275

NOTE: Add $250 for factory nickel; $350 for factory chrome; $1000 for engraving; $500 for NIROSTA marked barrel.

Two Line Slide Legend Variation (magazine release button)

C/N proofs, blued, magazine release button retained by a screw. RARE.

NIB	Exc.	V.G.	Good	Fair	Poor
—	2500	1500	900	500	275

NOTE: Add $250 for factory nickel; $350 for factory chrome; $1000 for engraving; $500 for NIROSTA marked barrel.

SA der NSDAP Gruppe Thuringen Marked Variation

Blued, C/N proofs, with magazine release button held by a screw. VERY RARE.

NIB	Exc.	V.G.	Good	Fair	Poor
—	5000	4000	2500	650	275

Model 38 pistols converted to H Models by Sauer factory

Currently there are fewer than 30 known examples in collections. The thumbsafety levers were added. Unique milling on the left side of the slide determines these pistols in the 262xxx, 263xxx and 264xxx ranges. This includes SA der NSDAP Gruppe Thüringen marked pistols.

MODEL 38-H OR H MODEL

This model has a thumbsafety on the slide, Crown N Nitro proof, high polish blued finish, a cocking/decocking lever, double-action, and is found in 7.65m/m caliber as the standard production pistol. This model is found only with the two line slide legend or logo. Type 1, variation 2.

Standard Commercial Variation

Blued, C/N proofs, with magazine release button held by a screw. VERY RARE.

NIB	Exc.	V.G.	Good	Fair	Poor
—	1200	900	600	300	175

NOTE: Add $100 for factory nickel (factory chromed has not been identified); $1000 for factory engraving; $250 for exotic grip material; $500 for NIROSTA marked stainless barrel.

SA der NSDAP Gruppe Thüringia Variation

Same as Standard. above except having SA markings on slide, with blued finish, VERY RARE.

NIB	Exc.	V.G.	Good	Fair	Poor
—	4000	3000	2500	900	400

NOTE: Add $700 for SA marked Akah holster in excellent condition.

L.M. Model

(Leicht Model-lightweight model); frame and slide made of DURAL (Duralumin), in the 264800 range, with thumb safety, and regular black Bakelite grips. EXTREMELY RARE.

NIB	Exc.	V.G.	Good	Fair	Poor
—	6500	5000	3000	1500	850

Flash Light Model

Only four known examples of this variation. Battery flash light attached by four screws to the pistol. Carried by the SS night partol at the Reich's chancellory in Berlin. No specific markings, but known serial numbers are 266814, 266842, 266845.

Too Rare To Price

Police Accepted Variation

Found with Police Eagle C acceptance on left trigger guard and having Crown N proofs. RARE.

NIB	Exc.	V.G.	Good	Fair	Poor
—	3000	2500	1850	500	175

TYPE TWO MODEL 38-H (H MODEL)

There are no Model 38 pistols in the Type Two description, only the H Model with thumbsafety. These begin at serial number 269100 and have the Eagle N Nitro proofs, with a blued high polish finish and black Bakelite grips. The normal caliber is 7.65mm.

A. H MODEL TYPE TWO

Standard Commercial

NIB	Exc.	V.G.	Good	Fair	Poor
—	1000	850	600	300	200

NOTE: Add $1500 for boxed examples complete with factory manual, clean ring rod, all accessories, extra magazine, etc. $250 for factory nickel, $350 for factory chrome, $1000 for factory engraving.

.22 Caliber Variation

Slide and magazines are marked CAL. .22 LANG. (Some with steel frame and slides; some with Dural frames and slides.) Found in 269900 range. Very Rare.

NIB	Exc.	V.G.	Good	Fair	Poor
—	6000	4500	3000	1000	600

Jager Model

A special order pistol in .22 caliber which is similar in appearance to Walther's 1936 Jagerschafts pistol. Very rare.

NIB	Exc.	V.G.	Good	Fair	Poor
—	6250	5000	3000	1000	400

Police Eagle C and Eagle F Acceptance Variations

These are the first Eagle N (post January 1940) police accepted pistols are found in the 270000 to 276000 ranges.

NIB	Exc.	V.G.	Good	Fair	Poor
—	1250	800	600	325	200

NOTE: Add 50 percent for E/F.

German Military Variation

This is the first official military accepted range of 2,000 pistols. It is in a range found between 271000 to 273000. Two Eagle 37 military acceptance marks are found on the trigger guard.

NIB	Exc.	V.G.	Good	Fair	Poor
—	2000	1500	1200	700	300

Second Military Variation

These pistols are found with the high polish finish but have only one Eagle 37 acceptance marks. The letter H is found on all small parts.

NIB	Exc.	V.G.	Good	Fair	Poor
—	1650	1450	800	400	200

Police Eagle C Acceptance

This variation includes the remainder of the high polish blued police accepted pistols.

NIB	Exc.	V.G.	Good	Fair	Poor
—	950	600	450	275	175

NOTE: Add $50 for matching magazine, $200 for both matching mags and correct police holster; $300 for both matching mags and correct matching numbered, police accepted and dated holster.

TYPE THREE 38-H MODEL (H MODEL)

This terminology is used because of the change of the exterior finish of the Sauer pistols. Due to the urgency of the war, the order was received to not polish the exterior surfaces of the pistols as had been done previously. There was also a change in the formulation of the grip's material. Later in this range there will be found stamped parts, zinc triggers and magazine bottoms, etc. used to increase the pistol's production. Type Three has a full slide legend.

A. H MODEL TYPE THREE

Military Accepted

One Eagle 37 Waffenamt mark.

NIB	Exc.	V.G.	Good	Fair	Poor
—	850	650	400	275	150

Commercial

Only Eagle N Nitro proof marks.

NIB	Exc.	V.G.	Good	Fair	Poor
—	725	500	400	250	150

NOTE: See Type Two Commercial, prices apply here also.

Police Accepted with the Police Eagle C Acceptance

NIB	Exc.	V.G.	Good	Fair	Poor
—	850	650	350	250	150

NOTE: See Type Two Police, prices apply here also.

TYPE FOUR 38-H MODEL (H MODEL)

This is a continuation of the pistol as described in Type Three except the J.P. Sauer & Sohn, Suhl legend is dropped from the slide and only CAL. 7.65 is found on the left side. The word PATENT may or may not appear on the right side. Many are found with a zinc trigger.

A. H MODEL TYPE FOUR

Military Accepted

One Eagle 37 Waffenamt mark.

NIB	Exc.	V.G.	Good	Fair	Poor
—	850	650	400	275	150

Commercial

Having only the Eagle N Nitro proofs.

NIB	Exc.	V.G.	Good	Fair	Poor
—	750	600	400	250	150

NOTE: See Type Two Commercial info, prices apply here also.

Police Accepted with the Police Eagle C Acceptance

NIB	Exc.	V.G.	Good	Fair	Poor
—	850	650	450	300	150

NOTE: See Type Two Price info, prices apply here also.

Eigentum NSDAP SA Gruppe Alpenland Slide Marked Pistols

These unique pistols are found in the 456000 and 457000 serial number ranges. They have thumb safety levers on the slides.

NIB	Exc.	V.G.	Good	Fair	Poor
—	4000	3000	2000	600	400

NSDAP SA Gruppe Alpenland Slide Marked Pistols

These unique pistols are found in the 465000 serial number range. They have thumbsafety levers on the slide.

NIB	Exc.	V.G.	Good	Fair	Poor
—	4000	3000	2000	600	400

Himmler Presentation Pistols

These desirable pistols have a high polish finish with DEM SCHARFSCHUTZEN - H. HIMMLER on the left side of the slide (with no other markings), and J.P. SAUER & SON over CAL. 7.65 on the right side (opposite of normal). These pistols came in imitation leather cover metal cases with cloth interiors having a cleaning brush, extra magazine and cartridges. Very rare pistols! Extremely rare if cased! Only 12 are known presently.

NIB	Exc.	V.G.	Good	Fair	Poor
—	25000	18500	12500	5000	1500

MODEL 38

To speed up production even more, the thumbsafety (Handsicherung-Hammer safety) was eliminated. The side continues to be marked only with CAL. 7,65. The frame's serial number changes from the right side to the left side at 472000 with overlaps up to 489000.

Military Accepted

One Eagle 37 Waffenamt mark.

NIB	Exc.	V.G.	Good	Fair	Poor
—	700	500	400	250	175

Commercial

Only the Eagle N Nitro proofs.

NIB	Exc.	V.G.	Good	Fair	Poor
—	600	475	350	250	175

NOTE: See Type Two Commercial info, prices apply here also.

Police Accepted with the Police Eagle C Acceptance

NIB	Exc.	V.G.	Good	Fair	Poor
—	700	500	400	300	200

Police Accepted with the Police Eagle F Acceptance

NIB	Exc.	V.G.	Good	Fair	Poor
—	750	600	500	250	175

NOTE: See Type Two Police info, prices apply here also.

TYPE FIVE MODEL 38 & H MODEL PISTOLS

There are two different basic variations of the Type Five Sauer pistols. Either may or may not have a thumbsafety lever on the slide. The main criteria is whether the frame is factory numbered as per normal and follows the chronological sequence of those pistols in the preceding model. After the frames were used which were already numbered and finished upon the arrival of the U.S. Army, the last variation came about. Neither variation has any Nitro proof marks.

NIB	Exc.	V.G.	Good	Fair	Poor
—	1800	750	450	250	175

First Variation

Factory numbered seequential frames starting on or near serial number 506800. Slides and breech blocks may or may not match.

NIB	Exc.	V.G.	Good	Fair	Poor
—	550	450	300	225	100

Second Variation

Started with serial number 1; made from mostly rejected parts, generally have notched trigger guards, may or may not be blued, no Nitro proofs, slides may or may not have factory legends, etc. Approximately 300 assembled. Defintely rare Sauer pistols!

NIB	Exc.	V.G.	Good	Fair	Poor
—	900	650	450	300	150

NOTE: There are some pistols which have post-war Russian Crown N Nitro proofs. The Russians assembled or refurbished a very few pistols after the U.S. Army left this section after the war. Several have been found with newly made barrels in 7.65mm with a C/N proof. A hard to find Sauer!

SAVAGE & NORTH
Middletown, Connecticut

FIGURE 8 REVOLVER

A .36 caliber percussion revolver with a 7" octagonal barrel and 6-shot cylinder. The barrel marked "E. Savage, Middletown. CT./ H.S. North. Patented June 17, 1856." The four models of this revolver are: (1) With a rounded brass frame, and the mouths of the chamber fitting into the end of the barrel breech; (2)

with a rounded iron frame and a modified loading lever that is marked "H.S. North, Patented April 6, 1858" ; (3) with a flat-sided brass frame having a round recoil shield; (4) with an iron frame. Approximately 400 of these revolvers were manufactured between 1856 and 1859.

First Model

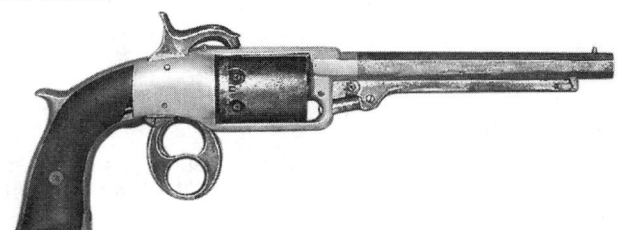

NIB	Exc.	V.G.	Good	Fair	Poor
—	—	16500	7250	1500	500

Second Model

NIB	Exc.	V.G.	Good	Fair	Poor
—	—	9900	3850	850	400

Third Model

NIB	Exc.	V.G.	Good	Fair	Poor
—	—	9900	3850	850	400

Fourth Model

NIB	Exc.	V.G.	Good	Fair	Poor
—	—	11000	4400	1000	450

SAVAGE ARMS CORPORATION
Utica, New York
Westfield, Massachusetts

Elbert Searle was granted a patent on an automatic pistol which utilized the bullet's torque to twist the barrel into a locking position with the slide. The patent also featured a double-row staggered magazine which increased the capacity over ordinary pistols. The patent was sold to Savage and the first Savage automatic pistol, the Model 1907 was produced.NOTE: Savage automatic pistols with the original cardboard box will bring between $50 and $100 premium. If the instruction pamphlet, cleaning brush, or other advertising material is present the price will escalate.

Model 1907

A .32 or .380 semi-automatic pistol with a 3.75" or 4.25" barrel depending upon caliber and a 9- or 10-shot magazine. Blued with hard rubber rectangular grips. This model is often incorrectly termed the Model 1905 or Model 1910.

NIB	Exc.	V.G.	Good	Fair	Poor
—	525	350	250	150	100

NOTE: The .380 caliber model is worth approximately 30 percent more than the values listed.

Model 1907 Portugese Contract

Similar to the commerical guns but with a lanyard ring same as the French contract model. Original Portugese pistols will have the Portugese Crest on the grips. Only about 1,150 of these pistols were produced. Very rare. Proceed with caution.

NIB	Exc.	V.G.	Good	Fair	Poor
—	1700	1250	950	600	300

MODEL 1915

Similar to the Model 1907, except fitted with a grip safety and with an internal hammer. Approximately 6,500 pistols were produced in .32 caliber and 3,900 in the .380 caliber. Manufactured between 1915 and 1917. The rarest of the regular-production Savage automatic pistols.

Courtesy Orvel Reichert

.32 Caliber

NIB	Exc.	V.G.	Good	Fair	Poor
—	650	550	400	300	200

.380 Caliber

NIB	Exc.	V.G.	Good	Fair	Poor
—	1000	750	600	450	300

Model 1917

As above, with an external hammer and without the grip safety. The form of the grip frame widened in a kind of trapezoidal shape. Manufactured between 1917 and 1928.

Model 1917 with watch fob for salesmen samples
Courtesy Bailey Brower, Jr., Copyright 2005, Bailey Brower, Jr.

NIB	Exc.	V.G.	Good	Fair	Poor
—	395	275	225	175	100

Model 6.35mm

A small number of .25 caliber Savage pistols were manufactured between 1915 and 1919. Perhaps less than 25 were built. There are two major variations of this pistol. First, is the wide or 10-serrations grip, and second the 27-serrations grip variation. This change occured around 1917. Magazine capacity was 6 to 7 rounds. Very rare.

Courtesy James Rankin

NIB	Exc.	V.G.	Good	Fair	Poor
—	8000	7000	4000	2500	1000

Model 1907 Test Pistol

Manufactured in 1907 in .45 ACP this pistol was tested in the U.S. Army trials. About 290 pistols were produced for these trials. Double-stack magazine held 8 rounds.

Courtesy Bailey Brower, Jr., Copyright 2005, Bailey Brower, Jr

NIB	Exc.	V.G.	Good	Fair	Poor
—	13500	11000	9500	6000	4000

Model 1910 Test Pistol

This was a modified Model 1907 with a heavier slide that was not concave like the Model 1907. There was a total of nine Model 1910s built. Too Rare To Price.

Model 1911 Test Pistol

This example was completely modified with a longer and thinner grip. Checkered wood grips were attached by friction instead of screws, the slide release was modified, a full grip safety was added, and a heavier serrated hammer (cocking lever) was added.

Four of these pistols were built. Serial #1 has never been located. Too Rare To Price.

Model 101

.22 caliber single-shot pistol resembling a revolver with a 5.5" barrel. Blued with hardwood grips. This pistol was made in Chicopee Falls or Westfield, Mass. Manufactured between 1960 and 1968.

NIB	Exc.	V.G.	Good	Fair	Poor
—	225	175	125	100	75

500 HANDGUN SERIES

Introduced in 1998 this line of short action handguns feature a left-hand bolt and a right-hand ejection. All are fitted with an internal box magazine, composite stock and 14" barrel.

Model 501F—Sport Striker

This handgun is fitted with a left-hand bolt and 10" free floating barrel. Detachable clip holds 10 rounds of .22 LR cartridges. Drilled and tapped for scope mount. Weight is about 4 lbs. Introduced in 2000.

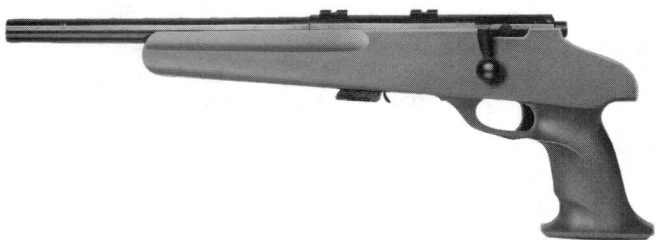

NIB	Exc.	V.G.	Good	Fair	Poor
350	295	250	175	150	100

Model 501FXP

Introduced in 2002 this model is similar to the one above but fitted with a 1.25-4x28mm scope with soft case.

NIB	Exc.	V.G.	Good	Fair	Poor
375	325	265	195	165	110

Model 502F—Sport Striker

Same as 501F but chambered for .22 WMR cartridge. Magazine capacity is 5 rounds. Introduced in 2000.

NIB	Exc.	V.G.	Good	Fair	Poor
375	325	265	195	165	110

Model 503F—Sport Striker

Same as the Model 502F-Sport Striker but chambered for the .17 HMR cartridge. Blued finish. Weight is about 4 lbs. Introduced in 2003.

NIB	Exc.	V.G.	Good	Fair	Poor
375	325	265	195	165	110

Model 503FSS—Sport Striker

As above but with stainless steel action and barrel.

NIB	Exc.	V.G.	Good	Fair	Poor
395	350	290	210	180	125

Model 510F Striker

Blued barrel action and chambered for .22-250, .243, or .308 calibers. Weight is approximately 5 lbs.

NIB	Exc.	V.G.	Good	Fair	Poor
475	400	350	295	175	150

Model 516FSS

Similar to the model above but with stainless steel barreled action.

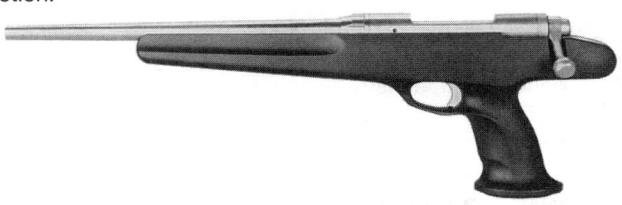

NIB	Exc.	V.G.	Good	Fair	Poor
495	425	365	310	195	150

Model 516FSAK

Features a stainless steel barreled action with adjustable muzzlebrake.

NIB	Exc.	V.G.	Good	Fair	Poor
525	450	395	345	225	165

Model 516FSAK Camo

As above but with Realtree Hardwood camo stock. Chambered for the .300 WSM cartridge. Weight is about 5.5 lbs. Introduced in 2002.

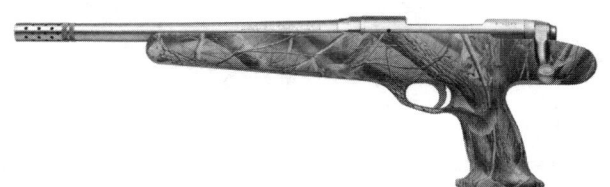

NIB	Exc.	V.G.	Good	Fair	Poor
600	525	450	300	235	75

Model 516BSS

Fitted with a laminated thumbhole stock, left-hand bolt for right-hand ejection, 14" barrel. This model is chambered for the .223, .243, 7mm-08 Rem., .260 Rem., and .308 Win. calibers. Magazine capacity is 2 rounds. Weight is about 5 lbs. Introduced in 1999.

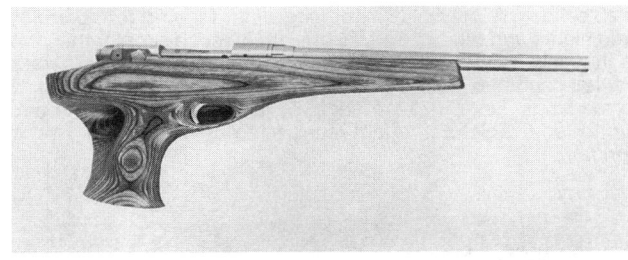

NIB	Exc.	V.G.	Good	Fair	Poor
600	525	450	300	235	75

Model 516BSAK

Similar to the model above but chambered for the .223 or .22-250 cartridges. The 14" barrel is fitted with an adjustable muzzlebrake. Introduced in 1999.

NIB	Exc.	V.G.	Good	Fair	Poor
600	525	450	300	235	75

SAVAGE REVOLVING FIREARMS CO.
Middletown, Connecticut

Navy Revolver

A .36 caliber double-action percussion revolver with a 7" octagonal barrel and 6-shot cylinder. The frame marked "Savage R.F.A. Co./H.S. North Patented June 17, 1856/Jan. 18, 1859, May 15, 1860." Approximately 20,000 were manufactured between 1861 and 1865, of which about 12,000 were purchased by the U.S. Government.

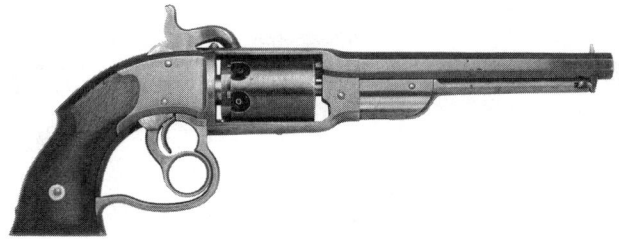

Courtesy Greg Martin Auctions

NIB	Exc.	V.G.	Good	Fair	Poor
—	—	4250	1750	700	500

SCHALL & CO.
New Haven, Connecticut

Manufactured the Fiala repeating pistol for Fiala. Later, after Fiala's bankruptcy, Schall provided parts, repair service, and produced repeating pistols with the Schall name. Marketed by Schall between about 1930 and 1935.

Repeating Pistol

A .22 caliber pistol with 10-shot magazine. Tapered 6.5" barrel with fixed sights and blued finish. Rear sight is much simpler than those on the Fiala. Grips are wood with ribs running lengthwise. Typically marked "schall & co./new haven, conn usa" but guns exist with no markings. Note that the original Fiala pistols had 7.5" barrels, but not so the Schalls (a fact revealed to us by our friend Jack in Florida).

Courtesy Dr. Jon Miller

NIB	Exc.	V.G.	Good	Fair	Poor
—	500	425	325	190	170

SCHMIDT, HERBERT
Ostheim, West Germany
Model 11, Liberty 11, and Eig Model E-8

A .22 caliber double-action revolver with a 2.5" barrel and 6-shot cylinder. Blued with plastic grips.

NIB	Exc.	V.G.	Good	Fair	Poor
—	125	80	60	40	25

Model 11 Target

As above, with a 5.5" barrel and adjustable sights.

NIB	Exc.	V.G.	Good	Fair	Poor
—	150	120	75	45	30

Frontier Model or Texas Scout

.22 caliber revolver with a 5" barrel and 6-shot cylinder. Blued with plastic grips.

NIB	Exc.	V.G.	Good	Fair	Poor
—	125	80	60	40	25

SCHMIDT & COMPANY, E.
Houston, Texas
Pocket Pistol

A .45 caliber percussion single-shot pistol with a 2.5" barrel, German silver mounts and walnut stock. The barrel marked "E. Schmidt & Co. Houston." Manufactured between 1866 and 1870.

NIB	Exc.	V.G.	Good	Fair	Poor
—	—	9000	4400	1000	350

SCHNEIDER & CO.
Memphis, Tennessee
Pocket Pistol

A .41 caliber single-shot percussion pocket pistol with a 3.5" octagonal barrel, iron or German silver mounts and a walnut stock.

The lock marked "Schneider & Co./Memphis, Tenn." Manufactured 1859 and 1860.

NIB	Exc.	V.G.	Good	Fair	Poor
—	—	4500	1850	650	300

SCHNEIDER & GLASSICK
Memphis, Tennessee
Pocket Pistols

A .41 caliber percussion pocket pistol with a 2.5" barrel, German silver mounts and walnut stock. The barrel marked "Schneider & Glassick, Memphis, Tenn." Manufactured 1860 to 1862.

NIB	Exc.	V.G.	Good	Fair	Poor
—	—	7000	5250	2500	800

SCHULER, AUGUST
Suhl, Germany
Reform

A 6.35mm caliber four-barreled pocket pistol with 2.5" barrels. The barrel unit rises as the trigger is pulled. Blued with walnut or hard rubber grips. Manufactured between 1907 and 1914.

NIB	Exc.	V.G.	Good	Fair	Poor
—	850	750	650	450	300

SCHWARZLOSE, ANDREAS
Berlin, Germany
Military Model 1898 (Standart)

A 7.63x25mm Borchardt or 7.63x25mm Mauser caliber semi-automatic pistol with a 6.5" barrel, rotary locked bolt, 7-shot magazine and adjustable rear sight. Weight is about 28 oz. Blued with walnut grips. The pistol was neither a commercial or military success, and fewer than 500 were made.

NIB	Exc.	V.G.	Good	Fair	Poor
—	—	20000	12000	5500	3000

SEAVER, E.R.
New York, New York
Pocket Pistol

A .41 caliber percussion pocket pistol with a 2.5" barrel, German silver mounts and a walnut stock.

NIB	Exc.	V.G.	Good	Fair	Poor
—	—	2300	1825	975	400

SECURITY INDUSTRIES
Little Ferry, New Jersey
Model PSS

A .38 Special double-action revolver with a 2" barrel, fixed sights and 5-shot cylinder. Stainless steel with walnut grips. Manufactured between 1973 and 1978.

NIB	Exc.	V.G.	Good	Fair	Poor
—	250	150	125	100	75

Model PM357

As above, with a 2.5" barrel and in .357 Magnum caliber. Manufactured between 1975 and 1978.

NIB	Exc.	V.G.	Good	Fair	Poor
—	300	200	175	150	100

Model PPM357

As above, with a 2" barrel and a hammer without a finger spur. Manufactured between 1975 and 1978.

NIB	Exc.	V.G.	Good	Fair	Poor
—	300	200	175	150	100

SEDCO INDUSTRIES, INC.
Lake Elsinore, California

This company was in business from 1988 to 1990.

Model SP22

A .22 caliber semi-automatic pistol with a 2.5" barrel. Blackened or nickel-plated with plastic grips. Introduced in 1989.

NIB	Exc.	V.G.	Good	Fair	Poor
125	90	65	50	35	25

SEECAMP, L. W. CO., INC.
Milford, Connecticut

LWS .25 ACP Model

A .25 caliber semi-automatic pistol with a 2" barrel, fixed sights and 7-shot magazine. Stainless steel with plastic grips. Approximately 5,000 were manufactured between 1982 and 1985.

NIB	Exc.	V.G.	Good	Fair	Poor
500	400	300	200	150	100

LWS .32 ACP Model

A .32 caliber double-action semi-automatic pistol with a 2" barrel and 6-shot magazine. Matte or polished stainless steel with plastic grips.

NIB	Exc.	V.G.	Good	Fair	Poor
525	450	400	350	200	150

Matched Pair

A matched set of the above, with identical serial numbers. A total of 200 sets were made prior to 1968.

NIB	Exc.	V.G.	Good	Fair	Poor
—	900	800	700	500	350

LWS .380 Model

Same as the .32 caliber but chambered for the .380 cartridge. Essentially the same weight and dimensions as the .32 caliber pistol. Introduced in 1999.

NIB	Exc.	V.G.	Good	Fair	Poor
900	650	500	400	300	100

SHARPS RIFLE MANUFACTURING COMPANY
Hartford, Connecticut

C. Sharps & Company and Sharps & Hankins Company Breechloading, Single-Shot Pistol

A .31, .34, or .36 caliber breechloading percussion pistol with 5" or 6.5" round barrels. Blued, case hardened with walnut stock.

Courtesy Buffalo Bill Historical Center, Cody, Wyoming

NIB	Exc.	V.G.	Good	Fair	Poor
—	—	7000	5000	2000	600

Percussion Revolver

A .25 caliber percussion revolver with a 3" octagonal barrel and

6-shot cylinder. Blued with walnut grips. The barrel marked "C. Sharps & Co., Phila. Pa." Approximately 2,000 were manufactured between 1857 and 1858.

NIB	Exc.	V.G.	Good	Fair	Poor
—	—	4250	3000	1250	500

4-SHOT PEPPERBOX PISTOLS

Between 1859 and 1874, these companies manufactured 4 barrel cartridge pocket pistols in a variety of calibers, barrel lengths and finishes. The barrels slide forward for loading. The major models are listed.

Courtesy Buffalo Bill Historical Center, Cody, Wyoming

Model 1

Manufactured by C. Sharps & Co. and in .22 rimfire caliber.

NIB	Exc.	V.G.	Good	Fair	Poor
—	—	800	600	250	100

Model 2

As above, in .30 rimfire caliber.

NIB	Exc.	V.G.	Good	Fair	Poor
—	—	800	600	250	100

Model 3

Manufactured by Sharps & Hankins and marked "Address Sharps & Hankins Philadelphia Penn." on the frame. Caliber. 32 short rimfire.

NIB	Exc.	V.G.	Good	Fair	Poor
—	—	950	750	300	150

Model 4

Similar to the above, in .32 Long rimfire and with a rounded bird's-head grip.

Courtesy John J. Stimson, Jr.

NIB	Exc.	V.G.	Good	Fair	Poor
—	—	950	750	300	150

SHATTUCK, C. S.
Hatfield, Massachusetts

Boom

A .22 caliber spur trigger revolver with a 2" octagonal barrel and 6-shot cylinder. Nickel-plated with rosewood or walnut grips. The barrel marked "Boom" and "Pat. Nov. 4. 1879." Manufactured during the 1880s.

NIB	Exc.	V.G.	Good	Fair	Poor
—	—	400	150	100	75

Pocket Revolver

A .32 caliber spur trigger revolver with a 3.5" octagonal barrel and 5-shot cylinder. Nickel-plated with hard rubber grips. The barrel marked "C. S. Shattuck Hatfield, Mass. Pat. Nov. 4, 1879." Manufactured during the 1880s.

NIB	Exc.	V.G.	Good	Fair	Poor
—	—	500	200	150	100

SHAW & LEDOYT
Stafford, Connecticut

Under Hammer Pistol

A .31 caliber under hammer percussion pistol with a 2.5" to 3.5" half-octagonal barrel. Blued with a brass mounted walnut grip. The frame marked "Shaw & LeDoyt/Stafford. Conn." Manufactured during the 1850s.

NIB	Exc.	V.G.	Good	Fair	Poor
—	—	1750	1300	550	150

SHAWK & McLANAHAN
St. Louis, Missouri

Navy Revolver

A .36 caliber percussion revolver with an 8" round barrel and 6-shot cylinder. Blued with a brass frame and walnut grips. Marked "Shawk & McLanahan, St. Louis, Carondelet, Mo." Produced in limited quantities prior to 1860.

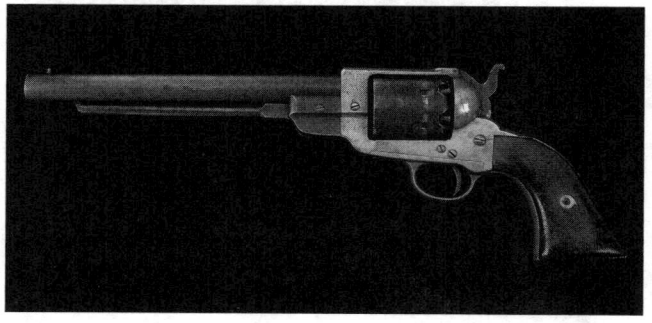

Courtesy Little John's Auction Service, Inc., Paul Goodwin photo

NIB	Exc.	V.G.	Good	Fair	Poor
—	—	15000	12000	5500	2000

SHERIDAN PRODUCTS, INC.
Racine, Wisconsin

Knockabout/Model D

A .22 caliber single-shot pistol with a 5" barrel having fixed sights. Blued with plastic grips. Manufactured between 1953 and 1960.

NIB	Exc.	V.G.	Good	Fair	Poor
—	350	225	175	100	50

SIG
Neuhausen, Switzerland

P 210

A 7.65mm or 9mm semi-automatic pistol with a 4.75" barrel and 8-shot magazine. Blued with plastic grips. In 1996 the 9mm version was the only one imported. Weight is about 32 oz.

NIB	Exc.	V.G.	Good	Fair	Poor
2300	1500	1300	1100	800	500

NOTE: For 1996 a .22 caliber conversion unit serialized to the gun was available. Add $600 for this option.

P 210-1

As above, with an adjustable rear sight, polished finish and walnut grips. Imported prior to 1987.

NIB	Exc.	V.G.	Good	Fair	Poor
2150	1700	1500	1150	800	400

P 210-2

NIB	Exc.	V.G.	Good	Fair	Poor
2000	1750	1350	1000	750	300

P 210-5

As above, with an extended length barrel, adjustable rear sight and walnut grips.

NIB	Exc.	V.G.	Good	Fair	Poor
2250	1850	1650	1000	800	400

P 210-6

As above, with a 4.75" barrel.

NIB	Exc.	V.G.	Good	Fair	Poor
2750	2250	1500	1150	800	400

SIG-HAMMERLI
Lenzburg, Switzerland

Model P240 Target Pistol

A .32 Smith & Wesson Long Wadcutter or .38 Midrange caliber semi-automatic pistol with a 5.9" barrel, adjustable rear sight, adjustable trigger and 5-shot magazine. Blued, with adjustable walnut grips. Imported prior 1987.

Courtesy John J. Stimson, Jr.

NIB	Exc.	V.G.	Good	Fair	Poor
—	1300	1150	950	750	600

.22 Conversion Unit

A barrel, slide, and magazine used to convert the above to .22 caliber.

NIB	Exc.	V.G.	Good	Fair	Poor
—	500	450	400	300	200

Model P208S

This is a semi-automatic target pistol chambered for the .22 LR cartridge. The barrel length is 5.9" long with adjustable sights. Sight radius is 8.2". Trigger has adjustable pull weight, travel, slack weight, and creep. Grips are stippled walnut with adjustable palm shelf. Weight is approximately 37 oz. empty.

NIB	Exc.	V.G.	Good	Fair	Poor
1900	1600	1300	1100	750	500

Model P280

This model is a semi-automatic pistol chambered for the .22 LR cartridge or the .32 S&W Long Wadcutter. Single-action-only. Barrel length is 4.6" with a sight radius of 8.7". Adjustable sights. Trigger is adjustable for pull weight, take-up, let-off, and creep. Stippled walnut grip with adjustable palm shelf. Weight is 35 oz. for the .22 caliber and 42 oz. for the .32 caliber. Magazine capacity is six .22 caliber rounds and five .32 caliber rounds.

NIB	Exc.	V.G.	Good	Fair	Poor
1200	10000	800	650	500	300

Model P160/162

This .22 LR single-shot pistol is designed for international free pistol competition. Barrel length is 11.3" with a sight radius of 14.6". Trigger is fully adjustable as are the sights. Stippled walnut grips with adjustable palm shelf and rake angle. The Model 160 has a mechanical trigger while the Model 162 is fitted with an electric trigger.

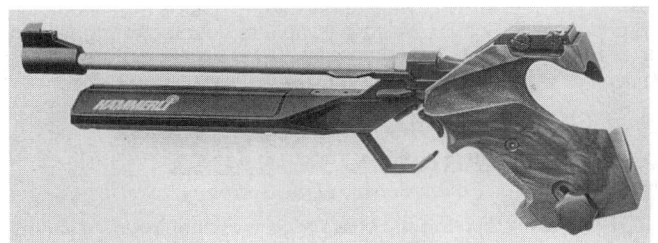

NIB	Exc.	V.G.	Good	Fair	Poor
2300	2000	1700	1250	800	400

Trailside PL 22

Introduced in 1999 this semi-automatic pistol is chambered for the .22 LR cartridge. Barrel length is 4.5" or 6" with fixed sights. Synthetic grips. Two-tone finish. Magazine capacity is 10 rounds. Weight is about 28 oz. with 4.5" barrel and 30 oz. with 6" barrel.

NIB	Exc.	V.G.	Good	Fair	Poor
575	500	375	295	200	100

NOTE: Add $90 for 6" barrel.

Trailside PL 22 Target

Similar to the PL 22 with the addition of adjustable sights and walnut grips. Introduced in 1999.

NIB	Exc.	V.G.	Good	Fair	Poor
595	525	400	325	225	125

NOTE: Add $25 for 6" barrel.

Trailside Competition

Introduced in 2004 this .22 caliber model features a 6" barrel with adjustable sights and adjustable competition grip, counterweights, and two-tone finish. Magazine capacity is 10 rounds. Weight is about 36 oz.

Similar to the above, with a checkered pistol grip stock and forend, a large Schuetzen style buttplate, double-set triggers and a vernier tang sight. Approximately 70 were manufactured.

NIB	Exc.	V.G.	Good	Fair	Poor
800	675	500	425	300	150

SIGARMS/SIG-SAUER
Eckernforde, West Germany

NOTE: SIGARMS currently offers an almost innumerable variety of semi-auto pistols. The main models are listed here. Values for similar models (i.e., those with similar model numbers) are generally comparable to the values given here with a 5-10 percent premium for scarce or desirable options.

CLASSIC SERIES

NOTE: For pistols with factory installed night sights add $90. Add $45 for pistols with K-Kote finish. Add $35 for nickel slides.

P210

This model was reintroduced into the U.S. in 2001 and is based on the Swiss military version first built in 1949. It is designed primarily as a target pistol and is furnished in four different variations. All variations are chambered for the 9mm cartridge. NOTE: Older P210 models imported before 1968 without importer stammps and pistols built during the late 1940s and early 1950s may bring a premium to the collector. Be aware that extra barrels, conversion kits, and other special order features will add additional value.

P210-8-9

This variation has adjustable target sights, select wood grips, lateral magazine catch, blued sandblasted finish, and adjustable trigger stop. Heavy frame. Barrel length is 4.8". Weight is about 37 oz.

NIB	Exc.	V.G.	Good	Fair	Poor
4275	3500	2750	2000	1000	500

P210-6-9

This variation has adjustable target sights, wood grips, target grade trigger, and blued sandblasted finish. Barrel length is 4.8". Weight is about 32 oz.

NIB	Exc.	V.G.	Good	Fair	Poor
2695	2000	1750	1400	800	500

P210-5-9

This variation has extended 5.85" barrel with compensator, ribbed front frame grip, wood grip plates, adjustable target sights, and target trigger. Weight is about 34 oz.

NIB	Exc.	V.G.	Good	Fair	Poor
4000	3500	3000	2400	1000	500

P210-2-9

This variation is similar to the Swiss Army service pistol and has wood grip plates and standard fixed sights. Barrel length is 4.8". Weight is about 32 oz.

NIB	Exc.	V.G.	Good	Fair	Poor
2200	1900	1600	1250	700	300

NOTE: A .22 LR conversion is available for the P210-2/5/6 series but not the P210-8. Retail price is $700.00.

P210-9-6S

This 9mm pistol is fitted with a heavy frame, target sights, wood grips, and U.S.-style magazine release. Introduced in 2004.

NIB	Exc.	V.G.	Good	Fair	Poor
3300	2950	2500	2000	1450	500

P220

This is a high-quality, double-action semi-automatic pistol chambered for .38 Super, .45 ACP, and 9mm Parabellum. It has a 4.41" barrel and fixed sights and features the de-cocking lever that was found originally on the Sauer Model 38H. There are two versions of this pistol—one with a bottom magazine release (commonly referred to as the European model) and the other with the release on the side (commonly referred to as the American model) as on the Model 1911 Colt. The frame is a lightweight alloy that is matte-finished and is available in either blue, nickel, or K-Kote finish with black plastic grips. The .45 ACP magazine capacity is 7 rounds and the pistol weighs 25.7 oz.; the .38 Super magazine capacity is 9 rounds and the pistol weighs 26.5 oz.; the 9mm magazine holds 9 rounds and the overall weight is 26.5 oz. This model was manufactured from 1976 and is still in production. The 9mm and .38 Super versions are no longer in production. The prices listed are for guns with a standard blue finish. **NOTE:** For the K-Kote finish add $40, for nickel slide add $40. Stainless steel add $100. In 2004 a blued version with tactical rail was offered.

NIB	Exc.	V.G.	Good	Fair	Poor
825	600	400	300	200	150

P220 .22

As above, chambered for the .22 LR cartridge.

NIB	Exc.	V.G.	Good	Fair	Poor
500	400	300	200	150	100

P220 ST

As above, chambered for the .45 ACP cartridge and features a stainless steel frame and slide with tactical rail. Also includes a SIGARMS tactical knife and aliminum carrying case. Weight is about 39 oz.

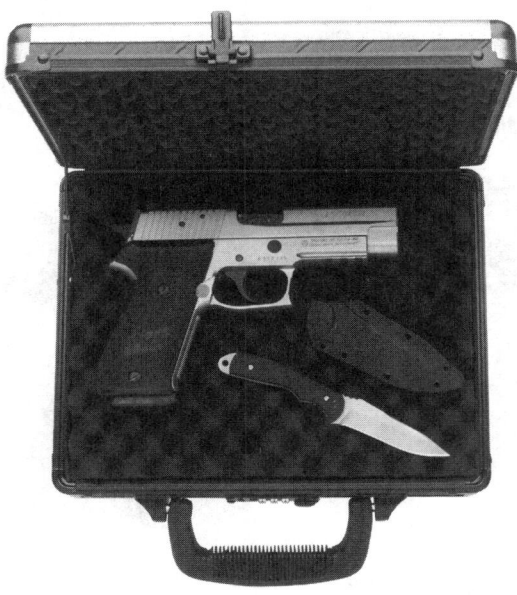

NIB	Exc.	V.G.	Good	Fair	Poor
875	700	550	425	300	150

P220 Sport

Introduced in 1999, this .45 ACP pistol is similar to the P220 with the addition of 5.5" barrel with stainless steel compensator. The frame and slide are stainless steel. Magazine capacity is 7 rounds. Weight is about 44 oz.

NIB	Exc.	V.G.	Good	Fair	Poor
1400	1250	1000	775	500	300

P220R SAO

An 8+1 or 10+1 capacity single-action semi-auto chambered for .45 ACP. Polymer grip and Nitron® finish, 4.4" barrel, 30.4 oz., 5-lb. trigger. Picatinny rail. Introduced 2006.

NIB	Exc.	V.G.	Good	Fair	Poor
750	600	475	350	200	150

P220R DAK

Semi-auto with 8+1 or 10+1 capacity chambered for .45 ACP. Polymer grip and Nitron® finish, 4.4" barrel, 30.4 oz., 7.5-lb. trigger. Picatinny rail. Introduced 2006.

NIB	Exc.	V.G.	Good	Fair	Poor
875	700	600	475	350	200

P220 SAS

An 8+1 capacity double-action semi-auto chambered for .45 ACP. Fixed sights, wood grips, 4.4" barrel, 30.4 oz., 6.5-lb. trigger. Introduced 2006.

NIB	Exc.	V.G.	Good	Fair	Poor
1000	875	725	600	400	200

P220 Carry SAS

An 8+1 capacity double-action semi-auto chambered for .45 ACP. Fixed sights, wood grips, 3.9" barrel, 30.4 oz., 6.5-lb. trigger. Introduced 2006.

NIB	Exc.	V.G.	Good	Fair	Poor
900	795	700	550	400	200

P220 Carry

An 8+1 or 10+1 capacity single/double-action semi-auto chambered for .45 ACP. Fixed sights, polymer grips, 3.9" barrel, 30.4 oz. Introduced 2006.

NIB	Exc.	V.G.	Good	Fair	Poor
875	725	600	450	350	200

P220R Equinox

An 8+1 or 10+1 capacity single/double-action semi-auto chambered for .45 ACP. Fixed sights, wood grips, 4.4" barrel, 30.4 oz. Introduced 2006.

NIB	Exc.	V.G.	Good	Fair	Poor
1200	1050	750	600	450	300

P220R Carry Equinox

An 8+1 or 10+1 capacity single/double-action semi-auto chambered for .45 ACP. Fixed sights, wood grips, 3.9" barrel, 30.4 oz. Introduced 2006.

NIB	Exc.	V.G.	Good	Fair	Poor
875	700	575	450	350	200

P220 Langdon Edition

This .45 ACP pistol, introduced in 2004, features a 4.4" barrel, Nill wood grips, fiber optic sight, competition rear sight, front serrations, short trigger and other special features. Two-tone finish. Magazine capacity is 8 rounds. Weight is about 41 oz. 500 manufactured.

NIB	Exc.	V.G.	Good	Fair	Poor
1300	1050	800	600	450	250

P220 Combat

Similar to P220 but with sand-colored alloy slide and steel frame. Available threaded barrel for suppressor. Capacity 8+1 or 10+1. Designed for SOCOM sidearm trials. Introduced in 2007.

NIB	Exc.	V.G.	Good	Fair	Poor
1100	950	750	600	400	200

P220 Match

Similar to P220 but with 5-inch barrel and adjustable sights. Introduced 2007.

NIB	Exc.	V.G.	Good	Fair	Poor
950	800	675	500	300	150

P220 Super Match

Super-accurized version of P220 Match with single-action-only trigger, beavertail safety and custom wood grips. Limited edition.

NIB	Exc.	V.G.	Good	Fair	Poor
1200	975	850	600	400	200

P220 Compact

Similar to P220 but with 3.9-inch barrel and 6+1 capacity. Single-action-only or single-/double-action. Various finishes, grip and sight options.

NIB	Exc.	V.G.	Good	Fair	Poor
950	800	675	500	375	200

P220 Elite

Similar to P220 but with SIG's new Short Reset Trigger or SRT. Beavertail safety, front cocking serrations, front strap checkering, SIGLITE® Night Sights and custom wood grips. Introduced in 2008. Also available in single action-only model.

NIB	Exc.	V.G.	Good	Fair	Poor
950	800	675	500	375	200

P220 Elite Stainless

Similar to above but in stainless. Introduced 2008.

NIB	Exc.	V.G.	Good	Fair	Poor
1250	1100	875	650	450	200

P220 Carry Elite Stainless

Compact version of above with 3.9-inch barrel; chambered in .45 ACP with 8-round capacity. Introduced 2008.

NIB	Exc.	V.G.	Good	Fair	Poor
1250	1100	875	650	450	200

P220 Platinum Elite

Fine-tuned, enhanced version of P220 Elite with front cocking serrations, front strap checkering, SIGLITE® Adjustable Combat Night Sights and custom aluminum grips.

NIB	Exc.	V.G.	Good	Fair	Poor
1000	825	700	550	400	200

P225

This is similar to the Model P220 except that it is chambered for 9mm cartridge. It is a more compact pistol, with a 3.86" barrel. It has an 8-shot detachable magazine and adjustable sights. The finish is matte blue. K-Kote, or electroless nickel plate with black plastic grips. The overall length is 7.1" with an overall height of 5.2". The pistol weighs 26.1 oz. No longer in production.

NIB	Exc.	V.G.	Good	Fair	Poor
625	575	500	400	200	150

NOTE: For K-Kote finish add $70. For nickel slide add $70.

P225 Limited

This 9mm 3.9" model features a Novak low-carry rear sight, three magazines, SIG-Sauer range bag. Introduced in 2004. Weight is about 26 oz.

NIB	Exc.	V.G.	Good	Fair	Poor
800	625	500	395	275	150

P226

This model is a full size, high-capacity pistol with a 4.41" barrel chambered for the 9mm or .40 S&W cartridge. In 1996 this model was also available chambered for the .357 SIG cartridge. It is available with a 15- or 20-round detachable magazine and high-contrast sights. It is either blued, electroless nickel plated, or has a polymer finish known as K-Kote. Overall length is 7.7" and overall height is 5.5". The pistol weighs 26.5 oz. This model was introduced in 1983. Add $50 for K-Kote finish and $50 for nickel slide. In 2003 this pistol was available with an integral rail system on the frame. In 2004 this pistol was offered with optional Crimson Trace laser grips.

NIB	Exc.	V.G.	Good	Fair	Poor
825	600	550	450	300	200

NOTE: Add $125 for Crimson Trace laser grips.

P226BR .22

Similar to above but in .22 LR.

NIB	Exc.	V.G.	Good	Fair	Poor
550	475	350	250	175	100

NOTE: Add $125 for Crimson Trace laser grips.

P226 Navy Seal

This special limited edition 9mm pistol is fitted with a 4.4" barrel and special serial numbers from "nsw0001" and above. Black finish.

NIB	Exc.	V.G.	Good	Fair	Poor
1400	900	750	550	400	300

P226 ST

Similar to P226 but with stainless steel frame and slide. Offered in 9mm, .40 S&W, and .357 SIG. Barrel length is 4.4". Magazine capacity is 10 rounds. Weight is about 39 oz. Introduced in 2002.

NIB	Exc.	V.G.	Good	Fair	Poor
1000	850	700	575	400	200

P226 Sport Stock

Introduced in 2002 this 9mm pistol features a heavy match barrel and adjustable rear sight. Hand tuned. Specifications are the same as the P226 ST. Available by special order only.

NIB	Exc.	V.G.	Good	Fair	Poor
1600	1450	1200	950	700	300

P226 Sport

Introduced in 2001 this model is similar to the other SIG Sport models and is chambered for the 9mm Luger cartridge. Stainless steel slide and frame with adjustable target sights and competition barrel weight.

NIB	Exc.	V.G.	Good	Fair	Poor
1350	1175	1000	850	700	300

JP226 Jubilee Pistol

This variation is a special limited edition of the P226. Each gun carries a special serial number prefixed JP. The grips are hand carved select European walnut. The slide and frame are covered with solid gold wire inlays, while the trigger, hammer, decocking lever, slide catch lever, and magazine catch are all gold plated. Each pistol comes in a custom fitted hard case of full leather. This pistol is no longer imported into the U.S. Fewer than 250 were imported between 1991 and 1992.

NIB	Exc.	V.G.	Good	Fair	Poor
1795	1500	1200	900	700	400

P226 ST

This .40 caliber model, introduced in 2004, features a reverse two-tone finish, 3-dot sights, and Hogue rubber grips. Weight is about 31 oz. Magazine capacity is 10 rounds.

NIB	Exc.	V.G.	Good	Fair	Poor
900	775	600	450	300	200

P226R DAK

Introduced in 2005 this model features double action only DAK trigger system with double strike capability. Chambered for the 9mm, .357 SIG, or .40 S&W cartridge with a 4.4" barrel. Fixed sights. Magazine capacity is 10, 12, or 15 rounds depending on caliber. Weight is about 32 oz. for 9mm and 34 oz. for .357 SIG or .40 S&W models.

NIB	Exc.	V.G.	Good	Fair	Poor
900	775	600	450	300	200

P226 X-Five

This single action model is chambered for the 9mm or .40 S&W cartridge and fitted with a 5" barrel. Adjustable rear sight and adjustable trigger pull. Slide has front cocking serrations. Checkered wood Null grips. Magazine capacity is 19 rounds for the 9mm and 14 rounds for the .40 S&W. Stainless steel finish. Weight is about 47 oz.

NIB	Exc.	V.G.	Good	Fair	Poor
1700	1525	1275	900	550	300

P226 Tactical

This 9mm pistol has a 4.98" extended threaded barrel. Fixed sights. Alloy frame. Magazine capacity is 15 rounds. Weight is about 32 oz. Black finish. Ellett Brothers exclusive. Introduced in 2005.

NIB	Exc.	V.G.	Good	Fair	Poor
900	795	600	450	300	150

P226 SAS

Double-action semi-auto with 12+1 capacity chambered for .40 S&W. Fixed sights, wood grips, 4.4" barrel, 34 oz., 6.5-lb. trigger. Introduced 2006.

NIB	Exc.	V.G.	Good	Fair	Poor
875	750	600	475	300	150

P226R Equinox

An 10+1 or 12+1 capacity single/double-action semi-auto chambered for .40 S&W. Fixed sights, wood grips, 4.4" barrel, 34 oz. Introduced 2006.

NIB	Exc.	V.G.	Good	Fair	Poor
1175	1025	875	700	550	350

P226 SCT

An all black, Nitron® finished P226 featuring front cocking serrations, a SIGLITE® rear night sight, a TRUGLO® tritium fiber optic front sight and comes with four newly designed 20-round magazines for the 9mm version or four 15-round magazines for the .40S&W version.

NIB	Exc.	V.G.	Good	Fair	Poor
950	825	700	575	400	200

P226 Elite

Introduced 2008. Similar to P226 but with redesigned short-reset trigger and improved ergonomics. Chambered in 9mm, .40 S&W and .357 SIG. Model P226 Enhanced Elite has same features as P226 Elite with the addition of ergonomic one-piece reduced-reach polymer grips.

NIB	Exc.	V.G.	Good	Fair	Poor
1050	900	825	675	450	250

P226 Elite Stainless

Similar to above but in stainless steel.

NIB	Exc.	V.G.	Good	Fair	Poor
1100	1000	900	750	475	275

P226 Platinum Elite

Fine-tuned, enhanced version of P226 Elite with front cocking serrations, front strap checkering, SIGLITE Adjustable Combat Night Sights and custom aluminum grips.

NIB	Exc.	V.G.	Good	Fair	Poor
1250	1175	950	775	500	300

Mosquito

This model is essentially a P226 reduced to 90 percent of its original size. Double action/single action trigger and fitted with a 3.98" barrel chambered for the .22 Long Rifle cartridge. Polymer frame with Picatinny rail. Fixed sights. Magazine capacity is 10 rounds. Weight is about 24.5 oz. Black finish. Introduced in 2005.

NIB	Exc.	V.G.	Good	Fair	Poor
325	300	250	200	150	100

P228

This model is a compact version of the P226 fitted with a 3.86" barrel and chambered for the 9mm cartridge. Like the P 226 it is available in blue, K-Kote, or nickel finish with black grips. Overall length is 7.1" and overall height is 5.4". Pistol weighs 26.1 oz. No longer in production.

NIB	Exc.	V.G.	Good	Fair	Poor
725	600	475	350	200	150

NOTE: For K-Kote finish add $50 and for nickel slide add $50.

P228 Limited (New Model)

Reintroduced in 2004 in a limited edition, this 9mm pistol features a Hi-Viz fiber optic front sight and 2-dot rear sight. One 15-round pre-ban magazine magazine included. Weight is about 26 oz.

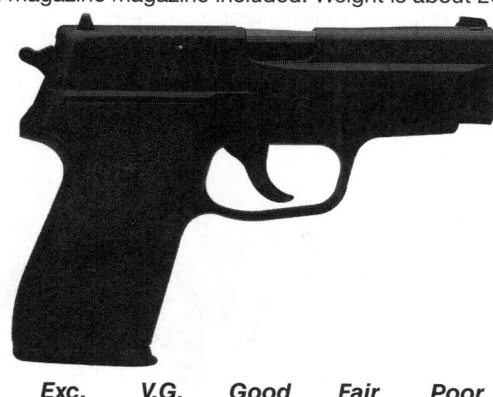

NIB	Exc.	V.G.	Good	Fair	Poor
800	675	550	400	250	150

P229

This model is similar to the P228 except that it is chambered for the .40 S&W cartridge and has a blackened stainless steel slide and lightweight aluminum alloy frame. The slide is slightly larger to accommodate the more powerful cartridge. In 1996 the 9mm chamber was also offered in this model. Its overall length is 7.1" and overall height is 5.4". Introduced in 1992. The pistol weighs 27.54 oz. and has a magazine capacity of 12 rounds. In 1994 the company introduced a new caliber for this model; the .357 SIG

developed by Federal. Magazine capacity is 12 rounds.

NIB	Exc.	V.G.	Good	Fair	Poor
800	675	550	400	250	150

P229 Nickel

Same as the standard P229 but with full nickel finish over a stainless steel slide and alloy frame. Weight is about 27.5 oz. Introduced in 1998.

NIB	Exc.	V.G.	Good	Fair	Poor
850	525	600	450	275	175

P229 Stainless

Introduced in 2005, has all the same features as the standard P229 except for the stainless steel slide and frame. Weight is about 41 oz. Magazine capacity is 12 rounds.

NIB	Exc.	V.G.	Good	Fair	Poor
900	775	600	475	300	150

P229 Sport

Chambered for the .357 SIG cartridge this model is fitted with a 4.8" barrel with a muzzle compensator. Adjustable target sights.

Both frame and slide are stainless steel. Magazine capacity is 10 rounds. Weight is approximately 41 oz. Introduced in 1998.

NIB	Exc.	V.G.	Good	Fair	Poor
1500	1350	1175	950	600	400

P229 Limited

This .40 S&W pistol features a 3.9" barrel with fixed sights. Stainless steel slide with Nitron® finish. Scroll engraving on top of slide, high polished 24 kt gold accents on trigger, hammer, magazine catch, and grip screws. Hardwood grips.

NIB	Exc.	V.G.	Good	Fair	Poor
950	825	675	500	350	200

P229 Combo

This pistol is chambered for the .40 S&W cartridge and fitted with a 3.9" barrel. Fixed sights. Black Nitron® finish. A spare barrel chambered for the .357 SIG is included. Magazine capacity is 10 rounds. Weight is about 30 oz. Introduced in 2004.

NIB	Exc.	V.G.	Good	Fair	Poor
900	775	625	450	300	175

P229 Elite

The P229 Elite features an ergonomic beavertail grip, front cocking serrations, front strap checkering, SIGLITE Night Sights, custom wood grips and the new Short Reset Trigger or SRT. Available in 9mm and .40 S&W. Model P229 Enhanced Elite has same features as P229 Elite with the addition of ergonomic one-piece reduced-reach polymer grips.

NIB	Exc.	V.G.	Good	Fair	Poor
1100	900	825	675	450	250

P229 Platinum Elite

Fine-tuned, enhanced version of P229 Elite with front cocking serrations, front strap checkering, SIGLITE® Adjustable Combat Night Sights and custom aluminum grips.

NIB	Exc.	V.G.	Good	Fair	Poor
1100	900	800	695	475	300

1911 C3

1911-style 6+1 autoloader in .45 ACP. 4-2/4-inch barrel, alloy frame. Introduced in 2008.

NIB	Exc.	V.G.	Good	Fair	Poor
900	775	600	475	300	150

1911 Platinum Elite

1911-style 8+1 autoloader in .45 ACP. 5-inch barrel, Nitron® frame, aluminum grips. Introduced in 2008.

NIB	Exc.	V.G.	Good	Fair	Poor
1100	950	800	675	500	300

1911 Platinum Elite Carry

Compact version of the above with 4.5-inch barrel. Introduced in 2008.

NIB	Exc.	V.G.	Good	Fair	Poor
1250	1025	875	750	575	350

Sig Sauer 1911-22

Same dimensions as standard 1911 pistol. Caliber .22 LR, alloy frame and slide, 10-round magazine, blowback operated, extended thumb safety, extended beavertail grip safety, magazine disconnect safety, skeletonized hammer and trigger. Weight: 18 ounces, Nitron® finish.

NIB	Exc.	V.G.	Good	Fair	Poor
340	285	235	200	165	100

Sig Sauer 1911 Scorpion

Caliber .45 ACP, stainless steel slide and frame, 8-round magazine, extended thumb safety, extended beavertail grip safety, skeletonized hammer and flat trigger, checkered front strap and mainspring housing, Low-Mount night sights and accessory rail. Frame and slide has Cerkote desert tan finish, grips are Hogue G10 Magwell with Piranha texture.

NIB	Exc.	V.G.	Good	Fair	Poor
975	850	700	500	300	150

Model GSR

This .45 ACP pistol was introduced in 2004. Fitted with a 5" barrel. Single-action only. It is offered with white stainless steel frame and slide or blued frame and slide. Also offered with black Nitron® finish. Tac rail standard. Hand fitted. Magazine capacity is 8 rounds. Weight is about 39 oz.

NIB	Exc.	V.G.	Good	Fair	Poor
775	650	500	375	250	150

REVOLUTION SERIES

Revolution

All-stainless frames and slides in four configurations. Novak Night Sights, Rose- or Diamond Wood custom grips. Stainless or Nitron® finish. 8+1 capacity, 45 ACP, single-action, 5" barrel, 40.3 oz. Introduced 2006.

NIB	Exc.	V.G.	Good	Fair	Poor
900	775	600	475	300	150

Revolution Custom STX

Single-action .45 ACP stainless semi-auto with 8+1 capacity. Adjustable combat night sights and custom wood grip panels, 5" barrel, 40.6 oz. Introduced 2006.

NIB	Exc.	V.G.	Good	Fair	Poor
1100	950	800	675	500	300

Revolution TTT

Stainless semi-auto with 8+1 capacity. Single-action .45 ACP. Adjustable combat night sights and custom wood grip panels, 5" barrel, 40.3 oz. Introduced 2006.

NIB	Exc.	V.G.	Good	Fair	Poor
1000	850	675	575	425	300

Revolution XO

Single-action .45 ACP stainless semi-auto with 8+1 capacity. Polymer grip panels. 8.65" LOA, 5" barrel, 40.3 oz. Introduced 2006.

NIB	Exc.	V.G.	Good	Fair	Poor
900	775	600	475	300	150

Revolution Target

Single-action .45 ACP stainless semi-auto with 8+1 capacity. Adjustable target night sights. Custom wood grip panels, 5" barrel, 40.3 oz. Stainless or Nitron® finish. Introduced 2006.

NIB	Exc.	V.G.	Good	Fair	Poor
950	825	650	495	325	150

Revolution Carry

Single-action .45 ACP stainless semi-auto with 8+1 capacity. Fixed sights. Custom wood grip panels, 4" barrel, 35.4 oz. Stainless or Nitron® finish. Introduced 2006.

NIB	Exc.	V.G.	Good	Fair	Poor
900	775	600	475	300	150

Revolution Compact

Stainless semi-auto single-action .45 ACP with 6+1 capacity. Fixed sights. Custom wood grip panels, 4" barrel, 30.3 oz. Stainless or Nitron finish. Introduced 2006.

NIB	Exc.	V.G.	Good	Fair	Poor
950	825	650	495	325	150

Revolution Compact SAS

Dehorned version of Revolution Compact.

NIB	Exc.	V.G.	Good	Fair	Poor
950	825	650	495	325	150

Revolution Compact C3

Similar to Revolution Compact but with black anodized alloy frame and stainless or Nitron®-finished slide.

NIB	Exc.	V.G.	Good	Fair	Poor
950	825	650	495	325	150

Revolution Custom Compact RCS

Stainless semi-auto single-action .45 ACP with 6+1 capacity. Fixed sights. Custom wood grip panels, 4" barrel, 30.3 oz. Stainless or Nitron® finish. Introduced 2006.

NIB	Exc.	V.G.	Good	Fair	Poor
950	825	650	495	325	150

P229R DAK

Introduced in 2005 this model features double action only DAK trigger system with double strike capability. Chambered for the 9mm, .357 SIG, or .40 S&W cartridge with a 4.4" barrel. Fixed sights. Magazine capacity is 10, 12, or 15 rounds depending on caliber. Weight is about 32 oz. for 9mm and 34 oz. for .357 SIG or .40 S&W models.

NIB	Exc.	V.G.	Good	Fair	Poor
850	525	600	450	275	175

P229 SCT

All black, Nitron® finished P229 featuring front cocking serrations, a SIGLITE® rear night sight, a TRUGLO® tritium fiber optic front sight and comes with four newly designed 17-round magazines for the 9mm version or four 14-round magazines for the .40S&W version.

NIB	Exc.	V.G.	Good	Fair	Poor
1100	950	800	675	500	300

P239

Introduced in 1996 this pistol is chambered for the 9mm, .40 S&W, or .357 SIG cartridge. It is double/single-action or double-action-only. The barrel is 3.6" long and the overall length is 6.6". Weight is 25 oz. It is fitted with a single column magazine with 7 rounds for the .357 SIG and 8 rounds for the 9mm.

NIB	Exc.	V.G.	Good	Fair	Poor
725	600	475	350	200	150

NOTE: All of the above SIG pistols from the P220 to the P239 are available with SIGLITE® night sights. Add $80 for these optional sights.

P239 Limited

This .40 S&W model features a rainbow titanium slide. Trigger, hammer, grip screws, and control levers also rainbow titanuim. Magazine capacity is 7 rounds. Weight is about 27 oz. Introduced in 2004.

NIB	Exc.	V.G.	Good	Fair	Poor
725	600	475	350	200	150

P230

This is a semi-automatic, compact, pocket-type pistol chambered for .22 LR, .32 ACP, .380 ACP, and 9mm Ultra. It has a 3.62" barrel and either a 10-, 8-, or 7-round magazine, depending on the caliber chambered. The pistol weighs between 16.2 oz. and 20.8 oz. The finish is blued or stainless, with black plastic grips; and it was manufactured from 1976. In 1996 a two-tone finish was offered. No longer in production.

NIB	Exc.	V.G.	Good	Fair	Poor
450	375	300	250	200	150

NOTE: For stainless steel finish add $85 and for stainless steel slide add $35.

P232

An improved model of the P230. Incorporates numerous changes to improve function and reliability. Basic features, operation, and dimensions remain the same as the P230.

NIB	Exc.	V.G.	Good	Fair	Poor
450	375	300	250	200	150

P232 (1998 Model)

In 1998 this model has as standard features night sights and Hogue grips with an all stainless steel finish. Chambered for .380 ACP, the pistol has a 7-round magazine capacity. Weight is about 21 oz.

NIB	Exc.	V.G.	Good	Fair	Poor
500	375	300	250	200	150

P232 Limited

This .380 pistol features a black finish, night sights, and satin nickel accents. Hogue rubber grips with finger grooves. Magazine capacity is 7 rounds. Weight is about 28 oz. Introduced in 2004.

NIB	Exc.	V.G.	Good	Fair	Poor
575	450	375	250	200	100

P245 Compact

Introduced in 1999 this model is chambered for the .45 ACP cartridge. It is fitted with a 3.9" barrel. Magazine capacity is 6 rounds. Overall length is 7.3". Weight is about 28 oz. Available finishes are blue and K-Kote. SIGLITE night sights are also available.

NIB	Exc.	V.G.	Good	Fair	Poor
775	650	500	375	250	150

P245 Custom Shop

Introduced in 2004 this .45 ACP pistol is limited to 75 guns. It features a Teflon-impregnated nickel slide, frame, trigger, hammer, etc. Hand-tuned action. Target crowned barrel. Novak low-carry sights, limited edition markings. Weight is about 27 oz.

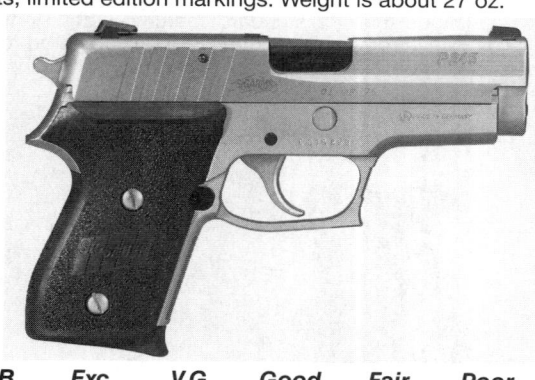

NIB	Exc.	V.G.	Good	Fair	Poor
2100	1700	1450	1000	600	350

P250 Compact

Introduced in 2008. A 9mm semiauto pistol of so-called "modular design" that enables the shooter to quickly remove the functional mechanism and place it into the polymer grip of his choice. This allows an immediate change in caliber and size; (subcompact, compact and full). And after any change the pistol delivers both outstanding accuracy and reliable functionality. Its modularity not only provides incredible ease of maintenance, but also provides a solution for accommodating different hand sizes— there are 6 different ergonomic combinations for each size, accomplished by changes in grip circumference and trigger style. Matte or duotone finish.

NIB	Exc.	V.G.	Good	Fair	Poor
650	525	450	375	300	150

Sig Sauer P290

New micro-compact pistol for concealed carry. Caliber 9mm Parabellum, is double-action only with stainless steel slide, polymer frame, 6-round magazine, three-dot sights and removable grip panels. Weight is 20.5 ounces, barrel length 2.9-inches. Finish is Nitron® or two-tone stainless. Available with detachable laser sight.

NIB	Exc.	V.G.	Good	Fair	Poor
650	550	465	400	325	150

NOTE: Add $70 for laser sight.

SIG PRO SERIES
SP2340

Introduced in 1998 this model is chambered for the .357 SIG or .40 S&W cartridge. It is built on a polymer frame with accessory rails on the dust cover. Barrel length is 3.9". Standard finish is blue. Weight is about 28 oz. Comes with two sets of interchangeable grips and two 10-round magazines. Available in single-action/double-action or double-action-only.

NIB	Exc.	V.G.	Good	Fair	Poor
650	525	450	375	300	150

SP2009

Similar to the SP2340 but chambered for the 9mm cartridge. Weight is about 25 oz. Magazine capacity is 10 rounds.

NIB	Exc.	V.G.	Good	Fair	Poor
500	425	350	225	175	100

SP2022

Chambered for the 9mm, .357 SIG, or .40 S&W cartridges and fitted with a 3.85" barrel with fixed sights. Polymer frame. Black finish. Weight is about 27 to 30 oz. depending on caliber. Magazine capacity is 10 or 12 rounds depending on caliber.

NIB	Exc.	V.G.	Good	Fair	Poor
575	450	325	250	200	150

SIMPLEX
Unknown

Simplex

A German design based on the Bergmann-Mars pistol. An 8mm caliber semi-automatic pistol with a 2.6" barrel and a front mounted 5-round magazine. Blued with hard rubber grips having the trade name "Simplex" cast in them. Manufactured from approximately 1901 to around 1906. Early samples may have come from Germany and later pistols are thought to have been produced in Belgium.

NIB	Exc.	V.G.	Good	Fair	Poor
—	1650	1050	550	400	200

SIMPSON, R. J.
New York, New York

Pocket Pistol

A .41 caliber single-shot percussion pocket pistol with a 2.5" barrel, German silver mounts and walnut stock. Manufactured during the 1850s and 1860s.

NIB	Exc.	V.G.	Good	Fair	Poor
—	—	2400	1750	700	300

SIMSON & COMPANY
Suhl, Germany

SEE—Luger

NOTE: The models listed are taken from a mid-1930s Simson catalog. Because the company was Jewish-owned the Nazis took control in the mid-1930s changing the name to "Berlin Suhler Waffen." Prices are estimates.

Model 1922

A 6.35mm semi-automatic pistol with a 2" barrel and 6-shot magazine. The slide marked "Selbstlade Pistole Simson DRP" and "Waffenfabrik Simson & Co Suhl." Blued, with black plastic grips.

NIB	Exc.	V.G.	Good	Fair	Poor
—	600	475	400	300	100

Model 1927

Similar to the above, with a slimmer frame stamped with the trademark of three overlapping triangles having the letter "S" enclosed.

NIB	Exc.	V.G.	Good	Fair	Poor
—	600	475	400	300	100

SIRKIS INDUSTRIES, LTD.
Ramat-Gan, Israel

SD9

A 9mm double-action semi-automatic pistol with a 3" barrel, fixed sights and 7-shot magazine. Blued with plastic grips. Also known as the Sardius.

NIB	Exc.	V.G.	Good	Fair	Poor
—	325	275	225	175	100

SLOTTER & CO.
Philadelphia, Pennsylvania

Pocket Pistol

A .41 caliber percussion pocket pistol with a 2.5" to 3.5" barrel, German silver mounts and walnut stock. Marked "Slotter & Co. Phila." Manufactured during 1860s.

NIB	Exc.	V.G.	Good	Fair	Poor
—	—	3000	2200	950	250

SMITH, OTIS
Rockfall, Connecticut

This company manufactured a line of single-action, spur-trigger revolvers that are chambered for .22, .32, .38, and .41 rimfire cartridges. The pistols have varying barrel lengths. The cylinder access pin is retained by a button on the left side of the frame. The cylinder usually holds five shots. The finishes are either blued or nickel-plated, with bird's-head grips. The quality was considered to be mediocre.

Model 1883 Shell-Ejector

A single-action, break-open, self ejecting revolver with a ribbed 3.5" barrel chambered for .32 centerfire. It has a 5-shot fluted cylinder and a spur trigger. It was quite well made. The finish is nickel-plated, with black plastic grips.

NIB	Exc.	V.G.	Good	Fair	Poor
—	—	500	275	100	75

Model 1892

A double-action, concealed-hammer revolver chambered for the .38 centerfire cartridge. It has a 4" barrel and, for the first time, a conventional trigger and trigger guard. It is gateloaded and has a solid frame. It is nickel-plated with black plastic grips and also appeared under the Maltby, Henley & Company banner marked "Spencer Safety Hammerless" or "Parker Safety Hammerless." The Otis Smith Company ceased operations in 1898.

NIB	Exc.	V.G.	Good	Fair	Poor
—	—	500	275	100	75

SMITH & WESSON
Springfield, Massachusetts

SMITH & WESSON ANTIQUE HANDGUNS

NOTE: A surprising number of pistols are still found in their original boxes, even for older models. This can add 100 percent to the value of the pistol.

MODEL 1, 1ST ISSUE REVOLVER

This was the first metallic-cartridge arm produced by Smith & Wesson. It is a small revolver that weighs approximately 10 oz. and is chambered for the .22 Short rimfire cartridge. The octagonal barrel is 3.25" long. It holds 7 cartridges. The barrel and nonfluted cylinder pivot upward upon release of the under the frame. This model has a square butt with rosewood grips. The oval brass frame is silver-plated. The barrel and cylinder are blued. The barrel is stamped with the company name and address; the patent dates also appear. The sides of the frame are rounded on the 1st issue.

Other characteristics which distinguish the more valuable 1st issue from later issues include a perfectly round side plate and a hinged hammer spur. Smith & Wesson manufactured approximately 11,000 of these revolvers between 1857 and 1860. Since this was the first of its kind, it is not difficult to understand the need for the number of variations within this model designation. Many small improvements were made on the way to the next model. These variations are as follows:

1st Type

Serial range 1 to low 200s, revolving recoil shield, bayonet type catch on frame.

NIB	Exc.	V.G.	Good	Fair	Poor
—	—	15000	10000	8000	1000

NOTE: Rarity makes valuation speculative.

2nd Type

Serial range low 200s to 1130, improved recoil plate.

NIB	Exc.	V.G.	Good	Fair	Poor
—	—	10000	6000	2500	500

3rd Type

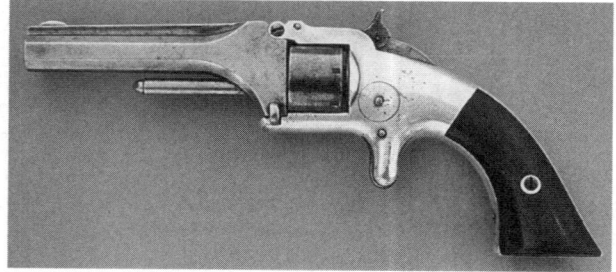

Serial range 1130 to low 3000s, bayonet catch dropped for spring-loaded side catch.

NIB	Exc.	V.G.	Good	Fair	Poor
—	—	5500	4000	2500	500

4th Type

Serial range low 3000s to low 4200s, recoil shield made much smaller.

NIB	Exc.	V.G.	Good	Fair	Poor
—	—	2250	1800	1250	300

5th Type

Serial range low 4200s to low 5500s, has 5-groove rifling instead of 3.

NIB	Exc.	V.G.	Good	Fair	Poor
—	—	2250	1800	1250	300

6th Type

Serial range low 5500s to end of production 11670. A cylinder ratchet replaced the revolving recoil shield.

NIB	Exc.	V.G.	Good	Fair	Poor
—	—	1600	1400	1000	250

Model 1 2nd Issue

Similar in appearance to the 1st Issue this 2nd Issue variation has several notable differences that make identification rather simple. The sides of the frame on the 2nd Issue are flat not rounded as on the 1st Issue. The sideplate is irregular in shape—not round like on the 1st Issue. The barrel was 3-3/16" in length. The barrel is stamped "Smith & Wesson" while the cylinder is marked with the three patent dates: April 3, 1858, July 5 1859, and December 18, 1860. There have been 2nd Issue noted with full silver or nickel-plating. Smith & Wesson manufactured approximately 115,000 of these revolvers between 1860 and 1868. The serial numbers started around 1100 where the 1st Issue left off and continued to 126400. There were approximately 4,400 revolvers marked "2D Quality" on the

barrels. These revolvers were slightly defective and were sold at a lesser price. They will bring an approximate 100 percent premium on today's market.

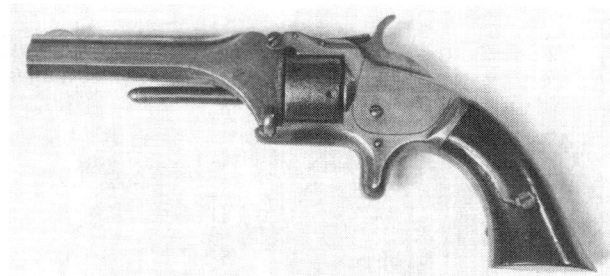

Courtesy Mike Stuckslager

NIB	Exc.	V.G.	Good	Fair	Poor
—	—	750	600	250	100

MODEL 1 3RD ISSUE

This is a redesigned version of its forerunners. Another .22 Short rimfire, 7-shot revolver, this model has a fluted cylinder and round barrel with a raised rib. This variation was manufactured totally from wrought iron. The three patent dates are stamped on top of the ribbed barrel as is "Smith & Wesson." It features bird's-head type grips of rosewood and is either fully blued nickel-plated, or two-toned with the frame nickel and the barrel and cylinder blued. There are two barrel lengths offered: 3.25" and 2-11/16". The shorter barrel was introduced in 1872. Serial numbering began with #1 and continued to 131163. They were manufactured between 1868 and 1882. The Model 1 3rd Issue was the last of the tip-up style produced by Smith & Wesson.

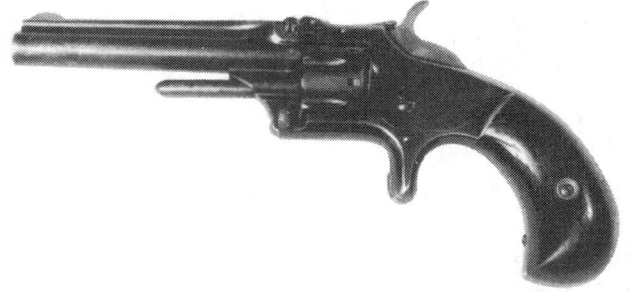

Courtesy Mike Stuckslager

Shorter Barreled Version

Rare.

NIB	Exc.	V.G.	Good	Fair	Poor
—	—	1350	800	400	100

Longer Barreled Version

Standard.

NIB	Exc.	V.G.	Good	Fair	Poor
—	—	500	275	200	100

Model 1-1/2 1st Issue (1-1/2 Old Model)

This model was the first of the .32-caliber Rimfire Short revolvers that S&W produced. It is a larger version of the Model 1 but is physically similar in appearance. The Model 1-1/2 was offered with a 3.5" octagonal barrel and has a 5-shot nonfluted cylinder and a square butt with rosewood grips. In 1866 a 4" barrel version was produced for a short time. It is estimated that about 200 were sold. The finish is blued or nickel-plated. The serial numbering on this model ran from serial number 1 to 26300; and, interestingly to note, S&W had most of the parts for this revolver manufactured on contract by King & Smith of Middletown, Connecticut. Smith & Wesson merely assembled and finished them. They were produced between 1865 and 1868.

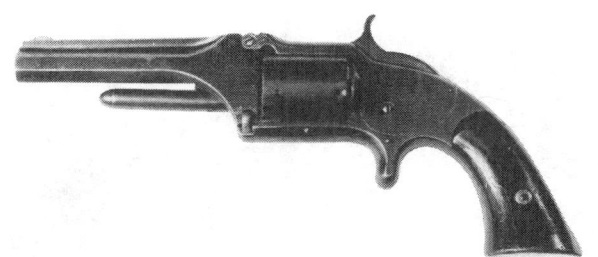

Courtesy Mike Stuckslager

NIB	Exc.	V.G.	Good	Fair	Poor
—	795	650	400	200	100

NOTE: Add a 50 percent premium for the 4" barrel variation.

MODEL 1-1/2 2ND ISSUE (1-1/2 NEW MODEL)

The factory referred to this model as the New Model 1-1/2 and it is an improved version of the 1st Issue. It is somewhat similar in appearance with a few notable exceptions. The barrel is 2.5" or 3.5" in length, round with a raised rib. The grip is of the bird's-head configuration, and the 5-shot cylinder is fluted and chambered for the .32 Long rimfire cartridge. The cylinder stop is located in the top frame instead of the bottom. The finish and grip material are the same as the 1st Issue. There were approximately 100,700 manufactured between 1868 and 1875.

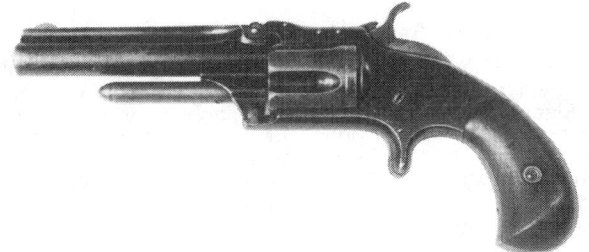

Courtesy Mike Stuckslager

3.5" Barrel

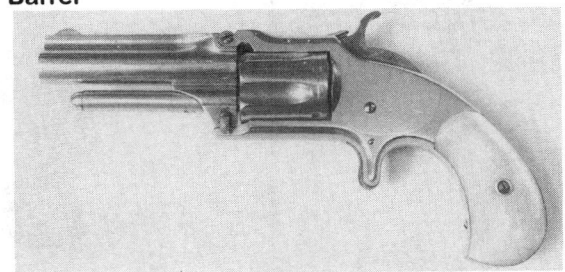

Courtesy Mike Stuckslager

NIB	Exc.	V.G.	Good	Fair	Poor
—	—	650	375	175	100

2.5" Barrel
Rare.

NIB	Exc.	V.G.	Good	Fair	Poor
—	—	1100	600	350	100

Model 1-1/2 Transitional Model

Approximately 650 of these were produced by fitting 1st Issue cylinders and barrels to 2nd Issue frames. They also have 1st Model octagon barrels with 2nd Model bird's-head grips. These revolvers fall into the serial number range 27200-28800.

NIB	Exc.	V.G.	Good	Fair	Poor
—	—	3000	1500	800	300

MODEL 2 ARMY OR OLD MODEL

Similar in appearance to the Model 1 2nd Issue, this revolver was extremely successful from a commercial standpoint. It was released just in time for the commencement of hostilities in the Civil War. Smith & Wesson had, in this revolver, the only weapon able to fire self-contained cartridges and be easily carried as a backup by soldiers going off to war. This resulted in a backlog of more than three years before the company finally stopped taking orders. This model is chambered for .32 Long rimfire cartridge and has a 6-shot nonfluted cylinder and 4", 5", or 6" barrel lengths. It has a square butt with rosewood grips and is either blued or nickel-plated. There were approximately 77,155 manufactured between 1861 and 1874.

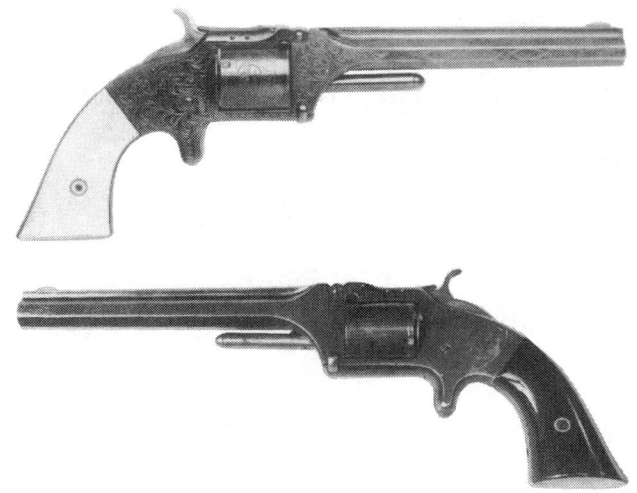

Courtesy Chester Krause

5" or 6" Barrel
Standard barrel.

NIB	Exc.	V.G.	Good	Fair	Poor
—	2450	1500	950	450	300

4" Barrel
Rare, use caution.

NIB	Exc.	V.G.	Good	Fair	Poor
—	—	6000	3650	1500	500

NOTE: A slight premium for early two-pin model. For rare 8-inch model add 800 percent.

.32 SINGLE-ACTION (SO-CALLED "1-1/2 FRAME" CENTERFIRE)

This model represented the first .32 S&W centerfire caliber top-break revolver that automatically ejected the spent cartridges upon opening. It is similar in appearance to the Model 1-1/2 2nd Issue. This model has a 5-shot fluted cylinder and a bird's-head grip of wood or checkered hard rubber and was offered with barrel lengths of 3", 3.5", 6", 8", and 10". The 8" and 10" barrel are rare and were not offered until 1887. This model pivots downward on opening and features a rebounding hammer that made the weapon much safer to fully load. There were approximately 97,599 manufactured between 1878 and 1892.

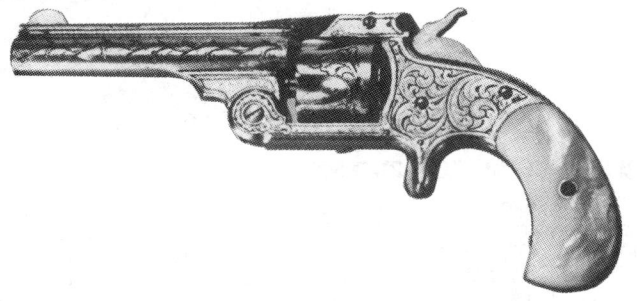

Courtesy W.P. Hallstein III and son Chip

Early Model w/o Strain Screw—Under #6500

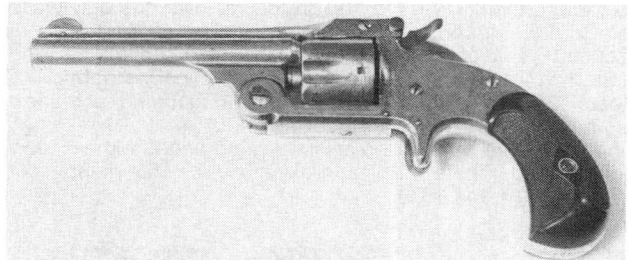

Courtesy Mike Stuckslager

NIB	Exc.	V.G.	Good	Fair	Poor
—	1200	600	300	175	75

Later Model with Strain Screw

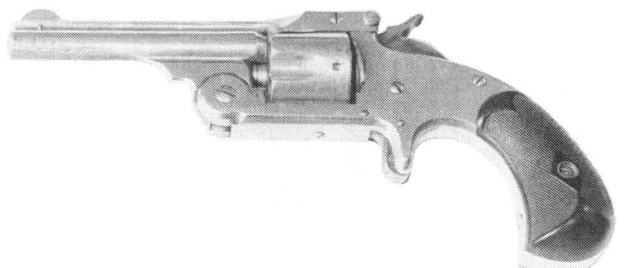

Courtesy Mike Stuckslager

NIB	Exc.	V.G.	Good	Fair	Poor
—	1000	450	300	150	75

8" or 10" Barrel

Very rare; use caution.

NIB	Exc.	V.G.	Good	Fair	Poor
—	—	4500	2500	800	400

.38 Single-Action 1st Model (Baby Russian)

This model is sometimes called the "Baby Russian." It is a top break, automatic-ejecting revolver chambered for the .38 S&W centerfire cartridge. Offered with either a 3.25" or 4" round barrel with a raised rib, has a 5-shot fluted cylinder, and finished in blue or nickel plating. A 5" barrel was added as an option a short time later. The butt is rounded, with wood or checkered hard rubber grips inlaid with the S&W medallion. It has a spur trigger. Approximately 25,548 were manufactured in 1876 and 1877, of which 16,046 were nickel and 6,502 were blued.

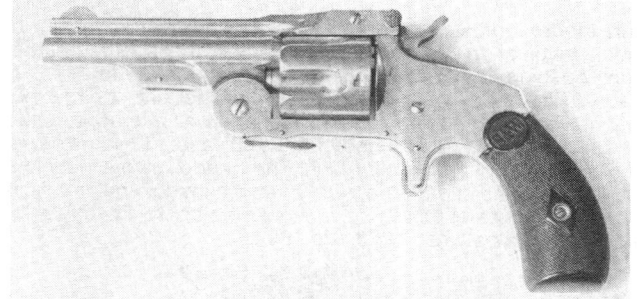

Courtesy Mike Stuckslager

NIB	Exc.	V.G.	Good	Fair	Poor
—	2000	1200	900	350	150

.38 SINGLE-ACTION 2ND MODEL

With the exception of an improved and shortened extractor assembly and the availability of additional barrel lengths of 3.25", 4", 5", 6", 8", and 10" with the 8" and 10" barrel lengths being the most rare, this model is quite similar in appearance to the 1st Model. There were approximately 108,225 manufactured between 1877 and 1891.

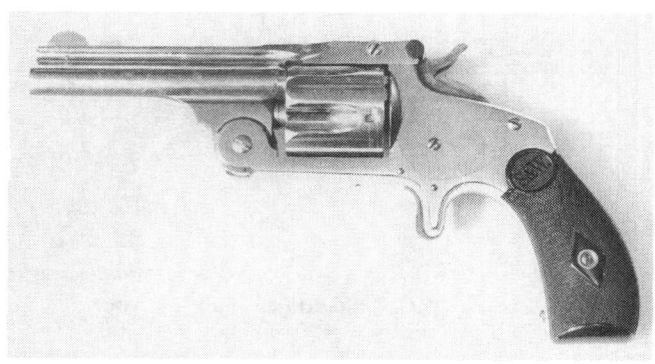

Courtesy Mike Stuckslager

8" and 10" Barrel

Very rare, use caution.

NIB	Exc.	V.G.	Good	Fair	Poor
—	—	4000	2250	950	500

3.25", 4", 5", and 6" Barrel Lengths

Small premium for 5" or 6" lengths.

NIB	Exc.	V.G.	Good	Fair	Poor
—	700	350	225	175	75

.38 Single-Action 3rd Model

This model differs from the first two models because it is fitted with a trigger guard. It is chambered for the .38 S&W centerfire cartridge, has a 5-shot fluted cylinder, and is a top break design with automatic ejection upon opening. The barrel lengths are 3.25", 4", and 6". The finish is blued or nickel-plated. The butt is rounded, with checkered hard rubber grips featuring S&W medallions. There were approximately 26,850 manufactured between 1891 and 1911.

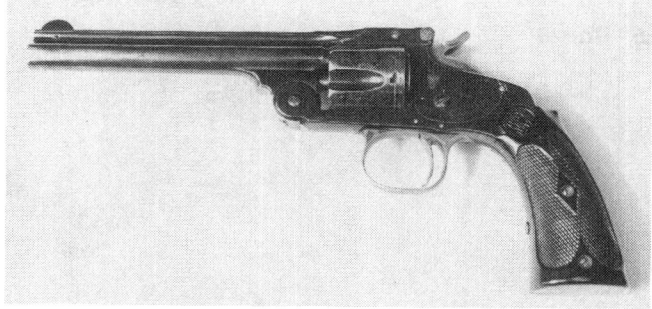

Courtesy Mike Stuckslager

NIB	Exc.	V.G.	Good	Fair	Poor
—	—	1300	1000	600	200

.38 Single-Action Mexican Model

This extremely rare model is quite similar in appearance to the 3rd Model Single-Action. The notable differences are the flat hammer sides with no outward flaring of the spur. The spur trigger assembly was not made integrally with the frame but is a separate part added to it. One must exercise extreme caution as S&W offered a kit that would convert the trigger guard assembly of the Third Model to the spur trigger of the Mexican Model. This, coupled with the fact that both models fall within the same serial range, can present a real identification problem. Another feature of the Mexican Model is the absence of a half cock. The exact number of Mexican Models manufactured between 1891 and 1911 is unknown but it is estimated that the number is small.

NIB	Exc.	V.G.	Good	Fair	Poor
—	—	3650	1500	950	400

.32 Double-Action 1st Model

This is one of the rarest of all S&W revolvers. There were only 30 manufactured. It also has a straight-sided sideplate that weakened the revolver frame. Perhaps this was the reason that so few were made. This model was the first break-open, double-action, automatic-ejecting .32 that S&W produced. It features a 3" round barrel with raised rib, a 5-shot fluted cylinder, and round butt with plain, uncheckered, black hard rubber grips. The finish is blued or nickel-plated. All 30 of these revolvers were manufactured in 1880.

NIB	Exc.	V.G.	Good	Fair	Poor
—	—	12000	7500	4000	1000

NOTE: Rarity makes valuation speculative.

.32 Double-Action 2nd Model

This revolver is chambered for the .32 S&W cartridge and has a 3" round barrel with a raised rib. The 5-shot cylinder is fluted, and the finish is blued or nickel-plated. It is a top break design with a round butt. The grips are either checkered or floral-embossed hard rubber with the S&W monogram. This model has an oval sideplate, eliminating the weakness of the 1st Model. There were approximately 22,142 manufactured between 1880 and 1882.

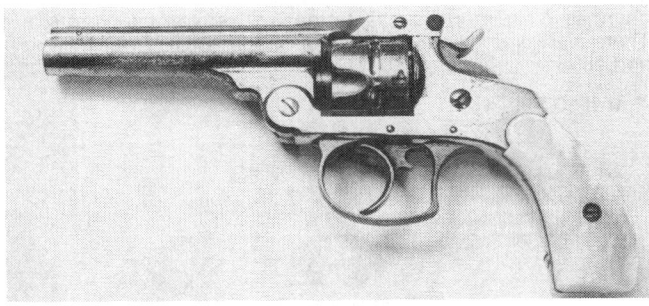

Courtesy Mike Stuckslager

NIB	Exc.	V.G.	Good	Fair	Poor
—	700	350	225	175	75

.32 Double-Action 3rd Model

This model incorporates internal improvements that are not evident in appearance. The most notable identifiable difference between this model and its predecessors is in the surface of the cylinder. The flutes are longer; there is only one set of stops instead of two; and the free groove is no longer present. There were approximately 21,232 manufactured in 1882 and 1883.

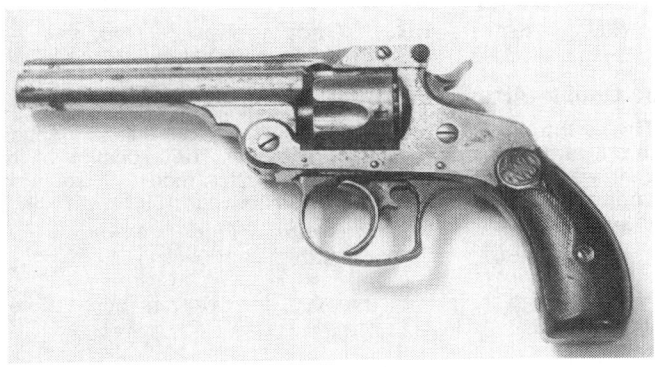

Courtesy Mike Stuckslager

NIB	Exc.	V.G.	Good	Fair	Poor
—	625	350	225	175	75

.32 Double-Action 4th Model

This model is quite similar in appearance to the 3rd Model except that the trigger guard is oval in shape instead of the squared back of the previous models. There were also internal improvements. There were approximately 239,600 manufactured between 1883 and 1909.

Courtesy Mike Stuckslager

NIB	Exc.	V.G.	Good	Fair	Poor
—	575	300	200	125	65

NOTE: Add a 50 percent premium for revolvers built before 1898.

.32 Double-Action 5th Model

The only difference between this model and its predecessors is that this model has the front sight machined as an integral part of the barrel rib. On the other models, the sight was pinned in place. There were approximately 44,641 manufactured between 1909 and 1919.

Courtesy Mike Stuckslager

NIB	Exc.	V.G.	Good	Fair	Poor
—	500	375	250	125	100

SAFETY HAMMERLESS

This model was a departure from what was commonly being produced at this time. Some attribute the Safety Hammerless design to D.B. Wesson's hearing that a child had been injured by cocking and firing one of the company's pistols. This story has never been proven. Nevertheless, the concealed hammer and grip safety make this an ideal pocket pistol for those needing concealability in a handgun. This is a small revolver chambered for .32 S&W and .38 S&W cartridges. It has a 5-shot fluted cylinder and is offered with a 2", 3", and 3.5" round barrel with a raised rib. The butt is rounded and has checkered hard rubber grips with the S&W logo. The finish is blue or nickel plated. The revolver is a top break, automatic-ejecting design; and the 1st Model has the latch for opening located in the rear center of the top strap instead of at the sides. The latch is checkered for a positive grip. This model is commonly referred to as the "Lemon Squeezer" because the grip safety must be squeezed as it is fired.

Courtesy Mike Stuckslager

.32 Safety Hammerless (aka .32 New Departure or .32 Lemon Squeezer) 1st Model

Push button latch serial number 1- 91417, built 1888-1902.

NIB	Exc.	V.G.	Good	Fair	Poor
—	475	275	165	100	50

NOTE: Add a 50 percent premium for revolvers built before 1898.

.32 Safety Hammerless 2nd Model

T-bar latch, pinned front sight, serial number 91418-169999, built 1902 to 1909.

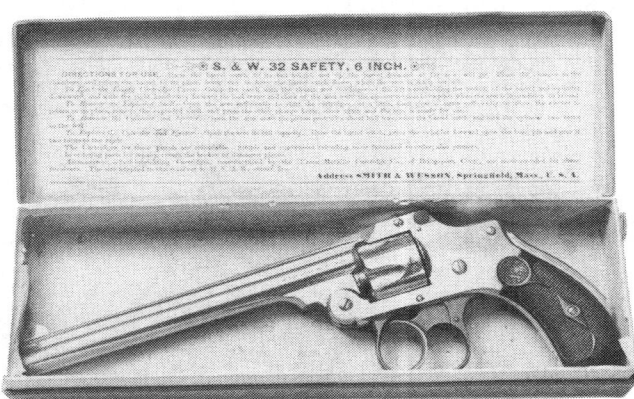

Courtesy Mike Stuckslager

NIB	Exc.	V.G.	Good	Fair	Poor
—	450	275	165	100	50

.32 Safety Hammerless 3rd Model

T-bar latch, integral forged front sight, serial number 170000-242981, built 1909 to 1937.

NIB	Exc.	V.G.	Good	Fair	Poor
—	450	325	265	150	50

NOTE: For 2" barrel, Bicycle Model add 200 percent.

.38 Double-Action 1st Model

This model is similar in appearance to the .32 1st Model, having a straight cut side-plate, but is chambered for the .38 S&W cartridge. The grips are checkered, and there were 4,000 manufactured in 1880.

NIB	Exc.	V.G.	Good	Fair	Poor
—	1200	650	400	250	75

.38 Double-Action 2nd Model

This is similar in appearance to the .32 2nd Model but is chambered for the .38 S&W cartridge. There were approximately 115,000 manufactured between 1880 and 1884.

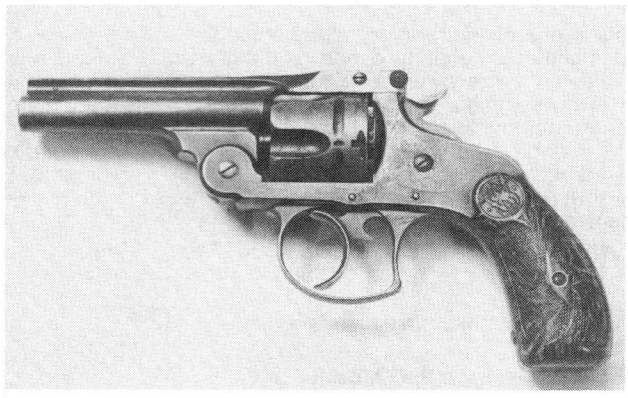

Courtesy Mike Stuckslager

NIB	Exc.	V.G.	Good	Fair	Poor
—	550	375	225	200	100

.38 DOUBLE-ACTION 3RD MODEL

Essentially the same in appearance as the .32 Model but chambered for the .38 S&W cartridge, it is also offered with a 3.25", 4", 5", 6", 8", and 10" barrel. There were numerous internal changes in this model similar to the .32 Double-Action 3rd Model. There were approximately 203,700 manufactured between 1884 and 1895.

8" and 10" Barrel

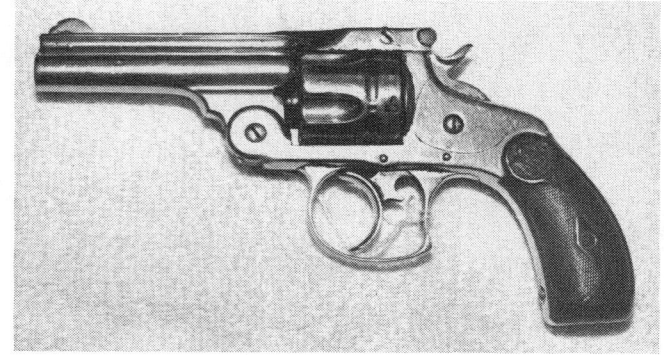

Courtesy Mike Stuckslager

Rare, use caution.

NIB	Exc.	V.G.	Good	Fair	Poor
—	—	2500	1500	800	200

Standard Barrel

NIB	Exc.	V.G.	Good	Fair	Poor
—	550	450	325	200	75

.38 Double-Action 4th Model

This is the .38 S&W version of the 4th Model and is identical in outward appearance to the 3rd Model. The relocation of the sear was the main design change in this model. There were approximately 216,300 manufactured between 1895 and 1909.

NIB	Exc.	V.G.	Good	Fair	Poor
—	495	230	225	150	75

NOTE: Add a 20 percent premium for revolvers built before 1898.

.38 Double-Action 5th Model

This model is the same as the .32 except that it is chambered for the .38 S&W cartridge. There were approximately 15,000 manufactured between 1909 and 1911.

Courtesy Mike Stuckslager

NIB	Exc.	V.G.	Good	Fair	Poor
—	525	385	225	150	75

.38 Double-Action Perfected

A unique top-break with both a barrel latch similar to the other top-breaks and a thumbpiece similar to the hand ejectors; also the only top-break where the trigger guard is integral to the frame rather than a separate piece. Produced from 1909 to 1911 in their own serial number range. About 59,400 were built.

NIB	Exc.	V.G.	Good	Fair	Poor
—	600	525	295	165	85

.38 Safety Hammerless 1st Model

Z-bar latch, serial number range 1 to 5250, made 1887 only.

NIB	Exc.	V.G.	Good	Fair	Poor
—	900	600	425	250	100

NOTE: Also offered with a 6" barrel. RARE! Add 50 percent.

.38 Safety Hammerless 2nd Model

Push button latch protrudes above frame, serial number 5251-42483, built 1887-1890.

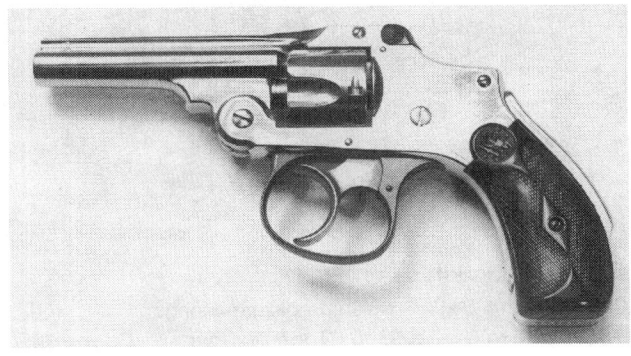

Courtesy Mike Stuckslager

NIB	Exc.	V.G.	Good	Fair	Poor
—	500	350	250	175	100

.38 Safety Hammerless 3rd Model

Push button latch flush with frame, serial number 42484-116002, 1890-1898.

NIB	Exc.	V.G.	Good	Fair	Poor
—	475	355	225	165	100

.38 Safety Hammerless Army Test Revolver

There were approximately 100 sold to U.S. government in 1890. They have 3rd Model features but are in the 2nd Model serial number range, 41333-41470. Fitted with 6" barrels and marked "US." CAUTION: Be wary of fakes.

NIB	Exc.	V.G.	Good	Fair	Poor
—	—	1000	7500	4000	—

NOTE: Rarity makes valuation speculative.

.38 Safety Hammerless 4th Model

This model was produced in .38 S&W only, and the only difference in the 4th Model and the 3rd Model is the adoption of the standard T-bar type of barrel latch as found on most of the top break revolvers. ".38 S&W Cartridge" was also added to the left side of the barrel. There were approximately 104,000 manufactured between 1898 and 1907; serial number range 116003 to 220000.

Courtesy Mike Stuckslager

NIB	Exc.	V.G.	Good	Fair	Poor
—	450	335	275	110	50

.38 Safety Hammerless 5th Model

This is the last of the "Lemon Squeezers," and the only appreciable difference between this model and the 4th Model is that the front sight blade on the 5th Model is an integral part of the barrel and not a separate blade pinned onto the barrel. There were approximately 41,500 manufactured between 1907 and 1940; serial number range 220001 to 261493.

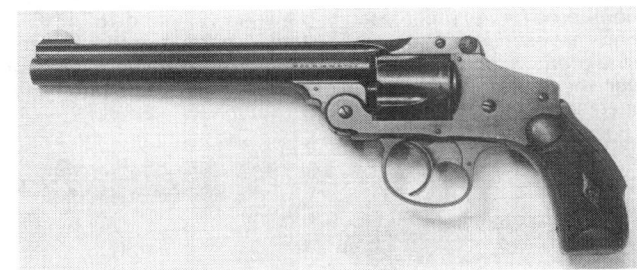

Courtesy Mike Stuckslager

NIB	Exc.	V.G.	Good	Fair	Poor
—	500	395	275	110	50

NOTE: 2" barrel version add 50 percent.

MODEL 3 AMERICAN 1ST MODEL

This model represented a number of firsts for the Smith & Wesson Company. It was the first of the top break, automatic ejection revolvers. It was also the first Smith & Wesson in a large caliber (it is chambered for the .44 S&W American cartridge as well as the .44 Henry rimfire on rare occasions). It was also known as the 1st Model American. This large revolver is offered with an 8" round barrel with a raised rib as standard. Barrel lengths of 6" and 7" were also available. It has a 6-shot fluted cylinder and a square butt with walnut grips. It is blued or nickel-plated. It is interesting to note that this model appeared three years before Colt's Single-Action Army and perhaps, more than any other model, was associated with the historic American West. There were only 8,000 manufactured between 1870 and 1872.

Standard Production Model

NIB	Exc.	V.G.	Good	Fair	Poor
—	—	7000	3500	1500	500

NOTE: Add 25 percent for "oil hole" variation found on approximately the first 1,500 guns. Add 50 percent for unusual barrel lengths other than standard 8". Original "Nashville Police" marked guns worth a substantial premium.

Transition Model

Serial number range 6466-6744. Shorter cylinder (1.423"), improved barrel catch.

NIB	Exc.	V.G.	Good	Fair	Poor
—	—	6000	3000	1500	500

U.S. Army Order

Serial number range 125-2199. One thousand (1,000) produced with "U.S." stamped on top of barrel; "OWA," on left grip.

NIB	Exc.	V.G.	Good	Fair	Poor
—	—	17500	7500	3000	500

.44 Rimfire Henry Model

Only 200 produced throughout serial range.

NIB	Exc.	V.G.	Good	Fair	Poor
—	—	12000	6000	3000	500

NOTE: Rarity makes valuation speculative.

MODEL 3 AMERICAN 2ND MODEL

An improved version of the 1st Model. The most notable difference is the larger diameter trigger pivot pin and the frame protrusions above the trigger to accommodate it. The front sight blade on this model is made of steel instead of nickel silver. Several internal improvements were also incorporated into this model. This model is commonly known as the American 2nd Model. The 8" barrel length was standard on this model. There were approximately 20,735 manufactured, including 3,014 chambered for .44 rimfire Henry, between 1872 and 1874.NOTE: There have been 5.5", 6", 6.5", and 7" barrels noted; but they are extremely scarce and would bring a 40 percent premium over the standard 8" model. Use caution when purchasing these short barrel revolvers.

Courtesy Buffalo Bill Historical Center, Cody, Wyoming

.44 Henry Rimfire

NIB	Exc.	V.G.	Good	Fair	Poor
—	—	6500	3250	1500	500

Standard 8" Model, .44 American Centerfire

NIB	Exc.	V.G.	Good	Fair	Poor
—	6750	5000	3000	1250	500

MODEL 3 RUSSIAN 1ST MODEL

This model is quite similar in appearance to the American 1st and 2nd Model revolvers. S&W made several internal changes to this model to satisfy the Russian government. The markings on this revolver are distinct; and the caliber for which it is chambered, .44 S&W Russian, is different. There were approximately 20,000 Russian-Contract revolvers. The serial number range is 1-20000. They are marked in Russian Cyrillic letters. The Russian double-headed eagle is stamped on the rear portion of the barrel with inspector's marks underneath it. All of the contract guns have 8" barrels and lanyard swivels on the butt. These are rarely encountered, as most were shipped to Russia. The commercial run of this model numbered

approximately 4,655. The barrels are stamped in English and include the words "Russian Model." Some are found with 6" and 7" barrels, as well as the standard 8". There were also 500 revolvers that were rejected from the Russian contract series and sold on the commercial market. Some of these are marked in English; some, Cyrillic. Some have the Cyrillic markings ground off and the English restamped. This model was manufactured from 1871 to 1874.

Russian Contract Model, Cyrillic Barrel Address

NIB	Exc.	V.G.	Good	Fair	Poor
—	—	7000	3500	2000	500

Commercial Model

NIB	Exc.	V.G.	Good	Fair	Poor
—	—	5000	2750	1250	500

Rejected Russian Contract Model

NIB	Exc.	V.G.	Good	Fair	Poor
—	—	5000	2750	1250	500

MODEL 3 RUSSIAN 2ND MODEL

This revolver was known as the "Old Model Russian." This is a complicated model to understand as there are many variations within the model designation. The serial numbering is quite complex as well, and values vary greatly due to relatively minor model differences. Before purchasing this model, it would be advisable to secure competent appraisal as well as to read reference materials solely devoted to this firearm. This model is chambered for the .44 S&W Russian, as well as the .44 Henry rimfire cartridge. It has a 7" barrel and a round butt featuring a projection on the frame that fits into the thumb web. The grips are walnut, and the finish is blue or nickel-plated. The trigger guard has a reverse curved spur on the bottom. There were approximately 85,200 manufactured between 1873 and 1878.

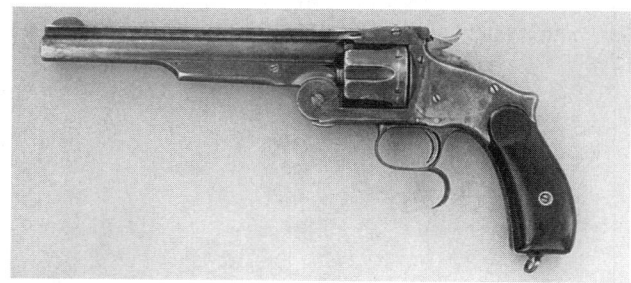

Courtesy Jim Supica, Old Town Station

Commercial Model

6,200 made, .44 S&W Russian, English markings.

NIB	Exc.	V.G.	Good	Fair	Poor
—	—	3250	1500	850	400

.44 Rimfire Henry Model

500 made.

NIB	Exc.	V.G.	Good	Fair	Poor
—	—	4750	2250	1000	500

Russian Contract Model

70,000 made; rare, as most were shipped to Russia. Cyrillic markings; lanyard swivel on butt.

NIB	Exc.	V.G.	Good	Fair	Poor
—	—	3500	1750	950	500

1st Model Turkish Contract

.44 rimfire Henry, special rimfire frames, serial-numbered in own serial number range 1-1000.

NIB	Exc.	V.G.	Good	Fair	Poor
—	—	6000	3750	1750	500

2nd Model Turkish Contract

Made from altered centerfire frames from the regular commercial serial number range. 1,000 made. Use caution with this model.

NIB	Exc.	V.G.	Good	Fair	Poor
—	—	4500	2250	1000	500

Japanese Govt. Contract

Five thousand made between the 1-9000 serial number range. The Japanese naval insignia, an anchor over two wavy lines, found on the butt. The barrel is Japanese proofed, and the words "Jan.19, 75 REISSUE July 25, 1871" are stamped on the barrel, as well.

NIB	Exc.	V.G.	Good	Fair	Poor
—	—	3500	1700	950	500

MODEL 3 RUSSIAN 3RD MODEL

This revolver is also known as the "New Model Russian." The factory referred to this model as the Model of 1874 or the Cavalry Model. It is chambered for the .44 S&W Russian and the .44 Henry rimfire cartridge. The barrel is 6.5", and the round butt is the same humped-back affair as the 2nd Model. The grips are walnut; and the finish, blue or nickel-plated. The most notable differences in appearance between this model and the 2nd Model are the shorter extractor housing under the barrel and the integral front sight blade instead of the pinned-on one found on the previous models. This is another model that bears careful research before attempting to evaluate. Minor variances can greatly affect values. Secure detailed reference materials and qualified appraisal. There were approximately 60,638 manufactured between 1874 and 1878.

Commercial Model

.44 S&W Russian, marked "Russian Model" in English, 13,500 made.

NIB	Exc.	V.G.	Good	Fair	Poor
—	—	9000	5000	2500	500

.44 Henry Rimfire Model

NIB	Exc.	V.G.	Good	Fair	Poor
—	—	4500	2700	900	500

Turkish Model

Five thousand made from altered centerfire frames. Made to fire .44 Henry rimfire. "W" inspector's mark on butt. Fakes have been noted; be aware.

NIB	Exc.	V.G.	Good	Fair	Poor
—	—	4500	2700	900	500

Japanese Contract Model

One thousand made; has the Japanese naval insignia, an anchor over two wavy lines, stamped on the butt.

NIB	Exc.	V.G.	Good	Fair	Poor
—	—	3100	1950	850	500

Russian Contract Model

Barrel markings are in Russian Cyrillic. Approximately 41,100 were produced.

NIB	Exc.	V.G.	Good	Fair	Poor
—	—	3100	1950	850	500

MODEL 3 RUSSIAN 3RD MODEL (LOEWE & TULA COPIES)

The German firm of Ludwig Loewe produced a copy of this model that is nearly identical to the S&W. This German revolver was made under Russian contract, as well as for commercial sales. The contract model has different Cyrillic markings than the S&W and the letters "HK" as inspector's marks. The commercial model has the markings in English. The Russian arsenal at Tula also produced a copy of this revolver with a different Cyrillic dated stamping on the barrel.

Courtesy Mike Stuckslager

Loewe

NIB	Exc.	V.G.	Good	Fair	Poor
—	—	2900	1750	700	400

Tula

NIB	Exc.	V.G.	Good	Fair	Poor
—	—	3350	2000	800	400

MODEL 3 SCHOFIELD 1ST MODEL

Barrel markings are in Russian Cyrillic. Approximately 41,100 were produced.

"US" Contract

3,000 issued.

NIB	Exc.	V.G.	Good	Fair	Poor
—	12500	7500	4250	2250	500

Civilian Model

No "US" markings, 35 made, Very Rare.

NOTE: Use caution. UNABLE TO PRICE. At least double the military model values. Expert appraisal needed.

MODEL 3 SCHOFIELD 2ND MODEL

"US" Contract

4,000 issued.

NIB	Exc.	V.G.	Good	Fair	Poor
—	10500	6500	4000	2250	500

Civilian Model

646 made.

NIB	Exc.	V.G.	Good	Fair	Poor
—	12000	7000	4000	2000	500

MODEL 3 SCHOFIELD—SURPLUS MODELS

After the government dropped the Schofield as an issue cavalry sidearm, the remaining U.S. inventory of these revolvers was sold off as military surplus. Many were sold to National Guard units; and the remainder were sold either to Bannerman's or to Schuyler, Hartley & Graham, two large gun dealers who then resold the guns to supply the growing need for guns on the Western frontier. Schuyler, Hartley & Graham sold a number of guns to the Wells Fargo Express Co. These weapons were nickel-plated and had the barrels shortened to 5", as were many others sold during this period. Beware of fakes when contemplating purchase of the Wells Fargo revolvers.

Wells Fargo & Co. Model

NIB	Exc.	V.G.	Good	Fair	Poor
—	—	8000	4000	2000	500

Surplus Cut Barrel—Not Wells Fargo

NIB	Exc.	V.G.	Good	Fair	Poor
—	—	3500	2000	1200	500

NEW MODEL NO. 3 SINGLE-ACTION

Always interested in perfecting the Model 3 revolver D.B. Wesson redesigned and improved the old Model 3 in the hopes of attracting more sales. The Russian contracts were almost filled so the company decided to devote the effort necessary to improve on this design. In 1877 this project was undertaken. The extractor housing was shortened; the cylinder retention system was improved; and the shape of the grip was changed to a more streamlined and attractive configuration. This New Model has a 3.5", 4", 5", 6", 6.5", 7", 7.5", or 8" barrel length with a 6-shot fluted cylinder. The 6.5" barrel and .44 S&W Russian chambering is the most often encountered variation of this model, but the factory considered the 3-1/2" and 8" barrels as standard and these were kept in stock as well. The New Model No. 3 was also chambered for .32 S&W, .32-44 S&W, .320 S&W Rev. Rifle, .38 S&W, .38-40, .38-44 S&W, .41 S&W, .44 Henry rimfire, .44 S&W American, .44-40, .45 S&W Schofield, .450 Rev., .45 Webley, .455 MkI and .455 MkII. They are either blued or nickel-plated and have checkered hard rubber grips with the S&W logo molded into them, or walnut grips. There are many sub-variations within this model designation, and the potential collector should secure detailed reference material that deals with this model. There were approximately 35,796 of these revolvers manufactured between 1878 and 1912. Nearly 40 percent were exported to fill contracts with Japan, Australia, Argentina, England, Spain, and Cuba. There were some sent to Asia, as well. The proofmarks of these countries will establish their provenance but will not add appreciably to standard values.

Standard Model

6.5" barrel, .44 S&W Russian.

NIB	Exc.	V.G.	Good	Fair	Poor
—	5000	3700	2000	1000	500

Japanese Naval Contract

This was the largest foreign purchaser of this model. There were more than 1,500 produced with the anchor insignia stamped on the frame.

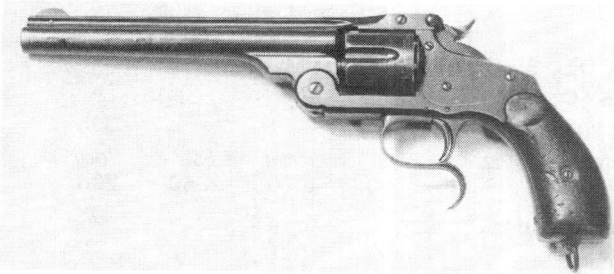

Courtesy Mike Stuckslager

NIB	Exc.	V.G.	Good	Fair	Poor
—	—	3700	2000	1000	500

Japanese Artillery Contract

This variation is numbered in the 25000 serial range. They are blued, with a 7" barrel and a lanyard swivel on the butt. Japanese characters are stamped on the extractor housing.

NIB	Exc.	V.G.	Good	Fair	Poor
—	—	5000	2500	1250	500

Maryland Militia Model

This variation is nickel-plated, has a 6.5" barrel, and is chambered for the .44 S&W Russian cartridge. The butt is stamped "U.S.," and the inspector's marks "HN" and "DAL" under the date 1878 appear on the revolver. There were 280 manufactured between serial-numbers 7126 and 7405.

NIB	Exc.	V.G.	Good	Fair	Poor
—	—	10000	6000	3000	500

NOTE: Rarity makes valuation speculative.

Argentine Model

This was essentially not a factory contract but a sale through Schuyler, Hartley and Graham. They are stamped "Ejercito/Argentino" in front of the trigger guard. The order amounted to some 2,000 revolvers between the serial numbers 50 and 3400.

NIB	Exc.	V.G.	Good	Fair	Poor
—	—	7000	3500	1750	500

Australian Contract

This variation is nickel-plated, is chambered for the .44 S&W Russian cartridge, and is marked with the Australian Colonial Police Broad Arrow on the buff. There were 250 manufactured with 7" barrels and detachable shoulder stocks. The stock has the Broad Arrow stamped on the lower tang. There were also 30 manufactured with 6.5" barrels without the stocks. They all are numbered in the 12000-13000 serial range.

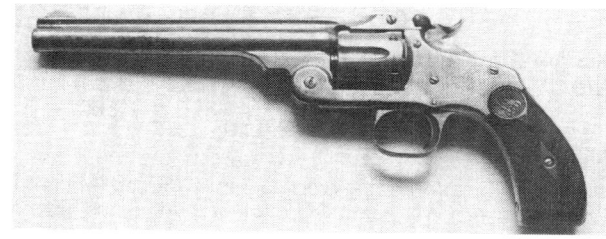

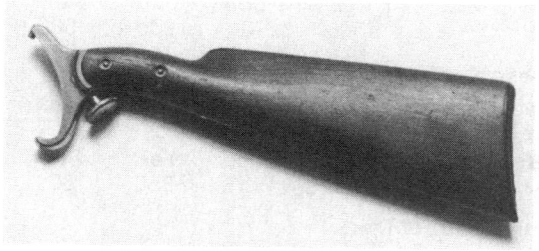

Courtesy Mike Stuckslager

Revolver with Stock and Holsters

NIB	Exc.	V.G.	Good	Fair	Poor
—	—	8000	4750	2750	500

NOTE: Deduct 40 percent for no stock.

Turkish Model

This is essentially the New Model No. 3 chambered for the .44 rimfire Henry cartridge. It is stamped with the letters "P," "U" and "AFC" on various parts of the revolver. The barrels are all 6.5"; the finish, blued with walnut grips. Lanyard swivels are found on the butt. There were 5,461 manufactured and serial numbered in their own range, starting at 1 through 5461 between 1879 and 1883.

Courtesy Mike Stuckslager

NIB	Exc.	V.G.	Good	Fair	Poor
—	—	7000	3500	1750	500

New Model No. 3 Target Single-Action

This revolver is similar in appearance to the standard New Model No. 3, but was the company's first production target model. It has a 6.5" round barrel with a raised rib and 6-shot fluted cylinder and is finished in blue or nickel-plated. The grips are either walnut or checkered hard rubber with the S&W logo molded into them. This model is chambered in either .32 S&W or .38 S&W. The company referred to these models as either the .32-44 Target or the .38-44 Target depending on the caliber. The designation of .44 referred to the frame size, i.e. a .32 caliber built on a .44 caliber frame. This model was offered with a detachable shoulder stock as an option. These stocks are extremely scarce on today's market. There were approximately 4,333 manufactured between 1887 and 1910.

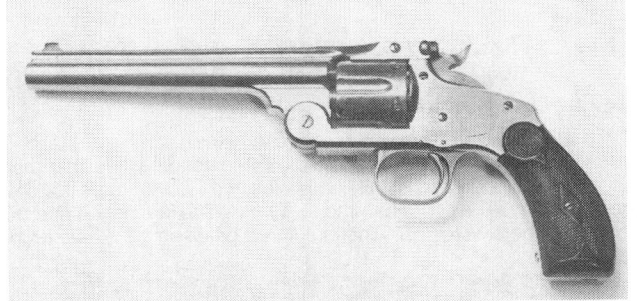

Courtesy Mike Stuckslager

NIB	Exc.	V.G.	Good	Fair	Poor
—	—	3100	1350	850	400

NOTE: Shoulder stock add 50 percent.

NEW MODEL NO. 3 FRONTIER SINGLE-ACTION

This is another model similar in appearance to the standard New Model No. 3. It has a 4", 5", or 6.5" barrel and is chambered for the .44-40 Winchester Centerfire cartridge. Because the original New Model No. 3 cylinder was 1-7/16" in length this would not accommodate the longer .44-40 cartridge. The cylinder on the No. 3 Frontier was changed to 1-9/16" in length. Later the company converted 786 revolvers to .44 S&W Russian and sold them to Japan. This model is either blued or nickel-plated and has checkered grips of walnut or hard rubber. They are serial numbered in their own range from 1 through 2072 and were

manufactured from 1885 until 1908. This model was designed to compete with the Colt Single-Action Army but was not successful.

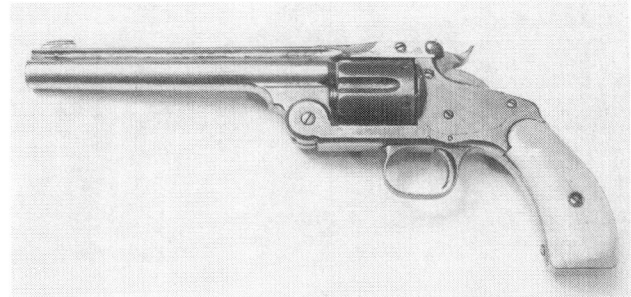

Courtesy Mike Stuckslager

.44-40—Commercial Model

NIB	Exc.	V.G.	Good	Fair	Poor
—	—	5000	2500	1250	500

Japanese Purchase Converted to .44 S&W Russian

NIB	Exc.	V.G.	Good	Fair	Poor
—	—	4000	2000	1000	500

New Model No. 3—.38 Winchester

This variation was the last of the New Model No. 3s to be introduced. It was offered in .38-40 Winchester as a separate model from 1900 until 1907. The finish is blue or nickel-plate, and the grips are checkered hard rubber or walnut. Barrel lengths of 4" or 6.5" were offered. This model was not at all popular, as only 74 were manufactured in their own serial range 1 through 74. Today's collectors are extremely interested in this extremely rare model.

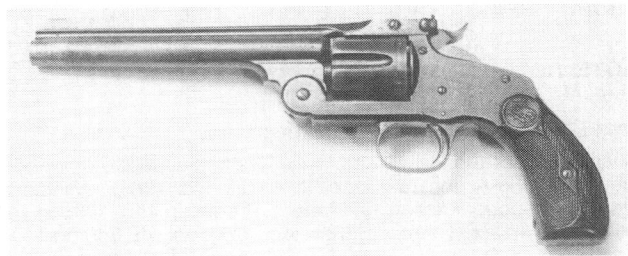

Courtesy Mike Stuckslager

NIB	Exc.	V.G.	Good	Fair	Poor
—	—	14000	8000	4000	500

NOTE: Rarity makes valuation speculative.

.44 Double-Action 1st Model

This model is a top break revolver that automatically ejects the spent cartridge cases upon opening. The barrel latch is located at the top and rear of the cylinder; the pivot, in front and at the bottom. This model was also known as "The D.A. Frontier" or "The New Model Navy." The revolver is chambered for the .44 S&W Russian and was built on a modified Model 3 frame. It is also found on rare occasions chambered for the .38-40 and the .44-40 Winchester. The barrel lengths are 4", 5", 6", and 6.5", round with a raised rib. A 3-1/2" barrel was produced on this model by special request. Collectors should be aware that the barrel for this model and the New Model No. 3 were interchangeable and the factory did in fact use barrels from either model. The serial number on the rear of the barrel should match the number on the butt, cylinder and barrel latch. The cylinder holds 6 shots and is fluted. It has double sets of stop notches and long free grooves between the stops. It is serial numbered in its own range, beginning at 1. There were approximately 54,000 manufactured between 1881 and 1913.

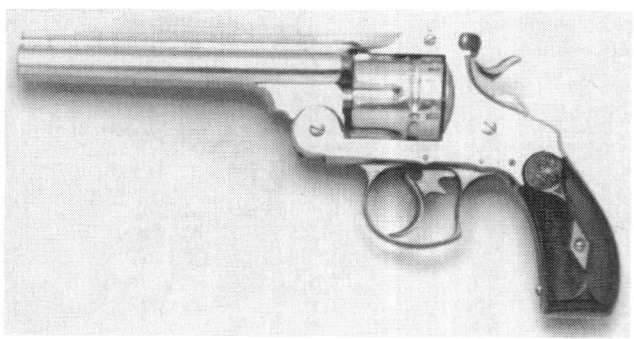

Courtesy Bonhams & Butterfields, San Francisco, California

Standard .44 S&W Russian

NIB	Exc.	V.G.	Good	Fair	Poor
—	—	2000	1300	700	400

Model .44 Double-Action Wesson Favorite

The Favorite is basically a lightened version of the 1st Model D.A. .44. The barrel is thinner and is offered in 5" length only. There are lightening cuts in the frame between the trigger guard and the cylinder; the cylinder diameter was smaller, and there is a groove milled along the barrel rib. The Favorite is chambered for the .44 S&W Russian cartridge and has a 6-shot fluted cylinder with the same double-cylinder stop notches and free grooves as the 1st Model Double-Action .44. The company name and address, as well as the patent dates, are stamped into the edge of the cylinder instead of on the barrel rib. It is serial-numbered in the same range, between 9000 and 10100. The revolver was most often nickel-plated but was also offered blued. The grips are walnut or checkered hard rubber with the S&W logo molded in. There were approximately 1,000 manufactured in 1882 and 1883. Use caution when purchasing a blued model.

NIB	Exc.	V.G.	Good	Fair	Poor
—	—	9000	5000	2500	500

NOTE: Rarity makes valuation speculative. Blued finish add 25 percent.

Model .44 Double-Action Frontier

Chambered for the .44-40 cartridge. This is a separate model from the .44 Double-Action 1st Model. It has a longer 19/16" cylinder like the later .44 double-action 1st Model's. Produced from 1886 to 1916 with their own serial number range. Approximately 15,340 built.

NIB	Exc.	V.G.	Good	Fair	Poor
—	—	1850	1200	750	400

Model .38 Winchester Double-Action

Similar to the .44 Double-Action 1st Model except for the chamber. Fitted with long cylinder. Approximately 276 produced in their own serial number range from 1900 to 1910.

NIB	Exc.	V.G.	Good	Fair	Poor
—	—	5500	3000	1250	500

1ST MODEL SINGLE-SHOT

This unusual pistol combines the frame of the .38 Single-Action 3rd Model with a single-shot barrel. This model is a top break and functions exactly as the revolver models do. The barrel length is 6", 8", or 10"; and the pistol is chambered for .22 LR, .32 S&W, and .38 S&W. The finish is blue or nickel plated, with a square butt. The grips are checkered hard rubber extension types for a proper target hold. This pistol is considered quite rare on today's market, as only 1,251 were manufactured between 1893 and 1905.

.22 L.R.

NIB	Exc.	V.G.	Good	Fair	Poor
—	—	1500	1000	600	400

.32 S&W

NIB	Exc.	V.G.	Good	Fair	Poor
—	—	1750	1275	700	500

.38 S&W

NIB	Exc.	V.G.	Good	Fair	Poor
—	—	1900	1400	750	50

2nd Model Single-Shot

The 2nd Model single-shot has a frame with the recoil shield removed, is chambered for the .22 LR only, and is offered with the 10" barrel. The finish is blue or nickel plated, and the grips are checkered hard rubber extension types. There were approximately 4,617 manufactured between 1905 and 1909.

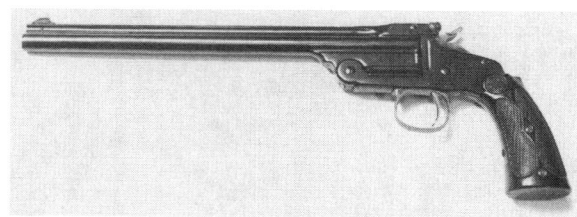

Courtesy Mike Stuckslager

NIB	Exc.	V.G.	Good	Fair	Poor
—	1000	875	650	350	175

3rd Model Single-Shot

The basic difference between this model and the 2nd Model is that this pistol could be fired double-action as well as single-action, and the frame came from the double-action perfected model. There were 6,949 manufactured between 1909 and 1923.

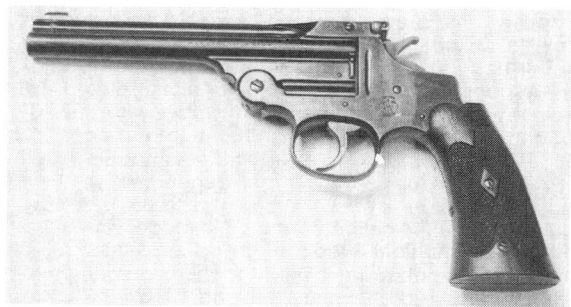

Courtesy Mike Stuckslager

NIB	Exc.	V.G.	Good	Fair	Poor
—	1050	875	650	450	275

Straight Line Single-Shot

This is a unique pistol that very much resembles a semi-automatic. The barrel is 10" in length and pivots to the left for loading. It is chambered for .22 LR cartridge and is finished in blue, with walnut grips inlaid with the S&W medallions. The hammer is straight-line in function and does not pivot. There were 1,870 manufactured between 1925 and 1936.

Courtesy Bonhams & Butterfields, San Francisco, California

NIB	Exc.	V.G.	Good	Fair	Poor
—	2500	1750	900	700	400

.32 Hand Ejector Model of 1896 or
.32 Hand Ejector 1st Model

This model was the first time S&W made a revolver with a swing-out cylinder. Interestingly, there is no cylinder latch; but the action opens by pulling forward on the exposed portion of the cylinder pin. This frees the spring tension and allows the cylinder to swing free. Another novel feature of this model is the cylinder stop location, which is located in the top of the frame over the cylinder. This model is chambered for the .32 S&W Long cartridge, has a 6-shot fluted cylinder, and is offered with 3.25", 4.25", and 6" long barrels. It is available with either a round or square butt, has checkered hard rubber grips, and is blued or nickel-plated. Factory installed target sights were available by special order. The company name, address, and patent dates are stamped on the cylinder instead of on the barrel. There were approximately 19,712 manufactured between 1896 and 1903.

Courtesy Mike Stuckslager

NIB	Exc.	V.G.	Good	Fair	Poor
—	650	425	350	200	150

Hand Ejector Model of 1903

This model is quite different from its predecessor. The cylinder locks front and back; the cylinder stop is located in the bottom of the frame, and the familiar sliding cylinder latch is found on the left side of the frame. The barrel lengths are 3.25", 4.25", and 6". The 6-shot cylinder is fluted, and the revolver is chambered for .32 S&W Long. It is offered either blued or nickel-plated, and the round butt grips are checkered hard rubber. There were approximately 19,425 manufactured in 1903 and 1904; serial number range 1 to 19425.

Courtesy Mike Stuckslager

NIB	Exc.	V.G.	Good	Fair	Poor
—	550	350	200	150	100

.32 Hand Ejector Model of 1903 1st Change

This model differs from the model of 1903 internally, and the serial number range 19426 to 51126 is really the only way to differentiate the two. There were approximately 31,700 manufactured between 1904 and 1906.

NIB	Exc.	V.G.	Good	Fair	Poor
—	475	325	200	150	100

.32 Hand Ejector Model of 1903 2nd Change

Produced from 1906 to 1909 in serial number range 51127 to 95500. A total of 44,373 manufactured.

.32 Hand Ejector Model of 1903 3rd Change

Produced from 1909 to 1910 in serial number range 95501 to 96125. A total of 624 manufactured.

.32 Hand Ejector Model of 1903 4th Change

Produced in 1910 in serial number range 96126 to 102500. A total of 6,374 manufactured.

.32 Hand Ejector Model of 1903 5th Change

Produced from 1910 to 1917 in serial number range 102500 to 263000. A total of 160,500 manufactured.

.32 Hand Ejector Third Model

Produced from 1911 to 1942 in serial number range 263001 to 536684. A total of 273,683 were manufactured.

NIB	Exc.	V.G.	Good	Fair	Poor
—	450	300	150	125	90

K-32 Hand Ejector First Model

This is one of the rarest pre-war K-frame revolvers. Chambered for the .32 S&W Long cartridge, less than 100 were made between 1936 and 1941. After WWII this model was part of the K-22/K-32/K-38 Masterpiece series of 6-inch barreled, target-sighted revolvers. Due to the rarity of this model, an expert appraisal is essential.

NIB	Exc.	V.G.	Good	Fair	Poor
—	14000	10000	6000	2000	500

.22 Ladysmith 1st Model

This model was designed primarily as a defensive weapon for women. Its small size and caliber made it ideal for that purpose. The 1st Model Ladysmith is chambered for .22 Long cartridge and has a 7-shot fluted cylinder and 3" and 3.5" barrel lengths. This little revolver weighed 9-5/8 ounces. It is either blued or nickel-plated and has a round butt with checkered hard rubber grips. The 1st Model has a checkered cylinder-latch button on the left side of the frame. There were approximately 4,575 manufactured between 1902 and 1906.

NIB	Exc.	V.G.	Good	Fair	Poor
—	2300	1550	1050	650	450

.22 Ladysmith 2nd Model

This is essentially quite similar in appearance to the 1st Model, the difference being in the pull-forward cylinder latch located under the barrel, replacing the button on the left side of the frame. The new method allowed lockup front and back for greater action strength. The 2.25" barrel length was dropped; caliber and finishes are the same. There were approximately 9,374 manufactured between 1906 and 1910; serial number range 4576 to 13950.

Courtesy Mike Stuckslager

NIB	Exc.	V.G.	Good	Fair	Poor
—	2000	1250	1000	600	400

.22 Ladysmith 3rd Model

This model is quite different in appearance to the 2nd Model, as it features a square butt and smooth walnut grips with inlaid S&W medallions. The barrel lengths remained the same, with the addition of a 2.25" and 6" variation. The under barrel cylinder lockup was not changed, nor were the caliber and finishes. There were approximately 12,200 manufactured between 1910 and 1921; serial number range 13951 to 26154.

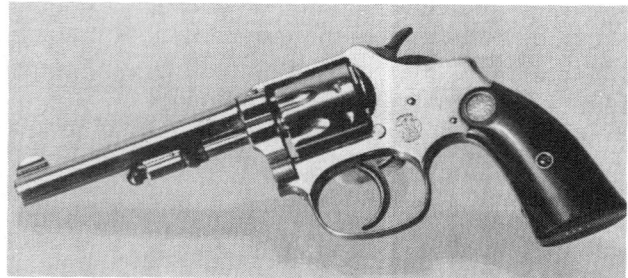

Courtesy W.P. Hallstein III and son Chip

NIB	Exc.	V.G.	Good	Fair	Poor
—	1750	1200	950	600	400

NOTE: Add a 50 percent premium for 2.25" and 6" barrel lengths.

K-22 Outdoorsman

Pre-war version of the K-22 K-frame, 6-inch barreled revolver chambered for the .22 Short, Long and Long Rifle. Walnut grips, adjustable rear sight, ribbed barrel. Manufactured from 1931 to 1940. In 1940 the name was changed to K-22 Masterpiece and an improved adjustable rear sight was added. The S&W short action was another improvement. Only about 1,000 K-22 Masterpieces were manufactured in 1940.

NIB	Exc.	V.G.	Good	Fair	Poor
—	2000	1600	1000	500	300

NOTE: Add 100 percent premium for 1940 manufacture in 682,420 - 696,952 serial number range.

.38 HAND EJECTOR MILITARY & POLICE 1ST MODEL OR MODEL OF 1899

This was an early swing-out cylinder revolver, and it has no front lockup for the action. The release is on the left side of the frame. This model is chambered for the .38 S&W Special cartridge and the .32 Winchester centerfire cartridge (.32-20), has a 6-shot fluted cylinder, and was offered with a 4", 5", 6", 6.5", or 8" barrel in .38 caliber and 4", 5", and 6-1/2" in .32-20 caliber. The finish is blued or nickel-plated; the grips, checkered walnut or hard rubber. There were approximately 20,975 manufactured between 1899 and 1902 in .38 caliber; serial number range 1 to 20975. In the .32-20 caliber 5,311 were sold between 1899 and 1902; serial number range 1 to 5311.

Commercial Model

NIB	Exc.	V.G.	Good	Fair	Poor
—	1500	1200	800	450	350

U.S. Navy Model

One thousand produced in 1900, .38 S&W, 6" barrel, blued with checkered walnut grips, "U.S.N." stamped on butt, serial number range 5000 to 6000.

NIB	Exc.	V.G.	Good	Fair	Poor
—	3000	2500	1200	500	300

U.S. Army Model

One thousand produced in 1901, same as Navy Model except that it is marked "U.S.Army/Model 1899" on butt, "K.S.M." and "J.T.T." on grips, serial number range 13001 to 14000.

NIB	Exc.	V.G.	Good	Fair	Poor
—	3000	2500	1200	500	300

.38 Hand Ejector M&P 2nd Model or Model of 1902

The 2nd Model is similar in appearance to the 1st Model. The major difference is the addition of the front lockup under the barrel, and the ejector rod was increased in diameter. Barrel lengths for the .38 S&W were 4", 5", 6", or 6-1/2" while the .32-20 was available in 4", 5", or 6-1/2" barrel lengths. Both calibers were offered in round butt only configuration. There were approximately 12,827 manufactured in .38 S&W in 1902 and 1903; serial number range 20976 to 33803. In the .32-20 caliber 4,499 were produced; serial number range 5312 to 9811.

NIB	Exc.	V.G.	Good	Fair	Poor
—	1200	900	500	250	100

.38 Hand Ejector M&P 2nd Model, 1st Change

Built between 1903 and 1905 this variation represents the change to the square butt, which made for better shooting control and standardized frame shape. Both the .38 S&W and the .32-20 were available in 4", 5", or 6-1/2" barrel lengths. The company manufactured 28,645 .38 calibers; serial number range 33804 to 62449 and produced 8,313 .32-20s; serial number 9812 to 18125.

NIB	Exc.	V.G.	Good	Fair	Poor
—	1100	800	400	250	100

.38 Hand Ejector Model of 1905

This model was a continuation of the .38 M&P Hand Ejector series. Built from 1905 to 1906 it was available in 4", 5", 6", and 6-1/2" barrels for both the .38 and .32-20 calibers. Finished in either blue or nickel with round or square butt the .38 caliber model serial number range was from 62450 to 73250 or about 10,800 produced. The .32-20 caliber serial number range spans 18126 to 22426 or 4,300 produced.

NIB	Exc.	V.G.	Good	Fair	Poor
—	1200	950	650	400	150

NOTE: Prices for the following four variations will be the same as those noted above.

.38 Hand Ejector Model of 1905, 1st Change

Produced from 1906 to 1908 this model is similar to the original model of 1905 with regard to barrel lengths, finish and butt styles. The 1st change in .38 caliber was produced in serial number range 73251 to 120000 with 46,749 sold. In .32-20 caliber the serial-number range was 22427 to 33500 with 11,073 sold.

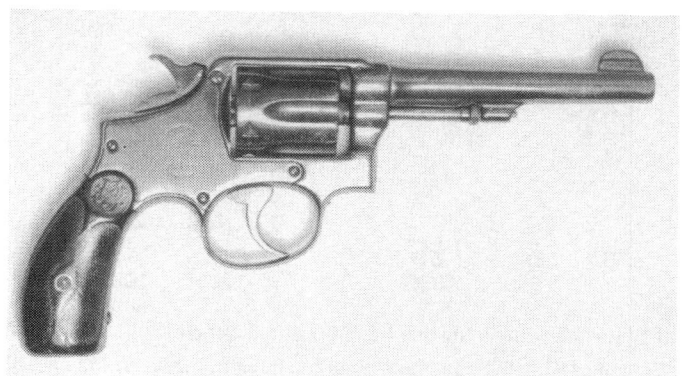

.38 Hand Ejector Model of 1905, 2nd Change

Produced from 1908 to 1909 only internal changes were made to this model. The best approach to differentiate this model is by serial number. The .38 caliber serial number range was from 120001 to 146899 with 26,898 produced. In the .32-20 caliber the serial number range is between 33501 and 45200 with 11,699 produced.

.38 Hand Ejector Model of 1905, 3rd Change

Produced from 1909 to 1915 the 3rd Change variation was available in only 4" or 6" barrel lengths for both the .38 and .32-20 models. The .38 caliber serial number range was between 146900 to 241703 with 94,803 sold.

Courtesy Mike Stuckslager

.38 Hand Ejector Model of 1905, 4th Change

This last variation was also the longest production run. Produced from 1915 to 1942 the .38 caliber model was available in 2", 4", 5", or 6", barrel lengths while the .32-20 caliber was offered in 4", 5", or 6" barrel lengths. The .38 caliber serial number range was from 241704 to 1000000. The .32-20 caliber model was produced from 1915 to 1940 in serial number range from 65701 to 144684.

Courtesy Mike Stuckslager

.22-32 Hand Ejector

This is a very interesting model from the collector's point of view. Phillip B. Bekeart, a San Francisco firearms dealer requested that S&W manufacture a .22 caliber target-grade revolver on the heavier .32 frame. He believed in his idea so passionately that he immediately ordered 1,000 of the guns for himself. This initial order is found within the serial number range 1 to 3000

and are known to collectors as the authentic Bekearts. The remainder of the extensive production run are simply .22-32 Hand Ejectors. This model is chambered for .22 LR cartridge and has a 6-shot fluted cylinder with 6" barrel. The finish is blue, with square butt and checkered extension-type walnut grips. There were only 292 revolvers of his initial order delivered to Mr. Bekeart, but the first 1,000 pistols are considered to be True Bekearts. The production number of each respective pistol is stamped into the base of the extended wooden grips. S&W went on to manufacture several hundred thousand of these revolvers between 1911 and 1953.

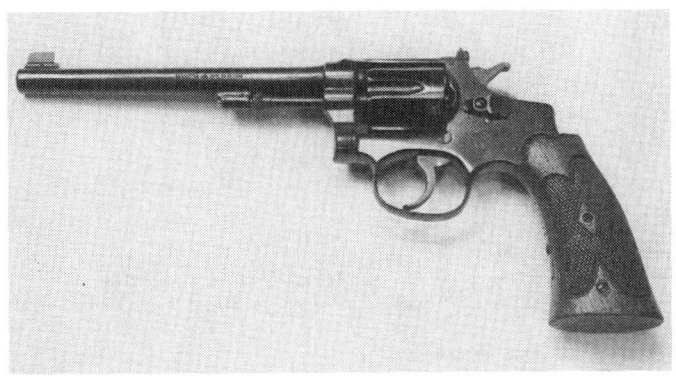

Courtesy Mike Stuckslager

"The True Bekeart"

Serial number range 138226 to 139275 in the .32 Hand Ejector series, production number stamped on butt. Professional appraisal should be secured.

NIB	Exc.	V.G.	Good	Fair	Poor
—	1500	1400	900	700	250

Standard Model

NIB	Exc.	V.G.	Good	Fair	Poor
—	600	400	250	200	125

.44 HAND EJECTOR 1ST MODEL

This model is also known by collectors as the ".44 Triple Lock" or "The New Century." The Triple Lock nickname came from a separate locking device located on the extractor rod shroud that is used in addition to the usual two locks. This model is chambered for the .44 S&W Special cartridge or the .44 S&W Russian. On a limited basis it is also chambered in .44-40, .45 Colt, and .38-40. The fluted cylinder holds 6 shots, and the barrel was offered in standard lengths of 5" or 6.5". A limited quantity of 4" barrel was produced. The finish is blued or nickel-plated; and the grips are checkered walnut, with the gold S&W medallion on later models. There were approximately 15,375 manufactured between 1908 and 1915.

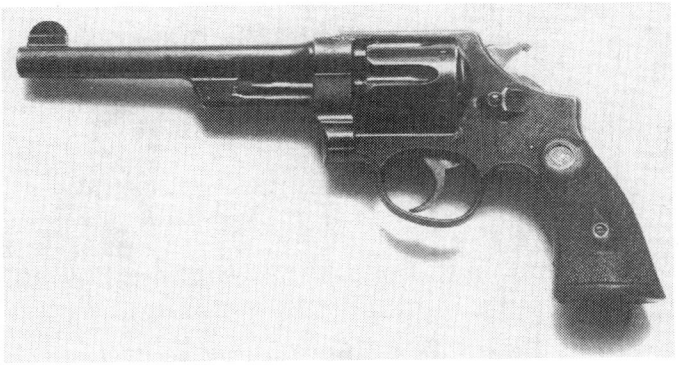

Courtesy Mike Stuckslager

.44 S&W Special

NIB	Exc.	V.G.	Good	Fair	Poor
—	3250	1800	1175	600	500

Other Calibers (Rare)

NIB	Exc.	V.G.	Good	Fair	Poor
—	4000	2000	1300	750	500

.44 HAND EJECTOR 2ND MODEL

This model is quite similar in appearance to the 1st Model. The major difference is the elimination of the third or triple lock device and the heavy ejector rod shroud. Other changes are internal and not readily apparent. This model is also standard in .44 S&W Special chambering but was offered rarely in .38-40, .44-40, and .45 Colt. Specimens have been noted with adjustable sights in 6-1/2" barrel lengths. Standard barrel lengths were 4", 5", and 6-1/2". There were approximately 17,510 manufactured between 1915 and 1937 in serial number range 15376 to 60000.

.44 S&W Special

NIB	Exc.	V.G.	Good	Fair	Poor
—	2300	1800	1250	500	200

.38-40, .44-40 or .45 Colt

NIB	Exc.	V.G.	Good	Fair	Poor
—	3700	3000	2400	1000	500

.44 HAND EJECTOR 3RD MODEL OR MODEL OF 1926

This model is similar in appearance to the 2nd Model but brought back the heavy ejector rod shroud of the 1st Model without the triple lock device. Barrel lengths were 4", 5", and 6-1/2". The .44 Hand Ejector Model was manufactured between 1926 and 1949.

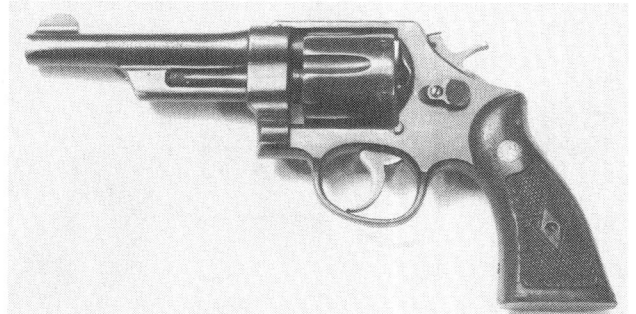

Courtesy Mike Stuckslager

.44 S&W Special

NIB	Exc.	V.G.	Good	Fair	Poor
—	3000	2400	2000	1000	500

.44-40 or .45 Colt

NIB	Exc.	V.G.	Good	Fair	Poor
—	4500	3500	3000	2000	500

.44 Hand Ejector 4th Model (Target Model)

The 4th Model featured a ribbed barrel, micrometer adjustable sight, and short throw hammer. Never a popular seller this model had only 5,050 pistol produced between 1950 and 1966.

NIB	Exc.	V.G.	Good	Fair	Poor
—	3000	2400	2000	1000	500

.45 HAND EJECTOR U.S. SERVICE MODEL OF 1917

WWI was on the horizon, and it seemed certain that the United States would become involved. The S&W people began to work with the Springfield Armory to develop a hand ejector model that would fire the .45-caliber Government cartridge. This was accomplished in 1916 by the use of half-moon clips. The new revolver is quite similar to the .44 Hand Ejector in appearance. It has a 5.5" barrel, blued finish with smooth walnut grips, and a lanyard ring on the butt. The designation "U.S.Army Model 1917" is stamped on the butt. After the war broke out, the government was not satisfied with S&W's production and actually took control of the company for the duration of the war. This was the first time that the company was not controlled by a Wesson. The factory records indicate that there were 163,476 Model 1917s manufactured between 1917 and 1919, the WWI years. After the war, the sale of these revolvers continued on a commercial and contract basis until 1949, when this model was finally dropped from the S&W product line.

Military Model

NIB	Exc.	V.G.	Good	Fair	Poor
—	1500	1200	1000	400	200

Brazilian Contract

25,000 produced for the Brazilian government in 1938. The Brazilian crest is stamped on the sideplate.

NIB	Exc.	V.G.	Good	Fair	Poor
—	1100	800	500	250	125

Commercial Model

Courtesy Mike Stuckslager

High gloss blue and checkered walnut grips.

NIB	Exc.	V.G.	Good	Fair	Poor
—	2000	1500	1000	475	300

.455 Mark II Hand Ejector 1st Model

This model was designed the same as the .44 Hand Ejector 1st Model with no caliber stamping on the barrel. It has a barrel length of 6.4". Of the 5,000 revolvers produced and sold only 100 were commercial guns, the rest were military. Produced between 1914 and 1915. The commercial model is worth a premium.

NIB	Exc.	V.G.	Good	Fair	Poor
—	1400	1150	700	400	200

.455 Mark II Hand Ejector 2nd Model

Similar to the first model without an extractor shroud. Barrel length was also 6.5". Serial number range was 5000 to 74755. Manufactured from 1915 to 1917.

NIB	Exc.	V.G.	Good	Fair	Poor
—	1300	1050	600	350	175

S&W .35 Automatic Pistol

Production of the .35 Automatic was S&W's first attempt at an auto-loading pistol. As was always the case, the company strived for maximum safety and dependability. This model has a 3.5" barrel and a 7-shot detachable magazine and is chambered in .35 S&W Automatic, a one-time-only cartridge that eventually proved to be the major downfall of this pistol from a commercial standpoint. There were two separate safety devices—a revolving cam on the backstrap and a grip safety on the front strap that had to be fully depressed simultaneously while squeezing the trigger. The finish is blue or nickel-plated; and the grips are walnut, with the S&W inlaid medallions. The magazine release slides from side to side and is checkered, expensive to manufacture, and destined to be modified. There were approximately 8,350 manufactured.

NIB	Exc.	V.G.	Good	Fair	Poor
—	750	450	300	200	150

S&W .32 Automatic Pistol

In 1921 it became apparent to the powers that controlled S&W that the .35-caliber automatic was never going to be a commercial success. Harold Wesson, the new president, began to redesign the pistol to accept the .32 ACP, a commercially accepted cartridge, and to streamline the appearance to be more competitive with the other pistols on the market, notably Colt's. This new pistol used as many parts from the older model as possible for economy's sake. The pivoting barrel was discontinued, as was the cam-type safety in the rear grip strap. A magazine disconnector and a reduced-strength recoil spring to ease cocking were employed. The barrel length was kept at 3.5", and the 7-shot magazine was retained. The finish is blued only, and the grips are smooth walnut. There were only 957 of these manufactured between 1924 and 1936. They are eagerly sought by collectors.

Courtesy James Rankin

NIB	Exc.	V.G.	Good	Fair	Poor
—	2500	1750	1100	700	500

SMITH & WESSON MODERN HANDGUNS

NOTE: A surprising number of pistols are still found in their original boxes even for older models. This can add 100 percent to the value of the pistol.With the development of the Hand Ejector Models and the swingout cylinders, Smith & Wesson opened the door to a number of new advancements in the revolver field. This new system allowed for a solid frame, making the weapon much stronger than the old top break design. The company also developed different basic frame sizes and gave them letter designations. The I frame, which later developed into the slightly larger J frame, was used for the .22-32 and the small, concealable .38 revolvers. The medium K frame was used for .38 duty- and target-type weapons. The N frame was the heavy-duty frame used for the larger .357 and .44 and .45 caliber revolvers. The hand ejector went through many evolutionary changes over the years. We strongly recommend that the collector secure a detailed volume that deals exclusively with Smith & Wesson (see the bibliography), and learn all that is available on this fascinating firearm. Models are catalogued the by their numerical designations, brief description are given, and current values offered. It is important to note that the S&W revolver that we see marketed by the company today has undergone many changes in reaching its present configuration. The early models featured five screws in their construction, not counting the grip screw. There were four screws fastening the sideplate and another through the front of the trigger guard that retained the cylinder stop plunger. The first change involved the elimination of the top sideplate screw, and the five-screw Smith & Wesson became the four-screw. Later the frame was changed to eliminate the cylinder stop plunger screw, and the three-screw was created. Some models were offered with a flat cylinder latch that was serrated instead of the familiar checkering. Recently in 1978, the method of attaching the barrel to the frame was changed; and the familiar pin was eliminated. At the same time, the recessed cylinder commonly found on magnum models was also eliminated. All of these factors have a definite affect on the value and collectibility of a particular S&W handgun.NOTE: The pre-model number designations are listed in parentheses after the model number.

IMPORTANT PRICING INFORMATION
Values reflected will be affected by the following factors:

Five Screw Models add 40 to 50 percent.
Four Screw Models add 30 percent.
Models with flat latches add 20 percent.
Models not pinned or recessed deduct 10 percent.

Courtesy Smith & Wesson

Model 10 (.38 Military & Police)

This model has been in production in one configuration or another since 1899. It was always the mainstay of the S&W line and was originally known as the .38 Military and Police Model. The Model

10 is built on the K, or medium frame, and was always meant as a duty gun. It was offered with a 2", 3", 4", 5", or 6" barrel. Currently only the 4" and 6" are available. A round or square butt is offered. It is chambered for the .38 Special and is offered in blue or nickel-plate, with checkered walnut grips. The model designation is stamped on the yoke on all S&W revolvers. This model, with many other modern S&W pistols, underwent several engineering changes. These changes may affect the value of the pistol and an expert should be consulted. The dates of these changes are as follows:

10-NONE-1957	10-1-1959	10-2-1961
10-3-1961	10-4-1962	10-5-1962
10-6-1962		

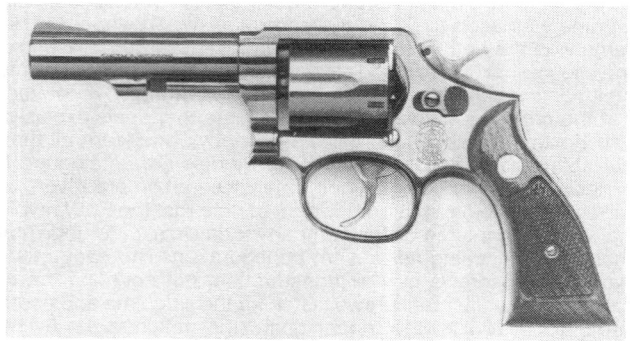

NIB	Exc.	V.G.	Good	Fair	Poor
500	300	200	150	125	90

Victory Model

Manufactured during WWII, this is a Model 10 with a sandblasted and parkerized finish, a lanyard swivel, and smooth walnut grips. The serial number has a V prefix. This model was available in only 2" and 4" barrel lengths. The Victory Model was discontinued on April 27, 1945, with serial number VS811119.

Victory Model marked "N.Y.M.I."   Courtesy Richard M. Kumor, Sr.

NIB	Exc.	V.G.	Good	Fair	Poor
—	600	395	250	100	75

NOTE: Top strap marked Navy will bring a 75 percent premium. Navy variation with both top strap and side plate marked will bring a 100 percent premium. Navy variation marked "N.Y.M.I." will bring a 125 percent premium. Revolvers marked "U.S.G.C." or "U.S.M.C." will bring a premium of unknown amount. Exercise caution.

Model 11 (.38/200 British)

First produced in 1947 S&W received many contracts for this service pistol. Nicknamed the .38/200 British Service Revolver, the company sold many of these models throughout the 1950s and 1960s. There are several rare variations of this model that will greatly affect its value. Consult an expert if special markings and barrel lengths are encountered.

NIB	Exc.	V.G.	Good	Fair	Poor
—	500	375	225	100	75

Model 12 (.38 Military & Police Airweight)

The Model 12 was introduced in 1952, starting serial number C223999, and is merely a Model 10 with a lightweight alloy frame and cylinder. In 1954 the alloy cylinder was replaced with one of steel that added an additional 4 ounces in weight. Discontinued in 1986.

NIB	Exc.	V.G.	Good	Fair	Poor
—	700	500	250	125	100

NOTE: Aluminum cylinder model add 40 percent.

USAF M-13 (Aircrewman)

In 1953 the Air Force purchased a large quantity of Model 12s with alloy frames and cylinders. They were intended for use by flight crews as survival weapons in emergencies. This model was not officially designated "13" by S&W, but the Air Force stamped "M13" on the top strap. This model was rejected by the Air Force in 1954 because of trouble with the alloy cylinder. Beware of fakes!

NIB	Exc.	V.G.	Good	Fair	Poor
—	1500	1150	800	650	300

Model 13 (.357 Military & Police)

This is simply the Model 10 M&P chambered for the .357 Magnum and fitted with a heavy barrel. It was introduced in 1974.

NIB	Exc.	V.G.	Good	Fair	Poor
—	525	350	275	175	125

Model 14 (K-38 Masterpiece)

This model is also known as the "K-38." In 1957 "Model 14" was stamped on the yoke. This model is offered in a 6" barrel with adjustable sights. In 1961 a single-action version with faster lock time was offered. This would be worth a small premium. This model was discontinued in 1981.

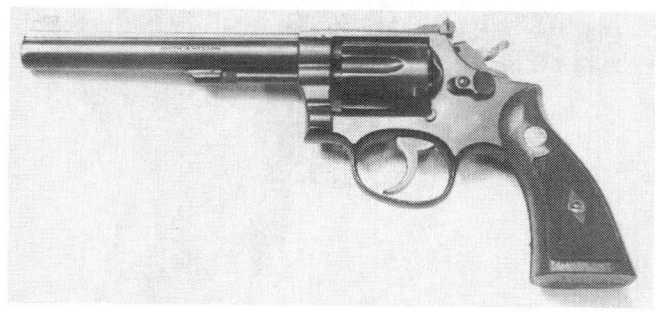

NIB	Exc.	V.G.	Good	Fair	Poor
—	600	450	200	175	125

NOTE: Single-action model add 25 percent.

Model 15 (K-38 Combat Masterpiece)

Also known as the "Combat Masterpiece" this model was produced at the request of law enforcement officers who wanted the "K-38" fitted with a 4" barrel. The model went into production in 1950 and was discontinued in 1987.

NIB	Exc.	V.G.	Good	Fair	Poor
—	475	350	200	175	125

Model 16 (K-32 Masterpiece)

Also known as the "K-32" until 1957, this model is identical in appearance to the Model 14 except that it is chambered for .32 S&W. The Model 16 did not enjoy the commercial popularity of the Model 14 and was dropped from the line in 1973. Only 3,630 K-32s/Model 16s were sold between 1947 and 1973. Reintroduced in 1990 in .32 Magnum and discontinued in 1993.

Courtesy Mike Stuckslager

NIB	Exc.	V.G.	Good	Fair	Poor
—	2200	1800	1200	400	200

NOTE: Add 25 percent for 1946 - 1957 production (no Model 16 marking).

Model 16 (.32 Magnum)

Reintroduced in 1990 in .32 Magnum and discontinued in 1993.

NIB	Exc.	V.G.	Good	Fair	Poor
1250	800	450	200	150	100

K-32 Combat Masterpiece

S&W produced a limited number of 4" barreled K-32 revolvers. They were never given a number designation, as they were discontinued before 1957 when the numbering system began.

NIB	Exc.	V.G.	Good	Fair	Poor
—	2000	1500	900	350	300

Model 17 (K-22)

This is the numerical designation that S&W placed on the "K-22" in 1957. This target model .22 rimfire revolver has always been popular since its introduction in 1946. It is offered in 4", 6", and 8-3/8" barrel lengths, with all target options. The 8-3/8" barrel was dropped from the product line in 1993. The finish is blued, and it has checkered walnut grips.

Courtesy Mike Stuckslager

NIB	Exc.	V.G.	Good	Fair	Poor
650	475	300	175	125	100

Model 17 Plus

Introduced in 1996 this new version of the old Model 17 has a 10-round cylinder for its .22 LR cartridges. It features a 6" full lug barrel with Patridge front sight and adjustable rear sight. The hammer is semi-target style and the trigger is a smooth combat style. Finish is matte black and the grips are Hogue black rubber. Drilled and tapped for scope mounts. Weight is about 42 oz. Discontinued.

NIB	Exc.	V.G.	Good	Fair	Poor
650	475	300	175	125	100

Model 617 Plus

Identical to the Model 17 but furnished with stainless steel frame and cylinder.

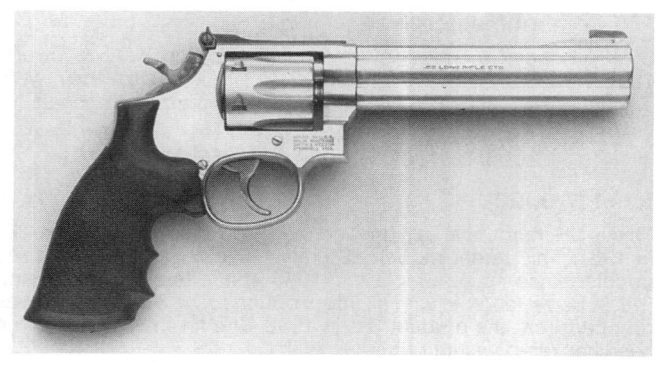

NIB	Exc.	V.G.	Good	Fair	Poor
575	400	250	200	150	100

Model 647

Introduced in 2003 this revolver is chambered for the .17 HMR cartridge. Fitted with a 8.375" barrel with full lug. Six-round cylinder capacity. Stainless steel finish. Adjustable rear sight. Hogue rubber grips. Fitted with a target trigger and hammer. Drilled and tapped for scope. Weight is about 52.5 oz. Discontinued.

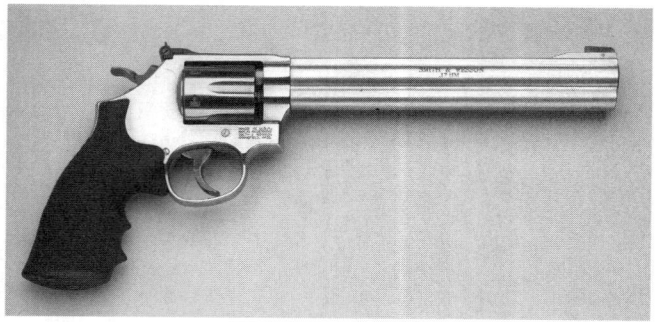

NIB	Exc.	V.G.	Good	Fair	Poor
775	525	375	225	175	100

Model 648

Identical to the Model 617 but chambered for the .22 Magnum rimfire cartridge.

NIB	Exc.	V.G.	Good	Fair	Poor
675	500	375	225	175	100

Model 648 (New Model)

Introduced in 2003 this medium frame revolver is chambered for the .22 WMR cartridge and fitted with a 6" full lug barrel. Pinned Patridge front sight and adjustable rear sight. New extractor system. Drilled and tapped for scope mount. Stainless steel finish. Weight is 45 oz.

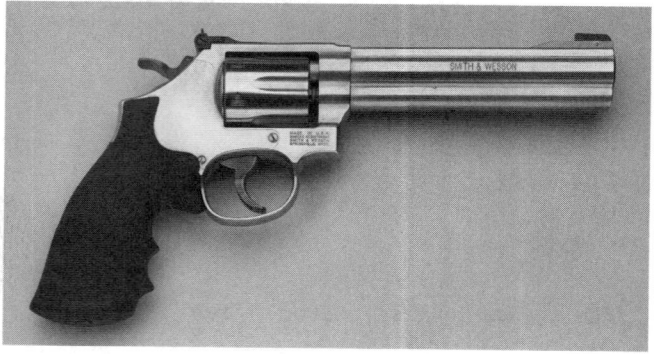

NIB	Exc.	V.G.	Good	Fair	Poor
700	525	395	250	200	125

Note On "K Frame" Target Models:

1. The factory eliminated the upper corner screw from the slide plate in 1955. The 5-screw became a 4-screw. This change occured around serial number K260000.

2. Model number designations were stamped on the yoke in 1957.

Model 18 (K-22 Combat Masterpiece)

This is the model designation for the 4"-barrel "Combat Masterpiece" chambered for the .22 rimfire.

NIB	Exc.	V.G.	Good	Fair	Poor
—	675	475	300	200	125

MODEL 19 (.357 COMBAT MAGNUM)

Introduced in 1954 at the urging of Bill Jordan, a competition shooter with the U.S. Border Patrol who went on to become a respected gun writer, this model is one of Smith and Wesson's most popular pistols. It was built on the "K-Frame" and was the first medium frame revolver chambered for the powerful .357 Magnum cartridge. Since its inception the Model 19 has been one of S&W's most popular revolvers. It was the first revolver to be introduced as a three-screw model. Originally it was offered with a 4" heavy barrel with extractor shroud; the 6" became available in 1963. The finish is blued or nickel plated, and the grips are checkered walnut. The Goncalo Alves target stocks first appeared in 1959. In 1968 a 2.5" round butt version was introduced. The Model 19 has been the basis for two commemoratives—the Texas Ranger/with Bowie Knife and the Oregon State Police/with Belt Buckle. This model is no longer in production.

NIB	Exc.	V.G.	Good	Fair	Poor
600	500	350	200	150	100

Texas Ranger Cased with Knife

NIB	Exc.	V.G.	Good	Fair	Poor
700	—	—	—	—	—

Oregon State Police Cased with Buckle

NIB	Exc.	V.G.	Good	Fair	Poor
900	—	—	—	—	—

Model 20 (.38/.44 Heavy Duty)

Known as the ".38/.44 Heavy Duty" before the change to numerical designations this model was brought out in 1930 in response to requests from law enforcement personnel for a more powerful sidearm. This model, along with the .38-44 S&W Special cartridge, was an attempt to solve the problem. The revolver was manufactured with a standard 5" long barrel but has been noted rarely as short as 3-1/2" and as long as 8-3/8". It was built on the large N-frame and is blued or nickel-plated, with checkered walnut grips. Eventually the popularity of the .357 Magnum made the Model 20 superfluous, and it was discontinued in 1966. Post-war production for this model was about 20,000 revolvers.

Courtesy Mike Stuckslager

NIB	Exc.	V.G.	Good	Fair	Poor
—	1000	850	600	450	200

NOTE: Pre-war add 50 percent.

Model 21 (1950 Military)

This model was known as the "1950 Military" and the "4th Model .44 Hand Ejector" before the Model 21 designation was applied in 1957. The Model 21 was chambered for the .44 Special cartridge and equipped with fixed sights. The Model 21 was built on the N frame and is quite rare, as only 1,200 were manufactured in 16 years of production. It was discontinued in 1966.

NIB	Exc.	V.G.	Good	Fair	Poor
—	2500	1800	950	650	500

Model 696

Introduced in 1997 this model features a 3" underlug barrel. chambered for the .44 Special and fitted on an L-frame, capacity is 5 rounds. Grips are Hogue black rubber. Finish is stainless steel. Weight is approximately 48 oz.

NIB	Exc.	V.G.	Good	Fair	Poor
850	725	600	450	300	—

Model 22 (1950 .45 Military)

This model was known as the "1950 .45 Military" before 1957. It was actually introduced in 1951 and is similar in appearance to the Model 21 except that it is chambered for the .45 Auto Rim or .45 ACP cartridge. Half-moon clips are used with the latter. There were 3,976 manufactured between 1951 and 1966. Beginning serial number for this model was S85,000.

NIB	Exc.	V.G.	Good	Fair	Poor
—	1550	1350	950	650	500

Model 23 (.38-44 Outdoorsman)

The .38-44 Outdoorsman was the model name of this N-frame revolver before the 1957 designation change. This is simply the Model 20 with adjustable sights. It was introduced in 1931 as a heavy-duty sporting handgun with hunters in mind. S&W produced 4,761 of these pre-war revolvers. It features a 6.5" barrel and blued finish and was the first S&W to have the new checkered walnut "Magna" grips. After 1949 this revolver was thoroughly modernized and had the later ribbed barrel. There were a total of 8,365 manufactured before the model was discontinued in 1966. 6,039 were of the modernized configuration.

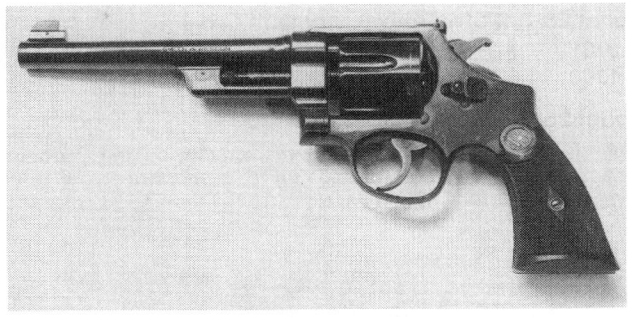

Courtesy Mike Stuckslager

NIB	Exc.	V.G.	Good	Fair	Poor
—	1700	1200	600	250	200

NOTE: Add 50 percent for pre-war production.

Model 22 – Thunder Ranch .45 ACP

Limited edition six-shot single/double-action chambered for .45 ACP. Blued with 4" tapered barrel, 37.5 oz. Cocobolo grips engraved with Thunder Ranch insignia. Fixed sights. SNs begin with TRR0000. Now a regular production item.

NIB	Exc.	V.G.	Good	Fair	Poor
—	850	675	500	250	200

Model 24 (.44 Target Model of 1950)

This model was introduced as the .44 Target Model of 1950. It is simply the N-frame Model 21 with adjustable target sights. This revolver was quite popular with the long-range handgunning devotees and their leader, Elmer Keith. The introduction of the .44 Magnum in 1956 began the death knell of the Model 24, and it was finally discontinued in 1966. S&W produced a total of 5,050 Model 24s. It was reintroduced in 1983 and 1984—and then was dropped again.

NIB	Exc.	V.G.	Good	Fair	Poor
—	2000	1600	1000	650	500

Model 25 (.45 Target Model of 1950)

Prior to the model designation change in 1957 this model was also known as the .45 Target Model of 1955, this was an improved version of the 1950 Target .45. The Model 25 features a heavier barrel 4", 6.5", or 8" in length with blued or nickel-plated finish. All target options were offered. The Model 25 is chambered for the .45 ACP or .45 Auto-rim cartridges. This model was later chambered for .45 Colt as the Model 25-5.

NIB	Exc.	V.G.	Good	Fair	Poor
—	1550	1350	950	650	500

NOTE: Add 100 percent premium for .45 Colt.

Model 25-3 125th Anniversary with Case

NIB	Exc.	V.G.	Good	Fair	Poor
1300	—	—	—	—	—

Model 25-2

This is the discontinued modern version of the Model 25 chambered in .45 ACP. The 6.5" barrel is shortened to 6" and is available in a presentation case.

NIB	Exc.	V.G.	Good	Fair	Poor
—	775	650	400	300	150

Model 25 Mountain Gun

Introduced in 2004 this .45 Colt N-frame round butt model features a 4" tapered barrel with black blade front sight and adjustable rear sight. Cocobolo wood grips. Blued finish. Weight is about 40 oz.

NIB	Exc.	V.G.	Good	Fair	Poor
750	625	500	425	300	150

Model 625-2

This is the stainless steel version of the Model 25-2. It is fitted with a 5" barrel and has Pachmayr SK/GR gripper stocks as standard. Designed for pin shooting. Weight is about 45 oz.

NIB	Exc.	V.G.	Good	Fair	Poor
750	625	500	425	300	150

Notes on N Frame Revolvers:

1. N-Frame models were changed from 5-screw to 4-screw between 1956 and 1958. Serial number SI75000.

2. Trigger guard screw was eliminated in 1961.

3. The pinned barrel and recessed cylinder were discontinued in 1978.

Model 625 IDPA

As above but fitted with a 4" barrel, adjustable rear sight, patridge front sight, and Hogue grips. Introduced in 2002. Weight is about 43 oz.

NIB	Exc.	V.G.	Good	Fair	Poor
1000	850	700	575	400	200

Model 625 JM (Jerry Miculek)

Introduced in 2005 this model is chambered for the .45 ACP cartridge and fitted with a 4" full lug barrel with adjustable rear sight and Patridge front sight. Capacity is 6 rounds. Wood grips. Weight is about 43 oz.

NIB	Exc.	V.G.	Good	Fair	Poor
750	625	500	425	300	150

Model 625 Mountain Gun

Offered for the first time in 1996 this model is chambered for the .45 Colt cartridge. It is fitted with a 4" tapered barrel with ramp front sight and adjustable rear sight. The frame is drilled and tapped for a scope mount. In 2000 this model was offered in .45 Colt caliber. NOTE: The Model 625 Mountain Gun is a limited production revolver limited to between 2,500 and 3,000 guns. When those units are sold the model is no longer in production until re-issued by S&W.

NIB	Exc.	V.G.	Good	Fair	Poor
650	500	400	300	200	125

Model 610

Introduced in 1998 this revolver is chambered for the 10mm cartridge. It is fitted with a 6.5" full-lug barrel and an unfluted cylinder. Hogue grips are standard. Adjustable rear sight. Interchangeable front sight. Weight is approximately 52 oz.

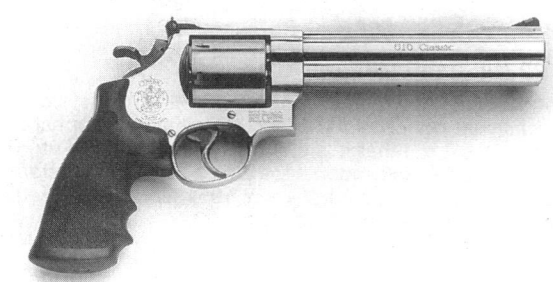

NIB	Exc.	V.G.	Good	Fair	Poor
750	625	500	425	300	150

Model 26 (1950 .45 Target)

This is the numerical designation of the 1950 .45 Target Model. This large N-frame revolver is basically the same as the Model

25 but has a lighter, thinner barrel. This caused its unpopularity among competitive shooters who wanted a heavier revolver. This brought about the Model 25 and the demise of the Model 26 in 1961 after only 2,768 were manufactured. The Model 26 also has two additional variations and are marked 26-1 and 26-2.

NIB	Exc.	V.G.	Good	Fair	Poor
—	2500	1800	1000	500	200

Factory Registered .357 Magnum

In the early 1930s, a gun writer named Phillip B. Sharpe became interested in the development of high performance loads to be used in the then-popular .38-44 S&W revolvers. He repeatedly urged the company to produce a revolver especially made to handle these high pressure loads. In 1934 S&W asked Winchester to produce a new cartridge that would create the ballistics that Sharpe was seeking. This new cartridge was made longer than the standard .38 Special case so that it could not inadvertently be fired in an older gun. The company never felt that this would be a commercially popular venture and from the onset visualized the ".357 Magnum" as a strictly deluxe hand-built item. They were to be individually numbered, in addition to the serial number, and registered to the new owner. The new Magnum was to be the most expensive revolver in the line. The gun went on the market in 1935, and the first one was presented to FBI Director J. Edgar Hoover. The gun was to become a tremendous success. S&W could only produce 120 per month, and this did not come close to filling orders. In 1938 the practice of numbering and registering each revolver was discontinued after 5,500 were produced. The ".357 Magnum," as it was designated, continued as one of the company's most popular items.

The Factory Registered Model was built on the N-frame. It could be custom ordered with any barrel length from 3.5" up to 8-3/8". The finish is blue, and the grips are checkered walnut. This model was virtually hand-built and test targeted. A certificate of registration was furnished with each revolver. The registration number was stamped on the yoke of the revolver with the prefix "Reg." This practice ceased in 1938 after 5,500 were produced.

Courtesy Mike Stuckslager

NIB	Exc.	V.G.	Good	Fair	Poor
—	13500	8500	500	2000	500

NOTE: For top dollar, all accessories and registration letter must be present.

Note: For top dollar, all accessories and registration letter must be present.

Pre-war .357 Magnum

This is the same as the Factory Registered Model without the certificate and the individual numbering. Approximately 1,150 were manufactured between 1938 and 1941. Production ceased for WWII weapons production.

NIB	Exc.	V.G.	Good	Fair	Poor
—	5000	4000	3000	600	300

Model 27 (.357 Magnum)

In 1948 after the end of WWII, production of this revolver commenced. The new rebound slide operated hammer block and short throw hammer were utilized, and the barrel lengths offered were 3.5", 5", 6", 6-1/2", and 8-3/8". In 1957 the model designation was changed to Model 27; and in 1975 the target trigger, hammer and Goncalo Alves target grips were made standard. This revolver is still available from S&W and has been in production longer than any other N-frame pistol. Some additional variations may be of interest to the collector. Around serial number SI71584 the three-screw side plate model was first produced. In 1960 the model designation -1 was added to the model to indicate the change to a left-hand thread to the extractor rod. In 1962 the cylinder stop was changed, which disposed of the need for a plunger spring hole in front of the trigger guard. This change was indicated by a -2 behind the model number. Add $1,000 premium for pre-1957 production.

NIB	Exc.	V.G.	Good	Fair	Poor
725	525	300	250	200	150

Model 627

This is special edition stainless steel version of the Model 27 and is offered with a 5-1/2" barrel. Manufactured in 1989 only. Approximately 4,500 produced.

NIB	Exc.	V.G.	Good	Fair	Poor
650	450	350	300	200	150

Model 627 Pro Series

Introduced in 2008. This is an eight-shot .357 revolver with stainless steel frame, adjustable sights, 4-inch barrel and various accurizing refinements.

NIB	Exc.	V.G.	Good	Fair	Poor
—	900	675	495	300	150

Model 28 (Highway Patrolman)

The Model 27 revolver was extremely popular among law enforcement officers, and many police agencies were interested in purchasing such a weapon—except for the cost. In 1954 S&W produced a new model called, at the time, the "Highway Patrolman." This model had all the desirable performance features of the deluxe Model 27 but lacked the cosmetic features that drove up the price. The finish is a matte blue; the rib is sandblasted instead of checkered or serrated, and the grips are the standard checkered walnut. Barrel lengths are 4" and 6.5". On late models the 6.5" barrel was reduced to 6", as on all S&Ws. The model designation was changed to Model 28 in 1957. S&W discontinued the Model 28 in 1986.

NIB	Exc.	V.G.	Good	Fair	Poor
—	625	475	325	250	100

Model 29 (.44 Magnum)

In the early 1950s, handgun writers, under the leadership of Elmer Keith, were in the habit of loading the .44 Special cartridge to high performance levels and firing them in the existing .44 Hand Ejectors. They urged S&W to produce a revolver strong enough to consistently fire these heavy loads. In 1954 Remington, at the request of S&W produced the .44 Magnum cartridge. As was the case with the .357 Magnum, the cases were longer so that they would not fit in the chambers of the older guns. The first .44 Magnum became available for sale in early 1956. The first 500 were made with the 6.5" barrel; the 4" became available later that year. In 1957 the model designation was changed to 29, and the 8-3/8" barrel was introduced. The Model 29 is available in blue or nickel-plate. It came standard with all target options and was offered in a fitted wood case. The Model 29 is considered by many knowledgeable people to be the finest revolver S&W has ever produced. The older Model 29 revolvers are in a different collector category than most modern S&W revolvers. The early four-screw models can be worth a 50 percent premium in excellent condition. These early models were produced from 1956 to 1958 and approximately 6,500 were sold. One must regard these revolvers on a separate basis and have them individually appraised for proper valuation. In 1993 the 4" barrel was dropped from production. This model is no longer in production.

NIB	Exc.	V.G.	Good	Fair	Poor
1500	1000	550	350	200	150

Early 5-Inch Barrel Model 29

This is the rarest of the Model 29s. A total of 500 were manufactured in 1958. Collectors are cautioned to exercise care before purchasing one of these rare Model 29 variations.

NIB	Exc.	V.G.	Good	Fair	Poor
4000	3200	2500	1500	500	300

Model 629

This revolver is simply a stainless steel version of the Model 29 chambered for the .44 Magnum. In 2002 this model was offered with HiViz sights.

NIB	Exc.	V.G.	Good	Fair	Poor
700	550	400	300	200	125

Model 629 Classic

This model has additional features that the standard Model 629 does not have such as: Chamfered cylinder, full lug barrel, interchangeable front sights, Hogue combat grips, and a drilled and tapped frame to accept scope mounts.

NIB	Exc.	V.G.	Good	Fair	Poor
700	550	400	300	200	125

Model 629 Classic DX

Has all of the features of the Model 629 Classic, introduced in 1991, plus two sets of grips and five interchangeable front sights. Available in 6.5" or 8-3/8" barrel. A 5" barrel option was offered in 1992 but dropped in 1993.

NIB	Exc.	V.G.	Good	Fair	Poor
750	600	500	400	300	200

Model 629 Mountain Gun

This limited edition 6-shot revolver, introduced in 1993, features a 4" barrel chambered for the .44 Magnum. Built on the large N frame this pistol is made from stainless steel and is drilled and tapped for scope mounts. It is equipped with a Hogue round butt rubber monogrip. Standard sights are a pinned black ramp front sight and an adjustable black rear blade. Weight is approximately 40 oz. Model was re-introduced in 1999.

NIB	Exc.	V.G.	Good	Fair	Poor
675	450	400	350	300	150

Model 629 Backpacker

This 1994 variation of the Model 629 is built on the N-frame with round butt. Cylinders are fluted and chamfered. Barrel length is 3" with adjustable rear sight. The finish is stainless steel and Hogue rubber grips are standard. Weight is approximately 40 oz.

NIB	Exc.	V.G.	Good	Fair	Poor
750	600	500	400	300	200

Model 629 Classic Powerport

Introduced in 1996 this model offers a integral compensator with a 6.5" full lug barrel. The Patridge front sight is pinned and the rear sight is fully adjustable. The frame is drilled and tapped for scope mounts. Synthetic Hogue combat-style grips are standard. Weight is approximately 52 oz.

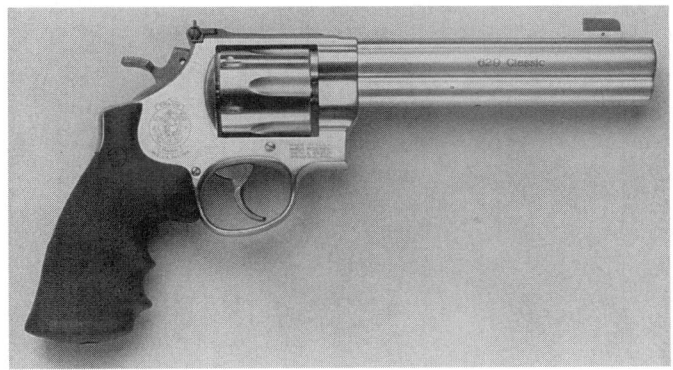

NIB	Exc.	V.G.	Good	Fair	Poor
700	550	400	300	200	125

Fiftieth Anniversary Model 29

A commemorative edition of the classic .44 Magnum. Carbon steel with polished blue finish. Double-action 6-shot. LOA 12", 6.5" barrel, 48.5 oz. Cocobolo wood grips with 24kt gold anniversary logo.

NIB	Exc.	V.G.	Good	Fair	Poor
1500	1000	550	350	200	150

NIGHT GUARD SERIES REVOLVERS

Model 310 Night Guard

Large-frame snubnose revolver chambered in 10mm/.40 S&W (interchangeable). Six-shot cylinder, 2.75" barrel, fixed tritium sights, synthetic grips. Scandium frame, stainless steel cylinder, matte black finish throughout. Weight 28 oz.

NIB	Exc.	V.G.	Good	Fair	Poor
900	775	600	475	300	150

Model 357 Night Guard

Don't let the model name fool you. Large-frame snubnose revolver chambered in .41 Magnum. Six-shot cylinder, 2.75" barrel, fixed tritium sights, synthetic grips. Scandium frame, stainless steel cylinder, matte black finish throughout. Weight 29.7 oz.

NIB	Exc.	V.G.	Good	Fair	Poor
900	775	600	475	300	150

Model 325 Night Guard

A 2-1/2" snubbie chambered for .45 ACP. Tritium sights, scandium alloy frame, matte black finish overall. Neoprene grips. Introduced 2008.

NIB	Exc.	V.G.	Good	Fair	Poor
900	775	600	475	300	150

Model 327 Night Guard

Large-frame snubnose revolver chambered in .357 Magnum/.38 Special +P (interchangeable). Six-shot cylinder, 2.5" barrel, fixed tritium sights, synthetic grips. Scandium frame, stainless steel cylinder, matte black finish throughout. Weight 27.6 oz.

NIB	Exc.	V.G.	Good	Fair	Poor
900	775	600	475	300	150

Model 329 Night Guard

Large-frame snubnose revolver chambered in .44 Magnum/.44 Special (interchangeable). Six-shot cylinder, 2.5" barrel, fixed tritium sights, synthetic grips. Scandium frame, stainless steel cylinder, matte black finish throughout. Weight 29.3 oz.

NIB	Exc.	V.G.	Good	Fair	Poor
900	775	600	475	300	150

Model 386 Night Guard

Medium-frame snubnose revolver chambered in .357 Magnum/.38 Special +P (interchangeable). Seven-shot cylinder, 2.5" barrel, fixed tritium sights, synthetic grips. Scandium frame, stainless steel cylinder, matte black finish throughout. Weight 24.5 oz.

NIB	Exc.	V.G.	Good	Fair	Poor
850	725	550	425	300	150

Model 396 Night Guard

Medium-frame snubnose revolver chambered in .44 Special. Five-shot cylinder, 2.5" barrel, fixed tritium sights, synthetic grips. Scandium frame, stainless steel cylinder, matte black finish throughout. Weight 24.2 oz.

NIB	Exc.	V.G.	Good	Fair	Poor
850	725	550	425	300	150

Model 315 Night Guard

Medium-frame snubnose revolver chambered in .38 Special +P. Six-shot cylinder, 2.5" barrel, fixed tritium sights, synthetic grips. Scandium frame, stainless steel cylinder, matte black finish throughout. Weight 24.0 oz.

NIB	Exc.	V.G.	Good	Fair	Poor
850	725	550	425	300	150

Model 30 (The .32 Hand Ejector)

This model was built on the small I frame and based on the .32 Hand Ejector Model of 1903. This older model was dropped from production in 1942. It was re-introduced in 1949 in a more modern version but still referred to as the .32 Hand Ejector. In 1957 the model designation was changed to Model 30. In 1960 this frame size was dropped, and the J frame, which had been in use since 1950, became standard for the Model 30. S&W stamped -1 behind the model number to designate this important change in frame size.

The Model 30 is chambered for the .32 S&W long cartridge. It has a 6-shot cylinder and 2", 3", 4", and 6" barrel lengths. It has fixed sights and is either blued or nickel-plated. The butt is round, with checkered walnut grips. It was discontinued in 1976.

Courtesy W.P. Hallstein III and son Chip

NIB	Exc.	V.G.	Good	Fair	Poor
—	425	300	200	150	100

Model 31 (.32 Regulation Police)

This model is the same as the Model 30 with a square butt. It was known as the .32 Regulation Police before 1957. Discontinued.

NIB	Exc.	V.G.	Good	Fair	Poor
—	425	300	200	150	100

Model 31 (.32 Regulation Police Target)

The Target model of the Regulation Police is rare. Only 196 of these special variations were produced in 1957. All specifications are the same as the Model 31 except for the addition of adjustable sights.

NIB	Exc.	V.G.	Good	Fair	Poor
—	1500	925	750	525	300

Model 32 (.38/.32 Terrier)

This model, known as the Terrier prior to 1957, was introduced in 1936. It is essentially a .38 Regulation Police chambered for .38 S&W and with a 2" barrel and round butt. Like the Model 30 and 31 this revolver was originally built on the I-frame, which was changed to the J frame in 1960. The -1 behind the model number signifies this change. It is offered in blue or nickel-plate and has a 5-shot cylinder, fixed sights, and checkered walnut grips. This model was discontinued in 1974.

NIB	Exc.	V.G.	Good	Fair	Poor
—	425	300	200	150	100

NOTE: A limited production version with alloy frame and steel cylinder was produced as the Model 032. Add 30 percent for this model.

Model 33 (.38 Regulation Police)

This model is simply the .38 Regulation Police with a square butt and 4" barrel chambered for the .38 S&W. The factory referred to this model as the .38-.32 revolver. It, too, was built on the small I frame and later changed to the J frame in 1960. The Model 33 was discontinued in 1974.

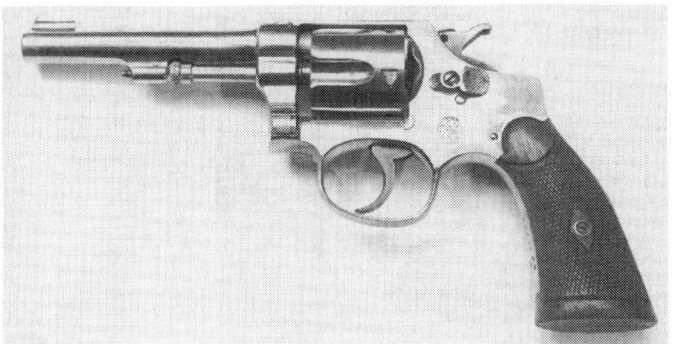

Courtesy Mike Stuckslager

NIB	Exc.	V.G.	Good	Fair	Poor
—	425	300	200	150	100

Model 34 (.22/.32 Kit Gun)

Introduced in 1936 as the .22-32 Kit Gun, it has a 2" or 4" barrel, either round or square butt, and adjustable sights. This model underwent several modifications before it reached its present form. S&W modernized this revolver in 1953 with the addition of a coil mainspring and micro-click sights. The Model 34 is built on this improved version. The revolver is a .32 Hand Ejector chambered for the .22 rimfire. It is built on the I frame until 1960 when the changeover to the improved J frame occurred. The -1 behind the model number indicates this variation. The Model 34 is offered blued or nickel-plate.

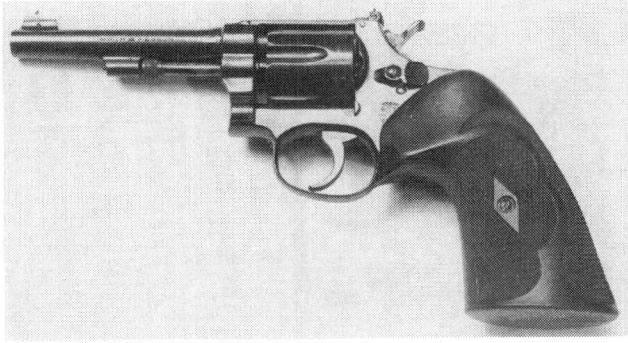

Courtesy Mike Stuckslager

NIB	Exc.	V.G.	Good	Fair	Poor
550	425	300	250	175	100

Model 35 (.22/.32 Target)

This is a square-butt, 6"-barreled version of the .22/32 Hand Ejector. It was known prior to 1957 as the .22/32 Target. It underwent the same changes as the Model 34 but was discontinued in 1973.

Courtesy Mike Stuckslager

NIB	Exc.	V.G.	Good	Fair	Poor
—	600	475	325	275	100

AIRLITE SERIES (TITANIUM CYLINDER—ALUMINUM ALLOY FRAME)

Model 317 AirLite

This 8-round revolver was introduced in 1997 and is chambered for the .22 LR cartridge. It is fitted with a 2" barrel, serrated ramp front sight, fixed rear sight, and Dymondwood boot grips. It is produced from carbon and stainless steel and also aluminum alloy on a J frame. Its weight is about 9.9 oz.

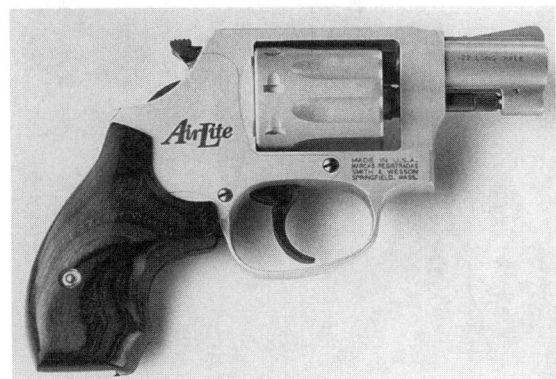

NIB	Exc.	V.G.	Good	Fair	Poor
550	400	375	295	175	100

Model 317 AirLite Kit Gun

This version of the Model 317 was introduced in 1998 and is fitted with a 3" barrel with adjustable rear sight. Choice of Dymondwood grips or Uncle Mike's Combat grips. Weight is about 12 oz. In 2001 this model was offered with HiViz green dot front sight.

NIB	Exc.	V.G.	Good	Fair	Poor
700	550	425	300	200	150

Model 317 AirLite Ladysmith

This model features a 2" barrel and Dymondwood grips. Display case is standard. Weight is about 10 oz.

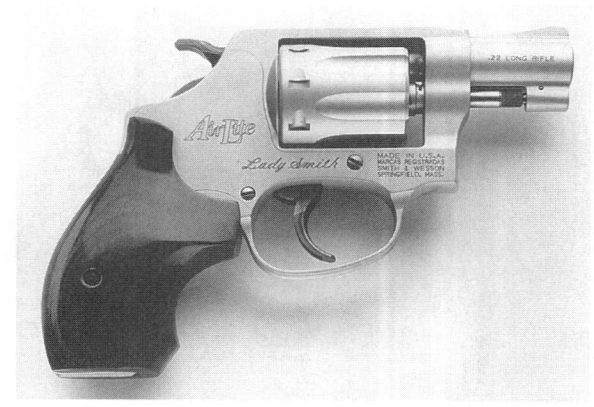

NIB	Exc.	V.G.	Good	Fair	Poor
700	550	425	300	200	150

Model 325PD

Introduced in 2004 this 6-round large frame revolver is chambered for the .45 ACP cartridge. Fitted with a 2.75" barrel. Wooden grips and HiViz sights. Black oxide finish. Weight is about 21.5 oz.

NIB	Exc.	V.G.	Good	Fair	Poor
900	775	600	450	300	150

Model 331 AirLite

This model is chambered for the .32 H&R Magnum cartridge on a J frame. Barrel length is 1-7/8". Exposed hammer offers single or double-action. The frame is aluminum, as is the barrel shroud and yoke. The cylinder is titanium. The barrel has a stainless steel liner. Matte finish. Because the revolver is made from aluminum and titanium it has a two-tone appearance because of the two different materials. Choice of wood or rubber boot grips. Capacity is 6 rounds. Weight is about 12 oz. with rubber grip and 11.2 oz. with wood grip. Introduced in 1999.

NIB	Exc.	V.G.	Good	Fair	Poor
700	550	425	300	200	150

Model 332 AirLite

This model is similar to the Model 331 above but with a concealed hammer, double-action configuration. Weight is 12 oz. with rubber grips and 11.3 oz. with wood grips.

NIB	Exc.	V.G.	Good	Fair	Poor
700	550	425	300	200	150

Model 337 AirLite

This model has an aluminum frame, exposed hammer, titanium cylinder. Front sight is black and pinned. Smooth trigger. Cylinder capacity is five rounds. Chambered for .38 Special +P ammo. Barrel length is 1-7/8". Wood or rubber grips. Weight with wood groups is about 11.2 oz., with rubber grips about 12 oz. Introduced in 1999.

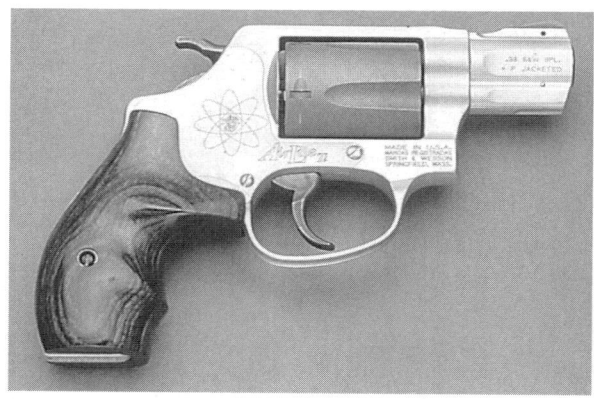

NIB	Exc.	V.G.	Good	Fair	Poor
600	450	325	250	175	100

Model 337 Kit Gun

Similar to the Model 337 but fitted with a 3" barrel. Adjustable rear sight. Weight is about 13.5 oz. In 2001 this model was offered with HiViz green dot front sight.

NIB	Exc.	V.G.	Good	Fair	Poor
650	475	325	250	175	100

Model 337 PD

Similar to the Model 337 but with a matte black finish over the aluminum frame and Hogue Bantam grips. Weight is 10.7 oz. Introduced in 2000.

NIB	Exc.	V.G.	Good	Fair	Poor
600	450	325	250	175	100

Model 340

Introduced in 2001 this hammerless model features a Scandium alloy frame and is fitted with a 1.875" barrel. Chambered for the .357 Magnum cartridge with a 5-round cylinder. Matte stainless gray finish. Pinned black front sight. Hogue Bantam grips standard. Weight is about 12 oz.

NIB	Exc.	V.G.	Good	Fair	Poor
700	550	425	300	200	150

Model 340 PD

Same as the Model 340 but with a gray/black finish. Also introduced in 2001.

NIB	Exc.	V.G.	Good	Fair	Poor
750	500	375	275	200	150

Model 342 AirLite

This is similar to the above model but with double-action-only concealed hammer. Weight is 11.3 oz. with wood grips and 12 oz. with rubber grips. Introduced in 1999.

NIB	Exc.	V.G.	Good	Fair	Poor
700	550	425	300	200	150

Model 342 PD

Similar to the Model 337 but with matte black finish over the aluminum frame and Hogue Bantam grips. Weight is about 10.8 oz. Introduced in 2000.

NIB	Exc.	V.G.	Good	Fair	Poor
700	550	425	300	200	150

Model 351PD

This 7-shot revolver is chambered for the .22 Magnum cartridge and fitted with a 1.875" barrel. Black oxide finish. Rubber grips. HiViz sights. Weight is about 10.6 oz.

NIB	Exc.	V.G.	Good	Fair	Poor
625	475	350	225	175	75

Model 360

This J frame model features a Scandium alloy frame with exposed hammer and 5-shot cylinder. Fixed sights on a 1.875" barrel. Matte stainless grey finish. Weight is about 12 oz. Introduced in 2001.

NIB	Exc.	V.G.	Good	Fair	Poor
700	550	425	300	200	150

Model 360 Kit Gun

This version of the M360 is fitted with a 3.125" barrel with HiViz green dot front sight and adjustable rear sight. Weight is about 14.5 oz. Introduced in 2001.

NIB	Exc.	V.G.	Good	Fair	Poor
700	550	425	300	200	150

Model 386

Introduced in 2001 this L frame model features a 6-shot cylinder chambered for the .357 Magnum cartridge. Fitted with a 3.125" barrel with HiViz green dot front sight and adjustable rear sight. Scandium alloy frame with matte stainless gray finish. Weight is about 18.5 oz. Hogue Bantam grips.

NIB	Exc.	V.G.	Good	Fair	Poor
800	675	500	400	300	200

Model 386 PD

Same as above but with gray/black finish and 2.5" barrel with red ramp front sight and adjustable rear sight. Weight is about 17.5 oz.

NIB	Exc.	V.G.	Good	Fair	Poor
800	675	500	400	300	200

Model 386 Sc/S

Single-/double-action L-frame revolver in .38/.357 Magnum. 7-shot cylinder, 2.5" barrel, Patridge front sight, adjustable rear, scandium/alloy frame, matte black finish, rubber grips. Introduced 2007.

NIB	Exc.	V.G.	Good	Fair	Poor
750	600	475	350	250	175

Model 386 XL Hunter

Single/double action L-frame revolver chambered in .357 Magnum. Features include 6-inch full-lug barrel, 7-round cylinder, Hi-Viz fiber optic front sight, adjustable rear sight, candium frame, stainless steel cylinder, black matte finish, synthetic grips.

NIB	Exc.	V.G.	Good	Fair	Poor
750	625	550	465	350	150

Model 396 Mountain Lite

This L frame revolver is chambered for the .44 Special cartridge. It is fitted with a five round titanium cylinder and aluminum alloy frame. Barrel length is 3" and has a green HiViz front sight and an adjustable rear sight. Introduced in 2000. Weight is approximately 19 oz.

NIB	Exc.	V.G.	Good	Fair	Poor
750	600	475	350	250	175

Model 242

This medium frame revolver is chambered for the .38 Special +P cartridge. Semi-concealed hammer and 2.5" barrel. Pinned black ramp front sight. Black rubber boot grips. Seven-round cylinder. Matte alloy and titanium finish. Weight is about 19 oz. Introduced in 1999. This model is no longer in production.

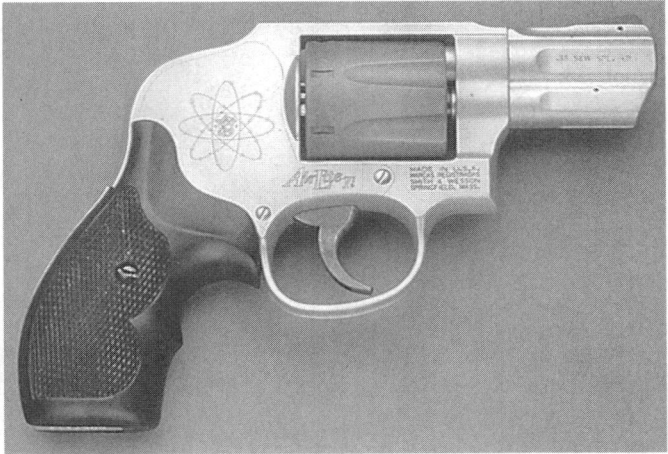

NIB	Exc.	V.G.	Good	Fair	Poor
550	450	300	225	175	75

Model 296

Also a medium frame revolver chambered for the .44 Special cartridge. Fitted with a 2.5" barrel. Concealed hammer. Cylinder capacity is 5 rounds. Weight is about 19 oz. Introduced in 1999.

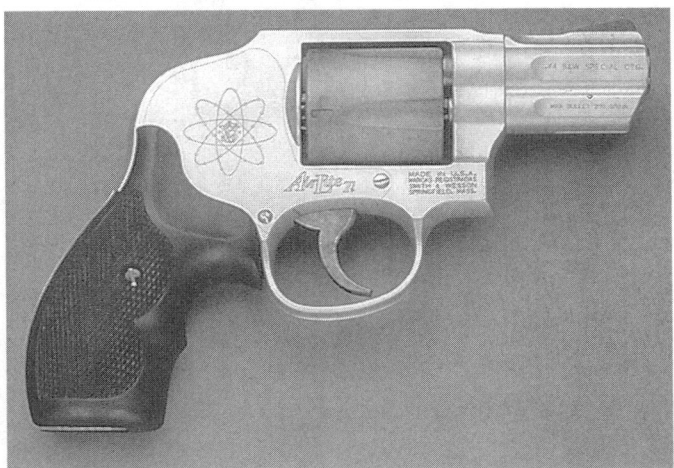

NIB	Exc.	V.G.	Good	Fair	Poor
700	550	425	300	200	150

Model 586

Six or seven shot double action revolver (L frame) chambered for the .357 Magnum cartridge. It will also chamber and fire .38 Special cartridges. The 686 has been available with 2-1/2-; 3-; 4-; 5- 6- and 8-3/8-inch barrel lengths. Blued frame and cylinder, adjustable sights, walnut Magna or rubber grips.

NIB	Exc.	V.G.	Good	Fair	Poor
550	425	300	200	150	100

Model 686

Six or seven shot double action revolver (L frame) chambered for the .357 Magnum cartridge. It will also chamber and fire .38 Special cartridges. The 686 has been available with 2-1/2-; 3-; 4-; 5- 6- and 8-3/8-inch barrel lengths. Stainless steel frame and cylinder, adjustable sights, walnut Magna or rubber grips. Introduced in 1980.The Performance Center also made a limited number of 686s in .38 Super for competitive shooters. Add 50% for Super.

NIB	Exc.	V.G.	Good	Fair	Poor
700	550	425	300	200	150

Model 329PD

Chambered for the .44 Magnum cartridge and fitted with a 4" barrel, this large frame revolver has a Scandium frame with matte black finish. Orange dot front sight and adjustable rear sight. Cylinder capacity is six rounds. Wood or rubber grips. Weight is approximately 26.5 oz. Introduced in 2003.

NIB	Exc.	V.G.	Good	Fair	Poor
800	675	500	400	300	200

Model 610 (2007 Reintroduction)

This N frame model is chambered for the 10mm cartridge and fitted with a variety of barrel lengths. Adjustable rear sight. Six-round non-fluted cylinder. Hogue rubber combat grips. Stainless steel finish. Weight is about 50 oz. for 4-inch model. Reintroduced in 2007.

NIB	Exc.	V.G.	Good	Fair	Poor
750	600	475	350	250	175

Model 36 (.38 Chief's Special)

This model, known as the Chief's Special, was introduced in 1950. It was built on the J frame and is chambered for the .38 Special cartridge. It holds 5 shots, has a 2" or 3" barrel, and was initially offered in a round butt. In 1952 a square-butt version was released. It is finished in blue or nickel-plate and has checkered walnut grips. A 3" heavy barrel was first produced in 1967 and became standard in 1975. The 2" barrel was dropped from production in 1993.

NIB	Exc.	V.G.	Good	Fair	Poor
575	375	275	200	150	100

Model 36LS (.38 Ladysmith)

This model is similar to the Model 36 with the exception that it is only offered with a 2" barrel, comes with rosewood grips and a soft carrying case. Weighs 20 oz.

NIB	Exc.	V.G.	Good	Fair	Poor
625	450	300	200	150	100

Model 36 (Chief's Special Target)

Since 1955 a limited number of Chief's Specials with adjustable sights have been manufactured. They have been offered with 2" or 3" barrels, round or square butts, and either blue or nickel-plated. Between 1957 and 1965, these target models were stamped Model 36 on the yoke. The revolvers manufactured between 1965 and the model discontinuance in 1975 were marked Model 50. This is a very collectible revolver. A total of 2,313 of these special target models were sold in various model designations. Some are more rare than others.

Courtesy W.P. Hallstein III and son Chip

NIB	Exc.	V.G.	Good	Fair	Poor
—	775	575	300	200	125

Model 37

Introduced in 1952 as the Chief's Special Airweight, this revolver initially had an alloy frame and cylinder. In 1954, following many complaints regarding damaged revolvers, the cylinders were made of steel. Barrel lengths, finishes, and grip options on the Airweight are the same as on the standard Chief Special. In 1957 the Model 37 designation was adopted. These early alloy frame and cylinder revolvers were designed to shoot only standard velocity .38 Special cartridges. The use of high velocity ammunition was not recommended by the factory.

NIB	Exc.	V.G.	Good	Fair	Poor
575	375	275	200	150	100

NOTE: All 1998 and later production models were rated for +P ammunition.

Model 637

Same as the model above but with aluminum frame and stainless steel finish.

NIB	Exc.	V.G.	Good	Fair	Poor
575	375	275	200	150	100

NOTE: Current production models are now rated for +P ammunition.

Model 637 Carry Combo

As above but supplied with Kydex carry holster. Introduced in 2004.

NIB	Exc.	V.G.	Good	Fair	Poor
575	375	275	200	150	100

Model 637 Power Port Pro Series

Aluminum J-frame 5-shot revolver with stainless steel cylinder chambered for .38 Special (5 shots). 2-1/8-inch ported black stainless barrel. Introduced 2008. Dealer sets pricing.

NIB	Exc.	V.G.	Good	Fair	Poor
575	375	275	200	150	100

Model 637CT

Same as Model 6377 but with Crimson Trace lasergrips.

NIB	Exc.	V.G.	Good	Fair	Poor
650	575	375	275	200	100

Model 38 (Airweight Bodyguard)

This model was introduced in 1955 as the Airweight Bodyguard. This was a departure from S&W's usual procedure in that the alloy-framed version came first. The Model 38 is chambered for .38 Special and is available with a 2" barrel standard. Although a 3" barrel was offered, it is rarely encountered. The frame of the Bodyguard is extended to conceal and shroud the hammer but at the same time allow the hammer to be cocked by the thumb. This makes this model an ideal pocket revolver, as it can be drawn without catching on clothing. It is available either blue or nickel-plated, with checkered walnut grips.

NIB	Exc.	V.G.	Good	Fair	Poor
525	350	225	175	125	100

NOTE: All 1998 and later production models were rated for +P ammunition.

Model 638

Same as the model above but with aluminum frame and stainless steel finish.

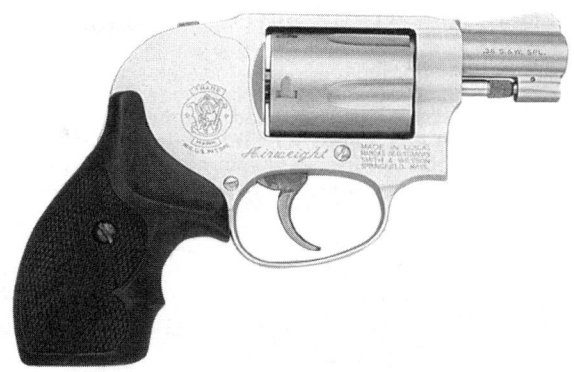

NIB	Exc.	V.G.	Good	Fair	Poor
475	375	300	225	175	125

NOTE: Current production models are now rated for +P ammunition.

Model 49 (Bodyguard)

This model was introduced in 1959 and is identical in configuration to the Model 38 except that the frame is made of steel.

NIB	Exc.	V.G.	Good	Fair	Poor
—	575	450	300	250	200

Model 649 (Bodyguard Stainless)

This stainless steel version of the Model 49 was introduced in 1985. It is also available in .357 Magnum. As of 1998 this model was also offered in a .38 Special-only version.

NIB	Exc.	V.G.	Good	Fair	Poor
500	350	225	200	175	125

Model 40 (aka Model 42) Centennial

This model was introduced in 1952 as Smith & Wesson's 100th anniversary and appropriately called the "Centennial Model." It is of the Safety Hammerless design. This model was built on the J frame and features a fully concealed hammer and a grip safety. The Model 40 is chambered for the .38 Special cartridge. It is offered with a 2" barrel in either blue or nickel plate. The grips are checkered walnut. The Centennial was discontinued in 1974.

Courtesy Mike Stuckslager

Model 42—Airweight Centennial

This model is identical in configuration to the Model 40 except that it was furnished with an aluminum alloy frame. It was also discontinued in 1974.Editors Note: The first 37 Model 42s were manufactured with aluminum alloy cylinders. They weigh 11-1/4 ounces compared to 13 ounces for the standard model. The balance of Model 42 production was with steel cylinders. Add 300 percent for this extremely rare variation.

NIB	Exc.	V.G.	Good	Fair	Poor
450	400	325	200	150	100

Model 640 Centennial

A stainless steel version of the Model 40 furnished with a 2" or 3" barrel. Both the frame and cylinder are stainless steel. The 3" barrel was no longer offered as of 1993. As of 1998 this model was also offered in a .38 Special-only version.

NIB	Exc.	V.G.	Good	Fair	Poor
500	375	250	200	150	100

Model 640 Centennial .357 Magnum

Introduced in 1995 this version of the Model 640 is chambered for the .357 cartridge and fitted with a 2-1/8" barrel. The gun is stainless steel with a fixed notch rear sight and pinned black ramp front sight. It is 6-3/4" in length and weighs 25 oz.

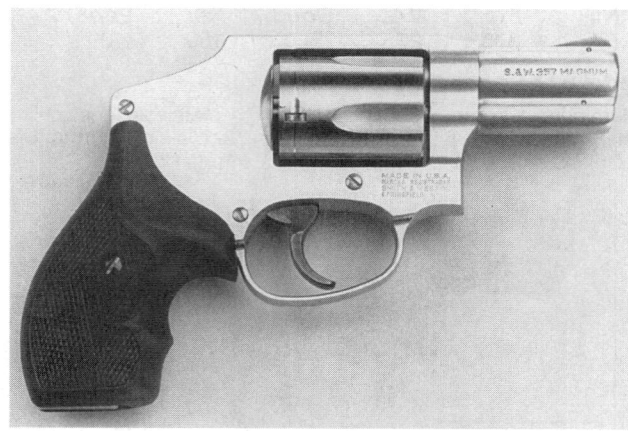

NIB	Exc.	V.G.	Good	Fair	Poor
525	400	250	200	150	100

Model 642 Centennial Airweight

Identical to the Model 640 with the exception of a stainless steel cylinder and aluminum alloy frame. Furnished with a 2" or 2.5" barrel. Discontinued in 1992. Replaced by the Model 442 which was introduced in 1993. This model was reintroduced in 1996.

NIB	Exc.	V.G.	Good	Fair	Poor
450	300	250	200	150	100

NOTE: Current production models are now rated for +P ammunition.

Model 642CT (Crimson Trace)

As above but fitted with Crimson Trace laser grips. Weight is about 15 oz. Introduced in 2004.

NIB	Exc.	V.G.	Good	Fair	Poor
650	575	375	275	200	100

Model 642LS Ladysmith

Similar to Model 642 but fitted with smooth combat wood grips and a softside carry case.

NIB	Exc.	V.G.	Good	Fair	Poor
575	450	325	275	175	100

NOTE: Current production models are now rated for +P ammunition.

Model 642 PowerPort Pro Series

Similar to Model 642 buit with gray aluminum frame and black stainless ported barrel. Dealer sets pricing. Introduced 2008.

NIB	Exc.	V.G.	Good	Fair	Poor
575	450	325	275	175	100

Model 631

This revolver is chambered for the .32 Magnum cartridge and is fitted with a 2" (fixed sights) or 4" (adjustable sights) barrel. Stainless steel finish. Weight with 23" barrel is 22 oz. Produced in 1990.

NIB	Exc.	V.G.	Good	Fair	Poor
650	575	375	275	200	100

Model 631 Lady Smith

Similar to the above model but with rosewood grips and laser etched. Fitted with 2" barrel.

NIB	Exc.	V.G.	Good	Fair	Poor
650	575	375	275	200	100

Model 632 Centennial

This model is similar to the other Centennial models but is chambered for the .32 H&R Magnum cartridge. It comes standard with a 2" barrel, stainless steel cylinder and aluminum alloy frame. Dropped from the product line in 1993.

NIB	Exc.	V.G.	Good	Fair	Poor
650	575	375	275	200	100

Smith & Wesson Model 632 PowerPort Pro Series

J-frame revolver chambered in .327 Federal Magnum. Six-shot cylinder, 3" full-lug ported barrel with full-length extractor. Pinned, serrated front sight, adjustable rear. Synthetic grips. Stainless steel frame and cylinder.

NIB	Exc.	V.G.	Good	Fair	Poor
775	650	495	350	250	175

Smith & Wesson Models 637 CT/638 CT/642 CT

Similar to Models 637, 638 and 642 but with Crimson Trace Laser Grips. Suggested retail price $920.

Model 042 Centennial Airweight

This model was produced in 1992 but is not catalogued. It is chambered for .38 Special and fitted with a 2" barrel. The frame is alloy. Marked "MOD 042." No grip safety. Blued finish. Weight is about 16 oz. Supposedly a reworked Model 642 "blemish gun" distributed through a national wholesaler.

NIB	Exc.	V.G.	Good	Fair	Poor
650	575	375	275	200	100

Model 442 Centennial Lightweight

This 5-shot revolver is chambered for the .38 Special and is equipped with a 2" barrel, aluminum alloy frame, and carbon steel cylinder. It has a fully concealed hammer and weighs 15.8 oz. The front ramp sight is serrated and the rear sight is a fixed square notch. Rubber combat grips from Michael's of Oregon are standard. Finish is either blue/black or satin nickel. Introduced in 1993.

NIB	Exc.	V.G.	Good	Fair	Poor
400	300	250	200	150	100

NOTE: Current production models are now rated for +P ammunition.

Smith & Wesson Model 442/642/640/632 Pro Series Revolvers

Double action only J-frame with concealed hammers chambered in .38 Special +P (442 & 642), .357 Magnum (640) or .327 Federal (632). Features include 5-round cylinder, matte stainless steel frame, fixed sights or dovetail night sights (632, 640), synthetic grips, cylinder cut for moon clips (442, 642, 640). Suggested retail price $640 (standard) to $916 (night sights).

Smith & Wesson Model 438

J-frame double-action-only revolver chambered in .38 Special +P. Five-shot cylinder, 1.87" barrel, fixed front and rear sights, synthetic grips. Aluminum alloy frame, stainless steel cylinder. Matte black finish throughout.

NIB	Exc.	V.G.	Good	Fair	Poor
575	450	325	275	175	100

Model 940

Styled like the other Centennial models, this model is chambered for the 9mm Parabellum cartridge. It has a stainless steel cylinder and frame and is furnished with a 2" or 3" barrel. The 3" barrel version was dropped from production in 1993.

Model 43 (.22/.32 Kit Gun Airweight)

This model was built on the J frame, is chambered for .22 rimfire, has a 3.5" barrel, and is offered in a round or square butt, with checkered walnut grips. It has adjustable sights and is either blued or nickel-plated. The frame is made of aluminum alloy. Except for this, it is identical to the Model 34 or .22/.32 Kit Gun. This model has a rare 2" barrel configuration as well as a .22 WRM model. The Model 43 was introduced in 1954 and was discontinued in 1974.

Courtesy Mike Stuckslager

NIB	Exc.	V.G.	Good	Fair	Poor
650	575	375	275	200	100

Model 51 (.22/.32 Kit Gun Magnum)

This model is simply the Model 34 chambered for the .22 Winchester Magnum rimfire. It was first introduced in 1960 beginning with serial number 52637. Available in both round and square butt with the round butt variation having a total production of only 600. The Model 51 was discontinued in 1974.

NIB	Exc.	V.G.	Good	Fair	Poor
—	675	400	250	200	125

Model 651

This stainless steel version of the Model 51 .22 Magnum Kit Gun was manufactured between 1983 and 1987.

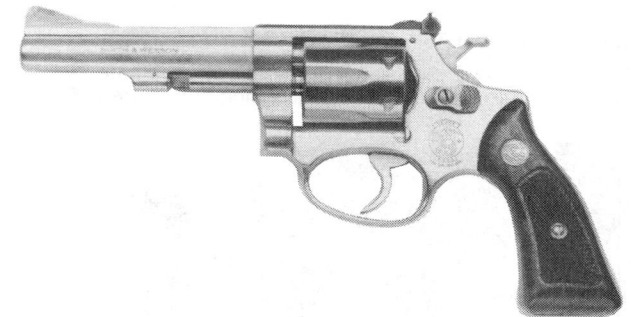

NIB	Exc.	V.G.	Good	Fair	Poor
—	675	400	250	200	125

Model 73

Produced in about 1973 this revolver was built on a special "C" size frame. Cylinder holds 6 rounds and is chambered for the .38 Special cartridge. Fitted with a 2" barrel. A total of 5,000 were built. All but 20 were destroyed. An extremely rare S&W revolver. Marked, "MOD 73" on yoke.

Courtesy Jim Supica, Old Town Station

NIB	Exc.	V.G.	Good	Fair	Poor
8500	—	—	—	—	—

Model 45 (Post Office)

This model is a special purpose K-frame Military & Police Model chambered for the .22 rimfire. It was designed as a training revolver for police departments and the U.S. Postal Service. This model was manufactured in limited quantities between 1948 and 1957. In 1963 production abruptly began and ended again. There were 500 of these revolvers released on a commercial basis, but they are rarely encountered.

NIB	Exc.	V.G.	Good	Fair	Poor
1250	800	650	450	300	100

Model 48 (K-22 Masterpiece Magnum)

Introduced in 1959 and is identical to the Model 17 or K-22 except that it is chambered for the .22 WRM cartridge. Offered in 4", 6", and 8-3/8" barrel lengths, it has a blued finish. Discontinued in 1986.

NIB	Exc.	V.G.	Good	Fair	Poor
700	500	275	225	150	100

Model 53 (Magnum Jet)

Introduced in 1961 and chambered for the .22 Jet, a Remington cartridge. The barrel lengths were 4", 6", and 8-3/8" and the finish is blued. Sights were adjustable and the revolver was furnished with cylinder inserts that would allow .22 rimfire cartridges to be fired. The frame had two firing pins. Approximately 15,000 were produced before it was discontinued in 1974. Price includes guns with individual chambered inserts.

NIB	Exc.	V.G.	Good	Fair	Poor
1500	750	450	350	250	200

NOTE: Add $150 for auxiliary .22 LR cylinder.

Model 57

This revolver was introduced in 1964 and is chambered for the .41 Magnum cartridge. It is built on the N frame. Offered in 4", 6", and 8-3/8" barrel lengths, it has a blued frame and adjustable sights. Model designations are: 57-1 1982; 57-2 1988; 57-3 1990; 57-4 1993.

NIB	Exc.	V.G.	Good	Fair	Poor
600	400	275	225	200	150

Model 657

This is a stainless steel version of the Model 57 and was introduced in 1980. Still in production. In 2001 this model was reintroduced again with a 7.5" barrel with pinned front sight and adjustable rear sight. Hogue rubber combat grips. Weight is about 52 oz.

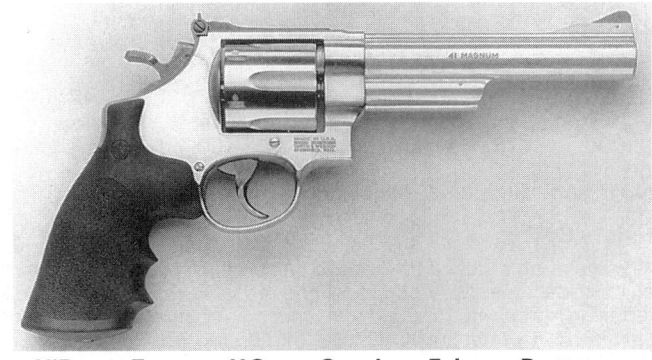

NIB	Exc.	V.G.	Good	Fair	Poor
670	525	425	295	200	150

Model 56 (KXT-38 USAF)

Introduced in 1962 this is a 2" heavy barrel built on the K frame. It is chambered for the .38 Special. There were approximately 15,000 of these revolvers built when it was discontinued in 1964. It was marked "US" on the backstrap. A total of 15,205 produced but most destroyed.

NIB	Exc.	V.G.	Good	Fair	Poor
4500	1750	1250	750	500	250

Model 58

This model is chambered for the .41 Magnum and is fitted with fixed sights. Offered in blued or nickel finish and with 4" barrel. Checkered walnut grips are standard. Introduced in 1964.

NIB	Exc.	V.G.	Good	Fair	Poor
1100	650	450	300	225	125

Model 547

Introduced in 1980 and chambered for the 9mm cartridge and offered with either 3" or 4" barrel. Finish is blued. Discontinued.

NIB	Exc.	V.G.	Good	Fair	Poor
650	475	375	275	200	125

Model 460 XVR

Introduced in 2005 this model is chambered for the .460 S&W magnum, which has the highest muzzle velocity of any production handgun. Fitted with a 8-3/8" barrel with interchangeable compensators. Frame size is extra large. Capacity is 5 rounds. Adjustable sights with Hi-Viz front sight. Finger groove grips. Satin stainless finish. Weight is about 72.5 oz.

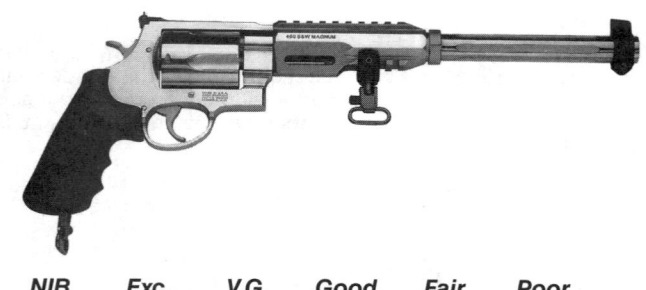

NIB	Exc.	V.G.	Good	Fair	Poor
1000	875	750	600	400	300

NOTE: Add $135 for 4" barrel model.

Model 460V

X-frame double-action trigger and 5" barrel in .460 S&W Magnum caliber. Also accepts .454 Casull and .45 Colt. Sorbothane recoil-reducing grip, interchangeable muzzle compensator. 5-shot, stainless with satin finish. 62.5 oz. Introduced 2006.

NIB	Exc.	V.G.	Good	Fair	Poor
1000	875	750	600	400	300

Model 500

Introduced in 2003 this revolver is chambered for the .500 S&W Magnum cartridge. Fitted with a 8.375" barrel with compensator and built on the X frame. Cylinder holds five rounds. Stainless steel frame and barrel. Interchangeable front blade sight and adjustable rear sight. K-frame size Hogue grips. Weight is about 72.5 oz. In 2004 this model was offered with a 4" barrel with compensator. Weight is about 56 oz. 6.5-inch model introduced 2008.

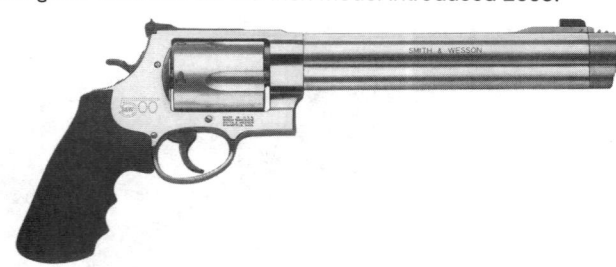

S&W Model 500 with 4" barrel

NIB	Exc.	V.G.	Good	Fair	Poor
1000	875	750	600	400	300

NOTE: Add $135 for 4" barrel model.

MODEL 60

Introduced in 1965 this model is similar to the Model 36 but in stainless steel. Offered in 2" barrel with fixed sights, walnut grips, and smooth trigger. Some 2" Model 60s were produced with adjustable sights add 50 percent. The 3" barrel version comes with a full underlug, adjustable sights, serrated trigger, and rubber grips. The 2" version weighs about 20 oz. while the 3" version weighs approximately 25 oz. In 1996 this model was offered chambered for the .357 Magnum cartridge. This new version is fitted with a 2-1/8" barrel. The 2-1/8" barrel weighs about 23 oz. This model was also offered in a .38 Special-only version.

2" Barrel

NIB	Exc.	V.G.	Good	Fair	Poor
450	350	300	200	125	100

3" Barrel

NIB	Exc.	V.G.	Good	Fair	Poor
475	375	350	250	150	100

5" Barrel

Introduced in 2005.

NIB	Exc.	V.G.	Good	Fair	Poor
550	475	375	295	200	125

Model 60LS (LadySmith)

Chambered for the .38 Special with 2" barrel and stainless steel frame and cylinder. This slightly smaller version of the Model 60 is made for small hands. A new version offered in 1996 is chambered for the .357 Magnum cartridge.

NIB	Exc.	V.G.	Good	Fair	Poor
450	350	300	200	125	100

Model 60 with Hi-Viz Sight

Similar to Model 60 but with light-gathering Hi-Viz red dot front sight and adjustable rear sight. Introduced 2007.

NIB	Exc.	V.G.	Good	Fair	Poor
525	400	300	225	175	100

Model 60 Pro Series

Similar to Model 60 but in .38/.357 with night front sights, "high-hold" enforcing walnut grips, 3-inch battel and matte stainless finish. Introduced 2008.

NIB	Exc.	V.G.	Good	Fair	Poor
650	475	375	275	200	125

Model 63

This model, introduced in 1977, is simply the Model 34 made of stainless steel.

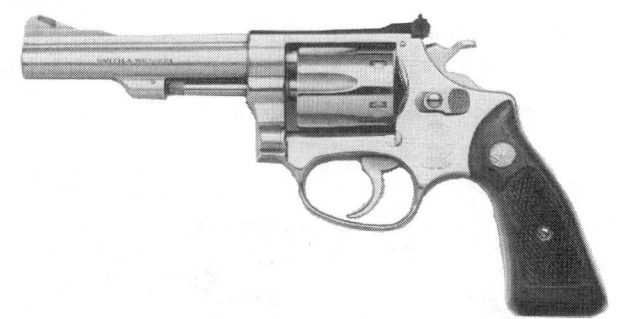

NIB	Exc.	V.G.	Good	Fair	Poor
500	375	250	225	200	150

Model 64 (Military & Police Stainless)

This model is the stainless steel version of the Model 10 M&P. It was introduced in 1970. The Model 64-1 variation was introduced in 1972 and is the heavy barrel version.

NIB	Exc.	V.G.	Good	Fair	Poor
500	325	275	225	175	125

Model 65 (.357 Military & Police Heavy Barrel Stainless)

This is the stainless steel version of the Model 13 M&P .357 Magnum. It was introduced in 1974.

NIB	Exc.	V.G.	Good	Fair	Poor
425	300	275	225	175	125

Model 66 (.357 Combat Magnum Stainless)

Released in 1970, this is the stainless steel version of the Model 19 or Combat Magnum. It is chambered for the .357 Magnum, has adjustable sights, a square butt with checkered walnut grips, and was initially offered with a 4" barrel. In 1974 a 2.5" barrel, round butt version was made available. It was available in a 6" barrel, as well as all target options until discontinued in 1993.

NIB	Exc.	V.G.	Good	Fair	Poor
575	400	250	200	150	125

Model 67 (.38 Combat Masterpiece Stainless)

Introduced in 1972 this is a stainless steel version of the Model 15 with a 4" barrel. It is chambered for the .38 Special cartridge. Model designation changes are as follows: {None} 1972 to 1977; {-1} 1977 to 1988; {-2} 1988 to 1993; {-3} 1993 to present.

NIB	Exc.	V.G.	Good	Fair	Poor
500	300	250	200	150	100

Model 650

Introduced in 1983 this stainless steel model is built on a J frame with a 3" heavy barrel chambered for the .22 WRM. It has a round butt and fixed sights. Discontinued in 1988.

NIB	Exc.	V.G.	Good	Fair	Poor
600	450	250	175	125	100

Model 651

This J-frame model was introduced in 1983 and chambered for the .22 WRM and fitted with a 4" barrel. Stainless steel finish and adjustable sights. Designation changes are: {None} 1983 to 1988; {-1} 1988 to 1990; {-2} 1988 to 1990.

NIB	Exc.	V.G.	Good	Fair	Poor
575	400	250	200	150	100

Model 686 Powerport

Introduced in 1995 this version of the Model 686 features a 6" full lug barrel with integral compensator. The frame is drilled and tapped for scope mounts. Hogue grips are furnished as standard.

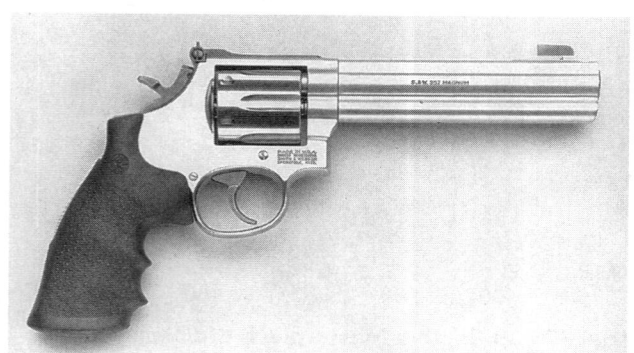

NIB	Exc.	V.G.	Good	Fair	Poor
650	550	450	400	300	200

Model 686 Plus Mountain Gun

This model is fitted with a 4" tapered barrel and chambered for the .357 Magnum cartridge. It has adjustable rear sights. Hogue rubber grips are standard. Stainless steel finish. Weight is about 44 oz.

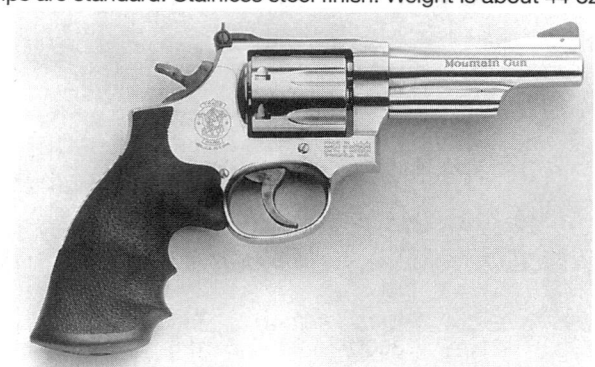

NIB	Exc.	V.G.	Good	Fair	Poor
650	475	450	400	300	200

Model 686 Magnum Plus

Offered for the first time in 1996 this model features a 7-shot cylinder. It is available with 2.5", 4", or 6" barrel lengths. It is fitted with a red ramp front sight and a fully adjustable rear sight. The frame is drilled and tapped for scope mounts. Hogue synthetic grips are standard. The stainless steel is satin finished. Weight is between 35 oz. and 45 oz. depending on barrel length.

NIB	Exc.	V.G.	Good	Fair	Poor
625	500	450	400	300	200

Model 686—5" Barrel

This .357 Magnum stainless steel model is fitted with a 5" barrel with HiViz front sight and adjustable rear sight. Cylinder holds 7 rounds. Cocobolo wood grips. Weight is about 41 oz. Introduced in 2004.

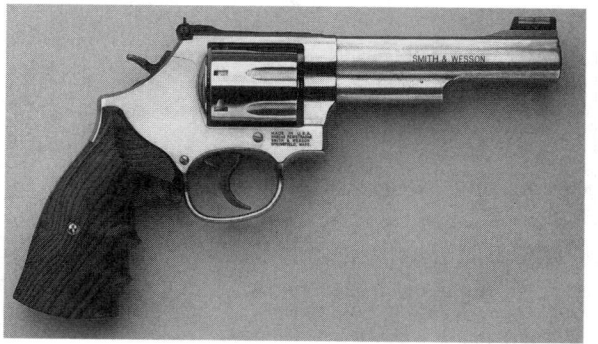

NIB	Exc.	V.G.	Good	Fair	Poor
575	475	395	300	200	100

Model 686 Plus

Single-/double-action L-frame revolver in .38/.357 Magnum. 7-shot cylinder, 3" barrel, Patridge front sight, adjustable rear, stainless finish, rubber grips. Introduced 2007.

NIB	Exc.	V.G.	Good	Fair	Poor
600	550	450	400	300	200

Smith & Wesson Model 686 Plus Pro Series

Single/double-action L-frame revolver chambered in .357 Magnum. Features include 5-inch barrel with tapered underlug, 7-round cylinder, satin stainless steel frame and cylinder, synthetic grips, interchangeable and adjustable sights. Suggested retail price $1,059.

Model 619

This model is chambered for the .357 Magnum cartridge and fitted with a 4" two-piece semi-lug barrel with fixed sights. Stainless steel frame and barrel. Capacity is 7 rounds. Medium frame. Weight is about 37.5 oz. Rubber grips. Introduced in 2005.

NIB	Exc.	V.G.	Good	Fair	Poor
575	475	395	300	200	100

Model 620

Similar to the model above but with a 4" barrel with adjustable rear sight and red ramp front sight. Weight is about 37.9 oz. Introduced in 2005.

NIB	Exc.	V.G.	Good	Fair	Poor
600	550	450	400	300	200

Model 3 Schofield

A reintroduction of the famous Schofield revolver. This is a single-action top-break model chambered for the .45 S&W cartridge. Barrel length is 7". Frame and barrel are blue while hammer and trigger are case hardened. Sights are a fixed rear notch and half moon post front. Walnut grips. Weight is 40 oz. Reintroduced in 2000. In 2002 this model was offered in a 7" nickel version as well as a 5" blue and 5" nickel configuration.

NIB	Exc.	V.G.	Good	Fair	Poor
1750	1400	1050	800	500	300

HERITAGE SERIES REVOLVERS

These revolvers are built by the S&W Performance Center and produced for Lew Horton Distributing Co. Each model is similar in appearance to the original but has modern internal features. These handguns are produced in limited runs of from 100 units to 350 units.

Model 1917

Chambered for the .45 ACP cartridge and fitted with a 5.5" heavy tapered barrel. High-profile front blade sight with fixed rear sight. Checkered service grips with lanyard ring. Offered in blue, case-colored, or military finish. Shipped in a S&W collectible box.

NIB	Exc.	V.G.	Good	Fair	Poor
900	775	600	450	300	150

NOTE: Add $60 for case color finish.

Model 15

This revolver is chambered for the .38 S&W Special. Fitted with a 4" barrel. Grips are S&W checkered target. Adjustable rear sight. Offered in nickel or color case hardened.

NIB	Exc.	V.G.	Good	Fair	Poor
800	675	550	400	250	125

Model 15 McGivern

Similar to the above model but fitted with 5" barrel and checkered diamond grips. Engraved sideplate of McGivern's speed record. Blue finish.

NIB	Exc.	V.G.	Good	Fair	Poor
900	775	600	450	300	150

Model 17

Chambered for the .22 caliber cartridge and fitted with a 6" barrel with patridge front sight and adjustable rear sight. Four screw sideplate. Diamond checkered S&W walnut grips. Blue or case colored finish.

NIB	Exc.	V.G.	Good	Fair	Poor
800	675	550	400	250	125

NOTE: Add $30 for case colored finish.

Model 24

This model is chambered for the .44 Special cartridge and fitted with a 6.5" tapered barrel. McGivern gold-bead front sight with adjustable rear sight. Four-screw sideplate, chamfered charge holes, checkered diamond grips.

NIB	Exc.	V.G.	Good	Fair	Poor
900	775	600	450	300	150

NOTE: Add $60 for case colored finish.

Model 25

Similar to the Model 24 but chambered for the .45 Colt cartridge. Blue or case colored finish.

NIB	Exc.	V.G.	Good	Fair	Poor
900	775	600	450	300	150

NOTE: Add $30 for case colored finish.

Model 29

Similar to the Model 24 and Model 25 but chambered for the .44 Magnum cartridge. Oversized wood grips. Blue or nickel finish. Was to be produced in 2002 only. Serial numbers to begin with "DBW2005."

NIB	Exc.	V.G.	Good	Fair	Poor
900	775	600	450	300	150

CLASSIC SERIES

Model 14 Classic

Recreation of the vintage Model 14 revolver chambered in .38 Special +P. Six-shot cylinder, 6" barrel with pinned Patridge front sight and micro-adjustable rear. Carbon steel frame and cylinder with blued finish. Weight 34.5 oz.

NIB	Exc.	V.G.	Good	Fair	Poor
800	675	525	400	275	150

Model 14 150253

Similar to above but with nickel finish.

NIB	Exc.	V.G.	Good	Fair	Poor
900	775	600	500	375	200

Model 36 Classic

Replica of vintage Model 36 Chief's Special in .38 Special. Five-shot cylinder. Carbon steel frame, 1-7/8" or 3" barrel, fixed sights. Blued, case colored, or nickel finish with Altamont wood grips. Introduced 2007.

NIB	Exc.	V.G.	Good	Fair	Poor
700	575	400	250	150	100

Model 21 Classic

Replica of vintage Model 21 N-frame revolver in .44 Special. Six-shot cylinder. Carbon steel frame, 4" barrel, fixed sights. Blued, case colored, or nickel finish with Altamont wood grips. Introduced 2007.

NIB	Exc.	V.G.	Good	Fair	Poor
800	675	525	400	275	150

Model 22 Classic

Replica of vintage Model 22 N-frame revolver in .45 ACP. Six-shot cylinder. Carbon steel frame, 4" barrel, fixed sights. Blued, case colored, or nickel finish with Altamont wood grips. Introduced 2007.

NIB	Exc.	V.G.	Good	Fair	Poor
800	675	525	400	275	150

Model 22 of 1917 Classic

Similar to Model 22 Classic but without ejector rod shroud and with lanyard ring on butt. Replica of U.S. Army WWI-era revolver. Introduced 2007.

NIB	Exc.	V.G.	Good	Fair	Poor
800	675	525	400	275	150

Model 27 Classic

Reintroduction of vintage Model 27. Available in blue or bright nickel finish. 6-1/2" barrel, walnut grips. Introduced 2008.

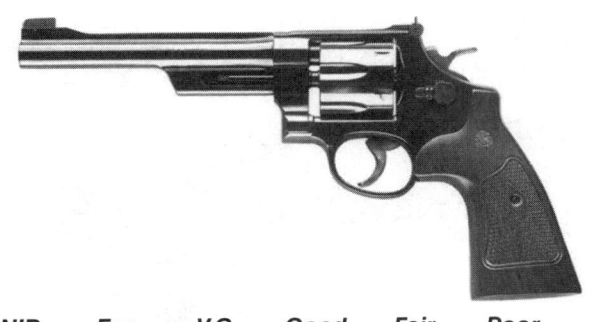

NIB	Exc.	V.G.	Good	Fair	Poor
800	675	525	400	275	150

Model 29 Classic

Replica of original (1956) Model 29 N-frame revolver in .44 Magnum. Six-shot cylinder. Carbon steel frame, 6.5" barrel, fixed sights. Blued or nickel finish with or without engraving. Altamont wood grips. Introduced 2007.

NIB	Exc.	V.G.	Good	Fair	Poor
900	775	600	500	375	200

Smith & Wesson Model 10 Classic

Single/double action K frame revolver chambered in .38 Special. Features include bright blue steel frame and cylinder, checkered wood grips, 4-inch barrel, adjustable patridge-style sights. Price: $814.

Smith & Wesson Model 48 Classic

Single/double action K frame revolver chambered in .22 Magnum Rimfire (.22 WMR). Features include bright blue steel frame and cylinder, checkered wood grips, 4- or 6-inch barrel, adjustable patridge-style sights. Price: $1,043 to $1,082.

MILITARY & POLICE (M&P) SERIES

M&P340

Double-action-only revolver built on Centennial (hammerless J) frame. .357 Magnum/.38 Special; five-shot cylinder; 1.87" barrel with fixed night sights. Matte black finish on scandium/alloy frame. Introduced 2007.

NIB	Exc.	V.G.	Good	Fair	Poor
700	575	400	250	150	100

M&P340CT

Similar to above but with Crimson Trace lasergrips. Introduced 2007.

NIB	Exc.	V.G.	Good	Fair	Poor
825	700	600	500	350	175

M&P360

Double-action-only revolver built on Chief's Special (hammered J) frame. .357 Magnum/.38 Special; five-shot cylinder; 1.87" barrel with fixed night sights. Matte black finish on scandium/alloy frame. Introduced 2007.

NIB	Exc.	V.G.	Good	Fair	Poor
700	575	400	250	150	100

M&PR8

Double-action-only revolver built on large (N) frame. .357 Magnum/.38 Special; eight-shot cylinder; 5" barrel with adjustable Patridge sights with interchangeable inserts. Matte black finish on scandium/alloy frame. Introduced 2007.

NIB	Exc.	V.G.	Good	Fair	Poor
900	775	600	500	375	200

Governor

Built on the Smith & Wesson L frame, this six-shot revolver can fire .410 shotshells, .45 Colt and .45 ACP (with moon clips) ammunition. Scandium alloy frame, stainless steel cylinder, Tritium night sight, internal security lock and Hogue synthetic grips. Barrel length is 2.75-inches, weight 29.6 ounces, overall length 8.5-inches with matte black finish. Available with Crimson Trace Laser grips. Introduced in 2011.

NIB	Exc.	V.G.	Good	Fair	Poor
575	525	425	365	250	150

NOTE: Add $200 for Crimson Trace Laser grips.

SEMI-AUTOMATIC PISTOLS

NOTE: For pistols with Smith and Wesson factory-installed night sights add $100 to NIB and Exc. prices. For S&W factory engraving add $1,000 for Class C (1/3 coverage), $1,250 for Class B (2/3 coverage), $1,500 for Class A (full coverage).

Model 39

This was the first double-action semi-automatic pistol produced in the United States. It was introduced in 1957. It had an alloy frame and was chambered for the 9mm Parabellum cartridge. The barrel was 4" and the finish was either blued or nickel with checkered walnut grips. The rear sight was adjustable. Magazine capacity is 8 rounds. Discontinued in 1982.

NIB	Exc.	V.G.	Good	Fair	Poor
600	450	250	200	150	100

Model 39 Steel Frame

A total of 927 steel frame Model 39s were produced. A rare pistol; use caution.

NIB	Exc.	V.G.	Good	Fair	Poor
1750	1200	700	550	400	250

Model 59

Introduced in 1971 this pistol is similar to the Model 39 but with a wide grip to hold a double column magazine of 14 rounds. Furnished with black checkered plastic grips. Discontinued in 1982.

NIB	Exc.	V.G.	Good	Fair	Poor
575	500	350	200	150	100

Model 439

Introduced in 1979 this is an improved version of the Model 39. Furnished with adjustable rear sight. Discontinued in 1988.

NIB	Exc.	V.G.	Good	Fair	Poor
600	450	350	325	250	100

Model 639

This is a stainless steel version of the Model 439. Introduced in 1984 and discontinued in 1988.

NIB	Exc.	V.G.	Good	Fair	Poor
600	450	350	325	250	100

Model 459

This improved-sight version of the 15-shot Model 59 9mm pistol was introduced in 1979 and discontinued in 1987.

NIB	Exc.	V.G.	Good	Fair	Poor
600	450	350	325	250	100

Model 659

This stainless steel version of the Model 459 9mm pistol features an ambidextrous safety and all other options of the Model 459. Introduced in 1982 and discontinued in 1988.

NIB	Exc.	V.G.	Good	Fair	Poor
550	425	350	300	250	150

Model 539

This is yet another version of the Model 439 9mm pistol. It incorporates all the features of the Model 439 with a steel frame instead of aluminum alloy. This model was introduced in 1980 and discontinued in 1983.

NIB	Exc.	V.G.	Good	Fair	Poor
525	400	350	300	250	200

Model 559

This variation of the Model 459 9mm pistol has a steel frame instead of aluminum alloy. It is identical in all other respects.

NIB	Exc.	V.G.	Good	Fair	Poor
475	400	350	300	250	200

Model 469

The Model 469 was brought out in answer to the need for a more concealable high-capacity pistol. It is essentially a "Mini" version of the Model 459. It is chambered for the 9mm Parabellum and has a 12-round detachable magazine with a finger-grip extension and a shortened frame. The barrel is 3.5" long; the hammer is bobbed and does not protrude; the safety is ambidextrous. The finish is matte blue, with black plastic grips. The Model 469 was introduced in 1983 and discontinued in 1988.

NIB	Exc.	V.G.	Good	Fair	Poor
450	375	325	275	200	150

Model 669

This is a stainless steel version of the Model 469 9mm pistol. All of the features of the 469 are incorporated. The Model 669 was manufactured from 1986 to 1988.

NIB	Exc.	V.G.	Good	Fair	Poor
475	425	350	300	250	200

Model 645

The Model 645 is a large-framed, stainless steel double-action pistol chambered for the .45 ACP cartridge. It has a 5" barrel, adjustable sights, and a detachable 8-shot magazine. It is offered with fixed or adjustable sights and an ambidextrous safety. The grips are molded black nylon. S&W manufactured this pistol between 1985 and 1988.

NIB	Exc.	V.G.	Good	Fair	Poor
600	450	375	325	250	150

Model 745—IPSC

This model is similar in outward appearance to the Model 645 but is quite a different pistol. The Model 745 is a single-action semi-automatic chambered for the .45 ACP cartridge. The frame is made of stainless steel, and the slide of blued carbon steel. The barrel is 5", and the detachable magazine holds eight rounds. The sights are fully adjustable target types. The grips are checkered walnut. Introduced in 1986 and discontinued in 1990.

Similar to above but with nickel finish.

NIB	Exc.	V.G.	Good	Fair	Poor
775	600	500	400	350	250

TARGET PISTOLS

Model 41

NOTE: For full set of steel and aluminum barrel weights add up to $500 depending on condition. For .22 Short conversion kit add $750 depending on condition. For military marked pistols add 400 percent.

Other Barrel Options:

5.5" with extended sight add $100. 5.5" heavy with extended sight add $100. 7.375" with muzzlebrake add $75.

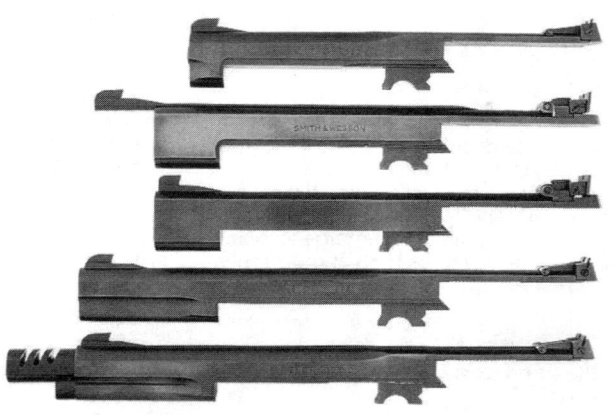

Courtesy John J. Stimson, Jr.

Model 41 barrel types

NIB	Exc.	V.G.	Good	Fair	Poor
1100	850	600	500	325	150

Model 41 (New Model)

This model was restyled in 1994 featuring recontoured hardwood stocks, a Millet adjustable rear sight, and a drilled and tapped barrel for scope mounting.

NIB	Exc.	V.G.	Good	Fair	Poor
775	600	500	400	350	250

Model 41-1

This model was introduced in 1960 and is chambered for the .22 Short rimfire only. It was developed for the International Rapid Fire competition. In appearance it is quite similar to the Model 41 except that the slide is made of aluminum alloy, as well as the frame, in order to lighten it to function with the .22 Short cartridge. This model was not a commercial success like the Model 41, so it was discontinued after fewer than 1,000 were manufactured.

NIB	Exc.	V.G.	Good	Fair	Poor
1200	900	725	500	375	225

Model 41 Fiftieth Anniversary Edition

Similar to original Model 41 but machine-engraved with Class A+ coverage, gold plated borders, and glass-topped presentation case. Introduced 2008. Serial Number Range: FYA0001 - FYA0500.

NIB	Exc.	V.G.	Good	Fair	Poor
1600	1400	1200	900	600	400

Model 46

This was a lower-cost version of the Model 41. It was developed for the Air Force in 1959. Its appearance was essentially the same as the Model 41 with a 7" barrel. Later a 5" barrel was introduced, and finally in 1964 a heavy 5.5" barrel was produced. This economy target pistol never had the popularity that the more expensive Model 41 had, and it was discontinued in 1968 after approximately 4,000 pistols were manufactured.

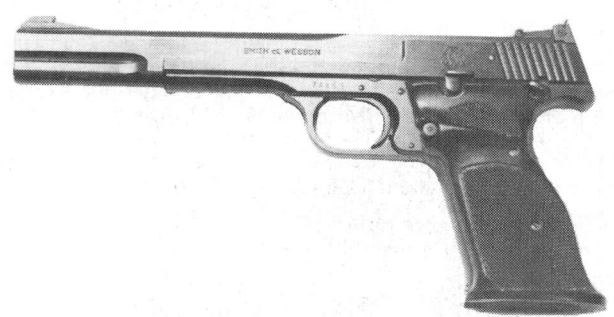

Courtesy Mike Stuckslager

NIB	Exc.	V.G.	Good	Fair	Poor
1100	900	800	650	400	200

Model 61 Escort

In 1970 the Model 61 was introduced as the only true pocket automatic that S&W produced. It was chambered for the .22 LR cartridge with a 2-1/2" barrel and 5-round magazine. It was offered in either blued or nickel finish with black checkered plastic grips. It was dropped from the product line in 1974.

NIB	Exc.	V.G.	Good	Fair	Poor
300	225	200	150	100	75

Model 52A

Introduced in 1961 in the .38 AMU caliber for the Army marksmanship training. Army rejected the pistol and the 87 units built were released to the public. The letter "A" is stamped behind the model designation. A rare find; only 87 were produced. Use caution.

NIB	Exc.	V.G.	Good	Fair	Poor
3000	2500	2000	1500	750	500

Model 52 (.38 Master)

Introduced in 1961 as a target pistol chambered for the .38 Special mid-range wad cutter cartridge. It is similar in appearance to the Model 39 but is single-action-only by virtue of a set screw. Fitted with a 5" barrel and a 5-round magazine. It has a blued finish with checkered walnut grips. About 3,500 of these pistols were produced in this configuration until discontinued in 1963.

NIB	Exc.	V.G.	Good	Fair	Poor
975	750	550	450	300	200

Model 52-1

In 1963 this variation featured a true single-action design and were produced until 1971.

NIB	Exc.	V.G.	Good	Fair	Poor
850	725	450	350	300	200

Model 52-2

Introduced in 1971 with a coil spring-style extractor. Model was discontinued in 1993.

NIB	Exc.	V.G.	Good	Fair	Poor
750	600	475	400	300	200

Model 2214 (The Sportsman)

This semi-automatic pistol is chambered for the .22 LR and designed for casual use. It is fitted with a 3" barrel and has a magazine capacity of 8 rounds. The slide is blued carbon steel and the frame is alloy. Introduced in 1990, discontinued 1997.

NIB	Exc.	V.G.	Good	Fair	Poor
250	200	150	125	100	50

Model 2206

This .22 LR pistol is offered with either a 4-1/2" or 6" barrel. Magazine capacity is 12 rounds. Adjustable rear sight. Stainless steel frame and slide.

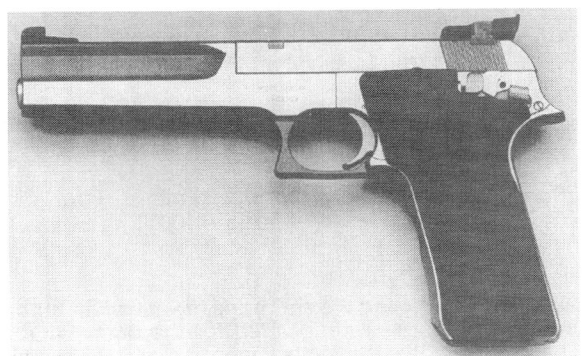

NIB	Exc.	V.G.	Good	Fair	Poor
300	250	175	125	100	50

Model 2206 TGT (Target)

Introduced in 1995 this version of the Model 2206 features a selected 6" barrel, bead blasted sighting plane and polished flat side surfaces. A Patridge front sight and Millet adjustable rear sight are standard. In addition the model has a serrated trigger with adjustable trigger stop and a 10-round magazine.

NIB	Exc.	V.G.	Good	Fair	Poor
350	300	250	200	150	100

Model 422 Field

Introduced in 1987 this .22 LR pistol has a 4-1/2" barrel or 6" barrel with an alloy frame and steel slide. The magazine capacity is 10 rounds. This model has fixed sights and black plastic grips. Finish is matte blue.

NIB	Exc.	V.G.	Good	Fair	Poor
350	275	225	125	100	50

Model 422 Target

Same as the Field model but fitted with adjustable sights and checkered walnut grips.

NIB	Exc.	V.G.	Good	Fair	Poor
350	275	225	125	100	50

Model 622 Field

This is a stainless steel version of the Model 422 Field.

NIB	Exc.	V.G.	Good	Fair	Poor
400	300	225	150	125	75

Model 622 Target

This is the stainless steel version of the Model 422 Target.

NIB	Exc.	V.G.	Good	Fair	Poor
400	300	225	150	125	75

Model 622VR

Redesigned in 1996 this .22 caliber model features a 6" ventilated rib barrel. It is fitted with a matte black trigger and a new trigger guard. The front sight is a serrated ramp style with an adjustable rear sight. Weight is approximately 23 oz. Grips are black polymer.

NIB	Exc.	V.G.	Good	Fair	Poor
375	275	200	150	100	75

Model 22A Sport

Introduced in 1997 this model features a choice of 4", 5.5", or 7" barrel. It is chambered for the .22 LR cartridge. Magazine capacity is 10 rounds. Rear sight is adjustable. Grips are either two-piece polymer or two-piece Soft Touch. Frame and slide are aluminum alloy and stainless steel. Finish is blue. Weight is approximately 28 oz. for 4" model and 32 oz. for 5.5" model. Weight of 7" model is about 33 oz. Prices quoted are for 4" model. In 2001 this model was furnished with a Hi-Viz green dot front sight. In 2008 a full-camo version was introduced (add $40).

NIB	Exc.	V.G.	Good	Fair	Poor
290	200	150	100	75	50

Model 22S Sport

This model, also introduced in 1997, is similar to the above model but with 5.5" and 7" barrel on stainless steel frames. Weight is about 41 oz. and 42 oz. respectively. In 2001 this model was furnished with a Hi-Viz green dot front sight.

NIB	Exc.	V.G.	Good	Fair	Poor
300	225	175	150	100	50

Model 22A Target

This .22 caliber target pistol has a 10-round magazine, adjustable rear sight, and target grips with thumb rest. The barrel is 5.5" bull barrel. Finish is blue. Weight is about 39 oz. Introduced in 1997.

NIB	Exc.	V.G.	Good	Fair	Poor
290	200	150	100	75	45

Model 22S Target

Same as above but with stainless steel frame and slide. Weight is approximately 48 oz.

NIB	Exc.	V.G.	Good	Fair	Poor
300	225	175	150	100	50

Model 22A Camo

Introduced in 2004 this .22 LR model features a Mossy Oak Break-Up finish. Weight is about 39 oz.

NIB	Exc.	V.G.	Good	Fair	Poor
325	250	175	150	100	50

Model 3904

In 1989 S&W redesigned the entire line of 9mm semi-automatic handguns. The 3904 is chambered for the 9mm Parabellum and has an 8-shot detachable magazine and 4" barrel with a fixed bushing. The frame is alloy, and the trigger guard is squared for two-hand hold. The magazine well is beveled, and the grips are one-piece wrap-around made of delrin. The three-dot sighting system is employed. This model has been discontinued.

NIB	Exc.	V.G.	Good	Fair	Poor
450	400	325	300	275	225

Model 3906

This is the stainless steel version of the Model 3904. The features are the same. It was introduced in 1989. This model has been discontinued.

NIB	Exc.	V.G.	Good	Fair	Poor
450	400	325	300	275	225

Model 3914

Offered as a slightly smaller alternative to the Model 3904, this 9mm pistol has a 3-1/2" barrel, 8-round magazine, and blued carbon steel slide and alloy frame.

NIB	Exc.	V.G.	Good	Fair	Poor
525	450	400	350	300	250

Model 3913

This version is similar to the Model 3914 but features a stainless steel slide and alloy frame.

NIB	Exc.	V.G.	Good	Fair	Poor
525	450	400	350	300	250

Model 3914LS

This is a redesigned Model 3914 that has a more modern appearance. The LS refers to LadySmith and is chambered for the 9mm cartridge. All other features are the same as the Model 3914 including the blued carbon slide and alloy frame.

NIB	Exc.	V.G.	Good	Fair	Poor
525	450	400	350	300	200

Model 3913LS

This model is identical to the Model 3914LS with the exception of the stainless steel slide.

NIB	Exc.	V.G.	Good	Fair	Poor
525	450	400	350	300	200

Model 3954

Similar to the Model 3914 but offered in double-action-only. Discontinued in 1993.

NIB	Exc.	V.G.	Good	Fair	Poor
525	450	400	350	300	200

Model 915

Introduced in 1993 this model is chambered for the 9mm cartridge and features a 4" barrel, matte blue finish, fixed rear sight, and wraparound rubber grips. Overall length is 7.5" and weight is about 28 oz.

NIB	Exc.	V.G.	Good	Fair	Poor
400	350	250	200	150	100

Model 5904

This is a full high capacity, 15-shot version of the Model 3904. It was introduced in 1989 and features a slide mounted decocking lever and 4" barrel. This version has a blued carbon steel slide and alloy frame. This model is no longer in production.

NIB	Exc.	V.G.	Good	Fair	Poor
525	450	375	325	275	200

Model 5903

The same caliber and features as the Model 5904 and Model 5906, but furnished with a stainless steel slide and alloy frame.

NIB	Exc.	V.G.	Good	Fair	Poor
525	450	400	350	300	250

Model 5906

This is a stainless steel version of the Model 5904. Both the slide and frame are stainless steel.

NIB	Exc.	V.G.	Good	Fair	Poor
525	450	375	275	200	—

Model 5906 Special Edition

A double-action semi-automatic pistol chambered for the 9mm with a 15-round magazine. The frame and slide have a special machine finish while the grips are one-piece wrap-around Xenoy. The front sight is a white dot post and the rear sight is a Novak L-Mount Carry with two white dots. This model has a manual safety/decocking lever and firing pin safety. Introduced in 1993.

NIB	Exc.	V.G.	Good	Fair	Poor
575	450	350	300	250	150

Model 5926

S&W offers a 9mm pistol similar to the 5906 but with a frame mounted decocking lever. Both the slide and frame are stainless steel. Discontinued in 1993.

NIB	Exc.	V.G.	Good	Fair	Poor
525	450	375	300	250	150

Model 5946

This 9mm pistol offers the same features as the Model 5926, but in a double-action-only mode. The hammer configuration on this model is semi-bobbed instead of serrated.

NIB	Exc.	V.G.	Good	Fair	Poor
525	450	400	350	300	250

Model 5967

This is a 9mm model with a M5906 frame and a 3914 slide. It has a stainless steel frame and blued slide. Novak Lo-Mount fixed sights. Introduced in 1990 and sold through Lew Horton.

NIB	Exc.	V.G.	Good	Fair	Poor
600	475	400	350	300	250

Model 6904

This is the concealable, shortened version of the Model 5904. It has a 12-shot magazine, fixed sights, bobbed hammer, and a 3.5" barrel.

NIB	Exc.	V.G.	Good	Fair	Poor
525	450	400	350	300	250

Model 6906

This version has a stainless steel slide and alloy frame but otherwise is similar to the Model 6904.

NIB	Exc.	V.G.	Good	Fair	Poor
525	450	400	350	300	200

Model 6946

This is a double-action version of the Model 6906.

NIB	Exc.	V.G.	Good	Fair	Poor
525	450	400	350	300	200

Model 4003

This pistol is chambered for the .40 S&W cartridge and is fitted with a 4" barrel, 11-round magazine, serrated hammer with a stainless steel slide and alloy frame.

NIB	Exc.	V.G.	Good	Fair	Poor
575	500	400	350	300	200

Model 4004

Identical to the Model 4003 except for a blue carbon steel slide and alloy frame. Discontinued in 1993.

NIB	Exc.	V.G.	Good	Fair	Poor
575	500	400	350	300	200

Model 4006

This model is identical to the Model 4003 except that both the slide and frame are made from stainless steel. This adds 8 oz. to the weight of the pistol.

NIB	Exc.	V.G.	Good	Fair	Poor
575	500	400	350	300	200

Model 4026

Similar to the Model 4006 this version has a frame-mounted decocking lever.

NIB	Exc.	V.G.	Good	Fair	Poor
575	500	400	350	300	200

Model 4046

Similar to the Model 4006 but with a double-action-only configuration.

NIB	Exc.	V.G.	Good	Fair	Poor
575	500	400	350	300	250

Model 4013

A compact version of the 4000 series, this .40 caliber model features a 3-1/2" barrel, eight-round magazine, and stainless steel slide and alloy frame.

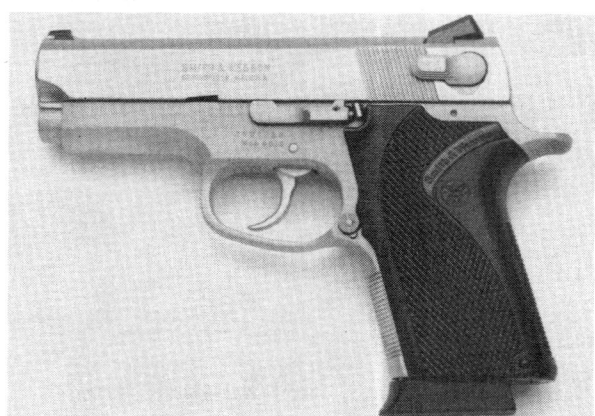

NIB	Exc.	V.G.	Good	Fair	Poor
575	500	400	350	300	200

Model 4013 TSW

Similar to the Model 4013 but traditional double-action-only with some improvements. Magazine capacity is 9 rounds of .40 S&W cartridges. Finish is satin stainless. Weight is approximately 26 oz. Introduced in 1997.

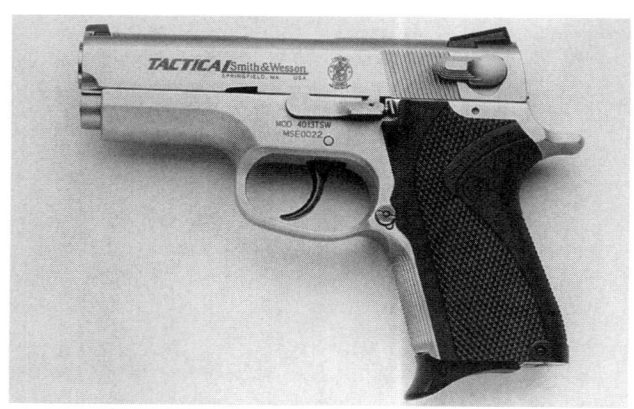

NIB	Exc.	V.G.	Good	Fair	Poor
700	575	400	325	250	150

Model 4014

Identical to the Model 4013 except for a blued carbon steel slide and alloy frame.

NIB	Exc.	V.G.	Good	Fair	Poor
575	500	400	350	300	200

Model 4053

Identical to the Model 4013, stainless steel slide and alloy frame, except offered in a double-action-only configuration.

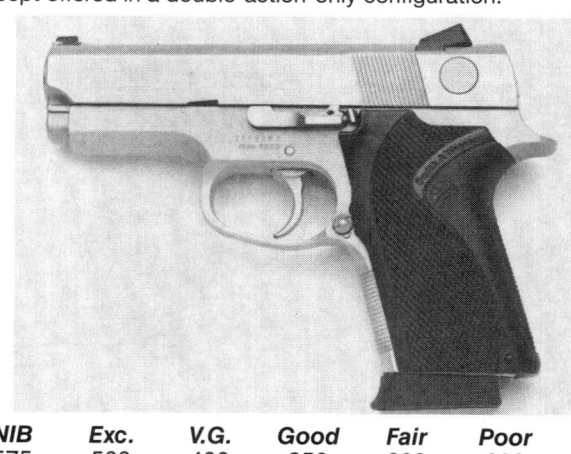

NIB	Exc.	V.G.	Good	Fair	Poor
575	500	400	350	300	200

Model 4054

This model is the same as the Model 4053 except for a blued carbon steel slide and alloy frame. Dropped from S&W product line in 1992.

NIB	Exc.	V.G.	Good	Fair	Poor
575	500	400	300	250	200

Model 411

This model was introduced in 1993 as a no frills model and features an alloy frame, 4" barrel, matte blue finish, fixed sights, and wrap-around rubber grips. Chambered for .40 S&W cartridge with 11-round magazine capacity. Overall length is 7.5" and weight is approximately 29 oz.

NIB	Exc.	V.G.	Good	Fair	Poor
400	350	300	250	200	150

Model 1006

This is a full-size 10mm pistol with a 5" barrel, nine-round magazine, and choice of fixed or adjustable sights. Both the slide and frame are stainless steel.

NIB	Exc.	V.G.	Good	Fair	Poor
675	550	400	350	300	200

NIB	Exc.	V.G.	Good	Fair	Poor
650	525	375	300	250	200

Model 1026

Similar to the Model 1006 with a 5" barrel this model has a frame mounted decocking lever.

Model 4056 TSW

This is a double-action-only pistol chambered for the .40 S&W cartridge. Fitted with a 3.5" barrel with white dot sights. Curved backstrap. Stainless steel and alloy frame. Stainless steel finish. Magazine capacity is nine rounds. Introduced in 1997. Weight is approximately 36 oz.

NIB	Exc.	V.G.	Good	Fair	Poor
700	575	400	325	250	150

NIB	Exc.	V.G.	Good	Fair	Poor
675	550	400	350	300	200

Model 1066

This is a slightly smaller version of the Model 1006 and is furnished with a 4-1/4" barrel. Discontinued in 1993.

Model 4506

This is the newly designed double-action .45 ACP pistol. It is all stainless steel and has a 5" barrel, 8-shot detachable magazine, and wrap-around black Delrin grips. This model is no longer in production.

NIB	Exc.	V.G.	Good	Fair	Poor
675	550	400	350	300	200

Model 1076

Identical to the Model 1066 with the exception of the frame mounted decocking lever.

NIB	Exc.	V.G.	Good	Fair	Poor
675	550	400	350	300	200

Model 1086

Similar to the Model 1066 but offered in double-action-only. This model was discontinued in 1993.

NIB	Exc.	V.G.	Good	Fair	Poor
550	475	400	350	300	250

Model 4505

This version is identical to the Model 4506 with the exception of a blued slide and frame.

NIB	Exc.	V.G.	Good	Fair	Poor
550	475	400	350	300	250

Model 4516

Offered in a .45 caliber this 4500 series is a compact version of the full size .45 caliber S&W autos. Furnished with a 3-3/4" barrel and a 7-round magazine this model has a stainless slide and frame. Discontinued in 1991. This model was reintroduced in 1994.

NIB	Exc.	V.G.	Good	Fair	Poor
550	475	425	375	300	250

Model 4536

A compact version and similar to the Model 4616 this pistol is offered with a decock lever on the frame.

NIB	Exc.	V.G.	Good	Fair	Poor
550	475	400	350	300	250

Model 4546

A full size version of the Model 4506 but offered in double-action-only.

NIB	Exc.	V.G.	Good	Fair	Poor
550	475	400	350	300	250

Model 4040PD

When introduced in 2003 this was the first Scandium frame S&W pistol. Chambered for the .40 S&W cartridge and fitted with a 3.5' barrel. White dot front sight with Novak Lo Mount rear sight. Matte black finish. Magazine capacity is seven rounds. Soft rubber grips. Weight is about 25.6 oz.

NIB	Exc.	V.G.	Good	Fair	Poor
700	575	400	325	250	150

Model SW1911

Introduced in 2003 this is a full size pistol chambered for the .45 ACP and 9mm Parabelluum cartridges. Fitted with a 5" barrel with white dot front sight and Novak Lo-Mount rear sight. Stainless steel frame and slide. Checkered black rubber grips. Magazine capacity is 8 rounds (9 in 9mm). Weight is about 39 oz. In 2005 this model was also offered with wood grips and black oxide finish.

NIB	Exc.	V.G.	Good	Fair	Poor
965	750	600	500	375	200

Model SW1911 Adjustable

As above but fitted with adjustable sights. Introduced in 2004.

NIB	Exc.	V.G.	Good	Fair	Poor
850	700	600	500	375	200

Model SW1911Sc

This .45 ACP model is fitted with a Commander size slide and Scandium frame. Fixed sights. Checkered wood grips. Black oxide finish. Weight is about 28 oz. Introduced in 2004.

NIB	Exc.	V.G.	Good	Fair	Poor
900	750	650	550	400	250

Model 1911 PD

This .45 ACP model is offered with either a 4.25" barrel or 5" barrel with Novak low mount sights. Wood grips. The frame is alloy with black finish. Magazine capacity is 8 rounds. Weight is about 28 oz. for 4.25" model and 29.5 oz. for the 5" model.

NIB	Exc.	V.G.	Good	Fair	Poor
850	700	600	500	375	200

Model SW1911 E Series

Full-size 1911-style pistol. Caliber .45 ACP, stainless steel frame and slide with "fish scale" scalloped slide serrations front and rear. Other features include checkered front strap and mainspring housing, oversized extractor, enlarged ejection port, titanium firing pin and laminated textured wood grips. Available with Crimson Trace Laser grips. Introduced in 2011.

NIB	Exc.	V.G.	Good	Fair	Poor
800	685	575	450	300	150

NOTE: Add 20 percent for Crimson Trace Laser grips. Add 30 percent for integral accessory rail.

TARGET PISTOLS

Model SW1911 DK (Doug Koenig)

Introduced in 2005 this .45 ACP model is fitted with a 5" stainless steel barrel. Adjustable rear sight with black blade front sight. Frame is stainless steel with black carbon steel slide. Wood grips. Magazine capacity is 8 rounds. Weight is about 41 oz.

NIB	Exc.	V.G.	Good	Fair	Poor
850	700	600	500	375	200

Model SW1911 Pro Series

Similar to Model SW1911 but with Novak fiber optic sights, skeletonized trigger and various tactical/performance enhancements. Introduced 2008.

NIB	Exc.	V.G.	Good	Fair	Poor
950	800	700	600	475	250

Smith & Wesson Model 1911 Sub-Compact Pro Series

Chopped 1911-style semi-auto pistol chambered for .45 ACP. 7+1 capacity, 3" barrel. Wood grips, scandium frame with stainless steel slide, matte black finish throughout. Overall length 6.9". Weight 26.5 oz.

NIB	Exc.	V.G.	Good	Fair	Poor
1100	950	700	600	475	250

TSW SERIES (TACTICAL SMITH & WESSON)

This series is an upgrade of the older Smith & Wesson pistol series, many of which have been discontinued. These pistols come with either a traditional double-action trigger or a double-action-only trigger. All TSW pistols have an equipment rail for mounting lights or lasers. All are marked "TACTICAL S&W" on the slide.

3913/3953 TSW

Chambered for 9mm cartridge and fitted with a 3.5" barrel. White dot front sight and Novak Lo-Mount rear sight. Aluminum alloy frame. Magazine capacity is 7 rounds. Weight is about 25 oz. Stainless steel finish. The 3913 is traditional double-action while the 3953 is double-action-only.

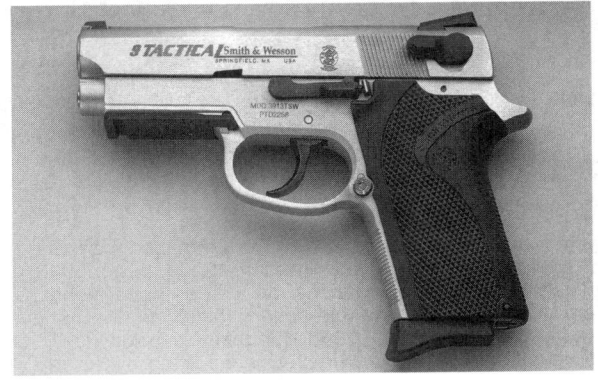

NIB	Exc.	V.G.	Good	Fair	Poor
650	525	475	400	325	125

4013/4053 TSW

This pistol is chambered for the .40 S&W cartridge and fitted with a 3.5" barrel. White dot front sight and Novak Lo-Mount rear sight. Aluminum alloy frame and stainless steel slide. Magazine capacity is 9 rounds. Weight is about 27 oz. The 4013 is traditional double-action while the 4053 is double-action-only.

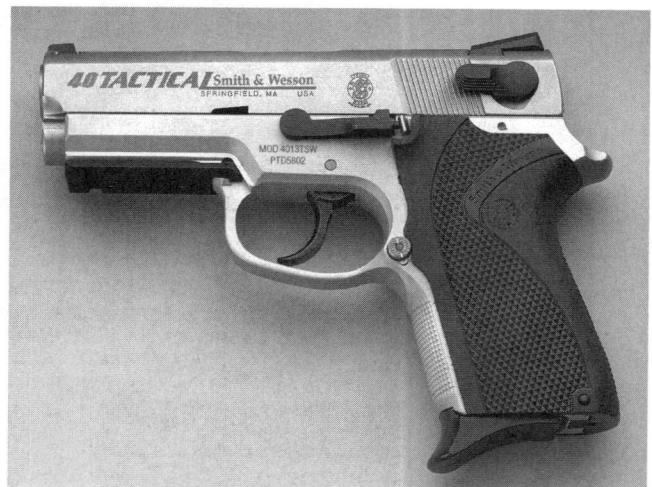

NIB	Exc.	V.G.	Good	Fair	Poor
650	525	475	400	325	125

4513/4553 TSW

This model is chambered for the .45 ACP cartridge and fitted with a 3.75" barrel. White dot front sight and Novak Lo-Mount rear sight. Aluminum alloy frame with stainless steel slide. Magazine capacity is 7 rounds. Weight is about 29 oz. The 4513 is traditional double-action while the 4553 is double-action-only.

NIB	Exc.	V.G.	Good	Fair	Poor
650	525	475	400	325	125

NOTE: The double-action-only model 4553 is $50 less.

5903/5906/5943/5946 TSW

These pistols are chambered for the 9mm cartridge and fitted with a 4" barrel. Fixed sights standard (5903, 5906, 5943, 5946) adjustable sights (5906) optional as well as night sights (5906). Offered in traditional double-action (5903, 5906) as well as double-action-only (5943, 5946). Magazine capacity is 10 rounds and weight is about 38 oz. Stainless steel finish.

NIB	Exc.	V.G.	Good	Fair	Poor
650	525	475	400	325	125

NOTE: Add $100 for night sights, add $50 for adjustable sights.

4003/4006/4043/4046 TSW

This model comes in the same configurations as the 5903 group except these pistols are chambered for the .40 S&W cartridge. Magazine capacity is 10 rounds. Weight is about 28 oz.

Similar to above but with nickel finish.

NIB	Exc.	V.G.	Good	Fair	Poor
650	525	475	400	325	125

NOTE: Add $100 for night sights, add $50 for adjustable sights.

4563/4566/4583/4586 TSW

Similar to the above model but chambered for the .45 ACP cartridge and fitted with a 4.25" barrel. Same configurations as above. Weight is about 31 oz.

NIB	Exc.	V.G.	Good	Fair	Poor
650	525	475	400	325	125

NOTE: Add $100 for night sights, add $50 for adjustable sights.

CHIEF'S SPECIAL SERIES
CS9

Chambered for 9mm cartridge and fitted with a 3" barrel, this model has a stainless steel slide and aluminum alloy frame. Also available in blued finish. Hogue wraparound grips are standard. Fixed sights. Magazine capacity is 7 rounds. Weight is approximately 21 oz.

NIB	Exc.	V.G.	Good	Fair	Poor
550	395	315	250	200	125

CS45

Similar to the model above but chambered for the .45 ACP cartridge. Barrel length is 3.25". Magazine capacity is six rounds. Weight is about 24 oz.

NIB	Exc.	V.G.	Good	Fair	Poor
575	400	315	250	200	125

CS40

This Chief's Special model is chambered for the .40 S&W cartridge. Barrel length is 3.25". Magazine capacity is seven rounds. Weight is about 24 oz.

NIB	Exc.	V.G.	Good	Fair	Poor
550	395	315	250	200	125

CS40 Two-Tone

Same as above but with alloy frame and stainless slide. Limited edition. Introduced in 2000.

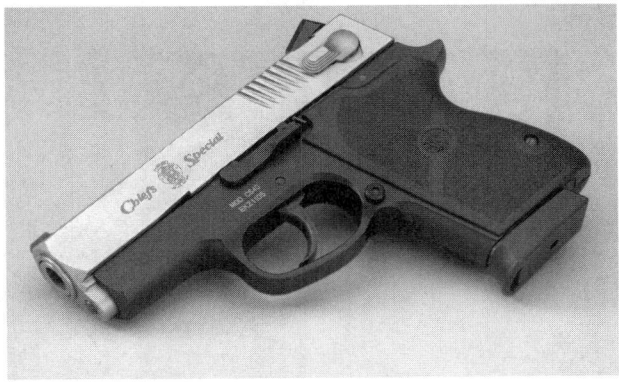

NIB	Exc.	V.G.	Good	Fair	Poor
575	400	315	250	200	125

SIGMA SERIES
SW40F

This new pistol was introduced in 1994 and was a departure from the traditional S&W pistol. The pistol features a stainless steel barrel, carbon steel slide, and polymer frame. Offered in .40 S&W and 9mm calibers with 15-round and 17-round capacities.

NIB	Exc.	V.G.	Good	Fair	Poor
450	400	350	300	250	200

Compact SW9C

Same as above but with barrel and slide 1/2" shorter than full size Sigma. Offered in both .40 S&W and 9mm.

NIB	Exc.	V.G.	Good	Fair	Poor
450	400	350	300	250	200

SW9M

Introduced in 1996 this pistol is chambered for the 9mm cartridge. It is fitted with a 3.25" barrel and has a magazine capacity of seven rounds. The frame is polymer and the slide carbon steel. Height is 4.5" and overall length is 6.25". Weight is 18 oz.

NIB	Exc.	V.G.	Good	Fair	Poor
450	400	350	300	250	200

SW9V

Chambered for the 9mm cartridge this model is fitted with a 4" barrel and 10-round magazine. It has a traditional double action. White dot sights are standard. Grips are integral to the frame. Stainless steel slide. Satin stainless finish with choice of gray or black frame. Weight is about 25 oz. Introduced in 1997.

NIB	Exc.	V.G.	Good	Fair	Poor
450	400	350	300	250	200

SW9P

Same as the Model SW9V with the addition of a ported barrel. Introduced in 2001.

NIB	Exc.	V.G.	Good	Fair	Poor
450	400	350	300	250	200

SW9G

Same as the standard SW9 but with a black Melonite stainless steel slide and NATO green polymer frame. Introduced in 2001.

NIB	Exc.	V.G.	Good	Fair	Poor
450	400	350	300	250	200

SW40V

Same as above but chambered for .40 S&W cartridge. Weight is 25 oz. Introduced in 1997.

NIB	Exc.	V.G.	Good	Fair	Poor
450	400	350	300	250	200

SW40P

Same as the Model SW40V but with the addition of a ported barrel. Introduced in 2001.

NIB	Exc.	V.G.	Good	Fair	Poor
450	400	350	300	250	200

SW40G

Same as the standard SW40 pistol but with a black Melonite stainless steel slide and NATO green polymer frame. Introduced in 2001.

NIB	Exc.	V.G.	Good	Fair	Poor
450	400	350	300	250	200

SW380

Introduced in 1995 this model is chambered for the .380 ACP cartridge. Barrel length is 3" with overall length 5.8". Empty weight is 14 oz. with a magazine capacity of 6 rounds.

NIB	Exc.	V.G.	Good	Fair	Poor
325	275	200	150	100	75

ENHANCED SIGMA SERIES

Introduced in 1999 this series features a shorter trigger pull, slide stop guard, redesigned extractor and ejector. The ejection port is also lower. These pistols are also fitted with an accessory groove. Checkering pattern is more aggressive.

SW9E

Chambered for the 9mm cartridge this model has a 4" barrel with Tritium sights. Stainless steel slide with black Melonite finish. Magazine capacity is 10 rounds. Weight is about 25 oz.

NIB	Exc.	V.G.	Good	Fair	Poor
375	300	225	175	150	75

SW40E

Similar to the above model but chambered for the .40 S&W cartridge. Weight is about 24 oz.

NIB	Exc.	V.G.	Good	Fair	Poor
375	300	225	175	150	75

SW9VE

This model is chambered for the 9mm cartridge and fitted with a 4" barrel. Fixed sights and stainless steel slide. Weight is about 25 oz.

NIB	Exc.	V.G.	Good	Fair	Poor
375	300	225	175	150	75

SW40VE

Similar to the model above but chambered for the .40 S&W cartridge. Weight is about 24 oz.

NIB	Exc.	V.G.	Good	Fair	Poor
375	300	225	175	150	75

SW99

This model features a polymer frame designed and manufactured in Germany by Walther. The slide and barrel are manufactured by S&W in the U.S. Chambered for either the 9mm or .40 S&W cartridge this model is fitted with a 4" barrel on the 9mm model and a 4.125" barrel on the .40 S&W model. Adjustable rear sights.

Decocking slide-mounted lever. Barrel and slide are stainless steel with black Melonite finish. Trigger is traditional double-action. Magazine capacity is 10 rounds. Weight is about 25 oz. Introduced in 1999.

NIB	Exc.	V.G.	Good	Fair	Poor
400	350	300	225	150	75

SW99 Compact

Introduced in 2003 this model is similar to the full size SW99 but with a 3.5" barrel and shorter grip frame. Chambered for both the 9mm or .40 S&W cartridge. Stainless steel barrel and slide with polymer frame. Magazine capacity is 10 rounds for 9mm and eight rounds for the .40 S&W. Weight is about 23 oz.

NIB	Exc.	V.G.	Good	Fair	Poor
400	350	300	225	150	75

SW99 .45 ACP

Same as the SW99 but chambered for the .45 ACP cartridge. Magazine is nine rounds. Weight is about 26 oz. Introduced in 2003.

NIB	Exc.	V.G.	Good	Fair	Poor
500	400	325	250	150	100

SW990L Compact

Introduced in 2005 this model is chambered for the 9mm or .40 S&W cartridge. Barrel length is 3.5". Adjustable rear sight with dot front sight. Polymer frame with stainless steel slide with Melonite finish. Plastic grips. Magazine capacity is 10 rounds for the 9mm and 8 rounds for the .40 S&W model. Weight is about 23 oz.

NIB	Exc.	V.G.	Good	Fair	Poor
475	400	300	225	150	100

SW990L Full Size

Similar to the above model but chambered for the 9mm, .40 S&W and .45 ACP cartridges. Barrel lengths are 4" for the 9mm; 4.125" for the .40 S and 4.25" for the .45 ACP. Magazine capacity is 16 rounds for the 9mm and 12 rounds for the .40 S&W model. Weight is about 25 oz. Introduced in 2005.

NIB	Exc.	V.G.	Good	Fair	Poor
500	400	325	250	150	100

NOTE: Add $40 for .45 ACP model.

410

This model was first introduced in 1996. It features an alloy frame with carbon steel slide. It is chambered for the .40 S&W cartridge. Barrel length is 4". The magazine capacity is 10 rounds and the overall length is 7.5". Weight is approximately 29 oz.

NIB	Exc.	V.G.	Good	Fair	Poor
450	400	325	250	150	100

410 Two-Tone

Same as the Model 410 but with alloy finish frame and black slide. Limited edition.

NIB	Exc.	V.G.	Good	Fair	Poor
475	400	325	250	150	100

410S

Introduced in 2003 this is a stainless steel version of the Model 410. Weight is about 28 oz.

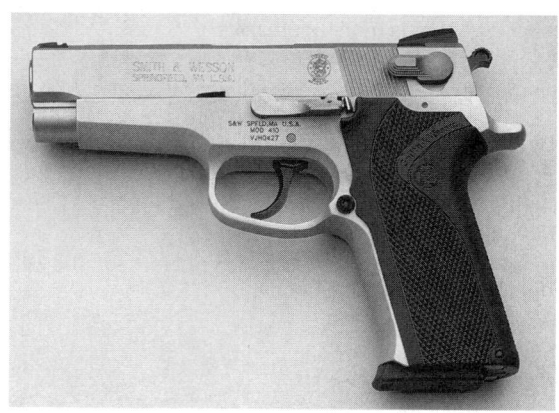

NIB	Exc.	V.G.	Good	Fair	Poor
475	400	300	250	150	100

457

Introduced in 1996 this .45 ACP model features a 3.75" barrel with rounded trigger guard and double-action. It is fitted with a single side decocker. Magazine capacity is seven rounds. Overall length is 7.25" and weight is about 29 oz. The frame is alloy and the slide a carbon steel. Finish is matte black.

NIB	Exc.	V.G.	Good	Fair	Poor
500	400	325	250	150	100

457S

Same as above but in stainless steel. Weight is about 29 oz. Introduced in 2003.

NIB	Exc.	V.G.	Good	Fair	Poor
500	400	325	250	150	100

908

Introduced in 1996 this is an economy compact pistol. It is chambered for the 9mm cartridge and is fitted with a 3.5" barrel. The action is traditional double-action. Fixed rear sight. Magazine capacity is eight rounds. Overall length is 6-7/8" and weight is about 26 oz.

NIB	Exc.	V.G.	Good	Fair	Poor
450	400	325	225	150	100

908S

Same as the Model 908 but in stainless steel. Weight is about 24 oz. Introduced in 2003.

NIB	Exc.	V.G.	Good	Fair	Poor
475	425	350	250	150	100

908S Carry Combo

Introduced in 2004 this model is the same as above with the addition of a Kydex carry holster.

NIB	Exc.	V.G.	Good	Fair	Poor
500	400	325	250	150	100

909

Introduced in 1995 this pistol is chambered for the 9mm cartridge. It has a blue carbon steel slide, aluminum alloy frame, and is double-action. It has a single column magazine and curved backstrap.

NIB	Exc.	V.G.	Good	Fair	Poor
405	350	250	150	100	75

910

Also introduced in 1995. Same as above model but with double-column magazine and straight backstrap.

NIB	Exc.	V.G.	Good	Fair	Poor
400	300	200	150	100	75

910S

Introduced in 2003 this is a stainless steel version of the Model 910. Weight is about 28 oz.

NIB	Exc.	V.G.	Good	Fair	Poor
400	325	250	150	100	75

MILITARY & POLICE (M&P) SERIES

M&P9m

Full-size Military and Police semi-auto chambered in 9mm. Capacity 17+1, 4.25" barrel, 6-1/2 lb. trigger, 24.25 oz. Picatinny rail and polymer frame. Optional tritium low-light sights. Introduced 2006.

NIB	Exc.	V.G.	Good	Fair	Poor
575	425	300	225	150	75

M&P9-JG

Similar to above but with interchangeable palmswell grip panels, including two pink ones. Dealer sets pricing. Introduced 2008.

NIB	Exc.	V.G.	Good	Fair	Poor
575	425	300	225	150	75

M&P9 Pro Series

Similar to M&P9 but with green fiber optic sights and interchangeable palmswell grip panels. Black Melonite finish. Introduced 2008.

NIB	Exc.	V.G.	Good	Fair	Poor
600	475	350	250	150	75

M&P9L

Similar to M&P9 but with 5-inch barrel. Introduced 2008.

NIB	Exc.	V.G.	Good	Fair	Poor
575	425	300	225	150	75

M&P9c

Striker-fired, double-action-only 9mm semi-auto pistol. Polymer frame with stainless steel black Melonite slide. Novak white dot dovetail front sight, Novak low profile carry rear. 3.5" barrel, 6.7" overall length. Unloaded weight 21.7 oz. Also available with Crimson Trace lasergrips.

NIB	Exc.	V.G.	Good	Fair	Poor
575	425	300	225	150	75

M&P 40

Full-size semi-auto chambered in .40 S this is the first of the new Military and Police series. Capacity 15+1, 4.25" barrel, .5 lb. trigger, 24.25 oz. Polymer frame and Picatinny rail. Optional tritium low-light sights. Introduced 2006.

NIB	Exc.	V.G.	Good	Fair	Poor
575	425	300	225	150	75

Pro Series Model M&P40

Striker-fired DAO semiauto pistol chambered in .40 S&W. Features include 4.25- or 5-inch barrel, matte black polymer frame and stainless steel slide, tactical rail, Novak front and rear sights or two-dot night sights, polymer grips, 15+1 capacity. Suggested retail price $830.

M&P .357 SIG

Full-size Military and Police semi-auto chambered in .357 Magnum. Capacity 15+1, 4.25" barrel, 6.5 lb. trigger, 24.25 oz. Polymer frame and Picatinny rail. Optional tritium low-light sights. Introduced 2006.

NIB	Exc.	V.G.	Good	Fair	Poor
575	425	300	225	150	75

M&P45

Semi-auto; similar to M&P40 but in .45 ACP. Black or Dark Earth Brown finish. Introduced 2007.

NIB	Exc.	V.G.	Good	Fair	Poor
575	425	300	225	150	75

M&P45 with Thumb Safety

Similar to above but with ambidextrous thumb safety. Introduced 2008.

NIB	Exc.	V.G.	Good	Fair	Poor
585	435	310	235	160	75

M&P40c

Semi-auto; compact model; similar to M&P9c but in .40 S&W. Black Melonite finish. Introduced 2007.

NIB	Exc.	V.G.	Good	Fair	Poor
575	425	300	225	150	75

M&P357c

Semi-auto; compact model; similar to M&P40c but in .357 SIG. Black Melonite finish. Introduced 2007.

NIB	Exc.	V.G.	Good	Fair	Poor
575	425	300	225	150	75

SW9VE Allied Forces

Similar to SW9VE but with black Melonite slide. Adopted by Afghanistan internal security and border forces. Introduced 2007. Add 75 percent for "Disaster Ready Kit" (case and emergency supplies).

NIB	Exc.	V.G.	Good	Fair	Poor
575	425	300	225	150	75

SW40VE Allied Forces

Similar to SW9VE Allied Forces but in .40 S&W. Introduced 2007. Add 75 percent for "Disaster Ready Kit" (case and emergency supplies).

NIB	Exc.	V.G.	Good	Fair	Poor
575	425	300	225	150	75

S&W M&P VTAC

Caliber 9mm Parabellum/.40 S&W. Magazine capacity: 19 (9mm), 17 (.40). Stainless steel slide, polymer frame, with Flat Dark Earth finish. Striker fired, double-action-only, ambidextrous slide release and reversible magazine catch. Weight is 24 ounces, 4.25-inch barrel with VTAC Warrior night sights.

NIB	Exc.	V.G.	Good	Fair	Poor
665	550	475	400	300	150

M&P22

Rimfire version of the M&P pistol. Striker-fired with aluminum alloy slide and polymer frame. Magazine capacity, 10 or 12 rounds. Ambidextrous thumb safety and slide release, and reversible magazine catch. Weight is 24 ounces, barrel length is 4.1-inches. Introduced in 2011.

NIB	Exc.	V.G.	Good	Fair	Poor
375	325	275	225	150	100

SMITH & WESSON COMMEMORATIVES (REFERENCE ONLY)

Smith & Wesson has, over the years, built many special edition handguns. These guns have been to commemorate some important national or regional event or group. The company has also built a large number of special edition handguns for certain distributors such as Lew Horton which is listed. There are well over 200 special production guns not reflected in this pricing guide. Not even Smith & Wesson has all of the information on these guns and with many the number is so small that a market price would not be possible to establish. Listed are a number of Smith & Wesson Commemoratives that we do have information on. Due to the difficulty in determining value only the original retail price is listed. Remember to receive full value for these guns they must be NIB, unfired with unturned cylinders.

Model 14 Texas Ranger Comm.

Introduced in 1973. Supplied with 4" barrel and cased. Edition limited to 10,000. 8,000 of these had knives. Serial numbers TR 1 to TR 10000.Original Retail Introductory Price: $250.00

Model 25-3 S&W 125th Anniversary Comm.

Introduced in 1977. Limited edition of 10,000. Serial numbers SW0000 to SW10000. Deluxe models marked 25-4.Original Retail Introductory Price: $350.00

Model 26-4 Georgia State Police Comm.

Introduced in 1988/1989 and supplied with a 5" barrel. Total production of 802 guns. Known Serial numbers BBY00354 to BBY0434.Original Retail Introductory Price: $405.00

Model 27 .357 50th Anniversary Comm.

Introduced in 1985 and supplied with a 5" barrel and cased. Limited edition to 2,500 guns. Serial numbers REG0001 to REG2500.Original Retail Introductory Price: N/A

Model 29-3 Elmer Keith Comm.

Introduced in 1986 and supplied with a 4" barrel. Gun etched in gold. Limited edition of 2,500 guns. Serial numbers EMK0000 to EMK0100 for Deluxe models and EMK 010 to EMK2500 for standard model.Original Retail Introductory Price: $850.00

Model 544 Texas Wagon Train 150 Anniversary Comm.

Introduced in 1986 and limited to 7801 guns. Serial numbers TWT0000 to TWT7800.Original Issue Introductory Price: N/A

Model 586 Mass. State Police Comm.

Introduced in 1986 and fitted with a 6" barrel. Limited to 631 guns. Serial numbers with ABT-AUC prefix.Original Retail Introductory Price: N/A

Model 629-1 Alaska 1988 Iditarod Comm.

Introduced in 1987 and limited to 545 guns. Serial numbers from AKI0001 to AKI0545.Original Retail Introductory Price: N/A

Model 745 IPSC Comm.

Introduced in 1986 and limited to 5362 guns. Serial numbers DVC0000 to DVC5362.Original Retail Introductory Price: N/A

Model 4516-1 U.S. Marshall Comm.

Introduced in 1990 and limited to 500 guns. Serial numbers USM0000 to USM0499.Original Retail Introductory Price: $599.95

Model SW1911 PD Gunsite Commemorative

Honors Lt. Col. Jeff Cooper's Gunsite Training Academy. Scandium alloy, single-action .45 ACP with 4.25" barrel and 8+1 capacity. Fixed sights. 28 oz. Introduced 2006.

NIB	Exc.	V.G.	Good	Fair	Poor
950	700	600	500	350	175

Model SW1911 – Rolling Thunder Commemorative

Limited edition commemorates American POW-MIAs. Rolling Thunder and POW-MIA logos in imitation bonded ivory grips. Chambered for .45 ACP. Blued, 8+1 capacity, 5" barrel, 38.5 oz. Introduced 2006.

NIB	Exc.	V.G.	Good	Fair	Poor
950	700	600	500	350	175

SMITH & WESSON PERFORMANCE CENTER HANDGUNS (REFERENCE ONLY)

The role of Smith & Wesson's Performance Center has changed since it was established in 1990. What was once a specialized tune-up and competition one-off production department has now become a separate facility in providing specialized and limited handguns to the public often with distributors participation. This change came about around 1991, when the Performance Center initiated its own limited edition designs. These editions are generally limited to between 300 and 600 pistols for each model. The Performance Center, in fact, has its own distinct product line. Performance Center pistols are made in its own shop using its own designers. One of these distributors that has played a major role in offering these special guns to the public is the Lew Horton Distribution Company. The Center still continues to offer action jobs and accurate work but no longer executes one-of-a-kind customizing. The Performance Center has built about eight to twelve different models in the last two years. Plans call for more of these unique handguns to be built in the future. Pistols that are available from a certain distributor or the Performance Center will be noted in the description of each pistol.

Limited Edition Pistols and Revolvers of 1990

One of the first limited special series of Performance Center handguns was this offering, which consisted of custom engraved S&W handguns limited to 15 units on any current (1990) production pistol or revolver. This Limited Edition featured: 24 karat gold and sterling inlays, special bright mirror finish, decorated in light scroll pattern, specially assigned serial number beginning with the prefix "PEC," tuned action, solid walnut presentation case inlaid with blue or burgundy leather insert, embossed with gold with performance center logo. Interior of case is custom fitted with a matching colored velvet. Each handgun is hand numbered and has a signed certificate of authenticity. Because of the unique nature of the Limited Edition offering it is strongly recommended to secure a professional appraisal.

.40 S&W Tactical

A limited edition semi-automatic handgun offered exclusively by Lew Horton through the Performance Center. This special pistol is fitted with a 5" match-grade barrel, hand fit spherical barrel bushing, custom tuned action, special trigger job, oversized frame and slide rails, wrap-around straight backstrap grip. Replaceable front and Novak rear sights. Special serial numbers. Offered in 1992 and limited to 200 units.

Suggested Retail Introductory Price: $1,500

.40 S&W Compensated

Similar to the .40 S&W Tactical but furnished with a 4.625" barrel and single chamber compensator. This is also a Lew Horton/Performance pistol. A production of 250 units. Offered in 1992.

Suggested Retail Introductory Price: $1,700

.40 S&W Performance Action Pistol

Offered in limited quantities in 1990, this Performance Center .40 S&W semi-automatic pistol was used by the Smith & Wesson shooting team. The frame and barrel are stainless steel with blued carbon steel slide, two port compensator, two fitted and numbered 13-round magazines, 5.25" match grade barrel extended frame beavertail, square combat trigger guard, oversize magazine release button, spherical barrel bushing, wrap-around straight backstrap grip, extended magazine funnel, and BoMar adjustable rear sight. The action is tuned for accuracy and precision.

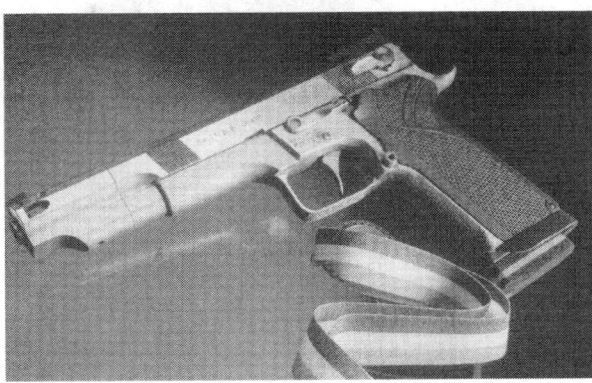

Suggested Retail Introductory Price: N/A

Model 681 Quadport

A Lew Horton revolver limited to 300 guns with special serial numbers. This 7-shot revolver has a 3" barrel underlug quadport barrel. The action is tuned, cylinders are chamfered and the trigger has an overtravel stop. Sights are fixed combat type. Suggested Retail Introductory Price: $675

Model 686 Competitor

Introduced by Lew Horton and the Performance Center for 1993 this limited edition revolver features a match grade barrel and unique under barrel weight system. The action has been custom tuned and the receiver is drilled and tapped for scope mounts. Charge holes are chambered, ejector rod housing is enclosed, and the grip is an extended competition type. Special serial numbers. Suggested Retail Introductory Price: $1,100

Model 686 Hunter

Similar to the Model 686 Competitor. This is also a limited edition Lew Horton revolver chambered for the .357 Magnum and features the under barrel weight system, internal scope mount, and custom tuned action. Special serial numbers. Suggest Retail Introductory Price: $1,154

Model 686 Carry Comp 4"

Offered in limited quantities by Lew Horton and the Performance Center in 1992 this new design features the unique single chamber integral barrel compensator. Front is windage adjustable and the action is custom tuned. Chambered for the .357 Magnum cartridge. Special serial numbers. Suggested Retail Introductory price: $1,000

Model 686 Carry Comp 3"

The 1993 Lew Horton limited edition version of the Model 686 Carry Comp 4" model with a 3" barrel. The same features apply to both models. Suggested Retail Introductory Price: $1,000

Model 686 Plus

This Lew Horton model features a 7-round cylinder with chamfered charge holes for use with full moon clips for both .38 Special and .357 Magnum cartridges. Fitted with a tapered 6" barrel with countersunk muzzle. Gold bead front sight and adjustable rear sight. Altamont wood grips are standard. Stainless steel finish. Weight is approximately 44 oz. Suggested Retail Introductory Price: $930

Model 686 - .38 Super

Introduced in 2003 this six-round revolver is chambered for the .38 Super cartridge and fitted with a 4" barrel with tapered lug. Interchangeable red ramp front sight and adjustable rear sight. Stainless steel with glass bead finish. Cocobolo grips. Weight is about 37 oz. Distributed by Bangers.

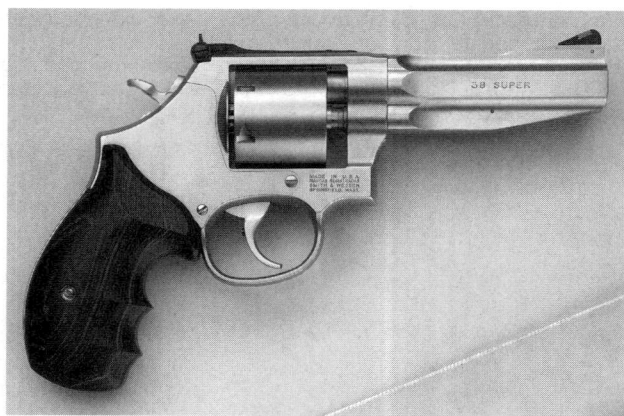

Suggested Retail Introductory Price: N/A

Model 629 Hunter

Introduced in 1992 by Lew Horton and the Performance Center this limited edition revolver features a new design that utilizes a 6" under barrel weight system, special integral barrel compensator. The action has been custom tuned and the receiver has an integral scope mount. Chambered for the .44 Magnum. Special finger groove grips are standard. Special serial numbers.

Suggested Retail Introductory Price: $1,234

Model 629 Hunter II

Another Lew Horton/Performance Center limited edition revolver that features 2x Nikon scope with steel see-through rings. The barrel is Mag-Na-Ported and incorporates the Performance Center's under barrel weight arrangement. The action is custom tuned and the revolver is supplied with a ballistic nylon range carry bag. Special serial numbers.Suggested Retail Introductory Price: $1,234

Model 629 Comped Hunter

Offered through RSR this model features a 6" barrel with 4-port detachable compensator. The cylinder is unfluted. Sights are adjustable, fitted with Altamount wood grips. Tuned action. Stainless steel. Weight is approximately 59 oz.Suggested Retail Introductory Price: $1,100

Model 629 12" Hunter/7.5" Hunter

Introduced in 2000 this Lou Horton revolver is fitted with a 12" barrel with Patridge front sight and Wilson silhouette adjustable rear sight. Hogue Combat grips. Finish is glassbead stainless steel. Comes with a Waller 21" gun rug. Weight is about 65 oz. A 7.5-inch version was introduced in 2008. Suggested Retail Introductory Price: $1,025

Model 629 Magnum Hunter Trail Boss

Exclusive to RSR this limited edition model is chambered for the .44 Magnum cartridge and is fitted with a 3" barrel. Stainless steel finish.Suggested Retail Introductory Price: $733

Model 629 Compensated Hunter

Chambered for the .44 Magnum cartridge and fitted with a 7.5" barrel with compensator. Barrel also has removable stainless steel scope mount. Open sights fitted with adjustable orange ramp front and adjustable rear sight. Rosewood grips. Six-round cylinder. Weight is 52 oz. Talo exclusive. Introduced in 2001.

Suggested Retail Introductory Price: $1190

Model 629 Stealth Hunter

Fitted with a 7.5" ported barrel and chambered for the .44 magnum cartridge. Six-round cylinder. The finish is black-T and NATO green. Red ramp Millett front sight and adjustable rear sight. Hogue rubber combat grips standard. Furnished with lockable aluminum case. Weight is about 56 oz. Introduced in 2001. Camfour Distributor exclusive.

Suggested Retail Introductory Price: $1,025

Model 629 Extreme

Chambered for the .44 Magnum cartridge and fitted with a 12" barrel with sling swivel. Bomar sights. Rubber grips.Suggested Retail Introductory Price: $1,025

Model 629 Carry Comp

Introduced in 1992 by Lew Horton and the Performance Center this limited edition revolver is chambered for the .44 Magnum cartridge. It features an integral ported 3" barrel, fluted cylinder, radiused charge holes, dovetail front and fixed groove rear sight. Fitted with a rubber combat grip. The action is custom by the Performance Center. Special serial numbers.

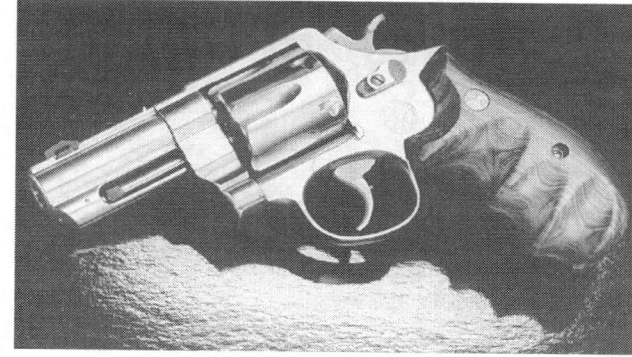

Suggested Retail Introductory Price: $1,000

Model 629 Carry Comp II

A limited edition 1993 offering by Lew Horton and the Performance Center similar to the 1992 Model 629 Carry Comp with the exception that this 1993 model has a special unfluted cylinder and fully adjustable rear sight. Special serial numbers.Suggested Retail Introductory Price: $1,000

Model 629 Comped Hunter

Chambered for the .44 Magnum cartridge and built with a 7.5" barrel with a tapered full length lug and compensator. Front sight is drift adjustable orange ramp. Adjustable rear sight. Stainless steel with glass bead finish. Removable scope mount. Rosewood grips. Weight is about 52 oz. Introduced in 2003.

Suggested Retail Introductory Price: $1,100

Model 610

Introduced in 1998 by Lew Horton this model features a 3" full lug barrel chambered for the 10mm cartridge. Nonfluted cylinder, red ramp front sight and white outline rear sight. Rosewood grips. Limited to 300 revolvers.Suggested Retail Introductory Price: $740

Model 640 Carry Comp

Introduced in 1991 by Lew Horton and the Performance Center this revolver is chambered for the .38 S&W Special, but with a strengthened action to handle +P loads. Fitted with a heavy 2.625" barrel with unique integral barrel compensator. The front sight is replaceable and adjustable for windage. The rear sight is a fixed groove. Custom trigger job and custom tuned action are also part of the package. Special serial numbers.Suggested Retail Introductory Price: $750

Model 640 .357 Quadport

Introduced in 1996. Similar to the model above but chambered for the .357 Magnum cartridge and quadported. Limited to 190 revolvers. Special serial numbers.Suggested Retail Introductory Price: $675

Model 460 Airweight

Chambered for the .38 Special cartridge, this model is fitted with a 2" Mag-Na-Ported barrel and a five-shot cylinder. Fixed sights. Eagle Secret Service grips. Weight is about 16 oz. Limited to 450 revolvers. Introduced in 1994.Suggested Retail Introductory Price: $580

Model 625 Light Hunter

This is a large frame revolver chambered for the .45 Colt. It is fitted with a 6" Mag-Na-Ported barrel with integral Weaver-style base. It has a stainless steel finish and black Hogue rubber grips. Drift adjustable Millet front and fully adjustable rear sight. Offered in limited quantities. Introduced in 1997 by RSR.Suggested Retail Introductory Price: $580

Model 625

Introduced in 1998 this model is chambered for the .45 ACP or .45 Colt cartridge. Fitted with a 3" full lug barrel, fluted cylinder, and rosewood grips. Limited to 150 revolvers in each chambering. Suggested Retail Introductory Price: $755

Model 625 V-Comp

Chambered for the .44 Magnum cartridge this model is fitted with a 4" barrel and removable three-port compensator. Front sight is a red ramp with black adjustable rear sight. Hogue wood combat grips. Furnished with aluminum case. Weight is about 43 oz. Finish is stainless steel. Distributed by RSR. Introduced in 1999.

Suggested Retail Introductory Price: $1,000

Model 625—5.25"

Introduced in 2001 this model features a special Jerry Miculek Hogue laminated combat grip. Chambered for the .45 ACP cartridge and fitted with a 5.25" barrel. Stainless steel finish. Interchangeable gold bead front sight and adjustable rear sight. Weight is about 42 oz. Camfour exclusive.

Suggested Retail Introductory Price: N/A

Model 627—8 Shot

Chambered for the .357 Magnum cartridge this revolver has an 8-round capacity. Drilled and tapped with adjustable sights on a 5" tapered and contoured barrel. Tuned action. Hogue wood grips. Satin stainless steel finish. Weight is approximately 44 oz. A Lew Horton exclusive. Introduced in 1997.Suggested Retail Introductory Price: $1,160

Model 627 Defensive—8 Shot

Chambered for the .357 Magnum this model is fitted with an eight-round unfluted cylinder recessed for full moon clips. Barrel length is 2-5/8". Adjustable rear sight and drift adjustable front sight. Wooden eagle boot grips. Weight is about 38 oz. Introduced in 1999. Furnished with aluminum case.

Suggested Retail Introductory Price: $1,025

Model 651

This is a limited edition revolver by RSR chambered for the .22 WMR cartridge. Fitted with a 2" barrel and boot grips. Stainless steel finish.Suggested Retail Introductory Price: $492

"Shorty-Forty" .40 S&W

Introduced in 1992 and available exclusively from Lew Horton, this limited edition Performance Center pistol features a light alloy frame, oversize slide rails, and spherical barrel bushing. A match grade barrel is joined to a custom tuned action. Special serial numbers.

Suggested Retail Introductory Price: $950

Model 647 Varminter

Introduced in 2003 this model is chambered for the .17 HMR cartridge and fitted with a 12" fluted barrel with a removable black Patridge front sight. Adjustable rear sight. Integral scope mount on barrel. Six-round cylinder. Stainless steel finish. Weight is about 54 oz.

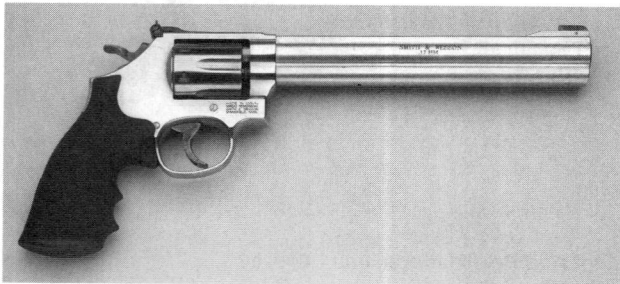

Suggested Retail Introductory Price: $1,100

Model 500 Magnum Hunter

Introduced in 2003 this revolver is chambered for the .500 S&W cartridge and fitted with a 10.5" barrel with compensator. Sling swivel studs and sling are standard. Orange dovetail ramp front sight and adjustable rear sight. Stainless steel with glass bead finish. Hogue rubber grips. Weight is approximately 82 oz.

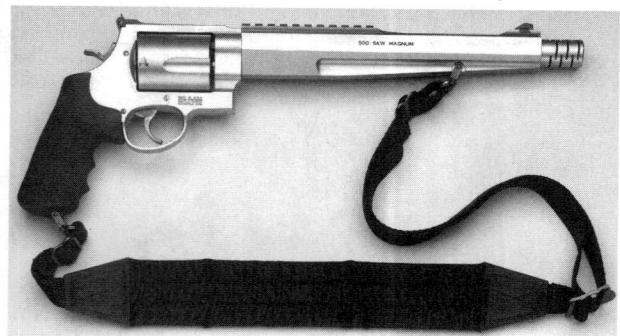

Suggested Retail Introductory Price: $1390

Model 460XVR

Built for serious handgun hunters. Chambered for the .460 S&W Magnum. Stainless steel cylinder, frame and barrel, 5-round capacity, adjustable rear and removable Partridge front sight. Other features include sling swivels, dual accessory rails and synthetic grips. Weight is a hefty 79.2 ounces, 12-inch fluted barrel with compensator. Re-introduced in 2011 by the Performance Center. Suggested Retail Introductory Price: $1,619.

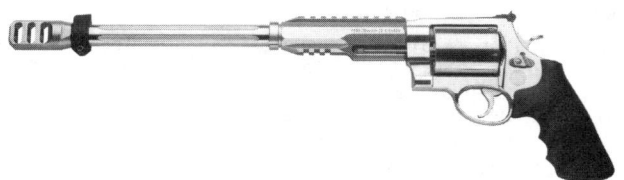

"Shorty Forty" Mark III

Offered in 1995 this Lew Horton exclusive features low-mount adjustable sights, hand-fitted titanium barrel bushing, checkered front strap. The action as been hand honed and the pistol is sold with two magazines; one 11 rounds and the other nine rounds. Suggested Retail Introductory Price: $1,000

Shorty .45

Introduced by Lew Horton in 1996 this .45 ACP pistol has a hand-fitted titanium barrel bushing, oversize frame and slide rails, match grade barrel, checkered front strap, hand honed double-action, and special serial numbers. Suggested Retail Introductory Price: $1,095

Shorty Nine

This Lew Horton exclusive is limited to 100 units. It features a hand-fitted titanium barrel bushing, oversize slide rails, action job, low mount adjustable sights, checkered front strap, match grade barrel, and two tone finish. Furnished with two 12-round magazines.Suggested Retail Introductory Price: $1,000

9 Recon

This is an RSR exclusive and introduced in 1999. Chambered for the 9mm cartridge this model is fitted with a 3.5" barrel. Rear sight is Novak Lo-Mount. Hogue wraparound rubber grips. The slide is black carbon steel with an alloy frame. Magazine capacity is 12 rounds. Weight is about 27 oz.

Suggested Retail Introductory Price: $1,178

Performance Center .45 Limited

This Lew Horton model is a full-size single-action pistol. Handfitted titanium barrel bushing, fitted slide lock, match grade barrel, adjustable sights, oversize magazine well, tuned action, and checkered front strap.Suggested Retail Introductory Price: $1,400

45 Recon

Another RSR pistol chambered for the .45 ACP cartridge, this model is an enhanced version of the "Shorty 45." The 4.25" barrel is ported with Novak Lo-Mount sights. Hogue wraparound rubber grips. Stainless steel slide and barrel with aluminum frame. Weight is about 28 oz. Magazine capacity is 7 rounds. Matte black or stainless finish. Furnished with aluminum case.

Suggested Retail Introductory Price: $1,221

Shorty .356 TSW

This new cartridge is also available in another Lew Horton/Performance Center limited edition pistol with a 4" barrel. It features a steel frame and hand-fitted slide, with spherical barrel bushing. The double-action is custom tuned by the Performance Center. Magazine holds 12 rounds. Similar in appearance to the "Shorty-Forty." Offered in 1993. Special serial numbers.

Suggested Retail Introductory Price: $1,000

Model .356 TSW "Limited" Series

This is a Lew Horton gun. This model is chambered for the new .356 TSW caliber (TSW stands for Team Smith & Wesson). This is a new caliber, actually a 9mm x 21.5mm cartridge, with ballistics of around 1,235 fps with a 147-grain bullet. Designed as a low-end .357 competition pistol. Built for the competitive shooter (IPSC) it features a 15-round magazine and distinctive profile and markings. The single-action trigger is adjustable for reach while the slide, frame, and barrel are custom fitted. The gun comes with a spherical barrel bushing and adjustable BoMar sights. The frame grip is checked 20 line to the inch, the magazine well is extended as is the magazine release. The magazine is fitted with a pad.

Suggested Retail Introductory Price: $1,350

Model 5906 Performance Center

Introduced in 1998 this 9mm pistol features front slide serrations, ambidextrous decocker, titanium coated barrel bushing, match grade barrel, and Novak Lo-Mount sights. Sold with one 15-round magazine and one 10-round magazine. Stainless steel finish.

Suggested Retail Introductory Price: $1,200

Model 845 of 1998

This .45 ACP caliber model has a 5" match grade barrel with hand lapped rails on frame and slide. Patridge front sight and adjustable Bomar rear sight. Single-action trigger is tuned and the slide has front serrations. Magazine capacity is 8 rounds. Stainless steel finish. Limited to 150 pistols.

Suggested Retail Introductory Price: $1,500

Model .45 CQB Combat

Introduced in 1998 this Lew Horton model features a 4" match grade barrel. Novak Lo-Mount sights. Double-action trigger with ambidextrous de-cocker. Available in both a matte black and stainless steel finish. Matte black model has alloy frame and weighs about 30 oz. Stainless steel version has stainless frame and weighs about 38 oz.

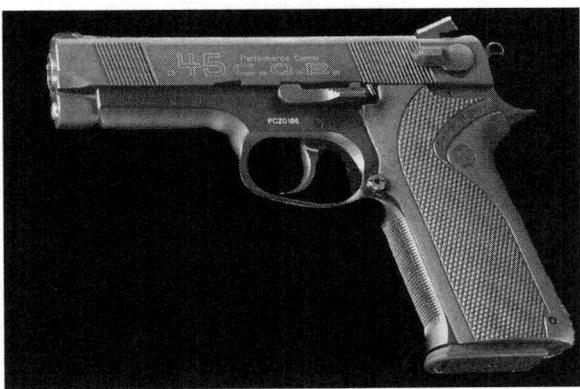

Suggested Retail Introductory Price: $1,200

Model 945

This is a single-action-only pistol chambered for the .45 ACP cartridge. Fitted with a 5" match grade barrel and Bomar adjustable rear sight. Grips are checkered black/silver wood laminate with matte stainless steel slide and frame. Magazine capacity is 8 rounds. Empty weight is approximately 44 oz. Introduced in 1998.

Suggested Retail Introductory Price: $1,600

Model 945 Black Model

This Performance Center Model features a 3.25" barrel with black stainless steel slide. Frame is aluminum. Novak Lo-Mount sights. Hogue checkered wood laminate grips. Furnished with two 6-round magazines and a locking aluminum gun case. Weight is about 24 oz. Exclusive with RSR.

Suggested Retail Introductory Price: $1,550

Model 945-40

This PC model is fitted with a 3.75" barrel chambered for the .40 S&W cartridge. Novak Lo-Mount sights and Hogue checkered wood laminate grips are standard. Furnished with two 7-round magazines and a locking aluminum case. Clear glassbead finish. Exclusive with Sports South.

Suggested Retail Introductory Price: $1,275

Model 945 Micro

Similar to the Model 945 Black Model but with stainless steel finish. Exclusive with Camfour Distributor.

Suggested Retail Introductory Price: $1,300

Model SW945

This .45 ACP pistol is fitted with a 5" barrel with Wilson Combat adjustable rear sight. Scalloped slide serrations both front and rear. Checkered wood grips. Many special features. Weight is about 40.5 oz.Suggested Retail Introductory Price: $2,085

Model SW1911

Chambered for the .45 ACP cartridge and fitted with a 5" barrel with adjustable rear sight. Checkered wood grips. Many special features. Scalloped slide serrations front and rear. Black Melonite finish. Magazine capacity is 8 rounds. Weight is about 41 oz. Also offered in a stainless steel version for $160 less.Suggested Retail Price: $2,270

Model SW1911 DK

This model is chambered for the .38 Super cartridge and fitted with a 5" barrel with adjustable rear sight. Smooth wood grips with DK logo. Stainless steel finish with scalloped serrations at rear of slide. Many special features. Magazine capacity is 10 rounds. Weight is about 41.5 oz. Introduced in 2005.Suggested Retail Price: $2,320

SW1911 Tactical Rail

One of Tactical Rail Series for SWAT Teams and tactical applications. Picatinny rail and fixed sights. Blued or stainless, single-action .45 ACP with 5" barrel and 8+1 capacity. 39 oz. Introduced 2006. MSRP: $1,057.

Model 66 .357 Magnum F-Comp

A Performance Center revolver designed as a carry gun. Furnished with a 3" ported barrel and full underlug. The thumbpiece has been cut down to accommodate all speed loaders and the charge holes are countersunk. The K-frame action has been custom tuned and the rear sight is a fully adjustable black blade while the front sight features a Tritium dot night sight. Furnished with a round butt combat-style rubber grip. This revolver has a stainless steel finish. Weight is about 35 oz. This is a Lew Horton special limited edition, 300 units. **NOTE:** In 2003 this revolver was produced for all S&W stocking dealers.

Suggested Retail Introductory Price: $800

Model 66

An RSR exclusive this model is chambered for the .357 Magnum cartridge and fitted with a 3" barrel. Red ramp front sight. Stainless steel finish. Limited edition.Suggested Retail Introductory Price: $490

Model 681 Quad Port

Chambered for the .357 Magnum cartridge and fitted with a 3" barrel with Quad porting. Fixed rear sight. Seven-round cylinder with moon clips. Two sets of grips are standard: Hogue Bantam and checkered wood laminate. Stainless steel finish. Weight is about 35 oz. Camfour exclusive. A 4" barrel version is also available.

Suggested Retail Introductory Price: $850

Model 25

This PC model is a reintroduction of the original Model 25. Chambered for the .45 Colt cartridge and fitted with a tapered 6" barrel with pinned gold bead patridge front sight. Four screw frame. Furnished with locking aluminum case. Weight is about 42 oz. Sports South exclusive.

NIB	Exc.	V.G.	Good	Fair	Poor
900	750	650	550	375	—

Model 657

This Lew Horton/Performance Center revolver is fitted with a 3" full lug barrel chambered for the .41 Magnum cartridge. Fluted cylinder with red ramp front sight and white outline rear. Rosewood grips. Limited to 150 revolvers in 1998.Suggested Retail Introductory Price: $720

Model 657 Classic

Offered in limited quantities of 350 units this Lew Horton/ Performance Center revolver features an unfluted cylinder and 6.5" barrel on a drilled and tapped N frame. Chambered for the .41 Magnum cartridge this handgun is fitted with adjustable rear sight. Special serial numbers.

Suggested Retail Introductory Price: $550

Model 657 Defensive

Introduced in 1999 by Lou Horton, this .41 Magnum revolver is fitted with a 2-5/8" barrel with drift adjustable Millet front sight and fully adjustable rear sight. Stainless steel finish with 6-shot nonfluted cylinder. Hogue combat grips. Weight is about 40 oz. Furnished with aluminum case.

Suggested Retail Introductory Price: $1,025

Model 657 Hunter

Introduced in 1995 this is an RSR Wholesale Guns exclusive. Fitted with an integral weaver base, Mag-Na-Ported 6" barrel with Millet red ramp front sight and adjustable rear sight. This model has a stainless steel finish, special serial numbers, chamfered charge holes, and adjustable trigger stop. Limited to 500 guns. Suggested Retail Introductory Price: $1,000

Model 19 .357 Magnum K-Comp

This is the same gun as the F-Comp but furnished with a black matte finish and is sold through stocking dealers on a unlimited basis.

Suggested Retail Introductory Price: $800

Model 60 Carry Comp

Introduced in the summer of 1993 this J-frame revolver is fitted with a 3" full underlug barrel with integral compensator. The charge holes are radiused for quick loading and the action is tuned by the Performance Center. The pistol is rated for +P ammunition. The grips are fancy wood contoured for speed loaders. This Lew Horton revolver is limited to 300 guns and has special serial numbers.

Suggested Retail Introductory Price: $795

Paxton Quigley Model 640

This is a Performance Center offering restricted to 300 revolvers. Built around the Model 640 this limited edition handgun has a 2" compensated barrel, windage adjustable front sight, specially tuned action, and a tapestry soft gun case. Each gun has a distinct serial number range.

Suggested Retail Introductory Price: $720

Model 640 Centennial Powerport

Introduced in 1996 this model is a Lew Horton exclusive. It is fitted with a 2-1/8" barrel with integral compensator. The front sight is a black blade with Tritium insert and the rear is a fixed notch. The cylinder holds five .357 or .38 rounds. Stainless steel with Pachmayr decelerator compact grips. Overall length is 6.75" and weight is about 25 oz. Limited to 300 units. Suggested Retail Introductory Price: $675

Model 327 Carry

Introduced in 2004 this 8-shot model is chambered for the .357 Magnum cartridge. Barrel length is 2" with dovetail .260 orange ramp. Scandium alloy frame with stainless steel barrel, titanium cylinder and shroud. Black oxide finish except for gray cylinder. Cocobolo wood grips. Weight is about 21 oz.

Suggested Retail Price: $1,226

Model 940 Centennial .356

Offered exclusively from Lew Horton this J-frame revolver is chambered for the new .356 cartridge and has a 2" compensated barrel. It will also fire the 9mm cartridge. This gun features a tuned action, radius hammer and trigger and special serial numbers. Suggested Retail Introductory Price: $760

Model 13 .357

This is a Lew Horton exclusive that features a 3" barrel with 4 Mag-Na-Ports, a bobbed hammer for double-action-only, chambered charge holes, beveled cylinder, contoured grip and thumb latch for speed loader clearance, overtravel trigger stop, and FBI grips. Limited to 300 guns. Suggested Retail Introductory Price: $730

Model 845 Single-Action

Offered by Lew Horton this pistol is chambered for the .45 ACP and is designed for the competitive shooter. Adjustable reach trigger precision fitted slide, frame and barrel are some of the special features. The barrel bushing is spherical and the front sight is dovetailed. The magazine well is extended as is the magazine release and safety. Both front and rear sight are adjustable. Suggested Retail Introductory Price: $1,470

Model 952

Chambered for the 9mm cartridge, this semi-automatic pistol has 5" barrel. Stainless steel frame and slide. Adjustable rear sight. Checkered wood grips. Magazine capacity is nine rounds. Weight is about 41 oz. Suggested Retail Introductory Price: $2,030

Model 1911

This .45 ACP PC model features a 5" barrel, micro-click adjustable black rear sight and dovetail black front sight. Checkered wine laminate grips. Stainless steel frame and slide with black oxide finish. Magazine capacity is 8 rounds. Weight is about 41 oz. Introduced in 2004.

Suggested Retail Price: $2,270

SNEIDER, CHARLES E.
Baltimore, Maryland

Two-Cylinder Revolver

A .22 caliber spur trigger revolver with a 2.75" octagonal barrel and twin seven-shot cylinders that can be pivoted. The barrel marked "E. Sneider Pat. March 1862." Produced in limited quantities during the 1860s.

NIB	Exc.	V.G.	Good	Fair	Poor
—	—	14000	11000	5500	1250

SOKOLOVSKY CORP. SPORT ARMS
Sunnyvale, California

.45 Automaster

A .45 caliber stainless steel semi-automatic pistol with a 6" barrel fitted with Millet adjustable sights and six-shot magazine. Approximately 50 of these pistols have been made since 1984.

NIB	Exc.	V.G.	Good	Fair	Poor
4850	3800	2750	2000	1500	500

SPALDING & FISHER
Worcester, Massachusetts

Double Barreled Pistol

A .36 caliber percussion double-barrel pocket pistol with 5.5" barrels, blued iron frame and walnut grips. The top of the barrels marked "Spalding & Fisher." Produced during the 1850s.

NIB	Exc.	V.G.	Good	Fair	Poor
—	—	1350	925	400	100

SPANG & WALLACE
Philadelphia, Pennsylvania

Pocket Pistol

A .36 caliber percussion pocket pistol with a 2.5" to 6" barrel, German silver furniture and checkered walnut stock. The barrel marked "Spang & Wallace/Phila." Manufactured during late 1840s and early 1850s.

Courtesy Bonhams & Butterfields

NIB	Exc.	V.G.	Good	Fair	Poor
—	—	2850	1500	750	200

SPENCER REVOLVER
Maltby, Henley & Company
New York, New York

Safety Hammerless Revolver

A .32 caliber hammerless double-action revolver with a 3" barrel. The frame and barrel made of brass, the cylinder of steel and the grips are of walnut. The barrel is marked "Spencer Safety Hammerless Pat. Jan. 24, 1888 & Oct. 29, 1889." Manufactured by the Norwich Pistol Company circa 1890.

NIB	Exc.	V.G.	Good	Fair	Poor
—	—	500	225	150	100

SPHINX
Sphinx Engineering SA
Porrentru, Switzerland
Imported by Sile Distributors Inc.

AT-380

This semi-automatic pistol is a small .380 caliber in double-action-only. The magazine capacity is 11 rounds. It is offered in stainless steel, blued, or two-tone finish. The barrel is 3.27" and overall length is 6.03". Sights are fixed and grips are black checkered plastic. Weight is 25 oz.

NIB	Exc.	V.G.	Good	Fair	Poor
600	550	400	300	200	100

AT-2000 SERIES PISTOLS

This is a series number applied to several different variations of the same basic design. Based on the CZ 75 pistol the AT-2000 is a semi-automatic pistol offered in 9mm and .40 S&W. Barrel lengths are different depending on variation, but the AT-2000 can be converted from double-action to double only in just a matter of minutes.

AT-2000S/SDA

This model is chambered for the 9mm or .40 S&W cartridge. The barrel length is 4.53" and overall length is 8.12". Magazine capacity is 15 rounds for 9mm and 13 rounds for .40 S&W. Available in double-action (S) or double-action-only (SDA). Offered with two-tone or all blued finish. Weighs 35 oz.

NIB	Exc.	V.G.	Good	Fair	Poor
1500	1150	875	675	600	300

AT-2000P/PDA

This is a slightly smaller of the AT-2000S. Magazine capacity is 13 rounds for 9mm and 11 rounds for .40 S&W. The features are the same except that the barrel length is 3.66", overall length 7.25", and weight is 31 oz.

NIB	Exc.	V.G.	Good	Fair	Poor
1500	1150	875	675	600	300

AT-2000PS

This version, sometimes referred to as the Police Special, features the shorter barrel of the AT-2000P model on the larger AT-2000S frame. Barrel length is 3.66" and magazine capacity is 15 rounds for 9mm and 13 rounds for the .40 S&W.

NIB	Exc.	V.G.	Good	Fair	Poor
1500	1150	875	675	600	300

AT-2000H/HDA

This is the smallest version of the AT-2000 series. Magazine capacity is 10 rounds for 9mm and 8 rounds for .40 S&W. The barrel length is 3.34" and overall length is 6.78". Weight is 26 oz.

NIB	Exc.	V.G.	Good	Fair	Poor
1500	1150	875	675	600	300

AT-2000C

This is the competitor model. It features a competition slide, dual port compensator, match barrel, and Sphinx scope mount. Offered in double-action/single-action. Available in 9mm, 9x21, and .40 S&W.

NIB	Exc.	V.G.	Good	Fair	Poor
2200	1600	1200	800	600	400

AT-2000CS

Same as above model but fitted with BoMar adjustable sights.

NIB	Exc.	V.G.	Good	Fair	Poor
2250	1650	1250	850	650	425

AT-2000GM

The Grand Master model. Features are similar to the AT-2000C but offered in single-action-only.

NIB	Exc.	V.G.	Good	Fair	Poor
3000	2550	2100	1750	1250	500

AT-2000GMS

Same as above but fitted with BoMar adjustable sights.

NIB	Exc.	V.G.	Good	Fair	Poor
3050	2600	2150	1800	1300	525

3000

16+1 autoloader chambered in 9mm or .45 ACP. Stainless steel frame and slide, manual safety, saingle/double/decocking action, weight 40.56 oz. Also available in compact version.

NIB	Exc.	V.G.	Good	Fair	Poor
2000	1650	1150	500	300	200

SPIES, A. W.
New York, New York

Pocket Pistol

A .41 caliber percussion pocket pistol with a 2.5" barrel, German silver furniture and a checkered walnut stock. Produced during the 1850s.

NIB	Exc.	V.G.	Good	Fair	Poor
—	—	1950	1775	900	300

SPILLER & BURR
Atlanta, Georgia

Navy Revolver

A .36 caliber percussion revolver with a 6" or 6.5" octagonal barrel and 6-shot cylinder. The barrel and cylinder blued, the frame of brass with walnut grips. Some pistols are marked "Spiller & Burr" while others are simply marked "C.S." Approximately 1,450 were made between 1862 and 1865.

Courtesy Milwaukee Public Museum, Milwaukee, Wisconsin

NIB	Exc.	V.G.	Good	Fair	Poor
—	—	45000	22500	15500	1500

SPITFIRE
JSL (Hereford) Ltd.
Hereford, England

This semi-automatic pistol is a design based on the CZ 75. This is a hand-built pistol designed by John Slough and built from a solid block of steel. The stainless steel frame and slide are cut with spark erosion and diamond grinding. Barrels are built and bored in the same factory. This is primarily a competition pistol. Manufactured 1992-1994.

Spitfire Standard Model (G1)

Chambered for the 9x21, 9mm Parabellum, or .40 S&W cartridges this pistol uses the locked breech concept. The trigger system is single and double-action and it is fitted with an ambidextrous safety. The barrel is 3.7" and the overall length is 7.1". Magazine capacity of the 9mm is 15 rounds. Sights are fixed. Empty weight is 35 oz. Finish is stainless steel. Comes supplied with presentation box, two magazines, and allen key. Discontinued.

NIB	Exc.	V.G.	Good	Fair	Poor
1300	900	700	500	300	200

Spitfire Master Model

This is similar to the Standard Model but without sights. It is fitted with a stainless steel bridge mount to take an Aimpoint sight. Also has a dual port compensator. Supplied with presentation box and two magazines. Discontinued.

NIB	Exc.	V.G.	Good	Fair	Poor
2100	1750	1250	800	400	200

Spitfire Squadron Model

This model has a Standard Model frame, adjustable rear sight slide, adjustable rear sight slide with compensator, Master Model slide and barrel with stainless steel bridge mount and Aimpoint sight, four magazines, screwdriver, allen key, oil bottle, spare springs, cleaning kit, and fitted leather case. Discontinued.

NIB	Exc.	V.G.	Good	Fair	Poor
6000	4800	2100	900	450	200

Spitfire Sterling Model (G2)

This model is chambered for the 9x21, 9mm Parabellum, or .40 S&W cartridges. Its features are the same as the Standard Model with the exception that it has adjustable sights. Discontinued.

NIB	Exc.	V.G.	Good	Fair	Poor
1400	1000	800	600	300	200

Spitfire Super Sterling (G7)

Also chambered for the 9x21, 9mm Parabellum, and .40 S&W this model features a single port compensator, 4.3" barrel, and overall length of 8.25". Weight is approximately 36 oz. Discontinued.

NIB	Exc.	V.G.	Good	Fair	Poor
1600	1200	900	700	350	200

Spitfire Competition Model (G3)

Chambered for 9x21, 9mm Parabellum, or .40 S&W cartridge this model features a tapered slide rib, adjustable rear sight, dual pod compensator, match hammer, adjustable trigger stop with presentation box. Barrel is 5.27" with compensator and weight is 40 oz. Discontinued.

NIB	Exc.	V.G.	Good	Fair	Poor
1800	1400	1000	800	400	200

Spitfire Battle of Britain Commemorative

This is a limited edition of 1,056 Spitfires in 9mm Parabellum. Each one represents one of the Spitfire aircraft. The stainless steel slide has the inscription "Battle of Britain-50th Anniversary," the grips are checkered walnut, log book of history of that particular aircraft, and a wooden presentation box with engraved plaque. Discontinued.

NIB	Exc.	V.G.	Good	Fair	Poor
1950	1400	1000	800	400	200

Westlake Britarms

This is a .22 LR Match pistol. Barrel length is 5.77", sight base is 8.42", magazine capacity is 5 rounds. Weight is approximately 47 oz. Trigger is adjustable for length, front and rear trigger stops, adjustable palm rest on contoured wood grips, take-down barrel design with removable weight. Limited importation.

NIB	Exc.	V.G.	Good	Fair	Poor
1850	1400	1000	800	400	200

SPRINGFIELD ARMORY INC.
Geneseo, Illinois

M6 Scout Pistol

As above but with 10" barrel and no folding stock. Parkerized or stainless steel finish. Weight is about 28 oz. Introduced in 2002. Discontinued.

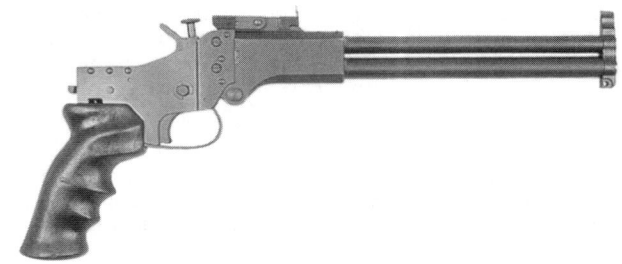

NIB	Exc.	V.G.	Good	Fair	Poor
575	425	295	200	100	50

NOTE: Add $30 for stainless steel.

Model 1911-A1

A 9mm, .38 Super or .45 caliber copy of the Colt Model 1911-A1 semi-automatic pistol. Blued or Parkerized. Introduced in 1985.

NIB	Exc.	V.G.	Good	Fair	Poor
625	425	375	350	300	250

Model 1911-A1 Service Model

Introduced in 2003 this .45 ACP pistol has a 5" barrel with Bo-Mar adjustable three-dot rear sight. This model also has a number of special features such as extended mag well, titanium firing pin, and beavertail grip safety. Stainless steel magazine capacity is seven rounds. Black stainless steel finish. Weight is about 35 oz.

NIB	Exc.	V.G.	Good	Fair	Poor
925	750	600	500	400	200

Model 1911-A1 Service Mil-Spec

Chambered for the .45 ACP cartridge and fitted with a 5" barrel. Fixed sights. Matte stainless steel finish. Black plastic grips. Weight is about 36 oz. Introduced in 2003.

NIB	Exc.	V.G.	Good	Fair	Poor
610	475	375	350	300	250

Model 1911-A1 Service Model Lightweight

This .45 ACP pistol has a 5" barrel with lightweight alloy frame and bi-tone finish. Novak Lo-Mount sights. A large number of special features. Checkered cocobolo grips. Magazine capacity is seven rounds. Weight is about 30 oz. Introduced in 2003.

NIB	Exc.	V.G.	Good	Fair	Poor
875	700	600	500	400	200

Model 1911-A1 Stainless

Similar to the standard Model 1911 but chambered for the .45 ACP cartridge and offered in stainless steel. Equipped with three-dot sights, beveled magazine well, and checkered walnut grips. Weighs about 39.2 oz.

NIB	Exc.	V.G.	Good	Fair	Poor
900	750	625	400	350	200

NOTE: For Bomar sights add $50.

Model 1911-A1 Factory Comp

Chambered for the .45 ACP or the .38 Super this pistol is fitted with a three chamber compensator. The rear sight is adjustable, an extended thumb safety and Videcki speed trigger are standard features. Also checkered walnut grips, beveled magazine well and Commander hammer are standard. Weighs 40 oz.

NIB	Exc.	V.G.	Good	Fair	Poor
1050	925	750	600	500	300

NOTE: Factory Comp pistols chambered for .38 Super may bring a small premium.

Model 1911-A1 Factory Comp High Capacity

Same as above but with 13-round magazine.

NIB	Exc.	V.G.	Good	Fair	Poor
1050	925	750	600	500	300

Model 1911-A2 S.A.S.S.

This is a single-shot pistol built on the Model 1911 frame. Available in two barrel lengths; 10.75" and 14.9". Offered in .22 LR, .223, 7mm-08, 7mmBR, .357 Magnum, .308, and .44 Magnum calibers. This conversion kit is available for those wishing to use it on their own Model 1911 pistol frames.

NIB	Exc.	V.G.	Good	Fair	Poor
225	200	175	150	100	50

Model 1911-A1 Defender

Chambered for the .45 ACP cartridge this pistol is fitted with a tapered cone dual port compensator. It also is fitted with reversed recoil plug, full length recoil spring guide, fully adjustable rear sight, serrated front strap, rubberized grips, and Commander-style hammer. Eight-round magazine capacity. The finish is bi-tone. Weighs 40.16 oz.

NIB	Exc.	V.G.	Good	Fair	Poor
875	700	600	500	400	200

Model 1911-A1 Loaded Defender Lightweight

As above but with loaded features: precision fit frames, slides and barrels, flat serrated mainspring housing, lowered and flared ejection port, Delta lightweight hammer, loaded chamber indicator, titanium firing pin, carry bevel treatment, ambidextrous thumb safety, high hand beavertail grip safety, dovetail front sight, Novak or adjustable rear sight, and adjustable speed trigger.

NIB	Exc.	V.G.	Good	Fair	Poor
950	775	675	550	450	250

Model 1911-A1 Compact

Available in blue or bi-tone this .45 ACP is fitted with a 4.5" barrel and compact compensator. It is equipped with Commander-style hammer and three-dot sights. Walnut grips are standard. Comes with 7-round magazine. Weighs 37.2 oz.

NIB	Exc.	V.G.	Good	Fair	Poor
900	750	625	400	350	200

NOTE: For stainless steel add $40.

Lightweight Compact Comp

Fitted with a 4-1/2" barrel and single port compensator. Magazine hold 8 rounds of .45 ACP. Frame is alloy and weight is 30 oz.

NIB	Exc.	V.G.	Good	Fair	Poor
900	750	625	400	350	200

Model 1911-A1 Compact Mil-Spec

This model is the same as the standard blued steel Compact model but with a Parkerized finish.

NIB	Exc.	V.G.	Good	Fair	Poor
850	700	575	350	300	200

Model 1911-A1 Long Slide

This model features a 6" barrel, 3-dot fixed sights, checkered wooden grips, and an 8-round magazine capacity. Finish is stainless steel. Weight is about 38 oz. Introduced in 1997.

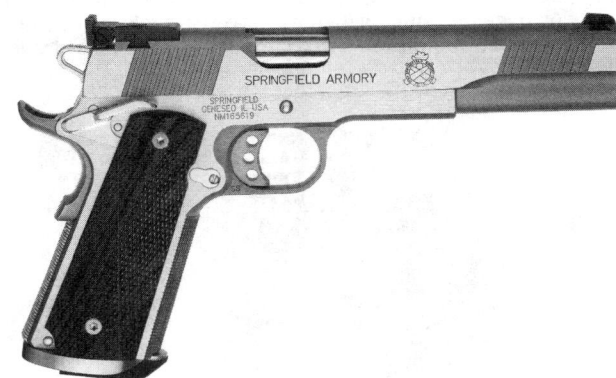

NIB	Exc.	V.G.	Good	Fair	Poor
950	775	675	550	450	250

Model 1911-A1 Loaded Long Slide

As above but with loaded features: precision fit frames, slides and barrels, flat serrated mainspring housing, lowered and flared ejection port, Delta lightweight hammer, loaded chamber indicator, titanium firing pin, carry bevel treatment, ambidextrous thumb safety, high hand beavertail grip safety, dovetail front sight, Novak or adjustable rear sight, and adjustable speed trigger.

NIB	Exc.	V.G.	Good	Fair	Poor
1100	950	775	600	475	350

Model 1911-A1 Champion

This .45 ACP pistol has a shortened slide, barrel, and reduced size frame. The Champion is fitted with 4" barrel, 8-round magazine,

Commander hammer, checkered walnut grips, and special 3-dot sights. Weighs 33.4 oz.

NIB	Exc.	V.G.	Good	Fair	Poor
795	650	500	400	295	150

Model 1911-A1 Champion Mil-Spec

Same as above but with a Parkerized finish.

NIB	Exc.	V.G.	Good	Fair	Poor
700	600	400	350	225	125

Model 1911-A1 Stainless Champion

Same as above but offered in stainless steel. Weighs about 33.4 oz.

NIB	Exc.	V.G.	Good	Fair	Poor
850	700	575	350	300	200

Model 1911-A1 Loaded Champion Stainless

As above but with loaded features: precision fit frames, slides and barrels, flat serrated mainspring housing, lowered and flared ejection port, Delta lightweight hammer, loaded chamber indicator, titanium firing pin, carry bevel treatment, ambidextrous thumb safety, high hand beavertail grip safety, dovetail front sight, Novak or adjustable rear sight, and adjustable speed trigger.

NIB	Exc.	V.G.	Good	Fair	Poor
1000	875	700	575	500	300

Champion Compact

Includes same features as Champion but with a shortened grip frame length and a 7-round magazine. Weighs 32 oz.

NIB	Exc.	V.G.	Good	Fair	Poor
850	700	575	350	300	200

Model 1911 Loaded Champion Lightweight

This model has a lightweight aluminum frame with Novak night sights. Checkered rubber grips. Finish is OD green and Black Armory Kote. Weight is about 28 oz. Introduced in 2004.

NIB	Exc.	V.G.	Good	Fair	Poor
850	700	575	350	300	200

Ultra Compact 1911-A1

This model features a 3-1/2" barrel with a 7-1/8" overall length. It has a stainless steel frame, beveled mag well, speed trigger, match grade barrel, and walnut grips. Weighs 31 oz.

NIB	Exc.	V.G.	Good	Fair	Poor
850	700	575	350	300	200

Ultra Compact Lightweight MD-1

Same as above but in .380 caliber with alloy frame. Weighs 24 oz.

NIB	Exc.	V.G.	Good	Fair	Poor
700	600	400	350	225	125

Ultra Compact 1911-A1 Mil-Spec

Same as the Ultra Compact Model but with a Parkerized or blued finish.

NIB	Exc.	V.G.	Good	Fair	Poor
750	650	450	350	225	125

V10 Ultra Compact 1911-A1

Same as the Ultra Compact 1911-A1 but fitted with a compensator built into the barrel and slide.

NIB	Exc.	V.G.	Good	Fair	Poor
900	750	625	400	350	200

V10 Ultra Compact 1911-A1 Mil-Spec

Same as above but with Parkerized finish.

NIB	Exc.	V.G.	Good	Fair	Poor
850	700	575	350	300	200

Model 1911-A1 High Capacity

This model is chambered in .45 ACP (10-round magazine) or 9mm caliber (16-round magazine). Standard features include Commander hammer, walnut grips, and beveled magazine well. Blued finish. Weighs 42 oz. In 1997 this model was offered in stainless steel and Parkerized finish.

NIB	Exc.	V.G.	Good	Fair	Poor
650	525	400	300	200	100

NOTE: For stainless steel add $40, for Parkerized finish deduct $25.

Compact High Capacity

Same as above but with an 11-round magazine.

NIB	Exc.	V.G.	Good	Fair	Poor
650	525	400	300	200	150

Ultra Compact High Capacity

This .45 ACP model is offered in three different 3.5" barrel variations: stainless steel, Parkerized, and ported. Standard magazine capacity is 10 rounds. Weight is about 31 oz.

NIB	Exc.	V.G.	Good	Fair	Poor
700	600	400	350	225	125

NOTE: Add $60 for stainless steel and $100 for ported models.

Micro Compact—Parkerized

Chambered for the .45 ACP cartridge and fitted with a 3" bull barrel. Aluminum frame with steel slide. Novak night sights. Cocobolo grips. Offered with Parkerized finish. Weight is about 24 oz. Magazine capacity is six rounds. Introduced in 2002.

NIB	Exc.	V.G.	Good	Fair	Poor
850	700	575	350	300	200

Micro Compact—Stainless

As above but with stainless steel frame and slide and Novak tritium night sights. Weight is about 24 oz. Introduced in 2003.

NIB	Exc.	V.G.	Good	Fair	Poor
900	750	625	400	350	200

Micro Compact—O.D. Green

As above but with Armory Kote green finish. Pearce grips. Introduced in 2003.

NIB	Exc.	V.G.	Good	Fair	Poor
900	750	625	400	350	200

Micro Compact—Black Stainless

As above but with black stainless steel finish and Slimline cocobolo grips. Weight is about 32 oz. Introduced in 2003.

NIB	Exc.	V.G.	Good	Fair	Poor
900	750	625	400	350	200

Micro Compact Lightweight

This model is similar to the other Micro models but is fitted with an aluminum frame and Novak night sights. Cocobolo wood grips. Bi-Tone finish. Equipped with XML Mini Light. Introduced in 2004. Weight is about 24 oz.

NIB	Exc.	V.G.	Good	Fair	Poor
900	750	625	400	350	200

Loaded Micro Compact Lightweight

As above but with loaded features: precision fit frames, slides and barrels, flat serrated mainspring housing, lowered and flared ejection port, Delta lightweight hammer, loaded chamber indicator, titanium firing pin, carry bevel treatment, ambidextrous thumb safety, high hand beavertail grip safety, dovetail front sight, Novak or adjustable rear sight, and adjustable speed trigger. Introduced in 2005.

NIB	Exc.	V.G.	Good	Fair	Poor
1000	975	775	600	475	300

Model 1911-A1 Mil-Spec Operator

Chambered for the .45 ACP and fitted with a 5" barrel. This model features a Picatinny rail system on the frame. Fixed sights. Magazine capacity is 7 rounds. Parkerized finish.

NIB	Exc.	V.G.	Good	Fair	Poor
900	750	625	400	350	200

Model 1911-A1 Loaded Operator

Introduced in 2002 this model features a integral Picatinny rail on the frame. Chambered for the .45 ACP cartridge and fitted with a 5" barrel. Novak night sights. Parkerized finish. Magazine capacity is 7 rounds.

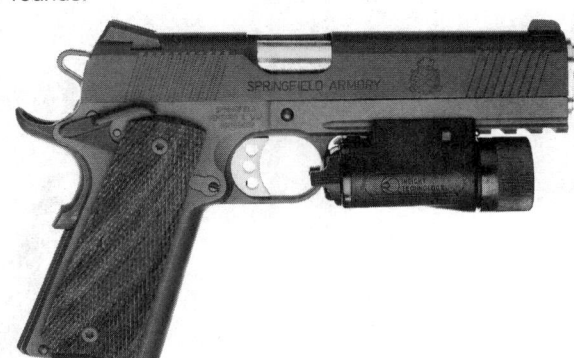

NIB	Exc.	V.G.	Good	Fair	Poor
950	800	675	450	375	250

Combat Commander

A copy of the Colt Model 1911-A1 Combat Commander chambered for .45 ACP only. Introduced in 1988.

NIB	Exc.	V.G.	Good	Fair	Poor
700	600	400	350	225	125

Trophy Match

This model has special features such as fully adjustable target sights, match grade 5" barrel, and special wide trigger. Weight is approximately 36 oz. Available in blue, stainless steel, or bi-tone finish. In 1997 this model was offered chambered for the 9mm cartridge. Values would be the same for both .45 ACP and the 9mm models.

NIB	Exc.	V.G.	Good	Fair	Poor
1000	975	775	600	475	300

NOTE: For stainless steel add $40.

Loaded Leatham Trophy Match

Introduced in 2005 this .40 S&W pistol is fitted with a 5" barrel with fully adjustable target sights. Black Polymer grips. Dawson magazine well, tuned trigger, match barrel and bushing, checkered front strap and other special features. Black finish. Weight is about 39 oz.

NIB	Exc.	V.G.	Good	Fair	Poor
1200	1075	900	700	575	300

1911 GI SERIES
GI Full Size

Chambered for the .45 ACP cartridge and fitted with a 5" barrel. Old style fixed sights. Standard checkered brown plastic grips. Lanyard loop on mainspring housing. Stainless steel frame and slide. Magazine capacity is 7 rounds. Weight is about 36 oz. Introduced in 2004. This model is also offered with Parkerized finish or OD green finish. Also offered in stainless steel.

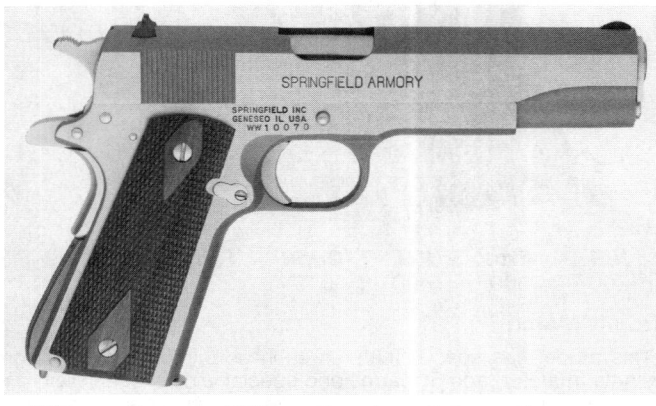

NIB	Exc.	V.G.	Good	Fair	Poor
560	450	375	325	250	125

NOTE: Deduct $45 for Parkerized or OD finish. Add $30 for stainless steel.

GI Full Size High-Capacity

As above but with 10-round magazine. Weight is about 38 oz. Introduced in 2005.

NIB	Exc.	V.G.	Good	Fair	Poor
600	500	425	375	295	175

GI Champion

This model is a scaled-down version of the full-size model above. Fitted with a 4" fully supported barrel and low-profile military sights. This model also has double diamond walnut grips. Black finish. Weight is about 34 oz. Introduced in 2004. Also offered with Parkerized finish.

NIB	Exc.	V.G.	Good	Fair	Poor
600	500	425	375	295	175

GI Champion Lightweight

Introduced in 2005 this .45 ACP model is fitted with a 4" barrel with fully supported ramp. Low profile military sights. Checkered walnut grips. Weight is about 28 oz.

NIB	Exc.	V.G.	Good	Fair	Poor
600	500	425	375	295	175

GI Micro-Compact

As above but fitted with a 3" fully supported and ramped barrel. Magazine capacity is 6 rounds. Weight is about 32 oz. Introduced in 2004.

NIB	Exc.	V.G.	Good	Fair	Poor
600	500	425	375	295	175

P9 Pistol

This is a double-action 9mm, .45 ACP, or .40 S&W pistol based on the Czech CZ 75 design. It incorporates several design features including: stainless steel trigger, sear safety mechanism, extended sear safety lever, redesigned back strap, lengthened beavertail grip area, and a new high strength slide stop. This model discontinued in 1993.

NIB	Exc.	V.G.	Good	Fair	Poor
600	500	425	375	295	1750

Model P9 Standard

This is the standard pistol fitted with a 4.7" barrel, low profile target sights, and a ribbed slide. The 9mm has a 16-round magazine, the .45 ACP has a 10-round magazine, and the .40 S&W holds 12 rounds. Offered in either blue or stainless finish. Weighs about 35 oz.

NIB	Exc.	V.G.	Good	Fair	Poor
600	500	425	375	295	175

Model P9 Factory Comp.

This is a competition pistol fitted with triple port compensator, extended magazine release, adjustable rear sight, slim competition wood grips, and bi-tone finish. Weighs 34 oz. Dropped from the Springfield product line in 1993.

NIB	Exc.	V.G.	Good	Fair	Poor
700	600	400	350	225	125

Model P9 Ultra (IPSC Approved)

This competition pistol features a longer slide and barrel, 5". Special target sights, rubberized competition grips. Pistol is engraved with IPSC logo. Available in bi-tone finish only. Weighs 34.5 oz. Dropped from production in 1993.

NIB	Exc.	V.G.	Good	Fair	Poor
775	575	425	350	250	200

Super Tuned Champion

Introduced in 1997 this model features a 4" barrel chambered for the .45 ACP cartridge, Novak fixed Lo-Mount sights. Tuned and polished extractor and ejector. Polished feed ramp and barrel throat. Magazine capacity is 7 rounds. Choice of blued or Parkerized finish. Weight is approximately 36 oz.

NIB	Exc.	V.G.	Good	Fair	Poor
850	700	575	350	300	200

Super Tuned V10

Similar to the model above but with 3.5" barrel. Finish is bi-tone or stainless steel. Weight is about 33 oz. Introduced in 1997. Add $100 for stainless steel.

NIB	Exc.	V.G.	Good	Fair	Poor
1000	895	700	600	400	250

Super Tuned Standard

This model features a 5" barrel with stainless steel finish. Weight is about 39 oz. Has all other super tune features. Introduced in 1997.

NIB	Exc.	V.G.	Good	Fair	Poor
1000	895	700	600	400	250

Armory Range Officer

A 1911 pistol ready to compete out of the box. Caliber: .45 ACP. Five-inch barrel with blue finish, forged steel slide and frame, 7-round magazine. Other features include adjustable rear sight, match grade barrel and bushing, checkered mainspring housing, lightweight Delta hammer, extended thumb safety and beavertail grip tang. Weight is 40 ounces.

NIB	Exc.	V.G.	Good	Fair	Poor
800	675	550	450	350	200

Tactical Response Pistol (TRP)

This .45 ACP pistol is fitted with a 5" barrel and choice of stainless steel or black Armory Kote finish. Fully checkered front strap and mainspring housing. Novak Lo-Mount sights. Magazine capacity 8 rounds. Weight is about 37 oz.

NIB	Exc.	V.G.	Good	Fair	Poor
1360	1150	850	600	400	250

TRP Champion

Same as above but with a 3.9" barrel and black Armory Kote finish. Weight is about 33 oz.

NIB	Exc.	V.G.	Good	Fair	Poor
1175	950	800	600	400	200

TRP Pro

This model is fitted with a 5" barrel and many special features including Novak Lo-Mount tritium sights. Magazine capacity is 7 rounds. Meets specifications for FBI SWAT team. Weight is 36 oz.

NIB	Exc.	V.G.	Good	Fair	Poor
2000	1750	1200	900	675	300

TRP Operator

This model has all the features of the TRP series with the addition of an integral light rail on the frame. Fitted with a 5" barrel. Adjustable night sights. Introduced in 2002.

NIB	Exc.	V.G.	Good	Fair	Poor
1350	1025	800	600	400	250

NOTE: Add $60 for night sights. Add $100 for OD green frame and slide.

Lightweight Operator

Blued, semi-auto .45 ACP with 5" bull barrel. Fixed sights, 5-6-lb. trigger pull, Cocobolo grips, 31 oz. Picatinny rail. Introduced 2006.

NIB	Exc.	V.G.	Good	Fair	Poor
850	700	575	350	300	200

Lightweight Champion Operator

Similar to above but with 4" bull barrel. Introduced 2006.

NIB	Exc.	V.G.	Good	Fair	Poor
850	700	575	350	300	200

XD PISTOLS

These pistols are fitted with a polymer frame, grip safety, chamber indicator, and raised firing pin indicator. Offered in black finish as well as O.D. green.

XD 4"

Chambered for the 9mm, .40 S&W, .357 SIG, or .45 GAP cartridges. Barrel length is 4". Magazine capacity for 9mm is 15 rounds; for .40 S&W 12 rounds, for the .357 SIG 12 rounds, and for the .45 GAP 9 rounds. Weight is about 23 oz.

NIB	Exc.	V.G.	Good	Fair	Poor
550	450	350	250	175	125

NOTE: Add $60 for night sights. Add $100 for OD green frame and slide.

XD 4" Bi-Tone

Offered in 9mm or .40 S&W this 4" pistol has a black polymer frame and stainless steel slide. Magazine capacity is 10 rounds. Weight is about 26 oz. Introduced in 2003.

NIB	Exc.	V.G.	Good	Fair	Poor
585	495	375	275	200	150

XD V-10 Ported 4"

Similar to XD but with 4" ported barrel chambered for the 9mm, .40 S&W or .357 SIG. Black finish. Weight is about 26 oz.

NIB	Exc.	V.G.	Good	Fair	Poor
550	450	350	250	175	125

XD 5" Tactical

This model is fitted with a 5" barrel and chambered for the 9mm, .40 S&W or .357 SIG cartridges. Magazine capacity is 10 rounds. Weight is about 26 oz. Offered in black or O.D. green finish. In 2005 the .45 GAP cartridge was also offered for this model. Magazine capacity for 9mm is 15 rounds; for .40 S&W 12 rounds, for the .357 SIG 12 rounds, and for the .45 GAP 9 rounds. Weight is about 31 oz.

NIB	Exc.	V.G.	Good	Fair	Poor
600	450	350	250	200	150

XD 5" Tactical Pro

Introduced in 2003 this model features a Robar NP3 finish, fiber optic front sight and fixed rear sight. The frame is built with an oversized beavertail frame extension of a higher grip. Chambered for the 9mm, .357 SIG., 40 S&W, or the .45 GAP cartridge. Magazine capacity for 9mm is 15 rounds; for .40 S&W 12 rounds, for the .357 SIG 12 rounds, and for the .45 GAP 9 rounds. Weight is about 31 oz.

NIB	Exc.	V.G.	Good	Fair	Poor
875	750	600	500	375	250

XD 5" Bi-Tone Tactical

Introduced in 2005 this model is chambered for the .45 GAP cartridge and fitted with a 5" barrel. Black polymer frame and stainless steel slide. Magazine capacity is 9 rounds. Weight is about 31 oz.

NIB	Exc.	V.G.	Good	Fair	Poor
600	500	400	300	200	125

XD Sub-Compact

Introduced in 2003 this polymer pistol is chambered for the 9mm or .40 S&W cartridge and fitted with a 3" barrel. Fitted with light rail on the dust cover. Grip safety and safe action trigger. Magazine capacity is 10 rounds. Weight is about 20 oz. Fixed sights.

NIB	Exc.	V.G.	Good	Fair	Poor
550	450	350	250	175	125

NOTE: For night sights add $60. Add $70 for XML Mini light.

XD 45 ACP

Polymer semi-auto in black, green or bi-tone holds 13+1 .45 ACP. Imported from Croatia. Fixed sights. Service model: 4" barrel, 30 oz. Tactical model: 5" barrel, 32 oz. Picatinny rail. Introduced 2006.

NIB	Exc.	V.G.	Good	Fair	Poor
585	495	375	275	200	150

LEATHAM LEGEND SERIES

This series was introduced in 2003 and will be identified with a unique series markings, serial number, and certificate of authenticity. Two sets of grips will come with each pistol: one cocobolo with lazer engraved signature of Rob Leatham and the other a black micarta double diamond slimline grips. A custom aluminum case is standard for this series.

TGO 1

This is a full custom pistol from the Springfield Custom Shop with Nowlin Match Grade throated barrel and bushing, Robar bi-tone finish, Bomar low-mount adjustable sights, and a number of other custom features. Chambered for the .45 ACP cartridge. Weight is about 38 oz. Four magazines are standard.

NIB	Exc.	V.G.	Good	Fair	Poor
2400	1875	1500	—	—	—

TGO 2

Similar to the TGO 1, but hand-built by the Springfield Armory.

NIB	Exc.	V.G.	Good	Fair	Poor
1900	1500	1200	—	—	—

TGO 3

This model is an enhanced high-end production model with a lightweight aluminum slide. Bi-tone finish. Weight is about 30 oz.

NIB	Exc.	V.G.	Good	Fair	Poor
1295	1025	800	—	—	—

Enhanced Micro Pistol (EMP)

Tiny little 1911-style semi-auto chambered in 9mm Parabellum or .40 S&W. Short-action single-action design, 7-shot capacity, 3" bull barrel, fixed sights, stainless frame that is 1/8" shorter than the company\qs Compact models. Premium for night sights and other refinements.

NIB	Exc.	V.G.	Good	Fair	Poor
1175	950	800	600	400	200

XD(M)

Enhanced variation of XD series with interchangeable backstraps, improved magazine release and disassembly design. Offered in 9mm, .40 S&W or .45 ACP with 4.5-inch barrel. Three-dot sights with night sights available. Black or two-tone polymer frame Ultra Safety Assurance trigger, striker fired, grip safety, ambidextrous magazine releases, accessory rail, loaded chamber and cocked striker indicators. Weight is approx. 27 ounces with empty magazine. Also available in competition model (9mm only) with 5.25-inch barrel with lightening cut on top of slide

NIB	Exc.	V.G.	Good	Fair	Poor
650	525	400	300	200	100

XDM-3.8

Sub-compact model chambered in 9mm Parabellum (19+1) and .40 S&W (16+1). Features include 3.8-inch steel full-ramp barrel; dovetail front and rear 3-dot sights (tritium and fiber-optics sights available); polymer frame; stainless steel slide with slip-resistant slide serrations; loaded chamber indicator; grip safety. Black, bi-tone or stainless steel finish. Overall length 7 inches, weight 27.5 oz. (9mm).

NIB	Exc.	V.G.	Good	Fair	Poor
650	525	400	300	200	100

SPRINGFIELD CUSTOM SHOP

This specialty shop was formed to build custom pistols to the customer's own specifications. When these one-of-a-kind pistols are encountered it is advisable for the shooter or collector to get an independent appraisal. The Springfield Custom also offers standard custom and Racegun packages that are readily available and in stock. These pistols are commercially available.

Custom Carry

Chambered for the following cartridges: .45 ACP, 9mm Parabellum, .38 Super, 10mm, .40 S&W, 9mm x 21. Pistol is fitted with fixed 3-dot sights, speed trigger, Match barrel and bushing, extended thumb safety, beveled magazine well, Commander hammer, polished feed ramp and throated barrel, tuned extractor, lowered and flared ejection port, fitted slide to frame, full length spring guide rod, and walnut grips. Supplied with two magazines and plastic carrying case.

NIB	Exc.	V.G.	Good	Fair	Poor
1600	1450	1075	800	500	300

Basic Competition Model

Chambered for the .45 ACP this model features a variety of special options for the competition shooter. Special BoMar sights, match trigger, custom slide to frame fit, polished feed-ramp and throated barrel are just some of the features of this pistol.

NIB	Exc.	V.G.	Good	Fair	Poor
1800	1600	1275	1050	650	400

N.R.A. PPC

Designed to comply with NRA rules for PPC competition this pistol is chambered for the .45 ACP cartridge with a match grade barrel and chamber. It has a polished feedramp, throated barrel, recoil buffer system, walnut grips, and fully adjustable sights. It is sold with a custom carrying case.

NIB	Exc.	V.G.	Good	Fair	Poor
1600	1450	1075	800	500	300

Trophy Master Expert Limited Class

Chambered for .45 ACP Adjustable BoMar rear sight, match barrel, polished ramp and throated barrel, extended ambidextrous thumb safety, beveled and polished magazine well, full length recoil spring guide, match trigger, Commander hammer, lowered and flared ejection port, tuned extractor, fitted slide to frame, extended slide release, flat mainspring housing, Pachmayr wraparound grips, two magazines with slam pads and plastic carrying case.

NIB	Exc.	V.G.	Good	Fair	Poor
2100	1750	1300	950	600	400

Expert Pistol

Similar to the above model but progressive triple port compensator.

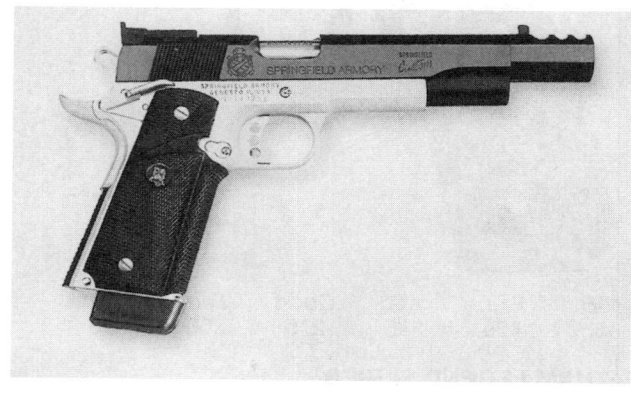

NIB	Exc.	V.G.	Good	Fair	Poor
2200	1850	1400	1000	650	400

Bureau Model 1911-A1

Introduced in 1998 this model features a 5" match barrel, a speed trigger, lowered and flared ejection port, beavertail grip safety, Lo-Mount Novak night sights, front strap checkering, Black T finish and special serial numbers with FBI prefix. Bureau Model markings on slide.

NIB	Exc.	V.G.	Good	Fair	Poor
2100	1750	1300	950	600	400

Springfield Formula "Squirtgun"

Chambered for .45 ACP, .38 Super, 9mmx19, 9mmx21, and 9mmx23. Fitted with a high capacity 20-round frame, customer specifications sights, hard chrome frame and slide, triple chambered tapered cone compensator, full recoil spring guide and reverse plug, shock butt, lowered and flared ejection port, fitted trigger, Commander hammer, polished feed ramp and throated barrel, flat checkered mainspring housing, extended ambidextrous thumb safety, tuned extractor, checkered front strap, bottom of trigger guard checkered, rear of slide serrated, cocking sensations on front of slide, built in beveled magazine well, and checkered wood grips.

NIB	Exc.	V.G.	Good	Fair	Poor
3500	2950	2500	2000	1400	700

Bullseye Wadcutter

Chambered for .45 ACP, .38 Super, 10mm, and .40 S&W. Slide is fitted with BoMar rib. Standard features include full length recoil spring guide rod, speed trigger, Commander hammer, lowered and flared ejection port, tuned extractor, fitted slide to frame, beveled magazine well, checkered front strap, checkered main spring housing, removable scope mount, match barrel and bushing, polished feed ramp and throated barrel, walnut grips, and two magazines with slam pads.

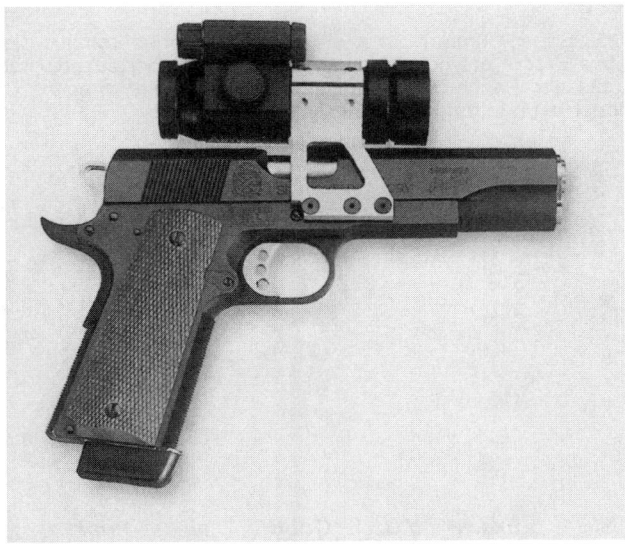

NIB	Exc.	V.G.	Good	Fair	Poor
1800	1600	1275	1050	650	400

Trophy Master Distinguished Pistol

This model is chambered for the following cartridges: .45 ACP, .38 Super, 10mm, .40 S&W, 9mmx21. Special BoMar adjustable rear sight with hidden rear leaf, triple port compensator on match barrel, full length recoil spring guide rod and recoil spring retainer, shock butt, lowered and flared ejection port, fitted speed trigger, Commander hammer, polished feed ramp and throated barrel, flat checkered magazine well and mainspring housing matched to beveled magazine well, extended ambidextrous thumb safety, tuned extractor, checkered front strap, flattened and checkered trigger guard, serrated slide top and compensator, cocking sensations on front of slide, checkered walnut grips, two magazines with slam pads, and carrying case.

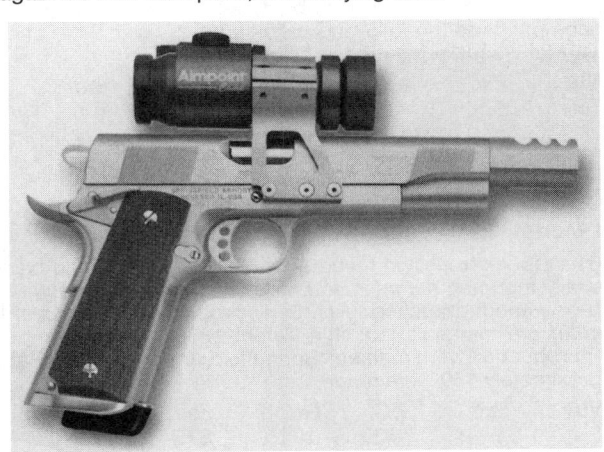

NIB	Exc.	V.G.	Good	Fair	Poor
2450	1900	1350	1000	650	500

Distinguished Limited Class

Similar to the above model but built to comply with USPSA "Limited Class" competition rules. This model has no compensator.

NIB	Exc.	V.G.	Good	Fair	Poor
2695	2000	1500	1000	650	500

CMC Formula "Squirtgun"

Chambered for .45 ACP, .38 Super, 9mmx19, 9mmx21, 9mmx23. This pistol has a 20-round magazine and a modular frame. All other features the same as the Trophy Master.

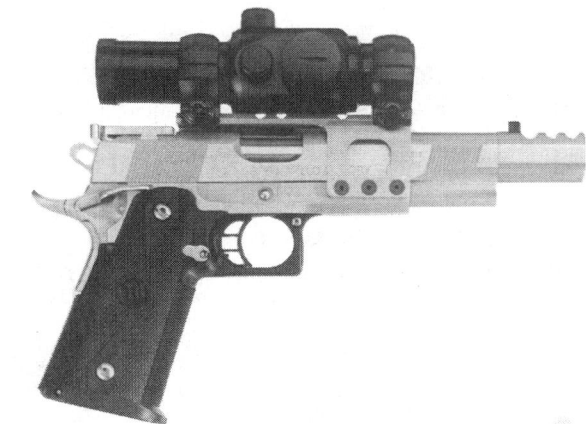

NIB	Exc.	V.G.	Good	Fair	Poor
2750	2000	1200	800	400	200

National Match Model

As above, with a National Match barrel and bushing, adjustable sights and checkered walnut grips. Introduced in 1988.

NIB	Exc.	V.G.	Good	Fair	Poor
1535	1150	850	600	400	300

Competition Grade

As above, hand-tuned, Match Grade trigger, low-profile combat sights, an ambidextrous safety, and a Commander-type hammer. Furnished with Pachmayr grips. Introduced in 1988.

NIB	Exc.	V.G.	Good	Fair	Poor
1600	1200	900	650	400	350

A Model Master Grade Competition Pistol

Similar to the Custom Carry Gun, with a National Match barrel and bushing. Introduced in 1988.

NIB	Exc.	V.G.	Good	Fair	Poor
1700	1500	1250	850	400	350

Model B-1 Master Grade Competition Pistol

Specially designed for USPSA/IPSC competition. Introduced in 1988.

NIB	Exc.	V.G.	Good	Fair	Poor
2000	1750	1250	850	400	350

High Capacity Full-House Race Gun

Built with all available race gun options. Offered in .45 ACP, 9x25 Dillon, .38 Super, and custom calibers on request.

NIB	Exc.	V.G.	Good	Fair	Poor
3085	2300	1700	1200	700	400

Night Light Standard

Introduced in 1996 as a limited edition from Springfield distributor Lew Horton this full size Model 1911A1 pistol is chambered for the .45 ACP. It has a lightweight frame and slide with Millett night sights with Hogue rubber wraparound grips. Fitted with extended beavertail safety. Weight 29 oz.

NIB	Exc.	V.G.	Good	Fair	Poor
620	500	400	300	200	100

Night Light Compact

This model was also introduced by Lew Horton in 1996 and is similar to the above model but fitted with a 4.25" barrel and lightweight frame and slide. Weight is 27 oz.

NIB	Exc.	V.G.	Good	Fair	Poor
620	500	400	300	200	100

Night Compact

Same as above but with a steel frame and slide.

NIB	Exc.	V.G.	Good	Fair	Poor
620	500	400	300	200	100

Omega

A .38 Super, 10mm Norma, or .45 caliber semi-automatic pistol with a 5" or 6" polygon rifled barrel, ported or unported, adjustable sights and Pachmayr grips. Patterned somewhat after the Colt Model 1911. Introduced in 1987.

NIB	Exc.	V.G.	Good	Fair	Poor
650	500	350	250	200	125

NOTE: Caliber Conversion Units add $400.

XD Custom Pro

This pistol is built in the Custom Shop and is available in service and tactical sizes. Tactical calibers offered are: 9mm, .40 S&W, and .45 GAP. In Tactical sizes the following calibers are offered: 9mm, .40 S&W, .357 SIG, and .45 GAP. Among some of the special features are: high hand frame relief, overtravel stop, low-mount Bomar sights. Extended magazine release. National Match barrel and special finish.

NIB	Exc.	V.G.	Good	Fair	Poor
1500	1100	825	675	500	300

XD Carry Pro

This model is offered in subcombact, service and tactical sizes. In subcompact size the following calibers are offered: 9mm and .40 S&W. Many special features as listed above.

NIB	Exc.	V.G.	Good	Fair	Poor
750	550	400	300	200	100

SPRINGFIELD ARMS COMPANY
Springfield, Massachusetts

Belt Model

A .31 caliber percussion revolver with 4", 5", or 6" round barrels, centrally mounted hammer, and an etched 6-shot cylinder. Made with or without a loading lever. Early production versions of this revolver are marked "Jaquith's Patent 1838" on the frame and later production were marked "Springfield Arms" on the top strap. Approximately 150 were made.

NIB	Exc.	V.G.	Good	Fair	Poor
—	—	2600	1925	875	200

Warner Model

As above, but is marked "Warner's Patent Jan. 1851." Approximately 150 of these were made.

NIB	Exc.	V.G.	Good	Fair	Poor
—	—	3200	2750	1325	250

Double Trigger Model

As above, with two triggers, one of which locks the cylinder. Approximately 100 were made in 1851.

NIB	Exc.	V.G.	Good	Fair	Poor
—	—	2750	2200	875	200

Pocket Model Revolver

A .28 caliber percussion revolver with 2.5" round barrel, centrally mounted hammer, no loading lever and etched 6-shot cylinder. Marked "Warner's Patent Jan. 1851" and "Springfield Arms Company." Blued, case hardened with walnut grips. Early production examples of this revolver do not have a groove on the cylinder and have a rounded frame. Approximately 525 were made in 1851.

Courtesy Milwaukee Public Museum, Milwaukee, Wisconsin

NIB	Exc.	V.G.	Good	Fair	Poor
—	—	1750	1250	585	150

Ring Trigger Model

As above, but fitted with a ring trigger that revolved the cylinder. Approximately 150 were made in 1851.

Courtesy Milwaukee Public Museum, Milwaukee, Wisconsin

NIB	Exc.	V.G.	Good	Fair	Poor
—	—	1725	1275	550	200

Double Trigger Model

As above, with two triggers set within a conventional trigger guard. The forward trigger revolves the cylinder. Approximately 350 were made in 1851.

Courtesy Milwaukee Public Museum, Milwaukee, Wisconsin

NIB	Exc.	V.G.	Good	Fair	Poor
—	—	1625	1275	550	200

Late Model Revolver

As above, except that the cylinder is automatically turned when the hammer is cocked. The top strap marked "Warner's Patent/

James Warner, Springfield, Mass." Approximately 500 were made in 1851.

NIB	Exc.	V.G.	Good	Fair	Poor
—	—	1300	875	325	100

Dragoon

A .40 caliber percussion revolver with either a 6" or 7.5" round barrel, some fitted with loading levers, others without. The top strap marked "Springfield Arms Company." Blued with walnut grips. Approximately 110 revolvers were manufactured in 1851.

NIB	Exc.	V.G.	Good	Fair	Poor
—	—	10000	8800	3850	950

Navy Model

A .36 caliber percussion revolver with a 6" round barrel, centrally mounted hammer, and 6-shot etched cylinder. The top strap marked "Springfield Arms Company." Blued, case hardened with walnut grips. This model was manufactured in two variations, one with a single trigger and the other with a double trigger, the forward one of which locks the cylinder. Both variations had loading levers. Approximately 250 of these pistols were made in 1851.

NIB	Exc.	V.G.	Good	Fair	Poor
—	—	6000	4250	1650	500

SQUIRES BINGHAM MFG. CO., INC.
Rizal, Philippine Islands

Firearms produced by this company are marketed under the trademark Squibbman.

Model 100D

A .38 Special caliber double-action swingout cylinder revolver with a 3", 4", or 6" ventilated rib barrel, adjustable sights, matte black finish and walnut grips.

NIB	Exc.	V.G.	Good	Fair	Poor
—	175	100	80	60	40

Model 100DC

As above, without the ventilated rib.

NIB	Exc.	V.G.	Good	Fair	Poor
—	200	100	80	60	40

Model 100

As above, with a tapered barrel and uncheckered walnut grips.

NIB	Exc.	V.G.	Good	Fair	Poor
—	200	100	80	60	40

Thunder Chief

As above, but in .22 or .22 Magnum caliber with a heavier ventilated rib barrel, shrouded ejector, and ebony grips.

NIB	Exc.	V.G.	Good	Fair	Poor
—	225	125	100	80	60

SSK INDUSTRIES
Bloomingdale, Ohio
SSK-Contender

A custom-made pistol available in 74 different calibers from .178 Bee to .588 JDJ and built on a Thompson/Center action.

NIB	Exc.	V.G.	Good	Fair	Poor
1250	1050	875	600	550	300

SSK-XP100

A custom-made pistol utilizing a Remington XP100 action. Available in a variety of calibers and sight configurations.

NIB	Exc.	V.G.	Good	Fair	Poor
1400	1225	900	625	575	400

.50 Caliber XP100

As above, with an integral muzzlebrake and reinforced composition stock.

NIB	Exc.	V.G.	Good	Fair	Poor
1750	1500	1250	1000	750	450

STAFFORD, T. J.
New Haven, Connecticut

Pocket Pistol

A .22 caliber single-shot spur trigger pistol with a 3.5" octagonal barrel marked "T.J. Stafford New Haven Ct.," silver-plated brass frame and walnut or rosewood grips.

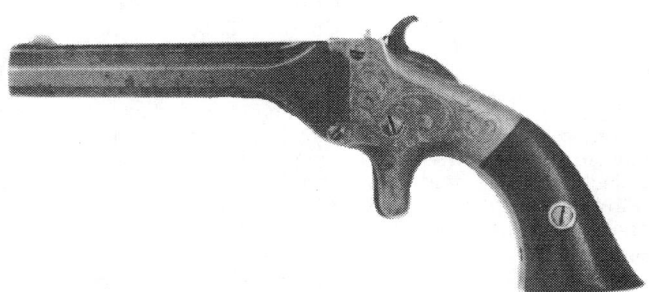

Courtesy W.P. Hallstein III and son Chip

NIB	Exc.	V.G.	Good	Fair	Poor
—	—	775	600	250	100

Large Frame Model

As above, but in .38 rimfire caliber with a 6" barrel.

NIB	Exc.	V.G.	Good	Fair	Poor
—	—	1050	850	400	200

STARR, EBAN T.
New York, New York

Single-Shot Derringer

A .41 caliber single-shot pistol with a pivoted 2.75" round barrel. The hammer mounted on the right side of the frame and the trigger formed in the shape of a button located at the front of the frame. The frame marked "Starr's Pat's May 10, 1864." The brass frame silver-plated, the barrel blued or silver-plated with checkered walnut grips. Manufactured from 1864 to 1869.

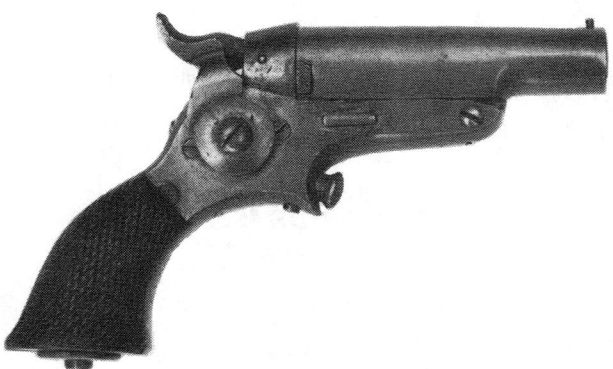

Courtesy Milwaukee Public Museum, Milwaukee, Wisconsin

NIB	Exc.	V.G.	Good	Fair	Poor
—	—	2300	1850	825	200

FOUR BARRELED PEPPERBOX

A .32 caliber 4 barreled pocket pistol with 2.75" to 3.25" barrels. The frame marked "Starr's Pat's May 10, 1864." Brass frames, silver-plated. The barrel is blued with plain walnut grips. This pistol was produced in six variations.

Courtesy Milwaukee Public Museum, Milwaukee, Wisconsin

First Model

Fluted breech and a barrel release mounted on the right side of the frame.

NIB	Exc.	V.G.	Good	Fair	Poor
—	—	3900	2750	875	200

Second Model

Flat breech.

NIB	Exc.	V.G.	Good	Fair	Poor
—	—	2500	1925	650	200

Third Model

Rounded breech with a visible firing-pin retaining spring.

NIB	Exc.	V.G.	Good	Fair	Poor
—	—	2350	1650	550	150

Fourth Model

Rounded breech without visible springs.

NIB	Exc.	V.G.	Good	Fair	Poor
—	—	2100	1650	550	150

Fifth Model

A larger, more angular grip.

NIB	Exc.	V.G.	Good	Fair	Poor
—	—	1950	1400	450	150

Sixth Model

The frame length of this variation is of increased size.

NIB	Exc.	V.G.	Good	Fair	Poor
—	—	2100	1650	550	150

STARR ARMS COMPANY
New York, New York

1858 NAVY REVOLVER

A .36 caliber double-action percussion revolver with a 6" barrel and 6-shot cylinder. Blued, case hardened with walnut grips. The frame marked "Starr Arms Co. New York." Approximately 3,000 were made between 1858 and 1860.

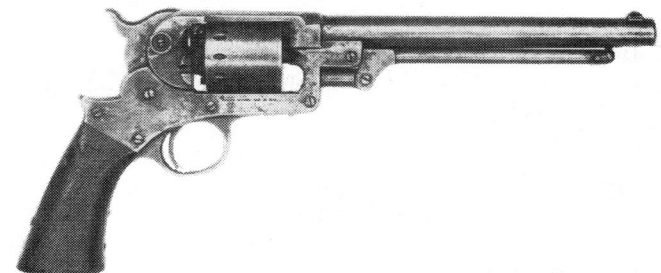

Courtesy Milwaukee Public Museum, Milwaukee, Wisconsin

Standard Model

NIB	Exc.	V.G.	Good	Fair	Poor
—	—	4100	3250	1100	350

Martially Marked (JT)

NIB	Exc.	V.G.	Good	Fair	Poor
—	—	5100	4250	1750	700

1858 Army Revolver

A .44 caliber double-action percussion revolver with a 6" barrel and 6-shot cylinder. Blued, case hardened with walnut grips. The frame marked "Starr Arms Co. New York." Approximately 23,000 were manufactured.

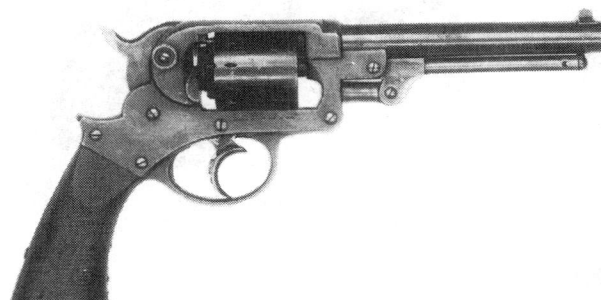

NIB	Exc.	V.G.	Good	Fair	Poor
—	6200	4300	2500	1100	300

1863 Army Revolver

Similar to the above, but single-action and with an 8" round barrel. Approximately 32,000 were manufactured between 1863 and 1865.

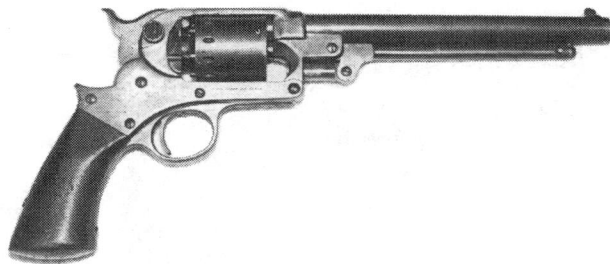

Courtesy Milwaukee Public Museum, Milwaukee, Wisconsin

NIB	Exc.	V.G.	Good	Fair	Poor
—	6750	4700	3250	1500	350

STEEL CITY ARMS, INC.
Pittsburgh, Pennsylvania

Double Deuce

A .22 caliber stainless steel double-action semi-automatic pistol with a 2.5" barrel, 7-shot magazine and plain rosewood grips. Introduced in 1984.

Courtesy J.B. Wood

NIB	Exc.	V.G.	Good	Fair	Poor
—	300	250	200	150	100

STENDA WAFFENFABRIK
Suhl, Germany

Pocket Pistol

A 7.65mm semi-automatic pistol similar to the "Beholla," the "Leonhardt," and the "Menta." Stenda took over the production of the Beholla pistol design at the close of WWI. The only major difference in the Stenda design was the elimination of the Beholla's worst feature, the pin that went through the slide and retained the barrel. It was replaced by a sliding catch that anchored it in place and unlocked the slide so that the barrel could be removed without the need of a vise and drift pin. The Stenda pistol can be identified by the fact that there are no holes through the slide and there is a catch on the frame above the trigger. The finish blued, with plastic grips; and the slide is marked "Waffenfabrik Stendawerke Suhl." Approximately 25,000 manufactured before production ceased in 1926.

NIB	Exc.	V.G.	Good	Fair	Poor
—	450	275	225	165	100

STERLING ARMAMENT LTD.
London, England

Parapistol MK 7 C4

A 9mm semi-automatic pistol with a 4" barrel, and detachable magazines of 10-round capacity. Black wrinkled paint finish with plastic grips.

NIB	Exc.	V.G.	Good	Fair	Poor
600	475	400	300	200	100

Parapistol MK 7 C8

As above, with a 7.8" barrel.

NIB	Exc.	V.G.	Good	Fair	Poor
625	500	400	300	200	100

STERLING ARMS CORPORATION
Gasport, New York

Model 283 Target 300

This pistol is similar in appearance to Hi-Standard semi-automatic pistols. Chambered for the .22 LR cartridge it was offered with 4", 4-1/2", or 8" barrels. Rear sight is adjustable and magazine holds 10 rounds. Grips are black plastic. Weight is approximately 36 oz.

NIB	Exc.	V.G.	Good	Fair	Poor
300	250	175	100	75	60

Model 284 Target 300L

Similar to the above model except for 4-1/2" or 6" tapered barrel with barrel band.

NIB	Exc.	V.G.	Good	Fair	Poor
325	275	175	100	75	60

Model 285 Husky

Similar to the Model 283 with the exception of fixed sights. Offered with 4-1/2" barrel only.

NIB	Exc.	V.G.	Good	Fair	Poor
300	250	175	100	75	60

Model 286 Trapper

Similar to the Model 284 except for fixed sights.

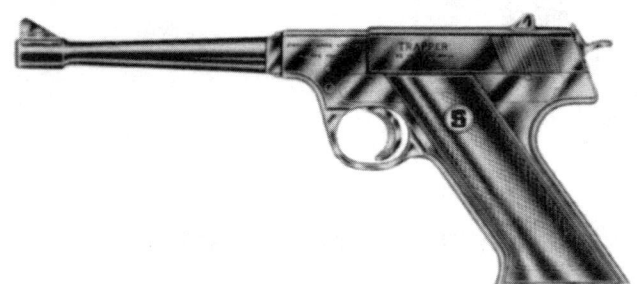

NIB	Exc.	V.G.	Good	Fair	Poor
300	250	175	100	75	60

Model 287 PPL .380

This is a pocket-size semi-automatic pistol chambered for the .380 ACP cartridge. Fitted with a 1" barrel it has a 5-1/4" length overall. Magazine holds 6 rounds. Weight is approximately 22 oz.

NIB	Exc.	V.G.	Good	Fair	Poor
225	175	125	75	50	25

Model PPL .22

This is a small pocket pistol similar to the Model 287 but chambered for the .22 LR cartridge. Barrel is 1" long. Pistol weighs about 24 oz.

NIB	Exc.	V.G.	Good	Fair	Poor
275	225	150	75	60	50

Model 300

Similar to the Model 287 but chambered for the .25 ACP cartridge. It has a 2-1/4" barrel with a 6-round magazine. Length is 5" overall and the weight is about 14 oz.

NIB	Exc.	V.G.	Good	Fair	Poor
250	225	150	75	50	40

Model 300S

This is the stainless steel version of the Model 300.

NIB	Exc.	V.G.	Good	Fair	Poor
265	235	165	75	50	40

Model 302

Identical to the Model 300 except that it is chambered for the .22 LR cartridge.

NIB	Exc.	V.G.	Good	Fair	Poor
250	225	150	75	50	40

Model 302S

Same as above but in stainless steel.

NIB	Exc.	V.G.	Good	Fair	Poor
265	235	165	75	60	50

Model 400

This is a double-action semi-automatic pistol chambered for the .380 ACP cartridge with a 3-1/2" barrel. Magazine holds 7 rounds. Pistol is 6-1/2" overall and the weight is approximately 24 oz.

NIB	Exc.	V.G.	Good	Fair	Poor
300	275	200	125	100	75

Model 400S

This is the stainless steel version of the Model 400.

NIB	Exc.	V.G.	Good	Fair	Poor
325	300	2255	125	100	75

Model 402

Similar to the Model 400 except chambered for the .22 LR cartridge.

NIB	Exc.	V.G.	Good	Fair	Poor
250	225	150	75	60	40

Model X-Caliber

A single-shot .22 LR, .22 WMR, .357 Magnum, or .44 Magnum pistol with interchangeable barrels from 8" and 10". Adjustable rear sight. Finger groove grips. Deduct 50 percent for rimfire.

NIB	Exc.	V.G.	Good	Fair	Poor
450	400	300	225	150	100

STEVENS ARMS CO., J.
Chicopee Falls, Massachusetts

The J. Stevens Arms Company also produced a series of utility-grade slide-action shotguns. They are chambered for various gauges with various barrel lengths and chokes. The finishes are blued, with walnut stocks. The values are similar, and are listed for reference purposes are listed.

Vest Pocket Pistol

This is a single-shot pocket pistol chambered for the .22 and the .30 rimfire cartridges. The .22 caliber version is rarely encountered and would be worth approximately 25 percent more than the values illustrated. It has a 2.75" part-octagonal barrel that pivots upward for loading. It has an external hammer and a spur-type trigger. The frame is nickel-plated or blued, with a blued barrel. The odd shaped flared grips are made of rosewood. The first models were marked "Vest Pocket Pistol" only. Later models have the barrels marked "J. Stevens & Co. Chicopee Falls, Mass." There were approximately 1,000 manufactured between 1864 and 1876.

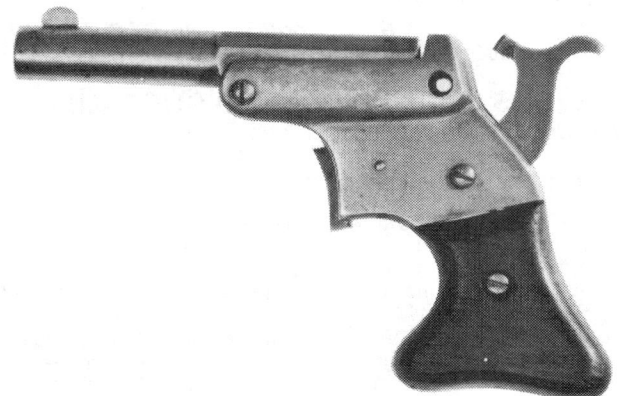

Courtesy Milwaukee Public Museum, Milwaukee, Wisconsin

NIB	Exc.	V.G.	Good	Fair	Poor
—	4600	3200	2100	1200	950

Pocket Pistol

This is a more conventional-appearing, single-shot pocket pistol chambered for either the .22 or the .30 rimfire cartridges. It has a 3.5" part-octagonal barrel that pivots upward for loading. It features a plated brass frame with either a blued or nickel-plated barrel and rosewood, two-piece grips. The barrel is marked "J. Stevens & Co. Chicopee Falls, Mass." There were approximately 15,000 manufactured between 1864 and 1886.

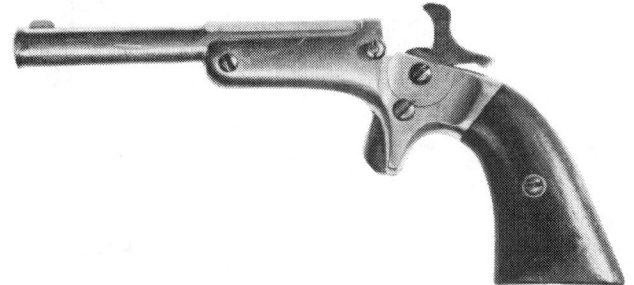

Courtesy Milwaukee Public Museum, Milwaukee, Wisconsin

NIB	Exc.	V.G.	Good	Fair	Poor
—	600	425	225	125	100

Gem Pocket Pistol

This is a single-shot, derringer-type pocket pistol chambered for either the .22 or .30 rimfire cartridges. It has a 3" part-octagonal barrel that pivots to the side for loading. It has a nickel-plated brass frame with either a blued or plated barrel. It has bird's-head grips made of walnut or rosewood. The barrel is marked "Gem." The Stevens name or address does not appear on this firearm. There were approximately 4,000 manufactured between 1872 and 1890.

NIB	Exc.	V.G.	Good	Fair	Poor
—	1000	800	550	425	300

.22 OR .41 CALIBER DERRINGER

This is a single-shot pocket pistol chambered for the .22 or .41 caliber rimfire cartridge. It has a 4" part-octagonal barrel that pivots upward for loading. It has a spur trigger and an external hammer. The frame is plated brass with a blued barrel. It has walnut bird's-head grips. This firearm is completely unmarked except for a serial number. There were approximately 100 manufactured in 1875.

.22 Caliber

NIB	Exc.	V.G.	Good	Fair	Poor
—	6000	5500	4000	2500	1400

.41 Caliber

NIB	Exc.	V.G.	Good	Fair	Poor
—	5700	5200	3700	2100	1300

No. 41 Pistol

This is a single-shot pocket pistol chambered for the .22 and .30 Short cartridges. It has a 3.5" part-octagonal barrel that pivots upward for loading. It features an external hammer and a spur-type trigger. It has an iron frame with the firing pin mounted in the recoil shield. It is either blued or nickel-plated, with square-butt walnut grips. There were approximately 90,000 manufactured between 1896 and 1916.

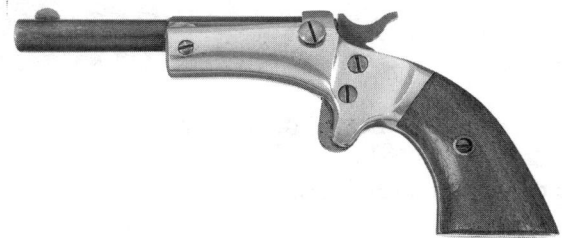

Courtesy Rock Island Auction Company

NIB	Exc.	V.G.	Good	Fair	Poor
—	450	400	300	250	135

Single-Shot Pistol

This is a single-shot pistol chambered for the .22 or .30 rimfire cartridges. It has a 3.5" part-octagonal barrel that pivots upward for loading. It is quite similar in appearance to the original pocket pistol. It has a plated brass frame and either a blued or nickel-plated barrel with walnut, square-butt grips. The barrel is marked "J. Stevens A&T Co." There were approximately 10,000 manufactured between 1886 and 1896.

NIB	Exc.	V.G.	Good	Fair	Poor
—	500	350	275	200	150

Six-inch Pocket Rifle

This version is chambered for the .22 rimfire cartridge and has a 6" part-octagonal barrel with open sights. The barrel is marked "J. Stevens & Co. Chicopee Falls, Mass." There were approximately 1,000 manufactured between 1869 and 1886.

NIB	Exc.	V.G.	Good	Fair	Poor
—	750	500	400	350	200

No. 36

This version is known as the Stevens-Lord pistol. It is chambered for various rimfire and centerfire calibers up to .44 Russian. It is offered with a 10" or 12" part-octagonal barrel and features a firing pin in the frame with a bushing. It has a conventional trigger with a spurred trigger guard. It features the standard Stevens barrel address. It was named after Frank Lord, a target shooter well-known at this time. There were approximately 3,500 manufactured from 1880 to 1911.

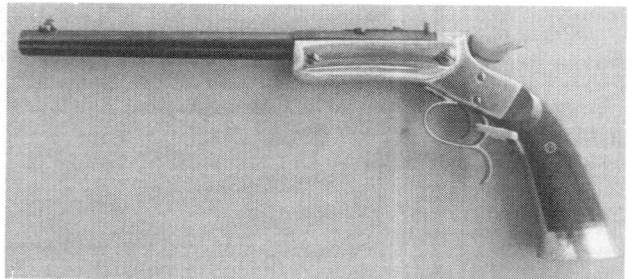

Courtesy J.B. Barnes

NIB	Exc.	V.G.	Good	Fair	Poor
—	1600	1300	950	650	400

First Issue Stevens-Conlin

This version is chambered for the .22 or.32 rimfire cartridges. It has a 10" or 12" part-octagonal barrel. It features a plated brass frame with a blued barrel and checkered walnut grips with a weighted buttcap. This version has a spur trigger either with or without a trigger guard. It was named after James Conlin, the owner of a shooting gallery located in New York City. There were approximately 500 manufactured between 1880 and 1884.

Courtesy J.B. Barnes

NIB	Exc.	V.G.	Good	Fair	Poor
—	2500	2100	1600	900	500

Second Issue Stevens-Conlin No. 38

This version is similar to the First Issue, with a conventional trigger and spurred trigger guard, as well as a fully adjustable rear sight. There were approximately 6,000 manufactured between 1884 and 1903.

NIB	Exc.	V.G.	Good	Fair	Poor
—	1700	1500	1200	800	450

No. 37

This version is also known as the Stevens-Gould and was named after a 19th century firearms writer. It resembles the No. 38 without the spur on the trigger guard. There were approximately 1,000 manufactured between 1889 and 1903.

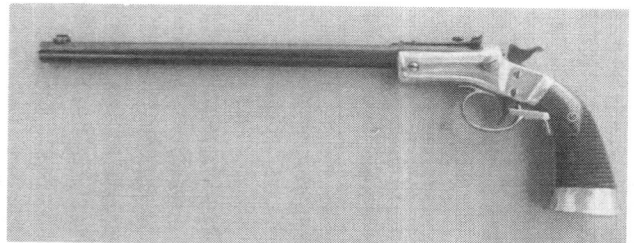

Courtesy J.B. Barnes

NIB	Exc.	V.G.	Good	Fair	Poor
—	2400	2000	1300	850	450

No. 35

This version is chambered for the .22 rimfire, the .22 Stevens-Pope, and the .25 Stevens cartridges. It is offered with a 6", 8", 10", or 12.25" part-octagonal barrel. The firing pin has no bushing. It features an iron frame that is either blued or plated with a blued

barrel. It has plain walnut grips with a weighted buttcap. It featured open sights. There were approximately 43,000 manufactured between 1923 and 1942.

NIB	Exc.	V.G.	Good	Fair	Poor
—	450	325	275	175	100

NOTE: Longer barrels worth a premium.

No. 35 Target

This version is similar to the No. 35 but has a better quality trigger guard and sights. There were approximately 35,000 manufactured between 1907 and 1916.

NIB	Exc.	V.G.	Good	Fair	Poor
—	500	400	325	200	100

STEVENS NO. 35 OFF-HAND SHOT GUN NFA, CURIO OR RELIC

STEVENS NO. 35 AUTO-SHOT

The Stevens No. 35 is a .410 bore pistol manufactured by the J. Stevens Arms Co., Chicopee Falls, Massachusetts. It was available with an 8" or 12.25" smoothbore barrel, for 2.5" shells only, in two variations: the Off-Hand Shot Gun (1923 to 1929) and the Auto-Shot (1929 to 1934). Total production is unknown because the .410 and .22 rimfire variations of the No. 35 share the same serial number range. Researcher Ken Cope estimates total Auto-Shot production was approximately 2,000, and Off-Hand production at 20,000 to 25,000. Production was halted after the government ruled the .410 Stevens to be a "firearm" in the "any other weapon" category under the NFA in 1934, when its retail price was about $12. The Stevens does not possess the same collector appeal as other .410 smoothbore pistols, because (1) its relatively light weight makes it an uncomfortable shooter, and (2) the gun is not well made.

Off-Hand Shot Gun

Serial range from 1 to 43357.

Courtesy John J. Stimson, Jr.

NIB	Exc.	V.G.	Good	Fair	Poor
—	400	250	200	100	75

Auto-Shot

NIB	Exc.	V.G.	Good	Fair	Poor
—	450	300	200	125	100

NOTE: 8" barrel commands a 25 to 50 percent premium.

No. 43

This version is also called the Diamond and was produced in two distinct variations called the First Issue and the Second Issue. The First Issue has a brass frame; and the Second Issue, an iron frame and no firing pin bushing. Otherwise they are quite similar and would be valued the same. They are chambered for the .22 rimfire cartridge and are offered with either a 6" or 10" part-octagonal barrel. The frames are either nickel-plated or blued with blued barrels and square-butt walnut grips. There were approximately 95,000 manufactured between 1886 and 1916.

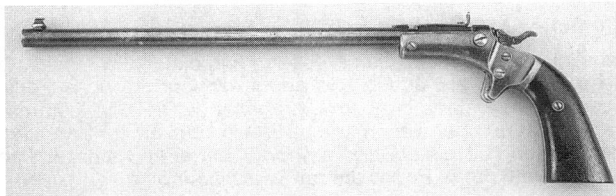

Paul Goodwin photo

NIB	Exc.	V.G.	Good	Fair	Poor
—	600	400	250	150	75

NOTE: Add a 25 percent premium for 10" barrels.

No. 10 Target Pistol

This version was a departure from its predecessors. It very much resembles a semi-automatic pistol but is, in reality, a single-shot. It is chambered for the .22 rimfire cartridge and has an 8" round barrel that pivots upward for loading. It has a steel frame and is blued, with checkered rubber grips. Instead of the usual exposed hammer, this version has a knurled cocking piece that extends through the rear of the frame. There were approximately 7,000 manufactured between 1919 and 1933.

Courtesy John J. Stimson, Jr.

NIB	Exc.	V.G.	Good	Fair	Poor
—	400	300	200	150	100

POCKET RIFLES

This series of pistols is similar to the target and sporting pistols except that these were produced with detachable shoulder stocks that bear the same serial number as the pistol with which they were sold. They are sometimes referred to as Bicycle rifles. The collector interest in these weapons is quite high; but it would behoove one to be familiar with the provisions of the Gun Control Act of 1968 when dealing in or collecting this variation—as when the stock is attached, they can fall into the category of a short-barreled rifle. Some are considered to be curios and relics, and others have been totally declassified; but some models may still be restricted. We strongly recommend securing a qualified, individual appraisal on these highly collectible firearms if a transaction is contemplated. **NOTE:** The values supplied include the matching shoulder stock. If the stock number does not match the pistol, the values would be approximately 25 percent less; and with no stock at all, 50 percent should be deducted.

Old Model Pocket Rifle

This version is chambered for the .22 rimfire cartridge and has an 8" or 10" part-octagonal barrel. It has a spur trigger and an external hammer on which the firing pin is mounted. The extractor is spring-loaded. It has a plated brass frame, blued barrel, and either walnut or rosewood grips. The shoulder stock is either nickel-plated or

black. The barrel is marked "J. Stevens & Co. Chicopee Falls, Mass." There were approximately 4,000 manufactured between 1869 and 1886.

NIB	Exc.	V.G.	Good	Fair	Poor
—	900	700	550	325	200

Reliable Pocket Rifle

This version is chambered for the .22 rimfire cartridge and in appearance is quite similar to the Old Model. The basic difference is that the extractor operates as a part of the pivoting barrel mechanism instead of being spring-loaded. The barrel is marked "J. Stevens A&T Co." There were approximately 4,000 manufactured between 1886 and 1896.

NIB	Exc.	V.G.	Good	Fair	Poor
—	800	625	500	400	300

No. 42 Reliable Pocket Rifle

This version is similar to the first issue Reliable except that it has an iron frame with the firing pin mounted in it without a bushing. The shoulder stock is shaped differently. There were approximately 8,000 manufactured between 1896 and 1916.

The frame length of this variation is of increased size.

NIB	Exc.	V.G.	Good	Fair	Poor
—	700	575	475	350	250

First Issue New Model Pocket Rifle

This version is the first of the medium-frame models with a frame width of 1". All of its predecessors have a 5/8" wide frame. This model is chambered for the .22 and .32 rimfire cartridges and is offered with barrel lengths of 10", 12", 15", or 18" that are part-octagonal in configuration. The external hammer has the firing pin mounted on it. It has a plated brass frame, blued barrel, and either walnut or rosewood grips. The shoulder stock is nickel-plated and fitted differently than the small-frame models in that there is a dovetail in the butt and the top leg is secured by a knurled screw. The barrel is marked "J. Stevens & Co. Chicopee Falls, Mass." There were approximately 8,000 manufactured between 1872 and 1875.

Courtesy Mike Stuckslager

NIB	Exc.	V.G.	Good	Fair	Poor
—	1000	900	650	500	400

Second Issue New Model Pocket Rifle

This version is similar to the First Issue except that the firing pin is mounted in the frame with a bushing. There were approximately 15,000 manufactured between 1875 and 1896.

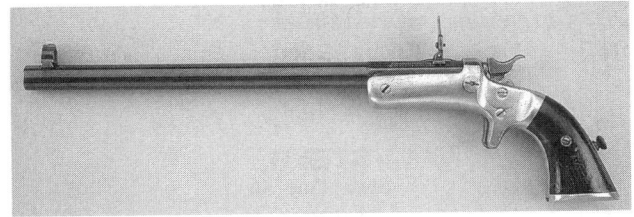

Paul Goodwin photo

NIB	Exc.	V.G.	Good	Fair	Poor
—	900	800	600	500	350

Vernier Model

This version is similar to the Second Issue except that it features a vernier tang sight located on the back strap. There were approximately 1,500 manufactured between 1884 and 1896.

Courtesy Rock Island Auction Company

NIB	Exc.	V.G.	Good	Fair	Poor
—	1100	800	650	525	300

No. 40

This version is similar to its medium-frame predecessors except that it has a longer grip frame and a conventional trigger with trigger guard. There were approximately 15,000 manufactured between 1896 and 1916.

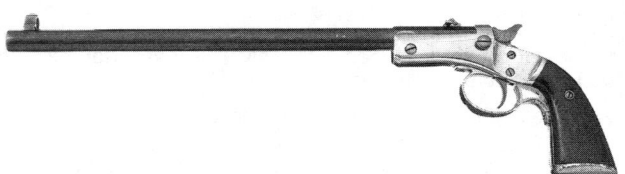

Courtesy Rock Island Auction Company

NIB	Exc.	V.G.	Good	Fair	Poor
—	900	800	650	400	300

No. 40-1/2

This version is similar to the No. 40, with a vernier tang sight mounted on the back strap. There were approximately 2,500 manufactured between 1896 and 1915.

NIB	Exc.	V.G.	Good	Fair	Poor
—	1000	900	700	550	400

No. 34 (Hunter's Pet)

This is the first of the heavy-frame pocket rifles that featured a 1.25" wide frame. This version is also known as the "Hunter's Pet." It is chambered for many popular cartridges from the .22 rimfire to the .44-40 centerfire. It is offered with a part-octagonal 18", 20", 22", or 24" barrel. It has a nickel-plated iron frame and blued barrel. The detachable stock is nickel-plated, and the grips are walnut. There were few produced with a brass frame; and if located, these would be worth twice the value indicated. The firing pin is mounted in the frame with the bushing, and it features a spur trigger. There were approximately 4,000 manufactured between 1872 and 1900.

NIB	Exc.	V.G.	Good	Fair	Poor
—	1150	1000	700	450	350

No. 34-1/2

This version is similar to the No. 34 except that it features a vernier tang sight mounted on the back strap. There were approximately 1,200 manufactured between 1884 and 1900.

NIB	Exc.	V.G.	Good	Fair	Poor
—	1300	1150	900	650	450

STEYR
Steyr, Austria

STEYR & MANNLICHER PISTOLS
Text by Joseph Schroeder

Not all Mannlicher pistols were made by Steyr, and many of the pistols made by Steyr were not designed by Mannlicher. However, since by far the greatest number of Mannlicher's pistols were made by Steyr we believe it will be appropriate to include all of Ferdinand Ritter von Mannlicher's pistols along with other Steyr designs under this heading.

Schoenberger

Considered by many to be the first "commercial" semi-automatic pistol even though apparently at the most only about two dozen were made in 1892. The Steyr-made 8mm Schoenberger was based on patents granted to Laumann in 1890-91 and had a magazine in front of the trigger guard. Too Rare to Price.

Mannlicher Model 1894

Mannlicher's first "successful" self-loading pistol, the Model 1894 had a blow-forward action and double-action lockwork. Earliest examples were made in Austria, probably by Steyr, in 7.6mm but the greatest number were made by SIG in 1896-97 for Swiss army tests. These 100 pistols had a shorter barrel and smaller frame and were in 6.5mm. Prices are for Swiss examples.

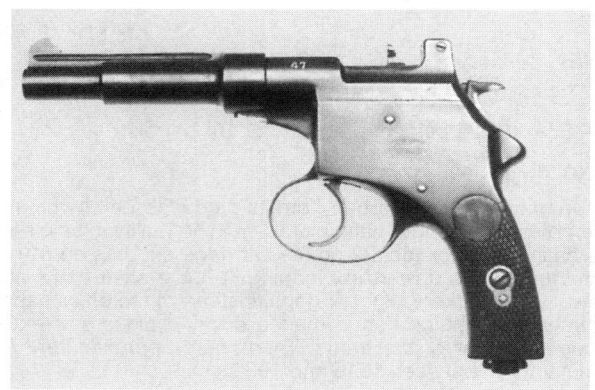

Courtesy Rock Island Auction Company

NIB	Exc.	V.G.	Good	Fair	Poor
—	13200	9900	6600	5500	3000

NOTE: Add 20 percent for 7.6mm pistols.

Mannlicher Model 1896/03

This is one of the most confusing of Mannlicher's pistols. Earliest examples, which have a fixed magazine and ribbed barrel, may have been made by Steyr and are very rare. Later versions, with a removable box magazine, have been called "Model 1896/03" and "Model 1901," and were made as both a pistol and pistol-carbine, possibly in Switzerland. Chambered for the 7.65mm Mannlicher cartridge, which is really a 7.65mm Borchardt. Prices listed are for the standard later model pistol or pistol-carbine (12" barrel, tangent sight); double prices for early pistol or late model pistol with detachable holster stock.

Courtesy Joseph Schroeder

NIB	Exc.	V.G.	Good	Fair	Poor
—	8250	5500	3850	2750	1500

Mannlicher Model 1899

Earliest version of Mannlicher's final semi-automatic pistol design, only about 250 were made by Dreyse in Soemmerda, Germany. Chambered for a tapered case 7.63mm Mannlicher cartridge. Distinguished by the large safety lever on the left side, takedown screw under the barrel, and the Dreyse markings.

Courtesy Joseph Schroeder

NIB	Exc.	V.G.	Good	Fair	Poor
—	9400	7150	4950	3850	2000

Mannlicher Model 1901

Marked "WAFFENFABRIK STEYR" on the left side and "SYSTEM MANNLICHER" on the right, the Model 1901 is distinguished by its checkered grips, rear sight located on the rear of the barrel, 8-round fixed magazine, and serial numbers to a little over 1000.

Courtesy Joseph Schroeder

NIB	Exc.	V.G.	Good	Fair	Poor
—	3300	2450	1750	900	700

Mannlicher Model 1905

Improved version of the Model 1901, with longer grip holding 10 rounds, grooved wooden grips, rear sight on rear of breechblock, and "MODEL 1905" added to right side. Later production moved all markings to the left side so Argentine crest could be placed on right side. Prices listed are for an original commercial Model 1905, NOT a reblued Argentine contract with the crest ground off. Subtract 60 percent for reworked examples.

Courtesy Joseph Schroeder

NIB	Exc.	V.G.	Good	Fair	Poor
—	2425	1875	1350	800	400

Mannlicher Model 1905 Argentine Contract

Original crest on right side.

NIB	Exc.	V.G.	Good	Fair	Poor
—	2750	2250	1650	900	500

Roth Steyr Model 1907

Based on the patents granted to Karel Krnka and Georg Roth, the 8mm Model 1907 had a rotating barrel locking system and was the first self-loading pistol adopted by the Austro-Hungarian Army.

Courtesy Joseph Schroeder

NIB	Exc.	V.G.	Good	Fair	Poor
—	1250	750	600	350	250

NOTE: Add 20 percent for early Steyr examples without a large pin visible on right side of frame, or for those made in Budapest instead of Steyr. Slight premium for correct stripper clips.

Steyr Model 1908 Pocket Pistol

Based on the Belgian patents of Nicholas Pieper, these .25 and .32 caliber pocket pistols featured tipping barrels were built by Steyr under license from Pieper in Liege. Production was suspended during WWI but may have resumed after the war ended. Prices are for either caliber.

NIB	Exc.	V.G.	Good	Fair	Poor
—	385	275	165	100	75

Steyr Hahn Model 1911 Commercially Marked

NIB	Exc.	V.G.	Good	Fair	Poor
—	2200	1650	1220	875	450

NOTE: For military versions of this model see the Standard Catalog of Military Firearms.

Steyr Model SP

Steyr's first post WWII pistol, the Model SP was a beautifully made .32 ACP which, being double-action-only and more expensive than most of its contemporaries, was not competitive and was discontinued in the early 1960s after fewer than 1,000 were made. Slide marked "STEYR-DAIMLER-PUCH A.G. MOD.SP KAL. 7.65mm."

Courtesy Joseph Schroeder

NIB	Exc.	V.G.	Good	Fair	Poor
—	950	825	550	385	200

STEYR MODEL GB

The GB was introduced in the mid-1970s as a 9mm Parabellum military pistol, large in size but with an 18-round magazine capacity. Other features included polygon rifling and a gas trap around the barrel to delay breech opening. Initially produced as the Rogak P-18 by L.E.S. of Morton Grove, Illinois, but discontinued due in part to quality control problems after just over 2,000 were made. Later production by Steyr as the GB was to much higher standards, but the GB never achieved much popularity and was discontinued in 1988.

Rogak P-18

NIB	Exc.	V.G.	Good	Fair	Poor
—	425	350	250	175	125

Steyr GB

NIB	Exc.	V.G.	Good	Fair	Poor
—	800	675	525	400	200

Model M

This model features the medium action and has the same barrel and stock configurations as the other two models listed above with the exception that it has no buttpad and it does have a forend tip on its half stock variation. Available in these calibers: 6.5x57,

.270 Win., 7x64, .30-06, 9.3x62, 6.5x55, 7.5 Swiss, 7x57, and 8x57JS. Weighs approximately 6.8 lbs. with full stock and 7 lbs. with half stock.

NIB	Exc.	V.G.	Good	Fair	Poor
2500	2100	1200	900	600	300

Model SPP

Introduced in 1993 this is a 9mm semi-automatic pistol. It is made from synthetic materials and operates on a delayed blowback, rotating barrel system. The magazine capacity is either 15 or 30 rounds. The barrel is 5.9" in length overall length is 12.75" and weight is about 42 oz. Due to its appearance and design this pistol was banned for importation into the United States shortly after its introduction. Because of this circumstance the price of this pistol may fluctuate widely.

NIB	Exc.	V.G.	Good	Fair	Poor
1000	900	750	600	500	400

Model S

This model is similar to the Model M but is fitted with a 3.58" barrel. Chambered for the .40 S&W, 9mm, or .357 SIG cartridges. Magazine capacity is 10 rounds. Weight is approximately 22 oz. Introduced in 2000.

NIB	Exc.	V.G.	Good	Fair	Poor
600	450	300	225	150	100

STI INTERNATIONAL
Georgetown, Texas

LS9 & LS40

Single stack pistol chambered for the 9mm or .40 S&W cartridge. Fitted with a 3.4" barrel and short grip. Heine Low Mount sights.

Rosewood grips. Matte blue finish. Magazine capacity is 7 rounds for 9mm and 6 rounds for .40 S&W. Weight is about 28 oz.

NIB	Exc.	V.G.	Good	Fair	Poor
850	675	550	400	300	200

BLS9 & BLS40

Same as above but with full length grip. Magazine capacity is 9 rounds for 9mm and 8 rounds for .40 S&W.

NIB	Exc.	V.G.	Good	Fair	Poor
825	650	525	375	275	200

Ranger

Chambered for the .45 ACP cartridge and fitted with a 3.9" barrel with short grip. Fixed STI sights. Blued frame with stainless steel slide. Weight is about 29 oz.

NIB	Exc.	V.G.	Good	Fair	Poor
950	775	600	500	400	200

Ranger II

Chambered for the .45 ACP cartridge and fitted with a 4.15" ramped bull barrel. Slide is flat top with rear serrations and chamfered fore end. Ambidextrous safety and high rise grip safety. Adjustable rear sight. Hard chrome upper with blued lower frame. Weight is about 39 oz.

NIB	Exc.	V.G.	Good	Fair	Poor
925	800	675	525	400	200

Trojan

Chambered for the .45 ACP, .40 Super, .40 S&W, and 9mm cartridge. Fitted with a 5" barrel. Rosewood grips. Matte blue finish. Eight-round magazine capacity. Weight is about 36 oz.

NIB	Exc.	V.G.	Good	Fair	Poor
1150	925	750	600	500	300

NOTE: For .40 Super with .45 ACP conversion add $275. For Trojan with 6" slide add $250.

Tactical 4.15

Chambered for the 9mm, .40 S&W, or the 45 ACP cartridge. Fully supported ramped 4.15" bull barrel. Frame has tactical rail. Slide has rear serrations. Fixed rear sight. Aluminum magazine well. Black polycoat finish. Weight is about 34.5 oz.

NIB	Exc.	V.G.	Good	Fair	Poor
1750	1475	1150	900	650	350

Tactical

As above but with 5" barrel. Flat blue finish. Weight is about 39 oz.

NIB	Exc.	V.G.	Good	Fair	Poor
1750	1475	1150	900	650	350

Trubor

Chambered for the 9mm major, 9x23, or .38 Super cartridges. Steel frame. Fully supported and ramped one piece with bull barrel with integral compensator. Slide has front and rear serrations. Sights are C-More or OK Red Dot reflix. Blued finish. Weight is about 42.5 oz. with scope.

NIB	Exc.	V.G.	Good	Fair	Poor
2500	2100	1600	1200	900	500

Lawman

This .45 ACP pistol has a 5" ramped barrel with match grade bushing. Aluminum trigger. Series 70 grip safety. Novak 3 dot sights. Checkered walnut grips. Polymer finish with brown slide over tan frame. Weight is about 36 oz.

NIB	Exc.	V.G.	Good	Fair	Poor
1200	975	825	675	500	250

Xcaliber Single Stack

Chambered for the .450 SMC cartridge and fitted with a 6" slide. Adjustable rear sight. Weight is about 38 oz. Blue finish. Single stack magazine. Discontinued.

NIB	Exc.	V.G.	Good	Fair	Poor
1475	1275	1050	775	500	350

Xcaliber Double Stack

Same as the Xcaliber Single Stack except that this model has a double stack magazine. Discontinued.

NIB	Exc.	V.G.	Good	Fair	Poor
1800	1600	1175	900	600	400

Executive

Chambered for the .40 S&W cartridge. Fitted with a 5" ramped bull barrel. Adjustable rear sight. Gray synthetic grip and hard chrome slide. Weight is about 39 oz. Double stack magazine.

NIB	Exc.	V.G.	Good	Fair	Poor
2350	2000	1650	1100	725	400

VIP

Chambered for the .45 ACP cartridge and fitted with a 3.9" ramped bull barrel. Stainless steel flat top slide. Fixed rear sight. Ten-round magazine capacity. Weight is about 25 oz.

NIB	Exc.	V.G.	Good	Fair	Poor
1400	1100	800	650	400	250

Edge

Chambered for the 9mm, 10mm, .40 S&W, and .45 ACP cartridge with 5" ramped bull barrel. Dual stack magazine. Bomar style sights. Blue finish. Weight is about 39 oz.

NIB	Exc.	V.G.	Good	Fair	Poor
1800	1400	1000	700	500	300

Eagle

Chambered for customer's choice of caliber and fitted with 5" ramped bull barrel. Fixed sights. Blued frame and stainless steel slide. Weight is about 30 oz.

NIB	Exc.	V.G.	Good	Fair	Poor
1700	1200	900	600	400	250

Duty One

Chambered for the 9mm, .40 S&W, or .45 ACP cartridges. Five-inch bull barrel is fully supported and ramped. Steel frame with single stack magazine with front strap checkering and tactical rail. Grips are rosewood. Slide has front and rear serrations. Adjustable sights. Finish is flat blue. Weight is about 38 oz.

NIB	Exc.	V.G.	Good	Fair	Poor
1100	900	750	500	400	250

Duty CT

1911-style steel frame single-stack with integral tactical rail and rosewood grips. 5" slide/barrel, fixed 2-dot tritium rear sight. 36.6 oz. Also available in 4.15" commander size. Blued.

NIB	Exc.	V.G.	Good	Fair	Poor
1100	900	750	500	400	250

Competitor

Chambered for the .38 Super cartridge and fitted with a 5.5" ramped bull barrel with compensator. Fitted with a C-More scope. Stainless steel slide. Weight is about 44 oz. with scope and mount. Discontinued.

NIB	Exc.	V.G.	Good	Fair	Poor
2350	2000	1650	1100	725	400

Grandmaster

Custom built to customer's specifications in 9mm major, 9x23, and .38 Super.

NIB	Exc.	V.G.	Good	Fair	Poor
2800	2500	2000	1500	850	500

Rangemaster

Fitted with a 5" fully supported and ramped bull barrel and chambered for the 9mm or .45 ACP cartridge, this pistol has a full length dust cover, checkered front strap and mainspring housing and square trigger guard. Front and rear slide serrations. Adjustable sights. Rose grips. Polished blue finish. Weight is about 38 oz.

NIB	Exc.	V.G.	Good	Fair	Poor
1500	1350	1100	800	500	250

Rangemaster II

Single-stack blued variation of Rangemaster. Chambered for 9mm, .40 S&W, .45 ACP. 5" slide/barrel, 37 oz. Introduced 2006.

NIB	Exc.	V.G.	Good	Fair	Poor
1300	1125	900	600	400	200

Targetmaster

As above but with 6" barrel.

NIB	Exc.	V.G.	Good	Fair	Poor
1650	1250	900	650	400	250

Stinger

Chambered for the 9mm or .38 Super cartridge. Fitted with a 3.9" barrel with compensator. Sights are OKO or C-More on STI mount. Blued finish. Weight is about 38 oz.

NIB	Exc.	V.G.	Good	Fair	Poor
2775	2275	1850	1450	900	500

Hawk 4.3

This pistol is modeled on the 1911 design and is equipped with a 4.3" barrel with steel slide. The frame of the pistol is made from polymer and features and increased magazine capacity while retaining the 1911 grip thickness. Chambered for .38 Super, .45 ACP, .40 S&W, 10mm, and 9x25 calibers. Built primarily for competition shooting. Discontinued.

NIB	Exc.	V.G.	Good	Fair	Poor
1700	1200	900	600	400	250

Night Hawk 4.3

Chambered for .45 ACP only with 4.3" bull barrel and a host of special features such a narrow tactical safety, front and rear slide serrations, and extended dust cover. Tritium sights optional. Blued finish. Weight is 33 oz. Discontinued.

NIB	Exc.	V.G.	Good	Fair	Poor
1925	1600	1300	1050	750	400

Falcon 3.9

Similar to the above model but fitted with a 3.9" barrel. Weight is approximately 30 oz. with steel frame and 25 oz. with aluminum frame. Discontinued.

NIB	Exc.	V.G.	Good	Fair	Poor
1925	1600	1300	1050	750	400

Sparrow 5.0

Chambered for the .22 LR cartridge only and fitted with a 5" bull barrel with fixed sights. Weight is approximately 30 oz. Discontinued.

NIB	Exc.	V.G.	Good	Fair	Poor
925	800	675	525	400	200

Edge 5.1

Chambered for .40 S&W only with 5" bull barrel and many special features. BoMar front and rear sights. Weight is 39 oz.

NIB	Exc.	V.G.	Good	Fair	Poor
1800	1400	1000	700	500	300

Eagle 5.1

Similar to the Model 2011 Hawk but furnished with a 5" barrel. Comes standard with BoMar adjustable sights.

NIB	Exc.	V.G.	Good	Fair	Poor
1925	1600	1300	1050	750	400

Eagle 5.5

Similar to above model but furnished with a 5-1/2" barrel with compensator.

NIB	Exc.	V.G.	Good	Fair	Poor
2395	1950	1600	1200	850	500

Eagle 6.0

Chambered for 9mm, .38 Super, .40 S&W, or .45 ACP cartridges. Fitted with a 6" bull barrel. Many special features. BoMar front and rear sights. Blued finish. Weight is about 42 oz.

NIB	Exc.	V.G.	Good	Fair	Poor
1925	1600	1300	1050	750	400

Hunter 6.0

Chambered for the 10mm cartridge only and fitted with a 6" bull barrel. Heavy extended frame. Many special features. Leupold 2x scope. Blued finish. Weight with scope 51 oz.

NIB	Exc.	V.G.	Good	Fair	Poor
2350	1900	1600	1200	850	500

Special Edition

Chambered for the 9mm, .40 S&W or .45 ACP cartridge and fitted with a fully supported and ramped 5" bull barrel. Hi-Rise grip. Sights are Dawson fiber optic with adjustable rear. Slide has Saber Tooth serrations and custom engraving. Finish is 24 karat gold on all steel parts except barrel. Weight is about 38 oz.

NIB	Exc.	V.G.	Good	Fair	Poor
2900	2500	1975	1600	1200	500

I.P.S.C. 30th Anniversary

Similar to the Special Edition but with hard chrome upper with color inlays and blued lower.

NIB	Exc.	V.G.	Good	Fair	Poor
2775	2400	1700	1400	950	450

TruSight

Semi-auto pistol chambered for 9mm, .40 S&W, .45 ACP; double-stack magazine. Steel frame, 4.15" slide/barrel. Dawson fiber optic front sight, adjustable rear sight. 36.1 oz. Blued with multiple options. IPSC, USPSA approved. Introduced 2006.

NIB	Exc.	V.G.	Good	Fair	Poor
1800	1575	1200	900	600	350

Legacy

Chambered for .45 ACP single-stack. 5" slide/barrel, LOA 8.5", 38 oz. with adjustable rear sight. Cocobola smooth grips. IDPA, USPSA approved. Introduced 2006.

NIB	Exc.	V.G.	Good	Fair	Poor
1500	1300	1050	750	600	300

GP6

Polymer-framed single/double action pistol with ambidextrous safeties and fized three-dot sight system. Chambered in 9mm Parabellum.

NIB	Exc.	V.G.	Good	Fair	Poor
650	500	375	250	175	75

Sentinel Premier

Top-of-the-line ISPC and IDPA competition 1911 with Dawson Precision/STI "Perfect Impact" style white outline tritium adjustable sights and the STI Tritium competition front; forged steel, government length, standard-width frame; and many other refinements. The Sentinel Premier comes standard with case, owner's manual, and one Wilson Combat \xa8 Elite Tactical magazine.

NIB	Exc.	V.G.	Good	Fair	Poor
1700	1500	1300	1000	800	450

Limited Edition 20th Anniversary

1911-style semi-auto pistol chambered in 9x19, .38 Super, .40 S&W, and .45 ACP to commemorate STI\qs 20th anniversary. Features include ambidextrous thumb safeties and knuckle relief high-rise beavertail grip safety; gold TiN (or Titanium Nitride) coating; full length steel bar stock slide with custom serrations specific to this model; 5-inch fully ramped and supported bull barrel; STI adjustable rear sight and a Dawson fiber optic front sight. STI will only build 200 of these pistols and the serial numbers reflect this (1 of 200, 2 of 200, etc.)

NIB	Exc.	V.G.	Good	Fair	Poor
3200	2900	2600	—	—	—

STI Duty One Pistol

1911-style semi-auto pistol chambered in .45 ACP. Features include government size frame with integral tactical rail and 30 lpi checkered front strap; milled tactical rail on the dust cover of the frame; ambidextrous thumb safeties; lowered and flared ejection port; fixed rear sight; front and rear cocking serrations; 5-inch fully supported STI International ramped bull barrel.

NIB	Exc.	V.G.	Good	Fair	Poor
1300	1100	850	700	300	200

STI Apeiro Pistol

1911-style semi-auto pistol chambered in 9x19, .40 S&W, and .45 ACP. Features include Schuemann "Island" barrel; patented modular steel frame with polymer grip; high capacity double-stack magazine; stainless steel ambidextrous thumb safeties and knuckle relief high-rise beavertail grip safety; unique sabertooth rear cocking serrations; 5-inch fully ramped, fully supported "island" bull barrel, with the sight milled in to allow faster recovery to point of aim; custom engraving on the polished sides of the (blued) stainless steel slide; stainless steel magwell; STI adjustable rear sight and Dawson fiber optic front sight; blued frame.

NIB	Exc.	V.G.	Good	Fair	Poor
2200	1850	1500	1200	800	400

STI Eclipse Pistol

Compact 1911-style semi-auto pistol chambered in 9x19, .40 S&W, and .45 ACP. Features include slide with rear cocking serrations, over-sized ejection port; 2-dot tritium night sights recessed into the slide; high-capacity polymer grip; single sided blued thumb safety;bobbed, high-rise, blued, knuckle relief beavertail grip safety; 3-inch barrel. Also comes with alloy frame as Escort model.

NIB	Exc.	V.G.	Good	Fair	Poor
1625	1400	1185	900	600	300

STI Texican Single Action Revolver

SAA-styled revolver chambered in .38 Special and .45 Colt. Features include 4.75- or 6.5-inch (.45) or 5.25-inch barrel (.38). Features include competition sights, springs, triggers and hammers; color case hardening and blued finish standard.

NIB	Exc.	V.G.	Good	Fair	Poor
1100	935	775	600	300	200

STOCK, FRANZ
Berlin, Germany

Stock

A .22, 6.35mm or 7.65mm semi-automatic pistol with an open topped slide. The frame marked "Franz Stock Berlin." Blued with black composition grips impressed with the name "Stock" at the top. Manufactured from 1918 to the early 1930s.

Courtesy J.B. Wood

NIB	Exc.	V.G.	Good	Fair	Poor
—	525	400	300	250	150

STOCKING & CO.
Worcester, Massachusetts

Pepperbox

A .28 or .316 barreled percussion pepperbox revolver with barrel lengths from 4" to 6". The hammer is fitted with a long cocking piece at the rear and the trigger guard may or may not be made with a spur at the rear. Blued with walnut grips. The barrel group marked "Stocking & Co., Worcester." Manufactured between 1846 and 1854.

NIB	Exc.	V.G.	Good	Fair	Poor
—	—	1950	1650	600	200

Single-Shot Pistol

A .36 caliber single-shot percussion pistol of the same pattern as the pepperbox with a 4" half octagonal barrel. Marked as above. Manufactured from 1849 to 1852.

NIB	Exc.	V.G.	Good	Fair	Poor
—	—	1200	850	350	100

STOEGER, A. F.
South Hackensack, New Jersey

.22 Luger

A .22 caliber simplified copy of the German Model P.08 semi-automatic pistol with a 4.5" or 5.5" barrel and an aluminum frame. The word "Luger" is roll engraved on the right side of the frame. Blued with checkered brown plastic grips. Made by Erma.

NIB	Exc.	V.G.	Good	Fair	Poor
—	350	275	200	150	100

Target Luger

As above, with adjustable target sights. Made by Erma.

NIB	Exc.	V.G.	Good	Fair	Poor
—	375	295	225	175	125

Luger Carbine

As above, with an 11" barrel, walnut forend and checkered walnut grips. Furnished with a red velvet lined black leatherette case. Manufactured during the 1970s. Made by Erma.

NIB	Exc.	V.G.	Good	Fair	Poor
—	1100	775	500	350	150

American Eagle Luger

This is identical to the German design. It is chambered for the 9mm with a 7-round magazine and fitted with a 4" barrel. Checkered walnut grips. Stainless steel. Weight is about 32 oz.

NIB	Exc.	V.G.	Good	Fair	Poor
1100	975	650	450	300	100

American Eagle Navy Model

Same as above but with a 6" barrel.

NIB	Exc.	V.G.	Good	Fair	Poor
1200	1075	700	450	300	100

STURM, RUGER & CO.
Southport, Connecticut

SEMI-AUTOMATIC RIMFIRE PISTOLS

Standard Model "Red Eagle Grips"

This is a blowback semi-automatic with a fixed, exposed, 4.75" barrel. The receiver is tubular, with a round bolt. There is a 9-shot detachable magazine, and the sights are fixed. The finish is blued, and the black hard rubber grips on this first model feature a red Ruger eagle or hawk medallion on the left side. There were approximately 25,600 manufactured before Alexander Sturm's death in 1951, but this model may be seen as high as the 35000 serial number range. Because variations of this model exist an expert opinion should be sought before a final price is established.

NIB	Exc.	V.G.	Good	Fair	Poor
750	550	450	325	250	150

NOTE: Factory verified plated pistols will bring between $2,500 and $5,000 depending on condition. For pistols in factory original wood "cod box" shipping carton add $2,000.

Standard Model

This model is identical to the Red Eagle except that after Sturm's death the grip medallions were changed from red to black and have remained so ever since. This pistol was produced from 1952-1982 in 4-3/4" and 6" barrels. There are a great many variations of this pistol, but a book dealing with this pistol alone should be consulted as the differences in variations are subtle and valuation of these variations is definitely a matter for individual appraisal.

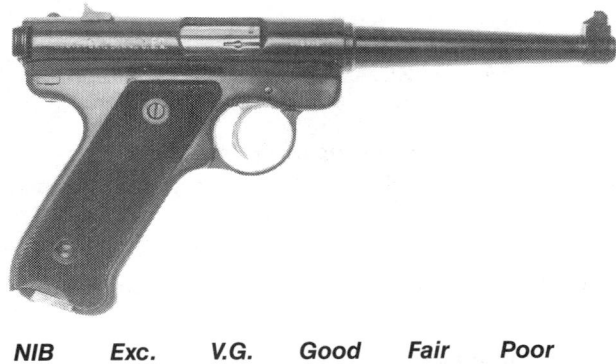

NIB	Exc.	V.G.	Good	Fair	Poor
—	350	275	125	100	85

Standard Model—Marked "Hecho en Mexico"

These pistols were assembled and sold in Mexico. Approximately 200 were built with 4-3/4" barrels and about 50 were produced with 6" barrels. Only a few of these pistols have been accounted for and for this reason an expert should be consulted.

NIB	Exc.	V.G.	Good	Fair	Poor
—	1500	1200	850	600	400

MARK I TARGET MODEL

The success of the Ruger Standard Model led quite naturally to a demand for a more accurate target model. In 1951 a pistol that utilized the same frame and receiver with a 6-7/8", target-type barrel and adjustable sights was introduced. Early target models number 15000 to 16999 and 25000 to 25300 have Red Eagle grips. In 1952 a 5-1/4" tapered barrel model was introduced, but was soon discontinued. In 1963 the popular 5-1/2" bull barrel model was introduced. These models enjoyed well deserved success and were manufactured from 1951-1982.

Red Eagle

6-7/8" barrel.

NIB	Exc.	V.G.	Good	Fair	Poor
—	675	500	250	200	150

Black or Silver Eagle

6-7/8" barrel.

NIB	Exc.	V.G.	Good	Fair	Poor
—	400	300	175	150	125

NOTE: For original hinged box add 35 percent. With factory supplied muzzlebrake add $75-100. For other Mark I Target models under serial number 72500 in original hinged box add 50 percent.

5-1/4" Tapered Barrel Model

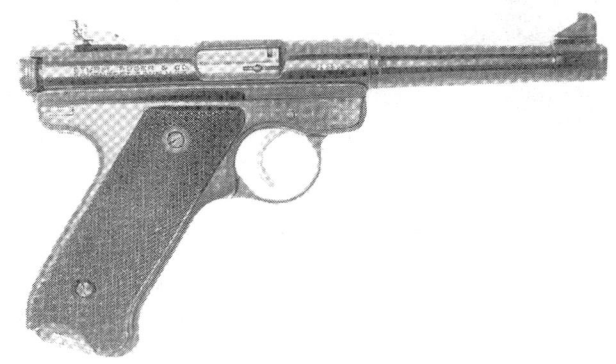

NIB	Exc.	V.G.	Good	Fair	Poor
—	700	600	400	250	125

NOTE: Add 50 percent if in original 5-1/4" marked hinged box.

5-1/2" Bull Barrel Model

NIB	Exc.	V.G.	Good	Fair	Poor
—	375	275	150	125	95

Rollmarked with U.S. on Top of Frame

These pistols will have either 1/16" or 1/8" high serial numbers.

NIB	Exc.	V.G.	Good	Fair	Poor
—	700	500	300	200	150

NOTE: Add 25 percent to price if pistol has 1/8" high serial numbers.

Stainless Steel 1 of 5,000

This model is a special commemorative version of the first standard with the "Red Eagle" grips. It is made of stainless steel and is rollmarked with Bill Ruger's signature on it. The pistol is encased in a wood "salt cod" case.

NIB	Exc.	V.G.	Good	Fair	Poor
395	350	300	225	175	125

MARK II .22 CALIBER PISTOL SPECIFICATIONS

Supplied in .22 LR with various barrel weights and lengths. Magazine capacity is 10 rounds. Trigger is grooved with curved finger surface. High speed hammer provides fast lock time. Grips are sharply checkered and made of black gloss delrin material. Stainless steel models have a brushed satin finish. Today, each model except the MK-10 and KMK-10, come from the factory with a lockable plastic case and Ruger lock. **NOTE:** Beginning n 2004 all Ruger adjustable sight .22 pistols were drilled and tapped for an included Weaver-type scope base adapter.

STANDARD MODEL MARK II

This is a generally improved version of the first Ruger pistol. There is a hold-open device, and the magazine holds 10 rounds. This model was introduced in 1982.

Model MK4

Blued finish with 4.75" barrel. Checkered composition grips. Weight about 35 oz.

NIB	Exc.	V.G.	Good	Fair	Poor
350	250	150	125	100	75

Model MK450

Introduced in 1999 to commemorate the 50th anniversary of the first Ruger rimfire pistol. Fitted with a 4.75" barrel with fixed sights. Chambered for the .22 LR cartridge. The pistols grips have a red Ruger medallion and Ruger crest on the barrel. Furnished in a red case. Weight is about 35 oz. Production limited to one year.

NIB	Exc.	V.G.	Good	Fair	Poor
385	350	250	175	125	75

Model MK6

Same as above but with 6" barrel. Weight 37 oz.

NIB	Exc.	V.G.	Good	Fair	Poor
350	275	225	125	100	75

Model KMK4

This model is the same as the Mark II Standard except that it is made of stainless steel.

NIB	Exc.	V.G.	Good	Fair	Poor
375	300	200	150	125	100

Model KMK6

Same as above but with 6" barrel. Weight is about 37 oz.NOTE: In 1997, Ruger produced 650 of the Model MK6 with special features for the "Friends of the NRA" auction of the same year. These guns have high polish blueing, faux ivory grips panels, a gold inlaid National Rifle Association inscription and a gold inlaid number of "1 of 650" to "650 of 650". The NIB price for these pistols is $550.

NIB	Exc.	V.G.	Good	Fair	Poor
375	300	200	150	125	100

Mark II Target Model

This model incorporates the same improvements as the Mark II Standard but is offered with 5.5" bull, 6-7/8" tapered and 10" heavy barrel. A 5-1/4" tapered barrel was added in 1990 but discontinued in 1994. Blued finish. This model has adjustable target sights and was introduced in 1982.NOTE: In 1989, approximately 2,000 5-1/2" bull barrel Mark II pistols with blue barreled receivers and stainless steel grip frames were produced by Ruger on order from a Ruger distributor. They exist in the 215-25xxx to 215-43xxx serial number range. The NIB price for these pistols is $375.

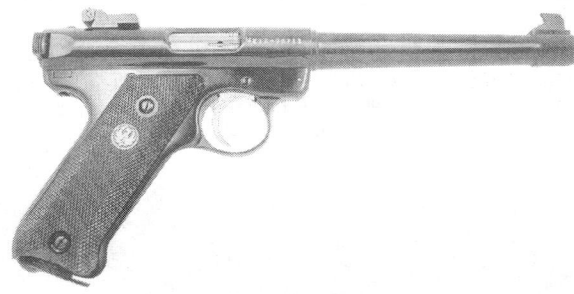

NIB	Exc.	V.G.	Good	Fair	Poor
315	275	200	150	125	100

Stainless Steel Mark II Target Model

This model is the same as the blued version but is made of stainless steel.

NIB	Exc.	V.G.	Good	Fair	Poor
350	285	250	200	175	125

Government Model

This model is similar to the blue Mark II Target, with a 6-7/8" bull barrel. It is the civilian version of a training pistol that the military is purchasing from Ruger. The only difference is that this model does not have the U.S. markings.

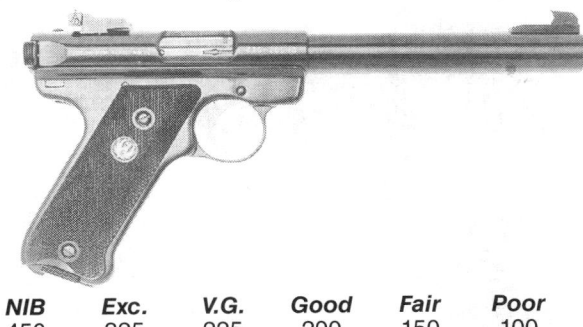

NIB	Exc.	V.G.	Good	Fair	Poor
450	325	225	200	150	100

Stainless Steel Government Model

Stainless steel version of the Government Model.NOTE: Same with U.S. markings. These are found in the serial number range of 210-00001 to 210-18600. Only a couple dozen are in civilian hands. The NIB price for these pistols is $1,000.00.

NIB	Exc.	V.G.	Good	Fair	Poor
475	350	250	225	175	125

Mark II Competition Model KMK678GC

The Competition model features a stainless steel frame with checkered laminated hardwood thumb rest grips, heavy 6-7/8" bull barrel factory drilled and tapped for scope mount, Partridge type front sight undercut to prevent glare and an adjustable rear sight. Pistol weighs 45 oz.NOTE: In 1997 Ruger produced 204 of these pistols in blue instead of stainless steel for one of their distributors. They are very scarce. The NIB for these pistols is $350.In 1995 Ruger produced a similar blued pistol (1,000 total, 500 each with or without scope rings) with 5-1/2" slab side barrels. These are not marked "Competition Target Model" like the previously described variation. The NIB price for these pistols was $350 and with rings $375.

NIB	Exc.	V.G.	Good	Fair	Poor
400	325	275	200	125	100

Mark II Bull Barrel Model MK4B

Introduced in 1996 this bull barrel variation has a blued finish with a 4" barrel. Grips are checkered composition. Weight is about 38 oz.

NIB	Exc.	V.G.	Good	Fair	Poor
400	325	275	200	125	100

RUGER 22/45 MODEL

This .22 LR caliber pistol has the same grip angle and magazine latch as the Model 1911 .45 ACP. The semi-automatic action is stainless steel and the grip frame is made from Zytel, a fiberglass reinforced lightweight composite material. Front sight is Patridge-type. This model is available in several different configurations. A 4" tapered barrel and standard model sights, a 5.25" tapered barrel with target sights, or a 5.5" bull barrel with target sights. The 5.25" barrel was discontinued in 1994.

KP4

This model features a 4.75" standard weight barrel with fixed sights. Pistol weighs 28 oz.

NIB	Exc.	V.G.	Good	Fair	Poor
300	275	250	200	125	75

KP514

Furnished with a target tapered barrel 5.25" in length. Comes with adjustable sights. Pistol weighs 38 oz. Model now discontinued.

NIB	Exc.	V.G.	Good	Fair	Poor
300	200	175	150	100	75

KP512 (22/45)

This model is equipped with a 5.5" bull barrel with adjustable sights. Weighs 42 oz. NOTE: In 1995 Ruger produced 500 22/45s with stainless steel 6-7/8" Government type barreled receivers for one of their distributors. They appear around the 220-59xxx serial number range. The NIB price for these pistols is $350.00. In 1997 another Ruger distributor succeeded in contracting Ruger to make a similar 22/45 only in blue and with 6-7/8" slab side bull barrels. Approximately 1,000 were produced with serial numbers extending to the 220-87xxx serial number range. The NIB price is $300.00.

NIB	Exc.	V.G.	Good	Fair	Poor
300	200	175	150	100	75

P4

A limited number, about 1,000, of this variation were produced in 1995 with a 4" bull barrel on a P frame. It was introduced into the product line as a production pistol in 1997. Weight is approximately 31 oz.

NIB	Exc.	V.G.	Good	Fair	Poor
350	200	150	100	75	50

22/45 Threaded Barrel

Variation of Model 22/45 with muzzle threaded to accept various accessories. Muzzle is capped to protect threads, receiver and barrel drilled and tapped to accept accessory rails. Weight is 32 ounces; 4.5-inch barrel with blue finish.

NIB	Exc.	V.G.	Good	Fair	Poor
375	325	285	200	135	100

P512

This variation of the stainless steel version has a blued receiver with P-style frame.

NIB	Exc.	V.G.	Good	Fair	Poor
350	250	150	100	75	60

MARK III .22 CALIBER PISTOL SPECIFICATIONS

The Mark III series was introduced in 2004. This series features a newly designed magazine release button located on the left side of the frame. Mark III pistols also have a visible loaded chamber indicator, an internal lock, magazine disconnect, re-contontured sights and ejection port.

Mark III Standard Pistol

Introduced in 2005 this .22 caliber pistol is fitted with a 4.75" or 6" barrel. Fixed rear sight. Blued finish. Magazine capacity is 10 rounds. Black checkered grips. Weight is about 35 oz. depending on barrel length.

NIB	Exc.	V.G.	Good	Fair	Poor
300	250	185	150	100	75

Mark III Hunter

This .22 caliber pistol is fitted with a 6.88" target crowned fluted stainless steel barrel. Adjustable rear sight with Hi-Viz front sight. Checkered Cocobolo grips. Drilled and tapped for scope mount. Supplied with green case, scope base adapter, and 6 interchangeable LitePipes for front sight. Weight is about 41 oz. Introduced in 2005. Add 50 percent for Crimson Trace lasergrips (limited edition for 2008).

NIB	Exc.	V.G.	Good	Fair	Poor
350	275	225	175	125	75

Mark III Competition

This .22 caliber model features a 6.88" flat sided heavy barrel with adjustable rear sight and Patridge front sight. Stainless steel finish. Checkered wood grips. Weight is about 45 oz. Introduced in 2005.

NIB	Exc.	V.G.	Good	Fair	Poor
425	315	245	200	150	75

Mark III 22/45 Standard Pistol

This .22 caliber pistol has a grip frame similar to the Colt 1911 pistol. The 4" bull barrel is flat sided. Blued steel frame. Fixed sights. Magazine capacity is 10 rounds. Grips are checkered black polymer. Weight is about 29 oz.

NIB	Exc.	V.G.	Good	Fair	Poor
300	225	175	125	100	75

Mark III 22/45 Stainless

Similar to above but with stainless barrel and receiver.

NIB	Exc.	V.G.	Good	Fair	Poor
425	375	325	250	175	125

Mark III 512 Pistol

This .22 LR pistol has a 5.5" bull barrel and adjustable rear sight. Steel frame is blued. Checkered black synthetic grips. Weaver-style scope base adapter included. Magazine capacity is 10 rounds. Weight is about 41 oz.

Ruger® Mark III Pistol
MKIII512

NIB	Exc.	V.G.	Good	Fair	Poor
350	300	225	175	125	100

22/45 Mark III Hunter

Similar to 22/45 .22 pistol but with Mark III-style improvements. 6-7/8" or 4-1/2" fluted barrel, HiViz front sight with six interchangeable inserts. Blued or stainless finish. Pricing is for stainless model. Introduced in 2007.

NIB	Exc.	V.G.	Good	Fair	Poor
465	395	300	225	150	100

22/45RP Mark III Pistol

Semiauto pistol chambered in .22 LR. Features include polymer frame with grip panels that recreate feel of 1911; 1911-style controls including magazine button, manual safety, and bolt stop locations as the classic 1911 pistol; slim polymer grip frame with serrated front strap and checkered back strap; blued alloy steel 5.5-inch bull barrel with a fixed front sight and micro-adjustable rear sight; adjustable sights, drilled/tapped for Weaver mounts. MSRP: $380.

Charger

Introduced in 2008. A 10-inch-barrel pistol version of the 10/22 .22 LR rifle. Black matte finish, black laminated stock (other colors available), bipod, and Weaver-style mounts. Includes one 10-round magazine.

NIB	Exc.	V.G.	Good	Fair	Poor
375	300	225	175	125	100

OLD MODEL SINGLE-ACTION REVOLVERS (PRE-TRANSFER BAR)

Single Six Revolver

This is a .22 rimfire, 6-shot, single-action revolver. It was first offered with a 5-1/2" barrel length and a fixed sight. In 1959 additional barrel lengths were offered for this model in 4-5/8", 6-1/2", and 9-1/2". It is based in appearance on the Colt Single-Action Army, but internally it is a new design that features coil springs instead of the old-style, flat leaf springs. It also features a floating firing pin and is generally a stronger action than what was previously available. The early model had a flat loading gate and was made this way from 1953-1957, when the contoured gate became standard. Early models had checkered hard rubber grips changed to smooth varnished walnut by 1962. Black eagle grip medallions were used from the beginning of production to 1971 when a silver eagle grip medallion replaced it. No "Red Eagle" single-sixes were ever produced. This model was manufactured from 1953-1972.

Flat Gate Model

60,000 produced. NOTE 1: Be aware that revolvers serial numbered under 2000 will bring a premium of 25 percent to 125 percent depending on condition, low serial number, and color of cylinder frame—bright reddish purple the most desirable. NOTE 2: Values cited belkow are for unconverted examples, and for converted examples with original parts present.

Courtesy John C. Dougan

NIB	Exc.	V.G.	Good	Fair	Poor
900	700	500	450	225	150

Contoured Gate Model

Introduced 1957. There were 258 5-1/2" barrel factory engraved pistols in this model. Add a 25 percent premium for 3-screw models.

NIB	Exc.	V.G.	Good	Fair	Poor
—	600	500	350	200	125

NOTE: Be aware that 4-5/8" and 9-1/2" barrel lengths will bring a premium. Add $3,500 to $6,000 for factory engraved and cased models.

Single Six Convertible

This model is similar to the Single Six but is furnished with an extra .22 rimfire Magnum cylinder.

NIB	Exc.	V.G.	Good	Fair	Poor
—	650	550	375	225	150

NOTE: Barrel lengths in 4-5/8" and 9-1/2" will bring a premium.

Single Six .22 Magnum Model

This model is similar to the Single Six except that it is chambered for the .22 rimfire Magnum and the frame was so marked. It was offered in the 6.5" barrel length only and was manufactured for three years. An extra long rifle cylinder was added later in production. The serial numbers are in the 300000-340000 range.

NIB	Exc.	V.G.	Good	Fair	Poor
—	600	500	350	200	125

LIGHTWEIGHT SINGLE SIX

This model is similar to the Single Six, with an aluminum alloy frame and 4-5/8" barrel. This variation was produced between 1956 and 1958 and was in the 200000-212000 serial number range.

Approximately the first 6,500 were produced with alloy cylinders with steel chamber inserts.NOTE: Stamped after the serial number or on the bottom of the frame. Varieties of "S" marked lightweights exist. Individual evaluation and appraisal is recommended. These are factory seconds and are verifiable.

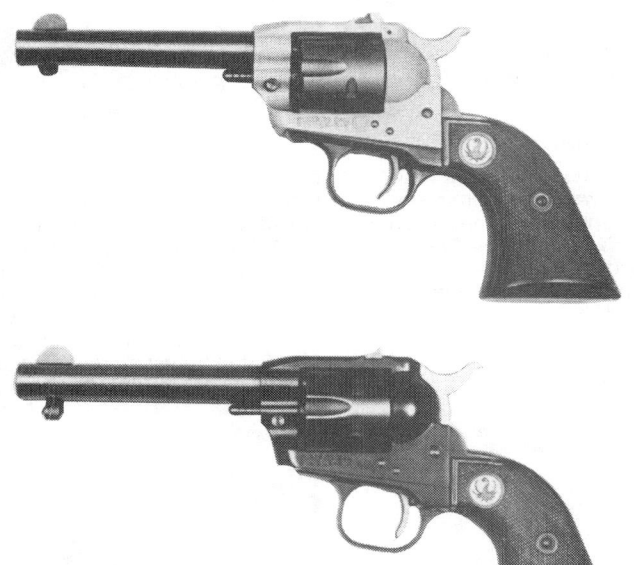

Courtesy Know Your Ruger Single-Action Revolvers 1953-63.
Blacksmith Corp.

Silver Anodized Frame with Aluminum Cylinder Model with Martin Hardcoat Finish

NIB	Exc.	V.G.	Good	Fair	Poor
—	775	550	400	225	195

Black Anodized Aluminum Frame and Cylinder Model

NIB	Exc.	V.G.	Good	Fair	Poor
—	850	600	500	300	250

Black Anodized Frame with Blue Steel Cylinder Model

NIB	Exc.	V.G.	Good	Fair	Poor
—	550	450	350	225	195

Silver Anodized with Blue Steel Cylinder Model

Only a few hundred pistols in this variation were produced by the factory with an "S" suffix.

NIB	Exc.	V.G.	Good	Fair	Poor
—	1100	850	600	400	200

NOTE: For original Lightweight Single-Six boxes add 25 percent to 40 percent.

SUPER SINGLE SIX

Introduced in 1964, this is the Single Six with adjustable sights. Prices listed are for pistols with 5-1/2" and 6-1/2" barrels.NOTE: The listed models are factory verifiable.

NIB	Exc.	V.G.	Good	Fair	Poor
—	600	500	350	200	125

4-5/8" Barrel

200 built.

NIB	Exc.	V.G.	Good	Fair	Poor
—	1100	900	750	—	400

Nickel-Plated Model

Approximately 100 built.

NIB	Exc.	V.G.	Good	Fair	Poor
—	2350	1600	1200	—	500

BEARCAT (OLD MODEL)

This is a scaled-down version of the single-action. It is chambered for .22 rimfire and has a 4" barrel and an unfluted, roll engraved cylinder. The frame is alloy, and it has a brass colored anodized alloy trigger guard. The finish is blue, and the grips are plastic impregnated wood until 1963, thereafter walnut with eagle medallions were used. This model was manufactured from 1958-1970.

Courtesy Know Your Ruger Single-Actions: The Second Decade.
Blacksmith Corp.

Serial Number under 30000

NIB	Exc.	V.G.	Good	Fair	Poor
—	500	350	225	150	125

Alphabet Model

NIB	Exc.	V.G.	Good	Fair	Poor
—	500	400	295	275	225

Black Anodized Trigger Guard Model

109 built.

NIB	Exc.	V.G.	Good	Fair	Poor
—	800	600	500	400	—

Serial Number over 30000 or with 90-prefix

NIB	Exc.	V.G.	Good	Fair	Poor
—	350	300	265	225	175

Super Bearcat (Old Model)

This model is similar to the with a steel frame and, on later models, a blued steel trigger guard and grip frame. The early examples still used brass. This model was manufactured from 1971 to 1974.

Courtesy W.P. Hallstein III and son Chip

NIB	Exc.	V.G.	Good	Fair	Poor
—	500	395	275	225	175

FLATTOP—.357 MAGNUM

The success of the Single Six led to the production of a larger version chambered for the .357 Magnum cartridge. This model is a single-action, with a 6-shot fluted cylinder and a flat top strap with adjustable "Micro sight." The barrel length is 4-5/8", 6.5", and 10". The finish is blue with checkered hard rubber grips on the early examples and smooth walnut on later ones. There were approximately 42,600 manufactured between 1955 and 1962.

Courtesy Know Your Ruger Single-Action Revolvers 1953-63.
Blacksmith Corp.

4-5/8" Barrel

NIB	Exc.	V.G.	Good	Fair	Poor
1200	1000	600	350	250	200

6-1/2" Barrel

NIB	Exc.	V.G.	Good	Fair	Poor
1000	850	600	450	350	250

10" Barrel

NIB	Exc.	V.G.	Good	Fair	Poor
2800	2500	1000	850	750	600

BLACKHAWK FLATTOP .44 MAGNUM

In 1956 the .44 Magnum was introduced, and Ruger jumped on the bandwagon. This is similar in appearance to the .357 but has a slightly heavier frame and a larger cylinder. It was available in a 6.5", 7.5", and 10" barrel. It was manufactured from 1956-1963. There were approximately 29,700 manufactured.

Courtesy Know Your Ruger Single-Action Revolvers 1953-63.
Blacksmith Corp.

6-1/2" Barrel

NIB	Exc.	V.G.	Good	Fair	Poor
1250	800	600	450	350	250

7-1/2" Barrel

NIB	Exc.	V.G.	Good	Fair	Poor
1325	950	700	600	450	300

10" Barrel

NIB	Exc.	V.G.	Good	Fair	Poor
3000	2000	1200	800	700	400

Blackhawk

This model is similar to the "Flattop," but the rear sight is protected by two raised protrusions—one on each side. It was available chambered for the .30 Carbine, .357 Magnum, .41 Magnum, or the .45 Colt cartridge. Barrel lengths are 4-5/8" or 6.5" in .357 Magnum and .41 Magnum. .45 Colt version has 4-5/8" and 7.5" barrel lengths. The .30 Carbine is furnished with a 7.5" barrel only. The finish is blue, and the grips are walnut with Ruger medallions. This model was produced from 1962 to 1972. Note that the "Old Style" Blackhawk (i.e., pre-transfer bar) is a popular platform for custom revolvers, so prices may exceed those shown depending on circumstances.

Courtesy Know Your Ruger Single-Action Revolvers 1953-63.
Blacksmith Corp.

NIB	Exc.	V.G.	Good	Fair	Poor
700	500	350	200	150	125

NOTE: Add 20 percent for .41 Mag. and 50 percent for .45 Colt and 35 percent for .30 Carbine. Original verified factory brass grip frame will add at least $200 to above prices. It was available chambered for the .357 Magnum or .41 Magnum (4-5/8" or 6-1/2" barrel), or .45 Long Colt (4-5/8" or 7-1/2" barrel). The .41 Magnum with factory installed brass frame will bring $800 to $1500 depending on condition.

BLACKHAWK CONVERTIBLE

This model is the same as the Blackhawk with an extra cylinder to change or convert calibers. The .357 Magnum has a 9mm cylinder, and the .45 Colt has a .45 ACP cylinder.

.357/9mm

NIB	Exc.	V.G.	Good	Fair	Poor
650	550	450	300	200	150

.45 L.C./.45 ACP

NIB	Exc.	V.G.	Good	Fair	Poor
1000	800	500	250	175	125

NOTE: The 4-5/8" barrel will bring a slight premium. Nonprefix serial numbered .357/9mm Blackhawks will bring a premium.

SUPER BLACKHAWK OLD MODEL

The formidable recoil of the .44 Magnum cartridge was difficult to handle in a revolver with a small grip such as found on the Blackhawk, so it was decided to produce a larger-framed revolver with increased size in the grip. The rear of the trigger guard was squared off, and the cylinder was left unfluted to increase mass. This model was offered with a 7.5" barrel; 600 6.5" barrel Super Blackhawks were produced by factory error. This model is blued and has smooth walnut grips with medallions. The first of these revolvers were offered in a fitted wood case and are rare today. The Super Blackhawk was made from 1959-1972. NOTE: For pistols with verified factory installed brass grip frame each example should be appraised.

NIB	Exc.	V.G.	Good	Fair	Poor
800	600	400	300	200	150

Early Model in Wood Presentation Case

NIB	Exc.	V.G.	Good	Fair	Poor
1000	850	650	475	400	300

Old Model In Fitted White Cardboard Case

NIB	Exc.	V.G.	Good	Fair	Poor
1200	1100	1000	950	875	675

Long Grip Frame in Wood Case

300 guns built.

NIB	Exc.	V.G.	Good	Fair	Poor
1500	1250	1150	1050	800	675

Factory Verified 6-1/2" Barrel

Approximately 600 guns built in the 23000-25000 serial number range.

NIB	Exc.	V.G.	Good	Fair	Poor
1200	1000	750	550	450	375

NOTE: For pistols with brass grip frames add $250 to the prices listed.

Hawkeye Single-Shot

The shooting public wanted a small-caliber, high-velocity handgun. The Smith & Wesson Model 53, chambered for the .22 Jet, appeared in 1961; and the cartridge created extraction problems for a revolver. Ruger solved the problem with the introduction of the Hawkeye—a single-shot that looked like a six shooter. In place of the cylinder was a breech block that cammed to the side for loading. This pistol was excellent from an engineering and performance standpoint but was not a commercial success. The Hawkeye is chambered for the .256 Magnum, a bottleneck cartridge, and has an 8.5" barrel and

adjustable sights. The finish is blued with walnut, medallion grips. The barrel is tapped at the factory for a 1" scope base. This pistol is quite rare as only 3,300 were produced in 1963 and 1964.

Courtesy John C. Dougan

NIB	Exc.	V.G.	Good	Fair	Poor
2500	1900	1400	850	600	500

EDITOR'S COMMENT: All of the above single-action Ruger pistols fitted with factory optional grips will bring a premium regardless of model. This premium applies to pistols manufactured from 1954 to 1962 only. For the optional grips the premium is: Ivory $800, Stag $400.

NEW MODEL SERIES

The Ruger firm in 1973 completely modified their single-action lockwork to accommodate a hammer block or transfer bar. This hammer block or transfer bar prevented accidental discharge should a revolver be dropped. In doing so, the company circumvented a great deal of potential legal problems and made collectibles out of the previous models.

Super Single Six Convertible (New Model)

This model is similar in appearance to the old model but has the new hammer block safety system. The frame has two pins instead of three screws, and opening the loading gate frees the cylinder stop for loading. Barrel lengths are 4-5/8", 5.5", 6.5", and 9.5". The sights are adjustable; the finish is blued. The grips are walnut with a medallion, and an interchangeable .22 Magnum cylinder is supplied. This model was introduced in 1973 and is currently in production.

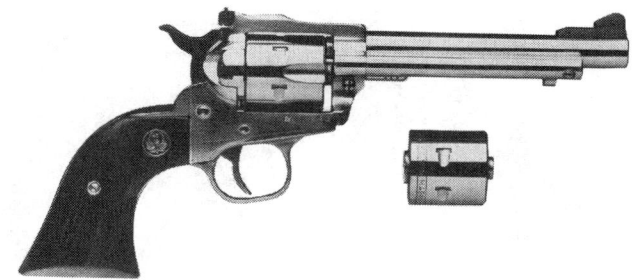

NIB	Exc.	V.G.	Good	Fair	Poor
400	325	250	200	175	125

Stainless Steel Single Six Convertible

The same as the standard blued model but made from stainless steel. Offered with a 4-5/8", 6-1/2", and 9-1/2" barrel.

NIB	Exc.	V.G.	Good	Fair	Poor
475	400	300	250	225	175

NOTE: Pre-warning pistols (1973-1976) with 4-5/8" or 9-1/2" barrel will bring an additional 40 percent premium. Pistols with 4-5/8" barrels with "made in the 200th year of American Liberty" rollmark on the barrel will bring at least 100 percent premium to the NIB prices.

NEW MODEL SINGLE SIX (.22 LR ONLY) "STAR" MODEL

This model was produced in blue and stainless for one year only in 4-5/8", 5-1/2", 6-1/2", and 9-1/2" barrel lengths. Very low production on this model.

Blue Variation 5.5" or 6.5" Barrel

NIB	Exc.	V.G.	Good	Fair	Poor
450	400	350	300	275	200

9.5" Barrel—Rare

NIB	Exc.	V.G.	Good	Fair	Poor
550	500	450	400	350	250

4.62" Barrel—Very Rare

NIB	Exc.	V.G.	Good	Fair	Poor
800	750	450	400	350	250

Stainless Variation 5.5" or 6.5" Barrel

NIB	Exc.	V.G.	Good	Fair	Poor
450	350	275	225	175	150

9.5" Barrel

NIB	Exc.	V.G.	Good	Fair	Poor
600	500	400	300	225	175

4.62" Barrel—Rare

NIB	Exc.	V.G.	Good	Fair	Poor
650	550	500	400	300	200

FIXED SIGHT NEW MODEL SINGLE SIX

First made as drift adjustable rear sight (500 each in 4-5/8", 5-1/2", and 6-1/2" blue) and now a catalogued item as a pinched frame style fixed rear sight. Barrel lengths are offered in 5-1/2" and 6-1/2" lengths. Finish is blued or glossy stainless steel. Rear sight is fixed. Weights are between 32 and 38 oz. depending on barrel length and cylinder.

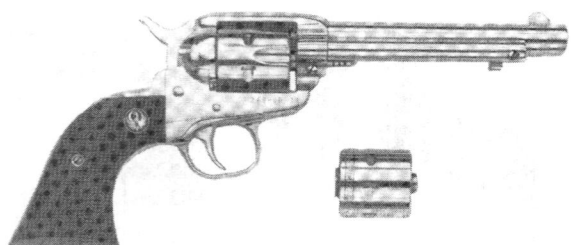

Blued Finish

NIB	Exc.	V.G.	Good	Fair	Poor
325	295	250	165	125	100

Stainless Steel

NIB	Exc.	V.G.	Good	Fair	Poor
395	300	250	200	150	125

Colorado Centennial Single Six

This model had a stainless steel grip frame, and the balance is blued. It has walnut grips with medallion insert. The barrel is 6-1/2", and the revolver is furnished with a walnut case with a centennial medal insert. There were 15,000 manufactured in 1975.

NIB	Exc.	V.G.	Good	Fair	Poor
500	400	300	200	125	100

Model "SSM" Single Six

This is the Single Six chambered for the .32 H&R Magnum cartridge. The first 800 pistols were marked with "SSM" on the cylinder frame and will bring a slight premium. Sold from 1984 to 1997. Adjustable sights.

NIB	Exc.	V.G.	Good	Fair	Poor
700	525	375	225	150	125

New Model Single Six Fixed Sight

Introduced in 2000 this revolver is chambered for the .32 H&R Magnum cartridge and fitted with a 4.625" barrel. Offered in blue or stainless steel. Short (1/4" shorter) simulated ivory grips. Vaquero-style frame with fixed sights. Values shown are for stainless. Deduct 25 percent for blued.

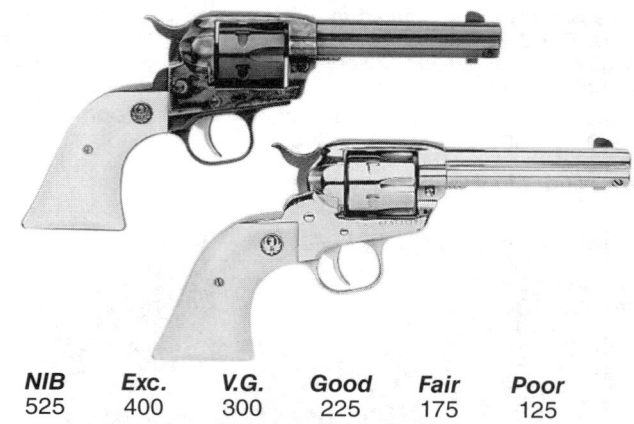

NIB	Exc.	V.G.	Good	Fair	Poor
525	400	300	225	175	125

New Model Single Six 50th Anniversary Model

Introduced in 2003 this model features a 4.625" barrel with blued finish. Top of barrel is rollmarked "50 years of single six 1953-2003". Comes standard with both .22 LR and .22 WMR cylinders. Cocobolo grips with red Ruger medallion. Packaged in a red plastic case with special "50 Year" label. Offered only in 2003.

NIB	Exc.	V.G.	Good	Fair	Poor
425	350	300	225	175	125

New Model Super Single Six

Chambered for the .22 LR and a separate cylinder for the .22 WMR cartridge. Barrel lengths are 4.625", 5.5", 6.5", and 9.5". Rosewood grips and adjustable or fixed sights. Blued finish except for optional stainless steel on 5.5" or 6.5" revolvers. Weight is about 35 oz. depending on barrel length.

NIB	Exc.	V.G.	Good	Fair	Poor
375	325	275	225	175	125

NOTE: For stainless steel models add $80.

New Model Super Single Six, .17 HMR

As above but with 6.5" barrel and chambered for the .17 HMR cartridge. Weight is about 35 oz. Introduced in 2003.

NIB	Exc.	V.G.	Good	Fair	Poor
400	350	275	225	175	125

New Model Single Six Hunter Convertible

This model is chambered for the .17 HMR/.17 Mach 2. Fitted with a 7.5" barrel with adjustable rear sight. Stainless steel finish with black laminate grips. The integral barrel rib machined for scope rings. Weight is about 45 oz. Introduced in 2005.

NIB	Exc.	V.G.	Good	Fair	Poor
675	500	500	300	250	175

Single-Ten

A 10-shot version of the Single-Six with a 5.5-inch barrel and walnut Gunfighter grips. Other features include a satin stainless finish and Williams adjustable fiber optic sights. Introduced in late 2011.

NIB	Exc.	V.G.	Good	Fair	Poor
525	450	385	300	220	150

NEW MODEL SERIES

Buckeye Special

This model was built in 1989 and 1990. It is chambered for the .38-40 or 10mm and .32-20 or .32 H&R cartridges.

NIB	Exc.	V.G.	Good	Fair	Poor
750	600	400	275	200	125

New Model Blackhawk

This model is similar in appearance to the old model Blackhawk, offered in the same calibers and barrel lengths. It has the transfer bar safety device. It was introduced in 1973 and is no longerin production.

NIB	Exc.	V.G.	Good	Fair	Poor
550	425	300	200	150	125

50th Anniversary New Model Blackhawk NVB34-50

Introduced in 2005 this model features a smaller, original size XR-3 grip and smaller main frame with checkered hard rubber grips. Adjustable rear sight. Special commemorative gold roll mark on top of barrel. Chambered for the .357 Mag and fitted with a 4.625" barrel. Weight is about 45 oz. All Blackhawk revolvers now featuure this new/old smaller main frame.

NIB	Exc.	V.G.	Good	Fair	Poor
575	425	300	200	150	125

New Model Blackhawk

Similar to above but without the fancy trimmings. Chambered in .327, .357, .44 Special, and .45 L.C.Weight is about 45 oz.

NIB	Exc.	V.G.	Good	Fair	Poor
575	425	300	200	150	125

Stainless Steel Blackhawk (New Model)

This is simply the New Model Blackhawk made from stainless steel. To date it has been offered in .357, .44, and .45 L.C. calibers.

NIB	Exc.	V.G.	Good	Fair	Poor
400	325	275	225	175	150

BLACKHAWK CONVERTIBLE (NEW MODEL)

This model is the same as the Blackhawk with interchangeable conversion cylinders—.357 Magnum/9mm and .45 Colt/.45 ACP. Prices listed are for blued model.

NIB	Exc.	V.G.	Good	Fair	Poor
465	350	250	175	150	125

.45 ACP & .45 Long Colt Convertible (1998)

NIB	Exc.	V.G.	Good	Fair	Poor
550	450	350	275	225	150

Stainless Model .357/9mm

300 guns built.

NIB	Exc.	V.G.	Good	Fair	Poor
925	700	600	500	375	250

Fiftieth Anniversary .44 Magnum Flattop New Model Blackhawk

Six-shot, single-action .44 Magnum (also accepts .44 Special) with 6.5" barrel and adjustable rear sight, 47 oz. Recreation of original .44 Falt-Top Blackhawk. Blued with checkered rubber grips. Gold, color-filled rollmark on top of barrel. Introduced 2006.

NIB	Exc.	V.G.	Good	Fair	Poor
525	400	300	225	175	150

Fiftieth Anniversary .44 Magnum New Model Ruger Blackhawk Flattop

Chambered for .44 Mag, blued single-action limited edition 6-shooter with gold-filled rollmark on barrel: "50 Years of .44 Magnum – 1956 to 2006." 6.5" barrel, hard rubber grips. Introduced 2006.

NIB	Exc.	V.G.	Good	Fair	Poor
500	400	300	225	150	125

Model SRM Blackhawk .357 Maximum

This is the New Model Blackhawk with a 7.5" or 10.5" barrel. It was chambered for the .357 Maximum and was intended for silhouette shooting. This model experienced problems with gas erosion in the forcing cone and under the top strap and was removed from production in 1984 after approximately 9200 were manufactured.

NIB	Exc.	V.G.	Good	Fair	Poor
—	675	575	400	275	250

Super Blackhawk (New Model)

This model is similar in appearance to the Old Model but has the transfer bar safety device. It was manufactured from 1973 to the present and commenced at serial number 81-00001.

NIB	Exc.	V.G.	Good	Fair	Poor
425	350	275	225	175	125

Super Blackhawk Stainless Steel

This model is the same as the blued version but is made of stainless steel. In 1998 this model was offered in 4-5/8" or 7-1/2" barrels with hunter grip frame and laminated grip panels.

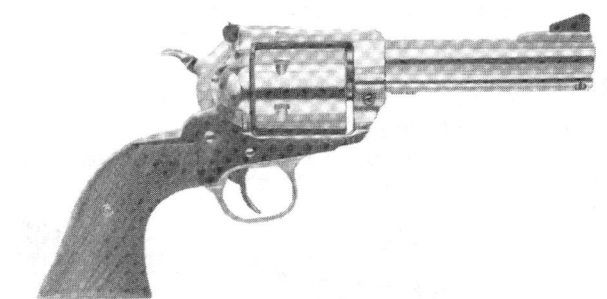

300 guns built.

NIB	Exc.	V.G.	Good	Fair	Poor
450	400	300	250	200	150

NOTE: Add $50 to prices for hunter grip frame and laminated grip panels.

Super Blackhawk Hunter

Introduced in 2002 this .44 or .41 Magnum model features a 7.5" barrel with integral full-length solid rib for scope mounts. Stainless steel. Adjustable rear sight. Scope rings included. Weight is about 52 oz.

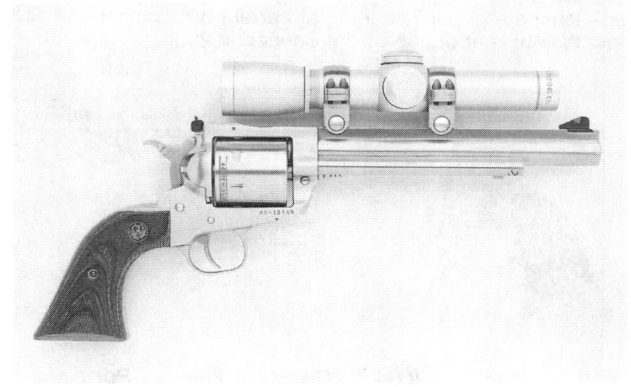

NIB	Exc.	V.G.	Good	Fair	Poor
675	575	485	400	300	175

50th Anniversary Matched Set .357 and .44 Magnum

Matched pair of Ruger New Blackhawks, one in .44 and the other in .357, commemorating 50th anniversary of Ruger Blackhawk revolver. Gold-filled rollmarked 6-1/2" and 4-5/8" barrels, respectively. Includes presentation case. Production limited. Introduced 2007.

NIB	Exc.	V.G.	Good	Fair	Poor
1350	1150	900	775	600	400

BISLEY MODEL

This model has the modified features found on the famous old Colt Bisley Target model—the flat top frame, fixed or adjustable sights, and the longer grip frame that has become the Bisley trademark. The Bisley is available chambered for .22 LR, .32 H&R Magnum, .357 Magnum, .41 Magnum, .44 Magnum, and .45 Long Colt. The barrel lengths are 6.5" and 7.5"; cylinders are either fluted or unfluted and roll engraved. The finish is a satin blue, and the grips are smooth Goncalo Alves with medallions. The Bisley was introduced in 1986.

.22 LR and .32 H&R Magnum

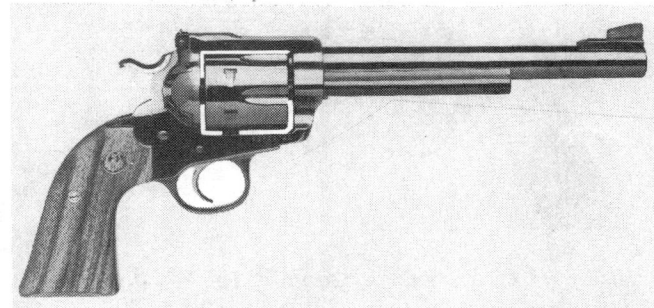

NIB	Exc.	V.G.	Good	Fair	Poor
425	375	225	200	150	125

NOTE: Add $100 for .32 Magnum Bisley.

.357 Magnum, .41 Magnum, .44 Magnum, and .45 Long Colt

NIB	Exc.	V.G.	Good	Fair	Poor
450	365	275	250	200	175

NOTE: Approximately 750 stainless grip frame .22 caliber Bisleys were made. These will demand a premium. Add $100 for stainless and $125 for convertible stainlesss.

Shootists Bisley

Produced in 1994 for the Shootist organization in memory of Tom Ruger. Chambered for the .22 cartridge these revolvers were limited to 52 total produced. They were stainless steel and were fitted with 4-5/8" barrels. The barrels were marked, "IN MEMORY OF OUR FRIEND TOM RUGER THE SHOOTIST 1994" . Some of these revolvers, but not all, have the name of the owner engraved on the backstrap.

Courtesy Jim Taylor

Old Army Percussion Revolver

This model is a .45 caliber percussion revolver with a 5" or 7-1/2" barrel. It has a 6-shot cylinder, with a blued finish and walnut grips. Beginning in 1994 this model was offered with fixed sights. Weight is about 46 oz. Add 20 percent for 5.5-inch model. All models now discontinued.

NIB	Exc.	V.G.	Good	Fair	Poor
575	475	375	250	175	150

NOTE: For pistols with original factory installed brass grip frame add $150 to prices listed.

Old Army Stainless Steel

This model is the same as the blued version except that it is made of stainless steel. Add 200 percent for stainless 200th Year model.

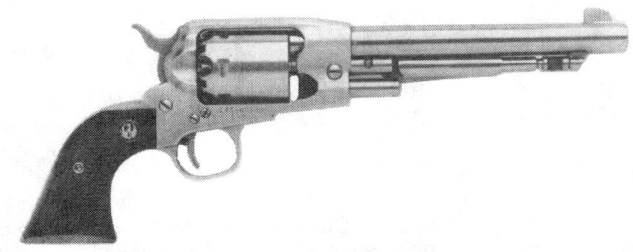

NIB	Exc.	V.G.	Good	Fair	Poor
650	525	400	275	225	150

Vaquero

This single-action pistol was introduced in 1993 and was voted handgun of the year by the shooting industry. It is a fixed sight version of the New Model Blackhawk. It is available in stainless steel or blued with case-colored frame. Offered in three different barrel lengths: 4.62", 5.5", and 7.5". Chambered for the .45 Long Colt. In 1994 the .44-40 and .44 Magnum calibers were added to the Vaquero line. Capacity is 6 rounds. Weighs between 39 and 41 oz. depending on barrel length. Discontinued; superseded by New Vaquero.

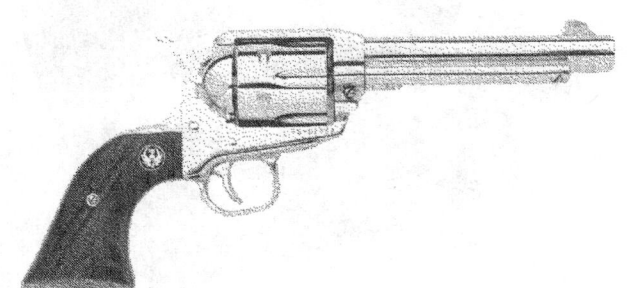

NIB	Exc.	V.G.	Good	Fair	Poor
500	425	325	200	150	100

NOTE: Vaqueros with 4-5/8" barrel chambered for .44 Magnum in both blue and stainless are uncatalogued, add 25 percent.

Bisley Vaquero

Introduced in 1997 this model features a 5.5" barrel chambered for .44 Magnum or .45 Long Colt. Grips are smooth rosewood. Finish is blued with case colored frame. Blade front sight and notch rear. Weight is about 40 oz. Discontinued.

NIB	Exc.	V.G.	Good	Fair	Poor
500	425	325	200	150	100

Vaquero Bird's-Head

Introduced in 2001 this model features a bird's-head grip. Chambered for the .45 Long Colt cartridge and fitted with a 5.5" barrel. Offered in stainless steel and blued finish. Weight is about 40 oz. Discontinued. NOTE: In 2002 this model was offered with 3.75" barrel and black Micarta grips. In 2003 this model was offered chambered for the .357 Magnum cartridge. Simulated ivory grips are also offered.

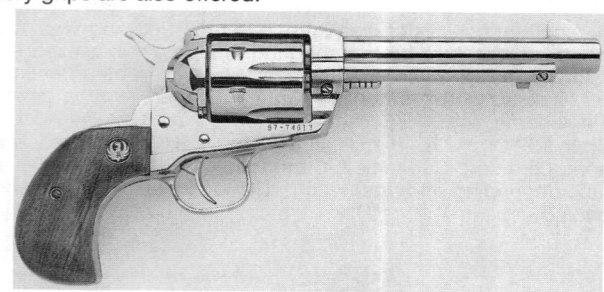

NIB	Exc.	V.G.	Good	Fair	Poor
575	450	350	225	175	125

"Cowboy Pair"

Matched pair of engraved and consecutively serial-numbered New Vaquero revolvers in .45 Colt. Includes lined wood collector case. Production limited to 500 sets. Introduced 2007.

NIB	Exc.	V.G.	Good	Fair	Poor
3500	3000	2500	1350	1000	600

New Vaquero ("Small Frame")

Introduced in 2005 this model features a slimmer pre-1962 XR-3 style grip frame with color case finish. The cylinder frame is mid-size. The cylinder is beveled. The ejector rod head is cresent shaped. Chambered for the .357 Mag or .45 Colt. Barrel lengths are 4.625", 5.5", and 7.5" (not in .357). Choice of case colored finish or stainless steel. Black checkered grips. Weight is about 37 oz depending on barrel length.

NIB	Exc.	V.G.	Good	Fair	Poor
475	350	250	175	125	100

New Vaquero Stainless

Similar to above but in stainless steel.

NIB	Exc.	V.G.	Good	Fair	Poor
585	450	350	250	175	150

Ruger New Model Bisley Vaquero

Similar to New Vaquero but with Bisley-style hammer and grip frame. Chambered in .357 and .45 Colt. Features include a 5.5" barrel, simulated ivory grips, fixed sights, six-shot cylinder. Overall length 11.12". Weight: 45 oz. Add 15 percent for stainless steel finish.

NIB	Exc.	V.G.	Good	Fair	Poor
565	425	325	225	165	150

NEW RUGER BEARCAT (SUPER BEARCAT)

This old favorite was reintroduced in 1994. This new version is furnished with a .22 LR cylinder and a .22 WMR cylinder. Barrel length is 4" with fixed sights. Grips are walnut. Offered with blued finish. NOTE: There was a factory recall on the magnum cylinders. Bearcats with both cylinders are very rare.

Blue

NIB	Exc.	V.G.	Good	Fair	Poor
425	325	250	175	125	100

Stainless Steel

NIB	Exc.	V.G.	Good	Fair	Poor
450	350	275	200	150	125

Convertible (Recalled)

NIB	Exc.	V.G.	Good	Fair	Poor
1100	1000	900	650	400	200

New Model Super Bearcat

Reintroduced in 2002 this .22 caliber model features a stainless steel or blued finish, 4" barrel with fixed sights and Rosewood grips. Weight is about 24 oz.

NIB	Exc.	V.G.	Good	Fair	Poor
425	325	250	175	125	100

NOTE: Add $50 for stainless steel version.

Fiftieth Anniversary New Bearcat

Gussied-up version of the New Bearcat (.22 LR only) commemorating the 50th anniversary of the original Bearcat. Blued finish with gold-filled anniversary script, gold-colored trigger guard and special box with anniversary booklet. Manufactured in 2008 only.

NIB	Exc.	V.G.	Good	Fair	Poor
700	600	500	—	—	—

DOUBLE-ACTION REVOLVERS

Security Six

This revolver, also known as the Model 117, is chambered for the .357 Magnum cartridge and has a 2.75", 4", or 6" barrel. It features adjustable sights and a square butt, with checkered walnut grips. It was manufactured between 1970 and 1985. Early guns with fixed sights and square butt were also marked "Security-Six". The model was later termed "Service-Six" and was so marked. The prices listed are only for the adjustable sight and square butt "Security-Six" models. Round butt Security-Sixes with adjustable are worth a premium.

NIB	Exc.	V.G.	Good	Fair	Poor
—	450	395	295	200	150

NOTE: Fixed sight guns marked Security-Six and round butt Security-Sixes with adjustable sights are worth a premium.

Stainless Steel Model 717

This model is the Security-Six made from stainless steel.

NIB	Exc.	V.G.	Good	Fair	Poor
—	50	0	400	225	125

Speed Six

This model is known as the Model 207, chambered for .357 Magnum; Model 208, chambered for .38 Special; and Model 209, chambered for 9mm. It has a 2.75" or 4" barrel, fixed sights, and a round butt with checkered walnut grips and was blued. There are some with factory bobbed hammers. This model was introduced in 1973. Discontinued. Add 200 percent for military (lanyard ring) and .38 S&W (not .38 Special) marked models.

NIB	Exc.	V.G.	Good	Fair	Poor
—	450	375	250	200	150

Models 737, 738, 739

These are the designations for the stainless steel versions of the Speed-Six. They are the same revolver except for the material used in the manufacture.

NIB	Exc.	V.G.	Good	Fair	Poor
—	47	5	350	225	125

GP-100

This model is chambered for the .327 Federal or .357 Magnum/.38 Special. It is available with fixed or adjustable sights in barrel lengths of 3", 4", or 6" barrel and has a frame designed for constant use of heavy magnum loads. The rear sight has a white outline, and the front sight features interchangeable colored inserts. The finish is blued, and the grips are a new design made of rubber with smooth Goncalo Alves inserts. This model was introduced in 1986. Discontinued.

NIB	Exc.	V.G.	Good	Fair	Poor
425	375	200	150	125	100

GP-100 Stainless

This model is the same as the GP-100 except that the material used is stainless steel.

NIB	Exc.	V.G.	Good	Fair	Poor
450	385	225	150	150	100

SP-101

This model is similar in appearance to the GP-100 but has a smaller frame and is chambered for the .22 LR (6-shot), .38 Special (5-shot), .357 Magnum (5-shot), and 9mm (5-shot). The grips are all black synthetic, and the sights are adjustable for windage. Barrel lengths are 2" or 3", and construction is of stainless steel. This model was introduced in 1989. 6" barrel is available for .22 caliber. .327 Federal Magnum chambering added 2008. Add $100 for Crimson Trace lasergrips (limited edition for 2008).

NIB	Exc.	V.G.	Good	Fair	Poor
525	425	300	200	150	125

SP-101 Spurless-Hammer

This model was introduced in 1993 and features an SP-101 without an exposed hammer spur. Available in two calibers: .38 Special and .357 Magnum with 2-1/4" barrel. This double-action revolver has fixed sights, holds 5 rounds and weighs about 26 oz.

NIB	Exc.	V.G.	Good	Fair	Poor
515	375	300	250	200	150

Redhawk

This model is a large-frame, double-action revolver which was chambered for the .357 and .41 Magnums until 1992, and currently for the .44 Magnum and .45 Colt cartridges. The barrel lengths are 5-1/2" and 7-1/2". The finish is blued, and the grips are smooth walnut. The Redhawk was introduced in 1979. Add 100 percent for .357 and 50 percent for .41.

NIB	Exc.	V.G.	Good	Fair	Poor
550	475	350	250	200	150

Redhawk Stainless Steel

The same as the blued version except constructed of stainless steel. It was chambered for .357 Magnum until 1985, the .41 Magnum until 1992, and currently for the .44 Magnum. In 1998 this model was offered chambered for .45 Long Colt cartridge in barrel lengths of 4", 5.5" and 7.5". Add 100 percent for .357 and 50 percent for .41.

NIB	Exc.	V.G.	Good	Fair	Poor
575	500	400	275	200	150

Redhawk 4-Inch .45 Colt (2008)

Similar to original stainless Redhawk but in .45 Colt only and with a 4-inch barrel. Hogue molded grips.

NIB	Exc.	V.G.	Good	Fair	Poor
600	500	375	250	175	150

Super Redhawk

This is a more massive version of the Redhawk. It weighs 53 oz. and is offered with a 7.5" or 9.5" barrel. It is made of stainless steel with either brushed or dull grey finish, and the barrel rib is milled to accept the Ruger scope-ring system. The grips are the combination rubber and Goncalo Alves-type found on the GP-100. This revolver was introduced in 1987. In 1999 this model was offered chambered for the .454 Casull cartridge with 7.5" or 9.5" barrel. In 2001 this model was offered in .480 Ruger caliber in 7.5" or 9.5" barrel. Also available ijn .44 Magnum.

NIB	Exc.	V.G.	Good	Fair	Poor
740	550	400	275	200	150

NOTE: Add $200 for .454 Casull or .480 Ruger caliber. Revolvers chambered for the .454 Casull also accept .45 Long Colt cartridges.

Super Redhawk Alaskan

This revolver is chambered for the .454 Casull and the .45 Colt interchangeable or the .480 Ruger cartridge. Barrel length is 2.5" with adjustable rear sight. Cylinder capacity is 6 rounds. Stainless steel finish. Hogue Tamer rubber grips. Weight is about 42 oz. Introduced in 2005. .44 Magnum chambering added 2007.

NIB	Exc.	V.G.	Good	Fair	Poor
850	700	500	375	250	200

Police Service-Six

This model is also known as the Model 107, chambered for .357 Magnum; the Model 108, chambered for the .38 Special; and the 109, chambered for the 9mm. The barrel is 2.75" or 4". A few 6" barrel Service-Sixes were also produced and these are worth a premium. It has fixed sights and a square butt, with checkered walnut grips. The finish is blued. The 9mm was discontinued in 1984; the other two calibers, in 1988. Add 60 percent for 9mm.

NIB	Exc.	V.G.	Good	Fair	Poor
—	375	300	200	150	100

LCR Lightweight Compact Revolver

Polymer-framer compact revolver chambered in .38 Special +P. Features include a five-shot stainless steel cylinder finished in Advanced Target Gray, 1.875" stainless steel barrel, fixed sights, Hogue or Crimson Trace grips, matte black frame. Overall length 6.5". Weight: 13 oz.

NIB	Exc.	V.G.	Good	Fair	Poor
450	400	325	200	150	100

LCR with Crimson Trace Grips

Similar to above but with CT laser grips.

NIB	Exc.	V.G.	Good	Fair	Poor
700	650	575	300	225	150

SEMI-AUTOMATIC CENTERFIRE HANDGUNS

P-85 or P-89

This model represents Ruger's entry into the wonder-nine market. The P-85 is a double-action, high-capacity (15-shot detachable magazine) semi-automatic, with an alloy frame and steel slide. It has a 4.5" barrel, ambidextrous safety, and three-dot sighting system. It has a matte black finish and black synthetic grips. The latest option for this model is a decocking device to replace the standard safety. There is also an optional molded locking case and extra magazine with loading tool available. It is more reasonably priced than many of its competitors. This pistol was introduced in 1987 and was sold at large premium for some time due to limited supply and great demand. As of this writing, Ruger is producing this pistol in a new plant in Prescott, Arizona; and the premium situation no longer exists. This model is also produced in a 9x21 cartridge for non-NATO countries. In 1991 the internal mechanism was changed slightly with the result that a name change occurred "P85 Mark II" .

NIB	Exc.	V.G.	Good	Fair	Poor
435	360	300	275	200	150

P85 Stainless Steel

This model is the same as the matte black version except that the receiver assembly is made of stainless steel.

NIB	Exc.	V.G.	Good	Fair	Poor
475	375	325	295	200	150

KP89X

Introduced in 1993 this pistol features a stainless steel convertible safety model which comes with both 9mm and .30 Luger barrels. The barrels are interchangeable without the use of tools. Magazine capacity is 15 rounds. Less than 6,000 produced.

NIB	Exc.	V.G.	Good	Fair	Poor
420	380	345	245	200	150

P89

Introduced in 1991 this semi-automatic pistol is chambered for the 9mm cartridge. It has a blued finish and a 15-round magazine. The safety is a manual ambidextrous lever type. The barrel is 4.5" and the empty weight is approximately 36 oz.

NIB	Exc.	V.G.	Good	Fair	Poor
350	300	200	150	100	80

KP89

This model is the same configuration as the P89 but furnished with a stainless steel finish. Introduced in 1991.

NIB	Exc.	V.G.	Good	Fair	Poor
400	300	250	200	150	100

P89DC

This model features a blued finish and is chambered for the 9mm Parabellum cartridge but is fitted with a decock-only lever (no manual safety). After decocking the gun can be fired by a double-action pull of the trigger.

NIB	Exc.	V.G.	Good	Fair	Poor
445	375	350	250	200	150

KP89DC

This is the stainless steel version of the P89DC with decock only.

NIB	Exc.	V.G.	Good	Fair	Poor
425	375	350	250	200	150

KP89DAO

Chambered for the 9mm cartridge this model is the stainless steel double-action-only version of the above model.

NIB	Exc.	V.G.	Good	Fair	Poor
425	375	350	250	200	150

KP90

Chambered for the .45 ACP cartridge, this model is in stainless steel and holds 7 rounds in the magazine. It is fitted with a manual safety. Introduced in 1991.

NIB	Exc.	V.G.	Good	Fair	Poor
475	375	275	200	150	100

KP90DC

This stainless steel version of the KP90 has a decock-only system. Chambered for the .45 ACP cartridge.

NIB	Exc.	V.G.	Good	Fair	Poor
475	375	275	200	150	100

P90

Same as above model but with blued finish. Introduced in 1998.

NIB	Exc.	V.G.	Good	Fair	Poor
450	350	275	200	150	100

KP91DC

This model features a stainless steel finish and is chambered for the .40 S&W cartridge. Magazine capacity is 11 rounds. It has a decock-only system. Introduced in 1992. Discontinued.

NIB	Exc.	V.G.	Good	Fair	Poor
475	375	325	295	200	150

KP91DAO

Chambered for the .40 S&W with stainless steel finish it features a double-action-only system. Discontinued.

NIB	Exc.	V.G.	Good	Fair	Poor
475	375	325	295	200	150

P93D

This is a blued version with ambidextrous decocker and 3.9" barrel. Introduced in 1998.

NIB	Exc.	V.G.	Good	Fair	Poor
400	300	250	200	150	100

KP93DC

Introduced in 1993 this pistol is a new addition to the P series as a compact model. Stainless steel and chambered for the 9mm cartridge it has a magazine capacity of 15 rounds. Available in decock-only configuration. Barrel length is 3.9" and the weight is about 24 oz. empty.

NIB	Exc.	V.G.	Good	Fair	Poor
500	400	300	250	150	100

KP93DAO

The double-action-only version of the KP93 compact series.

NIB	Exc.	V.G.	Good	Fair	Poor
490	400	300	250	150	100

KP94

Introduced in 1994 this model is smaller than the full-size P series pistols and the compact P93 pistols. Offered in 9mm or .40 S&W calibers this pistol has an aluminum alloy frame and stainless steel slide. Barrel length is 4-1/4" and magazine capacity for the 9mm is

15 rounds and for the .40 11 rounds. Weight is approximately 33 oz. It is offered in double-action-only as well as traditional double-action. A decock-only model is available also.

NIB	Exc.	V.G.	Good	Fair	Poor
415	350	300	250	200	150

KP94DC

This is similar to the model above but in decock only.

NIB	Exc.	V.G.	Good	Fair	Poor
415	350	300	250	200	150

P94

This is a blued version of the KP94. Introduced in 1998.

NIB	Exc.	V.G.	Good	Fair	Poor
400	300	250	200	150	100

KP94DAO

Same as the KP94 model but in double-action-only.

NIB	Exc.	V.G.	Good	Fair	Poor
400	350	300	250	200	150

KP944

Chambered for the .40 S&W cartridge this model has a stainless steel tapered slide, an 11-round magazine, and a manual safety. Models made after September 1994 have a 10-round magazine.

NIB	Exc.	V.G.	Good	Fair	Poor
415	350	300	250	200	150

KP944DC

Same as a model above but fitted with a decock-only system.

NIB	Exc.	V.G.	Good	Fair	Poor
415	350	300	250	200	150

KP944DAO

Same as model above but with a double-action-only model of fire.

NIB	Exc.	V.G.	Good	Fair	Poor
415	350	300	250	200	150

P95

Introduced in 1996 this 9mm pistol features a 3.9" barrel, polymer frame and stainless steel slide. Decocker only. Fixed 3-dot sights are standard. Overall length is 7.3". Empty weight is about 29 oz. In 2001 this model was offered with a manual safety and blued finish.

NIB	Exc.	V.G.	Good	Fair	Poor
450	350	300	225	150	100

KP95DC

This model is the same as the matte black version of the P95, only this is in stainless steel. It has a decock only safety.

NIB	Exc.	V.G.	Good	Fair	Poor
450	350	300	225	150	100

P95DAO

Same as above but in double-action-only.

NIB	Exc.	V.G.	Good	Fair	Poor
450	350	300	225	150	100

KP95DAO

Same as the model above but in double-action-only. In 2001 this model was offered with a manual safety and blued finish.

300 guns built.

NIB	Exc.	V.G.	Good	Fair	Poor
450	350	300	225	150	100

KP97D

Introduced in 1999 this decock-only model is chambered for the .45 ACP cartridge. It has a stainless steel slide. Magazine capacity is 7 rounds. Fixed sights. Weight is about 27 oz.

NIB	Exc.	V.G.	Good	Fair	Poor
450	350	300	225	150	100

KP97DAO

Same specifications as the model above but in double-action-only. Introduced in 1999.

NIB	Exc.	V.G.	Good	Fair	Poor
450	350	300	225	150	100

KP345

Introduced in 2004 this .45 ACP model features a 4.2" stainless steel barrel and stainless steel slide. Fixed sights. Internal lock, loaded chamber indicator, magazine disconnect, and a new cam block design to reduce recoil. Black polymer checkered grips. Magazine capacity is 8 rounds. Weight is about 29 oz. Available with ambidextrous safety or decocker.

NIB	Exc.	V.G.	Good	Fair	Poor
550	425	300	250	175	125

KP345PR

Similar to the model above but fitted with a Picatinny-style rail under the forward portion of the frame. Introduced in 2004.

NIB	Exc.	V.G.	Good	Fair	Poor
550	425	300	250	175	125

SR9 / SR40

Introduced in 2008. Ruger's first striker-fired semi-auto pistol. Chambered in 9mm Parabellum or .40 S&W. Double-action only with 4.14-inch barrel, 17+1 capacity. Available in three finish configurations: stainless steel slide with matte black frame; blackened stainless slide with matte black frame; and blackened stainless slide with matte black frame. Note: Ruger recalled all early-production SR9 pistols with a "330" serial number prefix because of a potential safety issue. SR40 has a 15-round magazine.

NIB	Exc.	V.G.	Good	Fair	Poor
450	350	300	225	150	100

SR9c Compact Pistol

Compact double action only semiauto pistol chambered in 9mm Parabellum. Features include 1911-style ambidextrous manual safety; internal trigger bar interlock and striker blocker; trigger safety; magazine disconnector; loaded chamber indicator; two magazines, one 10-round and the other 17-round; 3.5-inch barrel; 3-dot sights; accessory rail; brushed stainless or blackened alloy finish. Weight 23.40 oz. MSRP: $525.

LCP (Lightweight Compact Pistol)

Introduced in 2008. Ruger's first true pocket pistol. Chambered in .380 (6+1 capacity) with a 2.75-inch barrel. Double action only. Glass-filled nylon frame with steel barrel. Black matte finish.

NIB	Exc.	V.G.	Good	Fair	Poor
350	300	250	200	150	100

LCP Crimson Trace

Similar to above but with CT laser grips.

300 guns built.

NIB	Exc.	V.G.	Good	Fair	Poor
590	475	375	250	200	150

LC9

Subcompact 9mm pistol designed for concealed carry. Magazine capacity is seven rounds, barrel length is 3.12-inches and weight: 17.1 ounces. Steel slide, glass-filled nylon receiver, double-action-only trigger, hammer-fired operation. Three-dot sights, loaded-chamber indicator, manual safety, magazine disconnect and slide stop.

NIB	Exc.	V.G.	Good	Fair	Poor
385	335	285	200	150	100

NOTE: Add $100 for Crimson Trace LG-431 laser sight.

SR1911

After years of rumors, there is a Ruger 1911 pistol. Caliber .45 ACP, stainless steel slide and frame, 8-round magazine, extended thumb safety, grip tang and magazine release, Novak Lo-Mount 3-dot sights, checkered mainspring housing and hardwood grips. Standard 1911 dimensions and controls. Introduced in 2011.

NIB	Exc.	V.G.	Good	Fair	Poor
685	600	500	375	225	150

SUNDANCE INDUSTRIES, INC.
North Hollywood, California

This company was in business from 1989 to 2002.

Model D-22M

A .22 or .22 Magnum caliber double-barrel over-and-under pocket pistol with 2.5" barrels and an aluminum alloy frame. Blackened finish or chrome-plated with either simulated pearl or black grips. Introduced in 1989.

NIB	Exc.	V.G.	Good	Fair	Poor
—	225	175	125	100	75

Model BOA

Introduced in 1991 this semi-automatic pistol is chambered for the .25 ACP cartridge. Fitted with a 2.5" barrel with fixed sights. Grip safety. Choice of black or chrome finish. Magazine capacity is 7 rounds. Weight is about 16 oz.

NIB	Exc.	V.G.	Good	Fair	Poor
125	100	80	70	50	25

Model A-25

Similar to the BOA but without grip safety.

NIB	Exc.	V.G.	Good	Fair	Poor
125	100	80	70	50	25

Model Laser 25

Similar to the Model BOA with grip safety but equipped with a laser sight. Laser activated by squeezing grip safety. Weight with laser 18 oz. Introduced in 1995.

NIB	Exc.	V.G.	Good	Fair	Poor
220	175	125	100	75	50

Sundance Point Blank

This is an over-and-under derringer chambered for the .22 LR cartridge. It is fitted with a 3" barrel and double-action trigger. Enclosed hammer. Matte black finish. Weight is about 8 oz. Introduced in 1994.

NIB	Exc.	V.G.	Good	Fair	Poor
95	80	70	50	25	10

SUPER SIX LTD.
Fort Atkinson, Wisconsin

Bison Bull

Massive single-action .45-70 revolver with blued carbon steel (Bison Bull) or engraved molybdenum bronze (Golden Bison Bull) frame. Adjustable sights, 10.5" barrel, 17.5" overall length, weight 6 lbs. Introduced 2006. Value shown is for blued version. Add 350 percent for engraved version.

NIB	Exc.	V.G.	Good	Fair	Poor
1200	1050	900	775	600	500

SUTHERLAND, S.
Richmond, Virginia

Pocket Pistol

A .41 caliber percussion single-shot pistol with round barrels of 2.5" to 4" in length, German silver mounts and a walnut stock. The lock normally marked "S. Sutherland" or "S. Sutherland/Richmond" . Manufactured during the 1850s.

NIB	Exc.	V.G.	Good	Fair	Poor
—	—	2950	2200	800	300

SYMS, J. G.
New York, New York

Pocket Pistol

A .41 caliber single-shot percussion pistol with 1.5" to 3.5" barrels, German silver mounts and a walnut stock. The lock normally marked "Syms/New York" . Manufactured during the 1850s.

NIB	Exc.	V.G.	Good	Fair	Poor
—	—	2600	2150	825	300

T

TANFOGLIO
Valtrompia, Italy

The products of this company, which was established in the late 1940s, have been imported into the United States by various companies including Eig Corporation, F.I.E. of Hialeah, Florida, and Excam.

Sata

A .22 or 6.35mm caliber semi-automatic pistol with a 3" barrel. The slide marked "Pistola SATA Made in Italy" and the grips "SATA." Blued with black plastic grips.

NIB	Exc.	V.G.	Good	Fair	Poor
—	250	175	125	90	75

Titan

A 6.35mm caliber semi-automatic pistol with a 2.5" barrel and external hammer. The slide marked "Titan 6.35" and on U.S. imported examples, "EIG." Blued with plastic grips.

NIB	Exc.	V.G.	Good	Fair	Poor
—	250	175	125	90	75

Super Titan

Similar in design to above but with larger frame and in .380 ACP. Walnut grips.

NIB	Exc.	V.G.	Good	Fair	Poor
—	265	195	150	125	95

TA 90 or TZ-75

A 9mm caliber semi-automatic pistol with a 4.75" barrel and 15-shot magazine. Blued or chrome-plated with walnut or rubber grips. Those imported by Excam were known as the Model TA 90, while those imported by F.I.E. are known as the Model TZ-75.

NIB	Exc.	V.G.	Good	Fair	Poor
450	400	350	300	250	200

TA 90B

As above, with a 3.5" barrel, 12-shot magazine and Neoprene grips. Introduced in 1986.

NIB	Exc.	V.G.	Good	Fair	Poor
450	400	350	300	250	200

TA 90 SS

As above, with a ported 5" barrel, adjustable sights and two-tone finish. Introduced in 1989.

NIB	Exc.	V.G.	Good	Fair	Poor
650	600	500	450	400	300

TA 41 AE

As above, in .41 Action Express caliber. Introduced in 1989.

NIB	Exc.	V.G.	Good	Fair	Poor
500	450	400	350	300	250

TA 41 SS

As above, with a ported 5" barrel, adjustable sights and two-tone finish. Introduced in 1989.

NIB	Exc.	V.G.	Good	Fair	Poor
650	600	500	450	400	300

TA 76

A .22 caliber single-action revolver with a 4.75" barrel and 6-shot cylinder. Blued or chrome-plated with a brass back strap and trigger guard. Walnut grips.

NIB	Exc.	V.G.	Good	Fair	Poor
100	90	80	65	50	25

TA 76M Combo

As above, with a 6" or 9" barrel and an interchangeable .22 Magnum caliber cylinder.

NIB	Exc.	V.G.	Good	Fair	Poor
110	100	90	75	60	35

TA 38SB

A .38 Special caliber over-and-under double-barrel pocket pistol with 3" barrels and a hammer block safety. Blued with checkered nylon grips. Discontinued in 1985.

NIB	Exc.	V.G.	Good	Fair	Poor
—	100	90	80	60	40

TAURUS INTERNATIONAL MFG. CO.
Porto Alegre, Brazil

PISTOLS

PT-92C

This 9mm model is a large capacity semi-automatic pistol with a 4.25" barrel. Drift adjustable 3-dot combat rear sight. Magazine holds 13 rounds in a double column. Choice of blued, stain nickel, or stainless steel finish. Brazilian hardwood grips are standard. Weighs 31 oz.

NIB	Exc.	V.G.	Good	Fair	Poor
450	325	275	220	160	100

PT-92

A slightly larger and heavier version of the PT-92C. This model has a 5" barrel with drift adjustable 3-dot combat rear sight. Magazine capacity is 15 rounds. This model is 1" longer overall than the above model and weighs 34 oz. Also available in blued, nickel, and stainless steel.

NIB	Exc.	V.G.	Good	Fair	Poor
400	300	225	150	100	75

NOTE: Add $20 for stainless steel and $50 for blue with gold finish, $60 for stainless steel with gold accents. A blued or stainless steel .22 LR conversion kit will add $250.

PT-99

Similar in appearance and specifications to the PT-92, this version has the additional feature of fully adjustable 3-dot rear sight.

NIB	Exc.	V.G.	Good	Fair	Poor
425	325	250	150	100	75

NOTE: Add $20 for stainless steel finish.

PT-92AF

A 9mm caliber double-action semi-automatic pistol with a 4.92" barrel, exposed hammer, and 15-shot magazine. Blued or nickel-plated with plain walnut grips.

NIB	Exc.	V.G.	Good	Fair	Poor
400	350	300	250	200	150

PT-100

This model is similar to the other full-size Taurus semi-automatics except that it is chambered for the .40 S&W cartridge. Supplied with a 5" barrel, with drift adjustable rear sight, it has a magazine capacity of 11 rounds. Also available in blued, nickel, or stainless steel. Weighs 34 oz.

NIB	Exc.	V.G.	Good	Fair	Poor
500	400	300	200	150	100

NOTE: For Special Edition, blued steel with gold fixtures and rosewood grips add $50. For blued steel with gold fixtures and pearl grips add $110.

PT-101

Same as the model above but furnished with fully adjustable rear 3-dot combat sight.

NIB	Exc.	V.G.	Good	Fair	Poor
450	350	300	250	150	100

Deluxe Shooter's Pak

Offered by Taurus as a special package it consists of the pistol, with extra magazine, in a fitted custom hard case. Available for these models: PT-92, PT-99, PT-100, and PT-101.NOTE: Add approximately 10 percent to the prices of these models for this special feature.

PT-111

This is a double-action-only pistol chambered for the 9mm cartridge. Fitted with a 3.3" barrel and polymer frame. Magazine capacity is 10 rounds. Weight is about 16 oz. Choice of blue or stainless steel. Introduced in 1997.

NIB	Exc.	V.G.	Good	Fair	Poor
350	250	200	175	150	100

NOTE: Add $20 for stainless steel finish.

PT-138

Introduced in 1998 this polymer frame pistol is chambered for the .380 cartridge. It is fitted with a 4" barrel in either blue or stainless steel. Weight is about 16 oz. Magazine capacity is 10 rounds.

Blue

NIB	Exc.	V.G.	Good	Fair	Poor
350	250	200	175	125	100

Stainless Steel

NIB	Exc.	V.G.	Good	Fair	Poor
375	275	225	175	125	100

PT-908

A semi-automatic double-action pistol chambered for the 9mm Parabellum cartridge. It is fitted with a 3.8" barrel, with drift adjustable rear 3-dot combat sight. Magazine capacity is 8 rounds in a single column. Available in blued, satin nickel, or stainless steel. Stocks are black rubber. Pistol weighs 30 oz. Introduced in 1993.

NIB	Exc.	V.G.	Good	Fair	Poor
375	325	275	225	150	100

PT-911

This model was introduced in 1997 and is chambered for the 9mm cartridge. It is fitted with a 4" barrel and has a magazine capacity of 10 rounds. Choice of blue or stainless steel. Weight is about 28 oz. Black rubber grips are standard.

NIB	Exc.	V.G.	Good	Fair	Poor
450	350	275	225	175	125

NOTE: Add $20 for stainless steel.

PT-111

Chambered for the 9mm cartridge and fitted with a 3.25" barrel. Magazine is 10 rounds. Weight is about 19 oz.

NIB	Exc.	V.G.	Good	Fair	Poor
375	300	250	175	125	100

NOTE: For matte stainless steel finish add $15. For night sights add $80.

PT-140

Chambered for the .40 S&W cartridge and fitted with a 3.25" barrel. Magazine capacity is 10 rounds. Weight is about 19 oz.

NIB	Exc.	V.G.	Good	Fair	Poor
350	300	265	1\xd4 80	125	100

NOTE: For matte stainless steel finish add $15. For night sights add $80.

PT-140 MILLENNIUM

Chambered for the .40 S&W cartridge and fitted with a 3.25" barrel, this model features a polymer frame and either a blue or stainless steel slide. Fixed sights. Magazine capacity is 10 rounds. Weight is about 19 oz.

Blue

NIB	Exc.	V.G.	Good	Fair	Poor
345	315	225	150	100	75

Stainless Steel

NIB	Exc.	V.G.	Good	Fair	Poor
375	325	250	175	100	75

NOTE: For night sights add $75.

PT-145 MILLENNIUM

Similar to the PT-140 but chambered for the .45 ACP cartridge. Barrel length is 3.27". Weight is about 23 oz. Magazine capacity is 10 rounds. Weight is about 19 oz.

Blue

NIB	Exc.	V.G.	Good	Fair	Poor
345	315	225	150	100	75

Stainless Steel

NIB	Exc.	V.G.	Good	Fair	Poor
375	325	250	175	100	75

NOTE: For night sights add $75.

Taurus Model 609TI-PRO

Similar to Millennium Pro but with titanium slide. Chambered in 9mm Parabellum. Features include 13+1 capacity, 3.25" barrel, checkered polymer grips, Heinie Straight-8 sights. Overall length 6.125". Weight: 19.7 oz.

NIB	Exc.	V.G.	Good	Fair	Poor
500	450	325	225	175	125

PT-400/400SS

Chambered for the .400 CorBon cartridge and fitted with a 4.25" ported barrel with fixed sights. Magazine capacity is 8 rounds. Offered in blue or stainless steel. Rubber grips. Weight is about 30 oz.

Blue

NIB	Exc.	V.G.	Good	Fair	Poor
375	300	200	150	100	75

Stainless Steel

NIB	Exc.	V.G.	Good	Fair	Poor
420	325	225	150	100	75

PT-132

Chambered for the .32 ACP cartridge and fitted with a 3.25" barrel. Magazine capacity is 10 rounds. Weight is about 20 oz.

NIB	Exc.	V.G.	Good	Fair	Poor
325	275	200	150	100	75

NOTE: For matte stainless steel finish add $15.

PT-58

This model was introduced in 1988. Chambered for the .380 ACP cartridge it is fitted with a 4" barrel with drift adjustable rear sight. It is a conventional double-action design. Available in blued, satin nickel, or stainless steel. It is fitted with Brazilian hardwood grips. Pistol weighs 30 oz.

NIB	Exc.	V.G.	Good	Fair	Poor
300	250	200	150	100	75

PT-138

Chambered for the .380 ACP cartridge and fitted with a 3.25" barrel. Magazine capacity is 10 rounds. Weight is about 19 oz.

NIB	Exc.	V.G.	Good	Fair	Poor
350	300	245	195	150	125

NOTE: For matte stainless steel finish add $15.

PT-145

Chambered for the .45 ACP cartridge and fitted with a 3.25" barrel. Magazine capacity is 10 rounds. Weight is about 23 oz.

NIB	Exc.	V.G.	Good	Fair	Poor
325	275	250	200	150	100

NOTE: For matte stainless steel finish add $15. For night sights add $80.

PT-45

Introduced in 1994 this semi-automatic double-action pistol is chambered for the .45 ACP cartridge. The barrel is 3-3/4" in length and the magazine capacity is 8 rounds. Offered in blued or stainless steel with grips of Brazilian hardwood. Fixed sights are standard. Overall length is 7.1" and weight is approximately 30 oz.

Blue

NIB	Exc.	V.G.	Good	Fair	Poor
350	275	200	150	100	75

Stainless Steel

NIB	Exc.	V.G.	Good	Fair	Poor
400	325	250	200	150	100

PT-745B/SS

Chambered for the .45 ACP cartridge and fitted with a 3.25" barrel. Fixed sights. Polymer grips. Blue or stainless steel. Magazine capacity is 6 rounds. Weight is about 21 oz. Introduced in 2004.

NIB	Exc.	V.G.	Good	Fair	Poor
375	315	275	225	125	175

NOTE: Add $15 for stainless steel.

PT-640B/SS

Similar to the above model but chambered for the .40 S&W cartridge. Magazine capacity is 10 rounds. Weight is about 24 oz. Introduced in in 2004.

NIB	Exc.	V.G.	Good	Fair	Poor
375	315	275	225	125	175

NOTE: Add $15 for stainless steel.

PT-24/7-45B

This .45 ACP pistol is fitted with a 4.25" barrel with fixed sights. Ribbed grips. Blued receiver. Magazine capacity is 12 rounds. Weight is about 27 oz. Introduced in 2004.

NIB	Exc.	V.G.	Good	Fair	Poor
400	300	285	225	150	100

NOTE: Add $15 for stainless steel slide.

24/7 G2

Double/single action sem-iauto pistol chambered in 9mm Parabellum (15+1), .40 S&W (13+1), and .45 ACP (10+1).

Features include blued or stainless finish; "Strike Two" capability; new trigger safety; low-profile adjustable rear sights for windage and elevation; ambidextrous magazine release; 4.2-inch barrel; Picatinny rail; polymer frame; polymer grip with metallic inserts and three interchangeable backstraps. Also offered in compact model with shorter grip frame and 3.5-inch barrel.

NIB	Exc.	V.G.	Good	Fair	Poor
425	350	300	250	175	125

24/7-PRO Standard Series

4" barrel; stainless, duotone or blued finish.

NIB	Exc.	V.G.	Good	Fair	Poor
400	300	285	225	150	100

24/7-PRO Compact Series

3.2" barrel; stainless, titanium or blued finish.

NIB	Exc.	V.G.	Good	Fair	Poor
400	300	285	225	150	100

24/7-PRO Long Slide Series

NIB	Exc.	V.G.	Good	Fair	Poor
400	300	285	225	150	100

PT-24/7-9B

As above but chambered for the 9mm cartridge. Magazine capacity is 17 rounds. Weight is about 27 oz. Introduced in 2005.

NIB	Exc.	V.G.	Good	Fair	Poor
400	300	285	225	150	100

NOTE: Add $15 for stainless steel slide.

PT-24/7-40B

As above but chambered for the .40 S&W cartridge. Magazine capacity is 15 rounds. Weight is about 27 oz. Introduced in 2005.

NIB	Exc.	V.G.	Good	Fair	Poor
400	300	285	225	150	100

NOTE: Add $15 for stainless steel slide.

PT-24/7LS-9SS-17

Full-size stainless semi-auto chambered for 9mm. Long grip, long slide. Capacity 17+1. Single/double action. 5" barrel, 27.2 oz. Fixed, 2-dot rear sight. Also in short grip 10+1 capacity. Introduced 2006. Price is for stainless.

NIB	Exc.	V.G.	Good	Fair	Poor
425	345	295	245	175	125

PT-24/79SSC-17

Compact stainless semi-auto chambered for 9mm, short grip, short slide. Capacity 15+1. Single/double action. 5" barrel, 27.2 oz. Fixed, 2-dot rear sight. Also in short grip 10+1 capacity. Introduced 2006. Price is for stainless.

NIB	Exc.	V.G.	Good	Fair	Poor
400	300	285	225	150	100

PT-24/7PLS-9SSPTi-17

Full-size semi-auto chambered for 9mm. Capacity 17+1 or 10+1. Single/double action. Titanium slide, 4" barrel, 27.2 oz. Introduced 2006.

NIB	Exc.	V.G.	Good	Fair	Poor
400	300	285	225	150	100

24/7 OSS

Introduced in 2007. Available in .45 ACP, .40 S&W and 9mm Parabellum. 12+1 capacity (.45), single-/double-action. Ambidextrous decock and safety, match grade barrel, polymer frame with steel upper. Claimed to exceed all requirements set by United States Special Operations Command and developed to compete is SOCOM pistol trials. Add 5 percent for stainless.

NIB	Exc.	V.G.	Good	Fair	Poor
425	345	295	245	175	125

PT-24/7PLS-9SSCTi-17

Compact semi-auto chambered for 9mm. Capacity 17+1. Single/double action. Titanium slide, 3.3" barrel, 25.4 oz. Introduced 2006.

NIB	Exc.	V.G.	Good	Fair	Poor
425	345	295	245	175	125

24/7PLS

Similar to above but with 5" barrel. Chambered in 9mm Parabellum, .38 Super, and .40 S&W.

NIB	Exc.	V.G.	Good	Fair	Poor
425	345	295	245	175	125

Taurus Model 2045 Large Frame Pistol

Similar to Taurus Model 24/7 but chambered in .45 ACP only. Features include polymer frame, blued or matte stainless steel slide, 4.2" barrel, ambidextrous "memory pads" to promote safe finger position during loading, ambi three-position safety/decocker, Picatinny rail system, fixed sights. Overall length 7.34". Weight: 31.5 oz.

NIB	Exc.	V.G.	Good	Fair	Poor
450	375	325	250	175	125

809-B 9mm

Introduced in 2008. Basically a Model 24/7 OSS but with an exposed hammer. 17+1 capacity, black Tenifer finish.

Ambidextrous Three-Position Safety and Decocker

17+1 Rounds

NIB	Exc.	V.G.	Good	Fair	Poor
550	425	350	275	200	150

Taurus 800 Series Compact

Compact double/single action semi-auto pistol chambered in 9mm (12+1), .357 SIG (10+1) and .40 cal (10+1). Features include 3.5-inch barrel; external hammer; loaded chamber indicator; polymer frame; blued or stainless slide.

NIB	Exc.	V.G.	Good	Fair	Poor
485	410	350	275	200	150

Taurus 822

Compact double/single action semi-auto pistol chambered in .22 LR (10+1). Features include ambidextrous magazine release; external hammer; checkered grip; adjustable sights; 4.5-inch or 6-inch barrel; loaded chamber indicator; and Picatinny rail. Centerfire-to-rimfire conversion kit also available. Introduced in 2010 with MSRP of $586. As of mid 2011, has not gone into production.

PT191140B

1911-style .40 caliber semi-auto. Blued or Stainless steel. 5" barrel, 8+1 capacity, 32 oz. Fixed Heinie two-dot straight-eight sight. Blue or stainless. Introduced 2006. Add 10 percent for stainless.

NIB	Exc.	V.G.	Good	Fair	Poor
675	550	425	300	200	125

PT1911

Blued or stainless 1911-style single action in .45 ACP. 8+1 capacity. LOA 8.5", 32 oz., 5" barrel, fixed Heinie two-dot straight-eight sight. Numerous options. Add 10 percent for stainless. Introduced 2006. Add 10 percent for alloy frame and picatinny rail versions (added 2007).

NIB	Exc.	V.G.	Good	Fair	Poor
675	550	425	300	200	125

Model 1911B-9

Similar to above but chambered in 9mm Parabellum (9+1).

NIB	Exc.	V.G.	Good	Fair	Poor
675	550	425	300	200	125

Model 1911B-38

Similar to above but chambered in .38 Super.

NIB	Exc.	V.G.	Good	Fair	Poor
675	550	425	300	200	125

Model 1911HC

Similar to Taurus Model 1911 but with 12+1 capacity; .45 ACP only.

NIB	Exc.	V.G.	Good	Fair	Poor
725	600	475	375	250	150

PT-745GB

Blued semi-auto in .45 GAP with 7+1 capacity. 3.25" barrel, fixed sights, 22 oz., polymer grip plates. Introduced 2006.

NIB	Exc.	V.G.	Good	Fair	Poor
375	300	225	175	125	100

PT745B/SS-LS

Blued or stainless semi-auto in .45 ACP. 4.25" barrel, 23.3 oz. 7+1 capacity, polymer grip plates. Introduced 2006.

NIB	Exc.	V.G.	Good	Fair	Poor
375	300	225	175	125	100

PT917B20

9mm blued or stainless semi-auto with 20+1 capacity. Fixed sights, 4" barrel, 31.8 oz. Introduced 2006.

NIB	Exc.	V.G.	Good	Fair	Poor
375	300	225	175	125	100

PT609Ti-13

This 9mm semi-auto has a titanium finish plus 13+1 capacity, 3.25" barrel. Fixed sights, 19.2 oz. Introduced 2006.

NIB	Exc.	V.G.	Good	Fair	Poor
500	425	300	225	150	100

PT138BP12 Millenium Pro

Blued or stainless SA/DA semi-auto in .380 ACP with 12+1 capacity. Fixed sights, 3-1/4" barrel, 18.7 oz. Introduced 2006. Also available in .32 ACP and .40 S&W.

NIB	Exc.	V.G.	Good	Fair	Poor
400	300	285	225	150	100

PT-38B/SS

Chambered for the .38 Super cartridge and fitted with a 4.25" barrel with fixed sights. Grips are checkered rubber. Blued or stainless steel. Magazine capacity is 10 rounds. Weight is about 30 oz. Introduced in 2004.

NIB	Exc.	V.G.	Good	Fair	Poor
425	345	295	245	175	125

NOTE: Add $15 for stainless steel.

PT-38SSSPRL

Introduced in 2005 this model is chambered for the .38 Super cartridge and fitted with a 4.25" barrel. Magazine capacity is 10 rounds. Finish is stainless steel and gold. Weight is about 30 oz.

NIB	Exc.	V.G.	Good	Fair	Poor
475	400	300	225	150	100

NOTE: Deduct $60 for stainless steel only.

Model 738 TCP Compact Pistol

Lightweight DAO semi-auto pistol chambered for .380 ACP. Features include a 3.35" barrel; polymer frame; blued (738B), stainless (738SS) or titanium (738Ti) slide; concealed hammer; low-profile fixed sight; ambi safety; loaded chamber indicator. Capacity 6+1 (standard magazine) or 8+1 (extended magazine). Overall length 5.195". Weight: 9 oz. (titanium slide) to 10.2 oz. Suggested retail price: To be announced.

Taurus Model 709 "Slim"

Semi-auto pistol chambered in 9mm Parabellum. Features include a streamlined profile, 3.25" barrel, 7+1 capacity, fixed sights, checkered polymer grips, choice of blued (709B) or stainless (709SS) slide. Single/double action. Overall length 6.25". Weight: 10 oz.

NIB	Exc.	V.G.	Good	Fair	Poor
400	300	285	225	150	100

Taurus 638 Pro Compact

Caliber .380 ACP, steel slide, polymer frame, 15-round magazine. Barrel length is 3.2 inches. Single-action trigger has integral safety. Other features include ambidextrous thumb safety, accessory rail, adjustable rear sight and loaded chamber and cocked striker indicators. Taurus Security System. Weight is 28 ounces. Blue or matte stainless finish.

NIB	Exc.	V.G.	Good	Fair	Poor
410	350	300	250	200	150

Taurus DT Hybrid

Caliber: 9mm Parabellum/.40 S&W, steel slide, polymer/steel frame, 3.2-inch barrel. Magazine capacity is 13 rounds, 11 for .40. Single-action trigger has Strike Two capability. Integral trigger safety, manual safety and Taurus Security System. Ambidextrous magazine release, adjustable rear sight and loaded-chamber indicator. Weight is 24 ounces. Finish is blue or matte stainless.

NIB	Exc.	V.G.	Good	Fair	Poor
465	400	350	285	200	150

PT911

Medium-frame SA semi-auto in 9mm or .40 S&W. Blued steel. 4" barrel, 10+1 capacity. Blue or stainless. Numerous options. Add 10 percent for stainless. Add $25 for tactical light rail.

NIB	Exc.	V.G.	Good	Fair	Poor
400	300	285	225	150	100

Model 917

Lightweight, compact semi-auto chambered in 9mm Parabellum. Matte blue or stainless finish, 17+1 or 20+1 capacity. Introduced 2007.

NIB	Exc.	V.G.	Good	Fair	Poor
400	300	285	225	150	100

PT-945C

Introduced in 1995 this .45 ACP double-action pistol features a 4" barrel with an 8-round magazine. The grips are black rubber. The sights are drift adjustable 3-dot combat style. Approximate weight is 30 oz. Offered in blue or stainless steel with or without ported barrel.

Blue

NIB	Exc.	V.G.	Good	Fair	Poor
450	350	250	200	150	100

NOTE: Add $45 for blued finish with gold accents and ported barrel. Add $35 for ported barrel and blue finish. Add $40 for ported barrel.

Stainless Steel

NIB	Exc.	V.G.	Good	Fair	Poor
475	400	300	250	150	100

NOTE: Add $40 for ported barrel with stainless steel finish or Stainless steel finish with gold accents.

PT-945S

Same as the model above but chambered for the .45 Super cartridge. Introduced in 1998.

Blue

NIB	Exc.	V.G.	Good	Fair	Poor
450	350	250	200	150	100

Stainless Steel

NIB	Exc.	V.G.	Good	Fair	Poor
475	375	275	225	150	100

PT-940

Similar to the PT-945 except chambered for the .40 S&W cartridge. Fitted with a 4" barrel. Magazine capacity is 10 rounds. Choice of blue or stainless steel. Black rubber grips. Weight is approximately 28 oz. Introduced in 1997.

NIB	Exc.	V.G.	Good	Fair	Poor
425	315	265	200	125	75

NOTE: Add $20 for stainless steel.

PT-938

This model is chambered for the .380 ACP cartridge and fitted with a 3" barrel. Black rubber grips and choice of blue or stainless steel. Weight is about 27 oz. Introduced in 1997.

NIB	Exc.	V.G.	Good	Fair	Poor
365	300	245	175	80	50

Model 922 Sport

Introduced in 2003 this semi-automatic .22 caliber pistol features a lightweight polymer frame. Single- or double-action trigger. Barrel length is 6". Magazine capacity is 10 rounds. Adjustable sights. Weight is about 25 oz.

NIB	Exc.	V.G.	Good	Fair	Poor
310	250	175	150	100	75

NOTE: For matte stainless steel finish add $15.

PT-22

This is a semi-automatic double-action-only pistol that features a 2.75" barrel with fixed sights and a manual safety. It is chambered for the .22 LR cartridge and has a magazine capacity of 8 rounds. The stocks are Brazilian hardwood and the finish is available in either blue, blue with gold trim, nickel, or two-tone. Pistol weighs 12.3 oz.

NIB	Exc.	V.G.	Good	Fair	Poor
250	175	250	75	60	50

NOTE: For Special Edition, blued steel with gold fixtures and rosewood grips, add $50. For blued steel with gold fixtures and pearl grips add $110.

PT-922

This .22 caliber pistol has a 6" barrel with fiber optic adjustable sights. Polymer grips. Ten-round magazine. Blued finish. Weight is about 29 oz. Introduced in 2004.

NIB	Exc.	V.G.	Good	Fair	Poor
365	300	245	175	80	50

PT-25

Similar in appearance to the PT-22, this model is chambered for the .25 ACP cartridge and has a magazine capacity of 9 rounds. This model is also fitted with a 2.75" barrel. Offered in blue, blue with gold trim, two-tone finish, or nickel.

NIB	Exc.	V.G.	Good	Fair	Poor
250	175	125	75	60	50

NOTE: For Special Edition, blued steel with gold fixtures and rosewood grips, add $50. For blued steel with gold fixtures and pearl grips add $110.

Model 22PLY/25PLY Small Polymer Frame Pistols

Similar to Taurus Models PT-22 and PT-25 but with lightweight polymer frame. Features include .22 Long Rifle (22PLY, 9+1) or .25 ACP (25PLY, 8+1) chambering, 2.33" tip-up barrel, matte black finish, extended magazine with finger lip, manual safety. Overall length 4.8". Weight 10.8 oz. Suggested retail price: To be announced.

REVOLVERS

Model 17MB2/MSS2

This 8-shot revolver is chambered for the .17 HMR cartridge and fitted with a 1.75" barrel with fixed sights. Blued or stainless steel. Hard rubber grips. Weight is about 22 oz. Introduced in 2004.

NIB	Exc.	V.G.	Good	Fair	Poor
360	280	225	175	150	100

NOTE: Add $45 for stainless steel.

Model 73

A .32 Smith & Wesson Long double-action swing-out cylinder revolver, with a 3" barrel and 6-shot cylinder. Blued or nickel plated with walnut grips.

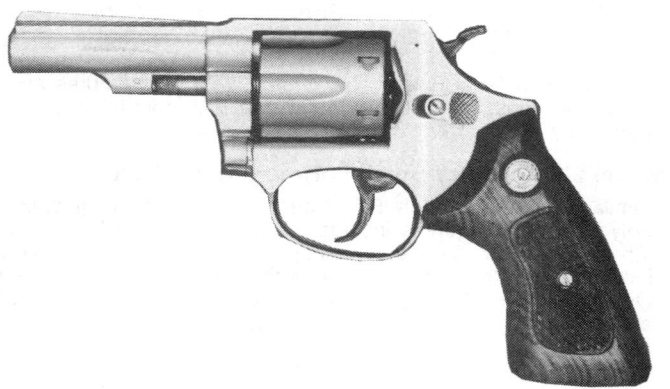

NIB	Exc.	V.G.	Good	Fair	Poor
250	195	150	125	100	75

Model 80

A full-size 6-round .38 Special with 3" or 4" heavy tapered barrel. Supplied with fixed sights and offered with blued or stainless steel (offered new in 1993) finish. Brazilian hardwood grips are standard. Weighs 30 oz.

NIB	Exc.	V.G.	Good	Fair	Poor
285	195	135	110	85	700

NOTE: Add $40 for stainless steel.

Model 82

Nearly identical to the Model 80, the Model 82 has a 3" or 4" heavy, solid rib barrel in place of the heavy tapered barrel. Pistol weighs 34 oz.

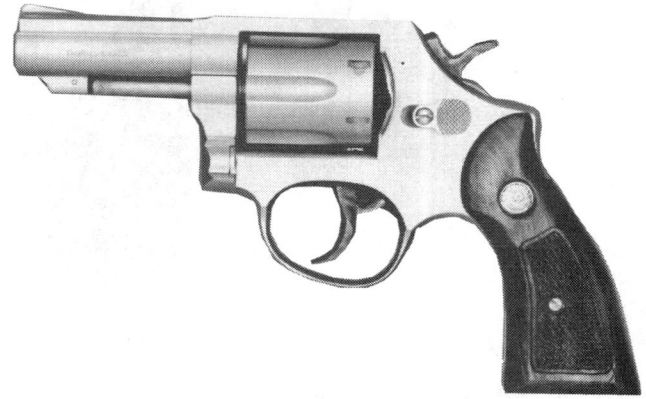

NIB	Exc.	V.G.	Good	Fair	Poor
285	195	135	110	85	70

NOTE: Add $40 for stainless steel.

Model 82B4

Chambered for the .38 Special +P cartridge and fitted with a 4" heavy solid rib barrel. Cylinder holds 6 rounds. Rubber grips. Fixed sights. Blue finish. Weight is about 37 oz.

NIB	Exc.	V.G.	Good	Fair	Poor
295	250	200	125	100	75

Model 82SS4

Same as above but with stainless steel finish. Weight is about 37 oz.

NIB	Exc.	V.G.	Good	Fair	Poor
315	265	185	125	100	75

Model 827B4

Chambered for the .38 Special +P cartridge and fitted with a 4" heavy barrel with solid rib. Cylinder is 7 shots. Rubber grips. Blued finish. Weight is about 37 oz. Fixed sights.

NIB	Exc.	V.G.	Good	Fair	Poor
300	250	200	150	100	75

Model 827SS4

Same as above but with stainless steel finish. Weight is about 35 oz.

NIB	Exc.	V.G.	Good	Fair	Poor
350	300	250	175	125	75

Model 83

Similar to the Model 82 except for a fully adjustable rear sight and Patridge-type front sight. Offered with 4" barrel only with blued or stainless steel (new for 1993) finish. Pistol weighs 34 oz.

NIB	Exc.	V.G.	Good	Fair	Poor
300	250	200	150	100	75

Model 86

Similar to the Model 83 with the exception of a 6" barrel, target hammer, adjustable trigger, and blue-only finish. Weighs 34 oz.

NIB	Exc.	V.G.	Good	Fair	Poor
325	275	225	175	125	75

Model 85

A double-action revolver chambered for the .38 Special. This model is available in either a 2" or 3" heavy, solid rib barrel fitted with ejector shroud. Sights are fixed. Blued finish and stainless steel (new for 1993) are offered with Brazilian hardwood grips. Pistol weighs 21 oz. with 2" barrel. Beginning in 1996 this model was furnished with Uncle Mike's Boot Grips.

NIB	Exc.	V.G.	Good	Fair	Poor
300	225	175	125	100	75

NOTE: For Special Edition, blued steel with gold fixtures and rosewood grips, add $50. For blued steel with gold fixtures and pearl grips add $110.

Model 85 Stainless

As above, in stainless steel. Beginning in 1996 this model was furnished with Uncle Mike's Boot Grips.

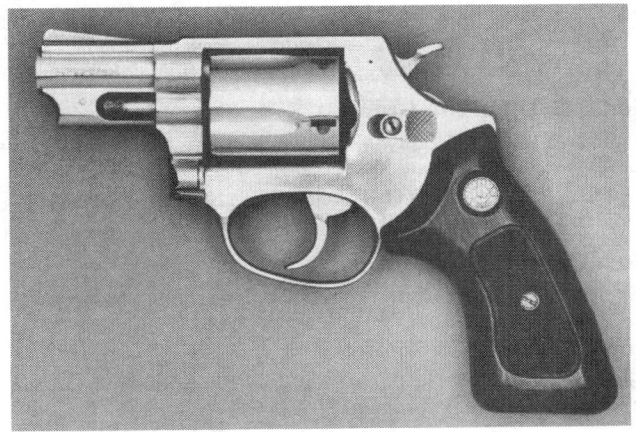

NIB	Exc.	V.G.	Good	Fair	Poor
350	275	225	200	150	100

Model 85CH

Same as above but offered in 2" or 3" barrel with shrouded hammer. Double-action-only.

NIB	Exc.	V.G.	Good	Fair	Poor
300	225	175	125	100	75

NOTE: Add $50 for stainless steel and $25 for ported barrel on 2" models.

Model 85 UL

This double-action revolver is built on a small aluminum frame and is chambered for the .38 Special cartridge. It is fitted with a 2" barrel. Choice of blue or stainless steel finish. Weight is approximately 17 oz. Introduced in 1997.

NIB	Exc.	V.G.	Good	Fair	Poor
325	250	195	150	125	100

NOTE: For Special Edition, blued steel with gold fixtures and rosewood grips add $50. For blued steel with gold fixtures and pearl grips add $110. Add $30.00 for stainless steel.

Model 85 Hy-Lite Magnesium

Similar to Model 85 but weighs only 13.8 oz. Gray alloy frame and Hy-Lite sights. Introduced 2007.

NIB	Exc.	V.G.	Good	Fair	Poor
375	300	250	200	175	125

Model 85 Ultra-Lite Gray

Similar to Model 85 but with lightweight magnesium frame. Fixed or fiber-optic front sight. Introduced 2007.

NIB	Exc.	V.G.	Good	Fair	Poor
375	300	250	200	175	125

Model 85 Ultra-Lite Scandium

Similar to Model 85 Magnesium but with scandium frame. Weighs 14.1 oz. Introduced 2007. Apparently never produced.

Model 85 Ultra-Lite Titanium

Similar to Model 85 Ultra-Lite Scandium but with titanium cylinder and barrel shroud. Introduced 2007.

NIB	Exc.	V.G.	Good	Fair	Poor
475	400	275	200	175	125

Model 850

Chambered for the .38 Special cartridge. Fitted with a 2" barrel with fixed sights. Hammerless with 5-round cylinder. Rubber grips. Weight is about 23 oz. Choice of blue or stainless steel.

NIB	Exc.	V.G.	Good	Fair	Poor
375	300	250	200	175	125

NOTE: Add $50 for stainless steel.

Model 850 Ultra-Lite Blue

Similar to Model 850 but with lightweight alloy frame. Introduced 2007.

NIB	Exc.	V.G.	Good	Fair	Poor
375	300	250	200	175	125

Model 850 Ultra-Lite Stainless Steel

Similar to Model 850 Ultra-Lite Blue but with stainless finish. Introduced 2007.

NIB	Exc.	V.G.	Good	Fair	Poor
375	300	250	200	175	125

Model 850 Ultra-Lite Scandium

Similar to Model 850 but with lightweight scandium frame. Introduced 2007. Announced but apparently never produced.

Model 605

Similar to Model 650 but with ultra-lightweight frame. Blue or stainless finish. Weight 23 oz. Introduced 2007.

NIB	Exc.	V.G.	Good	Fair	Poor
375	300	250	200	175	125

Polymer Protector

Single/double action revolver chambered in .38 Special +P. Features include 5-round cylinder; polymer frame; faux wood rubber-feel grips; fixed sights; shrouded hammer with cocking spur; blued finish; 2.5-inch barrel. Weight 18.2 oz.

NIB	Exc.	V.G.	Good	Fair	Poor
380	320	275	230	200	150

Model 650

Same as Model 850 but chambered for the .357 Magnum cartridge.

NIB	Exc.	V.G.	Good	Fair	Poor
375	300	250	200	175	125

NOTE: Add $50 for stainless steel.

Model 405/445

Chambered for .40 S&W with steel cylinder, alloy frame, 5-round capacity, two-inch barrel. Taurus Security System and Ribber grips. Weight is 29 ounces. Blue or matte stainless finish. Available in .44 Special as Model 445 with weight of 22 ounces.

NIB	Exc.	V.G.	Good	Fair	Poor
385	325	275	235	200	150

NOTE: Add 15 percent for stainless finish.

Model 851 and 651 Revolvers

Small-frame SA/DA revolvers similar to Taurus Model 85 but with Centennial-style concealed-hammer frame. Chambered in .38 Special +P (Model 851) or .357 Magnum (Model 651). Features include five-shot cylinder; 2" barrel; fixed sights; blue, matte blue, titanium or stainless finish; Taurus security lock. Overall length 6.5". Weight: 15.5 oz. (titanium) to 25 oz. (blued and stainless).

NIB	Exc.	V.G.	Good	Fair	Poor
400	300	285	225	150	100

MODEL 94

This double-action revolver is chambered for the .22 LR cartridge. The swing-out cylinder holds 9 rounds. It is available with a heavy, solid rib, 3" or 4" barrel. In 1996 a 5" barrel option was added to this model in both blue and stainless steel. Ramp front sight with fully adjustable rear sight. Offered in blued or stainless steel with Brazilian hardwood grips. Pistol weighs 25 oz. with 4" barrel.

94 Blue

NIB	Exc.	V.G.	Good	Fair	Poor
350	275	225	200	150	100

Stainless Steel

NIB	Exc.	V.G.	Good	Fair	Poor
375	300	250	225	175	125

Model 94 UL

Introduced in 1997 this model is built on a small aluminum frame with 2" barrel and chambered for the .22 LR cartridge. Choice of blue or stainless steel. Weight is approximately 14 oz.

NIB	Exc.	V.G.	Good	Fair	Poor
400	300	285	225	150	100

MODEL 941

Similar in appearance to the Model 94 this version is chambered for the .22 WMR. Available with a choice of 3" or 4" heavy, solid rib barrel. In 1996 a 5" barrel option was added to this model. This model holds 8 rounds. Ramp front sight with fully adjustable rear sight. Available in blued or stainless steel with Brazilian hardwood grips. Pistol weighs 27.5 oz.

Blue

NIB	Exc.	V.G.	Good	Fair	Poor
350	250	175	125	100	75

Stainless Steel

NIB	Exc.	V.G.	Good	Fair	Poor
375	275	200	150	100	75

Model 941 UL

Same as the standard Model 941 but with an aluminum frame and 2" barrel. Weight is about 18 oz. Introduced in 1997.

NIB	Exc.	V.G.	Good	Fair	Poor
400	300	285	225	150	100

Model 96

A full-size .22 LR revolver with 6" heavy, solid rib barrel. Fully adjustable rear sight with target hammer and adjustable target trigger. Cylinder holds 6 rounds. Available in blued only with Brazilian hardwood grips. Pistol weighs 34 oz.

NIB	Exc.	V.G.	Good	Fair	Poor
300	250	200	150	125	100

Model 741

This double-action revolver is chambered for the .32 H&R Mag. cartridge. It features a 3" or 4" heavy, solid rib barrel with fully adjustable rear sight. Swing-out cylinder holds 6 rounds. Available in either blued or stainless steel (stainless steel model introduced in 1993) with Brazilian hardwood grips. Pistol weighs 30 oz.

NIB	Exc.	V.G.	Good	Fair	Poor
200	175	150	125	100	75

NOTE: Add $40 for stainless steel.

Model 761

Similar to the Model 741 this version has a 6" barrel, target hammer, adjustable target trigger, and is available in blued only. Weighs 34 oz.

NIB	Exc.	V.G.	Good	Fair	Poor
350	250	175	125	100	75

Model 65

This double-action revolver is chambered for the .357 Magnum cartridge. It is offered with 2.5" or 4" heavy, solid rib barrel with ejector shroud. Fitted with fixed sights and Brazilian hardwood grips it is available in blued or stainless steel. The 2.5" barrel is a new addition to the Model 65 for 1993. Pistol weighs 34 oz. with 4" barrel.

NIB	Exc.	V.G.	Good	Fair	Poor
325	225	150	125	100	75

NOTE: Add $40 for stainless steel.

MODEL 605

Introduced in 1995 this revolver is chambered for the .357 Magnum cartridge. It is fitted with a 2-1/4" or 3" heavy barrel and is offered in blue or stainless steel. Weighs 25 oz.

Blue

NIB	Exc.	V.G.	Good	Fair	Poor
325	225	150	125	100	75

Stainless Steel

NIB	Exc.	V.G.	Good	Fair	Poor
375	275	200	150	100	75

MODEL 605 CUSTOM (B2C)

Same as above but offered with a 2-1/4" compensated barrel.

Blue

NIB	Exc.	V.G.	Good	Fair	Poor
400	300	285	225	150	100

Stainless Steel

NIB	Exc.	V.G.	Good	Fair	Poor
450	350	300	250	150	100

MODEL 605CHB2/SS2

Chambered for the .357 Magnum cartridge and fitted with a 2.25" solid rib barrel and 5-shot cylinder. This model is also offered with a concealed hammer. Weight is about 24 oz.

Blue

NIB	Exc.	V.G.	Good	Fair	Poor
350	250	175	125	100	75

Stainless Steel

NIB	Exc.	V.G.	Good	Fair	Poor
375	275	200	150	100	75

MODEL 605CHB2C/SS2C

Same as above but with concealed hammer and ported barrels.

Blue

NIB	Exc.	V.G.	Good	Fair	Poor
350	250	175	125	100	75

Stainless Steel

NIB	Exc.	V.G.	Good	Fair	Poor
375	275	200	150	100	75

Model 66

Similar to the Model 65 but offered with a choice of 2.5", 4", or 6" barrel with fully adjustable rear sight. Offered with either blued or stainless steel. Weighs 35 oz. with 4" barrel. The 2.5" barrel was introduced in 1993.

NIB	Exc.	V.G.	Good	Fair	Poor
225	200	175	150	125	100

Model 66CP

This model is similar to the Model 66 but features a compensated heavy, solid rib 4" or 6" ejector shroud barrel. Introduced in 1993. Pistol weighs 35 oz.

NIB	Exc.	V.G.	Good	Fair	Poor
250	225	200	150	125	100

MODEL 66B4/SS4

Chambered for the .357 Magnum cartridge with 4" solid rib barrel and 7-shot cylinder. Adjustable sights. Rubber grips. Weight is about 38 oz.

Blue

NIB	Exc.	V.G.	Good	Fair	Poor
350	275	225	150	125	100

Stainless Steel

NIB	Exc.	V.G.	Good	Fair	Poor
400	325	275	225	150	100

MODEL 607

Introduced in 1995 this .357 Magnum model features a choice of 4" or 6-1/2" integral compensated barrel in either blue or stainless steel. The 6-1/2" barrel is fitted with a vent rib.

Blue

NIB	Exc.	V.G.	Good	Fair	Poor
325	275	225	200	150	100

Stainless Steel

NIB	Exc.	V.G.	Good	Fair	Poor
400	350	300	200	150	100

Model 606

Introduced in 1997 this 6-round model is chambered for the .357 Magnum cartridge. Fitted with a 2" solid rib barrel with ramp front sight and notched rear sight. Available in double-action, single or double-action-only. Offered in blue or stainless steel. Rubber grips are standard. Weight is approximately 29 oz. A number of variations are offered on this model.

NIB	Exc.	V.G.	Good	Fair	Poor
375	275	200	150	100	75

NOTE: For stainless steel models add $50.

MODEL 608

Introduced in 1996 this revolver is chambered for the .357 Magnum cartridge. The cylinder is bored for 8 rounds. Offered in 4" and 6.5" barrel lengths with integral compensator. The front sight is serrated ramp with red insert and the rear is adjustable. Offered in both blued and stainless steel versions. Weight is approximately 51.5 oz. with 6.5" barrel.

Blue

NIB	Exc.	V.G.	Good	Fair	Poor
425	325	250	200	150	100

Stainless Steel

NIB	Exc.	V.G.	Good	Fair	Poor
450	350	300	200	150	100

Model 689

This model is chambered for the .357 Magnum cartridge and features a heavy, vent rib barrel in either 4" or 6" lengths. Fully adjustable rear sight is standard. Offered in blued or stainless steel. Pistol weighs 37 oz. In 1998 this model was fitted with a 7-round cylinder.

NIB	Exc.	V.G.	Good	Fair	Poor
375	275	200	150	100	75

MODEL 617

Chambered for the .357 Magnum cartridge with 7-round cylinder. It is fitted with a 2" barrel. Choice of blue or stainless steel finish. Some variations offered a ported barrel. Introduced in 1998.

Blue

Stainless Steel

NIB	Exc.	V.G.	Good	Fair	Poor
400	325	275	225	175	125

Ported Barrel

NIB	Exc.	V.G.	Good	Fair	Poor
425	325	250	200	150	100

NOTE: Add $20 for ported barrels.

Model 617 CHB2/SS2

Chambered for the .357 Magnum cartridge this model features a concealed hammer, 2" solid rib barrel, and fixed sights.

MODEL 617 CHB2/SS2 BLUE

NIB	Exc.	V.G.	Good	Fair	Poor
350	275	225	175	125	100

Stainless Steel

NIB	Exc.	V.G.	Good	Fair	Poor
425	325	250	200	150	100

Model 627 Tracker

This model is chambered for the .357 Magnum cartridge and has a 7-round cylinder. The 4" barrel is ported with a heavy underlug. Adjustable rear sight. Matte stainless steel finish. Introduced in 2000.

NIB	Exc.	V.G.	Good	Fair	Poor
450	325	275	225	175	125

Model 669

This model is chambered for the .357 Magnum cartridge and features a 4" or 6" heavy, solid rib barrel with full shroud. It has fully adjustable rear sight and is available with blued or stainless steel finish. Brazilian hardwood grips are standard. Pistol weighs 37 oz. with 4" barrel.

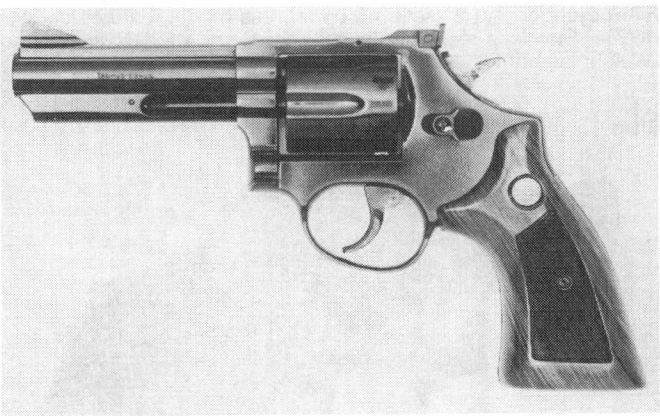

NIB	Exc.	V.G.	Good	Fair	Poor
375	275	200	150	100	75

NOTE: Add $60 for stainless steel.

Model 669CP

This variation of the Model 669 was introduced in 1993 and features a 4" or 6" compensated barrel. Fully adjustable rear sights are standard and it is offered with either blue or stainless steel finish. Weighs 37 oz. In 1998 this model was fitted with a 7-round cylinder.

NIB	Exc.	V.G.	Good	Fair	Poor
425	325	250	200	150	100

NOTE: Add $60 for stainless steel.

Model 415

Chambered for .41 Magnum cartridge and fitted with a 2.5" ported barrel. Fixed sights. Rubber grips. Matte stainless steel finish. Weight is about 30 oz.

NIB	Exc.	V.G.	Good	Fair	Poor
450	350	300	200	150	100

Model 431

Chambered for the .44 Special cartridge this double-action revolver is furnished with a 3" or 4" heavy, solid rib barrel with ejector shroud. Cylinder capacity is 5 rounds. Fixed sights are standard. Choice of blued or stainless steel finish. Pistol weighs 35 oz.

NIB	Exc.	V.G.	Good	Fair	Poor
450	350	300	200	150	100

NOTE: Add $60 for stainless steel.

MODEL 817 (ULTRA-LITE)

Chambered for the .357 Magnum cartridge and fitted with a 7-shot cylinder and 2" solid rib barrel, this model features an alloy frame. Stainless steel or blued finish. Some models are ported. Weight is about 21 oz.

Blue

NIB	Exc.	V.G.	Good	Fair	Poor
350	275	225	175	125	100

Stainless Steel

NIB	Exc.	V.G.	Good	Fair	Poor
390	325	275	225	175	100

NOTE: Add $20 for ported barrels.

Model 441

Similar to the Model 431 but furnished with an additional choice of a 6" barrel as well as a 3" or 4". Comes standard with fully adjustable rear sight. Cylinder capacity is 5 rounds. Blued or stainless steel finish. Pistol weighs 40.25 oz. with 6" barrel.

NIB	Exc.	V.G.	Good	Fair	Poor
395	300	240	150	125	100

NOTE: Add $60 for stainless steel.

Model 444 Multi

This model features a 4" barrel with adjustable sights chambered for the .44 Magnum cartridge. Cylinder holds 6 rounds. Frame is alloy with titanium cylinder. Grips have cushion inset. Weight is about 28 oz. Introduced in 2004.

NIB	Exc.	V.G.	Good	Fair	Poor
575	475	375	300	275	200

Model 905I-B1/SS1

Introduced in 2003 this revolver is chambered for the 9mm pistol cartridge. Barrel length is 2". Cylinder capacity is 5 rounds. Weight is about 21 oz. Blue or stainless steel finish.

NIB	Exc.	V.G.	Good	Fair	Poor
385	325	250	175	100	75

NOTE: For matte stainless steel finish add $45.

Model 951SH2

Chambered for the 9mm cartridge and fitted with a 2" barrel with adjustable sights. Cylinder holds 5 rounds. Titanium frame and finish. Rubber grips. Weight is about 16 oz.

NIB	Exc.	V.G.	Good	Fair	Poor
475	350	265	200	150	100

Model 907SH2

This 9mm revolver has a 7-shot cylinder, 2" barrel with fixed sights and rubber grips. Titanium frame and finish. Weight is about 17 oz. Introduced in 2004.

NIB	Exc.	V.G.	Good	Fair	Poor
475	350	265	200	150	100

Model 907B2/SS2

Chambered for the 9mm cartridge and fitted with a 2" barrel with fixed sights. Rubber grips. Ultra light alloy frame in blue or stainless steel. Weight is about 18.5 oz. Introduced in 2004.

NIB	Exc.	V.G.	Good	Fair	Poor
390	300	250	200	150	100

NOTE: Add $45 for stainless steel.

RAGING BULL SERIES

Model 22H (Raging Hornet)

This model is chambered for the .22 Hornet cartridge and has a 10" barrel with base mount and adjustable sights. Matte stainless steel finish. Cylinder holds 8 rounds. Rubber grips.

NIB	Exc.	V.G.	Good	Fair	Poor
750	675	550	400	300	200

Model 30C (Raging Thirty)

Chambered for the .30 Carbine cartridge and fitted with a 10" vent rib barrel with adjustable sights. Cylinder holds 8 rounds. Supplied with full moon clips. Matte stainless steel finish. Introduced in 2002.

NIB	Exc.	V.G.	Good	Fair	Poor
750	675	550	400	300	200

Model 416 (Raging Bull)

This model has a 6.5" vent rib ported barrel with adjustable sights. Chambered for the .41 Magnum cartridge. Matte stainless steel finish. Introduced in 2002. Cylinder holds 6 rounds.

NIB	Exc.	V.G.	Good	Fair	Poor
625	500	400	300	225	100

MODEL 454 (RAGING BULL)

This model is chambered for the .454 Casull. It is built on a large frame with a 5-round capacity. Barrel lengths are 5", 6.5" or 8.375". Barrels are fitted with a ventilated rib and integral compensator. Sights are adjustable. Finish is blue or stainless steel. Black rubber or walnut grips. Weight is 53 oz. with 6.5" barrel. Add $60 for stainless steel model. Introduced in 1997.

Blue

NIB	Exc.	V.G.	Good	Fair	Poor
700	650	575	450	325	175

Stainless Steel

NIB	Exc.	V.G.	Good	Fair	Poor
750	675	550	400	300	200

Black Stainless Steel

NIB	Exc.	V.G.	Good	Fair	Poor
750	675	550	400	300	200

Model 500 Magnum Raging Bull

Introduced in 2004 this revolver is chambered for the .500 Magnum cartridge. Ventilated barrel length is 10" with adjustable sights. Cushion inset grips. Stainless steel finish. Weight is about 72 oz.

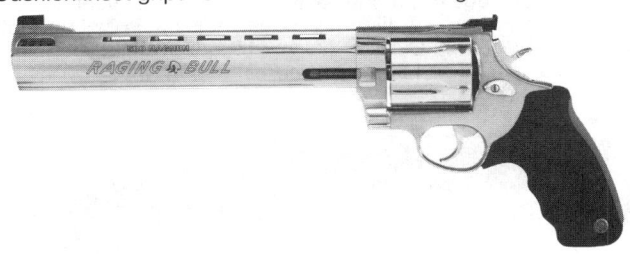

NIB	Exc.	V.G.	Good	Fair	Poor
900	775	600	475	350	200

Model 500, 500MSS2 Raging Bull

Stainless .500 S&W Magnum with 5-shot capacity, 2.25" or 10" barrel, soft rubber grips. 68 oz. Adjustable rear sight, single/double action. Introduced 2006.

NIB	Exc.	V.G.	Good	Fair	Poor
900	775	600	475	350	200

MODEL 44/444

Introduced in 1994 this heavy frame revolver is chambered for the .44 Magnum cartridge. Offered with choice of three barrel lengths: 4" with solid rib, 6-1/2" with vent rib, and 8-3/8" with vent rib. All Model 44s have a built in compensator. The front sight is a serrated ramp with adjustable rear sight. Offered in either blued or stainless finish. Weight of 6-1/2" barrel gun is 53 oz.

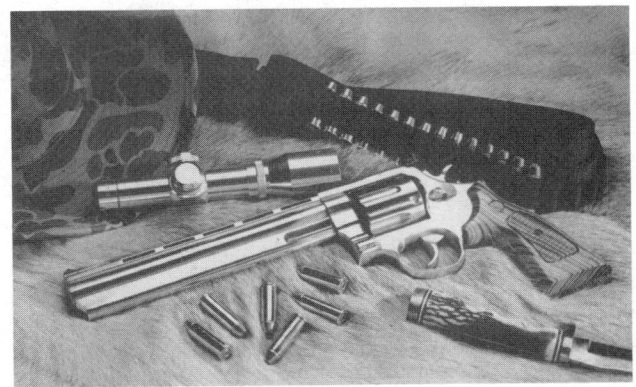

Blue

NIB	Exc.	V.G.	Good	Fair	Poor
—	425	300	200	150	100

Stainless Steel

NIB	Exc.	V.G.	Good	Fair	Poor
600	475	375	250	200	125

TRACKER SERIES

Model 17

Introduced in 2002 this model features a 6.5" or 12" vent rib barrel chambered for the .17 HMR cartridge. Adjustable sights. Matte stainless steel finish. Cylinder holds 7 rounds. Weight is about 41 oz. for 6.5" model and 50 oz. for the 12" model.

NIB	Exc.	V.G.	Good	Fair	Poor
375	300	225	175	125	100

Model 970

This model is chambered for the .22 LR cartridge and fitted with a 6.5" vent rib heavy barrel with adjustable sights. Matte stainless steel finish. Rubber grips. Cylinder holds 7 rounds. Introduced in 2002.

NIB	Exc.	V.G.	Good	Fair	Poor
300	200	165	125	100	75

Model 971

Same as the Model 970 but chambered for the .22 Magnum cartridge. Introduced in 2002.

NIB	Exc.	V.G.	Good	Fair	Poor
300	200	165	125	100	75

Tracker .22/.22 Mag.

Same as Model 971 except it is chambered for .22 LR with an interchangeable .22 WMR cylinder. Both cylinders hold 9 rounds. Weight: 38 to 44 ounces with 4.5 or 6-inch barrel. Blue or matte stainless finish.

NIB	Exc.	V.G.	Good	Fair	Poor
465	400	350	285	200	150

NOTE: Add 10 percent for stainless.

Model 425 Tracker

Chambered for the .41 Magnum cartridge this model features a 4" heavy underlug ported barrel. Adjustable rear sight. Cylinder is chambered for 5 rounds. Matte stainless steel finish. Introduced in 2000.

NIB	Exc.	V.G.	Good	Fair	Poor
425	325	250	200	150	100

Model 44 Tracker

This .44 Magnum revolver has a 4" barrel with adjustable sights and Ribber (ribbed) grips. Five-shot cylinder. Stainless steel finish. Weight is about 34 oz. Introduced in 2004.

NIB	Exc.	V.G.	Good	Fair	Poor
425	325	250	200	150	100

Tracker .45

Similar to other Tracker models but chambered in .45 ACP (via full-moon clips) with 5-shot cylinder. Four-inch barrel with Picatinny rail. Stainless steel frame and cylinder. Introduced 2007.

NIB	Exc.	V.G.	Good	Fair	Poor
450	350	275	225	175	125

Model 445

This small frame revolver is chambered for the .44 Special cartridge. It is fitted with a 2" barrel with ramp front sight and notched rear sight. Cylinder holds 5 rounds. Black rubber grips. Offered in blue or stainless steel. Weight is about 28 oz. Factory barrel porting, add $20, is optional. Introduced in 1997.

NIB	Exc.	V.G.	Good	Fair	Poor
425	325	250	200	150	100

NOTE: Add $50 for stainless steel.

Model 450

Chambered for the .45 Long Colt cartridge this model features a 2" heavy solid rib barrel with 5-shot cylinder and fixed sights. Ported barrel. Rubber grips. Stainless steel finish. Weight is about 28 oz.

NIB	Exc.	V.G.	Good	Fair	Poor
450	350	275	225	175	125

NOTE: Add $30 for Ultra Lite model.

Model 455

This model, introduced in 2002, is chambered for the .45 ACP cartridge. Offered with a choice of 2", 4", or 6.5" barrel. Barrels of 4" and 6.5" have adjustable sights. Matte stainless steel finish. Rubber grips. Supplied with full moon clips.

NIB	Exc.	V.G.	Good	Fair	Poor
450	350	275	225	175	125

Model 460

Chambered for the .45 Long Colt cartridge and fitted with either a 4" or 6.5" vent rib barrel with adjustable sights. Matte stainless steel finish. Introduced in 2002.

NIB	Exc.	V.G.	Good	Fair	Poor
450	350	275	225	175	125

MODEL 45

Chambered for the .45 Long Colt and fitted with a choice of 6.5" or 8-3/8" heavy vent rib barrels. Cylinder holds 6 rounds. Rubber grips, ported barrels, and adjustable sights are standard. Weight with 6.5" barrel is about 53 oz.

Blue

NIB	Exc.	V.G.	Good	Fair	Poor
450	350	275	225	175	125

Stainless Steel

NIB	Exc.	V.G.	Good	Fair	Poor
—	375	300	225	200	125

Model 627

This model is chambered for the .357 Magnum cartridge and fitted with a 4" ported or 6.5" vent rib ported barrel with adjustable sights. Rubber grips. Matte stainless steel finish. Introduced in 2002.

NIB	Exc.	V.G.	Good	Fair	Poor
425	350	275	225	150	100

NOTE: Add $200 for titanium model.

Tracker 10mm 10TSS4

Matte stainless 10mm with 4" barrel and fixed sights. Five-shot, 34.8 oz, rubber grip. Introduced 2006.

NIB	Exc.	V.G.	Good	Fair	Poor
500	400	295	250	175	125

Tracker 10SS8

10mm 6-shot matte stainless with either 6.5" (54.5 oz.) or 8.375" (59.5 oz.) barrel. Fixed sights and rubber grips. Introduced 2006.

NIB	Exc.	V.G.	Good	Fair	Poor
500	400	295	250	175	125

Tracker 4410 10TKR2SS

Shoots 2.5" .410 bore shells or .45 Colt. Holds 5 shots. Stainless or blued, 2.25" or 6.5" barrel, rubber grip. Single/double action, 32 oz., 9.1" LOA. Introduced 2006.

NIB	Exc.	V.G.	Good	Fair	Poor
500	400	295	250	175	125

Judge

Stainless steel- or lightweight alloy-frame version of Tracker Model 4410. Chambered in 3" .410/.45 Colt (4510TKR-3MAG) or 2.5" .410/.45 Colt (4510TKR-3UL) with 3" (3" Magnum) or 2.5" barrel (2.5"). Introduced 2007.

MAGNUM Stopping-Power
Fires both .410 GA 3-inch Magnum or 2.5-inch Shotshells and .45 Colt Ammunition

NIB	Exc.	V.G.	Good	Fair	Poor
525	425	300	265	195	150

Model 4510TKR-SSR

Similar to Taurus Judge but with ported barrel and tactical rail.

NIB	Exc.	V.G.	Good	Fair	Poor
600	525	425	300	265	175

Judge Public Defender Polymer

Single/double action revolver chambered in .45 Colt/.410 (2-1/2). Features include 5-round cylinder; polymer frame; Ribber rubber-feel grips; fiber-optic front sight; adjustable rear sight; blued or stainless cylinder; shrouded hammer with cocking spur; blued finish; 2.5-inch barrel. Weight 27 oz. MSRP: N/A.

Judge Public Defender Ultra-Lite

Single/double action revolver chambered in .45 Colt/.410 (2-1/2). Features include 5-round cylinder; lightweight aluminum frame; Ribber rubber-feel grips; fiber-optic front sight; adjustable rear sight; blued or stainless cylinder; shrouded hammer with cocking spur; blued finish; 2.5-inch barrel. Weight 20.7 oz. MSRP: N/A.

Raging Judge Magnum

Single/double action revolver chambered for .454 Casull, .45 Colt, 2.5-inch and 3-inch .410. Features include 3- or 6-inch barrel; fixed sights with fiber-optic front; blued or stainless steel finish; vent rib for scope mounting (6-inch only); cushioned Raging Bull grips. MSRP: N/A.

Raging Judge Magnum Ultra-Lite

Single/double action revolver chambered for .454 Casull, .45 Colt, 2.5-inch and 3-inch .410. Features include 3- or 6-inch barrel; aluminum alloy frame; fixed sights with fiber-optic front; blued or stainless steel finish; cushioned Raging Bull grips. Weight: 41.4 oz. (3-inch barrel). MSRP: N/A.

SILHOUETTE SERIES

Model 17-12

Chambered for the .17 HMR cartridge and fitted with a 12" vent rib silhouette barrel. Adjustable sights. Cylinder holds 7 rounds. Matte stainless steel finish. Introduced in 2002.

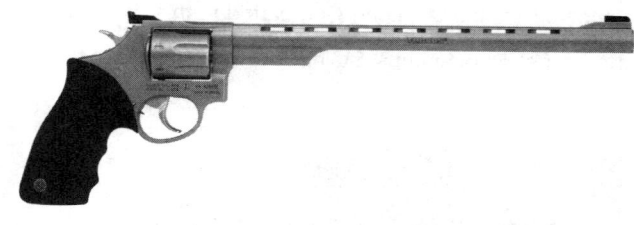

NIB	Exc.	V.G.	Good	Fair	Poor
700	600	475	350	200	150

Model 66

Chambered for the .357 Magnum cartridge and fitted with a 12" barrel with adjustable sights. Choice of blue or stainless steel finish. Rubber grips. Introduced in 2002.

NIB	Exc.	V.G.	Good	Fair	Poor
525	425	300	265	195	150

NOTE: Add $60 for stainless steel.

Model 980

This model is chambered for the .22 LR cartridge. Fitted with a 12" target barrel with adjustable sights. Cylinder holds 7 rounds. Matted stainless steel finish. Rubber grips. Introduced in 2002.

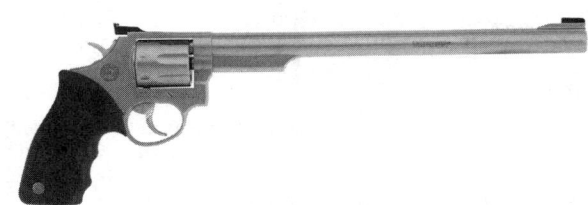

NIB	Exc.	V.G.	Good	Fair	Poor
375	350	300	250	200	150

Model 981

This model is the same as the Model 980 but chambered for the .22 Magnum cartridge.

NIB	Exc.	V.G.	Good	Fair	Poor
375	350	300	250	200	150

Model 217

This model is chambered for the .218 Bee cartridge and fitted with a 12" vent rib barrel with adjustable sights. Cylinder holds 7 rounds. Matte stainless steel finish. Introduced in 2002.

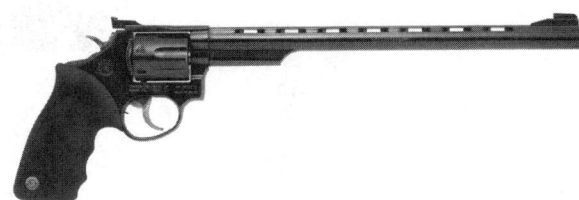

NIB	Exc.	V.G.	Good	Fair	Poor
900	775	600	475	350	200

TITANIUM SERIES REVOLVERS

Introduced in 1999 this series of revolvers feature titanium barrels with stainless steel bore liners, titanium frames and cylinders. Hammers, triggers, latches, ejector rod and other small parts are made from case hardened chrome moly steel. All Taurus Titanium revolvers have factory porting and are rated for +P ammunition. Rubber grips are standard. Three different finishes are offered: Bright Spectrum blue, Matte Spectrum blue, and Matte Spectrum gold.

Model 85Ti

Chambered for .38 Special and fitted with a 2" barrel with 5-shot cylinder. Fixed sights.

NIB	Exc.	V.G.	Good	Fair	Poor
525	425	300	200	150	100

Model 731Ti

Chambered for the .32 H&R Magnum and fitted with a 2" barrel with 6-shot cylinder. Fixed sights.

NIB	Exc.	V.G.	Good	Fair	Poor
525	425	300	200	150	100

Model 617Ti

Chambered for .357 Magnum and fitted with a 2" barrel and 7-shot cylinder. Fixed sights. Weight is about 20 oz.

NIB	Exc.	V.G.	Good	Fair	Poor
600	525	425	300	265	175

Model 627Ti

This model features a 7-round cylinder chambered for the .357 Magnum cartridge. Fitted with a ported 4" barrel with adjustable sights. Gray finish. Weight is about 28 oz. depending on barrel length.

NIB	Exc.	V.G.	Good	Fair	Poor
700	600	475	350	200	150

Model 415Ti

Chambered for the .41 Magnum and fitted with a 2.5" barrel with 5-shot cylinder. Fixed sights. Weight is about 21 oz.

NIB	Exc.	V.G.	Good	Fair	Poor
600	475	350	250	150	125

Model 425Ti

This model is chambered for the .41 Magnum cartridge and has a 5-round cylinder. The barrel is ported and 4" with adjustable rear sight. Gray finish. Introduced in 2000.

NIB	Exc.	V.G.	Good	Fair	Poor
600	475	350	250	150	125

Model 450Ti

Chambered for the .45 Long Colt and fitted with a 2" barrel with 5-shot cylinder. Fixed sights. Weight is about 19 oz.

NIB	Exc.	V.G.	Good	Fair	Poor
600	475	350	250	150	125

Model 445Ti

Chambered for the .44 Special and fitted with a 2" barrel with 5-shot cylinder. Fixed sights. Weight is about 20 oz.

NIB	Exc.	V.G.	Good	Fair	Poor
600	475	350	250	150	125

Model UL/Ti

Chambered for the .38 Special this model has a Titanium cylinder and alloy frame. Fitted with a 2" unported barrel. Cylinder is 5 shot. Fixed sights.

NIB	Exc.	V.G.	Good	Fair	Poor
525	425	300	200	150	100

GAUCHO SERIES

S/A-45, B/S/SM

Chambered for the .45 Colt cartridge and fitted with a 5.5" barrel with fixed sights. Checkered wood grips. Blued or stainless steel finish. Weight is about 37 oz. Introduced in 2004. Discontinued.

NIB	Exc.	V.G.	Good	Fair	Poor
400	325	275	225	175	125

NOTE: Add $15 for stainless steel.

S/A-45, S/S/CH

Chambered for the .45 Colt cartridge and fitted with a 5.5" barrel with fixed sights. Choice of Sundance stainless steel finish or case hardened blued finish. Weight is about 37 oz. Introduced in 2004.

NIB	Exc.	V.G.	Good	Fair	Poor
400	325	275	225	175	125

S/A-357-B, S/SM, S/S, CHSA

Single action 6-shot chambered for .357/.38 caliber. Barrel lengths 4.75" (36.2 oz.), 5.5" (36.7 oz.), 7.5" (37.7 oz.). Fixed sights. Blued, matte stainless, polished stainless or blued/case hardened receiver. Introduced 2006. Pricing is for blued.

NIB	Exc.	V.G.	Good	Fair	Poor
400	325	275	225	175	125

S/A-44-40-B, S/SM, S/S, CHSA

Single action 6-shot chambered for .44-40 caliber. Barrel lengths 4.75" (36.2 oz.), 5.5" (36.7 oz.), 7.5" (37.7 oz.). Fixed sights. Blued, matte stainless, polished stainless or blued/case hardened receiver. Introduced 2006.

NIB	Exc.	V.G.	Good	Fair	Poor
400	325	275	225	175	125

S/A-45-B12, S/SM12, S/S12, CHSA12

Single action Buntline-style 6-shot revolver chambered for .45 Colt. Barrel length 12" (41.5 oz.). Fixed sights. Blued, matte stainless, polished stainless or blued/case hardened receiver. Introduced 2006. Pricing is for blued.

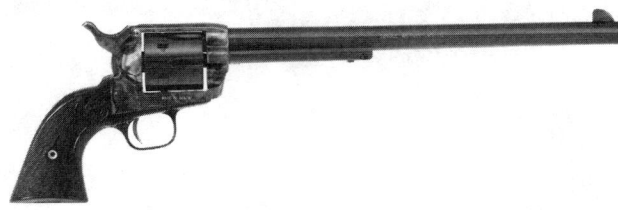

NIB	Exc.	V.G.	Good	Fair	Poor
450	375	300	250	195	10

NOTE: Add 15 percent for stainless.

TAYLOR, L.B.
Chicopee, Massachusetts

Pocket Pistol

A .32 caliber spur trigger single-shot pocket pistol with a 3.5" octagonal barrel marked "L. B. Taylor & Co. Chicopee Mass." Silver-plated brass frame, blued barrel and walnut grips. Manufactured during the late 1860s and early 1870s.

NIB	Exc.	V.G.	Good	Fair	Poor
—	—	1150	875	385	100

TAYLOR'S & CO., INC.
Winchester, Virginia

Napoleon Le Page Pistol (Model 551)

A percussion French-style duelling pistol. Chambered for .45 caliber and fitted with a 10" octagon barrel. Walnut stock silver plated buttcap and trigger guard. Double set triggers. Made by Uberti.

NIB	Exc.	V.G.	Good	Fair	Poor
450	375	300	250	200	100

Kentucky Pistol (Model 550)

Chambered for the .45 caliber ball and fitted with a 10" barrel. Bird's-head grip with brass ramrod thimbles and case hardened sidelock. Made by Uberti.

NIB	Exc.	V.G.	Good	Fair	Poor
295	225	200	125	85	60

Colt Model 1847 Walker (Model 500A)

Fitted with a 9" round barrel and chambered for .44 caliber. This model has a 6-round engraved cylinder. Steel frame and backstrap and brass trigger guard. One-piece walnut grips. Made by Uberti.

NIB	Exc.	V.G.	Good	Fair	Poor
400	325	275	250	200	100

COLT MODEL 1851 NAVY

Offered with either brass or steel frame with brass backstrap and trigger guard. Chambered for .36 caliber and fitted with a 7.5" barrel. Cylinder holds 6 rounds. One-piece walnut grip. Brass frame model made by Armi San Marco. Steel frame model made by F.lli Pietta.

Brass Frame (Model 210)

NIB	Exc.	V.G.	Good	Fair	Poor
295	225	200	125	85	60

Steel Frame (Model 245)

NIB	Exc.	V.G.	Good	Fair	Poor
350	250	200	150	100	75

REMINGTON MODEL 1858

This is a .44 caliber either a brass frame or steel frame and brass trigger guard model with 8" octagon barrel. Cylinder holds 6 rounds. Two-piece walnut grips. Brass frame made by F.lli Pietta. Steel frame made by Armi San Marco.

Brass Frame (Model 410)

NIB	Exc.	V.G.	Good	Fair	Poor
295	225	200	125	85	60

Steel Frame (Model 430)

NIB	Exc.	V.G.	Good	Fair	Poor
350	250	200	150	100	75

Colt Model 1848 Baby Dragoon (Models 470, 471, 472)

Chambered for the .31 caliber and fitted with a 5-round cylinder. Barrel length is 4". Choice of blued or white steel frame. Brass backstrap and trigger guard. One-piece walnut grip. Made by Uberti.

NIB	Exc.	V.G.	Good	Fair	Poor
350	250	200	150	100	75

Starr Model 1858 (Model 510, 511)

This model is offered in either double-action or single-action. Chambered for the .44 caliber and fitted with a 6" round barrel. Made by F.lli Pietta.

NIB	Exc.	V.G.	Good	Fair	Poor
350	250	200	150	100	75

COLT MODEL 1860 ARMY

This model features an 8" round barrel except for the Sheriff's model which is 5.5". Choice of brass or steel frame with brass backstrap and trigger guard. Chambered for .44 caliber. One-piece walnut grip. Brass frame model made by Armi San Marco and steel frame by Uberti.

Brass Frame (Model 300)

NIB	Exc.	V.G.	Good	Fair	Poor
295	225	200	125	85	60

Steel Frame (Model 310, 312, 315)

NIB	Exc.	V.G.	Good	Fair	Poor
350	250	200	150	100	75

NOTE: A half-fluted cylinder model is also offered.

Colt Dragoon (Models 485A, 490A, 495A)

Offered in 1st, 2nd, and 3rd models each is fitted with a 7.5" barrel and chambered for .44 caliber. Steel frame and brass backstrap and trigger guard. The 2nd and 3rd models have a square cylinder stop. The loading lever is inverted on the 3rd model. All have one-piece walnut grip. Made by Uberti.

NIB	Exc.	V.G.	Good	Fair	Poor
350	250	200	150	100	75

NOTE: Add $15 for 3rd model.

Colt Model 1861 Navy (Model 210)

This model is chambered for the .36 caliber and fitted with a 7.5" round barrel. Cylinder is 6 rounds. Brass frame and backstrap and trigger guard. One-piece walnut grip. Made by Uberti.

NIB	Exc.	V.G.	Good	Fair	Poor
295	225	200	125	85	60

Colt Model 1862 Police (Model 315B)

Fitted with a 6.5" round barrel and chambered for .36 caliber. Case hardened frame with brass backstrap and trigger guard. Made by Uberti.

NIB	Exc.	V.G.	Good	Fair	Poor
350	250	200	150	100	75

Colt Model 1862 Pocket (Model 315C)

Similar to the above model but fitted with a 6.5" octagonal barrel. Made by Uberti.

NIB	Exc.	V.G.	Good	Fair	Poor
350	250	200	150	100	75

Remington Model 1863 Pocket (Model 435)

This revolver is chambered for the .31 caliber ball and fitted with a 3.5" barrel. Cylinder is 5 rounds. Frame, backstrap and trigger guard are brass. Walnut grip. Made by Armi San Marco.

NIB	Exc.	V.G.	Good	Fair	Poor
295	225	200	125	85	60

Colt Model 1873 Cattleman (Models 700, 701, 702)

This famous replica is made in several different configurations. Offered in barrel lengths of 4.75", 5.5", and 7.5". Calibers are: .45 Colt, .44-40, .44 Special, .38-40, .357 Magnum, and .45 ACP. Frame is case hardened with steel backstrap. One-piece walnut grip. Made by Uberti.

NIB	Exc.	V.G.	Good	Fair	Poor
500	375	225	175	150	125

NOTE: Add $80 for dual cylinder and $80 for nickel finish.

Colt Model 1873 Bird's-head (Models 703A, 703B, 703C)

Same as above but offered with bird's-head grip.

NIB	Exc.	V.G.	Good	Fair	Poor
500	375	225	175	150	125

Colt Model 1873 "Outfitter"

Chambered for the .45 Colt or .357 Magnum cartridge and fitted with a 4.75", 5.5", or 7.5" barrel. Stainless steel finish and walnut grips.

NIB	Exc.	V.G.	Good	Fair	Poor
500	375	225	175	150	125

HARTFORD ARMORY MODELS

Introduced to the Taylor product line in 2004, this company produces revolvers made entirely in the U.S. Each gun comes with a lifetime warranty. All Hartford Armory revolvers come in a numbered wooden case with brass snap caps and brass plaque.

Remington Model 1875

This model is offered in these calibers: .38/.357, .44-40, .44 Special/Magnum, or .45 Colt. Barrel lengths are 5.75" or 7.5". Walnut grips. Armory dark blue finish.

NIB	Exc.	V.G.	Good	Fair	Poor
900	800	700	600	450	300

Remington Model 1890

This model is offered in .38/.357, .44-40, .44 Special/Magnum, or .45 Colt. Choice of 5.5" or 7.5" barrel. Armory dark blue finish. Walnut grips.

NIB	Exc.	V.G.	Good	Fair	Poor
900	800	700	600	450	300

TERRIER ONE

Terrier One

A .32 caliber double-action swing-out cylinder revolver with a 2.25" barrel and 5-shot cylinder. Nickel-plated with checkered walnut grips. Manufactured from 1984 to 1987.

NIB	Exc.	V.G.	Good	Fair	Poor
—	100	75	50	30	25

TERRY, J. C.
New York City, New York

Pocket Pistol

A .22 caliber spur trigger single-shot pocket pistol with a 3.75" round barrel. The back strap marked "J.C. Terry/Patent Pending." Silver-plated brass frame, blued barrel and rosewood or walnut grips. Manufactured in the late 1860s.

NIB	Exc.	V.G.	Good	Fair	Poor
—	—	1300	950	475	100

TEXAS GUNFIGHTERS
Ponte Zanano, Italy

Shootist Single-Action

A .45 Long Colt caliber single-action revolver with a 4.75" barrel. Nickel-plated with one-piece walnut grips. This model is made by Aldo Uberti. Introduced in 1988.

NIB	Exc.	V.G.	Good	Fair	Poor
400	350	250	200	150	75

1-of-100 Edition

As above, with one-piece mother-of-pearl grips fitted in a case with an additional set of walnut grips. 100 were made in 1988.

NIB	Exc.	V.G.	Good	Fair	Poor
450	375	295	225	175	100

TEXAS LONGHORN ARMS, INC.
Richmond, Texas

Jezebel

A .22 or .22 Magnum single-shot pistol with a 6" barrel. Stainless steel with a walnut stock and forend. Introduced in 1987.

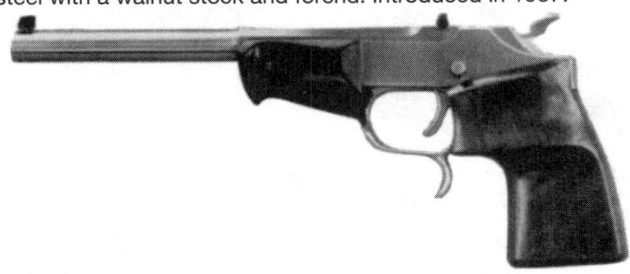

NIB	Exc.	V.G.	Good	Fair	Poor
750	675	600	550	500	350

Texas Border Special

A .44 Special or .45 Colt caliber single-action revolver with a 3.5" barrel and Pope-style rifling. Blued, case hardened with one-piece walnut grips.

NIB	Exc.	V.G.	Good	Fair	Poor
1500	1250	1000	800	600	300

Mason Commemorative

As above, in .45 Colt with a 4.75" barrel and the Mason's insignia. Gold inlaid. Introduced in 1987.

NIB	Exc.	V.G.	Good	Fair	Poor
1500	1250	1000	800	600	300

South Texas Army

As above, but with a 4.75" barrel also chambered for the .357 Magnum cartridge and fitted with conventional one-piece walnut grips.

NIB	Exc.	V.G.	Good	Fair	Poor
1500	1250	1000	800	600	300

West Texas Target

As above, with a 7.5" barrel, flat top frame and in .32-20 caliber in addition to the calibers noted above.

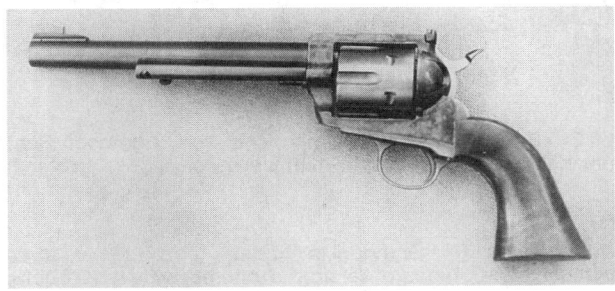

NIB	Exc.	V.G.	Good	Fair	Poor
1500	1250	1000	800	600	300

Grover's Improved Number Five

Similar to the above, in .44 Magnum with a 5.5" barrel. Serial Numbered K1 to K1200. Introduced in 1988.

NIB	Exc.	V.G.	Good	Fair	Poor
2300	1350	800	—	—	—

Texas Sesquicentennial Commemorative

As above, engraved in the style of Louis D. Nimschke with one-piece ivory grips and a fitted case.

NIB	Exc.	V.G.	Good	Fair	Poor
2500	2000	1500	900	750	400

THAMES ARMS CO.
Norwich, Connecticut

A .22, .32, or .38 caliber double-action top break revolver with varying length barrels normally marked "Automatic Revolver," which refers to the cartridge ejector. Nickel-plated with walnut grips.

NIB	Exc.	V.G.	Good	Fair	Poor
—	500	200	100	75	50

THIEME & EDELER
Eibar, Spain

Pocket Pistol

A 7.65mm caliber semi-automatic pistol with a 3" barrel marked "T E." Blued with black plastic grips. Manufactured prior to 1936.

NIB	Exc.	V.G.	Good	Fair	Poor
—	250	150	100	75	50

THOMPSON/CENTER ARMS
Rochester, New Hampshire

NOTE: In late 2006 it was announced that Thompson/Center Arms had been acquired by Smith & Wesson.

CONTENDER

Introduced in 1967 this model is the basis for all past and present variations. The standard version is offered with a 10" octagon barrel and is available in 10" Bull barrel, 10" vent rib barrel, 14" Super models, 14" Super with vent rib, 16" Super models, and 16" Super models with vent rib. A stainless steel finish is available on all models except the 10" octagon barrel. The action on these handguns is a single-shot, break open design. Unless otherwise stated the barrels are blued. The Competitor grip is walnut with rubber insert mounted on back of grip. A finger groove grip is also available made from walnut with finger notching and thumb rest. Forend is American black walnut in various length and designs depending on barrel size. Stainless steel models have rubber grips with finger grooves. Standard sights are standard Patridge rear with ramp front. An adjustable rear sight is offered as an option. Barrels with vent ribs are furnished with fixed rear sight and bead front sight. Due to the numerous variations of the Contender several breakdowns will be listed to help the reader find the closest possible handgun he may be looking for.

NOTE: Early frames with no engraving, called flatsides, and those with eagle engraving bring between $2,000 and $2,500 on the collector market.

10" Octagon Barrel Model

This was the first Contender design and is offered in .22 LR only. It is supplied with adjustable rear sight and mounting holes for scope. Grips are Competitor or rubber. Weighs about 44 oz.

NIB	Exc.	V.G.	Good	Fair	Poor
375	300	250	200	150	100

10" Bull Barrel Model

Comes standard with adjustable rear sight, mounting holes for scope mounts, and Competitor grips for blued models and rubber grips on stainless models. Available in blued or stainless steel. Offered in these calibers as complete pistols: .22 LR, .22 LR Match, .22 Win. Mag. (blued only), .22 Hornet, .223, 7mm T.C.U. (blued only), .30-30, .32-20 (blued only), .357 Mag., .357 Rem. Max (blued only), .44 Mag., .45 Colt, .410 bore. In 1994 Thompson/Center introduced the .300 Whisper cartridge to its Contender product line. Weighs approximately 50 oz.

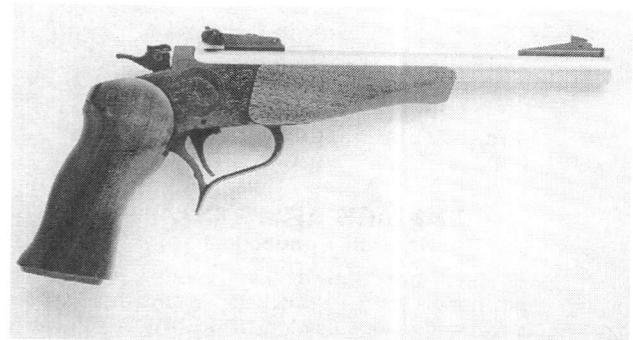

NIB	Exc.	V.G.	Good	Fair	Poor
375	300	250	200	150	100

10" Vent Rib Model

This features a raised vent rib and is chambered for the .45 Long Colt/.410 bore. The rear sight is fixed and the front sight is a bead. A detachable choke screws into the muzzle for use with the .410 shell. Furnished with Competitor grips or rubber grips.

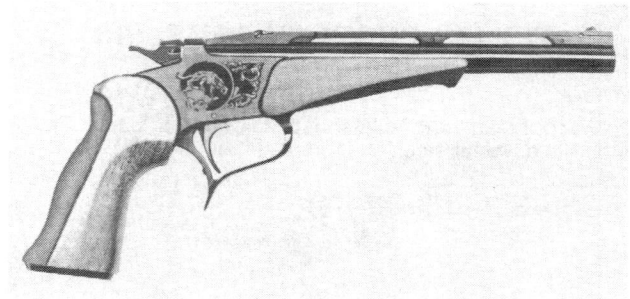

NIB	Exc.	V.G.	Good	Fair	Poor
370	320	270	220	150	100

Super 14" Model

This model features a 14" bull barrel. Furnished with adjustable rear sight and ramp front sight. Drilled and tapped for scope mounts. Competitor or rubber grips are offered. Available in blued or stainless steel finish. Furnished in these calibers in a complete pistol only: .22 LR, .22 LR Match, .17 Rem. (blued only), .22 Hornet, .222 Rem. (blued only), .223 Rem., 7mm T.C.U. (blued only), 7-30 Waters, .30-30, .357 Rem. Max (blued only), .35 Rem., .375 Win. (blued only), .44 Mag. (blued only). Weighs approximately 56 oz.

NIB	Exc.	V.G.	Good	Fair	Poor
400	360	300	250	200	150

Super 14" Vent Rib Model

Similar to the 10" vent rib model chambered for the .45 Long Colt/.410 bore but furnished with a 14" vent rib barrel.

NIB	Exc.	V.G.	Good	Fair	Poor
475	385	325	275	215	150

Super 16" Model

Fitted with a 16.25" tapered barrel, two position adjustable rear sight. Drilled and tapped for scope mount. Furnished with Competitor grips or rubber grips and choice of blued or stainless steel finish. Available in these calibers as complete pistols only: .22 LR, .22 Hornet, .223 Rem., 7-30 Waters, .30-30, .35 Rem., .45-70 Government. Weighs approximately 56 oz.

NIB	Exc.	V.G.	Good	Fair	Poor
370	320	275	215	150	100

Super 16" Vent Rib Model

Chambered for .45 Long Colt/.410 bore this model was offered for the first time in 1993. All other features are the same as the other Contender .45/.410 bore pistols.

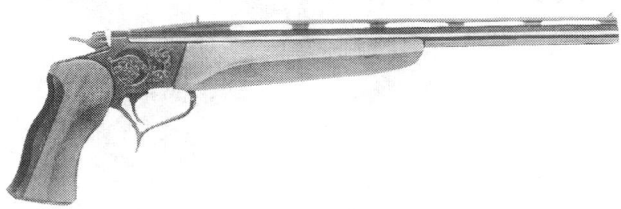

NIB	Exc.	V.G.	Good	Fair	Poor
390	350	300	250	175	125

G2 CONTENDER SERIES

Introduced in 2003, this is a second generation Contender that features a slightly different look, a simplified internal design that allows re-cocking the hammer without having to break open the action, and differently shaped grips that give more clearance between the grip and the finger guard. These G2 firearms will accept previously manufactured Contender barrels and forends but not grips.

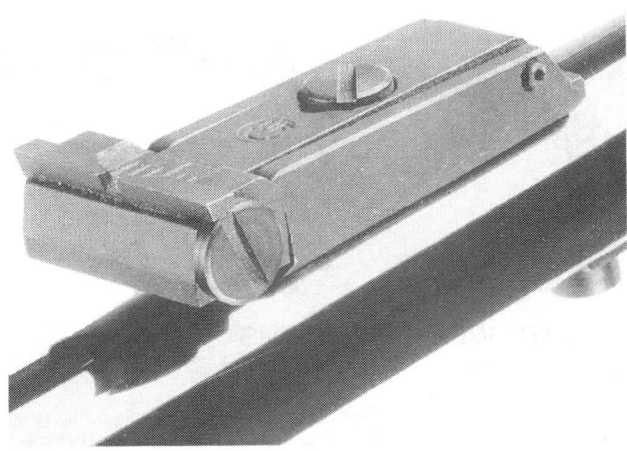

G2 Contender

Offered with both 12" and 14" barrels. Chambered for .22 Hornet, .357 Mag., .44 Mag., .45 Colt/.410 in 12" barrels. In 14" barrel chambered for the .17 HMR, .22 LR, .22 Hornet, .223 Rem., 7-30 Waters, .30-30, .44 Mag., .45 Colt/.410 and the .45-70. Adjustable sights and drilled and tapped for scope mounts. Walnut grips. Weight for 12" barreled guns is about 3.5 lbs., for 14" barreled guns about 3.75 lbs. In 2004 the .204 Ruger and .375 JDJ calibers were added.

NIB	Exc.	V.G.	Good	Fair	Poor
560	450	375	300	250	175

Encore Pistol

Introduced in 1996 this single-shot pistol will feature barrels chambered for the .30-06, .308 Win., 7mm-08 Rem., .223 Rem., .22-250 Rem., .44 Magnum, and 7mmBR. Offered with 10.625", 15", or 24" barrels this new handgun is designed for use with higher pressure cartridges. Barrels will not interchange with the Contender. Weight with 10.625" barrel is 56 oz., with 15" barrel about 4 lbs. and with 24" barrel about 6.75 lbs.

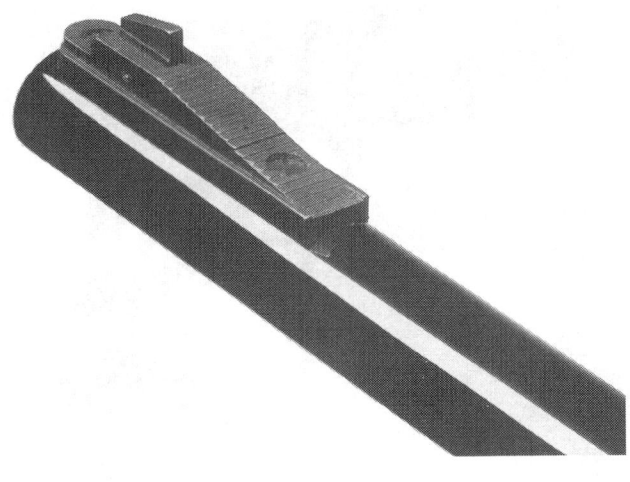

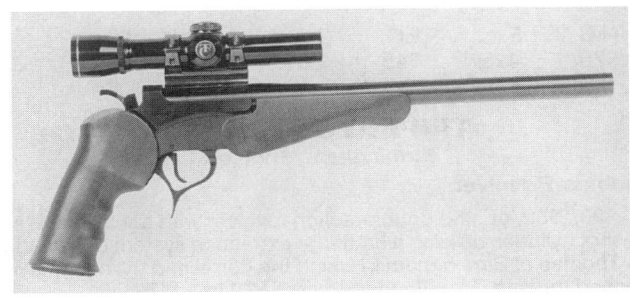

NIB	Exc.	V.G.	Good	Fair	Poor
550	450	375	300	250	175

NOTE: Add $60 for stainless steel frame and barrels.

Encore 209x50 Pistol

This model features a 15" barrel chambered for .50 caliber. Walnut stock and blued finish. Approximate weight is 16 oz. Introduced in 2000.

NIB	Exc.	V.G.	Good	Fair	Poor
550	450	375	300	250	175

BLACKPOWDER FIREARMS

Scout Pistol

The same design as the Scout carbine this single-action pistol is available in .45, .50, or .54 caliber. Fitted with a 12" barrel, adjustable rear sight, and blued finish with brass trigger guard. Black walnut grips. Weighs 4 lbs. 6 oz. Discontinued.

NIB	Exc.	V.G.	Good	Fair	Poor
250	225	200	175	100	75

THUNDER FIVE
MIL Inc.
Piney Flats, Tennessee

Five shot, double-action, 2" rifled barrel, matte finish, ambidextrous hammer block safety, Pachmayr grips, chambered in .45 Long Colt/.410 shotgun.

NIB	Exc.	V.G.	Good	Fair	Poor
575	425	345	250	200	150

TIPPING & LAWDEN
Birmingham, England

Thomas Revolver

A .320, .380, or .450 double-action revolver with a 4.5" barrel and 5-shot cylinder, utilizing a cartridge extraction system designed by J. Thomas of Birmingham in which the barrel and cylinder may be moved forward. Manufactured from 1870 to 1877.

NIB	Exc.	V.G.	Good	Fair	Poor
—	—	1400	950	400	175

TISAS (TRABZON GUN INDUSTRY CORP.)
Trabzon, Turkey

Fatih 13

Beretta-style autopistol clone chambered in .32 ACP. Introduced 1994.

NIB	Exc.	V.G.	Good	Fair	Poor
300	225	150	125	75	50

Kanuni 16

Single-/double-action autopistol chambered in 9mm Parabellum with 15- or 17-shot capacity. Black, chrome or chrome/gold finish. Introduced 1999.

NIB	Exc.	V.G.	Good	Fair	Poor
325	225	150	125	75	50

Kanuni S

Lightweight version of Kanuni 16. Black, chrome or chrome/black finish. Introduced 2000.

NIB	Exc.	V.G.	Good	Fair	Poor
325	225	150	125	75	50

Zigana M16

Single-/double-action autopistol chambered in 9mm Parabellum with 15- or 17-shot capacity and 5" barrel. Introduced 2000.

NIB	Exc.	V.G.	Good	Fair	Poor
395	300	225	195	150	75

Zigana K

Compact version of Zigana M16 with 4" barrel. Introduced 2002.

NIB	Exc.	V.G.	Good	Fair	Poor
395	300	225	195	150	75

Zigana T

Longer (5.5") barrel version of Zigana M16. Introduced 2002.

NIB	Exc.	V.G.	Good	Fair	Poor
395	300	225	195	150	75

Zigana Sport

Compensated version of Zigana K with 4.5" barrel. Introduced 2005.

NIB	Exc.	V.G.	Good	Fair	Poor
395	300	225	195	150	75

Zigana C45

Similar to Zigana M16 but chambered in .45 ACP with 4.75" barrel. Introduced 2005.

NIB	Exc.	V.G.	Good	Fair	Poor
395	300	225	195	150	75

Zigana F

"Meltdown" version of Zigana M16 with radiused edges and improved ergonomics. Introduced 2007.

NIB	Exc.	V.G.	Good	Fair	Poor
395	300	225	195	150	75

TOMISKA, ALOIS
Pilsen, Czechoslovakia

Little Tom

A 6.35mm or 7.65mm caliber semi-automatic pistol with a 2.5" barrel. The slide marked "Alois Tomiska Plzen Patent Little Tom" and the grips inlaid with a medallion bearing the monogram "AT." Blued with checkered walnut grips. Manufactured from 1908 to 1918. Subsequently produced by the Wiener Waffenfabrik.

NIB	Exc.	V.G.	Good	Fair	Poor
—	550	425	350	250	125

TRANTER, WILLIAM
Birmingham, England

William Tranter produced a variety of revolvers on his own and a number of other makers produced revolvers based upon his designs. Consequently, "Tranter's Patent" is to be found on revolvers made by such firms as Deane, Adams and Deane, etc.

Model 1872

A .38 caliber double-action revolver with a 6" octagonal barrel and 6-shot cylinder. Blued with walnut grips.

Courtesy Wallis & Wallis, Lewes, Sussex, England

NIB	Exc.	V.G.	Good	Fair	Poor
—	—	2200	975	400	200

Model 1878

A .450 caliber double-action revolver with a 6" octagonal barrel. Blued with a walnut grip. Manufactured from 1878 to 1887.

NIB	Exc.	V.G.	Good	Fair	Poor
—	—	2750	1350	500	250

TROCAOLA (TAC)
Eibar, Spain

This maker produced a variety of .32, .38, and .44 caliber top break revolvers between approximately 1900 and 1936. These pistols can be identified by the monogram "TAC" stamped on the left side of the frame. The value of all these revolvers is listed. Fifty percent premium for .44 models.

NIB	Exc.	V.G.	Good	Fair	Poor
—	275	175	125	100	75

TRYON, EDWARD K. & COMPANY
Philadelphia, Pennsylvania

Pocket Pistol

A .41 caliber single-shot percussion pocket pistol with a 2" or 4" barrel, German silver mounts and a walnut stock. The lock marked "Tryon/Philada." Manufactured during the 1860s and 1870s.

NIB	Exc.	V.G.	Good	Fair	Poor
—	—	2550	1900	750	200

TUCKER SHERARD & COMPANY
Lancaster, Texas

Dragoon

A .44 caliber percussion revolver with a 7.75" round barrel fitted with a loading lever and a 6-shot cylinder. The barrel marked "Clark, Sherard & Co., Lancaster, Texas," and the cylinder etched in two panels with crossed cannons and the legend "Texas Arms." Approximately 400 revolvers of this type were made between 1862 and 1867. Prospective purchasers are advised to secure a qualified appraisal prior to acquisition.

NIB	Exc.	V.G.	Good	Fair	Poor
—	—	60000	55000	22000	13000

TUFTS & COLLEY
New York, New York

Pocket Pistol

A .44 caliber single-shot percussion pocket pistol with a 3.5" barrel, German silver mounts and walnut stock. The lock marked "Tufts & Colley" and the barrel "Deringer/Pattn." Manufactured during the 1860s.

NIB	Exc.	V.G.	Good	Fair	Poor
—	—	2450	1900	825	200

TURNER, THOMAS
Redding, England

Pepperbox

A .476 double-action percussion pepperbox having 6 barrels. Blued, case hardened with walnut grips. The left side of the frame is engraved in an oval "Thomas Turner, Redding."

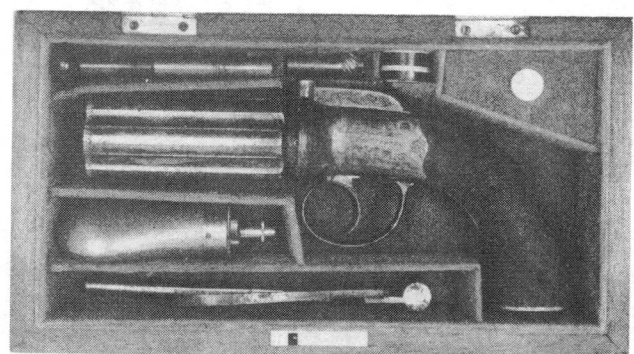

Courtesy Bonhams & Butterfields, San Francisco, California

NIB	Exc.	V.G.	Good	Fair	Poor
—	—	5500	1900	975	400

U

UBERTI, ALDO/UBERTI USA
Ponte Zanano, Italy

This company manufactures high-grade reproductions of famous Western-style American firearms. Their products have been imported over the years by a number of different companies. They produce both blackpowder guns and the cartridge firearms that are included in this section. This Italian manufacturer builds high quality firearms of the American West. Featured are Colt, Winchester, and Remington. Each importer stamps its name on the firearm in addition to the Uberti address.NOTE: In 2000 Beretta Holding Company purchased Uberti.

Paterson Revolver

This is an exact copy of the famous and rare Colt pistol. Offered in .36 caliber with engraved 5-shot cylinder, the barrel is 7.5" long and octagonal forward of the lug. The frame is casehardened steel as is the backstrap. Grips are one-piece walnut. Overall length is 11.5" and weight is about 2.5 lbs.

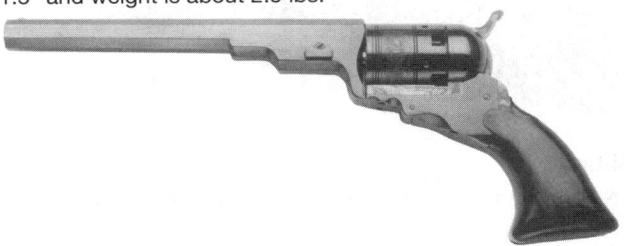

NIB	Exc.	V.G.	Good	Fair	Poor
400	300	200	125	100	75

Walker Colt Revolver

This is a faithful reproduction of the famous and highly sought-after Colts. Caliber is .44 and the round barrel is 9" in length. The frame is case hardened steel and the trigger guard is brass. The 6-shot cylinder is engraved with fighting dragoons scene. Grip is one-piece walnut. Overall length is 15.75" and weight is a hefty 70 oz.

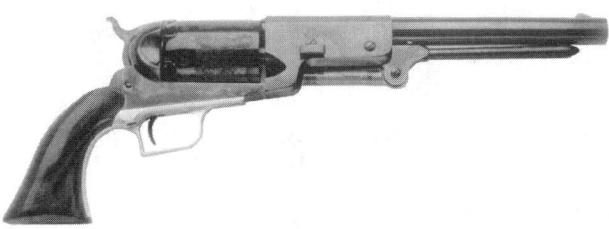

NIB	Exc.	V.G.	Good	Fair	Poor
500	400	300	200	125	100

Colt Whitneyville Dragoon

This was the transition Walker. A reduced version of the Model 1847 Walker. Fitted with a 7.5" barrel and chambered for the .44 caliber.

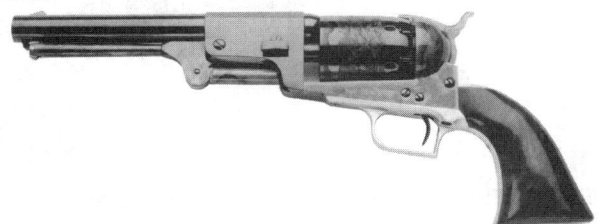

NIB	Exc.	V.G.	Good	Fair	Poor
475	375	200	125	100	75

Colt 1st Model Dragoon Revolver

This was a shorter version of the Walker and evolved directly from that original design. This model is a 6-shot .44 caliber with a 7.5" barrel. The frame is color case hardened steel while the backstrap and trigger guard are brass. Grips are one-piece walnut. Overall length is 13.5" and weight is about 63 oz.

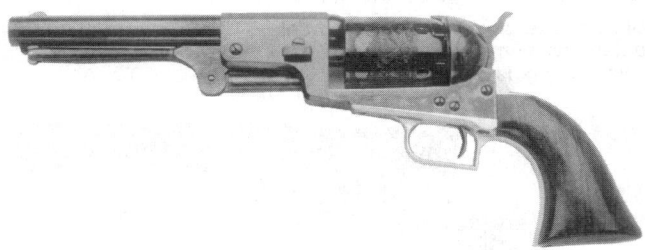

NIB	Exc.	V.G.	Good	Fair	Poor
400	300	250	125	100	75

Colt 2nd Model Dragoon Revolver

This differs from the 1st model in that the cylinder bolt slot is square instead of oval.

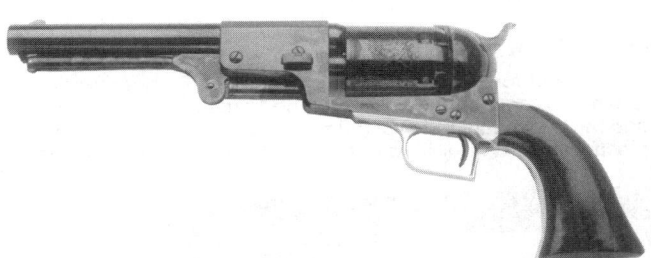

NIB	Exc.	V.G.	Good	Fair	Poor
400	300	250	125	100	75

Colt 3rd Model Dragoon Revolver

This model varies from the 2nd model as follows:
 a:Loading lever taper is inverted.
 b:Loading lever latch hook is different shape.
 c:Loading lever latch.
 d:Backstrap is steel and trigger guard is brass oval.
 e:Frame is cut for a shoulder stock.

NIB	Exc.	V.G.	Good	Fair	Poor
350	225	175	125	100	75

Colt Model 1849 Wells Fargo

This model has no loading lever. Chambered for .31 caliber cartridge. The barrel is octagonal. The frame is case colored and hardened steel while the backstrap and trigger guard are brass. Cylinder is engraved and holds 5 rounds. Grip is one-piece walnut. Overall length is 9.5" and weight is 34 oz.

NIB	Exc.	V.G.	Good	Fair	Poor
325	200	150	125	100	75

Colt Model 1849 Pocket Revolver

Same as the Wells Fargo with the addition of a loading lever.

NIB	Exc.	V.G.	Good	Fair	Poor
325	200	150	125	100	75

Colt Model 1848 Baby Dragoon

Similar is appearance to the Model 1849 but with a 4" tapered octagonal barrel and a square back trigger guard. No loading lever. Weight is about 23 oz.

NIB	Exc.	V.G.	Good	Fair	Poor
325	200	150	125	100	75

Model 1851 Navy Colt

Chambered for .36 caliber with an engraved 6-shot cylinder. The tapered octagonal barrel is 7.5". The frame is case colored steel and the backstrap and oval trigger guard are brass. Grips are one-piece walnut. Overall length is 13" and weight is about 44 oz.

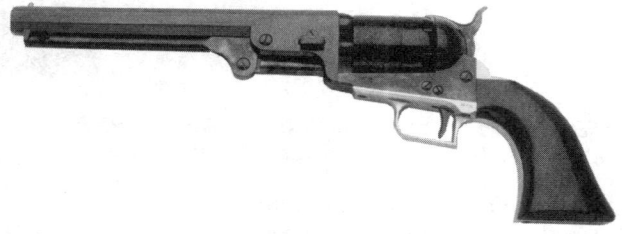

NIB	Exc.	V.G.	Good	Fair	Poor
400	300	250	125	100	75

MODEL 1861 NAVY COLT

Sometimes referred to as the "New Navy" this model is similar in appearance to the Model 1851. Offered in two variations. The military version has a steel backstrap and trigger guard and is cut for a shoulder stock. The civilian version has a Military Model

NIB	Exc.	V.G.	Good	Fair	Poor
400	300	250	125	100	75

Civilian Model

NIB	Exc.	V.G.	Good	Fair	Poor
400	300	250	125	100	75

COLT MODEL 1860 ARMY

Chambered for the .44 caliber ball and fitted with a round tapered 8" barrel, this revolver has a 6-shot engraved cylinder. Grips are one-piece walnut. Overall length is 13.75" and weight is approximately 42 oz.

Military

Steel backstrap and brass trigger guard and is cut for a shoulder stock.

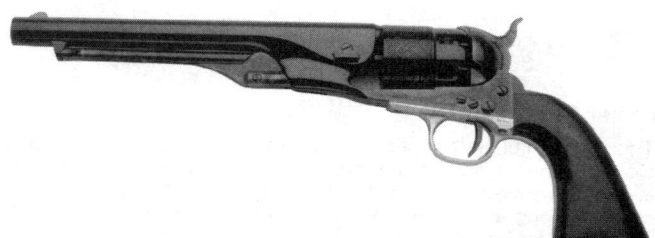

NIB	Exc.	V.G.	Good	Fair	Poor
400	300	250	125	100	75

Civilian

NIB	Exc.	V.G.	Good	Fair	Poor
400	300	250	125	100	75

Fluted Cylinder

NIB	Exc.	V.G.	Good	Fair	Poor
400	300	250	125	100	75

Fluted Cylinder Civilian

NIB	Exc.	V.G.	Good	Fair	Poor
400	300	250	125	100	75

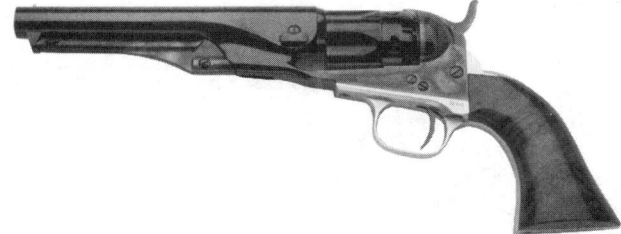

Colt Model 1862 Police Revolvers

Chambered for .36 caliber and fitted with a round tapered barrel in 4.5", 5.5", or 6.5" barrel. The 5-shot cylinder is fluted, the frame color case hardened, and the backstrap and trigger guard are brass. Grips are one-piece walnut. Weight is about 25 oz.

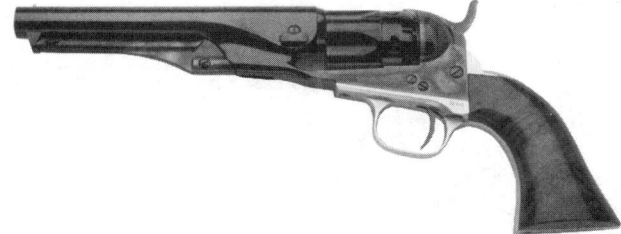

NIB	Exc.	V.G.	Good	Fair	Poor
400	300	250	125	100	75

Colt Model 1862 Pocket Navy Revolver

Similar to the Model 1862 Police model but fitted with a 5-shot engraved nonfluted cylinder. Barrel lengths are 4.5", 5.5", and 6.5". Weight is about 27 oz.

NIB	Exc.	V.G.	Good	Fair	Poor
400	300	250	125	100	75

Colt Model 1868 Army Thuer Conversion

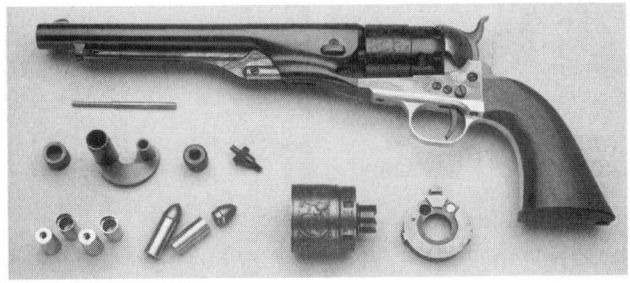

NIB	Exc.	V.G.	Good	Fair	Poor
450	325	225	175	150	100

Remington Model 1858 New Army .44 Caliber

Chambered for .44 caliber and fitted with a tapered octagonal 8" barrel. Cylinder holds 6 shots and the frame is blued steel. trigger guard is brass. Grips are two-piece walnut. Overall length is 13.75" and weight is about 42 oz.

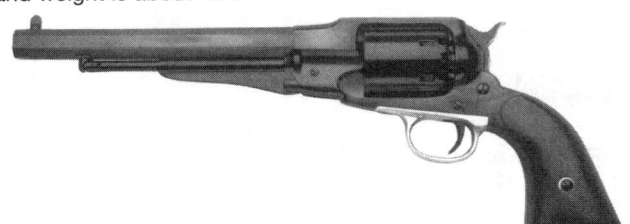

NIB	Exc.	V.G.	Good	Fair	Poor
300	200	150	125	100	75

Remington Model 1858 New Army .36 Caliber

Similar to above model but fitted with a 7-3/8" tapered octagonal barrel. Weight is approximately 40 oz.

NIB	Exc.	V.G.	Good	Fair	Poor
400	300	250	125	100	75

Remington Model 1858 New Army .44 Caliber Target

This version is fitted with a fully adjustable rear sight and ramp front sight.

NIB	Exc.	V.G.	Good	Fair	Poor
425	325	275	150	125	75

Remington Model 1858 New Army .44 Caliber Stainless Steel

All parts are stainless steel.

NIB	Exc.	V.G.	Good	Fair	Poor
425	325	275	150	125	75

Remington Model 1858 New Army .44 Cal. SS Target

Same as Target Model but all parts are stainless steel.

NIB	Exc.	V.G.	Good	Fair	Poor
450	325	250	200	125	75

1875 Remington "Outlaw"

This is a replica of the original Remington cartridge pistol chambered for .357 Magnum, .44-40, .45 ACP, .45 ACP/.45 L.C. conversion, and .45 Colt. The frame is case colored steel and the trigger guard is brass. It is offered with a 7.5" round barrel and is either blued or nickel-plated, with two-piece walnut grips. Overall length is 13.75" and weight is about 44 oz.

NIB	Exc.	V.G.	Good	Fair	Poor
450	325	250	200	125	75

Remington Model 1875 Frontier

Introduced in 2005 this model features a 5.5" barrel chambered for the .45 Colt cartridge. Case colored frame with blued barrel, backstrap, and trigger guard. Two-piece walnut grips. Weight is about 40 oz.

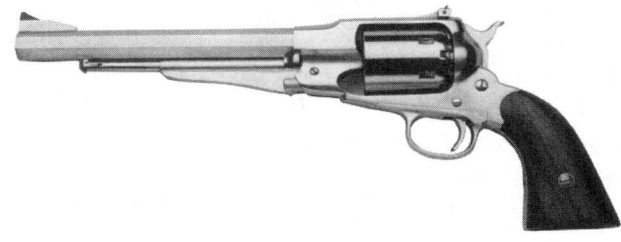

NIB	Exc.	V.G.	Good	Fair	Poor
500	375	250	175	150	100

Remington Model 1890 Police

This is a 5.5"-barreled replica of the original Remington Pistol. It is chambered for .357 Magnum, .44-40, .45 ACP, .45 ACP/.45 L.C. conversion, and .45 Colt. The frame is case colored steel and the trigger guard is brass. It was available in either blued or nickel-plate. Grips are two-piece walnut and are fitted with a grip ring. Overall length is 11.75" and weight is about 41 oz.

NIB	Exc.	V.G.	Good	Fair	Poor
500	375	250	175	150	100

Model 1871 Rolling Block Pistol

This is a single-shot target pistol chambered for .22 LR, .22 Magnum, .22 Hornet, .222 Rem., 223 Rem., .45 Long Colt, or .357 Magnum. It has a 9.5" half-octagonal, half-round barrel and is blued, with a case colored receiver and walnut grip and forearm. The trigger guard is brass. Overall length is 14" and weight is about 44 oz.

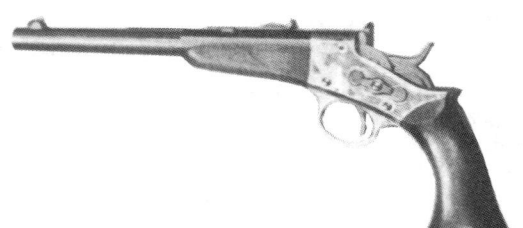

NIB	Exc.	V.G.	Good	Fair	Poor
500	375	250	175	150	100

Cattleman

This is a single-action revolver patterned closely after the Colt Single-Action Army. It is chambered in various popular calibers: .357 Magnum, .44-40, .44 Special, .45 ACP, .45 L.C./.45 ACP convertible, and .45 Colt. It is offered with barrel lengths of 4.75", 5.5", and 7.5". It is offered with either a modern or black powder-type frame and brass or steel backstraps. The finish is blued, with walnut grips. A Sheriff's Model with a 3" barrel and no ejector rod chambered for .44-40 and .45 Colt is also available and is valued the same. Weight is approximately 38 oz. for 5.5" barrel gun.

NIB	Exc.	V.G.	Good	Fair	Poor
400	275	225	150	100	75

Cattleman Flattop Target Model

This model is similar to the standard Cattleman, with an adjustable rear sight.

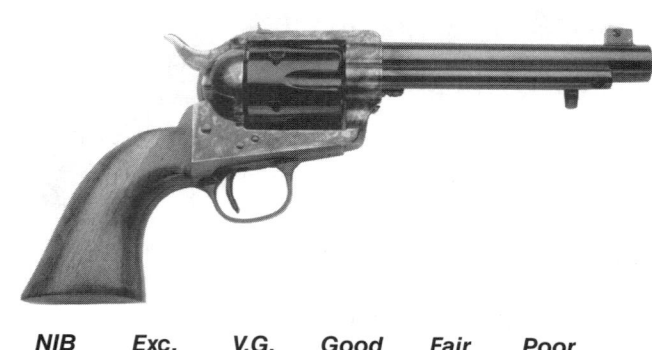

NIB	Exc.	V.G.	Good	Fair	Poor
435	350	275	225	175	125

Cattleman Gunfighter NM

Chambered for the .45 Colt cartridge and fitted with a 4.75", 5.5", or 7.5" barrel. Black checkered grip with matte blued finish. Weight is around 37 oz. Introduced in 2005.

NIB	Exc.	V.G.	Good	Fair	Poor
400	275	225	150	100	75

Cattleman Cody NM

As above but with nickel finish and ivory-style grips.

NIB	Exc.	V.G.	Good	Fair	Poor
500	375	250	175	150	100

Cattleman Frisco NM

As above but with charcoal blued barrel and case colored frame. Pearl grips.

NIB	Exc.	V.G.	Good	Fair	Poor
500	375	250	175	150	100

Cattleman El Patron CMS

Designed for Cowboy Mounted Shooter (CMS) competition. Caliber .357 Magnum or .45 Colt, steel cylinder, frame and barrel, 6-round capacity, single action trigger, low profile hammer, fixed sights and wood grips. Weight 36.8 ounces, 3.5 or 4-inch barrel with blue/casehardened or stainless finish.

NIB	Exc.	V.G.	Good	Fair	Poor
525	425	350	300	225	150

NOTE: Add 25 percent for stainless finish.

Bisley

Chambered for the .32-20, .38 Special, .357 Mag, .38-40, .44-40, and .44 Special and fitted with either 4.75", 5.5", or 7.5" barrel. Case hardened frame with two-piece walnut grips.

NIB	Exc.	V.G.	Good	Fair	Poor
435	350	275	225	175	125

Bisley Flattop

As above but with adjustable rear sight.

NIB	Exc.	V.G.	Good	Fair	Poor
435	350	275	225	175	125

Buckhorn Buntline

This version is chambered for the .44 Magnum. It has an 18" round barrel, and it is cut for attaching a shoulder stock. Steel backstrap and trigger guard. Overall length is 23" and weight is about 57 oz.

NIB	Exc.	V.G.	Good	Fair	Poor
400	325	300	250	200	100

NOTE: Detachable shoulder stock add 25 percent.

Buckhorn Target

Same as above but fitted with an adjustable rear sight and ramp front sight. Has a flat upper frame.

NIB	Exc.	V.G.	Good	Fair	Poor
450	350	300	250	200	100

Phantom

Similar to the Buckhorn, but chambered for the .44 Magnum and the .357 Magnum. The barrel is a round 10.5" and the frame is blued with blued steel backstrap. One-piece walnut grips with anatomic profile. Adjustable sight. Weight is approximately 53 oz.

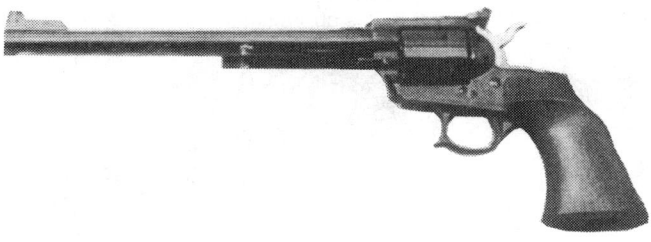

NIB	Exc.	V.G.	Good	Fair	Poor
400	275	225	150	100	75

New Thunderer Model

Designed and imported exclusively by Cimarron Arms for single-action shooting competition. Fitted with bird's-head grip with hard rubber, this model is chambered for the .357 Magnum, .44 Special, .44 WCF, and .45 Colt. Offered in barrel lengths of 3.5" and 4.75". Finish in nickel or blued with case colored frame.

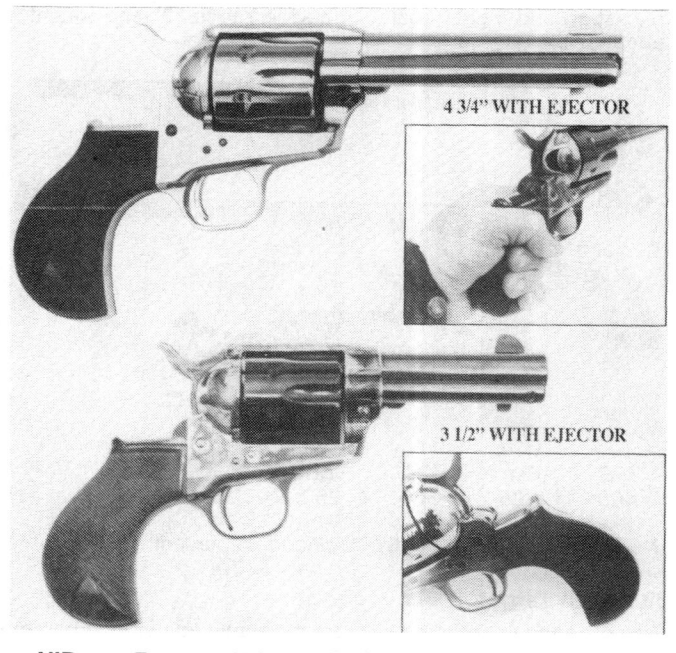

4 3/4" WITH EJECTOR

3 1/2" WITH EJECTOR

NIB	Exc.	V.G.	Good	Fair	Poor
450	350	300	250	200	100

Tornado

This five-shot revolver is chambered for the .454 Casull and fitted with a 4.75", 5.5" or 7.5" with ported barrel. Sandblasted nickel finish. Weight is about 47 oz.

NIB	Exc.	V.G.	Good	Fair	Poor
1000	900	750	600	500	400

No. 3 Schofield Revolver

Patterned after the original S&W revolver this model is chambered for the .44-40 or .45 Colt cartridge. It is fitted with a 7", 5", or 3.5" barrel. Weight with 7" barrel is approximately 40 oz.

NIB	Exc.	V.G.	Good	Fair	Poor
800	700	600	475	325	200

No. 3 New Model Russian

Chambered for the .44 Russian cartridge and fitted with a 6" or 7" barrel.

NIB	Exc.	V.G.	Good	Fair	Poor
900	800	700	575	400	300

Inspector Model

This is a double-action revolver built on the same general lines as the Colt Detective model. Cylinder holds six cartridges and is chambered for the .38 Special. Offered in these barrel lengths with fixed sights: 2", 2.125", 2.5", 3", 4", 6" and also offered in 4" and 6" barrel lengths with adjustable sights. Grips are walnut and finish is blued or chrome. With the 3" barrel the weight is about 24 oz.

NIB	Exc.	V.G.	Good	Fair	Poor
275	200	150	125	100	75

UHLINGER, WILLIAM P.
Philadelphia, Pennsylvania

POCKET REVOLVER

A .32 caliber spur trigger revolver with a 2.75" or 3" octagonal barrel and an unfluted 6-shot cylinder. Blued with rosewood or walnut grips. Manufactured during the late 1860s and early 1870s. **NOTE:** Uhlinger-manufactured pistols will often be found with retailer's names on them, such as D.D. Cone, Washington, D.C.; J.P. Lower; and W.L. Grant.

Long Cylinder (1-3/16")

NIB	Exc.	V.G.	Good	Fair	Poor
—	—	800	600	250	100

Short Cylinder (1")

NIB	Exc.	V.G.	Good	Fair	Poor
—	—	650	425	175	75

.32 Rimfire Model (5", 6", or 7" Barrel)

NIB	Exc.	V.G.	Good	Fair	Poor
—	—	800	600	250	100

ULTRA LIGHT ARMS, INC./NEW ULTRA LIGHT ARMS
Granville, West Virginia

This maker manufactures a variety of bolt-action rifles fitted with Douglas barrels of varying lengths, custom triggers, and reinforced graphite stocks. The values for standard production models are listed.

Model 20 Hunter's Pistol

A bolt-action repeating pistol designed with the serious hunter in mind. It is offered in various popular calibers with a 14", high-quality Douglas heavy barrel. It has a 5-shot magazine and is matte blued, with a reinforced graphite Kevlar stock. It was introduced in 1987.

NIB	Exc.	V.G.	Good	Fair	Poor
1250	1000	800	625	500	300

UNION
Unknown

Pocket Pistol

.22 caliber spur trigger single-shot pistol with a 2.75" barrel marked "Union." Nickel-plated with walnut grips.

NIB	Exc.	V.G.	Good	Fair	Poor
—	—	650	400	100	75

UNION FIRE ARMS COMPANY
Toledo, Ohio

This company was incorporated in 1902 and used the names of Union Fire Arms, Union Arms Company, Illinois Arms Company (made for Sears) and Bee Be Arms Company. In 1917 the company was either bought up or absorbed by Ithaca Gun Company.

Reifngraber

A .32 or .38 S&W caliber gas operated semi-automatic pistol, with a 3" barrel. Blued with walnut grips, approximately 100 of these pistols were manufactured.

NIB	Exc.	V.G.	Good	Fair	Poor
—	—	2250	1100	500	350

Automatic Revolver

.32 S&W caliber, similar to the Webley Fosbery semi-automatic revolver with a 3" barrel. Blued with either walnut or hard rubber grips. The cylinder has zigzag grooves.

NIB	Exc.	V.G.	Good	Fair	Poor
—	—	3250	1250	500	250

UNIQUE
Hendaye, France
SEE—Pyrenees

UNITED SPORTING ARMS, INC.
Tucson, Arizona

Blued Guns (Seville, etc.)

NIB	Exc.	V.G.	Good	Fair	Poor
N/A	500	450	350	—	—

Blue Silhouette (10.5" barrels)

NIB	Exc.	V.G.	Good	Fair	Poor
N/A	600	550	500	—	—

NOTE: Add $100 for stainless, $250 for stainless long-frame models (calibers .357 Maximum/Super Mag. and .357 USA/Super Mag).

Silver Sevilles

NIB	Exc.	V.G.	Good	Fair	Poor
N/A	550	475	400	—	—

Stainless Steel Guns

NIB	Exc.	V.G.	Good	Fair	Poor
N/A	600	525	450	—	—

Tombstone Commemorative

NIB	Exc.	V.G.	Good	Fair	Poor
1000	750	625	525	—	—

Quik-Kit Stainless Steel

NIB	Exc.	V.G.	Good	Fair	Poor
1500	1250	800	—	—	—

Quik-Kit Blued

NIB	Exc.	V.G.	Good	Fair	Poor
1200	1000	650	—	—	—

NOTE: For Quik-Kit guns with extra barrel and cylinder add $200 for each barrel and cylinder. Deduct 10 percent if United Sporting Arms, Hauppauge, N.Y. Deduct 20 percent if United Sporting Arms, Post Falls, ID. Add 20 percent if El Dorado Arms (either N.Y. or N.C.). Add 10 percent for 1-1/2" barrel Sheriff\qs Model. Add 20 percent for 10-1/2" barrel. Add 20 percent for bird's-head grip frame. Add 20 percent if brass grip frame.

UNITED STATES ARMS
Otis A. Smith Company
Rockfall, Connecticut

Single-Action Revolver

A .44 rimfire and centerfire single-action revolver with a 7" barrel and integral ejector. The hammer nose is fitted with two firing pins so that rimfire or centerfire cartridges can be used interchangeably. The barrel marked "United States Arms Company - New York," the top strap "No. 44." Blued with either hard rubber or rosewood grips. Manufactured in limited quantities. Circa 1870 to 1875.

NIB	Exc.	V.G.	Good	Fair	Poor
—	—	4750	3250	1250	500

UNITED STATES FIRE ARMS MFG.
(Formerly United States Patent Firearms Mfg. Co.)
Hartford, Connecticut

This company began business in 1992. The company uses parts manufactured in the U.S. and fits, finishes, and assembles the gun in Hartford. Produces a wide variety of extremely high-quality replica arms. **NOTE:** This company offers a wide variety of special order options on its revolvers, from special bluing to grips to engraving. These special order options will affect price to a significant degree.

Single-Action Army Revolver

Offered in a wide variety of calibers including .22 rimfire, .32 WCF, .38 S&W, .357 Magnum, .38-40, .41 Colt, .44 Russian, .44-40, .45 Colt, and .45 ACP. Barrel lengths are 4.75", 5.5", and 7.5" with or without ejector. A modern cross pin frame is available for an additional $10. Prices listed are for standard grips and finish, Armory bone case finish, and Dome blue finish.

NIB	Exc.	V.G.	Good	Fair	Poor
975	900	800	675	525	300

Single-Action Army Revolver Pre-War

As above but with pre-war "P" frame.

NIB	Exc.	V.G.	Good	Fair	Poor
1395	1150	950	700	550	300

Shooting Master

A large-frame model in .357 Magnum with 7.5-inch barrel, U.S. hard rubber grips, blue finish and enlarged trigger guard. Adjustable rear sight, six-round cylinder. Introduced in 2011. Also, available in .327 Federal with 8-shot cylinder (Sparrowhawk model).

NIB	Exc.	V.G.	Good	Fair	Poor
1300	1100	950	800	525	250

Flattop Target Model

This model is offered with the same calibers as the Single-Action Army above. Barrel lengths are 4.75", 5.5", and 7.5". Grips are two-piece hard rubber. Prices listed are given for standard finish. Introduced in 1997.

NIB	Exc.	V.G.	Good	Fair	Poor
1665	1450	1200	900	675	400

Rodeo

This single-action revolver is offered in .45 Colt, .44-40 and .38 Special calibers with a choice of 4.75" or 5.50" barrel. Satin blue finish with bone case hammer. "US" hard rubber grips are standard.

NIB	Exc.	V.G.	Good	Fair	Poor
625	550	450	350	250	175

Rodeo II

Similar to the Rodeo but with matte nickel finish and Burlwood grips.

NIB	Exc.	V.G.	Good	Fair	Poor
575	475	350	275	225	200

China Camp Cowboy Action Gun

Chambered for .45 Colt cartridge but other calibers also available from .32 WCF to .44 WCF. Barrel lengths are 4.75", 5.5", and 7.5". Special action job. Two-piece hard rubber grips standard. Finish is silver steel.

NIB	Exc.	V.G.	Good	Fair	Poor
1395	1150	950	700	550	300

Henry Nettleton Revolver

This is an exact reproduction of the U.S. Government inspector model produced in the Springfield Armory. Offered in 7.5" and 5.5" models. Introduced in 1997. Discontinued.

NIB	Exc.	V.G.	Good	Fair	Poor
1575	1450	1200	900	600	350

.22 Plinker

Chambered for the .22 cartridge and fitted with a choice of barrel lengths of 4.75", 5.5", or 7.5". An extra .22 WMR cylinder is included.

NIB	Exc.	V.G.	Good	Fair	Poor
975	875	725	550	300	150

.22 Target

As above but with adjustable rear sight and replaceable front sight blade.

NIB	Exc.	V.G.	Good	Fair	Poor
1665	1450	1200	900	675	400

Gunslinger

Offered in .45 Colt, .44 Special, .44 WCF, .38 Special, .38 WCF, or .32 WCF and choice of 4.75", .5.5",or 7.5" barrel. Cross pin frame. Hard rubber grips. Aged bluing finish. Black style frame optional.

NIB	Exc.	V.G.	Good	Fair	Poor
1145	1025	800	625	500	250

NOTE: Add $135 for black powder frame.

Custer Battlefield Gun

Replica of 1873 revolver used during height of Indian Wars, including Custer's Last Stand. Limited edition with cartouche of Ordnance Sub-inspector Orville W. Ainsworth; serial range 200-14,343. 7.5" barrel, six shot. Antique Patina aged blue. One-piece walnut stock.

NIB	Exc.	V.G.	Good	Fair	Poor
1625	1450	1200	900	675	400

Hunter

This revolver is chambered for the .17 HMR cartridge and fitted with a 7.5" barrel with adjustable rear sight and replaceable front sight blade. Finish is matte blue. Discontinued.

NIB	Exc.	V.G.	Good	Fair	Poor
975	875	725	550	300	150

Sheriff's Model

Chambered for a wide variety of calibers from the .45 Colt to the .32 WCF. Choice of 2.5", 3", 3.5", or 4" barrel. No ejector.

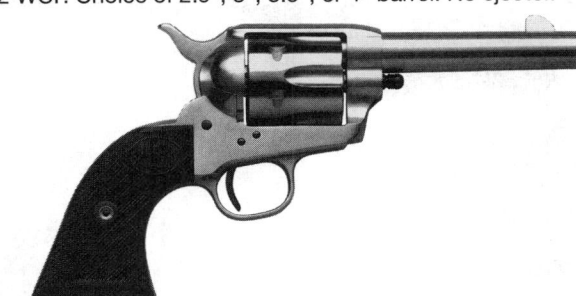

NIB	Exc.	V.G.	Good	Fair	Poor
975	875	725	550	300	150

NOTE: Add $250 for nickel finish.

Omni-Potent Bird's-Head Model

Chambered for the .45 Colt, .45 ACP, .44 Special, .44 WCF, .38 Special, .38 WCF, or the .32 WCF cartridges. Offered with bird's-head grips and available with 3.5", 4", or 4.75" barrel lengths.

NIB	Exc.	V.G.	Good	Fair	Poor
1625	1450	1200	900	675	400

Omni-Potent Snubnose

As above but with 2", 3", or 4" barrel without ejector.

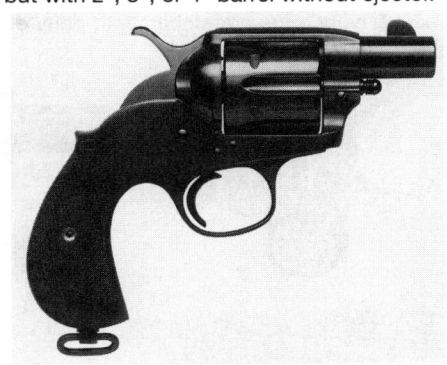

NIB	Exc.	V.G.	Good	Fair	Poor
1475	1300	1050	800	575	400

Omni-Potent Target

Choice of 4.75", 5.5", or 7.5" barrel with adjustable rear sight and replaceable front blade sight.

NIB	Exc.	V.G.	Good	Fair	Poor
1395	1150	950	700	550	300

Bisley Model

Based on the famous Bisley model this reproduction features barrel lengths of 4.75", 5.5", 7.5", and 10". The .45 Colt caliber is standard but .32 WCF, .38 S&W, .44 S&W, .41 Colt, .38 WCF, .44 WCF are optional. Introduced in 1997.

NIB	Exc.	V.G.	Good	Fair	Poor
1575	1450	1200	900	600	350

NOTE: Add $60 for 10" models.

Bisley Target

As above but with adjustable rear sight and replaceable blade front sight.

NIB	Exc.	V.G.	Good	Fair	Poor
1625	1450	1200	900	675	400

Pony Express

This model features a 5.50" barrel with special finish and engraved frame and barrel. Ivory grips are etched with pony express rider. Custom gun.

NIB	Exc.	V.G.	Good	Fair	Poor
3895	3500	2950	2200	1500	700

Sears 1902 Colt

This model is a replica of the Sears 1902 Colt SAA. Fitted with a 5.50" barrel, pearl grips, and full coverage engraving with gold line work on the cylinder and barrel. Custom gun.

NIB	Exc.	V.G.	Good	Fair	Poor
8995	7500	6000	500	4000	1000

Model 1910

This model is a stylized version of the early Colt Model 1910 .45 ACP pistol.

NIB	Exc.	V.G.	Good	Fair	Poor
1895	1700	1550	1200	900	500

Model 1911 Army or Navy

This model is a faithful version of the early Colt Model 1911 military model.

NIB	Exc.	V.G.	Good	Fair	Poor
1875	1725	1500	1200	900	600

Ace .22 LR

Recreation of 1911-style Colt Ace. .22 LR with 10+1 capacity. Walnut grips. Introduced 2006.

NIB	Exc.	V.G.	Good	Fair	Poor
1995	1825	1600	1250	950	650

Super .38

1911-style semi-auto. Blued finish; chambered for .38 Super Auto with 9+1 capacity. Walnut grips. Introduced 2006.

NIB	Exc.	V.G.	Good	Fair	Poor
1875	1725	1500	1200	900	600

UNITED STATES SMALL ARMS CO.
Chicago, Illinois

Huntsman Model Knife Pistol

Made from approximately 1918-1930. Too Rare To Price

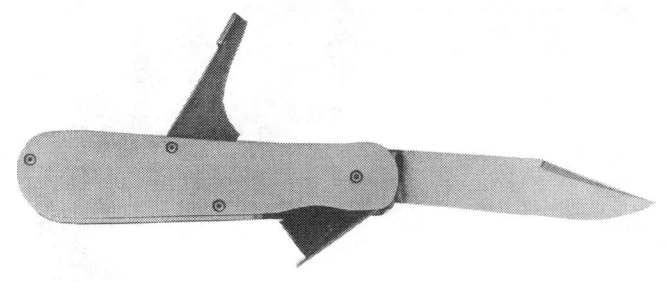

UNIVERSAL FIREARMS
Hialeah, Florida/Jacksonville, Arkansas

NOTE: Universal merged with Iver-Johnson in 1985 and relocated to Arkansas in 1986. Universal operated out of Florida from the late 1950s to 1985.

Model 3000 Enforcer Blued

A pistol version of the Model 1000 with an 11.25" barrel and 15- or 30-shot magazines.

Model 3000 Enforcer

NIB	Exc.	V.G.	Good	Fair	Poor
—	375	225	200	150	100

NOTE: Nickel finish add 20 percent. Gold-plated add 40 percent. Stainless steel add 30 percent. Teflon-S add 20 percent.

URIZAR, TOMAS
Eibar, Spain

Celta, J. Cesar, Premier, Puma, and Union

A 6.35mm semi-automatic pistol with a 3" barrel. The slide marked with the trade names listed above. Blued with black plastic grips, cast with a wild man carrying a club.

NIB	Exc.	V.G.	Good	Fair	Poor
—	250	150	125	90	75

Dek-Du

A 5.5mm folding trigger double-action revolver with a 12-shot cylinder. Later versions were made in 6.35mm. Manufactured from 1905 to 1912.

NIB	Exc.	V.G.	Good	Fair	Poor
—	225	125	100	75	50

Express

A 6.35mm semi-automatic pistol with a 2" barrel. The slide marked "The Best Automatic Pistol Express." Blued with walnut grips. A 7.65mm variety exists with a 4" barrel.

NIB	Exc.	V.G.	Good	Fair	Poor
—	225	125	100	75	50

Imperial

A 6.35mm caliber semi-automatic pistol with a 2.5" barrel. This model was actually made by Aldazabal. Manufactured circa 1914.

NIB	Exc.	V.G.	Good	Fair	Poor
—	225	125	100	75	50

Le Secours or Phoenix

A 7.65mm semi-automatic pistol marked with either of the trade names listed above.

NIB	Exc.	V.G.	Good	Fair	Poor
—	225	125	100	75	50

Princeps

A 6.35mm or 7.65mm semi-automatic pistol marked on the slide "Made in Spain Princeps Patent."

NIB	Exc.	V.G.	Good	Fair	Poor
—	225	125	100	75	50

Venus

A 7.65mm semi-automatic pistol with the grips having the trade name "Venus" cast in them.

NIB	Exc.	V.G.	Good	Fair	Poor
—	225	125	100	75	50

USELTON ARMS INC.
Goodlettsville, Tennessee

NOTE: Values shown are for base models. The sky's the limit.

Compact Classic

This model is chambered for the .45 ACP cartridge and has a 5" barrel. Checkered rosewood grips. Low-profile sights. Back and gray finish. Magazine capacity is 7 rounds. Weight is about 32 oz.

NIB	Exc.	V.G.	Good	Fair	Poor
1995	1700	1500	1100	800	500

Ultra Compact Classic

1911-style semi-auto .45 with fixed sights. 4.25" barrel, 34 oz. 3-4 lb. trigger pull, 7+1 capacity. Rosewood or imitation ivory grips. Introduced 2006. Pricing shown for basic model.

NIB	Exc.	V.G.	Good	Fair	Poor
1995	1700	1500	1100	800	500

Compact Classic Companion

Chambered for the .357 Sig or .40 S&W cartridge and fitted with a 5" barrel. Low-profile sights. Black or polymer ivory grips. Stainless or gray finish. Magazine capacity is 7 rounds. Weight is about 32 oz.

NIB	Exc.	V.G.	Good	Fair	Poor
2250	1900	1700	1250	900	600

Carry Classic

Chambered for the .45 ACP cartridge and fitted with a 4.25" barrel with low-profile sights. Rosewood or polymer ivory grips, gray and black finish. Magazine capacity is 7 rounds. Weight is about 34 oz.

NIB	Exc.	V.G.	Good	Fair	Poor
1995	1700	1500	1100	800	500

Ultra Carry

This .45 ACP model features a Damascus slide and titanium frame. Fitted with a 3" barrel with low-profile sights. Magazine capacity is 7 rounds. Weight is about 27 oz.

NIB	Exc.	V.G.	Good	Fair	Poor
3250	2900	2500	2000	1500	800

NOTE: This model is also offered in titanium and stainless for $2350 and stainless and black for $1850.

Tactical 1911

Chambered for the .45 ACP cartridge and fitted with as 5" barrel with Caspian adjustable sights. Rubber grips and moly coat finish. Magazine capacity is 8 rounds. Weight is about 40 oz.

NIB	Exc.	V.G.	Good	Fair	Poor
2200	1975	1600	1200	1000	500

Classic National Match

This .45 ACP pistol has a 5" barrel with Caspian adjustable sights. Black aluma grips and black finish. Magazine capacity is 8 rounds. Weight is about 40 oz.

NIB	Exc.	V.G.	Good	Fair	Poor
2200	1975	1600	1200	1000	500

NOTE: Add $300 for compensator.

UZI ISRAELI MILITARY INDUSTRIES
SEE—Vector Arms, Inc.

Uzi Pistol

Simular to the Uzi Carbine models in 9mm or .45 ACP, with a 4.5" barrel, pistol grip, no rear stock and a 20-shot magazine. This model is no longer imported.

NIB	Exc.	V.G.	Good	Fair	Poor
850	700	550	450	350	250

UZI EAGLE PISTOLS

NOTE: As of 1999 these pistols were no longer imported into the U.S.

Full Size Model

Introduced in 1997 this is a double-action pistol chambered for the 9mm and .40 S&W cartridge. Barrel length is 4.4". Overall length is 8.1". Tritium night sights are standard.

NIB	Exc.	V.G.	Good	Fair	Poor
550	425	350	275	200	150

Short Slide Model

Introduced in 1997 this is a double-action pistol chambered for the 9mm, .40 S&W and .45 ACP cartridge. Barrel length is 3.7". Overall length is 7.5". Tritium night sights are standard.

NIB	Exc.	V.G.	Good	Fair	Poor
600	475	400	325	250	200

Compact Model

Introduced in 1997 this is a double-action pistol chambered for the 9mm, .40 S&W and .45 ACP cartridge. Barrel length is 3.5". Overall length is 7.2". Tritium night sights are standard. Magazine capacity is 8 rounds for the .45 ACP and 10 rounds for the other calibers. Double-action-only is an option for this model.

NIB	Exc.	V.G.	Good	Fair	Poor
600	475	400	325	250	200

Polymer Compact Model

Introduced in 1997 this is a double-action pistol chambered for the 9mm and .40 S&W cartridge. Barrel length is 3.5". Overall length is 7.2". Tritium night sights are standard.

NIB	Exc.	V.G.	Good	Fair	Poor
550	425	350	275	200	150

V

VALTRO
Italy

1998 A1

A Model 1911 clone chambered for .45 ACP and fitted with a match grade 5" barrel. Many special features include a checkered front strap, beavertail grip safety, deluxe wood grips, serrated slide front and back, beveled magazine well. Weight is approximately 40 oz. Introduced in 1998.

NIB	Exc.	V.G.	Good	Fair	Poor
2250	1950	1600	1275	800	500

VEKTOR
South Africa

No longer in business.

Model Z88

This is a semi-automatic pistol chambered for the 9mm cartridge. It has a 5" barrel and fixed sights. Weight is about 35 oz. Blue finish. Magazine capacity is 15 rounds or 10 in U.S. Clone of the Beretta 92.

NIB	Exc.	V.G.	Good	Fair	Poor
600	475	350	250	175	100

Model SP1 Service Pistol

This model is chambered for the 9mm cartridge and is fitted with a 4-5/8" barrel. Fixed sights. Weight is 35 oz. Blue finish. Magazine capacity is 15 rounds or 10 in U.S.

NIB	Exc.	V.G.	Good	Fair	Poor
600	475	350	250	175	100

NOTE: Add $30 for anodized or nickel finish.

Model SP1 Sport

Similar to the SP1 this model features a 5" barrel with 3 chamber compensator. Blue finish. Weight is about 38 oz.

NIB	Exc.	V.G.	Good	Fair	Poor
725	575	450	350	275	175

Model SP1 Tuned Sport

This model also has a three-chamber compensator on a 5" barrel but it has an adjustable straight trigger and LPA 3-dot sighting system. Nickel finish. Weight is about 38 oz.

NIB	Exc.	V.G.	Good	Fair	Poor
1200	950	800	575	400	300

Model SP1 Target

This 9mm model is fitted with a 6" barrel with adjustable straight trigger. LPA 3 dot sighting system. Weight is about 40.5 oz. Two-tone finish.

NIB	Exc.	V.G.	Good	Fair	Poor
1200	950	800	575	400	300

Model SP1 Compact (General's Model)

A compact version of the 9mm pistol fitted with a 4" barrel. Fixed sights. Blue finish. Magazine capacity is 15 rounds or 10 for U.S. Weight is about 31.5 oz.

NIB	Exc.	V.G.	Good	Fair	Poor
650	525	400	300	200	75

Model SP2

A full size service pistol chambered for the .40 S&W cartridge. fitted with a 4-5/8" barrel. Fixed sights. Magazine capacity is 11 rounds or 10 for U.S. Blued finish. Weight is about 35 oz.

NIB	Exc.	V.G.	Good	Fair	Poor
650	525	400	300	200	75

Model SP2 Compact (General's Model)

A compact .40 S&W pistol with 4" barrel. Magazine capacity is 11 rounds or 10 for U.S. Weight is about 31.5 oz. Blue finish. Fixed sights.

NIB	Exc.	V.G.	Good	Fair	Poor
650	525	400	300	200	75

Model SP2 Competition

This model is chambered for the .40 S&W cartridge and fitted with a 5.88" barrel. It features enlarged safety levers and magazine catch. The frame has been thickened for scope mount. Beavertail grip and straight trigger. Weight is about 42 oz.

NIB	Exc.	V.G.	Good	Fair	Poor
1000	750	600	450	325	200

Model SP1 Ultra Sport

This model is designed for IPSC open-class competition. Barrel length is 6" with 3 chamber compensator. Chambered for 9mm cartridge. Optical scope mount with Weaver rails. Magazine capacity is 19 rounds or 10 for U.S. Weight is about 41.5 oz. Priced with Lynx scope.

NIB	Exc.	V.G.	Good	Fair	Poor
2150	1800	1575	1200	800	500

Model SP2 Ultra Sport

Same as model above but chambered for .40 S&W cartridge. Magazine capacity is 14 rounds or 10 for U.S.

NIB	Exc.	V.G.	Good	Fair	Poor
2150	1800	1575	1200	800	500

Model SP2 Conversion Kit

Made for the SP2 this is a 9mm conversion kit that consists of a 9mm barrel, recoil spring, and 9mm magazine.

NIB	Exc.	V.G.	Good	Fair	Poor
200	150	100	75	50	25

Model CP-1 Compact

Chambered for the 9mm cartridge and fitted with a 4" barrel this model has a polymer frame. Fixed sights. Weight is about 25 oz. Magazine capacity is 13 rounds standard, 12 rounds compact or 10 rounds for U.S. Offered with black or nickel slide.

NIB	Exc.	V.G.	Good	Fair	Poor
475	375	250	150	100	50

NOTE: Add $20 for nickel slide.

VENUS WAFFENWERKE
Zella Mehlis, Germany

Venus

A 6.35mm, 7.65mm, or 9mm semi-automatic pistol with a 3.5" barrel. Slide is marked "Original Venus Patent" and the grips bear the monogram "OW." Designed by Oskar Will. Blued, plastic grips. Manufactured from 1912 to 1914.

NIB	Exc.	V.G.	Good	Fair	Poor
—	700	550	400	250	100

VICTORY ARMS CO., LTD.
Northhampton, England

Model MC5

A 9mm, .38 Super, .41 Action Express, 10mm, or .45 caliber semi-automatic pistol with a 4.25", 5.75", or 7.5" barrel, 10-, 12-, or 17-shot magazine, decocking lever and Millett sights. Interchangeable barrels were available. Introduced in 1989.

NIB	Exc.	V.G.	Good	Fair	Poor
500	400	300	250	200	150

VOLQUARTSEN CUSTOM
Carroll, Iowa

This company was started in 1973, and began specializing in Ruger 10/22 aftermarket conversions. In 1997 the company began producing its own receivers. **NOTE:** Volquartsen offers beaucoup options on a wide variety of rifles. The values shown below are for the more-or-less base models.

PISTOLS

These pistols are based on the Ruger MK II design.

Black Cheetah Pistol

Special order only. Discontinued, Value speculative.

Compact

Fitted with a 3.5" bull barrel and Hogue Monogrip. Adjustable rear sight and target front sight. Stainless steel finish. Weight is about 42 oz.

NIB	Exc.	V.G.	Good	Fair	Poor
1000	850	700	525	400	300

Masters

The Masters features a 6.5" barrel with aluminum alloy-finned underlug. The top rib has a front blade sight with an adjustable rear sight. Rib is cut to accommodate optics. Integral compensator. Weight is about 56 oz.

NIB	Exc.	V.G.	Good	Fair	Poor
1600	1350	1200	900	650	500

Olympic

The Olympic is designed for NRA or UIT competitive shooting. It has a 7.5" match barrel with a unique gas chamber for recoil-free shooting. Target front sight and adjustable rear sight. Weight is about 36 oz.

NIB	Exc.	V.G.	Good	Fair	Poor
1750	1450	1300	1000	650	500

Stingray

Fitted with a 7.5" match-grade barrel with radial flutes. Compensator standard. Supplied with either a Ultra Dot red dot optic or TL rear optic. Weight is about 56 oz.

NIB	Exc.	V.G.	Good	Fair	Poor
1600	1350	1200	900	650	500

Terminator

This model is fitted with a 7.5" match barrel with integral compensator. Choice of Weaver-style or 3/8" tip-off scope mounting system.

NIB	Exc.	V.G.	Good	Fair	Poor
1600	1350	1200	900	650	500

NOTE: Add $150 for Ultra Dot optics.

Ultra-Lite Match

NIB	Exc.	V.G.	Good	Fair	Poor
1600	1350	1200	900	650	500

V-6

The V-6 has a 6" vent-rib triangular-shaped match barrel with full-length underlug. Adjustable rear sight and target front sight. Rubber target grips. Weight is about 36 oz.

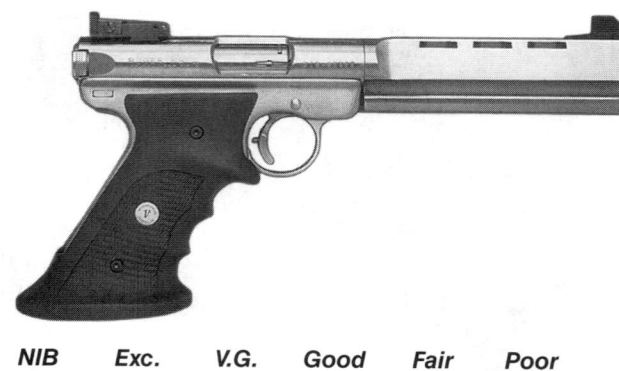

NIB	Exc.	V.G.	Good	Fair	Poor
1350	1200	950	700	550	300

V-2000

Fitted with a 6" match barrel with alloy-finned underlug. Rubber target grips and adjustable rear sight with target front sight. Weight is about 37 oz.

NIB	Exc.	V.G.	Good	Fair	Poor
1350	1200	950	700	550	300

V-Magic II

This model has an 8" fluted match barrel with integral compensator. Rubber target grips and Ultra Dot red dot optic. No open sights. Weight is about 46 oz.

NIB	Exc.	V.G.	Good	Fair	Poor
1350	1200	950	700	550	300

WALCH, JOHN
New York, New York

Navy Revolver

A .36 caliber superimposed load percussion revolver with a 6" octagonal barrel and a 6-shot cylinder fitted with 12 nipples, two hammers, and two triggers. The barrel marked "Walch Firearms Co. NY." and "Patented Feb. 8, 1859." Blued with walnut grips.

NIB	Exc.	V.G.	Good	Fair	Poor
—	—	13000	9000	4000	950

Pocket Revolver

A spur trigger .31 caliber 10-shot percussion revolver with either a brass or iron frame and walnut grips. The iron frame version is worth approximately 50 percent more than the brass variety.

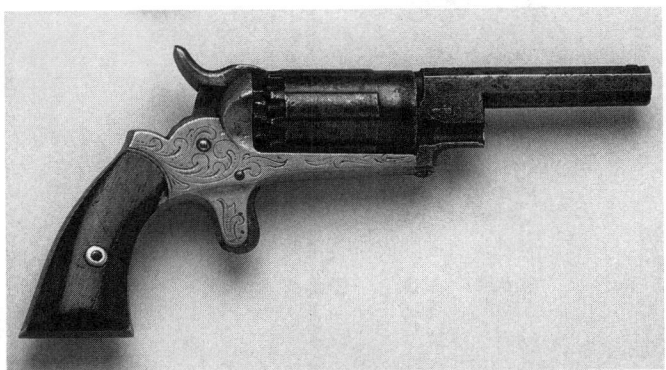

Courtesy Greg Martin Auctions

NIB	Exc.	V.G.	Good	Fair	Poor
—	—	5000	2750	1000	300

WALDMAN
Germany

Waldman

A 7.65mm semi-automatic pistol with a 3.5" barrel and 8-shot magazine. The slide marked "1913 Model Automatic Pistol" and some examples are marked "American Automatic Pistol." Blued with checkered walnut grips inlaid with a brass insert marked "Waldman."

NIB	Exc.	V.G.	Good	Fair	Poor
—	300	225	200	150	100

WALLIS & BIRCH
Philadelphia, Pennsylvania

Pocket Pistol

A .41 caliber single-shot percussion pocket pistol with a 2.5" or 3" barrel, German silver furniture and walnut stock. The barrel is marked "Wallis & Birch Phila." Produced during the 1850s.

NIB	Exc.	V.G.	Good	Fair	Poor
—	—	4050	2250	800	250

WALTHER, CARL
Zella Mehilis and Ulm/Donau, Germany

Model 1

A 6.35mm semi-automatic pistol barrel lengths of 2"-6". Blued with checkered hard rubber grips with the Walther logo on each grip. Introduced in 1908.

Courtesy James Rankin

NIB	Exc.	V.G.	Good	Fair	Poor
—	1000	700	400	200	200

MODEL 2

A 6.35mm semi-automatic pistol with a knurled bushing at the muzzle that retains the mainspring. There are two variations: one with a fixed rear sight, and one with a pop-up rear sight. Blued with checkered hard rubber grips with the Walther logo on each grip. Introduced in 1909.

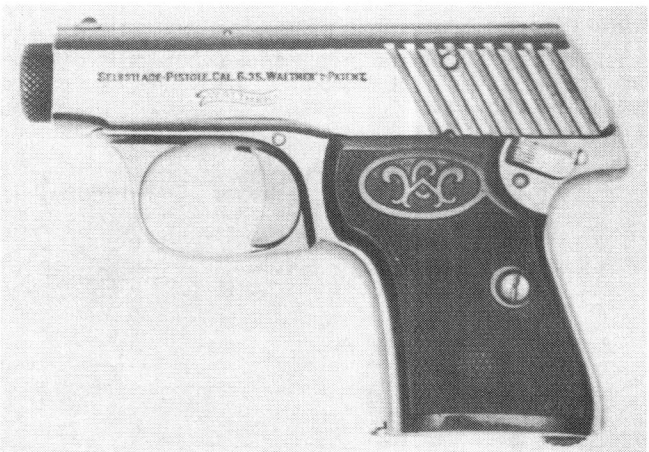

Courtesy James Rankin

Courtesy James Rankin

NIB	Exc.	V.G.	Good	Fair	Poor
—	1500	1000	600	350	200

Model 4

A 7.65mm semi-automatic pistol larger than the preceding models. There were many variations of this model produced. Blued with checkered hard rubber grips with the Walther logo on each grip. Introduced 1910.

Courtesy James Rankin

NIB	Exc.	V.G.	Good	Fair	Poor
—	650	525	400	275	150

Model 5

A 6.35mm semi-automatic pistol that is almost identical to the Model 2. Fixed sights. Blued with checkered hard rubber grips with the Walther logo on each grip.

Model 2 Fixed Sights

NIB	Exc.	V.G.	Good	Fair	Poor
—	800	600	300	200	150

Model 2 Pop Up Sights

NIB	Exc.	V.G.	Good	Fair	Poor
—	1800	1000	600	400	300

Model 3

A 7.65mm semi-automatic pistol having a smooth barrel bushing. Blued with checkered hard rubber grips with the Walther logo on each. Introduced in 1910.

Courtesy James Rankin

NIB	Exc.	V.G.	Good	Fair	Poor
—	500	400	300	200	150

Model 6

A 9mm semi-automatic pistol. The largest of the Walther numbered pistols. Approximately 1,500 manufactured. Blued with checkered hard rubber grips with the Walther logo on each grip. Sometimes seen with plain checkered wood grips. Introduced 1915.

NIB	Exc.	V.G.	Good	Fair	Poor
—	7000	5000	3000	1500	700

Model 7

A 6.35mm semi-automatic pistol in the same style as the Model 4. Blued with checkered hard rubber grips with the Walther logo on each side. Introduced in 1917.

Courtesy James Rankin

NIB	Exc.	V.G.	Good	Fair	Poor
—	700	500	300	200	150

MODEL 8

A 6.35mm semi-automatic pistol. Finish is either blue, silver, or gold. Most were unengraved, but three types of engraving coverage were available from the factory: slide only, slide and frame and complete coverage overall. The grips are checkered hard rubber with the WC logo on one grip, and 6.35mm on the opposite side. Ivory grips are seen with many of the engraved models. Introduced in 1920 and produced until 1944.

Courtesy James Rankin

Blue, Silver

NIB	Exc.	V.G.	Good	Fair	Poor
—	750	600	300	200	150

Engraved Slide

NIB	Exc.	V.G.	Good	Fair	Poor
—	1000	700	500	300	200

Engraved Slide and Frame

NIB	Exc.	V.G.	Good	Fair	Poor
—	2500	2000	1100	450	300

Engraved, Complete Coverage

NIB	Exc.	V.G.	Good	Fair	Poor
—	4000	3500	1400	500	300

NOTE: Add $500 for factory case.

Model 9

A 6.35mm semi-automatic pistol. Smaller than the Model 8, but built as the Model 1 with exposed barrel. Same finishes and engraving as the Model 8. Introduced 1921 and produced until 1944. All values the same as the Model 8.

Courtesy James Rankin

Sport Model 1926, Walther Hammerless, Target 22, Walther Standard Sport, Walther 1932 Olympia, Sport Model Target, Special Stoeger Model

All of these .22 LR caliber semi-automatic pistols are the same target pistol introduced by Walther in 1926. A well-made pistol with a barrel length of between 6"-16". It has one-piece checkered wrap-around wood grips. There was also a .22 Short version of the Olympia model produced for rapid fire Olympic shooting. There was also a torpedo-shape target weight available for shooters.

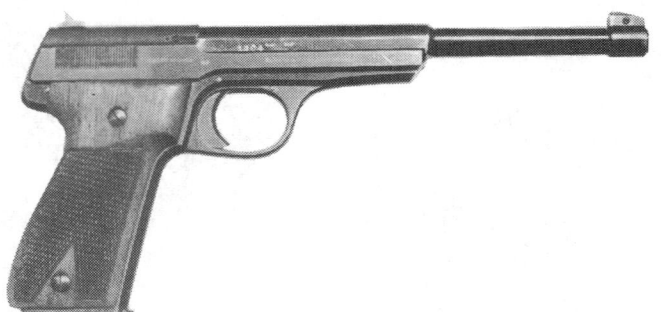

Courtesy Orvel Reichert

NIB	Exc.	V.G.	Good	Fair	Poor
—	1000	850	550	350	250

NOTE: Add $200 for target weight. Add $500 for case.

Walther 1936 Olympia

This semi-automatic target pistol in .22 caliber resembled the earlier 1932 Olympia, but with many improvements. There were four standard models produced with many variations of each one. These variations included many barrel lengths, and both round and octagon barrels. There were duraluminum slides, frames and triggers. Various weight configurations to as many as four separate weights to one gun. One-piece wrap-around checkered wood grips in different configurations for the individual shooter. Produced until 1944. The four models were:

1. Funfklamph Pentathlon
2. Jagerschafts—Hunter
3. Sport or Standard Model
4. Schnellfeur—Rapid Fire

NIB	Exc.	V.G.	Good	Fair	Poor
—	1500	1300	750	475	250

NOTE: Prices are for Standard Model. Add $100 for Pentathlon or Hunter, $200 for Rapid Fire. Add $250 for weights.Model MP

A 9mm semi-automatic pistol that was the forerunner of the Model AP and P.38 series. Found in variations that resemble a large Model PP or the P.38. Blued finish with one-piece wrap-around checkered wood grips.

Courtesy James Rankin

NIB	Exc.	V.G.	Good	Fair	Poor
—	35000	30000	25000	20000	15000

Model AP

A 9mm semi-automatic pistol that was the forerunner of the Model P.38. A hammerless pistol in various barrel lengths. Sometimes with duraluminum frames, and some with stocks. Blued finish with one-piece wraparound checkered wood grips.

NIB	Exc.	V.G.	Good	Fair	Poor
—	28000	25000	20000	15000	10000

NOTE: With stock add $4000.

MODEL PP

A semi-automatic pistol in .22, .25, .32 and .380 caliber. Introduced in 1928. It was the first successful commercial double-action pistol. It was manufactured in finishes of blue, silver, and gold, and with three different types of engraving. Grips were generally two-piece black or white plastic with the Walther banner on each grip. Grips in wood or ivory are seen, but usually on engraved guns. There are many variations of the Model PP and numerous NSDAP markings seen on the pre-1946 models that were produced during the Nazi regime. All reflect various prices.

.22 Caliber

NIB	Exc.	V.G.	Good	Fair	Poor
—	800	600	350	250	150

.25 Caliber

NIB	Exc.	V.G.	Good	Fair	Poor
—	5000	4500	2500	1500	600

.32 Caliber High Polished Finish

NIB	Exc.	V.G.	Good	Fair	Poor
—	850	650	325	225	175

.32 Caliber Milled Finish

NIB	Exc.	V.G.	Good	Fair	Poor
—	700	500	250	200	125

.380 Caliber

NIB	Exc.	V.G.	Good	Fair	Poor
—	1600	1300	800	475	350

.32 Caliber with Duraluminum Frame

NIB	Exc.	V.G.	Good	Fair	Poor
—	900	700	550	400	200

.32 Caliber with Bottom Magazine Release

NIB	Exc.	V.G.	Good	Fair	Poor
—	1400	1000	600	400	200

.32 Caliber with Verchromt Finish

NIB	Exc.	V.G.	Good	Fair	Poor
—	2800	2500	1200	700	400

.32 Caliber, Allemagne Marked

NIB	Exc.	V.G.	Good	Fair	Poor
—	850	700	550	325	250

.32 Caliber, A. F. Stoeger Contract

NIB	Exc.	V.G.	Good	Fair	Poor
—	2500	1750	1050	700	400

.32 Caliber with Waffenampt Proofs, High Polished Finish

NIB	Exc.	V.G.	Good	Fair	Poor
—	1500	1200	600	275	150

.32 Caliber with Waffenampt Proofs, Milled Finish

NIB	Exc.	V.G.	Good	Fair	Poor
—	700	500	325	250	150

.32 CALIBER IN BLUE, SILVER OR GOLD FINISH AND FULL COVERAGE ENGRAVING

Courtesy James Rankin

Blue

NIB	Exc.	V.G.	Good	Fair	Poor
—	5000	4000	3000	1200	700

Silver

NIB	Exc.	V.G.	Good	Fair	Poor
—	5500	4500	3000	1200	700

Gold

NIB	Exc.	V.G.	Good	Fair	Poor
—	5800	5000	3500	1500	700

NOTE: Add $500 for ivory grips with any of the three above. Add $700 for leather presentation cases. Add $1000 for .380 caliber.

.32 Caliber, Police Eagle/C Proofed, High Polished Finish

NIB	Exc.	V.G.	Good	Fair	Poor
—	1200	800	375	250	150

.32 Caliber, Police Eagle/C and Police Eagle/F Proofed, Milled Finish

NIB	Exc.	V.G.	Good	Fair	Poor
—	900	600	375	275	150

32 Caliber, NSKK Marked on the Slide

NIB	Exc.	V.G.	Good	Fair	Poor
—	3500	2700	850	550	300

NOTE: Add $1,000 with proper NSKK DRGM AKAH holster.

.32 Caliber, NSDAP Gruppe Markings

NIB	Exc.	V.G.	Good	Fair	Poor
—	2500	2000	1000	500	300

NOTE: Add $1,000 with proper SA DRGM AKAH holster.

.32 Caliber, PDM Marked with Bottom Magazine Release

NIB	Exc.	V.G.	Good	Fair	Poor
—	1500	1300	700	475	300

.32 Caliber, RJ Marked

NIB	Exc.	V.G.	Good	Fair	Poor
—	900	700	475	400	150

.32 Caliber, RFV Marked, High Polished or Milled Finish

NIB	Exc.	V.G.	Good	Fair	Poor
—	900	700	475	400	150

.32 Caliber, RBD Munster Marked

NIB	Exc.	V.G.	Good	Fair	Poor
—	2200	1750	1200	650	400

.32 Caliber, RpLt Marked

NIB	Exc.	V.G.	Good	Fair	Poor
—	1500	1200	700	375	200

.32 Caliber, Statens Vattenfallsverk Marked

NIB	Exc.	V.G.	Good	Fair	Poor
—	1500	1200	700	375	200

.32 Caliber, AC Marked

NIB	Exc.	V.G.	Good	Fair	Poor
—	700	500	300	250	150

.32 Caliber, Duraluminum Frame

NIB	Exc.	V.G.	Good	Fair	Poor
—	900	700	500	400	150

.380 Caliber, Bottom Magazine Release and Waffenampt Proofs

NIB	Exc.	V.G.	Good	Fair	Poor
—	2000	1500	700	500	300

MODEL PPK

A semi-automatic pistol in .22, .25, .32 and .380 caliber. Introduced six months after the Model PP in 1929. A more compact version of the Model PP with one less round in the magazine and one-piece wraparound checkered plastic grips in brown, black, and white with the Walther banner on each side of the grips. The Model PPK will be found with the same types of finishes as the Model PP as well as the same styles of engraving. Grips in wood or ivory are seen with some of the engraved models. As with the Model PP there are many variations of the Model PPK and numerous NSDAP markings seen on the pre-1946 models that were produced during the Nazi regime. All reflect various prices.

Courtesy James Rankin

.22 Caliber

NIB	Exc.	V.G.	Good	Fair	Poor
—	1700	1500	750	325	175

.25 Caliber

NIB	Exc.	V.G.	Good	Fair	Poor
—	6000	4000	1850	1000	500

.32 Caliber, High Polished Finish

NIB	Exc.	V.G.	Good	Fair	Poor
—	950	750	450	250	150

.32 Caliber, Milled Finish

NIB	Exc.	V.G.	Good	Fair	Poor
—	900	700	400	250	150

.380 Caliber

Courtesy Orvel Reichert

NIB	Exc.	V.G.	Good	Fair	Poor
—	3000	2500	1600	750	375

.32 Caliber with Duraluminum Frame

NIB	Exc.	V.G.	Good	Fair	Poor
—	1500	1300	600	400	200

.32 Caliber Marked Mod. PP on Slide

NIB	Exc.	V.G.	Good	Fair	Poor
—	5000	4000	2500	1500	1000

.32 Caliber with Panagraphed Slide

NIB	Exc.	V.G.	Good	Fair	Poor
—	950	750	450	300	200

.32 Caliber with Verchromt Finish

NIB	Exc.	V.G.	Good	Fair	Poor
—	2800	2500	1200	700	350

.32 CALIBER IN BLUE, SILVER OR GOLD FINISH AND FULL COVERAGE ENGRAVING

Blue NIB	Exc.	V.G.	Good	Fair	Poor
—	5000	3500	2500	1200	700

Silver NIB	Exc.	V.G.	Good	Fair	Poor
—	6000	4000	3000	1500	700

Gold NIB	Exc.	V.G.	Good	Fair	Poor
—	6500	5500	3500	1500	700

NOTE: Add $1,000 for ivory grips with any of the three above. Add $1,000 for leather presentation cases. Add $1,000 for .380 caliber.

.32 Caliber, Czechoslovakian Contract

NIB	Exc.	V.G.	Good	Fair	Poor
—	1850	1500	1000	550	300

.32 Caliber, Allemagne Marked

NIB	Exc.	V.G.	Good	Fair	Poor
—	1000	800	600	400	250

.32 Caliber with Waffenampt Proofs and a High Polished Finish

NIB	Exc.	V.G.	Good	Fair	Poor
—	1900	1600	900	400	250

.32 Caliber with Waffenampt Proofs and a Milled Finish

NIB	Exc.	V.G.	Good	Fair	Poor
—	1500	1300	750	300	175

.32 Caliber, Police Eagle/C Proofed, High Polished Finish

NIB	Exc.	V.G.	Good	Fair	Poor
—	1200	1000	500	300	175

.32 Caliber, Police Eagle/C Proofed. Milled Finish

NIB	Exc.	V.G.	Good	Fair	Poor
—	900	700	375	275	175

.32 Caliber, Police Eagle/F Proofed, Duraluminum Frame, Milled Finish

NIB	Exc.	V.G.	Good	Fair	Poor
—	1300	1000	550	350	225

.22 Caliber, Late War, Black Grips

NIB	Exc.	V.G.	Good	Fair	Poor
—	1800	1500	600	450	300

.32 Caliber, Party Leader Grips, Brown

NIB	Exc.	V.G.	Good	Fair	Poor
—	6000	5500	3000	2250	2000

.32 Caliber, Party Leader Grips, Black

NIB	Exc.	V.G.	Good	Fair	Poor
—	6000	5500	3200	2550	2500

NOTE: Add $1,500 with proper Party Leader DRGM AKAH holster.

.32 Caliber, RZM Marked

NIB	Exc.	V.G.	Good	Fair	Poor
—	2000	1700	800	400	300

.32 Caliber, PDM Marked with Duraluminum Frame and Bottom Magazine Release

NIB	Exc.	V.G.	Good	Fair	Poor
—	3200	2800	1300	750	450

.32 Caliber, RFV Marked

NIB	Exc.	V.G.	Good	Fair	Poor
—	2500	2000	1150	650	400

.32 Caliber, DRP Marked

NIB	Exc.	V.G.	Good	Fair	Poor
—	1200	900	550	450	275

.32 Caliber, Statens Vattenfallsverk

NIB	Exc.	V.G.	Good	Fair	Poor
—	1500	1200	700	450	300

WALTHER POST-WORLD WAR II

Models PP and PPK

Manufactured by the firm of Manufacture de Machines du Haut Rhin at Mulhouse, France under license by Walther.

Model PP Some with Duraluminum Frames, Model PP

.22 Caliber

NIB	Exc.	V.G.	Good	Fair	Poor
—	750	600	400	275	175

Model PP .32 Caliber

NIB	Exc.	V.G.	Good	Fair	Poor
—	500	375	350	275	175

Model PP .380Caliber

NIB	Exc.	V.G.	Good	Fair	Poor
—	750	600	400	275	175

Model PP, All Three Calibers Finished In Blue, Silver and Gold with Full Coverage EngravingBlue

NIB	Exc.	V.G.	Good	Fair	Poor
—	1900	1500	900	600	300

Silver

NIB	Exc.	V.G.	Good	Fair	Poor
—	1900	1500	900	600	300

Gold

NIB	Exc.	V.G.	Good	Fair	Poor
—	1900	1500	900	600	300

Model PP Mark II

These Walthers were manufactured under license by Walther and produced by the Manurhin Company. They were sold exclusively by Interarms, Alexandria, Virginia. The Mark IIs were the same pistols as those above and have the same types of finish and engraving as well as the same value.

Model PP Manurhin

Manurhin Company manufactured with Manurhin logo and inscription. Usually "licensed by Walther" somewhere on the pistol. The same pistols as those above, bearing the same types of finish and engraving, and having the same values.

Model PP Sport, Manurhin

.22 caliber. This is the same gun as the Model PP with different barrel lengths running from 5-3/4" to 7-3/4". It is basically a target .22 with adjustable rear sights for elevation and windage. The front sight is also adjustable. There is a barrel bushing at the muzzle that attaches the front sight to the barrel. The grips are contoured checkered plastic and are either squared at the bottom of the grips or are in the shape of an inverted bird's-head.

NIB	Exc.	V.G.	Good	Fair	Poor
—	900	600	450	375	275

Model PP Sport C, Manurhin

.22 caliber. This is the same gun as the Model PP Sport but in single-action with a spur hammer. It has front and rear adjustable sights and squared target grips in checkered black, brown and plastic. Blued and silver finish.

NIB	Exc.	V.G.	Good	Fair	Poor
—	900	600	450	375	275

Model PP Sport, Walther

A .22 caliber Sport was manufactured by Manurhin, but sold by Walther with the Walther logo and inscription. This is the same gun as the Model PP Sport, Manurhin. Only sold for a period of two years.

NIB	Exc.	V.G.	Good	Fair	Poor
—	900	600	450	375	275

Model PP 50th Anniversary Commemorative Model

In .22 or .380 caliber. Blued with gold inlays and hand-carved grips with oak leaves and acorns. Walther banner carved into each side of the grips. Wood presentation case.

NIB	Exc.	V.G.	Good	Fair	Poor
—	1500	1000	750	500	300

MODEL PPK, SOME WITH DURALUMINUM FRAMES

.22 Caliber

NIB	Exc.	V.G.	Good	Fair	Poor
—	750	600	400	275	175

.32 Caliber

NIB	Exc.	V.G.	Good	Fair	Poor
—	550	400	350	275	175

.380 Caliber

NIB	Exc.	V.G.	Good	Fair	Poor
—	750	600	400	275	175

Model PPK, All Three Calibers Finished In Blue, Silver and Gold With Full Coverage Engraving

1st Model

NIB	Exc.	V.G.	Good	Fair	Poor
—	1900	1500	750	450	300

2nd Model

NIB	Exc.	V.G.	Good	Fair	Poor
—	1900	1500	750	450	300

3rd Model

NIB	Exc.	V.G.	Good	Fair	Poor
—	1900	1500	750	450	300

Model PPK Mark II

These Walthers were manufactured under license by Walther and produced by the Manurhin Company. They were sold exclusively by Interarms, Alexandria, Virginia. The Mark IIs were the same pistols as those above and have the same types of finish and engraving as well as the same value.

Model PPK Manurhin

Manurhin Company manufactured with Manurhin logo and inscription. Usually "Licensed by Walther" somewhere on the pistol. The same pistols as above, bearing the same types of finish and engraving, and having the same value.

Courtesy James Rankin

Model PPK 50th Anniversary Commemorative Model

In .22 or .380 caliber. Blued with gold inlays and hand-carved grips with oak leaves and acorns. Walther banner carved into each side of the grips. Wood presentation case.

NIB	Exc.	V.G.	Good	Fair	Poor
—	2100	1800	1250	1000	500

Model PPK American

In 1986 the Model PPK was licensed by the Walther Company to be manufactured in the United States. The finish is stainless steel. Caliber is .380.

NIB	Exc.	V.G.	Good	Fair	Poor
—	500	375	300	200	150

Model PPK/S

This Walther was manufactured in .22, .32 and .380 caliber for sale in the United States market after the introduction of the United States Gun Control Act of 1968. It is basically a Model PP with a cut-off muzzle and slide. It has two-piece black checkered plastic grips as seen on the Model PP. It was finished in blue, nickel, dull gold and verchromt.

NIB	Exc.	V.G.	Good	Fair	Poor
—	550	475	375	300	200

Model PPK/S American

Manufactured in the United States. The same as the German Model PPK/S. This pistol is finished in blue and stainless steel. Caliber is .380.

NIB	Exc.	V.G.	Good	Fair	Poor
—	500	375	300	200	150

Model TP

A Walther-manufactured semi-automatic pistol in .22 and .25 calibers patterned after the earlier Model 9. Finish is blue and silver black plastic checkered grips with Walther banner medallions in each grip.

NIB	Exc.	V.G.	Good	Fair	Poor
—	900	700	500	375	250

Model TPH

A Walther-manufactured semi-automatic pistol in .22 and .25 calibers. This is a double-action pistol with a duraluminum frame. Finished in blue or silver. Two-piece black checkered plastic grips. Full coverage engraving available.

NIB	Exc.	V.G.	Good	Fair	Poor
—	650	500	450	350	250

NOTE: Add $300 for the engraved model.

Model TPH American

This semi-automatic is produced in both .22 and .25 calibers. It is licensed by Walther and manufactured in the United States. It is produced in stainless steel and has two-piece black plastic checkered grips. It is a double-action pistol.

NIB	Exc.	V.G.	Good	Fair	Poor
—	400	300	200	150	100

Model PP Super

This is a .380 and 9x18 caliber, double-action semi-automatic manufactured by Walther. It is similar in design to the Model PP, but with a P.38 type of mechanism. Finish is blue and the grips are wraparound black checkered plastic or a type of molded wood colored plastic.

Courtesy Orvel Reichert

NIB	Exc.	V.G.	Good	Fair	Poor
—	750	500	350	250	150

MODEL P.38

Following WWII, the P.38 was reintroduced in variety of calibers with a 5" barrel and alloy or steel frame.

.22 Caliber

NIB	Exc.	V.G.	Good	Fair	Poor
1200	850	650	500	350	200

Other Calibers

NIB	Exc.	V.G.	Good	Fair	Poor
750	600	500	400	300	200

Model P.38 Steel-Framed (Introduced 1987)

Factory-engraved versions of the P.38 pistol were blued, chrome, or silver or gold-plated. We suggest that a qualified appraisal be secured when contemplating purchase.

NIB	Exc.	V.G.	Good	Fair	Poor
1400	1250	1000	750	500	400

Model P.38K

As above, with a 2.8" barrel and front sight is mounted on the slide. Imported between 1974 and 1980.

NIB	Exc.	V.G.	Good	Fair	Poor
—	900	650	450	300	200

Model P.38 II

NIB	Exc.	V.G.	Good	Fair	Poor
—	800	550	350	250	200

Model P.38 IV

A redesigned version of the above, with a 4.5" barrel and 8-shot magazine. Fitted with a decocking lever and adjustable sights. Imported prior to 1983.

NIB	Exc.	V.G.	Good	Fair	Poor
—	900	650	450	300	200

CURRENTLY IMPORTED WALTHER PISTOLS—WALTHER USA

In 1999 Carl Walther Gmbh of Germany and Smith & Wesson entered into a joint agreement to import and distribute Walther-branded firearms and accessories into the U.S. beginning August 1, 1999.

Model PP Limited Edition

This model was introduced in 2000 and is a limited edition of 100 pistols chambered in .380 ACP and 50 pistols chambered in .32 ACP. The finish is a high-polish blue with the slide marked "LAST EDITION 1929-1999." Supplied with a special case with certificate and video of history of Walther.

NIB	Exc.	V.G.	Good	Fair	Poor
1350	1100	900	700	500	300

Model PPK/E—Walther USA

Introduced in 2000 this pistol is chambered for the .380 or .32 ACP cartridges and later in that year the .22 LR. It has a double-action trigger. Produced in Hungary by Walther. Barrel length is 3.4". Magazine capacity is seven rounds for the .380 and eight rounds for the .32 ACP and .22 LR. Blued finish and plastic grips.

NIB	Exc.	V.G.	Good	Fair	Poor
400	325	250	195	125	75

Model PPK

Chambered for the .380 ACP or .32 ACP cartridge and fitted with a 3.35" barrel. Offered in blue or stainless steel. Black plastic grips. Fixed red-dot sights. Magazine capacity is six for the .380 ACP and seven for the .32 ACP. Weight is about 21 oz.

NIB	Exc.	V.G.	Good	Fair	Poor
550	425	300	250	175	75

Model PPK/S

Same as the PPK but with .25" longer grip. Magazine capacity is seven rounds for the .380 ACP and eight rounds for the .32 ACP. Weight is about 23 oz. Offered in blue, stainless steel and two-tone finish.

NIB	Exc.	V.G.	Good	Fair	Poor
550	425	300	250	175	75

Model PPS

Striker-fired compact DAO semi-auto pistol. Chambered in .40 S&W (6 rounds) or 9mm Parabellum (7 rounds). Features include polymer frame and grip, decocker button, loaded chamber indicator, 3.2-inch stainless steel barrel, integral Weaver-style accessory rail, black Tenifer finish overall.

NIB	Exc.	V.G.	Good	Fair	Poor
625	535	450	350	250	150

Seventy-fifth Anniversary PPK

Blued with wood grips, machine engraving and available in .380 ACP with 6+1 capacity. Special SN beginning with 0000PPK, shipped with glass-top display case. Single/double-action, 3.3" barrel, 20.8 oz. Windage-adjustable rear sight. Introduced 2006.

NIB	Exc.	V.G.	Good	Fair	Poor
675	525	400	275	175	100

Model P5

A 9mm semi-automatic pistol with a double-action firing mechanism. One of the first Walthers to have a decocker lever.

Finish is a combination of black matte and high polish. It has black plastic checkered grips.

NIB	Exc.	V.G.	Good	Fair	Poor
1000	850	650	500	300	200

Model P5 Compact

A shorter version of the standard Model P5.

NIB	Exc.	V.G.	Good	Fair	Poor
1200	850	700	600	375	250

Model P5 One Hundred Year Commemorative

Blued with gold inlays and hand-carved grips with oak leaves and acorns. Walther banner carved into each side of the grips.

PRESENTATION CASE

NIB	Exc.	V.G.	Good	Fair	Poor
2750	1950	1600	1000	750	400

Model P88

A 9mm semi-automatic in double-action with ambidextrous decocking lever. Fifteen-shot magazine and two-piece black checkered plastic grips. Combination of high polish and black matte finish.

NIB	Exc.	V.G.	Good	Fair	Poor
1700	1525	1275	975	700	400

Model P88 Compact

A shorter version of the standard Model P88.

NIB	Exc.	V.G.	Good	Fair	Poor
1600	1425	1135	850	600	400

Model P99

Introduced in 1997, this is a single- and double-action design with a 4" barrel and polymer frame. Chambered for 9mm or .40 S&W cartridge it has a magazine capacity of 10 rounds (16 rounds in 9mm and 12 rounds in .40 S&W for law enforcement). Front sight is interchangeable and rear sight is windage adjustable. Total length of pistol is 7" and weight is approximately 25 oz. Finish is blue tenifer.

NIB	Exc.	V.G.	Good	Fair	Poor
800	700	550	450	300	200

Model P99 Compact AS/QA

This model is chambered for the 9mm cartridge with a double action trigger and 9mm or .40 S&W cartridges. Quick action, striker fired. Barrel length is 3.5" with fixed sights. Magazine capacity is 10 rounds for 9mm and 8 rounds for .40 S&W models. Weight is about 19 oz.

NIB	Exc.	V.G.	Good	Fair	Poor
675	575	400	325	200	175

Model P990

A double-action-only version of the P99.

NIB	Exc.	V.G.	Good	Fair	Poor
675	550	400	325	200	175

Model P99 QPQ

Similar to the P99 but with silver tenifer finish.

NIB	Exc.	V.G.	Good	Fair	Poor
750	625	475	375	275	250

Model P990 QPQ

A double-action-only silver tenifer finish version of the P99 QPQ.

NIB	Exc.	V.G.	Good	Fair	Poor
750	625	475	375	275	250

Model P99 QA

Similar to the P99 pistol but with a constant short trigger pull. Trigger pull is approximately 6.5 lbs. Offered in both 9mm and .40 S&W calibers. Introduced in 2000.

NIB	Exc.	V.G.	Good	Fair	Poor
675	575	400	325	200	175

Model P99 Military

Similar to the P99 but with military finish.

NIB	Exc.	V.G.	Good	Fair	Poor
675	575	400	325	200	175

Model P99 La Chasse DU

This model features laser engraving on the blue tenifer slide.

NIB	Exc.	V.G.	Good	Fair	Poor
750	625	475	375	275	250

Model P99 La Chasse

This model features hand engraving on a gray tenifer slide.

NIB	Exc.	V.G.	Good	Fair	Poor
1675	1350	1100	750	500	300

Model P99 Commemorative

This is a limited edition P99 that features a high polish blue slide with a special serial number and the marking" COMMEMORATIVE FOR THE YEAR 2000." Offered in both 9mm and .40 S&W calibers. Each handgun comes with a special certificate and video of the history of Walther.

NIB	Exc.	V.G.	Good	Fair	Poor
750	625	475	375	275	250

Walther PPQ

Caliber: 9mm Parabellum or .40 S&W. Steel slide, polymer frame with interchangeable backstraps. Magazine capacity, 15/12 (9mm) and 17/14 (.40). Other features include front slide serrations, Quick Defense Trigger with integral safety, ambidextrous slide and magazine release, adjustable rear sight and loaded-chamber indicator. Weight is 24.5 ounces, barrel length is 4.0-inches, finish matte black.

NIB	Exc.	V.G.	Good	Fair	Poor
625	525	450	380	325	200

Model P22 Standard

Introduced in 2002 this .22 caliber pistol is chambered for the LR cartridge. Barrel length is 3.4". Polymer frame with double-action trigger. Adjustable rear sight. Magazine capacity is 10 rounds. Weight is about 20 oz.NOTE: In 2003 this model was offered with a military black slide and green frame or a silver slide with black frame. A carbon fiber-framed model is also available at about the same price as standard models.

NIB	Exc.	V.G.	Good	Fair	Poor
400	325	250	200	150	75

Model P22 Target

Similar to the standard P22 model but with a 5" barrel with barrel weight. Weight is about 21 oz.

NIB	Exc.	V.G.	Good	Fair	Poor
425	350	275	225	175	75

NOTE: Barrels are interchangeable on both P22 pistols.

Model FP

A .22 LR caliber, single-shot target pistol that fires electrically. It has micro-adjustable electric firing system along with micrometer sights and contoured wooden grips that are adjustable. The barrel is 11.7" and the finish is blued.

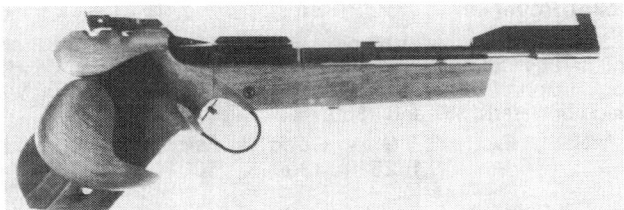

NIB	Exc.	V.G.	Good	Fair	Poor
—	2000	1600	1000	500	400

Model GSP

A semi-automatic target pistol in .22 LR and .32 calibers. This target pistol has a 4-1/2" barrel, 5-shot magazine and contoured wood target grips. Blued finish and sold with attache extra barrel, case and accessories.

Courtesy John J. Stimson, Jr.

NIB	Exc.	V.G.	Good	Fair	Poor
—	1600	1200	750	650	300

Model GSP-C

Almost the same pistol as the Model GSP, but in .32 caliber S&W wadcutter.

NIB	Exc.	V.G.	Good	Fair	Poor
—	1500	1100	750	650	300

Model OSP

A .22 Short semi-automatic target pistol that is similar to the Model GSP. This pistol is made for rapid fire target shooting. Blued finish with contoured wood grips.

NIB	Exc.	V.G.	Good	Fair	Poor
—	1800	1200	750	650	300

Free Pistol

A .22 caliber single-shot target pistol with an 11.7" barrel, micrometer sights, adjustable grips and an electronic trigger. Blued.

NIB	Exc.	V.G.	Good	Fair	Poor
1900	1600	1200	900	700	550

Model R99

This 6-shot revolver is chambered for the .357 Magnum cartridge. Barrel length is 3". Weight is about 28 oz. Offered in blue or stainless steel. Introduced in 1999. Said to be a close ringer for the S&W M19 but with different grips.

NIB	Exc.	V.G.	Good	Fair	Poor
1500	1300	1100	950	700	500

Model SP22-M1

.22 LR autoloader with aluminum frame and 4-inch barrel.

NIB	Exc.	V.G.	Good	Fair	Poor
400	325	350	150	100	75

Model SP22-M2

Similar to above but with a 6-inch barrel.

NIB	Exc.	V.G.	Good	Fair	Poor
400	325	250	150	100	75

Model SP22-M3

Similar to above but with match-grade barrel and adjustable trigger.

NIB	Exc.	V.G.	Good	Fair	Poor
475	400	325	200	150	100

Model SP22-M4

Similar to above but with wooden free-style grip assembly.

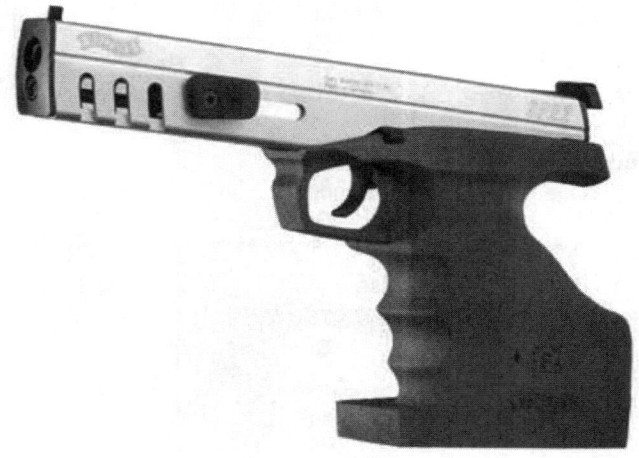

NIB	Exc.	V.G.	Good	Fair	Poor
750	675	550	400	250	150

WARNANT, L. AND J.
Ognee, Belgium

Revolver

Modeled after pistols manufactured by Smith & Wesson, the Warnants produced a variety of revolvers in .32, .38, or .45 caliber, between 1870 and 1890.

NIB	Exc.	V.G.	Good	Fair	Poor
—	—	250	175	100	50

Semi-Automatic Pistol

A 6.35mm semi-automatic pistol with a 2.5" barrel and 5-shot magazine. The slide marked "L&J Warnant Bte 6.35mm." Blued with black plastic grips bearing the monogram "L&JW." Manufactured after 1908.

NIB	Exc.	V.G.	Good	Fair	Poor
—	350	200	150	100	75

1912 Model

A 7.65mm caliber semi-automatic pistol with a 3" barrel and 7-shot magazine. The slide marked "L&J Warnant Brevetes Pist Auto 7.65mm." Manufactured prior to 1915.

NIB	Exc.	V.G.	Good	Fair	Poor
—	350	200	150	100	75

WARNER, CHAS.
Windsor Locks, Connecticut

Pocket Revolver

A .31 caliber percussion revolver with a 3" round barrel and 6-shot unfluted cylinder. The cylinder marked "Charles Warner. Windsor Locks, Conn." Blued with walnut grips. Approximately 600 were made between 1857 and 1860.

NIB	Exc.	V.G.	Good	Fair	Poor
—	—	1625	1300	500	100

Belt Revolver

A .31 caliber double-action percussion revolver with a 4" or 5" round barrel and 6-shot etched cylinder. Blued with walnut grips. No markings appear on this model except for the serial number. Manufactured in 1851.

Courtesy Milwaukee Public Museum, Milwaukee, Wisconsin

NIB	Exc.	V.G.	Good	Fair	Poor
—	—	2100	1650	675	100

Pocket Revolver

A .28 caliber percussion revolver with a 3" octagonal barrel marked "James Warner, Springfield, Mass., USA" and a 6-shot cylinder. Blued with walnut grips. Approximately 500 were made.

NIB	Exc.	V.G.	Good	Fair	Poor
—	—	1050	725	275	100

Second Model

As above, with either a 3" or 4" barrel and marked "Warner's Patent 1857."

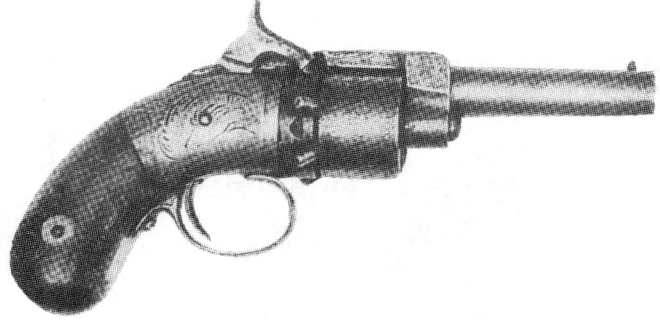

Courtesy Wallis & Wallis, Lewes, Sussex, England

NIB	Exc.	V.G.	Good	Fair	Poor
—	—	1100	750	325	100

Third Model

As above, but in .31 caliber.

NIB	Exc.	V.G.	Good	Fair	Poor
—	—	1000	650	300	100

Single-Shot Derringer

A .41 caliber rimfire single-shot pocket pistol with a 2.75" round barrel, brass frame and walnut grips. As this model is unmarked, it can only be identified by the large breechblock which lifts upward and to the left for loading.

NIB	Exc.	V.G.	Good	Fair	Poor
—	—	22500	19000	7250	1000

Pocket Revolver

A .30 caliber rimfire revolver with a 3" barrel marked "Warner's Patent 1857" and 5-shot cylinder. Blued or nickel-plated with walnut grips. Approximately 1,000 were made during the late 1860s.

NIB	Exc.	V.G.	Good	Fair	Poor
—	—	975	600	165	75

WARNER ARMS CORPORATION
Brooklyn, New York and Norwich, Connecticut

Established in 1912, this firm marketed revolvers, rifles, semi-automatic pistols and shotguns made for them by other companies (including N.R. Davis & Sons, Ithaca Gun Company and so forth). In 1917, the company was purchased by N.R. Davis & Company. See also Davis-Warner.The arms marketed by Warner prior to 1917 are listed.

REVOLVERS

Double-Action

.32 and .38 caliber with 4" or 5" barrels.

Double-Action Hammerless

.32 and .38 caliber with 4" or 5" barrels.

SEMI-AUTOMATIC PISTOLS

"Faultless" : Warner-Schwarzlose Model C, .32 ACP

NIB	Exc.	V.G.	Good	Fair	Poor
—	—	500	300	200	100

WEATHERBY
Atascadero, California

HANDGUNS

Mark V – CFP (Compact Firing Platform)

Bolt-action handgun with 5+1 capacity. 16" barrel, adjustable trigger, composite stock. Available in .223, .22-250, .243 and 7mm-08. 5.25 lb. Introduced 2006.

NIB	Exc.	V.G.	Good	Fair	Poor
1300	1050	800	600	400	200

Mark V Accumark CFP

This model is similar to the Accumark rifle and features a synthetic stock of Kevlar and fiberglass. The stock has a matte black gel-coat finish. Offered in .223 Rem., .22-250, .243 Win., 7mm-08, and .308 Win. calibers. Fluted barrel length is 15". Weight is about 5 lbs. Introduced in 2000.

NIB	Exc.	V.G.	Good	Fair	Poor
1050	800	600	400	225	150

WEAVER ARMS
Escondido, California

Nighthawk Assault Pistol

A 9mm semi-automatic pistol with a 10" or 12" barrel, alloy receiver and ambidextrous safety. Blackened with plastic grips. Introduced in 1987.

NIB	Exc.	V.G.	Good	Fair	Poor
550	450	400	350	300	150

WEBLEY & SCOTT, LTD.
Birmingham, England

Established in 1860, this firm has produced a wide variety of firearms over the years and has been known as Webley & Scott, Ltd. since 1906.NOTE: For all Webley .455 revolvers deduct 35 percent if converted to .45 ACP/.45 Auto Rim.

Model 1872 Royal Irish Constabulary

A .450 double-action revolver with a 3.25" barrel, 5-shot cylinder and rotating ejector. This model was also offered with 2.5" and 3.5" barrels. Blued with checkered walnut grips.

NIB	Exc.	V.G.	Good	Fair	Poor
—	1000	750	475	250	150

Model 1880 Metropolitan Police

As above, with a 2.5" barrel and 6-shot cylinder.

NIB	Exc.	V.G.	Good	Fair	Poor
—	1000	750	475	250	150

Model 1878 Webley-Pryse

Chambered for the .455 and .476 Eley cartridge.

NIB	Exc.	V.G.	Good	Fair	Poor
—	2100	1500	950	550	300

NOTE: Add 200 percent premium for revolvers chambered for .577. Deduct 50 percent for revolvers chambered for cartridges below .442.

New Model 1883 R.I.C.

Similar to the Model 1880, but in .455 caliber with a 4.5" barrel. Also made with a 2.5" barrel.

NIB	Exc.	V.G.	Good	Fair	Poor
—	900	750	425	250	100

Model 1884 R.I.C. Naval

As above, with a brass frame and oxidized finish. Barrel length 2.75" and of octagonal form.

NIB	Exc.	V.G.	Good	Fair	Poor
—	2250	1650	1225	600	500

British Bulldog

Similar to the new Model 1883 R.I.C. blued, checkered walnut grips. Those engraved on the back strap "W.R.A. Co." were sold through the Winchester Repeating Arms Company's New York sales agency and are worth a considerable premium over the values listed. Manufactured from 1878 to 1914.

NIB	Exc.	V.G.	Good	Fair	Poor
—	900	550	325	200	150

NOTE: Add a premium for U.S. dealer markings, see model description.

Pug

Similar to the British Bulldog but somewhat smaller. Interesting in that it has a manual safety. Chambered in .450, .442, and possibly others as well.

NIB	Exc.	V.G.	Good	Fair	Poor
—	800	500	325	200	150

Model 1878 Army Express Revolver

A .455 caliber double-action revolver with a 6" barrel and integral ejector. Blued with one-piece walnut grips.

NIB	Exc.	V.G.	Good	Fair	Poor
—	2100	1500	850	500	350

NOTE: Add 100 percent premium for single-action version. Add 25 percent for .450 Long (.45 Colt) markings.

Webley Kaufmann Model 1880

A top break, hinged-frame double-action revolver chambered for the .450 centerfire cartridge, with a 5.75" barrel and a curved bird's-head butt. Blued, with walnut grips.

NIB	Exc.	V.G.	Good	Fair	Poor
—	2300	1000	800	600	300

Webley-Green Model

A double-action, top break revolver chambered for the .455 cartridge, with a 6" ribbed barrel and a 6-shot cylinder. The cylinder flutes on this model are angular and not rounded in shape. Blued, with checkered walnut, squared butt grips with a lanyard ring on the butt. Introduced in 1882 and manufactured until 1896. Also known as the "WG" model.

NIB	Exc.	V.G.	Good	Fair	Poor
—	1900	1350	700	500	200

Mark I

A .442, .455, or .476 double-action top break revolver with a 4" barrel and 6-shot cylinder. Blued with checkered walnut grips. Manufactured from 1887 to 1894.

Courtesy Faintich Auction Services, Inc., Paul Goodwin photo

NIB	Exc.	V.G.	Good	Fair	Poor
—	950	550	375	250	150

Mark II

As above, with a larger hammer spur and improved barrel catch.

Manufactured from 1894 to 1897.

NIB	Exc.	V.G.	Good	Fair	Poor
—	925	550	350	225	100

Mark III

As above, with internal improvements. Introduced in 1897.

NIB	Exc.	V.G.	Good	Fair	Poor
—	975	600	325	200	75

Mark IV

As above, with a .455 caliber 3", 4", 5", or 6" barrel. This model was also available in .22 caliber with 6" barrel, .32 caliber with 3" barrel, and .38 caliber with 3", 4", or 5" barrel.

Courtesy Faintich Auction Services, Inc., Paul Goodwin photo

NIB	Exc.	V.G.	Good	Fair	Poor
—	900	575	375	200	75

Mark IV Target

Chambered for the .22 caliber cartridge and fitted with a 6" barrel with target sights.

Courtesy Rock Island Auction Company

NIB	Exc.	V.G.	Good	Fair	Poor
—	1450	1000	800	500	300

Mark V

Similar to Mark IV, with a 4" or 6" barrel. Manufactured from 1913 to 1915.

Courtesy Faintich Auction Services, Inc., Paul Goodwin photo

NIB	Exc.	V.G.	Good	Fair	Poor
—	1000	695	395	250	150

Mark VI

Similar to Mark V in design but with a smaller frame, 4" or 6" barrel and modified grip. Chambered for .38/200 (.38 S&W). Pricing is for commercial version. Subtract 40 percent for WAR FINISH-marked examples.

Courtesy Faintich Auction Services, Inc., Paul Goodwin photo

NIB	Exc.	V.G.	Good	Fair	Poor
—	800	600	375	225	150

WEBLEY SEMI-AUTOMATIC PISTOLS

WEBLEY-FOSBERY AUTOMATIC REVOLVER

Text by Jodeph Schroeder:

Recoil forces the top half of this unusual pistol back to cock the hammer, while a stud in the frame cams the cylinder around to bring a fresh chamber into position. Early examples under serial number 75 or so appear to be hand-made as no two seem to be identical; these bring a 100 percent premium over late-model pistols. Other low-number guns, under serial number 300 or so, also differ in appearance from the later production and bring a 25 percent premium. Early production was all in .455 Webley with a 6-round cylinder; a .38 ACP version with an 8-round cylinder was introduced about 1903 but is much scarcer than the .455.

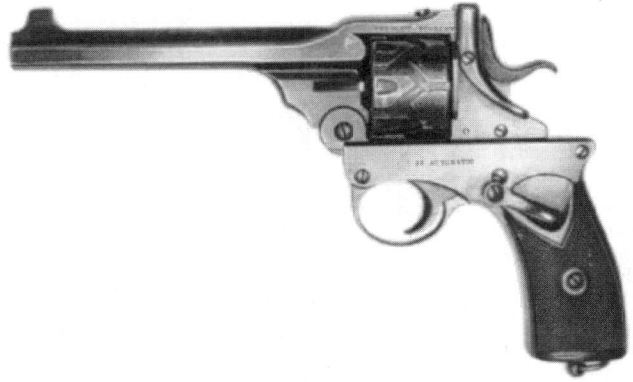

Courtesy Joseph Schroeder

.455 Caliber

NIB	Exc.	V.G.	Good	Fair	Poor
—	9000	4500	3000	2000	1250

.38 Caliber

NIB	Exc.	V.G.	Good	Fair	Poor
—	10000	7250	4500	3000	2000

Model 1904

Made experimentally in both .38 ACP and .455 calibers, the highest serial numbered 1904 known is in the 30s and very few seem to have survived. A later Webley experimental, the Model

1906, made in .45 for the U.S. Army trial but apparently never submitted. Either model is too rare to price.

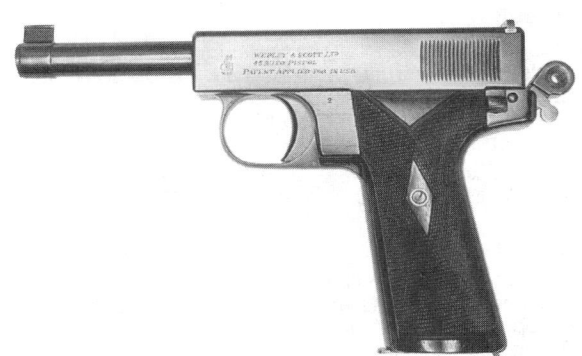

Courtesy Joseph Schroeder

Model 1905

Webley's first commercial semi-automatic pistol was this compact .32 caliber. The earliest Model 1905s have a diagonal flat machined on the slide and a hammer-mounted safety; these bring about a 50 percent premium. The Model 1905 was replaced by the Model 1908 after about perhaps 20,000 were made.

Courtesy Joseph Schroeder

NIB	Exc.	V.G.	Good	Fair	Poor
—	1200	1000	750	400	250

Model 1907

The 1907 is a .25 caliber pistol with an outside hammer and was one of Webley's most popular handguns; it remained in production until WWII and over 50,000 were made.

Courtesy Joseph Schroeder

NIB	Exc.	V.G.	Good	Fair	Poor
—	800	600	400	200	100

Model 1908

The Model 1908 is a slight redesign of the Model 1905. Webley's most popular self-loading pistol, it remained in production until WWII. Examples bearing a crown and the letters "MP" were made for the Metropolitan Police and bring a slight premium.

NIB	Exc.	V.G.	Good	Fair	Poor
—	650	550	350	175	125

Model 1909

The Model 1909 is a modified and enlarged version of the Model 1908, chambered for the 9mm Browning Long cartridge. It was never popular, and manufacture ended in 1914 with just under 1,700 made. Its most unusual feature was the slide release on top of the slide.

NIB	Exc.	V.G.	Good	Fair	Poor
—	1475	850	500	300	200

Model 1910 .380

The Model 1910 .380 was simply a Model 1908 modified to accept the .380 cartridge. Never very popular, under 2,000 were sold.

Courtesy Joseph Schroeder

NIB	Exc.	V.G.	Good	Fair	Poor
—	1500	875	525	—	—

Model 1910 .38 ACP

This was Webley's first locked-breech pistol, based closely on the experimental Model 1906 design and chambered for the .38 ACP cartridge. There are two models, both with internal hammers, but one with a grip safety and the later without. Total production for both was under 1,000, so both are rare.

Courtesy Joseph Schroeder

NIB	Exc.	V.G.	Good	Fair	Poor
—	2250	1500	900	500	350

Model 1911

The Model 1911 is a single-shot .22 caliber training version of the Model 1908, and developed specifically for the Metropolitan Police. It features a "blow open" action that ejects the fired cartridge but remains open for reloading, and the bottom of the frame is slotted for attaching a shoulder stock. Stocks are quite rare, and will probably add more than 100 percent to the value of the pistol.

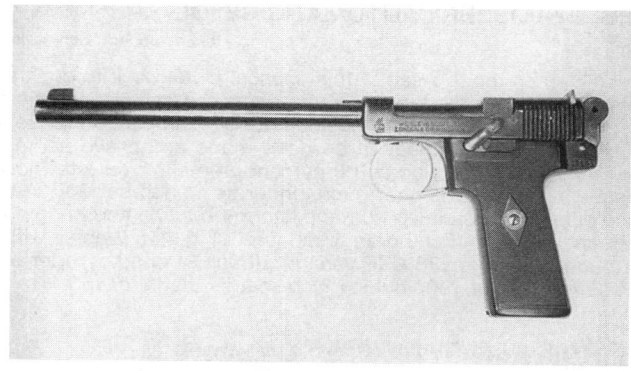

Courtesy Joseph Schroeder

NIB	Exc.	V.G.	Good	Fair	Poor
—	1750	1400	1100	800	300

Model 1912

A perceived need for a hammerless version of the Model 1907 .25 caliber led to the introduction of the Model 1912. It actually does have an internal hammer, but the recoil spring is two coils in the slide instead of the large V-spring under the right grip frame found in all other Webley semi-automatic pistols. Not as popular as the Model 1907, production totaled almost 15,000 vs. over 50,000 for the hammer model.

NIB	Exc.	V.G.	Good	Fair	Poor
—	1200	1000	750	400	200

Model 1913

The Model 1913 was the result of years of development in conjunction with the British government and was finally adopted in 1913 as the Model 1913 MK1N for Royal Navy issue. It has the same breech-locking system as the Model 1910, but has an external hammer and is chambered for the .455 Webley Self-Loading cartridge. About 1,000 Model 1913s were sold commercially and serial-numbered along with the smaller-caliber pistols. In 1915 a variation of the Model 1913 with butt slotted for a shoulder stock, an adjustable rear sight, and a hammer safety adopted for use by the Royal Horse Artillery. Shoulder stocks are very rare, and will double values listed for the RHA model. All militaries were numbered in their own series; about 10,000 made in both variations.

NIB	Exc.	V.G.	Good	Fair	Poor
—	1950	1200	800	500	300

Model 1913 (RHA model)

Courtesy Joseph Schroeder

NIB	Exc.	V.G.	Good	Fair	Poor
—	5000	4000	3000	1000	600

Model 1922

The Model 1922 was a redesign of the Model 1909 in hopes of military adoption. The grip safety was replaced by a manual safety mounted on the slide, the grip angle was changed, and a lanyard ring added to the butt. Unfortunately for Webley its only official use was by the Union Defense Force of South Africa (1,000 pistols). South African guns are marked with a large "U" with an arrow in it and bring a 20 percent premium.

NIB	Exc.	V.G.	Good	Fair	Poor
—	3000	2500	2000	1000	600

WEIHRAUCH, HANS HERMANN
Melrichstadt, West Germany

Model HW-3

A double-action, solid-frame, swing-out cylinder revolver chambered for .22 LR or .32 Smith & Wesson long cartridges with a barrel length of 2.75", and a cylinder holding either seven or eight cartridges. Blued, with walnut grips. In America, this revolver was known as the Dickson Bulldog. In Europe it was known as the Gecado.

NIB	Exc.	V.G.	Good	Fair	Poor
—	100	75	50	35	25

Model HW-5

As above, with a 4" barrel. Sold in the United States under the trade name "Omega."

NIB	Exc.	V.G.	Good	Fair	Poor
—	100	75	50	35	25

Model HW-7

As above, in .22 caliber with a 6" barrel and 8-shot cylinder. Sold in the United States as the "Herter's Guide Model." Also available with target sights and thumbrest grips as the Model HW-7S.

NIB	Exc.	V.G.	Good	Fair	Poor
—	100	75	50	35	25

Model HW-9

These pistols all carry the Arminius trademark, a bearded head wearing a winged helmet. The model number will be found on the cylinder crane; the caliber, on the barrel; and the words "Made in Germany" on the frame.

NIB	Exc.	V.G.	Good	Fair	Poor
—	100	75	50	35	25

WEISBURGER, A.
Memphis, Tennessee

Pocket Pistol

A .41 caliber percussion single-shot pocket pistol with 2.5" barrel, German silver furniture and a walnut stock. Manufactured during the 1850s.

NIB	Exc.	V.G.	Good	Fair	Poor
—	—	6500	5100	3250	1800

WESSON, EDWIN
Hartford, Connecticut

Dragoon

A .45 caliber percussion revolver with a 7" round barrel and 6-shot unfluted cylinder. The barrel blued, the frame case hardened and the walnut grips fitted with a brass buttcap. Manufactured in 1848 and 1849.

NIB	Exc.	V.G.	Good	Fair	Poor
—	—	13500	9500	5000	1750

WESSON, FRANK
Worcester & Springfield, Massachusetts

Manual Extractor Model

A .22 caliber spur trigger single-shot pistol with a 4" octagonal barrel and thin brass frame. The barrel release is located in the front of the trigger. No markings. Approximately 200 were made in 1856 and 1857.

NIB	Exc.	V.G.	Good	Fair	Poor
—	—	1400	950	400	100

First Model Small Frame

As above, with a 3", 3.5", or 6" half-octagonal barrel. Blued with rosewood or walnut grips. The barrel marked "Frank Wesson Worcester Mass/Pat'd Oct. 25, 1859 & Nov. 11, 1862." Serial numbered from 1 to 2500.

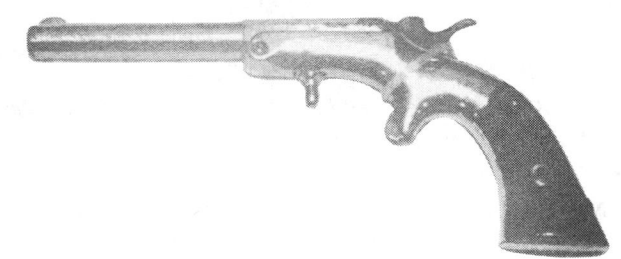

NIB	Exc.	V.G.	Good	Fair	Poor
—	—	900	575	225	75

Medium Frame Second Model

As above, with a longer spur trigger and a slightly wider frame at the barrel hinge. Manufactured from 1862 to 1870.

NIB	Exc.	V.G.	Good	Fair	Poor
—	—	950	600	225	75

Small Frame Pocket Rifle, Pistol Only

A .22 caliber spur trigger single-shot pistol with a 6" half octagonal barrel and narrow brass frame. This model is adopted for use with a detachable skeleton shoulder stock. The barrel marked "Frank Wesson Worcester, Mass." Manufactured from 1865 to 1875 with approximately 5,000 made.

NOTE: Matching shoulder stock add 100 percent.

NIB	Exc.	V.G.	Good	Fair	Poor
—	—	1500	925	350	100

Medium Frame Pocket Rifle, Pistol Only

As above, in .22, .30, or .32 rimfire with a 10" or 12" half octagonal barrel. Approximately 1,000 were made from 1862 to 1870.

NOTE: Matching shoulder stock add 100 percent.

NIB	Exc.	V.G.	Good	Fair	Poor
—	—	1000	650	200	75

Model 1870 Small Frame Pocket Rifle, Pistol Only

As above, in .22 caliber with a 10", 12", 15", or 18" or 20" half octagonal barrel that rotates to the side for loading. This model was made with either a brass or iron frame. It has a half cocked notch on the hammer.

NOTE: Matching shoulder stock add 100 percent.

NIB	Exc.	V.G.	Good	Fair	Poor
—	—	1000	650	200	75

1870 Medium Frame Pocket Rifle First Type, Pistol Only

NOTE: Matching shoulder stock add 100 percent.

NIB	Exc.	V.G.	Good	Fair	Poor
—	—	1000	650	200	75

1870 Medium Frame Pocket Rifle Second Type, Pistol Only

As above, with an iron frame and a push-button half cocked safety.

NOTE: Match shoulder stock add 100 percent.

NIB	Exc.	V.G.	Good	Fair	Poor
—	—	900	475	175	75

1870 Medium Frame Pocket Rifle Third Type, Pistol Only

As above, with three screws on the left side of the frame.

NOTE: Matching shoulder stock add 100 percent.

NIB	Exc.	V.G.	Good	Fair	Poor
—	—	900	475	175	75

1870 Large Frame Pocket Rifle First Type, Pistol Only

NIB	Exc.	V.G.	Good	Fair	Poor
—	—	2750	1500	550	200

NOTE: Matching shoulder stock add 100 percent.

1870 Large Frame Pocket Rifle Second Type, Pistol Only

As above, with a sliding extractor.

NOTE: Matching shoulder stock add 100 percent.

NIB	Exc.	V.G.	Good	Fair	Poor
—	—	2750	1500	550	200

Small Frame Superposed Pistol

A .22 caliber spur trigger over/under pocket pistol with 2" or 2.5" octagonal barrels that revolve. Approximately 3,500 were made between 1868 and 1880. On occasion. this pistol is found with a sliding knife blade mounted on the side of the barrels. The presence of this feature would add approximately 25 percent to the values listed.

NIB	Exc.	V.G.	Good	Fair	Poor
—	—	3000	1750	850	250

Medium Frame Superposed Pistol

As above, in .32 rimfire with 2.5" or 3.5" barrels. As with the smaller version, this pistol is occasionally found with a sliding knife blade mounted on the barrels that would add 25 percent to the values listed. Manufactured from 1868 to 1880.

Medium Frame Superposed Pistol First Type Marked "Patent Applied For"

NIB	Exc.	V.G.	Good	Fair	Poor
—	—	2500	1250	400	100

Medium Frame Superposed Pistol Second Type Marked "Patent December 15, 1868"

NIB	Exc.	V.G.	Good	Fair	Poor
—	—	2450	1200	400	100

Medium Frame Superposed Pistol Third Type Full-Length Fluted Barrels

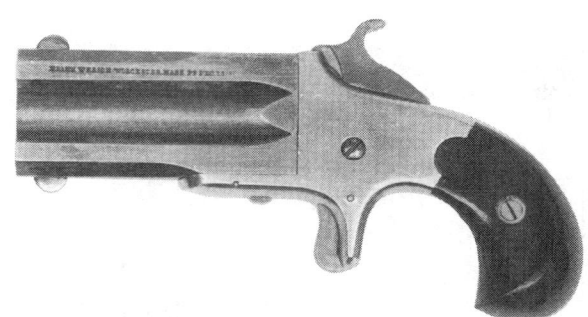

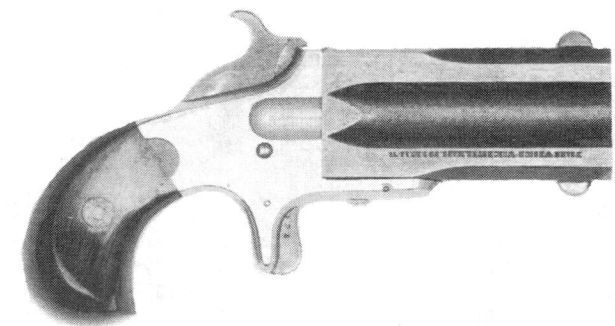

Courtesy W.P. Hallstein III and son Chip

NIB	Exc.	V.G.	Good	Fair	Poor
—	—	2750	1500	450	150

Large Frame Superposed Pistol

As above, in .41 rimfire with a 3" octagonal barrel fitted with a sliding knife blade. Approximately 2,000 were made from 1868 to 1880.

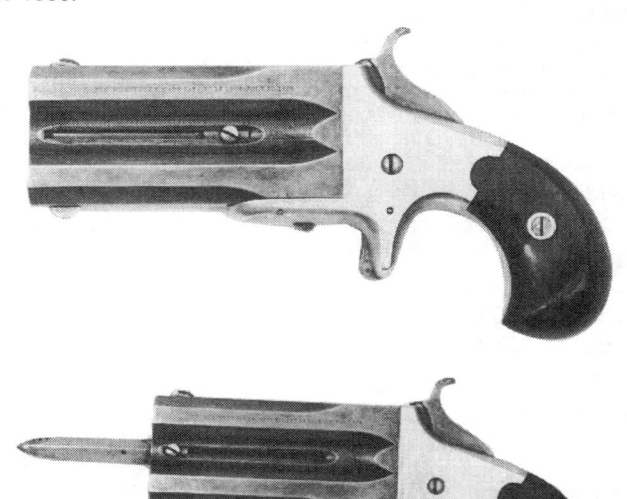

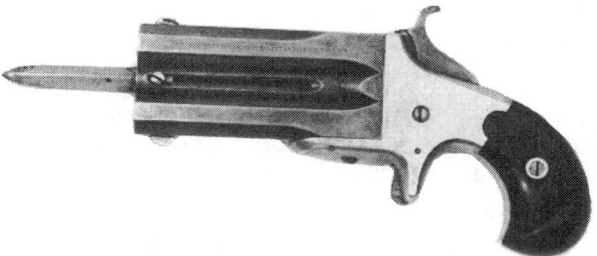

Courtesy W.P. Hallstein III and son Chip

NIB	Exc.	V.G.	Good	Fair	Poor
—	—	4200	2750	1250	400

WESSON & LEAVITT
Chicopee Falls, Massachusetts

Dragoon

A .40 caliber percussion revolver with a 6.25" or 7" round barrel and 6-shot cylinder. These pistols are marked "Mass. Arms Co./ Chicopee Falls." Approximately 30 were made with the 6.25" barrel and 750 with the 7" barrel. Manufactured in 1850 and 1851.

Courtesy Milwaukee Public Museum, Milwaukee, Wisconsin

NIB	Exc.	V.G.	Good	Fair	Poor
—	—	9000	4750	2000	500

WESSON FIREARMS, DAN
Norwich, New York

In 1996 the assets of the Wesson Firearms Co. were purchased by the New York International Corp. All interchangeable barrel models were produced. There are no plans at this time to build fixed barrel models. At the present time, parts and service for original Dan Wesson revolvers are available from the new company. Full production of new models occurred in 1997. These firearms are laser marked on the barrel or frame with: "NYI" in an oval and below "DAN WESSON FIREARMS" on the next line "NORWICH, NEW YORK USA." NOTE: In April, 2005 Dan Wesson Firearms was acquired by CZ-USA. Production continues (somewhat irregularly) at the Norwich, New York, facility.

NEW GENERATION SMALL-FRAME SERIES

NOTE: The "7" prefix denotes stainless steel frame and barrel. For models listed add between 4 percent and 9 percent depending on barrel length and for stainless steel.

Model 22/722

This is a 6-shot revolver chambered for .22 caliber cartridge. Interchangeable barrel lengths are 2.5", 4", 5.6", 8", and 10". Adjustable rear sight and interchangeable front sight. Hogue finger groove rubber grips. Weight is 36 oz. for 2.5" barrel and 58 oz. for 10" barrel.

NIB	Exc.	V.G.	Good	Fair	Poor
485	375	300	250	200	145

Model 32/732

Same as above. Chambered for .32 H&R cartridge.

NIB	Exc.	V.G.	Good	Fair	Poor
550	425	325	250	195	165

Model 3220/73220

Same as above but chambered for the .32-20 cartridge.

NIB	Exc.	V.G.	Good	Fair	Poor
550	425	325	250	195	165

Model 15/715

Same as above but chambered for the .38 Special and .357 Magnum cartridges.

NIB	Exc.	V.G.	Good	Fair	Poor
525	400	300	225	175	145

Model 715 (Current Production)

Made from 100 percent stainless steel and chambered in .357 Magnum. Traditional double-action with dual cylinder lockup, six-round capacity, fully adjustable rear sight, transfer bar ignition and interchangeable barrel with ventilated rib. Includes barrel wrench kit. Weight 46 ounces, 6-inch barrel, bright stainless finish. Reintroduced in 2011.

NIB	Exc.	V.G.	Good	Fair	Poor
975	850	700	500	350	200

NEW GENERATION LARGE-FRAME SERIES

NOTE: The "7" prefix denotes stainless steel frame and barrel. For models listed add between 4 percent and 9 percent depending on barrel length and for stainless steel.

Model 41/741

This is a large-frame revolver with 6-shot cylinder. Interchangeable barrels in 4", 6", 8", and 10". Adjustable rear sight with interchangeable front sight. Hogue finger grip rubber grips standard. Weight is from 49 oz. for 4" barrel to 69 oz. for 10" barrels.

NIB	Exc.	V.G.	Good	Fair	Poor
575	475	350	225	175	125

Model 44/744

Same as above but chambered for .44 Magnum cartridge.

NIB	Exc.	V.G.	Good	Fair	Poor
575	475	350	225	175	125

Model 45/745

Same as above but chambered for .45 Colt cartridge.

NIB	Exc.	V.G.	Good	Fair	Poor
600	500	375	250	200	125

Model 360/7360

Same as above but chambered for .357 Magnum cartridge.

NIB	Exc.	V.G.	Good	Fair	Poor
575	475	350	225	175	125

Model 460/7460

Same as above but chambered for the .45 ACP, .45 Auto Rim, .45 Super, .45 Win. Mag, or .460 Rowland.

NIB	Exc.	V.G.	Good	Fair	Poor
750	625	500	400	300	200

NEW GENERATION SUPERMAG-FRAME SERIES

NOTE: The "7" prefix denotes stainless steel frame and barrel. For models listed add between 4 percent and 9 percent depending on barrel length and for stainless steel.

Model 40/740

This is a 6-shot revolver chambered for .the .357 Magnum, .357 Super Magnum/Maximum cartridges with interchangeable barrels in 4", 6", 8", or 10" lengths. Adjustable rear sight and interchangeable front sights. Hogue finger groove rubber grips standard. Weight range from 51 oz. for 4" barrel to 76 oz. for 10" barrel.

NIB	Exc.	V.G.	Good	Fair	Poor
1300	1125	850	675	400	250

Model 414/7414

Same as above but chambered for .414 Super Magnum cartridge.

NIB	Exc.	V.G.	Good	Fair	Poor
1300	1125	850	675	400	250

Model 445/7445

Same as above but chambered for .445 Super Mag. cartridge.

NIB	Exc.	V.G.	Good	Fair	Poor
1500	1325	1050	875	550	350

NEW GENERATION COMPENSATED SERIES

NOTE: The "7" prefix denotes stainless steel frame and barrel. For models listed add between 4 percent and 9 percent depending on barrel length and for stainless steel.

Model 15/715

This is a 6-shot revolver that is chambered for the .357 Magnum cartridge and offered with interchangeable barrels in 4", 6", or 10" lengths. Barrels have an integral compensator. Adjustable rear sight and interchangeable front sight. Hogue finger groove rubber grips.

NIB	Exc.	V.G.	Good	Fair	Poor
575	450	325	250	175	100

Model 41/741

Same as above but chambered for .41 Magnum cartridge.

NIB	Exc.	V.G.	Good	Fair	Poor
675	550	425	350	250	125

Model 44/744

Same as above but chambered for .44 Magnum cartridge.

NIB	Exc.	V.G.	Good	Fair	Poor
675	550	425	350	250	125

Model 45/745

Same as above but chambered for .45 Colt cartridge.

NIB	Exc.	V.G.	Good	Fair	Poor
675	550	425	350	250	125

Model 360/7360

Same as above but chambered for .357 Magnum on large frame.

NIB	Exc.	V.G.	Good	Fair	Poor
675	550	425	350	250	125

Model 445/7445 (Alaskan Guide)

Chambered for the .445 SuperMag cartridge. Fitted with a 4" heavy ported barrel. Special matte black coating over stainless steel. Introduced in 2002.

NIB	Exc.	V.G.	Good	Fair	Poor
1000	800	675	500	375	250

Model 460/7460

Same as above but chambered for the .45 ACP, .45 Auto Rim, .45 Super, .45 Win. Mag., or the .460 Rowland cartridgs.

NIB	Exc.	V.G.	Good	Fair	Poor
825	650	500	375	200	125

STANDARD SILHOUETTE SERIES

NOTE: All Standard Silhouette series revolvers are stainless steel.

Model 722 VH10

This is a 6-shot revolver chambered for the .22 caliber cartridge. Interchangeable barrel system. Choice of fluted or non-fluted cylinders. Patridge front sight and adjustable rear sight. Hogue finger groove rubber grips standard. Lightweight slotted 8" shroud.

NIB	Exc.	V.G.	Good	Fair	Poor
825	650	500	375	200	125

Model 7360 V8S

Same as above but chambered for the .357 Magnum cartridge.

NIB	Exc.	V.G.	Good	Fair	Poor
825	650	500	375	200	125

Model 741 V8S

Same as above but chambered for the .41 Magnum cartridge with 8" slotted shroud.

NIB	Exc.	V.G.	Good	Fair	Poor
825	650	500	375	200	125

Model 741 V10S

Same as above but with 10" slotted shroud.

NIB	Exc.	V.G.	Good	Fair	Poor
925	750	600	475	300	175

Model 744 V8S

Chambered for .44 Magnum cartridge and fitted with an 8" slotted shroud.

NIB	Exc.	V.G.	Good	Fair	Poor
825	650	500	375	200	125

Model 744 V10S

Same as above but fitted with a 10" slotted shroud.

NIB	Exc.	V.G.	Good	Fair	Poor
925	750	600	475	300	175

Model 740 V8S

Chambered for the .357 Super Mag. and fitted with an 8" slotted shroud.

NIB	Exc.	V.G.	Good	Fair	Poor
925	750	600	475	300	175

Model 7414 V8S

Chambered for the .414 Super Mag and fitted with an 8" slotted shroud.

NIB	Exc.	V.G.	Good	Fair	Poor
925	750	600	475	300	175

Model 7445 V8S

Chambered for the .445 Super Mag. and fitted with an 8" slotted shroud.

NIB	Exc.	V.G.	Good	Fair	Poor
925	750	600	475	300	175

Dan Wesson VH8

.445 SuperMag revolver designed for barrel interchangeability. Also fires standard .44-caliber rounds. Stainless, 6-shot; 8" barrel, 4.1 lb. Single/double action. Introduced 2006.

NIB	Exc.	V.G.	Good	Fair	Poor
1100	950	775	600	450	275

SUPER RAM SILHOUETTE SERIES

NOTE: All Super Ram Silhouette series revolvers are stainless steel.

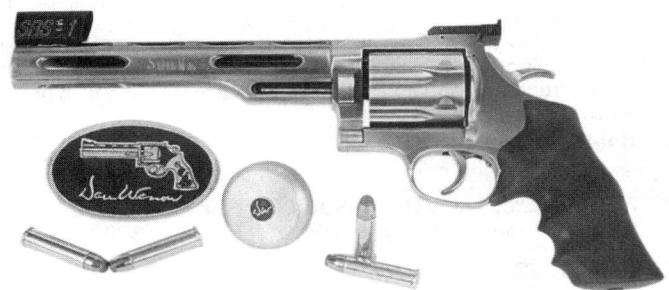

Model 722 VH10 SRS1

This model is chambered for the .22 caliber cartridge and is fitted with a 10" slotted shroud barrel. Interchangeable barrel system. Adjustable Bomar rear sight. Bomar SRS-1 hood front sight. Fluted or non-fluted cylinders. Hogue finger groove rubber grips.

NIB	Exc.	V.G.	Good	Fair	Poor
925	750	600	475	300	175

Model 7360 V8S SRS1

Same as above but chambered for .357 Magnum cartridge. Fitted with an 8" slotted shroud.

NIB	Exc.	V.G.	Good	Fair	Poor
1100	950	775	600	450	275

Model 741 V8S SRS1

Same as above but chambered for .41 Magnum cartridge and fitted with an 8" slotted shroud.

NIB	Exc.	V.G.	Good	Fair	Poor
1100	950	775	600	450	275

Model 741 V10S SRS1

Same as above but fitted with a 10" slotted shroud.

NIB	Exc.	V.G.	Good	Fair	Poor
1100	950	775	600	450	275

Model 744 V8S SRS1

Same as above but chambered for the .44 Magnum cartridge and fitted with an 8" slotted shroud.

NIB	Exc.	V.G.	Good	Fair	Poor
1100	950	775	600	450	275

Model 744 V10S SRS1

Same as above but fitted with a 10" slotted shroud.

NIB	Exc.	V.G.	Good	Fair	Poor
1100	950	775	600	450	275

Model 740 V8S SRS1

Same as above but chambered for .357 Super Mag. and fitted with an 8" slotted shroud.

NIB	Exc.	V.G.	Good	Fair	Poor
1200	1050	875	700	550	300

Model 7414 V8S SRS1

Same as above but chambered for .414 Super Mag. and fitted with an 8" slotted shroud.

NIB	Exc.	V.G.	Good	Fair	Poor
1200	1050	875	700	550	300

Model 7445 V8S SS1

Same as above but chambered for .445 Super Mag. and fitted with an 8" slotted shroud.

NIB	Exc.	V.G.	Good	Fair	Poor
1200	1050	875	700	550	300

PISTOL PACK SERIES

This series consists of a Dan Wesson revolver of the customer's choice with adjustable rear sight and four barrel assemblies in the small-frame calibers (2.5", 4", 6", and 8"); the large frame and supermag frame have three barrel assemblies (4", 6", and 8"). Also included is a cleaning kit, wrench kit, extra exotic wood grips, instruction manual and fitted hard case. Choice of blue or stainless steel finish ("7" prefix).

Model 22/722

Chambered for .22 LR.

NIB	Exc.	V.G.	Good	Fair	Poor
1200	1050	875	700	550	300

Model 32/732

Chambered for .32 H&R Magnum.

NIB	Exc.	V.G.	Good	Fair	Poor
1200	1050	875	700	550	300

Model 3220/73220

Chambered for the .32-20.

NIB	Exc.	V.G.	Good	Fair	Poor
1200	1050	875	700	550	300

Model 15/715

Chambered for the .357 Magnum.

NIB	Exc.	V.G.	Good	Fair	Poor
1200	1050	875	700	550	300

Model 41/741

Chambered for the .41 Magnum.

NIB	Exc.	V.G.	Good	Fair	Poor
1450	1250	1050	850	650	350

Model 44/744

Chambered for the .44 Magnum.

NIB	Exc.	V.G.	Good	Fair	Poor
1450	1250	1050	850	650	350

Model 45/745

Chambered for the .45 Colt.

NIB	Exc.	V.G.	Good	Fair	Poor
1450	1250	1050	850	650	350

Model 460/7460

Chambered for the .45 ACP, .45 Auto Rim, .45 Super, .45 Win. Mag, .460 Rowland.

NIB	Exc.	V.G.	Good	Fair	Poor
1450	1250	1050	850	650	350

Model 40/740

Chambered for the .357 Maximum.

NIB	Exc.	V.G.	Good	Fair	Poor
1650	1300	1150	950	750	450

Model 414/7414

Chambered for the .414 Super Mag.

NIB	Exc.	V.G.	Good	Fair	Poor
1650	1300	1150	950	750	450

Model 445/7445

Chambered for the .445 Super Mag.

NIB	Exc.	V.G.	Good	Fair	Poor
1650	1300	—	—	—	—

HUNTER PACK SERIES

The Hunter Pack comes with a Dan Wesson revolver of the customer's choice with adjustable rear sight and two 8" barrel assemblies, one with open sights and one drilled and tapped with Burris or Weaver mount installed. Extra set of exotic wood grips, wrench kit, cleaning kit, and manual. Offered in blue or stainless steel ("7" prefix).

Model 22/722

Chambered for .22 LR.

NIB	Exc.	V.G.	Good	Fair	Poor
1200	950	—	—	—	—

Model 32/732

Chambered for .32 H&R Magnum.

NIB	Exc.	V.G.	Good	Fair	Poor
1200	950	—	—	—	—

Model 3220/73220

Chambered for .32-20.

NIB	Exc.	V.G.	Good	Fair	Poor
1200	1050	875	700	550	300

Model 15/715

Chambered for .357 Mag.

NIB	Exc.	V.G.	Good	Fair	Poor
1200	1050	875	700	550	300

Model 41/741

Chambered for the .41 Mag.

NIB	Exc.	V.G.	Good	Fair	Poor
1450	1250	1050	850	650	350

Model 44/744

Chambered for the .44 Mag.

NIB	Exc.	V.G.	Good	Fair	Poor
1450	1250	1050	850	650	350

Model 45/745

Chambered for the .45 Colt.

NIB	Exc.	V.G.	Good	Fair	Poor
1450	1250	1050	850	650	350

Model 460/7460

Chambered for the .45 ACP, .45 Auto Rim, .45 Super, .45 Win. Mag., .460 Rowland.

NIB	Exc.	V.G.	Good	Fair	Poor
1450	1250	1050	850	650	350

Model 40/740

Chambered for the .357 Maximum.

NIB	Exc.	V.G.	Good	Fair	Poor
1650	1300	1150	950	750	450

Model 414/7414

Chambered for the .414 Super Mag.

NIB	Exc.	V.G.	Good	Fair	Poor
1650	1300	1150	950	750	450

Model 445/7445

Chambered for the .445 Super Mag.

NIB	Exc.	V.G.	Good	Fair	Poor
1650	1300	1150	950	750	450

PISTOLS

Pointman Major

This is a semi-auto pistol chambered for the .45 ACP cartridge. Many special features including interchangeable front sight, Jarvis match barrel, adjustable rear sight, beveled magazine well, and others. Stainless steel slide and frame. Rosewood checkered grips. Slide serrations both front and rear. A high sighting rib with interchangeable sights. Introduced in 2000.

NIB	Exc.	V.G.	Good	Fair	Poor
1200	1050	800	625	500	300

Pointman Seven

Has many of the same features as the Pointman Major with blued slide and frame and no sighting rib.

NIB	Exc.	V.G.	Good	Fair	Poor
1100	950	700	525	400	300

Pointman Minor

Same as above except blued slide and frame and no match barrel.

NIB	Exc.	V.G.	Good	Fair	Poor
1100	950	700	525	400	300

Pointman Seven Stainless

Same as above with stainless steel frame and slide.

NIB	Exc.	V.G.	Good	Fair	Poor
1200	1050	800	625	500	300

Pointman Guardian

This model is fitted with a 4.25" barrel and match trigger group. Adjustable rear sight, plus many other special features. Blued frame and slide with sighting rib.

NIB	Exc.	V.G.	Good	Fair	Poor
1200	1050	800	625	500	300

Pointman Guardian Duce

Same as above but with blued steel slide and stainless steel frame.

NIB	Exc.	V.G.	Good	Fair	Poor
825	675	525	400	300	175

Pointman Major Australian

Introduced in 2002 this model features a fully adjustable Bomar-style target sight. Unique slide top configuration that features a rounded radius with lengthwise sight serrations. Slide has Southern Cross engraved on right side. Chambered for the .45 ACP cartridge only.

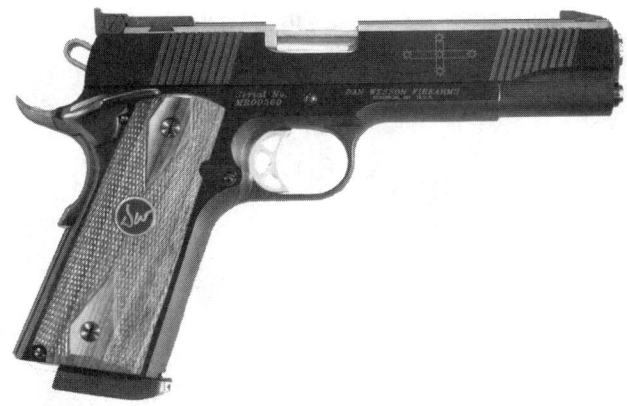

NIB	Exc.	V.G.	Good	Fair	Poor
1200	1050	800	625	500	300

Pointman Hi-Cap

This .45 ACP pistol is fitted with a 5" barrel and blued carbon alloy wide-body frame with a 10-round magazine. Fixed rear target sight. Extended thumb safety as well as other special features.

NIB	Exc.	V.G.	Good	Fair	Poor
1100	950	700	525	400	300

Pointman Dave Pruitt Signature Series

This pistol is fitted with a 5" match-grade barrel with a rounded top slide with bead blast matte finish. Chevron-style cocking serrations. Fixed rear sight with tactical/target ramp front sight. Many special features.

NIB	Exc.	V.G.	Good	Fair	Poor
1100	950	700	525	400	300

RZ-10

10mm single-action semi-auto with 8+1 capacity. 5" barrel, 2.4 lb. Fixed sights. Introduced 2006.

NIB	Exc.	V.G.	Good	Fair	Poor
1100	950	700	525	400	300

RZ-45 Heritage

Same as the discontinued RZ-10 except in .45 ACP. The RZ refers to "Razorback" which is based on the serrated Clark-

style target rib machined onto the top of the slide. Introduced in 2010.

NIB	Exc.	V.G.	Good	Fair	Poor
1100	950	700	525	400	200

Guardian

Designed for concealed carry with Bobtail frame. Caliber is .45 ACP with steel slide, alloy frame, Novak Lo-Mount night sights, extended thumb and grip safeties, 8-round magazine and stippled Shadow grips. Weight 28.8 ounces, 4.3-inch barrel and black Duty finish.

NIB	Exc.	V.G.	Good	Fair	Poor
1300	1100	850	600	450	300

Valor

Full-size 1911-style .45 ACP with black ceramic coated or matte stainless finish. Slimline G10 grips, Heinie Ledge Straight-Eight Night Sights.

NIB	Exc.	V.G.	Good	Fair	Poor
1675	1350	1050	800	500	400

Pointman Nine

Full-size 1911-style in 9mm with 9+1 capacity. Front and rear slide serrations, adjustable rear sight, fiber optic front.

NIB	Exc.	V.G.	Good	Fair	Poor
1300	1100	850	600	450	300

PATRIOT SERIES
Patriot Marksman

Introduced in 2002 this .45 ACP pistol has a 5" match grade barrel. Fixed sights. Many special features such as a beveled mag well, lowered and flared ejection port. Checkered wood grips. Magazine capacity is 8 rounds. Weight is about 38 oz.

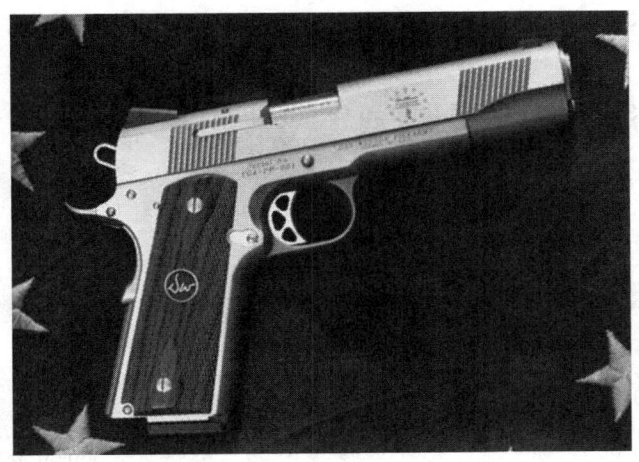

NIB	Exc.	V.G.	Good	Fair	Poor
795	650	525	400	300	175

Patriot Expert

As above but fitted with a Bomar target-style adjustable rear sight.

NIB	Exc.	V.G.	Good	Fair	Poor
900	750	625	500	400	225

WESSON FIREARMS CO., INC.
Palmer, Massachusetts

The company was founded in 1968 by Daniel B. Wesson, the great-grandson of D.B. Wesson, co-founder of Smith & Wesson. This line of handguns is unique for its barrel/shroud interchangeability. Dan Wesson revolvers have established themselves as champion metallic silhouette competition guns. The company offers a comprehensive line of handguns for almost every use. The company will also custom build a handgun to customer specifications. Dan Wesson Arms was restructured on January 4, 1991, and identified as Wesson Firearms Company, Inc. Wesson handguns made after this date will be stamped with this new corporate name. In 1995 the company declared bankruptcy. (See WESSON FIREARMS, DAN)

Model 11

A .357 Magnum caliber double-action swing-out cylinder revolver with interchangeable 2.5", 4", or 6" barrels and a 6-shot cylinder. Blued with walnut grips. Manufactured in 1970 and 1971.

NIB	Exc.	V.G.	Good	Fair	Poor
300	275	150	125	100	75

NOTE: Extra barrels add 25 percent per barrel.

Model 12

As above, with adjustable target sights.

NIB	Exc.	V.G.	Good	Fair	Poor
350	27	200	175	125	100

Model 14

As above, with a recessed barrel locking nut and furnished with a spanner wrench. Manufactured from 1971 to 1975.

NIB	Exc.	V.G.	Good	Fair	Poor
350	250	175	150	100	75

Model 15

As above, with adjustable target sights.

NIB	Exc.	V.G.	Good	Fair	Poor
375	275	200	175	125	100

Model 8

As above, in .38 Special caliber.

NIB	Exc.	V.G.	Good	Fair	Poor
325	225	150	125	100	75

Model 9

As the Model 15, with adjustable sights and in .38 Special caliber. Manufactured from 1971 to 1975.

NIB	Exc.	V.G.	Good	Fair	Poor
350	275	200	175	125	100

.22 CALIBER REVOLVERS

Model 22

This is a double-action target revolver chambered for the .22 LR cartridge. It is available in 2", 4", 6", and 8" barrel length with a choice of standard rib shroud, ventilated rib shroud, or ventilated heavy rib shroud. All variations feature an adjustable rear sight, red ramp interchangeable front sight and target grips. Offered in bright blue or stainless steel finish. For revolvers with standard barrel assembly weights are: 2"—36 oz., 4"—40 oz., 6"—44 oz., and 8"—49 oz.

Model 722

Same as above but with stainless steel finish.

Model 22M

Same as above but chambered for .22 Magnum with blued finish.

MODEL 722M

Same as above but chambered for .22 Magnum with stainless steel finish.

Model 722M Standard Rib Shroud

NIB	Exc.	V.G.	Good	Fair	Poor
375	300	200	150	100	75

Ventilated Rib Shroud

NIB	Exc.	V.G.	Good	Fair	Poor
400	325	225	150	100	75

Ventilated Heavy Rib Shroud

NIB	Exc.	V.G.	Good	Fair	Poor
425	330	240	200	125	100

NOTE: Add 10 percent to prices for stainless steel finish.

P22 PISTOL PAC

This model is also a target revolver similar to the Model 22 and its variations. Chambered for the .22 LR or .22 Magnum, it is also offered with three types of barrel shrouds: standard, ventilated, or ventilated heavy. It is available in blued or stainless steel finish. The principal feature of the Pistol Pac is the three barrel assemblies in 2.5", 4", 6", and 8" with extra grips, four additional front sights, and a fitted carrying case.

Standard Rib Shroud

NIB	Exc.	V.G.	Good	Fair	Poor
750	550	400	350	300	150

Ventilated Rib Shroud

NIB	Exc.	V.G.	Good	Fair	Poor
800	600	500	450	350	150

Ventilated Heavy Rib Shroud

NIB	Exc.	V.G.	Good	Fair	Poor
800	600	500	450	350	150

NOTE: Add 10 percent to prices for stainless steel finish.

HP22 Hunter Pac

This model is chambered for the .22 Magnum cartridge. The set includes a ventilated heavy 8" shroud, a ventilated 8" shroud only with Burris scope mounts and Burris 1.5x4X variable or fixed 2X, a barrel changing tool, and fitted carrying case. Finish is blued or stainless steel. NOTE: Hunter Pacs are a special order item and should be evaluated at the time of sale.

.32 CALIBER REVOLVERS

Model 32

This model is a target revolver chambered for the .32 H&R Magnum cartridge. It is offered in 2", 4", 6", or 8" barrel lengths with choice of rib shrouds. All variations are fitted with adjustable rear sight, red ramp interchangeable front sight, and target grips. Available in blued or stainless steel finish. Weights depend on barrel length and shroud type but are between 35 oz. and 53 oz.

Model 732

Same as above but with stainless steel finish.

Model 322

Same as above but chambered for .32-20 cartridge with blued finish.

MODEL 7322

Same as above but chambered for .32-20 cartridge with stainless steel finish.

Standard Rib Shroud

NIB	Exc.	V.G.	Good	Fair	Poor
475	325	200	150	100	75

Ventilated Rib Shroud

NIB	Exc.	V.G.	Good	Fair	Poor
500	350	225	150	100	75

Ventilated Heavy Rib Shroud

NIB	Exc.	V.G.	Good	Fair	Poor
525	375	250	150	100	75

P32 PISTOL PAC

This set offers the same calibers, barrel shrouds, and finishes as the above models but in a set consisting of 2", 4", 6", and 8" barrels with extra grips, four additional sights, and fitted case.

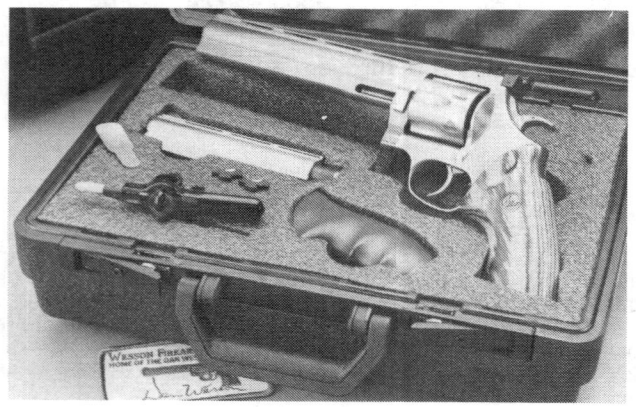

P32 Pistol Pac Standard Rib Shroud

NIB	Exc.	V.G.	Good	Fair	Poor
1200	1000	650	500	400	300

P32 Pistol Pac Ventilated Rib Shroud

NIB	Exc.	V.G.	Good	Fair	Poor
1200	1000	650	500	400	300

P32 Pistol Pac Ventilated Heavy Rib Shroud

NIB	Exc.	V.G.	Good	Fair	Poor
1200	1000	650	500	400	300

NOTE: Add 10 percent to prices for stainless steel finish.

329HP32 Hunter Pac

This model is chambered for the .32 H&R Magnum or .32-20 cartridge. The set includes a ventilated heavy 8" shroud, a ventilated 8" shroud only with Burris scope mounts and Burris scope in either 1.5x4X variable or fixed 2X, a barrel-changing tool, and fitted carrying case. Finish is blued or stainless steel. NOTE: Hunter Pacs are a special order item and should be evaluated at the time of sale.

.357 MAGNUM AND .38 CALIBER REVOLVERS

Model 14

This is a double-action service revolver chambered for the .357 Magnum cartridge. Available with 2", 4", or 6" barrel with service shroud. It has fixed sights, service grip, and is offered in blued or stainless steel finish.

Model 714

Same as above but with stainless steel finish.

Model 8

Same as above but chambered for .38 Special cartridge with blued finish.

Model 708

Same as above but chambered for .38 Special with stainless steel finish.

NIB	Exc.	V.G.	Good	Fair	Poor
400	350	250	125	100	75

P14/8 Pistol Pac

This set consists of a 2", 4", and 6" barrel with service shroud and fixed sights. It has an extra grip and fitted carrying case. The P14 is chambered for the .357 Mag. and the P8 is chambered for the .38 Special.

NIB	Exc.	V.G.	Good	Fair	Poor
800	700	600	500	400	300

Model 15

This model is designed as a double-action target revolver chambered for the .357 Magnum cartridge. It is available with 2", 4", 6", 8", and 10" barrel lengths with standard rib shroud. It features adjustable rear sight, red ramp interchangeable front sight, and target grips. Offered with blued finish. Weights according to barrel length are: 2"-32 oz., 4"-36 oz., 6"-40 oz., 8"-44 oz., 10"-50 oz.

Model 715

Same as above but with stainless steel finish.

Model 9

Same as above but chambered for .38 Special cartridge with blued finish.

MODEL 709

Same as above but with stainless steel finish.

Standard Rib Shroud

NIB	Exc.	V.G.	Good	Fair	Poor
800	700	600	500	400	300

Ventilated Rib Shroud

NIB	Exc.	V.G.	Good	Fair	Poor
800	700	600	500	400	300

Ventilated Heavy Rib Shroud

NIB	Exc.	V.G.	Good	Fair	Poor
800	700	600	500	400	300

330HP15 Hunter Pac

This model is chambered for the .357 Magnum cartridge. The set includes a ventilated heavy 8" shroud, a ventilated 8" shroud only with Burris scope mounts and Burris scope in either 1.5x4X variable or fixed 2X, a barrel changing tool, and fitted carrying case. Finish is blued or stainless steel.

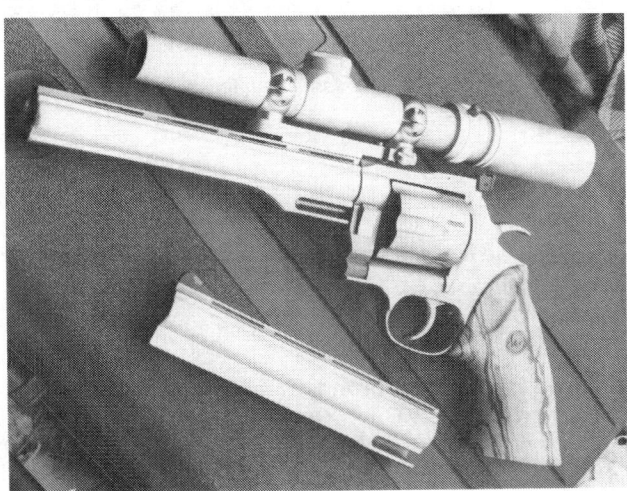

NOTE: Hunter Pacs are a special order item and should be evaluated at the time of sale.

331MODEL 40/SUPERMAG

This model is a target revolver chambered for the .357 Maximum cartridge. It has an adjustable rear sight, red ramp interchangeable front sight, ventilated rib shroud, and target grip. Barrel lengths are 4", 6", 8", or 10". A ventilated slotted shroud is available in 8" only. For 1993 a compensated barrel assembly, "CBA," was added to the product line as a complete gun. Finish is blued. Weighs approximately 64 oz. with ventilated rib shroud barrel. Add 20 percent for Model 740 in stainless steel.

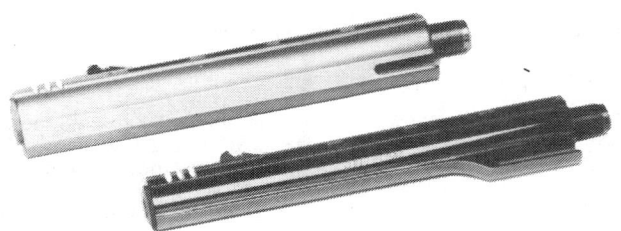

Ventilated Rib Shroud

NIB	Exc.	V.G.	Good	Fair	Poor
1100	950	750	600	450	300

Ventilated Slotted Shroud—8" barrel only

NIB	Exc.	V.G.	Good	Fair	Poor
1100	950	750	600	450	300

Ventilated Heavy Rib Shroud

NIB	Exc.	V.G.	Good	Fair	Poor
1100	950	750	600	450	300

NOTE: Add 10 percent to prices for stainless steel finish. For .357 Supermag with compensated barrel assembly add $30.

332HP40 Hunter Pac

This model is chambered for the .357 Supermag cartridge. The set includes a ventilated heavy 8" shroud, a ventilated 8" shroud only with Burris scope mounts and Burris scope in either 1.5x4X variable or fixed 2X, a barrel changing tool, and fitted carrying case. Finish is blued or stainless steel.NOTE: Hunter Pacs are a special order item and should be evaluated at the time of sale.

MODEL 375

This model, also known as the .375 Supermag, is chambered for the .375 Maximum cartridge, based on the .375 Winchester cartridge. Offered in 6", 8", 10" barrels in ventilated, ventilated heavy, or ventilated slotted rib barrels. Sights are interchangeable and adjustable. Available in bright blue finish only. Weighs approximately 64 oz. with ventilated rib shroud barrel.

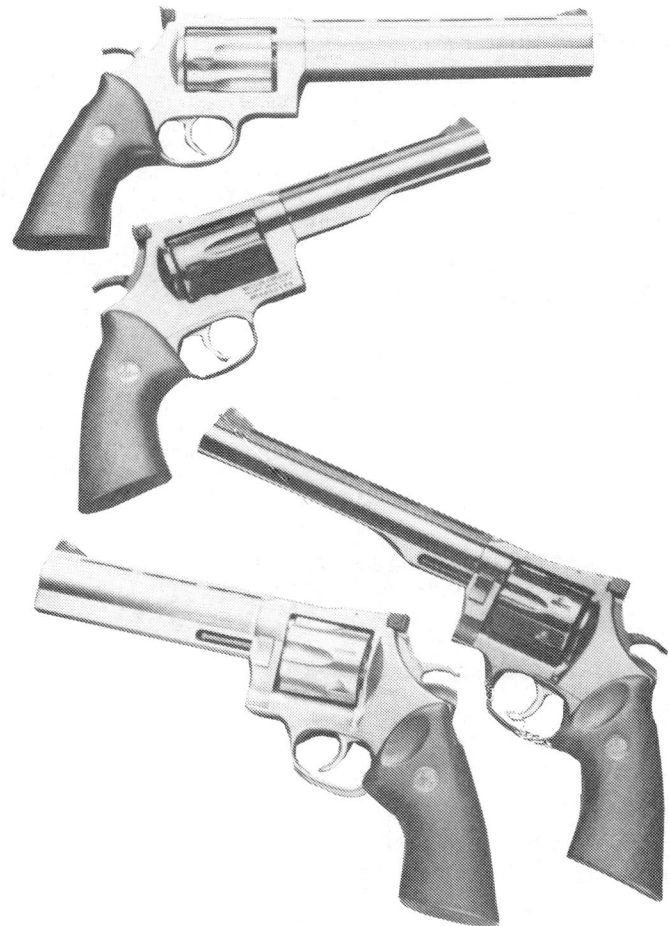

Ventilated Rib Shroud

NIB	Exc.	V.G.	Good	Fair	Poor
1100	950	750	600	450	300

Ventilated Heavy Rib Shroud

NIB	Exc.	V.G.	Good	Fair	Poor
1100	950	750	600	450	300

Ventilated Slotted Shroud—8" barrel only

NIB	Exc.	V.G.	Good	Fair	Poor
1100	950	750	600	450	300

P15/9 PISTOL PAC

This model is a set with 2", 4", 6", and 8" barrels with standard rib shroud. Chambered for the .357 or .38 Special with standard rib shroud, four additional sights, and extra grip, and carrying case. The P15 is chambered for the .357 Mag. while the P9 is chambered for the .38 Special.

Standard Rib Shroud

NIB	Exc.	V.G.	Good	Fair	Poor
800	700	600	500	400	300

Ventilated Rib Shroud

NIB	Exc.	V.G.	Good	Fair	Poor
800	700	600	500	400	300

Ventilated Heavy Rib Shroud

NIB	Exc.	V.G.	Good	Fair	Poor
800	700	600	500	400	300

NOTE: Add 10 percent to prices for stainless steel finish.

354HP375 Hunter Pac

This model is chambered for the .375 Supermag cartridge. The set includes a ventilated heavy 8" shroud, a ventilated 8" shroud only with Burris scope mounts and Burris scope in either 1.5x4X variable or fixed 2X, a barrel changing tool, and fitted carrying case. Finish is blued or stainless steel. NOTE: Hunter Pacs are a special order item and should be evaluated at the time of sale.

.41, .44 MAGNUM, AND .45 LONG COLT REVOLVERS

Model 44

This model is a target double-action revolver chambered for the .44 Magnum. It has 4", 6", 8", or 10" barrels with ventilated rib shrouds. Other features include: adjustable rear sight, red ramp interchangeable front sight, and target grips. Finish is bright blue. Weights with 4" barrel—40 oz., 6"—56 oz., 8"—64 oz., and 10"—69 oz.

Model 744

Same as above but with stainless steel finish.

Model 41

Same as above but chambered for .41 Magnum with blued finish.

Model 741

Same as above but with stainless steel finish.

MODEL 45

Same as above but chambered for .45 Long Colt with bright blue finish.

Model 745

Same as above but with stainless steel finish.

Ventilated Rib Shroud

NIB	Exc.	V.G.	Good	Fair	Poor
1000	850	550	450	300	200

Ventilated Heavy Rib Shroud

NIB	Exc.	V.G.	Good	Fair	Poor
1000	850	550	450	300	200

NOTE: Add 10 percent to prices for stainless steel finish.

P44/P41/P45 PISTOL PAC

This set features a 6" and 8" barrel assembly with ventilated rib shroud, an extra grip, two additional front sights, and a fitted carrying case. Chambered for .41 Magnum, .44 Magnum, or .45 Long Colt.

Ventilated Rib Shroud

NIB	Exc.	V.G.	Good	Fair	Poor
1000	850	550	450	300	200

Ventilated Heavy Rib Shroud

NIB	Exc.	V.G.	Good	Fair	Poor
1000	850	550	450	300	200

NOTE: Add 10 percent to prices for stainless steel finish.

HP41/44 Hunter Pac

This model is chambered for either the .41 or .44 Magnum cartridge. The set includes a ventilated heavy 8" shroud, a ventilated 8" shroud only with Burris scope mounts and Burris scope in either 1.5x4X variable or fixed 2X, a barrel changing tool, and fitted carrying case. Finish is blued or stainless steel. NOTE: Hunter Pacs are a special order item and should be evaluated at the time of sale.

Model 445

This double-action target revolver is chambered for the .445 Supermag cartridge. Barrel lengths offered are 8" with ventilated slotted rib shroud, 8" ventilated heavy slotted rib shroud, or 10" ventilated slotted rib shroud. Barrel lengths are also available in 4", 6", 8", and 10" with choice of ventilated rib or ventilated heavy rib shrouds. Introduced in 1993 is a compensated barrel assembly available as a complete gun. This is designated the "CBA." Fitted with adjustable rear sights, red ramp interchangeable front sight, and target grips. Finish is bright blue. Typical weight with 8" ventilated rib shroud barrel is about 62 oz.

MODEL 7445

Same as above but with stainless steel finish.

Ventilated Rib Shroud

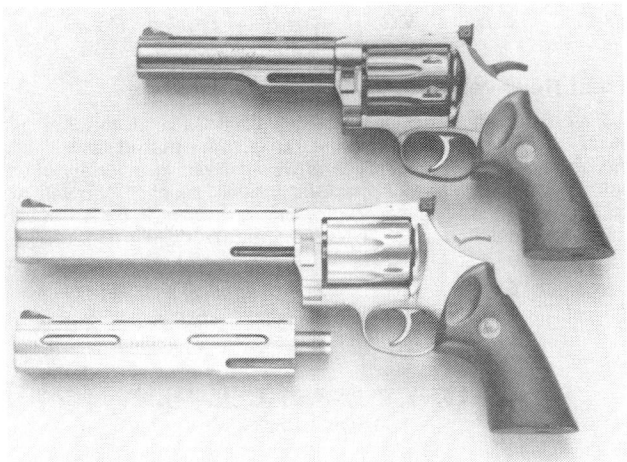

NIB	Exc.	V.G.	Good	Fair	Poor
1100	950	750	600	450	300

Ventilated Heavy Rib Shroud

NIB	Exc.	V.G.	Good	Fair	Poor
1100	950	750	600	450	300

NOTE: Add 10 percent to prices for stainless steel finish. For .44 Magnum and .445 Supermag with compensated barrel assembly add $30.

Model 7445 Alaskan Guide Special

This limited edition model (only 500 were produced) is chambered for the .445 Supermag cartridge. It features a 4" ventilated heavy compensated shroud barrel assembly, synthetic grips, and a matte black titanium nitride finish. Overall barrel length is 5.5" and the revolver weighs 56 oz.

NIB	Exc.	V.G.	Good	Fair	Poor
950	700	600	350	200	100

HP455 Hunter Pac

This model is chambered for the .445 Supermag cartridge. The set includes a ventilated heavy 8" shroud, a ventilated 8" shroud only with Burris scope mounts and Burris scope in either 1.5x4X variable or fixed 2X, a barrel changing tool, and fitted carrying case. Finish is blued or stainless steel. NOTE: Hunter Pacs are a special order item and should be evaluated at the time of sale.

FIXED BARREL HANDGUNS

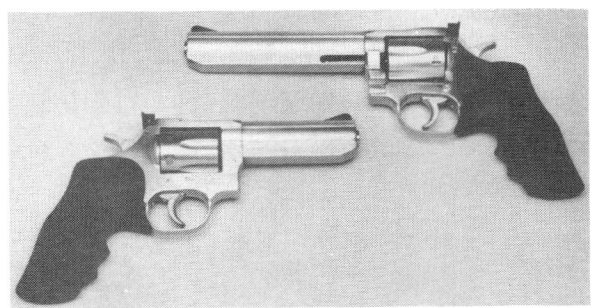

Model 38P

This model is a 5-shot double-action revolver designed for the .38 Special cartridge. Barrel is 2.5" with fixed sights. Choice of wood or rubber grips. Finish is blued. Weighs 24.6 oz.

NIB	Exc.	V.G.	Good	Fair	Poor
350	225	150	125	100	75

WESSON FIREARMS SILHOUETTE .22

This model is a 6-shot .22 LR single-action-only revolver with a 10" barrel. Fitted with compact-style grips, narrow notch rear sight with choice of ventilated or ventilated heavy rib shroud. Finish is blued or stainless steel. Weighs 55 oz. with ventilated rib shroud and 62 oz. with ventilated heavy rib shroud.

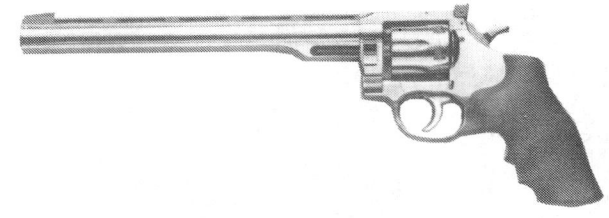

Ventilated Rib Shroud

NIB	Exc.	V.G.	Good	Fair	Poor
495	325	275	200	150	100

Ventilated Heavy Rib Shroud

NIB	Exc.	V.G.	Good	Fair	Poor
495	350	285	200	150	100

NOTE: Add 10 percent to prices for stainless steel finish.

Model 738P

Same as above but with stainless steel finish and 2" barrel.

NIB	Exc.	V.G.	Good	Fair	Poor
525	350	285	200	150	100

MODEL 45/745 PIN GUN

This model uses a .44 Magnum frame with 5" barrel with two-stage compensator. Choice of ventilated or ventilated heavy rib shroud configuration. Chambered for .45 ACP with or without half moon clips. Finish is blued or stainless steel. Weighs 54 oz.

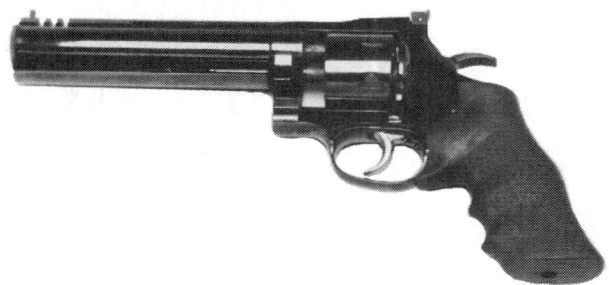

Ventilated Rib Shroud

NIB	Exc.	V.G.	Good	Fair	Poor
1100	950	750	600	450	300

Ventilated Heavy Rib Shroud

NIB	Exc.	V.G.	Good	Fair	Poor
1100	950	750	600	450	300

NOTE: Add 10 percent to prices for stainless steel finish.

Model 14/714 Fixed Barrel Service

Same features as the .357 Magnum Model 14 without the interchangeable barrels. Barrel length are either 2.5" or 4" with fixed sights. Offered in either blued or stainless steel. Weighs 30 oz. with 2.5" barrel and 34 oz. with 4" barrel.

NIB	Exc.	V.G.	Good	Fair	Poor
275	235	150	125	100	75

NOTE: Add 10 percent to prices for stainless steel finish.

Model 15/715 Fixed Barrel Target

Same as the .357 Magnum Model 15 with target sights and grips. Fixed barrel lengths are either 3" or 5". Available in blued or stainless steel. Weighs 37 oz. with 3" barrel and 42 oz. with 5" barrel.

NIB	Exc.	V.G.	Good	Fair	Poor
300	250	160	125	100	75

NOTE: Add 10 percent to prices for stainless steel finish.

WHITE, ROLLIN
Lowell, Massachusetts

Pocket Pistol

A .32 or .38 rimfire spur trigger single-shot pistol with a 3" or 5" octagonal barrel. Brass or iron frames with walnut grips. The .38 caliber version with the 5" barrel was not produced in large quantities and therefore is worth approximately 25 percent more than the values listed. The barrels are marked "Rollin White Arms Co., Lowell, Mass."

NIB	Exc.	V.G.	Good	Fair	Poor
—	—	900	750	350	150

Pocket Revolver

A .22 caliber spur trigger revolver with a 3.25" octagonal barrel and 7-shot cylinder. The brass frame silver-plated, barrel blued and grips of walnut. This revolver was marked in a variety of ways including "Rollin White Arms Co., Lowell, Mass.," "Lowell Arms Co., Lowell, Mass.," or "Made for Smith & Wesson by Rollin White Arms Co., Lowell, Mass." Approximately 10,000 were made during the late 1860s.

NIB	Exc.	V.G.	Good	Fair	Poor
—	—	775	600	250	75

WHITNEY ARMS COMPANY
INCLUDING

ELI WHITNEY, SR. / P. & E.W. BLAKE /

ELI WHITNEY, JR.

As the United States' first major commercial arms maker, Eli Whitney's New Haven plant, which began production in 1798 and continued under family control for the next 90 years, was one of the more important American arms manufactories of the 19th century. Its products, accordingly, are eminently collectible. Moreover, during its 90 years of operation, the Whitney clan produced a number of unusual arms, some exact copies of regulation U.S. martial longarms, others variations and derivatives of U.S. and foreign longarms, a variety of percussion revolvers, and finally a variety of single-shot and repeating breechloading rifles in an attempt to capture a portion of the burgeoning market in these cartridge arms during the post-Civil War period. Contrary to the prevailing myth, Eli Whitney, Sr., who also invented the cotton gin, did NOT perfect a system of interchangeability of parts in the arms industry. His contributions in this line were more as a propagandist for the concept that was brought to fruition by others, notably Simeon North and John Hall.

Hooded Cylinder Pocket Revolver

This is an unusual revolver that is chambered for .28 caliber percussion. It has a manually rotated, 6-shot hooded cylinder that has etched decorations. The octagonal barrel is offered in lengths of 3" to 6". There is a button at the back of the frame that unlocks the cylinder so that it can be rotated. The finish is blued, with a brass frame and two-piece rounded walnut grips. It is marked "E. Whitney N. Haven Ct." There were approximately 200 manufactured between 1850 and 1853.

NIB	Exc.	V.G.	Good	Fair	Poor
—	—	5750	3250	1500	600

Two Trigger Pocket Revolver

This is a conventional-appearing pocket revolver with a manually rotated cylinder. There is a second trigger located in front of the conventional trigger guard that releases the cylinder so that it can be turned. It is chambered for .32 caliber percussion and has an octagonal barrel from 3" to 6" in length. It has a 5-shot unfluted cylinder that is etched and a brass frame. The remainder is blued, with squared walnut two-piece grips. An iron-frame version is also available, but only 50 were produced. It would bring approximately 60 percent additional. There were approximately 650 total manufactured between 1852 and 1854.

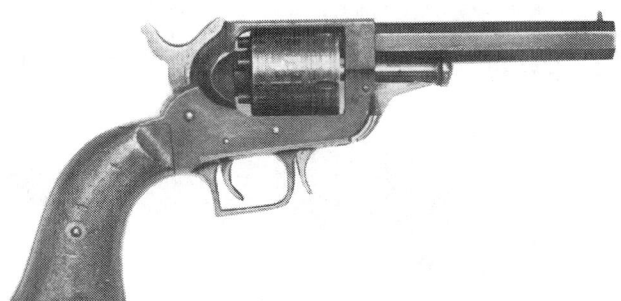

Courtesy Milwaukee Public Museum, Milwaukee, Wisconsin

NIB	Exc.	V.G.	Good	Fair	Poor
—	—	2750	2000	850	300

WHITNEY-BEALS PATENT REVOLVER

This was an unusual, ring-trigger pocket pistol that was made in three basic variations.

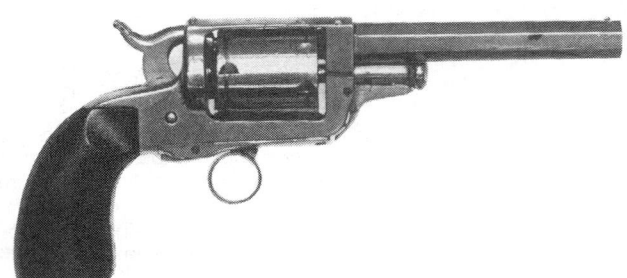

Courtesy Milwaukee Public Museum, Milwaukee, Wisconsin

First Model

This version is chambered for .31-caliber percussion and has barrels of octagonal configuration from 2" to 6" in length. It has a brass frame and a 6-shot cylinder. It is marked "F. Beals/New Haven, Ct." There were only 50 manufactured.

NIB	Exc.	V.G.	Good	Fair	Poor
—	—	5000	3500	1500	450

.31 Caliber Model

This version has an iron frame and a 7-shot cylinder. The octagonal barrels are from 2" to 6" in length. It is marked "Address E. Whitney/Whitneyville, Ct." There were approximately 2,300 manufactured.

NIB	Exc.	V.G.	Good	Fair	Poor
—	—	2500	1500	600	200

.28 Caliber Model

Except for the caliber, this model is similar to the .31 Caliber Model. There were approximately 850 manufactured.

NIB	Exc.	V.G.	Good	Fair	Poor
—	—	2750	1750	700	300

WHITNEY 1851 NAVY

This is a faithful copy of the 1851 Colt Revolver. It is virtually identical. There is a possibility that surplus Colt parts were utilized in the construction of this revolver. There were approximately 400 manufactured in 1857 and 1858.

NIB	Exc.	V.G.	Good	Fair	Poor
—	—	9000	4250	1750	650

Revolver

This is a single-action revolver chambered for .36 caliber percussion. It has a standard octagonal barrel length of 7.5". It has an iron frame and a 6-shot unfluted cylinder that is roll engraved. The finish is blued, with a case colored loading lever and two-piece walnut grips. The barrel is marked either "E. Whitney/N. Haven" or "Eagle Co." There are a number of minor variations on this revolver, and we strongly urge competent appraisal if contemplating a transaction. There were 33,000 total manufactured between 1858 and 1862.

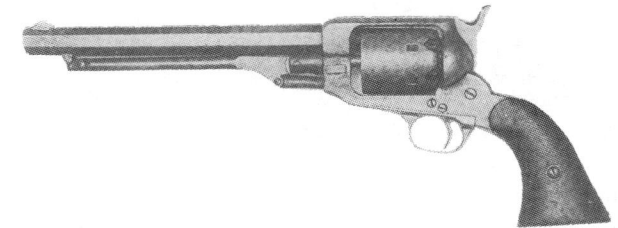

Courtesy Wallis & Wallis, Lewes, Sussex, England

FIRST MODEL

Nearly the entire production of the First Model is marked "Eagle Co." The reason for this marking is unknown. There are four distinct variations of this model.

First Variation

This model has no integral loading-lever assembly and has a thin top strap. There were only 100 manufactured.

NIB	Exc.	V.G.	Good	Fair	Poor
—	—	5400	3750	1500	550

Second Variation

This version is similar to the First Variation, with an integral loading lever. There were approximately 200 manufactured.

NIB	Exc.	V.G.	Good	Fair	Poor
—	—	5000	3000	1200	400

Third Variation

This is similar to the Second, with a three-screw frame instead of four screws. The loading lever is also modified. There were approximately 500 manufactured.

NIB	Exc.	V.G.	Good	Fair	Poor
—	—	4800	2500	1000	300

Fourth Variation

This version has a rounded frame and a safety notch between the nipples on the rear of the cylinder. There have been examples noted marked "E. Whitney/N. Haven." There were approximately 700 manufactured.

NIB	Exc.	V.G.	Good	Fair	Poor
—	—	4800	2500	1000	300

SECOND MODEL

First Variation

This version features a more robust frame with a brass trigger guard. The barrel is marked "E. Whitney/N. Haven." The cylinder pin is secured by a wing nut, and there is an integral loading lever. There were approximately 1,200 manufactured.

NIB	Exc.	V.G.	Good	Fair	Poor
—	—	3750	2000	900	300

Second Variation

This version has six improved safety notches on the rear of the cylinder. There were approximately 10,000 manufactured.

NIB	Exc.	V.G.	Good	Fair	Poor
—	—	3200	1750	750	250

Third Variation

This version has an improved, Colt-type loading-lever latch. There were approximately 2,000 manufactured.

NIB	Exc.	V.G.	Good	Fair	Poor
—	—	3200	1750	750	250

Fourth Variation

This is similar to the Third except the cylinder is marked "Whitneyville." There were approximately 10,000 manufactured.

NIB	Exc.	V.G.	Good	Fair	Poor
—	—	3200	1750	750	250

Fifth Variation

This version has a larger trigger guard. There were approximately 4,000 manufactured.

NIB	Exc.	V.G.	Good	Fair	Poor
—	—	3200	1750	750	250

Sixth Variation

This version has the larger trigger guard and five-groove rifling instead of the usual seven-groove. There were approximately 2,500 manufactured.

NIB	Exc.	V.G.	Good	Fair	Poor
—	—	3200	1750	750	250

WHITNEY POCKET REVOLVER

This is a single-action revolver chambered for .31 caliber percussion. It has octagonal barrels between 3" and 6" in length. It has a 5-shot unfluted cylinder that is roll engraved and marked "Whitneyville." The frame is iron with a blued finish and a case colored integral loading lever. The grips are two-piece walnut. The development of this model, as far as models and variations go, is identical to that which we described in the Navy Model designation. The values are different, and we list them for reference. Again, we recommend securing qualified appraisal if a transaction is contemplated. There were approximately 32,500 manufactured from 1858 to 1862.

FIRST MODEL

First Variation

NIB	Exc.	V.G.	Good	Fair	Poor
—	—	3750	2000	900	300

Second Variation

NIB	Exc.	V.G.	Good	Fair	Poor
—	—	2200	1250	500	200

Third Variation

NIB	Exc.	V.G.	Good	Fair	Poor
—	—	1900	1000	400	150

Fourth Variation

NIB	Exc.	V.G.	Good	Fair	Poor
—	—	1900	1000	400	150

Fifth Variation

NIB	Exc.	V.G.	Good	Fair	Poor
—	—	1900	1000	400	150

SECOND MODEL

First Variation

NIB	Exc.	V.G.	Good	Fair	Poor
—	—	1700	900	400	100

Second Variation

NIB	Exc.	V.G.	Good	Fair	Poor
—	—	1700	900	400	100

Third Variation

NIB	Exc.	V.G.	Good	Fair	Poor
—	—	1700	900	400	100

Fourth Variation

NIB	Exc.	V.G.	Good	Fair	Poor
—	—	1700	1000	425	125

New Model Pocket Revolver

This is a single-action, spur-triggered pocket revolver chambered for .28-caliber percussion. It has a 3.5" octagonal barrel and a 6-shot roll engraved cylinder. It features an iron frame with a blued finish and two-piece walnut grips. The barrel is marked "E. Whitney/N. Haven." There were approximately 2,000 manufactured between 1860 and 1867.

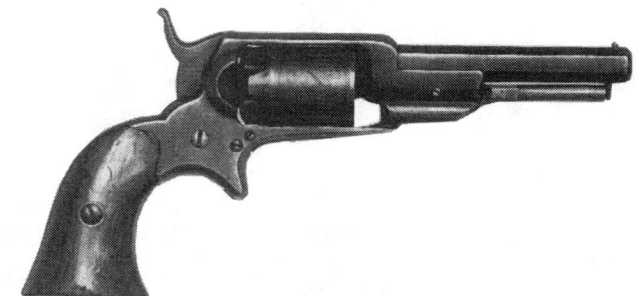

Courtesy Milwaukee Public Museum, Milwaukee, Wisconsin

NIB	Exc.	V.G.	Good	Fair	Poor
—	—	2000	1250	500	200

Rimfire Pocket Revolver

This is a spur-trigger, single-action, solid-frame pocket revolver that was produced in three frame sizes, depending on the caliber. It is chambered for the .22, .32, and .38 rimfire cartridges. The frame is brass, and it is found in a variety of finishes- nickel-plated or blued, or a combination thereof. The bird's-head grips are rosewood or hard rubber; ivory or pearl grips are sometimes encountered and will bring a slight premium in value. The barrels are octagonal and from 1.5" to 5" in length. The barrels are marked "Whitneyville Armory Ct. USA." They have also been noted with the trade names "Monitor," "Defender," or "Eagle." They were commonly referred to as the Model No. 1, No. 1.5, Model 2, or Model 2.5. The values for all are quite similar. There were approximately 30,000 manufactured of all types between 1871 and 1879.

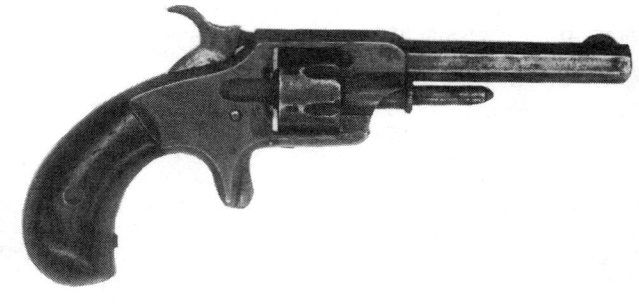

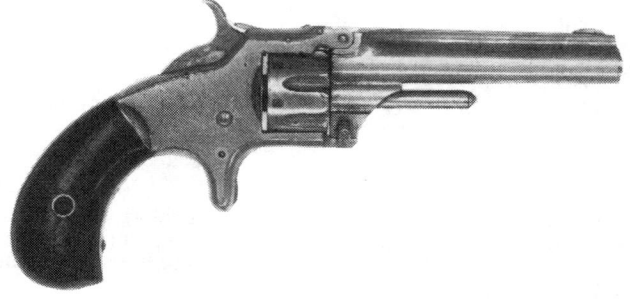

Courtesy Milwaukee Public Museum, Milwaukee, Wisconsin

NIB	Exc.	V.G.	Good	Fair	Poor
—	—	750	500	200	75

WHITNEY FIREARMS COMPANY
Hartford, Connecticut

WOLVERINE

A .22 caliber semi-automatic pistol with a 4.75" barrel. Blued or nickel-plated with plastic grips and an aluminum alloy frame. This pistol is readily distinguishable by its streamlined form. Approximately 13,000 examples were made with the blue finish and 900 with a nickel-plated finish. Some slides are marked "Wolverine Whitney Firearms Inc., New Haven, Conn USA." Others are marked "Whitney" only. The Wolverine-marked pistols are considered more rare. Pistol were produced in two locations: New Haven, Connecticut and Hartford, Connecticut. Manufactured from 1955 to 1962. Now being reproduced by Olympic Arms. Pricing is for original version.

Blue Finish

Blued pistols most often have brown or black grips.

NIB	Exc.	V.G.	Good	Fair	Poor
750	550	400	350	250	200

Nickel-Plated

Nickeled pistols most often have white plastic grips.

NIB	Exc.	V.G.	Good	Fair	Poor
4000	2750	1800	1250	800	500

WICHITA ARMS, INC.
Wichita, Kansas

Wichita International Pistol

A single-shot pivoted barrel target pistol produced in a variety of calibers from .22 to .357 Magnum with a 10.5" or 14" barrel fitted with either adjustable sights or telescopic sight mounts. Stainless steel with walnut forestock and grips.

NIB	Exc.	V.G.	Good	Fair	Poor
800	650	400	350	300	200

Wichita Classic Pistol

A bolt action single-shot pistol chambered for a variety of calibers up to .308, with a left-hand action and 11.25" barrel. Blued with a walnut stock.

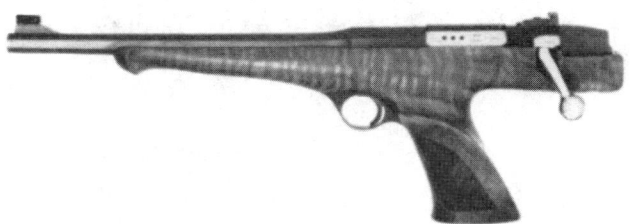

NIB	Exc.	V.G.	Good	Fair	Poor
3000	2500	2250	1850	1250	1000

Wichita Silhouette Pistol

As above, in 7mm HMSA or .308 with a 15" barrel. The walnut stock is made so that the pistol grip is located beneath the forward end of the bolt.

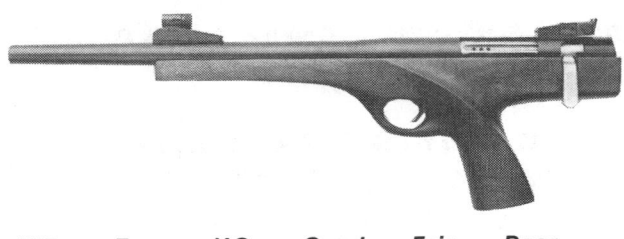

NIB	Exc.	V.G.	Good	Fair	Poor
1100	950	750	600	500	400

Wichita MK40

As above, with a 13" barrel, multi-range sights and either a composition or walnut stock. Standard finish is blued, however, this model was also made in stainless steel.

NIB	Exc.	V.G.	Good	Fair	Poor
1100	950	750	600	500	400

WIENER WAFFENFABRIK
Vienna, Austria

Little Tom

A 6.35mm or 7.65mm double-action semi-automatic pistol with a 2.5" barrel. The slide marked "Wiener Waffenfabrik Patent Little Tom," and the caliber. Blued with either walnut or plastic grips inlaid with a medallion bearing the company's trademark. Approximately 10,000 were made from 1919 to 1925.

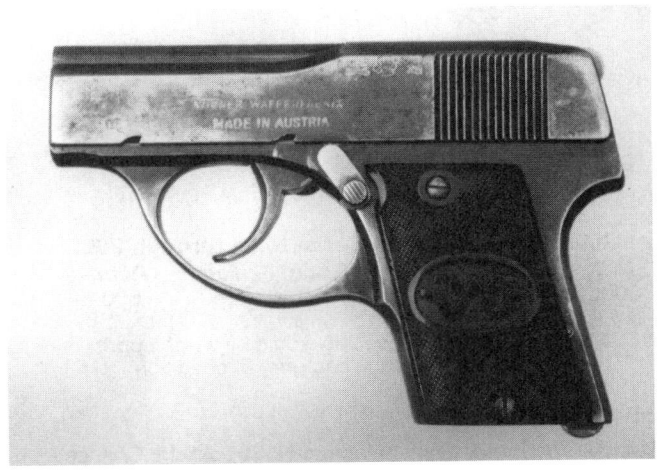

Courtesy J.B. Wood

Little Tom—6.35mm

NIB	Exc.	V.G.	Good	Fair	Poor
—	500	450	400	250	175

WILDEY FIREARMS CO., INC.
Cheshire, Connecticut
Newburg, New York
Warren, Connecticut

WILDEY AUTO PISTOL

A gas-operated, rotary-bolt, double-action semi-automatic pistol chambered for the .357 Peterbuilt, the .45 Winchester Magnum, or the .475 Wildey Magnum cartridges. with 5", 6", 7", 8", or 10" ventilated rib barrels. The gas-operated action is adjustable and features a single-shot cutoff. The rotary bolt has three heavy locking lugs. Constructed of stainless steel with adjustable sights and wood grips. The values of this rarely encountered pistol are based on not only the condition, but the caliber—as well the serial-number range, with earlier-numbered guns being worth a good deal more than the later or current production models.

Cheshire, Conn., Address

Produced in .45 Winchester Magnum only and is serial numbered from No. 1 through 2489.

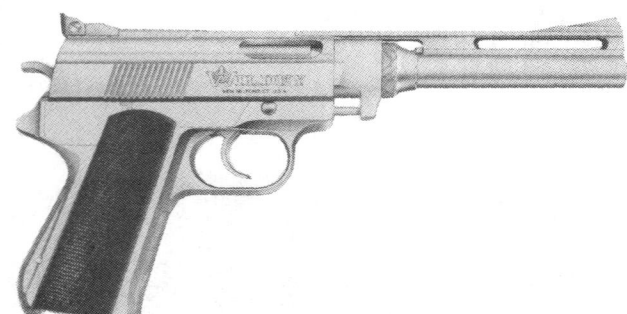

Cheshire, Conn., Address Serial No. 1 through 200
NIB	Exc.	V.G.	Good	Fair	Poor
2000	1500	1200	950	750	500

NOTE: Serial numbers above 200 would be worth approximately $200 less respectively in each category of condition.

Survivor Model

This pistol is presently manufactured in Brookfield, Connecticut.

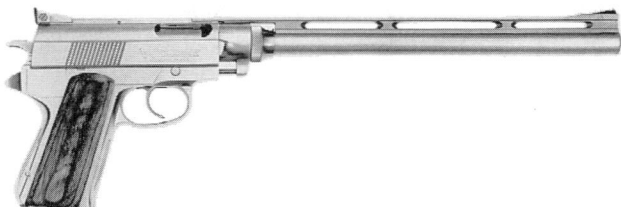

NIB	Exc.	V.G.	Good	Fair	Poor
1500	1000	750	550	450	300

NOTE: Add $100 for 12" barrel, $500 for 14" barrel, and $1,100 for 18" Silhouette model.

Hunter Model

As above but with matte stainless steel finish.

NIB	Exc.	V.G.	Good	Fair	Poor
1775	1250	900	700	600	450

Pin Gun

Gas-operated auto-loading pistol in polished or matte stainless for competition shooting. With muzzle brake; variety of calibers and barrel lengths (7", 8", 10", 12", 14"). 4.09 lb. (8" barrel).

NIB	Exc.	V.G.	Good	Fair	Poor
2000	1500	1200	950	750	500

Presentation Model

As above, but engraved and fitted with hand-checkered walnut grips.

NIB	Exc.	V.G.	Good	Fair	Poor
3000	2500	1950	1400	900	600

JAWS Viper

Jordanian Arms & Weapons System manufactured in Jordan. Semi-auto chambered for 9mm, .40 S&W, 45 ACP. Barrels: 4.4" and 5". 10-round magazine. Stainless finish with rubberized grip.

NIB	Exc.	V.G.	Good	Fair	Poor
—	725	500	375	250	150

WILKINSON ARMS CO.
Covina, California

Diane

A .25 caliber semi-automatic pistol with a 2.25" barrel and 6-shot magazine. Blued with plastic grips.

NIB	Exc.	V.G.	Good	Fair	Poor
—	400	325	200	150	100

WILLIAMSON
New York, New York

Derringer

A .41 caliber single-shot pocket pistol with a 2.5" sliding barrel. Blued, with a silver-plated furniture and a checkered walnut grip. Barrel marked "Williamson's Pat. Oct. 2, 1866 New York." This pistol was fitted with an auxiliary percussion cap chamber adaptor. Manufactured from 1866 to approximately 1870.

NIB	Exc.	V.G.	Good	Fair	Poor
—	—	—	1250	500	100

WILSON COMBAT
Berryville, Arkansas

Wilson's began making custom 1911-style pistols using Colt slides and frames in 1977. This company produces a wide range of quality components for the 1911 pistol, such as slides, triggers, safeties, barrels, etc. The models listed are for complete factory-built-and-assembled guns. These factory-built pistols are sold with a lifetime warranty, even to subsequent buyers. The pistols listed are divided into two categories. Semi-custom pistols are off-the-shelf guns available through participating dealers. Custom pistols are special order guns. The models listed below are representative, not inclusive.

POLYMER FRAME PISTOLS

Tactical Carry (KZ-45)

Chambered for .45 ACP cartridge and fitted with a 5" stainless steel match barrel, this model has numerous special features such as night sights and front and rear slide serrations. Frame is stainless steel and reinforced polymer. Magazine capacity is 10 rounds. Finish is black polymer. Weight is approximately 31 oz. Introduced in 1999.

NIB	Exc.	V.G.	Good	Fair	Poor
1050	900	750	600	500	300

KZ 9mm

Polymer-frame 1911 chambered for 9mm. Full size is 16+1 capacity with 5" barrel at 33 oz. Compact size is 14+1 capacity with 4.1" barrel at 31 oz. Introduced 2006.

NIB	Exc.	V.G.	Good	Fair	Poor
1500	1350	1200	900	750	300

ADP 9mm

11-round capacity, polymer frame. 19.5 oz. 6.3" overall length, 3.75" barrel. Introduced 2006.

NIB	Exc.	V.G.	Good	Fair	Poor
675	525	400	300	200	125

SEMI-CUSTOM PISTOLS

These pistols were first built in 1996 using Springfield Armory pistols as the base gun. The Protector Compact was built on the Springfield Compact pistol. In 1997 all Service Grade pistols are built on the new Wilson Combat slide and frame with the exception of the Protector compact which is built on a Colt commander slide and a Colt Officer Model frame. The semi-custom pistols are all marked with 1996A2 on the left-hand side of the slide. Service Grade pistols bear the name Protector, Protector Compact, or Classic on the rights side of the frame's dust cover.

Model 1996A2

This pistol, introduced in 1996, is offered in a number of different configurations. These configurations affect price. The base pistol is chambered for the .45 ACP cartridge, has snag-free sights and blue finish. Barrel length is 5", magazine capacity is 8 rounds, and weight is approximately 38 oz. There are numerous special features on the standard pistol.

NIB	Exc.	V.G.	Good	Fair	Poor
1450	1150	1000	800	625	300

NOTE: Add $70 for tritium night sights, $125 for Wilson adjustable sights, $275 for nights sights, ambi safety, hard chrome frame, $325 for Wilson adjustable sights, ambi safety, hard chrome frame.

Protector

This model is fitted to a 5" slide with match barrel adjustable sights, and numerous other special features. Weight is about 38 oz. Black polymer finish on slide and frame. Introduced in 1996.

NIB	Exc.	V.G.	Good	Fair	Poor
1795	1450	1150	900	650	400

NOTE: Add $100 for stainless steel.

Protector Compact

Same as above but fitted with a 4.25" match-grade barrel. Weight is about 34 oz. Introduced in 1996.

NIB	Exc.	V.G.	Good	Fair	Poor
1795	1450	1150	900	650	400

Sentinel Ultra Compact

This .45 ACP pistol is fitted with a 3.6" heavy tapered cone handfitted barrel, night sights, high-ride beavertail and numerous special features. Magazine capacity is 6 rounds. Weight is about 29 oz. Finish is a black polymer.

NIB	Exc.	V.G.	Good	Fair	Poor
2100	1675	1300	950	700	450

Tactical

This .45 ACP pistol is fitted with a 5" tapered cone handfitted barrel. Cocking serrations on front and rear of slide. High-ride beavertail safety and other special features. Night sights are standard. Cocobolo grips. Weight is about 38 oz. finish is black polymer. Magazine capacity is 8 rounds. Introduced in 1999.

NIB	Exc.	V.G.	Good	Fair	Poor
1825	1450	1100	900	700	400

Classic

This model has a 5" barrel, adjustable sights, hard chrome finish on frame, and other special features. Weight is about 38 oz. Introduced in 1996.

NIB	Exc.	V.G.	Good	Fair	Poor
1895	1500	1200	900	700	400

NOTE: Add $100 for stainless steel.

Service Grade Target

Chambered for the .45 ACP cartridge, this model features a 5" stainless steel match handfitted barrel with full length guide rod. Front and rear cocking serrations. Magazine well is beveled and grips are cocobolo. Numerous other special features. Weight is about 38 oz. Finish is black polymer. Magazine capacity is 8 rounds.

NIB	Exc.	V.G.	Good	Fair	Poor
1825	1450	1150	850	650	350

Custom Carry Revolver

Built on a Smith & Wesson .357 Magnum Model 66, this model features a 2.5" barrel with adjustable night sights. Cylinder is chambered and grip is black nylon with smooth finish. Stainless steel finish. Weight is about 30 oz.

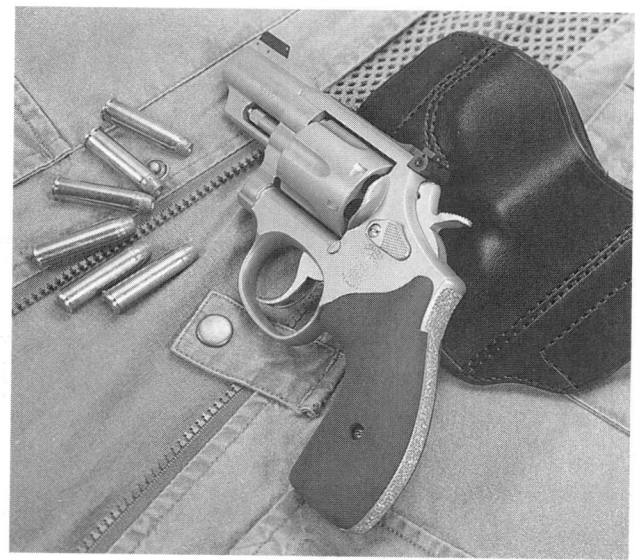

NIB	Exc.	V.G.	Good	Fair	Poor
1175	950	800	650	500	300

.22 Classic Rimfire Pistol

Chambered for the .22 caliber rimfire cartridge and fitted with a

5" barrel. Hard chrome frame and black anodized slide. Weight is less than standard .45 caliber pistol. Introduced in 1996.

NIB	Exc.	V.G.	Good	Fair	Poor
1125	975	800	625	500	250

CUSTOM-BUILT PISTOLS

Wilson Custom pistols bear the Wilson Combat or Wilson Custom label on the right side of the frame on the dust cover. Full custom guns are typically built on a Colt, Springfield Armory, Norinco, STI, Strayer Voight or Wilson Combat gun.

Combat Classic Super Grade (Tactical Super Grade)

Fitted with a 5" match-grade handfit stainless steel barrel. Adjustable sights, high ride beavertail safety, contoured magazine well and polymer slide with hard chrome frame. Weight is approximately 45 oz. In 9mm, .38 Super, .40 S&W, 10mm and .45 ACP.

NIB	Exc.	V.G.	Good	Fair	Poor
3595	2850	2300	1900	1500	600

Tactical Super Grade Compact

Similar to the above model but with a 4.1" match grade barrel. Magazine capacity is 7 rounds. Weight is about 40 oz. Introduced in 2003. Available in 9mm, .38 Super, .45 ACP.

NIB	Exc.	V.G.	Good	Fair	Poor
4475	3900	3200	2500	1850	650

Wilson X-TAC

Caliber .45 ACP, steel frame and slide, 8-round magazine, special XTAC-pattern slide serrations and texturing on front strap and mainspring housing, stainless match-grade barrel and bushing, extended thumb safety, beavertail tang, G10 grips and contoured mag well. Weight 38.1 ounces, 5-inch barrel with black Parkerized finish.

NIB	Exc.	V.G.	Good	Fair	Poor
2000	1700	1450	1150	750	300

CQB Light-Rail Lightweight

Calibers: 9mm Parabellum, .38 Super, .45 ACP. Compact size with 4-inch barrel, steel slide, alloy round butt frame. Weight is 27.34 ounces. Comes with two 8-round and one 7-round magazine, fiber optic front sight, integral accessory rail, G10 grips, extended thumb safety, beavertail tang, checkered front strap and mainspring housing. Several other sizes and variations available in CQB series.

NIB	Exc.	V.G.	Good	Fair	Poor
2300	1976	1650	1300	850	300

Ultralight Carry Series

A full-size 1911 with aluminum frame, steel slide. Chambered in 9mm Parabellum, .38 Super or .45 ACP. Stainless fluted 5-inch barrel. Comes with one 7- and two 8-round magazines. Other features include countersunk slide stop, integral accessory rail,

contoured mag well, G10 grips, extended thumb safety, beavertail tang, checkered front strap and mainspring housing. Weight is 26.5 ounces. Several Armor-Tuff finish options including black, O.D., silver, tan or two-tone. Compact model has a 4-inch barrel (all calibers), Sentinel has 3.6-inch barrel (9mm only).

NIB	Exc.	V.G.	Good	Fair	Poor
2900	2400	2000	1600	1000	500

Stealth Defense System

Built with a 4.25" slide with match-grade stainless steel barrel. This model features night sights, checkered front strap and mainspring spring housing with numerous special features. Black polymer finish. Weight is approximately 34 oz. Offered in 9mm, .38 Super, .40 S&W, .45 ACP.

NIB	Exc.	V.G.	Good	Fair	Poor
2895	2250	1700	1300	900	400

Defensive Combat Pistol

This .45 ACP pistol is built with a 5" match-grade stainless steel barrel, night sights, and numerous special features. Finish is black polymer. Weight 38 oz.

NIB	Exc.	V.G.	Good	Fair	Poor
2395	1850	1250	1000	600	300

Classic Master Grade

This .45 ACP pistol is fitted with a 5" stainless steel handfitted match-grade barrel. Numerous special features such as ultralight hammer, ambidextrous safety, etc. Finish is stainless steel frame and black polymer slide. Weight is about 38 oz. and magazine capacity is 8 rounds.

NIB	Exc.	V.G.	Good	Fair	Poor
2895	2250	1700	1300	900	400

Tactical Elite

This is similar to other Wilson pistols with the addition of the special tactical heavy tapered cone barrel.

NIB	Exc.	V.G.	Good	Fair	Poor
2895	2250	1700	1300	900	400

Defensive Combat Pistol Deluxe

This model has a 5" match-grade stainless steel barrel and numerous special features. Fitted with adjustable sights. Weight is about 38 oz. Finish is black polymer.

NIB	Exc.	V.G.	Good	Fair	Poor
2595	2000	1350	1050	700	300

Professional Model Pistol

Introduced in 2004 this .45 ACP pistol features a 4.1" stainless steel match barrel, tactical combat sights with tritium inserts. Many custom features. Magazine capacity is 8 rounds. Offered in gray/black, green/black, or all-black finish. Weight is about 35 oz.

NIB	Exc.	V.G.	Good	Fair	Poor
1215	1650	1375	1100	750	450

Competition Pistols

Wilson Combat offers a custom-built pistol to the customer's specifications. An expert appraisal is recommended prior to sale.

WINCHESTER REPEATING ARMS
New Haven, Connecticut

The prices given here are for the most part standard guns without optional features that were so often furnished by the factory. These optional or extra-cost features are too numerous to list and can affect the price of a shotgun or rifle to an enormous degree. In some cases these options are one of a kind. Collectors and those interested in Winchester firearms have the benefit of some of the original factory records. These records are now stored in the Cody Firearms Museum, Buffalo Bill Historical Center, P.O. Box 1000, Cody, Wyoming (307) 587-4771. For a $25 fee the museum will provide factory letters containing the original specifications of certain Winchester models using the original factory records. CAUTION: Buyers should confirm by Cody letter any special-order feature on any Winchester within the Cody record range before paying a premium for a scarce feature.

SMITH & WESSON VOLCANIC FIREARMS

An interesting connection in the evolution of the lever-action repeating firearm is found in the production of a small group of pistols and rifles built in Norwich, Connecticut, by Horace Smith and Daniel Wesson under the firm name of Smith & Wesson. The company built two types of Volcanic pistols. One was a large-frame model with an 8" barrel and chambered in .41 caliber. About 500 of these large frames were produced. The other pistol was a small-frame version with a 4" barrel chambered in .31 caliber. Slightly more of these small-frame pistols were built, about 700, than the large-frame version. In both variations the barrel, magazine, and frame were blued.

Courtesy Buffalo Bill Historical Center, Cody, Wyoming

4" Pistol

NIB	Exc.	V.G.	Good	Fair	Poor
—	—	—	11000	4000	1000

8" Pistol

Courtesy Buffalo Bill Historical Center, Cody, Wyoming

NIB	Exc.	V.G.	Good	Fair	Poor
—	—	—	13000	6000	1500

Volcanic Firearms (Volcanic Repeating Arms Company)

With the incorporation of the Volcanic Repeating Arms Company, a new and important individual was introduced who would have an impact on the American arms industry for the next 100 years: Oliver F. Winchester. This new company introduced the Volcanic pistol using the improvements made by Horace Smith and Daniel Wesson. Volcanic firearms are marked on the barrel, "THE VOLCANIC REPEATING ARMS CO. PATENT NEW HAVEN, CONN. FEB. 14, 1854." The Volcanic was offered as a .38 caliber breechloading tubular magazine repeater with blued barrel and bronze frame. These pistols were available in three barrel lengths.

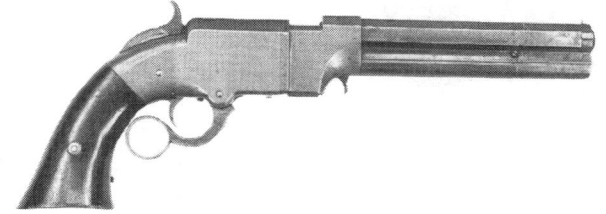

Courtesy Milwaukee Public Museum, Milwaukee, Wisconsin

6" Barrel

NIB	Exc.	V.G.	Good	Fair	Poor
—	—	—	7000	3500	1500

8" Barrel

NIB	Exc.	V.G.	Good	Fair	Poor
—	—	—	7000	3500	1500

VOLCANIC FIREARMS (NEW HAVEN ARMS COMPANY)

In 1857 the New Haven Arms Company was formed to continue the production of the former Volcanic Repeating Arms Company. Volcanic firearms continued to be built but were now marked on the barrel, "NEW HAVEN, CONN. PATENT FEB. 14, 1854." The

Volcanic pistols produced by the New Haven Arms Company were built in .30 caliber and used the same basic frame as the original Volcanic. These pistols were produced in 3-1/2" and 6" barrel lengths.

3-1/2" Barrel

NIB	Exc.	V.G.	Good	Fair	Poor
—	—	6500	5000	2500	1500

6" Barrel

NIB	Exc.	V.G.	Good	Fair	Poor
—	—	7500	5750	3000	1500

Silhouette Pistol

A custom made single-shot pistol produced in a variety of calibers with a 14" fluted stainless steel barrel and laminated pistol-grip stock. Furnished without sights. Introduced in 1989.

NIB	Exc.	V.G.	Good	Fair	Poor
—	1750	1450	1100	800	600

WOLF SPORTING PISTOLS
Importer—Handgunner Gunshop
Topton, Pennsylvania

Wolf SV Target

Chambered for 9x19, 9x21, 9x23, .38 Super, .40 S&W, or .45 ACP. Barrel is 4.5" long. Weight is 44 oz. Many special features. Built in Austria. Price listed is for basic pistol. A number of special order items are offered. Check with importer before a sale. First imported in 1998.

NIB	Exc.	V.G.	Good	Fair	Poor
2000	1600	1250	1000	750	600

Wolf SV Match

Chambered for 9x19, 9x21, 9x23, .38 Super, .40 S&W, or .45 ACP. Barrel is 5.5" long. Weight is 44 oz. Many special features. Built in Austria. Price listed is for basic pistol. A number of special order items are offered. Check with importer before a sale. First imported in 1998.

NIB	Exc.	V.G.	Good	Fair	Poor
2000	1600	1250	1000	750	600

WURFFLEIN, ANDREW & WILLIAM
Philadelphia, Pennsylvania

Pocket Pistol

A .41 caliber percussion single-shot pocket pistol with either a 2.5" or 3" barrel, German silver furniture and checkered walnut stock. The lock marked "A. Wurfflein / Phila." Manufactured during the 1850s and 1860s.

NIB	Exc.	V.G.	Good	Fair	Poor
—	—	2600	1750	700	200

Single-Shot Target Pistol

A .22 caliber single-shot pistol with half-octagonal barrels measuring from 8" to 16" in length. The barrel pivots downward for loading and is marked "W. Wurfflein Philad'a Pa. U.S.A. Patented June 24th, 1884." Blued with walnut grips. This model is also available with a detachable shoulder stock, which if present, would add approximately 35 percent to the values listed. Manufactured from 1884 to 1890.

NIB	Exc.	V.G.	Good	Fair	Poor
—	—	2600	1750	700	200

XL
HOPKINS & ALLEN
Norwich, Connecticut

Derringer

A .41 caliber spur trigger single-shot pistol with a 2.75" octagonal barrel and either iron or brass frame. Blued, nickel-plated with rosewood grips. The barrel marked "XL Derringer." Manufactured during the 1870s.

NIB	Exc.	V.G.	Good	Fair	Poor
—	1650	1295	950	500	150

Vest Pocket Derringer

As above, in .22 caliber with a 2.25" round barrel and normally full nickel-plated. The barrel marked "XL Vest Pocket." Manufactured from 1870s to 1890s.

NIB	Exc.	V.G.	Good	Fair	Poor
—	—	1350	750	325	125

XPERT
HOPKINS & ALLEN
Norwich, Connecticut

Xpert Derringer

A .22 or .30 caliber spur trigger single-shot pistol with round barrels, 2.25" to 6" in length and a nickel-plated finish with rosewood grips. The breechblock pivots to the left side for loading. The barrel marked "Xpert-Pat. Sep. 23. 1878." Manufactured during the 1870s.

NIB	Exc.	V.G.	Good	Fair	Poor
—	—	875	700	400	125

Z

ZEHNER, E. WAFFENFABRIK
Suhl, Germany

Zehna

A 6.35mm semi-automatic pistol with a 2.5" barrel and 5-shot magazine. The slide marked "Zehna DRPA," and the caliber on later production models. Blued with a black plastic grips bearing the monogram "EZ." Approximately 20,000 were made from 1921 to 1927.

NIB	Exc.	V.G.	Good	Fair	Poor
—	395	300	250	175	100

ZULAICA, M.
Eibar, Spain

Zulaica

A solid-frame .22 caliber revolver with a 6-shot cylinder that has zigzag grooves on its exterior surface. It is fired by an external hammer and the frame is hollow with a rod inside of it that connects to the breechblock. There is a serrated cocking piece connected to this rod that is found at the top rear of the frame. When fired, the cartridge case blows from the cylinder and activates the breechblock similar to a semi-automatic pistol.

NIB	Exc.	V.G.	Good	Fair	Poor
—	1000	800	600	350	250

ROYAL

The name Royal was applied to a number of pistols produced by this company, as listed.

Royal

A 6.35mm or 7.65mm semi-automatic pistol that is normally marked on the slide "Automatic Pistol 6.35 Royal" or "Automatic Pistol 7.65 Royal."

NIB	Exc.	V.G.	Good	Fair	Poor
—	300	175	100	75	50

Royal

As above, in 7.65mm caliber with a 5.5" barrel and 12-shot magazine.

NIB	Exc.	V.G.	Good	Fair	Poor
—	325	200	125	100	75

Royal

A rather poor copy of the Mauser Model C/96 semi-automatic pistol with fixed lockwork.

NIB	Exc.	V.G.	Good	Fair	Poor
—	900	700	500	300	150

Vincitor

A 6.35mm or 7.65mm caliber semi-automatic pistol patterned after the Model 1906 Browning. The slide marked "SA Royal Vincitor." Blued with plastic grips.

NIB	Exc.	V.G.	Good	Fair	Poor
—	300	175	100	75	50

FIREARMS TRADE NAMES

A.A. Co.: Inexpensive pocket revolvers of unknown manufacture.

Acme:
a) Trade name used by the W.H. Davenport Firearms Co. on shotguns.
b) Trade name used by the Hopkins and Allen Co. on revolvers produced for the Merwin, Hulbert and Co. and the Herman Boker Co. of New York.
c) Trade name used by the Maltby, Henley and Co. of New York on inexpensive pocket revolvers.

Acme Arms Company: Trade name used by the J. Stevens Arms and Tool Co. on pistols and shotguns produced for the Cornwall Hardware Co. of New York.

Aetna: Trade name used by the firm of Harrington and Richardson on inexpensive pocket revolvers.

Alamo Ranger: The name found on inexpensive Spanish revolvers.

Alaska: Trade name used by the Hood Firearms Co. on inexpensive pocket revolvers.

Alert: Trade name used by the Hood Firearms Co. on inexpensive pocket revolvers.

Alexander Gun Company: Trade name believed to have been used by E.K. Tryon of Philadelphia on imported shotguns.

Alexis: Trade name used by the Hood Firearms Co. on inexpensive pocket revolvers.

Allen 22: Trade name used by the Hopkins and Allen Co. on inexpensive pocket revolvers.

America: Trade name used by the Crescent Firearms Co. on inexpensive pocket revolvers.

American: Trade name used by the Ely and Wray on inexpensive pocket revolvers.

American Barlock Wonder: Trade name used by the H. & D. Folsom Arms Co. on shotguns made for the Sears, Roebuck Co. of Chicago.

American Boy: Trade name used on firearms retailed by the Townley Metal and Hardware Co. of Kansas City, Missouri.

American Bulldog: Trade name used by the Iver Johnson Arms and Cycle Works on inexpensive pocket revolvers.

American Bulldog Revolver: Trade name used by Harrington and Richardson Arms Co. on an inexpensive pocket revolver.

American Eagle: Trade name used by the Hopkins and Allen Co. on inexpensive pocket revolvers.

American Gun Company: Trade name used by H. & D. Folsom Arms Co. on pistols and shotguns that firm retailed.

American Gun Barrel Company: Trade name used by R. Avis of West Haven, Connecticut, between 1916 and 1920.

American Nitro: Trade name used by H. & D. Folsom Arms Co. on shotguns.

Americus: Trade name used by the Hopkins and Allen Co. on inexpensive pocket revolvers.

Angel: Trade name found on inexpensive pocket revolvers of unknown manufacture.

Arab, The: Trade name used by the Harrington and Richardson Arms Co. on shotguns.

Aristocrat:
a) Trade name used by the Hopkins and Allen Co. on inexpensive pocket revolvers.
b) Trade name used by the Supplee-Biddle Hardware Co. of Philadelphia on firearms they retailed.

Armory Gun Company: Trade name used by H. & D. Folsom Arms Co. on shotguns.

Aubrey Shotgun: Trade name found on shotguns made for the Sears, Roebuck and Co. of Chicago by Albert Aubrey of Meriden, Connecticut.

Audax: Trade name used by the Manufacture d'Armes Pyrenees on semiautomatic pistols.

Aurora: Trade name found on inexpensive Spanish semiautomatic pistols.

Autogarde: Trade name used by the Societe Francaise des Munitions on semiautomatic pistols.

Automatic:
a) Trade name used by the Forehand and Wadsworth Co. on inexpensive pocket revolvers.
b) Trade name used by the Harrington and Richardson Arms Co. on inexpensive pocket revolvers.
c) Trade name used by the Iver Johnson Arms and Cycle Works on inexpensive pocket revolvers.

Auto Stand: Trade name used by the Manufacture Francaise d'Armes et Cycles, St. Etiene on semiautomatic pistols.

Avenger: Trade name found on inexpensive pocket revolvers of unknown manufacture.

Baby Hammerless: Trade mark used successively by Henry Kolb and R.F. Sedgley on pocket revolvers they manufactured.

Baby Russian: Trade name used by the American Arms Co. on revolvers they manufactured.

Baker Gun Company: Trade name used by the H. & D. Folsom Arms Co. on shotguns they retailed.

Baker Gun and Forging Company: Trade name used by the H. & D. Folsom Arms Co. on shotguns they retailed.

Bang: Trade name found on inexpensive pocket revolvers of unknown manufacture.

Bang Up: Trade name used on inexpensive pocket revolvers retailed by the Graham and Haines Co. of New York.

Bartlett Field: Trade name used on shotguns retailed by Hibbard, Spencer, Bartlett and Co. of Chicago.

Batavia: Trade name used on shotguns produced by the Baker Gun Co.

Batavia Leader: Trade name used on shotguns produced by the Baker Gun Co.

Bay State: Trade name used by the Harrington and Richardson Arms Co. on both inexpensive pocket revolvers and shotguns.

Belknap: Trade name used by the Belknap Hardware Co. of Louisville, Kentucky, on shotguns made by the Crescent Fire Arms Co., which they retailed.

Bellmore Gun Company: Trade name used by the H. & D. Folsom Arms Co. on shotguns made for them by the Crescent Fire Arms Co.

Berkshire: Trade name used by the H. & D. Folsom Arms Co. on shotguns made for the Shapleigh Hardware Co. of St. Louis, Missouri.

Bicycle: Trade name used on firearms made by the Harrington and Richardson Arms Co.

Big All Right: Trade name used on shotguns manufactured by the Wright Arms Co.

Big Bonanza: Trade name found on inexpensive pocket revolvers of unknown manufacture.

Bismarck: Trade name found on inexpensive pocket revolvers of unknown manufacture.

Black Beauty: Trade name used by the Sears, Roebuck and Co. on imported shotguns they retailed.

Black Diamond: Trade name found on Belgian made shotguns retailed by an unknown American wholesale house.

Black Diana: Trade name used by the Baker Gun Co. on shotguns.

Blackfield: Trade name used by the Hibbard, Spencer, Bartlett and Co. of Chicago on shotguns they retailed.

Blackhawk: Trade name found on inexpensive pocket revolvers of unknown manufacture.

Black Prince: Trade name used by the Hopkins and Allen Co. on inexpensive pocket revolvers.

Bliss: Trade name believed to have been used by the Norwich Arms Co.

Blood Hound: Trade name found on inexpensive pocket revolvers of unknown manufacture.

Bluefield: Trade name used by the W.H. Davenport Firearms Co. on shotguns.

Bluegrass: Trade name used by the Belknap Hardware Co. of Louisville, Kentucky, on shotguns they retailed.

Bluegrass Arms Company: Trade name of shotguns made by H. & D. Folsom Arms Co. for Belknap Hardware of Louisville, Kentucky.

Blue Jacket: Trade name used by the Hopkins and Allen Co. on inexpensive pocket revolvers they made for the Merwin, Hulbert and Co. of New York.

Blue Leader: Trade name found on inexpensive pocket revolvers of unknown manufacture.

Blue Whistler: Trade name used by the Hopkins and Allen Co. on inexpensive pocket revolvers they made for the Merwin, Hulbert and Co. of New York.

Bogardus Club Gun: Trade name found on Belgian made shotguns retailed by an unknown American wholesaler (possibly B. Kittredge and Co. of Cincinnati, Ohio).

Boltun: Trade name used by F. Arizmendi on semiautomatic pistols.

Bonanza: Trade name used by the Bacon Arms Co. on inexpensive pocket revolvers.

Boom: Trade name used by the Shattuck Arms Co. on inexpensive pocket revolvers.

Boone Gun Company: Trade name used by the Belknap Hardware Co. of Louisville, Kentucky, on firearms they retailed.

Boss:
a) Trade name used by E.H. and A.A. Buckland of Springfield, Massachusetts, on single-shot derringers designed by Holt & Marshall.
b) Trade name used on inexpensive pocket revolvers of unknown American manufacture.

Boys Choice: Trade name used by the Hood Firearms Co. on inexpensive pocket revolvers.

Bride Black Prince: Trade name used by H. & D. Folsom Arms Co. on shotguns.

Bridge Gun Company: Registered trade name of the Shapleigh Hardware Co., St. Louis, Missouri.

Bridgeport Arms Company: Trade name used by H. & D. Folsom Arms Co. on shotguns.

Bright Arms Company: Trade name used by H. & D. Folsom Arms Co.

British Bulldog: Trade name found on inexpensive pocket revolvers of unknown American and English manufacture.

Brownie:
a) Trade name used by the W.H. Davenport Firearms Co. on shotguns.
b) Trade name used by the O.F. Mossberg Firearms Co. on a four-shot pocket pistol.

Brutus: Trade name used by the Hood Firearms Co. on inexpensive pocket revolvers.

Buckeye: Trade name used by the Hopkins and Allen Co. on inexpensive pocket revolvers.

Buffalo: Trade name used by Gabilongo y Urresti on semiautomatic pistols.

Buffalo: Trade name found on bolt action rifles made in France.

Buffalo: Trade name used by the Western Arms Co. on an inexpensive pocket revolver.

Buffalo Bill: Trade name used by the Iver Johnson Arms and Cycle Works on an inexpensive pocket revolver.

Buffalo Stand: Trade name used by the Manufacture Francaise d'Armes et Cycles on target pistols.

Bull Dog: Trade name used by the Forehand and Wadsworth Co. on inexpensive pocket revolvers.

Bull Dozer:
a) Trade name used by the Norwich Pistol Co. on inexpensive pocket revolvers.
b) Trade name used by the Forehand and Wadsworth Co. on inexpensive pocket revolvers.
c) Trade name on Hammond Patent pistols made by the Connecticut Arms and Manufacturing Co.

Bull Frog: Trade name used by the Hopkins and Allen Co. on rifles.

Bulls Eye: Trade name used by the Norwich Falls Pistol Co. (O.A. Smith) on inexpensive pocket revolvers.

Burdick: Trade name used by the H. & D. Folsom Arms Co. on shotguns made for the Sears, Roebuck and Co. of Chicago.

Cadet: Trade name used by the Crescent Firearms Co. on rifles.

Canadian Belle: Trade name used by H. & D. Folsom Arms Co. on shotguns.

Cannon Breech: Trade name used by the Hopkins and Allen Co. on shotguns.

Captain: Trade name used by Manufacture d'Armes de Pyrenees on semiautomatic pistols.

Captain Jack: Trade name used by Hopkins & Allen on inexpensive pocket revolvers.

Carolina Arms Company: Trade name used by the H. & D. Folsom Arms Co. on shotguns produced for the Smith, Wadsworth Hardware Co. of Charlotte, North Carolina.

Caroline Arms: Trade name used by the H. & D. Folsom Arms Co.

Caruso: Trade name used by the Crescent Firearms Co. on shotguns made for the Hibbard, Spencer, Bartlett and Co. of Chicago.

Centennial 1876:
a) Trade name used by the Deringer Pistol Co. on inexpensive pocket revolvers.

b) Trade name used by the Hood Firearms Co. on inexpensive pocket revolvers.

Central Arms Company: Trade name used by the W. H. Davenport Firearms Co. on shotguns made for the Shapleigh Hardware Co. of St. Louis, Missouri.

Century Arms Company: Trade name used by the W. H. Davenport Firearms Co. on shotguns made for the Shapleigh Hardware Co. of St. Louis, Missouri.

Challenge:
a) Trade name found on inexpensive pocket revolvers of unknown manufacture.
b) Trade name used by the Sears, Roebuck and Co. of Chicago on shotguns made by Albert Aubrey of Meriden, Connecticut.

Challenge Ejector: Trade name used by the Sears, Roebuck and Co. of Chicago on shotguns made by Albert Aubrey of Meriden, Connecticut.

Champion:
a) Trade name used by H.C. Squires on shotguns.
b) Trade name used by J.P. Lovell on shotguns.
c) Trade name used by the Iver Johnson Arms and Cycle Works on shotguns and inexpensive pocket revolvers.
d) Trade name used by the Norwich Arms Co. on inexpensive pocket revolvers.

Chantecler: Trade name used by Manufacture d'Armes de Pyrenees on semiautomatic pistols.

Charles Richter Company: Trade name used by the H. & D. Folsom Arms Co. on firearms made for the New York Sporting Goods Co. of New York.

Chatham Arms Company: Trade name used by H. & D. Folsom Arms Co. used on shotguns.

Cherokee Arms Company: Trade name used by the H. & D. Folsom Arms Co. on shotguns made for C.M. McLung and Co. of Knoxville, Tennessee.

Chesapeake Gun Company: Trade name used by the H. & D. Folsom Arms Co. of New York.

Chicago: Trade name found on shotguns retailed by the Hibbard, Spencer, Bartlett and Co. of Chicago.

Chicago Ledger: Trade name used by the Chicago Firearms Co. on inexpensive pocket revolvers.

Chicago Long Range Wonder: Trade name used by the H. & D. Folsom Arms Co. on shotguns made for the Sears, Roebuck and Co. of Chicago.

Chichester: Trade name used by Hopkins & Allen on inexpensive pocket revolvers.

Chicopee Arms Company: Trade name used by the H. & D. Folsom Arms Co. of New York.

Chieftan: Trade name found on inexpensive pocket revolvers of unknown manufacture.

Christian Protector: Trade name found on inexpensive pocket revolvers of unknown manufacture.

Climax XL: Trade name used by Herman Boker and Co. of New York on revolvers, rifles and shotguns.

Club Gun: Trade name used by B. Kittredge and Co. of Cincinnati, Ohio, on shotguns they retailed.

Cock Robin: Trade name used by the Hood Firearms Co. on inexpensive pocket revolvers.

Colonial: Trade name used by Manufacture d'Armes de Pyrenees on semiautomatic pistols.

Colonial: Trade name used by H. & D. Folsom Co. on shotguns.

Columbian Automatic: Trade name used by Foehl & Weeks on inexpensive pocket revolvers.

Colton Arms Company: Trade name used by the Shapleigh Hardware Co. of St. Louis, Missouri, on imported shotguns they retailed.

Colton Firearms Company: Trade name used by the Sears, Roebuck and Co. of Chicago on shotguns they retailed.

Columbia:
a) Trade name found on inexpensive pocket revolvers of unknown manufacture.
b) Trade name used by H.C. Squires on shotguns.

Columbia Arms Company: Registered trade name of Henry Keidel, Baltimore, Maryland.

Columbian: Trade name found on inexpensive pocket revolvers of unknown manufacture.

Columbian Firearms Company:
a) Trade name used by the Maltby, Henly and Co. on inexpensive pocket revolvers.
b) Trade name used by the Crescent Firearms Co. on shotguns.

Combat: Trade name used by Randall Firearms Co. for its service model with a flat rib top and fixed sights.

Comet: Trade name used by the Prescott Pistol Co. on inexpensive pocket revolvers.

Commander: Trade name used by the Norwich Arms Co. on inexpensive pocket revolvers.

Commercial: Trade name used by the Norwich Falls Pistol Co. (O.A. Smith) on inexpensive pocket revolvers.

Compeer: Trade name used by the H. & D. Folsom Arms Co. on firearms made for the Van Camp Hardware and Iron Co. of Indianapolis, Indiana.

Competition: Trade name used by John Meunier of Milwaukee, Wisconsin, on rifles.

Conestoga Rifle Works: Trade name of Henry Leman, Philadelphia, Pennsylvania.

Connecticut Arms Company: Trade name used by H. & D. Folsom Arms Co. on shotguns.

Constable: Trade name used by Astra on semiautomatic pistols.

Constabulary: Trade name used by L. Ancion-Marx of Liege on revolvers.

Continental: Trade name used by the Great Western Gun Works of Pittsburgh, Pennsylvania, on firearms they retailed.

Continental Arms Company: Trade name used by the Marshall Wells Co. of Duluth, Minnesota, on firearms they retailed.

Cotton King: Trade name found on inexpensive pocket revolvers of unknown manufacture.

Cowboy: Trade name used by the Hibbard, Spencer, Bartlett and Co. of Chicago on imported, inexpensive pocket revolvers they retailed.

Cowboy Ranger: Trade name used by the Rohde Spencer Co. of Chicago on inexpensive pocket revolvers.

Crack Shot: Trade name used by the J. Stevens Arms and Tool Co. on rifles.

Cracker Jack: Trade name used by the J. Stevens Arms and Tool Co. on pistols.

Creedmoore:
a) Trade name used by the Hopkins and Allen

Co. on inexpensive pocket revolvers.

b) Trade name used by the Chicago Firearms Co. on inexpensive pocket revolvers.

c) Trade name used by William Wurflein on rifles.

Creedmoore Armory: Trade name used by A.D. McAusland of Omaha, Nebraska on rifles.

Creedmoore Arms Company: Trade name found on imported shotguns retailed by an unknown American wholesaler.

Crescent: Trade name used by the Crescent Arms Co. on inexpensive pocket revolvers.

Crescent International 1XL: Trade name used by Herman Boker and Co. of New York on shotguns.

Creve Coeur: Trade name used by the Isaac Walker Hardware Co. of Peoria, Illinois, on imported shotguns they retailed.

Crown: Trade name used by the Harrington and Richardson Arms Co. on inexpensive pocket revolvers.

Crown Jewel: Trade name used by the Norwich Arms Co. on inexpensive pocket revolvers.

Cruso: Trade name used by the H. & D. Folsom Arms Co. on shotguns made for Hibbard, Spencer, Bartlett and Co. of Chicago.

Cumberland Arms Company: Trade name used by the H. & D. Folsom Arms Co. on shotguns made for the Gray and Dudley Hardware Co. of Nashville, Tennessee.

Czar:
a) Trade name used by the Hopkins and Allen Co. on inexpensive pocket revolvers.
b) Trade name used by the Hood Firearms Co. on inexpensive pocket revolvers.

Daisy:
a) Trade name used by the Bacon Arms Co. on inexpensive pocket revolvers.
b) Registered proprietary trade name engraved on firearms made by the Winchester Repeating Arms Co. for the F. Lassetter and Co., Limited of Sydney, Australia.

Daniel Boone Gun Company: Trade name used by H. & D. Folsom Arms Co. on shotguns made for Belknap Hardware Co. of Louisville, Kentucky.

Daredevel: Trade name used by Lou J. Eppinger of Detroit, Michigan, on pistols.

Dash: Trade name found on inexpensive pocket revolvers of unknown manufacture.

Davis Guns: Trade names used successively by N.R. Davis, Davis Warner, and the Crescent-Davis Arms Co. on various firearms.

Dead Shot:
a) Trade name found on inexpensive pocket revolvers of unknown manufacture.
b) Trade name used by the Meriden Firearms Co. on rifles.

Deer Slayer: Trade name used by J. Henry and Son of Boulton, Pennsylvania on rifles.

Defender:
a) Trade name used by the Iver Johnson Arms and Cycle Works on inexpensive pocket revolvers.
b) Trade name used by the U.S. Small Arms Co. on knife pistols.

Defiance: Trade name used by the Norwich Arms Co. on inexpensive pocket revolvers.

Delphian Arms Company:
a) Trade name used by the Supplee-Biddle Hardware Co. of Philadelphia, Pennsylvania, on shotguns they retailed that were supplied by the H. & D. Folsom Co. of New York.
b) Trade name used by the H. & D. Folsom Arms Co. of New York on shotguns.

Delphian Manufacturing Company: Trade name used by the H. & D. Folsom Arms Co. of New York on shotguns.

Demon: Trade name used by Manufacture d'Armes de Pyrenees on semiautomatic pistols.

Demon Marine: As above.

Dexter: Trade name found on inexpensive pocket revolvers of unknown manufacture.

Diamond Arms Company: Trade name used by the Shapleigh Hardware Co. of St. Louis, Missouri, on imported shotguns they retailed.

Dictator: Trade name used by the Hopkins and Allen Co. on inexpensive pocket revolvers.

Dominion Pistol: Trade name found on inexpensive pocket revolvers of unknown manufacture.

Double Header: Trade name used by E.S. Renwick on Perry and Goddard Patent derringers.

Douglas Arms Company: Trade name used by the Hopkins and Allen Co. on shotguns.

Dreadnought: Trade name used by the Hopkins and Allen Co. on shotguns and inexpensive pocket revolvers.

Duchess: Trade name used by the Hopkins and Allen Co. on inexpensive pocket revolvers.

Duke: Trade name found on inexpensive pocket revolvers which may have been made by the Hopkins and Allen Co.

Dunlop Special: Trade name used by the Davis Warner Arms Co. on shotguns made for the Dunlop Hardware Co. of Macon, Georgia.

Duplex: Trade name used by the Osgood Gun Works of Norwich, Connecticut.

E.B.A.C.: Trade name used by Manufacture d'Armes de Pyrenees on semiautomatic pistols.

Eagle: Trade name used by the Iver Johnson Arms and Cycle Works on inexpensive pocket revolvers.

Eagle Arms Company: Trade name used by the Iver Johnson Arms and Cycle Works on inexpensive pocket revolvers.

Earlhood: Trade name used by E.L. Dickinson on inexpensive pocket revolvers.

Earnest Companion: Trade name found on inexpensive pocket revolvers of unknown manufacture.

Earthquake: Trade name used by E.L. Dickinson on inexpensive pocket revolvers.

Eastern Arms Company: Trade name used by the Sears, Roebuck and Co. of Chicago on both shotguns and inexpensive revolvers made by the Iver Johnson Arms and Cycle Works.

Eclipse:
a) Trade name found on single-shot derringers of unknown manufacture.
b) Trade name used by E.C. Meacham on imported shotguns.

Electric: Trade name found on inexpensive pocket revolvers of unknown manufacture.

Electric City Single Hammer: Trade name found on single-shot shotguns retailed by the Wyeth Hardware and Manufacturing Co. of St. Joseph, Missouri.

Elector: Trade name found on inexpensive pocket revolvers of unknown manufacture.

Elgin Arms Company: Trade name used by the H. & D. Folsom Arms Co. on shotguns made for the Strauss and Schram Co. of Chicago.

Elita: Trade name used by the W.H. Davenport Fire Arms Co. on shotguns.

Empire:
a) Trade name used by the Rupertus Patented Pistol Manufacturing Co. on inexpensive pocket revolvers.
b) Trade name used by the Crescent Firearms Co. on shotguns.

Empire Arms Company: Trade name used by the H. & D. Folsom Arms Co. on firearms made for the Sears, Roebuck and Co. of Chicago.

Enders Royal Shotgun: Trade name used by the Crescent Davis Firearms Co. on shotguns made for the Simmons Hardware Co. of St. Louis, Missouri.

Enders Special Service: Trade name used by the Crescent Davis Firearms Co. on shotguns made for the Simmons Hardware Co. of St. Louis, Missouri.

Enterprise: Trade name used by the Enterprise Gun Works on inexpensive pocket revolvers.

Essex Gun Works: Trade name used by the Crescent - Davis Firearms Co. on shotguns made for the Belknap Hardware Co. of Louisville, Kentucky.

Eureka: Trade name used by the Iver Johnson Arms and Cycle Works on inexpensive pocket revolvers.

Excel: Trade name used by both the H. & D. Folsom Arms Co. and the Iver Johnson Arms and Cycle Works on shotguns made for the Montgomery Ward and Co. of Chicago.

Excelsior:
a) Trade name found on inexpensive pocket revolvers of unknown manufacture.
b) Trade name used by the Iver Johnson Arms and Cycle Works on shotguns.

Expert:
a) Trade name found on single-shot derringers of unknown manufacture.
b) Trade name used by the W.J. Davenport Firearms Co. on shotguns made for the Witte Hardware Co. of St. Louis, Missouri.

Express: Trade name used by the Bacon Arms Co. on inexpensive pocket revolvers.

Express: Trade name used by Tomas de Urizar on a variety of semiautomatic pistols.

Farwell Arms Company: Trade name used by the Farwell, Ozmun, Kirk and Co. of St. Paul, Minnesota, on shotguns.

Fashion: Trade name found on inexpensive pocket revolvers of unknown manufacture.

Faultless: Trade name used by the H. & D. Folsom Arms Co. on shotguns made for the John M. Smythe Merchandise Co. of Chicago.

Faultless Goose Gun: Trade name used by the H. & D. Folsom Arms Co. on shotguns made for the John M. Smythe Merchandise Co. of Chicago.

Favorite:
a) Trade name used by the J. Stevens Arms and Tool Co. on rifles.
b) Trade name used by the Iver Johnson Arms and Cycle Works on inexpensive pocket revolvers.

Favorite Navy: Trade name used by the Iver Johnson Arms and Cycle Works on inexpensive pocket revolvers.

Featherlight: Trade name used by the Sears, Roebuck and Co. of Chicago on firearms they retailed.

Federal Arms Company: Trade name used by Meriden Firearms Co.

Folks Gun Works: Trade name of William and Samuel Folk of Bryan, Ohio on rifles and shotguns.

Frank Harrison Arms Company: Trade name used by the Sickles and Preston Co. of Davenport, Iowa, on firearms they retailed.

Freemont Arms Company: Trade name found on shotguns distributed by an unknown retailer.

Frontier: Trade name used by the Norwich Falls Pistol Co. (O.A. Smith) on inexpensive pocket revolvers made for the firm of Maltby, Curtis and Co. of New York.

Fulton: Trade name used by the Hunter Arms Co. on shotguns.

Fulton Arms Company: Trade name used by the W.H. Davenport Firearms Co. on shotguns.

Furor: Trade name used by Manufacture d'Armes de Pyrenees on semiautomatic pistols.

Gallia: Trade name used by Manufacture d'Armes de Pyrenees on semiautomatic pistols.

Game Getter: Registered trade mark of the Marble Arms and Manufacturing Co. on combination rifle-shotguns.

Gaulois: Trade name used by Manufacture d'Armes et Cycles on squeezer type pistols (see also Mitrailleuse).

Gem:
a) Trade name used by the J. Stevens Arms and Tool Co. on single-shot pocket pistols.
b) Trade name used by the Bacon Arms Co. on inexpensive pocket revolvers.

Gen Curtis E. LeMay: Trade name used for Randall Firearms Co. for its small compact pistol made from the General's own gun.

General: Trade name used by the Rupertus Patented Pistol Manufacturing Co. on inexpensive pocket revolvers.

General Butler: Trade name found on inexpensive pocket revolvers of unknown manufacture.

Gerrish: Trade name of G.W. Gerrish of Twin Falls, Idaho, used on shotguns.

Gibralter: Trade name of Albert Aubrey on shotguns made for the Sears, Roebuck and Co. of Chicago.

Gladiator: Trade name of Albert Aubrey on shotguns made for the Sears, Roebuck and Co. of Chicago.

Gold Field: Trade name found on inexpensive pocket revolvers of unknown manufacture.

Gold Hibbard: Trade name used by Hibbard, Spencer, Bartlett and Co. of Chicago on firearms they retailed.

Gold Medal Wonder: Trade name used by H. & D. Folsom Arms Co. on shotguns.

Governor: Trade name used by the Bacon Arms Co. on inexpensive pocket revolvers.

Guardian: Trade name used by the Bacon Arms Co. on inexpensive pocket revolvers.

Gut Buster: Trade name found on inexpensive pocket revolvers of unknown manufacture.

Gypsy: Trade name found on inexpensive pocket revolvers of unknown manufacture.

Half Breed: Trade name found on inexpensive pocket revolvers of unknown manufacture.

Hamilton Arms: Registered trade name of the Wiebusch and Hilger Co., New York.

Hammerless Auto Ejecting Revolver: Trade name of the Meriden Firearms Co. used on revolvers made for the Sears, Roebuck and Co. of New York.

Hanover Arms Co.: If no foreign proofmarks then trade name used by H. & D. Folsom Arms Co.

Hardpan: Trade name found on inexpensive American pocket revolver.

Hard Pan: Trade name used by Hood Arms Co. on inexpensive pocket revolvers.

Hart Arms Company: Trade name used by a Cleveland, Ohio, wholesaler (possibly the George Worthington Co.).

Hartford Arms Company: Trade name used by the H. & D. Folsom Arms on shotguns made for the Simmons Hardware Co. of St. Louis, Missouri.

Harvard: Trade name used by the H. & D. Folsom Arms Co. on shotguns made for the George Worthington Co. of Cleveland, Ohio.

Hercules: Trade name used by the Iver Johnson Arms and Cycle Works on shotguns made for the Montgomery Ward and Co. of Chicago.

Hermitage Arms Company: Trade name used by the H. & D. Folsom Arms Co. on shotguns made for the Gray and Dudley Hardware Co. of Nashville, Tennessee.

Hero:
a) Trade name used by the American Standard Tool Co. on percussion pistols.
b) Trade name used by the Manhattan Firearms Manufacturing Co. on percussion pistols.

Hexagon: Trade name used by the Sears, Roebuck and Co. of Chicago on shotguns they retailed.

Hinsdale: Trade name used by the Hopkins and Allen Co. on inexpensive pocket revolvers.

Hornet: Trade name used by the Prescott Pistol Co. on inexpensive pocket revolvers.

Howard Arms Company: Trade name used by the H. & D. Folsom Arms Co. on shotguns they distributed.

Hudson: Trade name used by the Hibbard, Spencer, Bartlett and Co. of Chicago on shotguns they retailed.

Hunter: Trade name used by the H. & D. Folsom Arms Co. on shotguns made for the Belknap Hardware Co. of Louisville, Kentucky.

Hunter, The: Trade name used by the Hunter Arms Co. on shotguns.

Hurricane: Trade name found on inexpensive pocket revolvers of unknown manufacture.

I.O.A.: Trade name used by the Brown, Camp Hardware Co. of Des Moines, Iowa on firearms they retailed.

I.X.L.:
a) Trade name used by B.J. Hart on percussion revolvers.
b) Trade name used by the W.H. Davenport Firearms Co. on shotguns made for the Witte Hardware Co. of St. Louis, Missouri.

Illinois Arms Company: Trade name used by the Rohde, Spencer Co. of Chicago on firearms they retailed.

Imperial: Trade name used by the Lee Arms Co. on inexpensive pocket revolvers.

Imperial Arms Company: Trade name used by the Hopkins and Allen Co. on inexpensive pocket revolvers.

Infallible: Trade name used by the Lancaster Arms Co. of Lancaster, Pennsylvania on shotguns they retailed.

Infallible Automatic Pistol: Trade name used by the Kirtland Brothers Co. of New York on inexpensive pistols they retailed.

International:
a) Trade name found on inexpensive pocket revolvers of unknown manufacture.
b) Trade name used by E.C. Meacham on shotguns.

Interstate Arms Company: Trade name used by the H. & D. Folsom Arms Co. on shotguns made for the Townley Metal and Hardware Co. of Kansas City, Missouri.

Invincible: Trade name used by the Iver Johnson Arms and Cycle Works on both shotguns and inexpensive pocket revolvers.

Ixor: Trade name used by Manufacture d'Armes de Pyrenees on semiautomatic pistols.

J.J. Weston: Trade name used by the H. & D. Folsom Arms Co. on shotguns.

J.S.T. & Company: Trade name used by the Iver Johnson Arms and Cycle Works on inexpensive pocket revolvers.

Jackson Arms Company: Trade name used by the H. & D. Folsom Arms Co. on shotguns made for C.M. McLung and Co. of Knoxville, Tennessee.

Jewel: Trade name used by the Hood Fire Arms Co. on inexpensive pocket revolvers.

John M. Smythe & Company: Trade name used by H. & D. Folsom Arms Co. for shotguns made for John M. Smythe Hardware Co. of Chicago.

John W. Price: Trade name used by the Belknap Hardware Co. of Louisville, Kentucky, on firearms they retailed.

Joker: Trade name used by the Marlin Firearms Co. on inexpensive pocket revolvers.

Joseph Arms Company (Norwich, Connecticut): Trade name used by H. & D. Folsom Arms Co.

Judge: Trade name found on inexpensive pocket revolvers of unknown manufacture.

Jupitor: Trade name used by Fabrique d'Armes de Grand Precision, Eibar, Spain, on semiautomatic pistols.

K.K.: Trade name used by the Hopkins and Allen Co. on shotguns made for the Shapleigh Hardware Co. of St. Louis, Missouri.

Keno: Trade name found on inexpensive pocket revolvers of unknown manufacture.

Kentucky: Trade name used by the Iver Johnson Arms and Cycle Works on inexpensive pocket revolvers.

Keystone Arms Company: Trade name used by the W.H. Davenport Firearms Co. on shotguns made for the E.K. Tryon Co. of Philadelphia, Pennsylvania.

Kill Buck: Trade name of the Enterprise Gun Works (James Bown), Pittsburgh, Pennsylvania.

Killdeer: Trade name used by the Sears, Roebuck and Co. of Chicago on firearms bearing their trade name Western Arms Co.

King Nitro: Trade name used by the W.H. Davenport Firearms Co. on shotguns made for the Shapleigh Hardware Co. of St. Louis, Missouri.

King Pin: Trade name found on inexpensive single-shot and revolving pocket pistols.

Kingsland Gun Company: Trade name used by the H. & D. Folsom Arms Co. on shotguns made for the Geller, Ward and Hasner Co. of St. Louis, Missouri.

Kirk Gun Company: Trade name used by Farwell, Ozmun, and Kirk Co. of St. Paul, Minnesota.

Knickerbocker: Trade name used by the Crescent-Davis Firearms Co. on shotguns.

Knickerbocker Club Gun: Trade name used by Charles Godfrey of New York on imported shotguns he retailed.

Knockabout: Trade name used by the Montgomery Ward and Co. of Chicago on shotguns they retailed.

Knox-All: Trade name used by the Iver Johnson Arms and Cycle Works on firearms they made for the H. & D. Folsom Arms Co. of New York.

L'Agent: Trade name used by Manufacture Francaises d'Armes et Cycles on revolvers.

Lakeside: Trade name used by the H. & D. Folsom Arms Co. on firearms they made for the Montgomery Ward and Co. of Chicago.

Le Colonial: Trade name used by Manufacture Francaises d'Armes et Cycles on revolvers.

Le Colonial: As above.

Le Francais: Trade name used by Manufacture Francaises d'Armes et Cycles on semiautomatic pistols.

Le Francais: As above on semiautomatic pistols.

Le Petit Forminable: Trade name used by Manufacture Francaises d'Armes et Cycles on revolvers.

Le Petit Forminable: As above on revolvers.

Le Protecteur: Trade name used by J.E. Turbiaux of Paris on squeezer pistols of the type later made by the Ames Sword Co.

Le Terrible: Trade name used by Manufacture Francaises d'Armes et Cycles on revolvers.

Leader:
a) Trade name used by the Shattuck Arms Co. on inexpensive pocket revolvers.
b) Trade name used by the Harrington and Richardson Arms Co. on inexpensive pocket revolvers.

Leader Gun Company: Trade name used by the H. & D. Folsom Arms Co. on shotguns they made for the Charles Williams Stores, Inc. of New York.

Lee's Hummer: Trade name used by the H. & D. Folsom Arms Co. on firearms they made for the Lee Hardware Co. of Salina, Kansas.

Lee's Special: Trade name used by the H. & D. Folsom Arms Co. on firearms they made for the Lee Hardware Co. of Salina, Kansas.

Liberty: Trade name used by the Norwich Falls Pistol Co. (O.A. Smith) on inexpensive pocket revolvers.

Liege Gun Company: Trade name used by the Hibbard, Spencer, Bartlett and Co. of Chicago on imported shotguns they retailed.

Lion: Trade name used by the Iver Johnson Arms and Cycle Works on inexpensive pocket revolvers.

Little Giant: Trade name used by the Bacon Arms Co. on inexpensive pocket revolvers.

Little John: Trade name used by the Hood Firearms Co. on inexpensive pocket revolvers.

Little Joker: Trade name found on inexpensive pocket revolvers of unknown manufacture.

Little Pal: Registered trade name for knife pistols made by L.E. Pulhemus.

Little Pet: Trade name used by the Sears, Roebuck and Co. of Chicago on inexpensive pocket revolvers they retailed.

London Revolver: Trade name found on inexpensive pocket revolvers of unknown manufacture.

Lone Star: Trade name found on inexpensive pocket revolvers of unknown manufacture.

Long Range Winner: Trade name used by the Sears, Roebuck and Co. of Chicago on shotguns they retailed.

Long Range Wonder: Trade name used by the Sears, Roebuck and Co. of Chicago on shotguns they retailed.

Long Tom: Trade name used by the Sears, Roebuck and Co. of Chicago on shotguns they retailed.

Looking Glass: Trade name used on semiautomatic pistols of unknown Spanish manufacture.

Marquis of Horne: Trade name used by Hood Arms Co. on inexpensive pocket revolvers.

Mars: Trade name used by Manufacture d'Armes de Pyrenees on semiautomatic pistols.

Marshwood: Trade name used by the H. & D. Folsom Arms Co. on shotguns they made for the Charles Williams Stores Inc. of New York.

Marvel: Trade name used by the J. Stevens Arms and Tool Co. on various firearms.

Massachusetts Arms Company: Trade name used by both the J. Stevens Arms and Tool Co. and the H. & D. Folsom Arms Co. on firearms made for the Blish, Mizet and Silliman Hardware Co. of Atchison, Kansas.

Maximum: Trade name found on inexpensive pocket revolvers of unknown manufacture.

Metropolitan: Trade name used by the H. & D. Folsom Arms Co. on firearms they made for the Siegal-Cooper Co. of New York.

Metropolitan Police:
a) Trade name used by the Maltby, Curtiss and Co. on inexpensive pocket revolvers.
b) Trade name used by the Rohde-Spencer Co. of Chicago on inexpensive pocket revolvers.

Midget Hammerless: Trade name used by the Rohde-Spencer Co. of Chicago on inexpensive pocket revolvers.

Mikros: Trade name used by Manufacture d'Armes de Pyrenees on semiautomatic pistols.

Minnesota Arms Company: Trade name used by the H. & D. Folsom Arms Co. on shotguns they made for the Farwell, Ozmun, Kirk and Co. of St. Paul, Minnesota.

Missaubi Arms Company: Trade name used by the Hunter Arms Co., possibly for the Farwell, Ozmun, Kirk and Co. of St. Paul, Minnesota.

Mississippi Arms Company: Trade name used by the H. & D. Folsom Arms Co. on firearms made for the Shapleigh Hardware Co. of St. Louis, Missouri.

Mississippi Valley Arms Company: Trade name used by the H. & D. Folsom Arms Co. on firearms made for the Shapleigh Hardware Co. of St. Louis, Missouri.

Mitrailleuse: Alternate trade name of the Gauluis squeezer pistol.

Mohawk: Trade name used by the H. & D. Folsom Arms Co. on firearms made for the Blish, Mizet and Silliman Hardware Co. of Atchison, Kansas.

Mohegan: Trade name used by the Hood Firearms Co. on inexpensive pocket revolvers.

Monarch:
a) Trade name used by the Hopkins and Allen Co. on inexpensive pocket revolvers.
b) Trade name used by the Osgood Gun Works on Duplex revolvers.

Monitor:
a) Trade name used by the Whitneyville Armory on inexpensive pocket revolvers.
b) Trade name used by the H. & D. Folsom Arms Co. on firearms made for the Paxton and Gallagher Co. of Omaha, Nebraska.

Montgomery Arms Company: Trade name used by the H. & D. Folsom Arms Co. on a variety of firearms.

Mountain Eagle: Trade name used by the Hopkins and Allen Co. on inexpensive pocket revolvers.

Mount Vernon Arms Company: Trade name used by the H. & D. Folsom Arms Co. on firearms made for the Carlin, Hullfish Co. of Alexandria, Virginia.

My Companion: Trade name found on inexpensive pocket revolvers of unknown manufacture.

My Friend: Trade name used by James Reid of New York.

N.R. Adams: Trade name used by the N.R. Davis and Co. on shotguns.

Napoleon: Trade name used by the Thomas J. Ryan Pistol Manufacturing Co. of Norwich, Connecticut, on inexpensive pocket revolvers.

National Arms Company: Trade name used by the H. & D. Folsom Arms Co. on firearms made both for the May Hardware Co. of Washington, D.C., and the Moskowitz and Herbach Co. of Philadelphia, Pennsylvania.

Nevermiss: Trade name used by the Marlin Firearms Co. on single-shot pocket pistols.

New Aubrey: Trade name used by Albert Aubrey of Meriden, Connecticut, on both revolvers and shotguns made for the Sears, Roebuck and Co. of Chicago.

New Britain Arms Company: Trade name used by H. & D. Folsom Arms Co.

New Defender: Trade name used by Harrington & Richardson on revolvers.

New Elgin Arms Company: Trade name used by H. & D. Folsom Arms Co.

New Empire: Trade name used by H. & D. Folsom Arms Co.

New England Arms Company: Trade name believed to have been used by Charles Godfrey on shotguns made for the Rohde-Spencer Co. of Chicago.

New Era Gun Works: Trade name used by the Baker Gun Co. on firearms made for an unknown retailer.

New Haven Arms Company: Trade name found on Belgian shotguns imported by either E.K. Tryon of Philadelphia or the Great Western Gun Works of Pittsburgh, Pennsylvania.

New Liberty: Trade name used by the Sears, Roebuck and Co. of Chicago on inexpensive pocket revolvers they retailed.

New Rival: Trade name used by the H. & D. Folsom Arms Co. on firearms made for the Van Camp Hardware and Iron Co. of Indianapolis, Indiana.

New Worcester: Trade name used by the Torkalson Manufacturing Co. of Worcester, Massachusetts.

New York Arms Company: Trade name used by the H. & D. Folsom Arms Co. on firearms made for the Garnet Carter Co. of Chattanooga, Tennessee.

New York Gun Company: Trade name used by the H. & D. Folsom Arms Co. on firearms made for the Garnet Carter Co. of Chattanooga, Tennessee.

New York Club: Trade name used by the H. & D. Folsom Arms Co. on rifles.

New York Machine Made: Trade name used by the H. & D. Folsom Arms Co.

New York Pistol Company: Trade name used by the Norwich Falls Pistol Co. (O.A. Smith) on inexpensive pocket revolvers.

Newport:
a) Trade name found on inexpensive pocket revolvers of unknown manufacture.
b) Trade name used by the H. & D. Folsom Arms Co. on shotguns made for Hibbard, Spencer, Bartlett and Co. of Chicago.

Nightingale: Trade name found on inexpensive pocket revolvers of unknown manufacture.

Nitro Bird: Trade name used by the Richards and Conover Hardware Co. of Kansas City, Missouri.

Nitro Hunter: Trade name used by the H. & D. Folsom Arms Co. on shotguns made for the Belknap Hardware Co. of Louisville, Kentucky.

Nitro King: Trade name used by the Sears, Roebuck and Co. of Chicago on shotguns of unknown manufacture.

Nitro Special: Trade name used by the J. Stevens Arms and Tool Co. on shotguns.

Northfield Knife Company: Trade name used by the Rome Revolver and Novelty Works of Rome, New York, on inexpensive pocket revolvers.

Norwich Arms Company:
a) Trade name used by the Hood Firearms Co. on inexpensive pocket revolvers.
b) Trade name found on shotguns retailed by the Marshall, Wells Co. of Duluth, Minnesota, and Winnipeg, Manitoba, Canada.

Norwich Falls Pistol Company: Trade name used by the O.A. Smith Co. on inexpensive pocket revolvers made for Maltby, Curtis and Co. of New York.

Norwich Lock Manufacturing Company: Trade name used by F.W. Hood Firearms Co. on inexpensive pocket revolvers.

Not-Nac Manufacturing Company: Trade name used by the H. & D. Folsom Arms Co. on firearms made for the Canton Hardware Co. of Canton, Ohio.

Novelty: Trade name used by D.F. Mossberg & Sons on Shattuck Unique pistols.

OK:
a) Trade name used by the Marlin Firearms Co. on single-shot pocket pistols.
b) Trade name used by Cowles and Son of Chicopee Falls, Massachusetts, on single-shot pocket pistols.
c) Trade name found on inexpensive pocket revolvers of unknown manufacture.

Old Hickory:
a) Trade name found on inexpensive pocket revolvers of unknown manufacture.
b) Trade name used by the Hibbard, Spencer, Bartlett and Co. of Chicago on shotguns they retailed.

Old Reliable: Trade name used by the Sharps Rifle Co.

Olympic:
a) Trade name used by the J. Stevens Arms and Tool Co. on rifles and pistols.
b) Trade name used by the Morley and Murphy Hardware Co. of Green Bay, Wisconsin, on firearms they retailed (possibly made by the J. Stevens Arms and Tool Co.).

Osprey: Trade name used by Lou J. Eppinger of Detroit, Michigan, on firearms he made.

Our Jake: Trade name used by E.L. and J. Dickinson of Springfield, Massachusetts, on inexpensive pocket revolvers.

Oxford Arms Company: Trade name used by the H. & D. Folsom Arms Co. on firearms made for the Belknap Hardware Co. of Louisville, Kentucky.

Pagoma: Trade name used by the H. & D. Folsom Arms Co. on firearms made for the Paxton and Gallagher Co. of Omaha, Nebraska.

Peoria Chief: Trade name found on inexpensive pocket revolvers.

Perfect: Trade name used by the Foehl and Weeks Firearms Manufacturing Co. of Philadelphia, Pennsylvania, on inexpensive pocket revolvers.

Perfect: Trade name used by Manufacture d'Armes de Pyrenees on semiautomatic pistols.

Perfection:
a) Trade name used by the H. & D. Folsom Arms Co. on firearms made for the H.G. Lipscomb and Co. of Nashville, Tennessee.
b) Trade name used by the John M. Smythe Merchandise Co. of Chicago on firearms they retailed.

Pet: Trade name found on inexpensive pocket revolvers of unknown manufacture.

Petrel: Trade name found on inexpensive pocket revolvers of unknown manufacture.

Phenix: Trade name used by J. Reid of New York on revolvers.

Phoenix:
a) Trade name used by J. Reid of New York on revolvers.
b) Trade name used by the Whitneyville Armory on percussion revolvers.

Piedmont: Trade name used by the H. & D. Folsom Arms Co. on firearms made for the Piedmont Hardware Co. of Danville, Pennsylvania.

Pinafore: Trade name used by the Norwich Falls Pistol Co. (O.A. Smith) on inexpensive pocket revolvers.

Pioneer: Trade name found on inexpensive pocket revolvers of unknown manufacture.

Pioneer Arms Company: Trade name used by the H. & D. Folsom Arms Co. on firearms made for the Kruse and Baklmann Hardware Co. of Cincinnati, Ohio.

Pittsfield: Trade name used by the Hibbard, Spencer, Bartlett and Co. of Chicago on firearms probably made by the H. & D. Folsom Arms Co.

Plug Ugly: Trade name found on inexpensive pocket revolvers of unknown manufacture.

Plymouth: Trade name used by Spear and Co. of Pittsburgh, Pennsylvania, on firearms they retailed.

Pocahontas: Trade name found on inexpensive pocket revolvers of unknown manufacture.

Pointer: Trade name found on single-shot pocket pistols of unknown manufacture.

Prairie Fire: Trade name found on inexpensive pocket revolvers of unknown manufacture.

Prairie King:
a) Trade name used by the Bacon Arms Co. on inexpensive pocket revolvers.
b) Trade name used by the H. & D. Folsom Arms Co. on inexpensive pocket revolvers.

Premier:
a) Trade name used by the Thomas E. Ryan Co. on inexpensive pocket revolvers.
b) Trade name used by the Harrington and Richardson Arms Co. on revolvers.
c) Trade name used by the Montgomery Ward and Co. of Chicago on firearms they retailed.
d) Registered trade name of Edward K. Tryon and Co. of Philadelphia, Pennsylvania.

Premium: Trade name used by the Iver Johnson Arms and Cycle Works on inexpensive pocket revolvers.

Princess: Trade name found on inexpensive pocket revolvers of unknown American manufacture.

Progress: Trade name used by Charles J. Godfrey of New York on shotguns.

Protection: Trade name used by the Whitneyville Armory on revolvers.

Protector:
a) Trade name found on inexpensive pocket revolvers of unknown manufacture.
b) Trade name used by the Chicago Firearms Co. on inexpensive pocket revolvers.

Protector Arms Company: Trade name used by the Rupertus Patented Pistol Manufacturing Co. on inexpensive pocket revolvers.

Providence: Trade name found on inexpensive pocket revolvers of unknown manufacture.

Puppy: Trade name found on inexpensive pocket revolvers made by several European makers.

Quail: Trade name used by the Crescent-Davis Arms Co. on shotguns.

Queen:
a) Trade name used by the Hood Firearms Co. on inexpensive pocket revolvers.
b) Trade name used by the Hyde and Shattuck Co. on inexpensive single-shot pocket pistols.

Queen City: Trade name used by the H. & D. Folsom Arms Co. on firearms made for the Elmira Arms Co. of Elmira, New York.

Raider: Randall Firearms Co. Commander size pistol named after Gen Randall's flight squadron; "Randall's Raiders".

Ranger:
a) Trade name found on inexpensive pocket revolvers of unknown manufacture.
b) Trade name used by the Eastern Arms Co. on various firearms made for the Sears, Roebuck and Co. of Chicago.
c) Trade name of the Sears, Roebuck and Co. of Chicago on a wide variety of firearms marketed by that firm.

Rapid-Maxim: Trade name used by Manufacture d'Armes de Pyrenees on semiautomatic pistols.

Reassurance: Trade name found on inexpensive pocket revolvers of unknown manufacture.

Red Chieftan: Trade name used by the Supplee Biddle Hardware Co. of Philadelphia, Pennsylvania, on inexpensive pocket pistols they retailed.

Red Cloud: Trade name used by the Ryan Pistol Manufacturing Co. on inexpensive pocket revolvers.

Red Hot: Trade name found on inexpensive pocket revolvers of unknown manufacture.

Red Jacket:
a) Trade name used by the Lee Arms Co. on inexpensive pocket revolvers.
b) Trade name used by the Hopkins and Allen Co. on inexpensive pocket revolvers.

Reliable: Trade name found on inexpensive pocket revolvers of unknown manufacture.

Reliance: Trade name used by John Meunier of Milwaukee, Wisconsin, on rifles.

Rev-O-Noc: Trade name used by the H. & D. Folsom Arms Co. on firearms made for the Hibbard, Spencer, Bartlett and Co. of Chicago.

Rich-Con: Trade name used by the H. & D. Folsom Arms Co. for shotguns made for Richardson & Conover Hardware Co.

Richmond Arms Company: Trade name used by the H. & D. Folsom Arms Co. on firearms made for an unknown retailer.

Rickard Arms Company: Trade name used by the H. & D. Folsom Arms Co. on firearms made for the J.A. Rickard Co. of Schenectady, New York.

Rip Rap: Trade name used by the Bacon Arms Co. on inexpensive pocket revolvers.

Rival: Trade name used by the H. & D. Folsom Arms Co. on firearms made for the Van Camp Hardware and Iron Co. of Indianapolis, Indiana.

Riverside Arms Company: Trade name used by the J. Stevens Arms and Tool Co. on various types of firearms.

Robin Hood: Trade name used by the Hood Firearms Co. on inexpensive pocket revolvers.

Rocky Hill: Trade name found on inexpensive cast iron percussion pocket pistols made in Rocky Hill, Connecticut.

Rodgers Arms Company: Trade name used by the Hood Firearms Co. on firearms made for an unknown retailer.

Royal Gun Company: Trade name used by the Three Barrel Gun Co.

Royal Service: Trade name used by the Shapleigh Hardware Co. of St. Louis, Missouri, on firearms they retailed.

Rummel Arms Company: Trade name used by the H. & D. Folsom Arms Co. on firearms made for the A.J. Rummel Arms Co. of Toledo, Ohio.

Russel Arms Company: Registered trade name of the Wiebusch and Hilger Co. of New York.

Russian Model: Trade name used by the Forehand and Wadsworth Co. on inexpensive pocket revolvers.

S. Holt Arms Company: Trade name used by the Sears, Roebuck and Co. of Chicago on shotguns they retailed.

S.A.: Trade mark of the Societe d'Armes Francaises.

S.H. Harrington: If no foreign proofmarks then trade name used by H. & D. Folsom Arms Co.

Safe Guard: Trade name found on inexpensive pocket revolvers of unknown manufacture.

Safety Police: Trade name used by the Hopkins and Allen Co. on inexpensive pocket revolvers.

Scott: Trade name used by the Hopkins and Allen Co. on inexpensive pocket revolvers.

Secret Service Special: Trade name used by the Rohde-Spencer Co. of Chicago on inexpensive pocket revolvers.

Selecta: Trade name used by Manufacture d'Armes de Pyrenees on semiautomatic pistols.

Senator: Trade name found on inexpensive pocket revolvers of unknown manufacture.

Sentinal: Trade name found on inexpensive pocket revolvers of unknown manufacture.

Service Model C: The predecessor to the "Raider" pistol.

Sheffield, The: Trade name used by the A. Baldwin and Co., Limited of New Orleans, Louisiana, on shotguns they retailed.

Sickels-Arms Company: Trade name used by the Sickels and Preston Co. of Davenport, Iowa, on firearms they retailed.

Simson: Trade name used by the Iver Johnson Arms and Cycle Works on firearms made for the Iver Johnson Sporting Goods Co. of Boston, Massachusetts.

Sitting Bull: Trade name found on inexpensive pocket revolvers of unknown manufacture.

Skue's Special: Trade name used by Ira M. Skue of Hanover, Pennsylvania, on shotguns.

Smoker: Trade name used by the Iver Johnson Arms and Cycle Works on inexpensive pocket revolvers.

Southern Arms Company: Trade name used by the H. & D. Folsom Arms Co. on firearms made for an unknown retailer.

Southerner:
a) Trade name used by the Brown Manufacturing Co. and the Merrimac Arms Manufacturing Co. on single-shot pocket pistols.
b) Registered trade name of Asa Farr of New York on pistols.

Southron: Trade name found on inexpensive pocket pistols of unknown manufacture.

Special Service: Trade name used by the Shapleigh Hardware Co. of St. Louis, Missouri, on inexpensive pocket revolvers.

Spencer Gun Company: Trade name used by the H. & D. Folsom Arms Co.

Splendor: Trade name found on inexpensive pocket revolvers of unknown manufacture.

Sportsman, The: Trade name used by the H. & D. Folsom Arms Co. on firearms made for the W. Bingham Co. of Cleveland, Ohio.

Springfield Arms Company: Trade name used by the J. Stevens Arms and Tool Co.

Spy: Trade name found on inexpensive pocket revolvers of unknown manufacture.

Square Deal: Trade name used by the H. & D. Folsom Arms Co. on firearms made for the Stratton, Warren Hardware Co. of Memphis, Tennessee.

St. Louis Arms Company: Trade name used by the H. & D. Folsom Arms Co. on firearms made for the Shapleigh Hardware Co. of St. Louis, Missouri.

Standard: Trade name used by the Marlin Firearms Co. on revolvers.

Stanley Arms: Registered trade name of the Wiebusch and Hilger Co. of New York on firearms they retailed.

Stanley Double Gun: Trade name used by the H. & D. Folsom Arms Co. on shotguns they retailed.

Star:
a) Trade name found on inexpensive single-shot pocket pistols of unknown manufacture.
b) Trade name used by the Prescott Pistol Co. on inexpensive pocket revolvers.
c) Trade name used by Johnson & Bye on single-shot cartridge derringers.

State Arms Company: Trade name used by the H. & D. Folsom Arms Co. on firearms made for the J.H. Lau and Co. of New York.

Sterling:
a) Trade name used by E.L. and J. Dickinson of Springfield, Massachusetts, on single-shot pistols.
b) Trade name used by the H. & D. Folsom Arms Co. on shotguns they retailed.

Stinger: Registered proprietary trade name engraved on firearms made by the Winchester Repeating Arms Co. for the Perry Brothers Limited of Brisbane, Australia.

Stonewall:
a) Trade name used by the Marlin Firearms Co. on single-shot derringers.
b) Trade name used by T.F. Guion of Lycoming, Pennsylvania, on single-shot percussion pistols he retailed.

Striker: Trade name found on inexpensive pocket revolvers of unknown manufacture.

Sullivan Arms Company: Trade name used by the H. & D. Folsom Arms Co. on firearms made for the Sullivan Hardware Co. of Anderson, South Carolina.

Superior: Trade name of the Paxton and Gallagher Co. of Omaha, Nebraska, on revolvers and shotguns.

Super Range: Trade name of the Sears, Roebuck and Co. of Chicago on shotguns.

Sure Fire: Trade name found on inexpensive pocket revolvers of unknown manufacture.

Swamp Angel: Trade name used by the Forehand and Wadsworth Co. on inexpensive pocket revolvers.

Swift: Trade name used by the Iver Johnson Arms and Cycle Works on firearms made for the John P. Lovell & Sons, Boston, Massachusetts.

Syco: Trade name used by the Wyeth Hardware Co. of St. Joseph, Missouri, on firearms they retailed.

Sympathique: Trade name used by Manufacture d'Armes de Pyrenees on semiautomatic pistols.

T. Barker: Trade name used by the H. & D. Folsom Arms Co. of New York on shotguns they retailed.

Ten Star: Trade name used by the H. & D. Folsom Arms Co. on firearms made for the Geller, Ward and Hasner Co. of St. Louis, Missouri.

Terrier: Trade name used by the Rupertus Patented Pistol Manufacturing Co. on inexpensive pocket revolvers.

Terror: Trade name used by the Forehand and Wadsworth Co. on inexpensive pocket revolvers.

Texas Ranger: Trade name used by the Montgomery Ward and Co. of Chicago on inexpensive pocket revolvers they retailed.

Thames Arms Company: Trade name used by the Harrington and Richardson Arms Co. on firearms they made for an unknown wholesaler.

Tiger:
a) Trade name used by the Iver Johnson Arms and Cycle Works on inexpensive pocket revolvers.
b) Trade name used by the J.H. Hall and Co. of Nashville, Tennessee, on shotguns they retailed.

Tobin Simplex: Trade name used on shotguns of unknown manufacture that were retailed by the G.B. Crandall Co., Limited of Woodstock, Ontario, Canada.

Toledo Firearms Company:
a) Trade name used by the Hopkins and Allen Co. on inexpensive pocket revolvers.
b) Trade name used by E.L. and J. Dickinson on inexpensive pocket revolvers.

Toronto Belle: Trade name found on inexpensive pocket revolvers of unknown manufacture.

Touriste: Trade name used by Manufacture d'Armes de Pyrenees on semiautomatic pistols.

Tower's Police Safety: Trade name used by Hopkins & Allen on inexpensive pocket revolvers.

Townley's Pal and Townley's American Boy: Trade name used by H. & D. Folsom Arms Co. for shotguns made for Townley Metal and Hardware Co. of Kansas City, Missouri.

Tramps Terror: Trade name used by the Forehand and Wadsworth Co. on inexpensive pocket revolvers.

Traps Best: Trade name believed to have been used by the H. & D. Folsom Arms Co. on firearms made for the Watkins, Cottrell Co. of Richmond, Virginia.

Triumph: Trade name used by the H. & D. Folsom Arms Co. on shotguns.

Trojan: Trade name found on inexpensive pocket revolvers of unknown manufacture.

True Blue: Trade name found on inexpensive pocket revolvers of unknown manufacture.

Tryon Special: Trade name used by the Edward K. Tryon Co. of Philadelphia, Pennsylvania, on shotguns they retailed.

Tycoon: Trade name used by the Iver Johnson Arms and Cycle Works on inexpensive pocket revolvers.

U.S. Arms Company: Trade name used successively by the Alexander Waller and Co. (1877), the Barton and Co. (1878) and the H. & D. Folsom Arms Co. (1879 forward) on a variety of firearms.

U.S. Revolver: Trade name used by the Iver Johnson Arms and Cycle Works on inexpensive pocket revolvers.

U.S. Single Gun: Trade name used by the Iver Johnson Arms and Cycle Works on single barrel shotguns.

Uncle Sam: Trade name used by Johnson & Bye on percussion pocket pistols.

Union:
a) Trade name found on inexpensive single-shot pocket pistols of unknown manufacture.
b) Trade name used by the Hood Firearms Co. on inexpensive pocket revolvers.
c) Trade name used by the Prescott Pistol Co. on inexpensive pocket revolvers.

Union Arms Company: Trade name used by the H. & D. Folsom Arms Co. on firearms made for the Bostwick, Braun Co. of Toledo, Ohio.

Union Jack: Trade name found on inexpensive pocket revolvers of unknown manufacture.

Union N.Y.: Trade name used by the Whitneyville Armory on inexpensive pocket revolvers.

Unique: Trade name used by the C.S. Shattuck Arms Co. on revolvers and four barrel pocket pistols.

United States Arms Company: Trade name used by Norwich Falls Pistol Co. (O.A. Smith) on inexpensive pocket revolvers.

Universal: Trade name used by the Hopkins and Allen Co. on inexpensive pocket revolvers.

Utica Firearms Company: Trade name used by the Simmons Hardware Co. of St. Louis, Missouri, on firearms they retailed.

Valient: Trade name used by the Spear and Co. of Pittsburgh, Pennsylvania, on firearms they retailed.

Veiled Prophet: Trade name used by the T.E. Ryan Pistol Manufacturing Co. on inexpensive pocket revolvers.

Venus: Trade name used by the American Novelty Co. of Chicago on inexpensive pocket revolvers.

Veteran: Trade name found on inexpensive pocket revolvers of unknown manufacture.

Veto: Trade name found on inexpensive pocket revolvers of unknown manufacture.

Victor:
a) Trade name used by the Marlin Firearms Co. on single-shot pocket pistols.
b) Trade name used by the Harrington and Richardson Arms Co. on inexpensive pocket revolvers.
c) Trade name used by the H. & D. Folsom Arms Co. on inexpensive pocket pistols and revolvers.

Victor Arms Company: Trade name used by the H. & D. Folsom Arms Co. on firearms made for the Hibbard, Spencer, Bartlett and Co. of Chicago.

Victor Special: Trade name used by the H. & D. Folsom Arms Co. on firearms made for the Hibbard, Spencer, Bartlett and Co. of Chicago.

Victoria: Trade name used by the Hood Firearms Co. on inexpensive pocket revolvers.

Vindix: Trade name used by Manufacture d'Armes de Pyrenees on semiautomatic pistols.

Viper: Trade name used on inexpensive pocket revolvers of unknown American manufacture.

Virginia Arms Company: Trade name used by the H. & D. Folsom Arms Co. and later the Davis-Warner Arms Co. on firearms made for the Virginia-Carolina Co. of Richmond, Virginia.

Volunteer: Trade name used by the H. & D. Folsom Arms Co. on inexpensive pocket revolvers made for the Belknap Hardware Co. of Louisville, Kentucky.

Vulcan: Trade name used by the H. & D. Folsom Arms Co. on firearms made for the Edward K. Tryon Co. of Philadelphia, Pennsylvania.

Walnut Hill: Trade name used by the J. Stevens Arms and Tool Co. on rifles.

Warner Arms Corporation: Trade name used by the H. & D. Folsom Arms Co. on firearms made for the Kirtland Brothers, Inc. of New York.

Wasp: Trade name found on inexpensive pocket revolvers of unknown manufacture.

Wautauga: Trade name used by the Whitaker, Holtsinger Hardware Co. of Morristown, Tennessee on firearms they retailed.

Western: Trade name used by the H. & D. Folsom Arms Co. on firearms made for the Paxton and Gallagher Co. of Omaha, Nebraska.

Western Arms Company:
a) Trade name used by the Bacon Arms on various types of firearms.
b) Trade name used by W.W. Marston on revolvers.
c) Trade name used by Henry Kolb and later R.F. Sedgly of Philadelphia, Pennsylvania, on Baby Hammerless revolvers.
d) Trade name used by the Ithaca Gun Co. on shotguns believed to have been made for the Montgomery Ward and Co. of Chicago.

Western Field: Trade name used by Montgomery Ward and Co. of Chicago on shotguns of various makes that they retailed.

Western Field: Trade name used by Manufacture d'Armes de Pyrenees on revolvers.

Whippet: Trade name used by the H. & D. Folsom Arms Co. on firearms made for the Hibbard, Spencer, Bartlett and Co. of Chicago.

Whistler: Trade name used by the Hood Firearms Co. on inexpensive pocket revolvers.

White Powder Wonder: Trade name used by Albert Aubrey of Meriden, Connecticut on shotguns made for the Sears, Roebuck and Co. of Chicago.

Wildwood: Trade name used by the H. & D. Folsom Arms Co. for shotguns made for Sears, Roebuck & Co.

Wilkinson Arms Company: Trade name used by the H. & D. Folsom Arms Co. on firearms made for the Richmond Hardware Co. of Richmond, Virginia.

Wiltshire Arms Company: Trade name used by the H. & D. Folsom Arms Co. on firearms made for the Stauffer, Eshleman and Co. of New Orleans, Louisiana.

Winfield Arms Company: Trade name used by the H. & D. Folsom Arms Co. on various types of firearms.

Winner: Trade name found on inexpensive pocket revolvers of unknown manufacture.

Winoca Arms Company: Trade name used by the H. & D. Folsom Arms Co. on firearms made for the N. Jacobi Hardware Co. of Wilmington, North Carolina.

Witte's Expert: Trade name used by the Witte Hardware Co. of St. Louis, Missouri, on shotguns they retailed.

Witte's IXL: Trade name used by the Witte Hardware Co. of St. Louis, Missouri, on shotguns they retailed.

Wolverine Arms Company: Trade name used by the H. & D. Folsom Arms Co. on firearms made for the Fletcher Hardware Co. of Wilmington, North Carolina.

Woodmaster: Trade name found on Belgian shotguns imported by an unknown wholesaler.

Worlds Fair: Trade name used by the Hopkins and Allen Co. on shotguns.

Worthington Arms Company: Trade name used by the H. & D. Folsom Arms Co. on various types of firearms.

Wyco: Trade name used by the Wyeth Hardware and Manufacturing Co. of St. Joseph, Missouri, on firearms they retailed.

XL:
a) Trade name used by the Hopkins and Allen Co. on inexpensive pocket revolvers.
b) Trade name used by the Marlin Firearms Co. on single-shot pocket pistols.

Xpert:
a) Trade name used by the Hopkins and Allen Co. on inexpensive pocket revolvers.
b) Trade name used by the Iver Johnson Arms and Cycle Works on inexpensive single-shot pocket pistols.

XXX Standard: Trade name used by the Marlin Firearms Co. on revolvers.

You Bet: Trade name used on inexpensive pocket revolvers of unknown American manufacture.

Young America: Trade name used by J.P. Lindsay of New York on superimposed - load percussion pistols.

Young American: Trade name used by the Harrington and Richardson Arms Co. on revolvers.

FIREARMS MANUFACTURERS AND IMPORTERS

Accu-Tek
4510 Carter Ct.
Chino, CA 91710
909-627-2404
FAX: 909-627-7817
www.accu-tekfirearms.com

AcuSport Corporation
One Hunter Place
Bellefontaine, OH 43311
513-593-7010
FAX: 513-592-5625
www.acusport.com

American Derringer Corp.
127 N. Lacy Drive
Waco, TX 76715
254-799-9111
FAX: 254-799-7935
www.amderringer.com

American Frontier Firearms
40725 Brook Trails Way
Aguanga, CA 92536
909-763-0014
FAX: 909-763-0014

AR-7 Industries
998 N. Colony Rd.
Meriden, CT 06450
203-630-3536
FAX: 203-630-3637
www.ar-7.com

ArmaLite, Inc.
P.O. Box 299
Geneseo, IL 61254
309-944-6939
FAX: 309-944-6949
www.armalite.com

Armscorp USA Inc.
4424 John Avenue
Baltimore, MA 21227
410-247-6200
FAX: 410-247-6205

A-Square Co. Inc.
205 Fairfield Avenue
Jeffersonville, IN 47130
812-283-0577
FAX: 812-283-0375

Austin & Halleck
2150 South 950 East
Provo, UT 84606
877-543-3256
FAX: 801-374-9998
www.austinhalleck.com

Autauga Arms
Pratt Plaza Mall No. 13
Pratville, AL 36067
800-262-9563
FAX: 334-361-2961

Auto-Ordnance Corp.
P.O. Box 220
Blauvelt, NY 10913
845-735-4500
FAX: 845-735-4610
www.auto-ordnance.com

Axtell Rifle Company
Riflesmith, Inc.
353 Mill Creek Road
Sheridan, MT 59749
406-842-5814
www.riflesmith.com

Aya-Agiurre Y Aranzabal, S.A.L.
P.O. Box 45
Eibar (Guipuzcoa), Spain
+34 943 82 04 37
FAX: +34 943 20 01 33

B.C. Outdoors
P.O. Box 61497
Boulder City, NV 89005
702-294-3056
FAX: 702-294-0413

Ballard Rifle and Cartridge Co.
113 W. Yellowstone Ave.
Cody, WY 82414
307-587-4914
FAX: 307-527-6097
www.ballardrifles.com

Barrett Firearms Mfg.
P.O.Box 1077
Murfreesboro, TN 37133
615-896-2938
FAX: 615-896-7313

Benelli U.S.A.
17603 Indian Head Highway
Accokeek, MD 20607
301-283-6981
FAX: 301-283-6988
www.benelliusa.com

Beretta U.S.A. Corp.
17601 Beretta Drive
Accokeek, MD 20607
301-283-2191
FAX: 301-283-0435
www.berettausa.com

Bernardelli Vincenzo, S.P.A.
Via Grande, 10
Sede Legale Torbole Casaglia
Brescia, Italy
+39 30 8912851-2-3
FAX: +39 030 215 0963

Bond Arms
P.O. Box 1296
Grandbury, TX 76048
817-573-4445
FAX: 817-573-5636
www.bondarms.com

Briley Mfg. Company
1230 Lumpkin Road
Houston, TX 77043
800-331-5718
FAX: 713-932-1043

Brown, E. Arthur Co.
4353 State Highway 27 East
Alexandria, MN 56308
320-762-8847
FAX: 320-763-4310
www.eabco.com

Brown Precision Inc.
7786 Molinos Ave.
P.O. Box 270 W.
Los Molinos, CA 96055
530-384-2506
FAX: 530-384-1638
www.brownprecision.com

Brown, Ed Products
P.O. Box 492
Perry, MO 63462
573-565-3261
FAX: 573-565-2791
www.edbrown.com

Browning
One Browning Place
Morgan, UT 84050
801-876-2711
Parts & Service
800-322-4626
www.browning.com

Bushmaster Firearms
999 Roosevelt Trail
Windham, ME 04062
800-998-7928
FAX: 207-892-8068
www.bushmaster.com

Caspian Arms, Ltd.
14 N. Main St.
Hardwick, VT 05843
802-472-6454
FAX: 802-472-6709

Casull Arms Company, Inc.
P.O. Box 1629
Afton, WY 83110
307-886-0200
www.casullarms.com

Century International Arms
430 S. Congress Ave., Suite 1.
Delray Beach, FL 33445-4701
800-527-1252
FAX: 561-265-4520
www.centuryarms.com

Champlin Firearms
P.O. Box 3191/Woodring Airport
Enid, OK 73702
580-237-7388
FAX: 580-242-6922

Charter 2000, Inc.
273 Canal Street
Shelton, CT 06484
203-922-1652
FAX: 203-922-1469

Cimarron Arms
P.O. Box 906
105 Winding Oak Road
Fredericksburg, TX 78624
830-997-9090
FAX: 830-997-0802
www.cimarron-firearms.com

Cobra Enterprises
1960 S. Milestone Dr., Suite F
Salt Lake City, UT 84104
801-908-8300
FAX: 801-908-8301
www.cobrapistols.com

Colt Firearms
P.O. Box 1868
Hartford, CT 06144
800-962-COLT
FAX: 860-244-1449
www.colt.com

Colt Blackpowder Arms Co.
110 8th Street
Brooklyn, NY 11215
212-925-2159
FAX: 212-966-4986

Competitor Corporation Inc.
26 Knight Street, Unit 3
Jaffrey, NH 03452
603-532-9483
FAX: 603-532-8209
www.competitor-pistol.com

Connecticut Shotgun Manufacturing Co.
A. H. Fox Shotguns
35 Woodland Street
Box 1692
New Britain, CT 06051
860-225-6581
FAX: 860-832-8708

Connecticut Valley Arms, Inc. (CVA)
5988 Peachtree Corners East
Norcross, GA 30071
770-449-4687
FAX: 770-242-8546
www.cva.com

Cooper Arms
P.O. Box 114
Stevensville, MT 59870
406-777-0373
FAX: 406-777-5228

CZ-U.S.A.
P.O. Box 171073
Kansas City, KS 66117- 0073
913-321-1811
FAX: 913-321-2251
www.cz-usa.com

Dakota Arms, Inc.
130 Industry Rd.
Sturgis, SD 57785
605-347-4686
FAX: 605-347-4459
www.dakotaarms.com

Daly, Charles Inc.
P.O. Box 6625
Harrisburg, PA 17112
866-325-9486
FAX: 717-540-8567
www.charlesdaly.com

Dixie Gun Works
P.O. Box 130
Union City, TN 38281
731-885-0700
FAX: 731-885-0440

Downsizer Corp.
P.O. Box 710316
Santee, CA 92072
619-448-5510
www.downsizer.com

DSA, Inc.
P.O. Box 370
27 West 990 Industrial Ave.
Barrington, IL 600110
847-277-7258
FAX: 847-277-7259
www.dsarms.com

Dumoulin, Ernst
Rue Florent Boclinville 8-10
13-4041 Votten, Beligium
41 27 78 78 92

Eagle Imports
1750 Brielle Ave., Unit B1
Wanamassa, NJ 07712
908-493-0333

Ellett Bros.
P.O. Box 128
Chapin, SC 29036
803-345-3751
FAX: 803-345-1820

EMF Co., Inc.
1900 E. Warner Ave. Suite 1-D
Santa Ana, CA 92705
949-261-6611
FAX: 949-756-0133

Entreprise Arms Inc.
5321 Irwindale Ave.
Irwindale, CA 91706
626-962-8712
FAX: 626-962-4692
www.entreprise.com

Euro-Imports
412 Slayden St.
Yoakum, TX 77995
361-293-9353
FAX: 361-293-9353

European American Armory
P.O. Box 1299
Sharpes, FL 32959
321-639-4842
FAX: 321-639-7006
www.eacorp.com

F.N. Manufacturing, Inc.
P.O. Box 24257
Columbia, SC 29224
803-736-0522

Fieldsport
3313 W. South Airport Road
Traverse City, MI 49684
616-933-0767

Fiocchi Of America
5030 Fremont Road
Ozark, MO 65721
417-725-4118
FAX: 417-725-1039

Fletcher-Bidwell
305 E. Terhune Street
Viroqua, WI 54665
866-637-1860
FAX: 608-637-6922

Francotte, Aug.
Rue du 3 Juin, 109
4400 Herstal-Liege, Belgium
32-4-948-11-79

Freedom Arms
P.O. Box 150
Freedom, WY 83120
307-883-2468
FAX: 307-883-2005
www.freedomarms.com

Furr Arms
91 North 970 West
Orem, UT 84057
801-226-3877
FAX: 801-226-3877

Galaxy Imports
P.O. Box 3361
Victoria, TX 77903
361-573-4867
FAX: 361-576-9622

Gamba, Renato
Via Artigiana 93
25063 Gardone Val Trompia
    Brescia, Italy
+39 30 8911640
FAX: +39 30 8912180

Gamba, U.S.A.
P.O. Box 60452
Colorado Springs, CO 80960
719-578-1145
FAX: 719-444-0731

Glock, Inc.
6000 Highlands Parkway
Smyrna, GA 30082
770-432-1202
FAX: 770-433-8719
www.glock.com

Griffin & Howe, Inc.
33 Claremont Road
Bernardsville, NJ 07924
908-766-2287
FAX: 908-766-1068
www.griffinhowe.com

GSI, Inc. (Merkel)
7661 Commerce Lane
P.O. Box 129
Trussville, AL 35173
205-655-8299
FAX: 205-655-7078
www.gsifirearms.com

H-S Precision, Inc.
1301 Turbine Drive
Rapid City, SD 57703
605-341-3006
FAX: 605-342-8964
www.hsprecision.com

Hammerli USA
19296 Oak Grove Circle
Groveland, CA 95321
209-962-5311
FAX: 209-962-5931
www.hammerliusa.com

Hanus, Bill Birdguns
P.O. Box 533
Newport, OR 97365
541-265-7433
FAX: 541-265-7400

**Harrington & Richardson
 (H&R 1871)**
60 Industrial Rowe
Gardner, MA 01440
508-632-9393
FAX: 508-632-2300
www.hr1871.com

Heckler & Koch, Inc.
21480 Pacific Boulevard
Sterling, VA 20166
703-450-1900
FAX: 703-450-8160
www.hecklerkoch-usa.com

Henry Repeating Arms Co
110 8th Street
Brooklyn, NY 11215
718-499-5600
FAX: 718-768-8056

Heritage Manufacturing, Inc.
4600 NW 135th St.
Opa Locka, FL 30054
305-685-5966
FAX: 305-687-6721

High Standard Mfg. Co.
5200 Mitchelldale, Suite E-17
Houston, TX 77092
713-462-4200
FAX: 713-681-5665
www.highstandard.com

**Horton, Lew, Distributing Co.,
 Inc.**
15 Walkup Drive
Westboro, MA 01581
508-366-7400
FAX: 508-366-5332

Ithaca Classic Doubles
No. 5 Railroad Street
Victor, NY 14564
716-924-2710
FAX: 716-924-2737

Ithaca Gun/Ithaca Acq. Corp.
901 Route 34B
King Ferry, NY 13081
315-364-7171
FAX: 315-364-5134
www.ithacagun.com

KDF
2485 Highway 46 North
Seguin, TX 78155
830-379-8141
FAX: 830-379-5420

Kahr Arms
P.O. Box 220
Blauvelt, NY 10913
845-735-4500
FAX: 845-735-4610
www.kahr.com

Kel-Tec CNC, Inc.
1475 Cox Rd.
Cocoa, FL 32926
321-631-0068
FAX: 321-631-1169
www.kel-tec.com

Kimber
1 Lawton Street
Yonkers, NY 10705
800-880-2418
www.kimberamerica.com

**Knight Rifles/Modern
 Muzzleloading, Inc.**
21852 Hwy. J46
P.O. Box 130
Centerville, IA 52544
641-856-2626
www.knightrifles.com

Knight's Manufacturing Co.
701 Columbia Blvd.
Titusville, FL 32780
321-607-9900
FAX: 321-268-1498

Krieghoff International
P.O. Box 549
7528 Easton Rd.
Ottsville, PA 18942
610-847-5173
FAX: 610-847-8691
www.krieghoff.com

L.A.R. Manufacturing
4133 West Farm Road
West Jordan, UT 84088
801-280-3505
FAX: 801-280-1972

Laurona
P.O. Box 260
20600 Eibar (Guipuzcoa), Spain
34-43-700600
FAX: 34-43-700616

Lazzeroni Arms Co.
P.O. Box 26696
Tucson, AZ 85726
888-492-7247
FAX: 520-624-4250
www.lazzeroni.com

Legacy Sports International
206 South Union Street
Alexandria, VA 22314
703-548-4837

FAX: 549-7826
www.legacysports.com

Les Baer Custom Inc.
29601 34th Ave.
Hillsdale, IL 61257
309-658-2716
FAX: 309-658-2610
www.lesbaer.com

Ljutic Industries
732 N. 16th Ave. Suite 22
Yakima, WA 98902
509-248-0476
FAX: 509-576-8233
www.ljuticgun.com

Lone Star Rifle Company
11231 Rose Road
Conroe, TX 77303
936-856-3363
FAX: 936-856-3363

Lyman
475 Smith Street
Middletown, CT 06457
860-632-2020
FAX: 860-632-1699

Magnum Research, Inc.
7110 University Avenue N.E.
Minneapolis, MN 55432
763-574-1868
FAX: 763-574-0109
www.magnumresearch.com

Marlin Firearms
P.O. Box 248
North Haven, CT 06473
800-544-8892
www.marlinfirearms.com

Maverick Arms Inc.
7 Grasso Ave.
P.O. Box 497
North Haven, CT 06473
203-230-5300
FAX: 203-230-5420

McMillan (McBros Rifles)
1638 W. Knudsen No. 102
Phoenix, AZ 85027
623-582-3713
FAX: 623-582-3930
www.mcmfamily.com

M.O.A. Corp.
285 Government Valley Rd.
Sundance, WY 82729
307-283-3030
www.moaguns.com

Moore, William Larkin & Co.
8340 E. Raintree Dr., Suite B-7
Scottsdale, AZ 85260
480-951-8913
FAX: 480-951-3677

Mossberg, O. F., & Sons, Inc.
7 Grasso Avenue
North Haven, CT 06473
203-230-5300
FAX: 203-230-5420
www.mossberg.com

Navy Arms Co.
219 Lawn St.
Martinsburg, WV 25401
304-262-9870
FAX: 304-262-1658
www.navyarms.com

New England Arms Co.
Lawrence Lane
Box 278
Kittery Point, ME 03905
207-439-0593
FAX: 207-439-6726
www.newenglandarms.com

New England Custom Gun Service
438 Willow Brook Road
Plainfield, NH 03781
603-469-3450
FAX: 603-469-3471

New England Firearms
60 Industrial Rowe
Gardner, MA 01440
978-632-9393
FAX: 978-632-2300

North American Arms
2150 South 950 East
Provo, UT 84606
801-374-9990
FAX: 801-374-9998
www.naaminis.com

Northwest Arms
26884 Pearl Road
Parma, ID 83660
208-722-6771
FAX: 208-722-1062
www.northwest-arms.com

Nowlin Manufacturing Co.
20622 South 4092 Road
Claremore, OK 74019
918-342-0689
FAX: 918-342-0624
www.nowlinguns.com

Ohio Ordnance Works
P.O. Box 687
310 Park Drive
Chardon, Ohio 44024
440-285-3481
FAX: 286-8571

Olympic Arms, Inc.
624 Old Pacific Highway SE
Olympia, WA 98513
360-459-7940
FAX: 360-491-3447
www.olyarms.com

Para-Ordnance
980 Tapscott Rd.
Toronto, Ontario M1X 1C3
416-297-7855
FAX: 416-297-1289
www.paraord.com

Pedersoli Davide & Co.
Via Artigiani, 57-25063
Gardone Val Trompia, Brescia
Italy 25063

Perazzi U.S.A. Inc.
1010 West Tenth
Azusa, CA 91702
626-334-1234
FAX: 626-334-0344

Phoenix Arms
4231 Brickell St.
Ontario, CA 91761
909-937-6900
FAX: 909-937-0060

Prairie Gun Works
1-761 Marion Street
Winnipeg, Manitoba
Canada R2J OK6
204-231-2976
FAX: 204-231-8566

Reeder, Gary Custom Guns
2601 7th Avenue East
Flagstaff, AZ 86004
928-526-3313
FAX: 928-526-1287
www.reedercustomguns.com

Remington Arms Co., Inc.
P.O. Box 700
870 Remington Drive
Madison, NC 27025-0700
800-243-9700
FAX: 336-548-7801
www.remington.com

Rock River Arms Inc.
1042 Cleveland Rd.
Colona, IL 61241
866-980-7625
FAX: 309-792-5781
www.rockriverarms.com

Rogue Rifle Co.
1140 36th Street N, Suite B
Lewiston, ID 83501
208-743-4355
FAX: 208-743-4163
www.roguerifle.com

Rogue River Rifleworks
500 Linne Rd., Suite D
Paso Robles, CA 93446
805-227-4706
FAX: 805-227-4723

Savage Arms
100 Springdale Road
Westfield, MA 01085
413-568-7001
FAX: 413-568-8386
www.savagearms.com

Seecamp, L.W.C.
301 Brewster Rd.
Milford, CT 06460
203-877-3429

Shiloh Rifle Mfg. Co., Inc.
P.O. Box 279
201 Centennial Drive
Big Timber, MT 59011
406-932-4454
FAX: 406-932-5627
www.shilohrifle.com

SIGARMS, Inc.
18 Industrial Drive
Exeter, NH 03833
603-772-2302
FAX: 603-772-9082
www.sigarms.com

SKB Shotguns
4325 South 120th St.
Omaha, NE 68137
800-752-2767
FAX: 402-330-8029
www.skbshotguns.com

Smith & Wesson
2100 Roosevelt Road
Springfield, MA 01104
800-331-0852
FAX: 413-747-3317
www.smith-wesson.com

Springfield Armory, Inc.
420 West Main Street
Geneseo, IL 61254
309-944-5631
FAX: 309-944-3676
www.springfield-armory.com

SSK Industries
590 Woodvue Lane
Wintersville, OH 43953
740-264-0176
FAX: 740-264-2257
www.sskindustries.com

S.T.I. International, Inc.
114 Halmar Cove
Georgetown, TX 78628
800-959-8201
FAX: 512-819-0465
www.stiguns.com

Stoeger Industries
17603 Indian Head Highway
Accokeek, MD 20607
301-283-6300
FAX: 301-283-6986

Sturm Ruger & Co., Inc
Lacey Place
Southport, CT 06890
203-259-7843
FAX: 203-256-3367
www.ruger-firearms.com

Taconic Firearms Ltd.
P.O. Box 553
Perry Lane
Cambridge, NY 12816
518-677-2704
FAX: 518-677-5974

Taurus International
16175 NW 49th Av.
Miami, FL 33014
305-624-1115
FAX: 305-623-1126
www.taurususa.com

Thompson/Center Arms Co.
Farmington Road
P.O. Box 5002
Rochester, NH 03867
603-332-2394
FAX: 603-332-5133
www.tcarms.com

Traditions Performance Firearms
1375 Boston Post Road
P.O. Box 776
Old Saybrook, CT 06475
860-388-4656
FAX: 860-388-4657

Tristar Sporting Arms
P.O. Box 7496
18116 Linn St.
North Kansas City, MO 64116
816-421-1400
FAX: 816-421-4182
www.tristarsportingarms.com

Turnbull, Doug Restoration, Inc.
6680 Route 5 & 20
P.O. Box 471
Bloomfield, NY 14469
585-657-6338
FAX: 585-657-6338
www.turnbullrestoration.com

U.S. Repeating Arms/ Winchester
275 Winchester Ave.

New Haven, CT 06511
800-333-3288
www.winchester-guns.com

United States Fire Arms Manufacturing Co.
55 Van Dyke Av.
Hartford, CT 06106
877-277-6901
FAX: 860-724-6809
www.usfirearms.com

Valtro U.S.A.
24800 Mission Blvd.
Hayward, CA 94544
510-489-8477
FAX: 510-489-8477

Vector Arms, Inc.
270 W. 500 N.
North Salt Lake, UT 84054
801-295-1917
FAX: 801-295-9316
www.vectorarms.com

Volquartsen Custom
24276 240th Street
Carroll, IA 51401
712-792-4238
FAX: 712-792-2542
www.volquartsen.com

Weatherby, Inc.
3100 El Comino Real
Atascadero, CA 93422
805-466-1767
FAX: 805-466-2527
www.weatherby.com

Wesson, Dan Firearms
5169 Highway 12 South
Norwich, NY 13815
607-336-1174
FAX: 607-336-2730
www.danwessonfirearms.com

Westley Richards & Co. Ltd.
40 Grange Road, Bournbrook
Birmingham, England B29 5A
44 121 472 2953
FAX: 44 121 414 1138

Wichita Arms
923 E. Gilbert
Wichita, KS 67211
316-265-0061
FAX: 316-265-0760
www.wichitaarms.com

Wildey, Inc.
45 Angevine Rd.
Warren, CT 06754
860-355-9000
FAX: 860-354-7759
www.wildeyguns.com

Wilson Combat
2234 CR 719
P.O. Box 578
Berryville, AR 72616
870-545-3635
FAX: 870-545-3310
www.wilsoncombat.com

ZM Weapons
203 South Street
Bernardston, MA 01337
413-648-9501
FAX: 413-648-0219

Zoli, Antonio
Via Zanardelli, 39
I-25063 Gardone V.T. (BS) Italy

GUN COLLECTORS ASSOCIATIONS

Alabama Gun Collectors
P.O. Box 70965
Tuscalossa, AL 35407

Alaska Gun Collectors Association
5240 Litte Tree
Anchorage, AK 99507

American Society of Arms Collectors
P.O. Box 2567
Waxahachie, TX 75165

Arizona Arms Association
4837 Bryce Ave.
Glendale, AZ 85301

Ark-La-Tex Gun Collectors Association
919 Hamilton Road
Bossier City, LA 71111

Bay Colony Weapons Collectors, Inc.
Box 111
Hingham, MA 02043

Boardman Valley Collectors Guild
County Road 600
Manton, MI 49663

Browning Collectors Association
2749 Keith Dr.
Villa Ridge, MO 63089

**California Arms and
Collectors Assoc.**
8290 Carburton St.
Long Beach, CA 90808

Colorado Gun Collectors
2553 South Quitman Street
Denver, CO 80219

Colt Collectors Association
25000 Highland Way
Los Gatos, CA 95030

Derringer Collectors Association
500 E. Old 66
Shamrock, TX 79079

Florida Gun Collectors Association
P.O. Box 43
Branford, FL 32008

Freedom Arms Collectors Association
P.O. Box 160302
Miami, FL 33116

High Standard Collectors Association
540 W 92nd Street
Indianapolis, In 46260

Houston Gun Collectors Association
P.O. Box 741429
Houston, TX 77274

Indianhead Firearms Association
Route 9, Box 186
Chippewa Falls, WI 54729

**Indian Territory Gun Collectors
Association**
Box 4491
Tulsa, OK 74159

**International Society of Mauser
Arms Collectors**
P.O. Box 277
Alpharetta, GA 30239

Iroquois Arms Collectors Association
P.O.Box 142
Ransomville, NY 14131

Jefferson State Arms Collectors
521 South Grape
Medford, OR 97501

Jersey Shore Antique Arms Collectors
P.O. Box 100
Bayville, NJ 08721

Kentuckiana Arms Collectors Association
P.O. Box 1776
Louisville, KY 40201

Kentucky Gun Collectors Association
P.O. Box 64
Owensboro, KY 42376

**Lehigh Valley Military Collectors
Association**
P.O. Box 72
Whitehall, PA 18052

**Long Island Antique Gun Collectors
Association**
35 Beach Street
Farmingdale, L.I., NY 11735

Marlin Firearms Collectors Association
44 Main Street
Champaign, IL 61820

Maryland Arms Collectors Association
P.O. Box 20388
Baltimore, MD
21284-0388

Memphis Antique Weapons Association
4672 Barfield Road
Memphis, TN 38117

Minnesota Weapons Collectors Association
P.O. Box 662
Hopkins, MN 55343

Missouri Valley Arms Collectors Association
P.O. Box 33033
Kansas City, MO 64114

Montana Arms Collectors Association
308 Riverview Drive
East Great Falls, MT 59404

National Automatic Pistol Collectors Association
Box 15738-TOGS
St. Louis, MO 63163

National Rifle Association
11250 Waples Mill Rd.
Fairfax, VA 22030

New Hampshire Arms Collectors, Inc.
P.O. Box 5
Cambridge, MA 02139

Northeastern Arms Collectors Association, Inc.
P.O. Box 185
Amityville, NY 11701

Ohio Gun Collectors Association
P.O. Box 9007
Maumee, OH 43537

Oregon Arms Collectors
P.O. Box 13000-A
Portland, OR 97213

Pelican Arms Collectors Association
P.O. Box 747
Clinton, LA 70722

Pennsylvania Antique Gun Collectors Association
28 Fulmer Avenue

Havertown, PA 19083

Pikes Peak Gun Collectors Guild
406 E. Uintah
Colorado Springs, CO 80903

Potomac Arms Collectors Association
P.O. Box 1812
Wheaton, MD 20915

Randall Collectors Club
228 Columbine Dr.
Casper WY 82609-3948

Remington Society of America
8267 Lone Feather
Las Vegas, NV 89123

Ruger Collectors Association, Inc.
P.O. Box 240
Greens Farms, CT 06436

Sako Collectors Association, Inc.
202 N. Locust
Whitewater, KS 67154

Santa Barbara Antique Arms Collectors Association
P.O. Box 6291
Santa Barbara, CA 93160-6291

San Bernardino Valley Arms Collectors
1970 Mesa Street
San Bernardino, CA 92405

Santa Fe Gun Collectors Association
1085 Nugget
Los Alamos, NM 87544

San Fernando Valley Arms Collectors Association
P.O. Box 65
North Hollywood, CA 91603

Shasta Arms Collectors Association
P.O. Box 3292
Redding, CA 96049

Smith & Wesson Collectors Association
2711 Miami St.
St. Louis, MO 63118

Tampa Bay Arms Collectors Association
2461 67th Avenue South
St. Petersburg, FL 33712

Texas Gun Collectors Association
P.O. Box 12067
El Paso, TX 79913

Washington Arms Collectors, Inc.
P.O. Box 7335
Tacoma, WA 98407

Weapons Collectors Society of Montana
3100 Bancroft
Missoula, MT 59801

Weatherby Collectors Association, Inc.
21569 448th Avenue
Oldham, SD 57051

Willamette Valley Arms Collectors Association, Inc.
P.O. Box 5191
Eugene, OR 97405

Winchester Arms Collectors Association
P.O. Box 6754
Great Falls, MT 59406.

Ye Connecticut Gun Guild
U.S. Route 7
Kent Road
Cornwall Bridge, CT 06754

Zumbro Valley Arms Collectors, Inc.
Box 6621
Rochester, MN 55901

BIBLIOGRAPHY

Bady, Donald *Colt Automatic Pistols.* Alhambra, California: Borden Publishing Company, 1973.

Baer, Larry L. *The Parker Gun.* Los Angeles, California: Beinfeld Publications, 1980.

Bailey, D. and Nie, D. *English Gunmakers.* London: Arms and Armour Press, 1978.

Ball, W.D., *Remington Firearms: The Golden Age of Collecting,* Iola, WI: Krause Publications, 1995.

Ball, W.D., *Mauser Military Rifles of the World.* Iola, WI: Krause Publications, 1996.

Belford, James & Dunlap, Jack *The Mauser Self-Loading Pistol.* Alhambra, California: Borden Publishing, 1969.

Bishop, Chris and Drury, Ian *Combat Guns.* Secaucus, New Jersey: Chartwell Books, 1987.

Blackmore, H. *Gunmakers of London.* York, Pennsylvania: Geo. Shumway, 1986.

Blackmore, H. *Guns and Rifles of the World.* New York, New York: Viking Press, 1965.

Blair, C. *Pistols of the World.* London: B.T. Batsford, Ltd., 1968.

Bogdanovic & Valencak *The Great Century of Guns.* New York, New York: Gallery Books, 1986.

Bowen, T.G. *James Reid and his Catskill Knuckledusters.* Lincoln, Rhode Island: Andrew Mowbray, Inc., 1989.

Breathed, J. and Schroeder, J. *System Mauser.* Glenview, Illinois: Handgun Press, 1967.

Brophy, Lt. Col. William S., USAR, Ret. *The Krag Rifle.* Los Angeles, California: Beinfeld Publications, 1980.

Brophy, Lt. Col. William S., USAR, Ret. *L.C. Smith Shotguns.* Los Angeles, California: Beinfeld Publications, 1977.

Brophy, W. *Marlin Firearms.* Harrisburg, Pennsylvania: Stackpole Books, 1989.

Browning, J. and Gentry, C. *John M. Browning; American Gunmaker.* Ogden, Utah: Browning, 1989.

Butler, David F. *The American Shotgun.* New York, New York: Winchester Press, 1973.

Buxton, Warren *The P 38 Pistol.* Dallas, Texas: Taylor Publishing Company, 1978.

Carr, J. *Savage Automatic Pistols.*

Chant, Christopher *The New Encyclopedia of Handguns.* New York, New York: Gallery Books.

Conley, F.F. *The American Single Barrel Trap Gun.* Carmel Valley, California: F.F. Conley, 1989.

Cope, K.L. *Stevens Pistols and Pocket*

Rifles. Ottawa, Ontario: Museum Restoration Service.

Cormack, A.J.R. *Small Arms, a Concise History of Their Development.* Profile Publications, Ltd.

Cormack, A.J.R. *Small Arms in Profile, Volume I.* Garden City, New York: Doubleday & Company, Inc.,1973.

deHass, Frank *Bolt Action Rifles.* Northfield, Illinois: Digest Books, Inc., 1971.

deHass, Frank *Single-shot Rifles and Actions.* Northfield, Illinois: Digest Books, Inc., 1969.

Eastman, Matt, *Browning Sporting Arms of Distinction*; 1903-1992. Fitzgerald, Georgia, 1994.

Eberhart, L. D. & Wilson, R. L. *The Deringer in America: Volume Two - The Cartridge Era.* Lincoln, RI: Andrew Mowbray Inc., 1993.

Dance, T. *High Standard: A Collector's Guide to the Hamden & Hartford Target Pistols.* Lincoln, RI: Andrew Mowbray Inc., 1991.

Dunlap, J. *Pepperbox Firearms.* Palo Alto, California: Pacific Books, 1964.

Ezell, Edward C. *Small Arms Today.* Harrisburg, Pennsylvania: Stackpole Books.

Frasca & Hill *The 45-70 Springfield.* Northridge, California: Springfield Publishing Company, 1980.

Fuller, C. *The Whitney Firearms.* Huntington, West Virginia: Standard Pub., Inc., 1946.

Gaier & Francotte, *FN 100 Years; The Story of a Great Liege Company, 1889-1989.* Brussels, Belgium, 1989.

Gander, Terry, editor, *Janes Infantry Weapons,* 23rd edition, Surry, England, 1997.

Goddard, W. H. D. *The Government Models. The Development of the Colt Model of 1911.* Lincoln, RI: Andrew Mowbray Inc., 1988.

Graham, R., Kopec, J., Moore, C. *A Study of the Colt Single Action Army Revolver.* Dallas, Texas: Taylor Publishing Co., 1978.

Greener, W. *The Gun and Its Development.* Secaucus, New Jersey: Chartwell Books, 1988.

Gun Digest 1967 through 1989 Editions. Northfield, Illinois: DBI Books.

Guns of the World Los Angeles, California: Petersen Publishing Company, 1972.

Hayward, J.F. *Art of the Gunmaker, Vol.* 1. London: Barrie & Rockliff, 1962; Vol. 2. London: Barrie & Rockliff, 1963.

Henshaw, Thomas, et. al., *The History of*

Winchester Firearms 1866-1992, 6th Ed. Winchester Press, 1993.

Hiddleson, C. *Encyclopedia of Ruger Semi-Automatic Pistols: 1949-1992.* Iola, WI: Krause Publications, 1993.

Hinman, Bob *The Golden Age of Shotgunning,* New York, N.Y., Winchester Press, 1975.

Hoff, A. *Airguns and Other Pneumatic Arms.* London: Barrie & Jenkins, 1972.

Hoffschmidt, E.J. *Know Your. 45 Auto Pistols Models 1911 & AI.* Southport, Connecticut: Blacksmith Corporation, 1974.

Hoffschmidt, E.J. *Know Your Walther PP & PPK Pistols.* Southport, Connecticut: Blacksmith Corporation, 1975.

Hogg, Ian V. *German Pistols and Revolvers 1871-1945.* Harrisburg, Pennsylvania: Stackpole Books, 1971.

Hogg, Ian V. and Weeks, John *Military Small Arms of the 20th Century.* Fifth Edition. Northfield, Illinois: DBI Books, 1985.

Hogg, Ian V. and Weeks, John *Pistols of the World. Revised Edition.* Northfield, Illinois: DBI Books, 1982.

Honeycutt, Fred L., Jr. *Military Pistols of Japan.* Lake Park, Florida: Julin Books, 1982.

Houze, H. *The Winchester Model 52: Perfection in Design,* Iola, WI: Krause Publications, 1997.

Houze, H. *To The Dreams Of Youth: Winchester .22 Caliber Single-shot Rifle.* Iola, WI: Krause Publications, 1993.

Houze, H. *Winchester Repeating Arms Company Its History and Development 1865 to 1981.* Iola, WI: Krause Publications, 1994.

Houze, H. *Colt Rifles & Muskets: 1847-1870.* Iola, WI: Krause Publications, 1996.

Jamieson, G. Scott *Bullard Arms.* Erin, Ontario: Boston Mills Press, 1988.

Jinks, R.G. *History of Smith A. Wesson.* Beinfeld Pub., Inc., 1977.

Karr, C.L. and C.R. *Remington Handguns.* Harrisburg, Pennsylvania: Stackpole Co., 1956.

Kenyon, C. *Lugers at Random.* Glenview, Illinois: Handgun Press, 1990.

Kindig, J., Jr. *Thoughts on the Kentucky Rifle in its Golden Age.* New York, New York: Bonanza Books, 1964.

Laidacker, John S. *Collected Notes Concerning Developmental Cartridge Handguns In .22 Calibre As Produced in the United States and Abroad From 1855 to 1875.* Bloomsburg, PA: J.S. Laidacker, 1994.

Larson, Eric *Variations of the Smooth Bore H&R Handy-Gun.* Takoma Park, Maryland: 1993.

Leithe, Frederick E. *Japanese Handguns.* Alhambra, California: Borden Publishing Company, 1968.

Lenk, T. *The Flintlock, Its Origins and Development.* New York, New York: Bramhall House, 1965.

Lewis, Jack, editor, *Gun Digest Book of Assault Weapons*, 4th edition, Krause Publications, Iola, WI, 1996.

Lippard, K. *Fabbri Shotguns*, Colorado Springs, Colorado, VM Publications, 1998.

Lippard, K, *Perazzi Shotguns*, Colorado Springs, Colorado, VM Publications, 1996.

Lugs, J. *Firearms Past and Present.* London: Grenville, 1975.

Madis, George *The Winchester Model 12.* Brownsboro, Texas: Art & Reference House, 1982.

Madis, George *The Winchester Book.* Brownsboro, Texas: Art & Reference House, 1977.

Marcot, R. *Spencer Repeating Firearms.* Irvine, California: Northwood Heritage Press, 1990.

Markham, George *Japanese Infantry Weapons of World War Two.* New York, New York: Hippocrene Books, Inc., 1976.

McDowell, R. *Evolution of the Winchester.* Tacoma, Washington: Armory Pub., 1985.

McDowell, R. *A Study of Colt Conversions and Other Percussion Revolvers,* Iola, WI; Krause Publications, 1997.

McIntosh, Michael *A.H. Fox; The Finest Gun in the World.* Countrysport Press, 1992.

Moller, G. D. *American Military Shoulder Arms, Volume 1, Colonial and Revolutionary War Arms.* Niwot, CO: University Press of Colorado, 1993.

Murphy, J. M.D. *Confederate Carbines & Musketoons.* J. Murphy, M.D., n.p.: 1986.

Murray, Douglas P. *The 99: A History of the Savage Model 99 Rifle.* Murray, 1976.

Myatt, Major Frederick, M.D. *Pistols and Revolvers.* New York, New York: Crescent Books, 1980.

Nutter, W.E. *Manhattan Firearms.* Harrisburg, Pennsylvania: Stackpole Co., 1958.

Olson, Ludwig *Mauser Bolt Rifles.* Third Edition. Montezuma, Iowa: Brownell & Sons, 1976.

Parsons, J. E. *Henry Deringer's Pocket Pistol.* New York, New York: Wm. Morrow & Co., 1952.

Pender, Roy G. *III Mauser Pocket Pistols 1910-1946.* Houston, Texas: Collectors Press, 1971.

Peterson, H.L. *Arms and Armor in Colonial America.* New York, New York: Brandhall House, 1956.

Petty, Charles E. *High Standard Automatic Pistols 1932-1950.* Highland Park, NJ: The Gun Room Press, 1989.

Rankin, J. *Walther Models PP and PPK.* Coral Gables, Florida: Rankin, 1989.

Rankin, J. *Walther Volume III, 1908-1980.* Coral Gables, Florida: Rankin, 1981.

Reese, Michael *11 Luger Tips.* Union City, Tennessee: Pioneer Press, 1976.

Reilly, R. *United States Martial Flintlocks.* Lincoln, Rhode Island: Andrew Mowbray, Inc., 1986.

Reilly, R. *United States Military Small Arms 1816-1865.* Baton Rouge, Louisiana: Eagle Press, Inc., 1970.

Renneberg, R.C. *The Winchester Model 94: The First 100 Years.* Iola, WI: Krause Publications, 1992.

Riling, R. *The Powder Flask Book.* New York, New York: Bonanza Books, 1953.

Rosenberger, R.F.& Kaufmann, C. *The Long Rifles of Western Pennsylvania-Allegheny and Westmoreland Counties.* Pittsburgh, PA: University of Pittsburgh Press, 1993.

Rule, R. *The Rifleman's Rifle: Winchester's Model 70, 1936-1963.* Northridge, California: Alliance Books, 1982.

Ruth, L. *War Baby! Comes Home-The U.S. Caliber .30 Caliber Carbine Volume II.* Toronto, Ontario: Collector Grade Publications, Inc., 1993.

Ruth, L. *War Baby! The U.S. Caliber .30 Carbine.* Toronto, Ontario: Collector Grade Publications, Inc., 1992.

Schroeder, Joseph J. *Gun Collector's Digest, Volume II* Northfield, Illinois: Digest Books, Inc., 1977.

Schwing, N. *Winchester's Finest, The Model 21.* Iola, WI: Krause Pub., 1990.

Schwing, N. *The Winchester Model 42.* Iola, WI: Krause Pub., 1990.

Schwing, N. *Winchester Slide Action Rifles, Vol. Model 1890 and Model 1906.* Iola, WI: Krause Publications, 1992.

Schwing, N. *Winchester Slide Action Rifles, Vol. Model 61 and Model 62.* Iola, WI: Krause Publications, 1993.

Schwing, N. *The Browning Superposed: John Browning's Last Legacy.* Iola, WI: Krause Publications, 1996.

Sellers, F. *Sharps Firearms.* North Hollywood, California: Beinfeld Pub., Inc., 1978.

Sellers, F. *American Gunsmiths.* Highland Park, New Jersey: Gun Room Press, 1983.

Sellers, F. and Smith, S. *American Percussion Revolvers.* Ottawa, Ontario: Museum Restoration Service, 1971.

Serven, James E. *200 Years of American Firearms.* Chicago, Illinois: Follett Publishing Company, 1975.

Serven, J. *Collecting of Guns.*

Sharpe, P. *The Rifle in America.* Funk and Wagnalls Co., 1953.

Sheldon, Douglas G. *A Collector's Guide to Colt's. 38 Automatic Pistols.* Sheldon, 1987.

Smith, W. *The Book of Pistols and Revolvers.* Harrisburg, Pennsylvania: Stackpole Co., 1962.

Stadt, R.W. *Winchester Shotguns and Shotshells.* Tacoma, Washington: Armory Publications, 1984.

Stevens, R. *The Browning High Power Automatic Pistol.* Toronto, Canada: Collector Grade Publications, 1990.

Stoeger's Catalog & Handbook. 1939 Issue. Hackensack, New Jersey: Stoeger Arms Corporation.

Supica J. & Nahas R., *Standard Catalog of Smith & Wesson.* Iola, WI: Krause Publications, 1996.

Sutherland, R.Q. & Wilson, R. L. *The Book of Colt Firearms.* Kansas City, Missouri: R.Q. Sutherland, 1971.

Tivey, T. *The Colt Rifle, 1884-1902.* N.S.W. Australia: Couston & Hall, 1984.

Vorisek, Joseph T *Shotgun Markings:* 1865 to 1940, Canton, CT: Armsco Press 1990.

Wahl, Paul *Wahl's Big Gun Catalog II.* Cut And Shoot, Texas: Paul Wahl Corporation, 1988.

Walter, John *The German Rifle.* Ontario, Canada: Fortress Publishing, Inc., 1979.

Whitaker, Dean H. *The Winchester Model 70 1937-1964.* Dallas, Texas: Taylor Publishing Company, 1978.

Wilkerson, Don *The Post War Colt Single Action Army Revolver.* Dallas, Texas: Taylor Publishing Company, 1978.

Wilson, R.L. *Colt An American Legend.* New York, New York: Abbeville Press, 1985.

Wilson, R.L. *Colt Engraving.* Beinfeld Publishing, Inc., n.p., 1982.

Wilson, R.L. *Winchester Engraving.* Palm Springs, California: Beinfeld Books, 1989.

Wilson, R.L. *The Colt Heritage.* New York, New York: Simon & Schuster, 1979.

Wilson, R.L. *Winchester An American Legend.* New York, New York: 1991.

Winant, L. *Early Percussion Firearms.* New York, New York: Wm. Morrow & Co., 1959.

Winant, L. *Firearms Curiosa.* New York, New York: Greenburg Pub., 1955.

Workman, W.E. *The Ruger 10/22,* Iola, WI: Krause Publications, 1994.

Zhuk, A.B. *The Illustrated Encyclopedia of Handguns.* London, England, Greenhill Books, 1995.

MANUFACTURER & MODEL INDEX

COLT BLACKPOWDER ARMS 164

M

P

U

More Great Titles From Gun Digest® Books

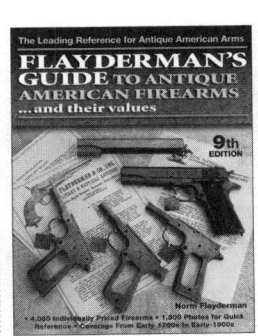

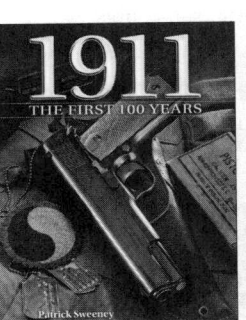

Be Your Own Gunsmith
Product Code: W0931
ISBN-13: 978-1-4402-1769-2

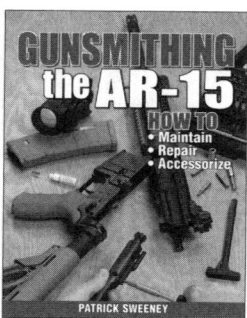

Gunsmithing the AR-15
Product Code: Z6613
ISBN-13: 978-1-4402-0899-7

Gunsmithing: Pistols & Revolvers
Product Code: Z5056
ISBN-13: 978 1 4402-0389-3

Gunsmithing: Rifles
Product Code: GRIF
ISBN-13: 978-0-8734-1665-8

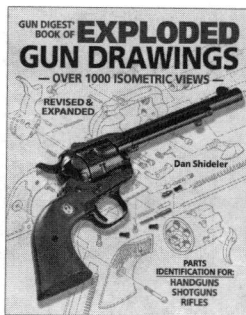

Gun Digest® Book of Exploded Gun Drawings
Product Code: Y0047
ISBN-13: 978-1-4402-14336

Gun Digest® Book of Revolvers Assembly/Disassembly
Product Code: Y0773
ISBN-13: 978-1-4402-1452-3

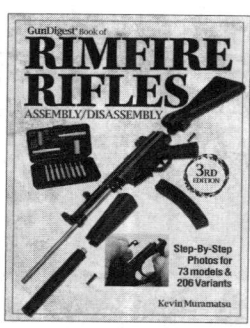

Gun Digest® Book of Rimfire Rifles Assembly/Disassembly
Product Code: W1577
ISBN-13: 978-1-4402-1813-7

Automatic Pistols Assembly/Disassembly
Product Code: Z0737
ISBN-13: 978-0-89689-473-0

The Gun Digest® Book of Tactical Weapons Assembly/Disassembly
Product Code: Z2297
ISBN-13: 978-0-89689-692-5

The Gun Digest® Book of Firearms Assembly/Disassembly Part V: Shotguns
Product Code: AS5R2
978-0-87349-400-7

Mauser Military Rifles of the World
Product Code: Y1287
ISBN-13: 978-1-4402-1544-5

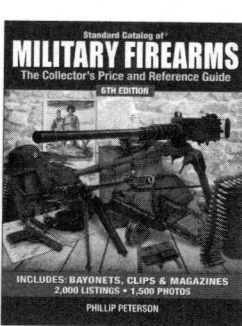

Standard Catalog of Military Firearms
Product Code: Y0772
ISBN-13: 978-1-4402-1451-6

The Gun Digest® Book of the AK & SKS
Product Code: Z2207
ISBN-13: 978-0-89689-678-9

The Gun Digest® Book of Assault Weapons
Product Code: Z0769
ISBN-13: 978-0-89689-498-3

The Gun Digest® Book of Firearms Assembly/Disassembly Part IV: Centerfire Rifles
Product Code: AS4R2
ISBN-13: 978-0-87349-631-5

Military Small Arms of the 20th Century
Product Code: MSA7
ISBN-13: 978-0-87341-824-9

Standard Catalog of® Civil War Firearms
Product Code: Z1784
ISBN-13: 978-0-89689-613-0

The Complete Gun Owner
Product Code: Z2614
ISBN-13: 978-0-89689-715-1

The Gun Digest® Buyer's Guide to Guns
Product Code: Z3048
ISBN-13: 978-0-89689-844-8

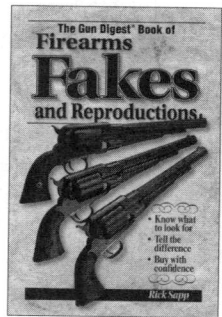

The Gun Digest® Book of Firearms Fakes & Reproductions
Product Code: Z2208
ISBN-13: 978-0-89689-679-6

**Gun Digest® Book of
Long-Range Shooting**
Product Code: Z0735
ISBN 13: 978-0-89689-471-6

**The Gun Digest® Book of
Combat Handgunnery**
Product Code: Z0880
ISBN-13: 978-0-89689-525-6

Personal Defense for Women
Product Code: Z5057
ISBN 13: 978-1-4402-0390-9

**The Gun Digest®
Book of Concealed Carry**
Product Code: Z1782
ISBN-13: 978-0-89689-611-6

Combat Shooting with Massad Ayoob
Product Code: W1983
ISBN-13: 978-1-4402-1857-6

Guns of the New West
Product Code: GNW
ISBN-13: 978-0-87349-768-8

Effective Handgun Defense
Product Code: CCFH
ISBN-13: 978-0-87349-899-9

Own the Night
Selection & Use of Tactical Lights
& Laser Sights
Product Code: Z5015
ISBN 13: 978-1-4402-0371-8

Defensive Handgun Skills
Product Code: Z8888
ISBN 13: 978-1-4402-1381-6

Armed for Personal Defense
Product Code: Z9404
ISBN-13: 978-1-4402-1408-0

**The Gun Digest® Book of
Personal Protection & Home
Defense**
Product Code: Z3653
ISBN-13: 978-0-89689-938-4

**Gun Digest® Buyer's
Guide to Assault Weapons**
Product Code: Z2209
ISBN-13: 978-0-89689-680-2

**Gun Digest® Book of the
Tactical Rifle**
Product Code: Y0046
978-1-4402-1432--5

Tactical Pistol Shooting
Product Code: Z5954
ISBN 13: 978-1-4402-0436-4

**Gun Digest® Buyer's
Guide to Tactical Rifles**
Product Code: Y0625
ISBN-13: 978-1-4402-1446-2

**The Gun Digest® Book of
Tactical Gear**
Product Code: Z2251
ISBN-13: 978-0-89689-684-0

**The Gun Digest® Book of the
AR-15**
Product Code: GDAR
ISBN-13: 978-0-87349-947-7

**Gun Digest® Book of the
AR-15 Volume II**
Product Code: Z0738
ISBN-13: 978-0-89689-474--7

**Gun Digest® Book of the
AR-15, Volume 3**
Product Code: Z8816
ISBN-13: 978-1-4402-137-6-2

**Gun Digest® Book of the
Tactical Shotgun**
Product Code: Y1448
ISBN-13: 978-1-4402-1553-7

www.gundigeststore.com

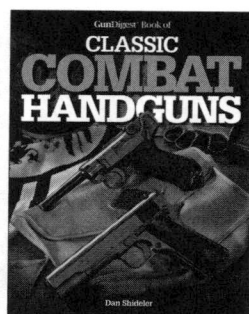

Gun Digest® Book of Classic Combat Handguns
Product Code: W4464
ISBN-13: 978-1-4402-2384-6

Massad Ayoob's Greatest Handguns of the World
Product Code: Z6495
ISBN-13: 978-1-4402-0825-6

Gun Digest® Buyer's Guide to Concealed Carry Handguns
Product Code: Z8905
ISBN-13: 978-1-4402-0825-6

The Gun Digest® Book of the Glock
Product Code: Z1926
ISBN-13: 978-0-89689-642-0

The Gun Digest® Book of the 1911
Product Code: PITO
ISBN-13: 978-0-87349-281-2

The Gun Digest® Book of the 1911, Volume 2
Product Code: VIIPT
ISBN-13: 978-0-89689-269-9

Reloading for Handgunners
Product Code: W0932
ISBN-13: 978-1-4402-1770-8

ABCs of Reloading
Product Code: Z9165
ISBN-13: 978-1-4402-1396-0

Reloading for Shotgunners
Product Code: Z7241
ISBN-13: 978-0-87349-813-5

The Complete Blackpowder Handbook
Product Code: Z7241
ISBN-13: 978-0-89689-390-0

Cartridges of the World
Product Code: Z3651
ISBN 13: 978-0-89689-936-0

Gun Digest® Book of the .22 Rifle
Product Code: Z8581
ISBN-13: 978-1-4402-1372-4

Gun Digest® Book of Green Shootings
Product Code: Z8039
ISBN-13: 978-1-4402-1362-5

Gun Digest® Big Fat Book of the .45 ACP
Product Code: Z4204
ISBN 13: 978-1-4402-0219-3

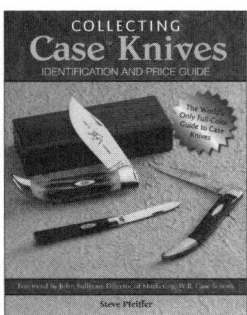

Collecting Case Knives
Product Code: Z4387
ISBN-13: 978-1-4402-0238-4

Blade's Guide to Knives & Their Values
Product Code: Z5054
ISBN-13: 978-1-4402-0387-9

The Wonder of Knifemaking
Product Code: Z7241
ISBN-13: 978-1-4402-1156-0

Bladesmithing with Murray Carter
Product Code: W1852
ISBN-13: 978-1-4402-1838-5

Knifemaking with Bob Loveless
Product Code: Z7240
ISBN-13: 978-1-4402-1155-3

American Premium Guide to Knives & Razors
Product Code: Z2189
ISBN-13: 978-0-89689-672-7

Wayne Goddard's $50 Knife Shop, Revised
Product Code: WGBW2
ISBN-13: 978-0-89689-295-8

The Tactical Knife
Product Code: Z6614
ISBN-13: 978-1-4402-0900-0

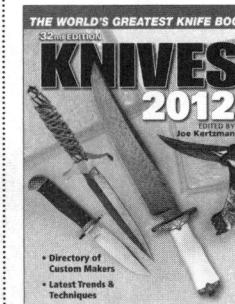

The Wonder of Knifemaking
Product Code: X3269
ISBN-13: 978-1-4402-1684-8

Knives 2012
Product Code: Z4713
ISBN-13: 978-1-4402-1687-9

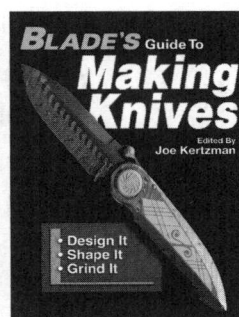

How to Knifes
Product Code: KHM01
ISBN-13: 978-0-87341-389-3

BLADE's Guide to Making Knives
Product Code: BGKFM
ISBN-13: 978-0-89689-240-8

Art of the Knife
Product Code: Z0733
ISBN-13: 978-0-89689-470-9

Calendars

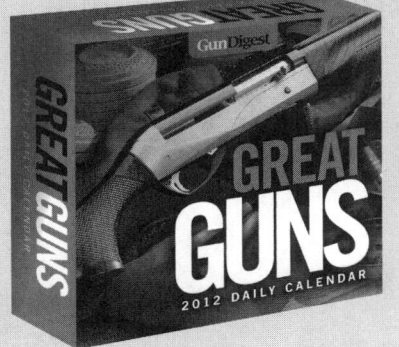

Whitetails 2012 Daily Calendar
Product Code: W4539
ISBN-13: 978-1-4402-2388-4

Gun Digest® **Great Guns 2012 Daily Calendar**
Product Code: W4556
ISBN-13: 978-1-4402-2395-5

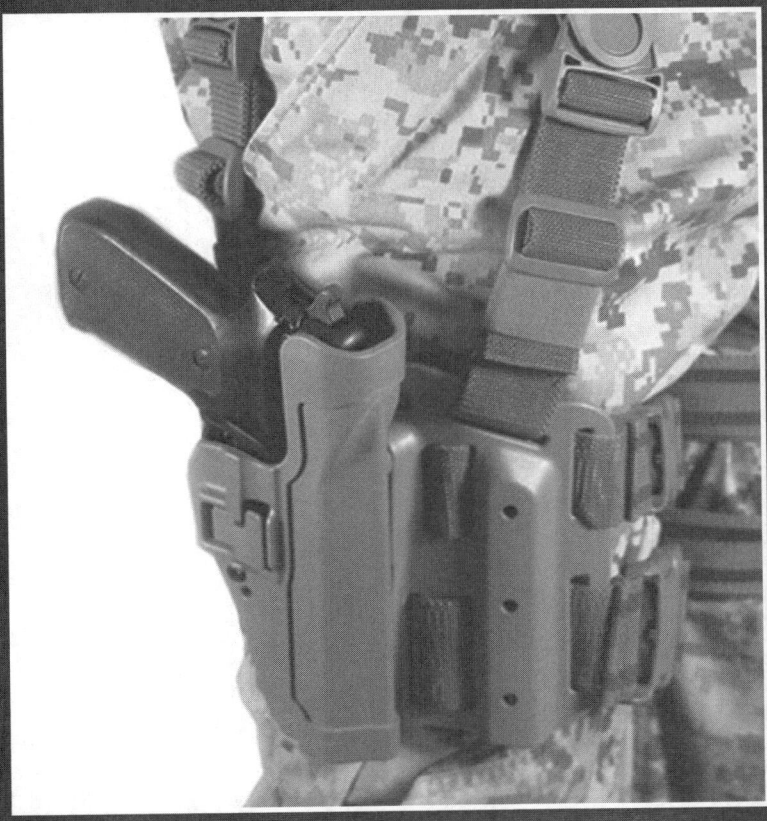